# Strategic Management

# Strategic Management

## Fourth Edition

## John L. Thompson

*University of Huddersfield*

THOMSON
LEARNING

Australia   Canada   Mexico   Singapore   Spain   United Kingdom   United States

**Strategic Management – Fourth Edition**

For more information, contact Thomson Learning, Berkshire House, 168–173 High Holborn, London, WC1V 7AA or visit us on the World Wide Web at: http://www.thomsonlearning.co.uk

*British Library Cataloguing-in-Publication Data*
A catalogue record for this book is available from the British Library

**ISBN 1-86152-587-7**

**First edition 1990**
**Second edition 1993**
**Third edition 1997, reprinted 1997**

Text design by Malcolm Harvey Young
Produced by Gray Publishing, Tunbridge Wells

Printed in Italy by G. Canale & C.

# Contents

# List of Minicases

# Preface

## About This Book

This book is about strategic awareness, strategic analysis and the management of strategic change. It is designed for use by students who will become future managers and for managers in practice; after all, in some way or another, '*all managers are strategy makers*'. It looks at how managers become strategically aware of their company's position and potential opportunities for change, at how changes often happen in reality, and at how the process might be managed more effectively.

Strategic management is concerned with the actions that organizations take to deal with the changes, opportunities, threats, challenges and surprises in their external and internal environments. Put simply, strategies are means to ends. How, then, do organizations:

- determine desired outcomes?
- understand the circumstances and events affecting these outcomes and the means of attaining them?
- decide upon actions that they intend to take?
- implement these desired strategies through a series of tactical moves and changes?
- evaluate progress and relative success?

These are the broad themes addressed in this book.

Since the first edition was written over 10 years ago the subject of strategic management has been developed and our understanding of certain aspects has changed. In addition, the 'world of business' has been transformed by the rapid growth of the Internet and the emergence of the new and entrepreneurial 'dot.com' organizations. Indeed, entrepreneurship as a subject has also increased in popularity and significance and it is not realistic to treat it as completely divorced from strategy as the two are very clearly related. While some of these changes were reflected in the second and third editions, this fourth edition sees major revisions to both the structure and content to bring both the text and the case material fully up to date.

## How To Use This Book

### Structure and content

The content follows the established Analysis, Choice, Implementation model and is structured in five parts, which systematically deal with a series of 12 key questions. These questions are illustrated in Figure 1, a chart that is reproduced at the beginning of every part of the book to illustrate how our understanding is developing.

Part One: *Understanding Strategy and Strategic Management* looks at the strategy process as a whole and includes a comprehensive framework of the process around which the book is structured in Chapter 2. This chapter also incorporates an introduction to the key strategic themes which are developed throughout the book and, for this reason, it could be seen in part as a reference chapter. This part also includes chapters on mission and objectives, strategic success, and culture and values. Culture is a vital element of

*Figure 1.* The 12-question figure.

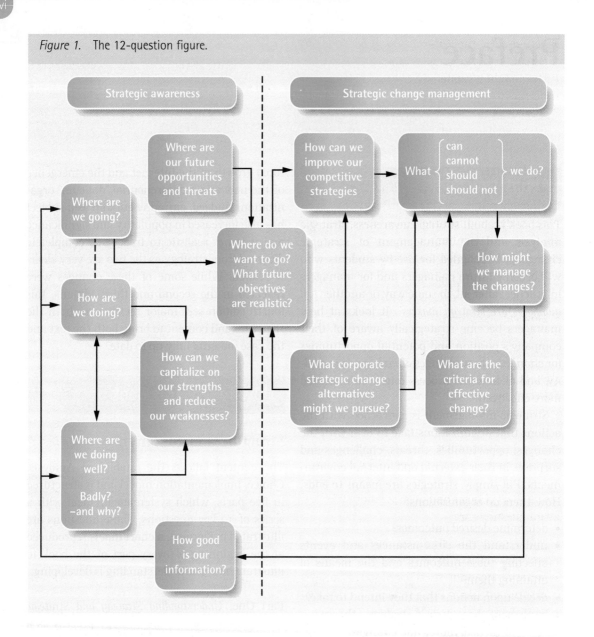

our study as it determines how strategies and changes are determined and implemented.

Part One thus addresses the following questions:

- How is the organization doing? Where is it doing well and where is it doing less well?
- Where is the organization going – and how might this have to be changed?

Part Two: *Environmental Analysis, Resources and Competitiveness* looks at two distinct but clearly related approaches to strategy, opportunity-driven and resource-based strategic management. Part Two includes a number of tools and techniques which help us to understand the current competitive situation. This part also looks at strategic positioning and competitive advantage. We ask:

- Where are the future opportunities and threats for the organization?
- How might it capitalize on its strengths, competencies and capabilities, and reduce any key weaknesses?
- How can its competitiveness be improved and strengthened?

Part Three: *Strategy Creation* describes and evaluates the different ways in which strategies are formulated and created. Several valuable planning models and techniques are discussed. We also look at both entrepreneurship and intrapreneurship. We therefore continue to ask:

- How might the organization be developed in the future?
- How can its competitiveness be strengthened?
- How good is the organization's information management?

Part Four: *Strategic Alternatives and Strategy Selection* begins with a study of the various strategic alternatives that a firm might consider and ends with the determinants of a good choice. It incorporates changes in both corporate and competitive strategies, and it deals with both growth and retrenchment issues. There is also a short chapter on business failure. The relevant questions are:

- What corporate strategic alternatives are available and worthy of serious consideration?
- What can, cannot, should and should not the organization do in the future?

Part Five: *Strategy Implementation and Strategic Management – Managing and Changing the Corporation* evaluates the issues involved in strategy implementation. Organization structures, resource management and the complexities of managing change are included, as are issues of risk and crisis management. The following questions are therefore addressed:

- What criteria affect the proposed change decisions, how and why?

- How might the proposed changes be implemented and managed?

Strategic management is a complex and dynamic subject and, as we said at the beginning of this Preface, since the first three editions of this book were published a number of new ideas and views has emerged. In addition, certain practices and priorities have changed to reflect developments around the world. Consequently, the whole text has been reviewed and restructured. Most chapters have been substantially rewritten and some have been consolidated. Existing readers will appreciate how the basic structure of the book has also been changed. The new content of individual chapters is explained below.

Chapters 1 and 2 have been rewritten; new material has been added and the content of the two chapters has been switched around. Chapter 1 now introduces strategy and strategic management, explores the scope of the subject and explains the differences between prescribed (intended) strategy and emergent strategy. It concludes by looking at strategy in different organizational contexts. Chapter 2 defines a number of key concepts and it has been designed to serve, in part, as a reference chapter for these important strategic ideas. It also contains a section on the paradoxes which pervade strategic decision making, which we develop throughout the text and then return to in Chapter 25.

Chapter 3 is a reworked chapter on Mission and Objectives.

Chapter 4 is a more extensive treatment of strategic success. It incorporates a new, holistic model and explores the relevance of reputation. Financial measures are included as a supplement.

Chapter 5 is a reworked chapter on Culture and Values.

Chapter 6 introduces Part Two by exploring the important themes of strategic thinking and synergy. The distinction between the opportunity-driven and resource-based approaches to strategy is explained.

Chapters 7, 8 and 9 all represent major revisions. Chapter 7, on the strategic environment, now includes our discussion of competition regulation and it introduces strategic positioning and added value. Chapter 8 discusses generic strategies, competitive advantage, activities and activity mapping, and competitive dynamics. Chapter 9, on strategic resources, incorporates a discussion of competency and capability, strategic architecture, the supply chain, the value chain and branding.

Chapter 10 introduces Part Three by explaining modes of strategy creation. Chapter 11 then follows with a review of planning and planning techniques. The new Chapter 12 includes material on strategic leadership (from Chapter 3 of the previous edition) and supplements it with an exploration of entrepreneurs and entrepreneurship.

Chapter 13 takes emergent strategy as its theme and looks at intrapreneurship in organizations. Human resource and information strategies are now included in this chapter, whereas previously they were looked at more independently.

Chapter 14 concentrates on strategic alternatives and strategic means and includes an extended treatment of international strategy. Chapters 15 and 16 now separate two important growth themes: diversification and acquisition, and strategic alliances and joint ventures. Chapter 17 discusses business failure before Chapter 18 explores strategic consolidation and recovery. Chapter 19 includes a framework for effective strategic choice and, in a new section, explores strategic decision-making processes in some detail. It includes a section on judgement.

Chapter 20 provides an introduction to strategy implementation and provides two models which explain the implementation of intended strategy and the process of emergent strategy. Chapter 21 explains alternative organization structures and discusses the underpinning issues. Chapter 22, on corporate strategy and style, has

been substantially rewritten. The diversification/focus dilemma, corporate parenting and strategic heartlands are discussed in detail.

Chapter 23 takes strategic resource management as its basic theme but includes an extended discussion of crisis avoidance and crisis management. It also includes a new discussion on strategic risks and risk management.

Chapter 24 explores strategic change management.

The final chapter (Chapter 25) explores the theme 'What is strategy?' and pulls the content of the book together in a new framework. This chapter also extends an earlier introduction to strategic competency (Chapter 2) and concludes with a review of the strategic paradoxes also presented in Chapter 2.

## Key Themes

### Strategy in practice

The book contains a selection of long cases at the end and over 100 minicases within the various chapters. These cover large and small businesses, both national and international in scope, manufacturing and service, and the private, public and non-profit sectors. The retail, leisure, financial and transport service industries are included, as are several non-profit and charity organizations. New long cases for this edition include Amazon.com, Kwik Fit Insurance and Princess Cruises. Contemporary short cases include the Concorde crash in Paris in summer 2000 and strategic issues at London's Millennium Dome. Some of the cases have been included in earlier editions of this book, but all of them have been either updated or rewritten for this new edition.

### Differing perspectives

It must be emphasized that no single approach, model or theory can explain the realities of strategic change in practice for all organizations; different organizations and managers will find certain approaches much more relevant to their circumstances and style. All approaches will have both supporters and critics. It is therefore important to study the various approaches within a sound intellectual framework so that they can be evaluated by students and other readers.

Students of business and management and practising managers must work out for themselves the intricacies and difficulties of managing organizations at the corporate level and of managing strategic change at all levels of the organization. It is no good being told how to be prescriptive when it is patently obvious that there is no universal model. Observations of practice in isolation are equally limited in their usefulness. However, an attempt to find explanations that can be utilized does make sense. Testing and evaluating reality against a theoretical framework helps this process.

## Key features

### Cases and examples

In addition to numerous references in the main text to organizations and events, over 100 short case examples are included. These relate to a wide variety of organization types throughout the world. The cases are designed to illustrate points in the main text. They are also intended to supplement the reader's own experiences and investigation. Each chapter begins with a carefully written minicase which represents the main themes of the chapter. For the first time there are specific questions at the end of every minicase and relevant website addresses are provided to enable easy follow-up. Inevitably some of the cases will 'date' in the sense that the strategies and fortunes of the companies featured in the examples will change. Strategies have lifecycles, and strategies that prove effective at certain times will not always remain so. Companies that fail to change their strategies at the right time are likely

to experience declining fortunes. Questions are included at the ends of chapters to encourage the reader to research and analyse the subsequent fortunes of companies included as cases. At the back of the book is a longer set of full-length case studies which can be used to supplement the text and develop a deeper insight into strategic issues. The cases have been written and selected to provide a comprehensive coverage of the material in the text and also to illustrate strategy in a wide range of different types and size of organization, both national and international.

Additional case examples and updates to the long cases are also included on the accompanying website.

### Boxes

Three types of box are used in the text and featured separately within the relevant chapter for special emphasis and easy reference:

*Key Concepts* boxes define and explain significant concepts and contributions which underpin an understanding of strategic management.

*Discussion* boxes feature particular debates where there are differing opinions.

*Strategy in Action* boxes provide annotated applications of particular ideas and concepts.

### Figures

A comprehensive set of figures, which are either new or redrawn, illustrates and explains the issues covered in the text.

### Pause for thought

Short and pithy quotations from a variety of senior managers in the private and the public sectors are sprinkled throughout the text to illustrate a spectrum of opinions. These are useful for provoking class discussion and examination questions.

### Chapter summary

An outline summary of the content and main

points is given at the end of every chapter. This can help readers to check that they appreciate the main points and issues before reading on.

### Questions and research projects

These are included at the end of each chapter. Some questions relate to the ideas contained in the text and the illustrative cases, and some are examples of the type that feature in non-case study examinations of this subject.

Several research projects, both library and Internet based, are included to encourage the reader to develop his or her knowledge and understanding further. The library-based assignments assume access to a library in the UK; lecturers in other countries will be able to advise students on similar, more local, companies that can be substituted and researched. The website provides a gateway of links to sites that are helpful in researching the Internet projects.

### Glossary

The book also includes a glossary for the first time, including definitions of over 100 key terms. For ease of reference words that are included in the glossary are highlighted in colour in the text.

### Concise version

For those readers studying or teaching a one-semester strategy course focusing on the analytical aspects of the subject a shorter version of this book is also available. *Understanding Corporate Strategy* (also published by Thomson Learning) comprises 13 analytical chapters from this book and does not include the long case studies.

### Website

An extensive accompanying website (accessible from http://www.thomsonlearning.co.uk) provides a comprehensive set of additional resources for both students and lecturers. It includes additional material and examples about strategic management, links to companies and further information sources, guidance for lecturers and interactive resources for students. Full details are given in the following sections.

## Advice for Lecturers

### Teaching aims

The main purpose of the book is to help students who aim to become managers, and managers in practice, to:

- develop their strategic awareness
- increase their understanding of how the functional areas of management (in which they are most likely to work) contribute to strategic management and to strategic changes within organizations
- appreciate how strategic change is managed in organizations.

The content is broad and the treatment is both academic and practical, in order to provide value for practising managers as well as full- and part-time students. The subject matter included is taught in a wide variety of courses, including undergraduate courses in business studies and related areas, MBA and other post-graduate master's degrees, post-experience management courses and courses for a number of professional qualifications. The subject can be entitled strategic management, business policy, corporate strategy or business planning.

The material is relevant for all types of organization: large and small businesses, manufacturing and service organizations, and both the public and private sectors. The examples included relate to all of these. Although the topics discussed are broadly applicable, certain issues are sector specific, and these are discussed individually.

This edition has been written and structured in 25 chapters to support courses that last a full academic year. Clearly, some lecturers will opt to spend longer on some topics than others or possibly switch the order of the chapters marginally. Neither of these should present any problems and suggested course outlines are provided on the website for different types of course. Some courses in strategy run for a only single semester, focusing more on the analytical aspects of the subject. A careful selection of chapters, in a logical sequence, can underpin such courses quite readily and a suggested outline is provided on the web. Alternatively, the Corporate Strategy text outlined above may be an ideal coursebook for such a module.

## The website

Lecturers who adopt this book for their course can gain access to the protected section of the accompanying website (contact your local Thomson Learning representative for access details), which includes:

- suggested course structures for different levels and lengths of courses
- learning outcomes for each chapter
- lecture notes to accompany each chapter
- guidance on using the Internet exercises with students
- guidance on teaching using case studies
- additional case studies
- teaching notes for the long case studies with suggested answers to the case questions
- a test bank of questions containing over 100 exercises
- Powerpoint slides for each chapter.

This replaces the paper-based Lecturer's Resource Manual that accompanied the previous edition. In addition, lecturers can access all the material that is freely available to students (outlined below).

## Advice for Students

### Studying strategy

Strategic management is concerned with understanding, as well as choosing and implementing, the strategy or strategies that an organization follows. It is a complex process that can be considered from a number of different perspectives. For example, one can design prescriptive models based on a series of logical stages that look at how to choose and implement strategies aimed at achieving some form of long-term success for the organization. This is a systematic approach designed to bring about optimum results. An alternative paradigm, or conceptual framework, is a systemic approach that concerns understanding what is happening in reality and thinking about how things might be improved. The emphasis is on learning about how strategic management is practised by looking at what organizations actually do and by examining the decisions that they make and carry out.

In this book both perspectives are considered and linked together. While it is always useful to develop models that attempt to provide optimizing solutions, this approach is inadequate if it fails to explain reality. Strategic management and strategic change are dynamic, often the result of responses to environmental pressures, and frequently not the product of extensive deliberations involving all affected managers.

Managers should be aware of the issues and questions that must be addressed if changes in strategy are to be formulated and implemented effectively. At the same time, they should be aware of the managerial and behavioural processes taking place within organizations in order that they can understand how changes actually come about.

Prescriptive models are found quite frequently in business and management teaching. For example, there are models for rational decision making built around the clear recognition and definition of a problem and the careful and objective analysis and evaluation of the alternative solutions. There are economic models of various market structures showing how an organization can maximize profit. However, decision making invariably involves subjectivity and short cuts, and organizations do not always seek profit maximization as their top priority. Although organizations and individuals rarely follow these models slavishly – quite often they cannot, and sometimes they choose not to – this does not render them worthless. Far from it: they provide an excellent framework or yardstick for evaluating how people reach their decisions, what objectives are being pursued and how situations might be improved. The argument is that if managers observe what is happening and seek to explain it and evaluate it against some more ideal state then they will see ways of managing things more effectively. In this way managerial performance can be improved. Note the use of the expression 'more effectively'. For a whole variety of reasons situations cannot be managed 'perfectly'.

The reader with personal experience of organizations, management and change (whether it is limited or extensive, broad or specialized) should use this experience to complement the examples and cases described in the book. Ideally the experience and the cases will be used jointly to evaluate the theories and concepts discussed. There is no universal approach to the management of strategy and strategic change. An individual must establish what approaches and decisions are likely to prove most effective in particular circumstances, and why. This learning experience can be enhanced:

- by evaluating the theoretical and conceptual contributions of various authors
- by considering practical examples of what has proved successful and unsuccessful for organizations

- by examining these two aspects in combination to see which theories and concepts best help an understanding of reality.

Managers perform a number of activities, including planning and organizing the work of their subordinates, motivating them, controlling what happens and evaluating results. All managers are planners to some degree; and it is extremely useful if they can develop an ability to observe clearly what is really happening in organizations and reflect on how things might be improved. Kolb (1979) calls this the learning cycle, and it can be usefully applied to a study of strategic management and change.

Students and managers build on their own experiences when they read about theories and concepts and think about case-study examples. They should reflect upon these experiences continually and seek to develop personal concepts that best explain for them what happens in practice. Wherever appropriate they should experiment with, and test out, these concepts to establish how robust they are. This, of course, constitutes added experience for further reflection. In other words:

This approach is illustrated in more detail in Figure 2.

Experiences, theories and concepts generate awareness. This, with reflection, improves understanding. Constant evaluation helps one to develop a personal perspective of effective management. This process is enhanced by trying out ideas which generate new experiences.

*The manager's job is change. It is what we live with. It is what we are to create. If we cannot do that, then we are not good at the job. It is our basic job to have the nerve to keep changing and changing and changing again.*

Sir Peter Parker

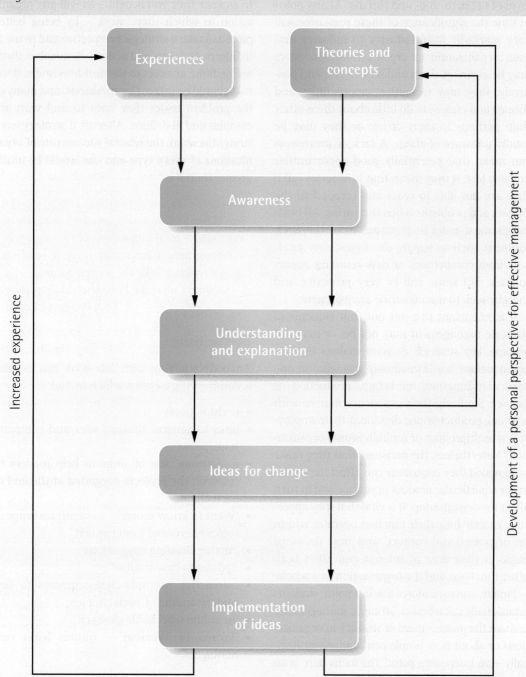

Figure 2

Development of a personal perspective for effective management

Pressures to change are always present in the form of opportunities and threats. At any point in time the significance of these pressures will vary markedly from industry to industry and from organization to organization. Managers may be aware of them and seek to respond positively; they may recognize opportunities and threats and choose to do little about them other than perhaps to avert crises; or they may be totally unaware of them. A lack of awareness can mean that potentially good opportunities are also lost; it may mean that businesses fail if they are not able to react and respond to the threats and problems when they arise. All businesses must react to pressures from the environment such as supply shortages, new products from competitors or new retailing opportunities, but some will be very proactive and thereby seek to manage their environment.

It is important to point out that students of strategic management may not be, or may not become, key strategic decision makers in their organizations but instead may specialize in one particular function, marketing, production or finance. Similarly, their experience may be with only one product or one division if their employer is a multiproduct or multidivisional organization. Nevertheless, the decisions that they make or to which they contribute can affect the strategy for a particular product or service and in turn affect the organization. It is vital that they appreciate exactly how their function operates within an organizational context, and how decisions made in their area of interest can affect both other functions and the organization as a whole.

Finally, and to reinforce this last point, students occasionally ask whether 'strategic management' is about the management of strategy in organizations or about how people can manage strategically – an interesting point! The focus here is on the management of strategy in organizations but, by studying and applying the theory, and reflecting on its relevance in the context of personal observations and experience, readers should be able to improve their effectiveness as managers. In essence they will benefit – as will any organization in which they work – by being better placed to take a strategic perspective and to use it to inform decisions and actions. Remember, there are no finite answers to the decisions and actions that should be taken. Organizations, and many of the problem issues they have to deal with are complex and ill-defined. After all, if strategy were straightforward, the relative success rate of organizations of every type and size would be much greater than it is.

*Experience is a wonderful thing, but not a useful one. When you are young, you don't trust others' experience – for if you do, this can paralyse you. When you get old, it is too late to use it – and you cannot transmit it for the reasons outlined.*
Jacques Calvet, Le President du Directoire,
PSA Peugeot Citroën.

## The website

Anybody studying with this book can use the accompanying website, which includes:

- revision notes
- links to general strategy sites and company homepages
- a 'gateway' site of links to help readers to research the projects suggested at the end of each chapter
- 'Want to know more?' – in-depth coverage of topics referenced from the text
- Further Reading suggestions
- updates to case studies
- interactive multiple-choice quizzes to test understanding of each chapter
- an online searchable glossary
- 'Words of Wisdom' – quotes from real managers.

## Reference

Kolb, DA (1979) *Organizational Psychology*, Prentice Hall.

## Acknowledgements

It is impossible to acknowledge individually everyone who has contributed to this book – and to the three earlier editions. I remain indebted to numerous teachers, colleagues and past and present students for providing me with ideas and for helping me to develop the perspective for, and revise the content of, *Strategic Management*.

I would, though, like to single out three people. Anna Faherty at Thomson Learning persuaded me to undertake a fourth edition and provided constant support and encouragement throughout the process of revision. Jim Gallagher at Napier University was generous in allowing me to use three of his case studies. My wife Hilary has been particularly understanding as 'jobs around the house' have been neglected.

The publishers wish to thank the following companies for their co-operation in supplying images for use in this book: Ben & Jerry's Homemade, Inc.; Glaxo Wellcome PLC; The Coca-Cola Company; Dyson; Wal-Mart Stores, Inc.; Richer Sounds PLC; Granada Media PLC; Nantucket Allserve, Inc.; Imperial Chemical Industries PLC; Apple Computer, Inc; and Walt Disney Company.

Figure 3.2 on p. 98. Reprinted by permission of the publisher. From *The Pillars of Success*, copyright © 2000 by Blanchard and O'Connor, Berrett-Koehler Publishers, Inc., San Francisco, CA. All right reserved. 1-800-929-2929.

Table 4.2 on p. 150. Reprinted by permission of Financial Times Ltd. 'The World's Most Successful Companies', *Financial Times Survey*, 7 December 1999.

Figures 8.4, 8.6a, 8.6b on pp. 292 and 305. Reprinted by permission from *Competitive Advantage: Creating and Sustaining Superior Performance*, Free Press, New York.

Figure 8.10 on p. 317. Reprinted by permission of Harvard Business School Press. From *Hidden Champions: Lessons from 500 of the World's Best Unknown Companies*, by Simon Hermann. Boston, MA 1996, p. 152. Copyright © 1996 by the President and Fellows of Harvard College; all rights reserved.

Figure 11.2 on p. 381. By kind permission of the author. From *Corporate Strategy*, by H. Igor Ansoff.

# Understanding Strategy and Strategic Management

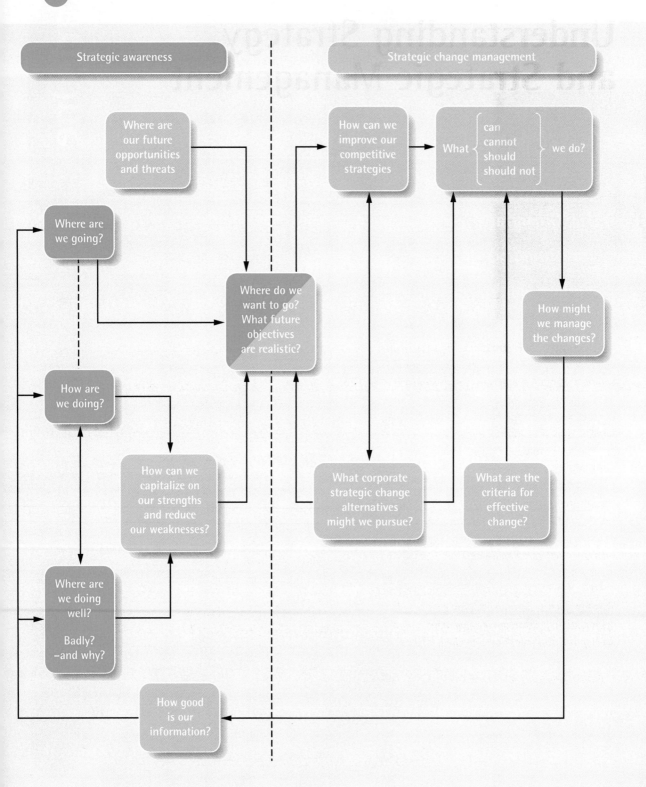

Strategic awareness

Strategic change management

Where are our future opportunities and threats

Where are we going?

Where do we want to go? What future objectives are realistic?

How are we doing?

How can we capitalize on our strengths and reduce our weaknesses?

Where are we doing well? Badly? –and why?

How good is our information?

How can we improve our competitive strategies

What { can / cannot / should / should not } we do?

How might we manage the changes?

What corporate strategic change alternatives might we pursue?

What are the criteria for effective change?

# Understanding Strategy and Strategic Management

1 Introducing Strategy and Strategic Management

2 The Strategic Management Process

3 The Organizational Mission and Objectives

4 Measuring Success

5 Culture and Values

*Organizations, their strategies, their structures and the management of them become ever more complex. Among the reasons for this are the increasing turbulence and propensity to change in the business environment, and the tendency for multiproduct multinational organizations to become commonplace. Organizations need to know where they are, where they are going and how to manage the changes. Managers in these organizations need to know where their roles fit in relation to the whole and how they can contribute to strategic developments and changes. These are the issues addressed by a study of strategic management.*

*This first part is designed to provide a broad appreciation of strategic management and to develop the framework used in the book in order to:*

- *outline the scope and complexity of the study area*

- *provide an initial overview of some major contributors to the subject in order to illustrate what is meant by, and included in, strategic management, and to show that there is no single universally accepted approach*
- *develop a framework which will provide a model for the structure and content of the book*
- *examine what is meant by purpose, direction and objectives, and consider how these might be set and used*
- *consider how we might evaluate the relative success of an organization*
- *explain how culture and values impact on every aspect of strategic management.*

*A number of issues and topics will be raised and discussed in brief in Chapters 1 and 2 and will then be explored in depth in the following chapters.*

# Introducing Strategy and Strategic Management

*Strategies are means to ends. All organizations, large and small, profit-seeking and not-for-profit, private and public sector, have a purpose, which may or may not be articulated in the form of a mission statement. Strategies relate to the pursuit of this purpose. Strategies must be created and implemented, and it is these issues which are addressed by our study of strategic management. This opening chapter begins by outlining how successful organizations manage their strategies, and what they achieve, before exploring the meaning of strategy in greater detail. It then continues by describing how the subject of strategic management has been developed in the last 30 years, before explaining the different ways in which strategies are created. It concludes with a brief consideration of the similarities and differences in strategic management in various types of organization.*

# Minicase 1.1 The Low-Price, No-Frills Airlines

Herb Kelleher began Southwest Air in 1971 with a simple intention – 'fly people safely, cheaply and conveniently between Dallas, Houston and San Antonio', three key cities in Texas. Kelleher set out to compete against coach and car travel rather than the other airlines. He had been a champion college athlete and a successful Texas lawyer before he started the airline when he was 40 years old. The idea for Southwest, however, had come from a client (and co-founder of the business) who spotted the gap in the market.

In nearly 30 years as a low-price, no-frills airline, Southwest has prospered and grown to become the fifth largest carrier in the USA. It serves over 50 cities in 27 states and has some 2500 flights every day. Kelleher's strategy, competitive advantage and success is based on a number of factors:

- frequent and reliable departures
- relatively short journeys by American standards, now averaging 450 miles but with the average having increased as the airline has grown in size and destinations
- the choice of smaller airports nearer to city centres where relevant, in preference to international airports which are further away from the centre
- very low prices
- automated ticketing and direct bookings (without travel agents), and now using the Internet extensively
- limited *frills*, with no seat assignments, no videos and just one class of seating
- fast gate turnarounds, to maximize the time the planes are in the air
- a standardized fleet of Boeing 737s, to simplify maintenance.

Southwest is now America's only significant short-distance, point-to-point carrier. Others have certainly tried to compete, but have been unable to make the equivalent impact. It has won the

US Department of Transport's coveted 'Triple Crown' award of best on-time record, best baggage handling and fewest customer complaints on several occasions. Every new route and destination is immediately popular and, as a result, Southwest has been consistently profitable for over 25 years, a unique record for an airline anywhere in the world.

Kelleher is a renowned 'people person'. Through profit-sharing schemes, employees own over 10% of the company's stock, and he has made 'working in the airline industry an adventure'. Southwest is dynamic and responsive; employees accept empowerment and are motivated to work hard and deliver high levels of service consistently. Rules and regulations are minimized to allow staff the freedom to deal with issues as they arise. 'Ask employees what's important to them. Ask customers what's important to them. Then do it. It's that simple', says Kelleher. The frequent flyer programme, unusually, rewards passengers for the number of individual flights, not the miles flown.

But it is never that simple! Southwest is also renowned as 'one of the zaniest companies in history'. From the very beginning, Kelleher encouraged flight attendants to crack jokes during in-flight emergency briefings, but, at the same time, operate with very high safety standards. He was determined that passengers would enjoy their flights. Some of the planes are decorated externally to reinforce the fun image. Three of them, promoting major sponsor Sea World, are flying killer whales; one is painted with the Texas flag; another is christened Arizona One, a spoof of Air Force One. Flight attendants have been known to hide in the overhead lockers as passengers come on board, startling them as they open up the lockers. Kelleher often appears in fancy dress for certain flights and special occasions. A special prize for the passenger with the biggest hole in his sock is quite typical.

Consequently, a sense of humour has become a key element in the recruitment process. During their training, employees are given a book with sections on jokes, games and songs – but they are all encouraged to develop an individual style. 'At Southwest we don't want clones – everyone is expected to colour outside the lines'. Kelleher is dedicated and focused and in possession of a strong ego drive. He is creative and innovative and he understands the contribution that people can make. He has always had the courage to be different. When he was introduced to an idea he appreciated the opportunity and activated it. Truly profit orientated, he has been extremely successful in a dynamic and cruel industry, where many competing airlines have failed.

The best-known European low price, no-frills airline is Easyjet, begun in 1995 by a 28-year-old Greek entrepreneur, Stelios Haji-Ioannou, the son of a wealthy shipping magnate. He intended to 'make flying in Europe affordable for more and more people'. Parodying British Airways' claim to be 'The World's Favourite Airline', EasyJet now calls itself 'The Web's Favourite Airline'. Some 75% of its bookings come via the Internet; the rest are direct over the telephone. There are no commissioned travel agency bookings, no tickets and no on-board meals. When passengers with a reservation check in at the airport, they are allocated a number, based on their time of check in, not when they prebooked, and this determines the order in which they board the aircraft. There are no seat reservations. Hub airports in the UK are the relatively uncongested and quick turnaround Luton and Liverpool; and destinations are concentrated in Scotland and continental Europe, including Athens, Barcelona, Geneva and Nice. All the aeroplanes are relatively new Boeing 737s, painted white and orange and featuring EasyJet's telephone number on the side. The airline became profitable for the first time in 1998.

Stelios had studied in the UK, at the London School of Economics and City University, and then worked for his father for a short while. He began his first business, Stelmar Tankers, in 1992. EasyJet's strategy was modelled on Southwest Air, but Stelios claimed he had been inspired by Richard Branson and Virgin Atlantic (see Minicase 1.4). His approach to customers and people mirrors that of Branson. He flies on his own planes some three or four times a week and talks to the passengers. A television 'docusoap' on EasyJet in 1998 and 1999 showed that Stelios was regularly present at Luton (his headquarters) and willing to help resolve passenger problems.

*A lot of my thinking is reactionary. I lead by example. I believe that people will do things if they see their boss doing exactly the same things . . . the best way to motivate a team is to convince them they're always under attack . . . having an external enemy is the best way of focusing their mind on results, rather than fighting each other and becoming complacent . . . I'm keen that important information is available to everybody in the company . . . there are no secrets.*

The EasyJet product is, in reality, a package of services, many subcontracted in. EasyJet provides the planes and their crews, and markets and sells the flights. As a company, it is focused. Check-in and information services, snacks (for passengers to buy before they board the aeroplane), baggage handling and fleet maintenance are all bought in from specialists.

Competition for customers in this sector of the market is intense. Both British Airways (with Go) and Virgin (with Virgin Express) have low-price, no-frills subsidiaries, neither of which is reputed to be profitable. The largest of the rivals is Ryanair, 15 years old and based in Dublin, which carries some 6 million passengers every year, and has grown recently at around 20% per year. If its success continues it will soon overtake smaller National airlines, such as KLM and Sabena, and become Europe's fifth largest airline. Ryanair again uses only Boeing 737s. There are just three cabin crew on every flight, low for an aircraft of this size, but they are not there to serve food and drinks but to look after passenger safety. One other significant competitor, Debonair, collapsed in 1999.

More recently, the serial entrepreneur Stelios Haji-Ioannou has personally diversified into other activities. EasyEverything, when it opened in London, was the world's largest Internet café; in 1999 he announced plans for an Internet bank, provisionally named Easy Money; and in early 2000 he unveiled Easy RentaCar, where cars can be rented only via a website.

QUESTION: What strategic issues and lessons does this case raise?

The quotations from Stelios Haji-Ioannou are extracted from: Maitland, A (1998) No frills and lots of feedback, *Financial Times*, 17 September.

*Easy Jet*   http://www.easyjet.com
*Southwest Airlines*   http://www.southwest.com

Photographer: Charles Falk

## Introducing Strategy

At their simplest, strategies help to explain the things that managers and organizations do. These actions or activities are designed and carried out in order to fulfil certain designated purposes, some of them short term in nature, others longer term. The organization has a direction and broad purpose, which should always be clear, articulated and understood, and which sometimes will be summarized in the form of a mission statement. More specific milestones and targets (objectives) can help to guide specific actions and measure progress. Strategies, then, are means to ends. They are relevant for the organization as a whole, and for the individual businesses and/or functions that comprise the organization. They are created and changed in a variety of ways. They have, however, one common feature: they all have lifecycles and need changing, either marginally or dramatically, at certain times.

The need for all managers to be able to think strategically was stressed in the Preface, and the approach taken in this book concentrates on the development of strategic awareness. While strategic management incorporates major changes of direction for the whole business, such as diversification and growth overseas, it also involves smaller changes in strategies for individual products and services and in particular functions such as marketing and operations. Decisions by managers in relation to their particular areas of product or functional responsibility have a strategic impact and contribute to strategic change.

> To some extent all managers
> are strategy makers.

Strategic management is a complex and fascinating subject with straightforward underlying principles but no 'right answers'. Companies succeed if their strategies are appropriate for the circumstances they face, feasible in respect of their resources, skills and capabilities, and desirable to their important stakeholders – those individuals and groups, both internal and external, who have a stake in, and an influence over, the business. Simply, strategy is fundamentally about a fit between the organization's resources and the markets it targets – plus, of course, the ability to sustain fit over time and in changing circumstances.

Companies fail when their strategies fail to meet the expectations of these stakeholders or produce outcomes which are undesirable to them. To succeed long term, companies must compete effectively and outperform their rivals in a dynamic, and often turbulent, environment. To accomplish this they must find suitable ways for creating and adding value for their customers. A culture of internal co-operation and customer orientation, together with a willingness to learn, adapt and change, is ideal. Alliances and good working relationships with suppliers, distributors and customers are often critically important as well.

While strategy is a complex topic, the underlying principles are essentially simple. There is, however, no 'one best way' of managing strategic change; and no single technique or model can provide either the right answer concerning what an organization should do, or superior and crystal-clear insight into a situation. Instead, managers should utilize the range of theories and concepts which are available, adapting them to meet their own situation and circumstances.

At the same time, a study of strategic changes in a variety of different organizations is valuable. An examination of outcomes, followed by an analysis of the decisions which led to these relative successes and failures, is rich in learning potential. Examples should not be confined to just one sector. Manufacturing and service businesses, the private and public sectors and not-for-profit organizations are all relevant.

Everyone who can make or influence decisions which impact on the strategic effectiveness of the business should have at least a basic understanding of the concepts and processes of strategy. The processes will often be informal, and the outcomes not documented clearly. But they still exist, and managing the processes effectively determines the organization's future.

Without this understanding people often fail to appreciate the impact of their decisions and actions for other people within the business. They are less likely to be able to learn from observing and reflecting upon the actions of others. They are also more likely to miss or misjudge new opportunities and growing threats in the organization's environment.

As a starting point, key terms used in this book are defined in Box 1.1 and examples of strategic change in a number of different organizations are illustrated in Box 1.2.

KEY CONCEPT – Box 1.1
Key Terms

**Mission** is the essential purpose of the organization, concerning particularly why it is in existence, the nature of the business(es) it is in, and the customers it seeks to serve and satisfy.

**Objectives (or goals)** are desired states or results linked to particular time-scales and concerning such things as size or type of organization, the nature and variety of the areas of interest and levels of success.

**Strategies** are means to ends, and these ends concern the purpose and objectives of the organization. They are the things that businesses do, the paths they follow, and the decisions they take, in order to reach certain points and levels of success.

**Tactics** are the specific activities which deliver and implement the strategies in order to fulfil objectives and pursue

the mission. Often short term, they can be changed frequently if necessary.

**Strategic management** is a process which needs to be understood more than it is a discipline which can be taught. It is the process by which organizations determine their purpose, objectives and desired levels of attainment; decide on actions for achieving these objectives in an appropriate time-scale, and frequently in a changing environment; implement the actions; and assess progress and results. Whenever and wherever necessary the actions may be changed or modified. The magnitude of these changes can be dramatic and revolutionary, or more gradual and evolutionary.

**Strategic change** concerns changes which take place over time to the strategies and objectives of the organization. Change can be gradual or evolutionary; or more dramatic, even revolutionary.

**Strategic awareness** is the understanding of managers within the organization about: (a) the strategies being followed by the organization and its competitors, (b) how the effectiveness of these strategies might be improved, and (c) the need for, and suitability of, opportunities for change.

**Synergy** is the term used for the added value or additional benefits which ideally accrue from the linkage or fusion of two businesses, or from increased co-operation either between different parts of the same organization or between a company and its suppliers, distributors and customers. Internal co-operation may represent linkages between either different divisions or different functions.

**STRATEGY IN ACTION – Box 1.2**
**Examples of Strategy Changes**

**Lex Service Group**, sizeable distributor of Rover, Rolls Royce and Volvo cars in the main, felt too dependent on one area of business and sought to find suitable diversification opportunities. Lex chose four- and five-star hotels in the UK and USA but later chose to sell them when the results were below those desired. This took place in the 1970s and 1980s, since when Lex entered and exited the distribution of electronics parts. More recently Lex has acquired related businesses to become the UK's largest car distribution and leasing company. In 1995 Lex bought Multipart, a distributor of commercial vehicle parts; and more recently it has acquired the roadside assistance business, the RAC.

*Lex Service Group*   http://www.lex.co.uk

**WH Smith**, desiring growth beyond the scope offered from its (then) current business lines (wholesaling and retailing newspapers and magazines, stationery, books and sounds), diversified into do-it-yourself with a chain of Do-It-All stores, introduced travel agencies into a number of its existing stores and acquired related interests in Canada and America. Travel was later divested, along with investments in cable television, to enable greater concentration on sounds, videos and consumer and office stationery. Important acquisitions included the Our Price and Virgin music stores and the Waterstone's chain of specialist booksellers. Do-It-All became a joint venture with Boots, but it struggled to be profitable with strong competition from B & Q (owned by Kingfisher) and Texas, acquired by Sainsbury's in the mid-1990s. In 1996 WH Smith divested Do-It-All and its office stationery businesses. Later in the 1990s both Waterstone's and Our Price were also divested, and the book publisher, Hodder Headline, was acquired. These are all examples of corporate strategic change.

In October 1995 WH Smith, responding to the willingness of the leading supermarket chains to sell newspapers, magazines and a carefully selected range of books – with discounted prices for current bestsellers – began to discount books from a number of publishers. This was an important change of competitive strategy as, previously, Smiths had been a staunch supporter of the Net Book Agreement. This longstanding agreement between publishers and booksellers was designed to prevent intense price competition.

*WH Smith*   http://www.whsmith.co.uk

**The Burton Group** sold the last of its manufacturing interests in 1988. Once one of the leading men's clothing manufacturers in Europe the group, by a series of acquisitions and divestments, has become essentially a major retailer of fashion goods for both men and women. In recent years Burton acquired – and later divested – Debenham's.

*Arcadia (Burton Group)*
http://www.arcadia.co.uk

**UK building societies**, restrained by legislation until the mid-1980s, expanded their financial services to include current accounts with cheque books and cash-dispensing machines – to compete more aggressively with the high-street banks – and diversified into such linked activities as estate agencies and insurance. Mergers took place between, for example, the Halifax and Leeds Permanent societies and Abbey National and National & Provincial, to strengthen their positions as diversified financial institutions. Moreover, the largest ones (notably Abbey National and the Halifax) have given up their mutual status and become quoted companies.

In a quite different (and more evolutionary way) the decision by high-street banks to open on Saturdays for a limited range of services was strategic change. Here the banks were copying the building societies.

*Abbey National*
http://www.abbeynational.co.uk
*Halifax* http://www.halifax.co.uk

**National Bus Company** was privatized during the mid-1980s, mostly by splitting it up into small local or regional companies which were bought out by their existing management teams. The sector has since become more concentrated as certain growth-orientated operators such as Stagecoach and

First Bus (a name change from Badgerline) have bought out other smaller companies. One major challenge for these aggressive companies has been to try and avoid intervention from the UK regulatory authorities, concerned with competition in the industry. Having acquired a number of local bus franchises in the UK, Stagecoach has also expanded overseas and bought a minority shareholding (49%) in Virgin Rail.

*Stagecoach*
http://www.stagecoachholdings.com

There is a number of aspects to strategic management. First, the strategy itself, which is concerned with the establishment of a clear direction for the organization and for every business, product and service, and a means for getting there, and which requires the creation of strong competitive positions. Second, excellence in the implementation of strategies in order to yield effective performance. Third, creativity and innovation to ensure that the organization is responsive to pressures for change, and that strategies are improved and renewed. Fourth, the ability to manage strategic change, both continuous, gradual, incremental changes and more dramatic, discontinuous changes. Innovation and change concern the strategy process in an organization. Excellence and innovation should enable an organization to thrive and prosper in a dynamic, global environment, but in turn they depend on competencies in strategic awareness and learning. Organizations must understand the strategic value of the resources that they employ and deploy, and how they can be used to satisfy the needs and expectations of customers and other stakeholders while outperforming competitors.

Many of these points were evident in Minicase 1.1, The Low-Price, No-Frills Airlines, which showed that:

- newcomers can change an industry – by being creative, innovative and different
- new competitors can, and will, find ways of breaking down apparent barriers to entry
- companies need to find some clear and distinct competitive advantage, something which is both attractive to customers and profitable
- this advantage will come from what organizations do, their distinctive competencies and capabilities
- charismatic and visible strategic leaders often have a major impact on the choice and implementation of key strategies
- people are critically important if strategies are to be implemented effectively
- the Internet is becoming increasingly important; and
- business can be fun!

It is, however, also important to realize that in many organizations certain parts may be *world class* and highly profitable while other businesses are not. Good practices in the strong businesses can be discerned, transferred and learned, but this may not be enough. Some industries and competitive environments are simply less *friendly* and premium profits are unlikely. The real danger occurs if the weaker businesses threaten to bring down the strong

# Minicase 1.2 Marks and Spencer plc

Marks & Spencer (M&S) is a well-known and revered high-street retailer in the UK. The early growth of M&S was built around clothing, and its reputation owes much to the popularity of its underwear! It built a second reputation for foods, pioneering chilled fresh varieties. Always gradually, other ranges such as cosmetics, homewear, gifts and furniture have been added systematically. A home-delivery service for furniture has been expanded to include other items. Every shopping centre developer wants M&S to open a store, as they always attract customers.

The original foundations of the business lay with a young, Jewish immigrant and his Leeds market stall. Michael Marks had a poor grasp of English, a clear disadvantage for a trader in a noisy street market! Opportunistically, he turned his disadvantage into a strength. He had a sign on his stall: *Don't Ask The Price – It's a Penny*, and for a penny he provided the widest range and best-quality items he could find. This philosophy of *value for money* has pervaded through the generations and been sustained with innovation and change – but the focus on value has never been lost. The market stall led to a store, and then to stores on most high streets in Britain.

The strategy of M&S then, is concerned with diversification of their product ranges within these broad product groups, but at the same time seeking to specialize where their own St Michael label could be used effectively. All M&S products have traditionally carried the M&S name and quite often the St Michael brand. At the beginning of the new millennium a decision has been made to reduce the emphasis on using the St Michael brand name and emphasize the company name more prominently. M&S seeks to innovate whilst upgrading and adding value to its existing ranges. Over the years, M&S has found that many of its long-established stores in town and city centres are simply too small. An expansion programme has therefore developed along several lines. Adjacent units have been acquired when practical and new larger stores created, especially in new out-of-town shopping centres; if land has been available, buildings have been extended; and new sales floors have been opened up by converting stockrooms and moving stock to outside warehouses. This brings its own logistics problems. Satellite stores – smaller branches some distance away from the main branch – have been opened in certain towns. These satellites typically carry complete ranges – it might be men's fashions, ladies' clothes or children's items. The choice depends on the square footage available and the local prospects for particular lines. In a similar vein, in towns considered too small to support a full branch, specialist stores, perhaps just for food, have been opened. The selection of products within the whole M&S range varies between stores.

Other strategic changes are:

- Constant improvements in displays, partly to present products better, and also to get more items into the stores. 'Sales per square foot' is a vital measure of success.
- Electronic point-of-sale (EPOS). Information technology has been harnessed to improve productivity and to enable M&S to respond more quickly to market changes,

particularly relevant for fashion items. Thanks in part to technology, M&S staff costs as a percentage of their turnover are less than those of many competitors, but the quality of service has remained high.

- The development of support financial services, such as unit trusts, building upon the success of the M&S Chargecard, the third most popular credit card in the UK.
- International growth in, for example, France, Belgium, Canada, the USA and Hong Kong. The development has been gradual, with one of the objectives being to introduce new types of competition. Some mistakes have been made as part of the learning process, and sales in some countries have been disappointing, but the risks have been contained in order not to threaten the UK interests.

In the 1930s M&S pioneered a new form of inventory control when it designed perforated tags in two identical halves. Half was torn off at the point-of-sale, dropped in a box and then sent to the Baker Street (London) head office, where it was used to direct store replenishment. Over time this enabled M&S to introduce sophisticated replenishment from out-of-town warehouses and reduce the in-store stockrooms in favour of more direct selling space.

M&S possesses a number of identifiable strategic resources which have been instrumental in meeting customer key success factors, and thereby providing long-term profitable returns for shareholders. They include:

Physical resources     –     The wide range of value-for-money, own-brand products
                                        The sites and store displays

Intangible resources     –     Image and reputation
                                        Staff knowledge, expertise and commitment to service

Capabilities/processes     –     Supply-chain management.

While there have been, and continue to be, strategic changes, the fundamental principles or values of the business have remained constant. These are:

- high-quality, dependable products, styled conservatively and offering good value for money
- good relations with employees, customers, suppliers and other stakeholders
- simple operations
- comfortable stores
- financial prudence (most properties, for example, are freehold – they have not been sold and leased back to fund the expansion).

The foundation for the unique (St Michael) products and competitive prices is the M&S system of supply-chain relationships, a considerable proportion of these being with UK manufacturers for much of its history. In recent years M&S has, somewhat controversially, included more and more goods sourced overseas, sometimes for particular quality issues, but mostly for lower costs. In general, where they have been successful, the arrangements with suppliers have been long term and non-contractual.

They are based on mutual trust and common understanding. M&S is actively involved in product specification, input management (to their suppliers), quality control and production scheduling. M&S is frequently the supplier's most important customer. Why has it worked so effectively? The M&S reputation for fair dealing – with its suppliers, customers and employees – has been seen as too valuable to put at risk.

But, at the end of the 1990s, this long-established business was suffering declines in sales and profits. Critics argued that too many product ranges were no longer the winners that people associated with the company, and its management needed strengthening at all levels. Interestingly, this setback occurred in the decade when the company had, for the first time in its history, a chief executive who was not a descendant of one of the founding Marks, Sieff or Sacher families.

Peter Drucker (1985) had earlier summarized M&S as 'probably more entrepreneurial and innovative than any other company is Western Europe these last fifty years . . . may have had a greater impact on the British economy, and even on British society, than any other change agent in Britain, and arguably more than government or laws'.

Was it conceivable that this visible and successful business was under real threat for the first time? One executive, Clara Freeman (2000) admitted that M&S 'lost the pace, lost the focus . . . no-one saw it coming. It was the classic management story – everything is going swimmingly and you don't tinker with a successful formula. After sales and profits declined, M&S put the magnifying lens on the business and asked what was wrong. Staff and customers told us that the quality was not as consistent as it used to be, and the service needs to be better than it is'.

In 1999 the current Chairman and Chief Executive, Richard Greenbury, announced he would retire early and, after a very visible and acrimonious internal wrangle, a new Chief Executive (Peter Salsbury) was appointed from inside the business. Later, a new Executive Chairman, Luc Van de Velde, previously the head of a major French supermarket chain, was recruited. Several ranges were quickly revamped and successful stock trials accelerated. M&S began to use more demographic and customer data to determine the product ranges for each store – previously stores of roughly the same size had carried similar ranges, regardless of their location. Sales did not pick up as rapidly as had been hoped, and rumours of possible takeover bids appeared in the press. Salsbury has now resigned as Chief Executive.

## References

Drucker, PF (1985) *Innovation and Entrepreneurship*, Heinemann.
Freeman, C (2000) Interview, *Management Today*, January.

QUESTIONS: Why do you think Marks and Spencer's fortunes changed as quickly as they did?
How might such a decline have been avoided?
(If you are an M&S customer . . .) Did you notice many changes during 2000 and 2001?

*Marks and Spencer* http://www.marks-and-spencer.co.uk

ones that are forced to subsidize them. It is an irony that companies in real difficulty, possibly through strategic weaknesses, need to turn in an excellent performance if they are to survive.

Finally, it must be realized that past and current success is no guarantee of success in the future. Companies are not guaranteed, or entitled to, continued prosperity. They must adapt and change in a dynamic environment. Many fail to do this, for all sorts of reasons, and disappear. Some close down; others are acquired. Minicase 1.2, Marks and Spencer, shows how this previously outstanding company has lost its way in recent years.

## Strategic thinking

It is worth mentioning that strategic management is not something that many companies are thought to be very good at. For example, by measuring factors such as relative world and European market shares won by companies, investment expenditure, productivity and the proportion of revenue allocated for research and development, Britain has performed less well industrially than many of her major competitors in a number of key sectors over the past 40 years. A lack of marketing skills, low productivity, inadequate investment and poor management generally have all been identified as causes, but in many cases these have improved in recent years. Another important aspect is the general failure to assess properly how to compete best.

Discussing this theme, a few years ago Peter Beck, the Chairman of the British Strategic Planning Society during 1984–1986, was critical of British companies as a whole:

*Far too many companies either have no goals at all, other than cost reduction, or their boss hides them in his head. There's no hope for companies in Britain unless more top managements accept the need for a widely communicated set of clear objectives*                    (Beck, 1987)

The flame of competition has changed from smokey yellow to intense white heat. For companies to survive and prosper they will have to have a vision, a mission and strategy. They will pursue the action arising from that strategy with entrepreneurial skill and total dedication and commitment to win.
*Peter B Ellwood, Chief Executive,*
*Lloyds TSB Group*

Many of Beck's points are still pertinent in Britain and elsewhere. Strategic clarity is absent, Beck argues, for essentially three reasons: the difficulties of forecasting in today's business environment (but difficulty is no excuse for not trying!); the lack of managerial competence in many companies; and above all the frequent absence of strong leadership from the top.

Part of the problem is the distinction between established views hostile towards the formal and elaborate strategic planning systems that were in vogue during the 1960s and 1970s, but which failed to work in many cases, and the idea of strategic thinking. It is perfectly possible for any organization to address a number of key questions about how well the company is doing, and why, and where it should seek to develop in the future, and how. It will be argued in this book that the most successful companies strategically are likely to be those that are aware of where they are and of what lies ahead, those that understand their environment and those that seek to achieve and maintain competitive advantage. By way of illustration the following points have been developed from a *Financial Times* article (Morrison and Lee, 1979).

Whatever their strategy, companies that are adept at strategic thinking seem to be distinguished from their less successful competitors by a common pattern of management practices.

First, they identify more effectively than their competitors the key success factors inherent in the economics of each business. For example, in the airline industry, with its high fixed costs and relatively inflexible route allocations, a high load factor is critical to success. It is important, though, that high load factors are not at the expense of healthy sales of more expensive seats, and this requires skilful marketing.

Secondly, they segment their markets so as to gain decisive competitive advantage. The strategic thinker bases his or her market segmentation on competitive analysis and thus may separate segments according to the strengths and weaknesses of different competitors. This enables him or her to concentrate on segments where he or she can both maximize his or her competitive advantage and avoid head-on competition with stronger competitors.

Thirdly, successful companies base their strategies on the measurement and analysis of competitive advantage. Essential to this is a sound basis for assessing a company's advantages relative to its competitors.

Fourthly, they anticipate their competitors' responses. Good strategic thinking also implies an understanding of how situations will change over time. Business strategy, like military strategy, is a matter of manoeuvring for superior position and anticipating how competitors will respond, and with what measure of success.

Fifthly, they exploit more, or different, degrees of freedom than their competitors. They seek to stay ahead of their rivals by looking for new competitive opportunities. Whilst innovation and constant improvement are essential, there are also potentially huge rewards for organizations which are first to reach the new *competitive high ground* by changing the currently practised *rules of competition.*

Finally, they give investment priority to businesses or areas that promise a competitive advantage.

## Strategic success

In order to be successful, organizations must be strategically aware. They must understand how changes in their competitive environment – some of which they may have started and others to which they will have to react – are unfolding. The implied and simultaneous proactivity and reactivity require strong and appropriate resources which continue to ensure that the organization is able to meet the needs and expectations of its external stakeholders, including customers, suppliers and shareholders. Employees are a key resource for delivering this satisfaction and also an important internal stakeholder.

The UK Department of Trade and Industry recently carried out research in an attempt to clarify the 'winning characteristics' of the most successful companies. The findings, published in 1995, are summarized in Table 1.1.

Satisfying the changing needs of stakeholders in a dynamic environment demands flexibility and sound control measures. Employees should be empowered to make and carry out decisions but, to be strategically effective, this must be within a clear and co-ordinated directed framework. Hamel and Prahalad (1989) use the term 'strategic intent' to describe this directional vision. Coca-Cola, for example, intend 'to put a Coke within arms' reach of every consumer in the world', while the growth of Canon in the photocopying market was driven by a desire to 'beat Xerox'. Taking up an earlier point, Canon successfully rewrote the rules of competition. Xerox had become the market leader with a strategy based on large, high-capability machines which organizations leased from them; Canon sold smaller machines designed for the individual office.

In Chapter 2 it will be shown how these three themes of environment, resources and organizational management and control can be synthesized into a useful model.

Table 1.1   Ingredients for strategic success

| Characteristics | Requirements |
|---|---|
| *The most successful UK companies are:* | |
| Led by visionary, enthusiastic champions of change | Communicated vision |
| Able to use the potential of employees | Empowerment |
| in a customer-focused culture | Benchmarking good practice |
| in a flattened structure | Team working |
| Aware of customer needs and expectations | Awareness of key success factors |
| by constant learning and | Networking |
| innovating in response to competitive pressures | Competitor awareness |
| Constantly introducing new, differentiated products and services | Total quality management |
| because they understand their competitors | |
| because they are innovative and | |
| because they use strategic alliances to enable them to focus | Supplier alliances |
| on core businesses | |
| Able to exceed their customers' expectations with these new products and services | |

*Source: DTI (1995) Competitiveness – How the Best UK Companies are Winning, Department of Trade and Industry, London.*

*Department of Trade and Industry   http://www.dti.gov.uk*

## Functional, competitive and corporate strategies

Figure 1.1 summarizes three distinct, but inter-related and interdependent, levels of strategy: corporate (the whole organization), competitive (the distinct strategy for each constituent business, product or service in the organization) and functional (the activities which underpin the competitive strategies).

Simply, most organizations choose to produce one or more related or unrelated products or services for one or more markets or market segments. Consequently, the organization should be structured to encompass this range of product markets or service markets. As the number and diversity of products increases the structure is likely to be centred on divisions which are sometimes referred to as strategic business units (SBUs). Such SBUs are responsible individually for developing, manufacturing

and marketing their own product or group of products. Each SBU will therefore have a strategy, which Porter (1980) calls a competitive strategy. Competitive strategy is concerned with 'creating and maintaining a competitive advantage in each and every area of business' (Porter, 1980). It can be achieved through any one function, although it is likely to be achieved through a unique and distinctive combination of functional activities. For each functional area of the business, such as production, marketing and human resources the company will have a functional strategy. It is important that functional strategies are designed and managed in a co-ordinated way so that they interrelate with each other and at the same time collectively allow the competitive strategy to be implemented properly.

Successful competitive and functional strategies add value in ways which are perceived to be important by the company's stakeholders, especially

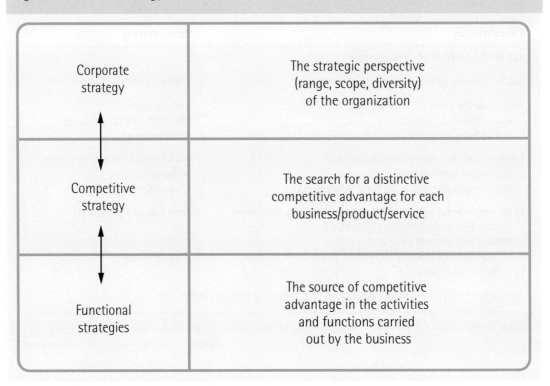

*Figure 1.1*   Levels of strategy.

its customers, and which help to distinguish the company from its competitors. Adding value is explained and discussed further in Chapter 2. Mathur and Kenyon (1997) reinforce these points and contend that competitive advantage is fundamentally about the positioning and fit of an organization in its industry or market, and that success is based on distinct differences and sound cost management.

Corporate strategy, essentially and simply, is deciding what businesses the organization should be in and how the overall group of activities should be structured and managed. It has been described by Porter as 'the overall plan for a diversified business', although it is perfectly acceptable for a business to elect to stay focused on only one product or service range. This does happen in many companies, especially small businesses. In this case the corporate and com-

petitive strategies are synonymous. Corporate strategy for a multibusiness group is concerned with maintaining or improving overall growth and profit performance through acquisition, organic investment (internally funded growth), divestment and closure. The term strategic perspective is often used to describe the range and diversity of activities, in other words the corporate strategy. Each activity then has a competitive position or strategy. The management of corporate strategy concerns the creation and safeguarding of *synergies* from the portfolio of businesses and activities.

## Synergy

Synergy (defined in Box 1.1) is a critical aspect of both corporate and competitive strategies. It is important that the functions and businesses

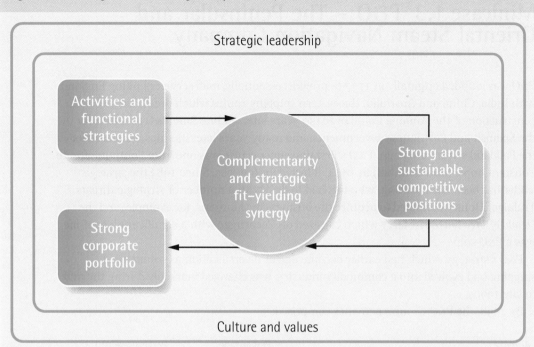

*Figure 1.2* Strategic success through complementary activities.

within an organization work collectively and support each other to improve effectiveness and outcomes.

All the time, companies should carry out efficiently those activities which are essential for creating a distinctive or differentiated competitive position, and avoid incurring unnecessary costs by providing non-essential values. This implies that they clearly understand their markets, their customers and the key success factors that they must meet, i.e. their defined competitive strategy. Moreover, they should constantly seek improvement by driving their operating efficiencies. These activities will be encapsulated in the organization's functional strategies, as illustrated in Figure 1.2.

Figure 1.2 highlights that these functional strategies must fit a defined, clear competitive strategic position and complement each other to achieve internal synergy. Where they fail to complement each other the company's compet-

itive position will inevitably be weakened. The outcome will be a strong competitive position which can only be sustained by innovation and improvement, and sometimes by the move to a new competitive paradigm. Managing these changes effectively is very dependent upon the style and approach of the strategic leader and the culture and values of the organization. These arguments accord with the latest ideas of Michael Porter (1996).

People, however, are often naturally competitive and their competitive energy should be directed against external rivals rather than members of their own organization; although, carefully managed, internal competition for scarce resources can sharpen managerial skills.

Taking the logic a stage further: where the organization's various competitive strategies are also complementary, based around a fitting heartland of activities to which the corporation

# Minicase 1.3  P&O – The Peninsular and Oriental Steam Navigation Company

P&O was founded originally in 1737 to provide, essentially, mail services linking England with India, China and Australia, the eastern shipping routes which pre-dated the construction of the Panama Canal over 150 years later. At one time P&O ran guns for the Spanish and Portuguese governments, and many years later its ships were used for the Falkland's War campaign. P&O's first passenger cruise was one from Southampton to Constantinople (now Istanbul) in 1844; it lasted for 6 weeks. Since 1983 the strategic leader has been Lord Sterling, who has had to deal with a number of strategic threats. Trafalgar House attempted to acquire the business in the 1980s, for example, and the *Herald of Free Enterprise* ferry which capsized off Zeebrugge with a significant loss of life was a P&O ship.

P&O's strategy, which had earlier become one of diversification as commercial shipping had evolved into a commodity industry, was changed markedly during the mid to late 1990s.

By 1998, the P&O Group's activities comprised:

| Activity | Percentage of turnover | Percentage of operating profits |
|---|---|---|
| **Cruises** – the P&O (UK) and Princess (US) lines | 19 | 37 |
| **Ports and Logistics** – managing ports around the world plus the land transportation of containers | 26 | 14 |
| **Ferries** – P&O is the largest ferry operator In Western Europe | 8 | 14 |
| **Cargo shipping** – both containers and bulk | 1 | 1 |
| **Property** – P&O owns and manages property in various places, including the Arndale Shopping Centre in Manchester and the Olympia and Earls Court exhibitions and entertainment venues in London | 46 | 34 |

Two years earlier, cargo shipping, dominated by containers, had been the main revenue earner.

By the mid to late 1990s, the important cross-channel ferry services between France and England were experiencing new competition from Eurotunnel and trains through the Channel Tunnel. Cruising had at this time become the fastest growing segment of the travel industry, and was experiencing annual growth rates of 20% in the UK and 9% in the USA, its largest market.

## Strategic changes in the 1990s

First, the decision was taken to focus on shipping and related activities and systematically to divest property and construction. Property holdings were put up for sale, and plans were announced for floating off the Bovis Homes subsidiary as an independent company.

Then P&O Ferries was merged with rival Stena.

The container shipping activities were merged with those of Dutch rival Nedloyd to create the world's largest container line as a separate joint venture. Major cost savings have accrued through this consolidation and it is widely forecast that 'at an appropriate time' this joint-venture business will be floated off to become truly independent.

In 1999 it was announced that the high-profile and profitable cruising businesses would be separated from other P&O activities (in 2000), and the Group divided into two discrete businesses. At around the same time an order for five new megaliners was placed, the largest ever at any one time. In early spring 2000, Carnival Group, the US-owned cruise holiday market leader, announced that advance bookings were slower than they had been a year earlier. With the relevant shipyards around the world all busy with orders for new cruise ships, some commentators suggested the industry might be heading for a situation of oversupply.

QUESTIONS: Do the consolidation and split strategies both make sense strategically? Will the two new parts be stronger as separate businesses than they would be combined? What skills and capabilities are required to succeed in cruising and ferry operations, and are any synergy possibilities being sacrificed?

*P&O Group*   http://www.p-and-o.com

can add value, the organization will be able to maintain a strong corporate portfolio. Individual businesses should, therefore, benefit from being part of the organization; membership should reduce their costs or help to provide other competitive advantages. At the same time, the organization as a whole should derive benefit from the particular mix of businesses which should, in some way, complement each other. There may be intergroup trading, for example, with one business unit supplying another; equally, skills could be transferred, factory units could be shared or the businesses could join together to purchase common requirements with substantial discounts.

Minicase 1.3 looks at possible synergies from the various activities embraced by the P&O Group.

Major changes to the corporate perspective will invariably be board-level decisions and actively involve the organization's strategic leader. Changes at the competitive and functional levels are more likely to be delegated to other managers in the business. The nature and extent of such delegation will vary from organization to organization and should reflect a careful balance between, on the one hand, the need to maintain effective control and integrate the businesses to create synergy and, on the other hand, the benefits that can be gained from

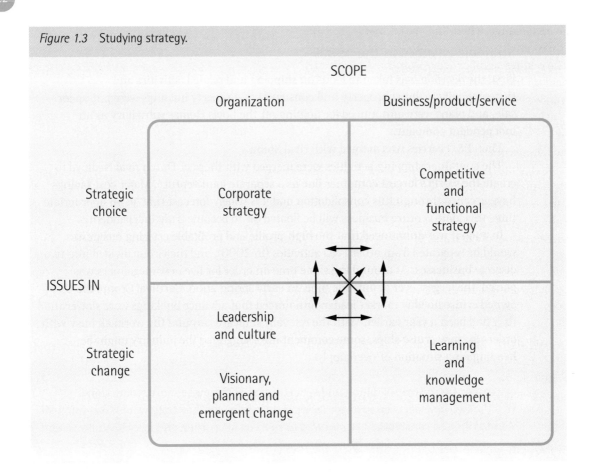

*Figure 1.3*    Studying strategy.

empowering those managers who are most aware of environmental changes and new competitive opportunities.

## Studying strategy

The study of strategy should embrace both its scope (the different levels discussed in the previous section) and issues of choice and change, and this is emphasized by Figure 1.3, developed from ideas in Whittington (1999).

Taking each box in turn, the choice of corporate strategy will first relate to the debate about focus and diversification, which in turn is really a debate over sources of potential organization-level synergy. Global ambitions are also a key element here. Competitive strategy concerns

activities, fit and positioning, as we have discussed. Competitive advantage is typically built around differentiation and cost management. Analysing the nature and logic of these choices, then, comprises a significant proportion of this book, but this type of analysis provides only a partial understanding of strategic management in organizations. We must also seek to understand how strategies are chosen and changed.

Some strategies are changed reactively when companies are surprised by their competitors or other events in their environment; in other instances there is evidence of proactive attempts to shape, mould and manage the business environment. We see later in this chapter (p. 28) how strategic change involves *entrepreneurial* leadership, planning and analysis and *intrapre-*

*neurial* change where individual managers are empowered to act in a dynamic environment. The relative significance of each mode is dependent on the preference and style of the strategic leader and the culture of the organization, and it helps to determine the extent to which power and responsibility are centralized or decentralized. Consequently, and towards the end of the book (Chapter 21), we study organizational structure and consider the link between structure and strategy implementation. As stated earlier, strategy concerns people, and their influence on choice and change. While their willingness (or not) to accept empowerment in a devolved structure is critical, so too is the ability of the organization to share its knowledge and learn collectively if it is to enjoy the synergies discussed above. Hence, we must also examine the way in which individual managers influence strategy, especially at the functional and competitive level.

## Five perspectives on strategy

More than anyone else, Henry Mintzberg has been responsible for drawing attention to alternative views and perspectives on strategy, all of them legitimate. Mintzberg *et al.* (1998) provide an excellent summary of his work on this topic.

The top oval in Figure 1.4 suggests that strategies can be seen in a visionary context. Here it is implied that strategy can be considered as a clear strategic purpose, intent and direction for the organization, but without the detail worked out. In a dynamic environment, managers would then determine more detailed and specific strategies in *real time* rather than exclusively in advance. However, they would always have a framework of direction to guide their decision making and help them to determine what is appropriate. In addition, some strategies come from a visionary input from an entrepreneurial manager, or strategic leader, who spots an opportunity and is minded to act on it.

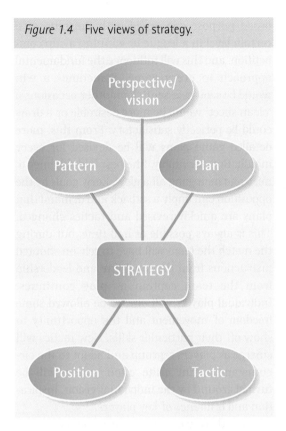

Figure 1.4   Five views of strategy.

This contrasts with some people's thinking that strategy and planning are synonymous. Certainly, as we shall see later in this chapter (p. 28), strategic planning has a crucial role in strategy creation, but it does not fully explain how strategies are changed. Both the visionary and planning perspective are concerned with thinking ahead as far as it might be sensible to think and plan. While the tactical view is also about the future, it is really about the immediate future. The assumption being made here is that competitors in a dynamic market will constantly adopt new ploys in an attempt to steal a short-term gain or advantage. Their tactics may be easily copied, but there can be some temporary advantage when rivals are caught by surprise and need time to react.

Metaphorically, we can relate these ideas to a game of competitive football. There will be a broad purpose concerned with finishing at a certain level in a league or winning a cup competition, and this will influence the fundamental approach to every game. Sometimes a win would be seen as essential; on other occasions a 'clean sheet' would be more desirable or a draw could be perfectly satisfactory. From this, more detailed game plans will be devised for every match. But, inevitably, 'the best laid schemes o' mice and men gang aft a gley'. Early goals by the opposition can imply a setback and demand that plans are quickly revised and tactics changed. This is always possible at half-time, but during the match the team will have to rely on shouted instructions from the touchline and leadership from the team captain as play continues. Individual players will always be allowed some freedom of movement and the opportunity to show off their particular skills. New tactics will emerge as players regroup and adapt to the circumstances, but quite often games will be turned around by the individual vision, inspiration and brilliance of key players.

These three views all concern the future and imply change; the notion of *position* is akin to the idea of freezing time momentarily. It relates to *strategic fit* and the organization's competitive position at the present time. It is, in effect, a statement of what is happening; and it can be vital for *taking stock*, realizing and clarifying a situation so that future changes are based on clear knowledge rather than assumption.

Of course, organizations come to their present position as a result of decisions taken previously; plans have been implemented and tactics adjusted as events have unfolded. It is again crucial to analyse and understand this evolving *pattern*, appreciating just what has happened, why and how. This can be a valuable foundation for future decisions, plans and actions but, although history can be a guide to the future, rarely in strategy are events repeated without some amendment. The importance of clarifying the pattern from the various decisions and

changes also explains why strategy has irreverently been described as a 'series of, mindless, random events, rationalized in retrospect'!

The next section of this chapter builds our understanding of these alternative perspectives by looking at how strategies are created and changed.

## The Strategic Management Process

### The strategic planning approach

Traditionally, courses in strategic management have been built around three important elements:

- strategic *analysis*
- strategy *creation and choice*
- strategy *implementation*.

Relevant frameworks for studying strategy, such as the one featured in Figure 1.5(a), tend to follow a pattern:

- appraisal of the current situation and current strategies, invariably using a SWOT (strengths, weaknesses, opportunities and threats) analysis
- determination of desirable changes to objectives and/or strategies
- a search for, and choice of, suitable courses of action
- implementation of the changes
- monitoring progress; ongoing appraisal.

Strategic management involves *awareness* of how successful and strong the organization and its strategies are, and of how circumstances are changing. At any time, previously sound products, services and strategies are likely to be in decline, or threatened by competition. As this happens, new 'windows of opportunity' are opening for the vigilant and proactive companies.

New strategies must be created which may be changes to the corporate portfolio or changes at

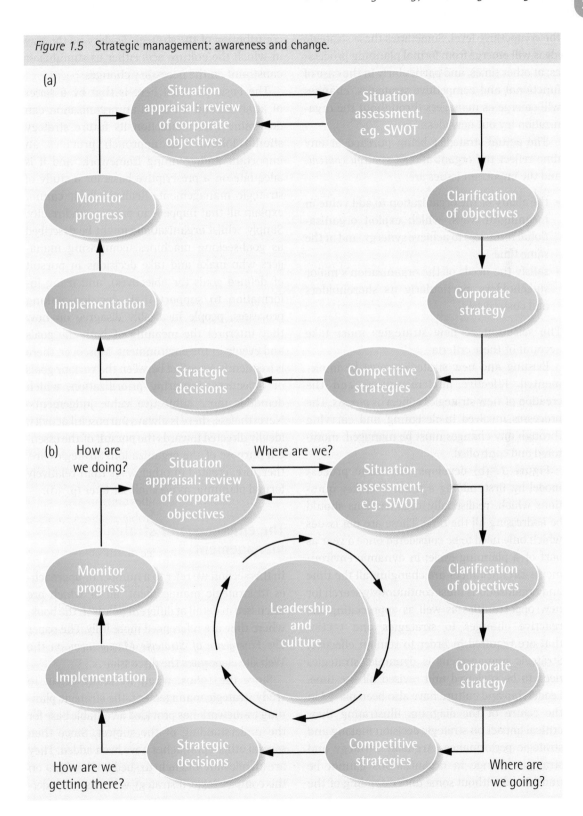

*Figure 1.5*  Strategic management: awareness and change.

(a)

Situation appraisal: review of corporate objectives

Situation assessment, e.g. SWOT

Clarification of objectives

Monitor progress

Corporate strategy

Implementation

Strategic decisions

Competitive strategies

(b)   How are we doing?

Where are we?

Situation appraisal: review of corporate objectives

Situation assessment, e.g. SWOT

Clarification of objectives

Monitor progress

Leadership and culture

Corporate strategy

Implementation

Competitive strategies

Where are we going?

How are we getting there?

Strategic decisions

the competitive level. Sometimes these strategic ideas will emerge from formal planning processes; at other times, and particularly in the case of functional and competitive strategies, changes will emerge as managers throughout the organization try out new ideas.

The actual strategies being pursued at any time reflect the organization's *strategy content*, and the important issues are:

- the ability of the organization to add value in meaningful ways, which exploit organizational resources to achieve synergy, and at the same time
- satisfy the needs of the organization's major stakeholders, particularly its shareholders and customers.

The selection of new strategies must take account of these criteria.

Existing and new strategies must be implemented. Effective implementation and the creation of new strategies concerns *process*. The processes involved in designing and carrying through any changes must be managed, monitored and controlled.

Figure 1.5(b) develops this basic process model by, first, adding a number of key questions which, realistically, organizations should be addressing all the time. These are not issues which only need to be considered once a year as part of a planning cycle; in dynamic environments circumstances are changing all the time and organizations must continuously search for new opportunities as well as appreciating the reactive changes to strategies and tactics that are required in order to remain effective. Strategic management is dynamic; strategies need to be reviewed and revised all the time. Leadership and culture have also been placed in the centre of the diagram, illustrating their critical impact on strategic decision making and strategic performance. Arguably, strategy and strategic change in organizations cannot be understood without some understanding of the

contribution of the strategic leader and the way in which the culture acts either as stimulus or constraint on the necessary changes.

The basic proposal here is that by a series of analyses and decisions an organization can determine which direction its future strategy should follow. This approach provides an important underpinning framework, and it is adequate on a prescriptive basis for a study of strategic management. Realistically it cannot explain all that happens in practice and reality. Simply, whilst organizations might be described as goal-seeking machines, comprising managers who make and take decisions in pursuit of defined goals (or objectives), and using information to support their decision-making processes, people invariably disagree on how they interpret the meaning of both the goals and events in the environment. Moreover, there is frequently a conflict between the various goals or objectives, requiring prioritization, which demands more subjective value judgements. Nevertheless, there is always purposeful activity, ideally directed towards the pursuit of the essential purpose of the organization. Strategies are, therefore, created in other ways than relatively formal planning, as we shall see later (p. 30).

## The emergence of strategic management

In this section we refer to a number of approaches to strategic management, all of which are discussed in detail at different points in the book, where they are referenced more fully. The paper *The Emergence of Strategic Management* on the Web site elaborates the discussion.

Since the 1960s, when we really began to study strategic management, the strategic planning framework has provided a valuable base for the understanding of the subject. Since then several other approaches have been added. They are all relevant and help to shed further light on this complex topic. If strategy were easy to under-

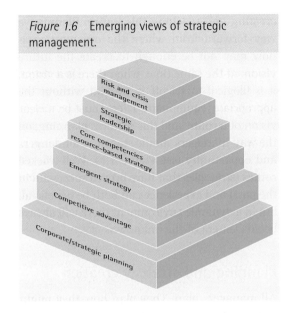

*Figure 1.6* Emerging views of strategic management.

stand and practise, then more organizations would be successful and sustain this success over time. However, although it is based in many ways on some simple points and common sense, strategy remains enigmatic.

Figure 1.6 shows that when Porter (1980, 1985) drew attention to the subject of competitive advantage, and the significance of strategic positioning, an important second layer was added to the planning foundation. The next important contribution was the clarification that many strategies emerge as decisions are taken all the time in dynamic circumstances, highlighting that while planning plays an important role, it is a partial one.

The general thrust of these approaches is market driven, based on the argument that organizations must react in a dynamic environment, seizing new opportunities and avoiding major potential threats. Responding to customers, suppliers and competitors will always be vital, but an alternative perspective is also relevant. This resource-based strategy argues that organizations must discern their critical strategic strengths and look for ways of building and

exploiting them in order to mould the competitive environment. In Chapter 2 we look at the relevant issues of core competency and strategic capability. Successful organizations will blend both the market and resource perspectives so that they do not overlook potentially good opportunities.

In recent years the subject of strategic leadership has received greater prominence, stimulated in part by the media. Business success stories have been popular items for newspapers and magazines, especially where there is a high-profile figure who can be identified with the organization and the story. In addition, the 'falls from grace' of some very high-profile business people have proved newsworthy. The accompanying autobiographies of some of these people have added to this understanding. It should be pointed out, however, that academically rigorous research on the subject has also been carried out. When the themes of leadership and entrepreneurship are incorporated the dimension of aspiration is added to strategy creation, to accompany the analysis of the strategic planning model (Figure 1.5).

Most recently, risk management and crisis management have joined the debate. Organizations have recognized that scenario building can help their understanding of uncertainty, where the future may depend in part on the past but will not replicate it. For some industries, such as pharmaceuticals (where huge investments in new drugs are required but carry no guarantee of success) and electronic commerce (which is changing by the day) serious risk assessment is vital. The environment is busy with information and triggers, never more so than now, thanks to the Internet, but discerning the real commercial opportunities is probably harder rather than easier than it was in the past. Organizational fortunes can, therefore, change rapidly, and crises can arise suddenly to catch out the unwary organization. The study of learning, and the involvement of people in an empowered and intrapreneurial culture, is a key element both of this topic and of emergent strategy.

## Strategy Creation

Points discussed in the earlier sections are now taken up. This section looks in greater detail at how strategies are changed and new strategies created.

### Opportunities for change

It is vital that managers are strategically aware both of potentially threatening developments and of opportunities for profitable change, and that they seek to match and improve the fit between the environment and the organization's resources.

> *A wise man will make more opportunities than he finds.* (Francis Bacon)

There is, however, no single recommended approach for seeking out and pursuing new opportunities. There is a broad spectrum ranging from what might be termed entrepreneurial opportunism to what Quinn (1980) calls 'logical incrementalism'. These are analogous to the Bird and Squirrel approaches described in Box 1.3.

Strategic change can be relatively evolutionary or gradual, or much more dramatic or revolutionary. The nature of the opportunities (and threats) is directly related to both the general and the specific industry environments; and the approach that particular organizations take in seeking to match resources to the environment is dependent on the basic values of the organization and the style of the strategic leader. However, as will be seen, it does not follow that the strategic leader is the sole manager of strategic change.

Effectively managed change requires a vision of the future – where the organization is heading or wants to go – together with the means for creating and reaching this future. Planning a way forward from where the organization is now may not be enough to create the future vision; at the same time, when there is a vision, it is illogical to set off in pursuit without the appropriate 'equipment'. There must be a clear vision of a route, and this requires planning; on the way, managers should stay alert for dangers and opportunity (see Figure 1.7). Well-tracked routes (strategies that have proved successful in the past) and experience can both be beneficial, but in a dynamic environment there will always be an element of the unknown.

### Planning and strategy creation

All managers plan. They plan how they might achieve objectives. Planning is essential to provide direction and to ensure that the appropriate resources are available where and when they are needed for the pursuit of objectives. Sometimes the planning process is detailed and formal; on other occasions planning may be informal, unstructured and essentially 'in the mind'. In the context of strategy formulation a clear distinction needs to be made between the cerebral activity of informal planning ('planning strategy') and formalized planning systems ('strategic planning').

Formal strategic planning systems are most useful in stable conditions. Environmental opportunities and threats are forecast, and then, as we saw earlier, strategies are planned and implemented. Strategies which are appropriate, feasible and desirable are most likely to help the organization to achieve its mission and objectives.

Where the environment is more turbulent and less predictable, strategic success requires flexibility, and the ability to learn about new opportunities and introduce appropriate changes continuously. Planning systems can still make a valuable contribution but the plans must not be inflexible.

## DISCUSSION – Box 1.3
## Approaches to Strategic Management

### The bird approach

Start with the entire world – scan it for opportunities to seize upon, trying to make the best of what you find.

You will resemble a bird, searching for a branch to land on in a large tree. You will see more opportunities than you can think of. You will have an almost unlimited choice.

But your decision, because you cannot stay up in the air for ever, is likely to be arbitrary, and because it is arbitrary, it will be risky.

### The squirrel approach

Start with yourself and your company – where you are at with the skills and the experience you have – and what you can do best.

In this approach you will resemble a squirrel climbing that same large tree. But this time you are starting from the trunk, from familiar territory, working your way up cautiously, treefork by treefork, deciding on the branch that suits you best at each fork.

You will only have one or two alternatives to choose from at a time – but your decision, because it is made on a limited number of options, is likely to be more informed and less risky.

In contrast to the bird who makes single big decisions, the squirrel makes many small ones. The squirrel may never become aware of some of the opportunities that the bird sees, but he is more likely to know where he is going.

Adapted from Cohen, P (1974) *The Gospel According to the Harvard Business School*, Penguin. Originally published by Doubleday, New York, 1973.

In addition, it is important not to discount the contribution of visionary strategic leaders who become aware of opportunities – and on occasions, create new opportunities – and take risks based on their awareness and insight of markets and customers.

Formal strategic planning implies determined actions for achieving stated and desired objectives. For many organizations these objectives will focus on sales growth and profitability. A detailed analysis of the strategic situation will be used to create a number of strategic

*Figure 1.7*   Strategic change.

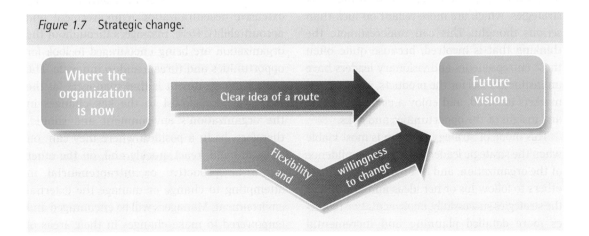

alternatives, and then certain options will be chosen and implemented.

Planning systems are useful, and arguably essential, for complex or diversified organizations with a large number of businesses that need integrating. There are several possible approaches. Head office can delegate the detailed planning to each division, offering advice and making sure that the plans can be co-ordinated into a sensible total package. Alternatively, the planning system can be controlled centrally in order to establish priorities for resource allocation.

While the discipline of planning and setting priorities is valuable, the plans must not be inflexible and incapable of being changed in a dynamic competitive environment. During implementation it is quite likely that some plans will be discarded and others modified.

## Visionary leadership

Planning systems imply that strategies are selected carefully and systematically from an analytical process. In other instances major strategic changes will be decided upon without lengthy formal analysis. Typically such changes will reflect strong, entrepreneurial leadership and be visionary and discontinuous: I have seen the future and this is it!

To an outsider it can often appear that the organization is pursuing growth with high-risk strategies, which are more reliant on luck than serious thought. This can underestimate the thinking that is involved, because quite often these entrepreneurs and visionary leaders have an instinctive feel for the products, services and markets involved, and enjoy a clear awareness and insight of the opportunities and risks.

This mode of strategy creation is most viable when the strategic leader has the full confidence of the organization, and he or she can persuade others to follow his or her ideas and implement the strategies successfully. Implementation requires more detailed planning and incremental

changes with learning: initially it is the broad strategic idea that is formulated entrepreneurially.

Formal planning and/or visionary leadership will invariably determine important changes to corporate strategies; competitive and functional level changes are more likely to involve emergent strategy in the form of adaptive and incremental changes. The actual implementation of corporate level decisions is also likely to be incremental.

All newly appointed chief executives should ask five key questions:

- What are the basic goals of the company?
- What is the strategy for achieving these goals?
- What are the fundamental issues facing the company?
- What is its culture?
- And is the company organized in a way to support the goals, issues and culture?

*Bob Bauman, ex-chief executive of*
*SmithKline Beecham*

## Adaptive strategic change

Some organizations will be characterized by extensive decentralization, empowerment and accountability. Here, managers throughout the organization are being encouraged to look for opportunities and threats and to innovate. The underlying argument is that managers 'at the coal face' are closest to the key changes in the organization's environment and should, therefore, be in a position where they can, on the one hand, react quickly and, on the other hand, be proactive or intrapreneurial in attempting to change or manage the external environment. Managers will be encouraged and empowered to make changes in their areas of responsibility and, ideally, rewarded for their initiatives. The implication is that functional changes will impact upon competitive strategies in a positive way as the organization adapts to its changing environment. Conceptually this is similar to incremental change.

Proponents of chaos theory such as Ralph Stacey (1993) argue that intentional strategies are, per se, 'too inflexible for unknown futures'. Relying on this approach is a 'recipe for stagnation and failure because of the extent of the complexity'. Companies must seek to 'achieve a state of creative tension on the edge of instability'. These theorists accept that organizational hierarchies and planning are needed to control day-to-day operations but, in the long-term, strategies must be allowed to emerge from the 'self-organizing activities of loose, informal, destabilizing networks'.

## Incremental strategic change

In dynamic and turbulent competitive environments, detailed formal planning is problematic. The plans are only as good as any forecasts, which must be uncertain. It can make sense, therefore, not to rely on detailed plans, but instead to plan broad strategies within a clearly defined mission and purpose.

Having provided this direction the strategic leader will allow strategies to emerge in a decentralized organization structure. Managers will meet regularly, both formally and informally, to discuss progress and changing trends; they will plan new courses of action and then try them out: a form of 'real-time planning'.

*When I was younger I always conceived of a room where all these [strategic] concepts were worked out for the whole company. Later I didn't find any such room. . . . The strategy [of the company] may not even exist in the mind of one man. I certainly don't know where it is written down. It is simply transmitted in the series of decisions made.* (James B Quinn, 1980)

Quinn argues that organizations test out relatively small changes and develop with this approach rather than go for major changes. An example would be Marks and Spencer testing a proposed new line in a selected and limited number of stores before deciding to launch it nationally. Lex Group (see Box 1.2) followed an incremental approach when it diversified into hotels, building and buying properties one by one rather than acquiring a chain of hotels.

An organization can use more than one means of bringing about strategic changes at any one time. During the 1980s, for example, Asda, the major food retailer, acquired, and later sold, the kitchen furniture group MFI. At the same time it was actively developing and pursuing growth strategies, involving opening new stores, re-designing and refurbishing existing stores, developing own-label goods, introducing more fresh foods and non-food items, using information technology and streamlining the distribution system.

Strategy, therefore, can result from a stream of decisions and information fed upwards from the lower management levels of the organization. Quinn contends that this is sensible, logical and positive:

*The most effective strategies of major enterprises tend to emerge step by step from an iterative process in which the organization probes the future, experiments and learns from a series of partial (incremental) commitments rather than through global formulations of total strategies. Good managers are aware of this process and they consciously intervene in it. They use it to improve the information available for decisions and to build the psychological identification essential to successful strategies. The process is both logical and incremental. Such logical incrementalism is not 'muddling' as most people understand that word. Properly managed it is a conscious, purposeful, proactive, executive practice.*

Teamworking and learning are at the heart of the adaptive and incremental modes. Managers must learn about new opportunities and threats; they should also learn from the successes and mistakes of other managers. Managers must be willing to take measured risks; for this to happen understandable mistakes and errors of judgement should not be sanctioned harshly.

Change is gradual and comes from experimentation; new strategies involve an element of trial and error. Success is very dependent upon communications. Managers must know of the opportunities and threats facing them; the organization must be able to synthesize all changes into a meaningful pattern, and spread learning and best practice.

Mintzberg (1989) argues that organizations should be structured and managed to ensure that formulators of strategies (managers whose decisions lead to strategic changes) have information, and that the implementers of strategies and changes have the appropriate degree of power to ensure that the desired changes are brought about.

It is quite normal to find all of these modes in evidence simultaneously in an organization, although there is likely to be one dominant mode. Moreover different managers in the same organization will not necessarily agree on the relative significance of each mode; their perceptions of what is actually happening will vary.

## The place of corporate planning today

Since the 1960s, a number of books has been written on the subject of corporate planning, where it is generally agreed that strategic change is the outcome of objective, systematic decision making which establishes objectives and then seeks and chooses ways of achieving them. As change is a planned activity, corporate planning is therefore prescriptive in its approach. It would be churlish to argue that formal planning has no role to play in strategic management but, quite simply, there is more to strategic management and strategic change than planning.

Planning activity will consider opportunities and threats (although this is not the only way that they should be spotted); it will allow a thorough evaluation of strengths and weaknesses; it will allow an assessment of where competitive advantage is or is not and how it might be achieved; and future scenarios can be tested. Planning can be used to help in deciding where the organization's scarce resources (e.g. future investment capital) should be concentrated; and it can be used to establish tactics (actions) for carrying out strategies.

There is a number of useful planning techniques and these will be considered in Chapter 11. However, the overall role and relative importance of planning remain a controversial and disputed issue. As mentioned by Mintzberg (1982), 'strategy need not always be a conscious and precise plan'.

Finally, it is quite plausible to argue that the outcome of planning need not be a plan. Rather than trying to produce a watertight document covering the next 10 years, planning, as an exercise, should concentrate on identifying and evaluating alternative courses of action for the business, so that more opportunities are created. Planning therefore increases awareness.

In this section the views of a number of contributors on strategy have been outlined. They can usefully be summarized as follows. Strategic management is concerned with:

- deciding the future direction and scope of the business, in line with perceived opportunities and threats. This will clearly require awareness and planning. The planning, however, may be more cerebral and visionary than detailed, formal and quantitative
- ensuring that the required resources are, or will be, available in order that the chosen strategies can be implemented
- ensuring that there is innovation and change. These changes can be in relation to corporate, competitive or functional strategies. Equally, innovation can take place throughout the

*Figure 1.8* Strategy creation.

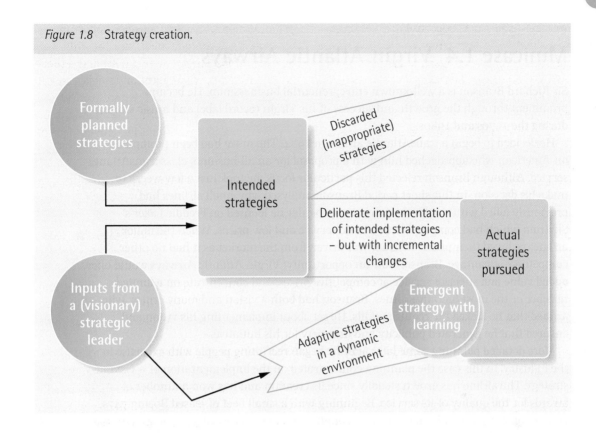

organization. If this is to happen then an appropriate organization structure and culture must be in place.

Figure 1.8 summarizes these ideas and Minicase 1.4 applies them to Virgin Atlantic Airways. Figure 1.8 indicates that intended strategies can be the outcome of both a formal planning process and visionary leadership. On implementation some of these intended strategies will be discarded: they turn out to be based on misjudgements, or changing circumstances make them less viable. Meanwhile, in this changing environment, the organization does two other things as a result of learning. First, it incrementally changes the intended strategies as they are implemented. Secondly, it introduces new adaptive strategies when fresh opportunities are spotted. Consequently, the actual strategies pursued will relate to, but differ from, the intended strategies.

## Mission, strategy, objectives and tactics

These four terms were all defined in Box 1.1 and they have either been introduced in brief or discussed in detail in this chapter. Figure 1.9 shows how they interrelate hierarchically, and looks at them in the context of intended and emergent strategy creation.

Strategies are means to ends. Where they are planned in some detail they will relate to specific objectives or targets. Both objectives and strategies set and pursued should help to achieve, or at least to pursue, the purpose or mission of the organization. Tactics and actions, carried out everywhere in the organization by various managers and other staff, represent on the one hand, the implementation of intended strategies and, on the other hand, new strategic ideas being tried out by empowered managers.

# Minicase 1.4  Virgin Atlantic Airways

Sir Richard Branson is a well-known entrepreneurial businessman. He became prominent through the growth and success of his Virgin record label and music stores during the 1970s and 1980s.

He decided to begin a transAtlantic airline in 1984. The move had been prompted by an American who approached him with a proposal for an all-business-class transAtlantic service. Although Branson rejected this particular focus, he took just a few weeks to make his decision. In this short period Branson analysed why small airlines had previously failed with similar ventures. In particular he focused on Freddie Laker's Skytrain which had competed with a basic service and low prices. When the major airlines reduced their prices Skytrain was driven from the market as it had no other competitive advantage. Branson saw an opportunity: Virgin Atlantic Airways would offer added value and superior service at competitive prices, and concentrate on a limited number of the most lucrative routes. Branson had both a vision and many critics, who argued that he lacked the requisite skills. He set about implementing his vision and ensured that he generated publicity and notoriety for his initiative.

More detailed planning came later after he began recruiting people with expertise in the industry. In this case the planning concentrated on the implementation of a visionary strategy. The airline has grown steadily since its creation and has won a number of awards for the quality of its service. Beginning with a small fleet of leased Boeing 747s, additional aircraft have been leased and bought, and new routes added. The growth has been in limited, incremental steps as Virgin Atlantic has learnt from experience in a very dynamic environment. The major carriers such as British Airways have clearly seen Virgin as a threat – but realistically only after Branson's early successes – and have been forced to respond. Simply, when Virgin broke into the transAtlantic market with its innovative new service, it took the existing carriers by surprise; this was competition from an unexpected source.

A successful holiday business has also been developed alongside the airline.

QUESTIONS: What are the similarities and differences between the Branson/Virgin Atlantic strategy and those of the low-price, no-frills airlines such as Southwest and EasyJet?

What routes has Branson added to his original transAtlantic services?

*Virgin Atlantic*  http://www.virgin-atlantic.com

*Figure 1.9* The strategy process.

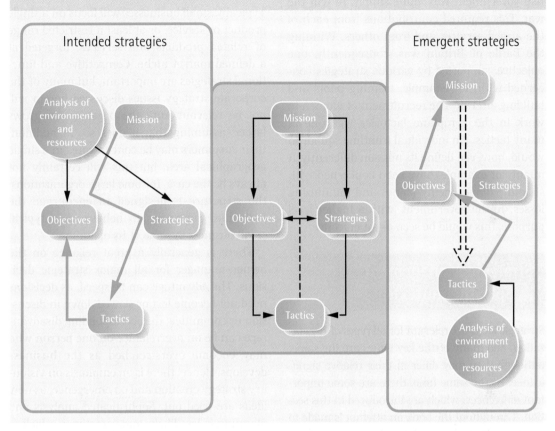

*Figure 1.9* The strategy process.

The left-hand section of Figure 1.9 highlights how, with intended strategies, the mission is used to establish objectives, which in turn lead to strategies and tactics. With emergent strategy – the right-hand section of the diagram – managers are expected to appreciate and support the broad purpose and direction of the organization, and it is a key role of the strategic leader to ensure that they actually do this. Within this context they are then empowered to decide upon, and try out, new strategic ideas. What they do determines the level of achievement and performance of the organization. In both cases environmental and resource considerations will guide decision making, but the information will be used by different people at different levels in the hierarchy.

With intended strategies, performance evaluation straightforwardly concerns the achievement (or not) of stated objectives with the strategies and tactics used. In the case of emergent strategy, performance evaluation is really an assessment of what has been achieved in the context of the mission.

Finally, it is important to recognize that specific issues and events will be perceived differently at different levels of the organizational hierarchy, partly because individual businesses in a diverse organization can – and often will – have their own mission statements. While they may differ, they should be complementary.

The subject of strategy has its origins in ancient warfare, and a more recent military example provides a useful illustration of these points. In World War II the mission of the British government was, quite simply, to win the war. This required contributions from each of the armed services and from others. Winning the Battle of Britain was, consequently, one objective, supported by various strategies concerned with, for example, training pilots and building aircraft. The recruitment of women to work in the aeroplane factories was one of many tactics. An individual frontline squadron would, however, define its mission differently. It might, for example, have been concerned with shooting down enemy planes and minimizing losses. To the government, with a higher level purpose, this would be seen as an objective.

## Strategic Management in Specific Contexts

Strategic ideas are relevant for all types of organization, and many of the key issues are the same, although they may differ in their relative significance. At the same time, there are some important differences, which are introduced in this section. Throughout the book an attempt is made to use examples and cases that reflect a range of different types and size of organization but, inevitably, large manufacturing and service businesses feature most prominently, largely because they are the organizations and brand names that most readers will recognize and relate to easily.

All men can see the tactics by which I conquer, but what none can see is the strategy out of which great victory is evolved.

*SunTzu, The Art of War, 400 BC*

Strategy is the evolution of the original guiding idea according to continually changing circumstance.

*Helmuth Moltke, Prussian General Chief of Staff, 1858–1888*

## Small businesses

Typically, small businesses will focus on a single product or service, or at least a restricted range of related products and services, targeted at a defined market niche. Competitive and functional strategies are important, but many of the corporate strategy issues discussed herein will not be relevant until the organization grows larger, assuming that it does so. In addition, their customers may be concentrated in a single geographical area, but this will certainly not always be the case. In some large organizations, the structure is designed to encourage the individual businesses to behave as a typical small business in some of its operations.

There is generally a great reliance on the owner–manager for all major strategic decisions. The advantage can be speed, as decisions need not become lost or slowed down in discussion or committee; the corresponding disadvantage can be an overreliance on one person who may become overstretched as the business develops. Hence, there is an emphasis on visionary strategy creation and on emergence, as new ideas are tried out. Sophisticated analysis and planning is less likely, and sometimes a lack of attention to detail can constitute another weakness.

The real challenge for small businesses is to develop and strengthen their resources once they start growing; if they fail they will lose their competitiveness. Some never possess any real competitive advantage in the first place and, while they may survive if they are run efficiently, they are unlikely to grow to any significant size.

Where a small business fails to grow it will always be dependent on the actions of others. Both its suppliers and customers could be larger and consequently more powerful. In this case it could be paying cash for its supplies and giving extended credit to its customers, resulting in cash-flow problems. It is also likely to be very reactive to competitor initiatives until it can become more prominent and proactive. The helpful publicity and visibility given to larger organizations may be withheld, even at a local level. High-quality managers and employees, who could fuel the growth, may not find a small, and perceptually inconsequential company, attractive to work for. Nevertheless, all companies start small: they are, after all, the seedbed for those successful entrepreneurs who create growth businesses.

The success, or lack of it, then, will be hugely dependent on the strategic leader, and his or her culture and style. The future will be dictated by their skill and also by their ability to acquire resources, particularly in terms of finance. A lack of capital can often be a real restraint to growth. Banks often demand security and collateral and venture capitalists often only become interested once the business has reached a certain size and proved itself. This traditional logic concerning small businesses, however, is being turned on its head in the case of many new Internet or 'dot.com' companies who are raising millions of pounds on the strength of a barely proven idea that appears to offer a golden opportunity. Financiers are taking risks that they have previously shunned because of the speed and growth of this sector and its inherent uncertainty. This point is developed in the cases featured in Minicase 2.1.

## Global companies

Here the emphasis is very much on corporate strategy: diversity, geographical scope and co-ordinating the countries where products are made with the countries where they are sold. Using low-cost labour factories in Eastern Europe and the Far East can prove controversial while still being an economic necessity. In addition, these are often very powerful companies whose annual turnover exceeds the gross national product (GNP) of many of the world's smaller countries. Nevertheless, issues of competitiveness and competitive advantage are as

relevant as they are for a small business. One key complication can be currency fluctuations when component supplies and finished goods are moved around the world.

The major dilemma for many global companies concerns their need to achieve global scale economies from concentrating production in large plants whilst not sacrificing their local identity and relevance in the various markets. To accomplish this they must stay close to their customers and markets, whose specific tastes and preferences may differ markedly, even though they are buying essentially the same product.

The organizational structure can be, and often is, just as important as the strategy. This, in turn, raises a number of important people issues. People may be switched from business to business and from country to country as part of their personal progression. This movement also helps the whole organization to transfer skills and knowledge and to learn good practices from different parts of the business.

Global corporations also need to develop expertise in financial management. Attractive development grants and packages will be available in certain countries and influence strategic developments. Interest rates are not the same around the world and consequently loans can be more attractive in certain countries and not in others. Moreover, tax rates vary and it can be very beneficial to be seen to be earning profits in low-tax countries instead of high-tax ones.

## Not–for–profit organizations

Organizations such as churches and charities clearly fit into this sector very well, but certain other profit-generating businesses, such as museums, zoos and local theatres, are relatively closely aligned. In the case of the latter examples, the profit objective is often designed to create a 'war chest' for future investment rather than to reward an owner or a group of investors. For this reason there are many common characteristics. Money may be perceived differently in not-for-profit organizations than in profit-seeking businesses, but there is still a need to create a positive cash flow. A charity, for example, can only spend on good causes if it can generate funds. For this reason, churches and charities can legitimately appear very commercial in their outlook, and this must be accepted alongside the cause that they are targeting.

These not-for-profit organizations need social entrepreneurs or strategic leaders who, in many ways, will be similar to those found in the profit-seeking sector. They will possess similar entrepreneurial and leadership qualities, but they will be driven by a cause, which attracts them to the particular organization and sector. This, in turn, guides the mission, purpose and culture. In addition, there is likely to be a greater reliance on voluntary helpers and possibly managers and others who readily accept salaries and wages below those that they might earn in the profit sector.

There are likely to be variations on the modes of strategy creation discussed herein. There is likely to be some committee structure, involving both salaried employees and unpaid volunteers, the latter often in senior roles. Decision making can be slow and political in nature, although clearly it does not have to be this way. However, strong and dominant leaders (either paid or unpaid) quite often emerge and are at the heart of strategy making. Because there is a need for accountability for the funds raised, planning systems are likely to be prominent.

## Public-sector organizations

In many countries around the world the composition of this sector has changed over recent years. Typically, essential service industries, such as telecommunications, gas, electricity, water, and air, bus and rail transport, have been privatized, often resulting in the creation of a number of complementary or even competing businesses. The outcome in each industry has been one or more private company, some of which have since merged or been acquired, sometimes by overseas parents. In the case of the UK this privatization programme has also included individual companies such as British Airports Authority (BAA), which manages several airports but is largely a retail organization. Outside direct government control, BAA has expanded overseas and now manages a number of other airports around the world.

In every case there is some form of regulation and government influence, as distinct from the direct government control of the past. The trend towards privatization has gathered momentum for many reasons, one factor in Europe being the stronger stance on government subsidies to individual industries by the European Commission. The key appears to lie in the effectiveness of the regulation, which must attempt to balance the needs of all key stakeholders: customers, employees and investors.

As a result, we now tend to think of local authorities and public health and emergency services as the archetypal public sector organizations. Clearly these are service businesses, and ones which will always have to choose and prioritize between different needs and stakeholders. In general, they will always be able to achieve more outcomes if they can acquire more resources. However, they remain largely dependent on central government for their resources and are therefore influenced by the political agenda of the day. Increasingly, some have greater involvement with the private sector than was the case in the past. The British National Health Service works alongside the private health-care sector and, although their roles and remits differ, the same consultants operate in both sectors. Many services in local communities were subjected to compulsory competitive tendering (CCT) and, as a result, have been outsourced to providers in the private, profit-seeking sector.

Decision making and style features some element of bureaucracy, in part because of the role of governing bodies, be they elected (local councillors) or appointed (e.g. NHS Trust Boards). As accountability has become increasingly public in recent years, analysis and planning will also be very prominent. Again, however, strong leaders can, and will, make an impact; and, as the public sector environment is no more stable than the one affecting commercial businesses, emergent strategy is also very important.

## Summary

Strategies are means to ends – they are the means through which organizations seek to achieve objectives and fulfil their mission or purpose.

All managers can be strategy makers because of their influence in both strategy creation and strategy implementation.

Strategic management is a process which embraces the strategies together with the themes of excellence in their implementation, creativity and innovation when they are changed and the effective and timely management of these changes.

There is evidence that strategic thinking, and hence strategic management, could be improved in many companies by:

- *segmenting* and *targeting* markets more crisply and definitively
- appreciating clearly what the *key success factors* are in the targeted markets and segments
- creating real *competitive advantage*
- out-thinking rivals.

There are three levels of strategy:

- *corporate* – the overall portfolio of businesses within an organization
- *competitive* – the search for, and maintenance of, competitive advantage in each and every business, product and/or service

- *functional* – the activities that deliver the competitive advantage.

These activities, products, services and businesses should not be analysed exclusively at an individual 'ring-fenced' level, but also in terms of the whole organization. Links should be forged wherever possible to generate *synergies*.

Strategies should not be thought of as having one single definition or perspective. Five have been discussed: visionary strategies, planned strategies and tactics, all of which address the future; present strategic positions, and patterns that have emerged with past decisions and strategies.

The strategic management process comprises three broad stages: analysis; creation and choice, and implementation. This three-stage approach can be linked to the popular and well-established concept of *strategic planning*.

Additional themes complement, but do not replace, strategic planning in the understanding of the realities of strategic management and strategic change, namely competitive advantage, emergent strategy creation, strategic competency, strategic leadership, and risk and crisis management.

There are three ways in which strategies are created: with visionary leadership, from a planning process, and adaptively and incrementally as new decisions are taken in real time.

Strategy and strategic management in different sectors, such as small and global businesses, the public sector and not-for-profit organizations, have many similarities, but there are clear differences, especially of emphasis.

## References

Beck, P, quoted in Lorenz, C (1987) Crusading for a clear strategy, *Financial Times*, 25 February.

Hamel, G and Prahalad, CK (1989) Strategic intent, *Harvard Business Review*, May–June.

Mathur, SS and Kenyon, A (1998) *Creating Value: Shaping Tomorrow's Business*, Butterworth-Heinemann.

Mintzberg, H, Ahlstrand, B and Lampel, J (1998) *Strategy Safari*, Prentice Hall.

Mintzberg, H, quoted in Lorenz, C (1982) Strategic doctrine under fire, *Financial Times*, 15 October. The themes are developed extensively in Quinn, JB, Mintzberg, H and James, RM (1987) *The Strategy Process*, Prentice-Hall.

Mintzberg, H (1989) *Mintzberg on Management*, Free Press.

Morrison, R and Lee, J (1979) From planning to clearer strategic thinking, *Financial Times*, 27 July.

Porter, ME (1980) *Competitive Strategy*, Free Press.

Porter, ME (1985) *Competitive Advantage*, Free Press.

Porter, ME (1996) What is strategy? *Harvard Business Review*, November–December.

Quinn, JB (1980) *Strategies for Change: Logical Incrementalism*, Irwin.

Stacey, RD (1993) *Strategic Management and Organizational Dynamics*, Pitman.

Whittington, R (1999) The 'how' is more important than the 'where', *Financial Times (Mastering Strategy Supplement)*, 25 October.

## Additional material on the website

Reference was made in the text to the paper *The Emergence of Strategic Management*. In addition to this paper there is one additional case on Rubbermaid which, like Marks and Spencer (Minicase 1.2) charts the progress of a successful business which, in part, lost its edge.

Test your knowledge of this chapter with our online quiz at http://www.thomsonlearning.co.uk

Explore Strategy and Strategic Management further at:

*The Financial Times*   http://www.news.ft.com

*Harvard Business Review*   http://www.hbsp.harvard.edu/products/hbr/index.html

*Management Today*   http://www.managementtoday.haynet.com/magazines/mantod

*Strategic Management Journal*   http://www.interscience.wiley.com/jpages/0143-2095

*Strategy and Business*   http://www.strategy-business.com

*The Strategic Management Society*   http://www.smsweb.org

*Strategic Planning Society*   http://www.sps.org/uk

## Questions and Research Assignments

### TEXT RELATED

1. What exactly is a strategy? What have you learned about different perspectives, levels and ways in which they are changed?

2. What are the key elements in the strategic management process?

3. How have Marks and Spencer sought to attain and maintain competitive advantage? What do you think their objectives might have been?

4. From your background knowledge, what might be the key success factors required for success in the airline business? How do you feel Virgin and EasyJet have embraced these? How important a factor is 'risk taking'?

## Internet and Library Project

Sainsbury's first became UK market leader for 'packaged groceries' in 1983, with some 16% market share. Tesco and the Co-op each had 14.5% and Asda 8%.

The company's shares continued to outperform the Financial Times Index of top shares throughout the 1980s, and an editorial in the Financial Times commented that Sainsbury's 'performance combines profitability, productivity and a sense of social purpose.'

However, there did not appear to be any 'grand strategy'.

> *We did not sit down in the early 70s and work out any corporate plan, or say that by a particular time we intended to be in a particular business, or to be of a particular size.*
>
> (Roy Griffiths, Managing Director)

Rather, Griffiths claimed, Sainsbury's had 'identified and obsessively pursued' opportunities that fitted the company's corporate values, the 'basics of the business'.

These were:
- selling quality-products at competitive (although not necessarily the cheapest) prices
- exacting quality-control standards
- extensive research into competitors and customers
- strict financial management
- tight control of suppliers
- planned staff involvement.

In recent years Tesco has overtaken Sainsbury to become the UK market leader. Why?

Try to identify the successful strategies pursued by Tesco and the comparative shortcomings in the Sainsbury strategy.

Can you identify any influence from changes in strategic leadership?

*Asda* http://www.asda.com
*J. Sainsbury plc* http://www.j-sainsbury.co.uk
*Sainsbury's* http://www.sainsbury.com
*Tesco* http://www.tesco.com

# 2

# The Strategic Management Process

Strategic Management

Key Strategic Concerns

The Strategic Challenge

*This chapter begins with an explanation of the strategic management process in the context of the framework upon which this book is structured. The framework is presented first as a series of issues and activities and then recrafted as a set of questions which, we can argue, organizations should be addressing all the time. This is followed by an introduction to a number of important strategic concepts which affect strategy creation and implementation in every organization, and which crop up in numerous places throughout the book. This part of the chapter thus constitutes a valuable reference section if readers need to recheck the meaning of key strategic concepts. The chapter concludes with an introduction to some of the important issues, dilemmas and challenges in strategy which affect many of the decisions that must be taken. It is the existence of these dilemmas that ensures there are no 'right answers' in the world of strategy.*

# Minicase 2.1 McDonald's

McDonald's, built by a visionary, the late Ray Kroc, has become a very successful international company, with outlets in nearly 120 countries. Its products are popular with large numbers of customers, and certainly not just children. In 1996, according to Interbrand consultants, McDonald's ousted Coca-Cola as the world's best-known brand.

Ray Kroc has been described by *Time Magazine* as 'one of the most influential builders of the twentieth century'. Few children refuse a McDonald's burger – and its golden arches logo symbolizes American enterprise. Kroc was a truly opportunistic and focused entrepreneur who built an organizational network of dedicated franchisees. Yet his entrepreneurial contribution began late in life and the McDonald's chain of hamburger restaurants was certainly not his own invention. Instead he saw – really he stumbled on – an opportunity where others missed the true potential for an idea. Once he had seen the opportunity he rigorously applied business acumen and techniques to focus on providing value for his customers. By standardizing his product and restaurants he was able to guarantee high and consistent quality at relatively low cost. Kroc was also wise enough to use the expertise that his franchisees were developing.

In 1955, at the age of 52, Ray Kroc completed 30 years as a salesman, mainly selling milkshake machines to various types of restaurant across America, including hamburger joints. His customers included the McDonald brothers who, having moved from New Hampshire to Hollywood but failing to make any headway in the movie business, had opened a small drive-through restaurant in San Bernadino, California. They offered a limited menu, paper plates and plastic cups, and guaranteed the food in 60 seconds. When their success drove them to buy eight milkshake machines, instead of the two their small size would logically suggest, Ray Kroc's interest was alerted and he set off to see the restaurant. Kroc's vision was for a national chain which could benefit from organization and business techniques. He bought out the McDonald brothers and set about building a global empire. After he officially retired from running the business, and until his death in 1984, Ray Kroc stayed on as President and visited two or three different restaurants every week. He saw himself as the 'company's conscience', checking standards against his QSCV vision – Quality food, fast and friendly service, clean restaurants and value for money.

By the late 1990s McDonald's had well over 20,000 restaurants worldwide; approximately 60% are in America. Up to 3000 new ones have been opened in a single year. The basic formula works as well in Moscow and Beijing as it does in the USA. Although the products available are broadly similar in the USA and Europe, menus are seen as flexible in other parts of the world. Japanese stores, for example, feature Teriyaki Burgers, sausage patties with teriyaki sauce. Half the stores are franchises; the rest are mainly joint ventures but some 2500 are company owned.

The growth and success in an industry where 'fast food is a by-word for low wages and an unskilled temporary workforce' is not accidental. It has been very carefully planned and managed, although McDonald's relies a lot on the people at the sharp end. Employees are often young; they work a closely prescribed system, operating internationally established rules and procedures for preparing, storing and selling food. Various incentive schemes are practised. Labour turnover is high, however, and consequently McDonald's has its critics as well as its supporters. Nevertheless, it is obvious that some competitors seek to emulate McDonald's in a number of ways: products, systems and employee attitudes.

*Our competitors can copy many of our secrets, but they cannot duplicate our pride, our enthusiasm and our dedication for this business.*

McDonald's is profitable because it is efficient and productive; and it stays ahead of its competitors by being innovative and looking for new opportunities.

A lot of the developments are planned and imaginative. McDonald's does not move into new countries without thorough investigation of the potential; the same is true for new locations. There are now McDonald's branches in American hospitals, military bases and zoos; worldwide they can be found in airport terminals, motorway service stations, supermarkets (Tesco), and on board cruise ships and Swiss trains.

McDonald's relies heavily on its suppliers for fresh food; again, arrangements are carefully planned, monitored and controlled. The in-store systems for cooking and running branches are very tight, to ensure that products and service standards are the same worldwide. New product development has utilized all of the group's resources. The Big Mac, which was introduced nationally in the USA in 1968, was the idea of a Pittsburgh franchisee who had seen a similar product elsewhere. The aim was to broaden the customer base and make McDonald's more adult orientated. The company allowed the franchisee to try the product in his restaurant in 1967, although there was some initial resistance amongst executives who wished to retain a narrow product line, and it proved highly successful.

Egg McMuffins in the early 1970s were a response to a perceived opportunity – a breakfast menu and earlier opening times. Previously the restaurants opened at 11.00 am. Although the opportunity was appreciated the development of the product took place over 4 years, and the final launch version was created by a Santa Barbara franchisee who had to invent a new cooking utensil.

When Chicken McNuggets were launched in 1982 it was the first time that small boneless pieces of chicken had been mass produced. The difficult development of the product was carried out in conjunction with a supplier and there was immediate competitive advantage. The product was not readily copied. From being essentially a hamburger chain McDonald's quickly became number 2 to Kentucky Fried Chicken for fast-food chicken meals.

McDonald's continually tries out new menus, such as pizzas, in order to extend its share of the overall fast-food market, but for many years it avoided any diversification, nor did it offer any different 'food concept'. To enhance its image of good value, and to compete in a very dynamic industry, McDonald's offers 'extra-value meals', special combinations at low prices. There is innovation and the ability to create and adapt strategies to capitalize on opportunities.

In addition, McDonald's is a 'penny profit' business. It takes hard work and attention to detail to be financially successful. Store managers must do two things well: control costs and increase sales. Increased sales come from the products, certainly, but also from service. Cost control is vital, but it must not be achieved by compromising product quality, customer service or restaurant appearance. Instead, it requires a focus on productivity and attention to detail. Success with these strategies has been achieved partly through serious attempts to share learning and best practice throughout the global network.

The company is an industry leader and contends there are six main reasons behind this:

- Visibility: to this end substantial resources are devoted to marketing. The golden arches symbol is instantly recognizable.
- Ownership or control of real-estate sites: McDonald's argues that this factor differentiates it from its competitors who lease more.
- Its commitment to franchising and supplier partnerships.
- It is worldwide, with restaurants in some 118 countries, and uses local managers and employees.
- The structure is very decentralized but lines of responsibility and accountability are clear.
- It is a growth company.

By the mid 1990s, the company held 40% of the US market for its products, and yet its burgers were not coming out as superior to Wendy's and Burger King in taste tests. In addition, a special promotion in America, based around burgers for 55 cents each, had not proved successful because of the conditions attached to the offer. A new spicier – and premium price – burger for adults, the Arch Deluxe, had not taken off. New restaurants in the USA were beginning to take sales away from existing ones, rather than generating new business. Established franchisees were hardly delighted! A leading franchisee pressure group expressed the view that the entrepreneurial drive of founder Ray Kroc (who died in 1984) had been lost and replaced by a non-entrepreneurial bureaucracy. This change of culture was one reason why McDonald's recently pursued a libel action in the UK against two environmentalists: a case where McDonald's won the legal argument but lost the accompanying public-relations battle.

After a period of criticism and disappointing results McDonald's has, however, fought back courageously. With franchisees paying half the costs, new computerized kitchen equipment has been systematically installed in its 25,000 restaurants, allowing fast cooking to order. Ready-to-serve meals no longer have to stand for a few minutes on heated trays. In addition, McDonald's has begun to experiment with new low-risk opportunities for its competencies in supply-chain management, franchising, promotion and merchandising by acquiring new restaurant chains. Included are a group of 18 Mexican restaurants in Colorado, 143 pizza outlets in Ohio, a chain of 23 Aroma coffee shops in London and the Boston Market chain of chicken restaurants. The US operations have been split into five independent geographical regions.

Ray Kroc has been dead for over 15 years but his legacy lives on in a brand name that is recognized and revered around the world.

QUESTIONS: How does McDonald's create value for its customers?
What are its important competencies and capabilities?
To what extent do you think issues of strategic leadership and culture have influenced its growth and prosperity?

*McDonald's*   http://www.mcdonalds.com

## Strategic Management

Addressing how well an organization is doing involves a number of themes. If the organization is meeting the needs and expectations of its stakeholders, and achieving its objectives, then arguably it is successful. When it does not meet objectives and expectations, then it is failing. Good strategic awareness involves a clear appreciation of events and trends in the external environment, and the overall competitive situation. Companies should monitor and benchmark competitors to ensure that they create and sustain some form of competitive edge.

From this awareness should come new strategies. Ideas must be generated and evaluated, and this process is multistranded as it is likely to be different at the corporate and competitive strategy levels. We must understand how competitive advantage can be created and sustained for each business or activity – through a variety of functional strategies and opportunities for adding customer value – and how each business must add value for the organization if the portfolio of activities is to generate beneficial synergies.

The creation and implementation of strategy are both linked irrevocably to the structure of the organization and the way in which it operates in practice.

There is a variety of ways in which the process of strategic change can be managed. No two organizations are completely alike in their behaviour and there is no 'single best way' of managing strategic change. What is essential is that the processes are co-ordinated and managed, and this requires sound monitoring systems, and the necessary information to sustain these systems.

Many of these points can be seen clearly in Minicase 2.1 on McDonald's, which shows how strategic competencies and capabilities have been developed and exploited to create value for customers. This value has provided a competitive edge and advantage which has been sustained with changes.

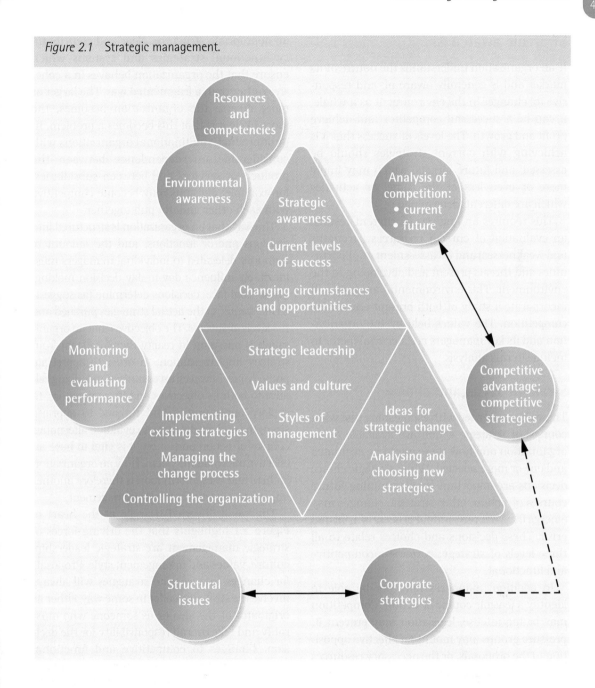

*Figure 2.1*   Strategic management.

The outer (full) triangle in Figure 2.1 provides a model of the strategic management process based on three areas of decision: strategic analysis (or strategic awareness), strategic ideas and choice, and strategy implementation, which should be seen as interrelated and linked to a monitoring and information system. However, the process of strategic management should not be thought of as having a linear form exclusively.

## Strategic awareness

If an organization understands the nature of its market and is generally aware of, and responsive to, changes in the environment as a whole, it can be a successful competitor and achieve profit and growth. The levels of success that it is achieving with current strategies should be assessed, and future targets, which may imply more or even less of the same, or activities which are different, determined.

This requires an analysis of current results, an evaluation of current resources (strengths and weaknesses) and an assessment of opportunities and threats present and developing in the environment. This environmental analysis will incorporate a study of both present and future competition. The values held by the organization and its key managers are a crucial factor to include in this analysis.

## Strategic ideas and choice

These are concerned with establishing just what courses of strategic action are available to an organization and how these might be evaluated and one or more selected. While strategic choice decisions are important for determining future courses of action, other strategic changes may emerge from a more gradual process of trial and error. These decisions and choices relate to all three levels of strategy: corporate, competitive and functional.

In addition, managers may not be able to identify a feasible course of action. Competition may be too intense, legislation may prevent it, pressure groups may mount an effective opposition to the proposals, or the necessary resources may not be available. It would then be necessary for the organization to reappraise its target objectives and set new ones.

## Strategy implementation

A strategy is only useful when it has been implemented, and hence the organization must have an appropriate structure, clear and contributory functional strategies and systems which ensure that the organization behaves in a cohesive rather than a fragmented way. The larger or more diverse the organization becomes, the more likely it is that this becomes a problem. In multiproduct, multinational organizations with considerable interdependence between the products or services and between subsidiaries, for example, divisions may become competitive with each other and not pull together.

The way that an organization is structured into divisions and/or functions, and the amount of authority delegated to individual managers must inevitably influence day-to-day decision making. These 'coal-face' decisions determine (as suggested in Chapter 1) the actual strategies pursued and the levels of success. The objectives that an organization is pursuing in reality therefore stem from strategy implementation. In order to appreciate properly just how well an organization is doing relative to both its objectives and its competitors, to explore opportunities and threats, to appraise strengths and weaknesses, to evaluate alternative courses of action and so on, it is vital to have an effective information system. How an organization gathers and uses information is therefore another important aspect of strategic management.

The small, inverted triangle at the heart of Figure 2.1 highlights that the driving forces of strategic management are strategic leadership, culture, values and management style. Proposals for changes to corporate strategies will always involve the strategic leader in some way, either as originator of the idea or as someone who must ratify and take overall responsibility for the decision. Changes to competitive and functional strategies will reflect the structure of the organization and styles of managing it. These again stem from choices made by the strategic leader and the prevailing culture that the leader drives or accepts. Change proposals at every level should take account of the existing culture and values, as they will affect the implementation of new strategies, and consequently their feasibility.

Figure 2.2 A strategy framework based on a series of questions.

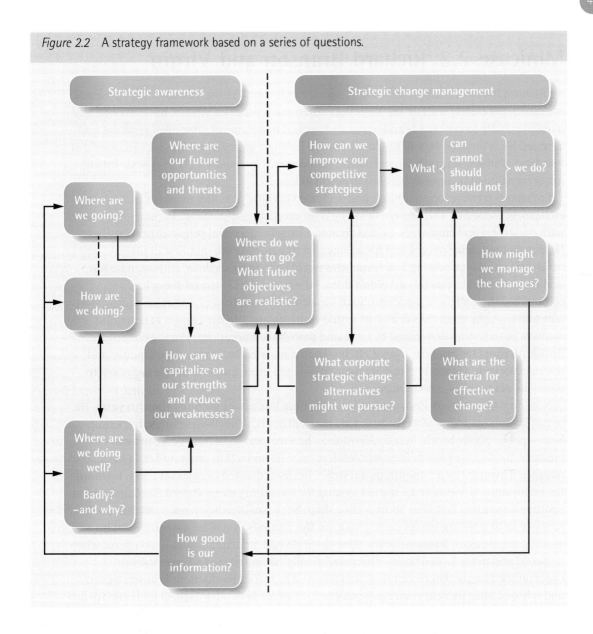

## Strategic management: awareness and change

*The most important management technique is to understand the real situation in which you are operating.*

(Sir Paul Girolami, Chairman, Glaxo, 1987)

*The best way to predict the future is to invent it.*

(John Sculley, when Chairman, Apple Computers)

Figure 2.2, which is used at the beginning of each part of this book to summarize the content and explain how the text and subject are developing, absorbs the themes of 'ideas for change' and 'implementation' from Figure 2.1 into a single

# Minicase 2.2  Richard Branson and Virgin

Sir Richard Branson is unquestionably a legend in his own lifetime. His name and presence are associated closely with all the Virgin activities and businesses, and he has demonstrated a unique ability to exploit a brand name and apply it to a range of diversified products and services. He *is* Virgin – so, will he leave a lasting business legacy like Ray Kroc (McDonald's) has done? Can this diverse business outlive its founder? Or would Virgin be split up into its many constituent businesses without Branson to lead it?

Branson is creative, opportunistic and dedicated to those activities in which he engages. Possessed of a strong ego drive, he is an excellent self-publicist. Popular with customers and employees, he has created a hugely successful people-driven business. His determination to succeed and his willingness to take risks are manifest in his trans-Atlantic power boating and round-the-world ballooning exploits. Although he has said that he 'wouldn't do this if I didn't think I'd survive', the *Financial Times* has commented that 'all those associated with Mr. Branson have to accept that he is an adventurer . . . he takes risks few of us would contemplate'. He has chosen to enter and compete in industries dominated by large and powerful corporations. Having challenged British Airways, for example, Coca-Cola has been a more recent target. Significantly, and not unexpectedly, his name comes up frequently when other business people are asked to name the person they most admire.

Now over 50 years old, Branson has been running businesses for more than 30 years. He began *Student* magazine when he was a 16-year-old public schoolboy, selling advertising from a public phone booth. Ever opportunistic, he incorporated a mail-order record business, buying the records from wholesalers once he had a firm order and cash in advance. Thwarted by a 2-month postal strike, Branson decided to enter retailing. Realizing the importance of location, he started looking for something along Oxford Street in London. Spotting an unused first floor above a shoe shop, he persuaded the owner to let him use it rent free until a paying tenant came along, on the grounds that if he was successful he would generate extra business for the shoe shop! He had a queue stretching 100 yards when it opened and never looked back – characteristically, he had turned a threat into an opportunity. The London record shop was followed by record production: Branson signed and released Mike Oldfield's extremely successful *Tubular Bells* after Oldfield had been turned down by all of the leading record companies. Branson was always an astute and visionary businessman, carefully recruiting people with the necessary expertise to manage the detail of his various enterprises. His main skill has been in networking, finding opportunities and securing the resources necessary for their exploitation. In this he has had to show courage and flexibility.

Virgin Atlantic Airways was started after an American businessman suggested the idea of an all-business-class transAtlantic airline. Branson rejected this particular strategy but was hooked on the idea. Initially he minimized the risk by leasing everything, and he was able to compete with the larger airlines by offering a perceived higher level of service at attractive prices. Over many years he has successfully marketed a range of products and services by systematically applying the Virgin brand name. The products and services may have been diversified – holidays, consumer products such as Virgin Vodka and Virgin Cola, cinemas, a radio station, financial services and Virgin Railways are examples – but the customer-focused brand image has remained constant.

Virgin was floated in 1986 but later reprivatized; Branson had been uncomfortable with the accountability expectations of institutional shareholders. Since then he has used joint ventures, minority partners and divestments (such as the sales of his music business and record shops) to raise money for new ventures and changes of direction. In 1999 Branson sold a 49% stake in the airline to Singapore Airlines, partly to strengthen its competitiveness, but also to raise money for investment in further new ventures. Describing itself as a 'branded venture capital company', Virgin had already created over 200 businesses; and Branson had decided to target electronic commerce and the Internet, believing that a vast range of products and services could be sold this way under the Virgin umbrella. Another new venture, wine, was to be included.

Branson's business philosophy is built around quality products and services, value for money, innovation and an element of fun. 'I never let accountants get in the way of business. You only live once and you might as well have a fun time while you're living.' By focusing on customers and service he has frequently been able to add value where larger competitors have developed a degree of complacency. 'The challenge of learning and trying to do something better than in the past is irresistible.' Branson always realized that this would be impossible without the appropriate people and created an organization with a devolved and informal culture. Business ideas can, and do, come from anywhere in Virgin. Employees with ideas that Branson likes will be given encouragement and development capital. Once a venture reaches a certain size it is freed to operate as an independent business within the Virgin Group, and the intrapreneur retains an equity stake. Branson runs Virgin from a large house in London's Holland Park, having outgrown the canal narrow boat that he used for many years. There has never been a traditional head office infrastructure.

QUESTIONS: What are Richard Branson's strengths and limitations as a strategic leader? How have they been manifested as Virgin has developed? Can this diverse business outlive its founder? Or would Virgin be split up into its many constituent businesses without Branson to lead it?

*Virgin Group*  http://www.virgin.com

theme of 'strategic change management', and represents the constituent elements as a set of 12 questions concerning strategic awareness and strategic change.

Moving from left to right, the questions follow a logical sequence. If an organization needs to take stock of just where it is placed at the moment, evaluate emerging opportunities and threats before clarifying a set of objectives for which strategies, both corporate and competitive, can be evaluated, selected and implemented, then the model can be used in a sequential, and possibly iterative, way. It will be seen that information (the bottom box) implies monitoring and continuity.

However, these questions can also be thought of as a set of important issues that managers everywhere in the organization should be addressing all the time in a turbulent environment. Nevertheless, they still need to be presented in a clear framework to ensure that any issues emerging can be placed in context, and any proposed changes assessed for their impact on other issues.

If managers seek answers to these questions continuously, and make and carry out appropriate strategic decisions, they will improve the performance and effectiveness of their organization by:

- generating increased strategic awareness
- ensuring that functional managers appreciate the strategic environment and the implications of decisions concerning individual products, services and markets; and
- making decisions about the need for, and appropriateness of, particular change opportunities.

The Margaret Brooke case study on the website provides an annotated application of the 12 questions in Figure 2.2.

## Key Strategic Concerns

The purpose of this section is to introduce, outline and explain a number of key terms, themes and concepts which run through the book and help our understanding of strategy and strategic management. They will all be taken up and developed in greater detail at various points in the text.

## Strategic leadership

It has been pointed out that a major aim of this book is to encourage readers to be more strategically aware. Long-term strategic success requires that the efforts of managers are co-ordinated. This is the task of the chief executive or managing director of the whole organization and in turn of general managers of subsidiaries or divisions in the case of large complex organizations. For simplicity in this book the term *strategic leader* is used to refer to this role.

The role is analogous to that of the captain of a ship. In a sailing race, for example, the captain must sail the ship possibly in uncertain or dangerous waters, with one or more clear goals in sight. The chosen strategy or strategies will be decided upon in the light of these goals, and the risks of any actions will be assessed. Nevertheless the captain's success will depend on the crew. It is essential that the crew acts in a co-ordinated way, and therefore it is crucial that the strategies are communicated and understood.

Lee Iacocca, who became chairman of the Chrysler Corporation in the USA in the early 1980s and succeeded in turning it round, provides a useful example. Chrysler, faced with competition from General Motors, Ford and Japan, was nearly bankrupt and had lost its way. Iacocca changed some of his crew, but essentially his success lay in persuading his managers to think about how to succeed in the 1980s and to forget the strategies of the 1960s and 1970s. Cars were redesigned, marketing was improved, labour costs were lowered, productivity and quality were improved and government support was obtained. Chrysler recovered.

The strategic leader must build and lead a team of managers, and establish the goals or objectives. Styles will vary enormously, as will the scope of the objectives. Some leaders will be autocratic, others entrepreneurial. Some, arguably like Henry Ford of Ford Motor Company and Ray Kroc who started McDonald's, will be visionaries, whereas others will set more modest goals. Others, such as Richard Branson (Minicase 2.2) are not only idiosyncratic role models, they *are* their organization. The person and the business cannot be realistically separated.

The leader and his or her managers should be clear about where the organization is going, where they want to go and how they are going to get there. This requires an appreciation of the environment and an understanding of the organization's resources.

## Culture and values

Schein (1985) defines culture as 'the deeper level of basic assumptions and beliefs that are shared by members of an organization, that operate unconsciously, and that define in a basic "taken for granted" fashion an organization's view of itself and its environment'.

Culture is 'a pattern of basic assumptions that works well enough to be considered valid, and therefore is taught to new [organization] members as the correct way to perceive, think and feel in relation to problems of external adaptation and internal integration. ... [it is] learned, evolves with new experiences, and can be changed if one understands the dynamics of the learning process'.

In the simplest terms it is the way that organizational members behave and the values that are important to them and it dictates the way that decisions are made, the objectives of the organization, the type of competitive advantage sought, the organization structure and systems of management, functional strategies and policies, attitudes towards managing people and information systems. Many of these are inter-related.

In the late 1980s, Woolworth's (the high-street retailer which is now part of the Kingfisher Group) identified that customer service, when compared with their main rivals, was a relative weakness and a major contributor to their disappointing performance. People, they concluded, are a major strategic resource, and they reflect the values of the organization. In common with many other service organizations, Woolworth's introduced a customer-care training programme entitled 'Excellence', and linked it to staff rewards. There have been two achievements: customer perception of staff helpfulness increased, and there were immediate financial gains.

For these reasons, styles of corporate decision making, leadership and values are a central driving force in the model in Figure 2.1. They are always important, and they are not easily changed without the appointment of a new chief executive.

## Environmental fit and stakeholder satisfaction

Several authors have defined strategy in terms of the relationship between an organization and its environment. One such definition is:

*The positioning and relating of the firm/organization to its environment in a way which will assure its continued success and make it secure from surprises.* (Ansoff, 1984)

Figure 2.3 considers the organization in the context of its environment. Influenced by the strategic leader, and in the context of an ideally clear vision and direction, the organization draws its resources (employees, managers, plant, supplies, finance, etc.) from a competitive business environment. It has to compete with other firms for labour, supplies, loans, etc., and it oper-

*Figure 2.3* The strategic perspective.

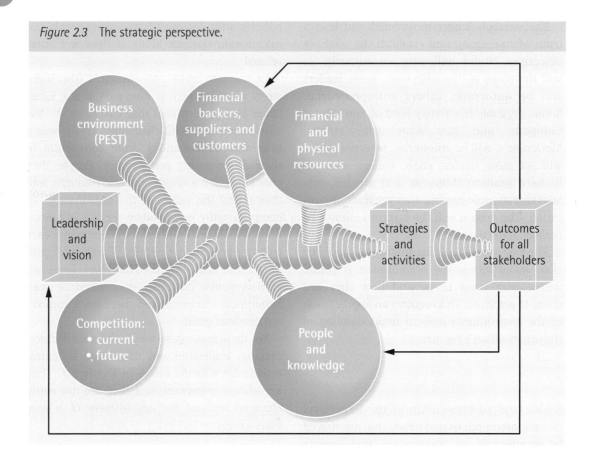

ates in a network which includes its suppliers and financial backers, with whom one would expect it to have strong and robust relationships. With strategies and activities, it must then use these inputs in some organized way to produce products and services which can be marketed effectively and, where appropriate, profitably – thus generating outcomes which satisfy all key stakeholders. It must invariably succeed in a competitive marketplace. As well as appreciating market demand and the strengths, weaknesses and strategies of its competitors, it must respond to fundamental changes in society and the economy. Over time people's tastes change, their discretionary purchasing power rises and falls, luxuries can become necessities and previously popular products

can become unfashionable. The economy is not static, and it is strongly affected by government policy. Whilst some companies influence government policy, many do not. A PEST (political, economic, social and technical) analysis can provide a straightforward and useful framework for analysing the external environment (see Chapter 7).

Therefore, strategic management involves the following:

• a clear awareness of environmental forces and the ways in which they are changing
• an appreciation of potential and future threats and opportunities
• decisions on appropriate products and services for clearly defined markets

- the effective management of resources to develop and produce these products for the market, achieving the right quality for the right price at the right time
- appreciating how key strategic resources might be redeployed and exploited to create new market opportunities.

Strategic management, then, is effective when resources match stakeholder needs and expectations and change to maintain a fit in a turbulent environment. As we have seen, the external environment consists of suppliers, distributors and customers as well as bankers and other financial institutions and shareholders. It also includes competitors and sometimes the government. These stakeholders all expect something from a business in return for their support. If organizations are to be successful – and in many cases, profitable – they have to meet the needs and expectations of all their external stakeholders. It is also essential that the interests, needs and expectations of internal stakeholders, the employees, are not overlooked; after all, it is these employees who create the outcomes that satisfy external stakeholders. The relative demands of all the stakeholders determine what it is that a business must do well, and invariably their different requirements imply some difficult choices and trade-offs.

Innovation is an important element in maintaining fit as environmental forces and competitor strategies change. An innovative organization fosters learning which leads to continuous, managed change to products, services and processes. In turn, this demands an organization-wide commitment to improvement and change, together with the ability and willingness of managers to spot and seize change opportunities, factors again dependent upon leadership and cultural issues. Effective innovation is thus about people and the exploitation of the organization's knowledge and intelligence.

## Strategic positioning

A straightforward, popular and well-known technique, a SWOT (strengths, weaknesses, opportunities, threats) analysis, implies that an organization's resources (which constitute its strengths and weaknesses) should match the demands and pressures from its external environment (manifest as a set of opportunities and threats) as effectively as possible and, with change, stay matched in dynamic and turbulent times. The overlap of products and services (the outcome of the use of the organization's resources) with market needs is shown as strategic fit in Figure 2.4.

Here we can see illustrated two different, but complementary, approaches to strategy creation and strategic change. Market-driven strategy (or opportunity-driven strategy) reflects the adoption of the marketing concept, and implies that strategies are designed – and resources developed and deployed – with customer and consumer needs in mind. Carefully and creatively defining the industry or industries in which an organization competes can influence its perspective on the products and services it supplies. Marketing students will always remember that railway companies are in the transportation business! The approach is market-pull, and the value of a distinct competitive advantage is clearly synonymous with this approach. It should, however, never be forgotten that different sectors of the same industry require different competencies, and that the demands of creating new competencies may be readily underestimated. Minicase 1.3 (in the previous chapter) invited you to consider whether the competencies that P&O needed to run its ferries effectively were the same as those required in the cruise industry.

Although it is convenient to see resources as organizational strengths and weaknesses (which they very clearly are) and the environment as the source of opportunities and threats,

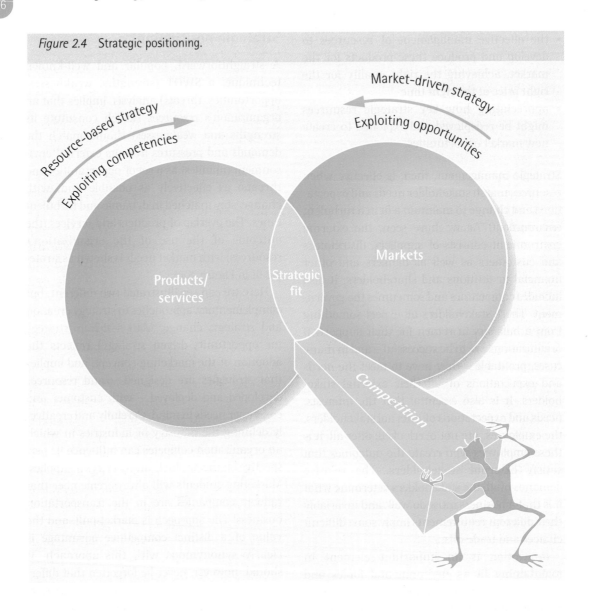

*Figure 2.4* Strategic positioning.

this is too simplistic. Resources can also constitute both opportunities and strengths. Resource-based strategy implies that the organization clarifies its core strategic competencies and capabilities and seeks to exploit these by finding new market opportunities where they can be used to create new values and competitive advantage. The assumption is that the organization can mould and develop its market with innovatory new ideas, sometimes changing the

rules of competition in an industry. This can imply the creation of new customer preferences and perspectives in the process.

Resources which are central to an organization's success can be a threat if they could be lost. Particular people can be a major asset, and a key reason for organizational success, and people can be lost. Although rare, one reality is that they could die, but more realistically they could leave and join a competitor. Obvious instances are professional sport and restaurant chefs. Some football clubs lose star players to rivals, sometimes for a transfer fee, sometimes when they are out of contract. Although this can affect the playing fortunes of the club, it is unlikely that fans will follow them. Loyalty goes too deep. The same cannot be said of chefs, however. Top-quality chefs can be the reason customers frequent a particular restaurant, and if they move, customers may well go with them.

All the time competitors will be attempting to accomplish the same ends. Hence, while a company is trying to create a stronger fit between itself and its customers, its competitors will be attempting to force them apart by offering something superior which draws customers away and destroys fit. Moreover, emerging opportunities can attract competitors with different backgrounds and motives. Developments in computer software and hardware (high-quality monitors, scanners and printers) have opened up an opportunity for digital cameras. Kodak were interested because of their dependency on the photographic industry and the potential long-term threat to film-based photography. Canon and Hewlett-Packard were both interested as they could see a new opportunity for exploiting technological competencies that they already possessed. The challenge for each rival was quite different.

It is now appropriate to look further at market needs as key success factors for an organization, and at resources in the context of competency and capability. From that the concept of added value can be explored. It is this value that provides strategic fit and competitive advantage.

## Key success factors

A company will have to produce to high and consistent quality levels and meet delivery promises to customers. Delivery times have been reducing gradually in very competitive industries. Suppliers and subcontractors expect regular orders and accurate forecasting when very quick deliveries are demanded from them. Without such support just-in-time production systems are impractical. Just-in-time systems rely on regular and reliable deliveries from suppliers in order to maintain constant production without the need for high parts inventories.

Companies will try to minimize their stockholding because this helps both cash flow and costs. Conglomerate subsidiaries will have to generate a positive cash flow in order to meet the financial expectations of the parent company who, in effect, act as its bankers. Costs have to be controlled so that companies remain price competitive, although low prices are not always a marketing weapon.

These stakeholder requirements represent *key success factors*, those things that an organization must do well if it is to be an effective competitor and thrive. In addition, many companies have to be innovative and improve both their product range and their customer service if they are to remain a leading competitor in a changing industry.

Some key success factors will be industry and sector specific. For example, successful consumer goods manufacturers will need skills in brand management. Charities need skills in fund raising and public relations. There is intense competition between charities for donations, and consequently they must be run as businesses. They can only spend what they can raise. It is also essential that they use their money appropriately, are seen to be doing so and are recognized for their efforts. The differing demands of fund raising and aid provision lead to complex cultures and organizations.

BUPA, a private medical organization based in the UK, has a similar dilemma. Typical of such organizations around the world, the business comprises two parts: insurance, with a strong commercial culture and orientation, and hospitals, which are naturally more of a caring community.

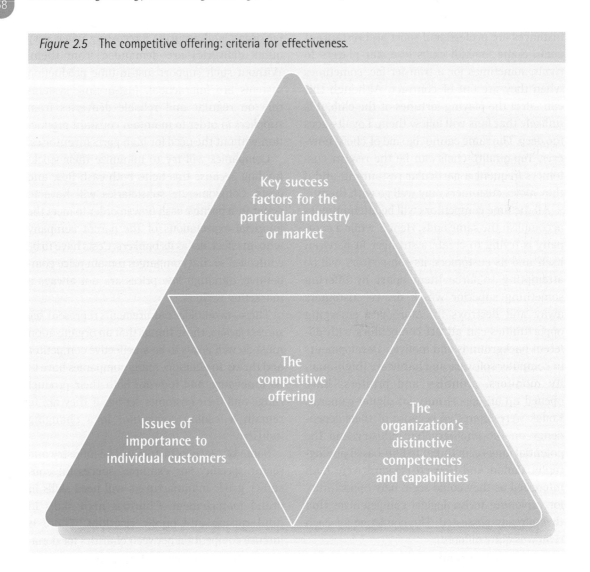

*Figure 2.5*   The competitive offering: criteria for effectiveness.

Resources must be managed with stakeholder needs in mind. Consequently, it is important that everyone in the organization recognizes and is committed to meeting key success factors, and is additionally responsive to change pressures in a dynamic and competitive environment. Without this commitment companies will be unable to sustain a match with the environment as it changes.

Figure 2.5 illustrates that if organizations are to satisfy their stakeholders, especially their customers, while outperforming their rivals, their competitive offering should comprise:

- the ability to meet the recognized key success factors for the relevant industry or market
- distinctive competencies and capabilities which yield some form of competitive advantage, and
- the ability and willingness to deploy these competencies and capabilities to satisfy the special requirements of individual customers, for which a premium price can often be charged. Hall (1992) suggests using the term 'customerizing' instead of marketing to reflect

the importance of customers as individuals rather than as a generic group who constitute a market.

## Core competencies

In order to meet their key success factors organizations must develop core competencies (Prahalad and Hamel, 1990). These are distinctive skills which yield competitive advantage, and ideally they:

- provide access to important market areas or segments
- make a significant contribution to the perceived customer benefits of the product or service
- prove difficult for competitors to imitate.

Once developed they should be exploited as, for example, Honda have exploited their skills at engine design and technology. Core competencies must, however, be flexible and responsive to changing customer demands and expectations. Canon have developed core competencies in precision mechanics, fibre optics and microelectronics, and these are spread across a range of products, including cameras, calculators, printers and photocopiers. There is constant product innovation.

Successful products and services, then, are the manifestation of important, underlying core competencies; and the true competition between organizations is at this competency level.

Prahalad and Hamel (1990) acknowledge that there are three strands to core competency:

- technologies
- processes (or capabilities) and
- strategic architecture.

Different competitors in the same industry may well build their success by emphasizing different key competencies. While the particular expertise may be different, they all need to be competent in a number of key activities, the key success

factors. In the global oil industry, for example, Exxon has long been renowned for its financial expertise, crucial when huge speculative and high-risk investments are required for exploration and developing new fields. In contrast, British Petroleum (BP) has historically relied heavily on its exploration skills. It was BP who developed the huge Forties Field in the North Sea and the fields off the hostile North Coast of Alaska, aided by the imaginative trans-Alaska pipeline. Royal Dutch Shell, a joint Anglo-Dutch company with two head offices in the UK and The Netherlands, has developed a valuable competency in managing a decentralized and diversified global business. Mobil's outstanding competency was in the related field of lubricants produced from the oil. Later in the book (Chapter 15) we will look at how the oil industry has been consolidating in recent years as the industry environment has become more demanding.

## Strategic capabilities

Stalk *et al.* (1992) argue that strategic success is based on capabilities – processes that enable the company to be an effective competitor. Distribution networks that achieve both high service levels (effectiveness) and low costs (efficiency) would be an example. Typically these processes will cut across whole organizations, rather than be product specific, and they will rely heavily on information systems and technology. In many respects Stalk's capabilities are the processes embedded in Hamel and Prahalad's core competencies. However, this author thinks that a valuable distinction can be made between *competencies* largely rooted in technologies and process-based *capabilities*. Although delivering similar outcomes, conceptually they are very different.

Retailers such as Boots in the UK (which has encompassed high-street department stores, specialist pharmacies, optical retailing, Halfords car products and service bays, Fads, Homestyle and Do-It-All DIY at various times) operate a number of different retail formats, capitalizing on their expertise in supply-chain, information and service management.

Hamel and Prahalad (1993) developed these ideas further when they argued that understanding processes should generate intelligence that can be used to create added or greater value from resources, in order to strengthen or enhance competitiveness. They refer to this as stretching resources. The ability to stretch resources is very dependent on strategic architecture, which is discussed next.

Kay (1993) further stresses that, to be beneficial, both core competencies and strategic capabilities must be capable of exploitation and be *appropriable*. In other words, the firm must be able to realize the benefits of the competencies and capabilities for the company itself, rather than the main beneficiaries being its suppliers, customers or competitors.

## Strategic architecture competencies

Strategic success requires:

- the organization to behave in a co-ordinated, synergy-creating manner, integrating functions and businesses
- the value-adding network (links between manufacturers, retailers, suppliers and intermediate distributors) to be managed as an effective, integrated, system.

Kay (1993) refers to the ability to achieve these demands as strategic architecture. The ability to build and control a successful architecture is facilitated by strong technological competency and effective functional process competencies.

Honda is renowned for its expertise in engine design and technology. However, its success as an international company has also been dependent on its ability to establish an effective distribution (dealer) network for all of its products. This has been enhanced by sound, information

technology (IT)-supported, communications and control systems. As another example, Marks and Spencer's functional competencies and brand technology create both an image and a capability which enable it to trade in clothes, foods, cosmetics, household furnishings and credit. These competencies also bestow on the company the power to demand and obtain from its suppliers worldwide both a strict adherence to Marks' technological specifications and very keen prices.

The important themes in architecture are:

- internally: 'systemic thinking', which leads to synergy from the fostering of interdependencies between people, functions and divisions in organizations; and
- externally: the establishment of linkages or even alliances between organizations at different stages of the added value chain.

Successful internal architecture requires that managers think 'organizationally' rather than put themselves first or promote their particular part of the organization to the detriment of other parts. Synergy from internal architecture also depends on the ability of the divisions or businesses in a conglomerate to support each other, transferring skills, competencies and capabilities, and sometimes sharing common resources. This, in turn, is partially dependent on the ability of the organization to learn, and share learning. It is also affected by the actual portfolio of businesses managed by a corporation. Goold *et al.* (1994) use the term heartland to describe that range of businesses to which a corporate head office can add value, rather than see value destroyed through too much complexity and diversity.

Alliances enable companies to focus on their core skills and competencies. Nike, for example, a leading company in sporting and leisure footwear, focuses on product design, marketing and personality endorsements; it avoids manufacturing, which it subcontracts to specialists worldwide. Partners have to support each other, however, and understand each other's various needs and expectations. The main benefits will come from sharing information, which in turn should enable companies to respond more quickly to new opportunities and threats. Alliance partners can also be an excellent means of overcoming relative weaknesses.

## Leveraging resources

Hamel and Prahalad (1993) also emphasize the need to manage the organization's strategic resources to achieve ambitious, stretching objectives. Productivity can be improved by gaining the same output from fewer resources – this is downsizing (sometimes called rightsizing) – and by leveraging, achieving more output from given resources.

Clearly, internal and external architecture are both important for leveraging resources. In addition, organizations can benefit by ensuring that there is a clear and understood focus for the efforts. This could take the form of a properly communicated mission or purpose, which is acknowledged and understood. British Airways would claim that much of its success historically has been based around a commitment to the slogan 'The World's Favourite Airline'. This example again emphasizes the significance of corporate image.

## Adding value

A business must add value if it is to be successful. As supply potential has grown to exceed global demand in the majority of industries, adding value has become increasingly important. In simple terms the extent of the value added is the difference between the value of the outputs from an organization and the cost of the inputs or resources used. Two fundamental questions are being addressed: what is the value created and what is the cost?

The traditional paradigm, based on the accountancy measure, is that prices reflect costs plus a profit margin. The lack of differentiation, for which a higher price can be charged, implies enormous downward pressures on costs. Performance measurement is then based upon economy of scale (low input costs) and efficiency (minimizing the actual and attributed costs of the resources used for adding further value).

While it is important to use all resources efficiently and properly, it is also critical to ensure that the potential value of the outputs is maximized by ensuring that they fully meet the needs of the customers for whom they are intended. An organization achieves this when it sees its customers' objectives as its own objectives and enables its customers to easily add more value or, in the case of final consumers, feel that they are gaining true value for money.

In the new paradigm, the key is value for the customer; if resources are used to provide real value for customers, they will pay a price which reflects its worth to them.

John Kay (1993) researched the most successful European companies during the 1980s, measured by their average costs per unit of net output. He found that each company had developed an individual strategy for adding value and creating competitive success. Glaxo (number 1 in the 10) successfully exploited the international potential for its patented antiulcer drug Zantac. LVMH (Louis Vuitton, Moët Hennessy), sixth in the list, generated synergy from the global distribution of a diverse range of high-quality, premium-brand products. Benetton, second, enjoyed beneficially close links with its suppliers and distributors, again worldwide. Marks and Spencer (tenth, and Minicase 1.2 in the previous chapter) was also expert at supply-chain management and further benefited from its value-for-money image and reputation. In contrast, low-price food retailer Kwik Save, fifth in the list, was selling its products with a low margin but enjoying a relatively very high turnover to capital employed. BTR (number nine) had expertise in the management of a diversified conglomerate. Many of Kay's leading companies are featured in minicases in this book, and it is important to emphasize that the relative fortunes of some of these organizations have declined. It was shown in Chapter 1 that Marks and Spencer has recently fallen from grace; the demise of both BTR and Kwik Save has been greater. Simply, it cannot be assumed that what constitutes value for customers at some point in time will always constitute value. When needs and requirements change, companies must find new ways of creating high added value.

The important elements in adding value are:

- understanding and being close to customers, in particular understanding their perception of value
- a commitment to quality
- a high level of all-round service
- speedy reaction to competitive opportunities and threats
- innovation.

Organizations can seek to add value by, first, adding positive features, such as air conditioning, comfortable bucket seats and CD players in cars and, secondly, by removing any features perceived as negatives or drawbacks. Antilock braking systems and four-wheel drive gearboxes reduce the concerns that some people have about driving in bad weather, while extended warranty schemes remove the fear of unknown future repair costs. Each of these additions has a value for which some customers, not all, will pay a premium.

It is quite conceivable that organizations are pursuing strategies or policies which make life harder for their customers. Minimum order quantities and, possibly, volume discounts, may force or encourage customers to buy more than they need or can afford to stock. Obsolescence can then become an issue. Organizations could evaluate the merit of discounts based on annual sales rather than only on individual orders. Simply, organizations should be looking to ensure that they follow the top loop of Figure 2.6 and not the bottom one.

Organizations that truly understand their customers can create competitive advantage and thereby benefit from higher prices and loyalty. High-capacity utilization can then help to reduce costs.

As an example, the prices of airline seats are related to the value that they have for customers and the benefits they offer, not simply the airline's cost for providing the seat and the associated service. The first-class cabin has traditionally offered space, comfortable seats which can be reclined almost to the horizontal, and high-quality food and service. Business class is based on similar principles but to a more limited degree. Now airlines are beginning to introduce sleeper seats, which can be converted into a horizontal bed, in these cabins for long-haul overnight flights. Both classes are quieter than the economy section, offering some opportunity for business travellers to work, and reservations can be changed. Economy seats at full fare allow for late bookings, open tickets to allow for flexible return schedules, upstairs seats on Boeing 747s with some airlines and, clearly, more chance of an upgrade when a flight is not fully booked. Reduced apex fares can be very good value for money, but they are inflexible. Travellers must stay for a prescribed period, flights and tickets cannot be altered and sometimes payment must be made early and in full.

One important key success factor for an airline is the ability to sell the right mix of tickets to maximize the revenue potential from every flight. Empty seats imply lost revenue; at the same time, if every ticket is sold at a discounted price, the flight is unlikely to be profitable. After flipping from profit to loss at the end of the 1990s, British Airways switched its emphasis and increased the size of its premium-price business class cabins at the expense of low-margin

*Figure 2.6* Adding value for customers.

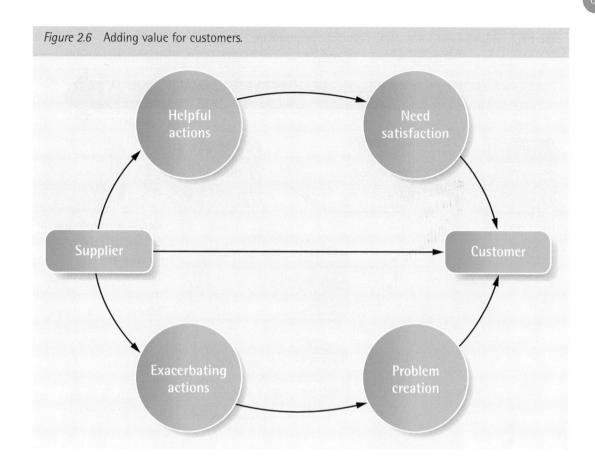

economy seating. Consequently, the airline performance measures include: load factors, passenger kilometres (the numbers of passengers multiplied by the distance flown), and the revenue per passenger kilometre.

Opportunities for adding value which attracts customers must be sought and exploited. Numerous possible opportunities exist at corporate, competitive and functional strategy levels. Resources must be deployed to exploit these opportunities. Pümpin (1991) argues that multiplication, i.e. strategic consistency and performance improvement by concentrating on certain important strategies and learning how to implement them more effectively, promotes growth. The matching process is led and championed by the strategic leader, who is responsible for establishing the key values. While striving to

improve performance with existing strategies the organization must constantly search for new windows of opportunity. McDonald's (Minicase 2.1) provides an excellent example. Ray Kroc spotted an opportunity in the growing fast-food market and exploited it by concentrating on new product ideas and franchised outlets, supported by a culture that promoted 'quality, service, cleanliness and value'.

Figures 2.7 and 2.8 summarize these arguments about strategic competency and competitive success. Figure 2.7 shows that organizations must add value, and continue to find new ways of adding fresh value, for their customers. They achieve this by developing, changing and exploiting core resource-based technological competencies. This exploitation involves organizational processes and capabilities, together with

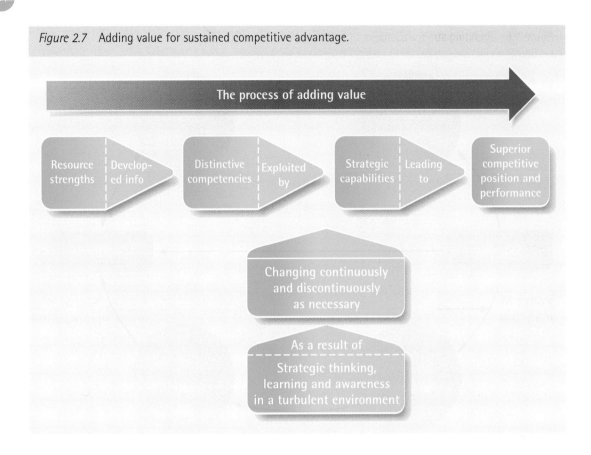

*Figure 2.7* Adding value for sustained competitive advantage.

The process of adding value

| Resource strengths | Develop-ed info | Distinctive competencies | Exploited by | Strategic capabilities | Leading to | Superior competitive position and performance |

Changing continuously and discontinuously as necessary

As a result of

Strategic thinking, learning and awareness in a turbulent environment

strong linkages with other companies in the supply chain (strategic architecture), in order to create differentiation and effective cost control and, thus, establish a superior competitive position. The situation is always fluid, though; organizations cannot assume that currently successful products, services and competitive strategies will be equally successful in the future. They must be changed at appropriate times. In turn, this requires competency in awareness, thinking and learning. Realizing which competencies are most important for long-term success, concentrating attention on them, developing them and measuring the desired improvements is a critically important task for the strategic leader.

All the time, companies should carry out efficiently those activities which are essential for creating a distinctive or differentiated competitive position, and avoid incurring unnecessary costs by providing non-essential values. This implies that they clearly understand their markets, their customers and the key success factors that they must meet – their defined competitive strategy. Moreover, they should constantly seek improvement by driving their operating efficiencies.

Figure 2.8 combines the market- and resource-based views of strategy with the analytical (planning) and aspirational (visionary and emergent) approaches to strategy creation introduced and explained in Chapter 1. The market-based approach can be manifest in either an analytical insight into the competitive environment or an endeavour to envision new opportunities for building value through an instinctive understanding of customers and their needs. The resource-based approach can build analytically on core competencies and capabilities. At the same time, real breakthroughs

*Figure 2.8* Changing strategies. Based on ideas in KPMG (1999) Change the Game, Change the Rules of the Game, www.kpmg.co.uk/kpmg/uk/services/manage/ebook/change

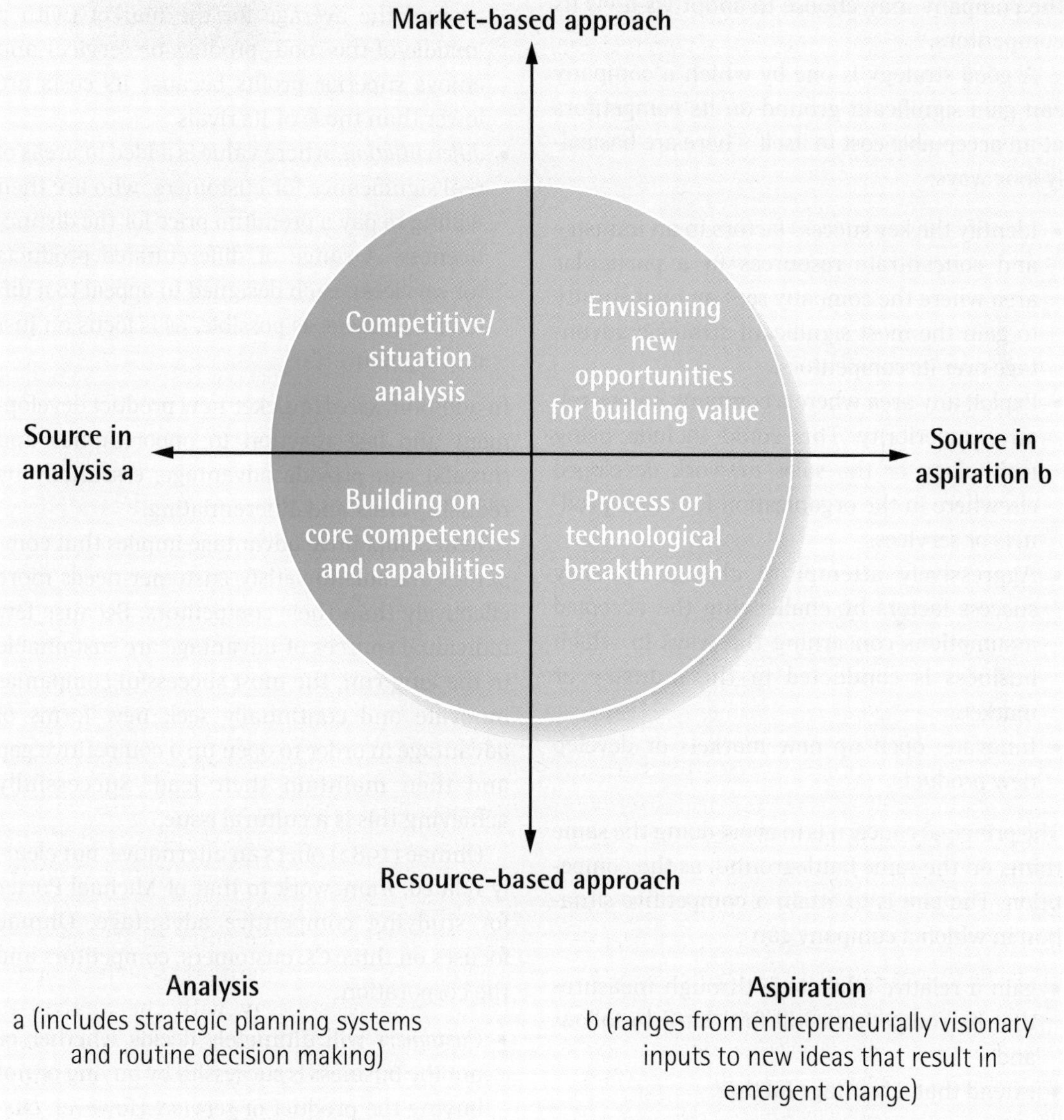

**Market-based approach**

Competitive/
situation
analysis

Envisioning
new
opportunities
for building value

**Source in
analysis a**

**Source in
aspiration b**

Building on
core competencies
and capabilities

Process or
technological
breakthrough

**Resource-based approach**

| **Analysis** | **Aspiration** |
|---|---|
| a (includes strategic planning systems and routine decision making) | b (ranges from entrepreneurially visionary inputs to new ideas that result in emergent change) |

in processes or technologies can help to rewrite the rules of competition in an industry.

## Competitive advantage

Ohmae (1982) contends that business strategy is all about competitive advantage. He argues that without competitors there would be no need for strategy, for the sole purpose of strategic management is to enable the company to gain, as effectively as possible, a sustainable edge over its competitors – to alter a company's strength relative to that of its competitors in the most efficient way. Actions affecting the health of a business (value engineering or improved cash flow which improve profitability) widen the range of alternative strategies that the company may choose to adopt *vis-à-vis* its competitors.

A good strategy is one by which a company can gain significant ground on its competitors at an acceptable cost to itself. There are basically four ways:

- Identify the key success factors in an industry and concentrate resources in a particular area where the company sees an opportunity to gain the most significant strategic advantage over its competitors.
- Exploit any area where a company enjoys relative superiority. This could include using technology or the sales network developed elsewhere in the organization for other products or services.
- Aggressively attempt to change the key success factors by challenging the accepted assumptions concerning the ways in which business is conducted in the industry or market.
- Innovate: open up new markets or develop new products.

The principal concern is to avoid doing the same thing, on the same battleground, as the competition. The aim is to attain a competitive situation in which a company can

- gain a relative advantage through measures that its competitors will find hard to follow, and
- extend that advantage further.

Competitive advantage is more than the idea of a competitive strategy, which may or may not prove distinctive. Porter (1985), the author most commonly associated with this topic, has shown how companies can seek broad advantage within an industry or focus on one or a number of distinct segments. He argues that advantage can accrue from particular generic strategies which are available to all competitors in an industry:

- *cost leadership*, whereby a company prices around the average for the market (with a 'middle-of-the-road' product or service) and enjoys superior profits because its costs are lower than those of its rivals
- *differentiation*, where value is added in areas of real significance for customers, who are then willing to pay a premium price for the distinctiveness. A range of differentiated products (or services), each designed to appeal to a different segment, is possible, as is focus on just one segment.

In addition, *speed* (quicker new product development and fast reaction to opportunities and threats) can provide advantage, essentially by reducing costs and differentiating.

Real competitive advantage implies that companies are able to satisfy customer needs more effectively than their competitors. Because few individual sources of advantage are sustainable in the long run, the most successful companies innovate and continually seek new forms of advantage in order to open up a competitive gap and then maintain their lead. Successfully achieving this is a cultural issue.

Ohmae (1982) offers an alternative, but clearly related, framework to that of Michael Porter for studying competitive advantage. Ohmae focuses on three Cs: customers, competitors and the corporation.

- *Customers* will ultimately decide whether or not the business is successful by buying or not buying the product or service. However, customers cannot be treated *en masse*. Specific preferences should be sought and targeted. Products should be differentiated to appeal to defined market segments.
- *Competitors* will similarly differentiate their products, goods and services, and again incur costs in doing so. Competition can be based on price, image, reputation, proven

quality, particular performance characteristics, distribution or after-sales service, for example.

- *Corporations* are organized around particular functions (production, marketing, etc.). The way that they are structured and managed determines the cost of the product or service.

There are opportunities to create competitive advantage in several areas of business, such as product design, packaging, delivery, service and customizing. Such opportunities achieve differentiation, but they can increase costs. Costs must be related to the price that customers are willing to pay for the particular product, based to some extent upon how they perceive its qualities, again in relation to competitors.

Strategic success, in the end, requires a clear understanding of the needs of the market, especially its segments, and the satisfaction of targeted customers more effectively and more profitably than by competitors.

## Achieving competitive advantage

Competitive advantage, then, does not come from simply being different. It is achieved if and when real value is added for customers. This often requires companies to *stretch their resources* to achieve higher returns (Hamel and Prahalad, 1993; see also p. 60). Improved productivity may be involved; ideally employees will come up with innovations, new and better ways of doing things for customers.

This innovation can result in lower costs, differentiation or a faster response to opportunities and threats, the bases of competitive advantage; and it is most likely to happen when the organization succeeds in harnessing and exploiting its core competencies and capabilities.

It also requires that employees are empowered. Authority, responsibility and accountability will be decentralized, allowing employees to make decisions for themselves. They should be able and willing to look for improvements. When this is managed well, a company may succeed in changing the rules of competition. Basically, organizations should seek to encourage 'ordinary people to achieve extraordinary results'.

This will only happen if achievement is properly recognized, and initiative and success are rewarded. Some people are naturally reticent about taking risks. 3M, which developed Post-It Notes, Sony, Hewlett-Packard and Motorola are four organizations which are recognized as being highly creative and innovative. In each case employees are actively encouraged to look for, and try out, new ideas. In such businesses the majority of products in the corporate portfolio will have only existed for a few years. Effective empowerment can bring continual growth to successful companies and also provide ideas for turning around companies in decline.

Competitive advantage is also facilitated by good internal and external communications, achieving one of the potential benefits of linkages. Without this businesses cannot share and *learn* best practice. Moreover, information is a fundamental aspect of organizational control. Companies can learn from suppliers, from distributors, from customers, from other members of a large organization, and from competitors.

Companies should never overlook opportunities for communicating their achievements, strengths and successes. Image and reputation are vitally important, as they help to retain business.

## E–V–R congruence

If one wished to claim that an organization was being managed effectively from a strategic point of view, one would have to show, first, that its managers appreciated fully the dynamics, opportunities and threats present in their competitive environment, and that they were paying due regard to wider societal issues; and, secondly, that the organization's resources (inputs) were being managed strategically, taking into account its strengths and weaknesses, and that the organization was taking advantage of its opportunities. Key success factors and core competencies would be matched. This will not just happen, it needs to be managed. Moreover, potential new opportunities need to be sought and resources developed. It is also important, therefore, that the values of the organization match the needs of the environment and the key success factors. It is the values and culture that determine whether the environment and resources are currently matched, and whether they stay congruent in changing circumstances.

Values are traditionally subsumed as a resource in a SWOT (strengths, weaknesses, opportunities, threats) analysis, but it is useful to separate them out. The notion of E–V–R (environment–values–resources) congruence then is an integration of these issues. Basically, there is an overlap between the environment (key success factors) and resources (competencies and capabilities), and the organization is committed to sustaining this overlap with effective strategic change initiatives. This notion of E–V–R congruence is illustrated in the top left diagram in Figure 2.9 and Minicase 2.3 on The National Trust.

The value of E–V–R analysis is that it provides a straightforward framework for assessing the organization's existing strategies and strategic needs. It is crystal clear at a conceptual level what organizations have to achieve and sustain strategically; the challenge then is to use the logic to explore and create opportunities and ways for achieving and sustaining congruence by dealing with the various, but different, risks that organizations have to manage if they are to avoid crises in the face of uncertainty.

The other four illustrations in Figure 2.9 illustrate alternative instances of incongruence. E–V–R analysis can be applied at more than one level; and consequently different managers should be in positions where they can address which of the alternatives in Figure 2.9 best repre-

sents their organization and their individual business. Having selected the one that they feel best sums up the present situation, they can immediately see the direction and thrust of the changes that are needed to create or restore congruency.

Working downwards from the top left in the figure, a 'lost organization' is seen next. Possibly there was congruency at some time, but now products, services and markets are out of alignment and the values inappropriate. Without major changes to strategy, structure and style, almost certainly involving a change of strategic leader, an organization in this situation has no future. This degree of incongruence would be relatively unusual, but the other three possibilities are not.

The 'consciously incompetent' organization is aware of the needs for success in its marketplace, and managers appreciate the importance of satisfying its customers, but it is simply not achieving the desired level of service and quality. Managers may well have some insight into what might be improved but not be in a position to achieve this improvement. Maybe there is a key resource shortage of some form or a lack of investment, or a person or people with key skills have left and not been replaced. Possibly too many managers are unwilling to grasp the changes that are needed and accept empowerment and responsibility. It is typical for a company in this situation to be constantly fighting crises and problems. Because of the customer orientation, there will be a commitment to resolving the problems and difficulties and, for this reason, some customers may be somewhat tolerant. However, the organization is likely to be highly reactive and, consequently, again the position cannot be sustained indefinitely. A more proactive and entrepreneurial approach will be required to strengthen the resource base and restore congruency with a fresh strategic position.

In contrast, the 'unconsciously competent' organization enjoys strategic positioning without

*Figure 2.9* E–V–R congruence and incongruence.

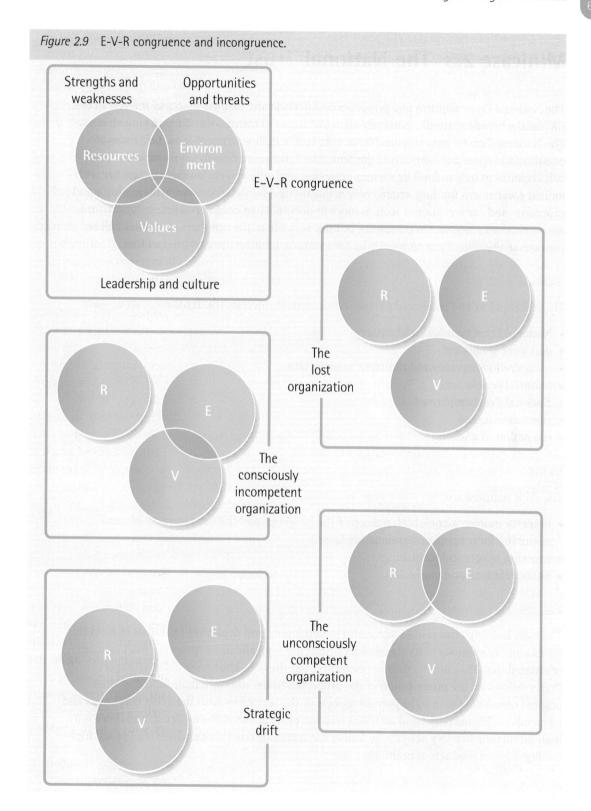

Strengths and weaknesses

Opportunities and threats

Resources

Environment

Values

E–V–R congruence

Leadership and culture

The lost organization

The consciously incompetent organization

The unconsciously competent organization

Strategic drift

# Minicase 2.3 The National Trust

The National Trust acquires and preserves countryside and historic places of interest in the UK 'for the benefit of us all', generally allowing access to members and fee-paying visitors. The National Trust is now responsible for over half a million acres of land, 600 miles of coastline and some 250 houses and gardens. The Trust relies heavily on members' subscriptions to help to fund its various activities; and gifts and endowments, together with limited government funding, enable new acquisitions. Maintenance standards are high and expensive, and conservation is seen as more important than commercial exploitation, and, where necessary, access. On occasions, but not very often, the numbers of visitors will be restricted either directly or indirectly by, for example, limiting the parking facilities.

## Stakeholders

The stakeholders and interested parties – those whose interests the Trust must serve – are:

- National Trust members and visitors
- donors of properties
- conservation agencies and ramblers' associations
- financial benefactors
- National Trust employees
- Government, and
- the nation as a whole.

## Skills

The skills required are:

- property management – both upkeep of the buildings and the management of land resources; large areas of farmland are leased
- expertise in arts and furnishings
- public relations and marketing.

## Values

The National Trust has proved successful in developing and deploying resources to meet the needs and expectations of its stakeholders. Staff are typically more 'property management' orientated than they are marketing orientated, but they are knowledgeable and expert. Preservation and the presentation of the properties to the standard maintained by their original owners are seen as important aspects of the service by both the Trust employees and its members. Theme parks and activities have no place in the National Trust; and there is a high moral tone to every activity, including the National Trust shops which tend to sell high-quality selected products at premium prices.

In addition, Trust staff appear to share an ethos (typically shared by people who work for other charities) which combines the feeling of working for a good cause, clear identification with its purpose and principles, and a certain readiness to accept lower rewards than those normally earned in manufacturing and service businesses.

National Trust membership doubled from 1 million to 2 million during the 1980s. A dilemma and a new challenge for the National Trust would arise if a more commercial orientation became necessary in order to fund desired activities.

QUESTION: Does the National Trust appear to enjoy E–V–R congruence? If not, which other alternative in Figure 2.9 best explains the situation?

*The National Trust* http://www.nationaltrust.org.uk

any real commitment, especially to improvement and change. Things are working, at a surface level and possibly with some element of luck. Any success is taken for granted. The organization is unable to exploit its strengths and, if it fails to address this, then E and R will drift apart over time, possibly sooner rather than later, to create a lost organization. The required change in culture and values probably implies a change of leadership, certainly of leadership style, to increase decentralization and empowerment.

'Strategic drift' is commonplace. An organization which is internally cohesive simply loses touch with its environment. Demands may change, and fresh competition may make the company's products and services less attractive than in the past. The challenge then concerns realignment in a dynamic environment, which certainly requires a change in management style and, possibly again, leadership. This organization desperately needs new ideas, which may already be available inside the organization, but have not been captured.

An article by Peter Drucker (1994) complements both this model and these arguments when he states that all organizations have implicit or explicit 'theories' for their business, incorporating:

- assumptions about the environment, specifically markets, customers and important technologies
- assumptions about its mission or purpose, and
- assumptions about the core (content) competencies required to fulfil the mission.

These assumptions, at any time, must be realistic, congruent, communicated and understood; to achieve this they must be evaluated regularly and rigorously.

Pümpin (1987) uses the term strategic excellence positions (SEPs) to describe 'capabilities which enable an organization to produce better-than-average results over the longer term compared with its competitors'. SEPs imply that organizations appreciate the views of customers and develop the capabilities required to satisfy these needs. Moreover, they are perceived by their customers to be a superior competitor because of their skills and accomplishments.

It is important to deploy resources and to focus the drive for excellence (an aspect of the organization's culture) on issues which matter to customers. IBM, for example, have succeeded historically by concentrating on service, Rolls Royce motor cars on image and quality, and Procter and Gamble on advertising and branding.

Businesses should seek to develop competitive advantage and a strategic excellence position for each product and service. Overall E–V–R congruence then depends on these SEPs together with any corporate benefits from linkages and interrelationships.

The development of SEPs and E–V–R congruence takes time, and requires that all functional areas of the business appreciate which factors are most significant to customers. Once achieved, however, it cannot be assumed that long-term success is guaranteed. Situations change and new windows of opportunity open (Abell, 1978). The demand for guaranteed overnight parcel deliveries anywhere in the country, and immediate services within cities, opened up the opportunity for couriers; new technologies used in laptop computers, facsimile machines and the Internet have created demand and behaviour changes. Competitors may behave unexpectedly, and consequently there is a need for strategic awareness and for monitoring potential change situations.

Handy (1994) also stresses that timing plays a crucial role in the management of strategic change. He uses the sigmoid curve (Figure 2.10) to illustrate that organizations must change when they are successful, not when it is too late.

His argument is that change should be initiated at point A, not point B. At point A there is time to be positive and embed change before a situation deteriorates, thus maintaining a positive momentum. If the change is delayed to point B, then there is a real chance that the organization will go into decline, albeit temporarily, and appear very reactive. The shaded area thus represents a period of uncertainty and turbulence, with 'old' and 'new' operating side by side.

Vigilance should help an organization to decide where it should be concentrating its resources at the moment, how it might usefully invest for the future, and where it needs to divest as existing windows of opportunity start to close. New market needs may imply a change of values, and this again will take time and prove challenging. It is not easy, for instance, to change a strong cost culture into one that is more innovatory.

Bettis and Prahalad (1995) argue that business decisions are affected by a 'dominant logic', championed by the strategic leader and communicated through the organization. This could be an articulated vision or a culturally integrated paradigm concerning 'what the business is about and how things get done'. It is shown next how strategic regeneration implies that this

*Figure 2.10*   Timing strategic change.

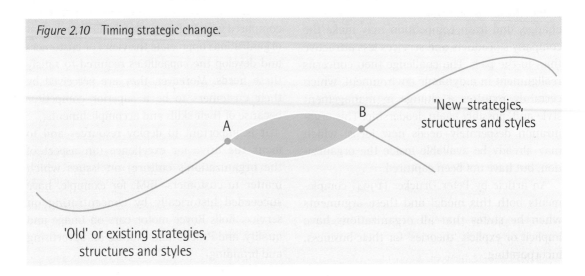

'New' strategies, structures and styles

'Old' or existing strategies, structures and styles

logic needs to be changed. IBM's growth and early industry dominance was built on a belief that mainframe computers were essential for organizations. Competitors such as Microsoft, which concentrated on software, highlighted that IBM's logic was outdated and it needed to be 'unlearned'. New products and new processes alone would prove inadequate. The new logic is one of decentralized personal computers in the hands of knowledgeable workers.

Organizations, therefore, should build on their past successes while always realizing that the past may not be the best guide to the future.

## Strategic regeneration

Organizations have to deal with dynamic and uncertain environments, some of which are more turbulent than others, as Minicase 2.4 illustrates. Organizations should actively and continuously look for opportunities to exploit their competencies and strategic abilities, adapt and seek improvements in every area of the business: gradual change, building on an awareness and understanding of current strategies and successes. One difficulty is the fact that organizations are not always able to clarify exactly why they are successful. At the same time it is also valuable if they can think ahead discontinuously, trying to understand future demand, needs and expectations. By doing this they will be aiming to be the first competitor with solutions. Enormous benefits are available to the companies which succeed by, in effect, rewriting the rules of competition in an industry.

*The future was predictable – though very few predicted it!*

(Allen Kay, when Research Fellow, Apple Computers)

Hamel (1997) argues that a changing business (or external) environment opens up the possibility for finding new business and competitive

opportunities all the time. There are opportunities for entrepreneurs and the entrepreneurially minded organization; for the others there are threats. He cites globalization, shorter product and service lifecycles (linked to technology improvements and to consumer willingness to change more frequently than in the past) and faster, more sophisticated communication networks as typical sources of opportunity. He explains that there are known and visible areas of opportunity, such as gene-engineered drugs, non-branch banking and multimedia, but stresses that the secret lies in finding the 'right' strategic position to exploit the opportunity. Because of the constant environmental turbulence any strategic position must be seen as temporary and sensitive to unexpected events; innovation is needed to reinforce and defend a position of strength.

Without constant improvement, renewal and intrapreneurship there are obvious dangers in this changing environment, but alone this may well prove inadequate. The most entrepreneurial companies will, at the same time, be searching for new ways of competing. Linked to this is the difficulty for many organizations that future competitive threats are as likely to come from unknown or unexpected organizations currently outside the industry as they are from existing, known rivals. In the early 1980s it is highly likely that British Airways (BA) was particularly concerned with the possible actions over routes and fares by its main American and European rivals; it seems much more improbable that they anticipated the threat that Richard Branson and Virgin Atlantic was going to pose. BA may well have recognized the potential for new competitors as deregulation changed the air-travel environment, but predicting the source was another matter. The outsider Direct Line had the same impact on the insurance industry.

In a sense this process is an attempt to invent the future, and the resources of the organiza-

# Minicase 2.4  Revolutionary Changes: The Toy Industry and the Internet

This case considers two industries where revolutionary change has become commonplace, and caused the relative fortunes of different competitors to change markedly.

## Toys

In the 1950s and 1960s boys seemed to crave electric train sets and die-cast toy vehicles (such as Matchbox and Dinky toys), whereas girls were often satisfied with dolls. These products all still exist, but largely confined to niches rather than mainstream market segments. Adult enthusiasts are more likely than their children to be found maintaining the railway layout. Model cars, typically resembling the original Matchbox toys, often feature as special corporate marketing promotions. Barbie dolls have, however, prospered and a special set of boxed collectables has grown to supplement the 'standard' model. Lego has also prospered while Meccano has declined in relative terms. Realistically, however, many of these toys and their makers have been overtaken by, first, battery-powered toys and, more recently, sophisticated computer games. In addition, toys and models of varying types and cost linked to film and television characters have had periods of great popularity, but fashion changes have a major impact. Many manufacturers and stores overestimated the commercial prospects for Star Wars products during 1999, despite the general popularity of the new film.

Technology has clearly played a major role in this, but so too have changing tastes and behaviours. Children have become computer literate at very young ages, and, linked to this, have been losing interest in 'traditional' toys at younger ages. As well as providing prospects for computer games designers, this created a niche for the Teletubbies. This TV programme, with a wide range of associated books and products, was the first specifically to identify children aged 3 years and under as a distinct market niche and target them directly.

The outcome has been the decline of many established manufacturers and the emergence of new ones. Once prominent UK names such as Hornby, Triang and Dinky are no longer high profile. Matchbox toys are still produced, but not in the UK and no longer under British ownership. Many 'character' toys are manufactured in the Far East, under licence from the American and British owners of the design and name. The Danish Lego remains successful, but its prosperity has not been without occasional setbacks. The US manufacturer of Barbie, Mattel, struggled in 1999 and its strategic leader resigned. Meanwhile, manufacturers of games consols and software, such as the Japanese Sony, Nintendo and Sega, have all seized sizeable market shares.

The same trend has been apparent in toy retailing. Independent toy shops now make little impact. Toys R Us, the American toy supermarket, grew to prominence but has declined in recent years as discount stores such as Wal-Mart have become increasingly significant. Sales via the Internet are also taking market share.

> *Matchbox*   http://www.matchbox.com
> *Mattel*   http://www.mattel.com
> *Sony*   http://www.sony.com
> *Toys R Us (Toysrus.com is now part of Amazon.com)*   http://www.toysrus.com

## The Internet

To make use of the potential offered by the Internet, users have to have means of access. The first requirement is a web browser, a program that enables a personal computer (PC) user to access and view data on the web. The pioneer was Netscape, with Navigator, but once Microsoft's Bill Gates realized the commercial value of its dominant position in the market, he developed a rival browser, Explorer, which he provided with Windows software. The way that he tied the two together created hostility from both his rivals and the US anti-trust authorities.

The second essential is a modem which provides access to the telephony that links computers around the world.

The third fundamental requirement is a service provider, whose software, once installed on a PC, will provide a gateway on to the web. The original business model was based around a fee for the service plus the cost of telephone calls. Typically, service providers (unless they are a telephone company) reach an agreement with the telephone company for a share of the call revenues. The early leader was America On-Line (AOL), which has since acquired its main rival, Compuserve, and also merged with Netscape.

The business model changed in the UK with the emergence of companies such as Freeserve, begun by retailer Dixons. The company was floated as an independent business in 1998 and its shares have fluctuated dramatically. Freeserve has yet to make a profit and it is now owned by a French competitor. The initial Freeserve model was free access but with a charge for phone calls, which were metered and charged by the minute. The revenue comes from a share of the phone revenues, supplemented by fees charged to companies who can be persuaded to advertise on the site. Other retailers with an interest in e-commerce also provided access under similar arrangements, attempting to attract customers to their own retail pages every time they log on to the Internet.

Prompted by fresh competition from newer service providers, such as ntl, the American cable business, the business model in the UK has changed again. Now access is free and phone time is provided unmetered for a fixed monthly or annual rate. Competitors such as Freeserve may now have to pay British Telecom (BT) a fee, rather than share BT's revenue. Hence, their income is more dependent than ever on advertising charges and a negotiated share of the profits of any electronic sales by companies whose Web pages are accessed via the service provider.

The dominant service provider globally is Yahoo! This was built around the concept of a search engine, which enables users to find their way around the World Wide Web and track down the sites and information that they are seeking.

In the film *Field of Dreams*, the phrase 'If you build it, they will come' features prominently. This cannot realistically be the case with the Internet. There are millions of main domain sites, and the number grows every day. There are no real barriers to putting a new site on the Web. Consequently, new e-commerce businesses rely heavily on publicity and advertising off the Web to generate interest in their sites. The leading e-commerce business worldwide, Amazon.com, like high-profile British companies, Boo.com and Lastminute.com (which are the subject of Minicase 4.1), has yet to make a profit. The argument is that continuous investment is required to build a truly powerful base from which future fortunes can be generated, but critics argue that at some stage the bubble must burst and that floated companies which are overvalued must collapse.

QUESTIONS: From your experience as a consumer, which toy products have enjoyed huge but only temporary successes?
Have their manufacturers been able to move on with fresh, new ideas or have they collapsed?
Given the uncertainties of the Internet, why are more and more companies attempting to stimulate electronic sales, and why does venture capital continue to be available for new ventures, when existing ones are still trading at a loss?

*AOL*  http://www.aol.com
*Freeserve*  http://www.freeserve.com
*Microsoft*  http://www.microsoft.com
*Yahoo!*  http://www.yahoo.com

tion, its people and technologies, will need to be applied creatively. Companies should imagine new product opportunities and strive to develop new products and services because they believe that customers will value them if they are available (Hamel and Prahalad, 1991). Sony, for example, developed a sketch pad for children, allowing them to project their drawings directly onto a TV screen as they create them. Developments like this are based on ideas and 'dreams' rather than merely attempting to improve existing products. Asking customers is not enough: companies must be able both to understand them and to think at least one jump ahead. There is a danger when companies 'follow their nose' but fail to truly understand their markets. In such cases, research and development may drive product development down an inappropriate track. In addition, caution is necessary when ideas are implemented, because markets and customers are likely to resist changes that seem too radical.

To minimize the risk, 'expeditionary marketing' – low-risk incursions into the market to test out new features or new performances – can be useful. Here, organizations are really attempting to create markets ahead of competitors and just slightly ahead of customers.

In summary, organizations are searching for:

- long-term product or service leadership, which is dictated by the *environment*
- long-term cost leadership, which is *resource dependent*
- product and service excellence, doing things more quickly than competitors without sacrificing quality – essential *values.*

Strategic regeneration refers to simultaneous changes to strategies and structures (organizational processes) in this search.

Strategies have to be reinvented. New products and services should be created by questioning how and why existing ones are popular and successful, and looking for new ways of adding extra value. Electronic publishing and CD-ROM technology, for example, have offered enormous potential for dramatically changing the ways in which people learn. Rewards have been available for those companies which have learnt how to exploit these environmental opportunities.

In thinking ahead, companies should consider both products (or services) and core competencies. Concentrating on products encourages a search for new competitive opportunities; thinking creatively about competencies (which transcend individual products and businesses) can generate radically new opportunities for adding value and establishing a different, future 'competitive high ground'.

*Structural* changes are designed to improve resource efficiency and effectiveness. Trends in the late 1990s have been:

- downsizing – splitting the organization into small, autonomous, decentralized units. Those organizations that have taken this too far have inadvertently lost key resources which were critical for their competitiveness. Consequently, the notion of 'rightsizing' is the important one.
- delayering – using the power and potential of IT to reduce the number of layers of managers, in order to speed up decision making, and

- process re-engineering – reviewing and redesigning processes in order that tasks can be performed better and more rapidly.

Simply, changes are required to the structure of the organization, the nature and scope of jobs and the network of communications.

*Empowerment and teamworking* are also seen as essential for creating the values necessary to enable this degree of change.

On paper, the idea of strategic regeneration can be justified as essential, exciting and rewarding but, not unexpectedly, there are likely to be major barriers when applying the ideas. The most obvious hurdles are:

- the quality of leadership required to provide the necessary drive and direction
- an inability to create an internal culture of change – the most powerful inhibitors will be experienced, established managers who have become out of date
- uncertainty about changing needs and competitor activities.

Pascale (1992) uses the word transformational to describe organizations which succeed with simultaneous strategic and structural change. They become learning organizations which 'encourage continuous learning and knowledge generation at all levels, have processes which can move knowledge around the organization easily to where it is needed, and can translate that knowledge quickly into changes in the way the organization acts, both internally and externally' (Senge, 1991).

Successful entrepreneurs and entrepreneurial organizations often find new products and new needs ahead of both their rivals and their customers. Market research can tap into issues that are important for customers, but it is unlikely to provide the answers. Creativity, insight and innovation stimulated within the organization are more likely to achieve this. Entrepreneurs and entrepreneurial organizations thus create proprietary foresight from public knowledge by synthesizing information and environmental signals and creating new patterns and opportunities.

This intellectual foresight has a number of possible sources according to Hamel and Prahalad (1994):

- It can be a personal restlessness with the existing status quo.
- It can be a natural curiosity (which the education system does not manage to stifle!) that leads to creativity. Sometimes the entrepreneurial people concerned have a childlike innocence in the questions they ask, and the process is stimulated by a wide network of contacts.
- It may be a willingness on the part of certain individuals to speculate and manage the risk of investigation. Invention has to precede learning.
- It is sometimes a desire to change things and 'leave footprints'.

- Often there is an empathy with the industry and market concerned, coupled with
- The ability to conceptualize what does not yet exist: 'you can't create a future you can't imagine'.

## The Strategic Challenge

Organizations must manage and change their strategies within the context of a set of strategic issues and dilemmas. The stances that they choose to deal with these issues and dilemmas, and the strategies, structures and styles that result from their decisions, will determine their overall effectiveness.

Table 2.1 lists 16 issues which are developed at various stages throughout the text, and the commentary below explains the dilemmas that they imply for managers and organizations. While this discussion introduces the topic, it is

*Table 2.1*   Strategic issues and dilemmas

|  | | |
|---|---|---|
| 1. Build on the past | or | Learn from the past and realign |
| 2. Deliberate strategy | or | Emergent strategy |
| 3. Hands-on leadership | or | Direction-only leadership |
| 4. Build on strengths: resource based | or | Search out new opportunities: market driven |
| 5. Differentiate for high added value | or | Beat competitors on cost |
| 6. Diversify | or | Focus |
| 7. Size for critical mass | or | Small and entrepreneurial |
| 8. Profit for shareholders | or | Consensus outcomes for multiple stakeholders |
| 9. Mass market | or | Niche market |
| 10. Global | or | Local |
| 11. Culture of stability | or | Culture of chaos |
| 12. Centralized for control | or | Decentralized for flexibility |
| 13. Constant change, acting quickly | or | Limited and controlled change to protect reliability and quality |
| 14. Relying on logic and investing when others have gone before | or | Being creative, innovative and pioneering: accepting the risks |
| 15. Reacting to competition and events | or | Shaping events and markets |
| 16. Revolutionary change | or | Incremental, emergent change |

not intended to be fully comprehensive of all the issues and dilemmas faced by an organization.

## Strategic issues and dilemmas

Organizations and managers must be able to clarify the learning from their past experiences, and pass this on to help future decisions (Issue 1). Successes can be built on; past mistakes and misjudgements should not be repeated. For many organizations, however, it would be a dangerous assumption that history will be repeated in the future. Things change too quickly, and in many industries future success will come from 'breaking past rules' and being different. Future competition may come from unexpected sources such as organizations currently outside the industry. The dilemma concerns just what knowledge from the past provides ideal building blocks, and how it should be used. Ironically, those organizations which are most successful in sustaining a strong competitive position with constant improvement may be the ones who find that radical, discontinuous change is not synonymous with their culture (Issue 16).

In was shown in Chapter 1 that strategic change decisions come from entrepreneurial (or visionary) inputs, planning and emergence. Finding the 'right' balance between these, and for managers to share a common perspective on their relative significance, constitutes a second dilemma (Issue 2). This leads on to a debate about strategic leadership style, something that will be taken up later. To what extent should the strategic leader be hands-on and actively involved in strategic decision making, and at what level of detail, and how much should he or she step back, provide clear direction and delegate responsibility (Issue 3)?

The need to take both a *market and a resource-based view of strategy* simultaneously (Issue 4) was discussed earlier in this chapter. Also in this chapter differentiation and effective cost management were discussed as two key approaches

to *competitive advantage* (Issue 5). Although the two are clearly linked, it is important that organizations are clear about whether they are attempting to compete on clear differences or superior cost management.

Another crucial issue is *size*. It is now quite normal to read that 'big is no longer beautiful', that it implies too much diversity and complexity. However, the issue of *diversity* (Issue 7) is itself complex. Clearly, many large, diverse conglomerates have chosen to divest and focus or, in cases such as ICI, split the organization into separate 'medium-sized' parts. The question remains: is a strategy of conglomerate diversification by nature a poor choice, or is it that many organizations are unable to *implement* the strategy and create a structure whereby corporate headquarters can add value and foster the synergies which they believe exist? Focus can be achieved by concentrating on a limited number of clearly related (by marketing or technology) businesses. Some organizations are choosing to go further and divest activities and processes which are seen as non-core or non-essential. This is unlikely to mean they are no longer required at all, and consequently this strategy implies a need to develop a capability in managing networks and alliances.

'Small' meanwhile is dubbed innovative, creative and entrepreneurial. Small companies, though, are often fragile financially, often (not always) using low technology and featuring relatively poor working conditions. Successful ones grow to become 'medium-sized'. The challenge for large organizations, searching for power, market share and critical mass is not to lose the creativity, flexibility and *spontaneity of the small organization* as they become bigger and more formal (Issue 7), such that they are able to manage the demands for discontinuous change and corporate renewal.

A further challenge is the attempt to *balance* and satisfy *the needs* and expectations *of* all the *stakeholders* (Issue 8). Shareholders, customers and employees have requirements which may conflict; moreover, they can sometimes sharpen the tension between the short- and long-term perspectives. Most people would agree that a business must ensure that it looks after its shareholders' investments and financial interests, but it would appear that organizations which balance the needs of all their stakeholders perform better (for their shareholders) in the long run. While thinking about the various internal and external stakeholders, the organization must never lose sight of what competitors are doing.

Other tensions concern the marketing issues of *mass or niche* markets (Issue 9), and, in the case of larger businesses, how to balance *global and local* issues (Issue 10). Here, again, one challenge for larger companies concerns the potential benefits to be gained from thinking and behaving like fast-moving, flexible small organizations while obtaining the scale and synergy benefits that can accrue from size.

Many businesses need to develop a *culture of change orientation* without losing internal *cohesion and stability* (Issue 11). This implies an explicit and shared vision of where the organization is heading.

There is also a need to *decentralize* and give managers more delegated authority while not losing sight (at chief executive level) of the changes that they are introducing. This involves a difficult trade-off between such empowerment (delegating real responsibility in order to make the business more effective in its relations with all of its stakeholders) and the greater efficiencies often yielded by *centralized control* and systems which harness the latest IT (Issue 12). The revelation, in September 1995, that the estate agency subsidiary of the Halifax Building Society was paying its staff a bonus if they could sell houses by persuading clients to accept reduced prices, sparked an outcry. The incident provoked an internal investigation and the outcome was likely to lead to changes in the autonomy given to subsidiaries or stronger guidance on policy making.

Organizations must be able to *act quickly* in response to opportunities and threats, but not at the expense of product and service *quality*: achieving high quality at the same time as cutting costs and improving efficiency (Issue 13). On occasions there will always be the dilemma of a recession. Organizations must cut back, control their costs and accept lower margins when supply potential exceeds demand in an economic downturn. Profits fall. Paradoxically, those competitors which are able to consolidate and invest strategically during a recession will be best prepared for the economic upturn. Some organizations will always be reticent about 'blue sky' investment in radical and innovatory ideas, while others will be willing to pioneer such change (Issue 14).

Finally, the organization must be able simultaneously to be *reactive and proactive*, planned and flexible, able to deal with pressures for both continuous and discontinuous change (Issue 15).

These issues reinforce the paradox of stability and instability. Stability concerns running existing businesses efficiently and effectively, exploiting strategic abilities and continually looking to create higher returns from the committed resources. Instability refers to the search for the new competitive high ground ahead of one's rivals. Stable organizations may come to rely on their ability to manage issues and potential crises as they arise. The danger for them is that they can easily become complacent and maybe even change resistant. When this happens there is an argument that an internal crisis should be created in order to provoke action and renewal before the situation becomes unrecoverable.

Dealing with these issues and dilemmas in a dynamic and unpredictable environment is clearly difficult; there are no easy answers and the situation is always fluid. Achieving success, therefore, again implies the creation and exploitation of key strategic competencies. All of these issues are dealt with at various stages in the book and the implications are also reviewed in the final chapter.

Collins and Porras (1995) analysed a number of American companies which have proved to be resilient to the problems which hit them from time to time. Many Western companies have a life expectancy of less than 50 years; a select minority not only survives but thrives on change pressures. We appear to be able to take for granted that successful companies will be dedicated to customer service and all-round quality; they also typically feature an open culture with 'restless enquiry, learning and constant innovation'. Underpinning this is a strategic leader who is able to build an organization with appropriate values, principles and ways of thinking that will last through generations of shifting strategies. He or she need not be individually charismatic, although some clearly are.

Collins and Porras cite Walt Disney Corporation as a leading example. Walt Disney himself was charismatic, but the organization has survived and prospered since his death. The success of its theme parks, recent box-office blockbusters such as *The Lion King*, *Pocahontas* and *Hercules* and the 1995 acquisition of ABC, one of the USA's leading three television networks, are testimony to this. But there have been major setbacks at the same time, which Disney has had to weather. Jeffrey Katzenberg, head of the studios and the man responsible for several major film successes, left in 1994 when he was passed over for a promotion; he sought the number two post of President, vacant after the incumbent was killed in a helicopter accident. This happened shortly after the chief executive, Michael Eisner, had major heart surgery. Katzenberg later sued Disney for a settlement which reflected the value of future earnings from strategies pursued whilst he was employed and for which he was responsible. In 1995 Disney abandoned its plans for a new Civil War theme park in Virginia, following an intensive protest

campaign by environmentalists. During the early 1990s EuroDisney experienced severe financial difficulties before being turned around.

Disney, according to Collins and Porras, relies more on experimentation than formal strategic planning; moreover, it effectively balances stability and change, integration and autonomy.

## Summary

The three themes of strategic *awareness*, ideas and strategic *choice*, and strategy *implementation* provide a valuable framework for studying strategic management.

These themes can be restated as a set of key questions that managers and organizations should be addressing all the time. While there is a systematic order to the themes, and hence a logical order for our study of the subject, strategic *decision making* should not always be thought of as a similarly systematic process.

Strategic *leadership*, *culture* and *values* are at the heart of all strategic decision making. The role, style and contribution of the strategic leader affect both strategy creation and implementation. The culture can, and should, act as a spur to, and facilitator of, change; however, in some organizations the culture will successfully frustrate important change initiatives.

*Strategic management* can be conceptualized as a process through which internal and external resources are brought together to produce products and services, and through these satisfactory (at least) outcomes for all the organization's stakeholders. Related to this there are two approaches to strategy – market-driven and resource based – but these should not be seen as mutually exclusive. They are complementary.

The *market-driven approach* requires that organizations understand and satisfy key success factors. These relate to general industry requirements, organizational distinctiveness and specific efforts for individual customers.

The *resource-based approach* implies that organizations identify and exploit their core competencies and strategic capabilities.

Linked to both is the importance of *strategic architecture* – linkages and synergy between the activities, functions and businesses inside the organization, and also between the organization and other members of its supply chain, such as suppliers and distributors.

The common theme to all of these approaches is the recognition that the organization must find suitable ways of creating and building value for its customers. This naturally impacts on the degree of *competitive advantage* (real differences) that it enjoys.

The *environment–values–resources* (E–V–R) model provides an ideal framework for pulling most of these ideas together. It is relevant at both the organization and individual business level.

On some occasions in turbulent environments, *organizational renewal and regeneration* will become essential, when strategies, structure and style will all need changing simultaneously. This level of change can be traumatic, especially if it is forced on the organization.

There are, however, no black-and-white answers to strategic management, no right and wrong answers. Organizations must make a number of choices in relation to a range of issues and dilemmas. The ways in which they deal with these challenges affect strategy creation and strategy implementation.

## References

Abell, DF (1978) Strategic windows, *Journal of Marketing*, 42 (July).

Ansoff, HI (1984) *Implanting Strategic Management*, Prentice Hall.

Bettis, R and Prahalad, CK (1995) The dominant logic: retrospective and extension, *Strategic Management Journal*, Volume 16, January.

Collins, J and Porras, J (1995) *Built to Last*, Century Business.

Drucker, PF (1994) The theory of business, *Harvard Business Review*, September–October.

Goold, M, Campbell, A and Alexander, M (1994) *Corporate Level Strategy*, John Wiley.

Hall, D (1992) *The Hallmarks for Successful Business*, Mercury Books.

Hamel, G (1997) Address to a Strategic Planning Society Conference, London.

Hamel, G and Prahalad, CK (1991) Corporate imagination and expeditionary marketing, *Harvard Business Review*, July–August.

Hamel, G and Prahalad, CK (1993) Strategy as stretch and leverage, *Harvard Business Review*, March–April.

Hamel, G and Prahalad, CK (1994) *Competing for the Future*, Harvard Business School Press.

Handy, C (1994) *The Empty Raincoat*, Hutchinson.

Kay, JA (1993) *Foundations of Corporate Success*, Oxford University Press.

Ohmae, K (1982) *The Mind of the Strategist*, McGraw-Hill.

Pascale, RT (1992) Paper presented at the *Strategic Renaissance Conference*, Strategic Planning Society, London, October.

Porter, ME (1985) *Competitive Advantage*, Free Press.

Prahalad, CK and Hamel, G (1990) The core competence of the corporation, *Harvard Business Review*, May/June.

Pümpin, C (1987) *The Essence of Corporate Strategy*, Gower.

Pümpin, C (1991) *Corporate Dynamism*, Gower.

Schein, EH (1985) *Organization Culture and Leadership*, Jossey Bass.

Senge, P (1991) *The Fifth Discipline: The Art and Practise of the Learning Organization*, Doubleday

Stalk, G, Evans, P and Shulman, LE (1992) Competing on capabilities: the new rules of corporate strategy, *Harvard Business Review*, March–April.

## Additional material on the website

The Margaret Brooke case study on the Web site provides an annotated application of the 12 questions in Figure 2.2.

As well as the Margaret Brooke case, there is a paper entitled *Effective Strategies for the 1990s* which expands on a number of the points discussed in this chapter.

Test your knowledge of this chapter with our online quiz at http://www.thomsonlearning.co.uk

Explore the Strategic Management Process further at:

*Journal of Marketing*   http://www.ama.org/pubs/jm

## Questions and Research Assignments

### TEXT RELATED

1. What is 'added value'? In what ways might an organization add value for its customers?

2. What are key success factors and core competencies? How are they related?

3. Taking any organization with which you are familiar:
   (a)  use the E–V–R framework to assess its current situation
   (b)  apply the 12 questions included in Figure 2.2.

## Internet and Library Projects

The American engineering contractor, Bechtel, has acquired a reputation for its ability to rescue major public-sector projects which have either been in difficulty or behind schedule, or had cost over-runs. Specific examples of successful intervention by Bechtel as project managers include the following.

| Appointment date | Project | Cost |
|---|---|---|
| 1990 | Channel Tunnel | £10 billion |
| 1993 | Cardiff Bay Barrage | £200 million |
| 1996 | Channel Tunnel Rail Link | £5.8 billion |
| 1998 | Jubilee Line Extension | £3.5 billion |

What are the competencies and capabilities possessed and exploited by Bechtel to create this record of success?

*Bechtel*   http://www.bechtel.com
*Cardiff Bay Barrage*   http://www.uwc.ca/pearson/ensy/mega/stephen/stephen.htm
*Channel Tunnel Rail Link*   http://www.ctrl.co.uk
*Eurotunnel*   http://www.eurotunnel.co.uk
*Jubilee Line Extension*   http://www.railway-technology.com/projects/jubilee

# 3

# The Organizational Mission and Objectives

*Strategies are means to ends; this chapter is about these ends. Organizations undertake purposeful activity; what they do is not without purpose. Ideally, that purpose will be understood, shared and supported by everyone in the organization such that there is a clear, if broad, direction for the activities and strategies. Establishing the purpose and direction is a key role of the strategic leader; and it will provide a basis for the more detailed objectives and performance targets for individual managers and employees. This does not imply that everyone always shares the more detailed objectives; indeed, there can often be internal conflicts over these. Moreover, what individual people actually do and achieve affects organizational performance. Hence, this chapter looks at the idea of purposeful activity by considering the organizational mission and objectives.*

*A number of economic and behavioural theories contributes to our understanding of this subject. Considered here are the potentially conflicting expectations of different stakeholders, the role of institutional shareholders, and whether the profit motive should be the key driving force. A separate section looks at inherent conflicts of interest in certain not-for-profit organizations and later at issues of social responsibility and business ethics which also affect behaviour, performance and outcomes in a variety of ways. The chapter begins with a case on Ben and Jerry's ice cream, a company which has always been proud of its commitment to social and environmental causes and which has recently been acquired by the Anglo-Dutch multinational corporation Unilever.*

# Minicase 3.1 Ben and Jerry's Ice Cream

This idiosyncratic business was founded and developed by two partners, both entrepreneurs but, at face value, unlikely businessmen. Ben Cohen was a college dropout who had become a potter. His friend from his schooldays was Jerry Greenfield, a laboratory assistant who had failed to make it into medical school. They had become 'seventies hippies with few real job prospects'. They decided they wanted to do something themselves and 'looked for something they might succeed at'. They 'liked food, so food it was!' They could not afford the machinery for making bagels, their first choice, but ice cream was affordable. In 1977 they opened an ice-cream parlour in Burlington, Vermont, where there were 'lots of students and no real competition'. They fostered a relaxed, hippy atmosphere and employed a blues pianist. Their ice cream was different, with large and unusual chunks.

They were instantly successful in their first summer, but sales fell off in the fall and winter when the snow arrived. They realized they would have to find outlets outside Vermont if they were to survive. Ben went on the road. Always dressed casually, he would arrive somewhere around 4.00 am and then sleep in his car until a potential distributor opened. He was able to 'charm the distributors' and the business began to grow. Ben and Jerry's success provoked a response from the dominant market leader, Häagen Dazs, owned by Pillsbury. Their market share was 70% of the luxury ice-cream market. Häagen Dazs threatened to withdraw their product from any distributors who also handled Ben and Jerry's. The two partners employed a lawyer and threatened legal action, but their real weapon was a publicity campaign targeted at Pillsbury itself, and its famous 'dough boy' logo. 'What's the Dough Boy afraid of?' they asked. Their gimmicks generated massive publicity and they received an out-of-court settlement. More significantly, the publicity created new demand for luxury ice cream, and the company began to grow more rapidly than had ever been envisaged. A threat had been turned into a massive opportunity. Soon Ben and Jerry's had a segment market share of 39%, just 4% behind Häagen

Dazs. The company has expanded internationally with mixed success. They have enjoyed only limited success in the UK 'because there was only limited marketing support'.

Perhaps not unexpectedly, given their background, Ben and Jerry have created a values-driven business; some of their ice creams have been linked to causes and interests they support and promote. Rainforest Crunch ice cream features nuts from Brazil; the key ingredients for Chocolate Fudge Brownie are produced by an inner-city bakery in Yonkers, New York; and they favour Vermont's dairy-farming industry. When the business needed equity capital to support its growth, local Vermont residents were given priority treatment. Ben and Jerry argue they are committed to their employees who 'bring their hearts and souls as well as their bodies and minds to work' but acknowledge that their internal opinion surveys show a degree of dissatisfaction with the amount of profits (7.5%) given away every year to good causes.

The two realists with an unusual but definite ego drive later dropped out of day-to-day management '. . . the company needed a greater breadth of management than we had . . .' and were content to be 'two casual, portly, middle-aged hippies'.

In early Spring 2000 the business was acquired by Unilever, the multinational foods, detergents and cosmetics business. Unilever already owned the UK market leader, Walls ice cream. Unilever and Walls had recently been investigated by the UK competition authorities because of their strategy of insisting that retailers only stock Walls ice cream if Unilever provide them with a freezer cabinet on loan.

QUESTIONS: Do you think the objectives of Ben and Jerry's will have to change after this acquisition?
Do you think it will feel like 'a different place to work', with different priorities?

*Ben and Jerry's*   http://www.benjerry.com

If you don't know where you are going, any road will take you there.
*Raymond G Viault,*
*when Chief Executive Officer,*
*Jacobs Suchard, Switzerland*

A voyage of a thousand miles begins with a single step. It is important that that step is in the right direction.
*Old Chinese saying, updated*

How can we go forward when we don't know which way we are facing?
*John Lennon, 1972*

Life can only be understood backward, but it must be lived forward.
*S Kierkegaard*

# Introduction

This chapter is about the idea of strategic direction and objectives – what is meant by the terminology used and the implications. Objectives (in some form or another) should be set and communicated so that people know where the strategic leader wants the organization to be at some time in the future. At the same time it is essential that the objectives currently being pursued are clearly understood. Because of incremental changes in strategies the actual or implicit objectives may have changed from those that were established and made explicit sometime in the past. Objectives, therefore, establish direction, and in some cases set specific end-points. They should have time-scales or end-dates attached to them. The attainment of them should be measurable in some way, and ideally they will encourage and motivate people.

It is important, straight away, to distinguish between the idea of a broad purpose and specific, measurable, milestones. The organization needs direction in terms of where the strategic leader wants it to go, and how he or she would wish it to develop. This is really related to the *mission* of the organization, and/or possibly a visionary statement concerning the future. This mission is likely to be stated broadly and generally, and it is unlikely that it can ever be achieved completely. Thus, the organization pursues the mission, looking for new opportunities and new ways of building value for customers, dealing with problems and seeking to progress continually in the chosen direction. Improvements in the overall situation towards the stated mission are the appropriate measure of performance.

Managers at all levels are likely to be set specific objectives to achieve. These, logically, are quantifiable targets for sales, profit, productivity or output, and performance against them is measured and evaluated. Objectives then become measurable points which indicate how the organization is making definite progress towards its broad purpose or mission.

Intended strategies are developed from the mission and the desired objectives as they are the means of achieving them. Hence, a change of objectives is likely to result in changes of strategy. At the same time it is important to realize that incremental, adaptive and emergent changes in strategy, whether the result of internal or external pressure, affect the levels of performance of the organization, i.e. the growth, profit or market share, and these performance levels should be related to the objectives actually being pursued.

The central theme of the chapter is that it is essential that the most senior managers in an organization understand clearly where their company is going, and why. Ideally, all managers will appreciate the overall mission and how their own role contributes to its attainment. The strategies being followed may be different to those that were originally stated, and there may be good reasons for this. Thus, the situation should be reviewed constantly and the strategic leader should seek to remain informed and aware of what is happening.

## Definitions, Terminology and Examples

Box 3.1 defines the terms *vision*, *mission* and *objectives* and provides a range of examples from the private and public sectors. Figure 3.1 shows the relationships between these terms, highlighting their key constituents. The examples in Box 3.1 were selected to illustrate the relevant points, not because they are superior or inferior to those of other organizations; they should be evaluated in this light.

The expression *aims* is sometimes used as an alternative to mission. The term *goals* is seen as synonymous with objectives, and in this book the terms are used interchangeably. Specifically, where other works are being referred to and those authors have used the term goal as opposed to objective, their terminology is retained. It is also important to distinguish between long-term and short-term objectives or goals. Thompson and Strickland (1980) provide a useful distinction. They argue that objectives overall define the specific kinds of performance and results that the organization seeks to produce through its activities. The *long-term objectives* relate to the desired performance and results on an ongoing basis; *short-term objectives* are concerned with the near-term performance targets that the organization desires to reach in progressing towards its long-term objectives. Making use of such techniques as management

STRATEGY IN ACTION – Box 3.1
Examples of Vision, Mission and
Objectives Statements

## Vision statements

A *vision statement* describes what the company is to become in the (long-term) future.

### The Sony spirit

Sony is a trail blazer, always a seeker of the unknown. Sony will never follow old trails, yet to be trod. Through this progress Sony wants to serve mankind.

*Sony*  http://www.sony.com

### WH Smith (1995)

There's nowhere quite like WH Smith. It's full of energy and colour and excitement.

Just when you think you know them, they surprise you. Everywhere you look there are fresh, inspired ideas.

Smith's is an essential part of life. It's a unique blend of information, inspiration and just plain fun.

Everything is chosen with thought, designed with care and presented with imagination.

Customer service is instinctive. It's the right help at the right time, by people who know what they're saying and love what they're doing.

Smith's builds its reputation day by day, product by product and customer by customer.

Always in Front.

We can see represented here: adding new values, innovation, products which match customer needs, effective presentation, service and constant improvement.

*WH Smith*
http://www.whsmith.co.uk

### British Airways

The world's favourite airline.

This vision focuses on employees and customers. The related mission emphasized BA's desire to be the world's first truly global airline, which in turn generated a corporate strategy of carefully selected alliances. To be feasible, however, it has always been essential that BA staff believe in the vision and act accordingly. In recent years staff trust and morale has declined as costs have been cut dramatically and the airline's profitability has declined.

*British Airways*
http://www.britishairways.com

## Mission statements

The *mission* reflects the essential purpose of the organization, concerning particularly why it is in existence, the nature of the business(es) it is in, and the customers it seeks to serve and satisfy.

### The Girl Guides Association

To help a girl reach her highest potential.

These eight words cut straight to the heart of the movement; there is a clear and direct statement of purpose.

*Girl Guides Association*
http://www.wagggsworld.org

### Financial Times Conferences

The mission of the FTC is to organize conferences on subjects of interest to the international business community, using the highest calibre speakers and providing attending delegates with the finest service, thereby providing a low-cost and time efficient means of both obtaining impartial quality information and making senior-level industry contacts.

We can see a clear definition of the business, a formulation of objectives, delivery strategies, means of differentiating the service and stakeholder relevance.

*Financial Times*
http://www.news.ft.com

### Virgin Atlantic Airways

As the UK's second long-haul carrier, to build an intercontinental network concentrating on those routes with a substantial established market and clear indication of growth potential, by offering the highest possible service and lowest possible cost.

Not particularly elegant in style, but it does clarify both the target markets and the source of competitive advantage.

*Virgin Atlantic*
http://www.virgin-atlantic.com

### Long-term objectives

*Objectives* are desired states or results linked to particular time scales and concerning such things as size or type of organization, the nature and variety of the areas of interest and levels of success.

### BAA – British Airports Authority: Open objectives

BAA aims to enhance the value of the shareholders' investments by achieving steady and remunerative long-term growth. Its strategy for developing and operating world-class international airports that are safe, secure, efficient and profitable is based on a commitment to continuously enhancing the quality of service to passengers and business partners alike. This process of constant improvement includes cost-effective investment in new airport facilities closely matched to customer demand.

These are in the context of a stated mission to 'make BAA the most successful airport company in the world'.

*British Airports Authority*
http://www.baa.co.uk

### HP Bulmer Holdings: Multiple stakeholder objectives

Our mission is to remain the world's most successful cider company. We will continue to measure our success in terms of market leadership, product quality, increasing shareholder value, and rewarding employment opportunities for our employees. This will be achieved by attaining the following objectives:

1. Lead and grow the UK and international cider markets through meeting consumer needs by superior marketing and sustained high levels of customer service.
2. Maintain lowest industry costs and ensure the most economical supply of essential and quality raw materials.
3. Be dedicated to fulfilling the requirements of all our customers through achieving excellence in our products, operations and service.
4. Adopt best practice across all of our activities through an innovative approach to product, process development and information technology.
5. Foster a culture of continuous improvement through self-motivation, team work and acceptance of change.
6. Provide competitive pay, employee share ownership and single status employment while achieving a link between performance. reward and shareholder interests.

7. Give all employees the opportunity to develop skills and potential through actively improving their own and the company's performance. Promote from within whenever appropriate.

8. Keep employees informed of policy, plans and performance. Invite comments and feedback and, through employee involvement, show how individual and team efforts contribute towards the company's success.

9. Provide a high quality working environment taking all appropriate steps to ensure the health and safety of our employees, customers and the community.

10. Preserve the quality of life and environment in our everyday work and to benefit our local communities whenever an affordable opportunity arises.

(Reproduced with permission.)

Multiple objectives, stated in this form, will demand priorities and trade-offs at different times, but their value is that they draw attention to the potentially conflicting needs of all the major stakeholders.

*HP Bulmer Holdings*
http://www.bulmer.co.uk

**Kirin Brewery (Japan): Closed objectives**
For the decade of the 1990s:

• Increase sales from 1250 billion yen (1990) to 1700 billion (2000)
• Increase sales of non-beer products to 60% of total revenue by
• Diversifying (further) into biotechnology, construction engineering, information systems and service industries
• Become a global corporation.

*Kirin Brewery*
http://www.kirin.co.jp/english/index.html

by objectives, these performance targets can be agreed with individual managers, who are then given responsibility for their attainment and held accountable.

Measurement can be straightforward for an objective such as 'the achievement of a minimum return of 20% of net capital employed in the business, but with a target of 25%, in the next 12 months'. If the objective is less specific, for example, 'continued customer satisfaction, a competitive return on capital employed and real growth in earnings per share next year', measurement is still possible but requires a comparison of competitor returns and the monitoring of customer satisfaction through, say, the number of complaints received. Richards (1978) uses the terms 'open' and 'closed' to distinguish between objectives that are clearly measurable and typically finance based (closed) and those that are less specific and essentially continuing.

## Vision statements

While mission statements have become increasingly popular for organizations, vision *statements* are less prevalent. The lack of a published statement, of course, is not necessarily an indication of a lack of vision. Where they exist they reflect the company's vision of some future state, which ideally the organization will achieve. Terminology and themes such as a world-class manufacturer, a quality organization, a provider of legendary service and a stimulating, rewarding place to work might well appear. The essential elements focus on those values to which the organization is committed

*Figure 3.1* Vision and mission statements and objectives.

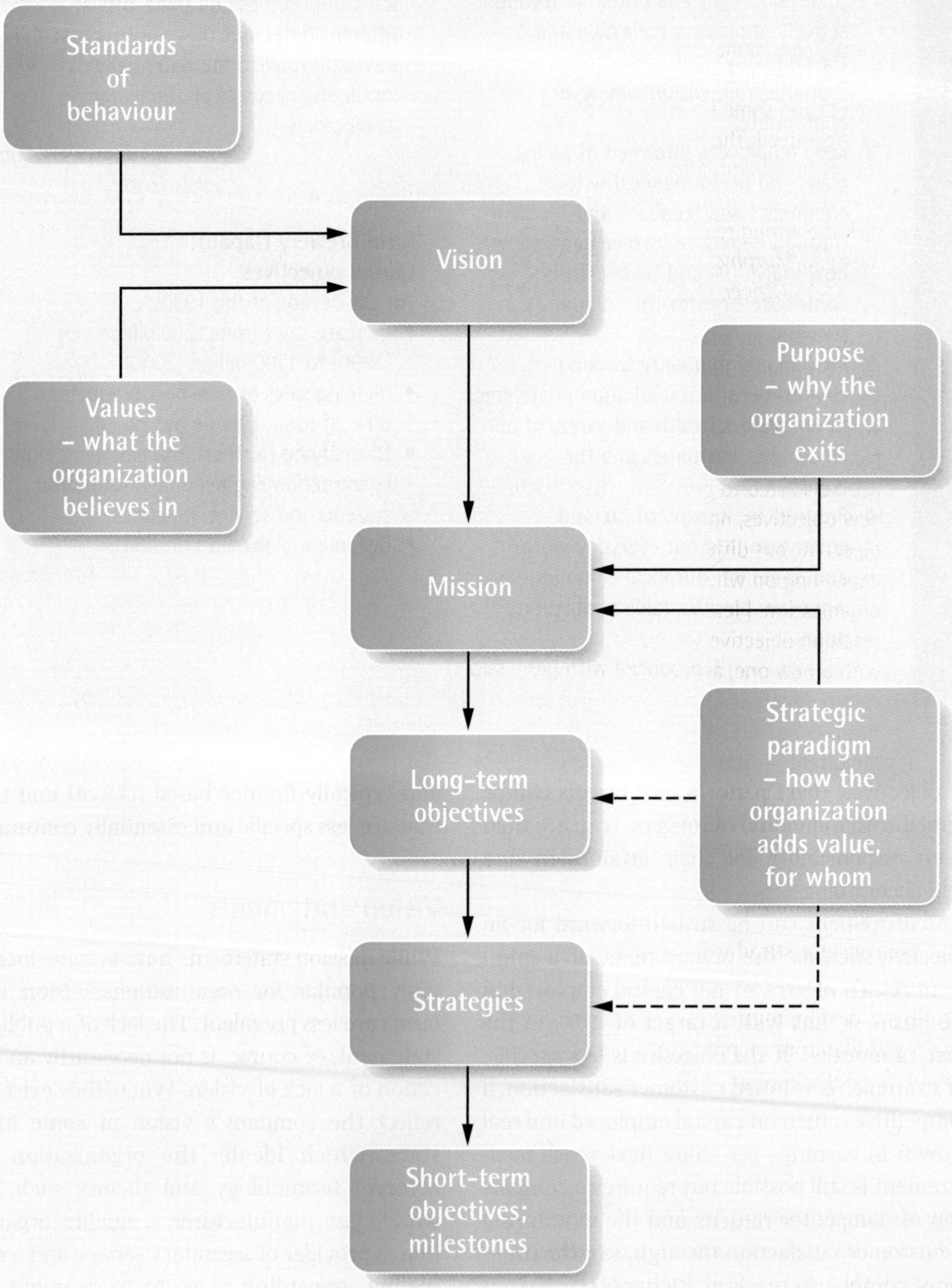

Strategy development is like driving around a roundabout. The signposts are only useful if you know where you want to go. Some exits lead uphill, some downhill – most are one-way streets and some have very heavy traffic indeed. The trick is in picking the journey's end before you set out – otherwise you go around in circles or pick the wrong road.

*Gerry M Murphy, when Chief Executive Officer, Greencore plc, Ireland*

Arne Ness said, when he climbed Everest: I had a dream. I reached it. I lost the dream and I miss it.
When we reached our dream we didn't have another long-term objective. So people started to produce their own new objectives, not a common objective, but different objectives depending on where they were in the organization. I learned that before you reach an objective you must be ready with a new one, and you must start to communicate it to the organization. But it is not the goal itself that is important . . . it is the fight to get there.

*Jan Carlzon, when Chairman and Chief Executive Officer, Scandinavian Airlines System*

and appropriate standards of behaviour for all employees. Possible improvement paths, employee development programmes and measures or indicators of progress should be established for each element of the vision.

## Mission statements

The corporate mission is the overriding *raison d'être* for the business. Ackoff (1986), however, claimed that many corporate mission statements prove worthless, one reason being that they consist of loose expressions such as 'maxi-

mize growth potential' or 'provide products of the highest quality'. How, he queries, can a company determine whether it has attained its maximum growth potential or highest quality? His points are still valid today. Primarily, the mission statement should not address what an organization must do in order to survive, but what it has chosen to do in order to thrive. It should be positive, visionary and motivating.

Ackoff suggests that a good mission statement has five characteristics.

- It will contain a formulation of objectives that enables progress towards them to be measured.
- It differentiates the company from its competitors.
- It defines the business(es) that the company wants to be in, not necessarily is in.
- It is relevant to all stakeholders in the firm, not just shareholders and managers.
- It is exciting and inspiring.

Campbell (1989) argues that to be valuable mission statements must reflect corporate values, and the strategic leader and the organization as a whole should be visibly pursuing the mission. He takes a wider perspective than Ackoff by including aspects of the corporate vision and arguing that there are four key issues involved in developing a useful mission.

First, it is important to clarify the purpose of the organization – why it exists. Hanson plc, for example, which is referred to at various stages in this book, was led by Lord James Hanson for some 25 years and he stated:

*It is the central tenet of my faith that the shareholder is king. My aim is to advance the shareholder's interest by increasing earnings per share.*

By contrast, and at the same time, Lex Service published an alternative view:

*We will exercise responsibility in our dealings with all our stakeholders and, in the case of conflict, balance the interest of the employees and share-holders on an equal basis over time.*

The implications of these contrasting perspectives are discussed in the next section of this chapter.

Secondly, the mission statement should describe the business and its activities, and the position that it wants to achieve in its field. Thirdly, the organization's values should be stated. How does the company intend to treat its employees, customers and suppliers, for example? Finally, it is important to ensure that the organization behaves in the way that it promises it will. This is important because it can inspire trust in employees and others who significantly influence the organization.

It is generally accepted that in successful companies middle and junior managers know where the strategic leaders are taking the company and why. In less successful organizations there is often confusion about this.

Mission statements, like vision statements, can all-too-easily just 'state the obvious' and as a result have little real value. The secret lies in clarifying what makes a company different and a more effective competitor, rather than simply restating those requirements that are essential for meeting key success factors. A mission (or vision) statement which could easily be used by another business, whether in the same industry or not – as many can be – is, simply, of no great value. Companies that succeed long term are those which create competitive advantages and sustain their strong positions with flexibility and improvement. The vision and mission should support this.

The principal purpose of these statements is communication, both externally and internally and, arguably, a major benefit for organizations is the thinking they are forced to do in order to establish sound statements. Nevertheless, many are still worded poorly. In addition, it is essential that the mission (or vision) is more than a plaque in a foyer; employees have to make the words mean something through their actions. For this to happen, employees must feel that the organization actually means what it is saying in the mission and vision statements. There must be an element of trust, for without it the desired outcomes will not be achieved.

The mission clearly corresponds closely to the basic philosophy or vision underlying the business, and if there is a sound philosophy, strategies that generate success will be derived from it. Sock Shop was founded in 1983, with a simple vision. One newspaper has summarized it as, 'shopping in big stores for basic items like stockings is a fag, but nipping into an attractive kiosk at an Underground station, British Rail concourse or busy high street is quick, convenient and can be fun'. From this have emerged six key marketing features or strategies, which have become the foundations of the company's success and rapid growth:

- shops located within areas of heavy pedestrian traffic
- easily accessible products
- friendly and efficient service
- a wide range of quality products designed to meet the needs of customers
- attractive presentations
- competitive selling prices.

In 1989, after a number of years of growth and success, Sock Shop began to lose money. The hot summer weather and the London Underground strikes were blamed for falling sales. Increasing interest rates caused additional financial problems. Moreover, Sock Shop expanded into the USA and this had proved costly. However, in February 1990 Sock Shop founder, Sophie Mirman, commented: 'We provide everyday necessities in a fashionable manner . . . our concept remains sound. Our merchandise continues to be not merely "lifestyle".' Sophie Mirman has since lost control of Sock Shop but her vision prevails.

## Objectives: Issues and Perspectives

A full consideration of objectives incorporates three aspects:

- an appreciation of the objectives that the organization is actually pursuing and achieving – where it is going and why
- the objectives that it might pursue, and the freedom and opportunity it has to make changes
- specific objectives for the future.

This chapter looks at the issues that affect and determine the first two of these. Decisions about specific future objectives are considered later in the book (Chapter 11). We begin, though, by looking briefly at a number of theories of business organizations and considering the role and importance of stakeholders.

### Market models

Basic microeconomic theory states that firms should seek to maximize profits and that this is achieved where marginal revenue is equal to marginal cost. A number of assumptions underpin this theory, including the assumptions that firms clearly understand the nature of the demand for their products, and why people buy, and that they are willing and able to control production and sales as the model demands. In reality, decision makers do not have perfect knowledge and production and sales are affected by suppliers and distributors.

However, this basic theory has resulted in the development of four market models (Table 3.1), and the characteristics of these in respect of barriers to entry into the industry and the marketing opportunities (differentiation potential; price and non-price competition) determine whether or not there is a real opportunity to achieve significant profits.

In markets which approach pure competition (pure competition as such is theoretical), firms will only make 'normal' profits, the amount required for them to stay in the industry. Products are 'commodities', not differentiated, and so premium prices for certain brands are not possible. There are no major barriers to entry into the industry and so new suppliers are attracted if there are profits to be made. Competition results, and if supply exceeds demand the ruling market price is forced down and only the efficient firms survive.

In monopolistic competition there are again several suppliers, some large, many small, but products are differentiated. However, as there are once more no major barriers to entry the above situation concerning profits applies. Newcomers increase supply and although those firms with distinctive products can charge some premium they will still have to move in line with market prices generally, and this will have a dampening effect on profits.

Only in oligopoly and monopoly markets, where a small number of large firms is dominant, is there real opportunity for 'supernormal' profits, in excess of what is required to stay in business. However, in oligopoly the small number of large firms tend to be wary of each other and prices are held back to some extent for fear of losing market share. Suppliers are interdependent and fear that a price decrease will be met by competitors (thus reducing profits) and price increases will not (hence market share will be threatened). There are two types of oligopoly, depending on whether opportunities exist for significant differentiation. In all of these models competition is a major determinant of profit potential and therefore objectives must be set with competitors in mind. In a monopoly (again somewhat theoretical in a pure sense) excess profits could be made if government did not act as a restraint. In the UK, although such public-sector organizations as British Gas and British Telecom have been privatized their actions in

*Table 3.1*    Structural characteristics of four market models

| Market model | Number of firms | Type of product | Control over price by supplier | Entry conditions | Non-price competition* | Examples† |
|---|---|---|---|---|---|---|
| Pure competition | Large | Standardized Identical or almost identical | None | Free | None | Agricultural products; some chemicals; printing; laundry services |
| Monopolistic competition | Large | Differentiated | Some | Relatively easy | Yes | Clothing; furniture; soft drinks; plumbers; restaurants. |
| Oligopoly‡ | Few or a few dominant | Standardized or differentiated | Limited by mutual interdependence. Considerable if collusion takes place | Difficult | Yes | Standardized: cement; sugar; fertilizers. Differentiated: margarine; soaps; detergents. |
| Pure monopoly | One | Unique | Considerable | Blocked | Yes | British Gas (domestic consumers); water companies in their regions; local bus companies in certain towns. |

*Non-price competition occurs in many ways, e.g. by attempts to increase the extent of product differentiation and buyer preference through advertising, brand names, trade marks, promotions, distribution outlets; by new product launch and innovation, etc.

†Useful further reading: Doyle, P and Gidengil, ZB (1977) An empirical study of market structures. *Journal of Management Studies*, **14**(3), October, 316–28. Some of the examples are taken from this.

‡There are many oligopoly models of collusive and non-collusive type. They make varying behavioural and structural assumptions.

terms of supply and pricing are monitored and regulated.

## Stakeholder theory

The influence of external stakeholders will be examined again in Chapter 7, which looks at the business environment, but it is important to introduce the topic at this stage. A further assumption of profit-maximizing theory is that shareholders in the business should be given first priority and be the major consideration in decision making, and this arose because early economic theorists saw owners and managers as being synonymous. This assumption no longer holds, however. A study of market models demonstrates the important role played by competitors and by government as a restraining force, and it was also suggested that organizations must pay some regard to their suppliers and distributors. In addition, managers and employees must be considered. The decisions taken by managers which create incremental change will be influenced by the objectives and values that they believe are important. Managers are paid employees, and whilst concerned about profits, they will also regard growth and security as important.

These are all *stakeholders*. Freeman (1984) defines stakeholders as any group or individual who can affect, or is affected by, the performance of the organization. Newbould and Luffman (1979) argue that current and future strategies are affected by

- external pressures from the marketplace, including competitors, buyers and suppliers; shareholders; pressure groups; and government
- internal pressures from existing commitments, managers, employees and their trade unions

- the personal ethical and moral perspectives of senior managers.

Figure 3.2 re-presents these ideas and also highlights the need for a solid base in the form of corporate values and priorities.

Stakeholder theory, then, postulates that the objectives of an organization will take account of the various needs of these different interested parties who will represent some type of informal coalition. Their relative power will be a key variable, and the organization will on occasions 'trade off' one against the other, establishing a hierarchy of relative importance. Stakeholders see different things as being important and receive benefits or rewards in a variety of ways, as featured in Table 3.2.

Stakeholder interests are not always consistent. For example, investment in new technology might improve product quality and as a result lead to increased profits. While customers who are shareholders might perceptively benefit, if the investment implies lost jobs then employees, possibly managers, and their trade

*Table 3.2*   Examples of stakeholder interests

| | |
|---|---|
| Shareholders | Annual dividends; increasing the value of their investment in the company as the share price increases. Both are affected by growth and profits<br>Institutional shareholders may balance high-risk investments and their anticipated high returns with more stable investments in their portfolio |
| Managers | Salaries and bonuses; perks; status from working for a well-known and successful organization; responsibility; challenge; security |
| Employees | Wages; holidays; conditions and job satisfaction; security – influenced by trade union involvement |
| Consumers | Desirable and quality products; competitive prices – very much in relation to competition; new products at appropriate times |
| Distributors | On-time and reliable deliveries |
| Suppliers | Consistent orders; payment on time |
| Financiers | Interest payments and loan repayments; like payment for supplies, affected by cash flow |
| Government | Payment of taxes and provision of employment; contribution to the nation's exports |
| Society in general | Socially responsible actions – sometimes reflected in pressure groups |

NB. This is not intended to constitute a complete list.

*Figure 3.2* The pillars of success. From Blanchard, K and O'Connor, M (1997) *Managing by Values*, Berret-Koehler Publishers.

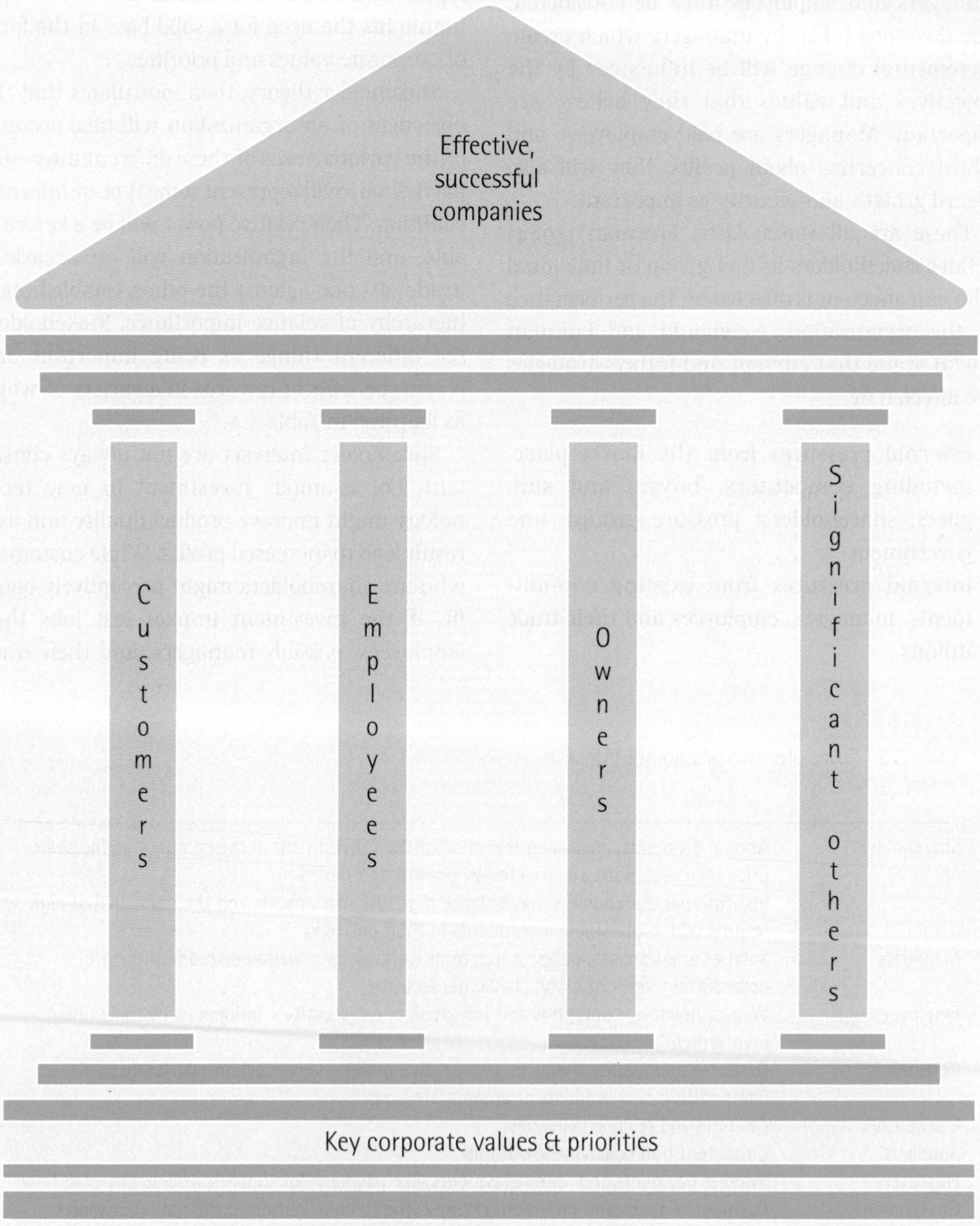

Effective,
successful
companies

C
u
s
t
o
m
e
r
s

E
m
p
l
o
y
e
e
s

O
w
n
e
r
s

S
i
g
n
i
f
i
c
a
n
t

o
t
h
e
r
s

Key corporate values & priorities

unions may be dissatisfied. If the scale of redundancy is large and results in militant resistance, the government may become involved.

The various stakeholders are not affected in the same way by every strategic decision and, consequently, their relative influence will vary from decision to decision. In 1995 Shell, one of Europe's most successful and respected companies, was forced to change an important strategic decision following a high-profile campaign by a leading pressure group. Shell wanted to sink its redundant Brent Spar oil platform in deep seas some 150 miles west of Scotland. It had reached an agreement with the UK government that, scientifically, this was the most appropriate means of disposal for the platform. Greenpeace objected and protesters boarded the platform, claiming that it still contained 5000 tonnes of oil which would eventually be released to pollute the sea. The ensuing and professionally orchestrated publicity fuelled public opinion, and there were protests in a number of European countries, including attacks on petrol stations in Germany. Shell backed down and agreed to investigate other possibilities for disposal. The UK government expressed both anger and disappointment with this decision. Independent inspectors later proved that Greenpeace's claims were gross exaggerations – the residual oil was much, much less than 5000 tonnes. The press concluded: 'Shell went wrong in spending too much time convincing government of the case for seabed dumping, but not attaching enough importance to consulting other stakeholder groups'.

Shell had been made to appear socially irresponsible, yet the ethics of the Greenpeace campaign are questionable; these issues are explored further at the end of this chapter.

Waterman (1994) contends that successful companies do not automatically make shareholders their first priority. Instead, they pay primary attention to employees and customers and, as a result, they perform more effectively than their rivals. The outcome is superior profits and wealth creation for the shareholders. Simon (1964) argues that one of the main reasons for an organization's collapse is a failure to incorporate the important motivational concerns of key stakeholders. Small businesses, for example, are generally weak in relation to their suppliers, especially if these are larger well-established concerns; and if they neglect managing their cash flow and fail to pay their accounts on time they will find their deliveries stopped. For any organization, if new products or services fail to provide consumers with what they are looking for, however well produced or low priced they might be, they will not sell.

A recent survey by Deloitte Consulting (1999) confirmed that 'customer-centric' manufacturing companies worldwide are 60% more profitable than those that are less committed to customers. In addition, they enjoy lower operating costs. Customer-centricity is seen as a 'systematic process which sets objectives for customer loyalty and retention and then tracks performance towards those goals'. It should facilitate the development of higher added value, premium-price products.

Figure 3.3 shows that shareholders, employees and customers are the three key stakeholders that the organization must satisfy, but invariably in a competitive environment: if they fail with any group long term they will place the organization in jeopardy through a spiral of decline. Figure 3.4 is an alternative presentation of the same points. On the left is a virtuous circle of growth and prosperity. Satisfied, perhaps even delighted, customers enable high financial returns, which can be used in part to reward employees. A perception of fairness here can be instrumental for motivating employees to keep customers satisfied and thus sustain the circle. The issues of measuring performance in relation to all of the stakeholders will be taken up in Chapter 4. The right-hand side clarifies that the needs of customers can sometimes conflict with the

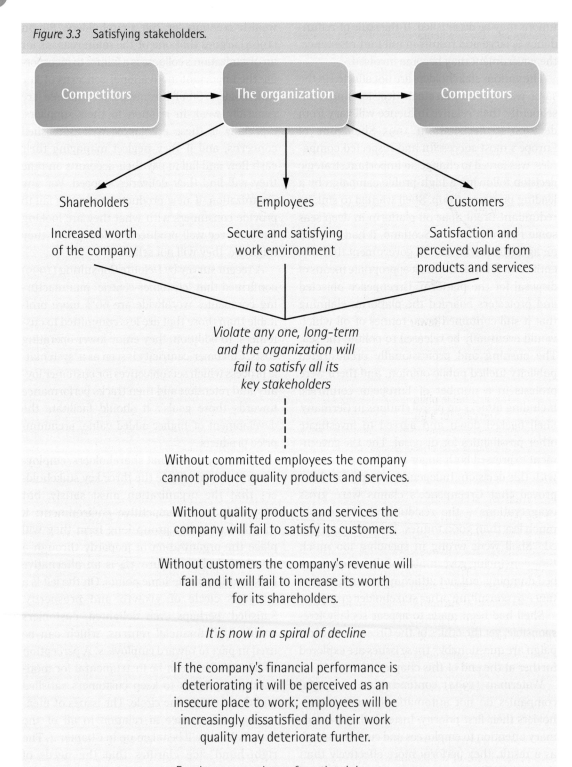

*Figure 3.3*  Satisfying stakeholders.

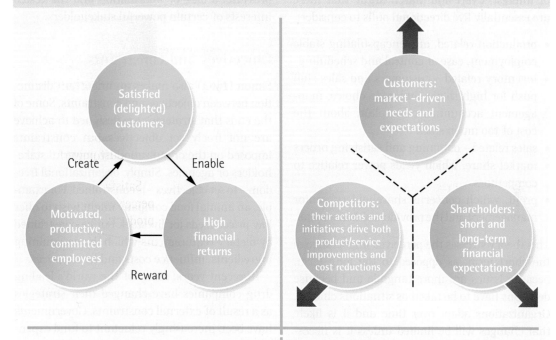

*Figure 3.4*  Complementary or conflicting measures.

This justifiable philosophy reinforces the case for a bundle of linked measures affecting all key stakeholders, e.g. the balanced scorecard.

However, time pressures and priority trade-offs frequently cause the measures to conflict. This is influenced by competitive pressures.

demands of some shareholders, especially those who are willing to trade off long-term achievement for short-term financial returns. Competitors are always trying to persuade customers to switch allegiance and thus impact on an organization's success.

While these arguments are, in themselves, convincing, many organizations still fail to satisfy their stakeholders long term. The following theories provide some insight into this reality.

## Cyert and March's behavioural theory

Stakeholder theory is closely related to the ideas in Cyert and March's *A Behavioural Theory of the Firm* (1963). Cyert and March argue that the

The investor and the employee are in the same position, but sometimes the employee is more important, because he will be there a long time, whereas an investor will often get in and out on a whim in order to make a profit. The worker's mission is to contribute to the company's welfare, and his own, every day. All of his working life he is really needed.

*Akio Morita, Joint Founder, Sony*

goals of an organization are a *compromise* between members of a coalition comprising the parties affecting an organization. The word compromise is used as the actual choice is linked to relative power and there are inevitably conflicts of interest. Cyert and March argue that there are essentially five directional pulls to consider:

- production related, and encapsulating stable employment, ease of control and scheduling
- inventory related – customers and sales staff push for high stocks and wide choice, management accountants complain about the cost of too much stock
- sales related – obtaining and satisfying orders
- market share, which yields power relative to competitors
- profit, which concerns shareholders, senior management and the providers of loan capital.

This theory stresses the perceived importance of the short term, as opposed to the long term, because issues are more tangible and because decisions have to be taken as situations change. Organizations adapt over time and it is likely that changes will be limited unless it is necessary to change things more radically. In other words, once a compromise situation is reached there is a tendency to seek to retain it rather than change it, and the goals will change as the values and relative importance of coalition members change. As a result, 'organizational slack' develops. This is 'payments to members of the coalition in excess of what is required to keep them in the coalition'. It is difficult, for example, to determine the minimum acceptable reward for employees; assets are generally underexploited since it is difficult to know the maximum productivity of a person or machine; and uncertainties mean that less-than-optimal price, product and promotional policies will be pursued. The existence of slack does allow for extra effort in times of emergency.

This theory can be usefully considered alongside Herbert Simon's (1964) theory of satisficing. Here he contends that managers seek courses of action which are acceptable in the light of known objectives. These actions may not be optimal but they are chosen because of internal and external constraints such as time pressure, a lack of information and the vested interests of certain powerful stakeholders.

## Objectives and constraints

Simon (1964) also makes an important distinction between objectives and constraints. Some of the ends that strategies are designed to achieve are not freely set objectives but constraints imposed on the organization by powerful stakeholders or agencies. Simply, organizational freedom – to set objectives – is constrained. For example, an animal food company might wish to offer low priced feeds for livestock but be constrained by dietary requirements which, by determining ingredients, influence costs and hence prices.

In recent years, many of the world's leading drug companies have changed their strategies as a result of external constraints. Governments have been increasingly reluctant to fund expensive drugs and treatments. Some companies have closed plants, while others have relocated for lower costs. There has been an increased research focus on treatments that are most likely to receive funding, arguably at the expense of potential breakthroughs in other areas. Priorities and strategies in the UK National Health Service (NHS) are affected by the Government's waiting-list targets. Although Railtrack (which manages and maintains the UK railway infrastructure) is a private-sector business, it has a Regulator who imposes specific requirements and targets for safety which inevitably affect costs and profits.

A number of other authors have offered theories in an attempt to explain the behaviour of organizations and the objectives they seek.

## Baumol's theory of sales maximization

Baumol (1959) argues that firms seek to maximize sales rather than profits, but within the constraint of a minimum acceptable profit level. It can be demonstrated that profit maximizing is achieved at a level of output below that which would maximize sales revenue and that, as sales and revenue increase beyond profit maximizing, profits are sacrificed. Firms will increase sales and revenue as long as they are making profits in excess of what they regard as an acceptable minimum. Businessmen, Baumol argues, attach great importance to sales as salaries are often linked to the scale of operations. 'Whenever executives are asked 'How's business?', the typical reply is that sales have been increasing or decreasing'.

## Williamson's model of managerial discretion

Williamson (1964) argues that managers can set their own objectives, that these will be different from those of shareholders and that managerial satisfaction is the key. Satisfaction increases if a manager has a large staff reporting to him or her, if there are 'lavish perks' and if profits exceed the level required for the essential development of the business and the necessary replacement of equipment. This extra profit can be used for pet projects or the pursuit of non-profit objectives. The manner in which managers reward themselves for success is discretionary.

## Marris's theory of managerial capitalism

Marris (1964) again postulates growth as a key concern, as managers derive utility from growth in the form of enhanced salaries, power and status. The constraint is one of security. If, as a result of growth strategies pursued by the firm, profits are held down, say because of interest charges, the market value of the firm's shares may fall relative to the book value of the assets. In such a case the firm may become increasingly vulnerable to take-over, and managers wish to avoid this situation.

## Penrose's theory of growth

Penrose (1959) has offered another growth theory, arguing that an organization will seek to achieve the full potential from all its resources. Firms grow as long as there are unused resources, diversifying when they can no longer grow with existing products, services and markets. Growth continues until it is halted. A major limit, for example, could be production facilities either in terms of total output or because of a bottleneck in one part of the operation. Changes can free the limit, and growth continues until the next limiting factor appears. Another limit is the capacity of managers to plan and implement growth strategies. If managers are stretched, extra people can be employed, but the remedy is not immediate. New people have to be trained and integrated, and this takes up some of the time of existing managers. Penrose refers to this issue as the 'receding managerial limit' because again the limiting factor decreases over a period of time. In a climate of reasonably constant growth and change managers learn how to cope with the dynamics of change; and properly managed, given that overambition is constrained and that market opportunities exist, firms can enjoy steady and continuous growth.

## Galbraith's views on technocracy

Finally, Galbraith (1969) highlighted the particular role of large corporations, whose pursuit of size requires very large investments associated with long-term commitments. Because of these financial commitments the corporations seek to control their environment as far as they possibly can, influencing both government and consumer, and they in turn are controlled by what Galbraith calls 'technocrats' – teams of powerful experts and specialists. Their purposes are, first, to protect as well as control the organization, and hence they seek financial security and profit, and, secondly, to 'affirm' the organization through growth, expansion and market share. As is typical of oligopolists, price competition is not seen to be in their interests, and hence aggressive marketing and non-price competition are stressed. In addition, such firms will seek to influence or even control (by acquisition) suppliers and distributors, and they may well see the world, rather than just the UK, as their market. These issues are all explored later in the book, but particularly in Chapter 15.

Galbraith (1963) also identified the growth of 'countervailing power' to limit this technocracy. The growth of trade unions in the past is an example of this, but, as seen in recent years, the technocrats have fought back successfully. The increasing size and power of grocery retailers such as Sainsbury and Tesco, and their success with own-label brands, has put pressure on all product manufacturers, especially those whose products are not the brand leader. As a conse-

quence the owners of the strongest brands have invested heavily to promote their brands and ensure that they are selected, even though there may be cheaper alternatives. Moreover, there have been mergers within retailing in an attempt to strengthen power bases. Tesco has expanded from the UK into Europe, while Wal-Mart has acquired ASDA. Simply, over time there are swings in relative power and, as a result, the potential for consumer exploitation is checked and available profits are shared more widely.

## Profit as an objective

Box 3.2 discusses whether profit is the ultimate objective of profit-seeking business organizations or whether it is merely a means to other ends, which themselves constitute the real objectives. Not-for-profit organizations are considered separately later in this chapter (p. 111).

Ackoff (1986) argues that both profit and growth are means to other ends rather than objectives in themselves. He argues that profit is necessary for the survival of a business enter-

---

**DISCUSSION – Box 3.2**
**Profit**

A business school is likely to teach that an organization must be good to people because then they will work harder; and if they work harder the business will make a profit.

They will also teach that a firm should strive to produce better products and services, because with better products the firm will make greater profits.

**What if they told the story the other way round?**
What if they taught managers: you have got to make a profit, because if you do not make a profit you cannot build offices that are pleasant to be in. Without profit you cannot pay decent

wages. Without profit you cannot satisfy a lot of the needs of your employees. You have got to make a profit because without a profit you will never be able to develop a better product.

The profit would still be made. People would still get decent wages. Most employers would still make an effort to improve their products as they do now.

'But you would have a whole new ball game.'

Adapted from Cohen, P (1974) *The Gospel According to the Harvard Business School*, Penguin. Originally published by Doubleday, New York, 1973.

*Harvard Business School*   http://www.hbs.edu

prise but is neither the reason for which the business is formed nor the reason why it stays in existence. Instead, Ackoff contends, 'those who manage organizations do so primarily to provide themselves with the quality of work life and standard of living they desire . . . their behaviour can be better understood by assuming this than by assuming that their objective is to maximize profit or growth'.

However, it is also important to consider the 'quality of life' of investors (shareholders), customers, suppliers and distributors, as well as other employees of the firm who are not involved in decision making. Developing earlier points, it can be argued that employees are the major stakeholders, because if the firm goes out of business they incur the greatest losses.

In many respects it does not matter whether profit is seen as an objective or as a means of providing service and satisfaction to stakeholders, as long as both are considered and not seen as mutually exclusive. However, the 'feel' and culture of an organization will be affected. In simple terms an organization will succeed if it survives and meets the expectations of its stakeholders. If its objectives relate to the stakeholders, it is successful if it attains its objectives.

The purpose of industry is to serve the public by creating services to meet their needs. It is not to make profits for shareholders, nor to create salaries and wages for the industrial community. These are necessary conditions for success, but not its purpose.

*Dr George Carey, Archbishop of Canterbury*

The responsibility of business is not to create profits but to create live, vibrant, honourable organizations with a real commitment to the community.

*Anita Roddick, The Body Shop*

## The influence of shareholders

Some commentators hold the view that too many companies are still encouraged to seek short-term profits in order to please their major institutional shareholders, and that it is only by considering the long term and the interests of all stakeholders that companies will become more effective competitors in world markets. In the UK, for example, Constable (1980) stated: 'Britain's steady relative industrial decline over the past 30 years is related to an insistence on setting purely financial objectives which have been operated in relatively short time scales'. Institutions such as pension funds effectively control the UK's largest companies through the sizeable blocks of shares that they own; in contested take-overs, for example, individual pension fund managers will be instrumental in determining the outcome. These managers have a remit to earn the best returns that they can obtain for their members. Since the mid-1990s there has been a drive to increase the 'transparency' of these large shareholder blocks, and companies have been required to publish more information.

The issue of short-termism is complex, however, and Box 3.3 investigates the debate. Companies, obviously, cannot disregard powerful institutional shareholders. What is crucial is to ensure that there is dialogue and mutual understanding and agreement concerning the best interests of the company, its shareholders and other stakeholders.

In his debate on the short- and long-term perspective, Constable, (Table 3.3), contrasts two sets of objectives, ranked in order of priority. He contends that company B is likely to grow at the expense of company A, and that these objective sets, A and B, are essentially those adopted by large UK and Japanese companies, respectively, for much of the period since World War II. To suggest that Japanese success rests solely on a particular set of objectives is oversimplifying reality, but it has certainly contributed.

## DISCUSSION – Box 3.3
## Long- and Short-termism: The Debate

Laing (1987) has argued that where owners and managers are the same people, the goals and means of achieving them are not in conflict; but institutional fund managers, themselves under pressure to perform in the short term, have often put pressure on public companies to pursue strategies that may be incompatible with sound long-term management. It is, however, generally acknowledged that companies must pursue strategies that increase the long-term value of the business for its shareholders, or eventually they are likely to be under threat of acquisition. It is also often argued that many companies believe that they are likely to be under threat from powerful institutional shareholders if short-term performance is poor, i.e. if sales and profits fail to grow. The result can be a reluctance to undertake costly and risky investments, say, in research and development (R&D), if the payback is uncertain.

Thus, it would follow that if a manufacturing business were seeking to boost short-term profits and earnings per share for reasons of expedience, it might well reduce quality and service and fail to invest adequately for the future. The price for this would be inevitable decline. This tendency could be worsened if the company were under threat of take-over and thus anxious to improve its immediate performance. For businesses in countries such as Germany and Japan, where historically 'the Damoclean sword of hostile take-overs was virtually unknown' (Laing, 1987) this has been less likely than in the UK.

Institutional shareholders must clearly want to be able to exercise some control or influence over large companies where they have substantial equity interests. One dilemma is that while they want to rein in powerful and risk-orientated strategic leaders, they do not want to forsake the potential benefits of strong, entrepreneurial leadership. They can exert influence by:

- pushing for the roles of chairman and chief executive to be separated, and arguing for a high proportion of carefully selected non-executive (external part-time) directors
- attempting to replace senior managers whose performance is poor or lacklustre, but this can be difficult (it is often argued that shareholders are too passive about this option)
- selling their shares to predatory bidders.

While this final option is a perpetual threat, and the biggest fear of many strategic leaders, not all companies are prevented from investing in R&D. Logically, those which are well managed are in command of where they are going to invest. In addition, institutions argue that they are objective about their investments and turn down more offers for their shares than they accept.

In essence, 'managers should not be discouraged by their owners, their shareholders, from taking risks, from undertaking research and from investing in innovation' (Laing, 1987).

A more recent analysis by the *Financial Times* (Martinson, 1998) suggests that large institutional shareholders do take a long-term view but rarely make helpful comments on strategy. When they exercise their voting power it is generally clear and visible, rather than covert. Many fund managers were seen as professional but, at the same time, 'ill-informed fund managers are making increasing demands on executive time'.

Undoubtedly more communication between directors and their shareholders concerning results, plans and philosophies would be desirable in many cases. Would this resolve the difficulties, or is something more drastic still required?

Lipton (1990) has controversially suggested that Boards should be subject to quinquennial reviews of their performance (partially conducted by independent outsiders) and their plans for the next five years. Hostile bids could be considered at the same time, but not between reviews. Boards may or may not be re-elected, depending on their relative performance. The idea is to generate more stability and to 'unite directors and shareholders behind the goal of maximizing long-term profits'.

The late Lord White of Hanson plc (1990) stated his disagreement, arguing that if institutional shareholders are willing to sell their shares it is usually the result of poor management generally, and not merely a reluctance to invest in R&D. 'Under-performing companies are frequently typified by high top salaries, share options confined to a handful of apparatchiks and generous golden parachutes'. Such companies are often legitimate take-over targets, and inevitably the bids are likely to be perceived as hostile.

In summary, long-term success requires that companies and their strategic leaders are properly accountable for their performance and, for many businesses, this really has to be to their shareholders. At the same time, shareholders must be objective and take a long-term perspective, and they must be active, not passive, about replacing poor managers and about intervening when they feel that the corporate strategy is wrong.

The dilemmas relate to the implementation of these ideas and to the issue of whether institutions have advisers with enough detailed, industry-specific, knowledge to make an objective judgement.

### Sources

Laing, H (1987) quoted in *First*, **1** (2).
Lipton, M (1990) An end to hostile takeovers and short-termism, *Financial Times*, 27 June.
Martinson, J (1998) Companies say big shareholders take long view, *Financial Times*, 27 April.
White, G (1990) Why management must be accountable, *Financial Times*, 12 July.

*Financial Times*   http://www.news.ft.com
*Hanson plc*   http://www.hansonplc.com

*Table 3.3*   Contrasting company objectives

| Company A | Company B |
| --- | --- |
| 1. Return on net assets, 1–3 year time horizon | 1. Maintenance and growth of market share |
| 2. Cash flow | 2. Maintenance and growth of employment |
| 3. Maintenance and growth of market share | 3. Cash flow |
| 4. Maintenance and growth of employment | 4. Return on net assets |

In Japan and Germany, however, shareholders do not exert pressure in the same way as they do in the UK. Cross shareholding between companies in Japan means that only 25% of shares in Japanese businesses are for trading and speculation, and this generates greater stability. In Germany the companies hold a higher proportion of their own shares, and banks act as proxy voters for private investors. Banks thereby control some 60% of the tradable shares, again generating stability. German companies also adopt a two-tier board structure. A supervisory board has overall control and reports to share-holders and employee unions; reporting to this board is a management board, elected for up to 5 years.

Table 3.4 pulls together a number of the points discussed here by showing how organizational strategic leaders and institutional investors do not share completely the same perspective on stakeholder priorities, although there are clear similarities with the most important stakehold-ers. Interestingly, suppliers, key partners in the supply chain, receive a higher priority from strategic leaders, while the institutions rate politi-cians more highly than do organizational leaders. It is both significant and realistic, that small, indi-vidual shareholders are not particularly power-ful, because they are generally too disparate to become organized. Individually, they may be able to embarrass an organization with difficult ques-tions at its Annual General Meeting, but this is far from an expression of ongoing power.

## The importance of the strategic leader

To conclude this section it is useful to emphasize the key role of the strategic leader, and his or her values, in establishing the main objectives and the direction in which they take the organiza-tion. Personal ambitions to build a large con-glomerate or a multinational company may fuel growth; a determination to be socially responsi-ble may restrain certain activities that other organizations would undertake; a commitment to high quality will influence the design, cost and marketing approach for products. A strong orientation towards employee welfare, as is illus-trated in Minicase 3.2 on Asda, will again influ-ence objectives quite markedly.

The objectives and values of the strategic leader are a particularly important consider-ation in the case of small firms. While it is possible for small firms to enjoy competitive advantage, say by providing products or services with values added to appeal to local

*Table 3.4*   Perceptions of stakeholder importance

| Stakeholder | Prioritization by industry strategic leaders | Prioritization by analysts with institutional investors |
|---|---|---|
| Existing customers | 1 | 1 |
| Existing employees | 2 | 3 |
| Potential customers | 3 | 2 |
| Institutional investors | 4 | 4 |
| Suppliers | 5 | 7 |
| Potential employees | 6 | 6 |
| City analysts | 7 | 5 |
| Private (individual) shareholders | 8 | 10 |
| Business media | 9 | 9 |
| General media | 10 | 11 |
| Local communities | 11 | 12 |
| Members of Parliament/Local Authorities | 12 | 8 |

Source: Based on research by MORI (2000).

*MORI*   http://www.mori.com

# Minicase 3.2  ASDA*

Archie Norman is the entrepreneurial strategic leader who 'made a difference' at Asda by pioneering change and instilling a new culture. ASDA, now owned by Wal-Mart of America (the world's largest retailer), is the UK's third largest supermarket group, behind Tesco and Sainsbury's. Its early growth and success came in the 1960s when it began to open out-of-town supermarkets – large stores for that time, but relatively small in today's terms – largely in the north of England, where the company has always been strongest. The Head Office is still in Leeds, but the company has now developed nationally. In the 1980s, Asda began to diversify, first into furniture retailing and then into carpets. This was followed by the acquisition of kitchen supplier MFI in 1985; 2 years later MFI became a management buyout when the promised synergies proved illusory. Shortly after this, ASDA bought 60 stores from Gateway and struck a deal with George Davies (the entrepreneur behind the growth and temporary fall of Next) which gave Asda the exclusive rights on a range of George-branded clothing. By the early 1990s ASDA was, however, trading at a loss. Analysts concluded that the company lacked a strong corporate identity and it had become a reactive follower in its main industry.

A new chairman was appointed in 1991 and he recruited Archie Norman to be the new Chief Executive. At this time Norman was 37 years old. Originally a McKinsey consultant, where he had worked with William Hague, he was then Group Finance Director with the retail group Kingfisher. When Norman became non-executive Chairman in 1997, after being elected a Conservative MP for Tunbridge Wells, ASDA had regained its popularity and profitability. Together with his deputy, and later successor, Allan Leighton, Norman had transformed the company. Although Norman 'took best practice from elsewhere and Asda-ised it', it was always believed that he used Wal-Mart as his model, and so perhaps it was no surprise when Wal-Mart acquired ASDA in 1999. David Glass, Chief Executive of Wal-Mart, commented of ASDA: 'I have not seen such passion for a company amongst its employees – except at Wal-Mart'.

What exactly had Norman done? Furniture and carpets had been divested at the earliest opportunity. The business had been split into two distinct parts: the (large) supermarkets – ASDA owns some of the largest food stores in the UK – where the non-food ranges were strengthened; and smaller, local, Dales stores with a limited range of grocery products. The whole business was refocused on 'ordinary working people who demand value': advertising used the slogan 'That's Asda Price!' to reinforce an average saving of some 5% against Tesco and Sainsbury prices.

High productivity and high levels of service have been derived from a committed and involved staff, who have seen many changes in their working lives. People are known as 'colleagues' and Julian Richer (of Richer Sounds – see Minicase 13.1) has advised the company on its suggestion scheme. The scheme, 'Tell Archie!', generated 45,000 suggestions in 5 years, and Norman read them all. Incentives are linked in to the scheme, and employees can also benefit from share options and training at the Asda Academy.

Since 1995, Colleague Circles have also provided an effective forum for staff involvement in customer service innovation. At Head Office there are no reserved car parking spaces and everyone works in large, open-plan offices. Staff are encouraged to wear ASDA baseball caps when they do not want to be disturbed by their colleagues. In relative terms, store management has grown at the expense of head-office staffing.

Norman initially became non-executive Chairman when he became an MP but once he had negotiated the sale to Wal-Mart he resigned.

*We return to ADSA later, first when we look at SWOT (strengths, weaknesses, opportunities, threats) analysis, and second, when we look at diversification – Chapters 7, 14 and 15.

QUESTION: How is ASDA attempting to ensure that its employees deliver the virtuous circle of growth and prosperity illustrated in Figure 3.4?

*ASDA*    http://www.asda.com

customers in a limited geographical area, many are not distinctive in any marked way. Where this is the case, and where competition is strong, small firms will be price takers, and their profits and growth will be influenced substantially by external forces. Some small-firm owners will be entrepreneurial, willing to take risks and determined to build a bigger business, whereas others will be content to stay small. Some small businesses are started by people who essentially want to work for themselves rather than for a larger corporation, and their objectives could well be concerned with survival and the establishment of a sound business which can be passed on to the next generation of their family.

Each of the ideas and theories discussed in this section provides food for thought, but individually none of them explains fully what happens, or what should happen, in organizations. In the author's experience certain organizations are highly growth orientated, willing to diversify and take risks, while others, constrained by the difficulties of coping with rapid growth and implementing diversification strategies, are less ambitious in this respect.

Each can be appropriate in certain circumstances and lead to high performance, but in different circumstances they may be the wrong strategy.

Stakeholder theory is extremely relevant conceptually, but organizations are affected by the stakeholders in a variety of ways. Priorities must be decided for companies on an individual basis. Moreover, the strategic leader, and in turn the organization, will seek to satisfy particular stakeholders rather than others because of their personal backgrounds and values. There is no right or wrong list of priorities. However, while priorities can and will be established, all stakeholders must be satisfied to some minimum level. In the final analysis the essential requirement is congruence among environment, values and resources.

So far this chapter has concentrated on profit-seeking organizations and considered just how important the profit motive might be. Not-for-profit organizations may be growth conscious, quality conscious or committed to employee welfare in the same way as profit seekers, but there are certain differences which require that they are considered separately.

## Objectives of Public-sector and Not-for-profit Organizations

In order to understand the objectives of not-for-profit organizations and appreciate where they are aiming to go, a number of points need to be considered.

- Stakeholders are important, particularly those who are providers of financial support.
- There will be a number of potentially conflicting objectives, and quite typically the financial ones will not be seen as the most essential in terms of the mission.
- While there will be a mix of quantitative (financial) and qualitative objectives, the former will be easier to measure, although the latter relate more closely to the mission of the organization.
- For this reason the efficient use of resources becomes an important objective.

These points will now be examined in greater depth, making reference to Minicases 3.3 and 3.4 (The National Theatre and London Zoo) together with a number of other examples, as public sector and not-for-profit organizations are many and varied.

Historically, and at one extreme, certainly in terms of size, *nationalized industries* with essentially monopoly markets have been seen as both public sector and non-profit. Throughout their existence different governments have strived to establish acceptable and effective measures of performance for them. At various times both breakeven and return on capital employed have been stressed. There has always been an in-built objectives conflict between social needs (many of them provided essential services) and a requirement that the very substantial resources involved were managed commercially in order to avoid waste. The Conservative government of the 1980s followed a policy of privatizing certain nationalized industries partly on the grounds that in some cases more competition will be stimulating and create greater efficiency.

In Britain, the NHS can be viewed similarly. Fundamentally, its purpose relates to the health and well-being of the nation, and attention can be focused on both prevention and cure. The role of the police in terms of crime prevention and the solution of crimes that have taken place can be seen as synonymous. The health service can spend any money it is offered, as science continually improves what can be done for people. In a sense it is a chicken-and-egg situation. Resources improve treatments and open up new opportunities for prevention; and these in turn stimulate demand, particularly where they concern illnesses or diseases which historically have not been easily treated. However, these developments are often very expensive, and decisions have then to be made about where funds should be allocated. Quite simply, the decisions relate to priorities.

Customers of the health service are concerned with such things as the waiting time for admission to hospital and for operations, the quality of care as affected by staff attitudes and numbers, and arguably privacy in small wards, cleanliness and food. Doctors generally are concerned with the amount of resources and their ability to cope with demand; some consultants are anxious to work at the leading edge of their specialism; while administrators must ensure that resources are used efficiently.

The government funds the NHS, and as the major source of funds it is a key influence. It is very concerned with the political fallout from perceived weaknesses in the service, and inevitably its priorities are affected by this. It has been reported that the Labour government's emphasis on waiting lists, a key pledge in its 1997 election manifesto, has distorted clinical priorities, such that many minor ailments have been given priority for treatment over more

Minicase

# Minicase 3.3  The National Theatre

The National Theatre is in fact three theatres in one building on the south bank of the Thames in London. A substantial proportion of revenue has to be allocated to cover the overheads on the building. The specially built theatre opened in 1976. Despite its name, and although its 'company' does at times tour the country, it does not attract a national audience. The plays it offers are generally different from those in the more commercial non-subsidized theatres in London's West End, and it attracts a mixture of regular theatre goers from the south-east of England, foreign tourists and occasional visitors.

The National receives a grant from the Arts Council, which is funded by the Treasury. At certain times during the 1980s and 1990s the grant increased at less than the rate of inflation, a reflection of government policy concerning support for the arts and their belief that more private support was required. In addition, the National receives private sponsorship and earns money from the box office, catering and other front-of-house sales. Sponsorship and subsidies allow ticket prices to be lower than they otherwise would.

Some stakeholders, such as directors and actors, might hold the view that as the National is prestigious it should seek to offer the 'best of everything' – plays, actors, costumes and scenery – and that it should experiment and seek to be innovative. At the same time it has at least to break even, although the types of play and musical which earn the most revenue at the box office are not necessarily those that the National will seek to produce.

Sir Peter Hall, Director from 1976 to 1988, has said that his main aim was to provide working conditions where actors can be at their most creative. Audiences and money matter, but they are not the primary goal.

How, then, is success measured? Audiences and revenue can certainly be measured, but 'success is something you can feel and smell when you are with an audience'.

QUESTIONS: Is it possible for the National Theatre to satisfy all of its stakeholders at any one time?
What do you think the priorities should be?

*National Theatre*  http://www.nt-online.org

# Minicase 3.4  London Zoo

London Zoo, in Regent's Park, is one of two zoological gardens which are controlled and administered by the Zoological Society of London. The other is Whipsnade Park, in Bedfordshire, and this covers 600 acres compared with 34 acres in London.

The Society's charter lays down its primary purpose as 'the advancement of zoology and animal physiology, and the introduction of new and curious subjects of the animal kingdom'. From this must stem a fundamental dilemma: although they have a scientific orientation, how much are zoos places of entertainment and relaxation, with customers paramount, and how much are they organizations with primarily educational and scientific purposes? One constraint for London Zoo is the fact that Regent's Park is a Royal Park, and that byelaws restrict certain activities such as on-site advertising.

At times the zoo has received a series of annual grants from the Department of the Environment, and in 1988 it was given £10 million as a one-off payment 'to put it on a firm financial footing'. It remains 'the only national collection in the world not publically funded on a regular basis'. Without these subsidies the zoo has a surplus of expenditure over income.

Income is essentially from visitors, the majority of whom live within comfortable travelling distance of London, and private sponsorship. Many of the visitors are on organized school trips, and weather conditions are very important in attracting or deterring people.

Many visitors are attracted by big animals, as evidenced by the commercial success of safari parks, but they are costly and dangerous, as well as well researched and relatively safe as far as endangered species go. Quite often the most endangered species are relatively unattractive. Whipsnade is regarded as more ideal for big animals. London Zoo for many years had no hippos (since the 1960s) and no bears (since 1986), but more recently these large animals have been brought back to counter visitor criticism. Visitors can drive around Whipsnade, parking in various places en route, but it is not a safari park.

Critics have argued that London Zoo's management has often failed to exploit the zoo's conservation work by featuring it in informative displays and that much of the zoo's important and scientifically renowned research is not recognized by the general public. This is correct, but the fact remains that much of the important conservation work involves species which are relatively uninteresting for many public visitors, for example the rare Rodriguez fruit bat.

The Department of the Environment paid for a report by independent consultants (1987–1988) and concluded that 'management at London Zoo did not reflect the commercial emphasis which was essential for survival and prosperity without a permanent subsidy'. They recommended the establishment of a new company to manage London and Whipsnade Zoos, separate from the scientific research of the Zoological Society. This company was established in October 1988, with the aim of reversing the falling trend in admissions and returning the zoo to profit in 3 years.

The numbers of visitors did increase in 1989 and 1990, but below the level required to break even. In April 1991 newspapers first reported that London Zoo might have to close, with some animals destroyed and others moved to Whipsnade. The Government refused further financial assistance, not wholly convinced of the need for urban zoos. Cost reduction per se was ruled out as this was likely to provoke a new fall in admissions. Instead, rescue plans concentrated on a smaller zoo with a new concept: natural habitats such as an African rainforest complete with gorillas, and a Chinese mountain featuring the pandas. There would be less emphasis on caged animals.

Changes were made but attendances fell. The zoo's closure was announced formally in June 1992. New external funding has since provided a reprieve.

Since 1992 the zoo has secured its survival by emphasizing its role as a conservation centre, breeding endangered species and returning them to the wild. It typically now breaks even using publicity more effectively to attract some 1 million visitors a year.

QUESTIONS: What should the objectives of London Zoo be?
Who are the major stakeholders, and how important are they?

*Zoological Society of London/London Zoo*   http://www.londonzoo.co.uk

major ones. Pfeffer (1981) has argued that the relative power of influencers is related to the funds that they provide. The less funding that is provided by customers, the weaker is their influence over decisions. Hence, a not-for-profit organization such as the NHS may be less customer orientated than a private competitive firm. Some would argue that the private medical sector is more marketing conscious. Without question, and in simple terms, the NHS is about patient care within imposed budgetary constraints. The issue really concerns whether patients perceive that it feels like a service driven by a culture of care or by a culture of resource management efficiency.

All organizations will seek to measure performance in some way. It was stated earlier in the chapter that performance against quantitative objectives can be measured directly, whereas performance against qualitative objectives is typically indirect and more difficult. If attention is focused on the aspects that are most easily measured there is a danger that these come to be perceived as the most important objectives.

Hospital administrators can easily measure the number of admissions, the utilization of beds and theatres, the cost of laundry and food and so on. Fundamentally more important is who is being treated relative to the real needs of the community. Are the most urgent and needy cases receiving the priorities they deserve? How is this measured? Performance measures therefore tend to concentrate on the *efficient use of resources* rather than the effectiveness of the organization. Although profit may not be an important consideration, costs are. In addition, these measures may well be a source of conflict between medical and administrative staff and this is a reflection of the fact that there is likely to be disagreement and confusion about what the key objectives are.

Given this, the objectives that are perceived as important and are pursued at any time are very dependent on the relative power of the influencers and their ability to exercise power. Linked to this point is the relationship between hospitals and area and regional health authorities. Similarly, where not-for-profit organizations have advisory bodies, or boards of trustees, the relationship and relative power are important.

Tourist attractions such as London Zoo (Minicase 3.3) and leading museums (including the British Museum, the Natural History Museum and the Victoria and Albert, which is the National Museum of Art and Design) have a potential conflict of objectives concerning their inevitable educational and scientific orientations and the requirement that they address commercial issues. Museums can earn money from shops and cafeterias and they receive some private funding, but to a great extent they are reliant on government grants. In the 1980s these grants did not keep pace with their monetary demands and hence it has been necessary for them to seek additional revenue as well as manage resources and costs more efficiently. Admission charges to museums have become a controversial issue in the UK. In November 1985 the Victoria and Albert Museum introduced voluntary admission charges, and in April 1987 the Natural History Museum started charging for entry. Some potential visitors are lost as they refuse to pay, and this has implications for the educational objective. It has been reported that by 1987 admissions to the Victoria and Albert had fallen to one million a year from a peak of 1.75 million in 1983, but they began to increase again after 1988. However, the museum was criticized by some arts lovers for a poster campaign describing it as 'an ace caff with quite a nice museum attached', although museum staff claimed that this was a major reason for the increase in attendances. Some museums, including the British Museum, adamantly opposed charging. The new Tate Modern, opened in 2000, does not charge for admission.

At *The National Theatre* (Minicase 3.4) the issue addresses art and finance. Subsidized theatres perceive their role to be different from that of commercial theatres and a number of them,

including the Royal Shakespeare Company, English National Opera and the Royal Opera House, Covent Garden, competes for a percentage of Arts Council funding. When the Arts Council, as a major stakeholder and provider of funds, attempts to influence the strategies of the theatres they are often accused of meddling. Again there is a potential chicken-and-egg situation. If the theatres, under pressure from reduced subsidies (in real terms), raise more revenue and reduce their costs, they may find that this results in permanently reduced subsidies. Hence, as an alternative, they may choose to restrain their commercial orientation.

*Cathedrals* face a similar dilemma. The costs of repairs and maintenance are forcing some to charge visitors fixed amounts rather than rely on voluntary donations. Their mission is concerned with religion and charity but they are not immune from commercial realities.

*Charities* frequently have sets of interdependent commercial and non-commercial objectives. Oxfam's mission concerns the provision of relief and the provision of aid where it is most needed throughout the world. Additional objectives relate to teaching people how to look after themselves better through, say, irrigation and better farming techniques and to obtaining publicity to draw public attention to the plight of the needy. Their ability to pursue these objectives is constrained by resource availability. Consequently, Oxfam have fund-raising objectives, and strategies (including retailing through Oxfam shops) to achieve them. It is difficult to say which receives most priority as they are so interdependent.

While the coverage of not-for-profit organizations in this section has been partial, as many other organizations, such as schools and universities, are fundamentally non-profitable, the points are representative of the sector.

The issue of the displacement of objectives has been discussed in some not-for-profit organizations. Attention is centred on quantitative measures as they are relatively easily carried out. The efficient use of resources replaces profit as the commercial objective, and while this may not be an essential aspect of the mission, it will be seen as important by certain stakeholders. In reality attention has switched from evaluating outputs and outcomes (the real objectives) to measuring inputs (resources) because it is easier to do. Where the stakeholders are major sponsors, and particularly in the case of government departments, there will be an insistence upon cost-effectiveness. Many of the organizations mentioned in this section are managed by people whose training and natural orientation is towards arts or science, and this can result in feelings of conflict with regard to objectives. Quite typically the organization will pursue certain objectives for a period of time, satisfying the most influential stakeholders in the coalition, and then change as the preferences of stakeholders, or their relative power and influence, change.

While profit-seeking and not-for-profit organizations have essentially different missions, the issue of profit making is complex. Some not-for-profit organizations rely on subsidies and these enable prices to be kept below what they would otherwise be. In nationalized industries the element of customer service has been seen to be important, with prices controlled or at least influenced by government. An independent regulator has been appointed when nationalized businesses have been privatized. However, unless the providers of grants and subsidies are willing to bear commercial trading losses and at the same time finance any necessary investment, there is a necessity for the organizations to generate revenue at least equal to the costs incurred. Where investment finance also needs to be generated a surplus of income over expenditure is important. This basically is profit. While profit may not therefore be an essential part of the mission it is still required.

## The Impact of Personal Objectives

The objectives pursued by organizations frequently differ from those proclaimed. Some years ago I assumed that the principal objective of universities was the education of students. Armed with this assumption I could make no sense of their behaviour. I learned that education, like profit, is a requirement not an objective and that the principal objective is to provide their faculties with the quality of work life and the standard of living they desire. That's why professors do so little teaching, give the same courses over and over again, arrange classes at their convenience, not that of their students, teach subjects they want to teach rather than students want to learn and skip classes to give lectures for a fee.

*Russell Ackoff (1986)*

It has already been established that organizations are generally too large and complex to have only one objective. As a result, and influenced by stakeholders, there are typically several objectives with varying degrees of relative importance. It is now appropriate to consider why organizations cannot be treated separately from the people who work in them.

Objectives can be set (and changed) in any one of three ways.

- The strategic leader decides.
- Managers throughout the organization are either consulted or influence the objectives by their decisions and actions.
- All or some of the external stakeholders influence or constrain the organization in some way.

The second of these is addressed in this section. With emergent strategy the decisions made by managers determine the actual strategies pursued, and in turn revised, implicit, objectives replace those that were previously declared as intended objectives. The incidence or likelihood of this is affected by the culture of the organization, the relative power bases of managers, communication systems, and whether or not there are rigid policies and procedures or more informal management processes that allow managers considerable freedom. Box 3.4 defines policies and discusses their role in strategy implementation. The following brief example illustrates the impact of policies. Consider a multiple store that sells compact discs as one of its products and has nearby a small independent competitor that appeals to different customers. If the small store

---

Key concept – Box 3.4
Policies

You must provide a framework in which people can act. For example, we have said that our first priority is safety, second is punctuality, and third is other services. So if you risk flight safety by leaving on time, you have acted outside the framework of your authority. The same is true if you don't leave on time because you are missing two catering boxes of meat. That's what I mean by a framework. You give people a framework, and within the framework you let people act.

*Jan Carlzon, when President and Chief Executive Officer, SAS (Scandinavian Airlines System)*

- *Policies* are guidelines relating to decisions and approaches which support organizational efforts to achieve *stated* and intended objectives.
- They are basically *guides to thoughts* (about how things might or should be done) *and actions.*
- They are therefore *guides to decision making.* For example, a policy which states that for supplies of a particular item three quotations should be sought and the cheapest selected, or a policy not to advertise in certain newspapers, or a policy not to trade with particular countries – all influence decisions. Policies are particularly useful for routine repetitive decisions.

- Policies can be at corporate, divisional [or strategic business unit (SBU)] or functional level, and they are normally stated in terms of management (of people), marketing, production, finance and research and development.
- If stated objectives are to be achieved, and the strategies designed to accomplish this implemented, the appropriate policies must be there in support. In other words, the behaviour of managers and the decisions that they make should be supportive of what the organization is seeking to achieve. Policies guide and constrain their actions.
- Policies can be mandatory (rules which allow little freedom for original thought or action) or advisory. The more rigid they are the less freedom managers have to change things with delegated authority, and this can be good or bad depending on change pressures from the environment.
- *It is vital to balance consistency and co-ordination* (between the various divisions, SBUs and departments in the organization) *with flexibility.*
- Policies need not be written down. They can be passed on verbally as part of the culture.
- Policies *must* be widely understood if they are to be useful.

closed down there could be new opportunities for the manager of the multiple store if he changed his competitive strategy for CDs by changing his displays, improved his stock levels and supported these moves with window displays promoting the changes. Head-office merchandising policies concerning stocks and displays may or may not allow him this freedom.

In the case of intended strategy, the strategic leader determines and states the objectives, strategies and proposed changes for the organization. In arriving at decisions he or she may be influenced in a minor or major way by stakeholders outside the organization and the managers consulted. In order to ensure that the strategies are implemented (and the objectives achieved) the strategic leader will design and build an organization structure – which may restrict managers or allow them considerable freedom – and will determine policies which may be mandatory or advisory. This will tie in to the culture of the organization and will be influenced by the style and values of the strategic leader, both of which were introduced earlier (p. 51).

However, the types of policy and the authority and freedom delegated to managers guide, influence and constrain decision making. The motives, values and relative power of individual managers, the relative importance of particular functions, divisions or strategic business units in the organization, and the system of communications are also influential. The stated or *official objectives* may or may not be achieved; there may be appropriate incremental decisions which reflect changes in the environment; or managers may be pursuing personal objectives, which Perrow (1961) has termed *operative goals*. This is happening when the behaviour taking place cannot be accounted for by official company objectives and policies. The aggregation of these various decisions determines the emergent strategic changes, the actual objectives followed and the results achieved.

Operative goals may complement official goals or they may conflict. A complementary situation would exist if the stated objective was in terms of a target return on capital employed, and if this was achieved through operative goals of managers and decisions taken by them regarding delivery times, quality and so on. If, however, a sales manager was favouring particular customers with discounts or priority deliveries on low-profit orders, or a production manager was setting unnecessarily high quality standards (as far as customers are concerned) which resulted in substantial rejections and high operating costs, profits would be threatened. In such cases operative goals would conflict with official goals.

In this context, a recent report from the Public Management Foundation (1999) highlights a dilemma. Arguing that the UK Government is feeling frustrated by the slow speed at which the public sector is embracing certain objectives and strategies from the profit-seeking private sector, the Foundation discovered a 'public-sector ethos' amongst its managers. They are driven to 'make a difference for the community'. Improving local services and increasing user satisfaction are their personal priorities. There are occasions when this conflicts with the prioritization, rather than the actual existence, of stated, intended objectives for cutting costs and improving efficiencies. There is also a perception among many public-sector managers that their funders prefer centralized management controls, while they would like more autonomy and delegated authority. The situation is confused further when changing political pressures and necessities impact upon objectives and priorities.

## Social Responsibility and Business Ethics

Having looked at some of the theories which are relevant for a study of objectives, and at typical objectives that organizations pursue and why, it is appropriate to conclude this chapter with a consideration of wider societal aspects. Objectives that relate to social responsibility may be affected by stakeholders; in some cases they result from legislation, but often they are voluntary actions. The issue is one of how responsible a firm might choose to be, and why. Again, the particular values of the strategic leader will be very influential.

There are numerous ways in which a firm can behave responsibly in the interests of society, and examples are given below. It should not be thought, however, that social responsibility is a one-way process; organizations can benefit considerably from it. Social responsibility and profitability can be improved simultaneously (The Performance Group, 1999).

- product safety: This can be the result of design or production and includes aspects of supply and supplier selection to obtain safe materials or components. Product safety will be influenced to an extent by legislation, but an organization can build in more safety features than the law requires. Some cars are an example of this, such as Volvo which is promoted and perceived as a relatively safe car. Product safety will have cost implications. Sometimes the safety is reflected in perceived higher quality, which adds value that the customer is willing to pay a premium for, but at other times it will be the result of the organization's choosing to sacrifice some potential profit.
- working conditions: Linked to the previous point, these can include safety at work, which again is affected by legislation which sets minimum standards. Aspects of job design to improve working conditions and training to improve employees' prospects are further examples.
- honesty, including not offering or accepting bribes.
- avoiding pollution.
- avoiding discrimination.

The above points are all subject to some legislation.

- community action: This is a very broad category with numerous opportunities, ranging from charitable activities to concerted action to promote industry and jobs in areas which have suffered from economic recession. Many large organizations release executives on a temporary basis to help with specific community projects.
- industry location: Organizations may locate new plants in areas of high unemployment for a variety of reasons. While aspects of social responsibility may be involved, the decision may well be more economic. Grants and rate concessions may be important.
- other environmental concerns: These include recycling, waste disposal, protecting the ozone layer and energy efficiency. Box 3.5 illustrates a number of specific examples.

Porter (1995) contends that many companies mistakenly see environmental legislation as a threat, something to be resisted. Instead, he argues, they should see regulation as an indication the company is not using its resources efficiently. Toxic materials and discarded packaging are waste. The costs incurred in eliminating a number of environmental problems can be more than offset by other savings and improvements in product quality. Companies should be innovative and not reluctantly just complying with their legal requirements.

However, the European chemical industry has argued that bulk chemical manufacture has been largely driven out of EC countries by the costs of complying with environmental regulation. Standards in many Far Eastern countries are less restrictive.

- attitude of food retailers: For example, accurate labelling (country of origin), free-range eggs, organic vegetables, biodegradable packaging, CFC-free aerosols and products containing certain dubious E-number additives. It is a moot point whether retailers or consumers should decide on these issues.

STRATEGY IN ACTION – Box 3.5
Examples of Environmental Strategies

1 **McDonald's** took an equity stake in a new venture for recycling the waste collected at their restaurants. Some plastic containers which cannot be recycled have been withdrawn; food scraps are used for making compost. **Sainsbury's** give a one-penny refund for every plastic carrier that customers reuse. This saves the retailer the cost of providing a new bag; it also reduces the amount of waste plastic.

2 **Electricity generating** has gradually switched to gas and cleaner coal (with a low sulphur content) because coal has been shown to cause acid rain.

3 **Packaging**. Smaller, lighter packages use fewer raw materials and they are cheaper to transport. Procter and Gamble and Unilever have both introduced more concentrated versions of their detergent brands which, ironically, many consumers have seen as poor value for money because they have been unconvinced by the instructions to use less of the product! Soft drinks manufacturers have switched to fully recyclable aluminium cans and plastic bottles.

4 **ICI** invested in the challenge to find a replacement for chlorofluorocarbons (CFCs), gases which are used extensively in aerosols and refrigeration equipment, and which are widely blamed for depleting the ozone layer.

5 **The Body Shop** produces a comprehensive, externally audited, environmental report, its *Green Book*. The emphasis on such factors as energy waste and product stewardship drives improvements. Among other initiatives, The Body Shop has sought to eliminate its use of polyvinylchloride (PVC) because of the environmental impact of such packaging.

6 **The motor vehicle industry**. Historically, car manufacturers exploited an opportunity very successfully: increased affluence and the desire for individual freedom had generated a demand for private cars. Their success in increasing levels of ownership created a number of threats: traffic density, pollution from exhaust emissions, material waste through obsolescence, the 'waste' of scarce resources in high-consumption, inefficient, engines, and safety problems arising from the sheer volume of traffic, congestion and hurry.

A response was needed, and this has involved both manufacturers and government:

- Legislation has made catalytic converters compulsory on all new cars after January 1993.
- New models invariably feature improvements in design and technology which reduce waste and increase fuel efficiency.
- New concept vehicles are being developed, including electric cars and others which mix the traditionally contradictory high performance with environmental friendliness. These have a long-term time scale.
- Links between different forms of transport (road, rail, air and water) are being strengthened. BMW, for example, has pioneered co-operative ventures in Munich, where research has shown that in one square kilometre of the city centre in busy periods drivers of 50% of the cars on the move are driving round looking for parking spaces.
- Old parts are being recycled. In France both Peugeot and Renault opened plants for this, followed by other

European manufacturers, but these initiatives remain small ventures in relation to the total numbers of cars being scrapped.

- In 1995 Vauxhall was the first UK car manufacturer to be awarded the new BS7750 for environmental management; it had successfully eliminated some packaging, segregated waste, reduced energy consumption and improved its waste water management.
- In 1998 Mazda promised to plant five trees for every Demio model it sold: more than enough to compensate for

the carbon emissions from the cars, as trees absorb carbon dioxide.
- Volvo has systematically introduced strategies for reducing energy consumption (achieving a 15% saving between 1995 and 1999), water consumption (a 24% saving in this same period) and solvent emissions (44% saving).

*Body Shop*   http://www.bodyshop.com
*ICI*   http://www.ici.com
*McDonald's*   http://www.mcdonalds.com
*Procter and Gamble*   http://www.pg.com
*Sainsbury's*   http://www.sainsburys.com

Objectives of this nature become part of the organization culture. Social responsibility is at the heart of activities and objectives because it is felt that the organization has an obligation both to the community and to society in general. However, it must not be assumed that the approach receives universal support. Milton Friedman (1979), the economist, argues that 'the business of business is business . . . the organization's only social responsibility is to increase its profit'. Friedman also comments that donations to charity and sponsorship of the arts are 'fundamentally subversive' and not in the best interests of the shareholders. Social responsibility would then be the result of legislation. Drucker (1974) argues businesses have a role in society which is 'to supply goods and services to customers and an economic surplus to society . . . rather than to supply jobs to workers and managers, or even dividends to shareholders'. The latter, he argues, are means not ends. Drucker contends that it is mismanagement to forget that a hospital exists for its patients and a university for its students. This contrasts with the comments by Russell Ackoff about university academics quoted earlier.

The topic is complex, and although the outcome of certain decisions can be seen to be bringing benefit to the community or employees the decision may have been influenced by legislation or perceived organizational benefit (enlightened self-interest) rather than a social conscience. One could argue that the organization will benefit if it looks after its employees; equally one could argue that it will suffer if it fails to consider employee welfare. The two approaches are philosophically different, but they may generate similar results. Some organizations feature their community role extensively in corporate advertising campaigns designed to bring them recognition and develop a caring, responsible image.

## Business ethics

Disasters such as the explosion at the chemical plant in Bhopal, India, in 1984 raise the question of how far companies should go in pursuit of profits. Ethics is defined as 'the discipline dealing with what is good and bad and right and wrong or with moral duty and obligation' (Webster's Third New International Dictionary). Houlden (1988) suggests that business ethics encompasses the views of people throughout society concerning the morality of business, and not just the views of the particular business and the people who work in it.

Issues such as golden handshakes, insider dealing and very substantial salary increases for company chairmen and chief executives are topical and controversial.

The high-profile case of British Airways and Virgin Atlantic, where BA was accused of using privileged information to evaluate Virgin's route profitability and to persuade Virgin customers to switch airlines, suggested that BA acted unethically. In contrast, Hewlett-Packard, the US electronics multinational which is widely regarded as being highly ethical, operates an internal ban on the use of improper means for obtaining competitor information. The company also insists that any statements about its competitors must be fair, factual and complete.

Public attention is drawn to these issues, and people's perceptions of businesses generally and individually are affected. However, their responses differ markedly. Some people feel disgruntled but do nothing, whereas others take more positive actions. Managers, however, should not ignore the potential for resistance or opposition by their customers, who may refuse to buy their products or use their services.

Another ethical concern is individual managers or employees who adopt practices which senior managers or the strategic leader would consider unethical. These need to be identified and stopped. If they remain unchecked they are likely to spread, with the argument that 'everyone does it'. Sales staff using questionable methods of persuasion, even lying, would be an example. However, it does not follow that such practices would always be seen as unethical by senior managers – in some organizations they will be at least condoned, and possibly even encouraged.

Minicase 3.5 on the Co-operative Bank highlights how one organization has used an ethical stance to create a competitive advantage.

## Ethical dilemmas

One classic ethical dilemma concerns the employee who works for a competitor, is interviewed for a job, and who promises to bring confidential information if he is offered the post. Should the proposition be accepted or not? The issue featured at the beginning of this section, is how far companies should go in pursuit of profits. In such a case as this, long-term considerations are important as well as potential short-term benefits. If the competitor who loses the confidential information realizes what has happened it may seek to retaliate in some way. Arguably, the best interests of the industry as a whole should be considered. Box 3.6 presents three more ethical dilemmas.

Another example is the company with a plant that is surplus to requirements and which it would like to sell. The company knows the land beneath the plant contains radioactive waste. Legally it need not disclose this fact to prospective buyers, but is it ethical to keep quiet? Research commissioned by the Rowntree Foundation (see Taylor, 1997) concluded that housebuilders and estate agents generally do not warn buyers when new homes are built on previously contaminated industrial land. Petfood manufacturers, looking to expand their sales, would logically seek to differentiate their products by featuring particular benefits and satisfied, friendly pets, but they will also hope to persuade more people to become owners. Given the publicity on potentially dangerous breeds of dog, and the numbers of abandoned pets, particularly after Christmas, what would constitute an ethical approach to promotion? In 1991 a small number of ministers in the Church of England questioned whether the Church Commissioners, with £3 billion to invest to cover the future salaries and pensions of clergy, should be free to invest the money anywhere (in an attempt to maximize earnings) or whether they should be restricted to organizations which

Minicase

# Minicase 3.5 The Co-operative Bank

Retail banking in the UK has become extremely competitive as traditional building societies and foreign banks have entered the sector. To compete, charges have been kept relatively low, leaving the banks with too many unprofitable accounts. Their challenge: attracting the 'right customers', those who will retain a sizeable current account balance and also purchase other products such as insurance policies. A typical 'good customer' would be 25–40 years old and a member of the ABC1 social groupings.

The Co-op Bank, owned by the Co-operative Wholesale Society, began an advertising campaign in the early 1990s which concentrated on the bank's ethical stance towards business. The bank stated it would not deal with tobacco companies, cosmetics companies which used animals for testing, companies involved in blood sports, factory farming and animal fur products, and any business which caused pollution. Some corporate accounts were closed.

Almost immediately, the volume of retail deposits increased by over 10%, with new customers actively citing the advertising campaign. Profits accrued after 2 years of losses. Many customers also took out the bank's new gold credit card.

The bank began to develop a customer profile which featured a disproportionate percentage of ABC1s. The Managing Director at the time, Terry Thomas, commented: 'After all, what bank would want to attract low income, badly-educated, ignorant people?'

QUESTIONS: Did it make sense for The Co-operative Bank to trade-off corporate clients for new personal accounts in this way?
Do you know whether the strategy is still in place?

*Co-operative Bank*   http://www.co-operativebank.co.uk

were known to be ethical in their business dealings. Interestingly, Martinson (1998) reported that the shares of companies widely perceived to be ethical in their strategies, policies and behaviour do not underperform when measured against the equity markets overall. In this context community involvement is seen as positive; any involvement with tobacco, alcohol or military equipment is negative.

Badaracco and Webb (1995) also highlight how internal decisions can be influenced by unethical practices. They quote instances of invented market-research findings, and altered investment returns which imply, erroneously, that the organization is meeting its published targets. They distinguish between 'expedient actions' and 'right actions'.

In contrast, a serious dilemma faces individuals in an organization who feel that their managers are pursuing unethical practices. There are several examples of individuals who have acted and suffered as a result of their actions. An accountant with an insurance company exposed a case of tax evasion by his bosses and jeopardized his career. Stanley Adams, an employee of Hoffman la Roche, the Swiss drug company, believed that his firm was making excessive profits and divulged commercially sensitive information to the European Commission. He also lost his career and suffered financially.

Strategy in action – Box 3.6
Three Ethical Dilemmas

A well-established European pharmaceutical company (X), in a country with a moderate but not large Catholic community, has developed and patented a new drug which safely induces abortion and has demonstrable health-care benefits for women seeking an abortion. For a variety of reasons, largely economic (health-care savings, benefit reductions and corporation tax revenues), its government is encouraging it to launch the drug in the home country and around the world at the earliest opportunity. Profits to the company would be good, but they would not have a dramatic impact on the company's overall profits. They would, however, ensure the future viability of a small production plant in an area of high unemployment. However, a sizeable block of the company's shares (but not a controlling interest) has recently been acquired by a foreign mini-conglomerate whose chief executive is a Catholic and opposed to the drug on religious grounds. As X's Managing Director you also know from your personal experience that if you launch the drug in America, one of your key export markets, you can expect protests from demonstrators opposed to abortion. What should you do?

A business manager for a well-known high street bank is told by her manager that her function is shortly to be moved to a new regional centre some 25 miles away and that her own position is secure. She is personally delighted as her travel-to-work commute will be reduced, but she knows that there will be redundancies. Under instruction that for the moment the news is embargoed from other staff, she is concerned when her personal assistant approaches her a few days later. She has heard unsubstantiated rumours on the bank's grapevine and she would, for family reasons, be unable to move. She wants to know what she should do as she is about to pay a deposit on a new house. What should the business manager do? What is 'right by her employer' and what is 'right by her subordinate'?

A young consultant with a relatively new and small but fast-growing management consultancy is invited out-of-the-blue to be joint presenter (with the senior partner) of a bid to a potentially very large client. He is surprised; he has had no involvement in preparing the bid. Moreover, it is not in his area of expertise. Flattered with the wonderful opportunity, but at the same time concerned, he discusses the request with his mentor in the consultancy. He is informed that the contact person in the client organization is, like him, from an ethnic minority background. The senior partner felt that the client would like to see that the consultancy's only non-white consultant was a key member of the team. How should he react?

Developed from material in: Badaracco, JL Jr (1997) *Defining Moments – When Managers Must Choose Between Right and Right*, Harvard Business School Press.

There are similar examples of engineers who felt that design compromises were threatening consumer safety, complained, and lost their jobs.

Many of the ethical issues that affect strategic decisions are regulated directly by legislation. Equally, many companies do not operate in sensitive environments where serious ethical issues require thought and attention. However, some companies and their strategic leaders do need a clear policy regarding business ethics. Often they have to decide whether to increase costs in the short run, say to improve safety factors, on the assumption that this will bring longer-term benefits. Short-term profitability, important to shareholders, could be affected. Increased safety beyond minimum legal requirements, for example, would increase the construction costs of a new chemical plant. If safety were compromised to save money, nothing might actually go wrong and profits would be higher. However, an explosion or other disaster results in loss of life, personal injury, compensation and legal costs, lost production, adverse publicity and tension between the business and local community. The long-term losses can be substantial.

Reidenbach and Robin (1994) have produced a spectrum of five ethical/unethical responses.

- *Amoral companies* seek to 'win at all costs'; anything is seen as acceptable. The secret lies in not being found out.
- *Legalistic companies* obey the law and no more. There is no code of ethics; companies act only when it is essential.
- *Responsive companies* accept that being ethical can pay off.
- *Ethically engaged companies* actively want to 'do the right thing' and to be seen to be doing so. Ethical codes will exist, but ethical behaviour will not necessarily be a planned activity and fully integrated into the culture.
- *Ethical companies* such as Body Shop have ethics as a core value, supported by appropriate strategies and actions which permeate the whole organization.

Because ethical standards and beliefs are aspects of the corporate culture, they are influenced markedly by the lead set by the strategic leader and his or her awareness of behaviour throughout the organization. If a proper lead is not provided, managers will be left to 'second guess' what would be seen as appropriate behaviour. Power, then, can be used ethically or unethically by individual managers.

Frederick (1988) contends that the corporate culture is the main source of any ethical problems. He argues that managers are encouraged to focus their professional energies on productivity, efficiency and leadership, and that their corporate values lead them to act in ways which place the company interests ahead of those of consumers or society

To guard against this it can be useful for a company to publish a corporate code of ethics, which all managers are expected to follow. Typically, large US companies have been more progressive with such codes than those in the UK. In the early 1990s, some 30% of large companies in the UK had published codes, but the number has since been growing all the time.

The typical issues covered in an ethics code include relationships with employees (the most prevalent factor in the UK codes of ethics), government (more important in the USA), the community and the environment.

Drawing on earlier points, attitudes towards bribery and inducement, and the use of privileged information, could also be incorporated in any code. Attention might also be paid to practices which are commonplace but arguably unethical. Examples would include a deliberate policy not to pay invoices on time, and creative accounting, presenting information in the most favourable light. The extent to which audited company accounts can be wholly relied upon is another interesting issue.

Business ethics is arguably important and worthy of serious attention. However, a consideration of ethical issues in strategic decisions typically requires that a long-term perspective is adopted. Objectives and strategies should be realistic and achievable rather than overambitious and very difficult to attain. In the latter case individual managers may be set high targets which encourage them to behave unethically, possibly making them feel uneasy. Results may be massaged, for instance, or deliberately presented with inaccuracies. Such practices spread quickly and dishonesty becomes acceptable. The longer-term perspective can reduce the need for immediate results and targets which managers feel have to be met at all costs. However, pressure from certain stakeholders, particularly institutional shareholders, may focus attention on the short term and on results which surpass those of the previous year. The longer-term perspective additionally allows for concern with processes and behaviour, and with how the results are obtained. The drive for results is not allowed to override ethical and behavioural concerns.

Houlden (1988) concludes that strategic leaders should be objective about how society views their company and its products, and wherever possible should avoid actions that can damage its image. If an action or decision that certain stakeholders might view as unethical is unavoidable, such as the closure of a plant, it is important to use public relations to explain fully why the decision has been taken. The need for a good corporate image should not be underestimated.

Later chapters (particularly Chapter 8) include discussions on how organizations might achieve competitive advantage. Ethical considerations can make a significant contribution to this. A commitment to keeping promises about quality standards and delivery times, or not making promises which cannot be met, would be one example. If employees are honest and committed, and rewarded appropriately for this, then costs

are likely to be contained and the overall level of customer service high, thereby improving profits.

To summarize briefly, this chapter has been about direction and about ends, the ends which help to determine the strategies that organizations select and pursue. A number of key terms have been defined and a number of important conflicts of interest explained. The next two chapters look first at how we might measure performance against these desired end-points and then at issues of organizational culture, which provide an important guide to why organizations pick particular strategies and follow certain routes.

## Summary

The corporate *mission* represents the overriding purpose for the business, and ideally it should explain why the organization is different and set it apart from its main rivals. It should not be a statement that other organizations can readily adopt. Its main purpose is communication.

It is useful to separate the mission statement from a statement of corporate *vision* which concerns 'what the organization is to become'.

Both can provide a valuable starting point for more specific *objectives* and strategies. Shorter term objectives will normally have time-scales or end-dates attached to them and ideally they will be 'owned' by individual managers.

It is, therefore, feasible to argue that organizations (as a whole) have a purpose and individual managers have objectives.

Mission, vision and objectives all relate to the *direction* that the organization is taking – the ends from which strategies are derived.

It is not, however, feasible to assume that the organization will always be free to set these objectives for its managers: there may be constraints from key stakeholders. A number of theories and models, mainly from a study of economics, can help us to understand why organizations do the things they do.

In addition, individuals will have *personal objectives* that they wish (and intend) to pursue, which should not be allowed to work against the best interests of the organization.

External *stakeholders* also have expectations for the organization. These will not always be in accord with each other, and important trade-offs and priorities must be established. There is always the potential for conflicts of interest. As a result, the organization will be seen to have a multitude of objectives, but all contributory to a single purpose.

Profit is necessary for profit-seeking businesses; a positive cash flow is essential for not-for-profit organizations. Profit (or cash) can, however, be seen as either a means or an end, and this will impact upon the 'feel' or culture of the organization.

Regardless, there is a virtuous circle of financial returns, motivated employees and satisfied customers.

Issues of *social responsibility* and *business ethics* are important for all organizations. They will be seen by some organizations as a threat or constraint and encourage a strategy of compliance. Other organizations will perceive them as an opportunity to create a difference and in turn a positive image. They are becoming increasingly visible, issues which organizations should take seriously and not ignore.

## References

Ackoff, RL (1986) *Management in Small Doses*, John Wiley.

Badaracco, JL and Webb, A (1995) Business ethics: a view from the trenches, *California Management Review*, 37.2, Winter.

Baumol, WJ (1959) *Business Behaviour, Value and Growth*, Macmillan.

Campbell, A (1989) Research findings discussed in Skapinker, M (1989) Mission accomplished or ignored? *Financial Times*, 11 January. See also: Campbell, A and Nash, L (1992) *A Sense of Mission: Defining Direction for the Large Corporation*, Addison-Wesley.

Constable, J (1980) The nature of company objectives. Unpublished paper, Cranfield School of Management.

Cyert, RM and March, JG (1963) *A Behavioural Theory of the Firm*, Prentice-Hall.

Deloitte (1999) *Making Customer Loyalty Real – A Global Manufacturing Study*, Deloitte Consulting and Deloitte & Touche, http://www.dc.com/research

Drucker, PF (1974) *Management: Tasks, Responsibilities, Practices*, Harper & Row.

Frederick, WC (1988) An ethics roundtable: the culprit is culture, *Management Review*, August.

Freeman, RE (1984) *Strategic Management: A Stakeholder Approach*, Pitman.

Friedman, M (1979) The social responsibility of business is to increase its profits. In *Business Policy and Strategy* (eds DJ McCarthy, RJ Minichiello and JR Curran), Irwin.

Galbraith, JK (1963) *American Capitalism. The Concept of Countervailing Power*, Penguin.

Galbraith, JK (1969) *The New Industrial State*, Penguin.

Houlden, B (1988) The corporate conscience, *Management Today*, August.

Marris, R (1964) *The Economic Theory of Managerial Capitalism*, Macmillan.

Martinson, J (1998) Ethical equities perform well, *Financial Times*, 21 July.

MORI (2000) See: Brown, K (2000) Survey exposes 'gulf' over the essentials for business success, *Financial Times*, 2 February.

Newbould, GD and Luffman, GA (1979) *Successful Business Policies*, Gower.

Penrose, E (1959) *The Theory of the Growth of the Firm*, Blackwell.

Performance Group, The (1999) *Sustainable Strategies for Value Creation*, Oslo, Norway.

Perrow, C (1961) The analysis of goals in complex organizations, *American Sociological Review*, 26, December.

Pfeffer, J (1981) *Power in Organizations*, Pitman.

Porter, ME (1995) Interviewed for the Green Management letter, *Euromanagement*, June.

Public Management Foundation (1999) *Wasted Values*, London.

Reidenbach, E and Robin, D (1995) Quoted in Drummond, J: Saints and sinners, *Financial Times*, 23 March.

Richards, MD (1978) *Organizational Goal Structures*, West.

Simon, HA (1964) On the concept of organizational goal, *Administrative Science Quarterly*, 9(1), June, 1–22.

Taylor, A (1997) Home buyers unaware of contamination, *Financial Times*, 24 October.

Thompson, AA and Strickland, AJ (1980) *Strategy Formulation and Implementation*, Irwin.

Waterman, R (1994) *The Frontiers of Excellence: Learning from Companies that Put People First*, Nicholas Brealey Publishing.

Williamson, OE (1964) *Economics of Discretionary Behaviour: Managerial Objectives in a Theory of the Firm*, Kershaw.

Test your knowledge of this chapter with our online quiz at http://www.thomsonlearning.co.uk

Explore The Organizational Mission and Objectives further at:

*Administrative Science Quarterly*   http://www.gsm.cornell.edu/ASQ/asq.html

*California Management Review*   http://www.haas.berkeley.edu/News/cmr/index.html

*Sociological Review*   http://www.blackwellpublishers.co.uk/journals/SOCREV/descript.htm

*Rowntree Foundation*   http://www.jrf.org.uk

## Questions and Research Assignments

### TEXT RELATED

1. Consider how the objectives of HP Bulmer Holdings, detailed in Box 3.1, might be ranked in order of priority. Is there a difference between an ideal ranking and the likely ranking in practice? Note: Members of the Bulmer family hold over 50% of the ordinary shares.

2. Thinking of any organization with which you have personal experience, do you believe that profit (or cash in the case of a non-profit organization) is seen as a means or an end by the key decision makers? Do they all agree on this?

3. What key issues do you believe should be incorporated in a company statement on ethics?

## Internet and Library Projects

1. When Tottenham Hotspur became the first English Football League club with a stock-exchange listing (in 1983) the issue prospectus said: 'The Directors intend to ensure that the Club remains one of the leading football clubs in the country. They will seek to increase the Group's income by improving the return from existing assets and by establishing new sources of revenue in the leisure field'.

   (A) Research the strategies followed by Tottenham Hotspur plc since 1983. Do you believe that the interests of a plc and a professional football club are compatible or inevitably conflicting?

   (B) Which other clubs have followed Tottenham? Have they chosen similar or different strategies? How have they performed as businesses?

   (C) In view of the comments about social responsibility, how do you view the fact that football clubs generally invest far more money in players (wages and transfer fees) than they do in their grounds (amenities and safety)?

2. Have the objectives (in particular the order of priorities) of the Natural History Museum changed since the introduction of compulsory admission charges in April 1987?

3. In view of the findings after the *Herald of Free Enterprise* disaster at Zeebrugge in March 1987 and the *Estonia* disaster in 1994, how does a company such as P&O (the owners of the *Herald*) balance the extra costs involved in additional safety measures with the need to be competitive internationally, and the time added on to voyages by more rigorous safety procedures with customer irritation if they are delayed unnecessarily?

*Natural History Museum*  http://www.nhm.ac.uk
*P&O Group*  http://www.p-and-o.com
*Tottenham Hotspur plc*  http://www.spurs.co.uk/corporatenew/index.html

# 4

# Measuring Success

*The performance of a company, the outcomes of the strategies that it is pursuing, is typically evaluated by financial ratios and other quantitative measures. In this chapter it is argued that while these are an essential element of the evaluation process, alone they are inadequate. To appreciate fully how well an organization is doing one needs to take a wider, more holistic, perspective, beginning with an assessment of the strategies themselves. We show how different measures and assessments can provide conflicting conclusions and finish the main body of the chapter with a comprehensive model based on E–V–R (environment–values–resources) congruence.*

*Financial ratio analysis is an important aspect of management case-study analysis and consequently a section explaining the main ratios is appended to this chapter.*

# Minicase 4.1 The New Internet Businesses

As we start the new millennium, cyberspace and e-commerce are providing another Klondike gold rush. Using the 'gold-rush' metaphor is interesting; it conjures up thoughts of huge fortunes and, without question, these fortunes are being made. There are 64 new millionaires every day in Silicon Valley alone, and Europe's first e-commerce millionaires have arrived. But we must not forget that only a small percentage of those prospectors attracted to Alaska really made their fortune. Most failed to find very much gold, and many perished in the harsh conditions. The Internet is a wonderful and attractive opportunity, but it will prove disappointing, even cruel, to many of those would-be entrepreneurs that it attracts. The commercial potential of new creative, innovative ideas is difficult to evaluate.

Brady (1999) argues that the success of any e-commerce business is dependent upon several factors. The idea must be innovatory, and while the business should be clearly focused it must be able to change and evolve speedily if it is to sustain growth. The people behind the business, their plans and their grasp of the issues, together with their ability to raise the necessary finance, are obviously critical issues. It is also essential that they develop a strong brand and, on the back of this, create and maintain very high levels of service. The site must be readily accessible, orders must be simple to place and then easily tracked while they are in the system, and deliveries should be on time.

How, then, might we evaluate these new businesses, remembering that at the moment only a minority is profitable? Partly concerned not to be left behind in this new gold rush, some financiers and venture capitalists seem willing to back some very high-risk proposals if they believe in the idea and the entrepreneur. Amazon.com, the most substantial and famous e-commerce company in the world, has secured enormous funding but has yet to declare a profit. The theoretical value of the company, a reflection of its current share price, varies dramatically – and many analysts have suggested that it is overvalued because of the relative uncertainty.

*Management Today* (see Gwyther, 1999) offers the following set of evaluation criteria.

### Three factors which determine the extent and value of the opportunity

1. *The concept or idea*
   - How *value* is created and built
   - The potential for profit, based on costs and revenues
   - The size of the potential market
   - The potential to establish an advantage and reap the rewards, specifically the presence of effective barriers to entry by direct competitors.

Minicase

2. *Innovation*
   - The initial difference and the potential to build new values and thus sustain any early advantage.
3. *Engagement and implementation*
   - The ability to set up the infrastructure and the business, which inevitably depends on the people behind the business.

## Three further factors which reflect the project or business outcomes

4. *Traffic*

   Numbers of customers generated – linked to the extent of repeat business, which in turn is dependent on service levels achieved. Although web congestion can be a constraint, the fact that people recommend websites by word of mouth is a major opportunity.

5. *Financing*

   Financial resources secured, to fund continued expansion as well as start-up. Setting up a robust business and infrastructure on the web is expensive.

6. *Visibility*

   The critically important brand identity and image, remembering that a strong public profile and visibility can also act as a barrier to entry. This will often be in the form of media coverage for either an exciting new idea or the recognition of a new, successful entrepreneur or even web millionaire.

   The following two examples feature a company which disappeared almost as quickly as it appeared and one which is prospering as this book is being written. Things, however, change quickly in this sector.

Boo.com had a physical base in London's Carnaby Street, home of 1960s' fashion, and it was set up to sell sportswear. The idea was to widen the availability of the more exclusive designer-label items, which are typically only available in large cities. Two of its three founders (who were all in their twenties) had previously created Books.com, an early on-line bookseller; the third was an ex-model. It has been estimated that Boo.com was able to raise £100 million in venture capital, but this is still far less than the amount required to set up a physical retail infrastructure which could provide customers with these items on a wide scale. After a number of well-publicized false starts, the company went on-line in November 1999, offering deliveries in 18 countries from warehouses in Cologne and Kentucky. Boo.com did not own these warehouses but had a dedicated staff working there and an alliance with the owners. Goods were delivered to the warehouses by their manufacturers and then repackaged in distinctive Boo boxes before being posted on.

The website offered 40,000 items. Each had been photographed at least 24 times such that browsers could examine them from every angle. Clothes could be seen on their own and on particular mannequin figures. Product descriptions were available in eight languages and sales were in local currencies. In reality, this level of detail proved too complex for the memories of many computers that were used to browse the site. In addition, there was a sophisticated internal checking system to ensure that customers were never sold anything which was not immediately available from the relevant manufacturer.

The delayed start, revelations about inadequate computer memories and an early sale when orders appeared to be below initial targets, all combined to ensure that Boo.com began to receive hostile publicity, having previously been heralded as a 'company of the future'. By May 2000 there were reports that the company needed refinancing with an additional £30 million. Rumours that Boo.com might be acquired by a leading sportswear company were also beginning to circulate. In the event the business went into liquidation within a year of its launch. Most of the invested millions were lost.

*Boo.com*   http://www.boo.com

Lastminute.com deals in products and services with a finite shelf-life that are close to their sell-by date and are sometimes candidates for distress pricing. Seats for flights, sporting events, theatres and holidays would all qualify. Events in the UK, France and Germany are included. Lastminute.com brokers a deal and then takes a commission. Clearly this web company is not the only potential outlet for the products in question, and consequently its success will depend on the variety it can offer, the extent of the business it can generate through its site and its ability to bring buyer and seller together. The target market is cash-rich, time-constrained professionals who would like a bargain but who cannot invest the time and effort to find it personally. In mid-1999 Lastminute.com was declaring 300,000 registered subscribers with an average of almost 15 site visits per month. Revenues amounted to some £6 million, and no direct American equivalent had been identified.

The company was founded in November 1998 by two ex-consultants in their late twenties, Brent Hoberman and Martha Lane Fox. The basic idea was Hoberman's, who had become increasingly irritated with the process of price haggling with individual hotels and airlines when he was travelling. Mid-way through 1999 the two partners had raised over £6 million from, amongst others, Intel and Deutsche Telekom, and they were constantly seeking new backers to help to develop the scope and extent of the business. At this time it was being speculated that the company would be floated in 2000. A potential valuation of £400 million was featured in the reports. The two partners would be able to retain 45% of the equity.

Having expanded its activities into France, Germany and Sweden, the company was floated in early 2000. The valuation was now some 50% higher than the 1999 indication and the shares were oversubscribed. Investor allocations had to be rationed and the price soared immediately. The uncertainty of this sector ensured that they fell just as quickly and soon they were trading at just one-third of their post-flotation high. After all, for some, Lastminute.com is 'nothing more than an up-market bucket shop'.

When the company published its results for the 6 month period October 1999 to March 2000, revenues had grown to £11.4 million for the half-year. From these the company received £1.2 million income, but lost £17 million. Like Amazon.com, Lastminute.com has yet to make a profit. In fact, the company is not forecasting a profit until 2004 at the earliest. In Spring 2000, Martha Lane Fox was placed fifth in a *Management Today* listing of the most powerful women in Britain.

Brent Hoberman reacted to the adverse publicity that the company was beginning to attract and commented: 'People have chosen to focus on personalities and the share price, but the results should focus people's minds on the business and we have shown real growth'.

In August 2000 Lastminute.com acquired its French rival, Dégriftour, for £59 million in a mixture of cash and shares. The proclaimed benefits were economies of scale and the likelihood of reaching break-even point in a shorter period. The potential downside was the reality that it could prove a distraction for a rapidly expanding company.

*Lastminute.com*    http://www.lastminute.com

## References

Brady, G (1999) The new rules for start-ups, *e-business*, December.
Gwyther, M (1999) Jewels in the web, *Management Today*, November.
Wheatcroft, P (2000) Britain's 50 most powerful women, *Management Today*, April.

QUESTIONS: Is Lastminute.com a successful company?
If yes, on what criteria are you judging it? If not, why not?
Do you know of any other companies which, like Boo.com, have failed?

## Introduction

An organization is successful if it is meeting the needs and expectations of its stakeholders. This implies a mixture of common sense and competency. These two simple, bold statements explain how we should seek to measure the success of an organization. We certainly need to know how well the stakeholder expectations are being met; we also need to understand the 'why' and 'how' behind the 'how well', as otherwise we will not be in a strong position to remedy weaknesses or sustain success.

We may feel that we know instinctively whether an organization is doing relatively well or relatively poorly, but realistically we need to be more precise than this. For one thing, we could be deluding ourselves or misjudging a situation. We could be seduced into feeling complacent and ignoring environmental changes. Success, assuming the success is real and not imagined, can be transient.

Figure 4.1 therefore implies that it is essential that organizations and their managers know where, how and why a company is doing relatively well or relatively poorly and that they use this information to sustain success by improve-

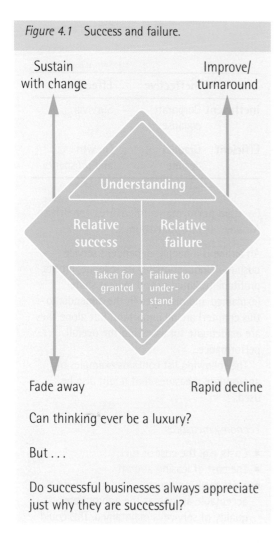

*Figure 4.1*    Success and failure.

Can thinking ever be a luxury?

But ...

Do successful businesses always appreciate just why they are successful?

ment and change or remedy weaknesses by remedial action. Otherwise, if relative success is taken for granted, or if relative failure is not understood, the organization will experience decline, whether this is slowly or rapidly.

It is quite normal to look for explanations when results or outcomes are disappointing or below target. Attention is quickly focused on failure. This is not always the case with success. It is not unusual for a group of managers proverbially to pat themselves on the back and assume that the success is a result of their personal abilities and brilliance. The reality could

be that the success lies more in good fortune and an absence of any strong, threatening competitors. Such advantages can prove very short lived. Success, when taken too much for granted, can quickly turn to failure.

It is also necessary to face up to the real issues and not attempt to 'spin' the figures to provide an attractive, but not entirely honest, explanation. Companies like to present and discuss their results in terms of absolute figures for revenue and profits, and the media seem happy to report these figures, frequently headlining any growth. Absolute growth in this form can – and can be used to – hide a deterioration in true performance. Profitability, for instance, is more important than profit per se for understanding how well a company is doing. Case 4.1 showed how growth alone could be a very dubious and misleading measure of success. Always remember – sales revenue is vanity,; cash flow is clarity; profits are sanity.

Taking this point further, it is also not unusual for companies to concentrate measurement on factors that can be measured most easily or readily. Typically, these will relate to inputs, resources and efficiencies as outcomes and effectiveness are more difficult to measure. Yet satisfying the needs and expectations of key stakeholders is critical for long-term prosperity as can be seen from the commentary in Box 4.1. Case 4.2 (p. 139) expands these points and looks at efficiency and effectiveness measurement for the British Tourist Authority.

## A Holistic Perspective of Performance Measurement

Thompson and Richardson (1996) argue that a strategically effective organization, driven by an able and aware strategic leader, is able to determine just which strategic competencies (from a set of over 30 generic competencies) are most important for that organization's competitive

## STRATEGY IN ACTION – Box 4.1
## Efficiency or Effectiveness?

There are three important measures of performance:

- Economy, which means 'doing things cost effectively'. Resources should be managed at the lowest possible cost consistent with achieving quantity and quality targets.
- Efficiency, which implies 'doing things right'. Resources should be deployed and utilized to maximize the returns from them.

    Economy and efficiency measures are essentially quantitative and objective.

- Effectiveness, or 'doing the right things'. Resources should be allocated to those activities which satisfy the needs, expectations and priorities of the various stakeholders in the business.

    Effectiveness relates to outcomes and need satisfaction, and consequently the measures are often qualitative and subjective.

Where economy, efficiency and effectiveness can be measured accurately and unambiguously it is appropriate to use the expression 'performance measures'. However, if, as is frequently the case with effectiveness, precise measures are not possible, it can be more useful to use the term 'performance indicators'.

As the following grid indicates, only efficient and effective organizations will grow and prosper. Effective but inefficient businesses will survive but underachieve because they are not using minimum resources; efficient but ineffective companies will decline as they cease to meet the expectations of their stakeholders – simply, the things they are doing are wrong, however well they might be doing them.

|  | Ineffective | Effective |
|---|---|---|
| **Inefficient** | Corporate collapse | Survival |
| **Efficient** | Gradual decline | Growth and prosperity |

### Possible performance measures for British Airways – an application

An airline is a people-dependent service business. Unquestionably its revenue, profits, profitability, liquidity and market share (explained and discussed in the appendix to this chapter) are all important. But alone they are inadequate for assessing the overall performance.

The following list contains examples of appropriate measures that might also be used.

*Economy measures*

- Costs, e.g. the cost of fuel
- The cost of leasing aircraft
- Staff levels and costs – slimming these is acceptable as long as the appropriate quality of service is maintained. This could be measured as an overhead cost per passenger.

*Efficiency measures*

- Timekeeping/punctuality
- Revenue passenger kilometres (RPK), the number of passengers carried multiplied by the distances flown
- Available seat kilometres (ASK), the number of seats available for sale multiplied by the distances flown
- The overall load factor = RPK/ASK. (Similar measures for freight are also relevant.)

Solid performance with these measures is essential if the airline is to run at all profitably, but increasing them requires the airline to be more effective in persuading more customers to fly, utilizing marketing and consistently good service.

A related measure is:

- Passenger revenue per RPK. Improving this implies increasing the return from each flight, given that on any aircraft there are likely to be several pricing schemes in operation. We shall see later how BA has changed its strategy to address this issue (Minicase 16.1).
- Income (from all sources) related to the numbers of employees
- Reliability of the aircraft, i.e. continuous flying without breakdown (as a result of efficient maintenance, see below)
- The average age of the aircraft in the fleet.

*Effectiveness*

- Ability to meet all legislative requirements
- Image – which is based on several of the factors listed in this section
- Staff attitudes and contributions – both on the ground and on board the aircraft: care, courtesy, enthusiasm, friendliness, respect and efficiency
- The aeroplane – does it look and feel new and properly looked after?
- Other aspects of the on-board service, such as the cleanliness of the seating and toilet areas, food and entertainment
- Innovation – new standards of passenger comfort
- Safety record
- The number of routes offered, the timing of flights and the general availability of seats (this requires good links with travel agents)

- Recognition of, and rewards for, regular and loyal customers, reflected in the accumulation of air miles by passengers and the numbers of passengers who become 'gold-card' holders in regular flier schemes
- Having seats available for all people with tickets who check in. While airlines, like hotels, often overbook deliberately, they must ensure that they are not 'bumping' people onto the next available flight at a level which is causing ill-will and a poor reputation
- The compensation package when people are delayed
- Time taken at check-in
- Reliability of baggage service, particularly making sure that bags go on the right flight. This also involves the issue of bags being switched from one flight to another for transit passengers
- The time taken for baggage to be unloaded (this is partially in the hands of the airport management)
- The absence of any damage to luggage
- The systems for allocating particular seats in advance of the flight and at check-in
- The number of complaints; the number in relation to the number of passengers
- The way in which complaints are handled
- The ability to balance the cost of maintenance with the costs incurred if things go wrong. If there is inadequate maintenance there are likely to be incidents or accidents which are costly in lost revenue and goodwill. At the same time airlines could 'overmaintain' to a level where they are no longer able to compete because of too-high costs.

The additional factors below are not wholly the responsibility of airlines as they also involve the airport owners:

- Terminal provisions and comfort – seating, escalators, restaurants, duty-free shopping and toilets
- Security – evidence of security and the perception that it is being taken seriously
- Availability of trolleys.

**Endnotes**

It is also important to consider how all these factors might be measured and evaluated. Observation, passenger surveys, complaints and comparisons with other airlines are all possibilities.

The distinction between indicators (aspects of service which are actually difficult to measure), measures and performance targets (standards to measure against) needs to be recognized.

The following points are also worth noting:

- it is sensible not to be overambitious with both measures and targets
- if something cannot be measured it is perhaps better to leave it out
- the chosen measures must be relevant and easily understood; hopefully the very act of measurement will foster improvements.

and strategic success. The full list is included in Chapter 25, Final Thoughts, where this topic is discussed more fully. These competencies then receive attention and priority treatment, and improvements are measured. One essential element is ensuring that people inside the organization understand this thinking and prioritization; they appreciate what matters and why. Many organizations possess strengths in competencies which do not yield any real competitive advantage; conversely, they do not target those factors which could make a real and significant difference to their relative success. The very act of visibly monitoring and measuring a particular factor or competency is likely to foster improvement, which again reinforces the need to diagnose where the real opportunities for improvement lie. Figure 4.2 reinforces these arguments, highlighting that organizations which fail to diagnose the strategically most important competencies risk underachievement, as do those which understand but fail to prioritize and measure.

Simply and fundamentally, the act of measurement affects the behaviour of individual managers.

What gets measured gets done. If you are looking for quick ways to change how an organization behaves, change the measurement system.
*Mason Haire, University of California Institute of Industrial Relations*

Measurement and review not only clarify how well an organization is doing, the process informs and guides change, both continuous, improvemental, emergent change and discontinuous change to new competitive paradigms, as explained in Figure 4.3.

Thompson and Richardson (1996) have also shown how these generic strategic competencies can be categorized into three broad groups which influence the organization's efficiency and effectiveness and have a relevance for all of

# Minicase 4.2  British Tourist Authority (BTA)

The *mission* of the BTA is 'to strengthen the performance of Britain's tourist industry in international markets by encouraging people to visit Britain and encouraging the improvement and provision of tourist amenities and facilities'.

## BTA objectives

The BTA has agreed the following long-term objectives:
1. Maximize the benefit to the economy of tourism to Britain from abroad.
2. Ensure that the Authority makes the most cost-effective use of resources in pursuing its objectives.

    Resources are constrained by grants and the ability to agree joint venture projects; and therefore the benefits generated are inevitably limited. With more money benefits could be increased, but when do they become less cost-effective to create?
3. Identify what visitors want and stimulate improvements in products and services to meet their needs.
4. Encourage off-peak tourism.
5. Spread the economic benefit of tourism more widely, and particularly to areas with tourism potential and higher than average levels of unemployment.

    Objectives 3, 4 and 5 may well prove contradictory. Moreover, there will always be considerable elements of subjectivity and value judgement in establishing priority areas.

## Measures of corporate performance

BTA could be judged to be successful if visitors (business people and tourists) come to Britain, if they come both off-season and in-season (objective 4), if they spend increasing amounts of money while they are in Britain, if they spend in the preferred places (objective 5), and if they go home and tell other people to come – and over a period this increases the number of visitors and their expenditure (objective 1 explicitly and objective 3 implicitly).

These are all measures of effectiveness, whilst objective 2 addresses resource efficiency. However, there is a problem of cause and effect. While the criteria listed above can all be measured, the net contribution of the BTA cannot be so easily ascertained. Tourists and business people would still come, regardless of the existence of the BTA. In addition, many of the reasons for them choosing to come, or not to come, are outside both the control and influence of the BTA. The cause and effect of BTA initiatives is consequently very difficult to ascertain without extensive tracking studies, which can be prohibitively expensive. However, research in the early 1990s showed that at that time 27% of all visitors to the UK had visited a BTA office abroad.

It is believed implicitly that the activities undertaken around the world contribute to corporate objectives and performance, but often it is the activities (efficiencies) which are measured rather than the outcomes. Are particular promotions actually implemented? Are planned brochures published? Are desirable workshops and seminars attended? In fairness, despite the difficulties, BTA does attempt to measure the impact of the special promotions that it undertakes on the numbers of visitors to the UK.

*British Tourist Authority*   http://www.visitbritain.com

QUESTIONS: Can you suggest any other/better measures of performance than those mentioned?
How difficult do you think it might be to track the effectiveness of the BTA?

*Figure 4.2*   Measuring strategic competencies.

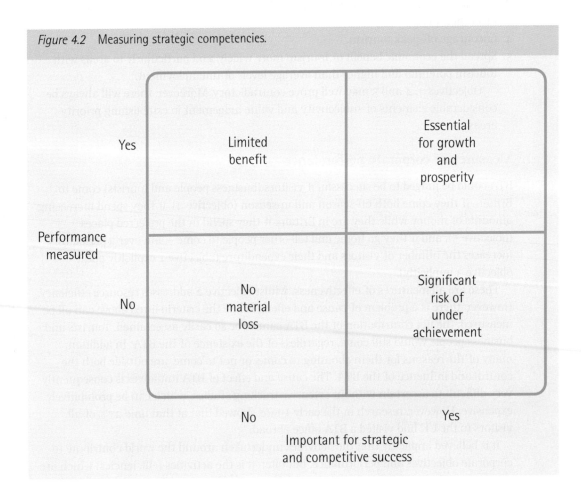

*Figure 4.3*   The measurement process.

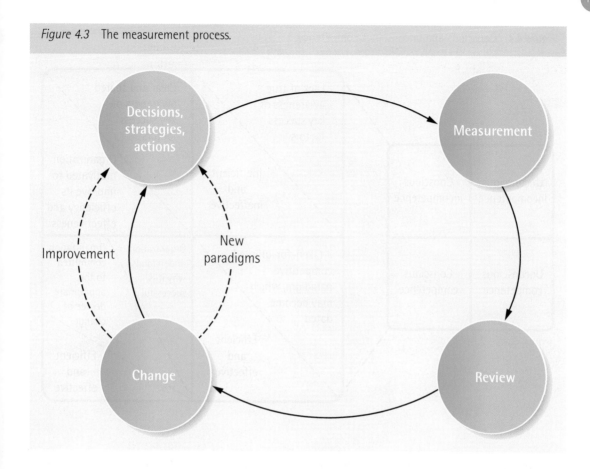

its stakeholders. *Content* competencies reflect the ways through which organizations add value, differentiate and manage their costs. They include functional and competitive strategies. *Process* competencies deal with the ways by which these content competencies are changed and improved in a dynamic and competitive environment, while *awareness and learning* competencies inform the change management process. Process competencies relate, for example, to strategy implementation and to quality and customer care; awareness and learning competencies include the ability to satisfy stakeholders, ethical and social issues and the ability to avoid and manage crises.

Each organization has its own particular mix of critical competencies, and this mix changes in dynamic and competitive environments. Consequently, the measurement systems must be flexible and capable of dealing with both hard and soft issues. Some competencies will need to be evaluated by indicators which are inevitably subjective in nature rather than by formalized, hard measures. The fact that this may be more difficult is no excuse for concentrating on measuring those factors which are simply easy to measure, as they may not be the ones which make a real difference.

## Improving competency

Where organizations need to become more successful and less crisis prone, it will be necessary for them to improve and/or reprioritize

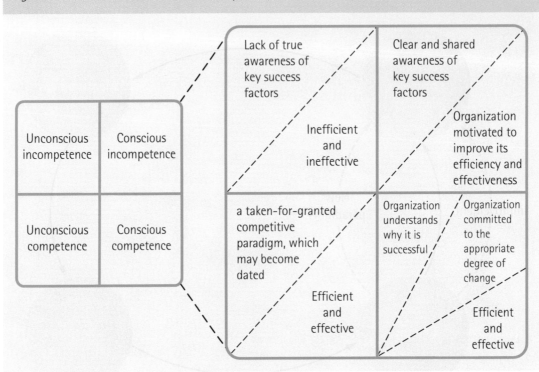

*Figure 4.4*    Conscious and unconscious competency.

their competencies. It was suggested above that it is necessary, first, to evaluate which competencies are critical for strategic and competitive success and, secondly, to ensure that the organization possesses these competencies at an appropriate level. To facilitate this, and to ensure that there is improvement and change, it will clearly be necessary for organizations to measure their competencies. Figures 4.4 and 4.5 expand the strategic implications of these points on competency for organizations.

The four-quadrant box on the left of Figure 4.4 has been adapted from May and Kruger (1988), whose ideas on personal competency have been extrapolated to an organizational context. An *unconsciously incompetent* organization does not appreciate just which factors are critical for competitive and strategic success; partly as a consequence of this it is both ineffi-

cient and ineffective. It is not deploying the right mix and measure of the generic competencies.

An *unconsciously competent* organization is efficient and effective, satisfying the needs and expectations of its stakeholders. However, there is an implication that it does not fully understand why it is successful, and when it might need to change. Consequently, it has a taken-for-granted paradigm of competitive and strategic success which may become out of date and no longer appropriate.

The *consciously incompetent* organization has a clear and shared awareness of key success factors. Managers recognize which issues and competencies are essential for success. Unfortunately, it is less efficient and effective than it needs to be, but it is motivated to improve.

Finally, the *consciously competent* organization understands why it is successful. It is efficient and

Figure 4.5   Improving competencies.

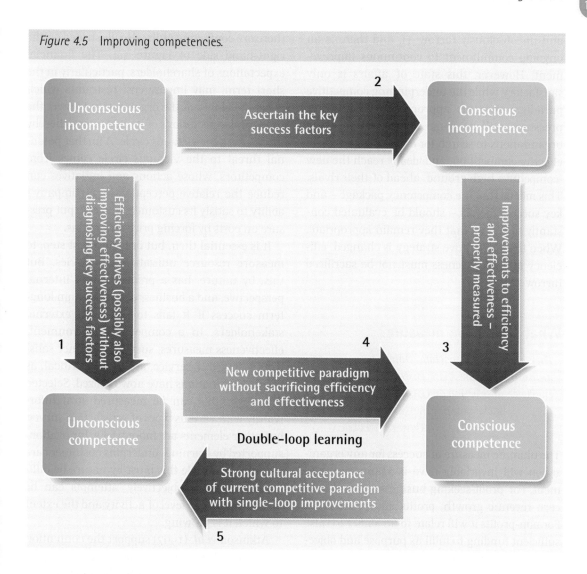

effective and it is motivated to manage both continuous and discontinuous change as necessary.

Figure 4.5 illustrates the requirements for moving from one quadrant to another. An unconsciously incompetent organization becomes more competent (arrow 1) by efficiency and productivity drives, which may also improve effectiveness to some extent, but it may not become properly effective because it fails to clarify its key success factors. The same organization, alternatively, may become more conscious by attempting to clarify the key success

factors (arrow 2). This, later, needs to be accompanied by a determined effort to improve efficiency and effectiveness (arrow 3) to generate competency.

Arrows 4 and 5, linking the bottom two quadrants, indicate an organization with E–V–R congruence. Once an organization has become consciously competent, these competencies and the associated competitive paradigm need to be fully accepted and absorbed into the organization's culture and values. Satisfying the key success factors happens almost automatically and unconsciously (arrow 4), and there is an ongoing commitment to continuous improvement. However, this state of affairs is only satisfactory while the underpinning competitive paradigm remains appropriate. Competitive pressures will at some stage require most organizations to search for a new perspective of effective competition, and ideally reach the new 'competitive high ground' ahead of their rivals. This means that the competency package – and key success factors – should be evaluated constantly to ensure that they remain appropriate. When the competitive strategy is changed, efficiency and effectiveness must not be sacrificed (arrow 5).

## What should we measure?

*The three most important things you need to measure in business are customer satisfaction, employee satisfaction and cash flow.*

Jack Welch, Chief Executive Officer,
General Electric (US)

The ultimate measure of success for any organization will invariably have a quantitative element. For profit-seeking businesses it will concern revenue growth, profits and profitability. For non-profits it will relate to an ability to raise sufficient funding to fulfil its purpose and objectives effectively. However, simply focusing on financial measures, important as they are, is woefully inadequate as they pay insufficient regard to issues of cause and outcome.

In the previous chapter, Figure 3.4 presented a virtuous circle whereby motivated, productive, committed employees create satisfied, maybe even 'delighted' customers, whose continued business enables high financial returns. To sustain the circle, this financial success must, in part, reward employees adequately and satisfactorily. While these dependencies are clear and obvious, measurement of the extent of the satisfaction is not always straightforward. Moreover,

there are conflicting pulls, also illustrated on the right-hand side of Figure 3.4. The financial expectations of shareholders, particularly in the short term, may impose cost restraints which affect the ability of the organization to meet the needs and expectations of its customers, thereby threatening the virtuous circle. A further potential threat to the virtuous circle comes from competitors, whose actions and initiatives can reduce the relative perception of a company's ability to satisfy its customers and also put pressure on costs by forcing price reductions.

It is essential then, but only as a first step, to measure resource utilization efficiencies. But this, by nature, has a predominantly internal perspective, and a business cannot sustain long-term success if it fails to satisfy its external stakeholders. In a competitive environment, effectiveness measures, such as customer satisfaction linked to service, are equally critical, as many organizations have now realized. Selected aspects of this can be measured straightforwardly with various types of satisfaction survey, but other elements are more tricky. Innovation, supported by learning, underpins customer care and service. While this must by nature be difficult to measure objectively, attempts can be made to judge the level of activity and the extent to which it is growing.

Atkinson *et al.* (1997) support the contention that satisfied employees are productive, and productive employees are essential for financial success. They suggest that employee satisfaction depends on four key variables: compensation schemes and rewards; the culture of the organization; the prevailing style of management; and job design and responsibility.

Research by Industrial Relations Services – IRS (1997) confirms that an increasing number of UK organizations now accepts that they must measure customer satisfaction, 'employee well-being' and the contributions made by people at both the individual and team levels. This in part explains the increasing influence of measurement 'packages' such as Kaplan and Norton's *balanced scorecard* (1992), which is discussed later in this chapter (p. 154).

Organizations are now just as likely to have stated and measured objectives covering customer relations and people-related issues as they are profit and profitability improvement. While it is acknowledged that elements of this are difficult, there is increasing evidence – but certainly not universal practice – of surveys of employee morale, satisfaction and opinion. Leadership and team behaviour, for example, can be usefully evaluated with 360° appraisals, but attempts at this by various organizations have enjoyed mixed success.

Consequently, Ruddle and Feeny (1997) have concluded that, for some organizations '. . . in spite of all the rhetoric and new ideas, it is very difficult to get people away from the financial numbers.'

Furthermore, parallel research in the USA by Towers Perrin (1997) concludes that employees who accepted and survived organizational restructuring and downsizing, together with the accompanying insecurity, do not feel that they are being rewarded justly now that the American economy is buoyant once again and corporate financial performances are generally improving. Productivity has increased and the satisfaction of employees with their individual jobs is relatively high and growing. People are accepting empowerment, responsibility and control of their jobs, but this is fuelling their expectations of higher rewards. However, there is only 'limited evidence of the partnerships employers have said they want to build with their workers'. The inherent danger is that the commitment level will plateau and turn down again, thus breaking the virtuous circle in Figure 3.4, instead of providing a platform for both corporate and personal growth now that the degree of job insecurity is reduced.

As a final qualification to this section, my own research suggests that even when softer issues are evaluated and measured, the results are not always communicated through the organization to an appropriate and desirable degree.

## A holistic model

Accepting these reservations, it is next important to look at performance measures within a comprehensive cause and outcome framework. Manfred Kets de Vries (1996) argues that strategic leaders have two key roles to play. First a charismatic one, through which they ensure that the organization has an understood vision and direction, people are empowered and as a consequence they energize, stimulate and galvanize change. Secondly, an architectural role of establishing an appropriate structure and style for both control and reward. Effective leaders succeed when strategies are owned by those who must implement them, customers are satisfied, people enjoy their work and things happen in the organization – specifically, the necessary changes are quick and timely. These issues will be explored more fully in Chapter 12.

Extending the themes, Figure 4.6 reinforces earlier comments about how strategic leadership is crucial for establishing (and changing) both competency and the corporate 'strategic logic' of the organization. With the latter we are considering whether or not the organization's corporate portfolio and its competitive strategy or strategies 'make sense' and can be justified, or appear to be a recipe for poor or disappointing performance.

A strong and well-managed portfolio will be reflected in successful and effective competitive and functional strategies and in operating efficiency. Also important and relevant manifestations are the image, visibility and reputation of the organization, its strategic leader and its products and services, factors which can be managed and can have a bearing on many things, but which are tricky to evaluate and

Figure 4.6    Strategic performance evaluation.

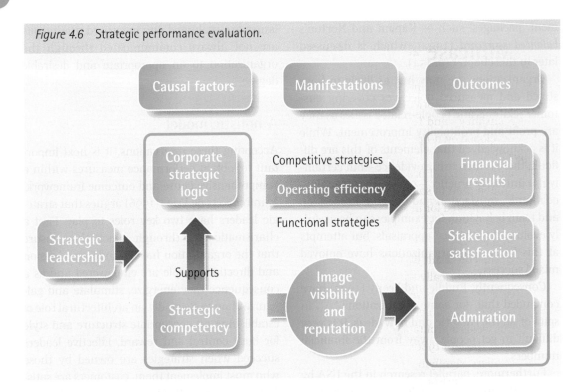

measure, particularly by the organization itself. Largely, they are the subjective opinion of external experts and stakeholders.

There are three distinctive broad approaches to measuring outcomes. These are:

- *Financial results* and other market-driven quantitative measures such as market share
- *Stakeholder satisfaction*, reflected in the balanced scorecard and similar packages
- *Admiration*, for example the annual reviews carried out by *Fortune* in the USA and *Management Today* in the UK.

This chapter now looks briefly at corporate logic, and then at admiration, image and reputation, financial measurement and stakeholder measures to explain the linkages in Figure 4.6.

## Corporate strategic logic

Caulkin (1995) stresses that the average life expectancy of successful UK companies is some 40–50 years. He has shown how only nine of the 30 companies used to make up the first Financial Times share index in 1935 still existed in their own right 60 years later. Several others were still in existence but under new ownership. Some had been liquidated; many had been acquired and absorbed by their new corporate parents. It is inevitable that every one of the companies will have seen major strategic and/or structural changes of some kind.

It has long been recognized that businesses which succeed in maintaining real growth over a number of years quickly abandon their early dependence on a single product or service. As they increase the range of activities in their portfolio, a key strategic issue is the extent of their diversity. Some will diversify only around related markets, processes and technologies; many others have historically chosen to move into completely unrelated areas. Although General Electric, a genuinely diversified conglomerate spanning manufacturing, television

# Minicase 4.3  Kwik Save

Kwik Save stores have always competed with grocery giants such as Sainsbury and Tesco, and historically they have prospered with an individual strategy. While ASDA, Sainsbury's and Tesco (together with other competitors) have built ever bigger stores, developed own-brand alternatives and introduced non-food items, Kwik Save concentrated on having a large number of smaller, well-located units selling mainly a limited range of branded products at competitive prices. Choice was therefore more limited than in some other stores, and less was invested in shopper comforts, but this was compensated for in the prices. Some products were in boxes rather than shelved, and aisles were relatively narrow, for example. The basic message was 'Everything is kept simple'.

The end result was lower overheads, which reduced the break-even level in every store. Historically Kwik Save turned over its assets approximately six – and sometimes eight – times per year, more times than their main rivals. Combined with a profit margin of some 5% (which compares quite favourably with other grocery supermarket chains) this yields a profitability of 30–40%. This was higher than most of their rivals. At this time, the late 1980s, Kwik Save's price to earnings ratio was also higher than most other retailers, signifying investor confidence in the future of the business.

In comparison, in a typical year, Marks and Spencer, for example, would have a profit margin much higher than that of Kwik Save but, because they were investing far more in their stores and offering a wide range of products (albeit under only one brand name), their net asset turnover would be around two times.

While the strategy proved very successful, Kwik Save became aware of a number of drawbacks. By concentrating on selling only food they were vulnerable to the introduction of Sunday trading. Stores offering a wider range of products were always likely to benefit far more than food stores. In addition, their success attracted direct competition from rivals such as Aldi, the German supermarket chain which has opened a number of stores in the UK, Netto and others. While Kwik Save offered some 4000 product lines (Sainsbury's and Tesco have over 20,000) and priced between 5% and 10% lower than the giants, Aldi offered just 600 lines and discounts of over 20%.

In 1993 Sainsbury's and Tesco both reduced the prices of their own-label products to widen the price gap between own-label and brand leader; this move put real pressure on Kwik Save's discounted prices for the leading brands. As a counter-measure, Kwik Save introduced own-label products for the first time. The extent was limited to some 15% of total shelf space, whereas Sainsbury's and Tesco would each feature at least 30%, but the amount of discount was huge. Shoppers could save around 50% of the main brand price. The strategy did not bring the hoped-for benefits. Overheads were increased without a compensating increase in sales revenue.

In 1994 Kwik Save acquired the Scottish discount chain, Shoprite; its 90 stores gave Kwik Save a much stronger presence in the north of Britain. Kwik Save now had some 900 stores.

Strong profits continued through 1994, but in 1995 Kwik Save suffered its first ever profits fall. The accumulated pressures from European discounters, stronger discounting by the giants, the need to revamp its older stores substantially and the investment required in Shoprite were all blamed. Further difficulties in 1996 led to shop closures. During 1996–97 Kwik Save's once buoyant shares underperformed against the stockmarket average by 68%.

In 1997 a second, higher quality, own-label was introduced alongside the existing one and priced between it and the branded items. A series of store refurbishments, costing £250,000 each, was begun. A year later Kwik Save was merged with Somerfield, another medium-size food retailer which had earlier acquired Gateway. The group, with 1400 stores, was now the fifth largest in the UK. All the stores were 'high street' rather than located in out-of-town shopping centres. There would be some savings from combining two purchasing operations, but analysts saw little strategic logic in the merger. They were to be proved right.

A £1 billion refurbishment programme was promised, designed to change the Kwik Save format to that of a more 'typical' supermarket. But did Kwik Save's customers, albeit a limited segment of the market, want these changes? If not, who would replace them?

Kwik Save's head office was closed prematurely, before the two businesses were properly consolidated; the distribution network was cut back, creating supply problems; the brand was neglected and not promoted. Kwik Save continued to decline; and in 1999 350 of its stores were offered for sale, alongside another 150 Somerfield stores. Before their merger the two companies, valued separately, were together worth £1.26 billion. Now the group was valued at £415 million.

*Kwik Save (now owned by Somerfield)*    http://www.somerfield.co.uk

QUESTION: Do you believe that Kwik Save, in the early 1990s, and facing new competition, could have preserved its earlier success if it had adopted different strategies?

and financial services, enjoys the status of one of the world's largest and most successful companies – due in no small way to the style of its chief executive, Jack Welch – the attractiveness of real diversity has waned. Sadtler *et al.* (1997) defend the case for a clear focus, built around a defensible core of related activities, and in this they reflect current practice. These issues are debated further in Chapter 22.

Minicase 4.3 on Kwik Save illustrates how easily fortunes can change if the underlying strategy for the business becomes outdated and fragile.

## Admired companies

Sound profits and a strong balance sheet are very important, but alone they will not necessarily lead to a company being 'admired'. In the 1980s, and based on research in the USA by *Fortune*, the *Economist* began to investigate which companies are most admired by other business people, particularly those with whom they compete directly. More recently, *Management Today* has taken over the project in the UK and the *Financial Times* in association with Price

Waterhouse later initiated a parallel European and then a global study. Business people are asked to allocate marks against certain criteria for their main rivals. The criteria used in the UK survey are as follows: quality of management; financial soundness; value as a long-term investment; quality of products and services; the ability to attract, develop and retain top talent; capacity to innovate; quality of marketing; and community and environmental responsibility. These reflect multiple perspectives and stakeholder interests; and consequently the *Economist* (1991) argues that admiration encourages customers to buy more and to stay loyal, employees to work harder, suppliers to be more supportive and shareholders also to remain loyal.

Table 4.1 features the most admired British companies for the period 1994–1999, tracking the relative progress in the charts of the top five businesses in both 1994 and 1999. The results for 2000 are listed at the end of the chapter. Tesco stands out as the one business which has been ranked consistently over a period of years; the other winners have enjoyed more mixed fortunes. In particular, Marks and Spencer has declined dramatically in 1999 (the explanation can be found in Case 1.2 earlier). In general, British service businesses also score very highly in the European poll but, significantly, the manufacturing sections are normally dominated by German, Swedish and Swiss companies. In a second vote, business people have often been asked for their views on all companies, not just those in their own industry sector. Marks and Spencer was the clear winner here for several years in the mid-1990s, reinforcing the extent of its recent fall from grace.

The ten most admired American companies (*Fortune*, 2000) in 1999 were:

1. General Electric
2. Microsoft
3. Dell Computers
4. Cisco Systems
5. Wal-Mart
6. Southwest Airlines
7. Berkshire Hathaway
8. Intel
9. Home Depot
10. Lucent Technologies.

*Table 4.1*  Britain's most admired companies, 1994–1999

| | Year | | | | | |
|---|---|---|---|---|---|---|
| | 1994 | 1995 | 1996 | 1997 | 1998 | 1999 |
| Company | | | Position | | | |
| Tesco | 31 | 4 | 1 | 2 | 1 | 1 |
| SmithKline Beecham | 4 | 14 | 7 | 8 | 5 | 2 |
| Glaxo (Wellcome) | 2 | 13 | 11 | 4 | 6 | 3 |
| Daily Mail | 28 | 47 | 43 | 40 | 12 | 4 |
| Cadbury Schweppes | 7 | 1 | 5 | 16 | 2 | 5 |
| Rentokil (Initial) | 1 | 11 | 30 | 14 | 37 | 56 |
| Marks & Spencer | 3 | 7 | 4 | 3 | 11 | > 125 |
| Unilever | 5 | 2 | 16 | 6 | 7 | 7 |

Covers the progress over 6 years of the top 5 in 1994 and top 5 in 1999.
Source: *Management Today* (every November issue).

A number of observations can be made:

- In an era of strategic focus, an extensively diversified company is the most admired – and globally as well (see Table 4.2). The important contribution of General Electric's strategic leader, Jack Welch, in ensuring that there is a cohesive and synergistic link between strategy, structure and style will emerge throughout this book.
- Unlike the UK, the chart of winners is dominated by computing, networks and semiconductor companies, of which there are five in the top ten.
- The extremely successful and remarkable Berkshire Hathaway is included. Run by entrepreneur, Warren Buffett, Berkshire Hathaway is neither a manufacturing nor a service business; instead it is an investment vehicle for its shareholders' funds. Minority shareholdings in a range of companies, including Coca-Cola, are typically held for the long term. Notably, high-technology companies are avoided because of their perceived inherent uncertainty.

It is also interesting that McDonald's is perceived by American business people to be their most socially responsible company, a view clearly not held by many environmental protest groups around the world.

Table 4.2 shows the world's most respected companies for 1998–2000. Notably, General Electric also tops this poll, with Microsoft following up. The other American giants included here, Coca-Cola, IBM and Daimler-Chrysler are, interestingly, not in the US top ten listed above. It is also noticeable that the British companies which enjoy the most respect globally are quite different from those admired 'at home'.

Another survey in the UK by BMRB/Mintel (see Summers, 1995) asked a sample of consumers which companies they perceive offer good value for money, understand their market, are trustworthy and care about the environment. Boots won every category except for environmental concern, where it came second to The Body Shop. Inevitably, the winning companies in a poll such as this will be those with high visibility and presence, especially retailing orga-

*Table 4.2* The world's most respected companies, 1998–2000

| | | | Year | | | |
|---|---|---|---|---|---|---|
| | | **1998** | | **1999** | | **2000** |
| **Position** | 1 | General Electric | | General Electric | | General Electric |
| | 2 | Microsoft | | Microsoft | | Microsoft |
| | 3 | Coca-Cola | | Coca-Cola | | Sony |
| | 4 | IBM | | IBM | | Coca-Cola |
| | 5 | Toyota | | Damler-Chrysler | | IBM |
| **Position of best-placed UK Companies** | | | | | | |
| | 12 | Royal Dutch Shell | 20 | Unilever | 21 | Vodaphone |
| | 27 | Body Shop | 21 | Royal Dutch Shell | 23 = | Royal Dutch Shell |
| | 35 = | British Airways | 28 | BP/Amoco | 23 = | BP/Amoco |
| | 35 = | Marks & Spencer | 32 | British Airways | 28 = | Virgin |
| | 35 = | Unilever | 41 | Lloyds/TSB | 37 | Unilever |

Sources: The World's Most Respected Companies, *Financial Times* Survey, 7 December 1999; 15 December 2000.
http://surveys.ft.com (past surveys) – www.globalarchive.ft.com

nizations, reflecting the value of a good corporate image. Ironically, Marks and Spencer did not appear in the top ten in any category.

Yet another related survey is the British Quality of Management awards (see Houlder, 1997), where Marks and Spencer were again placed first for three consecutive years in the mid-1990s, this time followed by British Airways and Glaxo Wellcome. The polling here is conducted by MORI, who seek opinions on a selection of key issues from institutional investors, company chief executives and business journalists. One significant fact to emerge is that different categories of judges prioritize the significant issues in different ways. Journalists see innovation as vitally important, whereas it receives much lower priority from industrialists in the MORI poll. By contrast, Price Waterhouse concluded that both industrialists and analysts see innovation as the most important factor of all. Interestingly, strategic leadership is not recorded as a particularly high priority for fund managers by MORI, but the following comment was made about ABB's success in the European poll:

*The biggest asset may well be the charismatic figure of its chairman [Percy Barnevik] . . . who is identified as an outstanding business leader.*
[Asea Brown Boveri (ABB) is a Swedish–Swiss engineering conglomerate]

Financial success alone certainly does not guarantee admiration from competitors and popularity with all the stakeholders; at the same time, as evidenced by The Body Shop over a period of years, deteriorating financial returns will bother shareholders far more than customers! Fisher (1996) has argued that admiration placings in the USA can certainly affect the stock price both positively and negatively, yet the extent to which financial performance affects the admiration marks remains less clear.

While several tentative conclusions might be drawn from these polls, prolonged debate is outside the scope of this book. However, it is worth emphasizing three points: first, fortunes can change very quickly; secondly, admiration seems to be affected by short-term changes of fortune; and thirdly, the various polls on the same themes are themselves not always consistent, although some patterns can be traced.

## Image, reputation and strategic panache

A well-recognized and positive image and reputation appear to improve the admiration rankings; and, correspondingly, linkage with a major corporate mistake or mishandled crisis has a negative effect, especially if social and ethical responsibilities are involved. The next issue to be addressed, therefore, concerns the relative value of a good reputation and high visibility. Could reputation, inevitably a subjective judgement, actually help to cover up a relatively poor financial performance, itself a more objective measurement? Fombrum (1996) contends that reputations create economic value, and that image, because it embodies the company's uniqueness, is a key competitive tool. He uses this as an argument in favour of benchmarking those companies perceived to be the leading performers, to ensure that no critical gaps are left open.

We have seen that General Electric, Microsoft and Coca-Cola are the world's most respected companies. It is significant that General Electric (Jack Welch) and Microsoft (Bill Gates) have highly respected strategic leaders and, if we accept Windows as a brand, two of the three have hugely popular and instantly recognizable *brands* that are systematically encircling the globe. Until his sudden, early death Coca-Cola's long time strategic leader, Roberto Goizueta, was also highly respected.

Brands can give a company visibility, sometimes international visibility. When a prominent brand becomes associated with trust and quality, its corporate owner should be in a position to command premium prices, although some of this is needed to cover the extra promotional costs required to sustain the brand's visibility. Companies are increasingly including their brands as balance-sheet assets and attempting to place a value on them. Usefully for consumers, sensible companies will invest in their brands in order to improve them and sustain their competitive leadership. We return to this issue in Chapter 9.

The relative value of a charismatic, high-profile and media-friendly – or even media-chasing – strategic leader is more difficult to quantify, although the reality of their impact is not in question.

The thinking behind Figure 4.7 recognizes that competency and reputation may or may not be aligned. Some companies enjoy a repu-

Virgin may be innovative and Body Shop may be ethical, but the main thing that distinguishes these companies from the pack is how hard they shout about their achievements.
*Columnist Lucy Kellaway writing in the Financial Times, 23 September 1996*

tation which exceeds their true competency if it is evaluated objectively; as long as they are not actually incompetent this must surely be good for them, but only in the short run! This situation could be the product of history, trading on past success, which clearly can only last for

*Figure 4.7    Competency, recognition and success.*

| Competency-driven success | | Low | Medium | High |
|---|---|---|---|---|
| | High | Unrecognized | Quiet, high performer | True strategic panache |
| | Medium | Under achieving | Neutral | Overhyped |
| | Low | Poor (struggling) performer | Tending to crisis proneness | Living dangerously on thin ice |
| | | Low | Medium | High |

Recognition and reputation

some finite time; it could equally be that they are simply very good publicists. Meanwhile, others fail to exploit their real worth and competency.

Figure 4.7 uses the phrase '*strategic panache companies*' to describe those organizations that are competent, successful, highly visible and widely recognized. Such companies are doing the right things (effectiveness), they know that they are doing them well (properly measured efficiency) and they are recognized for their achievements. Their challenge is to maintain both their competency and reputation, because otherwise their visibility could become their downfall. It is clearly a prized spot in the matrix, but it is not without a potential downside.

Quiet high performers are less visible and always really underachieving, but only to a limited degree. This is a lower-risk approach, but because the companies are less prominent, it could pay off in the long term. The secret lies in not becoming unrecognized.

Companies whose reputation exceeds their competency and success over a prolonged period must be in danger of becoming crisis prone as they increasingly fail to live up to the expectations of their stakeholders. Where success is drifting, but a company still enjoys a sound reputation, ideally this reputation should be used to 'buy time' and drive through competency improvements. Sadly, in a number of cases, it will not, and once-successful businesses will find themselves in need of major turnaround if they are to avoid liquidation. This frequently requires the creation of new strategic competencies, and is often associated with a change of leadership.

Admiration, image and reputation are not correlated closely with financial performance. While there are understandable reasons for this the implication has to be that no single 'measure' can be taken as a comprehensive assessment. This point is debated further in Thompson (1998).

## Financial measures

A plethora of financial performance measures has long been used to help evaluate the relative success and progress of a business; there is no suggestion here that this should cease to be the case. These measures include ratios such as return on capital employed and return on shareholders' funds, earnings per share, the share price itself and the price to earnings ratio. Typically, a company's share price performance will be evaluated against the relevant industry average and against one of the the Financial Times indices. While these are objective within the constraints of accounting practice and convention, there are two points to note. First, although analysts always seem to stress profitability, relating pre- or after-tax profits to either sales, capital employed or shareholders' funds, press headlines are more likely to focus on the specific growth or decline in revenues and actual profits made. Secondly, share prices are also affected by future expectation, and a plausible and convincing strategic leader can be persuasive about 'better times being on the way'.

An analysis of financial ratios is useful for a number of reasons.

- It enables a study of trends and progress over a number of years to be made.
- Comparisons with competitors and with general industry trends are possible.
- It can point the way towards possible or necessary improvements – necessary if the organization is performing less and less well than competitors, useful if new opportunities are spotted.
- It can reveal lost profit and growth potential.
- It can emphasize possible dangers – for example, if stock turnover is decreasing or ratios affecting cash flow are moving adversely.

Financial analysis concentrates on efficiency rather than effectiveness unless the objectives are essentially financial or economic ones. The real measures of success, as far as the strategic leader and the various stakeholders are concerned, is whether or not the objectives that they perceive as important are being achieved.

Outside analysts, such as students and interested readers, can gain some insight into the apparent objectives of an organization by reading annual reports, articles, press releases and so on, but only the people involved in decision making know the real objectives and whether they are being achieved. Financial analysis from the published (and easily obtained) results can be very informative and lead to conclusions about how well a company is performing, but certain aspects remain hidden. Decision makers inside an organization use financial analysis as part of the wider picture, but outsiders are more restricted. Financial analysis, then, is a very useful form of analysis, and it should be used, but the wider aspects should not be overlooked.

More recently, *economic value added* (EVA; see, for example, Lynn, 1995) has been adopted as another measure. EVA compares a company's after-tax operating profits with its cost of capital.

A more detailed treatment of financial measures is included as a Finance in Action supplement to this chapter.

## Stakeholder measures

The important *Tomorrow's Company* report (RSA, 1995), written in an attempt to improve the competitiveness of UK industry in global markets, concluded that there is:

- complacency and ignorance about world-class standards
- an overreliance on financial measures which often focus attention on the short rather than the long term
- a national adversarial culture which fails to integrate stakeholders into a cohesive network of interdependent organizations.

The preferred solution lies in a more holistic approach which incorporates the interests of multiple stakeholders. Implicit here is a clear realization that both measurement and organizational learning must encompass both what is happening inside an organization and what is emerging in the outside environment. This accords with the ideas behind the '*balanced scorecard*' approach of Kaplan and Norton (1992, 1996).

Kaplan and Norton suggest that organizations should focus their efforts on a limited number of specific, critical performance measures which reflect stakeholders' key success factors. In this way managers can readily concentrate on those issues which are essential for corporate and competitive success.

Kaplan and Norton use the term 'balanced scorecard' to describe a framework of four groups of measures, and argue that organizations should select critical measures for each one of these areas. The four groups, and examples of possible measures, are:

- financial – return on capital employed; cash flow
- customers – perceived value for money; competitive prices
- internal processes – enquiry response time; enquiry to order conversion rate
- growth and improvement – number of new products/services; extent of employee empowerment.

These measures encapsulate both efficiency and effectiveness. Figure 4.8 illustrates the synergistic dependencies and linkages between the four groups of measures. These have a close relationship with the competency linkages mentioned in the Introduction to this chapter, and featured on the right-hand side of the figure.

Measuring effectiveness requires a recognition that quality does not mean the same things for every customer. Organizations must determine what will generate repeat business and seek to provide it. Supermarkets, for example, can offer service in the form of a wide range of products,

Figure 4.8   Stakeholder measurements.

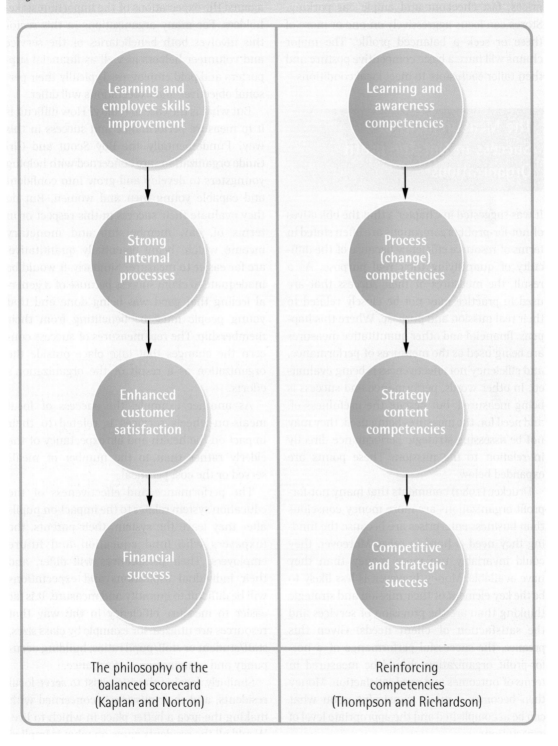

brand choice for each product in the range, low prices, fast checkout and ample car parking. Stores can focus aggressively on one or more of these or seek a balanced profile. The major chains will have a basic competitive posture and then tailor each store to meet local conditions.

## The Measurement of Success in Not-for-profit Organizations

It was suggested in Chapter 3 that the objectives of not-for-profit organizations are often stated in terms of resource efficiency because of the difficulty of quantifying their real purpose. As a result, the measures of their success that are used in practice may not be closely related to their real mission and purpose. Where this happens, financial and other quantitative measures are being used as the measures of performance, and efficiency not effectiveness is being evaluated. In other words, performance and success is being measured, but despite the usefulness of, and need for, the measures being used, they may not be assessing strategic performance directly in relation to the mission. These points are expanded below.

Drucker (1989) comments that many not-for-profit organizations are more money conscious than business enterprises are because the funding they need is hard to raise. Moreover, they could invariably use more money than they have available. Money, however, is less likely to be the key element of their mission and strategic thinking than are the provision of services and the satisfaction of client needs. Given this premise, the successful performance of a not-for-profit organization should be measured in terms of outcomes and need satisfaction. Money then becomes a major constraint upon what can be accomplished and the appropriate level of expectations.

The outcomes, in turn, must be analysed against the expectations of the important stakeholders. For many organizations in this sector this involves both beneficiaries of the service and volunteer helpers as well as financial supporters and paid employees. Typically their personal objectives and expectations will differ.

But what is the case in reality? How difficult is it to measure performance and success in this way? Fundamentally, the Boy Scout and Girl Guide organizations are concerned with helping youngsters to develop and grow into confident and capable young men and women. But do they evaluate their success in this respect or in terms of, say, membership and monetary income which, being essentially quantitative, are far easier to measure? Similarly, it would be inadequate to claim success because of a general feeling that good was being done and that young people must be benefiting from their membership. The real measures of success concern the changes that take place outside the organization as a result of the organization's efforts.

As another example, the success of local meals-on-wheels services is related to their impact on the health and life expectancy of the elderly rather than to the number of meals served or the cost per meal.

The performance and effectiveness of the education system relates to the impact on pupils after they leave the system, their parents, the taxpayers who fund education and future employers. Their perspectives will differ, and their individual aspirations and expectations will be difficult to quantify and measure. It is far easier to measure efficiency in the way that resources are utilized, for example by class sizes, staff/student or staff/pupil ratios, building occupancy and examination performance.

Similarly, local authorities exist to serve local residents, and their mission is concerned with making the area a better place in which to live. Would all the residents agree on what is implied by 'a better place in which to live', and could changes be objectively measured and evaluated? Because of the difficulties, value for money from the resources invested is more likely to be considered, and improvements in the efficiency of service provision sought.

If a charity seeks to save money by minimizing administration and promotion expenditures it is focusing on short-term efficiency. If it concentrates on long-term effectiveness it may well be able to justify investing in marketing and administration in order to raise even more money. A charity that spends some 60% of its current income on administration and marketing (and the rest on its directly charitable activities) could well, in the long run, be more effective than one that spends only 20% in this way. The aim is to establish the most appropriate structure, administration network and promotional expenditure to achieve the purpose, and then run it efficiently.

The not-for-profit sector is increasingly attempting to measure effectiveness in terms of impacts and outcomes rather than efficiency alone. The task is not straightforward.

Value for money looks at the relationship between the perceived value of the output (by the stakeholders involved) and the cost of inputs. Essentially it is used as a comparative measure. There are too many uncertainties for there to be any true agreement on the magnitude of 'very best value', and consequently one is seeking to ensure that good value is being provided, when measured against that of other similar, or competitive, providers.

If we consider both inputs and outcomes then we are considering the efficiency and effectiveness of the organization's transformation processes, its ability to add value. With certain non-profit organizations, such as the UK National Health Service (NHS), it is also tempting to make international comparisons. How much per head of the population is spent on health care? What percentage of gross domestic product does this represent? Again, these are input measures when it is outcomes that matter. The life expectancy of British people and the infant mortality rate are critically important outcomes but, while health care makes an important contribution, it is not the only causal factor.

Jackson and Palmer (1989) emphasize that if performance is to be measured more effectively in the public sector, then the implicit cultural and change issues must also be addressed, a point that was addressed in Chapter 3. The climate must be right, with managers committed to thinking clearly about what activities should be measured and what the objectives of these activities are. This may well involve different reward systems linked to revised expectations. This approach, they suggest, leads managers to move on from measuring the numbers of passengers on the railway network to analysing how many had seats and how punctual the trains were; and measuring and analysing the numbers of patients readmitted to hospital after treatment, rather than just the numbers of patients who are admitted and the rate of usage of hospital beds. Jackson and Palmer also emphasize the importance of asking users about how effective they perceive organizations to be.

## A Holistic Framework of Measures

Figure 4.9 offers an outline framework for reflecting on the measurement demands facing an organization. It is based on the premise that a competitive and strategically successful organization will achieve and, with changes, sustain, a congruency among its environment (key success factors), resources (competencies and capabilities) and values (the ability to manage appropriate and timely continuous and discon-

*Figure 4.9* A holistic framework of measures.

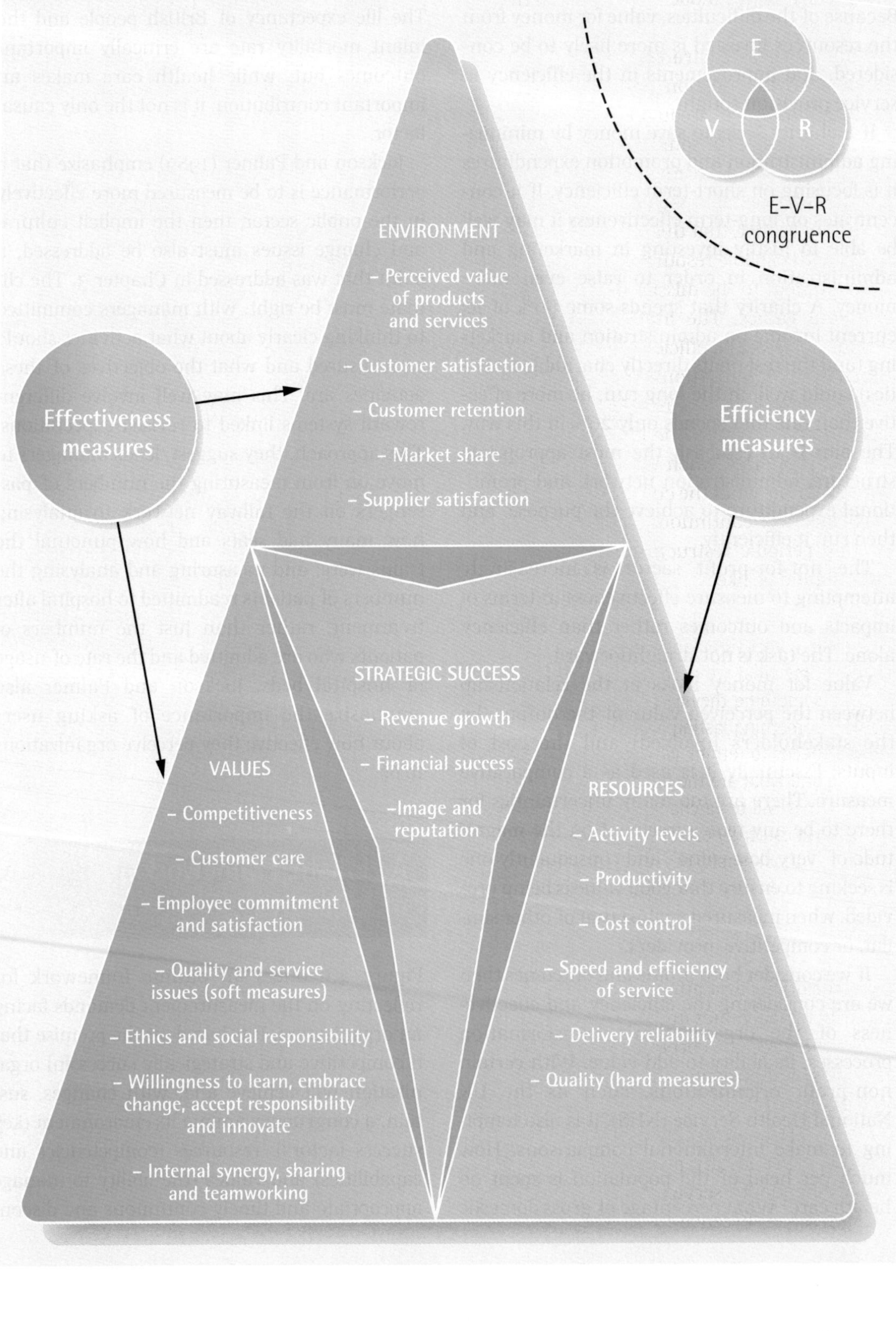

E–V–R congruence

**Effectiveness measures**

**Efficiency measures**

**ENVIRONMENT**

– Perceived value of products and services

– Customer satisfaction

– Customer retention

– Market share

– Supplier satisfaction

**STRATEGIC SUCCESS**

– Revenue growth

– Financial success

–Image and reputation

**VALUES**

– Competitiveness

– Customer care

– Employee commitment and satisfaction

– Quality and service issues (soft measures)

– Ethics and social responsibility

– Willingness to learn, embrace change, accept responsibility and innovate

– Internal synergy, sharing and teamworking

**RESOURCES**

– Activity levels

– Productivity

– Cost control

– Speed and efficiency of service

– Delivery reliability

– Quality (hard measures)

tinuous change). A small reminder of this E–V–R congruence model is provided in the top right corner.

While corporate strategic success is concerned with the mission and purpose of the organization, it will frequently be assessed by financial measures of some form, as highlighted earlier. Long-term strategic success requires that the interests of stakeholders are met, and are seen to be met, that this is accomplished efficiently with capable resources, and that there is a commitment to the mission reflected in organizational values. The implication is that in addition to resource efficiency and stakeholder satisfaction, organizations should attempt to measure values to ensure that the culture is appropriate. However, the true complexity of this task is realized when we question whether we really know what the culture of an organization in an era of continuous change – and incorporating periodic restructurings and downsizings – should be like.

In a very turbulent, rapidly changing time what we need to give people is something they can depend on, something lasting. Every company needs to rethink what are the values and what are the operating principles that will be unchanging in time so that we can truly establish a new contract with all employees.

*George Fisher, Chairman, Eastman Kodak*

Organizations that attempt this will first need to clarify which values and behaviours are critical for carrying out corporate and competitive strategies, and pursuing the mission, both now and in the future. In 1991, for example, Yorkshire Water determined that their key values were: trust, loyalty, pride, honesty, integrity, endeavour, quality, service/excellence and competitiveness. Adherence to these values would be manifested in a number of behaviour traits. It was seen as important that employees were committed to, and confident about, their roles, and that they were suitably empowered and rewarded. Effective communications networks were also thought to be vital.

Research can capture a snapshot of currently held values and the extent to which particular behaviours are being manifested. Some organizations will prefer to use volunteers from among the workforce rather than select a sample. The findings should be evaluated against a set of expectancies, and follow-up research can track both positive and negative developments. The organization must then decide what action to take if there is any deterioration or the initial absence of a critical value or behaviour pattern. Changing the culture of the organization is dealt with in Chapter 5.

It will, therefore, be realized that the Figure 4.9 framework implies a series of both hard and soft measures and indicators. Some will be straightforward, others far more difficult and subjective. Arguably the real key to success lies in those issues that are most difficult to assess. This is no excuse for not attempting a robust assessment of some form, even though it is sometimes easy to argue a case based on unsubstantiated opinion which, when rigorously probed, turns out to be a delusion. It is all too easy for senior managers to argue for what they would like to believe is a reality: that their company is competitive, that it is committed to quality and service, and that their employees are committed and supportive. They need to check these things out!

## Summary

At a most basic level of argument, an organization is successful if it is meeting the needs and expectations of its stakeholders, such that their support and commitment are maintained.

Strategically, this will imply a clear direction, from which are derived corporate, competitive and functional strategies, the implementation of which brings about the desired results. This needs both common sense and strategic competency.

*Measurement* matters. Apparent success cannot, and must not, be taken for granted. Nor must weaknesses be overlooked. We must measure those issues which really matter. The act of measurement focuses attention and endeavour on that which is being measured: being brilliant at things that do not really matter to stakeholders will not add and build value.

Some key elements will, through their very nature, be difficult to measure. They are essentially subjective and qualitative issues rather than objective and quantifiable. This is no excuse to avoid tackling them; instead we have to rely on indicators rather than measures of performance.

In some cases attention is focused on *efficiency* measures, which largely concern the utilization of resources. We are evaluating whether or not we are 'doing things right'. Measures and indicators of *effectiveness* look more at outcomes (for stakeholders) and provide a check on whether we are 'doing the right things'.

Most organizations use a raft of quantitative *measures*, embracing sales and production. Analysts external to the organization, such as students – and lecturers, come to that – will not normally have access to this information to draw conclusions from. However, financial data have to be published and can be used to calculate a number of valuable ratios which provide some insight into organizational performance. In the Appendix to this chapter investment, performance, solvency and liquidity ratios are explained.

The '*balanced scorecard*' approach provides a more comprehensive set of measures which cover stakeholders. The four categories for measurement are: finance; customers; internal processes; and growth and improvement.

It is also relevant to look at issues of *admiration*, *image* and *reputation*. These evaluations are normally by people inside the relevant industries and therefore provide an insight into how organizations are rated by their competitors and peers. There is, however, a short-term focus in this approach. Companies that are highly regarded will not necessarily be those with the strongest financial results. Although there is some link between the most admired American and the most respected global companies, those British companies that enjoy the greatest international admiration are not those held in the highest regard 'at home'.

The term '*strategic panache*' has been adopted to cover those companies that are not only successful but also seen to be successful and thus are highly regarded. Charismatic strategic leadership and strong brands are often major contributors to strategic pananche.

In isolation, therefore, any single measure or type of measure must be treated cautiously.

Consequently, the chapter concluded with a holistic framework of measures derived from the E–V–R congruence model.

## References

Atkinson, AA *et al.* (1997) A Stakeholder Approach to Strategic Performance Measurement, *Sloan Management Review*, Spring.

Caulkin, S (1995) The pursuit of immortality, *Management Today*, May.

Drucker, PF (1989) What businesses can learn from nonprofits, *Harvard Business Review*, July–August.

Economist (1991) Britain's Most Admired Companies, 26 January.

Fisher, AB (1996) Corporate reputations, *Fortune*, 4 March.

Fombrum, CJ (1996) *Reputation – Realising the Value from the Corporate Image*, Harvard Business School Press.

Houlder, V (1997) What makes a winner? *Financial Times*, 19 March.

IRS (1997) IRS Management Review No. 5, *Measuring Performance*, April.

Jackson, P and Palmer, R (1989) *First Steps in Measuring Performance in the Public Sector*, Public Finance Foundation, London.

Kaplan, RS and Norton DP (1996) *The Balanced Scorecard*, Harvard Business School Press. See also: The balanced scorecard – measures that drive performance, *Harvard Business Review*, January–February 1992.

Kets de Vries, M (1996) Leaders who make a difference, *European Management Journal*, 14, 5, October.

Lynn, M (1995) Creating wealth: the best and the worst, *Sunday Times*, 10 December.

May, GD and Kruger, MJ (1988) The manager within, *Personnel Journal*, 67, 2.

Reid, W and Myddelton, DR (1974) *The Meaning of Company Accounts*, 2nd edn, Gower. The quotation in the Appendix was taken from this second edition, but there are later editions.

RSA (1995) *Tomorrow's Company: The Role of Business in a Changing World*.

Ruddle, K and Feeny, D (1997) Transforming the Organization: New Approaches to Management, Measurement and Leadership, Research Report, Templeton College, Oxford.

Sadtler, D, Campbell, A and Koch, R (1997) *Break-up. When Large Companies are Worth More Dead Than Alive*, Capstone.

Summers, D (1995) Boots comes top in corporate image poll, *Financial Times*, 23 October.

Thompson, JL (1998) Competency and measured performance outcomes, *Journal of Workplace Learning –Employee Counselling Today*, 10, 5. This paper can be found in full on the Website accompanying this book.

Thompson, JL and Richardson, B (1996) Strategic and competitive success – towards a model of the comprehensively competent organization, *Management Decision*, 34, 2.

Towers Perrin (1997) Workplace index. Summarized in: Bolger, A (1997) Workers feel their just reward, *Financial Times*, 26 September.

*Notes*

Britain's most admired companies 2000 – see *Management Today*, December (2000).

1  Glaxo/Smith Kline (recently merged)
2  BP/Amoco
3  Shell Transport
4  Cadbury Schweppes
5  Tesco

Test your knowledge of this chapter with our online quiz at: http://www.thomsonlearning.co.uk

Explore Measuring Success further at:

*Economist*   http://www.economist.com

*Fortune*   http://www.fortune.com/fortune

*IRS Management Review*   http://www.irseclipse.co.uk/publications/irsmr.html

*Journal of workplace Learning*   http://www.mcb.co.uk/jurl.htm

*Management Decision*   http://www.mcb.co.uk/md.htm

*RSA Journal*   http://www.rsa.org.uk/publications/journal.html

*Sloan Management Review*   http://www.mitsloan.mit.edu/smr/main.html

*Sunday Times*   http://www.sunday-times.co.uk

## Questions and Research Assignments

### TEXT RELATED

1. The purpose of the Metropolitan Police Service is to: 'uphold the law fairly and firmly; to prevent crime; to pursue and bring to justice those who break the law; to keep the Queen's peace; to protect, help and reassure people in London; and to be seen to do all this with integrity, common sense and sound judgement'.
   How might they measure their success?

2. The Royal Charter for the Royal National Institute for the Blind (RNIB), granted originally in 1949, states that the RNIB exists in order to:
   - 'promote the better education, training, employment and welfare of the blind
   - protect the interests of the blind; and
   - prevent blindness.'
   How might they assess how well they are doing?

## Internet and Library Projects

1. In early 2000 Microsoft was judged by the American courts to have been operating as a monopoly and stifling competition. How have its reputation, respect and admiration been affected by this judgement and also by subsequent moves by both the company and the competition authorities?

   *Microsoft*    http://www.microsoft.com

2. Select a number of organizations from Tables 4.1 and/or 4.2 (or the *Fortune* list), picking out ones that interest you personally. Obtain their financial results for at least two years which correspond with the admiration rankings. To what extent are financial performance and admiration linked? By also checking the movements in the company's share prices over the same period, does the company's market valuation more closely reflect financial performance or a wider perception of its relative performance?

3. The National Health Service
   British Prime Minister John Major announced a new Citizen's Charter in July 1991. This implied a change of attitude for the NHS: patients should be seen as customers with rights, rather than people who should be grateful for treatment, however long the wait. From April 1992 hospitals would have to set standards for maximum waiting times.

This followed on from the 1989 NHS White Paper, *Working for Patients*, which was designed to achieve:

- raising the performance of all hospitals and general practitioners (GPs) to the level of the best (significant differences existed in measured performances)
- patients receiving better health care and a greater choice of services through improved efficiencies and effectiveness in the use of NHS resources
- greater satisfaction and rewards for NHS staff.

In subsequent years, how has this impacted on NHS strategies, and how have these also been affected by a change of government? How have performance measures and indicators been brought into line?

*Citizen's Charter*    http://www.cabinet-office.gov.uk/servicefirst

*NHS*    http://www.nhs50,nhs.uk

# Finance in Action

# Financial Analysis

The published financial accounts of a company, as long as they are interpreted carefully, can tell a good deal about the company's activities and about how well it is doing. This section concentrates on three main aspects, examining the financial measures and what they can tell us, and considers the strategic implications. The three aspects are as follows.

- *Investment*: How do the results relate to shareholders and the funds they have provided, and to the company's share price?
- *Performance*: How successfully is the business being run as a trading concern? Here we are concerned not so much with profit as with profitability. How well is the company using the capital it employs to generate sales and in turn profits?
- *Financial status*: Is the company solvent and liquid? Is it financially sound?

The ratios calculated in each of these categories have relevance for different stakeholders. Shareholders, and potential investors, are particularly concerned with the investment ratios. Performance ratios tell the strategic leader how well the company is doing as a business. Bankers and other providers of loan capital will want to know that the business is solvent and liquid in addition to how well it is performing.

This form of analysis is most relevant for profit-seeking businesses, although some of the measures can prove quite enlightening when applied to not-for-profit organizations.

Ratios are calculated from the published accounts of organizations, but an analysis of just one set of results will only be partly helpful. Trends are particularly important, and therefore the changes in results over a number of years should be evaluated. Care should be taken to ensure that the results are not considered in isolation of external trends in the economy or industry. For example, the company's sales may be growing quickly, but how do they compare with those of their competitors and the industry as a whole? Similarly, slow growth may be explained by industry contraction, although in turn this might indicate the need for diversification.

Hence, industry averages and competitor performance should be used for comparisons. One problem here is that different companies may present their accounts in different ways and the figures will have to be interpreted before any meaningful comparisons can be made. Furthermore, the industry may be composed of companies of varying sizes and various degrees of conglomeration and diversification. For this reason certain companies may be expected to behave differently from their competitors.

In addition, it can be useful to compare the actual results with forecasts, although these will not normally be available to people outside the organization. The usefulness is dependent on how well the forecasts and budgets were prepared.

## Financial Statements

The two most important statements used for calculating ratios are the profit and loss account

**Table 4.3**   Simplified profit and loss account

|  |  |  | £ |
|---|---|---|---|
|  | **Sales/turnover** |  |  |
| less: | Costs of goods sold |  |  |
|  |  | equals | Gross profit |
| less: | Depreciation<br>Selling costs<br>Administration costs |  |  |
|  |  | equals | Profit before interest and tax* |
| less: | Interest on loans |  |  |
|  |  | equals | Profit before tax |
| less: | Tax |  |  |
|  |  | equals | Profit after tax |
| less: | Dividends |  |  |
|  |  | equals | Retained earnings (transferred to balance sheet) |

*In published accounts this figure will not always be shown. It is required, however, for the calculation of certain ratios.

**Table 4.4**   Simplified balance sheet

| Information required for ratio calculations | | | Conventional presentation of figures in published accounts |
|---|---|---|---|
|  | **Fixed assets** | (Land; property buildings; plant and equipment) | **Fixed assets** |
| plus | **Current assets** | (Stock; debtors; cash and investments) | plus **Current assets** |
| less | **Current liabilities** | (Creditors: amounts falling due within one year; specifically trade creditors, overdraft, taxation not yet paid) | less **Current liabilities** |
| equals | **Net assets** |  | equals **Total assets** less **Current liabilities** |
|  | **Long-term loans** | Generally termed creditors: amounts falling due after more than one year) | plus **long-term loans** |
|  |  |  | equals **Total net assets** |
| plus | **Shareholders' funds** | (Called-up share capital: share premium account; revaluation reserve; profit and loss account) | **Shareholders' funds** |
| equals | **Total capital employed** |  |  |
| **Net assets** | equals | **Total capital employed** | Total net assets = Shareholders' funds |

and the balance sheet, simplified versions of which are illustrated in Tables 4.3 and 4.4. The full accounts may be required in order to make certain adjustments.

From the profit and loss account (Table 4.3) we wish to extract a number of figures. Gross profit is the trading profit before overheads are allocated. It is the difference between the value of sales (or turnover) and the direct costs involved in producing the product(s) or service(s), which is known as the contribution. In the case of multiproduct or multiservice organizations, where it may be difficult to attribute overheads to different products and services accurately, comparison should be made between the contributions from different divisions or strategic business units.

When depreciation and selling and administrative overheads are subtracted from gross profit the remainder is profit before interest and before tax. This is the net profit that the organization has achieved from its trading activities; no account has yet been taken of the cost of funding. This figure is not normally shown in published accounts; it has to be calculated by adding interest back onto profit before tax.

Profit before tax is the figure resulting when interest charges have been removed. Tax is levied on this profit figure, and when this is deducted profit after tax remains. This represents the profits left for shareholders, and a proportion will be paid over to them immediately in the form of dividends; the remainder will be reinvested in the future growth of the company. It will be transferred to the balance sheet as retained earnings (or profit and loss) and shown as a reserve attributable to shareholders.

This simplified outline excludes the need to, and value of, clearly separating the revenue and profits from ongoing businesses or continuing activities, recent acquisitions and discontinued activities.

Balance sheets are now normally laid out in the format illustrated on the right in Table 4.4.

Assets are shown at the top and the capital employed to finance the assets below.

Fixed assets comprise all the land, property, plant and equipment owned by the business. These will be depreciated annually at varying rates. Balance sheets generally reflect historical costs (the preferred accounting convention), but occasionally assets may be revalued to account for inflation (land and property values can increase significantly over a number of years) and any ratios calculated from an asset figure will be affected by this issue of up-to-date valuations.

Current assets, assets which are passing through the business rather than more permanent features and which comprise stocks (raw materials, work-in-progress and finished goods), debtors (customers who are allowed to buy on credit rather than for cash), investments and cash, are added on. Current liabilities, short-term financial commitments, are deducted. These include the overdraft, tax payments due and trade creditors (suppliers who have yet to be paid for goods and services supplied).

The left-hand column of Table 4.4 shows the resultant figure as net assets, which is equal to the total capital employed in the business, or the sum of long-term loans and shareholders' funds. The right-hand column differs slightly and presents net assets as total assets minus the sum of current liabilities and long-term loans – and therefore equal to shareholders' funds. This is the normal way in which a company will present its accounts, leaving us to calculate a figure for total capital employed.

Long-term loans are typically called 'creditors: amounts falling due after more than one year'. Shareholders' funds are made up of the called up share capital (the face value of the shares issued), the share premium account (money accrued as shareholders have bought shares for more than their face value, dependent on stock market prices at the time of sale), any revaluation reserve (resulting from revaluation of assets) and retained earnings (past profits reinvested in the business).

Balance sheets balance. Net assets are equal to the capital employed to finance them.

## Investment Ratios

The five key investment ratios are explained in Table 4.5, and the linkages between four of them are illustrated in Figure 4.10.

The return on shareholders' funds deals with the profit available for ordinary shareholders after all other commitments (including preference share dividends) have been met; and it is divided by all the funds provided both directly

and indirectly by ordinary shareholders. 'The return on shareholders' funds is probably the most important single measure of all. It takes into account the return on net assets, the company's tax position, and the extent to which capital employed has been supplied other than by the ordinary shareholders (for example by loans)' (Reid and Myddelton, 1974).

Earnings per share indicates how much money the company has earned in relation to the number of ordinary shares. Taken in isolation this measure is useful if considered over a number of years. Companies can be compared with each other if the ratio is linked to the current market price of shares. This calculation provides the price-to-earnings ratio $P/E$.

*Table 4.5*  Investment ratios

| Ratio | Calculation | Comments |
|---|---|---|
| Return on shareholders' funds (%) | $\dfrac{\text{Profit after tax}}{\text{Total shareholders' funds}}$ | Measures the return on investment by shareholders in the company |
| Earning per share (pence) | $\dfrac{\text{Profit after tax}}{\text{Number of ordinary shares issued}}$ | Profit after tax represents earnings for the shareholders. It can be returned to them immediately as dividends or reinvested as additional shareholders' funds (retained earnings) |
| Price-to-earnings ratio P/E | $\dfrac{\text{Current market price of ordinary shares}}{\text{Earnings per share}}$ | Indicates the multiple of earnings that investors are willing to pay for shares in the stock market<br>The higher the ratio, the more favourably the company is perceived |
| Dividend yield | $\dfrac{\text{Dividend per share}}{\text{Market price per share}}$ | Equivalent to rate of interest per cent paid on the investment<br>Shareholders will not expect it to equal say building society rates – reinvested profits should generate longer-term increases in the share price |
| Dividend cover (number of times) | $\dfrac{\text{Earnings per share}}{\text{Dividend per share}}$ | The number of times the dividends *could* have been paid from the earnings: the higher the better |

*Figure 4.10* Linkages between four investment rations: the squares represent the investment ratios; the circles the figures required for calculating ratios. (Note: the two figures required to calculate each ratio are shown leading into the box.)

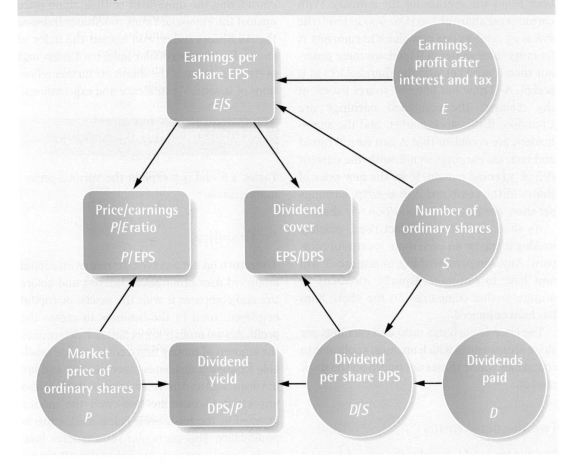

The *P/E* ratio indicates the amount (how many times the current earnings figure) that potential shareholders are willing to pay in order to buy shares in the company at a particular time. It is affected by previous success and profits, but really it is an indication of expectations. The more confidence the market has in a company, generally the higher will be its *P/E*. It can also indicate relatively how expensive borrowing is for the company. If the company opts to raise money from existing shareholders by offering new shares in a rights issue (the shareholders are invited to buy new shares in fixed

proportion to those they already hold) the higher the *P/E* is, the cheaper is the capital. A high *P/E* implies that shareholders will pay many times current earnings to obtain shares.

The *P/E* ratio is also very important in acquisition situations. Consider two companies as an example. Company A has issued 500,000 ordinary shares with a face value of 25p and their current market price is 600p. Current earnings per share are 20p (£100,000 in total). Hence, the *P/E* is 600/20 = 30. Company A looks attractive to the shareholders of company B when it makes a bid for their shares. B also has 500,000 shares issued, again with a face value of 25p, but they are trading at only 150p as company B has been relatively sleepy of late and growth has been below the average for the industry. With earnings per share of 10p (£50,000 in total) the *P/E* is 15. A offers one new share in company A for every three shares in B (perhaps more generous than it need be), and the shareholders in B accept. A–B now has 666,667 shares issued; at the moment the combined earnings are £150,000. If the stock market, and the shareholders, are confident that A can turn B round and increase earnings significantly the current *P/E* of 30 could remain. If so, the new price of shares in the combined A–B is 675p. Earnings per share are 22.5p (£150,000/666,667 shares).

A's share price has in effect risen, possibly making it appear an even more successful company. Any company wishing to acquire A will now have to pay more. Equally, A's ability to acquire further companies on the above lines has been enhanced.

The price-to-earnings ratio and earnings per share are measures which are most applicable to companies whose shares are traded on the stock market.

## Two dividend ratios

The dividend yield provides the rate of interest that shareholders are receiving in relation to the current market price for shares. It must be used cautiously as it takes no account of the price that people actually paid (historically) to buy their shares; and in any case shareholders are often more interested in long-term capital growth.

The dividend cover indicates the proportion of earnings paid out in dividends and the proportion reinvested. Company dividend policies will vary between companies and, for example, a decision to maintain or reduce dividends in the face of reduced earnings will be influenced by the predicted effect on share prices and in turn

the valuation of the company, which as we saw above can be an issue in acquisitions.

Quoted companies can also be analysed by considering the movement of their share price against the Financial Times 100 Shares Index or the All Shares Index, and against the index of shares for their particular industry. Under- and overperformance of the shares are further reflections of investors' confidence and expectations.

## Performance Ratios

Tables 4.6 and 4.7 explain the various performance ratios.

## Profitability

The return on net assets or the return on capital employed uses profit before interest and before tax and compares it with the assets, or capital employed, used in the business to create the profit. Actual profit is important as it determines the amount of money that a company has available for paying dividends (once interest and tax are deducted) and for reinvestment. But it is also important to examine how well the money invested in the business is being used – this is profitability. This particular ratio ignores how the business is actually funded, making it a measure of how well the business is performing as a trading concern. It was mentioned earlier that contributions from different products or strategic business units should be compared in the case of multiproduct organizations. The return on net assets should also be used to compare the profitabilities of products and strategic business units. In this way the ratio can be used for evaluating particular competitive strategies and the relative importance to the business of different products. However, this measure should not be used in isolation from an assessment of the relative importance of different products in terms of turnover. High-volume products or divisions

*Table 4.6* Performance ratios

| Ratio | Calculation | Comments |
| --- | --- | --- |
| Return on net assets Return on capital employed (%) | Profit before interest and before tax ——————— Total capital employed in the business | Measures the relative success of the business as a trading concern Trading profit less overheads is divided by shareholders' funds and other long-term loans Useful for measuring and comparing the relative performance of different divisions/strategic business units |
| Profit margin (%) | Profit before interest and before tax ——————— Sales (turnover) | Shows trading profit less overheads as a percentage of turnover Again useful for comparing divisions, products, markets |
| Net asset turnover (number of times) | Sales ——————— Total net assets or capital employed in the business | It measures the number of times the capital is 'turned over' in a year Or: the number of pounds of sales generated for every pound invested in the company |

*Table 4.7* Other useful performance ratios

| Ratio | Calculation | Comments |
| --- | --- | --- |
| Stock turnover (number of times) | Turnover ——— Stock | Shows how quickly stocks move through the business. Logically the quicker the better – as long as it does not result in stock shortages Most accurate measurement from *average* stock level over the year rather than the balance-sheet figure |
| Debtor turnover (number of times; or days of credit given) | Turnover ——— Debtors Debtors ——————— Turnover × 365 | Shows how quickly credit customers pay. Again, use *average* debtors. Retail organizations, such as Marks & Spencer, sell mostly for cash, or charge interest for credit through their credit cards A similar measure, credit purchases/average creditors, shows how much credit time is received by the company |
| Gross profit margin (%) and | Gross profit ——————— Turnover (sales) | Indicates percentage profit before overheads |
| Selling and administration costs to sales (%) | Selling and administration costs ——————— Turnover (sales) | Shows overheads (indirect costs) in relation to turnover |

may be less profitable than smaller volume ones for a variety of reasons, which are examined in the section on portfolio analysis.

This ratio is particularly useful when it is examined in the light of the two ratios that comprise it. The return on net assets is equal to the profit margin times the net asset turnover. The profit margin is the proportion of sales revenue represented by profits (before interest and tax); the net asset turnover illustrates how well the company is utilizing its assets in order to generate sales. Minicase 4.3 highlighted how Kwik Save's success in the 1980s was built around a high asset turnover.

Certain companies will adopt strategies that are designed to yield good profit margins on every item sold, and as a result probably add value into the product or service in such a way that their assets are not producing the same amount of sales per pound sterling as is the case for a company which uses assets more aggressively, adds less value and makes a lower profit margin. Particular industries and businesses may offer little choice in this respect; others offer considerable choice.

If a decision is reached that for the business as a whole, or some part of it, the return on net assets (profitability) must be improved, there are two approaches. Either profits must be increased, or assets reduced, or both. Figure 4.11 illustrates the alternatives available to the organization, and at the bottom the functional responsibilities. Hence, a corporate or competitive strategy change will result in changes to functional strategies.

## Other useful performance ratios

Table 4.7 explains stock turnover and debtor turnover, which both indicate how well the company is managing two of its current assets. The stock turnover will depend on how the company is managing its operations – different strategies will lead to higher or lower stocks. Low stocks (high stock turnover) save costs, but they can make the business vulnerable if they are reduced to too low a level in order to save money and result in production delays. Debtor turnover, for certain types of business, looked at over a period can show whether the company is successful at persuading credit customers to pay quickly. This can affect the marketing strategy if decisions have to be taken not to supply certain customers who are slow payers.

The gross profit margin and the selling and administration costs to sales ratio are useful for indicating the percentage of turnover attributable to overheads. If a company has a high gross profit margin but is relatively unprofitable after accounting for overheads it is a sign of poor management. The product or service is able to command a price comfortably in excess of direct costs (direct labour and materials) but this contribution is being swallowed by overheads which are possibly too high and in need of reduction. Such a company is appropriate for restructuring and perhaps acquisition. Again, these ratios should be examined over a period of years to ensure that the overhead burden is not creeping up without just cause. In terms of increasing profits (to improve profitability; Figure 4.11) it may be easier to reduce overheads than to reduce direct costs.

## Measures of Financial Status

Measures of financial status can be divided into two groups: solvency and liquidity. The ratios are explained in Table 4.8.

### Solvency

The major ratios are the debt ratio and interest cover. The debt ratio relates to the company's gearing – how much it is funded by equity capital (shareholders' funds) and how much by long-term loans. Loans generally carry fixed interest payments, and these must be met regardless of any profit fluctuations; a company

*Figure 4.11* Improving profitability.

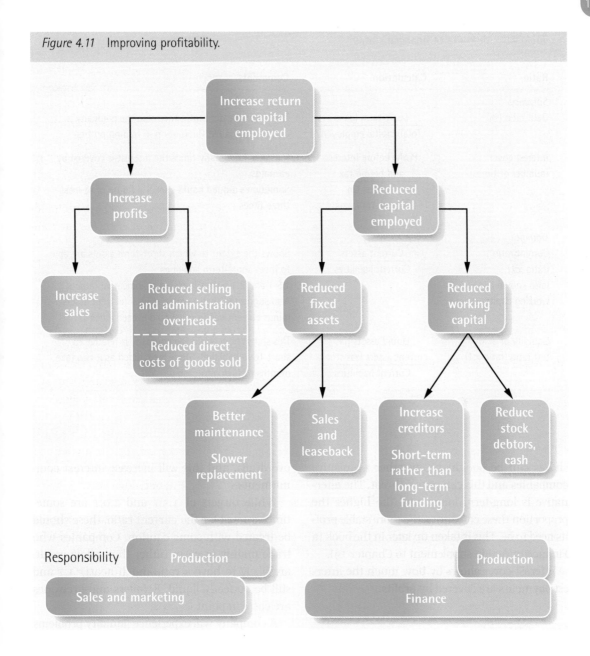

can elect not to pay dividends to shareholders if profits collapse, which gives it more flexibility.

Managers and investors will both be wary of the debt ratio creeping up, as it does when companies borrow money from the banking system to finance investment or acquisitions. In fact, acquisitive companies must relate their acquisi-tion strategies to their ability to finance them. Sometimes money can be raised from share holders, but the company must be confident that shareholders will subscribe to rights issues. If not, and the shares have to be sold to the banks who underwrite the issue (who then sell them when the price is appropriate), blocks of

*Table 4.8*   Measures of financial status

| Ratio | Calculation | Comments |
|---|---|---|
| *Solvency* | | |
| Debt ratio (%) | $\dfrac{\text{Long-term loans}}{\text{Total capital employed}}$ | The lower the debt ratio the more the company is cushioned against fluctuation in trading profits |
| Interest cover (number of times) | $\dfrac{\text{Profit before interest and before tax}}{\text{Interest on long-term loans}}$ | Indicates how many times the interest is covered by earnings<br>Sometimes argued banks expect a figure of at least three times |
| *Liquidity* | | |
| Current ratio (ratio *x*:1) (also known as working capital ratio) | $\dfrac{\text{Current assets}}{\text{Current liabilities}}$ | Shows the extent to which short-term assets are able to meet short-term liabilities<br>1.5:1 and 2:1 both suggested as indicative targets. Also suggested that working capital (current assets minus current liabilities) should exceed stock |
| Liquidity or acid test ratio (ratio *x*:1) | $\dfrac{\text{Liquid assets (i.e. current assets less stock)}}{\text{Current liabilities}}$ | This shows how liquid the company is relative to short-term liabilities. Stock is excluded as it can take months to turn into cash |

shares can be bought up by other acquisitive companies and this can pose a threat. The alternative is long-term loans, and the higher the proportion these constitute, the more stable profits need to be. This is taken up later in the book (a Finance in Action supplement to Chapter 19).

Interest cover shows by how much the interest payments are covered by profits.

## Liquidity

The two main liquidity ratios, the current ratio and the acid test (liquidity) ratio, relate to working capital. Has the company sufficient money available to meet its short-term commitments? They are determined by the flow of cash in and out of the business. A shortage of cash, and commitments to meet, will push the company towards increased borrowings (say a larger overdraft), and this will increase interest commitments.

While targets of 1.5:1 and 2.0:1 are sometimes quoted for the current ratio, these should be treated with some caution. Companies who trade mainly in cash, rather than allow credit, are likely to have a ratio much nearer 1:1 and still be perfectly liquid. Retailers and breweries are cases in point.

A company will experience liquidity problems if it invests in stock and then fails to win orders or if it fails to control its debtors. Conversely, a successful company can have cash problems. Success at winning orders may require investment in machinery or stocks and labour, and these may have to be paid for before and during production and before the goods are delivered and paid for by customers. This can lead to temporary illiquidity, and is known as overtrading.

## Managing Cash

Cash flow, therefore, can be just as important as profitability. Where demand is seasonal for certain products production may take place when sales are low, in advance of peak demand. This puts pressure on cash flow in the way outlined above. A perfect example of this is Standard Fireworks, a largely focused business, whose sales are concentrated in the weeks before bonfire night (5 November), but who produce all through the year.

Cash reserves built up in good years can be run down to finance a company during lean years or a recession.

Cash-flow issues affect corporate strategy in terms of the range of products, services and businesses selected, competitive strategies in terms of the way they are marketed (to avoid the worst implications of seasonal fluctuations) and functional production, marketing and financial strategies.

It is not unusual for companies to be slow in paying their bills when their performance is poor. This impacts upon their customers, and highlights the importance of cash flow, particularly in a recession. Table 4.9 shows how cash is generated and spent.

Cash flow can be improved in a number of ways, for example, by

- increased turnover – but only if linked to
- effective management of debtors and creditors
- higher operating profit margins
- reduced tax payments
- reduced investment in working capital and/or fixed assets
- improved gearing to reduce interest payments.

Simply, a company must be able to produce cash in order to finance future investments and acquisitions, meet outstanding payments on earlier acquisitions and cover any unexpected events requiring extraordinary charges.

*Table 4.9*  A typical cash-flow statement

Cash generated by operating activities (including operating profits, changes in stocks, debtors, and creditors and depreciation charged in the accounts)

| | |
|---|---|
| Add: | Interest from investments |
| | proceeds from any share issues |
| | receipts from any asset sales |
| | new loans taken out |
| Deduct: | interest paid on loans |
| | loans repaid |
| | tax paid |
| | dividend paid |
| | fixed assets purchased |
| Leaving: | money available for further investment |

## Accounting for Inflation

It is an accounting convention to use historical costs, and within the accountancy profession there is ongoing debate and disagreement about how best to treat inflation. This topic is outside the scope of this book. However, it is important to take some account of inflation when looking at growth rates for actual data such as turnover and profits as otherwise companies appear to be doing far better than in reality they are.

## Other Quantitative Performance Indicators

In addition to all of these financial ratios, businesses will typically collect and evaluate information concerning the performance of all the activities being undertaken. For each functional area there will be a number of measures, such as the value of orders acquired by every sales-person, machine utilization, turnover at every retail outlet, output per shift, productivity per employee and absenteeism. Performance will be evaluated against targets or objectives agreed with individual managers who should be held accountable. These are measures of resource efficiency. They are important control measures which evaluate the efficiency of each functional area of the business.

Similarly, individual sectors will favour particular measures. Retailers will typically consider sales per square foot of trading space, sales per employee, average shopping spend per trip and the number of new store openings or refits.

Improvements can strengthen the company's competitive capability. In isolation, however, these measures do not indicate how successful the company is strategically. This particular issue is very significant for not-for-profit organizations which cannot use the traditional profitability ratios sensibly and at the same time cannot readily measure their effectiveness in relation to their fundamental purpose. Consequently, they often rely more on quantitative measures of efficiency.

These measures are not developed in the same detail as the financial ones in this chapter and Appendix as they will not be available to students tackling management case studies, whereas key financial data are normally obtainable.

## Service Businesses

In addition to the above measures, the ability to retain customers is a key requirement for service businesses. Retention implies customer satisfaction and probably word-of-mouth recommendation. It is likely to result in higher profits because of the high costs incurred in attracting new business. Moreover, customers are likely to increase their level of spending over time. For insurance companies the cost of processing renewals is far cheaper than the cost of finding new clients; and many people will take out additional policies with a company on which they feel they can rely.

Key performance measures for solicitors are their ability to achieve results for their clients, and the service they offer, measurable by, for instance, the speed with which they respond to letters and telephone calls.

## Applying the Ratios – A Library/Internet Project

Table 4.10 provides selected financial data for British Airways in 1994–95, and Table 4.11 a worked analysis of the following ratios:

*Investment ratios:*
Return on shareholders' funds
Earnings per share
Price/earnings ratio
Dividend yield
Dividend cover

*Performance ratios:*
Return on net assets
Profit margin
Net asset turnover
Stock turnover
Debtor turnover
Gross profit margin

*Solvency ratios:*
Debt ratio
Interest cover

*Liquidity ratios:*
current ratio
liquidity ratio

Check how these ratios have been calculated. Then update the figures for subsequent years and calculate the relevant ratios. Consider the trends with what you know (or can find out) about BA's strategy and general fortunes since 1995.

*Table 4.10*  British Airways: Extracts from profit and loss account and balance sheet, 31 March 1995

| | £million | | £million | £million |
|---|---|---|---|---|
| Turnover | 7177 | Fixed assets | 6163 | |
| | | Investments | 471 | |
| Cost of sales | 6436 | | | 6634 |
| Gross profit | 741 | Current assets | | |
| | | Stock | 70 | |
| Overheads/administration | 123 | Debtors | 1182 | |
| | | Short-term loans | 1099 | |
| Operating profit | 618 | Cash | 64 | |
| Other income/provisions | (76) | | | 2415 |
| Interest | 215 | Current liabilities | 2320 | |
| Tax | 77 | Working capital | 95 | |
| Profit after interest and tax | 250 | Total net assets | | 6729 |
| Dividend paid | 119 | Long-term loans | 4582 | |
| Retained profit | 131 | Provisions for charges | 57 | |
| | | Shareholders' funds | 2090 | |
| Number of ordinary shares | 954,605,000 | | | |
| Year-end share price | 402 pence | Total capital employed | | 6729 |

*Table 4.11*  British Airways: worked ratio analysis for 1994–95

**Investment ratios**

| | | | | |
|---|---|---|---|---|
| Return on shareholders' funds | = | $\dfrac{250}{2090}$ | = | 11.96% |
| Earnings per share | = | $\dfrac{250}{954.605}$ | = | 26.2 pence |
| Price/earnings ratio | = | $\dfrac{402}{26.2}$ | = | 15.34 |
| Dividend yield | = | $\dfrac{12.46}{402}$ | = | 3.1% |
| Dividend cover | = | $\dfrac{26.2}{12.46}$ | = | 2.1 times |

**Performance ratios**

| | | | | |
|---|---|---|---|---|
| Return on net assets | = | $\dfrac{618}{6279}$ | = | 9.2% |
| Profit margin | = | $\dfrac{618}{7177}$ | = | 8.6% |
| Net asset turnover | = | $\dfrac{7177}{6729}$ | = | 1.07 times |
| Stock turnover | = | $\dfrac{7177}{70}$ | = | 102 times |
| Debtor turnover | = | $\dfrac{7177}{1182}$ | = | 6.1 times (or 60 days) |
| Gross profit margin | = | $\dfrac{741}{7177}$ | = | 10.3% |

**Solvency ratios**

| | | | | |
|---|---|---|---|---|
| Debt ratio | = | $\dfrac{4582}{6729}$ | = | 68% |
| Interest cover | = | $\dfrac{542}{215}$ | = | 2.5 times |

**Liquidity ratios**

| | | | | |
|---|---|---|---|---|
| Current ratio | = | 2415:2320 | = | 1.04:1 |
| Liquidity ratio | = | 2345:2320 | = | 1.01:1 |

# Culture and Values

*Culture affects every element of strategy and strategic management and consequently this topic is studied early in the book. The key decision elements of strategic management concern strategic choice (deciding what to do), and strategy implementation and change (making things happen). Chapter 2 showed briefly how strategic leadership and values are at the heart of the decision-making processes. Simply, they influence the choices that are made and the feasibility of change. Can ideas for change be implemented smoothly? Will there be major barriers and resistance? If we do not understand the culture of an organization, and the impact of the strategic leader who underpins the culture, we cannot understand strategic management in that organization. The culture varies between organizations, although some elements will be common and transferable. It also varies between countries, influencing the relative competitiveness of industries and organizations in different countries. This chapter looks into these implications and into the determinants of culture and cultural differences.*

# Minicase 5.1 The Body Shop

The Body Shop, which sources and retails (directly and through franchises) naturally inspired lotions and cosmetics, has been a highly successful business with a price to earnings ratio which stayed well above the retail sector average throughout the 1980s, before declining as a result of expansion and increased competition. Until 1999, The Body Shop also manufactured at least half of the products it sold.

The Body Shop was started in England in 1976 by Anita Roddick and her husband Gordon, as a means of supporting Anita and their two daughters while Gordon went to fulfil a dream, riding horseback across the Americas. Gordon helped Anita get a bank loan of £4000 to open the first shop and shortly afterwards while Gordon was away the first franchise was agreed. Stores have subsequently been opened in over 40 countries – there are now over 1700 stores – and The Body Shop was floated on the UK Stock Exchange in 1984. Well renowned for its environmental and ethical stance and strategies, The Body Shop has made an impact around the world. 'If you think you are too small to have an impact, try going to bed with a mosquito' (Anita Roddick).

Anita's motivation for starting her business was always influenced by her personal commitment to education and to the environment and social change. Simply, her talent for entrepreneurism was channelled into a cause. The business and its financial success has been a vehicle to achieve other, more important, objectives. 'Profits are perceived as boring, but business as exciting'. The Body Shop's declared 'reason for being', 'dedicates the business to the pursuit of social and environmental change'. Anita Roddick was concerned to do something that was 'economically, socially and ecologically sustainable, meeting the

needs of the present without compromising the future'. Her ideas were the outcome of her world travels. She had visited many developing countries, 'living native', and had seen how women used natural products efficaciously and effectively. She noticed how women in Tahiti rubbed their bodies with cocoa butter to produce soft, satin-like skin despite a hot climate. She realized that women in Morocco used mud to give their hair a silky sheen. She also saw Mexicans successfully treat burns with aloes, the slimy juice from cactus leaves. From these observations and experiences she conceptualized, and realized, her opportunity. She would use natural ingredients from around the world to produce a range of new products. People in villages
were asked to supply her with the natural ingredients she needed – a form of community trade.

The Body Shop has always aroused enthusiasm, commitment and loyalty amongst those involved with it. 'The company must never let itself become anything other than a human enterprise'. Much of this has developed from the ethical beliefs and values of Anita and Gordon Roddick, which have become manifested in a variety of distinctive policies. Gordon oversaw many of the operational aspects of the business.

The Body Shop adopts an environmentally responsible approach, offering products in minimal or no packaging. Posters in the shops have been used to campaign, among other things, to save whales and to stop the burning of rain forests. Packaging is simple, yet the shops are characterized by strong and distinctive aromas. The packages, together with posters and shelf cards, provide comprehensive information about the products and their origins and ingredients. This has created a competitive advantage which rivals have at times found difficult to replicate.

The sales staff are knowledgeable, but they are not forceful and do not sell aggressively, generally offering advice only if it is requested. Marketing themes concern 'health and well-being rather than glamour, and reality rather than instant rejuvenation'. The Body Shop chose to avoid advertising for many years, preferring in-store information and word of mouth to attempts at persuasion. More recently, and especially in the USA, informative advertising has been used. The Body Shop states that neither ingredients nor final products have been tested on animals. Despite the company's active stance on ethical issues, there have been accusations to the contrary, and The Body Shop was forced into litigation (which it won) in 1992. The business has always been controversial in some circles and attracted hostility. When the first shop opened local morticians were horrified at the name: The Body Shop!

Employees are provided with regular newsletters and training packages. Anita Roddick contributes regularly to the newsletters, which *concentrate* on The Body Shop campaigns and products. Employees are given time off during working hours, to do voluntary work in the community.

The Body Shop was initially able to integrate manufacturing and retailing effectively and was efficient and operationally strong. Fresh supplies could be delivered to its UK stores with a 24-hour lead time. These strategies, policies and beliefs generated substantial growth and profits in the 1980s. In the year ended 28 February 1991 turnover exceeded £100 million with trading profits of some £22 million. When these results were announced the UK share price exceeded 350 pence. Between 1984 and 1991, against the Financial Times All Share index of 100, The Body Shop shares rose from an index figure of 100 to 5500. However, by mid-1995 the share price had fallen to 150 pence. Profits had fallen; new professional senior managers had been brought in to add strength. One dilemma concerned whether the culture and quirky management style was still wholly appropriate as The Body Shop became a much bigger international business. Global scale brings global competition. As the business grew it lost some of its entrepreneurial spirit.

In addition, The Body Shop had attracted more and more competition. Leading UK retailers such as Boots, Marks and Spencer and Sainsbury's introduced natural ingredients in their own-label ranges; further competition arrived in the form of the US Bath and Body Works chain, whose early trial stores in the UK were a joint venture with Next. Bath and Body Works is renowned as a fast-moving organization, quick to innovate new ideas – and aggressive at advertising and promotion. Among its responses in the UK, The Body Shop began trials of a party plan operation. The first Values Report was published by The Body Shop in 1995 and detailed independently verified information relating to the company's social and ethical performance.

In October 1995 The Body Shop announced its intention to reprivatize the company by buying back shares. The shares would then be placed in a charitable trust, which would be able to make donations to humanitarian and environmental causes. The plan was abandoned in March 1996 because The Body Shop would have had to borrow heavily to finance the plan. In 1998, Anita joined Gordon as a co-chairman and a new chief executive was recruited from outside the company. The loss-making US business was separated out and a joint venture agreement was established; a non-executive director injected $1 million in exchange for an option to acquire 49% of the US business. Nevertheless, profits grew steadily throughout the 1990s, reaching almost £40 million in 1998. In 1999 The Body Shop withdrew from manufacturing and established a strong supply network instead, enabling it to concentrate on the retail end of the business.

The Body Shop is an idiosyncratic, unusual and high-profile business; Anita Roddick, like Richard Branson, is an entrepreneur who has made a very individual contribution. It has not been easy and has required courage in the face of criticism, hostility and setback.

QUESTIONS: How different do you believe it would feel to work for The Body Shop as distinct from a retailer without the same manifest commitment to environmental and ethical issues? In what ways might this commitment prove disadvantageous?

*The Body Shop*   http://www.bodyshop.com

Photo: Anita Roddick OBE, Founder & Co-Chair of The Body Shop International PLC.
© Sean McNenemy (April 2000)

## Introduction

When any group of people live and work together for any length of time, they form and share certain beliefs about what is right and proper. They establish behaviour patterns based on their beliefs, and their actions often become matters of habit which they follow routinely. These beliefs and ways of behaving constitute the organization's *culture*.

Culture is reflected in the way in which people in an organization perform tasks, set objectives and administer resources to achieve them. It affects the way that they make decisions, think, feel and act in response to opportunities and threats. Culture also influences the selection of people for particular jobs, which in turn affects the way in which tasks are carried out and decisions are made. Culture is so fundamental that it affects behaviour unconsciously. Managers do things in particular ways because it is expected behaviour.

The culture of an organization is therefore related to the people, their behaviour and the operation of the structure. It is encapsulated in beliefs, customs and values, and manifested in a number of symbolic ways.

The formation of, and any changes to, the culture of an organization is dependent on the leadership and example of particular individuals, and their ability to control or influence situations. This is itself dependent on a person's ability to obtain and use power.

Minicase 5.1, The Body Shop, shows how the values of the founder, Anita Roddick, inspired employees and attracted customers. The distinctive culture enabled The Body Shop to grow and prosper, but it was not totally appropriate for the large, international business that The Body Shop became. As a consequence, Anita Roddick has relinquished day-to-day control and a number of changes has been made to the strategies.

Culture and power, then, affect the choice, incidence and application of the modes of strategy creation, which will also reflect the values and preferences of the strategic leader. The preferred mode must, however, be appropriate for the organization's strategic needs, which are affected by competition. Moreover, culture and power are such strong forces that, if the prevailing culture is overlooked, implementation may not happen. Strong cultures can obstruct strategic change, particularly if companies are in decline and people feel vulnerable.

Quite simply, culture is at the heart of all strategy creation and implementation. Organizations are seeking to respond to perceived strategic issues. Resources must be deployed and committed, but successful change also requires the 'right' attitude, approach and commitment from people. This mindset, which might, for example, reflect a strong customer and service focus, could imply further empowerment and consequently cultural change.

In the early 1980s, Berry (1983) claimed that after some 20 years of emphasis on analytical techniques in strategic management, the concentration switched to the softer aspect of culture. The emphasis was no longer on the marketplace, but on what managers could do to resolve internal problems; by using culture, companies could become more strategically effective. The perspective of this book is that both the hard and soft aspects of strategy have important roles to play in strategic management.

Strong cultures, then, are an important strategic asset. Internalized beliefs can motivate people to exceptional levels of performance. An effective strategic leader will understand and mould the culture in order that a vision can be pursued and intended strategies implemented. Most successful companies develop strong cultures; the major doubt concerns an organization's ability to change the culture.

Moreover, large organizations formed by a series of acquisitions will frequently exhibit different cultures in the various divisions or businesses; in many international businesses this is inevitable. The challenge for corporate headquarters is to ensure that certain critically important values are reflected in all branches of the corporation and cultural differences do not inhibit internal architecture and synergy.

At the same time, cross-border mergers and alliances promise to fuse together the best features of different cultures, but this may prove more idealistic than realistic. For example, the acquisition of Rover by BMW appeared to offer an opportunity to bring together the longer-term German perspective on investment, training and employee consultation and the UK's flexibility in working practices and lower manufacturing costs. In the event the marketing aspects were ineffective and well-reviewed Rover cars did not sell in the showrooms. In spring 2000 Rover was resold by BMW to the specially formed Phoenix Group.

## Aspects of Culture

The points discussed in this section are summarized in Figure 5.1.

### Manifestations of culture

Edgar Schein (1985) contends that it is important to consider culture as having a number of levels, some of which are essentially manifestations of underlying beliefs.

The first and most visible level Schein terms '*artefacts*'. These include the physical and social environment and the outputs of the organization. Written communications, advertisements and the reception that visitors receive are all included.

*Values* are the second level, and they represent a sense of 'what ought to be' based on convictions held by certain key people. For example if an organization has a problem such as low sales

or a high level of rejections in production, decisions might be made to advertise more aggressively or to use high-quality but more expensive raw materials. These are seen initially as the decision maker's values, which can be debated or questioned. Many of the strategies followed by organizations start in this way, and many will reflect values held by the strategic leader.

If the alternative is successful it may well be tried again and again until it becomes common practice. In this way the value becomes a belief and ultimately an assumption about behaviour practised by the organization. These basic *underlying assumptions* are Schein's third level, and they represent the taken-for-granted ways of doing things or solutions to problems.

One belief accepted by employees within a bank might be that all lending must be secure. A football team could be committed to always playing attractive, open football. A university might be expected to have clear beliefs about the relative importance of research and teaching, but this is likely to be an issue where employees 'agree to disagree', leading to a fragmented culture. Examples of *behaviours* are speedy new product development, long working hours, formal management meetings and regular informal meetings or contacts with colleagues, suppliers and customers.

It is also important to appreciate that certain organizations may state that they have particular values but in reality these will be little more than verbal or written statements or aspirations for the future.

Schein argues that cultural paradigms are formed which determine how 'organization members perceive, think about, feel about, and judge situations and relationships' and these are based on a number of underlying assumptions.

### People and culture

For Schwartz and Davis (1981) culture is 'a pattern of beliefs and expectations shared by the

*Figure 5.1*    Aspects of culture – the culture grid.

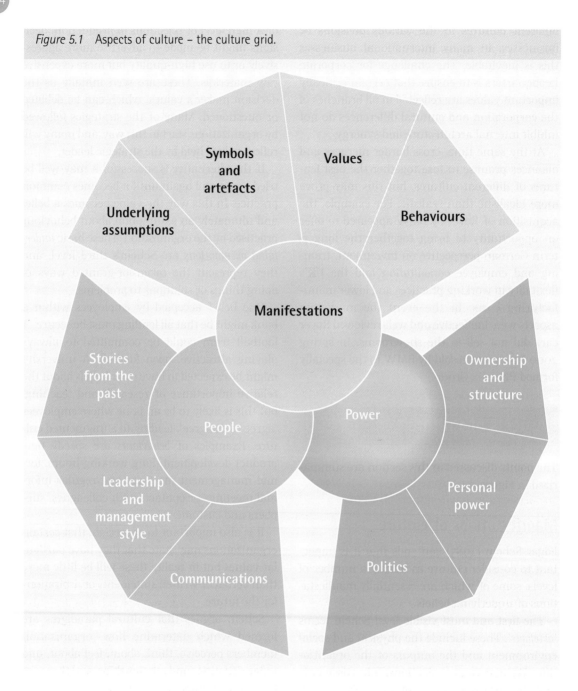

organization's members, and which produce norms that powerfully shape the behaviour of individuals and groups in the organization'. They argue that the beliefs held by the company are seen as major aspects of corporate policy as they evolve from interactions with, and in turn form policy towards, the marketplace. As a result, rules or norms for internal and external behaviour are developed and eventually both performance and reward systems will be affected. These aspects of the culture are often transmitted through *stories* of past events, glories and heroes.

Success is measured by, and culture therefore becomes based on, past activities. Current decisions by managers reflect the values, beliefs and norms that have proved beneficial in the past and in the development and growth of the organization. Moreover, they reinforce the corporate culture and expected behaviour throughout the organization.

The culture affects suppliers and customers, and their reactions are important. They will feed back impressions about the organization, and their views should be sought. Successful organizations will ensure that there is congruence between these environmental influences and the organization culture. In this way key success factors can be met if resources are administered, controlled and developed appropriately.

Organizations need a cohesive blend of the philosophies introduced earlier. A cohesive culture would exhibit strong leadership, whereby the strategic leader is sensitive to the degrees of decentralization and informality necessary for satisfying customer needs efficiently, and managing change pressures, in order to keep the business strong and profitable. At the same time a centralized information network will ensure that communications are effective and that managers are both kept aware and rewarded properly for their contributions. A fragmented culture, in contrast, would suggest that the needs of certain stakeholders were perhaps not being satisfied adequately, or that strategies and changes were not being co-ordinated, or that managers or business units were in conflict and working against each other, or that the most deserving people were not being rewarded.

Linked to this is *communication*, an essential aspect of culture. The organization might be seen as open or closed, formal or informal. Ideally, employees from different parts of the business, and at different levels in the hierarchy,

will feel willing and able to talk openly with each other, sharing problems, ideas and learning. 'Doors should be left open'. Employees should also be trusted and empowered to the appropriate degree. Good communications can 'stop nasty surprises'. It is helpful if employees know how well competitors are performing, where they are particularly strong, so they can commit themselves to high levels of achievement in order to outperform their rivals.

Communication is clearly essential for creating effective internal and external architecture.

Hampden-Turner (1990) argues that culture is based on communication and learning. The strategic leader's vision for the organization must be communicated and understood; events and changes affecting the organization also need to be communicated widely. Managers should be encouraged to seek out new opportunities by learning about new technology and customer expectations, and to innovate. The organization should help them to share their experiences and their learning.

## Power and culture

Power is reflected in the *ownership* of the business. It may be a family company with strong, concentrated power. A small group of institutional shareholders could control the business, in which case it is conceivable that short-term financial targets will dictate strategies. *Structural issues* include the extent to which the organization is centralized or decentralized, the role and contribution of corporate headquarters, and control and reward systems. *Personal power* is discussed later in this chapter; *politics* refers to the ways in which managers use power and influence to affect decisions and actions.

Minicase 5.2 analyses IKEA against this model. IKEA focuses on being a low-cost competitor and achieves this while maintaining a complex supply-chain network. IKEA also has an ability to be flexible in response to local

# Minicase 5.2  IKEA

IKEA was started in Sweden by Ingvar Kamprad, who pioneered the idea of self-assembly furniture in handy packs. His vision of 'a better, more beautiful, everyday life for the many' led to 'a wide range of home furnishings, of good function and style, at low prices, for mass consumer markets'. Kamprad began with a mail-order business in 1943; the first IKEA store was opened in 1958.

Growth has been carefully regulated. IKEA waited for seven years before opening a second branch; the first branch outside Sweden was in the early 1970s; the first US store opened in 1985, with typically one new store being added every year. This approach allows IKEA to establish local supply networks and ensures that it does not become stretched financially. The expansion programme has always been funded from cash generated by the retail activities. IKEA does not have a large market share in any single country; instead, it has a global brand and an intriguing reputation which draws customers from substantial distances away.

By the late 1990s, IKEA had some 150 shops in 30 countries. IKEA's strategy has always involved high-quality merchandise at prices which undercut the competition. In the mid-1990s IKEA's annual turnover passed the $5 billion mark; after-tax profits were estimated to be 8% of revenue. Reputedly worth at least $12.5 billion, IKEA has always been reticent about the financial data it releases.

IKEA stores focus on sales of self-assembly packs which customers take away themselves. IKEA will, however, deliver fully assembled pieces for a premium price. The stores have a wide range of facilities, typically including restaurants and games and video rooms for children; these are normally on the top floor, which is where customers come in. People are then routed carefully through a series of display areas to the downstairs purchase points which resemble a typical discount warehouse.

The furniture packs are commissioned from over 2300 suppliers in some 70 countries, many of them low labour cost countries in the Far East and Eastern Europe. IKEA has an equity stake in several of its suppliers and insists on tight stock control programmes to reduce costs through the whole supply chain. IKEA designs all its own products and aims to lead customer taste. There is just one range of products for the global market, but not every country and store stocks the full range. IKEA chooses not to have mini-ranges for specific countries and prides itself on an ability to respond to local fashion and opportunities by quickly adjusting the range in any one store. Sales per square foot invariably exceed industry averages.

## Manifestations of IKEA's distinctive culture

The *artefacts* clearly include the stores, the products and the prices. There are (like Marks and Spencer) no brands other than IKEA's own. There are no annual or seasonal sales; prices stay valid for a whole year. There is a plethora of in-store information and communications, but no commissioned sales people.

*Values* – IKEA use the word 'prosumers' to imply that value is added by both IKEA and their customers in partnership. Employees are empowered to be innovative and helpful and challenged to 'dare to be different'. IKEA recognizes that always offering prices substantially below those of its competitors places considerable pressure on its staff.

*Underlying assumptions* can be summarized in the following quotes:

*We do not need to do things in traditional ways* (window manufacturers have been approached to make table frames; shirt manufacturers for seat cushions).

*Break your chains and you are free; cut your roots and you die. IKEA should look for constant renewal. Experiments matter; mistakes (within reason) will be tolerated.*

*Behaviours* – Every IKEA manager flies economy class and uses taxis only if there is no suitable alternative. In The Netherlands, managers have been encouraged to stay with typical IKEA customer families to learn more about their needs.

## People

A variety of *stories* permeates the IKEA culture. Initially customers in the US stores were simply not buying any beds – there had been no market research into US tastes; it was IKEA's global product. Eventually, it was realized that Americans sleep in bigger beds than Swedes. Similarly, kitchen units had to be adjusted to handle extra-large pizza plates.

*Leadership and management style* – Kamprad rarely shows his face to the public. At one stage there was some adverse publicity concerning alleged wartime allegiances, but no lasting damage. The lack of published financial information reinforces this hidden aspect of IKEA.

The *organization* is structured as an inverted pyramid – employees are there to serve customers – and based on managers and co-workers. There are no directors, no formal titles and no dining rooms or reserved parking spaces for executives. Managers are quite likely to switch between functions and countries. The organization is fundamentally informal with 'few instructions'. Every year there is an 'anti-bureaucracy' week when everyone dresses casually.

*Communications* – Both customers and employees are encouraged to provide ideas and suggestions, which may be translated into new products. Information enters the system from several points.

## Ownership and structural issues

IKEA remains a private company which owns all of its sites. It pays for new sites in cash. 'We don't like to be in the hands of the banks'. There are no plans to become a limited company either; Kamprad has criticized the short-term interests of many investors.

The company operates as three distinct activities. The core retailing business is now a Dutch-registered charitable foundation. The profits of the operations are subjected to a top-slice of 3% to fund a separate business which has responsibility for managing the brand and IKEA's franchisees. The third arm is a banking and finance business; IKEA, for example, owns a majority shareholding in Habitat in the UK.

QUESTION: IKEA believes that fashionable and modern furniture and furnishings can be affordable for most families. It need not be prohibitively expensive. How does it achieve this?

*Ikea*   http://www.ikea.com

opportunities, which could easily add costs as well as value. The company is product and production driven, but able to capture and use ideas from customers and employees.

## Determinants of Culture

Deal and Kennedy (1982) have conducted research into US companies in an attempt to ascertain what factors lead to consistently outstanding (above average for the industry) performance. They found that over the long term the companies that are the most successful are those that believe in something and those where the belief or beliefs have permeated through the whole organization, i.e. they are communicated and understood. Examples quoted are progress via innovation and technology and 'excellence' in something that customers value, say service or delivery on time.

Deal and Kennedy argue that employees must be rewarded for compliance with the essential cultural aspects if these values are to be developed and retained over time; and they conclude that people who build, develop and run successful companies invariably work hard to create strong cultures within their organizations.

From their research Deal and Kennedy isolated five key elements or determinants of culture.

- The environment and key success factors: what the organization must do well if it is to be an effective competitor. Innovation and fast delivery are examples quoted.

- The values that the strategic leader considers important and wishes to see adopted and followed in the organization. These should relate to the key success factors, and to employee reward systems.

- Heroes: the visionaries who create the culture. They can come from any background and could be, for example, product or service innovators, engineers who build the appropriate quality into the product, or creative marketing people who provide the slogans which make the product or brand name a household word.

- Rites and rituals: the behaviour patterns in which the culture is manifest. Again there are any number of ways in which this can happen, including employees helping each other out when there are difficulties, the way in which sales people deal with customers, and the care and attention that go into production.

- The cultural network: the communications system around which the culture revolves and which determines just how aware employees are about the essential issues.

When the culture is strong, people know what is expected of them and they understand how to act and decide in particular circumstances. They appreciate the issues that are important. When it is weak, time can be wasted in trying to decide what should be done and how. Moreover, it is argued that employees feel better about their companies if they are recognized, known about and regarded as successful, and these aspects will be reflected in the culture.

There can be a number of separate strands to the culture in any organization, which should complement each other. For example, there can be aspects relating to the strategic leader, the environment and the employees. There could be a strong power culture related to an influential strategic leader who is firmly in charge of the organization and whose values are widely understood and followed. This could be linked to a culture of market orientation, which ensures that customer needs are considered and satisfied, and to a work culture if employees feel committed to the organization and wish to help in achieving success.

## Implications of Culture

Pümpin (1987) suggests that seven aspects comprise the culture of an organization, and that the relative significance of each of these will vary from industry to industry. The seven aspects are:

1. The extent to which the organization is marketing orientated, giving customers high priority.
2. The relationships between management and staff, manifested through communication and participation systems, for example.
3. The extent to which people are target orientated and committed to achieving agreed levels of performance.
4. Attitudes towards innovation. It is particularly important that the risks associated with failure are perceived as acceptable by all levels of management if innovation and entrepreneurship are to be fostered.
5. Attitudes towards costs and cost reduction.
6. The commitment and loyalty to the organization felt, and shown, by staff.
7. The impact of, and reaction to, technology and technological change and development. One major issue concerns whether or not the opportunities offered by information technology are being harnessed by the firm.

Many of these aspects are developed further in later chapters of the book.

Hampden-Turner (1990) believes that the culture is a manifestation of how the organization has chosen to deal with specific dilemmas and conflicts. Each of these can be viewed as a continuum, and the organization needs a clear position on each one. As shown in Chapter 2, one dilemma might be the conflict between, on the one hand, the need to develop new products and services quickly and ahead of competitors and, on the other hand, the need for thorough development and planning to ensure adequate quality and safety. Another dilemma is the need for managers to be adaptive and responsive in a changing environment, but not at the expense of organization-wide communication and awareness. Such change orientation may also conflict with a desire for continuity and consistency of strategy and policy.

Tables 5.1 and 5.2 take this idea further. Table 5.1 highlights how every apparent virtue also has a 'flip side', and consequently something which is positive at one point may suddenly prove disadvantageous. Table 5.2 looks at the advantages and drawbacks of three business paradigms: a market-orientated business, an organization focused on resource efficiency, and a growth-driven business. Taken together, these confirm that there can never be one best or ideal culture. The culture needs to be flexible and adaptive as circumstances change. The cultural factors that bring initial success may need to be changed if success is to be sustained. Similarly, it is not enough simply to look at what other successful organizations are doing and copy them.

**Table 5.1** Every coin, every virtue, has a flip side!

| | |
|---|---|
| Team players | May be indecisive and avoid risks |
| Customer focus | Can lead to reactivity and lack of innovation |
| Action orientation | Can become reckless and dictatorial |
| Analytical thinking | Can result in paralysis |
| Innovation | Which is impractical, unrealistic, ill thought through, wastes time and money |
| A global vision | May mean valuable local opportunities are missed |
| Being a good 'people manager' | May allow someone to become soft and walk away from tough decisions |

Developed from ideas in McCall, MW (1998) *High Flyers*, Harvard Business School Press.

**Table 5.2** The imperfect world of organizations

| A market-driven business is likely to be: | An efficient operations driven business is likely to be: | A growth-orientated business is likely to be: |
|---|---|---|
| Resourceful | Efficient | Competitive |
| Entrepreneurial | Strong on teamworking | Strong on targets and achieving results |
| Risk oriented | Good at executing plans | Full of hard-working people |
| Pragmatic in terms of getting things done | Sophisticated with its systems and procedures | Flexible |
| | | Changing quickly |
| **But it may not be:** | **But it may not be:** | **But it may not be:** |
| Consistent | Responsive to customers | Taking a long-term perspective |
| Disciplined in what it does | Good at managing change | Offering a balanced lifestyle for its employees |
| Adhering to systems and procedures | Able to see 'the big picture' | Sensitive to people's needs |
| Strong on teamworking | | |

Developed from ideas in McCall, MW (1998) *High-flyers*, Harvard Business School Press.

Benchmarking and teasing out good practices is both important and beneficial, but these practices again need customizing and adapting to the unique circumstances facing an individual organization.

## Culture and Strategy Creation

We have already seen that the essential cultural characteristics will dictate the preferred mode of strategy creation in an organization; all the modes are likely to be present to some degree.

The culture will influence the ability of a strategic visionary to 'sell' his or her ideas to other members of the organization and gain their support and commitment to change. The planning mode is most suitable in a reasonably stable and predictable environment, but a reliance on it in a more unstable situation can lead to missed opportunities. It is an ideal mode for a conservative, risk-averse, slow-to-change organization.

Where environmental opportunities and threats arise continuously in a situation of competitive chaos an organization must be able to deal with them if it is to survive. It is the culture, with its amalgam of attitudes, values, perceptions and experiences, which determines the outcomes and relative success. The structure must facilitate awareness, sharing and learning, and people must be willing and able to act. People 'learn by doing' and they must be able to learn from mistakes. Peters (1988) states that 'managers have to learn how to make mistakes

faster'. The reward system is critical here. Managers and employees should be praised and rewarded for exercising initiative and taking risks which prove successful; failures should not be sanctioned too harshly, as long as they are not repeated!

Berry (1983) argues that if a strategic leader really understands the company culture he or she must, by definition, be better equipped to make wise decisions. He or she might conclude that 'cultural change will be so difficult we had better be sure to select a business or strategy that our kind of company can handle well'. This is just as valid as, and perhaps more useful than, believing that one can accomplish cultural

*Table 5.3* Organizational values and strategies

| Type | Characteristics | Strategy formation |
|---|---|---|
| Defenders | Conservative beliefs | Emphasis on planning |
| | Low-risk strategies | |
| | Secure markets | |
| | Concentration on narrow segments | |
| | Considerable expertise in narrow areas of specialism | |
| | Preference for well-tried resolutions to problems | |
| | Little search for anything really 'new' | |
| | Attention given to improving efficiency of present operations | |
| Prospectors | Innovative | Visionary mode |
| | Looking to break new ground | |
| | High-risk strategies | |
| | Search for new opportunities | |
| | Can create change and uncertainty, forcing a response from competitors | |
| | More attention given to market changes than to improving internal efficiency | |
| Analysers | Two aspects: stable and changing | |
| | Stable: formal structures and search for efficiencies | Planning mode |
| | Changing: competitors monitored and strategies amended as promising ideas seen (followers) | Adaptive/Incremental mode |
| Reactors | Characterized by an inability to respond effectively to change pressures | Adaptive mode |
| | Adjustments are therefore forced on the firm in order to avert crises | |

change in order to shift the firm towards a new strategy.

Moreover, if business strategies and culture are intertwined, the ability to analyse and construct strategies and the ability to manage and inspire people are also intertwined. Hence, a good strategy acknowledges, 'where we are, what we have got, and what therefore managerially helps us to get where we want to be' and this is substantially different from selecting business options exclusively on their product/market dynamics. In other words, developing and implementing strategy is a human and political process that starts as much with the visions, hopes and aspirations of a company's leaders as it does with market or business analysis. Ideas drive organizations.

With ever-shortening product lifecycles, intense global competition and unstable economies and currencies the future is going to require organizations that are ready to commit themselves to change. Strategy is going to be about intertwining analysis and adaptation. The challenge is to develop more effective organizations.

Miles and Snow (1978), whose research has been used to develop Table 5.3, have suggested a typology of organizations which can be looked at in relation to culture and strategy formation. The typology distinguishes organizations in terms of their values and objectives, and different types will typically prefer particular approaches to strategy creation. Defenders, prospectors and analysers are all regarded by Miles and Snow as positive organizations; reactors must ultimately adopt one of the other three approaches or suffer long-term decline. Suggested examples of each type are as follows. GEC, despite being in high-technology industries, has been relatively conservative and a defender. The risk-oriented innovative Amstrad has always been a prospector. The respective strategic leaders of these organizations, Lord Weinstock (until his retirement

in 1996) and entrepreneur Sir Alan Sugar have adopted different styles of management and exhibited different corporate values. Historically, many public-sector bureaucracies have been stable analysers, while Marks and Spencer has long been a changing analyser. Prior to its decline and acquisition by BTR, Dunlop, in the 1970s, exhibited many of the characteristics of a reactor organization, and failed to change sufficiently in line with environmental changes.

Miles and Snow argue that, as well as being a classification, their typology can be used to predict behaviour. For example, a defender organization, in a search for greater operating efficiency, might consider investing in the latest technology, but reject the strategy if it has high risk attached.

The power of 'corporate culture' should not be underestimated, both for a company's success and, if it is inappropriate, in frustrating change. Values, strategies, systems, organization and accountabilities – the components of culture – are a very strong mix which can either make a company successful or, alternatively, lead to its decline. The task of corporate leadership is to apply energy and judgement to the corporate culture to ensure its relevance.

*Sir Allen Sheppard, when Chairman, Grand Metropolitan plc*

## Culture, Structure and Styles of Management

Charles Handy (1976), building on earlier work by Harrison (1972) has developed an alternative classification of organizations based on cultural differences, and this is illustrated in Figure 5.2.

*Figure 5.2* Handy's four cultures. Adapted from Handy, CB (1976) *Understanding Organizations*, Penguin.

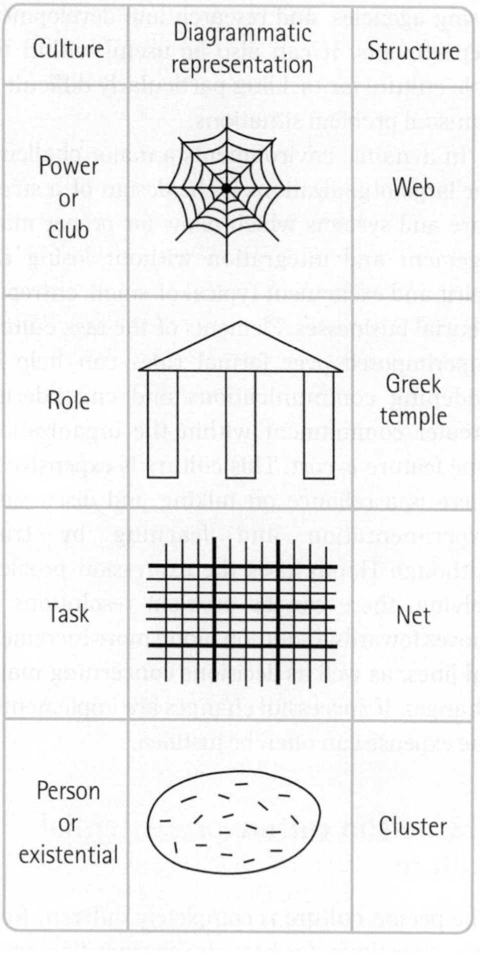

| Culture | Diagrammatic representation | Structure |
|---|---|---|
| Power or club | | Web |
| Role | | Greek temple |
| Task | | Net |
| Person or existential | | Cluster |

These functions or departments are represented in Handy's figure by the lines radiating out from the centre; but the essential point is that there are also concentric lines representing communications and power. The further away from the centre, the weaker is the power and influence. This structure is dominated from the centre and therefore is typical for small entrepreneurial organizations. Decisions can be taken quickly, but the quality of the decisions is very dependent on the abilities of managers in the inner circle.

In its heyday Hanson was described by a former director as a 'solar system, with everyone circling around the sun in the middle, Lord Hanson' (see Leadbeater and Rudd, 1991). This analogy suggests both movement and dependency. The Hanson story is discussed in detail in Chapter 22 and in a full-length case at the end.

Decisions depend a great deal on empathy, affinity and trust, both within the organization and with suppliers, customers and other key influences.

People learn to do instinctively what their boss and the organization expect and require. Consequently, they will prove reliable even if they are allowed to exercise a degree of initiative. Foreign-exchange dealers provide an illustration of this point.

For this reason the culture can be designated either 'club' or 'power'. Employees are rewarded for effort, success and compliance with essential values; and change is very much led from the centre in an entrepreneurial style.

A culture such as this may prevent individual managers from speaking their minds, but decisions are unlikely to get lost in committees.

## The role culture

The role culture is the more typical 'organization' as the culture is built around defined jobs, rules and procedures and not personalities. People fit into jobs, and are recruited for this purpose. Hence, rationality and logic are at the

## The club culture or power culture

In the club culture type of organization, work is divided by function or product and a diagram of the organization structure would be quite traditional. There would be departments for sales, production, finance and so on, and possibly product-based divisions or strategic business units if the organization was larger. However, this structure is mostly found in smaller firms.

heart of the culture, which is designed to be stable and predictable.

The design is the Greek temple because the strengths of the organization are deemed to lie in the pillars, which are joined managerially at the top. One essential role of top management is to co-ordinate activity, and consequently it will be seen that both planning systems and incremental changes can be a feature of this culture. Although the strength of the organization is in the pillars, power lies at the top.

As well as being designed for stability the structure is designed to allow for continuity and changes of personnel, and for this reason dramatic changes are less likely than more gradual ones.

High efficiency is possible in stable environments, but the structure can be slow to change and is therefore less suitable for dynamic situations.

Aspects of this culture can prove beneficial for transport businesses such as railways and airlines, where reliability and timekeeping are essential. Unfortunately, it is not by nature a flexible, service-orientated culture. Intrapreneurship or elements of the task culture are also required for effectiveness.

## The task culture

Management in the task culture is concerned with the continuous and successful solution of problems, and performance is judged by the success of the outcomes.

The challenge is more important than the routine.

The culture is shown as a net, because for particular problem situations people and other resources can be drawn from various parts of the organization on a temporary basis. Once the problem is dealt with people will move on to other tasks, and consequently discontinuity is a key element. Expertise is the major source of individual power and it will determine a per-

son's relative power in a given situation. Power basically lies in the interstices of the net, because of the reliance on task forces.

The culture is ideal for consultancies, advertising agencies, and research and development departments. It can also be useful within the role culture for tackling particularly difficult or unusual problem situations.

In dynamic environments a major challenge for large organizations is the design of a structure and systems which allow for proper management and integration without losing the spirit and excitement typical of small, entrepreneurial businesses. Elements of the task culture superimposed over formal roles can help by widening communications and engendering greater commitment within the organization. One feature is cost. This culture is expensive as there is a reliance on talking and discussion, experimentation and learning by trial. Although Handy uses the expression problem solving, there can be problem resolutions or moves towards a solution along more incremental lines, as well as decisions concerning major changes. If successful changes are implemented the expense can often be justified.

## The person culture or existential culture

The person culture is completely different from the other three, for here the organization exists to help the individual rather than the other way round. Groups of professional people, such as doctors, architects, dentists and solicitors, provide excellent examples. The organization with secretarial help, printing and telephone facilities and so on provides a service for individual specialists and reduces the need for costly duplication. If a member of the circle leaves or retires, he or she is replaced by another who may have to buy in.

Some professional groups exhibit interdependencies and collaboration, allocating work among the members, although management of such an organization is difficult because of individual expertise and because the rewards and sanctions are different from those found in most other situations.

However, in an environment where government is attempting to increase competition between professional organizations, and in some cases to reduce barriers to entering the profession, it is arguable that effective manage-

ment, particularly at the strategic level, will become increasingly necessary. Efforts will need co-ordinating and harnessing if organizations are to become strong competitors.

## Management philosophies

Press (1990) suggests that the culture of an organization is based upon one or more philosophies. His ideas are developed in Figure 5.3. The

*Figure 5.3* Organizational philosophies. Adapted from Press, G (1990) Assessing competitors' business philosophies, *Long Range Planning*, 23, 5.

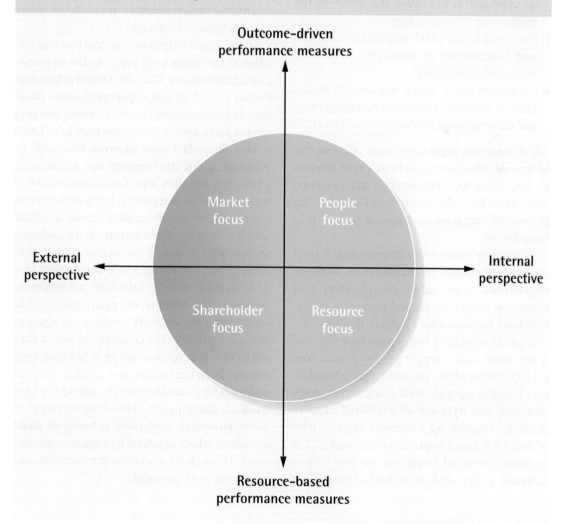

specific philosophies are related to the various stakeholders in the business, and are determined by two intersecting axes. One relates to whether the business is focused more internally or externally; the other is based on performance measures. Do they concentrate more on resource management and efficiency, or outcomes and effectiveness? This creates four discrete philosophies:

- the resource focus, which concentrates on internal efficiencies and cost management
- the shareholder focus, which sees the business as a portfolio of activities which should be managed to maximize the value of the business for its shareholders
- the people focus, which emphasizes the skills and contribution of employees, and their needs and expectations
- the market focus, which stresses the importance of satisfying customers by adding value and differentiating products and services.

All of these are important; none of them can be ignored. The culture can be analysed in terms of how these four philosophies are perceived and prioritized. As pointed out earlier, the philosophy may have to change if success is to be sustained.

A company which relies heavily upon formal strategic planning, for example, is likely to concentrate more upon shareholders and resources. It may be argued that, at a corporate level Hanson was similarly inclined; the individual subsidiary businesses typically had a resource focus supported by people and market philosophies. (Hanson was ultimately split into five separate businesses: the strategy, structure and style are all explained in more detail in Chapter 22.) General Electric (GE) of the USA (see Chapters 21, 22 and 24) is another diversified conglomerate but with a different policy and style from Hanson on

empowerment and decentralization. GE places most emphasis upon people and its style and culture has proved more enduring. Japanese companies, discussed later in this chapter, exhibit a particular blend of people, markets and resources.

## Styles of management

The style adopted by the strategic leader can have a strong influence on the culture of the organization. Individual leaders can, for example, be relatively autocratic or democratic, visionary or essentially champions of the past, orientated more towards markets or more towards financial controls.

Styles which differ from the 'normal and traditional' can prove to be very effective in particular circumstances. The John Lewis Partnership, Britain's third largest department store chain after Debenhams and House of Fraser, practises worker participation and democracy. John Lewis is also diversified into supermarkets with its Waitrose chain. The company has a chairman, a board of directors and a management structure, as do most companies, but parallel to this commercial structure stands a second structure which represents the interests of the ordinary worker who is also a partner in John Lewis. While a partner working in a department in a store cannot directly influence management decisions, as a result of the partnership and its constitution the ordinary workers are again in ultimate control of the company for which they work. This is supplemented by a profit-sharing scheme. Decision making and communications within the organization must be affected by high levels of participation. John Lewis's motto of 'never knowingly undersold' is based on value for money which is helped by employee involvement. Through its workforce the company can relate well to its customers.

Everyone in the business feels (and is) involved. Everyone also feels (and is) accountable, especially those at the top. Top management are given lots of freedom to determine and change strategy, but they can be questioned on anything by the rank-and-file partners ... this ... makes people think ahead and consider the consequences of their actions.

*Stuart Hampson, Chairman, John Lewis Partnership, since 1993. Hampson is only the fourth Chairman since the Partnership was formed in 1929*

## Culture and Power

In Charles Handy's classification of organizations in terms of their culture, power is an important element which needs further consideration. While an introduction to the topic is included here, the subject of power is explored more fully in Chapter 24 when its impact on strategy implementation and strategic change is considered.

Power is related to the potential or ability to do something. Consequently strategic change will be strongly influenced by the bases of power within an organization and by the power of the organization in relation to is environment.

### Internal power

Change is brought about if the necessary resources can be harnessed and if people can be persuaded to behave in a particular way. Both of these require power. Power results in part from the structure of the organization, and it needs exercising in different ways in different cultures if it is to be used effectively. At the same time power

can be a feature of an individual manager's personality, and managers who are personally powerful will be in a position to influence change.

The ways in which managers apply power are known as 'power levers'; Box 5.1 describes seven major sources of power. The classifications of power bases produced by a number of authors differ only slightly. Box 5.1 has been developed from a classification by Andrew Kakabadse (1982), who has built on the earlier work of French and Raven (1959).

In order to understand the reality of change in an organization and to examine how change might be managed, it is important to consider where power lies, which managers are powerful, and where their sources of power are. While a visible, powerful and influential strategic leader is often a feature of an entrepreneurial organization, the nature and direction of incremental change will be influenced significantly by which managers are powerful and how they choose to exercise their power.

A power culture has strong central leadership as a key feature and power lies with the individual or small group at the centre who controls most of the activity in the organization. In contrast, role cultures are based on the legitimacy of rules and procedures and individual managers are expected to work within these. Task cultures are dependent on the expertise of individuals, and their success, in some part, depends on the ability of the individuals to share their power and work as a team. Managers are expected to apply power levers in ways that are acceptable to the predominant culture of the organization, and at the same time the manner in which power levers are actually used affects what happens in the organization. Power is required for change; change results from the application of power. Hence the implementation of desired changes to strategies requires the effective use of power bases; but other strategic changes will

KEY CONCEPT – Box 5.1
Power Levers

- **Reward power** is the ability to influence the rewards given to others. These can be tangible (money) or intangible (status). Owner managers enjoy considerable reward power, managers in larger public-sector organizations very little. For reward power to be useful, the rewards being offered must be important to the potential recipients.

- **Coercive power** is power based on the threat of punishment for non-compliance, and the ability to impose the punishment. The source can be the person's role or position in the organization, or physical attributes and personality.

- **Legitimate power** is synonymous with authority, and relates to an individual manager's position within the structure of the organization. It is an entitlement from the role a person occupies. The effective use of legitimate power is dependent on three things: access to relevant information; access to other people and communication networks inside the organization; and approaches to setting priorities – this determines what is asked of others.

- **Personal power** depends on individual characteristics (personality) and physical characteristics. Charm, charisma and flair are terms used to describe people with personality-based power. Physical attributes such as height, size, weight and strength also affect personal power.

- **Expert power** is held by a person with specialist knowledge or skills in a particular field. It is particularly useful for tackling complex problem areas. It is possible for people to be attributed expert power through reputation rather than proven ability.

- **Information power** is the ability to access and use information to defend a stance or viewpoint – or to question an alternative view held by someone else – and is important as it can affect strategic choices.

- **Connection power** results from personal and professional access to key people inside and outside the organization, who themselves can influence what happens. This relates particularly to information power.

result from the exercise of power by individual managers. It is important for the organization to monitor such activity and ensure that such emergent changes and strategies are desirable or acceptable.

## The relative power of the organization

The ability of an organization to effect change within its environment will similarly depend on the exercise of power. A strong competitor with, say, a very distinctive product or service, or with substantial market share, may be more powerful than its rivals. A manufacturer who is able to influence distributors or suppliers will be similarly powerful. The issue is the relative power in relation to those other individuals, organizations and institutions – its stakeholders – on whom it relies, with whom it trades, or which influence it in some way.

## The Search for Excellence

### Research into US companies

McKinsey and Company, well-known US management consultants, initiated an investigation in the 1970s into why certain companies were more successful than their rivals. The findings were published in 1980 in a *Business Week* article and they eventually became the basis for the book *In Search of Excellence* (Peters and Waterman, 1982). The research emphasizes the important contribution of culture and values to organizational success.

At successful companies, strong cultures are clearly a strategic asset as internalized beliefs motivate people to unusual performance levels. We must, however, be cautious. While much may be known about the culture of a successful organization, we may not learn 'how to get it'. *In Search of Excellence* (in

*Table 5.4*   In search of excellence: characteristics of the most successful organizations

| | |
|---|---|
| A bias for action | Greater emphasis on trying things rather than talking about them and seeking 'solutions' rather than 'resolutions' |
| | Avoidance of long, complicated business plans |
| | Use of task forces to tackle special problems (Handy's task culture) |
| Close to the customer | Companies are 'customer-driven, not technology-driven, not product-driven, not strategy-driven' |
| | They 'know what the customer wants, and provide it – better than competitors' |
| Autonomy and entrepreneurship | Managers are authorized to act entrepreneurially rather than be tied too rigidly by rules and systems |
| Productivity through people | Productivity improvements by motivating and stimulating employees, using involvement and communications |
| | 'Corny merit awards, like badges and stars work' if they are properly managed and not just used as a gimmick |
| Hands on, value driven | Values are established with good communications |
| | People must 'believe' |
| | The power and personality of the strategic leader is crucial |
| Stick to the knitting | Successful companies know what they do well and concentrate on doing it well |
| Simple form, lean staff | Simple structures |
| Simultaneous loose–tight properties | An effective combination of central direction and individual autonomy |
| | Certain control variables, such as a particular financial return measure or the number of employees, are managed tightly; for other things managers are encouraged to be flexible |

Summarized from Peters, TJ and Waterman, RH Jr (1982) In *Search of Excellence*, Harper and Row.

common with similar books) is descriptive, not prescriptive.

Some 40 companies were surveyed in a cross-section of industries and included IBM, Texas Instruments, Hewlett-Packard, 3M, Procter and Gamble, Johnson and Johnson, and McDonald's. The companies were selected for being well-run and successful organizations. Most of the companies were well established and large. In the selection process 20 years of financial data were analysed and the companies under consideration were evaluated relative to competitors in their industry. In addition, a subjective assessment of their innovation records was used as a final screen. The research concluded that the most successful companies exhibited eight common attributes, which are featured in Table 5.4, and that their success was based primarily on good management practice. Managers had invested time, energy and thought into doing certain important things well, and those activities and values were understood by employees and appreciated by customers. In other words they had become part of the culture of the organization.

In most companies the role of one or more strategic leaders had proved to be very influential in establishing and developing the values, and in many cases the values had been established early in the company's history. In other words growth had been assisted by the culture. Peters and Waterman conclude that 'the real role of the chief executive is to manage the values of the organization'.

Peters and Waterman argued that 'excellent' companies are successful in their management of the basic fundamentals with respect to their environment: customer service; low-cost manufacturing; productivity improvement; innovation; and risk taking. In order to ensure that the key values are understood and practised throughout the organization there is an emphasis on simplicity: simple organization structures; simple strategies; simple goals; and simple communications systems.

The attributes featured in Table 5.4 are essentially basic rather than startling, and they are very much related to the contribution made by people. 'The excellent companies live their commitment to people'. Not all the attributes were visible in each of the companies studied, nor were they given the same priority in different organizations, but in every case there was a preponderance of the attributes and they were both visible and distinctive. In less successful companies, argue Peters and Waterman, 'far too many managers have lost sight of the basics: quick action, service to customers, practical innovation, and the fact that you can't get any of these without virtually everyone's commitment'.

Since the book was published some of the 'excellent' companies, most notably People Express and Caterpillar Tractor, have been less successful and so the findings of *In Search of Excellence* should be treated carefully. Basically, the research found a number of common attributes to be present in the organizations studied rather than providing a set of recommendations concerning how unsuccessful companies could be transformed. It provided food for thought rather than answers.

In a more recent book Robert Waterman (1988), writing independently, argued that in order to become and remain successful organizations must master the management of change. As will be seen later in this book (Chapter 24), there is often a fear of change and hostility towards it. These must be overcome, claims Waterman, because competition changes too quickly to allow companies to fall into what he calls the 'habit trap'. He further argues that strategies should be based on 'informed opportunism', developing from effective information systems which ensure that customers, suppliers and other key influences are consulted. Waterman emphasizes that for an information system to be effective it should not be allowed to become too rigid or bureaucratic.

Peters (1988) also asserts that there are no long-term excellent companies. 'The pace of change has become far too rapid to make any enterprise secure. Tomorrow's winners will have to view chaos, external and internal, not as a problem, but as a prime source of competitive advantage'. Peters quoted Ford of Europe as an example of a company which was dealing successfully with the challenge of change by stressing a new set of basic values: world-class quality and service; greater flexibility and responsiveness; continuous and rapid product and service innovation. Arguably, however, the change had been forced on Ford by strong Japanese competition and it has not prevented Ford having to reduce production capacity in Europe in recent years. Simply, we need companies that are flexible and innovative, companies that can learn from the past and find new opportunities and new ways of competing as markets and industries change.

After the success of *In Search of Excellence* it was inevitable that there would be a parallel study in the UK. This was reported originally by Goldsmith and Clutterbuck in *The Winning Streak* (1984), with the work updated in 1997. In this more recent book Goldsmith and Clutterbuck conclude that success lies not with specific strategies, structures and styles but with the dexterity with which organizations deal with the pressures they face. Their ability to do this, of course, is culture related and culture dependent. It is their ability to deal with the strategic issues and dilemmas introduced in Chapter 2, mentioned briefly earlier in this chapter and to which we return properly in Chapter 25.

It is, however, worth singling out four key cultural dilemmas discussed by Goldsmith and Clutterbuck:

- Pride and humility – realizing that internal self-belief and pride in what the organization is doing and achieving are crucial, but that they must not become arrogance and a belief the organization is untouchable
- Values and rules – finding the appropriate degree of effective empowerment
- Customer care versus customer count – finding new customers will always be important, but this should not be at the expense of looking after existing ones properly
- Challenging and nurturing people at the same time – setting stretching targets, but providing support.

There will never be straightforward answers to these issues and dilemmas, but the current style and approach of an organization will affect its relative fortunes.

## The limits to excellence

To summarize, some firms do appear to obtain superior financial performance from their cultures, but it does not follow that firms who succeed in copying these cultural attributes will necessarily also achieve superior financial results. Organizations which pursue the excellence factors must surely improve their chances of success, but clearly there can be no guarantees. Ignoring these issues will, however, increase the chances of failure.

However, the need to maintain E–V–R congruence in a dynamic, competitive environment must never be forgotten.

During the early 1980s Jan Carlzon turned around the struggling SAS (Scandinavian Airlines System) by focusing on improvements in service and communications. Profits were restored with improved revenues, but costs later increased as well. As a driving philosophy, the service culture had to give way to a focus strategy and rationalization.

*Everything that does not further the competitiveness of our airline activities must be removed, sold or turned into separate entities.*

(Jan Carlzon)

# Minicase 5.3  British Airways

Prior to privatization British Airways (BA) was fragmented. Leadership was, to some considerable extent, 'military', with strict rules and procedures, and top–down communications. Cabin staff were essentially powerless and insufficiently customer orientated. Customer attitudes and reactions were not fed back into the organization, and BA was seen as less friendly than many of its rivals.

When Colin Marshall (now Lord Marshall) became Chief Executive in 1983 he set 'giving the best service' as a key objective. He argued that this involved:

- appreciating what the market wants
- being able to respond quickly to changes in customer demand and expectations by
- having an appropriate organization structure and
- being adequately resourced.

These were to be achieved by ensuring that employees throughout BA were committed to providing a high level of customer service and that managers were equally aware of the needs and expectations of employees. Marshall sought to change the culture of BA to one of service orientation by:

- Issuing a new mission statement reflecting the revised objectives and values.
- A management training programme entitled 'Managing People First', designed to 'substantially enhance the participant's personal performance as a manager of others' by concentrating on developing a sense of urgency, vision, motivation, trust and a willingness to take responsibility.
- Improving both performance appraisal and a linked reward system.
- Customer service training for all employees who dealt directly with customers – entitled 'Putting People First'.
- Establishing 'Customer First' teams where groups of staff meet regularly to discuss their learning.

Front-line staff were given more authority to use initiative, on the assumption that they would behave more warmly to passengers. Positive and negative responses (complaints) were now fed through formalized channels, aided by increased use of information technology. Staff became more professional, and the organization more effective and more profitable.

New, revised service campaigns – 'Winning for Customers' and 'Managing Winners' – were introduced in the early and mid-1990s, after the Gulf War caused a slump in air travel and airline profits. A 'Leadership 2000' programme aimed to develop skills among BA's top 200 managers. Programmes looked at how to deal with international customers from different country backgrounds and cultures. At the same time, and very controversially, BA changed the tail-fins of some of its aircraft, abandoning the Union Jack and replacing it with colourful, ethnic designs from all round the world. These designs proved generally unpopular in the UK but were well received elsewhere. BA was trying to portray itself as an international airline, 'the world's favourite'. Internal research had been indicating that both employees and customers were not convinced that BA was a truly global airline.

In 1995, the company also created the post of 'Corporate Jester'. A long-serving but energetic and enthusiastic manager, who had worked in a wide range of different functions, was charged with roaming around and asking questions. The job was about creativity and challenge.

After Robert (Bob) Ayling succeeded Colin Marshall as chief executive in the late 1990s, global overcapacity affected load factors and profitability. In the subsequent drive for cost savings and improved efficiency BA lost the trust of its workforce. The implementation of the changes had been less than ideal. Morale fell and there were damaging high-profile strikes. The values the ongoing culture programmes had been intended to create and sustain were now being eroded. Continued trading difficulties finally led to the resignation of Ayling in early 2000.

His Australian successor, Rod Eddington, was charged with 'boosting morale and regaining BA's reputation for setting standards in customer service'.

QUESTION: How difficult do you think it is for cabin staff to create, deliver and sustain a high level of customer service in an environment of competitive pricing and efficiency gains?

*British Airways*   http://www.britishairways.com

Footnote: A later case (Minicase 16.1) looks at the emerging corporate and competitive strategies of BA over the same period.

Carlzon was successful for a period, but 'fell from grace' when SAS profits later declined again. BA, which followed SAS with a service culture, was, for a number of years, more successful in simultaneously controlling costs, and it became one of the world's most successful and admired airlines. Again fortunes have changed. Minicase 5.3 shows how the trust that is required to underpin a service culture can easily be lost when difficult strategies have to be implemented and are not handled well.

In my opinion effective strategic management requires:

- a sound strategy, which implies an effective match between the resources and the environment

- a well-managed execution and implementation of the strategy
- appropriate strategic change. While it can be important to 'stick to the knitting', firms must watch for signs indicating that strategies need to be improved or changed.

## Culture and competitive advantage

Barney (1986) has examined further the relationship between culture and 'superior financial performance'. He has used microeconomics for his definition of superior financial performance, arguing that firms record either below-normal returns (insufficient for long-term survival in the industry), normal returns (enough for survival, but no more) or superior results, which are more than those required for long-term survival. Superior results, which result from some form of competitive advantage, attract competitors who seek to copy whatever is thought to be the source of competitive advantage and generating the success. This in turn affects supply and margins and can reduce profitability to only normal returns and, in some cases, below normal. Therefore, sustained superior financial performance requires sustained competitive advantage. Barney concluded that culture can, and does, generate sustained competitive advantage, and hence long-term superior financial performance, when three conditions are met.

- The culture is valuable. The culture must enable things to happen which themselves result in high sales, low costs or high margins.
- The culture is rare.
- The culture is imperfectly imitable, i.e. it cannot be copied easily by competitors.

Hence, if the cultural factors identified by Peters and Waterman are in fact transferable easily to other organizations, can they be the source of superior financial performance? Barney contends that valuable and rare cultures may be difficult, if not impossible, to imitate. For one thing, it is very difficult to define culture clearly, particularly in respect of how it adds value to the product or service. For another, culture is often tied to historical aspects of company development and to the beliefs, personality and charisma of a particular strategic leader.

Minicase 5.4, Club Méditerranée, and Minicase 5.1 earlier (The Body Shop) provide examples of companies which have gained success and renown with a culture-based competitive advantage. While maintaining the underlying principles and values, both companies have had to rethink their strategies to remain competitive.

## Changing Culture

The culture of an organization may appear to be in need of change for any one of a number of reasons. It could be that the culture does not fit well with the needs of the environment or with the organization's resources, or that the company is not performing well and needs major strategic changes, or even that the company is growing rapidly in a changing environment and needs to adapt.

Ideally, the culture and strategies being pursued will complement each other and, again ideally, the organization will be flexible and adaptable to change when it is appropriate. But these ideals will not always be achieved.

The culture of an organization can be changed, but it may not be easy. Strong leadership and vision is always required to champion the change process. If an organization is in real difficulty, and the threat to its survival is clearly recognized, behaviour can be changed through fear and necessity. However, people may not feel comfortable and committed to the changes they accept or are coerced into accepting. Behaviour may change, but not attitudes and beliefs. When an organization is basically successful the process of change again needs careful management – changing attitudes and beliefs does not itself guarantee a change in behaviour. It is not unusual for a team of senior managers to spend time, frequently at a location away from the organization itself, discussing these issues and becoming excited about a set of new values that they proclaim are the way forward. After the workshop any commitment to the new values and to change can be easily lost once managers return to the 'daily grind' and they become caught up again in immediate problems and difficulties. Their behaviour does not change and so the culture remains largely untouched.

The potential for changing the culture is affected by:

# Minicase 5.4  Club Méditerranée

Club Med, founded in 1950 in France, is Europe's largest tour operator with a clearly distinguished product.

Club Med represents 'beautiful people playing all sorts of sports, white sand beaches, azure sky and sea, Polynesian thatched huts, free and flowing wine at meals, simple yet superb food' (*Economist*, 12 July 1986). It is an 'organized melange of hedonism and back to nature'.

The organization has spread around the world, opening over 100 holiday villages and over 60 holiday residences (hotel/sports complexes) for both summer and winter vacations. Organizers are present in a ratio of 1:5 with guests, for whom they provide sports tuition and organize evening entertainment. Traditionally all tuition, food and drinks with meals were paid for in advance in the holiday cost, and guests were provided with beads which they used as they chose to buy extra drinks and so on. Clothing is permanently casual.

Club Med has traditionally charged prices above the average for package holidays, its clientele have been mainly above-average income earners, and the organization has enjoyed a reputation for delivering customer service and satisfaction. The strategy has been developed and maintained by the founder of the business, Gilbert Trigano. Although Triagano was always an influential strategic leader, Club Med is a public company, with most of its equity held by institutional shareholders.

A culture of creativity and teamworking has long been encouraged at all levels in Club Med. Gilbert Trigano always saw the organization as 'one big, happy family'. No employee should feel as if they are simply a pawn; promotions are typically from within. The loyalty of Club Med staff is very high, making it difficult for outsiders to come in as managers. Trigano set up Club Med as an organization 'without rules – in a world where most companies operate with fixed rules and structures. Everyone is under an obligation to create, but, of course, not every idea is a success'.

The company grew successfully for over 30 years with little change to the basic strategy. By the mid-1980s, however, occupancy rates had fallen, and profits declined and then stagnated. While the underlying concept was still sound, people's tastes were changing. Holidaymakers increasingly sought higher quality facilities than the straw huts provided. Many Americans wanted televisions and telephones – yet it was the absence of these which helped make Club Med unique.

Building on the original concept and strategy, Club Med developed new products in order to better satisfy selected audiences around the world. In addition to the traditional villages, where in some cases straw huts were replaced by bungalows, Club Med introduced cheaper, half-board holidays in newly acquired hotels and villages, at the same time as it opened more expensive properties. This latter development was pioneered at Opio, near Cannes, which opened in 1989. Opio has expensive rooms with facilities, and, unusually, is open 12 months of the year. The international conference trade was being targeted. A limited number of villages experimented with a multilingual staffing policy to ensure that visitors from different European countries could all be greeted in their own language. Attempts have been made to attract more American visitors, but there has always been some scepticism. Americans are more puritanical in their tastes and expectations, and Club Med's sexy image has not proved as successful in the USA.

There have also been problems with certain other strategic developments:

- Profitability at the Vienna City Hotel and from two cruise ships was never adequate.
- New developments in Japan were delayed.
- In 1991 Club Med bought a controlling stake in a second charter airline – its first airline came when Club Med acquired a competitor in the 1980s. Combined the two could fly to 100 destinations spread over 20 countries on four continents. In reality, Club Med had too much capacity and ended up selling 80% stakes in both airlines.

In 1993, with European occupancy rates depressed, Club Med recorded its worst ever results. Gilbert Triagno (then aged 72) partially retired and was succeeded by his son, Serge, who was determined to:

- accelerate developments in new territories such as Asia and
- reduce costs to allow for more competitive prices, still with quality and innovation – it was 'time to realize people would not always come just because it is Club Med'.

'It is by focusing on our core business that we will return to profit'.

Nevertheless, Rosemary Astles, Marketing Director at Thomson Holidays, was quoted as saying 'Club Med has a reasonably unique formula that has worked well in a number of markets . . . but there will be [only] limited growth for the club concept in the future. It's a fairly mature market'.

Serge Trigano resigned after losses in 1995. Interestingly – and unusually – Serge Trigano had no personal shareholding; and his father owned just 0.8% of the business. He reflected: 'Perhaps I was not quick enough to take the necessary measures . . . perhaps we should have closed loss-making villages more quickly'. Club Med appointed a new Chief Executive in February 1997; Philippe Bourguignon had previously been Chairman of Euro Disney.

Club Med reportedly 'began preparing for a future of tougher professional management' while conscious of the need to retain the important aspects of its culture, image and strategy. After all, the company was still successful. There had been 20 million customers in its 47 years and 1.4 million of those holidayed at Club Med villages and hotels in 1995–96. New imitations were happening all the time as the idea of the 'all-inclusive' holiday has grown in popularity. Nevertheless, the emphasis has been changing. Telephones in rooms and tables for two instead of eight, for example, were becoming increasingly normal as the average age of customers increased.

The first main change announced by Bourguignon implied the abandonment of the ubiquitous beads (for purchasing extra drinks) in favour of smart cards, which would enable tighter management controls. The fully inclusive package concept was retained; earlier trials with à la carte alternatives had not proved successful. Bourguignon commented: 'Club Med is a well known product but with a fuzzy identity. It is far too French in an international context. We need a complete recreation of the group. The concept is not outdated but the image is stuck in the 1970s'.

After a period of review it was decided to abandon the Club Aquarius budget format, re-creating most of these villages in the traditional Club Med style. At the other end of the scale, the most luxurious five-star villages have been phased out in favour of the typical mid-range three-star village. Between 1998 and 2000 some 74 out of a remaining 120 villages were renovated. Some now have a more limited range of activities. Linked to this was a major price restructuring – low-season holidays in particular were discounted by up to 30% – and new advertising has been targeted directly at younger people.

QUESTIONS: Is Club Med now realistically a limited-appeal niche product? If so, what are the implications of this fact? If not, how might the business be expanded?

*Club Méditerranée* http://www.clubmed.com

- the strength and history of the existing culture
- how well the culture is understood
- the personality and beliefs of the strategic leader and
- the extent of the strategic need.

Lewin (1947) contends that there are three important stages in the process of change: unfreezing existing behaviour, changing attitudes and behaviour, and refreezing the new behaviour as accepted common practice.

The first steps in changing culture are recognizing and diagnosing the existing culture, highlighting any weaknesses and stressing the magnitude of the need to change.

One way of changing behaviour would be the establishment of internal groups to study and benchmark competitors and set new performance standards. This would lead to wider discussion throughout the organization, supported by skills training – possibly including communication, motivation and financial awareness skills. People must become committed to the changes, which requires persistence by those who are championing the change and an emphasis on the significance and the desired outcomes.

Unless the changes become established and part of the culture, there will be a steady drift back to the previous pattern. While critical aspects of the culture should remain rock solid and generate strategic consistency, this must not mean that the organization becomes resistant to change without some major upheaval. Competitive pressures require organizations to be vigilant, aware and constantly change orientated, not change resistant.

Resistance to change should always be expected. People may simply be afraid because they do not understand the reasons behind the proposed changes; they may mistrust colleagues or management because of previous experiences; communications may be poor; motivation and commitment may be missing; internal architecture may be weak, causing internal conflict and hostility; and the organization may simply not be good at sharing best practice and learning. This topic is revisited in Chapter 24, Strategic Change Management.

## Culture – An International Dimension

There are cultural differences between nations and ethnic groups. What constitutes acceptable behaviour in one country (for example, bribes) would be totally unacceptable in others. Ways of conducting discussions and deals vary – Indians always like and expect to negotiate, for instance. Some countries, such as France, have a high respect for tradition and the past, while others, such as the USA, are more interested in future prospects. This influences the extent to which both individuals and organizations are judged on their track record and on their promise. These differences are important because business is conducted across frontiers and because many organizations have bases in several countries. Organizations, therefore, have to adjust their style for different customers and markets and accept that there will be cultural differences between the various parts of the organization. This reality affects the ability of the strategic leader to synthesize the various parts of the organization and achieve the potential synergies.

Related to these issues, research by Kanter (1991) drew out different perspectives on competitive success between the leading nations, where she argued that these stemmed from national cultures and cultural differences. Her findings indicated the following priorities:

- Japan – Product development
  Management
  Product quality
- USA – Customer service
  Product quality
  Technology
- Germany – Workforce skills
  Problem solving
  Management.

These conclusions may be summarized by arguing that Japan is driven by a commitment to innovation, America by customers and Germany by engineering.

Interestingly, the report highlighted how UK competitiveness had been enhanced by its drive to privatize public services and other state-owned organizations, the opening up of its capital markets and its encouragement of inward investment. At the same time it is arguably inhibited by an education system which discourages rather than encourages creativity, individualism and entrepreneurship, by a general lack of language skills and, for many, a preference for leisure over work. While a case can be made that these issues are being addressed in various ways, they remain relative weaknesses.

Differences in international cultures have been examined by various authors, including Hofstede (1991), Kluckhohn and Strodtbeck (1961) and Trompenaars and Hampden-Turner (1997). The following points have been distilled from their findings. From these points general conclusions may be drawn about cultural differences between nations; but it must also be recognized that certain organizations in the same country do not automatically fit the national picture in every respect. In some respects, for example, Sony is typically Japanese. In other respects it behaves more like an American company, such that research has confirmed that many US citizens think that Sony is American!

- Some countries and cultures prefer a water-tight contractual approach while others are more comfortable with trust and 'a handshake'. The appropriate way of conducting business therefore varies accordingly.
- In some countries managers operate with individual freedom and responsibility, and negotiations are on a one-to-one basis. In others there will invariably be a team of people involved. Where there are multiple decision makers like this, there will sometimes be a clear hierarchy and recognition of the relative

power of various individuals. On other occasions such demarcations will be less obvious or visible.

- In addition, individual managers can be relatively selfish in their outlook, or far more corporate. This can have a particular bearing on where managers' natural competitive energy is channelled. Is it directed at outside competitors, as realistically it should be, or at perceived internal rivals? Simply, would a culture of internal rivalry inside an organization be typical or rare?

- There is also an issue of women managers. In some countries they will not be found, either at all, or at least in positions of real authority.

- Leisure activities can play a relatively minor or more prominent role in business. The image of the British bank manager who enjoys long lunches and regular golf matches with clients has been largely confined to history, but negotiations and networking away from the place of business can still be important. Corporate hospitality at major sporting events would be one example, but it is not practised universally.

- Senses of humour also vary, which begs the question: is creativity more likely to be found in some countries than others? Creativity implies elements of fun and irreverence, challenging existing ways and looking for new and different alternatives. Certainly humour, together with other issues, such as the symbolism of certain objects and colours, affects advertising and promotion. The same campaigns cannot necessarily be used on a global scale.

- This leads on to a final point: do managers in different countries have similar or different perspectives on uncertainty? Some countries, organizations and managers are relatively risk orientated and view environmental turbulence as a source of opportunity. They look to be proactive. Others seek to be more reactive and adaptive, attempting to find positions of stability amongst the perceived chaos.

Since the end of World War II Japan has risen to become a major economic force around the world, with some Japanese companies extremely prominent in certain industries. The Japanese style of management is very different in some respects from that found in most Western countries and, while it cannot simply be copied – largely because of cultural differences – it offers a number of important and valuable lessons. Consequently, this chapter finishes with a section on Japanese culture and management style.

## The Japanese Culture and Style of Management

Without question, Japanese companies have become formidable competitors in several industries. For many years they have been the principal challengers of Western firms serious about world markets. More recently domestic recession, a high yen and intensifying competition from other Pacific Rim countries (many with lower wages) have restrained Japan's global expansion. However, a study of the philosophies, strategies and tactics adopted by Japanese companies will yield a number of valuable insights into competitive strategy, even though it is impractical to suggest that Western businesses could simply learn to copy their Japanese rivals. This section looks at some of the reasons for Japan's economic rise and success; it has to be acknowledged that in the 1990s some of the practices have changed. 'In the long-run the only feasible response is to do better what the Japanese are doing well already – developing management systems that motivate employees from top to bottom to pursue growth-oriented, innovation-focused competitive strategies' (Pucik and Hatvany, 1983).

Deal and Kennedy (1982) have argued that 'Japan Inc.' is a culture, with considerable co-operation between industry, the banking systems and government. For this reason certain

*Understanding Strategy and Strategic Management*

aspects of the Japanese culture are difficult to imitate. For example, banks in the UK are public companies with their own shareholders and they borrow and lend money in order to make profit; this is their basic 'mission'.

Another key structural feature historically has been the keiretsu, or corporate families, whereby a unique mix of ownerships and alliances makes hostile takeovers very unlikely. At its height, for example, the powerful Mitsubishi keiretsu represented 216,000 employees in 29 organizations as diverse as banking, brewing, shipping, shipbuilding, property, oil, aerospace and textiles. The companies held, on average, 38% of each other's shares; directors were exchanged; and the fact that 15 of the companies were located together in one district of Tokyo facilitated linkages of various forms, including intertrading wherever this was practical. The keiretsu influence is fading as Japanese companies are locating more and more production overseas in their search for lower manufac-

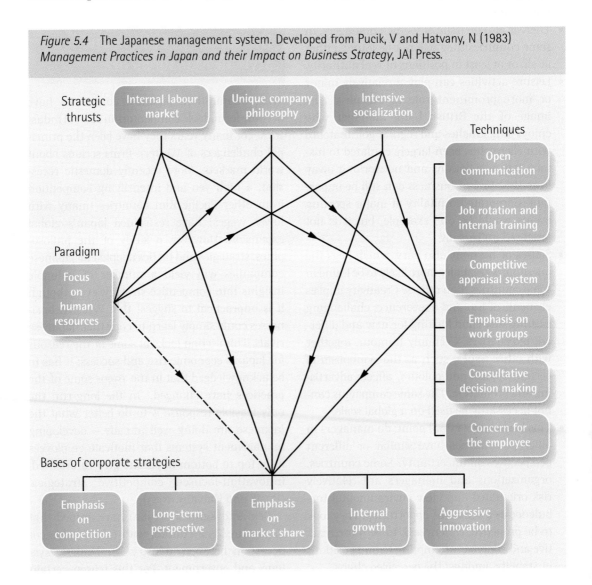

*Figure 5.4* The Japanese management system. Developed from Pucik, V and Hatvany, N (1983) *Management Practices in Japan and their Impact on Business Strategy*, JAI Press.

turing costs. Mitsubishi's shipping company, for instance, has begun to buy vessels manufactured in Korean yards; Japanese shipbuilders are no longer an automatic low-price competitor.

Culture plays a significant role at the heart of the Japanese strategy process.

In Japan the historic focus has been on human resources (Pucik and Hatvany, 1983) and this became the basis for three key strategic thrusts which are expressed as a number of management techniques. These have acted as key determinants of the actual strategies pursued (Figure 5.4). The three strategic thrusts are the notion of an internal labour market within the organization, a unique company philosophy, and intensive socialization throughout the working life.

The internal labour market is based on the tradition of lifetime employment whereby young men (not women) who joined large companies after school or university were expected to remain with them for life and in return were offered job security. Commitment and loyalty to

**STRATEGY IN ACTION – Box 5.2**
**The Cycle of Goodness**
**Attributed to Tadeo Yoshida, President, YKK**

YKK is the world's leading manufacturer of zip fasteners. YKK produces and markets zips throughout the world, and is vertically integrated, designing and manufacturing much of its own machinery.

I firmly believe in the spirit of social service.

Wages alone are not sufficient to assure our employees of a stable life and a rising standard of living. For this reason we return to them a large share of the fruits of their labour, so that they may also participate in capital accumulation and share in the profits of the firm. Each employee, depending on his means, deposits with the company at least ten per cent of his wages and monthly allowances, and 50 per cent of his bonus; the company, in turn, pays interest on these savings. Moreover, as this increases capital, the employees benefit further as stockholders of the firm. It is said that the accumulation of savings distinguishes man from animals. Yet, if the receipts of a day are spent within that day, there can be no such cycle of saving.

The savings of all YKK employees are used to improve production facilities, and contribute directly to the prosperity of the firm. Superior production facilities improve the quality of the goods produced. Lower prices increase demand. And both factors contribute to the prosperity of other industries that use our products.

As society prospers, the need for raw materials and machinery of all sorts increases, and the benefits of this cycle spread out not just to this firm, but to all related industries. Thus the savings of our employees, by enhancing the prosperity of the firm, are returned to them as dividends that enrich their lives. This results in increased savings which further advance the firm. Higher incomes mean higher tax payments, and higher tax payments enrich the lives of every citizen. In this manner, business income directly affects the prosperity of society; for businesses are not mere seekers after profit, but vital instruments for the improvement of society.

This cycle enriches our free society and contributes to the happiness of those who work within it. The perpetual working of this cycle produces perpetual prosperity for all. This is the cycle of goodness.

*YKK*  http://www.ykk.com

the employer result. With recession in recent years this practice has been less widespread.

The articulated and enacted unique philosophy is again designed to generate commitment and loyalty with the argument that familiarity with the goals of a company helps to establish values and provides direction for effort and behaviour. YKK's 'Cycle of Goodness' (Box 5.2) is an excellent example.

The potential benefits of a company philosophy will only be gained if the philosophy is communicated to employees and demonstrated by managers. Hence this is a key aspect of company socialization in Japan, which starts with initial training and continues with further training throughout the working life.

These three strategic thrusts are closely linked to six management techniques used extensively in Japanese firms.

Open communication and sharing information across departmental boundaries aims to develop a climate of trust and a team spirit within the organization. This is enhanced by close integration between managers and employees. Job rotation and the internal training programmes supplement this communication system because through them employees become more aware of what happens throughout the organization. Because of relatively low labour turnover, promotion opportunities are very limited and advancement is slow and often based on seniority. However, performance is essential, and employees are carefully and regularly appraised in their abilities to get things done and to co-operate with others.

This is particularly important as Japanese companies revolve around groups rather than individuals, with work being assigned to teams of employees. This, together with the use of quality circles (whereby groups of employees are encouraged to discuss issues and problems and suggest improvements), is seen as a key motivator. There is considerable emphasis on consultative decision making, involving these working groups, and a desire for consensus decisions. This generates greater loyalty to the decisions and to implementation. Finally, managers are encouraged to spend time with employees discussing both performance and personal problems. Companies have also frequently provided housing and various other services for employees.

Several Japanese companies have invested in manufacturing plants in the USA and Europe in recent years. In a number of cases they have selected industries where the country had already ceased to manufacture products because of an inability to compete (e.g. television sets and video recorders) or where the competitive edge had declined. Motor vehicles is an example of the latter. The British car industry fell behind the Japanese and German producers in terms of quality and productivity and has struggled to catch up. The first Japanese car plant was built by Nissan near Sunderland and, using a Japanese approach – rather than adopting all the techniques described in this section – it has become the most productive car plant in the UK, and one of Nissan's most efficient anywhere in the world.

Hill (1990) explains that the key human resources aspects of the Nissan UK strategy are as follows.

- There is a single union agreement, with the AEU.
- All employees (including managers) have the same conditions of employment, and wear similar blue overalls at work.
- There are no (inflexible) written job descriptions.
- There is no clocking on and no privileged parking.
- Absenteeism has remained very low.
- There are daily communications meetings – searching for continuous improvement.
- Employees often go to Japan for training – skilled workers learn both operational and maintenance skills.

- The training budget, equivalent to 14% of sales revenue, is exceptionally high for a British company. A typical employee will receive 9 days on-the-job and 12 days off-the-job training each year.
- Supervisors are empowered managers. They recruit and select their own staff (individually they are responsible for about 20 employees), and they control the layout and operation of their own part of the production line.

> The core of management is the art of mobilizing every ounce of intelligence in the organization and pulling together the intellectual resources of all employees in the service of the firm. We know that the intelligence of a handful of technocrats, however brilliant and smart they may be, is no longer enough. Only by drawing on the combined brain power of all its employees can a firm face up to the turbulence and constraints of today's environment.
>
> *Mr Konosuke Matsushita, Matsushita Electrical Industrial Company Ltd*

## Quality and competition

Although there are close supporting links between companies, government and the banking system, there is intense and aggressive competition between the individual firms in an industry, fostered by growth objectives and the loyalty of employees to their firm.

Prahalad and Hamel (1985) have suggested that the Japanese 'rewrite the rules of the game to take their competitors by surprise'. Through technology, design, production costs, distribution and selling arrangements, pricing and service they seek to build 'layers of competitive advantage' rather than concentrate on just one aspect. Many competitors in the West think more narrowly. Prahalad and Hamel suggest

that Japanese companies are successful in part because they have a clear mission and statement of strategic intent, and a culture which provides both opportunity and encouragement to change things incrementally. Getting things right first time and every time – total quality management – is endemic in the culture.

Internationally, Japanese companies may not be consistent with their strategies; instead they will seek the best competitive opportunities in different places and they will change continually as new opportunities arise and are created.

Japanese companies benchmark against the best in the world and willingly customize their products to meet local market demand.

## Long-term perspective

It was shown in Chapter 3 that while many Western companies concentrate on short-term strategies, influenced often by financial pressures, the Japanese take a long-term perspective.

## Emphasis on market share

Japanese companies are competitive, growth orientated and anxious to build and sustain high market shares in world markets. This will enable them to provide the job security that is a fundamental aspect of the culture. They often use their experience curve (which is examined in detail in the appendix to Chapter 7) to develop strategies aimed at market dominance with a long-term view of costs and prices.

## Internal growth

Mergers, acquisitions and divestitures are relatively uncommon in Japan – the Japanese favour the internal production system and innovation.

In a book on Japanese manufacturing techniques, Schonberger (1984) argued that a major reason for Japan's success has been its ability to use its resources well, better than many Western competitors. In many factories, he contends, the equipment is no better than that used elsewhere in the world, but wherever they can Japanese companies invest in the best equipment available. Managerial skills are used in improvement drives, a search for simple solutions and, in particular, a meticulous attention to detail. Simplicity is important since management and shopfloor can relate better to each other; and flexible techniques and workforces result in low stock production systems, efficiency and lower costs.

The ability to trust and establish close links with other companies in the supply chain allows focused specialization and just-in-time manufacturing with low inventories. However, this type of dependency can act as a hindrance to global expansion until comparative supplier links can be established.

### Innovation

Research and development is deemed important and funded appropriately. As a result much of Japan's technology has advanced quickly, and firms who fail to innovate go out of business. Ohmae (1985) has described Japan as a 'very unforgiving economy', with thousands of corporations destroyed every year through bankruptcy. He points out that Japan is selective about the industries in which research and development will be concentrated. Japan has, for example, spent a relatively high proportion of its research and development money in ceramics and steel, and as a result has become a world leader in fibre optics, ceramics and mass-produced large-scale integrated circuits. For similar reasons the USA is world leader in biotechnology and specialized semiconductors, and Europe in chemicals and pharmaceuticals.

Product innovation in Japan is fast and competitive. For example, Sony launched the first miniaturized camcorder (hand-held video camera and recorder) in June 1989. Weighing less than 700 g (1.5 lb) it was one-quarter of the size of existing camcorders. Within six months Matsushita and JVC had introduced lighter models. Within a further six months there was additional competition from Canon, Sanyo, Ricoh and Hitachi. Sony introduced two new models in Summer 1990. One was the lightest then available; the other had superior technical features. More recent models feature larger viewfinders and allow the user to hold the camcorder at arm's length instead of up-to-the-eye.

This faster model replacement is linked to an ability to break even financially with fewer sales of each model. Japan has achieved this with efficient and flexible manufacturing systems and a greater willingness to use common, rather than model-specific, components.

Individual Western companies have proved that it is possible, with determination and distinctive products, to penetrate Japanese markets successfully, but contenders can expect fierce resistance and defensive competition.

## Summary

*Culture* is the way in which an organization performs its tasks, the way its people think, feel and act in response to opportunities and threats, the ways in which objectives and strategies are set and decisions made. It reflects emotional issues and it is not easily analysed, quantified or changed. Nevertheless, it is a key influence on strategic choice, strategy implementation and strategic change – until we understand the culture of an organization we cannot understand strategic management in that organization.

A large organization is unlikely to be just one single, definable culture. It is more likely to be a loose or tight amalgam of different cultures.

It is quite normal for the culture to be influenced by a strong strategic leader and his or her beliefs and values.

In a very broad sense we can think of culture as a mixture of *behaviours* (manifestations) and underlying *attitudes and values*. It is easier to change one of these rather than both simultaneously.

There is no 'ideal culture' as such. Key elements typically have a 'flip side' and, therefore, a style and approach that is appropriate at a particular time can quickly become out of date and in need of change.

An useful grid for analysing the culture of any organization would comprise:

Manifestations – artefacts; values; underlying assumptions; behaviours
People      – stories; leadership; communications
Power      – ownership and structure; personal power; organizational politics.

Charles Handy proposes *four cultural types* which help to explain the culture, style and approach of different organizations. These are the power culture (typical of small, entrepreneurial organizations), the role culture (larger and more formal organizations), the task culture (the complex organization seeking to achieve internal synergies through effective linkages) and the person culture (built around the individual managers' needs).

In an alternative and equally significant contribution Miles and Snow differentiate among *defenders* (conservative and low-risk organizations), *prospectors* (innovative and entrepreneurial), *analysers* (limited change with measured steps) and *reactors* (followers). These can be readily linked to styles of strategy creation.

We can only understand culture when we understand power inside an organization. Who has power, how do they acquire it and how do they use it?

A number of books on the general theme of 'organizational excellence' has highlighted how it is culture that is at the heart of success. Although general themes and lessons can be teased out, an organization cannot simply replicate the culture of another successful organization and become successful itself.

There are important cultural differences between nations. This has implications for businesses which operate or trade globally.

## References

Barney, JB (1986) Organization culture: can it be a source of sustained competitive advantage? *Academy of Management Review*, 11 (3).

Berry, D (1983) The perils of trying to change corporate culture, *Financial Times*, 14 December.

Deal, T and Kennedy, A (1982) *Corporate Cultures. The Rites and Rituals of Corporate Life*, Addison-Wesley.

French, JRP and Raven, B (1959) The bases of social power. *In Studies in Social Power* (ed. D Cartwright), University of Michigan Press.

Goldsmith, W and Clutterbuck, D (1997) *The Winning Streak Mark II*, Orion Business. The first edition, *The Winning Streak*, was originally published in 1984 by Weidenfeld and Nicolson.

Hampden-Turner, C (1990) Corporate culture – from vicious to virtuous circles, *Economist*.

Handy, CB (1976) *Understanding Organizations*, Penguin. The ideas are elaborated in Handy, CB (1978) *Gods of Management*, Souvenir Press.

Harrison, R (1972) Understanding your organization's character, *Harvard Business Review*, May/June.

Hill, R (1990) Nissan and the art of people management, *Director*, March.

Hofstede, G (1991) *Cultures and Organization: Software of the Mind*, McGraw Hill.

Kakabadse, A (1982) *Culture of the Social Services*, Gower.

Kanter, RM (1991) Transcending business boundaries: 12000 world managers view change, *Harvard Business Review*, May–June.

Kluckhohn, C and Strodtbeck, F (1961) *Variations in Value Orientations*, Peterson.

Leadbeater, C and Rudd, R (1991) What drives the lords of the deal? *Financial Times*, 20 July.

Lewin, K (1947) Frontiers in group dynamics: concept, method and reality in social science, *Human Relations*, I.

Miles, RE and Snow, CC (1978) *Organization Strategy, Structure and Process*, McGraw-Hill.

Ohmae, K (1985) *Triad Power*, Free Press.

Peters, TJ (1988) *Thriving on Chaos*, Knopf.

Peters, TJ and Waterman, RH Jr (1982) In *Search of Excellence: Lessons from America's Best Run Companies*, Harper and Row. Original article: Peters, TJ (1980) Putting excellence into management, *Business Week*, 21 July.

Prahalad, CK and Hamel, G (1985) Address to the Annual Conference of the Strategic Management Society, Barcelona, October.

Press, G (1990) Assessing competitors' business philosophies, *Long Range Planning*, 23, 5.

Pucik, V and Hatvany, N (1983) Management practices in Japan and their impact on business strategy, *Advances in Strategic Management*, Vol. 1, JAI Press.

Pümpin, C (1987) *The Essence of Corporate Strategy*, Gower.

Schein, EH (1985) *Organizational Culture and Leadership*, Jossey Bass.

Schonberger, RJ (1984) *Japanese Manufacturing Techniques*, Free Press.

Schwartz, H and Davis, SM (1981) Matching corporate culture and business strategy, *Organizational Dynamics*, Summer.

Trompenaars, F and Hampden-Turner, C (1997) *Riding the Waves of Culture: Understanding Cultural Diversity in Business*, Nicholas Brealey Publishing.

Waterman, RH Jr (1988) *The Renewal Factor*, Bantam.

Test your knowledge of this chapter with our online quiz at: http://www.thomsonlearning.co.uk

Explore Culture and Values further at:

*Academy of Management Review*   http://www.aom.pace.edu/amr

*Business Week*   http://www.businessweek.com

*Long Range Planning*   http://www.lrp.ac

*Strategic Management Journal*   http://www.smsweb.org/about/SMJ/SMJ.html

## Questions and Research Assignments

TEXT RELATED

1. Use the text in Minicase 5.2 (IKEA) to complete a culture grid (Figure 5.1) for IKEA.

2. Take an organization with which you are familiar and evaluate it in terms of Handy's and Miles and Snow's typologies.

3. List other organizations that you know which would fit into the categories not covered in your answer to Question 2.

For both Questions 2 and 3 you should comment on whether or not you feel your categorization is appropriate.

4. Considering the organization that you used for Question 2, assess the power levers of the strategic leader and other identifiable managers.

5. Thinking of the identified cultural priorities for Japan, Germany and the USA, listed in the text, what do you think the cultural priorities of UK businesses are?

## Internet and Library Projects

1. From the 1980s to the mid-1990s Rover had a strategic alliance with Honda. When its then owner, British Aerospace, sold Rover to BMW this alliance was wound down and then terminated. A Japanese influence was replaced by a German one. Rover developed a number of new models but by early 2000 its trading losses were so significant that BMW decided to 'sell or close'. The Phoenix group was pulled together by a previous Rover manager, John Towers, and he acquired the business for a mere £10. Rover became British once more. How has the culture and style changed with these various changes of ownership?

   *Rover Group*   http://www.rovergroup.com
   *Honda*   http://www.honda.com
   *British Aerospace*   http://www.bae.co.uk
   *BMW*   http://www.bmw.com

2. Research how profitable John Lewis and Waitrose have been in comparison with their major competitors in the 1990s. What conclusions can you draw?

   *John Lewis Partnership*   http://www.johnlewis.co.uk
   *Waitrose*   http://www.waitrose.com

3. Find out where your nearest John Lewis or Waitrose store is and if possible visit it. Can you detect any differences in attitude between the John Lewis staff and those who work in similar stores?

   *John Lewis Partnership*   http://www.johnlewis.co.uk
   *Waitrose*   http://www.waitrose.com

4. Our Price, once part of WH Smith, is a leading specialist retailer of music and video products, including computer games – markets where the majority of competing products are identical. At the end of the 1980s, following years of growth, this market had flattened out. Our Price was acknowledged to be a company which provided excellent service but its stores were seen as 'dull, drab, boring and intimidating'.

WH Smith was determined to 'reposition the brand' to revitalize it while ensuring that it was easily distinguishable from its major competitors, especially the informal Virgin Megastores and the mainstream WH Smith stores, which are more formal and traditional. It was thought necessary to change the ways in which products are displayed and sold, media and in-store promotions, aspects of the service and, especially, staff attitudes and behaviour.

A new vision and values was defined 'to build an attitude and way of behaving in all that we do in the business that will support . . . the re-positioning of the brand'.

*The Our Price vision*
- The first place everybody thinks of for music
- The place its customers keep coming back to
- The place where the involvement and fulfilment of its people creates commercial success.

*The required values*
To pursue the vision effectively Our Price would need:
- To 'delight' its customers, who need to feel satisfied even if they leave the store without purchasing
- To empower its people
- To drive itself forward and embrace change . . . while recognizing the need to be commercially successful.

Visit your nearest Our Price store and evaluate whether this vision and values are still relevant. Compare and contrast Our Price with competing HMV stores (or Virgin Megastores) and sounds departments within WH Smith high-street stores. Do they seem and feel to be different? What are the implications of any differences?

*WH Smith*    http://www.whsmith.co.uk
*Virgin Megastores*    http://www.virginmega.com
*HMV*    http://www.hmv.co.uk

# Environmental Analysis, Resources and Competitiveness

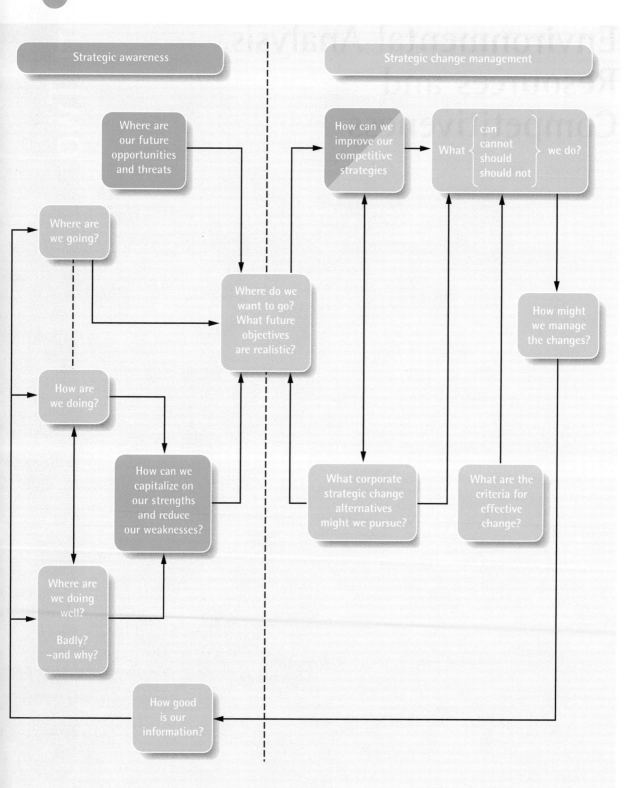

# Environmental Analysis, Resources and Competitiveness

6 Strategic Thinking and Synergy

7 Environmental Analysis and Strategic Positioning

8 The Dynamics of Competition

9 Strategic Resources

In Part One the concept of E–V–R (environment–values–resources) congruence was used to illustrate the presence, absence or loss of strategic positioning, competitiveness and strategic effectiveness. Later, culture and values were discussed and it was argued that they hold the key to the existence and sustenance of positioning, competitiveness and effectiveness. This part looks in much greater detail at positioning and competitiveness, and useful techniques for carrying out the appropriate analyses are explained. Chapter 6, which begins the part, discusses the important concepts of strategic thinking and synergy, which are relevant for the whole book.

Specifically, the following techniques are discussed in Part Two:

Chapter 7   A PEST (political, economic, social and technical) analysis for evaluating external environmental forces
A SWOT (strengths, weaknesses, opportunities and threats) analysis for combining resource competencies and environmental windows of opportunity

Chapter 8   The industry environment and forces which determine industry competitiveness
Generic strategies for competitive advantage
Activity maps which look at resource linkages and internal synergies

Chapter 9   A strategic resource audit Value chains which link the organization with its suppliers and customers.

In simple terms, an organization should be asking and addressing two questions simultaneously:

- What distinctive competencies and relative strengths does the organization possess – and where are there opportunities to exploit these further and more effectively? This is the resource-based approach.

- *What new opportunities can be spotted and identified for which the organization has, or can, obtain the strengths and competencies which would be needed to exploit them? This is the opportunity-driven approach.*

*It is important to hold these two approaches in mind when reading the four chapters in this part of the book. In essence, Chapter 7 (environmental analysis) and much of Chapter 8 (competitive dynamics) concentrate on the opportunity-driven approach. The resource-based approach is touched on in Chapter 8 when activity mapping is introduced and then it is developed in greater detail in Chapter 9. However, successful organizations do not adopt one approach rather than the other: they address both issues simultaneously and blend them together.*

# Strategic Thinking and Synergy

*This is a short introductory chapter to Part Two. It explains strategic thinking and synergy, two key strategic issues which impact upon the opportunity-driven and resource-based approaches to strategy. Like the other short introductory chapters at the beginning of subsequent parts, there is no summary or questions at the end.*

## Introduction

Good ideas for the future can either start inside the organization or be obtained from external contacts, and the ability to synthesize the answers to the two questions listed in the Introduction to this part of the book is a reflection of the organization's *strategic thinking* capabilities.

At one level, matching, exploiting and changing the linkages between resource competency and environmental opportunity is an expression of organizational competitiveness, and the presence (or absence) of competitive advantage. It was shown earlier (Chapter 2) how it is essential for organizations to seek competitive advantage for every product, service and business in their portfolios. Competitiveness comes from functions and activities, and the effectiveness of the links between them. This is one aspect of *synergy*. The second aspect of synergy is the relatedness and interdependency of the different products, services and businesses and their ability to support each other in some way. Synergy is covered in this chapter, although corporate strategic logic is not explored until Part Five.

Figure 6.1 illustrates the organization in the context of its external environment. Its suppliers and customers, upon whom it depends, and its competitors – both existing and new-in-the-future – are shown as having an immediate impact. Wider environmental forces bear on all the 'players' in the industry, and these are shown in the outer circle as political, economic, social and technological (PEST) forces.

The forces and influences have been deliberately shown in concentric circles. It is quite typical for us to think of the organization as a group of activities (and/or functions) and then to place everything and everyone else, including suppliers and customers, in a so-called external business environment. Increasingly, it makes considerable sense for the organization to see

*Figure 6.1*   The business environment.

itself working in partnership with its suppliers, distributors and customers. When this perspective is adopted, then only competitors from the middle ring would be placed in the external environment, together with the general forces which impact upon the whole industry.

Figure 6.2 extends this point, and shows the various concepts and techniques discussed in this part of the book in diagrammatic form.

## Strategic Thinking

Strategic thinking embraces the past, present and future. Understanding patterns and lessons from the past will certainly inform the future – but given the dynamic, turbulent and uncertain business environments that affect many industries and organizations, it would be dangerous to assume that the future will reflect the past and be a continuation of either past or existing trends.

Figure 6.3 shows (bottom right triangle) how strategies which link competencies with a strategic vision for the future embrace learning

*Figure 6.2*   Competitive strategy: a summary of techniques.

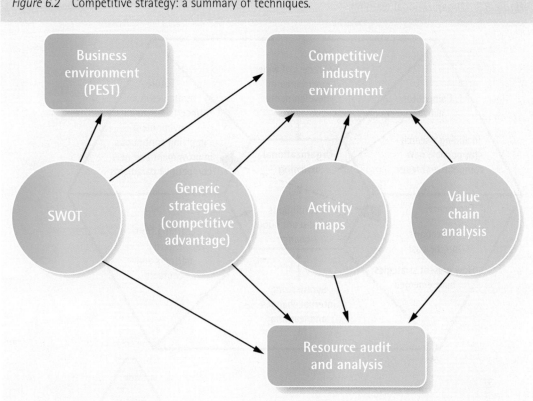

from the past, an awareness of existing competencies and some insight into likely future trends. The central part of the figure highlights that *organizational learning* is required to build the future and that it encompasses:

- a reflection on how present strategies have emerged over time
- an understanding of current competencies and the strategic value of particular resources and the linkages between them
- knowledge of existing competitors and what they are doing at the moment – and preparing to do in the future
- an appreciation of possible new sources of competition
- an awareness of wider environmental opportunities and threats

- an ability to share information with, and thus learn from, external partners and contacts, including suppliers, distributors and customers.

The effective organization will synthesize this learning into insightful strategies for dealing with future uncertainties.

Campbell and Alexander (1997) offer a different, but clearly related, approach to strategic thinking. They delineate three elements. First, insight into operating issues: with benchmarking other organizations (searching for good practices), process re-engineering and total quality management organizations should look for opportunities to improve continuously the way they do things. Secondly, future gazing: exponents of chaos theory warn

Figure 6.3    Organizational learning.

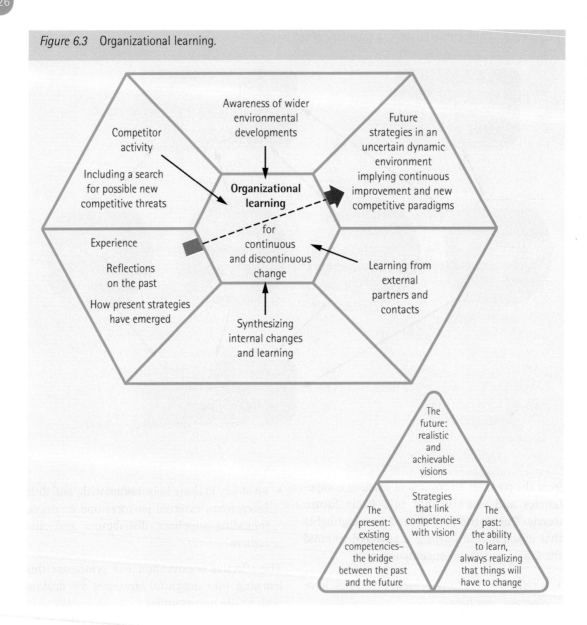

of the need always to be ready for the unexpected and unpredictable; and so here the emphasis is on discontinuous change, and the idea of reinventing and thus controlling developments in the industry. Put another way, establishing new rules of competition and seizing the 'high ground' ahead of any rivals. Scenario building (which is discussed in Chapter 7) plays an important role. The third element is behaviour and culture. Without a clear and communicated vision and direction, and with an absence of employees who are willing to engage the future and look for change opportunities, strategic thinking will be very limited and unimaginative. Simply, the organization must become

# Minicase 6.1 Kellogg's Cereals

Kellogg, with its well-known and very valuable brand name, had been the clear market leader for breakfast cereals throughout the world for many years when, at the end of the 1970s and into the early 1980s, it experienced declining market share in the USA for the first time. Between 1979 and 1983 market share in the USA fell from 42% to 38% in a market which was then growing at only 2% per year, compared with 7% a decade earlier. A key issue at the time was public pressure against foods with a high sugar content.

It was anticipated that Kellogg, like their main rivals in the cereals market, would choose to diversify into other foods. Kellogg did begin to diversify, but only on a relatively small scale, preferring to concentrate on grain-based products which it knows best. New products were developed and launched on a regular basis, some featuring artificial sweeteners. As well as new brands of breakfast cereal, these have included Nutri-Grain bars and fruit Pop Tarts, and more recently Rice Krispies snacks have been launched very successfully. Because of the declining birth rate, the new products were often aimed at adults as well as children. Fibre content was seen as an important factor for this. Kellogg, though, has been careful not to target products too narrowly on the grounds that once they are in a house any member of the family is likely to eat them. There have been a number of successes, and some failures.

As a result, Kellogg's market share of 42% was restored in 1985. Sometime later Kellogg, along with its main rivals, increased prices and provoked a consumer switch to supermarket own-label brands, which Kellogg refused to manufacture. Its share then declined again.

In the 1990s consumers in the USA began to turn away from breakfast cereals. Lifestyles were changing; many people were minded to skip breakfast or quickly eat a bagel, muffin or doughnut. They were in a hurry. Between 1995 and 2000 the US breakfast cereal market declined by 12.5%. Kellogg's main rival, General Mills, was closing the market share gap in America with successful new products and in 1998 it overtook the declining Kellogg for the first time. Its share of 32% was 1% higher than Kellogg's reduced share. Although Kellogg, with an overall share of 40% of the world market, remained global leader, its profits had been severely affected. In early 2000 Kellogg announced the closure of its plant in Battle Creek, Michigan, the city where the business began over 100 years ago.

## Breakfast cereals in Europe

In Europe, Kellogg is again market leader with six out of the ten best-selling brands. Its share has been as high as 50% in recent years. British consumers eat more cereal per head than any other country, including the USA, but other European countries, which tend to prefer breads, meats and cheeses for breakfast, have begun to provide a real opportunity as people have become more health conscious. In the 1990s, for example, the French market for breakfast cereals grew at over 20% per year.

British Weetabix has traditionally held second place, but this is no longer the case. The market has become more competitive and Kellogg has faced an important challenge from a joint venture between Nestlé and General Mills of the USA, known as Cereal Partners. General Mills has provided the brands – particularly Cheerio's, an oat cereal which helps to reduce cholesterol, and Golden Grahams, which compete with (and preceded) Kellogg's Golden Crackles – and Nestlé has provided the distribution network. At the same time, private-label brands have been enjoying the fastest rate of growth, especially for mueslis and bran products, which are particularly popular with adult consumers.

In February 2000 Kellogg agreed to produce a special range of cereals for the German discount retailer, Aldi – the first time it had ever produced own-label products.

The continuing challenge for Kellogg lies in creating new product ideas for a market which is growing in certain parts of the world and declining in others, and the generation of a strong enough cash flow to fund the necessary advertising budgets, both for supporting existing brands and for launching the new cereal products. Each cereal product needs to be promoted individually.

*Project: Visit a supermarket and look for the various Kellogg products. How many different breakfast cereal products can you spot? Do they all have directly competing brand alternatives? To what extent are they aimed at different market segments? What are the non-cereal products? Do they appear robust enough to compensate for any long-term decline in the breakfast cereal market?*

*Kelloggs*   http://www.kelloggs.com

more entrepreneurial in a dynamic environment, as discussed later in Chapters 12 and 13.

Courtney *et al.* (1997) distinguish four alternative future patterns and three broad approaches, which have different degrees of relevance for different situations.

The four futures are:

- a clear and definable future, which implies a continuation of present trends
- a limited and definable number of discrete alternatives which can be evaluated and judged

- a known range of possibilities, which can be defined only in more general terms
- real uncertainty, and with the possibility of major disruption and change.

The three broad approaches, which should not be seen as mutually exclusive, for utilizing organizational learning to deal with the relevant future pattern are:

- being relatively clear, or confident, about the direction, attempting to play an important influence and shape events

- accepting that there will be some uncertainty, staying vigilant and in close touch with events and happenings, and adapting to retain a strong position
- monitoring events and waiting for an appropriate opportunity to intervene in some way.

To reinforce the importance of strategic thinking and vigilance to changing circumstances, Minicase 6.1 discusses how Kellogg, the dominant company in breakfast cereals all round the world, has been adversely affected by increased competition combined with changing consumer tastes.

Figure 6.4 completes this section and summarizes the purposes and broad elements of strategic thinking.

Throughout this section on strategic thinking, the emphasis has been on the ability to take a holistic view and synthesize information. We need to synthesize information from the past and present and combine it with a view of the future. This embraces information which originates inside the organization and information that can be obtained from external partners and contacts. Synergy, which is discussed next, explains the importance of linkages and synthesis.

## Synergy

Synergy is either a path to sustained growth or a 'bridge too far' for organizations. It is concerned with the returns that are obtained from resources. Ansoff (1968) argues that resources should be combined and managed in such a way that the benefits which accrue exceed those which would result if the parts were kept separate, describing synergy as the 2 + 2 = 5 effect. Simply, the combination of the parts produces results of greater magnitude than would be the case if the parts operated independently.

*Figure 6.4*   Strategic thinking: purposes and elements.

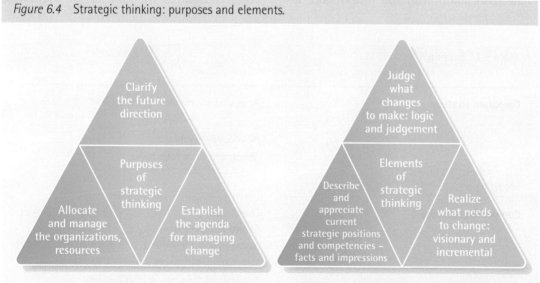

This figure is based on Rhodes, J and Thame, S (1988)
*Colours of Your Mind*, HarperCollins.

There are three basic synergy opportunities:

- *functional* – sharing facilities, competencies, ideas and best practice
- *strategic* – complementary competitive strategies across a corporate portfolio: even in a diversified conglomerate some sharing is possible
- *managerial* – compatible styles of management and values in different functions and businesses.

Sometimes the synergy is obtained by transferring people between different parts of an organization, possibly for a period of secondment, in order to facilitate the sharing.

In simple terms, if an organization manufactures and markets six different products, the organization should be structured to yield the benefits that might be possible from combining these different interests. For example, central purchasing for all products might yield economies of scale; factory rationalization might increase productivity or lower production costs; sales staff might be able to obtain more or larger orders if they are selling more than one product; each product might gain from name association with the others; and distributors might be more satisfied than if the company offered only a very limited range or a single product. Some of the benefits are clearly measurable, whereas others are more subjective; and the search for synergy clearly embraces structural as well as strategic decisions.

Similarly, if functions, products or business units were not co-ordinated, then efforts may well be duplicated, or delays might be built into the organization system because of a lack of understanding.

Table 6.1 explains how corporate strategy decisions, such as acquisitions, alliances or divestments, should be made in the light of the overall synergistic implications of the change. Some – strategically sound – changes imply increased synergy opportunities, while others imply complexity, fragmentation and lost synergy. The synergy impact is seen in the competitive strategies and competitive success for each relevant activity. Simply, where an organization is considering increasing its range of products and services, or merging with or acquiring another company, synergy is an important consideration. In the case of an acquisition

---

*Table 6.1*  Synergy

| | |
|---|---|
| **Corporate strategy** | Acquisitions – Horizontal |
| | – Vertical |
| | Alliances/joint ventures |
| | Divestment for greater focus |
| Impacting on | |
| **Competitive strategy** | Lower costs |
| | Shared resources |
| | 'Know-how' – transferable skills and learning |
| | Negotiating, bargaining power |
| | Foundations for a new spinoff business |

the combination of the companies should produce greater returns than the two on their own. Adding new products or services should not affect existing products or services in any adverse way, unless they are intended to be replacements. When such strategic changes take place the deployment of resources should be re-evaluated to ensure that they are being utilized both efficiently and effectively.

Obtaining synergy may well imply the sharing of knowledge and other resources between divisions or business units, possibly attempting to disseminate best practice. This is only feasible if resource efficiencies are measured and compared in order to identify which practices are best. Internal rivalries may prevent the attainment of the potential benefits from sharing. Synergy is more likely to occur if all the relevant activities are linked in such a way that the organization as a whole is managed effectively, which Drucker (1973) has defined as 'doing the right things'. Individual business units and functions must themselves be managed efficiently or, as Drucker would say, they must be 'doing things right'. As seen in Chapter 4, resource efficiency considers how well resources are being utilized and the returns being obtained from them. Effectiveness incorporates an evaluation of whether the resources are being deployed in the most beneficial manner.

There are four key elements which must come together if potential synergy is to be achieved:

- *effective leadership* – which emphasizes the importance of co-operation, sharing, transfer and learning throughout the organization
- *facilitative structure* – which allows co-operation and inhibits internal conflict
- *supportive systems* – which encourage sharing and transfer. Examples include cross-functional and cross-business project teams

and the provision of opportunities for managers to spend time in other parts of an organization
- *appropriate rewards* – such that parts of an organization can benefit from helping others.

Figure 6.5 pulls these themes together and shows how synergy potential must be examined inside a framework of strategic resources, strategic thinking and the relevant business environment. Potential exists from effectively combining the various functions and activities in each business, from sharing and learning between businesses and from the overall corporate strategic logic.

At the same time, though, it must be realized that the anticipated synergy from strategic changes is easily overestimated and quite frequently it does not accrue. Potential benefits from adding new activities may be misjudged. After all, there is always an element of subjective anticipation and promise – the synergy is justified with strategic logic but delivered through people and their behaviour – and this should not be an excuse for delusion. Admitting to strategic misjudgements rarely comes easy to strategic leaders and managers and, as a result, the appropriate exit or withdrawal when synergy is not obtained, may not happen when it should. Internal politics and conflicts, because businesses and divisions see themselves as rivals rather than partners, all too often inhibit synergy.

Box 1.2 mentioned one diversification by the Lex Service Group in the 1970s. Lex were successful and profitable essentially with car distribution and felt that their resources and skills would be ideally suitable for transfer into hotel management. They anticipated synergy because of their management skills. Their level of success from the change, however, was below their expectations and they withdrew from this industry.

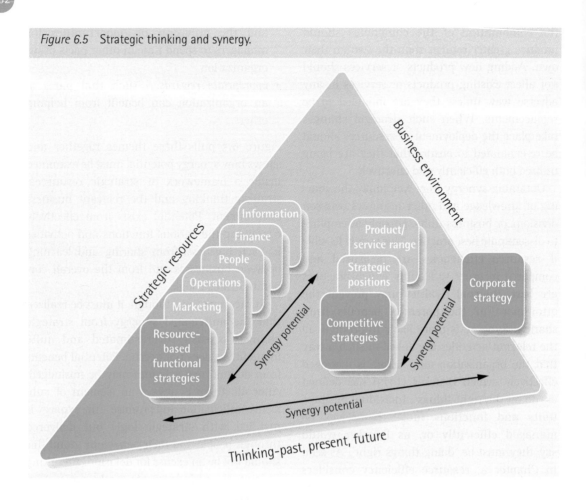

*Figure 6.5*    Strategic thinking and synergy.

## Searching for synergy – two examples

### Sony

A number of Japanese electronics companies (specifically manufacturers of 'hardware' – televisions, videos and hi-fi equipment) has sought links with the US makers of music and films, the related 'software', arguing that there is potential synergy from merging the two. An array of new products continues to become technologically feasible and the manufacturers want to secure their commercial exploitation. Such developments have included high-definition and digital televi-

sions, flat-screen TVs (both large and small for mounting on walls, like a picture, and carrying around), personal video disc players the same size as personal cassette players, miniaturized compact discs (CDs) and CD players and digital versatile discs (DVDs). Films can also be the basis for computer games. The large film companies have huge film libraries for video and games exploitation, both growth markets. The strategy is similar to that of the manufacturers of razors who have derived benefits and synergy from also manufacturing razor blades.

Not every product was a success, of course. Record companies were always reluctant to release music in the new high-technology digital audio tape (DAT) format when it was introduced. While Sony pioneered the hardware, its subsidiary CBS chose not to break industry ranks. DAT has never really taken off.

Sony acquired CBS Records in 1987 and Columbia Pictures from Coca-Cola in 1989. Previously, Coca-Cola had anticipated synergy from linking soft drinks and entertainment, but it had not accrued. Matsushita acquired MCA (Universal Pictures, record labels and part-ownership of a network TV station) in 1990. Toshiba negotiated a joint venture with Time Warner. Earlier, Rupert Murdoch had bought Twentieth Century Fox to exploit the film library on his cable and satellite TV networks worldwide.

The strategy has been defended with logical arguments. It has been suggested that if Sony had owned Columbia in the 1970s their Betamax video format would have proved more successful because more prerecorded videos would have been available in this format rather than the successful VHS – developed by Matsushita who were more resourceful in striking agreements with video makers. Similarly, CBS would prove a useful vehicle for forcing the pace of the switch from records to CDs.

Sceptics always argued that the synergy would not accrue, contending that the typical Japanese company and Hollywood film makers have dramatically different cultures which would not prove compatible. Moreover, Japan is not noted for creativity in entertainment.

In 1995 Matsushita divested MCA, selling it to Seagram. At this time, Sony was still not in a position to claim that it had effectively integrated its entertainments subsidiaries to deliver the anticipated benefits, profits and synergies. However, it has persevered and financial and other benefits have since accrued from the integration.

## LVMH – Moët Hennessy. Louis Vuitton

LVMH, which describes itself as the world's leading luxury products group, 'brings together a unique collection of crafts and brands well known in prestige circles: champagne, cognac, luggage, watches, jewellery, perfumes and haute couture'. LVMH brands include: Moët and Chandon, Veuve Clicquot, Hennessy, Hine, Tag Heuer, Zenith, Christian Dior, Givenchy and Christian Lacroix, as well as the Louis Vuitton leather products. In 1993 LVMH sold its Roc Skincare subsidiary to Johnson and Johnson, as its products did not fit properly since they sell exclusively through pharmacies. More recently LVMH expanded into selective retailing with chains such as Le Bon Marché and Sephora.

These are all products with a global appeal, albeit to relatively limited market niches. For such products, the marketing/selling network has to be extensive or it cannot support the global distribution; consequently, there can be major benefits from linking together an appropriate range of products and brands. LVMH's synergistic benefits are:

- name association, particularly with fashion and perfumes
- advertising – savings by advertising several brands in the same magazines
- distribution – although there are specialist outlets for different products, large department stores sell many LVMH brands. Because the LVMH range as a whole is vital for these stores, LVMH can command premium positions and displays
- sales – a worldwide sales force and network yields savings.

In November 1999 LVMH appeared to depart from its traditional pattern of acquisitions and bought Phillips, the world's third largest fine art auction house. Could it see hidden synergy potential?

## References

Ansoff, HI (1968) *Corporate Strategy*, Penguin (originally published by McGraw Hill in 1965).

Campbell, A and Alexander, M (1997), What's wrong with strategy? *Harvard Business Review*, November–December.

Courtney, H, Kirkland, J, and Viguerie, P (1997) Strategy under uncertainty, *Harvard Business Review*, November–December.

Drucker, PF (1973) *Management*, Harper and Row.

# Environmental Analysis and Strategic Positioning

Analysing the Business Environment

Competition and the Structure and Regulation of Industry

Strategic Positioning and Adding Value

SWOT (Strengths, Weaknesses, Opportunities and Threats) Analysis

Forecasting the Environment

Scenario Planning

*The notion of strategic positioning helps us understand the fit between an organization and its external environment. The opening case on the European Pharmaceutical Industry shows how company strategies have been influenced by such external environmental forces. Positions are related to the organization's ability to create and add value and consequently added value is discussed in relation to a SWOT (strengths, weaknesses, opportunities and threats) analysis. The chapter begins by examining the nature of the business environment, followed by a consideration of the impact of competition regulations on industry and company strategies. Positions, also, have to be changed, as seen in the discussion of E–V–R congruence. Sometimes the change is continuous and incremental; sometimes it is more dramatic or discontinuous. To help with the understanding of the latter the chapter concludes with a discussion of scenario building.*

Minicase

# Minicase 7.1  The European Pharmaceutical Industry

The global drugs industry is dominated by powerful American companies, perhaps not unexpectedly as the USA has the world's highest spending ratio for health as a proportion of gross domestic product. But no single company is in a truly dominant position, although individual companies dominate particular segments with patented treatments. There is, in addition, a number of sizeable pharmaceutical companies in the UK, Germany, Sweden, Switzerland and France.

Past, and inevitable, government interest and involvement makes pharmaceuticals a politically sensitive industry. Individual consumers have relatively little influence on the choice of a particular drug, which is prescribed by doctors who are often working under constraints or limitations imposed by their respective governments. This affects the research and marketing strategies of the drug manufacturers. Governments across Europe have frequently agreed favourable prices with international companies who locate and invest in their countries, which has led to the establishment of more plants than are really needed and some loss of production efficiencies. The total spend on prescription drugs rose throughout Western Europe in the 1980s and early 1990s. Between 1989 and 1992 it grew by nearly 50% in real terms. Almost all of the cost is borne by the public purse. The main reasons for the growth were ageing populations and medical advances.

However, in the economic recession, governments have become less and less willing to meet an ever-increasing bill; and in 1993 drug spending was deliberately curbed. The pharmaceutical companies have been forced to respond, and they have reacted in a number of ways. It will be seen in the following examples that national borders are no constraint in this industry.

- Workforces have been reduced and sites closed. Hoechst and Bayer (Germany), Glaxo Wellcome and Fisons (UK) and Ciba (Switzerland) have all followed this strategy.

- In addition, there has been a number of strategic acquisitions and divestments. Two of the UK's leasing companies were sold, Fisons to Rhône-Poulenc Rorer and the manufacturing interests of Boots to BASF. Wellcome was taken over by Glaxo, following a contested bid. In 1998, the two dominant UK companies, Glaxo Wellcome and SmithKline Beecham, were poised to merge, but the two chief executives could not reach agreement on strategic leadership of the new group. However, the strategic logic was always there and the merger went ahead in 2000. Other mergers include:
  Sandoz and CIBA (both Swiss)
  American Home Products, Monsanto and Pharmacia (in two stages)
  Pfizer and Warner Lambert (both US)
  Astra (Sweden) and Zeneca (UK and a spin-off from ICI)
  Astra-Zeneca and Novartis (Switzerland).

As a result, Glaxo SmithKline is 'number one' with a 7.5% share of the world market, followed by Pfizer-Warner Lambert with 6.5% and Merck (5%).

- As a form of industry restructuring both SmithKline Beecham (Anglo-American) and Merck (US) acquired leading American drugs wholesalers.
- New marketing strategies have been developed, actively promoting to doctors and hospitals those drugs that governments are still willing to pay for. This applies particularly to drugs which are differentiated, protected by patent and not subject to intense competition. Sales forces have also been rationalized
- Research and development has been redirected to focus on:
  (i) programmes which could lead to innovative and high-revenue drugs. The development of 'me-too' brands, which must be sold with lower margins in more competitive markets, is now seen as only low priority.
  (ii) generic (unbranded) drugs where patents have expired. Margins are low but generic drugs are popular with governments.
- European companies have forged alliances with US companies to obtain their greater expertise in cost management and in the research and development of generic products.
- New joint venture businesses have been set up, such as Rhône-Poulenc (France) and Merck's Animal Health Products division in London and then Rhône-Poulenc with Hoechst (Germany) for all the pharmaceutical interests of these two diversified conglomerates.

In the mid-1990s, the UK claimed 40% of those employed in contract research in Europe and was continuing to attract new investment by overseas companies. When Sweden's Pharmacia merged with Upjohn of the USA in 1995, a new corporate head office was opened in London. More recently, Pfizer opened a major research centre in Kent. There were four main reasons why London became 'the centre of the globe in terms of the pharmaceutical industry':

- UK scientists are as good as those in France, Germany, Switzerland and the USA, but the total cost of employing them is lower
- the UK government's regulatory scheme differs from those of certain other countries and allows the drug companies to make between 17% and 21% return on capital employed, thus encouraging more investment
- strong UK capital markets have supported the blossoming biotechnology industry and

- the UK is home to the European Medicines Evaluation Agency, which issues drug licences for the whole EU.

The general approach to regulation in the UK has typically been one of regulating company profits and not the price of individual drugs, ensuring that companies which do invest in research and development can recover their costs while enjoying patent protection for a period of years. However, the new Labour government (elected in 1997) threatened to rein in drug expenditure. The leading companies countered by saying they would relocate abroad. In addition, the formation of a National Institute for Clinical Excellence (NICE) which licenses new drugs provided a new opportunity (for more effective monitoring) but, at the same time, a threat. In 1999 NICE refused a licence for Glaxo Wellcome's new influenza drug, Relenza, as it had not been tested on enough elderly people, those most vulnerable to flu. The drug has since received approval from NICE.

QUESTIONS: How might the UK ensure it retains a leading position in this dynamic, turbulent but very important global industry?
What approach would you suggest any future British government should take?

*AstraZeneca* http://www.astrazeneca.com
*Fisons (Aventis)* http://www.aventis.com
*Glaxo Wellcome* http://www.glaxowellcome.co.uk
*ICI* http://www.ici.com
*Pfizer* http://www.pfizer.com
*Pharmacia & Upjohn* http://www.pharmacia.com
*SmithKline Beecham* http://www.sb.com

*Photograph: Apparatus used in combinational chemistry at the Glaxo Wellcome Medicines Research Centre, Stevenage UK*

One thing is clear. Even if you're on the right track, you'll get run over if you just sit there!
*Sir Allen Sheppard, when Chairman, Grand Metropolitan plc (now Diageo)*

## Analysing the Business Environment

### Managing in an increasingly turbulent world

This chapter examines in detail the environment in which the organization operates and considers how the forces present in the environment pose both opportunities and threats. The topic of stakeholders is developed further as several of the environmental forces which affect the organization clearly have a stake in the business. Simply, stakeholders should be categorized in terms of their power and their interest – a simple four-quadrant grid can easily be used for this, as shown in Figure 7.1. Those with power must be satisfied, especially if they are also interested in the activities of the organization. Those with relatively low power but high interest should certainly be kept informed. Competitors inevitably constitute a major influence on corporate, competitive and functional strategies and they are the subject of Chapter 8.

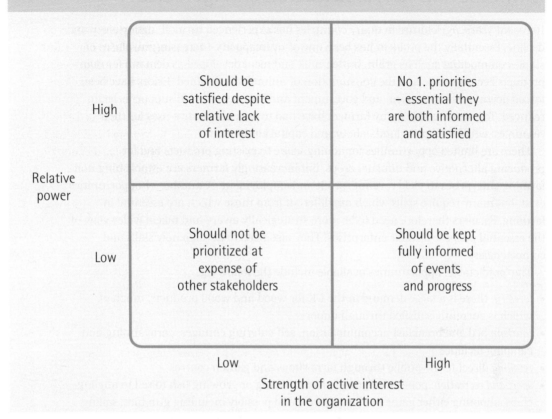

*Figure 7.1* Stakeholder significance grid. Developed from ideas in Mendelow, A. (1991) *Proceedings of 2nd International Conference on Information Systems*, Cambridge, MA.

If a firm is to control its growth, change and development it must seek to control the forces that provide the opportunities for growth and change, and those that pose threats and demand responses. Not only must managers be aware of environmental forces and environmental change, they must manage the organization's resources to take advantage of opportunities and counter threats. In turn, the strategic leader should ensure that this happens and that the values and culture of the organization are appropriate for satisfying the key success factors. Quite simply, the environment delivers shocks to an organization, and the way in which resources are deployed and managed determines the ability to handle these shocks. This relates to E–V–R (environment–values– resources) congruence.

Over time, paradigms concerning 'what will work' to bring about success in a particular industry or competitive environment will be created and maintained. However, as environmental and competitive forces change, the current reality (at any time) of what is required for competitive success may be drifting away from the organization's paradigm; consequently, a new paradigm will be essential. In an age of discontinuity, paradigms will need changing more frequently and more dramatically; expediting these changes is a key managerial task.

Put another way, in a turbulent environment, the organization must change its strategies and possibly its beliefs if it is to maintain E–V–R–congruence. Minicase 7.2 illustrates an important change of paradigm in UK agriculture.

# Minicase 7.2  Diversification in Agriculture

In recent years, agriculture in many countries has experienced turmoil, uncertainty and decline. Essentially the problem has been one of overcapacity. Increasing surpluses of staple commodities such as grain, butter, milk and meat developed as demand for many products became static and the consumption of animal fats declined. Prices have been forced down, costs have risen, and government and European Union support is being reduced. To remain viable many farmers have had to seek alternative uses for their resources, which comprise land, labour and capital equipment.

There are limited opportunities for adding value to existing products and for producing alternative and unusual crops, but increasingly farmers are establishing non-farming enterprises to yield revenue, profit and employment. A number of opportunities exist, but many require skills which are different from those which are essential in farming. Farmers therefore need to be more strategically aware and take a wider view of the essential purpose of their enterprises. They also need to develop new skills and competencies.

The 'predictable' opportunities available include the following:

- *forestry*: there is a large demand in the UK for wood and wood products, much of which is currently satisfied through imports
- *tourism*: bed and breakfast accommodation, self-catering cottages, caravanning and camping facilities
- *retailing* direct to the public through farm shops and garden centres
- *sport and recreation*: ponds and gravel pits for fishing or growing fish to sell to angling clubs; shooting either game or clay pigeons, and possibly including gun hire; sailing facilities; equestrian opportunities including horses for trekking and hunting, and stabling; golf courses on surplus land; and using rough terrain and woodland for simulated war games
- engineering, woodworking and craft workshops.

In recent years, more enterprising farmers have sought opportunities through the Internet. One farmer's wife in Sussex (UK) has developed a major electronic estate agency. Her husband travels around the properties when he is not active on the farm, photographing them with a digital camera and putting up the ubiquitous 'for sale' boards; his wife masterminds the IT side of the business. Because the business has been able to secure a number of properties in the high-price south-east and London area, the business is lucrative.

Quite different, but also very successful, is Ample Bosom, an on-line company which sells bras for the fuller figure from a farm in North Yorkshire (UK). The farmer's wife, Sally Robinson, was able to secure a £7500 diversification grant and she had access to a disused farm building. The site receives some 15,000 hits a week (in 2000) from buyers as far away as Singapore and New Zealand. The aim of the business is to supply a wide range of styles in unusual sizes, and which would not normally be readily available in a high-street shop, using products supplied by leading manufacturers.

QUESTION: Can you think of other 'good ideas' which would utilize the skills and spare resources of a farming business?

*Ample Bosom* http://www.amplebosom.com or www.bras-online.co.uk

Farmers now look at their farms as potentially diversified businesses.

A number of key themes underpins the issues discussed in this chapter:

- Traditional industries such as manufacturing and mining have given way to new, more technological – and frequently electronics-based – industries which demand new labour skills, and where 'knowledge workers' are of prime importance.
- New technologies can generate opportunities for substitutability, different forms of competition and the emergence of new competitors in an industry.
- In addition to changing skills demands, there have been other changes in the labour markets of developed countries. Many families have joint wage earners and more women are working. More and more people work from their homes, at least for part of their time.
- Many managers and employees are more time constrained and have less spare time than they would like. Not only does this imply less time for shopping (hence the potential for e-commerce), but demand has increased for convenient, time-saving products.
- People are living longer and, coupled with periods of lower birth rates, the average age of the population and the number of retired people are both increasing. These groups have more leisure time than working people.
- The Internet continues to change the way in which we access information in a quite remarkable way.

- Multinational businesses have grown in strength and significance and they have become the norm for manufacturing industries.
- Manufacturers from the UK, USA, Germany, Japan and other nations with a longstanding tradition in manufacturing have been willing to relocate factories in developing countries with lower wage costs. Technology which allows increasing levels of output from the same-size factory has facilitated these changes.
- Consequently, the competitive arena has been changing with, recently, the highest economic growth being enjoyed by the USA, although during the early and mid-1990s it was the Pacific Rim countries. In many industries, global supply potential exceeds demand, placing downward pressures on real prices.
- Product and service markets, supply chains, capital markets and communication systems have become global in nature.
- The speed of change in most industries and markets has increased and product lifecycles have shortened. For some companies, success can be very transient.
- Governments have masterminded increasing degrees of deregulation. Other countries have followed the UK's lead and privatized public-sector utilities; air travel and telecommunications markets have been opened up to more competition.
- Consumers are more aware and more knowledgeable; environmental groups have begun to wield increasing influence.

- Changes in politics and regimes in different parts of the world, such as Eastern Europe and the Far East, have introduced an element of chaos and greater unpredictability. Opportunities open up but carry a significant downside risk.

Simply, environments are more turbulent; managing them and managing *in* them demand more flexibility and more discontinuity than in the past.

There is no doubt that the world is becoming one marketplace. Capital markets, products and services, management and manufacturing techniques have all become global in nature. As a result, companies increasingly find that they must compete all over the world – in the global marketplace.

*Maurice Saatchi, when Chairman,*
*Saatchi and Saatchi Company plc*

In my experience, corporate life-threatening problems in large manufacturing companies have developed over a long period. These problems should never have been permitted to grow so large, but they were allowed to do so by top management who were lethargic and self-satisfied, who engaged in self-delusion and congratulated themselves on their exalted status. In short, the managements were the problem.

*Eugene Anderson,*
*ex-Chairman and Chief Executive,*
*Ferranti International plc*

How can we expect to succeed when we are playing cricket and the rest of the world is practising karate?

*Sir Edwin Nixon, when Chairman,*
*Amersham International*

Figure 7.2 emphasizes that as industries and markets become increasingly global, quality is more important than origin. People in Britain might like to claim 'British is best' – as might other people in other countries – but a statement such as this is meaningless unless it can be demonstrate that British (or other) products and services really are world class. To achieve world-class quality and reputation, companies must use knowledge and ideas to be innovative, operate at the level of the best in the world and form international networks and partnerships to access the best resources from around the world.

In this dynamic environment, the USA has become the most competitive nation because it has taken a lead in technically advanced industries and transformed itself into a service economy. It has found ways of generating the private-sector finances required for investment in new and relatively high-risk sectors, and it has ensured that regulations do not inhibit labour-force flexibility. Europe is generally more restrictive, although practices do vary between countries, even within the European Union.

Although the following examples are British in origin and used to illustrate an important theme, similar stories can readily be told of other parts of the world. When the former British Prime Minister, Margaret Thatcher, came to power in 1979 she quickly identified a wide productivity gap between many British companies and those perceived to be the best in the world. She set about reducing the gap for both large and small companies – and she was successful, although in many industries a gap remains, albeit smaller than it otherwise would have been. In some industries Britain does have 'best in the world' companies, but relatively few industry-wide centres of excellence. In motor cars, really only two truly British companies remain. These, Morgan and TVR, are very small niche players. Rover is manufacturing again, having recently been divested by BMW, but it is

*Figure 7.2* World-class strategic performance. Developed by John Thompson from ides in Moss Kanter, R (1996) *World Class – Thriving Locally in the Global Economy*, Simon and Schuster.

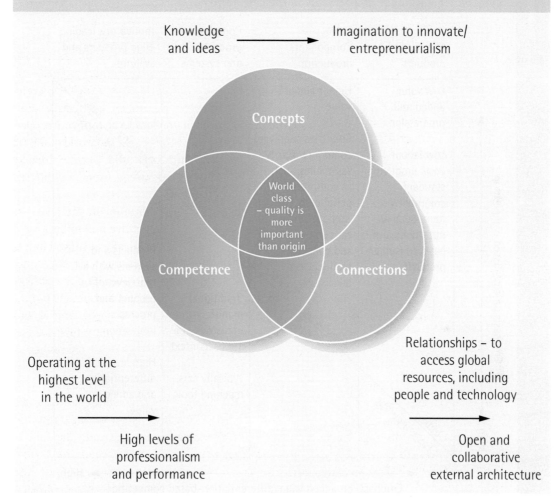

Knowledge and ideas ⟶ Imagination to innovate/ entrepreneurialism

Concepts

World class – quality is more important than origin

Competence

Connections

Operating at the highest level in the world ⟶ High levels of professionalism and performance

Relationships – to access global resources, including people and technology ⟶ Open and collaborative external architecture

financially weak with vehicles dependent upon competitors' technology. Ford now owns Jaguar and Land Rover; Vauxhall is a subsidiary of General Motors. Peugeot, Honda, Nissan and Toyota all assemble vehicles in UK factories. Nissan's Sunderland factory is their most productive plant. Yet, British companies are dominant in the high-profile, advanced technology, segment of Formula One racing. UK-based McLaren and Williams have only one serious rival, Ferrari. Television assembly is similar in principle, with British plants owned and operated by French and Japanese manufacturers.

Where there are individual world-class companies in an industry, there is also often a long tail of low performers. Most significantly, though, average productivity in Britain remains below the average for many of its leading competitors. Simply, while British companies have improved, so too have most others! Britain may have reduced the productivity gap, and may seem able and committed to it not widening again, but

KEY CONCEPT – Box 7.1
Competitive Advantage and Strategy in the Late 1990s

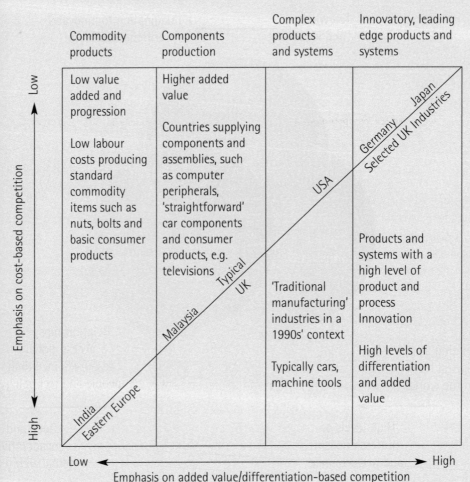

- Countries progress up and down the diagonal over time.
- Within each country different industries will be in different sectors. The position shown here on the diagonal is that with which the country is typically associated.
- The UK has drifted down to 'components' by offering incentives and relatively low labour costs to attract inward investments. However, with aerospace and

pharmaceuticals, for example, the UK is clearly in the 'innovatory' sector.
- Arguably, the UK should focus more intently on innovation to reverse the trend, otherwise it will increasingly become a mere supplier to the industry leaders and drivers. However, innovation requires managerial and workforce strengths and skills that the UK may not have.

- Innovation relates to products and services (radical improvements in value; reconceiving form and function) and market boundaries (attracting new customers; providing new values by satisfying individual needs more effectively).

Thompson, J (1997) based on ideas in Kruse, G and Berry, C (1997) A nation of shopkeepers, *Management Today*, April.

the gap has not been closed, and rivals have certainly not been overtaken.

The competitive future for the UK, however, does not lie in reducing wages to compete with the Far East and Eastern Europe, and thus creating a downward spiral of expectation; rather it lies in finding new ways of innovating, adding value, differentiating and *leading* consumers. Notwithstanding this, some cutting back to create and maintain trim and efficient organizations will always be essential.

These points are explored further in Box 7.1.

There are several frameworks for studying the environment of an organization. In addition to considering the company's *stakeholders* in terms of their relative power, influence, needs and expectations, a PEST analysis (discussed in detail on p. 247) can prove useful. This is an objective and straightforward consideration of changing POLITICAL, ECONOMIC, social and TECHNOLOGICAL influences. This review should help to clarify changing opportunities and threats.

The nature of the stakeholders and the environmental forces is a useful indicator of the most appropriate strategic approach for the organization to take. Where the environment is complex, turbulent and uncertain it will be necessary for the organization to be vigilant and speedily reactive. A carefully planned approach is ideal in stable and predictable circumstances; and a positive and proactive approach should be adopted where the environment can be changed or influenced.

## Understanding the environment

Although the constituent forces of the environment can be listed and assessed for opportunities and threats, and the forecasting of possible changes can be attempted, of most importance for managers is ongoing insight and awareness. The important issues might well be listed as part of a SWOT (strengths, weaknesses, opportunities and threats) analysis: they constitute an essential part of the planning process and can be used for developing and evaluating possible strategic changes. Managers, however, should always be attentive to changes and their decisions and actions should be both reactive and proactive as appropriate. In other words, their awareness should result from constant vigilance and attentiveness rather than from any isolated clinical analysis. This will in turn be dependent on the information system within the organization, sources of external information and the uses made of it, and the ability of individual managers to evaluate the importance and potential significance of events of which they become aware. While environmental forces and influences clearly exist and change, what matters is the perception that managers place on their observations and experiences, i.e. the meaning that they attribute to information. Manager capabilities are dependent on experience and basic understanding of the overall strategic process. It is particularly useful if managers are able to take a strategic perspective rather than a functional one because then they may perceive opportunities and threats in areas outside their own particular specialisms.

## Uncertainty, complexity and dynamism

Duncan (1972) argued that the environment is more uncertain the more complex it is or the more dynamic it is. An example of an organization facing a generally stable, non-dynamic and hence fairly certain environment is a small rural village post office. While most organizations face far more uncertainty, their managers also enjoy more challenges. In recent years the position of small village post offices has become more uncertain and many have closed. At the same time, however, The Post Office is looking at the possibility of offering a new range of banking services. The Post Office has realized that there is a window of opportunity as high-street banks consolidate and shut small branches. Moreover, they already have branches in every town and city that possess both spare capacity and a secure environment for handling cash. This development is not feasible without support and co-operation from the main clearing banks who, on the one hand, could benefit from the beneficial publicity, but, on the other hand, might see it constituting a new form of competition for some of their services. So far the banks have only co-operated reluctantly. The government has also announced plans for new computers which will allow post offices to become Internet centres with access to information of a variety of government services. If trials are successful this could enable more and more rural post offices to stay open.

While windows of opportunity are opening all the time, windows also close. In Spring 2000 the Dutch retail chain C & A announced that it was to close all its branches in the UK. The stores and their ranges had become unfashionable for many customers at a time when retail spending was pretty static, electronic commerce was increasing and new, more focused rivals, together with supermarkets such as Asda, were selling fashionable designs at low prices.

### The dynamic environment

Dynamism can be increased by a number of factors. Rapid technological change involving either products, processes or uses will mean that changes are likely to occur quickly and that organizations must stay aware of the activities of their suppliers and potential suppliers, customers and competitors. Where competition is on a global scale the pace of change may vary in different markets, and competition may be harder to monitor. In such cases the future is likely to be uncertain. Risk taking and creative entrepreneurial leadership may well be required as strategies pursued in the past, or modifications of them, may no longer be appropriate.

### The complex environment

An environment is complex where the forces and the changes involving them are difficult to understand. Quite often complexity and dynamism occur together. Technology-based industries and Internet-based businesses are excellent examples of this. The structure of the organization, the degree of decentralization and the responsibility and authority delegated to managers throughout the organization, and information systems can render complexity more manageable. Managers will need to be open and responsive to the need for change and flexible in their approach if they are to handle complexity successfully.

Managerial awareness and the approach to the management of change are therefore key issues in uncertain environments. If managers are strategically aware, and flexible and responsive concerning change, then they will perceive the complex and dynamic conditions as manageable. Other less aware managers may find the conditions so uncertain that they are always responding to pressures placed on the organization rather than appearing to be in control and managing the environment. Hence a crucial aspect of strategic management is understanding and negotiating with the environment in order to influence and ideally to control events.

## Environmental influences

Figure 6.1 showed how the organization is typically one of a number of competitors in an industry; and to a greater or lesser degree these competitors will be affected by the decisions, competitive strategies and innovation of the others. These interdependencies are crucial and consequently strategic decisions should always involve some assessment of their impact on other companies, and their likely reaction. Equally, a company should seek to be fully aware of what competitors are doing at any time.

Furthermore, this industry will be linked to, and dependent on, other industries: industries from which it buys supplies, and industries to which it markets products and services. Essentially this relates to Porter's model of the forces that determine industry profitability, which will be considered in Chapter 8. The relationships between a firm and its buyers and suppliers are again crucial for a number of reasons. Suppliers might be performing badly and as a result future supplies might be threatened; equally they might be working on innovations that will impact on organizations to which they supply. Buyers might be under pressure from competitors to switch suppliers. It is important to be strategically aware, and to seek to exert influence over organizations where there are dependencies.

These industries and the firms that comprise them are additionally part of a wider environment. This environment is composed of forces that influence the organizations, and which in turn can be influenced by them. Particular forces will be more or less important for individual organizations and in certain circumstances. It is important that managers appreciate the existence of these forces, how they might influence the organization, and how they might be influenced.

Mintzberg (1987) has used the term 'crafting strategy' to explain how managers learn by experience and by doing and adapting strategies to environmental needs. He sees the process as being analogous to a potter moulding clay and creating a finished object. If an organization embarks upon a determined change of strategy certain aspects of implementation will be changed as it becomes increasingly clear with experience how best to manage the environmental forces. Equally, managers adapt existing competitive and functional strategies as they see opportunities and threats and gradually change things. In each case the aim is to ensure that the organization's resources and values are matched with the changing environment.

## External forces: a PEST analysis

A PEST analysis is merely a framework that categorizes environmental influences as political, economic, social and technological forces. Sometimes two additional factors, environmental and legal, will be added to make a PESTEL analysis, but these themes can easily be subsumed in the others.

*Economic conditions* affect how easy or how difficult it is to be successful and profitable at any time because they affect both capital availability and cost, and demand. If demand is buoyant, for example, and the cost of capital is low, it will be attractive for firms to invest and grow with expectations of being profitable. In opposite circumstances firms might find that profitability throughout the industry is low. The timing and relative success of particular strategies can be influenced by economic conditions. When the economy as a whole or certain sectors of the economy are growing, demand may exist for a product or service which would not be in demand in more depressed circumstances. Similarly, the opportunity to exploit a particular strategy successfully may depend on demand which exists in growth conditions and does not in recession. Although a depressed economy will generally be a threat which results in a number of organizations going out of business, it can provide opportunities for some.

Economic conditions are influenced by *politics and government policy*; equally, they are a major influence affecting government decisions. The issue of whether European countries join, or remain outside, the single European currency is a case in point. At any one time either exported or imported goods can seem expensive or inexpensive, dependent upon currency exchange rates. There are many other ways, however, in which government decisions will affect organizations both directly and indirectly as they provide both opportunities and threats.

While economic conditions and government policy are closely related, they both influence a number of other environmental forces that can affect organizations. Capital markets determine the conditions for alternative types of funding for organizations; they can be subject to government controls, and they will be guided by the prevailing economic conditions. The rate of interest charged for loans will be affected by inflation and by international economics and, although the determining rate may be fixed by a central bank (as, for example, it is by the Bank of England) it will always be influenced by stated government priorities. Government spending can increase the money supply and make capital markets more buoyant. The expectations of shareholders with regard to company performance, their willingness to provide more equity funding or their willingness to sell their shares will also be affected.

The labour market reflects the availability of particular skills at national and regional levels; this is affected by training, which is influenced by government and other regional agencies. Labour costs will be influenced by inflation and by general trends in other industries, and by the role and power of trade unions.

The *sociocultural environment* encapsulates demand and tastes, which vary with fashion and disposable income, and general changes can again provide both opportunities and threats for particular firms. Over-time most products change from being a novelty to a situation of market saturation, and as this happens pricing and promotion strategies have to change. Similarly, some products and services will sell around the world with little variation, but these are relatively unusual. Figure 7.3 shows how washing-machine designs are different for different European countries to reflect consumer preferences. Organizations should be aware of demographic changes as the structure of the population by ages, affluence, regions, numbers working and so on can have an important bearing on demand as a whole and on demand for particular products and services. Threats to existing products might be increasing; opportunities for differentiation and market segmentation might be emerging.

*Technology* in one respect is part of the organization and the industry part of the model as it is used for the creation of competitive advantage. However, technology external to the industry can also be captured and used, and this again can be influenced by government support and encouragement. Technological breakthroughs can create new industries which might prove a threat to existing organizations whose products or services might be rendered redundant, and those firms which might be affected in this way should be alert to the possibility. Equally, new technology could provide a useful input, perhaps in both manufacturing and service industries, but in turn its purchase will require funding and possibly employee training before it can be used.

The examples referred to here are only a sample of many, and individual managers need to appreciate how these general forces affect their organization in particular ways. Table 7.1 provides a general list of environmental influences and forces. To provide a specific example, Box 7.2

*Figure 7.3* European preferences for washing machines.

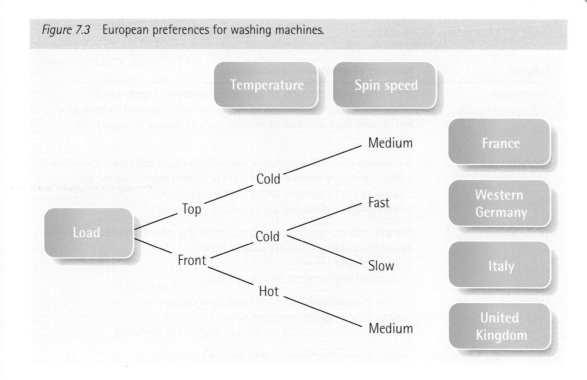

includes a short and very selective PEST analysis of environmental forces affecting the credit-card industry and picks out a number of key influences. It will be realized how such an analysis can be useful for helping to identify emerging opportunities and threats.

For any organization certain environmental influences will constitute powerful forces which affect decision making significantly. For some manufacturing and service businesses the most powerful force will be customers; for others it may be competition.

In some situations suppliers can be crucial. In the case of some small businesses external forces can dictate whether the business stays solvent or not. A major problem for many small businesses concerns the management of cash flow – being able to pay bills when they are due for payment and being strong enough to persuade customers to pay their invoices on time. A small subcontract metal-working business which works mostly for large car manufacturers and whose main supplier is a large organization such as Corus (previously British Steel) will have little power of persuasion. Payments may be delayed, and the customers will be too large and important to be threatened in any meaningful way, such as by the refusal to do any more work for them; meanwhile, the supplies will have to be paid for or future deliveries are likely to be suspended. While it is essential for all managers to have some insight into how their organization is affected by the environment, it is also desirable for them to consider how some of the environmental forces might be influenced and managed to gain benefits for the organization. This is less possible generally in the case of small businesses as they are less powerful. However, small companies should examine their environment for opportunities and threats in order to establish where they can gain competitive advantage and where their resources might most usefully be concentrated. For many not-for-profit organizations, such as subsidized theatres and major

*Table 7.1*   Environmental influences

| Influence | Examples of threats and opportunities |
|---|---|
| The economy | The strength of the economy influences the availability of credit and the willingness of people to borrow. This affects the level of demand. Interest rates and currency fluctuations affect both the cost and demand of imports and exports |
| Capital markets | This includes shareholders, and their satisfaction with company success. Are they willing to buy more shares if offered them to increase equity funding? Would they willingly sell if someone bid for the organization? Also included are the banking system, and the cost and availability of loan capital |
| Labour market | Changes in structure with an ageing population and more women seeking work<br>Availability of skills, possibly in particular regions<br>Influence of trade unions<br>Contribution of government training schemes |
| Technology | Robotics in manufacturing in such industries as car assembly<br>Computers for design and manufacturing<br>Information technology such as electronic point of sale in retailing |
| Sociocultural environment | Pressure groups affecting demand or industry location<br>Changing population – by age groups<br>Changing tastes and values<br>Regional movements |
| Government | Regional aid policies<br>Special industry initiatives, e.g. where high technology is involved<br>The legal environment is part of this, including the regulation of competition. Restraints on car exhaust emissions (pollution control) and labelling requirements would be other examples |
| Suppliers | Availability and cost of supplies, possibly involving vertical integration and decisions concerning whether to make or buy in essential components. |
| Customers | Changes in preferences and purchasing power<br>Changes in the distribution system |
| Competitors | Changes in competitive strategies<br>Innovation |
| The media | Effects of good and bad publicity, drawing attention to companies, products and services |

museums, the government constitutes a major environmental force because each of these organizations is dependent in different ways on government grants. In the UK, the National Health Service (NHS) is similarly very dependent upon government policies which affect all decision areas. Consultants' salaries, nurses' pay, new hospitals and wards, and new equipment are substantially determined by government decisions, which they will seek to influence.

STRATEGY IN ACTION – Box 7.2
A PEST Analysis of the Credit–card Industry

| | | | |
|---|---|---|---|
| **Political** | Legislation allowing young people to own credit cards | | Freedom for, or restrictions on, new entrants to the industry |
| | The threat of restrictions on Internet trading | **Social** | The willingness or reluctance to buy on credit – while credit is |
| **Economic** | The future presence – or not – of the UK, Denmark and Sweden in the Euro-Zone and the European single currency, and the impact of the single currency on interest rates generally | | readily available for many people, there can be a rebellion against high interest charges The increasing acceptance of Internet shopping, which depends on credit-card transactions – possibly affected by age profile of the population |
| | Future economic trends which will affect demand for consumption and credit | **Technical** | Internet and e-business possibilities – and security. |

## Ansoff's model

Ansoff (1987) contends that 'to survive and succeed in an industry, the firm must match the aggressiveness of its operating and strategic behaviours to the changeability of demands and opportunities in the market-place'. The extent to which the environment is changeable or turbulent depends on six factors:

- changeability of the market environment
- speed of change
- intensity of competition
- fertility of technology
- discrimination by customers
- pressures from governments and influence groups.

Ansoff suggests that the more turbulent the environment is, the more aggressive the firm must be in terms of competitive strategies and entrepreneurialism or change orientation if it is to succeed. The firms in an industry will be distributed such that a small number is insufficiently aggressive for the requirements of the industry, and as a result they are unprofitable or go out of business. Another small number will be above average in terms of success because they are best able to match the demands of the environment. Many will achieve results above average; and some others may also fail because they are too aggressive and try to change things too quickly through lack of awareness.

Where an organization is multiproduct or multinational the various parts of the business are likely to experience some common environmental influences and some which are distinctive, which reinforces the need for managers who are closest to the market and to competitors to be able to change things.

Ansoff suggests that the environment should be analysed in terms of competition and entrepreneurship or change. By attributing scores to various factors the degree of competitive and entrepreneurial turbulence can be calculated. The competitive environment is affected by market structure and profitability, the intensity of competitive rivalry and the degree of differentiation, market growth, the stage in the life of the products or services in question and the frequency of new product launches, capital intensity and economies of scale. Certain of these factors, namely market growth, the stage in the life of the product and profitability, also help to determine the extent to which the environment is entrepreneurial. Changes in structure and technology, social pressures and innovation are also influential.

The culture of the organization and managerial competencies should then be examined to see whether they match and be changed as appropriate if they do not. Again, scores are attributed to various factors. Culture encompasses factors such as values, reaction and response to change, and risk orientation. Problem-solving approaches, information systems, environmental forecasting and surveillance, and management systems are included in the competencies. Ansoff is really arguing that the resources of the organization and the values must be congruent with the needs of the environment.

## Competition and the Structure and Regulation of Industry

The four economic models of pure or perfect competition, monopolistic competition, oligopoly and monopoly were introduced in Chapter 3, when it was pointed out that the opportunity for substantial profits was most likely to be found in oligopoly and monopoly structures. Competition in the other models, resulting mainly from lower barriers to entry, has the effect of reducing profit margins. It is now useful to consider which models are dominant in the UK, and most other developed nations, as this influences the ways in which firms compete. Specifically, it affects the opportunities for differentiation and for the achievement of cost advantages which, as will be seen in Chapter 8, are major determinants of competitive advantage.

## Monopoly power

It is important to point out here that as far as the regulatory authorities are concerned a 25% market share offers opportunities for a company to exploit monopoly power, Hence, although the model of pure monopoly assumes only one producer with absolute power in the marketplace, a large producer with a substantial share will be regarded as having monopoly power. It does not follow that such power will be used against the consumer; on the contrary, it can be to the consumer's advantage. Large companies with market shares in excess of their rivals may be able to produce at lower cost (and sell at lower prices) for any one of several reasons, including the ability to invest in high-output, low unit cost technology; the ability to buy supplies in bulk and receive discounts; the ability to achieve distribution savings; and the opportunity to improve productivity as more and more units are produced. In fact, savings are possible in every area of the business. Economists call these savings economies of scale, and they are related to the notion of the experience or learning curve which is explained in a Finance in Action supplement to this chapter.

A cost advantage, then, can be a major source of competitive advantage, and this point will be developed in greater detail later. The producer who is able to produce at a lower cost than his or her rivals may choose to price very competitively with a view to driving competitors out of the market and thereby increasing market share. Equally he or she may not; and by charging a higher price can make a greater profit per unit and thereby seek profit in preference to market share. In the first case the consumer benefits from lower prices and therefore monopoly power is not being used against the consumer. However, once a firm has built up a truly dominant market share it might seek to change its strategy and exploit its power more. This is when governments need to intervene in some way.

## Concentration

Concentration is the measure of control exercised by organizations. There are two types.

*Aggregate concentration*, which will be mentioned only briefly, considers the power of the largest privately owned manufacturing firms in the economy as a whole.

*Sectoral or market concentration* traditionally considers the percentage of net output or employment (assets, sales or profits can also be measured) controlled by the largest firms in a particular industry, be it manufacturing or service. High concentration figures tend to encourage monopoly or oligopoly behaviour, most probably the latter, which implies substantial emphasis on differentiation and non-price competition, with rivals seeing themselves as interdependent.

Many industries world-wide are essentially oligopolistic in structure, with a limited number of major competitors and barriers to entry in individual countries. In general, competition will be non-price rather than price, but price competition will be seen in situations where supply exceeds demand and there is aggressive competition for market share.

There may well be marketing and distribution advantages for companies which belong to conglomerates and this could increase their relative market power. Similarly, products which dominate particular market segments will yield advantages. Consequently, there is still opportunity for smaller companies to compete successfully in certain oligopoly markets, especially if they can differentiate their product so that it has appeal for particular segments of the market.

In the chocolate industry Thornton's has been successful with a limited range of high-quality products distributed through the company's own specialist outlets. In contrast, certain industries exhibit very low concentration. Ladies' dresses are one example, and they are very much affected by fashion and the nature of the businesses which involve large numbers of part-time workers; leather goods are another, and here the barriers to entry are very low.

The UK exhibits higher concentration overall than is found in rival countries such as the USA and Germany, which have generally larger economies. However, UK companies, like many others around the world, have to compete in global markets, and therefore size is an important issue. After all, few British companies are dominant producers when considered in world terms.

The dilemma for government is to encourage firms to grow in size and become powerful competitive forces in world markets but at the same time to ensure that such size and power are not used to exploit consumers in the UK.

## The regulation of monopoly power

It is generally accepted in many countries that it is the state's role to monitor the forces of competition, to minimize any waste of resources due to economic inefficiency, to guard against any exploitation of relatively weak buyers or suppliers, and to ensure that powerful companies do not seek to eliminate their competitors purely to gain monopoly power.

Regulations are passed and implemented to police these issues. This section uses the situation in the UK to illustrate the point, but the principles and general approach are not unique to the UK. A new UK Competition Bill, passed in 1997 and operational in 1999, put the following structure in place.

In overall charge is the Department (or Minister) for Trade and Industry (DTI). Reporting to the DTI are two bodies. First, the Office of Fair Trading (OFT), headed by a Director-General, which has powers to carry out preliminary investigations of all proposed mergers or take-overs involving market shares of 25% or more, or combined assets in excess of £75 million. If the OFT believes that major competition concerns are present, then it can refer the proposal to a second body, the Competition Commission, for further investigation.

Each case is considered on merit, and the presumption is not automatically that monopoly power is against the public interest. High profitability is considered acceptable if it reflects efficiency, but not if it is sustained by artificial barriers to entry.

The delay involved in an investigation can be important strategically. The process is likely to take at least six months and in that time a company which opposes the take-over bid against it will work hard to improve its performance and prospects. If this results in a substantial increase in the share price the acquisitive company may withdraw on the grounds that the cost has become too high. Companies may seek to prevent a reference by undertaking to sell off part of the businesses involved in an acquisition if competition concerns are raised.

The DTI retains secondary powers to refer any bid directly to the Competition Commission.

In line with other countries in Europe, the OFT also polices a ban on anticompetitive agreements (such as price fixing or market share cartels) and anticompetitive behaviour such as predatory pricing by a dominant company. Offending firms can be fined up to 10% of their global turnover. Firms found guilty by the OFT have a right of appeal to the Competition Commission.

Since September 1990 the European Commission has also been able to influence the growing number of corporate mergers and acquisitions in the European Union (EU). Mergers are exempted, though, if each company has more than two-thirds of its EU-wide turnover in any one EU country.

## Examples of intervention

In February 2000 the Competition Commission in the UK ruled that Unilever should be banned from distributing its own Wall's ice cream direct to retailers. Wall's ice-cream products hold the largest market share in the UK, in excess of 50%. The argument was that a newly formed subsidiary, Wall's Direct, was undermining independent wholesalers and, as a consequence, competitors such as Nestlé and Mars were being squeezed out of the supply chain. The DTI chose to water down the ban and recommended a capping of the scope and extent of the distribution operation. Unilever, however, concluded that a cap was not feasible and it began to wind down its distribution.

In parallel with this investigation the Competition Commission had also looked at Unilever's practice of providing retailers with free freezer cabinets but insisting that they were used only for Wall's products. Small retailers, with room for just one freezer cabinet, were effectively prevented from stocking other brands. The Commission recommended that retailers should be allowed to fill up to half of the cabinet with rival products.

In 1998 BSkyB, part of the media group controlled by Rupert Murdoch, sought to buy a major shareholding in Manchester United, acknowledged to be the most valuable football club in the world. While the two activities may not appear to compete, the contractual arrangement between Sky Television and football's Premier League meant that there was a very clear relationship. It was felt that Manchester United and Sky could both benefit at the expense of rival football clubs and media companies, and consequently the OFT began an investigation. The concern was that Sky could be placed in a position where it could drive down the price that it paid for televising Premier League matches, particularly as Manchester United's matches are very popular with viewers as well as fans. The situation was compounded by the growing incidence of pay-per-view football. In the event the merger was not allowed to proceed. Instead, BSkyB, other media groups including Carlton and Granada, and the cable television company ntl, have all bought minority stakes in the most successful Premier League clubs.

Highlighting the global nature of competition regulation, Microsoft, dominant in personal computer operating systems, has been judged by an American court to be exploiting its monopoly power. In early 2000 it was ruled that the basic operating systems (based on Windows) and the applications (Microsoft Office and Internet Explorer) should be separated into two separate businesses, and that Microsoft should also be required to give away to its competitors some of its operating systems code. Inevitably the company has appealed against the ruling. The *Financial Times* commented: 'Surely, most seriously of all, is that at a time Microsoft should be

focusing all its talent on keeping up with technological innovation, it is hamstrung by this case'.

Minicase 7.3 describes the impact of regulation on the structure of the UK brewing industry over a period of years. Sometimes regulation produces unexpected and unpredicted outcomes; it is a grey world.

## Strategic Positioning and Adding Value

Strategic positioning and added value were defined and explained in Chapter 2, and this section builds on that introduction.

### Strategic positioning

Figure 7.4 emphasizes that effective strategic positions ensure that corporate strategic resources meet and satisfy key (or critical)

*Figure 7.4*  Strategic positioning revisited.

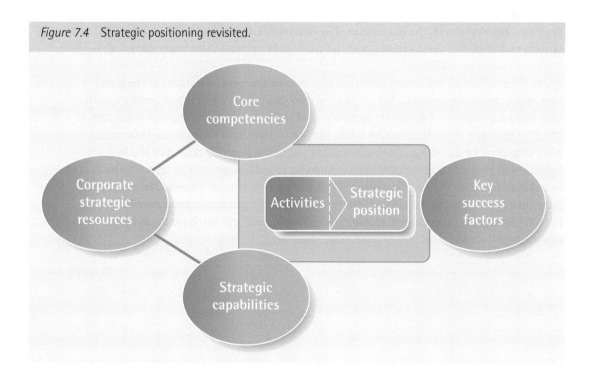

# Minicase 7.3 Regulation and the brewing industry

When governments interfere in industries, there will be forced changes which often open up new opportunities. After all, detailed reports from the UK Competition Commission often contain significant information which becomes freely available to competitors and industry outsiders.

An investigation by the Monopolies and Mergers Commission (the predecessor to the Competition Commission) into brewing resulted in the 1991 Beer Orders. The investigation was prompted by four brewers controlling 60% of brewing and 80% of the UK's 60,000 public houses. The Beer Orders required that brewers with over 2000 pubs had to divest half their estate. In addition, all pubs they retained had to offer 'guest beers', ones not produced by the owner–brewer. The intention was to break the tied link whereby particular beers could be forced on to tenants by the powerful brewers.

In response, the leading brewers set up independent companies to buy out their own pubs, typically with links back to the brewers who were loaning the money. Naturally, the brewers retained the most lucrative pubs in their estates. In reality, the tied link was never truly broken. At the same time, the brewers began to diversify into hotels and restaurants because they were unable to open any new pubs. Bass acquired Holiday Inn, for example. Bass also owns Harvester restaurants and Britvic soft drinks.Whitbread similarly built a portfolio which included Travel Inn, Marriott Hotels (in the UK), Beefeater, Brewers Fayre, the Bella Pasta, TGI Fridays (UK franchise) and Pizza Hut (another UK franchise) restaurants, and the wine and spirits retailers Wine Rack, Threshers and Victoria Wine.

The Beer Orders provided new opportunities for entrepreneurial outsiders. The guest beer requirement, for example, led to the growth of microbreweries, which produce only very limited quantities of generally very strong ales. Some pubs brew their own beer on-site. One manager with the Japanese bank, Nomura, came up with an idea to buy 2000 pubs from Bass for £2 billion. The bank had no interest in running pubs, but it was interested in property which could earn it some £300 million per year in rent. The bank raised the money for the deal by issuing bonds with a 10% annual interest. Simply, the bank raised £2 billion for an annual interest payment of £200 million and earned £300 million in rents – a £100 million annual profit. Simple, really, if you have the idea and the resources to back the deal!

By 1999 the situation was:

| | Percentage of UK beer sales | |
| --- | --- | --- |
| | On-trade | Take home |
| Scottish and Newcastle | 27 | 22 |
| Bass | 23 | 17 |
| Whitbread | 14 | 20 |
| Carlsberg–Tetley | 13 | 9 |
| Other companies | 23 | 32 |

The activity profile (percentages of total turnover) of the four leading brewers was as follows:

| | Bass | Whitbread | Scottish and Newcastle | Carlsberg–Tetley |
| --- | --- | --- | --- | --- |
| Brewing | 33 | 22 | 61 | 77 |
| Retail | 30 | 30 | 27 | 0 |
| Soft drinks | 11 | 10 | 0 | 8 |
| Other leisure activities | 26 | 38 | 12 | 15 |

Shortly afterwards, both Bass and Whitbread announced that they were to withdraw from brewing in favour of other leisure activities. The Belgian brewer of Stella Artois, Interbrew, expressed interest in acquiring breweries from both companies and thus became the UK market leader. Meanwhile, Scottish and Newcastle (S&N) acquired Kronenbourg to become Europe's second largest brewer, second only to Heineken. S&N also owns Lodge Inns, Chef and Brewer restaurants, and the Center Parcs and Pontin's holiday resorts. In 2000 S&N was looking to divest its least profitable pubs and Center Parcs.

QUESTION: Overall, have the Beer Orders really affected power and industry concentration in favour of the consumer?

*Bass*  http://www.bass-brewers.com
*Carlsberg-Tetley*  http://www.carlsberg.com
*Heineken*  http://www.heineken.com
*Interbrew*  http://www.interbrew.com
*Scottish and Newcastle*  http://www.scottish-newcastle.com
*Whitbread*  http://www.whitbread.co.uk

# Minicase 7.4  Flying Flowers

Flying Flowers, as the name suggests, sells flowers by post. The company was set up in Jersey in the Channel Islands in the early 1980s to save a struggling glasshouse business – a loss-making nursery needed and created a new opportunity. By 1996 turnover had grown to £35 million, with pre-tax profits of £4 million.

There are several key elements to the strategy and the success. First, the company holds only low stocks of the actual flowers, many of which it buys in cheaply from countries such as Colombia: flowers *from* Jersey does not have to mean flowers grown in Jersey!

Demand fluctuates markedly, peaking twice, at Christmas and Mother's Day, when the company typically receives 15,000 postal and 5000 telephone orders per day for a short period. Christmas sales amount to 5 million carnations in 330,000 boxed deliveries. Coping with this surge in demand is critical for success. The second key element therefore is staffing and staff management. As tourism is a leading source of employment in Jersey, and is strongest during the summer months, Flying Flowers is able to use casual hotel and restaurant staff. They are relatively plentiful on an island of scarce labour resources, and critically they are often laid off temporarily over Christmas and Mother's Day when tourism falls off.

Thirdly, the company uses a disused glasshouse to house a noisy, steam-breathing machine which produces polystyrene boxes every working day of the year. These are then piled high to ensure that any demand peak can be catered for.

Fourthly, and very critically, Flying Flowers has invested in IT to support both control and marketing. It holds a database on one million people and carefully targets its direct mail, analysing all responses and orders in detail. It has opened a telephone call centre in Witham, Essex.

Flying Flowers as a concept adds value for customers – high-quality, fresh flowers delivered directly to the door. Its operating costs are relatively low for the reasons described above and, of course, there are no returns to deal with.

The skills and competencies have been further exploited with the acquisition of other businesses. Flying Flowers bought Gardening Direct (mail-order bedding plants), Stanley Gibbons (publisher and stamp supplier) and another supplier of first-day covers.

QUESTIONS: How does Flying Flowers add value?
What is the nature of its strategic position?
Did the acquisitions make sense in relation to its competencies and capabilities?

*Flying Flowers*   http://www.jersey.co.uk/flyingflowers

## Minicase 7.5 Cargo Lifter

Cargo Lifter is a German manufacturer of airships. Mention of airships invariably brings to mind the tragic accident with the Hindenberg in 1937, such that airships have generally far more negative than positive connotations. In this disaster a passenger airship caught fire over New Jersey in the USA and 36 people died. While airships have been used ever since, mainly small ones for surveillance work and for advertising, they have been relatively low profile.

The new ships, scheduled to fly in 2003, will be different. They are to be 260 m long and carry a crew of ten. They can carry a payload of some 160 tonnes and fly non-stop for up to 10,000 km at speeds of 90 km per hour. Strong winds do not affect the flying, but they would affect take-off and landing. They are loaded and unloaded by special cranes and they can easily carry items such as power station turbines and railway carriages.

The opportunity that they satisfy is a need for worldwide movement of heavy payloads which are difficult to transport by road. Typically, very large loads move at less than 10 km per hour and so the airship implies a massive time saving on a long journey.

The hull is constructed from durable materials and filled with non-flammable helium, whereas the Hindenberg was filled with very flammable hydrogen! They have low-reviving diesel engines supplied by BMW and enjoy the benefits of satellite navigation systems.

QUESTIONS: Explain the strategic positioning of Cargo Lifter.
How is value added?
Can you think of other opportunities for this product?

*Cargo Lifter*   http://www.cargolifter.com

---

success factors for customers and markets. Strategically valuable resources translate into core competencies and strategic capabilities (as explained in Chapter 2), which are then manifest in a whole range of activities that the organization undertakes. The idea of activity mapping is developed in Chapter 8.

Competencies and capabilities can be separated by thinking of core competencies being built around technologies and technological skills, and strategic capabilities referring to processes and ways of doing things. Capabilities thus exploit the competencies; technology must, however, be developed to a particular level for a company to be influential in an industry or market. Hence, while the real competitive strength of an organization can be built around either competencies or capabilities, both must be present for relative success. Over time, both competency and capability must be improved with innovation. In Chapter 13 it is shown that people, learning and information are critical elements of this innovation. In addition, companies can benefit markedly from exploiting the linkages and relationships that they have with their suppliers and distributors.

It will be appreciated that an emphasis on key success factors – with a search for efficient, effective and imaginatively different ways of satisfying them – represents the market- or opportunity-driven approach to strategy, while exploiting competencies and capabilities is the resource-based approach. The market-driven approach places customers first, clarifying their needs and looking for new and different ways of satisfying them. The emphasis is on finding opportunities that competitors have yet to realize, and which ideally they will not be able to copy quickly. The resource-based approach is a search for better ways of utilizing and exploiting the strategic resources possessed by the organization. The two cases of Flying Flowers (Minicase 7.4) and Cargo Lifter (Minicase 7.5) illustrate the resource-based and opportunity-driven approaches. Flying Flowers shows how underutilized resources can be exploited to develop a new market; Cargo Lifter is a response to a perceived window of opportunity.

It should be understood that strategic positioning, per se, is not a source of competitive advantage. Any relative advantage enjoyed by the organization comes from the resources and activities which establish and support the posi-

In a fast-changing world where businesses are buffeted by external forces, managers need to be nimble to respond capably, to keep the company on track and to meet its objectives. They must be outwardly focused, aware of important trends that will impact on business or industry. They need to be opportunity-aware, without losing the more usual inward-looking focus on doing things better and responding to threats.

*Neville Bain, when Group Chief
Executive, Coats Viyella*

tion. This can be tangible or intangible in nature. It could come from specific technological skills, from the reputation that an organization enjoys or from the way that its people deliver service. Simply, these are the ways through which it creates and adds value.

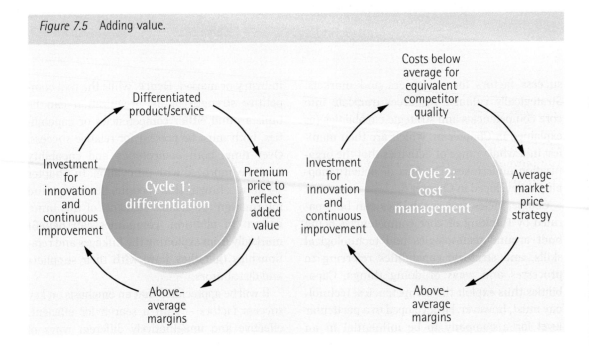

*Figure 7.5*   Adding value.

## Added value

Added value was introduced and explained in Chapter 2 (p. 61). In essence, an organization uses its various resources, tangible and intangible, to create value. In Chapter 9 it is shown how a value chain can be built which links the various internal activities and blends them with other key members of the whole supply chain. This value is then manifest in either differentiated products or services, or a cost advantage which can be partially passed on to customers in the form of lower prices. Figure 7.5 delineates two value-adding cycles, both of which can establish superior profits and allow for ongoing investment and innovation. They are not mutually exclusive, because whatever the competitive strategy, strong cost management is essential.

To be successful, products and services must fit into markets.[1] These could be global or local markets, mass or niche markets. The products could be essentially commodities or substantially customized. The market (or the relevant niche) could be growing, static or declining. Every one can be profitable, but in different ways, with different strategies. Companies which target new markets, segments or niches may find that they are hard to penetrate, unless they have developed something radically new and different which is seen as a valuable alternative by customers. After all, most successful companies have realized that it is more expensive to win new business than it is to retain existing customers and, as a result, look after their customers. While patents can provide a barrier to new entrants and new rivals, so too can loyal customers!

[1]Marketing and operations strategies are critical elements of competitive strategy but it is assumed that most readers will have already studied these topics elsewhere. However, a number of key points is included on the website to act as a reminder and reinforcement of the most significant aspects.

However, some markets may equally be difficult to defend. This would be the case where the wider business environment is dynamic and turbulent, where the organization enjoys only a relatively weak strategic fit and where the service being provided is below the level expected. Hence, positioning and fit can be improved with customer care, product and service innovation and improvement, and by developing new products. All of this requires that companies take their competitors seriously, defend against any initiatives that they start and, on occasion, attack them. This can imply any or all of the following:

- finding and opening new windows of opportunity
- product and service development, improvement and enhancement
- direct attacks, such as price wars, either 'all-out' and sustained or short-term and guerrilla. Special discount promotions would be an example of the latter
- attempting to change the 'rules of engagement or competition' either openly (with genuinely new ideas) or more deviously (lobbying government for new regulations or buying out a key supplier or competitor)
- a 'war of words', seeking publicity for your activities and carefully disparaging your competitors. Sir Richard Branson was able to strengthen the image and position of Virgin Atlantic when he drew attention to British Airways' so-called 'dirty tricks' campaign to win over Virgin customers
- networking and collaboration with key partners in the supply chain.

Minicase 7.6 (Sainsbury's) looks at opportunities for adding value and finding new windows of opportunity in a very competitive environment, and thus draws together many of these points.

To summarize this section, Markides (1999) provides a list of six factors for competitive and strategic success. These are:

# Minicase 7.6 Sainsbury's changing window of opportunity

Sainsbury's vies with Tesco for market leadership of the UK retail grocery industry. In the early 1990s Tesco increased its market share through a series of initiatives, including a loyalty card scheme, and both retailers reduced the prices of a large number of 'everyday' products. During the 1980s Sainsbury's, again like Tesco, had invested heavily in new superstores. A key challenge, critical for competitive advantage in the 1900s, was – and still is – customer service.

> *Our strategy is about giving better quality, about value for money. Our customers come in every week, perhaps twice a week, and buy a huge range of products. If we are not performing, that is seen very quickly.*
>
> (David Sainsbury, when Chairman)

Sainsbury began to address service more aggressively in the early 1990s. Head-office jobs were cut, but the number of staff in the stores was increased. Advertising was strengthened. A more extensive customer research programme revealed that shoppers were happy with Sainsbury's products but not its service. The major irritant was 'wonky' trolleys which prove difficult to steer in a straight line, followed by a lack of tills, the consequential long queues at the tills, product locations being changed too frequently, flimsy carrier bags, and fruit and vegetable bags which are difficult to open when they are removed from a roll. There were also complaints that check-out operators were scanning items more quickly than customers could pack them.

Sainsbury's introduced new policies. Once a check-out queue reached a certain size, another till would be opened. Customers asking about the location of a product were to be taken personally to the shelf rather than merely told where an item could be found. Staff were asked to cut the scanning speed from 22 to 18 items a minute.

Staff were involved extensively in the changes and £9 million was spent on retraining over an 18-month period.

However, Sainsbury's lost market leadership to Tesco in 1994 and has not regained it. Moreover, Asda (now Wal-Mart) has been closing the gap on the two leaders during the past five years. Sainsbury's profits have been affected – 1995 proved to be a 'high'.

Analysts contend that Sainsbury's costs are higher, reflected in margins of just 4%, while its rivals achieve 6%. They argue that the stores and distribution systems need streamlining. The average age of Sainsbury's retail depots is 21 years, and its IT systems are eight years old. Building and opening new stores is not enough.

Sainsbury still believes that it must retain a brand which stands for quality and value, and that these must be delivered and be seen to be delivered – but without any further price cuts, which would threaten margins further. Whether Sainsbury's can achieve and retain this, and stay a mainstream rather than a more niched competitor, is the key issue and the key challenge.

QUESTION: Tesco and Wal-Mart have been investing more aggressively and now enjoy a higher margin cushion. Is there a way back for Sainsbury's?

*Sainsbury's*   http://www.sainsburys.com

1. Choose a potentially winning position. This requires understanding *who* your customers are, *what* they require and expect and *how* they can be reached. This corresponds with Porter's (1996) view that it is essential to focus on certain activities and ignore others, not attempting to be 'all things to all people'.

2. Make this choice by a proper exploration of options, which implies.

3. An active search for opportunities to be different in a meaningful way, not just adopting a strategy because it seems to work.

4. Ensure all the support activities work together effectively and synergistically.

5. Create a real strategic fit and position which links the organization with its customers.

6. Ensure there is flexibility in both the activities and the fit so that innovation and change can sustain competitiveness.

## Appropriability

Kay (1993) uses the term 'appropriability' to make the point that organizations must seek to ensure that they see the benefits of the value which they create and add. After all, few things cannot be copied and some positions of advantage will be transient without improvement.

Value can be provided for customers in a whole variety of ways, but unless they are willing to pay a premium price which at least offsets the cost of adding the value, then it is the cus-

tomer and not the organization that benefits. Even if a premium price can be charged, if this is then used to reward suppliers and employees, additional profits may not accrue. Sometimes higher profits are used primarily to reward shareholders, or owner–managers in the case of small organizations. All of these possibilities imply that the organization is not creating and sustaining a position where it makes superior profits and uses these (at least in part) to reinvest and help to build new values through improvement and innovation. Quite simply, the ideal scenario is a virtuous one, where every stakeholder benefits.

Regulation of railways in the UK provides an excellent example of the inherent tensions. The network and infrastructure provider (Railtrack, which essentially maintains the lines, signalling and stations) and the train operating companies (such as Virgin Rail, GNER and the French company Connex and who provide the actual train services) are independent businesses with their own employees and shareholders. Sometimes customers travel on services provided by just one train operator, but many journeys mean that customers are shared. Standards of reliability and service do vary. The government wants more people to use the railways (and other forms of public transport) to reduce traffic on the roads. This will only happen if services are good and prices acceptable. But attractive wages, required to recruit and retain a high calibre of employee, impact on costs and prices. So too do requirements for investment in new infrastructure (to improve services) and safety, particularly after a series of high-profile crashes. If investment demands, together with restraints on prices and profits imposed by the rail regulator, result in reduced profits and dividends, the individual train companies will find it increasingly difficult to generate and raise the funds they need for ongoing investment and improvement. Without the improvement, of course, they are likely to be fined by the regulator, making the profit situation even more precarious. There could very easily be a vicious rather than a virtuous circle.

## SWOT (Strengths, Weaknesses, Opportunities and Threats) Analysis

Environmental opportunities are only potential opportunities unless the organization can utilize resources to take advantage of them and until the strategic leader decides that it is appropriate to pursue the opportunity. It is therefore important to evaluate environmental opportunities in relation to the strengths and weaknesses of the organization's resources, and in relation to the organizational culture. Real opportunities exist when there is a close fit between environment, values and resources. Similarly, the resources and culture will determine the extent to which any potential threat becomes a real threat. This is E–V–R congruence, which was explained in Chapter 2.

All of the resources at the disposal of the organization can be deployed strategically, including strategic leadership. It is therefore useful to consider the resources in terms of where they are strong and where they are weak as this will provide an indication of their strategic value. However, this should not be seen as a list of absolute strengths and weaknesses seen from an internal perspective; rather, the evaluation should consider the strengths and weaknesses in relation to the needs of the environment and in relation to competition. The views of external stakeholders may differ from those of internal managers (who in turn may disagree among themselves) when evaluating the relative strength of a particular product, resource or skill. Resources should be evaluated for their relative strengths and weaknesses in the light of key success factors.

Even though an organization may be strong or weak in a particular function, the corresponding position of its major competitors must also be taken into account. For example, it might have sophisticated computer-controlled machine tools in its factory, but if its competitors have the same or even better equipment, the plant should not be seen as a relative strength. This issue refers to distinctive competencies – relative strengths which can be used to create competitive advantage. As any resource can be deployed strategically, competitive advantage can be gained from any area of the total business.

An evaluation of an organization's strengths and weaknesses in relation to environmental opportunities and threats is generally referred to as a SWOT analysis.

As mentioned above, a mere list of absolute factors is of little use. The opportunities which matter are those that can be capitalized on because they fit the organization's values and resources; the threats which matter are those that the organization must deal with and which it is not well equipped to deal with; the key strengths are those where the organization enjoys a relatively strong competitive position and which relate to key success factors; the key weaknesses are those which prevent the organization from attaining competitive advantage.

Again, to be useful the lists of factors should be limited to those which matter the most, so that attention can be concentrated on them. In

| | | | |
|---|---|---|---|
| **Strengths** | Strong and visible brand and reputation Increasingly wide range of products and services Valuable database for cross-selling | | thus one of reach not further diversification Europe, where so far there has been only limited marketing effort to date |
| **Weaknesses** | Ill-judged move into the USA which reduced profits Late entrant into e-commerce – many over-50s do use the Internet! | **Threats** | Developing e-commerce may now prove to be too late, as others have targeted Saga's market – the power of the brand may, however, overcome the issue of the delay. |
| **Opportunities** | E-commerce, especially for deeper penetration into the USA. The issue for Saga is | | |

*Saga*   http://www.sagaholidays.com

arriving at such a summary SWOT statement it can therefore be useful to start by drawing up a large grid and using it for assessing relative importances.

The example in Box 7.3 (developed from Benoit, 1999) considers Saga, founded originally in 1951, which now provides a wide range of holidays and other services (including insurance and home shopping) for people over 50 years old, a clearly identified and targeted segment.

Figure 7.6 illustrates a popular and useful framework for a SWOT analysis applied to ASDA earlier in the 1990s, before the introduction of new strategies focusing on the product ranges, in-store layouts and a clear distinction between large ASDA superstores and smaller units with a limited range and discounted prices (called Dales), and finally its acquisition by Wal-Mart. The chart highlights how certain issues can be considered as either a strength or a weakness, an opportunity or a threat, depending on how they are managed in the future.

Once all of the important strategic issues have been teased out from a long list of strengths, weaknesses, opportunities and threats, the following questions should be asked.

- How can we either neutralize critical weaknesses or convert them into strengths?
- Similarly, can we neutralize critical threats or even build them into new opportunities?
- How can we best exploit our strengths in relation to our opportunities?
- What new markets and market segments might be suitable for our existing strengths and capabilities?
- Given the (changing) demands of our existing markets, what changes do we need to make to our products, processes and services?

Finally, alongside a general SWOT analysis, it is essential to evaluate the relative strengths and weaknesses of the company's leading competitors.

## Forecasting the Environment

A complex and dynamic modern environment is inevitably difficult to forecast; the inherent uncertainties can make it highly unpredictable and potentially chaotic. External events and competitor activities can trigger a chain

**Figure 7.6    ASDA: SWOT analysis, early 1990s.**

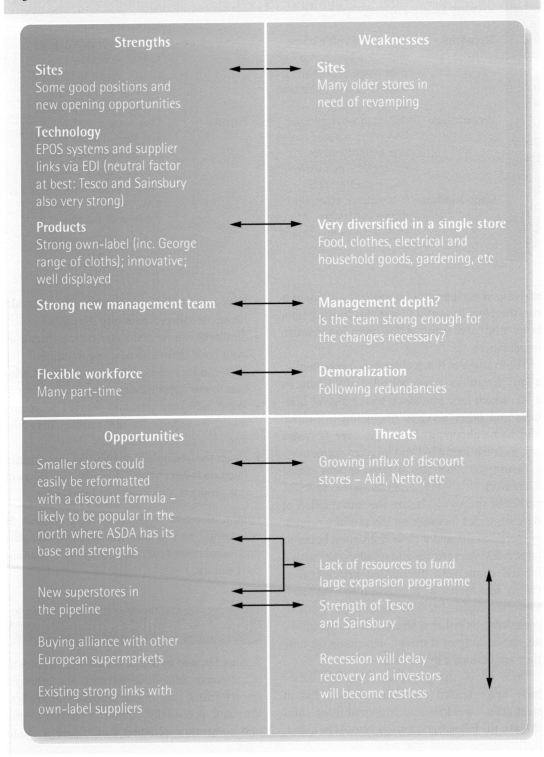

reaction of responses and new scenarios; but Handy (1989) contends that 'those who know why changes come waste less effort in protecting themselves or in fighting the inevitable'. Consequently, however difficult it may be to forecast environmental change, organizations must attempt to stay strategically aware. They should reflect upon their experiences and look for emerging patterns or trends in the industry and business environment. They should be vigilant in tracking technological and other developments which may affect, possibly radically, their industries and markets. They should look for, and maybe even borrow or 'steal', appropriate ideas. New management literature can help; so too can reports of good practice in a whole variety of different organizations.

In analysing the environment managers should seek to do the following.

- Identify which forces are most important, and why they are critical. This will reflect opportunities and threats.
- Forecast how these forces might change in the future, using whatever methods are appropriate.
- Incorporate these expectations and predictions into decision making and management thinking. Fahey and King (1983) have emphasized the usefulness of including line managers from the whole organization in any teams which are specifically charged with environmental analysis, as this can lead to more effective dissemination of information to enable it to be used in decision making. Managers will be individually aware of many changes in the environment. Where strategic change takes place incrementally through managers with delegated authority, this information can be easily incorporated in decisions. However, where major strategic change is being considered centrally by the strategic leader it is important to gather the relevant data together.

- Be honest and realistic when evaluating strengths and weaknesses relative to competitors, and when considering the organization's ability to respond to opportunities and threats. The environment should be managed wherever possible, and managers should seek to ensure that their resources are compatible with the organization's environment and the factors and forces that will influence and determine success.

This last factor implies that forecasts should be as realistic as possible; they should be used in decision making and for the determination of future strategy; and the implications of changes in the environment should be acted upon and not ignored.

Individual managers will develop their environmental and strategic awareness through experience and perception, and by thinking about their observations and experiences. It is particularly important to assess the significance of what happens and what can be observed to be happening. However, in considering future strategic changes there will be an additional need to forecast the changes that might take place in the environment concerning supplies, customers, competitors, demand, technology, government legislation and so on. Some of the future changes may be forecast through straightforward extrapolation of past events; many will not. Some of the environmental forces can be better quantified than others, and consequently some subjectivity will be involved. Hogarth and Makridakis (1981) have argued that the overall performance of organizations in predicting future changes is poor, and that the most sophisticated methods of forecasting are not necessarily the best. However, despite the difficulties, forecasting is important. Managers who are encouraged to think about future changes, to ask questions and to query assumptions will increase their insight and awareness and this should help decision making.

What, then, do managers need to forecast, and how might the forecasting be carried out?

*The economy* and the possible impact of economic changes can be assessed in a number of ways. Economic growth, inflation, government spending, interest rates, exchange rates, the money supply, investment and taxation may all be influential. The Treasury provides forecasts periodically, based on its own econometric model. Some universities and business schools also publish predictions based on their econometric models. Sometimes they are in agreement, but often they are not. Analysts from City institutions are regularly quoted on television and radio news programmes, and again there is often disagreement. The problem lies in the number of interrelationships and interdependencies amongst the economic variables and in imperfect understanding of the cause and effect relationships. In addition, economic forces and changes around the world, such as changes in the exchange value of key currencies, inflation rates in major markets such as the USA and balances of payments in different countries, can all affect the UK and organizations based in the UK, especially those with overseas interests. Although nor all changes can be forecast with great accuracy, managers should be aware of what is happening at the moment and the implications of any trends that can be observed.

*Demographic influences* include some that can be forecast reasonably well and some that are more unpredictable. Changes in population structure can be readily forecast; changes in tastes and values are more difficult. Again, it is essential to be able to appreciate the significance of observed events and changes. The government provides statistics on social trends, which give some insight, but organizations need to be continually aware rather than rely on statistics which are a little dated when published.

At one level this issue is relatively clear: there is a general breakdown of two-parent families, a growth in the number of older and retired people, and a decline in those aged 15–24. But what are the implications? Categorizing people into socioeconomic or house-type groupings has often been used to try and understand demand patterns, but the situation remains complex. Individual firms must conduct attitude and behavioural research. Why, for example, does a friend of the author drive a £30,000 car but wear a £20 wristwatch? Why does his wife buy premium-price luxury ice cream and the cheapest own-label toilet paper?

*Political influences* relate to changes in governments and their priorities and legislation programmes. Opinion polls help in forecasting the former, and indications of the latter are readily available. However, planned legislation is not always passed, for various reasons.

Developing from this is the need to forecast how certain laws and regulations might be implemented. Organizations considering mergers or acquisitions must try to predict whether a referral to the Competition Commission is likely before mounting their bid. Contacts within the so-called corridors of power can be of great benefit.

Demographic and political forecasting often relies on expert opinion, which can be obtained through personal contacts, commissioned research or published information in journals and newspapers. Outside opinions may well be biased or prejudiced because of strong views on certain issues or because of political perspectives, and this must be taken into account. Wilson (1977) has shown how probability-diffusion matrices can be useful here. Where opinions concerning the likelihood or probability of certain events are being gathered it is useful to plot both the strength of feeling (high or low probability of occurrence) and the diffusion of opinion (consistency or dispersion) among the sources or experts.

*Technological forecasting* covers changes in technology generally, and the possible impact of innovations which result from research and development by an organization, by its competitors and by other firms with which it is involved in some way. Expert opinion through scenario planning and from technical journals can be useful. Technological changes can have an impact throughout an organization and consequently it is useful for managers in various functions to consider the possible effects on them.

This issue has been manifested in the need for organizations to come to terms with the threats and opportunities posed by the Internet, both for information movement and for e-commerce. The Internet has expanded more rapidly than many people thought credible just a few years ago and many organizations are a long way from exploiting its potential. However, there are inbuilt dilemmas. For example, only one in seven German and Italian adults possesses a credit card, essential for buying on-line. Buying on-line for home delivery has varying degrees of relevance in different countries. Many Europeans live relatively close to the shops concerned and can easily fetch the goods themselves. In addition, relatively few Europeans have the larger, American-style, outside postboxes which can accept small parcel deliveries when people are out.

Don't try to eliminate uncertainty . . . embrace it. Despite overwhelming evidence to the contrary many of us still view the future as an extension of the past.

*Clem Sunter, Anglo American Corporation of South Africa (the world's largest mining group)*

The world's changing. People in the US and Europe aren't going to live the way they do 100 years from now unless they do a lot of things differently. Who says that because we have 240 million people on this big piece of land [USA] we should have two cars and second homes, while 800 million people in India and 1 billion in China should live the way they live? We've only been wealthy in this country for 70 years. Who said we ought to have all this? Is it ordained?

*John F. Welch, Chairman and CEO, General Electric*

## Scenario Planning

Scenarios are often used in strategic management to explore future possibilities. Possible happenings and events are considered by looking at potential outcomes from particular causes and seeking to explain why things might occur. The value is in increased awareness by exploring possibilities and asking and attempting to answer 'what if' questions. Although scenario planning can be predictive and can be used to plan strategic changes, it can also help decision making by providing managers with insight so that they can react better when things

happen or change. It can also be helpful for conceptualizing possible new competitive paradigms.

Environments for many organizations have become – and continue to become – increasingly dynamic, turbulent and uncertain. They feature an element of competitive chaos, where companies continually thrust and parry with new ploys and stratagems in an attempt to, at the very least, stay 'in the game' and, ideally, get ahead of their rivals. Scenarios and scenario planning concern the medium- or long-term future and they embrace the possibility of real and dramatic change. Anticipation and creativity can be invaluable in dealing with the turbulence and uncertainty. By considering and evaluating future possibilities, organizations can put themselves in positions where they might be better placed to deal with the unpredictable challenges of the future. Put another way: simply engaging in the process of acknowledging and anticipating change enables managers to be less shocked by whatever change does occur.

Three central themes underpin effective scenario planning:

- It is important to clarify just what a business can and cannot change. Small farmers, for example, cannot enjoy the scale economies of large farms, nor can they affect the climate. They can, within reason, improve their soil and they can change their crops.
- What seems trivial or a pipe-dream today could be crucial in the future. In 1874, Western Union in America turned down Alexander Graham Bell's prototype telephone!
- Multiple scenarios need to be explored and then *held* as real possibilities. Shell, which pioneered scenario planning, is arguably ready to respond quickly to shocks which affect supply or prevailing prices.

The scenarios considered may involve modified versions of current competitive paradigms (the future is not the past, but at least the two are related) or radically new paradigms (everything changes in the end). The implications of the scenarios will tend towards one of two themes: first, there will be environmental changes but organizations can learn to cope with, and influence or manage events, and thereby enjoy some degree of relative stability; secondly, the environmental turbulence will be so great that the competitive situation will become ever more chaotic in nature.

Readers might like to consider a number of emerging issues in the UK, evaluate their significance and implications and, where appropriate, consider how they might apply in their own countries.

- People are living longer; there is an ageing population. But will the more recent trend of people retiring earlier, many on good pen-

sions, continue? As people are healthier, is it not logical for them to work longer, as long as employers do not discriminate on age grounds? Of course, for some jobs skills can become outdated and people do become less useful. There is also the key dilemma of pensions. If people retire relatively early and live longer, there are two implications: one is that they will have to accept lower pensions; the other is that those people still in employment will have to pay far higher contributions to build up and sustain the pension funds.

- According to most published statistics, unemployment is coming down, yet, at the same time, there are growing skills shortages. Developing the point above, raising the retirement age could help here, but only for some jobs. In a knowledge-based society, does the need for skill retraining and updating become more critical through a person's working life?
- The NHS is stretched and private medicine is expensive. This could become more problematical as people live longer and especially if pensions are reduced. Hence, economically, people might need to work longer.
- However, if the relative balance between salaried and 'permanent' career posts and self-employed people who contract themselves to various organizations continues to change, this issue of the length of working lives could be exacerbated.
- In addition, it is becoming increasingly difficult for many families to prepare for retirement because of the increasing costs of educating their children. In turn, this increases the number of two-income families and creates a larger number of child-care positions.

## Developing useful scenarios

Organizations should really be looking to develop a number of scenarios that can be used to provoke debate among managers and possibly generate new creative ideas in the process – ideas that can be used as a basis for new strategies and action plans.

The first step is to clarify the *key strategic issues*, mainly external, which will impact on the future that the company will face. Internally, many managers will already have formed views, which may not always accord, and which may be partial rather than comprehensive, but these preliminary views will have caused the development of current working assumptions about future trends. It is invariably invaluable to also consult outside experts.

There are three types of issue to consider:

- *predetermined elements* – for example, *social* changes to the size and structure of the population, lifestyles and values
- *key uncertainties* – *political* changes and the inevitable *economic* changes which accompany it; the entry of new competitors; possible changes of corporate ownership
- *driving forces* – developments in *technology* and education.

The link to a PEST analysis will be clearly seen.

The next step is to examine a number of *plausible outcomes* from the various key issues. It is particularly important to debate issues of positive and negative synergy, specifically the impact of interconnectedness. The discussions should generate some consensus, or possibly, and more realistically, accommodation on priorities, in the form of *viable scenarios* to test further.

These will often be presented as *stories*, illustrated creatively to generate interest and enthusiasm.

The *tests* against which they will be ultimately evaluated are:

- What has been left out? – in effect, the extent of the comprehensiveness and the absence of key omissions – and

- Do they lead to clearer understanding which informs future decisions and actions, while winning the commitment of everyone involved?

Box 7.4 provides a number of examples.

## The dream society

Jensen (1999) contends that we shall soon be living in a 'dream society' where the stories attributed to products and services – their image and reputation – will be an increasingly significant aspect of competitive advantage. Examples might relate to free-range eggs, organic vegetables and celebrity-endorsed training shoes. Simply, the story adds value.

Jensen provides a number of themes for those organizations interested in creating 'dreams':

- adventure     Involvement in the 'great outdoors' or leisure activities. Manchester United branded clothing appears to combine both
- networks     BT (British Telecom) capitalized on this with its 'family and friends' name for its discounted call scheme as well as the television advertisements which feature ET and which, for example, link an absent father with his son for a game of chess
- self-discovery     Linked to products which allow people to say something about themselves. This theme has been exploited by VW (Volkswagen) with advertisements for the Golf which claim the only statement it needs to makes is 'gone shopping'

!

### British Airways (BA)

BA believes that annual planning meetings (which are valuable and have a role to play) 'do not help people think about what might happen a decade from now'. Moreover, 'people have difficulty envisaging dramatic change'.

Consequently, in the mid-1990s, BA created two scenarios for the period to 2005, which it used in management meetings to provoke discussion about the implications of possible changes. These are known as *Wild Gardens* and *New Structures*.

*Wild Gardens* postulates a world where market forces are unleashed. Asian markets in particular grow rapidly and, early in the twenty-first century, after a period of strong growth, the USA falls into a long recession. The 1996/97 general election in the UK is won for a fifth consecutive time by the Conservatives; the country remains divided over Europe. The EU is enlarged to bring in more Eastern countries, but there is no single currency. The European Commission takes over negotiation of airline agreements from member governments, and concludes an Atlantic open-skies agreement which gives free access to transatlantic routes to carriers from both Europe and the USA. Access to domestic airports in Europe and the USA is widened.

The *New Structures* scenario is more stable, and gives greater control to individual governments. Asia's rise proves to be slower than initially anticipated, and Asian investment is reduced. Labour comes to power in the UK and joins France and Germany in promoting stronger European integration. A single currency (the Euromarque) is agreed, together with integrated air-traffic control and a European high-speed rail network. There is increased commitment to the environment. In the USA,

President Clinton remains in power and reaches agreement with the Republicans to work together to increase investment and productivity. Taxes are increased; defence expenditure is reduced. North Korea provokes a security crisis in Asia and China suffers unrest after the death of Deng Xiaoping.

In discussions, BA managers believed that *New Structures* implied greater emphasis on ethical issues and customers who demand increased personal attention. *Wild Gardens* could mean that English ceases to be the international language and that fluency in Asian languages would inevitably be more important. As outcomes:

- BA decided to trial interactive television screens in airport lounges, allowing travellers to raise issues with an employee whose face they can see
- BA began investigating a single database covering its customers around the world
- there were discussions with partner, airlines Qantas and US Air, concerning the implications of *Wild Gardens*. Even if Asia developed more slowly, the language implications would not disappear.

*British Airways*
http://www.britishairways.com

### Motor vehicles

Historically, most car makers have seen engine and other technologies as key core competencies – and they have invested in research and development to enhance their competency. Many would argue they have placed less emphasis on marketing issues. This might well reflect a harder, male image of cars and, as a possible scenario, a softer and so-called female style might be envisioned. While technology improvements tend to be incremental, this might imply more radical changes of design.

Areas for debate might then include the following.

- Why not see the driver's side and the passenger side as quite separate instead of basically replicating the layout of one in the other? Do the seats need to be designed the same? Would passengers enjoy more working or reading space?
- Should optional and child-orientated rear seating areas be considered? Could these be flexible and easily changed when the car changes hands?
- Could doors which are ideal for older and more infirm people be another option?

The debate could be extended to consider cars as something more than a means of transport. For some, they are almost a mobile office in any case. Certain customized – and premium-price – cars already provide telecommunications links.

Can lessons be applied to less expensive cars? This could, of course, be tied in with the whole issue of how motorists might receive more accurate and timely information about road and weather conditions on both the route they are following and the alternative rerouting options open to them. As motorists, we often feel frustrated about the lack of hard information while realizing we are in an information age!

### References

Barnett, S (1996) Style and strategy: new metaphors, new insights, *European Management Journal*, **14**, 4, August.

Moyer, K (1996) Scenario planning at British Airways – a case study, *Long Range Planning*, **29**, 2.

| | |
|---|---|
| • peace of mind | Security, often linked to the perceived safety of the known past. Perhaps this explains why VW has been able to relaunch the Beetle model and BMW a new Mini (a model that it acquired when it owned Rover) |
| • caring | Businesses can exploit their community links and programmes |
| • convictions | Ethical and environmental concerns are prominent. The Body Shop built a successful business around this, as shown in Chapter 3. |

## Summary

Organizations operate with external environments that spring surprises on them from time to time. Indeed, many industries and markets are characterized by a form of 'competitive chaos' which arises from the natural dynamism, turbulence and uncertainty of both the industry and the environment.

It can make sense for the organization to see its boundary with the environment as relatively fluid. While suppliers, distributors and customers can be seen as outside the organizational boundary, they can also be identified as partners in a collaborative network which, more holistically, bounds with a number of external influences and forces.

Organizations must be able to react to the change pressures imposed by their environment (potential threats) and, at the same time, take advantage of opportunities which seem worthwhile. But this is arguably not enough. Leading organizations will create and sustain positions of strength by seeking to influence – and maybe even manage – their external environment.

A *PEST* (political, economic, social and technological forces) analysis provides a valuable framework for analysing relevant environmental forces.

Over time, strong competitors create and seek to hold positions of power in markets and industries. For this reason governments everywhere will seek to exercise some degree of control. In the UK the relevant bodies are the Office of Fair Trading and the Competition Commission. However, in certain instances, UK companies will also be subject to regulation by the European Union.

Regulation is rarely clear-cut or 'black and white' and sometimes the outcomes are not quite the ones desired.

To manage, and manage in, its environment an organization will need strong strategic positions. This implies finding and exploiting opportunities for adding value, in ways that consumers value and for which they will reward the organization with prices that imply superior margins.

Here we are talking about finding an effective blend between the opportunity-driven approach to strategy creation and the resource-based approach.

As organizations seek to exploit their *core competencies* and *strategic capabilities* to add value in this way, it is important that the value is appropriable. In other words, the benefits should not all go to shareholders (through high dividends), consumers (in, say, the form of relatively low prices) or employees (generous remuneration) such that the organization has inadequate resources for investment to build new ways of adding value for the future.

A *SWOT* (strengths, weaknesses, opportunities and threats) analysis is a second valuable framework for evaluating the position of an organization in relation to its environment. It is, however, important that the SWOT analysis is used to create ideas and is not just seen as a static statement of position.

Taking this further, it is important that organizations attempt to forecast their environment, however difficult this may prove. *Scenario planning* can make a very valuable contribution here.

## References

Ansoff, HI (1987) *Corporate Strategy*, Penguin.

Benoit, B (1999) Nearing 50, hale and hearty on home ground – a corporate profile of SAGA, *Financial Times*, 23 November.

Duncan, R (1972) Characteristics of organizational environments and perceived environmental uncertainty, *Administrative Science Quarterly*, 313–27.

Fahey, L and King, R (1983) Environmental scanning for corporate planning. In *Business Policy and Strategy: Concepts and Readings*, 3rd edn (eds DJ McCarthy *et al.*), Irwin.

Handy, C (1989) *The Age Of Unreason*, Hutchinson.

Hogarth, RM and Makridakis, S (1981) Forecasting and planning: an evaluation, *Management Science*, 27, 115–38.

Jensen, R (1999) *The Dream Society*, McGraw Hill.

Kay, JA (1993) *Foundations of Corporate Success*, Oxford University Press.

Markides, C (1999) Six principles of breakthrough strategy, *Business Strategy Review*, 10, 2, Summer.

Mintzberg, H (1987) Crafting strategy, *Harvard Business Review*, July–August.

Porter, ME (1996) What is strategy?, *Harvard Business Review*, November–December.

Wilson, IH (1977) Forecasting social and political trends. In *Corporate Strategy and Planning* (eds B Taylor and J Sparkes), Heinemann.

Test your knowledge of this chapter with our online quiz at: http://www.thomsonlearning.co.uk

Explore Environmental Analysis and Strategic Positioning further at:

*Business Strategy Review*   http://www.blackwellpublishers.co.uk/journals/BSR

## Questions and Research Assignments

### TEXT RELATED

1. Draw a diagram incorporating the environmental influences and stakeholders for any pub, discotheque or nightclub with which you are familiar.
   Do the same for London Zoo (Chapter 3, Minicase 3.4).

   *Zoological Society of London/London Zoo*   http://www.londonzoo.co.uk

2. Evaluate the threats and opportunities faced by any organization with which you are familiar.

3. From this evaluation, develop a SWOT analysis and consider the strategic implications.

4. Possibly in a group discussion, build a scenario relevant for the motor vehicle industry in ten years' time. How will people be using their cars? What will they expect in terms of size, performance, and external and interior design?

## Internet and Library Projects

1. How have changes in competition from around the world affected the UK footwear industry? What are the strategies of the leading, remaining manufacturers?
   You may wish to use a leading manufacturer such as C&J Clark as a key reference point. You should also look at a specialist such as Grenson or Church's. You might also investigate the source of your personal wardrobe of shoes, boots and trainers.

   *C&J Clark*   http://www.clarks.com
   *Church's*   http://www.churchsshoes.com
   *Grenson*   http://www.grenson.co.uk

2. How has Steve Pateman, owner of a family boot and shoe business in Northamptonshire, dealt with the pressures for change in this industry? How has the company diversified, and what do you think the implications are?

3. From your own experience, and from newspaper and other articles you have read or seen, list examples of where monopoly power and restrictive practices have been investigated, and where proposed mergers have been considered by the Competition Commission (or its predecessor the Monopolies and Mergers Commission). Evaluate the recommendations and outcomes. If you wish to follow up any of these investigations, all of the reports are published by HMSO.

   *Monopolies and Mergers Commission UK*   http://www.coi.gov.uk/coi/depts/GMM/GMM.html
   *HMSO UK*   http://www.hmso.gov.uk

# Finance in Action

# The Experience Curve

A large size, relative to competitors, can bring benefits. In particular, if a company has a market share substantially greater than its competitors it has opportunities to achieve greater profitability. Lower costs can be achieved if the company is managed well and takes advantage of the opportunities offered by being larger. These lower costs can be passed on to the consumer in the form of lower prices, which in turn puts pressure on competitors' profit margins and strengthens the position of the market leader.

Lower costs are achieved through economies of scale and the experience or learning effect. In the 1960s the Boston Consulting Group in the USA estimated that the cost of production decreases by between 10% and 30% each time that a company's experience in producing the product or service doubles, as long as the company is managed well. In other words, as cumulative production increases over time there is a potential cost reduction at a predictable rate. The company learns how to do things better. The savings are spread across all value-added costs: manufacturing, administration, sales, marketing and distribution. In addition, the cost of supplies decreases as suppliers experience the same learning benefits.

The experience effect has been observed in high- and low-technology industries, in new and mature industries, in both manufacturing and service businesses, and in relation to consumer and industrial markets. Specific examples are cars, semiconductors, petrochemicals, long-distance telephone calls, synthetic fibres, airline transportation, crushed limestone and the cost of administering life insurance.

The experience curve is illustrated by plotting on a graph the cumulative number of units produced over time (the horizontal axis) and the cost per unit (the vertical axis), as shown in Exhibit 1. This particular curve is called an '85% experience curve' as every time output is doubled the cost per unit falls to 85% of what it was. In reality, the plot will be of a least-squares line but the trend will be clear. However, it is more common to plot the data on logarithmic scales on both axes, and this shows the straight-line effect illustrated in Exhibit 2.

Sources of the experience effect

- increased labour efficiency through learning and consequent skills improvement
- the opportunity for greater specialization in production methods
- innovations in the production process
- greater productivity from equipment as people learn how to use it more efficiently
- improved resource mix as products are redesigned with cost savings in mind.

This is not an exhaustive list and the savings will not occur naturally. They result from good management.

## Pricing Decisions and the Experience Effect

A market leader or other large producer who enjoys a cost advantage as a result of accumulated experience will use this as the basis for a pricing strategy linked to his or her objectives, which might be profit or growth and market share orientated. Exhibit 3 illustrates one way in which industry prices might be forced down (in real terms, after accounting for inflation) as the market leader benefits from lower costs. Initially, prices are below costs incurred because of the cost of development. As demand, sales and production increase prices fall, but at a slower rate than costs; the producer is enjoying a higher profit margin. This will be attractive to any competitors or potential competitors who feel that they can compete at this price even if their costs are higher. If competition becomes intensive and the major producer(s) wish to assert authority over the market they will decrease prices quickly and force out manufacturers whose costs are substantially above theirs. Stability might then be restored.

Companies with large market shares can therefore dictate what happens in a market, but there is a need for caution. If a company ruthlessly chases a cost advantage via the experience effect the implication could be ever-increasing efficiency as a result of less flexibility. The whole operating system is geared towards efficiency and cost savings. If demand changes or competitors innovate unexpectedly the strategy will have run out of time, as we have already seen. Companies should ensure that they are flexible enough to respond.

*Exhibit 1*  An 85% experience curve plotted on a normal scale.

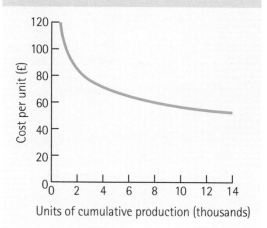

*Exhibit 2*  The same 85% experience curve plotted in log–log form.

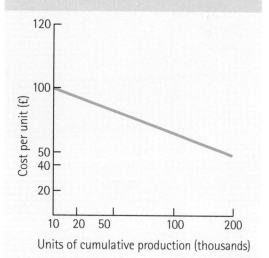

This material has mainly been summarized from Abell, DF and Hammond, JS (1979) *Strategic Market Planning: Problems, and Analytical Approaches*, Prentice-Hall.

Exhibit 3 is adapted from The Boston Consulting Group (1972) *Perspectives on Experience*.

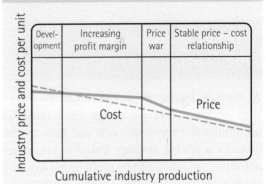

*Exhibit 3*   Pricing in relation to costs and the experience effect.

# The Dynamics of Competition

Competition: An Introduction

Analysing An Industry

Competitive Strategy

Competitive Advantage and Competitive Success

The Dynamics of Competition

Concluding Comments

*Few companies enjoy the luxury of having no serious competitors or little likelihood of any need to change their competitive strategy. It is essential for companies to look for opportunities to create – and sustain – a competitive edge over their rivals and build customer loyalty that provides something of a comfort zone. Logically this should lead to superior profits. However, competitive advantage, as a term, is easily misunderstood. Some organizations clearly believe, and thus delude themselves, that a clear competitive strategy constitutes advantage. It does not. Advantage comes from being better or different in some meaningful way. Even the strongest companies cannot afford to stand still, as shown in Minicase 8.1. A cynic would argue that a company must change more rapidly than its rivals can steal its ideas!*

*This chapter begins by looking at the nature of competition in general, before discussing models and frameworks which help us to understand industries, competitive strategy, competitive advantage and competitive dynamics.*

Minicase

# Minicase 8.1   Coca–Cola

Although it is typically priced higher than many competing products, Coca-Cola (Coke) remains the world's best-selling soft drink and the world's best-known brand name. Coca-Cola is reputed to see its only serious competitor as water! Ideally an adult requires a daily liquid intake of 64 ounces, and overall Coke provides just two of these. The Coca-Cola company was founded over 100 years ago, and today it remains largely focused; Columbia Pictures was acquired some years ago, but later sold to Sony. Seventy per cent of Coke's sales and 80% of its operating profits are now earned outside the USA. The company has a 50% share of the world market for carbonated drinks, including 44% of the US market. A typical American adult who drinks Coke will consume 400 eight-ounce servings in a year, just over one a day. Because Americans own very large refrigerators which can store the largest bottles available, this can work out relatively inexpensive. By contrast, a regular British Coke drinker consumes 120 eight-ounce servings in a year, from smaller and more expensive bottles and cans. The UK is still perceived to be a developing market for the product. Other 'established' territories, which include Switzerland, Chile and Mexico, have a consumption of 300 eight-ounce servings per year.

Over the years critics have predicted that something would happen to stem the continual and successful growth of the business, possibly changing tastes, stronger competition or market saturation. This really has not happened; Coca-Cola has continued to increase worldwide sales through clever marketing and occasional new products. In 1996 Coca-Cola was America's most admired company in the *Fortune* rankings but, as seen in Chapter 4, it has not sustained this position in the late-1990s, although it continues to enjoy high global admiration. In terms of increases in shareholder wealth, Coca-Cola was unrivalled in the USA throughout the leadership of its charismatic chief executive, Roberto Goizueta. Goizueta was the strategic leader from 1981 until his death in post in 1997. Nevertheless, Coca-Cola still made a number of strategic misjudgements.

## Competitive strategies

Coke had successfully established Fanta (the fizzy orange drink launched in 1960) and Tab (sugar-free Coca-Cola, 1963) when Goizueta took over. In 1982 Diet Coke was launched. Diet products are particularly important for the American market, but generally less significant elsewhere. However, in 1985, New Coke was launched to replace the original blending, but subsequently withdrawn after a consumer outcry. The Fresca range has also been launched. Sprite is another famous Coca-Cola brand, as are Minute Maid fruit juices. In 1998, an agreement to buy the Schweppes soft drinks businesses outside the USA from Cadbury's was thwarted by the European regulatory authorities. Coca-Cola has also been affected by economic crises and recessions in countries where it is particularly popular, especially Russia and Asia. In 1999 it was forced to withdraw the product in Belgium after a health scare resulting from minor contamination. Arguably, the company's public relations could have been better.

Coke really became popular overseas when it was shipped out to GIs during World War II, and systematically it has been introduced to more and more countries. For many years its stated goal was to 'always have Coca-Cola within an arm's reach of desire' and preferably in chilled storage, whether this was on retail shelves or through vending machines. It has benefited from being associated with the image and persona of America. When GIs drank it during World War II – and subsequent wars in Korea and Vietnam – it was seen as a reminder of exactly what they were fighting for. Early in 1999 Coca-Cola's name was linked to a line of fashion and sports clothing, the first significant extension of the brand.

Coca-Cola controls production of the concentrated syrup from Atlanta; mixing, bottling/canning and distribution is franchised to independent businesses worldwide. In truth, the issue of the 'secret formula' is more mystique than necessity, but it provides another valuable story to reinforce the brand and its image. Goizueta inherited a distribution network which was underperforming and he set about strengthening it with proper joint venture agreements and tight controls. Effective supply management is absolutely vital for the business.

Goizueta chose to acquire its smaller, underperforming bottlers, invested in them and, when they were turned around, sold them to stronger anchor bottlers – specifically those with the financial resources to invest in developing the business. 'Coca-Cola's distribution machine is [now] the most powerful and pervasive on the planet.'

Coca-Cola has always advertised heavily and prominently; and Goizueta has also negotiated a number of important promotional agreements. Coca-Cola has special aisles in Wal-Mart stores; Coke's Hi-C orange juice is supplied to McDonald's, for example. In recent years there has been increased emphasis on branding and packaging at the expense of pure advertising. 'We had really lost focus on who our customer was. We felt our customer was the bottler, as opposed to the McDonald's and the Wal-Marts' (Goizueta).

Faced with increased competition from retail own-label brands sold mainly through supermarket chains, Coca-Cola has carefully defended and strengthened its other distribution outlets such as convenience stores, fast-food restaurants and vending machines.

## Competition

Coca-Cola's main rival is Pepsi Cola, which has a 30% share of the US market and 20% of the world market. Its share has been growing since the 1993 introduction of Pepsi Max, a sugar-free product with the taste of the original Pepsi. Pepsi diversified into snack foods (Frito-Lay in the USA, Walkers and Smiths crisps in the UK) and restaurants (Pizza Hut, Taco Bell and Kentucky Fried in the USA); just one-third of global profits came from soft drinks in the mid-1990s. Pepsi also owns much of its bottling network. In 1996 the Pepsi brand was relaunched with a massive international promotional campaign. The new Pepsi colours, predominantly blue, were chosen to appeal to the younger buyer. In 1997 PepsiCo divested its restaurants into a separate business, and followed this up with the acquisition of the French company, Orangina – after the European competition regulators had prevented Coca-Cola from buying the business. A year later Pepsi acquired Tropicana, the world's largest marketer of branded juices, which it bought from the Canadian company Seagram. With this purchase, Pepsi controlled 40% of the US chilled orange juice market, twice the share of Coca-Cola.

Another significant competitor is Cott of Canada, which produces discounted colas with acceptable alternative tastes. Cott produces concentrate for Wal-Mart in the USA and for Sainsbury and Virgin in the UK.

QUESTIONS: Why is Coca-Cola 'number one' in its industry?

Where is its competitive advantage?

If it avoids *serious* mistakes, does it need to do anything radically different to retain its position?

Can you think of anything its leading rivals might do to 'upset the applecart'?

*Coca Cola*   http://www.coca-cola.com

One advantage when you're No. 1 or 2 in an industry is that you can really have a hell of a lot of say in what the future's going to be like by what you do. I'm not a believer in always forecasting the future. But if you take actions that can create that future, at least shape it, then you can benefit from it.

They say: 'Do you sleep well at night with all the competition?' I say: 'I sleep like a baby'. They say: 'That's wonderful'. I say: 'No, no. I wake up every two hours and cry!' Because its true, you know. You have to feel that restlessness.

*Roberto Goizueta,*
*late Chief Executive,*
*Coca-Cola Corporation*

## Competition: An Introduction

Causes generate effects. Actions lead to outcomes. On occasions companies may attempt to seize the competitive initiative and introduce an innovatory change. An action by one competitor which affects the relative success of rivals provokes responses. One action can therefore provoke several reactions, depending on the extent of the impact and the general nature of competition. Each reaction in turn further affects the other rival competitors in the industry. New responses will again follow. What we have in many markets and industries is a form of *competitive chaos*. Figure 8.1 shows a competitive business environment which is permanently fluid and unpredictable. For example, the Post

Office continues to experience new forms of competition from cheaper telephone calls, courier services and fax machines; it must adapt and respond to defend its place in the market.

In spring 2000, a proposed acquisition of US Air by market leader, United, was expected to provoke a hostile reaction by United's leading rivals, American and Delta Airlines. Quite the contrary – American and Delta both realized that if the United/US Air merger was allowed to proceed it would open up opportunities for further consolidation and rationalization. American was interested in linking with NorthWestern and Delta with Continental. This would, simply, create three larger and stronger companies from the current top six.

It is important to differentiate between two sets of similar, but nevertheless different, deci-

*Figure 8.1* Dynamic competition.

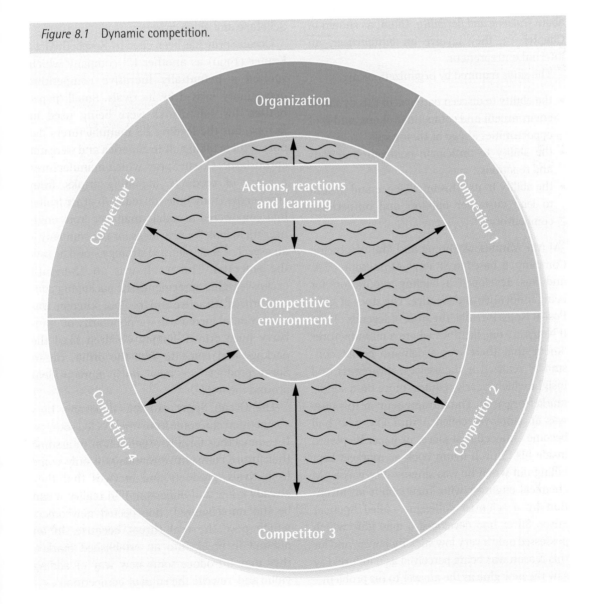

sions. First, some actions are innovatory and represent one competitor acting upon a perceived opportunity ahead of its rivals; other actions constitute reactions to these competitive initiatives. Secondly, some decisions imply incremental strategic change to existing, intended strategies; on different occasions companies are adapting their strategies (adaptive strategic change) as they see new opportunities which they can seize early, or possible future threats which they are seeking to avoid. The process is about *learning and flexibility*. Often, as shown in Chapter 13, they involve an *intrapreneur*, an internal entrepreneur.

The skills required by organizations are:

- the ability to discern patterns in this dynamic environment and competitive chaos, and spot opportunities ahead of their rivals
- the ability to anticipate competitor actions and reactions
- the ability to use this intelligence and insight to lead customer opinion and outperform competitors.

3M (the Minnesota Mining and Manufacturing Company) is based in St. Paul, Minnesota, USA, and has developed a leading reputation for being innovative and creative. The story of 3M's Post-It Notes is really 'the stuff of legends'. Post-It Notes are one instance where a manufacturer 'knew' that there was a demand before consumers realized it themselves, awareness and insight which clearly requires more than simple market research. The intrapreneur in this case was an employee called Arthur Fry, who had become annoyed that pieces of paper he placed inside his Church hymn book as markers kept falling out when he was singing. Fry was a 3M chemical engineer who knew about an invention by a scientist colleague called Spencer Silver. Silver had developed a new glue which possessed only a very low sticking power, and for this reason was being perceived as a failure! Fry saw the new glue as the answer to his problem –

when he applied it to his paper markers, they stayed put but they were easily removed. Realizing that many others also shared the same problem, Fry sought approval to commercialize his idea, but initially he met with scepticism. The idea took hold when he passed samples around to secretaries within 3M and other organizations. The rest, as they say, is history! Over the years the company has developed over 60,000 new products, including everything that bears the Scotch brand name, for example Sellotape and video cassettes.

Ocean Spray has been cited by Rosabeth Moss Kanter (1990) as another US company which spotted a potentially lucrative competitive opportunity missed by its rivals. Small 'paper bottles' for soft drinks were being used in Europe, but the leading US manufacturers did not see them taking off in America and were not enthusiastic. Ocean Spray, which manufactures a range of products, including drinks, from cranberries (sometimes mixed with other fruits) had empowered a middle manager from engineering to look for new ideas for the company – an aspect of their planned strategy – and he saw the potential. The result was an 18-month exclusive rights agreement. The packaging concept proved attractive and the final outcome was a substantial increase in the popularity of cranberry juice drinks. Simply, children liked the package and came to love the drink. Ocean Spray products are now much more evident around the world.

The Ocean Spray example illustrates how competition can come from unexpected sources. It is dangerous for any organization to assume that future competitive threats will only come from rivals, products and services that they already know and understand; in reality, it can be the unrecognized, unexpected newcomers which pose the real threat because, in an attempt to break into an established market, they may introduce some new way of adding value and 'rewrite the rules of competition'.

Bill Gates' 'view of the future', based on personal computers on every desk, was radically different from that of long-time industry leader, IBM, and it enabled Microsoft to enter and dominate the computer industry. British Airways was surprised by the entry and success of Virgin Atlantic Airways on profitable trans-Atlantic routes, as it perceived its main competition to come from the leading US carriers. Virgin was adding new values, offering high and differentiated levels of service at very competitive prices. The success of Direct Line, with telephone insurance services at very competitive prices, has provoked a response from existing companies; telephone banking is having a similar effect. In both cases the nature of the service has been changed dramatically, and improved for many customers.

Figure 8.2 shows how organizational resources need to be used to drive the competitive cycle. Constant, or ideally growing, sales and market share can lead to economies of scale and learning and, in turn, cost reductions and improved profits. The profits could, in a particularly competitive situation, be passed back to customers in the form of lower prices, but more normally they will be reinvested in the organization. This can generate productivity improvements, sometimes with new capacity and, then, lower prices and/or further cost reductions. The investment can also bring about new sources of added value and differentiation, possibly allowing higher prices and further profit growth. The improved competitiveness should also increase sales and market share and drive the cycle round again. These changes might take the form of gradual, continuous improvements or radical changes to establish new rules of competition.

To drive the cycle continuously, organizations will need a mix of steady-state managers to maintain efficiencies and more creative change agents to develop new initiatives.

## Competitive themes and frameworks

According to Michael Porter (1980) effective strategic management is the positioning of an organization, relative to its competitors, in such a way that it outperforms them. Marketing, operations and personnel, in fact all aspects of the business, are capable of providing a competitive edge – an advantage which leads to superior performance and superior profits for profit-orientated firms.

Two aspects of the current position of an organization are important: (1) the nature and structure of the industry and (2) the position of the organization within the industry.

1. The number of firms, their sizes and relative power, the ways they compete, and the rate of growth must be considered. An industry may be attractive or unattractive for an organization. This will depend on the prospects for the industry and what it can offer in terms of profit potential and growth potential. Different organizations have different objectives, and therefore where it is able an organization should be looking to compete in industries where it is able to achieve its objectives. In turn, its objectives and strategies are influenced by the nature of the industries in which it does compete. Porter has developed a model for analysing the structure of an industry, which is examined later in the chapter (p. 290). For the moment, the flow chart illustrated in Figure 8.3 explains the basic principles.

2. The position of a firm involves its size and market share, how it competes, whether it enjoys specific and recognized competitive advantage, and whether it has particular appeal to selected segments of the market. The extent of any differentiation, which is discussed below, is crucial here.

An effective and superior organization will be in the right industry and in the right position

*Figure 8.2* The competitive cycle.

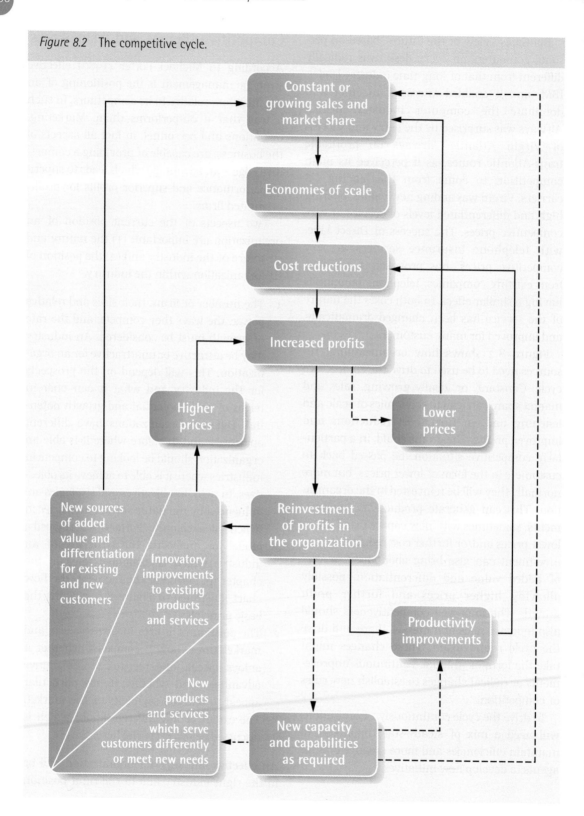

Figure 8.3   Industry growth prospects.

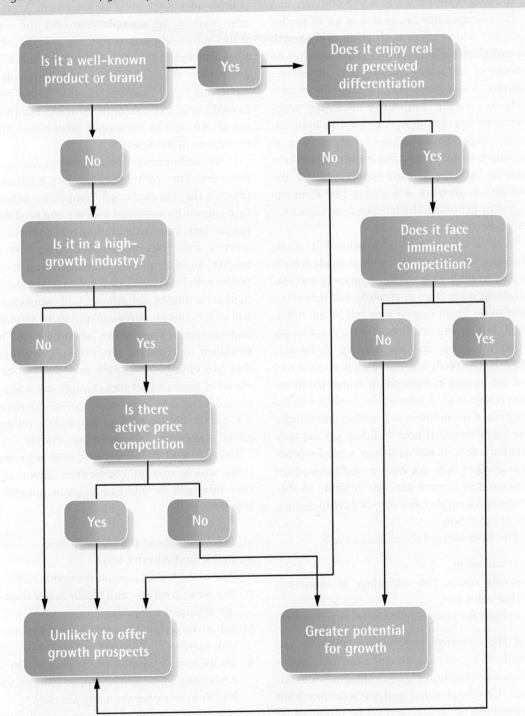

within that industry. An organization is unlikely to be successful if it chooses to compete in a particular industry because it is an attractive industry which offers both profit and growth potential but for which the organization has no means of obtaining competitive advantage. Equally, a company should not concentrate only on creating competitive advantage without assessing the prospects for the industry. With competitive advantage a company can be profitable in an unattractive industry, but there may be very few growth opportunities if the industry is growing at a slower rate than the economy generally. Much depends on objectives and expectations.

In the economy profit is the reward for creating value for consumers; and in individual businesses profits are earned by being more successful than competitors in creating and delivering that value. Profit may or may not be an end in itself, but profits are important for achieving other objectives and for helping to finance growth. The profit remaining after interest and tax can be paid in dividends or reinvested in the firm (Chapter 4). A firm will be healthier in the long run if it can invest as it wishes and finance the investments without building up too substantial a debt. In the same way, a not-for-profit organization may not have a profit-orientated mission, but it must generate revenue to stay viable and a surplus over expenditure to develop the organization.

The most successful competitors will:

- create value
- create competitive advantage in delivering that value and
- operate the business effectively and efficiently.

For above-average performance all three are required. It is possible to run a business well – efficiently – but never create competitive advantage. Certain products and services may have competitive advantage and yet be produced by organizations that are not run well. In both,

potential is not fully exploited. Moreover, competitive advantage must be sustained. A good new product, for example, may offer the consumer something new, something different, and thus add value; but if it is easily imitated by competitors there is no sustainable competitive advantage. For example, Freddie Laker pioneered cheap trans-Atlantic air travel but went out of business in the face of competition and management weaknesses.

In the author's experience sustaining competitive advantage, rather than creating it initially, presents the real challenge. Competitive advantage cannot be sustained for ever and probably not for very long without changes in products, services and strategies which take account of market demand, market saturation and competitor activity. People's tastes change, the size of markets is limited not infinite, and competitors will seek to imitate successful products, services and strategies. Competitive advantage can be sustained by constant innovation. Companies that are change orientated and seek to stay ahead of their competitors through innovatory ideas develop new forms of advantage. Minicase 8.1 earlier considers how Coca-Cola retains global leadership of the soft drinks market.

Heller (1998) has suggested that organizations which sustain competitive advantage over time will be addressing seven questions effectively:

1. Are we supplying the 'right' things?
2. In the most effective way?
3. And at the lowest possible economic cost?
4. Are we as good as – and ideally better than – our strongest competitor?
5. Are we targeting and serving the widest possible market?
6. Do we have a 'unique selling proposition' – something which will persuade customers to buy from us rather than anyone else?
7. Are we innovating to make sure the answer to all these questions will remain 'yes'?

## Differentiation and market segmentation

A product or service is said to be differentiated if consumers perceive it to have properties which make it distinct from rival products or services, and ideally unique in some particular way. Differentiation is most beneficial when consumers value the cause of the difference and will pay a premium price to obtain it, and where competitors are unable to emulate it.

Differentiation recognizes that customers are too numerous and widely scattered, and with heterogeneous needs and adequate spending power, for them all to prefer exactly the same product or service. Hence competitors will distinguish their brand, product or service in some way, perhaps size, quality or style, to give it greater appeal for certain customers. Those customers who value the difference will be willing to pay a premium price for it and ideally buy it consistently in preference to the alternatives.

Consequently, effective organizations will be both customer-driven (responsive) and customer-driving (innovative).

### Sources of differentiation

- *Speed* – High-street opticians and photo developers compete on their speed of service; courier businesses are successful because of the speed at which they can move items.
- *Reliability* – Consistent quality and the ability to keep promises: providing what customers want, where, when and how. One example is McDonald's.
- *Service* – Adding extra values to augment the service and thereby satisfy customers. Staff in certain hotels illustrate this point; some years ago Xerox provided a new level of service by incorporating a self-diagnostic computer chip in its copying machines.
- *Design* – both in the product itself (Bang and Olufsen hi-fi equipment, for instance) and in its reparability. This also relates to:

- *Features* – such as cordless irons, kettles and drills. The balance, though, is critical; some video cassette recorders now have too many features for most customers.
- *Technology* – which, say, led to the development of laser printers.
- *Corporate personality*. There is a value in certain corporate names and images, such as The Body Shop.
- *Relationships with customers* – through effective supply-chain management.

The differentiation need not be clearly tangible as long as customers believe that it exists.

Where specific groups of customers with broadly similar needs can be identified and targeted they are known as market segments, and often products and services are differentiated to appeal to specific segments. The segmentation might be based on ages, socioeconomic groups, lifestyle, income, benefits sought or usage rate for consumer markets, and size of buyer and reasons for buying in the case of industrial markets. To be viable the segment must be clearly identifiable, separated from other segments, easily reached with advertising and large enough to be profitable. Given these factors and a differentiated product, prices, distribution and advertising can all be targeted specifically at the segment.

Successful differentiation and segmentation require that products and services are clearly positioned. Toyota, for example, wanted to appeal to the lucrative executive market with a car that offered the 'ultimate in quality' and succeeded against BMW, Mercedes and Volvo. The car needed to be differentiated from the main Toyota brand and consequently it was named Lexus.

Both differentiation and market segmentation are key aspects of marketing strategy, a more detailed treatment of which can be found on the accompanying website.

## The importance of timing

Products and services have finite lives, and broadly speaking they follow a lifecycle pattern. Strategies also have lifecycles. Strategies which deliver value and competitive advantage will bring benefits to the organization in terms of success, growth and profits. However, if consumer preferences change, and the factors creating the advantage are no longer perceived as valuable, the advantage is lost. A change of competitive strategy is required. Similarly, if the advantage is cost based and the factors generating the cost advantage change, such that the advantage is lost, a new strategy is required. Again, any advantage is potentially vulnerable to copying or improvements in some way by competitors, particularly if it is seen to be generating success.

Referring back to E–V–R (environment–values–resources) congruence, at times particular strategies reflect a congruence between resources and the environment. However, demand can change, or investment resources to strengthen competitive advantage may not be available. The congruence may disappear and withdrawal or divestment may well be appropriate.

Towards the end of 1992 it was being claimed that Porsche sports cars had become 'an extravagance which increasingly few people are able to afford'. Sales were around half those of the mid-1980s. Production costs had to be slashed and the company rationalized. Fortunately, Porsche was a family company with no debt and a strong cash base; it was therefore able to survive on its reserves until a new range of sports models was ready (in 1996). Referring back to the Sigmoid curve (Figure 2.10), Porsche's timing was flawed; it was not ready to change at the most appropriate time.

The two classic cases from the 1960s, featured in Minicase 8.2, involve well-known companies which also illustrate the above point extremely well. Although dated, they are still relevant examples. One further message in these examples is that all strengths are potential weaknesses. Both Tizer and Lesney had failed to appreciate when the effective life of a particular strategy was coming to an end, as much as anything because it had proved so successful in the past. As a result, the strategy became a weakness.

## Analysing An Industry

Porter (1980) argues that five forces determine the profitability of an industry. They are featured in Figure 8.4. At the heart of the industry are rivals and their competitive strategies linked to, say, pricing or advertising; but, he contends, it is important to look beyond one's immediate competitors as there are other determinants of profitability. Specifically, there might be competition from substitute products or services. These alternatives may be perceived as substitutes by buyers even though they are part of a different industry. An example would be plastic bottles, cans and glass bottles for packaging soft drinks. There may also be a potential threat of new entrants, although some competitors will see this as an opportunity to strengthen their position in the market by ensuring, as far as they can, customer loyalty. Finally, it is important to appreciate that companies purchase from suppliers and sell to buyers. If they are powerful they are in a position to bargain profits away through reduced margins, by forcing either cost increases or price decreases. This relates to the strategic option of vertical integration, which will be considered in detail later in the book (Chapter 14). Vertical integration occurs where a company acquires, or merges with, a supplier or customer and thereby gains greater control over the chain of activities which leads from basic materials through to final consumption.

Any company must seek to understand the nature of its competitive environment if it is to be

# Minicase 8.2  Tizer and Lesney: The Importance of Strategic Lifecycles

## Tizer

Tizer was some 30 years old in the 1960s and it had become successful by producing its well-known fizzy drink in a number of regional plants and selling it direct to small corner shops and off-licences. Van driver salesmen collected returnable empty bottles as they sold new ones. However, customer shopping habits were changing with the growth of self-service stores and supermarkets, and corner shops were in decline. In addition, breweries were acquiring off-licences and insisting that they stocked only brewery products. The new retailers were often part of a national chain with central rather than local buying. In addition, returnable bottles were seen as outdated. Tizer's strategy, which had brought success to the company, was no longer appropriate; change was needed.

*Tizer*   http://www.tizer.co.uk

## Lesney

Lesney was one of the fastest growing companies in the UK in the 1960s as a result of the success of Matchbox toys. Large quantities of the small die-cast scale models of cars were produced cost effectively by using sophisticated production equipment and systems. They were priced very competitively and distributed widely through a variety of outlets rather than only toy shops. Buyers collected them, purchasing new models when they were introduced. Lesney was so busy meeting demand that they failed to innovate. An American competitor, Mattel, saw an opportunity based on how children played with the cars, and introduced a range of small cars with friction-free wheels on plastic bearings. These cars rolled further when pushed; they behaved differently in use and allowed such things as looping-the-loop. Mattel charged 30p for their cars (Matchbox cost 12 1/2p) and they sold. Lesney's competitive strategy, similar to that of Tizer, was no longer appropriate and it needed replacement. Lesney succeeded in responding to the competition, but early in the 1980s they went into receivership. As with many UK toy producers they had been unable to withstand foreign competition.

*Task: Using the Internet, check on the recent fortunes of these brands. Tizer has been owned by soft drinks manufacturer A G Barr for several years; Matchbox's most recent owner is Mattel.*

These examples have been developed from the Tizer (A) case, written by JM Stopford and P Edmonds, and the Lesney Products and Company Ltd (A) case, written by CJ Constable. Copies of both cases are available from the European Case Clearing House, Cranfield.

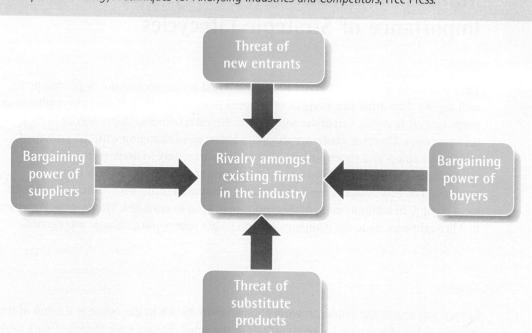

*Figure 8.4*   Determining industry profitability: the five forces. Adapted from Porter, ME (1980) *Competitive Strategy: Techniques for Analysing Industries and Competitors*, Free Press.

successful in achieving its objectives and in establishing appropriate strategies. If a company fully understands the nature of the five forces, and particularly appreciates which one is the most important, it will be in a stronger position to defend itself against any threats and to influence the forces with its strategy. The situation, of course, is fluid, and the nature and relative power of the forces will change. Consequently, the need to monitor and stay aware is continuous.

## The threat of new entrants: barriers to entry

Where barriers to entry are high new entrants are likely to be deterred, and if they do attempt entry they are likely to provoke a quick reaction from existing competitors. Low barriers generally mean that responses will be slower, offering more opportunities. A number of factors can create barriers:

- *Economies of scale* – Some of the possible ways of achieving economies of scale have been considered earlier. In addition, the experience curve (see the Finance in Action supplement to Chapter 7) can be important. If there is a need for substantial investment to allow a new entrant to achieve cost parity with existing firms this may well be a deterrent. In such a case if a newcomer enters the market with only limited investment and is not able to achieve comparable economies of scale, he or she will be at a cost disadvantage from the start, in which case substantial differentiation will be required, but this introduces another issue.
- *Product differentiation* – If consumers perceive rival products or services to be clearly differ-

entiated then newcomers must also seek to establish a distinct identity. Newcomers will therefore have to invest in advertising and promotion to establish their new brand, and this may be expensive. The major brewers and chocolate manufacturers, for example, spend millions of pounds each year promoting specific products and brands.

- *Capital requirements* – Any requirement for substantial investment capital in order to enter a market is a barrier to entry. The investment may be on capital equipment, research and development, or advertising to establish a market presence, and it may deter many aspiring competitors. However, large multi-product companies who wish to break into a market may finance the necessary investment with profits from other areas of the business. Drugs is one industry where huge investments are required to develop and test possible new products over several years. While *patent protection* allows the costs to be recouped through prices, the investment is all 'up front'.

- *Switching costs* – These are costs incurred not by the company wishing to enter the market but by the existing customers. If a buyer were to change his supplier from an established manufacturer to a newcomer costs may be incurred in a number of ways. New handling equipment and employee training are examples. Buyers may not be willing to change their suppliers because of these costs, thereby making it very difficult for any newcomer to poach existing business.

- *Access to distribution channels* – Existing relationships and agreements between manufacturers and the key distributors in a market may also create barriers to entry. Some manufacturers may be vertically integrated and own or control their distributors. Other distributors may have established and successful working relationships with particular manufacturers and have little incentive to change.

Companies aspiring to enter a market may look for unique distribution opportunities to provide both access and immediate differentiation.

- *Cost advantages independent of scale* – This represents factors which are valuable to existing companies in an industry and which newcomers may not be able to replicate. Essential technology may be protected by patent; the supply of necessary raw materials may be controlled; or favourable locations near to supplies or markets may not be accessible. Government restrictions on competition may apply in certain circumstances.

Minicase 8.3 discusses the powerful barriers to entry in two completely different industries.

Potential entrants, attracted by high margins in an industry and not detracted by any of the above barriers, must try to gauge any likely retaliation by existing manufacturers; and Porter argues that this can be assessed by examining:

- past behaviour when newcomers have entered or tried to enter the market
- the resource capabilities of existing companies which will affect their ability to retaliate
- the investment and commitment of existing companies which may make retaliation inevitable if they are to protect their investment and position
- the rate of growth of the industry – the faster it is the more possibilities for a newcomer to be absorbed.

Existing firms may be prepared to reduce prices to deter entry and protect their market shares, especially if supply already exceeds demand. As a result, even in an oligopoly, profitability can be contained.

## The bargaining power of suppliers

The behaviour of suppliers, and their relative power, can squeeze industry profits. Equally, the ability of a firm to control its supplies by vertical

# Minicase 8.3   Barriers to Entry: Glaxo's Zantac and Champagne

## Zantac

Sir Paul Girolami became the chief executive of Glaxo in 1980, and sequentially divested the non-pharmaceutical businesses: specialized chemicals and food, agricultural and horticultural products. In 1985 Glaxo was not in the leading ten world pharmaceutical companies; in 1988 it was number 2 to Merck. In 1990 half of Glaxo's worldwide revenue was contributed by Zantac, its antiulcer drug whose chemical name is ranitidin. Zantac enjoyed one important competitive advantage over its main rival Tagamet (SmithKline Beecham) – it was a twice-daily treatment rather than four times a day.

Glaxo exploited the product successfully with two unusual strategies. First, it registered ranitidin simultaneously in all major markets – typically drugs are registered first in their home market, followed by other countries sequentially. Secondly, Glaxo uniquely used other companies for manufacturing and distributing the product (including three separate companies in the USA), rather than building a world sales force. Turnover tripled in 1983/84 and then quadrupled during the next five years. As a result of these factors, Zantac was able to command a premium price and still become the world's biggest selling prescription medicine.

By 1995, after Glaxo's take-over of Wellcome, Zantac still accounted for 30% of the group's sales, but key patents were beginning to expire. Originally thought to be protected until 2002, basic Zantac came fully out of patent much earlier. Generic versions were already appearing in Europe, causing sales to fall.

Glaxo has retained a strong position in the global pharmaceutical industry through acquisitions and new products, but no single product has ever made the equivalent contribution to that made by Zantac.

*Glaxo Wellcome*   http://www.glaxowellcome.co.uk

## Champagne

Several barriers to entry have acted to preserve the exclusiveness of the champagne industry. In most countries, and with the notable exceptions of the USA and Russia, the term champagne can be applied only to wines made from grapes grown in one area, Champagne, in north-west France. The best grapes for champagne are grown on a particular type of chalky soil found only in this region. In addition, strict (and enforced) French government rules require that only three varieties of grape may be used; and after the first fermentation the wine must be matured in the bottle for at least a year to generate the bubbles.

The business is carefully regulated, generally in favour of the 19,000 growers. Growers, who operate in co-operatives, historically have accounted for approximately one-third of the champagne that is manufactured; the rest has been produced by merchants who buy the grapes from the growers at prices fixed contractually every six years.

During the early and mid-1980s demand and sales grew by some 70%. As a result grape prices rose and growers particularly started to manufacture more. These events attracted competitors who looked for ways of overcoming the entry barriers. The real threat came from other premium quality sparkling wines manufactured in countries such as Spain. The grower/merchant price agreement broke down in 1990, roughly at the time when demand fell back. In an attempt to reinforce the image of superiority and exclusivity, and in response to the competition from other sparkling wines, champagne prices were increased deliberately. 'Quality and image is more important than quantity'.

The most influential company in the industry is LVMH (Louis Vuitton Moët Hennessy) whose brands [including Moët & Chandon, Dom Perignon, Veuve Clicquot, Mercier and Pommery (very popular in Japan)] command around a 25% market share. LVMH own 1500 prime hectares out of the region's total of 35,000 hectares.

*Task: Using LVMH as a starting point, look into the barriers to entry in the perfumes industry. (Other companies to track are Estée Lauder, L'Oréal and Unilever.) How successful have these leading companies been in controlling the distribution of their products through selected retailers?*

*LVMH* http://www.lvmh.com

integration (acquiring its suppliers) or long-term supply arrangements can be very beneficial. The relative power is affected by five major factors.

- Concentration among suppliers *vis-à-vis* the industry they sell to – if the supply industry is very concentrated then buyers have little opportunity for bargaining on prices and deliveries as suppliers recognize that their opportunities for switching suppliers are limited.
- The degree of substitutability between the products of various suppliers and the amount of product differentiation – a buyer could be tied to a particular supplier if his or her requirements cannot be met by other suppliers.
- The amount of, and potential for, vertical integration which might be initiated by either the supplier or the buyer – again, government regulation on competition may prevent this.
- The extent to which the buyer is important to the supplier – if a buyer is regarded as a key

customer he or she may well receive preferential treatment.
- Any switching costs that might be incurred by buyers will strengthen the position of suppliers.

## The bargaining power of buyers

Any competitive action by buyers will act to depress industry profits, but specific arrangements with distributors or customers can be mutually beneficial. Vertical integration is again a possibility. The major supermarket grocery stores with their multiple outlets nationwide are in a very strong bargaining position with most of their suppliers.

This power has been strengthened by the success of private- label brands, whose prices can be up to 60% below those for the recognized major brands. Private labels have grown to over one-third of UK retail food sales. They have proved most successful with chilled meals, frozen vegetables, fruit juices and cheese; and least successful with pet foods, sugar, coffee and, for a long time, breakfast cereals. Barriers against private-label products are provided by innovation and aggressive marketing and promotion.

As the market for overseas travel grew in the UK, the power of the leading travel agency groups also grew *vis-à-vis* the tour operators – it is, after all, the travel agency that actually sells the holiday and has direct contact with customers, who they are able to influence. As a consequence the leading tour operators (Thomson and Airtours) sought to acquire their own agencies and exercise greater control over the supply chain. At the same time, industry rationalization has meant that a small number of tour operators (all of whom also own their own airline) dominates the market.

The bargaining power of buyers is determined by:

- the concentration and size of buyer
- the importance to the buyer of the purchase in terms of both cost and quality (the more important it is the more he or she must ensure good relations with the supplier)
- the degree of product standardization, which affects substitutability
- the costs, practicability and opportunity for buyers to switch supplier
- the possibility of vertical integration, initiated by either the supplier or the buyer.

## The threat of product substitutes

The existence or non-existence of close substitutes helps to determine the elasticity of demand for a product or service. In simple terms this is price sensitivity. If there are close substitutes, demand for a particular brand will increase or decrease as its price moves downwards or upwards relative to competitors. Price changes can be initiated by any firm, but other competitors will be affected and forced to react. If products are not seen as close substitutes then they will be less price sensitive to competitor price changes.

For this reason firms will seek to establish clear product or service differentiation in order to create customer preference and loyalty and thereby make their product or service less price sensitive. Where this is accomplished industry profits are likely to rise, which may be attractive to prospective newcomers who will seek to create further differentiation in order to encourage customers to switch to them and enable them to establish a presence in the market.

Products and services can be substituted for something completely different, reflecting the ever-present possibility that new competitors can change the 'rules of competition' in a market or industry.

## Rivalry among existing competitors

Porter terms rivalry amongst existing competitors 'jockeying for position'. Competition may take the form of price competition, advertising and promotion, innovation, or service during and after sale. Where competitive firms are mutually interdependent retaliation is a key issue. Before deciding upon aggressive competitive actions firms must attempt to predict how their competitors will react; when other firms are proactive an organization must at least be defensive in order to protect market share and profitability. The intensity of competition is affected by the market structure and depends on the following:

- the number of competitors and the degree of concentration
- the rate of growth of the industry – slow growth increases the pressure upon competitors to fight for market share
- the degree of differentiation – the less there is the more likely is price competition
- cost structures – where fixed costs are high relative to variable costs companies are very sensitive around the break-even point. Profits are very dependent upon volume.

As passenger aircraft become larger and more technologically sophisticated, the cost of buying (or leasing) and insuring them grows. The operating cost per seat mile – and break-even loadings – increases steadily, but with international overcapacity and competition, the revenue per seat mile has been falling. Some airlines have closed or been acquired; others have had to reduce salaries and numbers of employees.

- The implications of changing size or supply capability through investment – although demand may be increasing at a relatively gradual and consistent rate, supply provision may increase in sizeable blocks as a result of the necessary investment. If a firm wishes to increase output and it has exhausted the possibilities from increased usage of existing plant it will have to invest in new plant. When this is commissioned it may increase supply potential substantially and affect competitors as the company seeks orders to utilize its new capacity. Consider as examples a small charter airline which has three freight aeroplanes. If it buys a fourth it increases its capacity by 25% overnight. Similarly, if there are two three-star hotels in a medium-sized town and a third is opened, the competitive situation changes markedly.
- The extent to which competitors are aware of the strategies of their rivals – one issue in this is the relative importance of the product or service to the various competitors. If a product is a byproduct of another more important operation, for example, then the company concerned may compete very aggressively for sales and be far more concerned with volume than profits.
- The objectives of the competing firms – what matters to them. Are they more interested in profit, turnover or percentage market share? The objectives determine the strategies.
- Exit barriers, and the costs of leaving the industry – if these are high for any reason

firms may be willing to accept low margins and limited profit opportunities in order to remain in the industry. The types of factor that determine exit costs are dedicated assets which have no profitable alternative use; the costs of redundancy; interrelationships within a conglomerate, whereby a product may be either a byproduct or an essential component for another division; emotional ties related to the history of the product and its association with the business; and pressure from government not to close down.

An example of dedicated assets which have no obvious alternative use is multiplex cinema complexes. As the number of these has grown, cinema audiences have also grown, and an industry in decline has been given a new lease of life. In addition, it is quite normal for several fast-food and retail outlets to open alongside the cinemas, helping to boost their traffic. But what would happen to the cinema buildings if audiences declined again?

Manufacturers of consumer electronics products have to invest continually to maintain the technology required for the necessary product improvements. To generate revenues to fund further investment they need volume sales; to create these they price with low, competitive margins. Profits are very slim, but the sunk costs are such that the cycle continues; it is too costly to come out of the industry. The cycle is reinforced by consumer purchasing behaviour. Consumers know which brands they are happy to consider, their shortlist depending upon the quality and differentiation they are seeking. They then buy on price, seeing certain brands as interchangeable. Inevitably, the retailers also earn only low margins.

Table 8.1 provides a summary checklist of factors for industry analysis, and Box 8.1 analyses the supermarket industry against Porter's model of five forces.

---

*Table 8.1* Checklist for industry analysis

1. How many firms are in the industry, and what size are they?
2. How concentrated is the industry?
3. To what degree are products substitutes?
4. Is the industry growing or contracting?
5. What are the relative powers of suppliers, buyers and competitors?
6. What are the prevailing competitive strategies?
7. What entry barriers exist?
8. What economies of scale are present?
9. What experience/learning curve effects are important?
10. What exit barriers exist (if any)?
11. What important external factors affect competition?

---

## STRATEGY IN ACTION – Box 8.1
## Industry Analysis – Supermarkets

### Threat of new entrants

Barriers to entry are very high, because of the necessary supply network and distribution infrastructure. The continual investment in EPOS (electronic point-of-sale) and EDI (electronic data interchange) systems creates further barriers. In addition, it is very difficult and very expensive to acquire new sites in prime positions. It is possible, given financial reserves, to build a position in selected market niches. Of course, powerful companies, able to command huge financial resources, can break in with an acquisition, |as was seen when Wal-Mart bought ASDA.

### Relative strength of suppliers

Supply agreements with major retail chains, using EDI, make the leading suppliers and supermarkets more and more interdependent. Ownership of a leading brand yields power, but secondary and tertiary brands must be more vulnerable. There is further interdependency with own-label supply agreements.

### Relative strength of buyers

Most buyers will have more than one supermarket that they can access, especially if they are car owners. The power of the Internet to promote home deliveries also opens up choice. There will be some loyalty, but only if prices and service are competitive.

### Threat of substitutes

Small independent stores have a niche and a role, but the supermarkets are dominant. However, they are vulnerable on price for those products/brands offered by smaller, discount stores, especially where customers are willing to multishop. Home shopping via IT continues to be a sector of the market that supermarkets must develop rather than relinquish.

### Existing rivalries

The industry is very competitive, with four or five chains competing for the family shopping budget. Sainsbury's, Tesco, ASDA (Wal-Mart) and Safeway have different competitive strategies (product ranges, pricing strategies, etc.) and have differing appeals, but they remain largely interchangeable. These companies must all invest to try and create differences as well as pricing competitively. The relative speedy demise of the Co-op to a predominantly niche role illustrates how intense the rivalry is.

*Summary:*
Barriers to entry – high
Power of suppliers – medium
Power of buyers – medium/high
Threat of substitutes – medium
Existing rivalries – intense

The rivalry factors discussed above, and the rivalry strategies, are both affected by any slowing down in the rate of industry growth, by acquisitions, and by changes in the marketing strategy of any one competitor resulting from the perception of new opportunities for differentiation or segmentation.

To be an effective competitor, a company must:

- appreciate which of the five forces is the most significant (it can be different for different industries) and concentrate strategic attention in this area
- position itself for the best possible defence against any threats from rivals
- influence the forces detailed above through its own corporate and competitive strategies
- anticipate changes or shifts in the forces – the factors that are generating success in the short term may not succeed long term.

Much will depend upon the strategic leader, the quality of management in the organization and the prevailing culture.

## The role of government

Rather than incorporation as a separate sixth factor, Porter maintains that the importance of government lies in an ability to affect the other five forces through changes in policy and new legislation. The examples below are not exhaustive.

1. The introduction of competition and an internal market in the UK National Health Service, a Conservative policy abandoned by the Blair Labour government.
2. A series of privatizations during the 1980s and 1990s, including British Aerospace, Rolls Royce, British Airways, British Telecom (BT), British Rail and British Steel, along with the critically important gas, water and electricity utility industries.

To prevent the businesses becoming national or local monopolies in private ownership, with enormous potential to exploit their customers, industry regulators have been appointed in a number of cases. The regulators and the newly privatized businesses have at times disagreed over important strategic issues. Individual regulators are given freedom to establish specific guidelines within clear broad principles, and some would argue that this makes conflict between them and the regulated businesses inevitable. One of the reasons for the diversification strategies by privatized companies is that they create business activities which are outside the direct control of the regulator. Given a general trend away from diversification to a concentration on core businesses and competencies, this has sometimes proved to be risky. Maybe the impact of the regulators also needs regulating.

Regulation has also allowed, and even encouraged, acquisitions and the entry of new competitors into a market. A number of the regional water companies has been acquired by French rivals; some electricity suppliers are now owned by American energy businesses. With the emergence of mobile and cable telephony, BT has been subject to several new competitors, some with overseas financial backing. Customers can now buy their gas and electricity from several suppliers. Electricity companies can supply domestic gas, and vice versa. For example, someone living in Yorkshire can buy their electricity from Lancashire-based Norweb.

3. Deregulation of particular industries, such as air transport (see Minicase 8.4).

The lessening of restrictions and regulations unleashes new competitive forces and changes the nature of the industry. Some competitors will benefit, while others will suffer.

In the UK the changes in air transport created an interesting dilemma. British Airports Authority (BAA), which runs most of the major airports in the UK (the exception is Manchester), was privatized in 1987. Airport charges are regulated by the Civil Aviation Authority (CAA) which, for example, insisted on a new five-year formula covering the period April 1992 to March 1997. In years 1 and 2 charges would change by a figure 8% below retail price index (RPI), in year 3 by RPI less 4%, and in years 4 and 5 by RPI less 1%. These implied a need for major cost savings, together with greater efficiency and productivity. At the same time the need continues to grow for both a fifth runway in the London area (to add to two at Heathrow and one each at Gatwick and Stansted) and a fifth terminal at Heathrow. If either or both finally goes ahead, BAA will be the developers, assuming that their finances are sufficiently robust – because they have recently been further affected by the abolition of duty-free prices for travel inside the European Union.

The forces described above determine the profitability of an industry, and hence the attractiveness of the industry for companies already competing in it and for companies who might wish to enter it. As well as understanding the nature and structure of the industry it is important for organizations to decide how best to compete. In other words, firms must appreciate the opportunities for creating and sustaining competitive advantage.

## Competitive Strategy

As far as customers are concerned, the link between price and perceived quality must make sense. Products and services should be neither overpriced (resulting in a loss of goodwill and often lost business) nor underpriced. In this latter case, potential profits must be lost and, perversely, orders may be lost as well – people may become suspicious of the unexpectedly low price and begin to question their perception of the relative quality. Companies must, therefore, also be realistic about customer perception of the relative quality of their products and services and neither overestimate nor underestimate the situation. Companies may think, or wish to believe, that they are 'the best'; customers may disagree.

Figure 8.5 offers a simple matrix of competitive strategies developed from this reasoning.

Porter (1985) developed his work on industry analysis to examine how a company might compete in the industry in order to create and sustain a position of strength. In simple terms, he argued, there are two basic parameters:

- Parameter 1. A company can seek to compete:
  - by achieving lower costs than its rivals and, by charging comparable prices for its products or services, creating a superior position through superior profitability,
  or
  - through differentiation, adding value in an area that the customer regards as important, charging a premium price, and again creating a superior position through superior profitability.

# Minicase 8.4 Deregulation and the International Airline Industry

When governments regulated their airline industries, in order to control both national and international competition, new airlines were prevented from entering markets, existing companies could not simply offer flights into or out of any airport of their choice, routes could not be poached and prices for specified routes were fixed.

This regulation has been systematically reduced since the late 1970s. At this time in the *USA*, where flying is as commonplace as bus and train journeys, and airline seats are perceived as essentially a commodity product, domestic competition was opened up. This has unleashed the underlying competitive nature of the industry with dramatic effects. The industry is characterized by chaos.

It is relatively easy to break into the industry once companies are allowed to do so. Planes can be leased and funded from revenue; maintenance can be bought in. Normally both fuel and planes are easily obtained. A company can enter by offering a limited service and concentrating on particular cities. Deregulation in the USA attracted such companies, and existing large airlines sought to expand their routes. Buyers were generally willing to fly with the airline which offered a flight at the time they wanted to travel, not differentiating, rather than building their arrangements around the schedule of their first-choice airline.

The *British* government has sought competition rather than monopoly control in the UK, privatizing British Airways (BA) in 1987. In 1991 the Civil Aviation Authority (CAA) relaxed certain rules, allowing new airlines to fly into and out of Heathrow for the first time since 1977. This intensified transatlantic competition as two strong US airlines (American and United, the two largest airlines in the world), which were restricted to Gatwick, acquired Heathrow/America routes from two weaker competitors, TWA and Pan Am, respectively. At the same time Virgin Atlantic was allowed to operate from Heathrow as well as Gatwick, allowed to fly to more American destinations, and given a number of BA's slots on the lucrative Heathrow to Tokyo route. All of these changes increased the competition for BA.

In 1992 *European Union* transport ministers agreed plans for a new 'open skies' policy, eventually featuring:

- Freer access for airlines to new routes throughout Europe. Previously many routes have been protected by governments to prevent competition with their national carriers. One difficulty in implementing this is the ability of air-traffic controllers to cope with more flights; European air-traffic control is not fully co-ordinated and is overstretched.
- Greater freedom for airlines to set their own seat prices, within certain protective safeguards. This did not imply that prices would fall quickly because operating costs are already high, with many flights operating below capacity.
- Lower barriers to entry for new carriers.

Deregulation began in *Australia* in 1990, when controls on prices and schedules were removed, resulting in domestic price warfare, cost-cutting measures and the entry of a new national airline, 'the first for decades'. BA was allowed to buy a substantial shareholding in Qantas, Australia's leading international airline.

## Effects

- New route strategies based on a 'hub and spokes' – flights are concentrated around particular regional centres. American controL 65% of the slots at Dallas, United own 68% of the slots at Washington National and 48% of Chicago, and Delta 70% of Atlanta. Internationally, carriers expect the same control at the major airport in their home country, but many are now seeking to establish further hubs around the world.
- Company winners and losers. In 1991 in the USA, for example, two previously major competitors, Eastern and Pan Am, went out of business. Earlier, People Express, founded in the USA in the early 1980s (following deregulation) to offer cheaper price flights, also failed after rapid growth and profitability. Companies such as American, United and Delta, less well-known before deregulation, have grown dramatically. More recently United has opened negotiations to acquire their smaller rival, US Air.
- New, small, focused airlines have also proved successful. It was shown in Minicase 1.1 how Southwest Air, based in Dallas, flies point-to-point (not hub-and-spoke) on short-haul routes, offering low fares, no preassigned seating and calling at secondary airports. Empowered employees deliver high service – founder Herb Kelleher has 'made working in this business an adventure for the employees'. The company uses only one type of aircraft, Boeing 737s, and avoids computer reservation systems in travel agencies; it prefers direct sales to its customers. Southwest has been consistently profitable; its operating ratios confirm that it outperforms most other US airlines. The Southwest strategy has been followed to varying degrees in the UK and Europe by competitors such as EasyJet, Ryanair, Virgin Express, Go (BA) and Buzz (KLM of The Netherlands).
- New joint venture agreements and cross-shareholdings. In July 1992 BA reached an agreement with financially troubled US Air (the fourth largest US carrier) to acquire a shareholding, and thereby gain access to US domestic routes. This arrangement collapsed when BA and American began to discuss a strategic alliance.
- Increased competitiveness with job losses during recession. Events such as the 1991 Gulf War can have a major impact if people are deterred from flying.
- Greater reliance on information technology to allow pricing flexibility in order to maximize load factors. However, the increasing number of 'price wars' and special low-fare promotions has led to non-optimum fare mixes and unprofitable flights. In 1994 in the USA, for example, 92% of passengers flew on discount tickets and the average fare paid was just 35% of the published full fare. During the 1990s the real cost of trans-Atlantic flights halved. It is hardly surprising that customers have become increasingly confused. At the end of the 1990s BA chose to change its strategy and increase the number of its premium-price business and first-class seats (at the

expense of cheaper economy seats) in an attempt to increase the average fare and revenue yield of each flight.

At the same time . . .

- Greater emphasis on service quality, especially punctuality and reliability, to try and establish customer loyalty. After all, expectations continue to rise despite the low fares.
- The introduction of frequent flyer promotions (free flights on particular airlines for regular travellers who accumulate points for miles). This is also aimed at generating more loyalty.

The end result has been a potent mix of poor profits, leading to corporate failures, disgruntled employees who are either laid off or forced to accept pay cuts, and unhappy passengers who are affected by the inevitable overbooking as airlines try to ensure that every plane flies full.

- The industry has exhibited one aspect of classic oligopoly behaviour with deregulation. When American Airlines tried to lead fares back up, it failed.

Perversely, at the same time, there is considerable regulation. The alliance between BA and American has become embroiled in the long-running negotiations for an open-sky agreement between the UK and USA, whereby individual airlines are allowed freer access to routes and airports. A proposal (in early 2000) for the acquisition of KLM by BA was immediately seized upon by the European Union competition regulators. Almost immediately it was suggested that BA and KLM would be required to divest their respective low-cost carriers, Go and Buzz. The proposal has been abandoned.

QUESTIONS: Why, then, deregulate?
Are governments too readily impressed by the seductive cost savings for passengers?
Would some regulation be more sensible than full deregulation?

- Parameter 2. The arena in which the company seeks to compete can be a broad range of segments or a narrow range, perhaps just one.

This line of argument led Porter to develop his valuable model of generic strategies, which is discussed below. It also focused attention on the relevance of differentiation, adding value and cost management for helping to create – and sustain – competitive advantage. It is important, first, to appreciate that the generic strategy framework is a reflection of current (or targeted) positioning, and that competitive advantage is by nature a relative (to other competitors) and dynamic notion. Secondly, as mentioned briefly before, it is essential to realize that competitive strategy and competitive advantage, although clearly linked, are not one and the same. Competitive strategy concerns the way in which organizations choose to compete and position themselves – competitive advantage may or may not be an outcome of this. To achieve true advantage an organization must find opportunities to be different in ways which are meaningful for customers. The activities which create the position are the key to advantage (see p. 312).

*Figure 8.5*    Simple competitive strategy matrix. Based on an idea found on the Abram Hawkes plc web site.

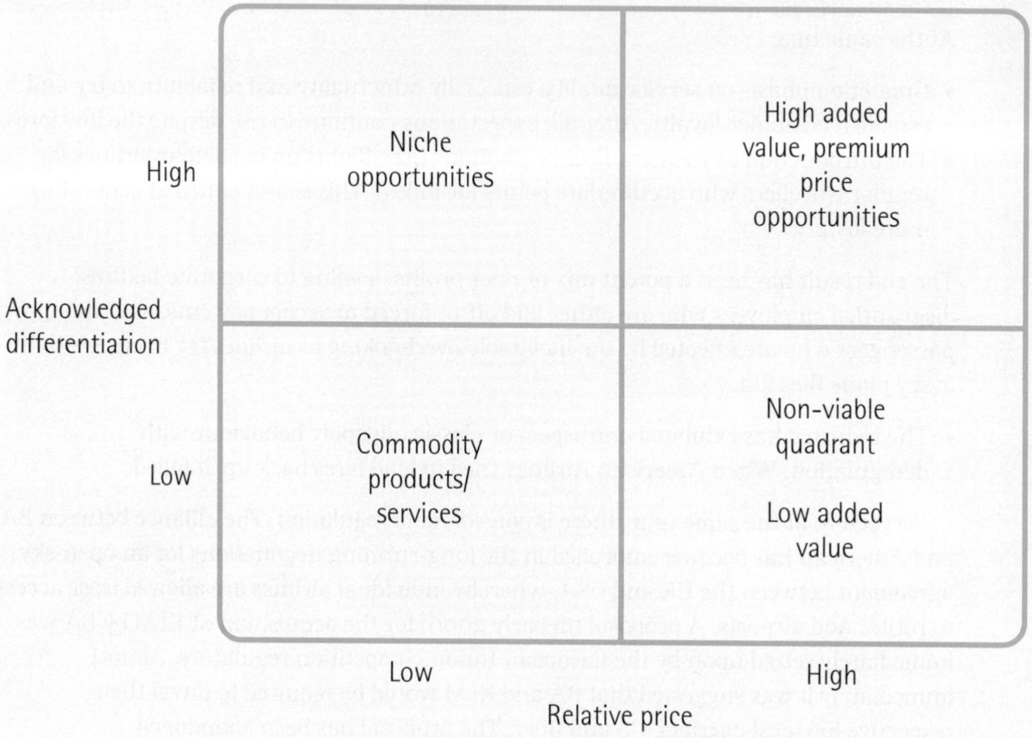

## Generic competitive strategies

Porter's two parameters lead to the three generic strategies illustrated in Figure 8.6(a). Cost leadership is where the company achieves lower costs than its rivals and competes across a broad range of segments. Differentiation occurs when the company has a range of clearly differentiated products which appeal to different segments of the market. Focus strategies are where a company chooses to concentrate on only one segment or a limited range of segments. With this approach it can again seek either lower costs or differentiation.

Before considering these generic strategies in greater detail it is useful to apply them to particular industries. Porter argues that in the motor vehicle industry (Figure 8.6(b)) Toyota became the overall cost leader. The company is successful in a number of segments with a full range of cars, and its mission is to be a low-cost producer. Minicase 8.5 outlines Toyota's competitive strategy. In contrast, General Motors (GM) also competes in most segments of the market but seeks to differentiate each of its products with superior styling and features. GM also offers a wider choice of models for each car in its range.

Hyundai became successful around the world with a restricted range of small and medium size cars which it produced at relatively low cost and priced competitively. It should be noted that neither Toyota nor Hyundai markets the *cheapest* cars available. BMW and Mercedes have both succeeded by producing a narrow line of

Figure 8.6    (a) Porter's model of generic strategies. Adapted with permission of the Free Press, a division of Macmillan Inc., from Porter, ME *Competitive Advantage: Creating and Sustaining Superior Performance.* © Michael E Porter, 1985. *(b)* Porter's model of generic strategies applied to the world motor industry. Source: Porter, ME (1985) *Competitive Advantage: Creating and Sustaining Superior Performance,* Free Press.

| | Competitive advantage | |
|---|---|---|
| Competitive scope | **Broad target** | 1 — Cost leadership | 2 — Differentiation |
| | **Narrow target** | 3a — Cost focus | 3b — Differentiation focus |

(a)

| | Competitive advantage | |
|---|---|---|
| Competitive scope | **Broad target** | *Cost leadership* — Toyota | *Differentiation* — General Motors |
| | **Narrow target** | *Cost focus* — Hyundai | *Differentiation focus* — BMW Mercedes Mazda |

(b)

more exclusive cars for the price-insensitive, quality-conscious customer. There are several cars available from both companies but they are clearly targeted at people who are willing to pay premium prices for perceived higher quality. Mazda was similarly successful with a narrow and sporty range.

It is never going to be easy to identify who the true cost leader is in any industry or segment. To ascertain this we need accurate information on gross margins and profitability together with an acceptance of the relevant segment boundaries. We can, nevertheless, make educated guesses.

Applying the same ideas to credit cards, it is quickly and readily appreciated that Barclaycard, by offering both Visa and Mastercard credit cards, together with platinum, gold and special business versions, is differentiated and covers most segments of the market. American Express, and the increasingly popular 'affinity cards', such as those linked to football clubs, are focused differentiators because they concentrate on identifiable interest groups. Some would argue that MBNA, because of its international coverage and strategy of persuading other cardholders to transfer, has become the overall cost leader. Egg, linked to Prudential's competitive but niched banking activity, is following a strategy of focused cost leadership.

In Chapter 7 the position of Unilever and its Wall's ice cream was discussed. This would appear to be the cost leader. Mars and Nestlé pursue differentiation strategies successfully; premium ice creams such as Ben and Jerry's and Häagen-Dazs are focused differentiators. Small,

# Minicase 8.5 Toyota's Cost Leadership Strategy

- Toyota historically has enjoyed a 40% plus market share in Japan, supplemented by 7.5% of the US market (where it also manufactures) and 3% of Europe – Toyota followed Nissan in manufacturing in the UK.
- Toyota has sought to sell a range of cars at prices marginally below those of comparable Ford and General Motors cars. Ford and GM both sell more cars than Toyota worldwide. However, Toyota's operating profits have exceeded those of its rivals because it has ruthlessly controlled its costs.
- Production systems, based on JIT (just-in-time supply of components), are very efficient. Toyota claims fewer defects than any other manufacturer, resulting from the vigilance of each worker on the assembly lines. The Lexus range of top-quality cars requires one-sixth of the labour hours used to build a Mercedes. During the mid-1990s the best Toyota plant was assembling a car in 13 person-hours, whereas Ford, Honda and Nissan all required 20.
- 'Toyota does not indulge in expensive executive facilities'.
- Toyota also spends 5% of sales revenue on research and development (as high as any major competitor), concentrating on a search for continuous improvements 'to inch apart from competitors', rather than major breakthroughs.
- There is a policy of fast new model development. In the 1990s Toyota models had an average age of two years; Ford and GM cars averaged five years.

Revenues, however, began to fall back in 1995. Sales of Toyota's new, revamped version of its best-selling Corolla saloon were disappointing. 'In its hot pursuit of cost savings, Toyota had produced a car that lacks character'.

Overall cost leaders, slicing through the competitive middle market, must still produce distinctive, differentiated products to justify their near-market-average pricing policy.

In addition, the growing popularity of four-wheel drive recreational vehicles affected saloon car sales, but Toyota responded with its own models, especially the popular Rav 4.

QUESTION: What do you believe the competitive position of Toyota to be now? (To answer this it would be useful to look at the margin and profitability figures for the leading manufacturers.)

*Toyota*    http://www.toyota.com

local retailers with low overheads will be following a cost focus strategy.

Using these ideas in a slightly different way, we can see that retailers seek to compete on either image or cost. Image-based retailers add value to either or both the product and the service provided to customers. Success in differentiating generates customer loyalty and premium prices. Cost-based retailers operate with competitive margins, searching for strategies that balance high turnover with low costs resulting from operating efficiencies.

Porter argues that a company cannot achieve superior profitability if it is 'stuck in the middle' with no clear strategy for competitive advantage and no clearly delineated position, a point that is debated later (see p. 309). Moreover, competitors seeking cost advantages should not lose sight of the need to maintain distinctiveness; and competitive differentiators should be vigilant in managing their costs. Otherwise, the potential for superior profits is lost.

## The cost leadership strategy

To achieve substantial rewards from this strategy Porter argues that the organization must be *the* cost leader, and unchallenged in this position. There is room for only one; and if there is competition for market leadership based on this strategy there will be price competition.

Cost leadership as a generic strategy does not imply that the company will market the lowest price product or service in the industry. Quite often the lowest price products are perceived as inferior, and as such appeal to only a proportion of the market. Consequently, low price related to lower quality is a differentiation strategy. Low cost therefore does not necessarily mean 'cheap' and low-cost companies can have upmarket rather than downmarket appeal. Equally, low cost does not imply lower rewards for employees or other stakeholders as successful cost leaders can be very profitable. Their aim is to secure a

cost advantage over their rivals, price competitively and relative to how their product is perceived by customers, and achieve a high profit margin. Where this applies across a broad range of segments turnover and market share should also be high for the industry. They are seeking above-average profits with industry-average prices.

Cost focus strategies can be based on finding a distinct group of customers whose needs are slightly below average. Costs are saved by meeting their needs specifically and avoiding unnecessary additional costs.

Figure 8.7 illustrates the above points and relates the generic strategies to efficiency and effectiveness.

There is little advantage in being only one of a number of low-cost producers. The advantage is gained by superior management, concentrating on cost-saving opportunities, minimizing waste, and not adding values which customers regard as unimportant to the product or service. Many products do have values added which are not regarded as necessary by the market. Cost savings can generally be achieved in any and every area of the business, and quite often they begin with the strategic leader. Senior executives who enjoy substantial perks are unlikely to pursue a cost leadership strategy. Porter suggests that it is a mistake to believe that cost savings are only possible in the manufacturing function and that this strategy is only applicable to the largest producers in an industry. However, where cost leadership generates market share and volume production opportunities, economies of scale in manufacturing do apply.

## The differentiation strategy

Cost leadership is usually traded off against differentiation, with the two regarded as pulling in opposite directions. Differentiation adds costs in order to add value for which customers are willing to pay premium prices. For a differentiation

*Figure 8.7*    Competitive strategies.

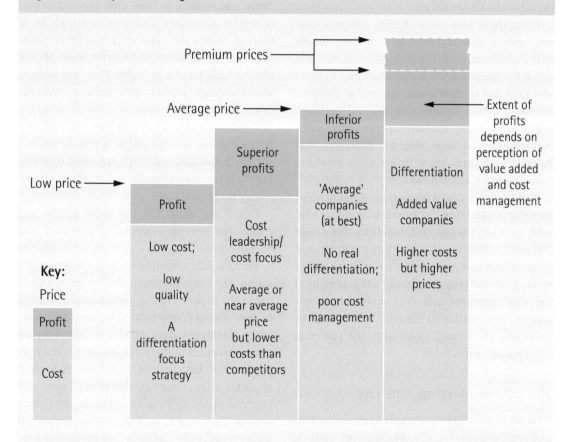

Efficiency, effectiveness and competitive strategies

|  | Cost leadership | Differentiation |
| --- | --- | --- |
| Efficiency via | Driving costs downwards | Doing things well |
| Effectiveness via | Knowing what is important and unimportant to customers – saving on latter | Finding and sustaining unique or different ways of competing |

focus strategy to be successful the market must be capable of clear segmentation, and the requirements for this were highlighted earlier (see p. 289).

With differentiation superior performance is achieved by serving customer needs differently, ideally uniquely. The more unique the difference, the more sustainable is any advantage which accrues. Differentiation must inevitably add costs, which can only be recouped if the market is willing to pay the necessary premium prices. It is crucial that costs are only added in areas that customers perceive as important, and again this can relate to any area of the operation. A solicitors' practice, for example, might find competitive advantage in the manner and promptness with which customer queries are dealt, both over the telephone and in person. A fuller list might include the following possibilities:

- quality of materials used (related to purchasing)
- superior performance (design)
- high quality (production; inspection)
- superior packaging (distribution)
- delivery (sales; production)
- prompt answer of queries (customer relations; sales)
- efficient paperwork (administration).

Furthermore, it is insufficient merely to add value; customers must recognize and appreciate the difference. If it cannot be seen easily it should be communicated, perhaps through advertising. Communication between manufacturer and customer is vital, for it is only by understanding customer needs that the most appropriate value can be added. Take as an example the supplier of a component to an assembly company. At face value the supplier will seek to help the assembler to lower his or her costs, or enhance the quality of his or her product, the choice depending upon the competitive strategy of the assembler. But this level

of thinking alone might overlook further worthwhile opportunities. How does the assembler handle and store the components? And so on. If a supplier understands fully his or her customers' operations he might find new ways of adding value.

The differentiation strategy can be easily misjudged, however, for a number of reasons, including:

- by choosing something that buyers fail to recognize, appreciate or value
- by over-fulfilling needs and as a consequence failing to achieve cost-effectiveness
- by selecting something that competitors can either improve on or undercut
- by attempting to overcharge for the differentiation
- by thinking too narrowly, missing opportunities and being outflanked by competitors.

Case 8.6 illustrates three differentiation strategies.

## A critique of Porter's generic strategies

Care must be taken not to misunderstand the implications of delineation. Porter has stated that successful organizations will select and concentrate their efforts on effectively implementing one of the generic strategies that he identified; they will avoid being 'stuck in the middle'. However, it does appear that while cost leadership and differentiation may be seen as mutually exclusive, successful strategies can be based on a mix of the two. YKK, the Japanese zip manufacturer and world market leader, achieves both cost leadership and significant differentiation. This case is explored in detail in Chapter 9.

At the same time, Sainsbury's has argued that its strategy has been based on providing good food at low cost for the broad middle ground in the market. They do not offer the

# Minicase 8.6 Three Differentiation Strategies: BMW, Bang & Olufsen and James Purdey

## BMW

BMW follows a number of strategies designed to protect its market niche, especially from Japanese competition. Notably, these cover both the cars and the overall service package provided by BMW for its customers.

- Cars can be tailored and customized substantially. Customers can choose any colour they want, a benefit normally restricted to Rolls Royce and Aston Martin; and there is a wide range of interior options and 'performance extras'.
- Safety, environment, economy and comfort are featured and stressed in every model.
- National BMW sales companies are wholly owned, together with strategically located parts warehouses. The independent distributors place their orders directly into BMW's central computer.
- There are fleets of specially equipped cars to assist BMW motorists who break down.
- In 1994 BMW became the first European car manufacturer to produce in the USA.
- Historically, BMW chose to ignore sports cars and hatchbacks, which it saw as downmarket from luxury saloon cars. However, market trends and preferences brought a change of heart. The 1994 BMW Compact was launched as a hatchback version of the successful 3-series; a BMW sports model was used for the James Bond film Goldeneye.

The acquisition of Rover gave BMW a range of successful, smaller hatchbacks, along with Land Rover recreational and multipurpose vehicles. But the two companies, with their very different histories and cultures, were not easily integrated. In 2000 Rover was bought back by a financial consortium and Land Rover was sold to Ford.

*BMW*    http://www.bmw.com

## Bang & Olufsen

Now 75 years old, Bang & Olufsen is a Danish manufacturer of hi-fi equipment and televisions, which enjoys an elite reputation and status worldwide for the quality of its products. Its customers tend to be very loyal.

The company has adopted sleek, tasteful designs, clever technologies and high standards of manufacture for many years. During the 1980s its performance deteriorated because it was seen as too much of a niche competitor. As a response, ranges of slightly less expensive – but still exceptionally high-quality – products were launched. From this a new philosophy has emerged – that the products are about lifestyle and technical excellence is more of a 'given'.

Company advertising uses the slogan 'a life less ordinary' to suggest that 'distinctiveness is a value in itself'. Clearly, this fits with the paradigm of the 'dream society' discussed in Chapter 7.

Bang & Olufsen never asks its customers about future designs and products. Instead, its 'free thinking designers plant their ideas in the marketplace'. The company sees itself as a fashion leader. In addition, the company is very concerned to maintain control over who retails its products and how they are displayed in stores.

The company's niche must be potentially under threat if its rivals are able to improve the quality and reliability of their designs and exploit the manufacturing competencies of lower-cost labour countries.

*Bang and Olufsen*   http://www.bang-olufsen.com

### James Purdey

Purdey firearms would be classified as a super-luxury product; they retail at 'prices more normally associated with small houses'. The company manufactures something in the order of 60 guns per year, 90% of which are sold abroad.

There is close attention to detail, and quality control is incredibly tight. Every order is perceived as a special; nothing is seen as standard. The stocks are oil polished rather than varnished in a lengthy, labour-intensive process; and buyers can choose almost any special, idiosyncratic feature as long as they are happy to pay the appropriate premium. Typically, orders are placed two years in advance of delivery.

Because they appeal to a very limited market segment, and because they literally last a lifetime (and sometimes longer), growth potential for James Purdey, without diversification, is clearly limited.

*James Purdey*   http://www.purdey.com

QUESTIONS: Are these companies successfully defending their differentiation focus strategies?
How much are they changing in a response to competitive pressures?

cheapest food; equally they do not offer the choice or range of a specialist delicatessen. Really what Sainsbury's was arguing was that it sought to ensure that it has relatively low costs but is seen as differentiated. However, Sainsbury has lower margins than its main rivals – it is not enjoying the benefits of relatively low costs. Sainsbury's has lost market leadership to Tesco.

Hendry (1990) has suggested that as there can be only one cost leader, cost leadership is not so much a strategy as a position that one company – which is almost certainly differentiated – enjoys. Toyota may be overall cost leader, but it still differentiates all of its cars. There are different models for different market segments, as well as the associated Lexus range. Because it is a position, and because competitors are always likely to be following cost reduction strategies, it can be a very risky and precarious position if other opportunities for adding value are ignored. Simply, cost leadership is based on efficiencies and sound cost management, but being different still matters.

Similarly, differentiation may be concerned with adding value, and therefore costs, but costs must still be managed. We must understand the cost drivers for any business, a topic taken up in the next chapter. It is important to incur and add costs only where they can be recouped in the form of premium prices. Yet, where a company is particularly concerned with issues of size and market share it may deliberately choose to charge relatively low prices and not attempt to recover the extra costs it has added in its search to be different. It sacrifices superior profits, at least in the shortterm while it builds a power base.

Hendry also questions the value of broad and narrow focus, arguing that internal industry boundaries are always changing, enhanced by the speed of technological change. New niches are emerging all the time, such that what appears to be a solid niche can quickly become a tomb.

To summarize, while the ideas of Michael Porter can be questioned and debated, they nevertheless provide an extremely useful framework for analysing industries and competitive strategy. It is important not to take them simply at face value and assume that the idea of generic strategies is the key which unlocks the secret of competitive advantage. They are not prescriptive.

## Competitive Advantage and Competitive Success

So far it has been argued that competitive strategies are *built around* differentiation and cost leadership. Competitive advantage is *reflected in* and accrues from perceived differences and real cost advantages, both of these relative to competitors. Hence, competitive advantage is *dependent upon* strategic positioning, but the two are not the same. Competitive advantage will normally, at least in the long term, result in superior margins. Table 8.2 shows that any individual functional area, or a combination of several functions, can be the actual source of the advantage.

Porter (1996) later reinforced these points, and attempted to answer some of the criticisms of his generic strategy approach, when he restated that competitive success is based on one of two alternatives. First, an organization can aim to be better than its rivals and focus on operating efficiencies to achieve this. Secondly, it can seek either to do different things, or to do things differently. This concerns effectiveness, and it relates to strategic positioning. He identified three broad approaches to positioning:

- An organization can focus on a particular product or service – or an identifiable and limited range – and sell it to every customer who is interested. This is the approach favoured by BMW and EasyJet.
- It can, alternatively, target a segment group and provide a wider range of products which can serve a variety of their needs. This is the IKEA approach.
- Thirdly, it can identify and focus on an carefully defined niche with a single product or service. James Purdey (Minicase 8.6) provides an ideal example.

Porter pointed out that it is activities – what the organization actually does both directly and indirectly for its customers, its functional strategies – that create and build value and, in turn, advantage. Together these activities determine the strategic position that an organization enjoys, and competitive advantage comes from the strength of the position. While being able to do something better or differently is essential, the way in which the activities are combined to generate synergy is also critical. Most individual activities can be copied, but it is much more difficult to replicate what might be a unique combination of activities.

Consequently, organizations must choose what to do and what not to do, which activities to undertake and which to ignore, and how they might be fused into a powerful mix. Activities that affect the value proposition must not be neglected, but those that have little impact should not consume resources. Critical trade-

*Table 8.2* Functional strategies and competitive advantage

| Functional strategy | Competitive strategy | |
| --- | --- | --- |
| | Low cost | Differentiation |
| Marketing | Large companies can obtain media discounts | Image – reinforced by well-known strategic leader |
| Operations | Efficient plant management and utilization (productivity) | Low defect rate and high quality |
| | Re-engineered processes which reduce costs | Re-engineered processes which add extra value |
| Human resources | Training to achieve low rejections and high-quality policies which keep turnover low | Incentives to encourage innovation |
| Research and development | Reformulated processes which reduce costs | New, patented breakthroughs |
| Finance | Low-cost loans (improves profit after interest and before tax) | Ability to finance corporate strategic change, investments and acquisitions |
| Information technology | Faster decision making in flatter organization structure | Creative use of information to understand customer needs, meet them and outperform competitors |
| Distribution logistics | Lower stock-holding costs | Alliances with suppliers and/or distributors which are long-term mutually supportive |

This list of examples is indicative only, and not an exhaustive set of possibilities.

offs must be made in an attempt to find a 'unique' position. It can be expensive, even self-destructive, to try and do too much and not focus on what does make a difference.

IKEA has chosen to trade-off in a number of ways, for example. It sacrifices being able to offer a wide range of bought-in products by designing and manufacturing its own. By choosing to hold stock in all of its stores and warehouses IKEA sacrifices the low inventory costs some of its competitors enjoy by only delivering against orders. It sacrifices the use of the highest quality materials in favour of function and affordable prices. IKEA also sacrifices sales assistance in favour of self-service; and it opts for only out-of-town locations.

## Activity mapping

Ideally, all of the selected activities will fit together and complement the corporate and competitive strategies in order to yield uniqueness and synergy. Porter uses the metaphor of a comparison of two people to make his point. They each have hands, feet, eyes, ears and so on which, by-and-large, perform similar functions. While there will be differences between two people's hands or feet, the real difference is in the way all the parts combine into a whole. Individual differences in parts, such as colour blindness or arthritis in a hand, do not in themselves explain

different behaviours and outcomes. To understand this we need to understand more about the workings of the brain. In a similar way, if we are to understand organizations and organizational differences, we must understand how different organizations acquire and use knowledge, which is frequently related to the synergy created by the interactions of the functions and activities.

*Figure 8.8*    Lilliput Lane activity system.

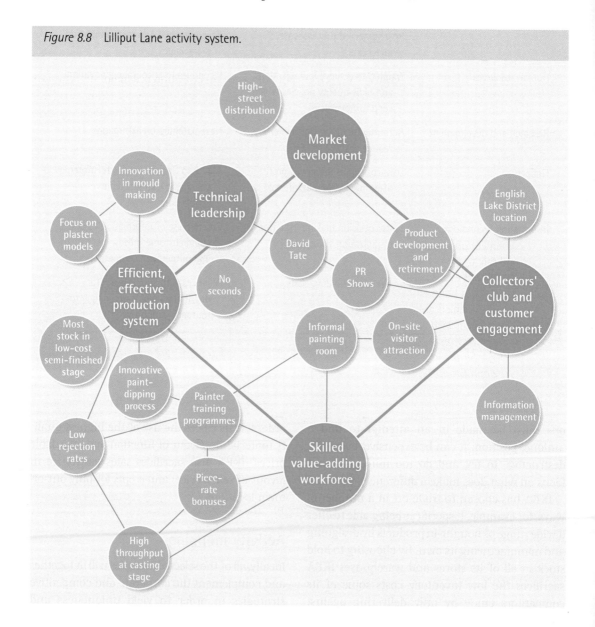

Figure 8.8 is an example of Porter's activity mapping idea. The organization selected is Lilliput Lane, manufacturer of plaster cottages and other collectable items. Using innovatory moulding technology, much of it invented by founder, David Tate, the company casts intricate figures and models out of plaster, a cheap and readily obtainable commodity. Individual painters then transform a relatively bland model into a unique finished article. A full-length case study of the company appears later in the book. Simply, the five larger circles represent what I believe are the key activities in terms of difference and competitive strength; the smaller circles are important support activities. It will be realized that the key activities are all linked and complementary and that the other activities often support more than one key activity.

Over time, activities will be abandoned, added or changed to affect the competitive position. To a large extent the way in which activities are carried out by people is crucially important and, consequently, the culture and style of management in the organization is a major determinant of the organization's ability to change and find new opportunities for creating different values for customers.

Activity mapping is clearly related to the value chain which is explained in Chapter 9 (p. 342)

## Sustaining competitive advantage

Few positions are defensible long term against rivals. Competitors will copy good ideas and maybe even improve on them. Change is the key. Competitors, having created a competitive advantage, will stay ahead if they innovate and look for improvements on a continuous basis and, at the same time, look for discontinuous opportunities to effect change on industries and markets.

Figure 8.9 combines a number of the points made here, emphasizing that successful companies create advantage and success by being committed to their customers through careful positioning and managed change. The differences and cost advantages which create a position must be supported by high levels of service in strategy implementation and ideally by a strong reputation and brand, as discussed further in Chapter 9.

Figure 8.10 shows that competitive advantage can be rooted in technology, organization and people, but that it is people and people-driven

Many companies spend a lot of time and money researching customers' views, but most spend nothing like enough on observing competitors. The main reason for change is to keep ahead of competitors or to catch up on the complacent market leaders. Companies must invest in development – it's a case of 'duck or no dinner'.

*Sir Simon Hornby,
ex-Chairman, WH Smith plc*

When I'm on a plane, I prowl around and talk to passengers and ask the staff about everything. I normally come back with a hundred notes in my pocket scribbled on little pieces of paper. Direct feedback is far better than market research.

*Sir Richard Branson, Chairman,
Virgin Group, quoted in Ferry (1989)*

The strategy of Virgin Atlantic Airways is built around quality service and differentiation. Virgin's 'Upper Class' aims to offer a first-class-equivalent service at business-class prices and has provided for a number of years, for example, electrostatic headphones that customers can keep afterwards, a large selection of films to watch on personal mini video-cassette players, and chauffeur-driven rides to and from airports.

*Figure 8.9*    Competitive advantage through customer commitment. Developed by John Thompson from material in de Kare-Silver, M (1997) *Strategy in Crisis*, Macmillan.

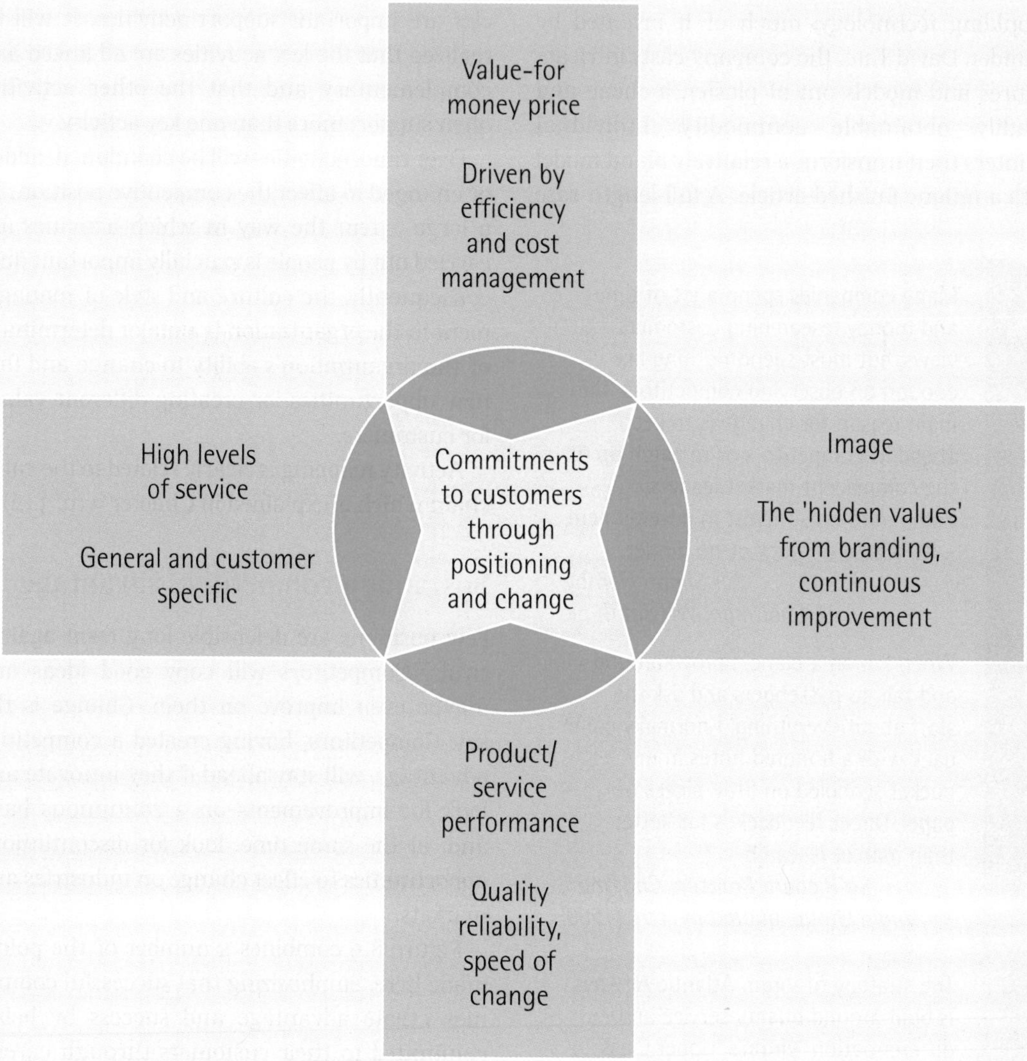

Value-for
money price

Driven by
efficiency
and cost
management

High levels
of service

General and customer
specific

Commitments
to customers
through
positioning
and change

Image

The 'hidden values'
from branding,
continuous
improvement

Product/
service
performance

Quality
reliability,
speed of
change

processes that are the real source of *sustained* advantage, because it is these that are most difficult for rivals to copy. People must be convinced that they are important, and that their contribution is valued – logically through an appropriate reward system – as otherwise they may not deliver and improve the all-important service. This will always prove difficult in a culture where cost management and resource savings have become dominant.

There are many examples where once-powerful and prominent companies have lost their edge and failed to sustain their competitive advantage:

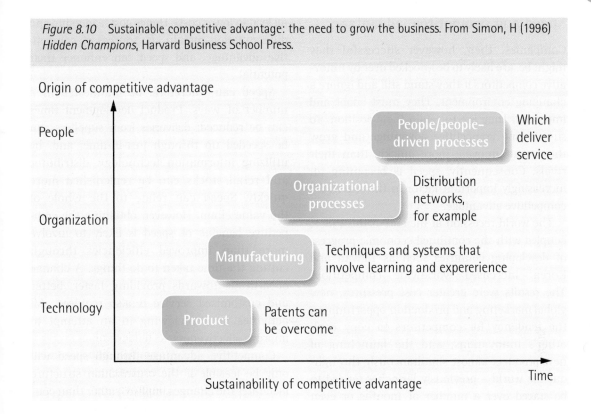

*Figure 8.10* Sustainable competitive advantage: the need to grow the business. From Simon, H (1996) *Hidden Champions*, Harvard Business School Press.

- Minicase 1.2 showed how Marks and Spencer 'took its eye off the ball' and allowed some of its ranges, particularly clothing, to become tired. Large retailers such as M&S normally control buying, product and range selection for every store centrally, because this can save costs. In an attempt to re-establish its position, M&S is allowing individual store managers to have more of an input than in the past. After all, they are closest to local customers.

- With Next, George Davies opened a niche for stylish clothing for slightly older age groups. However, once such a niche has been opened it is relatively easy for rivals to copy the broad strategy, and they did. When Next failed to defend its position by improvements, and instead committed resources to the acquisition of other retail brands and formats, its early advantage was lost. Davies was a corporate casualty, and Next has been turned around under different leadership.

- Toys R Us are the American toy superstores who grew at the expense of independent retailers. More recently, Toys R Us has suffered at the hands of Wal-Mart, which has used its purchasing power to compete on price and gain a significant market share. Wal-Mart simply focuses on the best-selling toys which it offers at rock-bottom prices. Toys R Us has a wider choice but that clearly is not what every customer wants. According to Tomkins(1998), 'the company's big mistake was complacency ... they stopped renewing and refreshing their stores', and thus provided a way in for Wal-Mart. Toys R Us became 'stuck in the middle'. The remaining high-street independents are often more convenient and the discounters are cheaper. Their demise was exacerbated by a reputation for relatively poor in-store service.

## Speed and competitive advantage

Companies, then, however successful they might be, are likely to be knocked over by innovative competitors if they stand still and ignore a changing environment. They must adapt and improve if they are to retain their position. To sustain any competitive advantage and grow they must innovate more quickly than their rivals. Consequently, speed is becoming an increasingly important factor in the search for competitive advantage.

The world recession at the end of the 1980s, coupled with the continued economic progress of developing countries such as Taiwan and Korea, increased worldwide competition. The results were greater cost pressures, new global marketing and production opportunities, the tendency for competitors to copy each other's innovations, and the launching of new products almost simultaneously throughout the world – previously launches tended to be staged over a number of months or even years.

Technological developments in electronics are leading to shorter lifecycles for many products and growing difficulties in establishing sustainable competitive advantage. Increasing research and development costs have focused attention on the strategic value of innovation and incremental change – the constant search for gradual improvements. This is enhanced by the possibilities of computer-aided design and manufacturing and, in turn, just-in-time systems.

The emergence of global markets and competition is opening up new segmentation opportunities. Companies that can capitalize on these through innovation and product and market development are often able to differentiate their products and services.

Shorter product development times, just-in-time manufacturing, together with the benefits of learning and incremental improvements, can all lead to lower costs. Hence cost leadership and differentiation remain key sources of competitive advantage, and speed can enhance their potential.

Speed can, therefore, be manifested in a number of ways. Product development times can be reduced; deliveries from suppliers can be speeded up through just-in-time; and, by utilizing information technology, distributor and retail stocks can be replenished more quickly. Speed can relate to the whole of the value chain. However, obtaining the competitive benefits of speed is likely to involve more than improved efficiencies through cutting the time taken to do things. A change of attitude towards providing faster, better and customized service is also required. All activities need reviewing in an attempt to improve effectiveness.

Competitive advantage through speed will only be feasible if the organization structure facilitates the changes implied, rather than constrains them. Ideas and information must be able to permeate quickly through the organization; and managers at the operational level must be empowered to make decisions. This implies decentralization and possibly fewer levels of management in the hierarchy.

Successful organizations will become fast learners, ideally finding out about changing customer preferences and expectations ahead of their competitors. They will also need to be able to respond quickly to changes in competitor strategies. This again emphasizes the importance of decentralization.

When speed was less important it was normal for products to be developed and tested in advance of any investment in the new plant which would eventually be required to produce them in volume. These must now be seen as parallel, not sequential, activities. This necessitates close co-operation between the various functional areas of the business, perhaps using special project teams. As shown in Chapter 21, such changes can prove difficult to implement.

Finally, the notion of speed must be considered very carefully in certain industries. The design and development of new drugs and new aeroplanes, for example, should not be hurried if safety and reliability could be compromised.

## The Dynamics of Competition

### Competitor benchmarking

Recapping key points from earlier in the chapter, a true cost leader will also enjoy some form of differentiation, and successful differentiators will be effective cost managers. Differentiation and cost control are compatible. All companies should continually search for innovatory differentiation opportunities and for ways of improving their cost efficiencies. As seen in earlier chapters, leveraging resources and setting stretching targets for employees can help to bring about innovation and savings; benchmarking good or best practice in other organizations (a process of measurement and comparison) can also provide new ideas and suggestions for reducing costs and improving efficiency. Organizations from different sectors and industries can be a useful source of ideas if they have developed a high level of expertise. It should be stressed that this process is a search for ideas that can be customized for a different organization rather than an exercise in simply copying. Managers should be open-minded and inquisitive and look 'everywhere' for ideas.

At the same time, it is vital for an organization to understand clearly its position relative to its competitors. Table 8.3 provides a general framework for considering competitive strategies and Figure 8.11 shows how we might benchmark

competitors for comparison with an organization and with customer preferences. The key order criteria – key success factors – are listed down the left-hand side and ranked in order of their importance to customers. Their relative significance is plotted against the horizontal axis. The ability of different competitors to meet these key success factors is illustrated by the dotted lines. Competitor A is clearly relying on its quality and technical back-up, for which it has a good reputation, but is it truly satisfying customer needs? Competitor B seems to offer an all-round better service, and in a number of areas is providing a service beyond that demanded. Given the areas, this may be good as it will indicate a reliable supplier.

How would our customers rank our products/services in relation to those of our competitors?

*Not as good as.* We must improve!

*No worse than.* This implies a general dissatisfaction, so there must be real opportunities to benefit from improvement and differentiation.

*As good as the others, no better, no worse.* Again opportunity to benefit if new values can be added and real differentiation perceived.

*Better than.* We must still work hard to retain our lead.

I subscribe absolutely to the concept of stealing shamelessly! Wherever you come across a good idea, if it's likely to work, pinch it. There's nothing wrong with that. There is a quite respectable word – benchmarking – which is the same thing if you think about it.

*Bill Cockburn, British Telecom, when Group Chief Executive, WH Smith plc*

*Table 8.3*   A framework for evaluating competitive strategies

| Scope | Global; industry-wide; niche |
|---|---|
| | Single or multiproduct/service |
| | Focused or diversified |
| | Vertical linkages with suppliers/distributors |
| Objectives | Ambitious for market or segment leadership |
| | Market presence just to support other (more important) activities |
| Success | Market share |
| | Image and reputation |
| | Profitability |
| Commitment | Aggressive – willing to acquire to grow |
| | Passive survivor |
| | Willing to divest if opportunity arises |
| Approach | Offensive – attacking other competitors |
| | Defending a strong position [note: the same strategy (new products, price cuts) can be used both offensively and defensively] |
| | Risk taking or risk averse |
| | Teasing out new segments or niches |
| Strategy | High quality – perhaps with technological support |
| | High service |
| | Low price |
| Position | Cost advantage or even cost leadership enjoyed |
| | Clearly differentiated |
| Competitive resources | High technology base; modern plant |
| | Location relative to markets |
| | Quality of people (ability to add value) |
| | Reputation |

The examples provided for each of the eight criteria are not offered as an exhaustive list.

## Changing competitive positions

A successful competitive position implies a match between customers' perceptions of the relative quality or value of a product or service – in comparison to rival offerings – and its price, again in relation to the prices of competing products or services. The relevant area of analysis is the segment or segments in which an organization chooses to compete; and, in addition, the 'total price' should be used for comparison purposes. Customers, for example, may willingly pay a premium purchase price initially for a particular brand of, say, an electrical good or car if they believe that over its life it will incur lower maintenance and service costs

*Figure 8.11*    Competitor gap analysis.

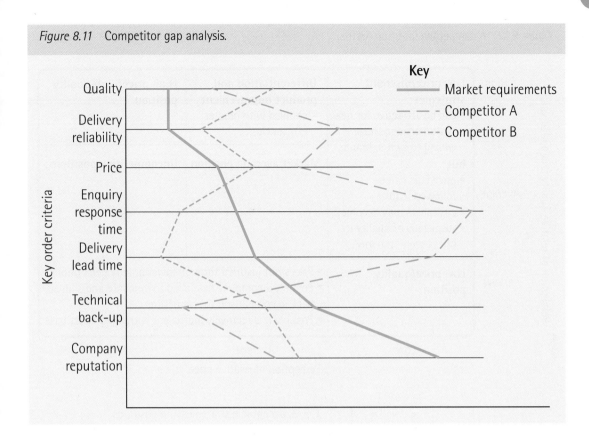

than competing brands. Products offered at initially lower prices may be perceived to be more expensive overall.

Figure 8.12 (which develops Figure 8.5) features a competitive positioning grid. Three basic positions are shown by sectors 1, 2 and 3. Sector 6, high perceived prices but only average (at best) quality, is an untenable position in the longrun. Sector 4 illustrates a company competing on price, which can be a successful strategy, but it can provoke competitive responses; in which case, it may only serve in driving down all prices and making all competitors less profitable. Do-it-yourself chains, such as B&Q, have come to believe that the key to survival in a crowded market is to offer permanently competitive prices as well as developing a unique identity. Sporadic high discounts are being replaced

by 'everyday low prices'; success is more dependent on volume sales than the actual margins on individual products.

Effective differentiators, commanding premium prices and earning superior profits with high margins, are shown as Sector 5. Their success is partially dependent upon sound cost management.

Figure 8.13 illustrates a number of possible competitive strategy changes for companies in selected positions in the matrix.

## Concluding Comments

This chapter has concentrated on how an organization can gain a deeper understanding of its competitive environment with a view to becom-

*Figure 8.12*    A competitive position matrix.

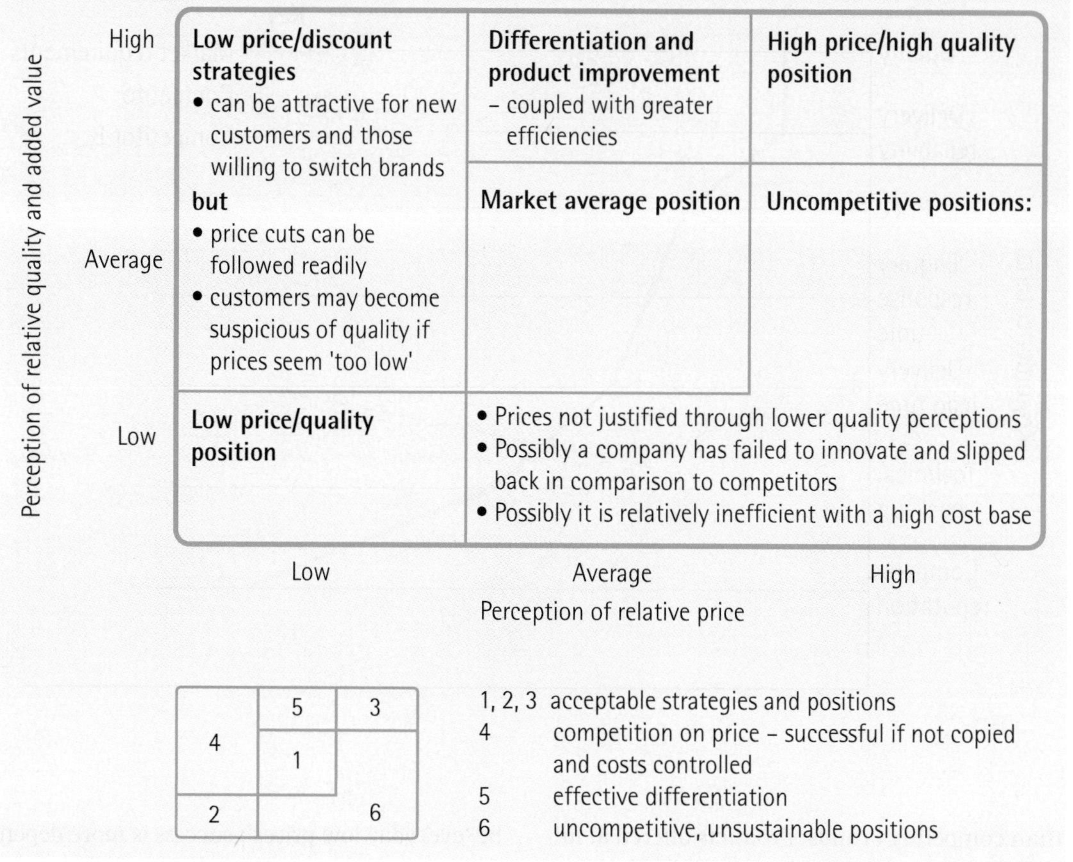

| Perception of relative quality and added value | | Low price/discount strategies | Differentiation and product improvement | High price/high quality position |
|---|---|---|---|---|
| | **High** | Low price/discount strategies<br>• can be attractive for new customers and those willing to switch brands<br>**but**<br>• price cuts can be followed readily<br>• customers may become suspicious of quality if prices seem 'too low' | Differentiation and product improvement<br>– coupled with greater efficiencies | High price/high quality position |
| | **Average** | | Market average position | Uncompetitive positions: |
| | **Low** | Low price/quality position | • Prices not justified through lower quality perceptions<br>• Possibly a company has failed to innovate and slipped back in comparison to competitors<br>• Possibly it is relatively inefficient with a high cost base | |

|  | Low | Average | High |
|---|---|---|---|

Perception of relative price

| | 5 | 3 |
|---|---|---|
| 4 | 1 | |
| 2 | | 6 |

1, 2, 3  acceptable strategies and positions
4       competition on price – successful if not copied
        and costs controlled
5       effective differentiation
6       uncompetitive, unsustainable positions

ing a stronger, more effective competitor through creating and sustaining competitive advantage. The closer a business is to its customers, the more it will understand the market and the industry. Competitive strategy, essential for every product and service that the organization makes and markets, involves a vision about how best to compete. There is a number of ways to generate competitive advantage, and the process is both logical and creative. The choice will also be influenced by the strategic leader and by the organization's culture. However, every employee contributes in some way to both lower costs and uniqueness, and therefore it is important that the competitive strategy is communicated and understood throughout the organization.

In the end, the most successful companies will be those with:

• differentiated products and services which are recognized for their ability to add value, and are
• produced efficiently
• upgraded over time through innovation and improvement, and which
• prove relevant for international markets.

Porter contends that competitors can be viewed as 'good' or 'bad'. Good ones differentiate, innovate and help to develop an industry; bad ones

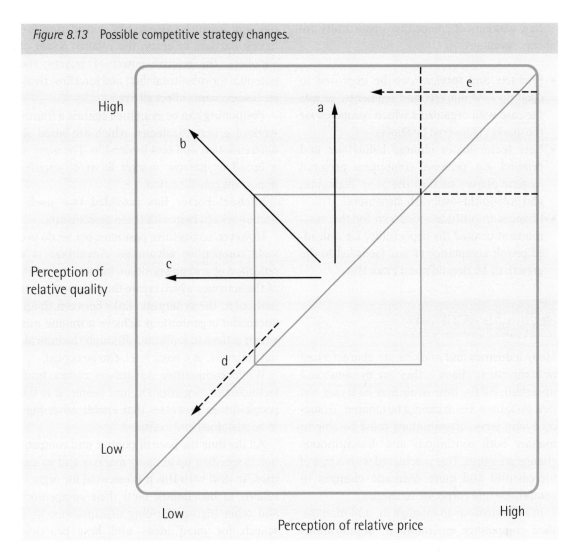

*Figure 8.13*  Possible competitive strategy changes.

just cut prices in an attempt to drive others out of business. Good competitors should be encouraged as they sharpen their rivals and help to set up barriers against bad competitors. A good competitor seeks to increase the market by improving products, not by cutting prices. An interesting example is Polaroid, who invented and patented the instant picture camera. Kodak introduced a rival product but Polaroid eventually succeeded in establishing that it broke their patent illegally. While both products were in competition Polaroid became a much more effective competitor as it was unable to

rely on its barrier to entry. By contrast, it has been argued that certain large Japanese companies have literally bought themselves into segments of the computer and semiconductor industries by accepting very low prices until volume sales have been achieved. Where this has the effect of driving rivals out of business, as has been the experience in random access memory (RAM) chips, the question arises of whether it is in the best long-term interests of consumers. Much depends upon the strategies of companies when they reach a stage of market domination.

New windows of competitive opportunity are always opening:

- Products and services can be improved to open up new markets and segments, as was the case with organizers which competed for the market pioneered by Filofax.
- New technologies change behaviour and demand, e.g. personal computers, personal cassette players such as the Sony Walkman, and hole-in-the-wall cash dispensers.
- Changes in attitude – concern for the environment created the opportunity for unleaded petrol; acceptance of fast foods led to the growth of McDonald's and Pizza Hut.

## Summary

Many industries and markets are characterized by competitive 'chaos' – they are dynamic and uncertain. All the time rivals may be trying out new initiatives which cannot be ignored. To succeed long term, organizations must be able to manage both continuous and discontinuous change pressures. This is achieved with a mix of incremental and more dramatic changes to competitive and corporate strategies.

In an endeavour to manage in, and manage, their competitive environment, organizations must understand the nature and attractiveness of their industry, and their relative position in it.

Industry attractiveness affects profit potential, and it can be assessed by considering five forces: barriers to entry; the relative power of suppliers; the relative power of buyers; the potential for substitutability; and interfirm rivalry. Governments affect all five.

Positioning can be examined against a framework of generic strategies, which are based on differentiation and cost leadership. The issue of a broad or narrow market focus is another important consideration.

Michael Porter has provided two useful frameworks to help with these assessments.

However, competitive positions, per se, do not yield competitive advantage. Advantage is a reflection of a strong position, but it is the result of the activities which create the position and, in particular, the synergistic links between them. Successful organizations achieve a unique mix which is hard to replicate, although the individual activities, at a basic level, can be copied.

While competitive advantage comes from technologies, organization and people, it is the people-driven processes that enable advantage to be sustained and extended.

All the time the pace of change and competition is speeding up in many markets and industries. To deal with this it is essential for organizations to benchmark both their competitors and other high-performing organizations in a search for good ideas and best practice. Specifically, they are looking for new opportunities to add or build value in ways that are meaningful for customers.

## References

Ferry, I (1989) Branson's misunderstood Midas touch, *Business*, November.

Heller, R (1998) *Goldfinger – How Entrepreneurs Grow Rich by Starting Small*, HarperCollins.

Hendry, J (1990) The problem with Porter's generic strategies, *European Management Journal*, December.

Kanter, RM (1990) Strategic alliances and new ventures, Harvard Business School Video Series.

Porter, ME (1980) *Competitive Strategy: Techniques for Analysing Industries and Competitors*, Free Press.

Porter, ME (1985) *Competitive Advantage: Creating and Sustaining Superior Performance*, Free Press.

Porter, ME (1996) What is strategy? *Harvard Business Review*, November–December.

Tomkins, R (1998) Trouble in toyland pushes Toys R Us on the defensive, *Financial Times*, 29 May.

## Additional material on the web site

The website contains extra material for readers who want reinforcement of key issues in:

- marketing strategy
- operations strategy
- management and strategy issues in service businesses.

There is also a summary and critique of Michael Porter's work on how we might analyse the relative competitive strengths of nations.

Test your knowledge of this chapter with our online quiz at http://www.thomsonlearning.co.uk

## Questions and Research Assignments

### TEXT RELATED

1. Study Figure 8.6(b) and consider where you would place other major car manufacturers and why. Where should Rover be categorized? Which companies appear to be 'struck in the middle' without a clear strategy for competitive advantage?

2. Apply the Competitor Grid (Figure 8.11) to this industry.

## Internet and Library Projects

1. Take an industry of your choice, perhaps the one in which you work, and assess it in terms of:
   (a) concentration
   (b) Porter's model of five forces.

From this, analyse one or more of the major competitors in terms of their chosen competitive strategies.

As well as the Internet the following library sources might prove useful sources of information:

- Business Monitors (PA and PQ series)
- Annual Report of the Director General of Fair Trading (as a source of ideas)
- Monopolies and Mergers Commission reports, and Competition Commission reports, which usually feature a comprehensive industry analysis
- McCarthy's (or similar) Index (press-cutting service for firms and industries).

2. How successful has Porsche been since the introduction of its new models? Do you believe that the size of its niche is viable, or might the company have to extend its range?

*Porsche*   http://www.porsche.com

3. Laura Ashley was started in the 1950s by the late Laura Ashley and her husband, Bernard. The company was very successful, with an instinctive approach to designs for fashions and fabrics. Laura Ashley designed, manufactured and retailed mostly clothes and furnishings. The company later diversified with a chain of perfume stores, leather goods stores and a knitwear business in Scotland. The company fared badly in the recession, and by 1991 was losing money.

The company's success has always depended upon the strength of the Laura Ashley name and brand, but the company has struggled after the death of Laura Ashley. In 1995 American Ann Iverson became the fourth chief executive of the decade. She inherited a company which was still clearly differentiated and popular with customers but where costs had escalated, resulting in margins of just 2%.

Ann Iverson declared she would tackle the cost base while 'preserving the mood and emotion, the countryside feeling' of the brand.

Her strategies have involved:

- selected store closures around the world, particularly in the USA
- a consolidation of the design, buying and merchandising functions
- a slimming of the product range.

The need for the company to manufacture, rather than focus on its core strengths of design and retailing, has been questioned.

Ann Iverson is no longer with the company; she too has been replaced.

What is the current position with Laura Ashley? Has the company been turned around or is it still struggling to find a strong competitive position?

*Laura Ashley*   http://www.laura-ashley.com

# Strategic Resources

9

Auditing Strategic Resources

Strategic Architecture

The Organization's Value Chain

The Value Chain and Competitive Advantage

Reputation and Branding

*The resource-based view of strategy gradually emerged during the 1980s and 1990s with a series of important contributions, in particular work on core competency from Prahalad and Hamel (1990) and on added value by Kay (1993). This view helps to explain why some organizations succeed in creating competitive advantage and earning superior profits, while others do not. Consequently, it looks at strategies which can be identified with an individual company as distinct from those that are available to all competitors through an understanding of industries and markets. In other words, market opportunities have to be identified and then satisfied in an individual and distinctive way.*

*Supporters of the resource-based view put forward a number of arguments. As long as there are opportunities which can be identified, it will normally be easier and less risky for organizations to exploit their existing resources in new ways than to seek to acquire and learn new skills and competencies. Innovation matters and new ways of exploiting resources must be found to sustain any competitive advantage. Relative differences which separate a company from its rivals are critical. Just having a resource is not enough. For this reason, it can be useful if particular strengths are not easily learned and imitated by rivals. The opening case on Dyson shows how innovation and new ways of creating and adding value through design can markedly change an industry. In this particular case, innovation allowed a newcomer to establish a position of market dominance and force a reaction from established manufacturers.*

*This chapter looks firstly and briefly at the idea of a resource audit before considering resource linkages and synergy through architecture and the notion of the value*

*chain. The idea of the activity maps, explained in Chapter 8, is developed here. The chapter concludes with a section on reputation and branding, key intangible assets.*

*Before reading this chapter you might usefully re-read the sections on core competencies and leveraging resources in Chapter 2 (pp 59–61).*

## Minicase 9.1  James Dyson

James Dyson is an entrepreneur who challenged the industry giants, in his case with a revolutionary vacuum cleaner. His dual cyclone cleaner now has a UK market share in excess of 50% and international sales are blooming. A Hoover spokesman has said on the *BBC Money Programme*: 'I regret Hoover as a company did not take the product technology of Dyson ... it would have been lain on a shelf and not been used'. Dyson has been compared by Professor Christopher Frayling, Rector of the Royal College of Art, with 'the great Victorian ironmasters ... a one-man attempt to revive British manufacturing industry through design'. Dyson is creative, innovative, totally focused on customers and driven by a desire to improve everyday products. His dedication and ego drive is reflected in the following comment: 'the only way to make a genuine breakthrough is to pursue a vision with a single-minded determination in the face of criticism ...' and this is exactly what he has done. Clearly a risk taker, he invested all of his resources in his venture. In the end his rise to fame and fortune came quickly, but the preceding years had been painful and protracted, and characterized by courage and persistence. They reflect the adage that 'instant success takes time.'

James Dyson's schoolmaster father died when he was just nine years old. The public school to which he was then sent 'made him a fighter'. At school he excelled in running, practising by running cross-countries on his own; and it was on these runs that he began to appreciate the magnificence of the railway bridges constructed by Brunel in the nineteenth century, an experience which helped to form his personal vision. An early leap in the dark came when he volunteered to play bassoon in the school orchestra, without ever having seen a bassoon! Naturally artistic, he won a painting competition sponsored by the *Eagle* comic when he was ten years old. Art became a passion and he later went on to complete a degree in interior design. Dyson may be an inventor, but he has no formal engineering background.

Dyson's first successful product and business was a flat-bottomed boat, the Sea Truck. At this time he learnt how a spherical plastic ball could be moulded, an idea that he turned to good use in the wild garden of his new home. His wheelbarrow was inadequate as the wheels sunk into the ground, so he substituted the wheel with a light plastic ball and thus invented the Ballbarrow. Backed by his brother-in-law on a 50:50 basis, Dyson invested in his new idea. Made of colourful, light plastic the barrow was offered to garden centres and the building trade, both of whom were less than enthusiastic. With a switch to direct mail via newspaper advertisements, the business took off. A new sales manager was appointed but his renewed attempt to sell the barrow through more traditional retail channels was again a failure. The financial penalty was the need for external investors, who later persuaded Dyson's brother-in-law to sell the business. A second painful experience came when the sales manager took the idea and design to the USA, where Dyson later failed with a legal action against him.

Dyson's idea for a dual cyclone household cleaner came in 1979, when he was 31 years old. Again, it was a case of a need creating an opportunity. He was converting his old house and becoming frustrated that his vacuum cleaner would not clear all of the dust that he was creating. Particles were clogging the pores of the dust bags and reducing the suction capability of the cleaner. Needing something to collect paint particles from his plastic spraying operation for the ballbarrows, Dyson had developed a smaller version of the large industrial cyclone machines, which separate particles from air by using centrifugal forces in spinning cylinders. He believed that this technology could be adapted for home vacuum cleaners, removing the need for bags, but his partners in the Ballbarrow business failed to share his enthusiasm. Out of work when the business was sold, his previous employer, Jeremy Fry (for whom he had developed the Sea Truck), loaned him £25,000. Dyson matched this by selling his vegetable garden for £18,000 and taking out an additional £7000 overdraft on his house. Working from home, risking everything and drawing just £10,000 a year to keep himself, his wife and three children, he pursued his idea. Over the years he produced 5000 different prototypes.

When he ultimately approached the established manufacturers his idea was, perhaps predictably, rejected. Replacement dust bags are an important source of additional revenue. A series of discussions with potential partners who might license his idea brought mixed results. Fresh legal actions in the USA for patent infringement – 'with hindsight I didn't patent enough features' – were only partially offset by a deal with Apex of Japan. Dyson designed the G-Force upright cleaner which Apex manufactured and sold to a niche in the Japanese market for the equivalent of £1200 per machine, from which Dyson received just £20. At least there was now an income stream, but this had taken seven years to achieve. Finally, in 1991 Lloyds Bank provided finance for the design and manufacture of a machine in the UK. Several venture capitalists and the Welsh Development Agency had turned him down. Dyson was determined to give his latest version the looks of NASA technology, but further setbacks were still to occur. Dyson was let down by the plastic moulder and assembler with whom he contracted, and was eventually forced to set up his own plant. Early sales through mail-order catalogues were followed by deals with John Lewis and eventually (in 1995) with Comet and Curry's. In this year a cylinder version joined the upright. Dyson continues to improve the designs to extend his patent protection. By 1999 his personal wealth was estimated to be £500 million.

Dyson has always seen himself as more of an inventor than a businessman. He runs two separate businesses, both in Malmesbury, Wiltshire, and he keeps Dyson Manufacturing and Dyson Research (design and patenting) apart. The dress code for employees is perpetually informal and communications are predominantly face-to-face. Memos are banned and even e-mails discouraged. Every employee is encouraged to be creative and contribute ideas. Most new employees are young – 'not contaminated by other employers' – and they all begin by assembling their own vacuum cleaner, which they can then buy for £20. There are over 60 designers, who work on improvements to the dual cyclone cleaners as well as new product ideas. In early 2000 Dyson launched a robot version of the dual cyclone cleaner, which is battery-powered, self-propelled and able to manoeuvre itself around furniture. It retails at some £2500, which may limit it to a select segment of the market. Later in 2000 Dyson launched a revolutionary super-fast washing machine with short wash cycles and an ability to spin clothes almost dry, presenting a challenge to the manufacturers of both washing machines and tumble dryers. This time, however, Dyson had his own resources to launch the product. Moreover Dyson controls 100% of the shares in the business. He has learnt some painful lessons but is now enjoying the rewards of his dogged determination.

QUESTIONS: Thinking about the issues of core competency and strategic capability, what is the 'secret' of James Dyson's competitive advantage?
Has he been able to appropriate the rewards of the value he has added?

*Dyson*   http://www.dyson.com

People feel the best about their work when they do a high-quality job! Getting a job done quickly is satisfying. Getting a job done at low cost is rewarding. But getting a job done quickly, at low cost and with high quality is exciting!
*Robert C Stempel, when Chairman, General Motors Corporation*

## Auditing Strategic Resources

Chapters 7 and 8 looked at organizations in the context of their environments, somewhat artificially separating their general and competitive environments. Environments spring surprises on organizations from time to time. Sometimes the surprises constitute opportunities; at other times, threats. The most vigilant and aware organizations will be better placed to respond. Success lies in seeing opportunities 'ahead of the game' and responding in some individual way, ideally one that is genuinely different, appreciated by customers and not easily copied by rivals. The ability to do this comes down to individual, specific to the organization, competencies and capabilities, which in turn emanate from the organization's resources. Resources, therefore, make the difference. In this chapter this argument is explored in greater depth and frameworks are provided which can help us to audit and evaluate strategic resources.

The relationship between environmental forces and internal resources is at the heart of Figure 9.1, which has been adapted from the Harvard Business School approach to strategy (Kelly and Kelly, 1987). Here, selected products, services and markets are seen as environment driven and the competitive environment and

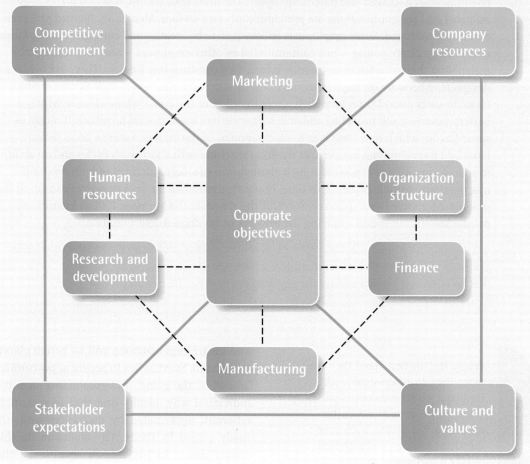

*Figure 9.1* Matching the organization and the environment. Adapted from Kelly, FJ and Kelly, HM (1987) *What They Really Teach You at the Harvard Business School*, Piatkus.

stakeholders are shown with resources and values as four key strategic elements linked to corporate objectives. These elements can be changed, but in many cases not readily and not quickly, and consequently at any point in time they are reasonably fixed.

Six operating elements are also incorporated. *Marketing* relates to how the various products and services are positioned in relation to competitors, and how they are priced, advertised and distributed. *Manufacturing* involves the types of production process, location issues and

technology utilization. *Finance* incorporates both performance targets and sources of funding. *Research and development* considers how much to spend on research and development and whether the perspective is short or long term. *Human resources* relates to the types of people utilized and how they are rewarded. The *organization structure* encompasses how these functions are co-ordinated and controlled.

These operating elements determine whether or not the corporate objectives are achieved. The different functions in the organization are affected to varying degrees by different stakeholders, and certain stakeholders who have a significant impact on certain functions may have little direct importance for others. Equally, the specific stakeholders may influence individual functions in quite different ways. Their impact upon the whole organization is therefore affected by the organization structure and relative power and influence within the firm. The figure also highlights the strategic value of functional managers taking a more holistic view of the organization and their role and contribution.

How, then, might we audit and evaluate these operating elements or strategic resources?

An internal analysis should be a three-stage process:

1. an evaluation of the profile of the principal skills and resources of an organization
2. a comparison of this resource base with the requirements for competitive success in the industry
3. a comparison with competitors to determine the relative strengths and weaknesses and any significant comparative advantage.

Where internal managers carry out this analysis, it is inevitable that there will be some subjective judgement and it will be affected by their position in the organization.

In a SWOT (strengths, weaknesses, opportunities and threats) analysis, then, the strengths and weaknesses of resources must be considered in relative and not absolute terms. It is important to consider whether they are being managed effectively as well as efficiently. Resources, therefore, are not strong or weak purely because they exist or do not exist. Rather, their value depends on how they are being managed, controlled and used.

In auditing resources we consider the functional areas of the business, as this is where the human, financial and physical resources are deployed. These areas might include finance, production, marketing, research and develop-

ment, procurement, personnel and administration. However, it is also important to consider how they are related together in the organization's structure and control systems. A brilliant and successful marketing manager, for example, might seem to represent a strength; however, if there is no adequate cover for him and he leaves or falls ill, it is arguable that the firm has a marketing weakness.

Control systems, such as production and financial control, and the ways in which managers co-operate within the organization influence how well resources are managed for efficiency and effectiveness. Table 9.1, which is not meant to be fully comprehensive, provides a sample of key resource considerations. In completing such an audit the various resources should be evaluated: their existence, the ways in which they are deployed and utilized, and the control systems that are used to manage them.

Efficiency measures of the salesforce might include sales per person or sales per region, but the effectiveness of the salesforce relates to their ability to sell the most profitable products or those products or services that the organization is keen to promote at a particular time, perhaps to reduce a high level of stocks. The efficiency of individual distribution outlets can be measured by sales revenue in a similar way. However, the effectiveness of the distribution activity relates to exactly which products are being sold and to whom, whether they are available where customers expect them, and how much investment in stock is required to maintain the outlets. The efficiency of plant and equipment is linked to percentage utilization. The effectiveness involves an assessment of which products are being manufactured in relation to orders and delivery requirements, to what quality and with what rejection levels.

It is also important to assess the relative strengths and weaknesses in relation to competition.

Managers must be aware of and must address strategic issues if the resources are to be used for

**Table 9.1**  Aspects of the resource audit

| Resource/function | Key considerations |
|---|---|
| **Marketing** | Products and services: range, brand names and stage in lifecycle |
| | Patents |
| | Strength of salesforce |
| | Distribution channels |
| | Market information |
| **Operations** | Location and plant |
| | Capital equipment |
| | Capacity |
| | Processes |
| | Planning and manufacturing systems |
| | Quality control |
| | Supplies |
| **Research and development** | Annual budget |
| | Technology support |
| | Quality of researchers |
| | Record of success and reputation |
| | Spending in relation to industry norm |
| **Information** | Organizational knowledge and extent of sharing |
| | Information systems |
| | Problem-solving capabilities and procedures |
| **Finance** | Capital structure |
| | Working capital |
| | Cash flow |
| | Costing systems and variances |
| | Nature of shareholders |
| | Relations with bankers |
| **Human resources** | Numbers and qualifications |
| | Skills and experience |
| | Age profile |
| | Labour turnover and absenteeism |
| | Flexibility |
| | Development and training record and policies |
| | Motivation and culture |
| | Managerial competencies and capacity |

creating and sustaining competitive advantage. *Marketing* can be looked at from the point of view of managing the activities which comprise the marketing function. Product design and pricing, advertising, selling and distribution would be included here. However, if an organization is marketing orientated there is an implication that employees throughout the organization are aware of consumers and customers, their needs, and how they might be satisfied effectively while enabling the organization to achieve its objectives. Consumer concern becomes part of the culture and values. Consumers and customers are mentioned separately because for many organizations, particularly the manufacturers of products for consumer markets, their customers are distributors and their ultimate consumers are customers of the retailers that they supply.

Innovation and quality can be seen as aspects of production or *operations management*. Again, it is helpful if these factors become part of the culture. An innovatory organization is ready for change, and looking to make positive changes, in order to get ahead and stay ahead of competition. A concern for quality in all activities will affect both costs and consumer satisfaction.

In *human resources management* values are communicated and spread throughout the organization.

*Financial management* includes the control of costs so that profit is achieved and value is added to products and services primarily in areas that matter to consumers. This should provide differentiation and competitive advantage.

Lower costs and differentiation are important themes in competitive strategy. They relate to both an awareness of consumer needs and the management of resources to satisfy these needs effectively and, where relevant, profitably. Marketing orientation and the effective management of production and operations, people and finance are all essential aspects of the creation

and maintenance of competitive strength and advantage.

Functional and competitive strategies are important for an understanding of strategic management in all types of organization, and they are especially important for a large proportion of small businesses and many not-for-profit organizations. Corporate strategic changes such as major diversification and acquisition, divestment of business units which are underperforming or international expansion may not be relevant for small firms with a limited range of products or services and a primarily local market, or for not-for-profit organizations with very specific missions. However, these organizations must compete effectively, operate efficiently and provide their customers and clients with products and services that satisfy their needs. Competitive and functional strategies are therefore the relevant issue.

As the Internet becomes more pervasive in our lives some organizations and industries are being presented with wonderful opportunities and, at the same time, real threats. Book retailing has changed with the growth of Amazon.com and the opening of on-line bookshops by the leading book retailers. Similarly, domestic banking has been changed with the growth of ATMs (automated teller machines or 'holes in the wall'), telephone call centres and Internet accounts. Competitors have had to develop new skills, competencies and capabilities in order to survive, let alone thrive. The challenge, though, did not stop here. It has also been necessary to clarify the key success factors for those customers who opted to avoid the Internet and stick with a personal service. What exactly are their needs and preferences? How can they be satisfied 'wonderfully well'? How can costs be trimmed in the process?

Success, then, depends upon understanding and linking with customers, and these points are explored further through the remainder of this chapter.

## Strategic Architecture

Kay (1993) adopted the word 'architecture' to emphasize the importance of corporate networks and relationships. He argued that companies depend upon their people for their competitiveness and success, but strong and capable individuals, while important, are not enough. They must work together well and synergistically. Football clubs, and their need for skilled individuals to be moulded into a strong, winning team, provide a valuable metaphor. In addition, people's natural energies should not be focused on internal rivalries but on managing external demands. Success here can be enhanced through effective links between an organization, its suppliers, its distributors and its ultimate customers.

In summary, we should consider:

- The way managers and other employees co-operate within the organization. Communications and co-operation should work both horizontally and vertically. Transfer pricing arrangements and poorly crafted internal performance measures can all too easily set division against division and department against department, and create real internal competition for resources. Where managers find delight when another manager, department or division finds itself in trouble, something is wrong. But it still happens. Similarly, in some organizations, there is a reliance on top–down communications for issuing instructions coupled with an ability for managers lower down the organization to feed only good news upwards and suppress bad news. The valuable ideas that some junior and middle managers have are, consequently, neither sought nor listened to by their superiors. Kay calls this 'internal architecture'.
- Suppliers, organizations, distributors and final customers and consumers working together supportively in a 'seamless' chain which builds and provides value for all the participants, or 'external architecture'. Members of this value chain can make life either relatively easy or problematical for the other members, depending on their philosophy. The ideal outcome is one where everyone feels they are gaining some benefit rather than they are being exploited by someone who is ruthless or selfish. It is a feeling of 'win–win' rather than 'I win, you lose' or 'you win at my expense', which happens in many negotiations and deals. Sometimes the members of such a value chain will establish formalized partnerships or alliances to seal the relationship more firmly.

The outcome should be shared knowledge, co-operation and the development of trust and trusted routines, as illustrated in Figure 9.2 and Minicase 9.2 on Benetton. All parties should feel that they can rely on each other.

The driving force in all the world's markets is competition. And the most aggressive drivers are the Japanese. Their competitive strength and ambitions are apparent around the world. Ultimately the only way to succeed is to be fully competitive in the marketplace. Fundamentally this means offering products with utility, style and value that the buyers want, making them with world-class productivity and quality, and serving the customers better than anyone else.

*John F Smith Jr, Vice Chairman*
*(International Operations),*
*General Motors Corporation*

A number of useful examples highlight the benefit of strong strategic architecture:

- For many years Japanese organizations have benefited from membership of corporate fam-

*Figure 9.2*    Effective supply chain management.

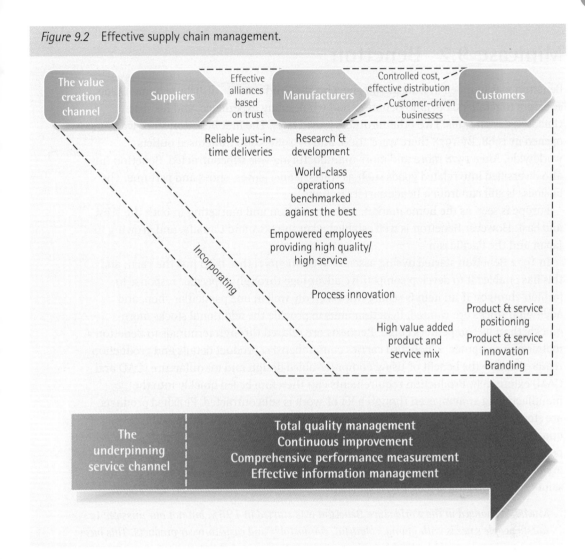

ilies or 'keiretsu'. Businesses, typically those clustered together in a geographical area, will all own shares in each other. Their directors will hold part-time directorships in other organizations in the keiretsu. The whole philosophy will be one of helping each other with either preferred supplier arrangements or the provision of help and advice. It will be realized how a base like this can foster benchmarking and the exchange of ideas and good practice, and the ability to exploit just-in-time supply arrangement. Here, manufacturers can avoid inventory costs by relying on their suppliers to deliver the quantities they need exactly when they are required for production.

- For many years Marks and Spencer was credited with having a valuable portfolio of key suppliers, many of them British, who were committed to it. Typically, M&S would take a substantial proportion of a supplier's annual output and would work with it on designs and quality. M&S knew that it was buying reliable, quality products; the suppliers knew

## Minicase 9.2   Benetton

Benetton was founded in Italy in 1965 by a brother and sister to distribute home-made sweaters to retailers. Luciano Benetton had wholesaling experience, and his sister, Guiliana, design skills. Two other brothers joined later. The first Benetton store was opened in 1968. By 1978 there were 1000, and by 1988 5000 franchised outlets worldwide. After 1978 more and more manufacturing was subcontracted. Benetton has also diversified into related goods such as shirts, jeans, gloves, shoes and perfume. The business is still run from a headquarters in Italy.

Europe is seen as the home market, with production and marketing in both the West and East. However Benetton is well established in the USA and Canada, and growing in Japan and the Pacific rim.

In 1972 Benetton started dyeing assembled garments rather than just the yarn; and this has enabled it to develop competitive advantage through a speedier response to fashion changes. If an item is selling unexpectedly well in one particular shop, and additional stocks are wanted, Benetton aims to provide the additional stocks more quickly than its competitors could. Requests are relayed through terminals to Benetton's mainframe computer, which also carries comprehensive product details and production requirements – the benefit of using computer-aided design and manufacture (CAD and CAM) extensively. Production requirements can therefore be fed quickly into the manufacturing system, even though a lot of work is subcontracted. Finished products are stored in one central warehouse, run by robots and just a handful of people. A quarter of a million items can be handled daily. Benetton aims to replenish its shops with popular items in one week ex-stock, four weeks including production. Production costs are increased by dyeing finished goods, but stock management overall (raw materials, semi-finished and finished items) is efficient.

> *Much has changed in the world since Benetton was started in 1965, but not our mission: to satisfy people's needs with young, colourful, comfortable and easy-to-wear products. This has been our route to world leadership in the design, production and distribution of clothing, accessories and footwear for men, women and children. Our range has been constantly enriched over time by intensive research into new materials and designs – and further additions will follow.*

Benetton is an international company with a global brand image, which has been built around the theme 'The United Colors of Benetton'. This international image is boosted by a strong association with motor racing. Benetton won both the Formula 1 drivers' and constructors' championships in 1995.

> *Colour makes Benetton unique. The secret lies in presenting a broad spectrum of shades, creatively mixed and matched – new and different every time. The study of colour is our greatest research commitment as we constantly seek out new tones.*

Advertising features the same central message and choice of media throughout the world, although the actual themes of the advertisements vary. On occasions, some examples have proved controversial in certain countries. Benetton's approach is based on the premise that customers in different countries use clothing and accessories to express personal lifestyle preferences, with a tendency to demand increasingly higher quality goods. Advertising campaigns 'feature simplified, unambiguous images that convey meaning to the largest possible number of people and cultures throughout the world'.

## Competencies and capabilities

Benetton provides a range of popular and attractive garments and achieves some 20% production cost savings compared with its main competitors. Its franchised retailers offer a high level of customer service with responsive and helpful employees. There is some local customization but, in the main, the same colourful, fashionable and classic garments are available worldwide. To achieve these outcomes, Benetton exploits a number of important competencies and capabilities:

- Dyeing skills are retained in-house.
- The basic grey colour lends itself readily to later colour changes.
- For many years Guiliana Benetton has controlled the design activities, which have again been retained in-house.
- Benetton retains classic designs and saves costs by avoiding too much variety.
- Eighty per cent of manufacturing is undertaken by independent suppliers.
- There are strong contractual arrangements with key suppliers around the world, some of whom work exclusively for Benetton.
- Benetton dictate tight technical specification for their supplies.
- Sophisticated IT systems are utilized in both design and manufacture.
- Most suppliers are small businesses, and in many instances Benetton loans money to finance them.
- Benetton's success is frequently seen by their suppliers as their own success, a relationship issue which clearly works in Benetton's favour.
- Periodically Benetton 'releases' suppliers, which keeps the rest 'on their toes'.
- Purchasing is centralized and in bulk.
- A 'small army' of agents oversees the franchised retailers and controls the company's image.
- Retailers are contracted to stock only Benetton's own brand products, although they have some local autonomy on ranges and colours.
- Benetton strictly controls the design, layout, ambience and prices in every store.
- Sophisticated IT systems link retailers with Benetton and in turn its suppliers to provide a fast response to demand patterns without unnecessary stockholding.
- Standard worldwide advertising features 'The United Colors of Benetton'.

- The company carefully sponsors events such as Formula One which have a young and smart image.

(Quotations extracted from Benetton Annual Reports.)

QUESTIONS: What is Benetton's competitive strategy?
How does it achieve competitive advantage?
How does Benetton use networks and partnerships to great effect?
In what ways would it be difficult for competitors to try and copy the success?

*Benetton*   http://www.benetton.com

they were working with one of the UK's strongest retailers. Customers were equally satisfied. M&S standards and expectations were exacting, but the mutual rewards were high and shared. Towards the end of the 1990s, as M&S was accused of having 'tired' ranges and manufacturing costs in Britain for many clothing and food products seemed relatively expensive, some of these arrangements broke down. One clothing supplier, William Baird, sued M&S for alleged breach of contract.

- The legendary Silicon Valley, heart of the American, and arguably the global, computer and semiconductor industries, has long benefited from networks and alliances. Companies spin-off from each other, sometimes as rivals, but more often to develop new products or to supply each other. In the early days of the industry young entrepreneurs readily shared their ideas and knowledge. As a result, Silicon Valley as a whole became an opportunity which attracted people with ideas and ambition.

Sometimes the value and constituency of these networks and partnerships can be hard to quantify or even explain. They owe a lot to people and to their history. They are relationships which emerge and strengthen over many years. They are dependent upon personal relations and interactions. This often serves to make them even more powerful as they are automatically difficult to replicate. Consequently, architecture can be a vital element of competitive advantage.

As more and more organizations opt to focus on core strengths, activities and competencies, and divest those that are peripheral, the significance of architecture is reinforced and increased. When companies outsource important services such as information technology (IT) or payroll management, or choose to buy in key components they once made for themselves, they need to be able to rely upon, and trust, their new suppliers. Managing relationships, therefore, becomes an important new capability.

Buckingham and Coffman (1999) also draw attention to the importance of architecture in their delineation of four levels of customer service. Level 1 is accuracy and level 2, availability. These, they argue, have to be seen as the relatively easy levels, and are generally taken for granted. In other words, without them, a company cannot hope to win repeated business. Levels 3 and 4 are working partnerships and the provision of advice and support. These relate to strategic architecture.

Porter also made a contribution to strategic architecture by providing a value chain framework for helping to identify valuable differences and manage cost drivers. This is looked at in the next section.

## Supply-chain partnerships

Developing his earlier work on industry structure (Porter, 1980), where he highlights the significance of the relative power of buyers and suppliers, Porter (1985) argues that in the search for competitive advantage a firm must be considered as part of a wider system:

suppliers → firm → distributors → consumers.

As well as seeking improvements in its own activities, a firm should assess the opportunities and potential benefits from improving its links with other organizations. A firm is linked to the marketing and selling activities of its suppliers, and to the purchasing and materials handling activities of its distributors or customers.

The supply chain, then, is a process, and managing it is a key *strategic capability*. Cost savings and service differentiation can be achieved.

Organizations can create synergy, and enjoy the appropriate benefits, if they can successfully link their value chain with those of their suppliers and distributors. Just-in-time (JIT) deliveries integrate a supplier's outbound logistics with the organization's inbound logistics. Stock and costs can be reduced for the manufacturer, whose delivery lead time and reliability should also be improved. Set up properly, a JIT system can enable suppliers to plan their work more effectively and reduce their uncertainty. This requires an open exchange of reliable, up-to-date information and medium- to long-term supply arrangements. When Nissan was developing the supply chain for its UK manufacturing plant in Sunderland, it deliberately forged links with its suppliers' suppliers in its search to control costs without sacrificing quality and service. A retail bookseller, taking orders for non-stock items,

needs to be sure of the delivery lead time from his publishers or wholesaler before quoting a date to the customer. This again demands accurate information, supported by reliable supply.

Carphone Warehouse, a leading retailer of mobile phones, retails telephones at prices ranging from 50p to over £300. Where the phone is sold as part of a package which involves a monthly line rental, the phone will typically have been provided free to the Carphone Warehouse by one of the major networks, such as BT Cellnet or Vodafone, who in turn will have a supply arrangement with a manufacturer, perhaps Nokia or Motorola. The retailer will later receive a share of the future call revenues, normally between 3 and 5%. The ultimate value to Carphone Warehouse of the sale will average £300, regardless of the apparent selling price. In the case of phones used for prepaid calls without any monthly line rental, a typical sale will yield £200.

Organizations looking to launch a new product need to ensure that their supply and distribution networks are properly in place; given this, all interested parties can benefit. Retailers will need to be convinced of a new product's viability and potential before they agree to stock it, normally at the expense of taking something else off their shelves. Manufacturers must be sure that stocks are available where customers expect to find them before they proceed with launch advertising.

The key lies in an integrated network, where all members of the supply chain see themselves as mutual beneficiaries from an effective total system; however, this does not always happen.

Supply-chain management issues become increasingly important where organizations seek to reduce the number of their suppliers, buying as many items as possible from each selected supplier. It is quite feasible that these major suppliers will have to buy-in products that they do not make themselves in order to create the 'basket' of items demanded by their customer. This strategy has been adopted by the leading oil companies and car manufacturers. In 1994 Ford in the USA included components from 700 US suppliers in its Tempo model; in 1995 the company's equivalent Mercury Mystique was using 227 suppliers worldwide. One supplier, for example, was now required to provide a fully assembled dashboard, ready for immediate installation; it is likely that the electronic instrumentation will be bought-in by the relevant supplier. In 1999 Ford of Brazil went further. For the first time a supplier was given responsibility for part of the production line in a Ford assembly plant. Simply, the workers are employed by the supplier but work inside a plant owned by Ford.

Preece *et al.* (1995) use the value chain to explain how Levi Strauss, producer of the internationally successful Levi's jeans, has created value and used its value-creating activities carefully to establish a distinctive corporate reputation, which is a form of competitive advantage. Key aspects include:

- established links with suppliers from around the world
- team manufacturing (underpinned by training and empowerment) and linked to high-technology equipment and sophisticated information support
- global advertising and branding
- alliances with retailers who concentrate on Levi's jeans and do not stock competitor products
- a programme of 'marketing revitalization' designed to reduce lead times and improve the availability of the products.

Strengthening the processes involved in managing the supply chain relates to the level of service that companies are able to offer their customers and to total quality management, topics which are discussed in the supplementary pages on the website.

Corporate restructuring to improve international competitiveness is a vital priority for British and European businesses in the 1990s. However, such restructuring must be a continual process of change and revitalization if we are to consistently satisfy the consumer's need for the highest quality products and services at the most competitive cost. The leadership of this process is the primary role of management in the modern company.
*Ian G McAllister, when Chairman and Managing Director, Ford Motor Company Limited, UK*

ICI Explosives Division, who manufacture a range of explosive products, have also developed expertise in detonating explosions; quarry managers, who buy the products, really want stones and rocks on a quarry floor rather than the explosives. As a consequence ICI offered to produce a three-dimensional map of a quarry for their customers, indicating where the charges need to be placed, and then, when suitable holes have been drilled in the quarry face (by the quarry owners), carry out controlled explosions. In this way they add value for their customers and link the two value chains

## The Organization's Value Chain

While strategic success depends upon the way in which the organization as a whole behaves, and the ways in which managers and functions are integrated, competitive advantage stems from the individual and discrete activities that a firm performs. A cost advantage can arise from low-cost distribution, efficient production or an excellent salesforce that succeeds in winning the most appropriate orders. Differentiation can be the result of having an excellent design team or being able to source high-quality materials or high-quality production. Value-chain analysis is a systematic way of studying the direct and support activities undertaken by a firm. From this analysis should arise greater awareness concerning costs and the potential for lower costs and for differentiation. Quite simply, argues Porter (1985), competitive advantage is created and sustained when a firm performs the most critical functions either more cheaply or better than its competitors. But what are the most critical factors? Why? How and where might costs be reduced? How and where might differentiation be created?

In this section we are extending the ideas behind activity mapping (Chapter 8, p. 313).

## Activities in the value chain

The value chain developed by Michael Porter is illustrated in Figure 9.3. There are five primary activities, namely inbound logistics, operations, outbound logistics, marketing and sales, and service. In the diagram they are illustrated as a chain moving from left to right, and they represent activities of physically creating the product or service and transferring it to the buyer, together with any necessary after-sale service. They are linked to four support activities: procurement, technology development, human resource management, and the firm's infrastructure. The support activities are drawn laterally as they can affect any one or more of the primary activities, although the firm's infrastructure generally supports the whole value chain. Every one of the primary and support activities incurs costs and should add value to the product or service in excess of these costs. It is important always to look for ways of reducing costs sensibly; cost reductions should not be at the expense of lost quality in areas that matter to customers and consumers. Equally, costs can be added justifiably if they add qualities that the customer values and is willing to pay for. The difference between the total costs and the selling price is the

**Figure 9.3** The value chain. Source: Porter, ME (1985) *Competitive Advantage: Creating and Sustaining Superior Performance*, Free Press. © Michael E Porter, 1985. Adapted with permission of the Free Press.

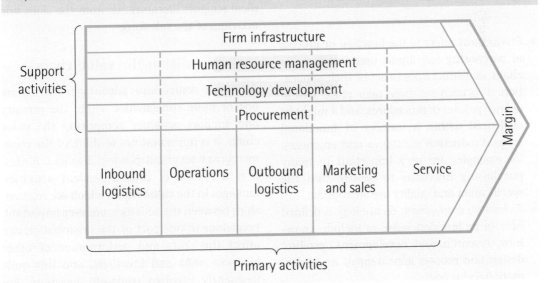

margin. The margin is increased by widening the gap between costs and price. The activities are described in greater depth below.

## Primary activities

- *Inbound logistics* are activities relating to receiving, storing and distributing internally the inputs to the product or service. They include warehousing, stock control and internal transportation systems.
- *Operations* are activities relating to the transformation of inputs into finished products and services. Operations includes machining, assembly and packaging.
- *Outbound logistics* are activities relating to the distribution of finished goods and services to customers.
- *Marketing and sales* includes such activities as advertising and promotion, pricing and salesforce activity.
- *Service* relates to the provision of any necessary service with a product, such as installation, repair, extended warranty or training in how to use the product.

Each of these might be crucial for competitive advantage. The nature of the industry will determine which factors are the most significant.

## Support activities

- *Procurement* refers to the function or process of purchasing any inputs used in the value chain, as distinct from issues of their application. Procurement may take place within defined policies or procedures, and it might be evidenced within a number of functional areas. Production managers and engineers, for example, are very important in many purchasing decisions to ensure that the specification and quality are appropriate.
- *Technology development*: technology is defined here in its broadest sense to include know-how, research and development, product design and process improvement and information technology.

- *Human resource management* involves all activities relating to recruiting, training, developing and rewarding people throughout the organization.
- *The firm's infrastructure* includes the structure of the organization, planning, financial controls and quality management designed to support the whole of the value chain.

Again, each of these support activities can be very important in creating and sustaining competitive advantage.

### Subactivities

Porter argues that it can often be valuable to subdivide the primary and support activities into their component parts when analysing costs and opportunities for differentiation. For example, it is less meaningful to argue that an organization provides good service than to explain it in terms of installation, repair or training. The competitive advantage is likely to result from a specific subactivity. Similarly, the marketing mix comprises a set of linked activities which should be managed to complement each other. However, competitive advantage can arise from just one activity in the mix, possibly the product design, its price or advertising, technical support literature, or from the skills and activities of the salesforce.

## Linkages within the value chain

Although competitive advantage arises from one or more subactivities within the primary and support activities comprising the value chain, it is important not to think of the chain merely as a set of independent activities. Rather, it is a system of inter-dependent activities. Linkages in the value chain, which are relationships between the activities, are very important. Behaviour in one part of the organization can affect the costs and performance of other business units and functions, and this quite frequently involves trade-off decisions. For example, more expensive materials and more stringent inspection will increase costs in the inbound logistics and operations activities, but the savings in service costs resulting from these strategies may be greater. The choice of functional strategies and where to concentrate efforts will relate to the organization's competitive and corporate strategies concerning competitive advantage.

Similarly, several activities and subactivities depend on each other. The extent to which operations, outbound logistics and installation are co-ordinated can be a source of competitive advantage through lower costs (reduced stockholding) or differentiation (high quality, customer-orientated service). This last example uses linkages between primary activities, but there are also clear linkages between primary and support activities. Product design affects manufacturing costs, purchasing policies affect operations and production costs, and so on.

Having introduced and discussed the concept of the value chain, it is now important to consider how it might be applied in the evaluation of costs and differentiation opportunities.

## The Value Chain and Competitive Advantage

### Cost leadership and differentiation strategies

#### Cost leadership

Chapter 8 discussed the argument of Porter (1985) that the lowest cost producer in either a broad or narrow competitive scope:

- delivers acceptable quality but produces the product or service with lower costs than competitors
- sustains this cost gap
- achieves above-average profits from industry-average prices.

This cost advantage will be achieved by the effective management of the key determinants of costs.

#### The differentiation strategy

Similarly, Porter argues that the successful application of a differentiation strategy involves:

- the selection of one or more key characteristics which are widely valued by buyers (there are any number of opportunities relating to different needs and market segments)
- adding costs selectively in the areas perceived to be important to buyers, and charging a premium price in excess of the added costs.

The success of this strategy lies in finding opportunities for differentiation which cannot be matched easily by competitors, and being clear about the costs involved and the price potential. Costs in areas not perceived to be significant to buyers must be controlled, and in line with competitor costs, for otherwise above-average profits will not be achieved.

The successful implementation of both of these strategies therefore requires an understanding of where costs are incurred throughout the organization. Understanding costs and the search for appropriate cost reductions involves an appreciation of how costs should be attributed to the various discrete activities which comprise the value chain. Table 9.2 compares a possible cost breakdown for a manufacturing firm with that for a firm of professional accountants. If an analysis of the value chain is to be meaningful, it is important that the costs are genuinely attributed to the activities that generate them, and not simply apportioned in some convenient way, however difficult this might prove in practice. Given the figures in Table 9.2 one might question whether the manufacturing firm is spending enough on human resources management and marketing, and the accountancy practice too much.

*Table 9.2*  Indicative cost breakdown of a manufacturing and a service business

|  | Manufacturing firm (% of total) | Professional firm of accountants (% of total) | |
|---|---|---|---|
| *Primary activities* | | | |
| Inbound logistics | 4 | 8 | (data collection for audits) |
| Operations | 64 | 26 | (actual auditing) |
| Outbound logistics | 1 | 5 | (report writing and presentations) |
| Marketing and sales | 7 | 21 | (getting new business) |
| Service | 1 | 3 | (general client liaison) |
|  | 77 | 63 | |
| *Support activities* | | | |
| Procurement | 1 | 1 | |
| Technology development | 10 | 8 | (IT development) |
| Human resources management | 2 | 16 | |
| Firm's infrastructure | 10 | 12 | |
|  | 100 | 100 | |

These figures are only indicative, and should not be seen as targets for any particular firm.

## Cost drivers

It is important to appreciate which cost drivers are the most significant. The following cost drivers can all influence the value chain.

- Economies of scale and potential experience and learning curve benefits.
- Capacity utilization, linked to production control and the existence of bottlenecks.
- Linkages – Time spent liaising with other departments can incur costs, but at the same time create savings and differentiation through interrelationships and shared activities.
- Interrelationships and shared activities – Shared activities, possibly a shared sales force, shared advertising or shared plant, can generate savings. Close links between activities or departments can increase quality and ensure that the needs of customers are matched more effectively.

- Integration – This incorporates the extent to which the organization is vertically integrated, say manufacturing its own component parts instead of assembling bought-in components, or even designing and manufacturing its own machinery. This again can influence costs and differentiation, and is an important element of the strategy of YKK, which is featured as an example later in this chapter (see p. 348).
- Timing – Buying and selling at the appropriate time. It is important to invest in stocks to ensure deliveries when customers want them, but at the same time stockholding costs must be monitored and controlled.
- Policies – Policy standards for procurement or production may be wrong. If they are set too low, quality may be lost and prove detrimental. If they are too high in relation to the actual needs of the market, costs are incurred unnecessarily.

A key challenge for motor car anufacturers is one of reducing new product development times and costs while increasing the number of models that they offer their customers. To succeed, a car must look and feel different from its rivals, but the manufacturers have found that they can save both time and cost if they share components which are hidden from view. Examples would include floor pans (or platforms), engines and chassis. As a consequence, in recent years, there has been a tendency for new partnerships to emerge, as well as a number of important mergers.

Fiat, for example, owns the Alfa Romeo and Lancia marques and uses the same platforms for similar-sized models with the Fiat, Alfa Romeo and Lancia names.

Similarly, Volkswagen has acquired Audi, Seat and Skoda and adopts similar strategies. The platforms account for one-third of the costs incurred in designing a new car.

Manufacturers trade engines. Ford, for example, sells engines to other companies, as well as sharing components across the businesses it owns, which now include Jaguar, Land Rover and Volvo. In the same way, Peugeot diesel engines are common to Citroën and Peugeot cars.

- Location issues – This includes wage costs, which can vary between different regions, and the costs of supporting a particular organization structure.
- Institutional factors – Specific regulations concerning materials content or usage would be an example.

Porter argues that sustained competitive advantage requires effective control of the cost drivers, and that scale economies, learning, linkages, interrelationships and timing provide the key opportunities for creating advantage. In the case of a cost leadership strategy, the cost advantage is relative to the costs of competitors, and over time these could change if competitors concentrate on their cost drivers. Consequently, it is useful to attempt to monitor and predict how competitor costs might change in the future linked to any changes in their competitive and functional strategies.

Box 9.1 provides details of some cost drivers in the car industry.

## Common problems in cost control through the value chain

It was mentioned above that it can prove difficult to assign costs to activities properly, and this is one of the difficulties likely to be encountered in using value-chain analysis as a basis for more effective cost management. Porter contends that there are several common pitfalls in managing costs for competitive advantage:

- misunderstanding of actual costs and misperceptions of the key cost drivers
- concentrating on manufacturing when cost savings are required. Often it is not the area to cut if quality is to be maintained, especially once a certain level of manufacturing efficiency has been achieved
- failing to take advantage of the potential gains from linkages
- ignoring competitor behaviour
- relying on small incremental cost savings when needs arise rather than introducing a long-term, permanently installed cost-management programme.

## Differentiation opportunities

It has been mentioned on a number of occasions that competitive advantage through differentiation can arise from any and every area of the business. In relation to the component parts of the value chain, the following are examples of where differentiation might originate.

## Primary activities

- *Inbound logistics* – careful and thoughtful handling to ensure that incoming materials are not damaged and are easily accessed when necessary, and the linking of purchases to production requirements, especially important in the case of JIT manufacturing systems.
- *Operations* – high quality; high-output levels and few rejections; and delivery on time.
- *Outbound logistics* – rapid delivery when and where customers need the product or service.
- *Marketing and sales* – advertising closely tied to defined market segments; a well-trained, knowledgeable and motivated salesforce; and good technical literature, especially for industrial products.
- *Service* – rapid installation; speedy after-sales service and repair; and immediate availability of spare parts.

## Support activities

- *Procurement* – purchasing high-quality materials (to assist operations); regional warehousing of finished products (to enable speedy delivery to customers).
- *Technology development* – the development of unique features, and new products and services; the use of IT to manage inbound and outbound logistics most effectively; and sophisticated market analyses to enable segmentation, targeting and positioning for differentiation.

- *Human resources management* – high-quality training and development; recruitment of the right people; and appropriate reward systems which help to motivate people.
- *Firm's infrastructure* – support from senior executives in customer relations; investment in suitable physical facilities to improve working conditions; and investment in carefully designed IT systems.

In searching for the most appropriate means of differentiating for competitive advantage it is important to look at which activities are the most essential as far as consumers and customers are concerned, and to isolate the key success factors. It is a search for opportunities to be different from competitors in ways which matter, and through this the creation of a superior competitive position. The Japanese zip manufacturer YKK, the world market leader, grew to enjoy a superior competitive position, and the company's strategy is analysed against the value chain in the next section. The underlying philosophy of YKK, the 'cycle of goodness', was illustrated in Chapter 5, Box 5.2.

## An application of the value chain

YKK has arguably succeeded in creating both cost leadership and substantial differentiation with its corporate, competitive and functional strategies, and these have resulted in effective barriers to entry into the industry and close relationships with customers. The idea might be illustrated in Figure 9.4.

The essential components of the strategy, summarized below, are illustrated in Figure 9.5, which places them in the context of the value chain and highlights the linkages.

YKK is structured as a multiplant multinational company with both wholly owned subsidiary companies and joint ventures throughout the world. The latter organizations are primarily the result of local politics, particularly in low labour cost countries in the Far East. While

Figure 9.4

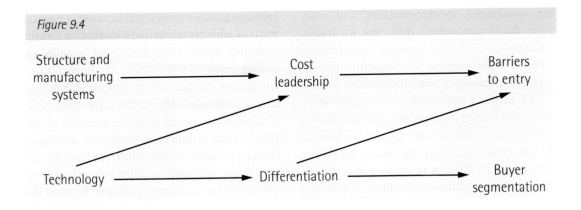

Figure 9.5   YKK's competitive advantage and the value chain. Developed from Channon, DF and Mayeda, K (1979) *Yoshida Kogyo KK'A' and 'B' Case Studies*. Available from the European Case Clearing House and Ireland. The dashed lines illustrate the linkages.

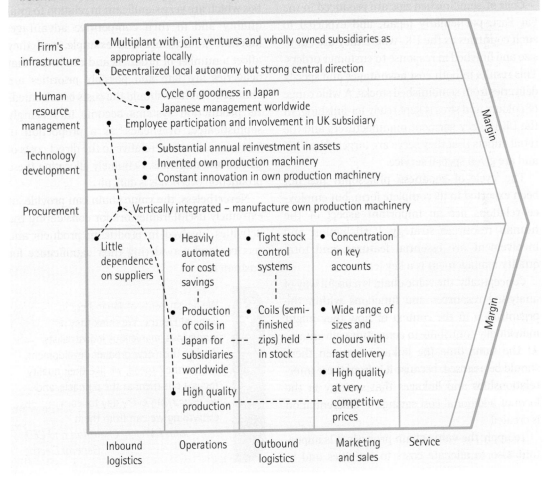

the subsidiaries are decentralized and enjoy some local autonomy, they are invariably managed at the top by Japanese executives on a period of secondment. Consequently, there is substantial influence from the Japanese parent.

YKK invests a significant percentage of after-tax profits back in the business, and as a result is heavily automated and able to enjoy the benefits of the experience/learning curve. Moreover, YKK prices its finished products very competitively both to generate customer satisfaction and to create barriers to entry. The company is vertically integrated, designing and manufacturing its own production machinery, and this gives it a unique competitive edge. It is also particularly innovative as far as both machinery and finished products are concerned.

Coils of semifinished zips are produced in the Far East, particularly Japan, and exported to such countries as the UK, where they are cut to size and finished in response to customer orders. This results in both cost advantages and speedy deliveries from semifinished stocks. A wide range of colours and sizes is kept ready for finishing. In the UK the key garment manufacturers and the retail outlets that they serve are targeted by YKK and are given special service.

The 'cycle of goodness' philosophy has not been exported in its complete form, but employee relations are an important aspect of the human resources strategy. Participation and involvement are essential features, and total quality management is a key feature.

Conceptually, the value chain is a useful way of analysing resources and functions within the organization in the context of how they might individually contribute to competitive advantage. At the same time the linkages between them should be assessed, because it is from these inter-relationships and linkages that synergy in the form of additional cost savings or differentiation is created.

To apply the value chain properly it is important also to allocate costs to activities and to evaluate whether costs could be saved in various areas or whether additional spending on certain activities might yield additional benefits by adding value in ways which are important to consumers. In practice it can be difficult to assign costs accurately. In this respect the actual application, rather than the concept, of the value chain is more applicable for managers than for students of this subject. In the author's experience, applications of the value chain pose difficulties for managers, primarily because the management accounting systems in many organizations not readily provide the data in the form required. Developing this theme, Johnson and Kaplan (1987) contend that certain costs are extremely difficult to allocate to certain individual products, but they are the costs of activities which are very significant in relation to total quality and in turn competitive advantage. Machine failures are one example, and they affect a number of products and can mean that deliveries are late and possibly priorities are changed. But how should the costs be allocated? As production systems become increasingly sophisticated, overheads, as a proportion of total costs, increase relative to the direct costs of labour and materials. Genuinely allocating these production overheads is difficult.

Nevertheless, the value chain can provide an extremely useful framework for considering the activities involved in producing products and services and considering their significance for customers.

We are students of Japan here in General Electric. We think they're marvellous, marvellous industrialists. We like their new product development, we like their speed, we like their quality focus. I put them at the pinnacle, and we're working every day to learn everything we can from them.

*John F Welch, Chairman and CEO, General Electric*

## Reputation and Branding

Reputation and branding are clearly linked but they are not one and the same. In a sense, a brand is a label that is attached to an organization's reputation. Kay (1993) contends that reputation is a key element of differentiation and that both reputation and branding are key intangible resources. What matters with differentiation is the customers' perception of the difference and what it means or conveys. It is, therefore, a qualitative indicator of quality; where quantitative measurement is difficult it can be a significant variable in decision making and choice.

The reputation of Sir Richard Branson's Virgin brand has allowed him to diversify into a wide range of activities – customer confidence in the brand provides reassurance and allows him entry into areas where he has little if any previous experience or expertise. It is critically important, therefore, never to disappoint customers in ways which tarnish a reputation; somewhat paradoxically, this means that there can be a huge downside risk for companies with the strongest reputations if they make strategic errors of judgement.

In similar vein, a strong reputation provides a 'safe choice' for customers who are new entrants to a market. A strong reputation therefore can help to sustain and build a strong position in a market. Moreover, it can sometimes be used to justify a premium price.

Famous-name endorsements provide an ideal opportunity for enhancing a company's reputation. Ownership of an endorsed product 'makes a statement' about a person. People hold certain personalities in very high regard and would find it hard to imagine that they would endorse anything that was not good, even the best in the market. Whether such people actually use the products and services that they endorse is an entirely different matter!

## Branding

Many differentiated products, and some services, are identified by brand names. These brand names, and/or the identity of the companies that own them, convey an image to customers. Simply, brands reflect reputations; and advertising is often used to create and reinforce this image and reputation. As competition intensifies, more and more products are perceived as commodities, sold essentially on price. When this happens, differentiation and branding become increasingly significant. The product needs a clear brand identity; a supportive corporate image, a company brand, is also valuable.

Minicase 9.3 illustrates how Britt Allcroft has built a very successful business by exploiting a number of children's character brands.

Brands add value, possibly the promise of some particular satisfaction or experience, a 'guarantee' of a specific level of quality, or reliability. Consequently, a brand can be seen as an actual product or service augmented by some additional added value. Branding is important and valuable; the drive to establish and maintain a recognized brand image can bring about differentiation and innovation. Nescafé, for example, has had several variants and improvements over the years. However, the value added must be real, as informed customers today will quickly see through any marketing hype. Moreover, the distinctiveness will not be achieved without investment, in both research and development and advertising, an issue which is taken up later.

Ideally, successful branding will generate customer loyalty and repeat purchases, enable higher prices and margins, and provide a springboard for additional products and services. Customers expect to find the leading brand names widely available in distribution outlets but, in the case of, say, grocery products,

# Minicase 9.3  Britt Allcroft

Britt Allcroft, who became a producer of television programmes, went to the same school at the same time as Anita Roddick, founder of The Body Shop. She always had a passion for storytelling. In her younger days she wrote several short stories, but none of them was ever published. Instead she found her way into television, and in 1978 she was asked to make a film about the British passion for steam engines.

There can be few better-loved children's characters than Thomas the Tank Engine, created originally by the Reverend W. Awdry in his spare time. As well as this series of illustrated books for children, Awdry wrote serious, adult books on steam railways. Although the Thomas books were no longer enjoying the popularity they initially had, Awdry was invited to appear in the film. He agreed, but inclement weather held up the project for several days. Awdry and Allcroft spent two days talking to each other. Although others had tried unsuccessfully to animate Awdry's characters – essentially a fleet of steam engines with distinctive faces and personalities – Britt Allcroft became determined to succeed where others had failed.

> *You need courage when people tell you are off your head . . . Thomas is much more than just a steam train having adventures – it is a way of life for me.*

Together with her business partner, who at the time was her husband, she approached venture capitalists, but the general reaction was that the time for Thomas had passed. Eventually, a bank loan from Barclays, supplemented by a second mortgage, allowed her to agree a licensing deal with publishers Reed Elsevier, who owned the master rights to the character, and to make her first film, which was broadcast on network television in 1984. Supported by a range of toys and clothing, the film was an instant success.

Her business now grew rapidly. More films were completed, with ex-Beatle Ringo Starr doing the narrating, the books were all reissued and character merchandising mushroomed. The films found an audience in 43 countries, including the USA where, for political correctness, the Fat Controller was renamed Sir Topham Hat! When Britt Allcroft's company went public in 1996, it was valued at £31 million. In 1998 she posted a profit of £3 million, roughly 10% of this coming from the films and 90% from merchandising. A total of 1800 different items – books, videos, toys, clothes, bags, party supplies, bakewear, computer games, puzzles, models and carpets – was being manufactured by 400 sublicensees. Thomas had become the seventh most valuable toy brand in the USA.

In 1997 Britt Allcroft acquired the worldwide rights to another past-glory character, Captain Pugwash, for £1.5 million, and set about resurrecting a programme that had first appeared on television in 1957 and disappeared in 1975. In the following year she bought all the rights to Thomas from Reed Elsevier (for £13.5 million) and no longer has to pay an annual licence fee. In 1999 Britt Allcroft formed an alliance with the two venture capital businesses which own the rights to Sooty, a hugely popular puppet character since its creation by Harry Corbett in 1952. Allcroft would merchandise the characters around the world and receive a management fee. In 2000 this deal was followed up with the acquisition of the company which produces Art Attack, the second most popular children's television programme in the UK.

Britt Allcroft has also opened a Thomas World theme park in Japan.

QUESTIONS: Character merchandising can clearly be very lucrative, but how would you set about putting a value on a particular character?
Can you think of other ways Britt Allcroft might exploit its brands and strengthen the synergy between them?
Were they to be available, what others could be usefully added to the portfolio?

*Thomas the Tank Engine*   http://www/thomasthetankengine.com

the supermarkets will typically only offer the number one and number two brands alongside their own-label competitor. In the case of groceries, strong branding has been essential for enabling the leading manufacturers to contain the growing power of the leading supermarket chains. Nevertheless, branding has not exempted them from tight pricing strategies. Edwin Artzt, until the mid-1990s a powerful and renowned Chief Executive of Procter and Gamble, has stated that 'winning companies offer lower prices, better quality, continuous improvement and/or high profits to retailers'.

The quality of own-label products has increased, and consequently the magnitude of the premium that customers will pay for the leading manufacturer brand has declined in recent years. Procter and Gamble, which is not alone in this strategy, has adopted perpetual 'everyday low prices' for all of its products. Marlboro cigarettes, the world's leading cigarette brand, were reduced in price dramatically in the mid-1990s. In the competitive food sector, product innovation, quality, specific features and, to a lesser extent, packaging are seen as the most effective means of distinguishing brands from own-label alternatives.

## Examples of leading brands

- *Persil* and *Pampers*: brand names not used in conjunction with the manufacturer's name – they are produced by Unilever and Procter and Gamble, respectively.
- *Coca-Cola*: manufacturer's name attributed to a product.
- *Cadbury's Dairy Milk* and *Barclaycard Visa*: the first is a combination of a company and a product name, the second a combination of an organization (Barclays) and a service provided by a separate business.
- *St Michael*: the personalized brand name used historically on all products sold by Marks and Spencer.
- *Hoover*: a company name which historically became irrevocably associated with a particular product, although it is just one of a range of products produced by Hoover.

Several large organizations have, through strategic acquisitions and investments in brands, established themselves as global corporations. Examples include:

- *Unilever*: now owns a variety of food (Bird's Eye, Batchelors, Walls, John West, Boursin, Blue Band, Flora), household goods (Shield soap, Persil, Lux and Surf detergents) and cosmetics (Brut, Fabergé and Calvin Klein) brands.

- *Philip Morris*: US tobacco company which has acquired General Foods (US; Maxwell House coffee) and Jacobs Suchard (Switzerland; confectionery and coffee).
- *Nestlé*: including Chambourcy (France), Rowntree (UK) and Buitoni (Italy).
- *LVMH*: discussed earlier, in Chapter 6.

These companies can afford substantial investments in research and development to innovate and:

- strengthen the brand, say by extending the range of products carrying the name
- develop new opportunities, for example, Mars Bars Ice Cream, which was launched simultaneously in 15 European countries and priced at a premium over normal ice-cream bars
- transform competition in the market. Pampers disposable nappies have been developed into a very successful range of segmented products selling throughout the USA and Europe.

Brand names are clearly an asset for an organization. The value of the brand, the so-called brand equity, relates to the totality of all the stored beliefs, likes/dislikes and behaviours associated with it. Customer attitudes are critical; so too are those of distributors. The fact that a brand can command a certain amount of shelf space in all leading stores carries a value. However, creating and maintaining the image is expensive. It has been estimated that manufacturers spend on average 7% of sales revenue to support the top ten leading brands, covering all product groups; this percentage increases as the brand recognition factor decreases. Because of this, manufacturers need to control the number of brands that they market at any

time; Procter and Gamble withdrew over 25% of their brands in the 1990s. Similarly, new product launches need to be managed effectively.

There is a so-far unresolved debate concerning how these assets might be properly valued in a company balance sheet. In the mid-1990s the US magazine *Financial Week* postulated that the world's most valuable brand name was Marlboro (owned by Philip Morris) and that it was then worth in excess of $30 million. In terms of monetary value, Coca-Cola was perceived to be second, although it is generally accepted that it is better known. The most valuable European brand is Nestlé's Nescafé; the three leading British brands (worldwide) are Johnnie Walker Red Label whisky (owned by Guinness), Guinness itself and Smirnoff Vodka (Diageo). Where the most recognized brand names are tied to high market shares and above-average margins, they are typically valued at over twice their annual revenues.

## Relationship marketing

Branding helps to establish, build and cement relationships among manufacturers, their customers and their distributors. The term 'relationship marketing' is used to reinforce the argument that marketing should be perceived as the management of a network of relationships between the brand and its various customers. Marketing, therefore, aims to enhance brand equity and thus ensure continued satisfaction for customers and increased profits for the brand owner. Implicit in this is the realization that new customers are harder, and more expensive, to find than existing ones are to retain. This potent mix of brand identity and customer care is clearly related to the whole service package offered by manufacturers to their customers, and to total quality management.

We always travel with our teddy bears. When we got back to our room at the hotel we saw that the maid had arranged our bears very comfortably in a chair. The bears were holding hands.

I needed a few more minutes to decide on dinner. The waitress said: 'If you would read the menu and not the road map, you would know what you want to order'.

*Binter et al. (1990)*

## Summary

The *opportunity-driven* approach to strategy starts with the environment, and the relevant markets, and looks into emerging trends, possible new opportunities and potential threats. All competitors in an industry can, should and invariably will carry out an analysis along these lines. Some will see opportunities where others, provided with the same data or information, will miss them. Critically, some will be in a better position than their rivals to deal with opportunities and threats.

Acquiring, deploying and exploiting key resources in an individual and effective way is the source of important differences and, in turn, competitive advantage. The resource-based view of strategy looks at how organizations *individually* respond, and at how their core competencies and strategic capabilities determine their success as a competitor.

A simple *resource audit* is an attempt to assess the strengths and weaknesses of an organization; typically it will be carried in conjunction with an assessment of opportunities and threats. However, any evaluation should be relative. The assessment should be in the context of, first, the key success factors for the markets and industries in question and, secondly, the comparable strengths and weaknesses of competitors for the same customers.

*Strategic architecture* refers to the linkages inside the organization (between different divisions, departments and managers) and the relationships, possibly partnerships, that an organization has with other members of the relevant value chain, such as suppliers and distributors. Synergy, mutual dependency and trust are key issues in the relationships.

Michael Porter has provided a useful value-chain framework for helping to understand where differences are created, where costs are incurred and how synergy might be generated through linkages. His value chain comprises:

five primary activities – inbound logistics; operations; outbound logistics; marketing and sales service; and

four support activities – procurement; technology; development; human resource; management; the firm's infrastructure.

Organizations must understand and manage their cost drivers. They should not attempt to 'cut corners' with things that really matter for customers; at the same time, they should not incur unnecessary costs with things that do not add value in ways that customers believe are important.

The value of a strong reputation must not be underestimated. A sound corporate reputation reassures customers. It generates sales and, very significantly, repeat sales. It can enable price premiums. It is a crucially important intangible resource. It is frequently manifested in a strong, visible and readily identified brand name.

## References

Binter, MJ, Booms, B and Tetreault, MS (1990) The service encounter: diagnosing favourable and unfavourable incidents, *Journal of Marketing*, 54, January.

Buckingham, M and Coffman, C (1999) *First, Break all the Rules*, Simon and Schuster.

Johnson, HT and Kaplan, RS (1987) *Relevance Lost: The Rise and Fall of Management Accounting*, Harvard Business School Press.

Kay, JA (1993) *Foundations of Corporate Success*, Oxford University Press.

Kelly, FJ and Kelly, HM (1987) *What they Really Teach you at the Harvard Business School*, Piatkus.

Porter, ME (1980) *Competitive Strategy: Techniques for Analysing Industries and Competitors*, Free Press.

Porter, ME (1985) *Competitive Advantage: Creating and Sustaining Superior Performance*, Free Press.

Prahalad, CK and Hamel, G (1990) The core competency of the corporation, *Harvard Business Review*, May/June.

Preece, S, Fleisher, C and Toccacelli, J (1995) Building a reputation along the value chain at Levi Strauss, *Long Range Planning*, 28, 6.

Test your knowledge of this chapter with our online quiz at http://www.thomsonlearning.co.uk

## Questions and Research Assignments

### TEXT RELATED

1. What are the opportunity-driven and resource-based views of strategy? Where and why are they different? Why is it important for organizations to embrace both views simultaneously?

2. Think about your own buying habits and choices. Where do you specifically choose high-profile branded items, and where are you less concerned? Why? What do you think this behaviour is saying about you?

## Internet and Library Projects

1. Using the Internet to look at the current status of Dyson and the other main manufacturers of vacuum cleaners, to what extent has James Dyson transformed an industry? How has he now extended the product range for his dual cyclone cleaners? In what ways are his washing machines different?

*Dyson*   http://www.dyson.com

2. Selecting an organization of your choice, and ideally one with which you are familiar, carry out a resource audit. Make sure that you take account of industry key success factors and competitors' relative strengths in your evaluation.

3. Using the same organization, apply Porter's value chain. As far as you are able, and accepting that there may be elements of subjectivity, allocate the costs and consider whether your breakdown matches your initial expectations. Where are the all-important linkages?

# Strategy Creation

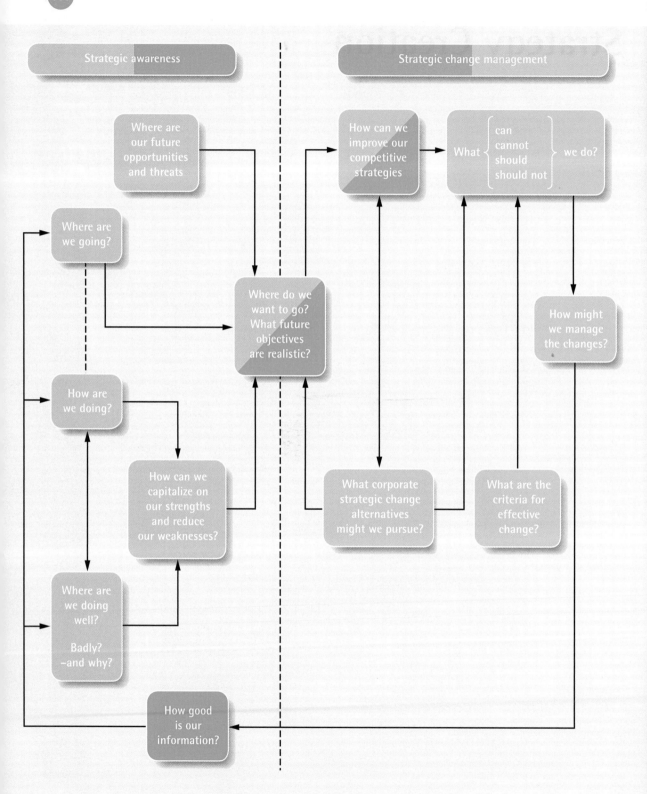

Strategic awareness

Strategic change management

Where are our future opportunities and threats

How can we improve our competitive strategies

What $\begin{cases} \text{can} \\ \text{cannot} \\ \text{should} \\ \text{should not} \end{cases}$ we do?

Where are we going?

Where do we want to go? What future objectives are realistic?

How might we manage the changes?

How are we doing?

How can we capitalize on our strengths and reduce our weaknesses?

What corporate strategic change alternatives might we pursue?

What are the criteria for effective change?

Where are we doing well?

Badly? –and why?

How good is our information?

# Strategy Creation

*This part of the book acts as a transition between the key themes of awareness and change. It looks at the ways in which organizations might, and in reality do, generate new ideas for future strategies.*

*There are three key elements:*

- *Planning* – *which in turn is dependent upon the quality of the available information*
- *Leadership* – *to provide both ideas and a clear framework in which other decision makers can operate effectively*
- *Innovation* – *intrapreneurship within the organization to ensure that new opportunities are found and*

*threats are avoided, such that the organization stays strong, competitive, effective and successful in a dynamic environment. This is again dependent upon communications and information.*

*The following chapters show why it is the case that every manager can be a strategy maker. Very broadly, Chapters 11, 12 and 13 examine these three elements systematically. Every organization will feature a blend of all three, although one may well be a dominant feature. Chapter 10 provides a short introduction to the whole topic of strategy creation.*

# An Introduction to Strategy Creation

Introduction

Strategy Creation

Changing Strategies

*This chapter recaps on themes introduced in Chapter 1. Figure 1.8 summarized the situation, by showing the linkages between the ideas of intended strategy (through strategic planning and entrepreneurial leadership) and emergent strategies when intended strategies are changed incrementally as they are implemented and new strategies are created as managers adapt in a changing environment.*

We're not necessarily great overall strategists [at Virgin] ... we often do things and then work out afterwards what the overall strategy was.
*Sir Richard Branson, Chairman, Virgin Group*

If you're in the penalty area and aren't quite sure what to do with the ball, just stick it in the net and we'll discuss your options afterwards.
*Bill Shankly (1914–1981), once Manager, Liverpool Football Club*

## Introduction

Football, or really any professional sport, provides a useful metaphor for understanding strategy creation. Teams – or, in the case of sports such as tennis, individuals – will begin all important matches with a game plan. They will have studied their opponents, assessed their relative strengths and weaknesses, thought about their natural game and about how they might approach this particular match, and worked out how they might be beaten. Led by the manager, coaches will have helped the players with the analysis and the tactics. Normally, the objective will be about winning. In some instances it can be about not losing (a subtle difference) or winning might be qualified by adding a 'means' objective related to approach and style. These game plans will undoubtedly *inform* the players, but it may be impossible to carry them out to the letter. Unexpected tactics from their opponents will ensure that this is the case.

Once the game is underway, the intended plans and strategies will be adjusted – there will be incremental changes. Broadly, however, they may well be implemented, certainly as long as the game is being won and not lost. At the same time, new, unexpected opportunities will be presented during the game, and good teams will be able to adapt.

Of course, 'the best laid plans o' mice and men gang aft a gley'. The opponents may prove stronger and more disciplined than predicted. They may take the lead and seize control of the game. In this case, there will be a need to adapt to the threats and change the tactics. When this happens, the ability to remain cohesive and disciplined as a team is essential.

At any time there is always the opportunity for individuals to show initiative and to shine. A strong, experienced and maybe visionary team manager (the strategic leader in this example) can act as a master tactician and an inspiration both beforehand and from the sidelines during the game. Talented players, with individual goals, spectacular saves or important tackles at key moments, will often make important contributions and, by doing so, encourage their colleagues also to make the extra effort that 'tips the balance'. As they always say, a game is not lost until the final whistle: teams often do go one or two goals down before recovering to win. Tennis players do not have to win the first set to win a match.

## Strategy Creation

Chapter 1 explained how strategy creation involves three strands:

- *planning*, both systematic and formal strategic planning systems and informal, cerebral planning
- *vision* and visionary leadership, and
- *emergent strategies* – incremental changes to predetermined, intended strategies and adaptive additions with learning and responsiveness to opportunities and threats.

Figure 10.1 reiterates that strategy and strategic management embrace the corporate portfolio of businesses and the search for competitiveness

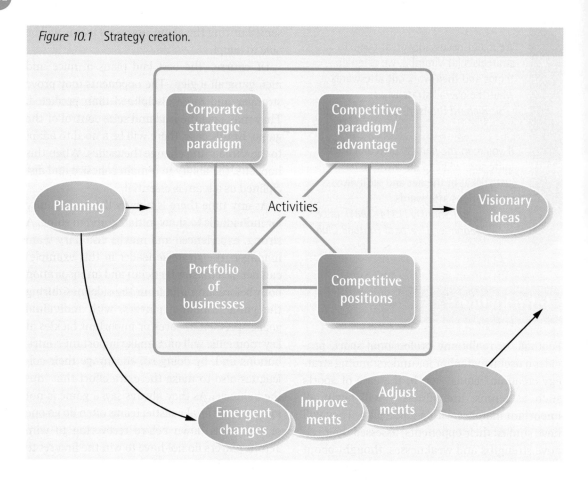

*Figure 10.1*    Strategy creation.

and competitive advantage with each business, product and service, and that this competitiveness arises from the functional activities that an organization undertakes. Visionary ideas pull the organization forward. Where these result in significant changes, they will often be associated with the strategic leader. Planning pushes everything forward. Emergent changes, improvements and adjustments – intrapreneurial changes initiated and implemented by individual managers throughout the organization – support and complete the process.

If all strategies were planned formally, then organizations would be able to look back and review the decisions that they had made over a period of time. At some stage in the past there would have been a clear recorded statement of

intent which matched these events closely. In reality, stated plans and actual events are unlikely to match closely. In addition to strategies that have emerged and been introduced entrepreneurially, there are likely to have been expectations and planned possible strategies that have not proved to be viable. However, broad directions can be established and planned and then detailed strategies allowed to emerge as part of an ongoing learning experience within the organization.

Idenburg (1993) presents these ideas in a slightly modified way, distinguishing between the following strategies.

- formal planning systems, through which clear objectives should lead to intended strategies.

- learning or real-time planning, which represents a formal approach to adaptive strategy creation. Managers meet regularly, both formally and informally, and debate how key strategic issues are changing and emerging. Objectives and strategies will be changed in a turbulent environment.
- incremental change and logical incrementalism. The organization will have a clear mission and directional objectives, and it will be recognized that pursuing these requires flexibility. Managers will be encouraged to experiment with new ideas and strategies, learning and adapting all the time. Internal politics and systems will play an important role in this mode.
- emergent strategies. Specific objectives will not be set; instead, organizations will be seen as fully flexible, 'muddling through' environmental turbulence. Opportunism, being ready and able to 'seize the main chance', is critical.

Mintzberg and Waters (1985) and Bailey and Johnson (1992) have also shown how the simple three-mode categorization might be extended, but the underlying implications remain unchanged. A number of points should be noted:

- Although it is not made explicit, some strategies, especially those formulated by a visionary entrepreneur, attempt to shape and change the environment, rather than react to changing circumstances.
- The organization structure and the actual planning process will affect the nature of planned objectives and strategies. Wherever a group of managers is involved in planning, their personal values and relative power will be reflected. See Cyert and March's behavioural theory in Chapter 4.
- Adaptive changes will also reflect the values, power and influence of managers.

It is important to appreciate that the three modes described above are not mutually exclusive, and that one mode frequently leads on from

another. The implementation of visionary ideas and strategies typically requires careful planning, for example, and this will invariably bring about incremental changes. In Chapter 1 it was confirmed that all three modes will be found in an organization simultaneously, but the mix and prioritization will be particular to an individual company. This key point is illustrated in Figure 10.2. It was also emphasized that individual managers, depending largely on their position within the organization, will not necessarily agree on the relative significance of each mode. It is essential that managers understand and support the processes.

The mixed approach is both sensible and justifiable. In some manufacturing industries the time taken from starting to plan a substantive innovatory change to peak profit performance can be ten years. This needs planning, although the concept may be visionary. Throughout the implementation there has to be adaptive and incremental learning and change. Where strategies are being changed in a dynamic environment it is also useful, on occasions, to evaluate the current situation and assess the implications. This could well be part of an annual planning cycle.

It is now appropriate to reread Minicase 2.1, which looked at how the three modes can be seen in practice in McDonald's. McDonald's has a clear and understood vision which also embraces its thousands of franchisees worldwide. In the late 1990s its annual rate of global expansion grew to over 3000 new restaurants; this requires careful planning. This planning, together with arrangements with building contractors and suppliers, has also allowed McDonald's to cut 30% off the cost of opening every new restaurant, through the use of more efficient building systems, standardized equipment and global sourcing. As a consequence, it can now afford to open restaurants in locations which, in the past, had been seen as uneconomical. Given the intense competition in the fast-food industry, it is also essential for McDonald's

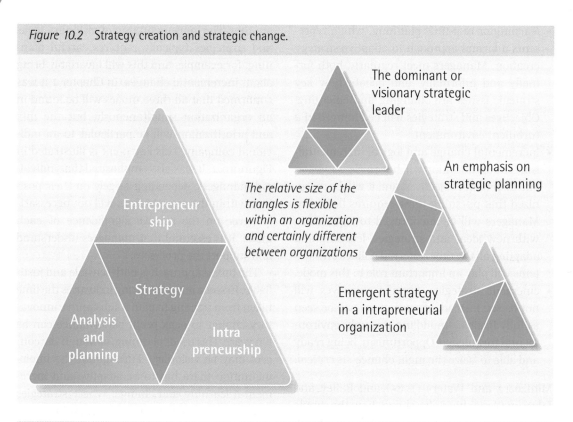

*Figure 10.2*    Strategy creation and strategic change.

*Table 10.1*    Levels of strategy and modes of strategy creation

| | Levels of strategy | |
|---|---|---|
| Modes of strategy creation | Corporate strategy | Competitive and functional strategies |
| Planning | Formal planning systems | Planning the detail for implementing corporate strategies |
| Visionary | Seizing opportunities – limited planning only | Innovation throughout the organization |
| Adaptive/Incremental | Reacting to environmental opportunities and threats, e.g. Businesses for sale; divestment opportunity | Reacting to competitor threats and new environmental opportunities<br>Learning and adjustment as planned and visionary strategies are implemented |

to remain flexible and responsive, international-ly, nationally and locally.

Table 10.1 further relates these themes to the three levels of strategy: corporate, competitive and functional. In large organizations much of

the responsibility for corporate strategic change will be centralized at the head office, although the businesses and divisions can be involved or consulted. Competitive and functional change decisions are more likely to be decentralized, but again, not exclusively. Corporate policies can require or constrain changes at these levels.

## Planning and strategy creation

Mintzberg (1989) contends that the strategic leader should be the chief architect, in conjunction with planners, of corporate plans; the process should be explicit, conscious and controlled; and issues of implementation should be incorporated. Essentially, analysis leads to choice, which leads on to implementation. The process is sequential:

Analysis → Choice → Implementation

Certain organizations might claim that detailed long-term planning is essential for them. An airline, for example, must plan capacity several years ahead because of the long delivery lead times for new aeroplanes and the related need to manage cash flow and funding. In addition, resources must be co-ordinated on an international scale. While planes are utilized on most days and fly as many hours in the day as possible, crews work only limited hours, and typically finish a flight or series of flights in a location which is different from their starting point.

However, Mintzberg argues that this is planning the implications and consequences of the strategic perspective, not necessarily the perspective itself. Detailed planning of this type should not inhibit creativity concerning the perspective.

Planning of some form will always be required in large organizations. It forces thinking and enables and supports resource allocation and budgeting. However, the extent and nature of the overall planning contribution will relate to the industry and the environment and be affected by both leadership and culture.

## The visionary mode

A visionary strategic leader who formulates strategic change in his or her mind may only be semiconscious of the process involved. He or she will clearly understand the current and desired strategic perspective, and ideally the culture of the organization will be one in which other managers are receptive of the changes in perspective. The personality and charisma of the leader, and the ability to sell his or her ideas, will be crucial issues, and as speed of action, timing and commitment are typical features the strategy can prove highly successful.

The visionary or entrepreneurial approach suggests that the strategic leader is very aware of the strengths, weaknesses and capabilities of the organization; the current matching with the environment; a wide range of possibly diverse opportunities for change; and the likely reaction of managers to certain changes. Similar to the 'bird approach' described in Chapter 1, Box 1.3, the selection is made somewhat arbitrarily without careful and detailed planning, and therefore an element of risk is involved. This informality in the process is important to allow for creativity and flair. The strategic leader then sells the idea to other managers, and the strategy is implemented and changed incrementally as experience is gained and learning takes place. In other words, the vision acts as an umbrella and within it specific decisions can be taken which lead to the emergence of more detailed strategies.

With this mode it is difficult to separate analysis and choice, so that

$$\left. \begin{array}{c} \text{analysis} \\ \text{(in the form of} \\ \text{ongoing awareness)} \\ \text{and} \\ \text{choice} \end{array} \right\} \rightarrow \text{implementation.}$$

### Dangers

The success of this mode in the long term depends on the continued strategic awareness and insight of the strategic leader, particularly if the organization revolves around a visionary leader and becomes heavily dependent upon him or her. People may be visionary for only a certain length of time, and then they become blinkered by the success of current strategies and adopt tunnel vision, or they somehow lose the ability to spot good new opportunities. It might also be argued that, if luck is involved, their luck runs out. The problems occur if the strategic leader has failed to develop a strong organization with other visionaries who can take over.

On a current basis the strategy requires management as well as leadership. In other words, managers within the organization must be able to capitalize on the new opportunities and develop successful competitive positions within the revised strategic perspective. This might involve an element of planning; equally it might rely more on the adaptive approach described below.

## The adaptive and incremental modes

Under the adaptive and incremental modes strategies are formed and evolve as managers throughout the organization learn from their experiences and adapt to changing circumstances. They perceive how tasks might be performed, and products and services managed, more effectively, and they make changes. They also respond to pressures and new strategic issues. There will again be elements of semiconsciousness and informality in the process. Some changes will be gradual, others spontaneous, and they will act collectively to alter and improve competitive positions. As individual decisions will often involve only limited change, little risk and possibly the opportunity to change back, this is essentially the 'squirrel approach' described in Chapter 1, Box 1.3. Managers learn whether their choice is successful or unsuccessful through implementation.

Hence this mode implies limited analysis preceding choice and implementation, which are intertwined and difficult to separate. A proper analysis follows in the form of an evaluation of the relative success:

Analysis → Choice and
(limited) implementation → Analysis.

Adaptive strategic change requires decentralization and clear support from the strategic leader, who also seeks to stay aware of progress and link the changes into an integrated pattern. It is often based on setting challenges for managers: challenging them to hit targets, improve competitiveness and stretch or exploit internal systems and policies to obtain the best possible returns. The greater the challenge, the more care needs to go into establishing a suitable reward system. When the structure enables effective adaptive change, then intrapreneurship can be fostered throughout the organization and individual managers can be allowed the necessary freedom. However, if adaptive changes are taking place in a highly centralized organization, and despite rigid policies, there is a problem which should be investigated. The major potential drawbacks concern the ability of the organization and the strategic leader to synthesize all the changes into a coherent pattern, and the willingness and ability of individual managers to take an organization-wide perspective. This latter point is examined later in Chapter 13.

Information technology provides opportunities for collecting and co-ordinating information and should be harnessed to support decentralization. In addition, team briefing can prove useful. Here, a strategic leader would regularly brief his or her senior executives, discussing progress and any proposed changes to the corporate strategy and policies. On a cascading basis managers would quickly and systematically communicate this information downwards and throughout the organization by meeting teams of people responsible to them. The secret lies in using team briefing meetings also

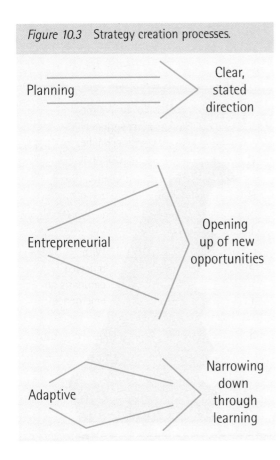

*Figure 10.3*   Strategy creation processes.

to communicate information upwards by reporting on new strategic issues and how they are being handled.

Figure 10.3 provides a short summary of the processes. Planning is shown at the top as a 'closed funnel' activity. The entrepreneurial, visionary style is more one of diverging and opening things up, widening the scope of the ideas considered. Adaptive strategy (responding to new opportunities) is, conversely, illustrated as a convergent process. Here, learning and synthesis are required to form cohesive patterns which bind the emerging strategies. In the entrepreneurial mode, planning is required during implementation; and in the adaptive mode, individual managers are doing their own planning, sometimes informally, sometimes more formally.

## Changing Strategies

Two important strategic pressures can leave the unprepared organization weakened: competitive and other environmental pressures, and focusing too much on controls at the expense of flexibility.

Hurst (1995) has shown how management and control becomes increasingly necessary as organizations grow and become more complex, but that this development contains the seeds of potential failure. Figure 10.4 shows that organizations often start life with an entrepreneurial vision but that the significance of this vision soon gives way to learning and emergence as the entrepreneur and the organization learns to cope with the pressures of a dynamic and competitive environment. This flexibility maintains the momentum and the organization grows and prospers. To ensure that the organization is managed efficiently, planning and control systems run by specialist professional managers become increasingly prominent, but this often reduces the flexibility which has proved so valuable. If the flexibility is lost, if the organization fails to address what it is doing wrong while it is still succeeding, some of the momentum for innovation is lost. Unless the entrepreneur and the organization foresee the impending problem and find a major new initiative, a crisis is likely to happen. If the organization is to survive the crisis it will need a substantial new opportunity, together with a renewed reliance on innovation and learning.

Businesses hit these crisis points when they run short of money, usually because they have failed to remain competitive and to attract sufficient resource contributions from customers and other important resource suppliers. Sometimes turnaround is possible, frequently accompanied by a change of strategic leader to input the new vision and inspiration. On other occasions the intervention is too late, and the

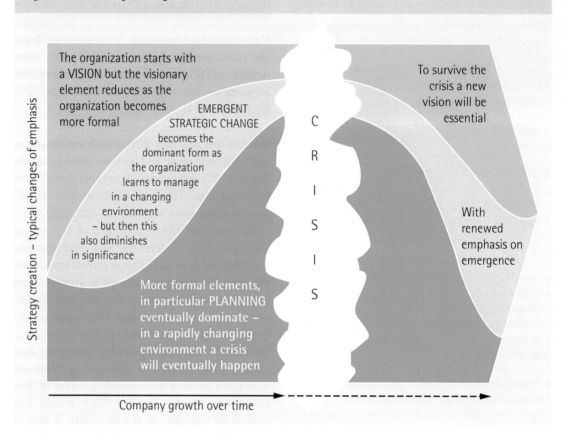

*Figure 10.4*    Strategic change.

organization either collapses or is taken over as a means of providing the necessary new leadership and resourcing.

Businesses in trouble, then, may be realistically irrecoverable, recoverable but only to a level of survival, or capable of genuine renewal. The immediate need is to stop any financial haemorrhaging before new opportunities are sought and pursued. The first step does not need someone with entrepreneurial talent and temperament – it is largely based on technique, backed by a willingness to take tough decisions – but the second stage does.

Hurst further argues that on occasions it can be valuable to engineer an internal crisis and upset in order to drive through major changes in an organization that has lost its dynamism and become too resistant to change. A controlled crisis is better than one resulting from external events as it can be used for positive change rather than constitute a more desperate reaction.

Stasis is less likely to happen if the company employs and encourages creative people who drive innovation and intrapreneurship. But if momentum is lost, the company may need more than creative people: it may need a 'maverick', perhaps someone who is normally ill-at-ease in a typical organization or a new strategic leader who will come in for just a short period. The maverick manager is unorthodox, individualistic and outspoken, someone who will challenge mediocrity and existing ways of doing things and someone who is not afraid to upset others in the drive for change.

Another way of presenting these arguments is the following four-stage model of organizational progression and development.

- The first step is a *creative* one, when new ideas are put forward.
- *Reflection and nurturing* follow as the idea is crafted into a winning opportunity. The person who has the original idea may not be the person who takes it forward in the most opportune way.
- The third stage is an *action* stage as the organizations grows by developing a business from the opportunity. As the business takes off, and more and more products are sold, some element of order becomes vital if the organization is to control events, manage its cash flow and deliver on time.
- The fourth stage then becomes one of *management* and administration with clear policies and procedures which deliver smooth running and efficiencies. This can become a dangerous stage if stasis sets in and new, creative ideas are not forthcoming.

Clearly, each stage has a downside. A constant stream of new ideas may not constitute entrepreneurial opportunities. Too much deliberation may inhibit action. An overemphasis on 'doing' and competitiveness may mean that inadequate attention is given to structural necessities. Finally, too much bureaucracy can mean missed opportunities. The organization begins to need a fresh input of creative ideas. Individually, we are all different and our affinity and fit with each of these stages varies; some of us are not able to switch styles. While the most successful and habitual entrepreneurs will ensure that there is a constant flow of activity between these stages and the potential downsides do not materialize, other strategic leaders will need to recognize their relative strengths and weaknesses and recruit other people carefully to ensure that there is a balance of skills and constant progression. Moreover, the positive organization implied here will be in a better position to exploit and retain its most talented intrapreneurial managers.

## References

Bailey, A and Johnson, G (1992) How strategies develop in organizations. In *The Challenge of Strategic Management* (eds G Johnson and D Faulkner), Kogan Page.

Hurst, DK (1995) *Crisis and Renewal – Meeting the Challenge of Organizational Change*, Harvard Business School Press.

Idenburg, PJ (1993) Four styles of strategy development, *Long Range Planning*, 26, 6.

Mintzberg, H (1973) Strategy making in three modes, *California Management Review*, 16(2), Winter.

Mintzberg, H (1989) Presentation to the Strategic Planning Society, London, 2 February. Further details can be found in Mintzberg, H (1973).

Mintzberg, H and Waters, JA (1985) Of strategy deliberate and emergent, *Strategic Management Journal*, 6(3).

# 11

# Strategic Planning

*Planning the future – thinking about the most appropriate strategies, and changes in strategic direction – is essential for organizations, particularly those experiencing turbulent environments. Rigid systematic planning – based on techniques and formalized procedures is, however, no longer as fashionable as it was, nor is it the only way in which strategic change decisions are made. There are dangers if organizations become reliant upon professional planners and where the only outcome of planning is a plan. This may not allow for effective strategic thinking, and may not result in a clear direction for the future.*

*There are dangers, then, in thinking that all strategic changes can be planned systematically and procedurally. Whether it is the result of formal and systematic planning, or much more informal and ad hoc leadership and management – which, paradoxically, still implies an element of planning – an organization will have strategies and processes whereby these strategies are changed. The processes need to be understood, and in many cases improved. It is important to assess where and how the organization should change and develop in the light of market opportunities and competitive threats, but there are lessons to be learnt about their appropriateness to certain strategic opportunities. Managers should know clearly where the organization is, and where it might sensibly go, and start making appropriate changes. They should then monitor progress and be aware of changes in the environment; in this way they can be flexible and responsive. After all, all managers are strategy makers.*

*In this context, this chapter considers what is meant by the term planning, and what is involved in the systematic planning cycle approach to the management of strategic change. The contribution of a number of planning techniques will be evaluated, and possible pitfalls and human issues in planning will be pinpointed.*

# Minicase 11.1 Unilever

Unilever is an Anglo-Dutch multinational corporation with manufacturing activities and markets all round the world. In 1999 50% of Unilever's turnover came from food products, 23% from personal care products and the remaining 27% from home care products and dry cleaning services. At this time the portfolio was restructured into 13 categories, which are listed later. The main brands include:

Food products – Wall's ice cream, sausages, etc.; Bird's Eye frozen foods; Stork, Flora and other margarines and spreads; Brooke Bond (PG Tips) and Lipton teas

Personal care – Timotei and Sunsilk shampoos
Sure deodorants
Signal and SR toothpastes
Brut, Fabergé and Calvin Klein fragrances

Home care – Persil, Lux, Fairy and Dove branded products.

Many of the products are subject to constant innovation. Persil washing powder, for example, lost its market leadership position to Procter and Gamble's Ariel brand in the 1980s and Unilever was determined to fight back. Liquids and concentrates had already taken market share from traditional powders when Unilever launched its new Persil Power in 1994 (branded Omo Power in Continental Europe). This new powder product was claimed to wash clothes cleaner than rival brands, which it did. Unfortunately, the special cleaning agent was particles of manganese, and Unilever misjudged the amount. Procter and Gamble were able to demonstrate that some clothes were damaged after multiple washes, and finally the product was abandoned. Other Persil products, specifically for colour and fine wool and silk garments, followed before Unilever pioneered its new – and this time very successful – Persil tablets.

In 1998 Unilever charged 20 of its younger managers (their average age was 32) to spend six months on a special project designed to identify new opportunities:

- One outcome was a new way of thinking about products and brands. Unilever, they concluded, was in 'the business of selling dreams of healthy eating, clean living and fragrant sex appeal'. People no longer really want soap powder, instead they want clean clothes, ideally without the hassle of using a washing machine! Unilever's future might well be in services rather than products.
- It was decided that Unilever should be seen as a brand marketing group that makes some of its products, as distinct from a manufacturing organization.

- The divestment of non-core products was completed. Over a period of years, Unilever has divested plantations, shipping lines and speciality chemical companies.
- The number of global manufacturing sites was reduced from 400 to fewer than 300. Of these 150 were designated key sites; the rest are ancillary. Most divestment was in food processing.
- At the same time, the number of suppliers was reduced to provide a more streamlined supply chain.
- The number of global brands was to be reduced from 1600. The top 400 (which, in classic 'Pareto' style, contribute 90% of annual turnover) would receive serious investment to generate a targeted annual growth rate of 6% and higher profit margins. Of the remaining 1200, some would be dropped altogether, some harvested and abandoned when they are no longer profitable, and others marketed without promotion of any consequence.

The 13 new product groups were classified as offering either superior growth (number 1 in the table below), steady growth (number 2) or selective growth only (number 3).

| Activity | Product category | Growth prospects |
|---|---|---|
| Food | Tea | 1 |
| | Culinary products | 1 |
| | Ice cream | 1 |
| | Spreads and cooking products | 2 |
| | Frozen foods | 3 |
| Personal care | Hair care products | 1 |
| | Skin care products | 1 |
| | Deodorants | 1 |
| | Toothpaste and oral products | 2 |
| | Fragrances | 3 |
| Home care | Laundry products (soap powders, etc.) | 2 |
| | Household care products | 2 |
| | Professional cleaning | 3 |

In 2000 Unilever acquired and divested a number of businesses. First it acquired Slimfast Foods, and followed this with Ben and Jerry's premium ice-cream business (featured in Minicase 3.1). Later it agreed to buy the American Bestfoods, which constituted the biggest global acquisition in the food industry for 12 years. With an annual turnover of $8 billion, Bestfoods was approximately one-fifth the size of Unilever. Bestfoods provided a number of important brands to complement Unilever's portfolio: Knorr soups, Hellmann's mayonnaise, Mazola oils and Bovril stock cubes and concentrate. To ensure that the acquisition was not blocked by the European competition authorities, Unilever agreed to seek a buyer for its Batchelor's and Oxo branded products. Unilever is now the world's second largest food business, second only to Nestlé. At the same time as acquiring new food brands, Unilever divested its main bakery business for £440 million. As Bestfoods also owns bakeries (producing, for example, Entemann's cakes) it was assumed these might later be sold as well.

Later in 2000 Unilever announced that it would split its businesses into two separate companies: foods and home products.

QUESTIONS: In the light of its new product prioritization, do the acquisitions of Ben and Jerry's and Bestfoods make strategic sense?
Can you identify any problems or risks in Unilever's strategy of focusing on just 400 of its previous 1600 brands?
Do you agree with the decision to split the business into two?

*Unilever* http://www.unilever.com

The planning era, if one may call it that, occurred some time ago, and has been discredited as we have moved on to the greater belief in the development of common values in the organization, and are rediscovering again today the necessity to be close to the market.
*Sir John Harvey-Jones, Past Chairman, ICI, 1987*

Planning is one of the most complex and difficult intellectual activities in which man can engage. Not to do it well is not a sin; but to settle for doing it less than well is.
*Russell Ackoff, 1970*

## Strategic Thinking and Strategic Planning

Robinson (1986) argues that the role of the planner should be not to plan but to enable good managers to plan. It is not the task of the planner to state the objectives; rather he or she should elicit and clarify them. Planning should concentrate on understanding the future, which is uncertain and unpredictable, and helping managers to make decisions about strategic changes. Thus, the aim of planning should be to force people to think and examine, not to produce a rigid plan.

It is worth reinforcing here that the real value of planning is not the plan which emerges, and which might be produced as a summary document which is worth little more than the paper it is printed on! Rather, the value lies in the thinking that the act and process of planning forces people to do.

Undoubtedly, planning techniques, used carefully, can provide a valuable description and analysis of the current situation. But the future is not necessarily the past extrapolated forwards, and while we can learn from past decisions, actions and events, companies must develop new competitive and corporate paradigms for managing the future and its inherent uncertainties. Vision and flexibility will be essential, alongside a clear direction and purpose. New thinking is essential for reaching the new competitive high ground first.

Strategic planning systems, popular and dominant in the 1960s and 1970s, became less fashionable in the 1980s and 1990s, but they still have an important contribution to make. In most companies planning had not contributed to strategic thinking and, because strategic thinking is essential, a new role has had to be found for strategic planning.

Strategic planning became fashionable for two basic reasons. First, it provided a means for allocating resources and managing budgets in complex multiproduct organizations and, second, it helped to pull together the disparate activities and businesses in organizations. These needs remain.

The outcome for many organizations was formal planning systems, heavily reliant on financial data, and supported by thick planning manuals. This was the downside.

On the positive side, planning can encourage managers to think about the need and opportunities for change, and to communicate strategy to those who must implement it. This was particularly important in the 1960s and early 1970s when there was an abundance of investment opportunities and a dearth of capital and key priorities needed to be established. In complex multiactivity organizations, decisions have to be made concerning where to concentrate investment capital in relation to future earnings potential, and this has generated a number of portfolio analysis techniques, some of which are studied later in the chapter. Rather than use these techniques for gaining greater awareness and insight, for which they are well suited, managers sought to use them prescriptively to determine future plans.

Formal strategic planning had become unfashionable by the 1980s for a number of reasons:

- Planning was often carried out by planners, rather than the managers who would be affected by the resultant plans.
- As a result, the outcome of planning was often a plan which in reality had little impact on actual management decisions, and therefore was not implemented.
- The planning techniques used were criticized primarily because of the way in which they were used.
- The important elements of culture and total quality management were usually left out.

However, many industries continue to experience turbulent environments caused by such factors as slower economic growth, globalization and technological change, and consequently strategic thinking is extremely important. The following questions must be addressed:

- What is the future direction of competition?
- What are the future needs of customers?
- How are competitors likely to behave?
- How might competitive advantage be gained and sustained?

Minicase 11.1 shows how Unilever has been addressing these issues.

Organizations must ensure that these questions are constantly addressed rather than addressed occasionally as part of an annual cycle. Line managers who implement plans must be involved throughout the process. 'Every executive needs to understand how to think strategically'. Rigorous frameworks and planning manuals are not necessary as long as the proper thinking takes place.

There should be a strategic plan for each business unit in a complex organization, i.e. clear competitive strategies built around an understanding of the nature of the industry in which the business competes, and sources of competitive advantage. Chosen strategies must have action plans for implementing them, including an assessment of the needs for finance and for staff training and development. This is generally less difficult than formulating a corporate strategy for the whole organization.

## Planning and Planning Systems

### What do we mean by planning?

All managers plan. They plan how they might achieve objectives. However, a clear distinction needs to be made between the cerebral activity of informal planning and formalized planning systems.

A visionary strategic leader, aware of strategic opportunities and convinced that they can be capitalized upon, may decide independently where the organization should go and how the strategies are to be implemented. Very little needs to be recorded formally. Conversations between managers may result in plans which again exist only in individual managers' heads or in the form of scribbled notes. Equally, time, money and other resources may be invested by the organization in the production of elaborate and formally documented plans.

In all cases planning is part of an ongoing continuous activity which addresses where the organization as a whole, or individual parts of it, should be going. At one level a plan may simply describe the activities and tasks that must be carried out in the next day or week in order to meet specific targets. At a much higher level the plan may seek to define the mission and objectives, and establish guidelines, strategies and policies that will enable the organization to adapt to, and to shape and exploit, its environment over a period of years. In both cases, if events turn out to be different from that which were forecast, the plans will need to be changed.

### The value of strategic planning

When managers and organizations plan strategies they are seeking to:

- be clearer about the business(es) that the organization is in, and should be in
- increase awareness about strengths and weaknesses
- be able to recognize and capitalize on opportunities, and to defend against threats
- be more effective in the allocation and use of resources.

Irrespective of the quality or format of the actual plans, engaging in the planning process can be valuable. It helps individual managers to establish priorities and address problems; it can bring managers together so that they can share their problems and perspectives. Ideally, the result will be improved communication, co-ordination and commitment. Hence there can be real benefit from planning or thinking about the future. What form should the thinking and planning take? Should it be part of a formalized system making use of strategic planning techniques?

### Corporate and functional plans

Corporate and strategic plans concern the number and variety of product markets and service markets in which the organization will compete, together with the development of the necessary resources (people, capacity, finance, research and so on) required to support the competitive strategies. Strategic plans, therefore, relate to the whole organization, cover several years and are generally not highly detailed. They are concerned with future needs and how to obtain and develop the desired businesses, products, services and resources. The actual time-scale involved will be affected by the nature of the industry and the number of years ahead that investments must be planned if growth and change are to be brought about.

Functional plans are derived from corporate strategy and strategic plans, and they relate to the implementation of functional strategies. They cover specific areas of the business; there can be plans relating to product development, production control and cash budgeting, for example. Functional plans will usually have shorter time horizons than is the case for strategic plans, and invariably they will incorporate greater detail. However, they will be reviewed and updated, and they may very well become ongoing rolling plans. While strategic plans are used to direct the whole organization, functional plans are used for the short-term management of parts of the organization.

Competitive strategies and functional strategies and plans are essential if products and services are to be managed effectively, but they should be flexible and capable of being changed if managers responsible for their implementation feel it necessary.

Ohmae (1982) emphasizes that individual products must be seen as part of wider systems or product groups/business units, and that although short-term plans must be drawn up for the effective management of individual products, it is important to ensure that thinking about the future is done at the appropriate level. As an example, a particular brand or type of shampoo targeted at a specific market segment would constitute a product market. The company's range of shampoos should be produced and marketed in a co-ordinated way, and consequently they might constitute a strategic planning unit. The relevant strategic business unit might incorporate all of the company's cosmetics products and there should be a competitive strategy to ensure that the various products are co-ordinated and support each other. In terms of strategic thinking Ohmae suggests that it is more important to consider listening devices as a whole than radios specifically, and that this type of thinking resulted in the Sony Walkman and similar products. In the same way, the Japanese realized a new opportunity for black and white television receivers in the form of small portable sets, when other manufacturers had switched all of their attention to the development of colour sets. If the level of thinking is appropriate, resources are likely to be allocated more effectively.

## Alternative approaches to planning

Taylor and Hussey (1982) feature seven different approaches to planning which are detailed briefly below.

- *Informal planning* takes place in someone's head, and the decisions reached may not be written down in any extensive form. It is often practised by managers with real entrepreneurial flair, and it can be highly successful. It is less likely to be effective if used by managers who lack flair and creativity.
- *Extended budgeting* is rarely used as it is only feasible if the environment is stable and predictable. Extended budgeting is primarily financial planning based on the extrapolation of past trends.
- *Top–down planning* relates to decisions taken at the top of the organization and passed down to other managers for implementation. These managers will have had little or no input into the planning process. Major change decisions reached informally may be incorporated here, and then a great deal depends upon the strength and personality of the strategic leader in persuading other managers to accept the changes. At the other extreme, top–down plans may emanate from professional planners using planning techniques extensively and reporting directly to the strategic leader. These are the type of plans that may not be implemented.
- *Strategic analysis/policy options* again uses planning techniques, and involves the creation and analytical evaluation of alternative options. Where future possible scenarios are explored for their implications, and possible courses of action are tested for sensitivity, this form of planning can be valuable for strategic thinking. It is an appropriate use of planning

techniques, but it is important to consider the potential impact on people.

- *Bottom–up planning* involves managers throughout the organization, and therefore ensures that people who will be involved in implementing plans are consulted. Specifically, functional and business unit managers are charged with evaluating the future potential for their areas of responsibility and are invited to make a case for future resources. All of the detail is analysed and the future allocation of resources is decided. In an extreme form thick planning manuals will be involved, and the process may be slow and rigid. Necessary changes may be inhibited if managerial freedom to act outside the plan is constrained. A formal system of this nature is likely to involve an annual planning cycle, which is discussed on p. 384.

- *Behavioural approaches* can take several forms, but essentially the behavioural approach requires that managers spend time discussing the future opportunities and threats and areas in which the organization might develop. The idea is that if managers are encouraged to discuss their problems and objectives for the business freely, and if they are able to reach agreement concerning future priorities and developments, then they will be committed to implementing the changes. However, it is quite likely that not all of the conflicts concerning resource allocation and priorities will be resolved. Clearly, scenario planning can be very useful here.

- The *strategic review* was developed to take the best features of the other six approaches and blend them together into a systematic and comprehensive planning system. A typical system is discussed in detail in the next section.

All of these approaches have individual advantages and disadvantages, and they are not mutually exclusive. The approach adopted will depend on the style and preferences of the strategic leader, who must, as seen in Chapter 12:

- clarify the mission and corporate objectives and establish the extent and nature of changes to the corporate perspective
- approve competitive and functional strategies and plans for each part of the business, however they might be created, and
- establish appropriate control mechanisms, which may or may not involve substantial decentralization.

It has been established that planning may be either informal or formal. Informal planning, as such, cannot be taught; but formal planning systems can. These are the subject of the next sections.

## The planning gap

A number of essentially similar models of systematic planning has been developed by such authors as Argenti (1980), Hussey (1976), Cohen and Cyert (1973) and Glueck and Jauch (1984). All of these models use the concept of gap analysis, which is extremely useful for strategic thinking purposes and which is explained in Box 11.1.

The concept of the planning gap relates very closely to issues which were raised in Chapter 3 on objectives. It addresses the following questions:

- Where do we want to go?
- Where can we go realistically?

When considering where and how an organization might develop in the future, both the desired and realistic objectives are essential considerations. Desired objectives relate to where the strategic leader and other decision makers would like to take the organization if it is possible to do so. Realistic objectives incorporate the influence of the various stakeholders in the

## DISCUSSION – Box 11.1
## The Planning Gap

The planning gap should be seen as an idea which can be adapted to suit particular circumstances, although gap analysis could be regarded as a planning technique.

An example of the planning gap is illustrated in Figure 11.1. The horizontal axis represents the planning time horizon, stretching forward from the present day; either sales volume or revenue, or profits, could be used on the vertical axis as a measure of anticipated performance. The lowest solid line on the graph indicates expected sales or profits if the organization continues with present corporate, competitive and functional strategies; it does not have to slope downwards. The top dashed line represents ideal objectives, which imply growth and which may or may not ultimately be realized. The difference between these two lines is the gap. The gap is the difference between the results that the organization can expect to achieve from present strategies continued forward and the results that the strategic leader would like to attain.

The example illustrated in Figure 11.1 shows the gap filled in by a series of alternative courses of strategic action ordered in an ascending hierarchy of risk. Risk is constituted by the extent to which future products and markets are related to existing ones; and this idea of increased risk and strategic alternatives is developed further in Figures 11.2 (p. 381) and 11.3 (p. 382).

The lowest risk alternative is to seek to manage present products and services more effectively, aiming to sell more of them and to reduce their costs in order to generate increased sales and profits. This is termed market penetration in the simple growth vector developed by H Igor Ansoff and illustrated in Figure 11.2. It can be extended to strategies of market and product development, which imply, respectively:

- new customers or even new market segments for existing products, which might be modified in some way to provide increased differentiation; and
- new products, ideally using related technology and skills, for sale to existing markets.

(In this context 'new' implies new to the firm rather than something that is necessarily completely new and innovative, although it could well be this.) Figure 11.1 distinguishes between market and product development strategies that are already under way and those that have yet to be started.

The highest risk alternative is diversification because this involves both new products and new markets. Figure 11.3 develops these simple themes further and distinguishes between the following:

- replacement products and product line extensions based on existing technologies and skills, which represent improved products for existing customers
- new products based on new or unrelated technologies and skills, which constitute concentric diversification (these may be sold to either existing or new customers)
- completely new and unrelated products for sale to new customers. This is known as conglomerate diversification and is regarded as a high-risk strategic alternative.

### Using the planning gap

Thinking about the extent of the initial gap between present strategies and ideal objectives enables managers to consider how much change and how much risk would be involved in closing the gap and achieving the target objectives. Some of the strategies considered might be neither feasible nor desirable, and consequently the gap might be too wide to close. Similarly, the degree of risk, especially if a number of changes is involved, might be greater than the strategic leader is willing to accept. In these cases it will

be necessary to revise the desired objectives downwards so that they finally represent realistic targets which should be achieved by strategic changes that are acceptable and achievable.

This type of thinking is related to specific objectives concerning growth and profitability. It does not follow, as was discussed in Chapter 3, that either growth or profitability maximization will be the major priority of the organization, or that the personal objectives of individual managers will not be an issue.

*Figure 11.1*   An example of the planning gap.

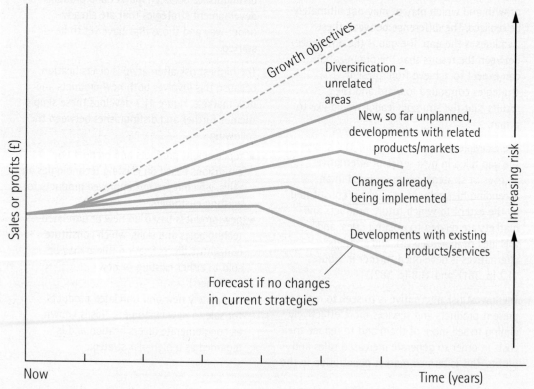

*Figure 11.2* Ansoff's growth vector. Source: Ansoff, HI (1987) *Corporate Strategy*, revised edition, Penguin.

*Figure 11.2* Ansoff's growth vector. Source: Ansoff, HI (1987) *Corporate Strategy*, revised edition, Penguin.

business, and their expectations; the existence of suitable opportunities; and the availability of the necessary resources. The issue of the risk involved in the alternative courses of action that might be considered is crucial. The discussion of the planning gap in Box 11.1 draws attention to the increasing risk typically associated with certain strategic alternatives, in particular diversification, which is often implemented through acquisition. Failure rates with diversification are high, as will be discussed in Chapter 15. However, diversification may be the only feasible route to the achievement of high growth targets or the maintenance of present rates of growth in profits and sales revenues. The strategic leader, perhaps under significant pressure from City investors, shareholders and analysts who expect growth rates to be at least maintained, may be forced to pursue high-risk strategies.

Table 11.1 looks at how three organizations, two of which have been featured in earlier cases

in the book, specifically Virgin, McDonald's and Sony, have pursued several different strategies over a period of years.

While undue risk should be avoided wherever possible, it is always important to accept a certain level of risk and set stretching targets for managers and businesses.

## A contemporary approach to strategic planning

In order to ensure that planning does not become an end in itself, and that planners facilitate management thinking, many large companies have evolved personalized contemporary planning systems along the lines of the one illustrated in Figure 11.4 (p. 384).

The organization's culture and the expectations of the strategic leader and the key stakeholders influence the whole process of analysis and decision making. The thinking starts with an assessment of the current position of the organization, its skills and resources, and an evaluation of whether there is a clear understanding of the 'mission', the broad objectives and directions for the future.

Then the business environment is analysed thoroughly, concentrating on the industries in which the organization currently competes and those in which it might apply its skills and resources. Feeding into this analysis are three other analyses:

- broad scenario planning – conceptualizing a range of different futures with which the organization might have to deal, to ensure that the less likely possibilities, threats and opportunities are not overlooked, and to encourage a high level of flair and creativity in strategic thinking (see Chapter 7)
- product portfolio analyses, which are discussed in greater detail in the next section; contingency and possible crisis planning considerations can be incorporated in this

*Figure 11.3*   An extended growth vector.

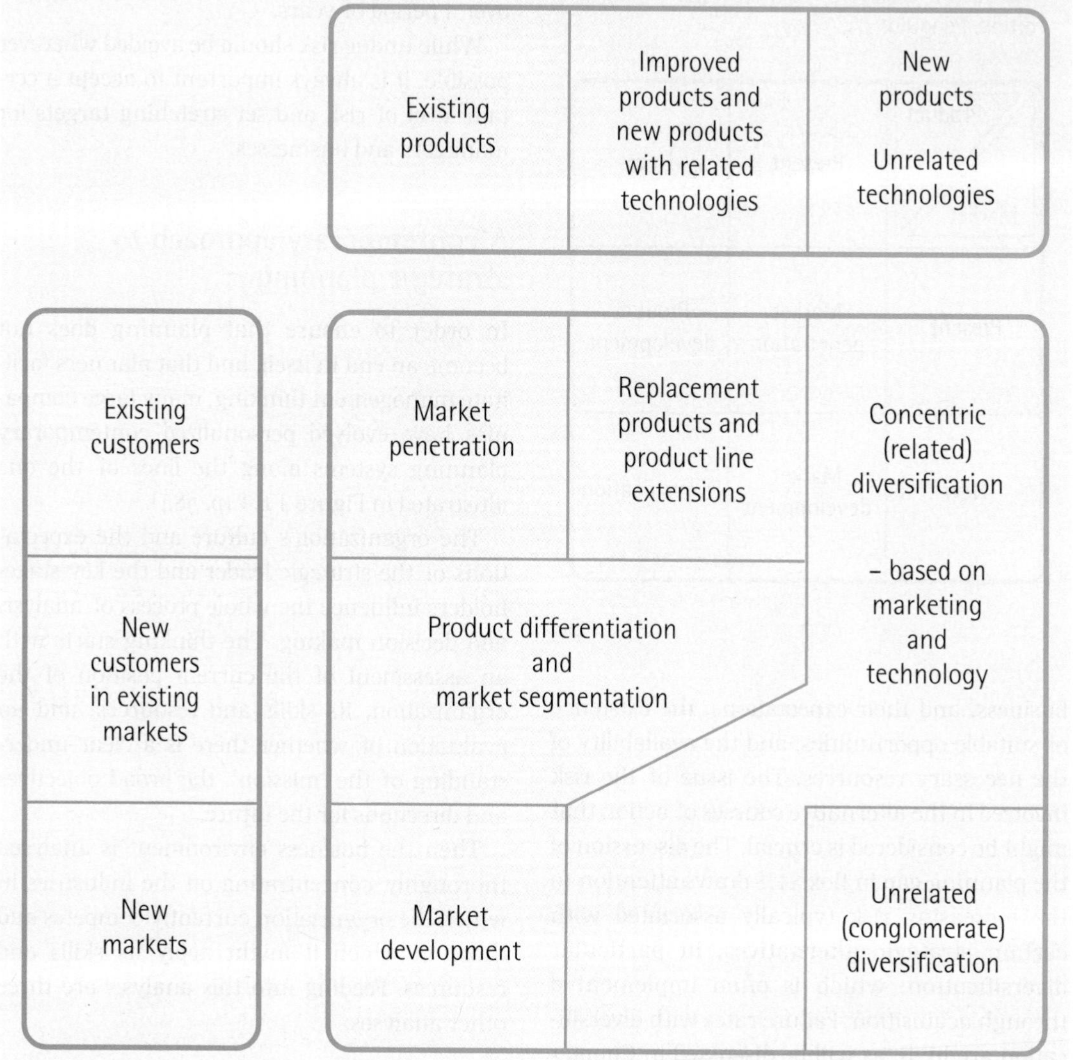

| | Existing products | Improved products and new products with related technologies | New products / Unrelated technologies |
|---|---|---|---|
| Existing customers | Market penetration | Replacement products and product line extensions | Concentric (related) diversification |
| New customers in existing markets | Product differentiation and market segmentation | | – based on marketing and technology |
| New markets | Market development | | Unrelated (conglomerate) diversification |

- industry analyses, following the Porter criteria for judging attractiveness and opportunities for competitive advantage (see p. 290).

This environmental analysis should focus on any *strategic issues* – current or forthcoming developments, inside or outside the organization, which will impact upon the ability of the organization to pursue its mission and meet its objectives. Ideally, these would be opportunities related to organizational strengths. Wherever possible any unwelcome, but significant, potential threats should be turned into competitive opportunities.

Minicase 11.2 looks at the strategic issues facing high-street banks in the 1990s and how they have affected strategic developments.

*Table 11.1*  Applications of the simple growth vector

| | Virgin | McDonald's | Sony |
|---|---|---|---|
| Market penetration | Publicity, self-publicity and exploitation of Virgin name, e.g. Branson's balloon challenges | Sponsorship of major sporting activities<br><br>Opening restaurants in different types of location: supermarkets, hospitals, military bases<br><br>Special value meals | |
| Market development | Before divesting the businesses: opening Virgin Megastores around the world and a music business in the USA | Opening new restaurants all round the world<br><br>The Big Mac, a hamburger for adults not children | The Sony Walkman and associated derivatives: – effectively existing products repackaged |
| Product development | Music retailing led to music production and publishing and later music videos | Chicken McNuggets, McChicken Sandwiches, Egg McMuffins, etc. | Tape recorders to videos Televisions Compact discs (some limited diversification involved) |
| Related diversification | Films, computer games | | Computers, Sony Playstation (related technologies) |
| Unrelated diversification | Virgin Atlantic Airways, Virgin Holidays, Virgin Cola, Virgin Financial Services | | CBS Records, Columbia Pictures |

From these analyses competitive strategy decisions must be reached concerning:

- the reinforcement or establishment of a superior competitive position, or competitive advantage, for each business within the existing portfolio of products and services
- product markets and service markets for future development, and the appropriate functional strategies for establishing a superior competitive position.

Amalgamated, these functional and competitive strategies constitute the corporate strategy for the future, which in turn needs to be broken down into resource development plans and any decisions relating to changes in the structure of the organization, i.e. decisions that reflect where the organization is going and how the inherent changes are to be managed. The band across the bottom of Figure 11.4 shows how this contemporary approach blends planning techniques with an intellectual input and later action plans for implementing strategic choices.

Simply, planning techniques and analyses are used to clarify the key strategic issues. Discerning the issues and deciding what should be done to

Figure 11.4   A contemporary approach to strategic planning.

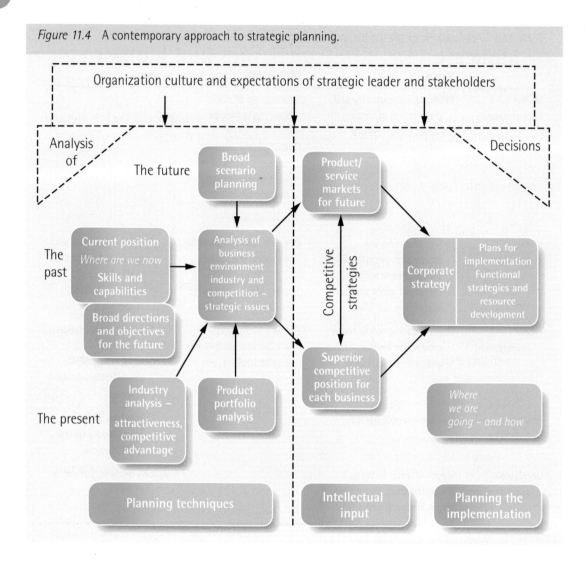

address them require creativity (the search for something different) and hence a more intellectual input. Once broad strategic directions are clarified, detailed implementation planning will follow. Like the strategies, these detailed implementation plans should not be seen as inflexible.

It is important that new strategic issues are spotted and dealt with continuously, and the organization structure must enable this to happen, either by decentralization and empowerment or by effective communications.

## An example of a systematic corporate planning system for a large organization

A corporate planning team for a large corporation, based at its head office, will typically comprise both planners and analysts. The analysts are responsible for monitoring the external environment, searching for new opportunities and threats. They also model the implications of possible future events and scenarios for the group.

# Minicase 11.2   Strategic issues and high-street banking

During the 1990s, and following the worldwide economic recession and the ensuing bad debts, the UK high-street clearing banks have changed their strategies as a response to a number of key challenges and issues.

## Strategic issues

- They faced a need to switch from a position of high overheads with an extensive branch infrastructure and the associated high-risk lending (required to cover the overheads) to one where their (lower) cost base is in equilibrium with the type and volume of lower risk business that can be more readily justified.
- Information technology, exploited effectively, offered opportunities for providing new and more efficient services without sacrificing either quality or reliability. In addition, the Internet was forecast to attract up to 10 million personal accounts by 2003.

Both of these issues implied restructuring and job losses, although there was always the possibility that once the banks had re-established strong controls and truly efficient systems they would reconsider taking higher risks again.

- The entry of new competitors, particularly linked to Internet banking (Prudential's Egg) and savings accounts (the leading supermarkets).
- A prediction that many personal customers would switch emphasis from borrowing to saving as the economy strengthened. The high-street banks were not perceived to be good for savers, offering relatively low rates of interest in comparison to the building societies and PEP-linked (subsequently ISA-linked) unit trusts.
- A possibility that customers would be more willing to switch bank accounts than has generally been the case historically. The reasoning was that the Internet was making everything, including comparable interest rates, much more visible.
- Changes in capital markets were taking away some of the bank's leading corporate customers.

## New strategies

- High-street banks now typically offer a wider range of financial services, which they promote aggressively, often using their extensive databases for direct-mail campaigns.
- Attempts by certain banks to charge customers from other banks who use their 'hole-in-the-wall' automated teller machines (ATMs) – this strategy provoked considerable controversy.
- Efforts to reinforce brand names and strengthen reputations – difficult for some who faced customer resistance to branch closures.

- Stronger credit controls for more effective loan management – implying both improved information and tracking and a reduction in the number of loans.
- Computerized credit and loan assessments to link charges with risks more closely than in the past. This has changed the role of individual bank managers and, for some businesses, made borrowing more difficult. Many business managers now offer counselling and advice rather than negotiate and track loans.
- A tighter focus on specific market segments, looking for positions of strength, rather than 'being involved in everything'. In particular, UK banks have reviewed their overseas exposure.
- A search for more attractive savings products in an increasingly competitive environment.
- New forms of service. Following the pioneering work of First Direct (a subsidiary of the old Midland, now owned by HSBC) other clearing banks have introduced telephone banking services. This would not have been possible without information technology. Some, such as the Co-op Bank with 'Smile', have started Internet bank accounts.
- Mergers between banks, building societies and insurance companies to create a more comprehensive financial services corporation. The systematic amalgamation of Lloyds, TSB, Cheltenham & Gloucester and Scottish Widows is an excellent example of this.

QUESTION: From your own experiences, what changes have you noticed in the service and the range of services offered by your bank?

The planners consolidate the individual plans for every business in the group to create the overall corporate plan. Group progress against the plan is continuously monitored and evaluated by the planners.

A timetable for a typical planning system is included in Table 11.2. Say the company's financial year end is 31 March: around this time, when the relative success of the group for the year is becoming clear, the planners will produce a final review of progress towards corporate objectives. They evaluate where the group is doing well and where it is less successful, and the extent to which it is satisfying its major stakeholders. To this is added a rigorous internal (corporate resources) and external (environmental developments) assessment of the group, provided by the analysts. They specifically high-light the important *strategic issues* facing the group – appropriate and feasible opportunities and critical threats – together with details about current and (if known) planned competitor strategies.

During April the group chief executive (the strategic leader) convenes his corporate strategy committee, which comprises senior board members and the head of the corporate planning group. The divisional managing directors are not members, although on occasions they will be asked to attend. They are excluded on the grounds that when bids from the divisions for additional investment capital are being considered later in the year, they would all support each other's projects. Any opposition by one divisional head would provoke counter-hostility from the others.

*Table 11.2*   A typical corporate planning timetable for a diversified organization

|  | Head–office corporate planning team | Individual businesses |
|---|---|---|
| March | Review of progress and corporate objectives |  |
| April | Strategic review for the group |  |
|  | ⟶ |  |
| May |  | Strategic review for each business and |
| June |  | Presentation to divisional boards |
|  | ⟵ |  |
|  | Divisional strategies and bids presented |  |
| July/August | Search for new strategies – growth and divestment |  |
| September | Final corporate plan agreed |  |
|  | ⟶ |  |
|  |  | Action plans and target milestones |
| October→March | Ongoing search for further strategic opportunities; monitoring, control and change |  |

The outcome of the April meeting is a preliminary statement of corporate objectives for the year ahead; these will normally reaffirm the company's mission statement, although it may be reviewed and amended. Typically, the objectives will summarize:

- growth and profit aspirations
- the company's strategy for exploiting core competencies and capabilities and its willingness to diversify (possible acquisition targets and divestments may be discussed but not announced)
- international/geographical objectives
- the commitment to, and standards for, quality, service and customer care
- the resources available to support expansion.

This is broadly equivalent to the top line of the planning gap illustrated in Box 11.1.

During May and early June each business unit finalizes its own strategic review, which is presented to the relevant divisional board of directors. Each company is likely to carry out comprehensive SWOT (strengths, weaknesses, opportunities and threats) competitor and portfolio analyses (portfolio analysis is explained on p. 395) and indicates:

(i)   the anticipated revenue and profit targets if there are no *major* changes to competitive and functional strategies.

(ii)  the requirements for the company to achieve or maintain competitive advantage

(iii) strategic changes that it would like to make, the anticipated returns and the resource implications.

Each business may be asked to submit proposals based on a range of financial assumptions, ranging from limitless resources to very tight funding. All significant investments will need to be justified in detail; the assistance of head-office planners could be enlisted in formulating proposals.

Items (i) and (ii) will be used immediately for updating the company's action plans and budgets, recognizing that these may have to be adjusted later.

The role of the divisional board is to question and challenge before reaching a set of recommendations for the chief executive. The strategy committee then meets for a second time at the end of June to discuss these recommendations, which may be accepted (and the necessary resources provided) or rejected. Portfolio analysis is again used to consider the current and emerging state of the group; and strategic opportunities for interdivisional support and internally generated synergies are sought.

At the same time the committee compares the promised returns from all the businesses with their own initial growth objectives. If a gap remains, and further resources are available or can be found, the corporate analysts will be asked for costed options and recommendations. The strategic leader may have ideas of his or her own to input. In addition, the analysts will be asked for recommendations concerning how the group might rationalize and achieve further cost savings, beyond those being offered by the divisions. Divisional boards may suggest the divestment of particular businesses, but this is unusual; such decisions are more likely to start with the strategic leader or the analysts.

This evaluation takes place throughout the summer, and the strategy committee meets for a third time in September to agree the corporate strategy. Final targets are issued to the divisions and business units, enabling them to review, and if necessary change, their current plans and budgets. It is these final plans which are co-ordinated by the head-office planners into the corporate plan and used for committing and managing the group's strategic resources.

Different reactions will be provoked by these strategic decisions. Business units that are allocated resources and given support for their proposed strategies tend to be euphoric, whereas those which see themselves as 'losers' are frequently demotivated, an inevitable drawback of this approach.

The divisions and individual businesses are not precluded from changing functional and competitive strategies at any time in response to competitive threats and opportunities, but if they require additional resources, outside their budgeted allocation, they have to apply to the chief executive.

A planning system along the lines of this example is basically a process which forces managers to address key questions and issues. Head office is likely to find that the detailed plan can be a useful document for explaining their basic intentions to the major institutional shareholders. The value of the finished plan to the individual subsidiaries, as distinct from the *process* of planning its content, is more questionable. They should see the document as a *summary of thinking* and a statement of intent, rather than a rigid plan that must be executed.

The corporate strategy may also be changed by the strategic leader at any time during the year if new windows of opportunity become available; such changes may imply either a visionary approach to major strategy additions or more emergent, opportunistic responses to events.

In addition, the planning exercise can be essential for providing a framework against which the strategic leader can monitor the commitment of resources and the emergent outcomes.

### Commentary

This approach to corporate planning may well succeed in the essential task of co-ordinating the plans for all the divisions and businesses, enabling the strategic leader to exercise control over a conglomerate. In addition, the system should not prohibit vision and learning within the corporation, which is important as these are the two modes of strategy creation most likely to take the organization forward in a competitive and uncertain environment. Unfortunately, the vision and learning may be concentrated within each division. Ideally, it will permeate the whole organization.

Typically, strategic planning systems used to be very formal. All ideas from the individual businesses had to be supported by comprehensive, documented analyses. Now it is frequently accepted that many proposals cannot be fully justified quantitatively; instead, the assumptions and justifications will be probed and challenged by divisional boards. Care must also be taken to ensure that the evaluation and resource allocation processes do not create too high a level of internal competition. Divisions and businesses should have to justify their intentions and proposals, and it is inevitable they will be competing for scarce resources. Nevertheless, the 'real enemy' is external competitors, not other parts of the organization, and this must never be forgotten.

In addition, some organizations still tend to use the performance targets as the primary means of control, which sometimes results in short-term thinking. Once a business drops below its target it is put under considerable pressure to reduce costs, and this may restrict its ability to be creative and innovative. Many strategic planning systems could be improved if the head office corporate planners had more contact and involvement with the businesses; they sometimes tend to be remote and detached.

In summary, formalized planning systems may be imperfect, but a system of some form remains essential for control and co-ordination. Alone it cannot enable the company to deal with competitive uncertainties and pressures. Vision and learning are essential, but planning must not be abandoned.

---

**STRATEGY IN ACTION – Box 11.2**
**Strategy and Local Government**

A typical UK local authority is likely to perceive the aim of the activities it carries out as the provision of more, and ideally better, services for the local community. These services fall into three broad categories: front-line (housing, education and leisure), regulatory (environmental health, planning and building control), and promotional (economic development and tourism).

How does local government 'work' strategically? Strategic decisions at the top policy level demand an input from two groups of people: the elected councillors who exert a controlling influence, and the salaried managers. The councillors may be politically very experienced and, working on behalf of their constituents, they should be in a position to reflect local needs. The specialist expertise is more likely to come from the salaried staff. There are, therefore, two strategic leaders – the Leader of the Council and the Chief Executive – who ideally will be able to work together harmoniously and synergistically. On occasions there will be clear evidence of visionary leadership. Some leaders, either individually or in partnership, will transform the character and infrastructure of a town or city. At the other extreme, other leaders really do little more than manage budgets and carry through central government initiatives.

There is an obvious role for strategic planning as local authorities have to work within guidelines and budget restraints set by central government. They have to decide upon how, at least, to maintain local services, improve efficiencies and implement any central government requirements.

Councillors will form into policy-making groups, and the salaried employees will operate with some degree of delegated authority in discrete service areas. Each service will have policy guidelines, output targets and a budget. Normally they will be free to develop and adapt strategies as long as they operate within their budget and achieve their outputs.

Many councils will want to increase spending wherever possible, as more or better services are popular with the electorate. In simple terms, spending minus income (including grants from central government) equals the sum to be raised from householders and businesses, and generally more spending is likely to lead to higher local taxes. The freedom to increase these is constrained by central government. Borrowing is used primarily to fund new capital programmes and for managing the cash flow on a temporary basis. It is, for example, being suggested that in the future local councils will borrow money to build new roads or improve existing ones and repay the money with congestion charges on motorists. Some councils establish partnerships with specific developers. An independent company might, for example, develop a new shopping centre in partnership with a local authority. Together they will put up or raise substantial sums of development capital which will be repaid later through rents and business rates.

It is very difficult to measure quantitatively the benefits that accrue from certain services, such as parks and gardens for public recreation. Information from the Audit Commission enables one authority to compare its costs and spending in total, and per head of the population, for individual services with those incurred by similar authorities in the UK. Where this is utilized it is basically a measure of efficiency, rather than an assessment of the overall effectiveness of the service provision, as shown in Chapter 4.

Until the 1980s it was usual for a local authority to carry out most of its activities in-house. External contractors were used for some building and engineering work, and in other instances where very specialized skills were required. However, the first Thatcher government required that councils put out to tender all major new build projects, together with significant projects in housing and highways maintenance. Later in the 1980s school catering, refuse collection, street cleaning and most white-collar services were also subject to compulsory competitive tendering (CCT). Where services were put out for tender an authority continued to determine the specific level of service to be provided, and then sought quotations for this provision. Tendering organizations neither suggested nor influenced the actual level of service. This power remained firmly with the local authority. As more and more services were compulsorily put out to tender local authorities essentially became purchasers of services on behalf of the local community.

The Blair Labour government, elected in 1997, was determined to abolish CCT and replace it with 'Best Value'. CCT was abandoned in 2000. Best Value requires a local authority to review each of its services over five-year periods, assessing whether it should be provided in-house, via the voluntary sector or by private-sector contractors. There are four key themes:

- challenge
- consult (stakeholders)
- compare (by benchmarking external and other local authority providers)
- compete (with the best providers that can be identified).

*Audit Commission UK*   http://www.audit-commission.gov.uk

This section has considered the important role and contribution of strategic planning in large, and possibly diverse, organizations. The next section considers strategic planning in small businesses. Box 11.2 examines a number of relevant planning issues in local government.

## Strategic planning and small businesses

Many small companies stay focused and do not diversify or acquire another business. Their corporate perspective stays the same, but they still need to create some form of competitive advantage and develop and integrate functional plans. In this respect, small business planning is similar to that for an individual business inside a conglomerate. Aram and Cowen (1990) believe that small businesses can improve their performance by limited investment in strategic planning and development, and returns well in excess of costs can be generated. Unfortunately, many small owner–managers misguidedly believe that:

- strategic planning is too expensive and only belongs in large organizations
- formalized processes, requiring expert planners, are essential
- the benefits are too long term and there are no immediate payoffs.

As a result they adopt a more seat-of-the-pants reactive approach. Both vision and flexibility are important features of most successful small businesses, but these can be built on to provide greater strength and stability. Simply, and reinforcing points made earlier in the chapter, small companies can benefit in the same way as large ones from discerning the important *strategic issues* and from involving managers from the various functions in deciding how they might best be tackled.

Aram and Cowen recommend that small companies should involve all relevant managers in discussions about priorities, opportunities, problems and preferences. They should look ahead and not just consider immediate problems and crises. Objective information and analyses (albeit limited in scope) are required to underpin the process, which must be actively and visibly supported by the owner–manager or strategic leader, who, in turn, must be willing to accept ideas from other managers. Adequate time must also be found, and sound financial systems should be in place to support the implementation of new strategies and plans.

## Strategic Planning Issues

### Who should plan?

Among the various authors on corporate planning who have been referred to earlier in this chapter, there is a consensus of opinion that strategic planning should not be undertaken by the chief executive alone, planning specialists divorced from operating managers, marketing executives or finance departments. An individual or specialist department may be biased and fail to produce a balanced plan. Instead, it is important to involve, in some way, all managers who will be affected by the plan, and who will be charged with implementing it. However, all of these managers together cannot constitute an effective working team, and therefore a small team representing the whole organization should be constituted, and other managers consulted. This will require a schedule for the planning activities and a formalized system for carrying out the tasks. As discussed above, it is important that planning systems do not inhibit ongoing strategic thinking by managers throughout the organization. Threats must still be spotted early and potential opportunities must not be lost.

## Planning traps

Ringbakk (1971) and Steiner (1972) have documented several reasons why formal planning might fail and have discussed the potential traps to avoid. Among their conclusions are the following.

- Planning should not be left exclusively to planners who might see their job as being the production of a plan and who might also concentrate on procedures and detail at the expense of wide strategic thinking.
- Planning should be seen as a support activity in strategic decision making and not a once-a-year ritual.
- There must be a commitment and an allocation of time from the strategic leader. Without this managers lower down the organization might not feel that planning matters within the firm.
- Planning is not likely to prove effective unless the broad directional objectives for the firm are agreed and communicated widely.
- Implementers must be involved, both in drawing up the plan (or essential information might be missed) and afterwards. The plan should be communicated throughout the organization, and efforts should be made to ensure that managers appreciate what is expected of them.
- Targets, once established, should be used as a measure of performance and variances should be analysed properly. However, there can be a danger in overconcentrating on targets and financial data at the expense of more creative strategic thinking.
- The organizational climate must be appropriate for the planning system adopted, and consequently structural and cultural issues have an important role to play.
- Inflexibility in drawing up and using the plan can be a trap. Inflexibility in drawing up the plan might be reflected in tunnel vision, a lack of flair and creativity, and in assuming that past trends can be extrapolated forwards.

- If planning is seen as an exercise rather than a support to strategy creation, it is quite possible that the plan will be ignored and not implemented.

## The impact of planning on managers

Unless the above traps are avoided and the human aspects of planning are considered, the planning activity is unlikely to prove effective. Abell and Hammond (1979) and Mills (1985) highlight the following important people considerations.

- Ensure the support of senior executives.
- Ensure that every manager who is involved understands what is expected of him or her and that any required training in planning techniques is provided.
- Use specialist planners carefully.
- Keep planning simple, and ensure that techniques never become a doctrine.
- Particularly where detailed planning is involved, ensure that the time horizon is appropriate. It is harder to forecast and plan detail the further into the future one looks.
- Never plan for the sake of planning.
- Link managerial rewards and sanctions to any targets for achievement which are established.
- Allow managers of business units and functions some freedom to develop their own planning systems rather than impose rigid ones, especially if they produce the desired results.

In summary, planning activities can take a number of forms, and organizations should seek to develop systems that provide the results they want. Ideally, these should encapsulate both strategic thinking and the establishment of realistic objectives and expectations and the strategies to achieve them. Planning techniques can be used supportively, and their potential contribution is evaluated in the next section. Systematic corporate planning, though, should not be seen as the only way in which strategic changes are formulated.

## The role of planning and planners

In the light of the comments above on strategy formulation, this section concludes by considering further the role of planning and planners. Planning and strategy creation are different in the sense that planners may or may not be strategists but strategists might be found anywhere in the organization. Mintzberg (1989) suggests that planning activities are likely to involve a series of different and very useful analyses, but it does not follow that these must be synthesized into a systematic planning system. Planners can make a valuable contribution to the organization and to strategic thinking by:

- programming strategies into finite detail to enable effective implementation (this will involve budgeting and ensuring that strategies are communicated properly, plus the establishment of monitoring and control processes)
- formalizing ongoing strategic awareness – carrying out SWOT analyses and establishing what strategic changes are emerging at any time
- using scenarios and planning techniques to stimulate and encourage thinking
- searching for new competitive opportunities and strategic alternatives, and scrutinizing and evaluating them

In other words, all of the activities incorporated in the planning systems discussed earlier in the chapter are seen to be making an important contribution, but they need not be component parts of a systematic model. Rather, they are contributors towards strategic thinking, awareness and insight.

Johnson (1992) further points out that on occasions plans are documented in detail only because particular stakeholders, say institutional shareholders or bankers, expect to see them as justification for proposals. There is never any real intention that they should be implemented in full.

Figure 11.5 draws together a number of these themes and illustrates the various contributions that planning and planners can make. In conjunction with this, the next section considers the relative value and contribution of selected planning techniques.

> The key macro and micro variables of our business are so dynamic that poker becomes more predictable than planning and reactivity more profitable than rumination.
> *Dr John White, ex-Managing Director, BBA, whose customers were involved in the motor vehicle industry*

> I have a saying: 'Every plan is an opportunity lost' . . . because I feel that if you try to plan the way your business will go, down to the last detail, you are no longer able to seize any opportunity that may arise unexpectedly.
> *Debbie Moore, Founder Chairman, Pineapple (dance studios) Ltd*

## Strategic Planning Techniques

It has already been explained that different strategists and authors of strategy texts adopt different stances on the significance of vision, culture and strategic planning techniques in effective strategic planning. In this book the view is held that the role of the strategic leader, styles of corporate decision making and organization culture are key driving forces in strategy

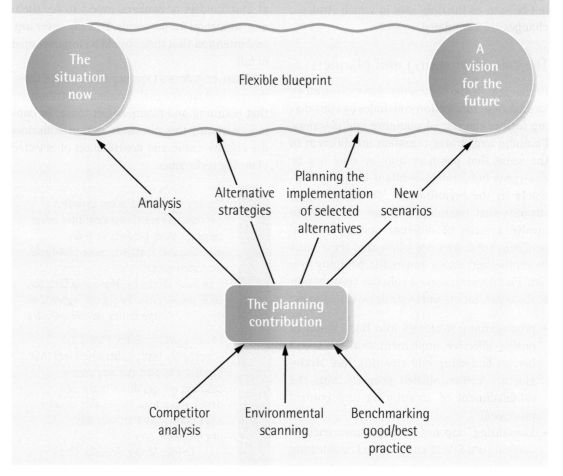

*Figure 11.5* The planning contribution. Systematic planning (in isolation) will not create a vision – but you can plan your own way towards a vision. Ideas generated through planning may well change the vision.

creation and implementation. However, strategic planning techniques, which rely heavily on the collection and analysis of quantitative data, do have an important contribution to make. They help to increase awareness, and thereby reduce the risk involved in certain decisions. They can indicate the incidence of potential threats and limitations which might reduce the future value and contribution of individual products and services. They can help in establishing priorities in large complex multiproduct multinational organizations. They can provide

appropriate frameworks for evaluating the relative importance of very different businesses in a portfolio.

However, their value is dependent on the validity and reliability of the information fed into them. Where comparisons with competitors are involved, the data for other companies may well involve 'guesstimation'.

Judgement is required for assessing the significance of events and competitor strategies; vision is essential in discontinuous change management.

In the author's opinion strategic planning techniques should be used to help and facilitate decision makers. They should not be used to make decisions without any necessary qualifications to the data and assumptions.

## Portfolio analysis

The Boston Consulting Group growth-share matrix (Box 11.3) can be very useful for positioning products in relation to their stage in the product lifecycle as long as one is both careful and honest in the use of data. It can provide insight into the likely cash needs and the potential for earnings generation. However, while a particular matrix position indicates potential needs and prospects it should not be seen as prescriptive for future strategy. In certain respects, all competitive positions are unique, and it is very important to consider the actual industry involved and the nature and behaviour of competitors. Business unit and product managers are likely to be able to do this with greater insight than specialist planners as they are in a better position to appreciate the peculiarities of the market.

KEY CONCEPT – Box 11.3
The Boston Consulting Group (BCG) Growth-share Matrix

### Basic premises

Bruce Henderson (1970) of BCG has suggested firstly that the margins earned by a product, and the cash generated by it, are a function of market share. The higher the market share, relative to competitors, the greater the earnings potential; high margins and market share are correlated. A second premise is that sales and revenue growth requires investment. Sales of a product will only increase if there is appropriate expenditure on advertising, distribution and development; and the rate of market growth determines the required investment. Third, high market share must be earned or bought, which requires additional investment. Finally, no business can grow indefinitely. As a result, products will at times not be profitable because the amount of money being spent to develop them exceeds their earnings potential; at other times, and particularly where the company has a high relative market share, earnings exceed expenditure and products are profitable.

Profitability is therefore affected by market growth, market share, and the stage in the product lifecycle. A company with a number of products might expect to have some that

are profitable and some that are not. In general, mature products, where growth has slowed down and the required investment has decreased, are the most profitable, and the profits they earn should not be reinvested in them but used instead to finance growth products that offer future earnings potential.

### The matrix

The matrix is illustrated in Figure 11.6. Chart (a) shows the composition of the axes and the names given to products or business units which fall in each of the four quadrants; chart (b) features 15 products or business units in a hypothetical company portfolio. The sterling-volume size of each product or business is proportional to the areas of the circles, and the positioning of each one is determined by its market growth rate and relative market share.

The *market growth rate* on the vertical axis is the annual growth rate of the market in which the company competes, and really any range starting with zero could be used. The problem is where to draw the horizontal dividing line which separates high-growth from low-growth markets.

## KEY CONCEPT – Box 11.3 (Continued)

The *relative market share* on the horizontal axis indicates market share in relation to the largest competitor in the market. A relative market share of 0.25 would indicate a market share one-quarter of that of the market leader; a figure of 2.5 would represent a market leader with a market share that is 2.5 times as big as that of the nearest rival. The vertical dividing line is normally 1.0, so that market leadership is found to the left-hand side of the divider. It is important to consider market segmentation when deciding upon the market share figure to use, rather than using the share of the total market.

The growth-share matrix is thus divided into four cells or quadrants, each representing a particular type of business.

- *Question marks* are products or businesses which compete in high growth markets but where market share is relatively low. A new product launched into a high growth market and with an existing market leader would normally constitute a question mark. High expenditure is required to develop and launch the product, and consequently it is unlikely to be profitable and may instead require subsidy from more profitable products. Once the product is established, further investment will be required if the company attempts to claim market leadership.

- Successful question marks become *stars*, market leaders in growth markets. However, investment is still required to maintain the rate of growth and to defend the leadership position. Stars are marginally profitable only, but as they reach a more mature market position as growth slows down they will become increasingly profitable.
- *Cash cows* are therefore mature products which are well-established market leaders. As market growth slows down there is less need for high investment, and hence they are the most profitable products in the portfolio. This is boosted by any economies of scale resulting from the position of market leadership. Cash cows are used to fund the businesses in the other three quadrants.
- *Dogs* describe businesses that have low market shares in slower growth markets. They may well be previous cash cows, which still enjoy some loyal market support although they have been replaced as market leader by a newer rival. They should be marginally profitable, and should be withdrawn when they become loss makers, if not before. The opportunity cost of the resources that they tie up is an important issue in this decision.

*Boston Consulting Group*
http://www.bcg.com

The product portfolio suggests the following strategies for products or business units falling into certain categories:

- cash cow – milk and redeploy the cash flow
- dog – liquidate or divest and redeploy the freed resources or proceeds
- star – strengthen competitive position in growth industry
- question – invest as appropriate to secure and improve competitive position.

Given that a dog represents a product or service in a relatively low-growth industry sector, and one which does not enjoy market segment leadership, it follows that many companies will have a number of dogs in their portfolios. Liquidation or divestment will not always be justified. Products which have a strong market position, even though they are not the market leader, and which have a distinctive competitive advantage can have a healthy cash flow and profitability.

*Figure 11.6* The Boston Consulting group growth-share mix.

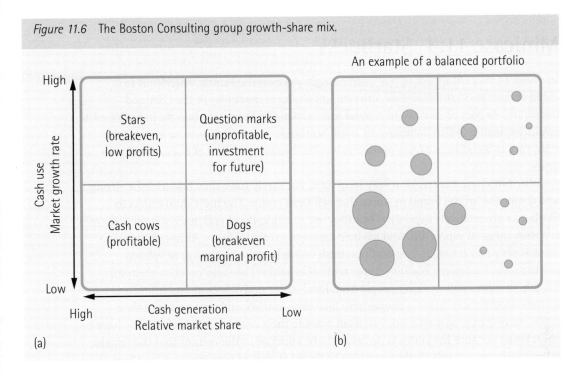

An example of a balanced portfolio

(a)

(b)

Such products are sometimes referred to as cash dogs. Divestment is most appropriate when the market position is weak and when there is no real opportunity to create sustainable competitive advantage, as long as a buyer can be found. Turnaround strategies for products which are performing very poorly are examined further in Chapter 18.

According to Hamermesch (1986) many businesses that are classified as cash cows should be managed for innovation and growth, especially if the industry is dynamic or volatile, or can be made so. In other words, strategies that succeed in extending the product lifecycle can move it from a state of maturity into further growth. One example quoted is coffee. This market experienced renewed growth when the success of automatic coffee makers increased demand for new varieties of fresh ground coffee. The success of Starbucks (Minicase 11.3) shows how a single organization which spots and seizes an opportunity can change an industry and provide an impetus for growth.

At one time in the ballpoint pen market Bic was the clear market leader and a cash cow when the market reached a stage of maturity. However, the introduction of rollerball pens and erasable ballpoint pens generated new growth and marketing opportunities for other competitors. Bic, meanwhile, has ensured its continued success by producing pens as 'give-away' corporate products for clients such as the main hotel chains, who mainly place them in hotel rooms and expect that guests will remove them.

When 'milking' products care also has to be taken not to reduce capacity if there is a chance that demand and growth opportunities might return as a result of scarcities or changes in taste. When restrictions on the import of Scotch whisky into Japan were eased in the late 1980s, the product enjoyed star status even though it was seen as a cash cow in the UK.

Strategic decisions based on portfolio positions may also ignore crucial issues of interdependence and synergy. Business units may

# Minicase 11.3  Starbucks

In under 15 years Starbucks grew from a single store on the Seattle waterfront to a chain of over 1600 stores across America, spawning competitors in the USA and elsewhere. As part of its drive to expand internationally, Starbucks bought its smaller UK rival, The Seattle Coffee Company, in 1998. Starbucks succeeded because it found the right way to blend sales of top-grade fresh coffee beans with sales of cups of coffee to drink.

Coffee bars have existed for a very long time, but rarely have they featured the strong and distinctive aroma found in stores that sell fresh coffee. The individual drinks in Starbucks are relatively expensive, but they are individualized and made to order. There is a wide range of piping-hot and ice-cold variants to choose from. Although coffee to drink is very much the leading product, fresh coffee beans and a range of related products, such as cakes, biscuits, mugs and coffee makers are also on offer. Customers include shoppers and working people from local stores and offices at lunchtime and teatime on their way home – people who take time to relax and converse over their coffee, as well as people who pop out from work to their nearest outlet when they have a short break because the coffee is perceived to be superior to the instant that they might otherwise have to drink. Outlets can also be found at airport terminals and in those bookstores where people go to browse and relax. Essentially, Starbucks 'sells an emotional experience' and not just a commodity product. It thus adds value.

The success is down to Howard Schulz, the son of a blue-collar worker in Brooklyn. Schulz became a salesman, and when he was working for a houseware products company he visited Seattle and was introduced to the Starbucks Coffee Company, a business that sold imported coffee beans. He joined the business in 1982 with the title of Marketing Director. Enthused by espresso bars on a business trip to Italy, and convinced that a similar concept could be developed for the USA, he attempted to sell the idea to his bosses. The family declined to go along with him and he left to start up on his own. He managed to raise enough money to open one outlet and within two years he was in a position to buy out Starbucks.

Schulz claims that his mission has always been to 'educate consumers everywhere about fine coffee'. Customers who visit Starbucks must feel relaxed and enjoy 'a sense of wonder and romance in the midst of their harried lives'. People will pay 'arguably outrageous prices' for their coffee as long as it is seen as an indulgence. If this is to be achieved, staff attitudes and behaviours are critical. Service, therefore, is everything. Schulz has created Starbucks as 'living proof that a company can lead with its heart and nurture its soul and still make money'. Employees are seen as partners. Including part-timers, they all enjoy free health insurance, stock options (known as bean stock), training programmes and wages above the industry average. Although many are young and fit, students who will not stay long enough to earn stock options and who will not need health care, they feel valued and consequently deliver the desired service. They matter. In addition, all unsold beans over eight days old are given away free to local food banks. Nevertheless, the company has also been criticized for exploiting cheap labour in coffee-growing countries.

QUESTIONS: How would you summarize the opportunity that Starbucks has identified and exploited?
How might the opportunity be developed further as new competitors enter the attractive market?

*Starbucks*   http://www.starbucks.com

*Table 11.3*   Glaxo Wellcome (1997)

| Area of treatment | Revenue contribution (%) | Current rate of growth/decline (%) |
|---|---|---|
| Gastrointestinal, including Zantac | 23 | −13 |
| Respiratory | 21 | +11 |
| Viral infections | 16 | +28 |
| Bacterial infections | 11 | +2 |
| Migraine-type drugs | 9 | +47 |
| Oncology | 6 | −3 |
| Others | 14 | +8 |

At this time (and prior to its merger with SmithKline Beecham), Glaxo Wellcome was focusing its research efforts on viral infections (two separate AIDS drugs), asthma, influenza and hepatitis B.

*Glaxo Wellcome*   http://www.glaxowellcome.co.uk

be treated as separate independent businesses for the purposes of planning, and this can increase the likelihood of the more qualitative contributions to other business units, and to the organization as a whole, being overlooked when decisions are made about possible liquidation or divestment.

Table 11.3 provides information on Glaxo Wellcome's product portfolio in 1997. The table shows the relative importance to Glaxo of each product area and the current growth that it was enjoying. At this time the company was beginning to lose revenue from its very successful Zantac antiulcer drug and was looking to replace it with other patented new successes. When an individual drug is seen as *the* treat-

ment for a particular condition, then the manufacturer of that drug will dominate the relevant segment of the industry.

## Directional policy matrices

The best-known directional policy matrices were developed in the 1970s by Shell and General Electric and the management consultants McKinsey. They are broadly similar and aim to assist large complex multiactivity enterprises with decisions concerning investment and divestment priorities. A version of the Shell matrix is illustrated in Figure 11.7; a fuller explanation can be found in Robinson *et al.* (1978).

Figure 11.7    The directional policy matrix developed by Shell: two presentations

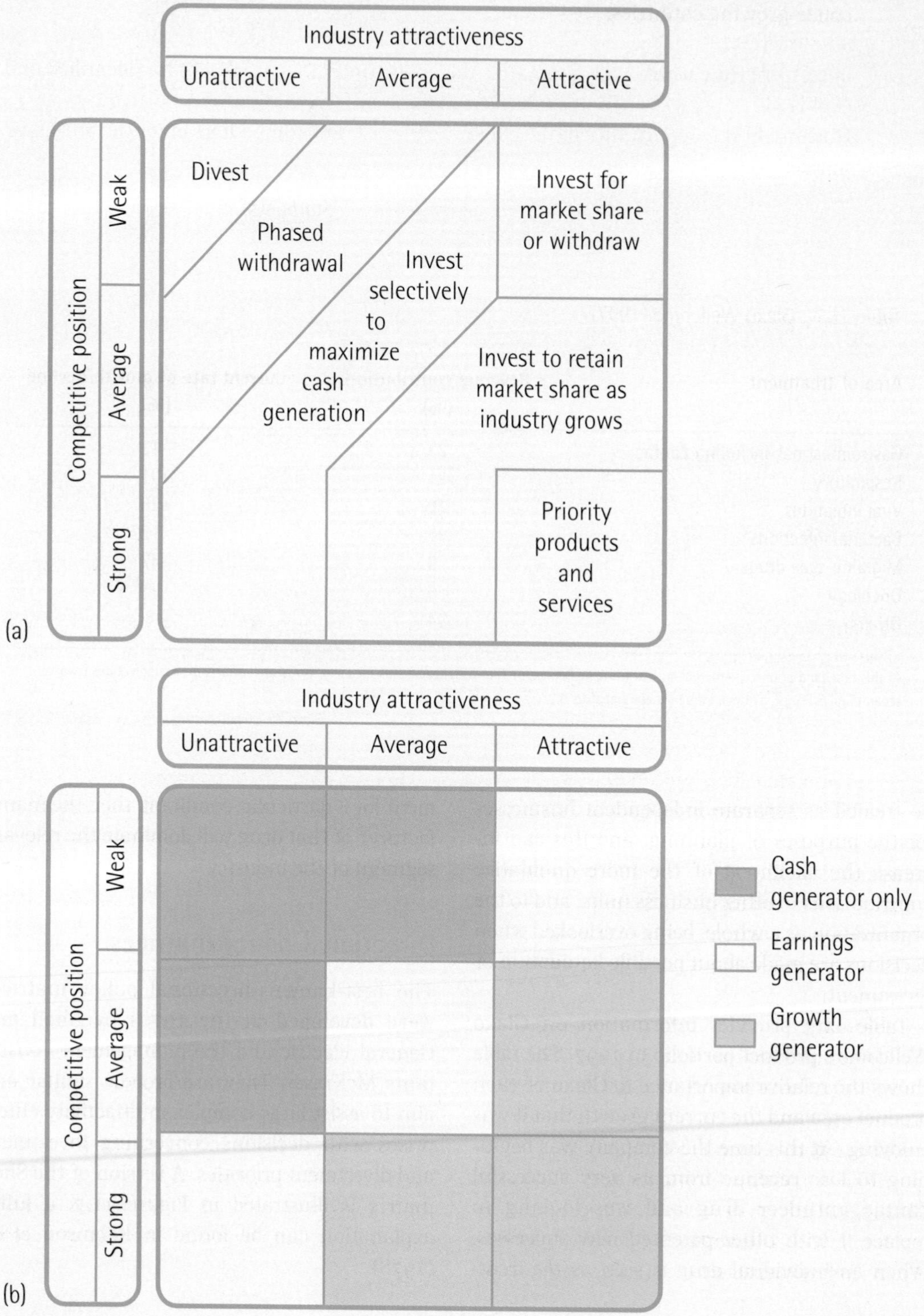

(a)

| Industry attractiveness | | |
|---|---|---|
| Unattractive | Average | Attractive |

Competitive position

Weak: Divest / Phased withdrawal / Invest selectively to maximize cash generation / Invest for market share or withdraw

Average: Invest to retain market share as industry grows

Strong: Priority products and services

(b)

| Industry attractiveness | | |
|---|---|---|
| Unattractive | Average | Attractive |

Competitive position: Weak / Average / Strong

■ Cash generator only

□ Earnings generator

■ Growth generator

*Table 11.4*   Factors in the directional policy matrix

| Industry attractiveness | Market growth |
| --- | --- |
| | Market quality, or the ability for new products to achieve higher or more stable profitability than other sectors |
| | Supplier pressure |
| | Customer pressure |
| | Substitute products |
| | Government action |
| | Entry barriers |
| | Competitive pressure |
| Competitive position and relative strength | Competition |
| | Relative market shares |
| | Competitive postures and opportunities |
| | Production capability |
| | Research and development record and strengths |
| | Success rate to date, measured in terms of market share and financial success (earnings in excess of the cost of capital) |

In using such a matrix there is an assumption that resources are scarce, and that there never will be, or should be, enough financial and other resources for the implementation of all the project ideas and opportunities which can be conceived in a successful, creative and innovative organization. Choices will always have to be made about investment priorities. The development of an effective corporate strategy therefore involves an evaluation of the potential for existing businesses together with new possibilities in order to determine the priorities.

The matrix is constructed within two axes: the horizontal axis represents industry attractiveness, or the prospects for profitable operation in the sector concerned; the vertical axis indicates the company's existing competitive position in relation to other companies in the industry. New possibilities can be evaluated initially along the vertical axis by considering their likely prospects for establishing competitive advantage. It will be appreciated that Michael Porter's work links closely to this.

In placing individual products in the matrix the factors shown in Table 11.4 are typical of those that might be used.

Each factor would be given a weighting relative to its perceived importance, and each product being evaluated would be given a score for every factor. The aggregate weighted scores for both axes determine the final position in the matrix.

### Using the matrix

Figure 11.7(a) illustrates that the overall attractiveness of products diminishes as one moves diagonally from the bottom right-hand corner of the matrix to the top left. Priority products, in the bottom right-hand corner, are those which score highly on both axes. As a result they should receive priority for development, and the resources necessary for this should be allocated to them.

Products bordering on the priority box should receive the appropriate level of investment to ensure that at the very least market share is retained as the industry grows.

Products currently with a weak competitive position in an attractive industry are placed in the top right-hand corner of the matrix. They should be evaluated in respect of the potential to establish and sustain real competitive advantage. If the prospects seem good, then carefully targeted investment should be considered seriously. If the prospects are poor it is appropriate to withdraw from the market. A weak position in an attractive industry might be remedied by the acquisition of an appropriate competitor.

Products across the middle diagonal should receive custodial treatment. It is argued that a good proportion of products is likely to fall into this strategic category, which implies attempting to maximize cash generation with only a limited commitment of additional resources.

Currently profitable products with little future potential should be withdrawn gradually, but retained as long as they are profitable and while the resources committed to them cannot be allocated more effectively elsewhere.

Products for divestment are likely already to be losing money if all of their costs are properly assigned.

Figure 11.7(b) provides an alternative presentation and flags that products should been seen as either cash generators at best, earnings generators or true growth generators, dependent upon their relative positioning.

The directional policy matrix, like other matrices, is only a technique which assists in determining the industry and product sectors that are most worthy of additional investment capital. Issues of synergy and overall strategic fit require further managerial judgement before final decisions are reached.

## SPACE (strategic position and action evaluation)

Rowe *et al.* (1989) have developed a model based on four important variables:

- the relative stability/turbulence of the environment
- industry attractiveness
- the extent of any competitive advantage
- the company's financial strengths – incorporating profitability, liquidity and current exposure to risk.

Scores are awarded for each factor, and then put into a diagram (see Box 11.4). This particular illustration features a financially strong company (or division or product) enjoying competitive advantage in an attractive industry with a relatively stable environment. The appropriate strategy is an aggressive one. The table shows the appropriate strategies for four clearly delineated positions, and judgement has to be applied when the situation is less clear cut.

This technique usefully incorporates finance, which will affect the feasibility of particular strategic alternatives and the ability of a company to implement them. It has similar limitations to directional policy matrices.

## PIMS (profit impact of market strategy)

According to Buzzell and Gale (1987) the profit impact of market strategy (PIMS) approach is similar to portfolio analysis in that industry characteristics and strategic position are seen as important determinants of strategy and strategic success. However, PIMS was designed to explore the impact of a wide variety of strategic and environmental issues on business performance, and to provide principles that will help managers to understand how market conditions and particular strategic choices might affect business performance.

## KEY CONCEPTS – Box 11.4
## SPACE: Strategic Position and Action Evaluation

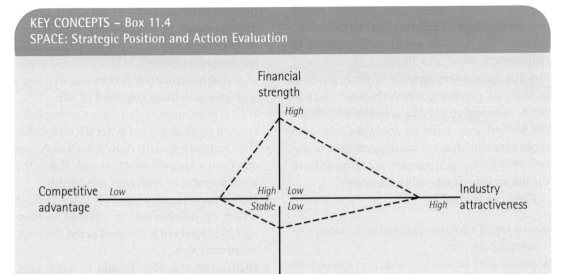

| Strategic thrust | Aggressive | Competitive | Conservative | Defensive |
|---|---|---|---|---|
| **Features:** | | | | |
| Environment | Stable | Unstable | Stable | Unstable |
| Industry | Attractive | Attractive | Unattractive | Unattractive |
| Competitiveness | Strong | Strong | Weak | Weak |
| Financial strength | High | Weak | High | Weak |
| **Appropriate strategies** | Growth, possibly by acquisition | Cost reduction, productivity improvement, raising more capital to follow opportunities and strengthen competitiveness | Cost reduction and product/service rationalization | Rationalization |
| | Capitalize on opportunities | | Invest in search for new products, services and competitive opportunities | Divestment as appropriate |
| | Innovate to sustain competitive advantage | | | |
| | | Possibly merge with a less competitive but cash-rich company | | |

Source: Rowe, AJ, Mason, RO, Dickel, KE and Snyder, NH (1989) *Strategic Management: A Methodological Approach*, 3rd edn, Addision-Wesley.

PIMS was invented by General Electric in the 1960s as an internal analysis technique to identify which strategic factors most influence cash flow and investment needs and success. Its scope was extended by the Harvard Business School and eventually in 1975 the Strategic Planning Institute (SPI) was established to develop PIMS for a variety of clients.

PIMS is a very sophisticated computer model and its database is information submitted by clients. They provide about a 100 pieces of information about the business environment and the competitive position of each product, production processes, research and development, sales and marketing activities and financial performance. From an analysis of the data those elements that are most significant to the performance for each business are identified and the information is relayed to the client.

PIMS can be used for:

- evaluating business performance relative to competitors, and
- establishing targets for return on investment and cash flow.

The SPI claims that variables in the PIMS models are able to explain some 80% of the variations in performance of the businesses included.

## Major findings

Among the most significant findings that have emerged from the PIMS models are the following.

- High investment intensity (investment as a percentage of sales) is associated with low profitability. Substantial investment creates additional production capacity which companies seek to use. Quite often this results in low prices and low margins for products. Japanese industry, in contrast, has been able to harness good management and labour practice with their high investment intensity, and this has resulted in high profitability. This links to the next conclusion from PIMS.
- High productivity (value added per employee) and high return on capital are associated. This appears to be an obvious conclusion, but the significance of the point is that, while the previous finding indicates that high investment in capital and the corresponding reduc-

tion in labour intensity do not create profits, improvements in working practices have a more positive impact on profitability.
- Additional investment in products and industries that are currently performing well is not guaranteed to bring increased profits.
- High relative market share has a strong influence on profitability but is not the only factor.
- High industry growth rates absorb cash, and can have a harmful effect on cash flow – this is made worse by high capital intensity.
- High relative product quality is related to high return on investment. An element of managerial judgement is involved in the data substantiating this.
- High relative quality is said to exist when managers in the organization believe that they have a superior competitive position.
- Product innovation and differentiation lead to profitability, especially in mature markets, but relative market share also has a considerable influence on this factor.
- Vertical integration is more likely to prove successful in stable industries than in unstable ones. Vertical integration tends to increase fixed costs, making the firm more vulnerable if there is intense competition or technological change.
- The conclusion of the experience curve is sound in that unit cost reductions over time prove profitable for companies with high market share.

## Limitations of PIMS

It is important to appreciate that there are certain drawbacks which Constable (1980), among others, has listed. These include the following.

- PIMS assumes that short-term profitability is the prime objective of the organization.
- The analysis is based on historical data and the model does not take account of future changes in the company's external environment.

- The model cannot take account of interdependencies and potential synergy within organizations. Each business unit is analysed in isolation.

Planning techniques, then can be extremely useful, particularly as they force managers and organizations to ask themselves many relevant and searching questions and compile and analyse important information. But the techniques do not, and cannot, provide answers; they merely generate the questions. The danger is that some managers may perceive the output of a technique such as PIMS or a matrix analysis as an answer to strategic issues.

## Summary

*Strategic planning* – using techniques and formalized procedures – is just one of the ways in which strategies are created. Strategies can also be provided by the strategic leader and be decided by managers 'in real time'. Intended strategies, say those selected by the leader or a formal planning system, have to be implemented, and during this implementation they may well be changed incrementally. After all, intended strategies imply forecasting, and, to some extent, all forecasts are wrong. In addition, flexible organizations will adapt all the time by responding to new opportunities and threats.

In the 1960s and 1970s the predominant view with academics and organizations was that formalized strategic planning was at the heart of strategy creation, and should be used to manage future direction. It became clear, however, that a planning approach that relies on quantitative data, forecasts and manuals, can restrict creativity, thinking, flexibility and, critically, the support and engagement of the managers who must implement strategy. Many organizations fell into the trap of believing the key outcome of planning is the plan!

Nevertheless, it is important to realize that all managers plan, all the time. Evaluating the current situation, and discussing possible changes and improvements with colleagues, implies planning. Simply, this is informal planning rather than the formalized systems implied by the term strategic planning.

There are at least seven approaches to planning, which should not necessarily be seen as mutually exclusive. Formal planning is separate from informal planning. The process can be largely top–down or bottom–up. It can take the form of extended budgeting and be numbers driven, or be more behavioural in approach, possibly using scenarios.

The '*planning gap*' is a very flexible concept and technique which can be used in a variety of ways. Broadly, it is used to clarify the extent of the revenue or profits gap that might emerge if current strategies are left largely unchanged. The more ambitious the objectives set by the company, the greater the risk that is likely to be involved in the strategies required to close the gap.

Our contemporary approach to strategic planning is based on a mixture of planning techniques, intellectual input and action plans for implementing strategies; and central to the whole process are current strategic issues.

With any form of strategic planning it is important to decide upon who should be involved and what they should contribute. Professional or specialist planners have an important role to play, but others must be involved as well. Where there is an overreliance on planners, or where there is inadequate flexibility with the plan itself, the organization is likely to fall into one of the obvious planning traps.

Planning has a number of important contributions to make and individual organizations will not all adopt the same approach.

There is a number of useful planning techniques, specifically:

- the Boston Consulting Group (BCG) 2 × 2 matrix
- directional policy matrices
- SPACE
- PIMS.

In various ways all of these techniques can be valuable. They will always be dangerous if they are used too rigidly and allowed to drive decisions without reference to, or qualification by, managerial judgement.

## References

Abell, DF and Hammond, JS (1979) *Strategic Market Planning*, Prentice-Hall.

Ackoff, RL (1970) *A Concept of Corporate Planning*, John Wiley.

Ansoff, HI (1987) *Corporate Strategy*, revised edn, Penguin.

Aram, JD and Cowen, SS (1990) Strategic planning for increased profit in the small business, *Long Range Planning*, 23, 6.

Argenti, J (1980) *Practical Corporate Planning*, George Allen & Unwin.

Buzzell, RD and Gale, BT (1987) *The PIMS Principles – Linking Strategy to Performance*, Free Press.

Cohen, KJ and Cyert, RM (1973) Strategy formulation, implementation and monitoring, *Journal of Business*, 46(3), 349–67.

Constable, J (1980) Business strategy. Unpublished paper, Cranfield School of Management.

Glueck, WF and Jauch, LR (1984) *Business Policy and Strategic Management*, 4th edn, McGraw-Hill.

Hamermesch, R (1986) Making planning strategic, *Harvard Business Review*, July–August.

Harvey-Jones, JH (1987) In an introduction to Ansoff, HI, *Corporate Strategy*, Penguin.

Henderson, B (1970) *The Product Portfolio*, Boston Consulting Group.

Hussey, D (1976) *Corporate Planning – Theory and Practice*, Pergamon.

Johnson, G (1992) Strategic direction and strategic decisions, presented at 'Managing Strategically: Gateways and Barriers', Strategic Planning Society Conference, 12 February.

Mills, DQ (1985) Planning with people in mind, *Harvard Business Review*, July–August.

Mintzberg, H (1989) Presentation to the Strategic Planning Society, London, 2 February. Further detail can be found in Mintzberg, H (1973).

Ohmae, K (1982) *The Mind of the Strategist*, McGraw-Hill.

Ringbakk, KA (1971) Why planning fails, *European Business*, Spring.

Robinson, J (1986) Paradoxes in planning, *Long Range Planning*, 19(6).

Robinson, SJQ, Hitchens, RE and Wade, DP (1978) The directional policy matrix – tool for strategic planning, *Long Range Planning*, 21, June.

Rowe, AJ, Mason, RO, Dickel, KE and Snyder, NH (1989) *Strategic Management: A Methodological Approach*, 3rd edn, Addison-Wesley.

Steiner, G (1972) *Pitfalls in Comprehensive Long Range Planning*, Planning Executives Institute.

Taylor, B and Hussey, DE (1982) *The Realities of Planning*, Pergamon.

Test your knowledge of this chapter with our online quiz at: http://www.thomsonlearning.co.uk

Explore Strategic Planning Further at:

*Journal of Business*    http://www.journals.uchicago.edu/JB

## Questions and Research Assignments

TEXT RELATED

1. Mintzberg has distinguished between 'grass-roots' strategies (which can take root anywhere in the organization but eventually proliferate once they become more widely adopted) and 'hothouse' strategies which are deliberately grown and cultured. What do you think he means?

2. Who should plan? What should they plan, how and when?

3. A manufacturer of industrial products is structured around five separate strategic business units (SBUs). Use the data below to construct a Boston matrix and assess how balanced the portfolio seems. Where are the strengths? Where are the weaknesses?

| SBU | Sales £ million | Number of competitors | Sales of top three companies £ million | Market growth rate % |
|-----|-----|-----|-----|-----|
| A | 0.4 | 6 | 0.8, 0.7, 0.4 | 16 |
| B | 1.8 | 20 | 1.8, 1.8, 1.2 | 18 |
| C | 1.7 | 16 | 1.7, 1.3, 0.9 | 8 |
| D | 3.5 | 3 | 3.5, 1.0, 0.8 | 5 |
| E | 0.6 | 8 | 2.8, 2.0, 1.5 | 2 |

4. In the context of the Boston matrix, is the Big Mac a cash cow? What do you feel McDonald's competitive strategy for the Big Mac should be?

## Internet and Library Projects

1. For an organization of your choice, ideally one with which you are familiar:
   (a) Ascertain how the planning, entrepreneurial and emergent modes might apply currently to strategic change in the organization. Which mode is predominant? Why do you think it is the preferred mode? How successful is it?
   (b) What would be the opportunities and concerns from greater utilization of the other modes?
   (c) As far as you are able, draw up a directional policy matrix for the products and services of the organization. (Use your own judgement in assigning weights to the various factors for assessing industry attractiveness and competitive position.)

2. Update Table 11.3 on Glaxo's 1997 portfolio of products. How strong and how balanced is the portfolio? To what extent has the merger with SmithKline Beecham strengthened the portfolio?
   *Glaxo Wellcome*   http://www.glaxowellcome.co.uk

3. In 1975 the Boston Consulting Group wrote a report for the British government concerning the penetration of Honda motorcycles in the USA. They concluded that the success was the result of meticulous staff work and planning.

Pascale (1984) disagrees and argues that the success was entirely due to learning and persistence, and that it was Honda's learning experience concerning operating in the USA that eventually led to a more rationally planned approach.

Both arguments are documented in Pascale, R (1984) Perspectives on strategy – the real story behind Honda's success, *California Management Review*, 26 (3). Read this article and assess the points that Pascale makes.

*Boston Consulting Group*    http://www.bcg.com
*Honda*    http://www.honda.com
*California Management Review*
http://www.has.berkeley.edu/News/cmr/index_.html

# Strategic Leadership and Entrepreneurship

*Strategic leaders 'come in all shapes and sizes'. They have to be able to think, make things happen, engage the support of other people and, on occasions, be the public face of the organization. It is optimistic to believe that all strategic leaders will be good at all four of these tasks. Some, such as Sir Richard Branson and Sir John Harvey-Jones are very visible and have an influence which extends well beyond the organizations that they run. Others are far more anonymous as far as the public are concerned but are excellent leaders of their organizations. There is no 'right' style or personality but there are certain roles that must be fulfilled effectively, regardless of the type or size of organization. The strategic leader has an overall responsibility for clarifying direction, for deciding upon strategies by dictating or influencing the relative significance of the modes of strategy creation discussed in this part of the book, and for ensuring that strategies are implemented through the decisions that he or she makes on structure, style and systems.*

*Some leaders are entrepreneurial and visionary, but this is not a requirement. In exploring these issues, this chapter also looks at how some leaders are perceived to fail and fall from grace, and at the vital issue of leadership succession. The important topic of corporate governance is also debated.*

# Minicase 12.1 Sam Walton and Wal-Mart

Sam Walton was a truly great retailer. His Wal-Mart stores provide huge ranges and choices of household goods. Prices are kept low through scale economies and a first-class supply chain network. Despite their size, the stores seem friendly and Walton employed people simply to answer customer queries and show them where particular goods were shelved. A visionary, he was focused and dedicated. He worked long hours and 'talked retailing outside work'. Strong on the people and team elements, and willing to take measured risks, Walton sought to learn from other organizations. In this respect he was opportunistic, but reflective. He never claimed to be an original thinker and he networked widely to find his new ideas.

Born in 1918 (in Missouri, USA) and raised in relative poverty, Walton started earning money from selling newspapers when he was very young. As a footballer he showed he was highly competitive, a trait which again proved valuable when he started his career in retailing. After he graduated in 1940 he began selling shirts in a J.C. Penney store. Because of a minor heart murmur he was not drafted for the war effort and instead worked in a gunpowder factory. Afterwards, and in partnership with his brother, he took on the franchise for a Ben Franklin five-and-dime store in Arkansas. The two brothers bought additional outlets, abandoned counters in favour of self-service, established central buying and promotion, and quickly became the most successful Ben Franklin franchisees in America. In 1962, the same year that K-Mart began opening discount stores in larger cities, Walton began with discount stores in small towns. Both had seen the concept pioneered elsewhere. Walton's principle was simple: mark everything up by 30%, regardless of the purchase cost. This proved to be a winning formula. He toured, observed, absorbed and learned to develop his 'buy it low, stack it high, sell it cheap' strategy. Walton's first Wal-Mart store opened in Arkansas in 1962; turnover now exceeds the figures for McDonald's, Coca-Cola and Walt Disney combined! With 3600 stores in the USA alone, and with annual sales of $85 billion, Wal-Mart is the world's largest retailer. It is exceeded by only the Indian National Railways, the Russian Army and the British National Health Service in terms of numbers employed. Yet the wealthy Sam Walton is alleged to have always driven himself around in a pick-up truck and to have been a mean tipper until the day he died!

Growth was gradual in the early years, but there were 30 Wal-Mart stores by 1970. Once Walton opened his own distribution warehouse (another idea that he copied) growth would explode. In addition, Wal-Mart was the first major retailer to share sales data electronically with its leading suppliers. 'We got big by replacing inventory with information'. Wal-Mart has always been careful to contain the risk 'by not investing more capital than is justified by results'. But Sam Walton was always willing to try out new ideas, quickly abandoning those that did not work. He successfully combined emergent strategy with his vision to create a potent organization and formula.

Walton's very strong ego drive was manifested in three guiding principles: respect for individual employees, service to customers ('exceed their expectations') and striving for excellence. An intuitive and inspirational retailer, Walton was also a cheer-leading orator and inspirer. He preached that 'extraordinary results can come from empowering ordinary people'. His showman style was also reflected in 'glitzy store openings'. He created a 'culture that in many ways represents a religion – in the devotion it inspires amongst its associates and in the Jesuit-like demands it makes on its executives'. Following the lead of the John Lewis Partnership in the UK, Walton called his employees 'associates' and personally spent much of his time in stores exchanging ideas with them. Profits were shared with employees. 'Ownership means people watch costs and push sales'. Sam Walton provided support for many good causes, but largely anonymously. Recognizing his own weaknesses, Walton recruited an analytical businessman, David Glass, to be his number two. Glass commented once that Walton 'wasn't organized – I saw one store he was running with water melons piled outside in temperatures of 115 degrees'. Glass has continued as Chief Executive after Walton's death.

Founded by a truly individual and visionary entrepreneur, Wal-Mart has become an entrepreneurial businesses; its growth and prosperity have continued after the death of the founder. Wal-Mart is now expanding selectively into other countries and, in 1999, it acquired ASDA in the UK.

QUESTIONS: In terms of leadership styles and characteristics, how would you describe Sam Walton?
Why do you think Wal-Mart has been able to grow into the world's largest retailer in a relatively short space of time? Is there a 'secret formula' which is hard to copy, and is it reflected in Wal-Mart's strategy creation?

*Wal-Mart*   http://www.walmart.com

The most important quality of a CEO (Chief Executive Officer) is communicating a clear vision of the company's strategy – and the reputation of the CEO directly contributes to the company's ability to attract investment, recruit talent and survive crises.

*Burson-Marsteller, US public relations business*

## Introduction

*The task of leadership, as well as providing the framework, values and motivation of people, and allocation of financial and other resources, is to set the overall direction which enables choices to be made so that the efforts of the company can be focused.*

In this quotation, Sir John Harvey-Jones emphasizes the need for a clear direction for the organization.

It is the responsibility of the chief executive to clarify the mission and objectives of the organization, to define the corporate strategy which is intended to achieve these and to establish and manage the organization's structure. Personal ideas, vision and planning systems are all involved in defining the strategy.

The corporate strategy will be implemented within the structure, and the ways in which people behave – and are allowed to behave – within the organization structure will impact upon changes in competitive and functional strategies. The chief executive will also be a major influence on the organization's culture and values, which are key determinants of the ways in which strategies are created and implemented.

However, the chief executive is not the only creator of strategic change. Managers who are in charge of divisions or strategic business units (normally referred to as 'general managers') are also responsible for strategic changes concerning their own products, services or geographical territories. Functional managers will make and carry out decisions which result in strategic change. In many firms the chief executive will also act as chairman of the board, but in others he or she will be supported by a part-time, non-executive chairman who will contribute actively to corporate strategy decisions and external relations. In a limited number of large companies, particularly those which are diverse and multinational, a chief operating officer will report directly to the chief executive. He or she will be responsible for ensuring that the operating parts of the business perform effectively, and consequently will influence changes in competitive and functional strategies. Throughout this book the term *strategic leader* is used to describe the managers who head the organization and who are primarily responsible for creating and implementing strategic change, particularly corporate strategic change.

While the strategic leader has overall responsibility for managing strategy in the organization it should not be thought that he or she is the sole source of thoughts and ideas. All employees can make a contribution, and should be encouraged to do so. The more that people are invited to participate in debate and discussions concerning products, services, markets and the future, the more likely they are to accept changes. Where people accept empowerment, emergent strategies can make the organization a strong competitor. Simply, leaders should not – and realistically cannot – do everything themselves, but they remain the catalyst for what does happen.

The strategic leader is in a unique position to gather and receive information about all aspects of the business, and it is incumbent on him or her to monitor the environment and the organization and watch for important opportunities and threats that could affect the whole business.

He or she will need both analytical skills and insight (or 'awareness') to provide an intuitive grasp of the situation that faces the organization.

The way in which the organization manages to grasp opportunities and overcome potential threats will be very dependent on the personal qualities and values of the strategic leader.

Power is irrevocably associated with leadership. Strategic leaders are put in a position of power, but they have discretion over how they use this power. Some leaders, but not all, will be very motivated by the power that the position gives them. However, as explained in Chapter 5, there are many sources of power and many ways in which it can be obtained and used. Some strategic leaders will use it to impose their own ideas; others will seek to share power and responsibility with others, empowering them and encouraging them to make decisions without always referring back for advice and guidance. Everyone who becomes a strategic leader will have some experiences and expertise on which they call. The nature of their background and experience will have some impact upon their relative preference for analysis and planning or for working through people and allowing them individual freedom in strategy creation.

These are the key themes of this chapter.

The strategic leader is responsible directly to the board of directors of the organization, and through the board, to the stakeholders in the business. The responsibilities of the board and, in effect, the strategic leader, could be summarized as follows.

1. Manage the business on behalf of all the stakeholders (or interested parties).
2. Provide direction in the form of a mission or purpose.
3. Formulate and implement changes to corporate strategies.
4. Monitor and control operations with special reference to financial results, produc-

tivity, quality, customer service, innovation, new products and services, and staff development.
5. Provide policies and guidelines for other managers to facilitate both the management of operations and changes in competitive and functional strategies.

Responsibility 5 is achieved through the organization structure; 2 and 4 are dependent on an effective communications network.

Figure 12.1 summarizes these points by explaining that, essentially, the strategic leader has a meta-level responsibility for deciding how strategies are to be created and implemented to pursue the mission and direction. He or she may impose strategies; at the same time decide upon the nature, scope and significance of strategic planning systems. The choices of structure and management style will affect emergent strategy making, as will be seen in Chapter 13. The structure, style and management systems provide the implementation framework, a subject explored in detail in Part Four. Minicase 12.1 shows how Sam Walton provided this meta-strategy for Wal-Mart and built the world's largest retail group.

## Strategic Leaders and Strategic Leadership

Kets de Vries (1996) concludes that the most successful strategic leaders perform two key roles, a charismatic role and an architectural one, effectively (see Figure 12.2). As a result, their strategies are owned, customers are satisfied, employees enjoy work and things can, and do, happen and change quickly. The charismatic role involves establishing and gaining support for a (winning) vision and direction, empowering employees and 'energizing' them, gaining their enthusiastic support for what has to be done. The architectural role concerns building

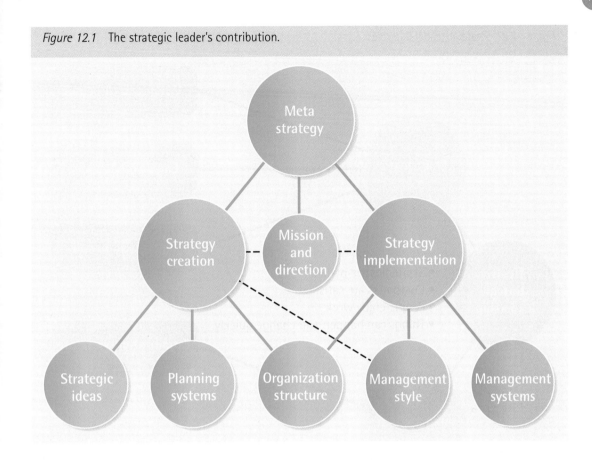

*Figure 12.1* The strategic leader's contribution.

an appropriate organization structure, together with systems for controlling and rewarding people. We can see that these arguments embrace visionary leaders, entrepreneurs and a process of intrapreneurship within the organization.

Related to this latter point, Hamel (1999) distinguishes between stewardship and entrepreneurship. Stewardship concerns the continued exploitation of opportunities spotted in the past. Costs will be managed for efficiencies; some incremental changes and improvements will be made to reinforce the strategic position in a competitive environment. On its own, however, in an increasingly dynamic environment, this may well prove inadequate. Hamel uses the metaphor of Silicon Valley to contend that organizations need to bring together new ideas, talented and entrepreneurial managers, and the

resources that they need in order to exploit new opportunities in an entrepreneurial way. The style of these people is dictated more by aspiration than it is by analysis.

By way of illustration, Table 12.1 features ten quite different strategic leaders who have made a real impact. They have made their difference in a variety of ways. Most of the companies are featured in minicases at various points in the book. Anita Roddick built The Body Shop around her personal vision and refused to abandon this vision when the company experienced trading difficulties. She accepted a new role in the organization which continues successfully. Another visionary, Sir Richard Branson, accepted that parts of the Virgin empire that he built up needed to be sold off at different times, partly to secure the future for

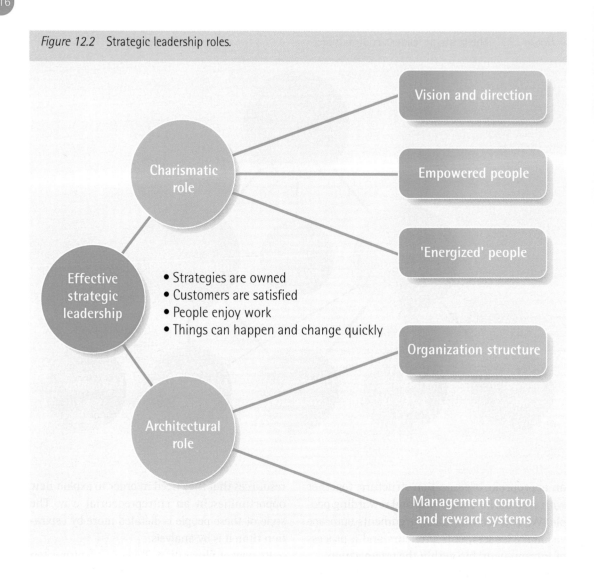

*Figure 12.2*    Strategic leadership roles.

that particular business and also to provide funding for new business ideas which he wished to pursue. Sir Alan Sugar similarly chose to separate Viglen from Amstrad, the company he founded – but this was a corporate split, not a sale, and he retained an influence over both businesses. Tim Waterstone, having been made redundant by WH Smith, opened the first Waterstone's store using ideas he spotted in the USA. Having built up a chain of bookshops he sold them all to WH Smith, with whom he stayed for a period of years. He resigned and, in

true entrepreneurial fashion, began a series of new ventures. When Waterstone's was merged with EMI's Dillons and HMV music stores, and then floated off as a separate business, Tim Waterstone returned as Chairman.

Archie Norman was recruited to ASDA when it was in trouble. Together with Allan Leighton, whom he recruited, ASDA was turned around and rejuvenated before being sold to Wal-Mart. Jack Welch similarly transformed General Electric in the USA, but GE is a hugely successful diversified conglomerate in an era when such

*Table 12.1* Ten strategic leaders, each of whom has or had a vision, and is linked irrevocably with his or her company's strategy, structure and performance

| | | |
|---|---|---|
| Anita Roddick | The Body Shop | Built up and 'stuck with it' |
| Richard Branson | Virgin | Built up and sold parts |
| Alan Sugar | Amstrad | Built up and split up |
| Tim Waterstone | Waterstone's | Built up, sold off and started again |
| Archie Norman | ASDA | Turned around and rejuvenated |
| Jack Welch | General Electric | Transformed |
| Lord John King | British Airways | Privatized |
| Percy Barnevik | ABB (Asea Brown Boveri) | Integrated |
| Gerald Ratner | Ratner's | Inherited, grew and lost |
| Freddie Laker | Laker Airways (Skytrain) | Built up, lost and retired temporarily |

conglomerates are unfashionable. John (Lord) King was the architect of British Airways' successful privatization. Percy Barnevik integrated the Swedish Asea engineering business with the Swiss Brown Boveri to create a powerful business that stretches around the globe.

Gerald Ratner inherited a family business, built it up rapidly and then fell from grace when he spoke out of turn at a conference and rubbished his company's products. Sir Freddie Laker built his Skytrain business and then went out of business through a series of strategic misjudgements and very aggressive competition. Both Ratner and Laker, again typical of a true entrepreneur, have made comebacks with smaller and less ambitious ventures.

The ideas in Figure 12.2 are extended in Figure 12.3. An underemphasis on the visionary, charismatic role and an overemphasis on structure and procedures results in a bureaucratic organization which is risk averse, likely to miss new opportunities and eventually, as a result, become crisis prone. At the other extreme, an overemphasis on the visionary role at the expense of adequate structure and systems implies an opportunistic 'cowboy' who takes unnecessarily high risks and again

The problem is not to get people to work. It is to get them working together for the same damn thing.
*Sir John Harvey-Jones, retired chairman, ICI*

Strategic awareness and change involves: becoming aware – listening, being on the shop floor more than in the office whilst, most important of all, staying humble – and taking action – sharing with others.
*Michel Bon, PDG, Carrefour SA*

As a strategic leader . . . one must organize oneself to have as much time as possible to see colleagues in the firm, and to be known to be available to them, for talking face-to-face is more valuable than a long memo. One must go and see others in their offices. This is the only way to stay in touch with what is going on and to ensure that an agreed plan is being carried out.
*François Michelin, PDG, Michelin et Cie*

becomes prone to crises. The term 'adventurer entrepreneurs' has been adopted by Derr (1982)

*Figure 12.3*    Leadership opportunity and risk.

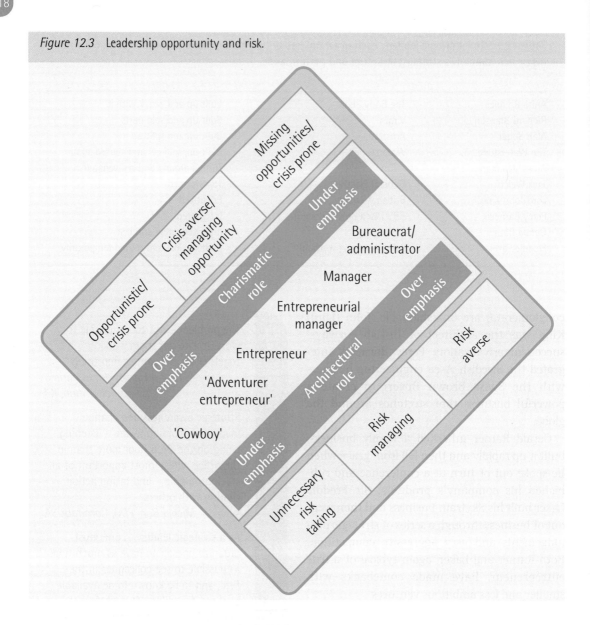

to describe people who take risks that others would perceive to be high ones. 'They live on adrenaline; those who work with them live on valium'. They are able to exercise some control over the risks that they perceive to be manageable. Entrepreneurs, entrepreneurial leaders and enterprising managers all balance the two roles in order to manage both opportunities and risks effectively.

## The role of the strategic leader

The strategic leader must *direct* the organization. He or she must ensure that long-term objectives and strategies have been determined and that they are understood and supported by managers within the organization who will be responsible for implementing them. The more feasible and achievable the objectives

*Figure 12.4*   Strategic leadership.

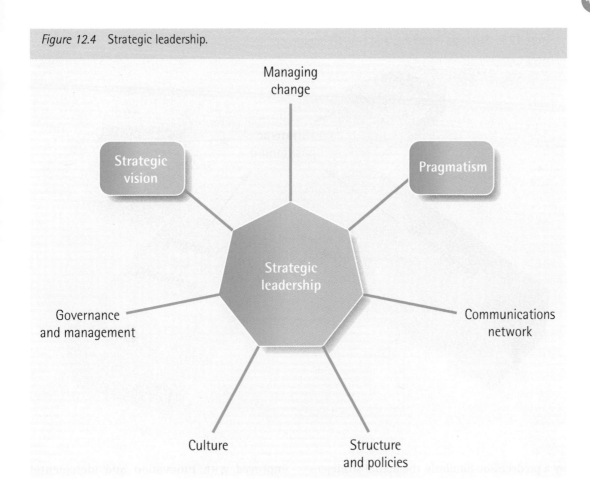

and strategies seem, the more likely they are to be supported.

These intended strategies will be implemented through the *organization structure* adopted by the strategic leader. Some intended strategies will prove not to be feasible, as the assumptions on which they are based may be wrong, and circumstances can change, and they will be discarded or postponed. Decisions taken by general and functional managers within a decentralized structure will lead to new, incremental and adaptive changes in competitive and functional strategies. A third major responsibility of the strategic leader is a system of *communications* which first enables managers throughout the organization to be strategically aware,

and secondly ensures that the strategic leader stays informed of the changes that are taking place.

Figure 12.4 extends these three contributions into seven themes which are discussed below.

### Strategic vision

At the heart of this is a clear, understood and supported mission for the organization. Employees must appreciate the fundamental purpose and be committed to its achievement; the mission will provide guidance and direction when managers make decisions and implement strategies determined by others. The mission and vision may be those of the current strategic leader; equally they may have been established

*Figure 12.5*  Strategic leadership and E–V–R congruence.

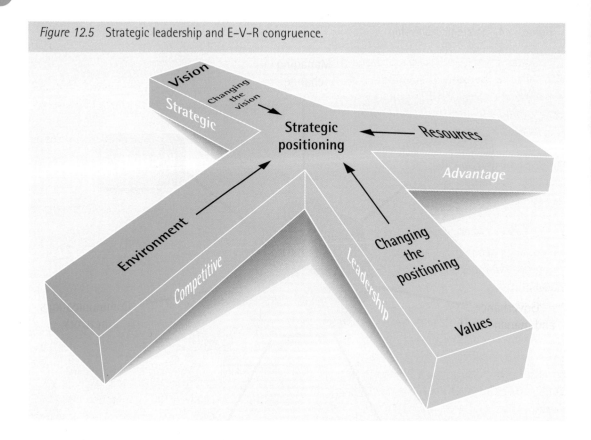

by a predecessor. Similarly, the actual strategies – corporate and competitive – for achieving long-term objectives may be created personally by a strong or visionary strategic leader, or they may be ideas from anywhere inside the organization.

It is important to appreciate that strategic leaders need not be personally visionary, the type of visionary leader discussed later, but they must ensure that the organization has a clear direction and resources are committed to its achievement.

Figure 12.5 develops the ideas behind the E–V–R (environment–values–resources) congruence framework introduced in Chapter 2. Effective strategic positioning is seen as being central and reflecting competitive advantage. It has to be recognized that positions have to be changed. Sometimes the situation will be

improved with innovation and incremental changes, and functional upon the culture and values, and the ways in which managers work and make decisions about possible changes. On other occasions the changes will be more dramatic and discontinuous and reflect a change in the vision. Hence, the strategic leader dictates changes to both the vision and values.

### Pragmatism

This is the ability to make things happen and bring positive results. This implies that the organization's resources are managed efficiently and effectively. Some strategic leaders will be *doers*, active in carrying strategies through; others will be delegators who rely instead on their skills for motivating and inspiring. Control systems for monitoring results and strategic effectiveness are also important.

Some corporate leaders, then, will be strategic visionaries who are also active in operations; others will contribute ideas and leadership but be happy to devolve operational responsibility. It is possible for pragmatic but non-visionary leaders to be highly effective as long as they ensure that the organization has a clear and appropriate purpose and direction. The dangers here are, first, that short-term success can sometimes be the result of efficient management against a background of friendly market forces (which can, of course, quickly become less friendly) and, secondly, that when previously successful strategies are in need of renewal, a non-visionary may fail to provide the appropriate leadership and champion the necessary changes. Consequently, Bennis (1988) suggests that vision is crucial and that the most effective leaders are those with ideas. This accords with the view of Sir Winston Churchill, who believed that the 'emperor of the future will be the emperor of ideas'.

The strategic leader's vision and his or her record of achievement are critical for obtaining and maintaining the confidence and support of influential stakeholders, especially the very important institutional shareholders. The willingness of large shareholders to hold or sell their shares, and their expressed support for company strategies, are essential for maintaining a healthy share price and reducing the likelihood of a take-over. Their confidence in the ability of the leader is a major determinant; on occasions it is shareholder pressure which forces a change of leadership.

As well as vision and pragmatism it is necessary for the leader to build a structure and culture that captures the abilities and contributions of other managers and employees.

## Structure and policies

It is the strategic leader who decides on the appropriate structure for carrying out existing strategies and ensuring that there is proper momentum for change.

The issues are as follows.

- Should the organization be relatively flat and informal or have several layers of management and more formality?
- Should it be split into individual businesses or divisions?
- How much power and responsibility should be delegated and decentralized?
- What is the appropriate role for the corporate headquarters?
- How might planning systems be used to direct and co-ordinate the various parts of the organization?
- To what extent should managers and other employees be empowered to take more responsibility?
- What structures and mechanisms are required to ensure that managers in different business areas and different functions integrate and plan how they can help each other? In other words, planning synergies through effective organizational teamworking.
- What policies are necessary and appropriate for guiding and directing decision making?

These issues are explored in greater detail in various parts of the book.

## Culture

To a great extent the culture of the organization is dictated by the strategic leader. The attitudes and behaviours of people are affected, as well as their willingness to accept responsibility and take measured risks.

The strategic leader may have very clear or specific values which influence his or her style, and the culture of the organization. For example, if the leader has a financial background and orientation, this may prove important. Financial targets and analysis may be crucial elements in the management of strategy. Similarly, if the leader has a marketing background this could result in a different style of leadership, with perhaps more concentration on consumers and competition. An engineer may be very committed to product design and quality. These comments are generalizations, and will not always prove to be true; over a period of time a strategic leader is likely to become

more of a generalist and less of a specialist. If a new strategic leader is appointed from another company it is inevitable that he or she will bring values which have been learned elsewhere, and these may involve change. Logically, the person will be chosen because of his or her successful record in one or more previous companies, and

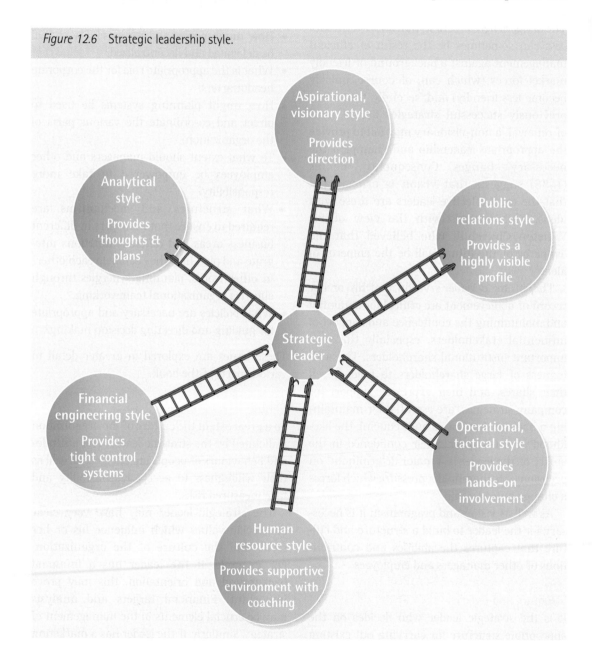

*Figure 12.6* Strategic leadership style.

the newcomer may be determined to establish his or her presence by introducing changes.

Figure 12.6 delineates six key leader styles, each of which makes an important contribution. It may be argued that every leader will have a dominant style, but must make sure that the others are not neglected because all of the contributions are required. The chart is illustrated with ladders to suggest that leaders might usefully evaluate themselves, or ask someone else to evaluate them, against the six elements. The balance between the six, which ones are strong relative to the others, will affect the culture and management style of the whole organization. Arguably, use of this framework can help us to understand why things happen as they do in any organization being analysed. It will certainly help to explain the relative balance between visionary, planned and emergent strategy creation.

## The communications network

Effective communication systems, both formal and informal, are required to share the strategic vision and inform people of priorities and strategies and to ensure that strategies and tasks are carried out expeditiously. Where the organization is decentralized an effective communications network is vital for feeding information *upwards and laterally* inside the organization; without this control will be lost. In quite different ways, both 'managing by wandering around' and budgetary control systems can help to achieve this co-ordination. Good lateral communications also help managers to learn from other parts of the business; this in turn can lead to 'best practices' being shared.

In addition, the strategic leader must champion the relationships between the organization and its important stakeholders, particularly its financiers, suppliers and major customers. Effective communications with government agencies and the media may also prove to be critically important.

Two-way communication is at the heart of successful management of change. Top management must beware of the conceit that it has all the answers. Having identified a problem, it will often be very rewarding to put to those in middle management a challenge to suggest a solution. Being nearer to the 'sharp-end' of the business in practical terms, it is surprising how frequently and rapidly they will provide an answer; and, since it comes from the heartland of the business, its implementation will find easier acceptance.

*Peter Smith OBE, when Chairman,*
*Securicor Group plc*

## Governance and management

Corporate governance relates to the location and exercise of power and responsibility at the head of the organization, and it is discussed in detail later in the chapter (p. 451). In simple terms, it is vital that the strategic leader ensures that there is a strong, competent and balanced executive team at the head of the organization.

## Managing change

The importance attached to formal planning processes and emergent strategy creation in an organization will depend upon the personal preferences and the style of management adopted by the strategic leader. The organization must be able to respond to the change pressures of a competitive environment. Curiosity, creativity and innovation become critically important values, and it is important for the strategic leader to ensure that they become part of the corporate culture. However, while learning and incremental change are crucially important they may not be sufficient. Discontinuous change and strategic regeneration will be necessary for organizations at certain stages in their lifecycles. When this is the case, and strategies, structures and styles of management need reinventing simultaneously, an effective, visionary leader will be essential.

The importance of an *effective* strategic leader cannot be stressed too highly, but an individual leader cannot and should not attempt to 'do everything'. An important skill is the ability to understand personal strengths and limitations and to appreciate the most appropriate ways of contributing.

There is no single, recommended behaviour for effective strategic leadership. Some leaders are autocratic, others democratic in the way they make decisions. Some rely on planning and analysis, while others are more intuitive and visionary. Leaders vary in the degree of risk they will accept willingly. Some look for consistency as far as is practicable in today's dynamic environments, while others are constantly opportunistic and driving change. Some pursue growth through efficiency and cost savings, others by adding new values in an innovatory climate. Some set very ambitious growth objectives, and others are more modest. All of these styles can prove effective; the challenge lies in creating and maintaining E–V–R congruence.

It is always important to evaluate the leader's position and situation. A strategic leader may be the founder of an organization and still in control, or he or she may be a later family generation. The leader may have 'risen through the ranks' to take control, or he or she may have been brought in specially, possibly to turn around a company in difficulty. The leader may be relatively new or have been in post for some time. The style of leadership adopted will depend upon the leader's preferred style, his or her background and the situational circumstances.

Box 12.1 provides a summary of the qualities and skills required for effective leadership,

## KEY CONCEPTS – Box 12.1
### Effective and Ineffective Leadership

### Qualities and skills for effective leadership

- A vision – articulated through the culture and value systems.
- The ability to build and control an effective team of managers.
- Belief in success and in corporate strengths and competencies that can be exploited.
- The ability to recognize and synthesize important developments, both inside and outside the organization. This requires strategic awareness, the ability to judge the significance of an observed event and conceptualization skills.
- Effective decentralization, delegation and motivation (the appropriate extent will vary).
- Credibility and competence. 'Knowing what you are doing' and having this recognized. This requires the abilities to exercise power and influence and to create change.
- Implementation skills; getting things done, which requires drive, decisiveness and dynamism.
- Perseverance and persistence in pursuing the mission or vision, plus mental and physical stamina.
- Flexibility; recognizing the need (on occasions) to change strategies, structures and style. Some leaders are single style and inflexible.

### Characteristics of ineffective leadership

After a period in office some leaders appear to coast, enjoying their power and status, but no longer adding any real value to the organization. Specifically:

- There are few new initiatives; instead there is a reliance on tinkering with existing strategies to try and update past successes.
- Good new products and services are not developed.
- The leader surrounds himself or herself with loyal supporters, rather than enjoying the stimulus of newcomers with fresh mindsets.
- Moreover, discordant views are either ignored or not tolerated.
- Cash reserves, beyond those needed to sustain a period of depressed sales, are allowed to accrue.
- The leader becomes out of touch with the views of customers and the activities of competitors.
- Too much time is spent by the leader on external activities, without ensuring that other managers are dealing with important organizational issues.

together with a list of the factors that typically characterize ineffective leadership. Figure 12.7 features those requirements that will determine the extent of the impact made by a strategic leader. The model presents the issues in three clusters:

- Drive – concerns motivation and ambition and a person's ability to accept demanding targets and achieve results
- Judgement – related to decision-making style and abilities. The 'softer' or more conceptual issues of opportunity spotting and problem framing (awareness and insight into a situation) blend with 'harder' analytical abilities
- Influence – a person's appreciation of how others might be influenced and their way of doing it. Networks and contacts are an important element of this.

A number of these themes is also illustrated in Minicase 12.2 on Sir Tom Farmer, founder of Kwik Fit. Tom Farmer imported his vision for Kwik Fit from the USA; success has involved opportunism and innovation backed up by sound business sense.

Sir Tom Farmer could legitimately be described as an entrepreneur. The next section looks at the link between entrepreneurs and strategy before examining visionary strategic leadership.

## Entrepreneurs and Entrepreneurship

Bolton and Thompson (2000) define an entrepreneur as a person who 'habitually creates and innovates to build something of recognized value around perceived opportunities'. Entrepreneurs can be found starting organizations, running organizations and working in organizations as employees. In the latter case they are typically called intrapreneurs, i.e. internal entrepreneurs. Two issues now need to be examined:

- the strategic leader as an entrepreneur
- whether the strategic leader has built an organization which fosters intrapreneurship.

Strategic management is concerned with environmental fit and it is important to achieve congruence between environment, values and resources for both existing and potential future products and services. Figure 12.8 revisits the model of E–V–R congruence and presents it in a marginally different way, one which implies action rather than being an expression of a state. The environment is presented as a number of windows of opportunity, and resources are represented by organizational competencies and capabilities. The argument is that entrepreneurship in the organization, both at the level of the

*Figure 12.7*   Leadership requirements. Based on a framework devised by Kingfisher plc in conjunction with occupational psychologists, YSC.

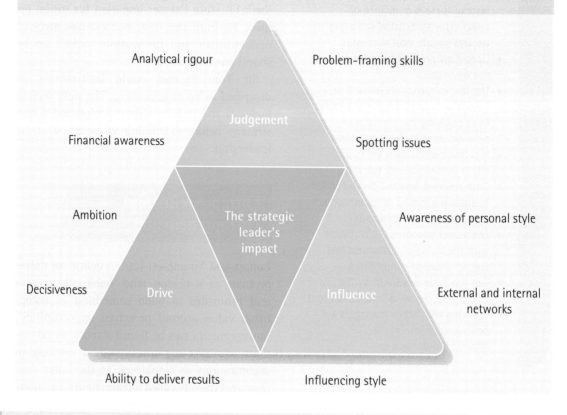

| Analytical rigour | | Problem-framing skills |
| Judgement | | |
| Financial awareness | | Spotting issues |
| Ambition | The strategic leader's impact | Awareness of personal style |
| Decisiveness | Drive    Influence | External and internal networks |
| Ability to deliver results | | Influencing style |

Minicase

# Minicase 12.2  Tom Farmer and Kwik Fit

Tom Farmer was born into a working-class family in Edinburgh, Scotland, in 1940; he was the seventh child. Brought up a Roman Catholic in a largely Protestant city, he left school at the age of 15 and began working in a tyre company. In 1964 he set up his own business, retailing tyres at discount prices. New legislation on minimum tyre depths opened a window of opportunity and he quickly expanded from one to four outlets. After four years he sold the whole business for £450,000 to Albany Tyres, 'retired' and went to live in California. Within three years he and his wife were bored. He returned to Scotland but, because of his agreement with Albany, he could not start a new tyre-retailing business until a number of years had elapsed.

Instead, he brought over an idea he had seen in the USA: a fast-change exhaust shop. Again, he quickly expanded from one to four outlets, so that he could re-employ a number of his old friends! Tyres were added later. As for the Kwik Fit name, he just dreamed it up. The distinctive blue and yellow colours, pervasive to this day, were chosen because these were the colours of some paint that someone would give him free of charge!

Farmer is a workaholic, very committed to his business and his employees. All of Tom Farmer's employees were put on profit-share schemes; about half became individual shareholders in the business. Private garages and repair shops are often thought to involve dubious commercial practices; one of Tom Farmer's major achievements has been to bring a high level of perceived (and real) integrity into the industry. He places a strong emphasis on good customer service and friendliness, attributes which are featured in distinctive Kwik Fit advertisements.

By the early 1980s there were 200 depots; arguably the business grew too quickly. Inadequate management control left the company vulnerable to take-over for a while, but it managed to retain its independence. For 29 years the company grew organically and stayed focused. There was some geographical expansion, successfully in Belgium and the Netherlands, but Kwik Fit entered and then withdrew from France. 'There are cultural differences. The French want to close for lunch. French managers are reluctant to bond with their employees. These are key Kwik Fit values'.

In 1994 Kwik Fit acquired 125 Superdrive Motoring Centres from Shell, a related business. In 1995 Kwik Fit Insurance was launched, exploiting Kwik Fit's large customer database. Farmer argues that it is based on the same principles: high service using someone else's products. In 1999 Kwik Fit was sold to Ford for £1 billion. By this time there were 1900 outlets, 10,000 employees and 8 million customers a year. Tom Farmer, by this time Sir Tom, has stayed active in the business. He has yet to retire for a second time. Yet Farmer has always been seen as a demanding man to work for, and many employees are 'rather frightened of him'.

In an interview with *Management Today* (August 1995) Tom Farmer made the following comments.

*If the customer is king, the staff are emperors.*

*We don't have a head office; we have a support office. We don't have senior management; we have support management.*

*All sound businesses are built on good Christian ethics: don't steal, don't exploit your customers or your people, always use your profits for the benefit of your people and the community.*

*We are in business to make a profit and we should not be ashamed of that, provided we stick to sound principles, and, at the end of the day, do proper things with that profit.*

QUESTIONS: Why is Kwik Fit so successful?
Is Tom Farmer a visionary leader, an entrepreneur or both?
Does the fact that he lives in a large house and owns both a corporate jet and a helicopter contradict any of his stated beliefs?

*Kwik Fit* http://www.kwik-fit.com

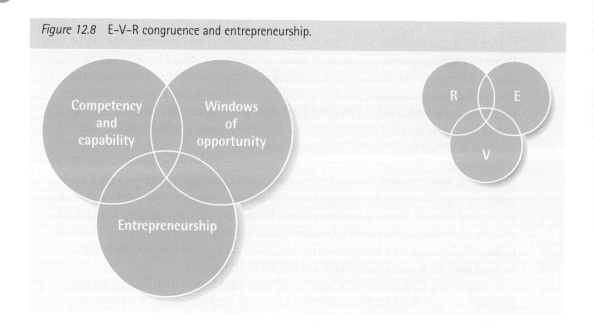

*Figure 12.8*    E–V–R congruence and entrepreneurship.

leader and throughout the whole organization, is required to ensure that resources are developed and changed and used to exploit the windows of opportunity ahead of rival organizations.

The management of existing businesses should ensure that attention is focused on costs and prices (as they determine profits) and on ways of reducing costs by improving productivity. Technology changes, and new operating systems, may reduce costs; equally they may improve product quality for which premium prices might be charged.

Future developments might concern new products (or services) or new markets or both, and they might involve diversification. For different alternatives the magnitude of the change implied and the risk involved will vary.

For both areas the changes that take place can be gradual or incremental, or they can be more dynamic or individually significant. Real innovation can be costly in terms of investment required, and consequently can involve a high level of risk, but sometimes it is necessary.

Figure 12.9 shows alternative development paths for a business. We normally think of entre-

preneurs as the people who develop new ideas and new businesses, but there are different views on the implications of an entrepreneurial start-up. Schumpeter (1949), for example, argues that entrepreneurs bring innovative ideas into a situation of some stability and create disequilibrium. The so-called Austrian School of economists (see Kirzner, 1973) suggests that entrepreneurs create equilibrium (in the form of E–V–R congruence) by matching demand and supply in a creative way. However, it is the path of future progress that really matters.

From its initial position the business could at first be successful but then fade away without further innovation and renewal (path I). The original window of opportunity closes and the business fails to find or capitalize on a new one.

Some businesses never really improve and grow (path II), sometimes by deliberate choice, sometimes through lack of insight and awareness; however, they survive as long as they can satisfy a particular niche or localized market. If one window of opportunity closes they find a new one, but in this respect they are more likely to be reactive rather than proactive. It is quite

*Figure 12.9* Business development paths.

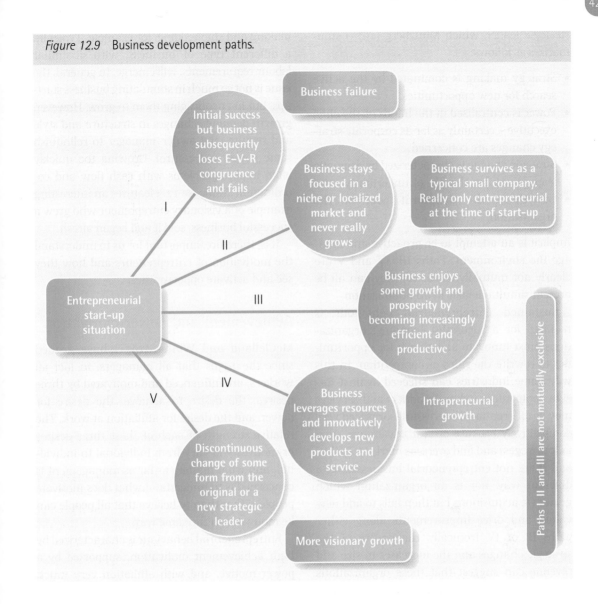

feasible for path II businesses to *expand*, as distinct from true growth based on improvement and excellence. In reality, many businesses fall in this category. They are the archetypal small business – and they are not run by 'real' entrepreneurs as they fail the 'habitual' requirement included in the definition. They can legitimately be called 'lifestyle businesses' and their founders are sometimes described as lifestyle entrepreneurs.

Paths III and IV feature more proactive entrepreneurial businesses which *grow* via productivity improvements and/or by leveraging their resources to develop new products and service opportunities. Sometimes, but certainly not always, such businesses will be decentralized, empowered and *intrapreneurial*.

Path V implies discontinuous change and requires visionary leadership, either from the original founding entrepreneur or a new strategic leader, which Mintzberg (1973) summarizes as follows:

- Strategy making is dominated by the active search for new opportunities.
- Power is centralized in the hands of the chief executive – certainly as far as corporate strategy changes are concerned.
- Strategic change is characterized by dramatic leaps forward in the face of uncertainty.
- Growth is the dominant goal of the organization.

Implicit is an attempt to be proactive and manage the environment. Paths III, IV and V are clearly not mutually exclusive; they can all be present simultaneously in an organization.

Sustained entrepreneurial behaviour is required for a successful economy; organizations must innovate and search for opportunities to rewrite the rules of competition. In this way home industries can succeed against foreign competitors (whose products and services may be differentiated successfully or priced very competitively because of cost advantages such as low wages) and find overseas markets. Paths I and II are not entrepreneurial businesses; in a different way, nor is an organization which grows via acquisitions but then fails to add new values and drive improvements along either paths III or IV. Ironically, the nature of the strategic changes and the increases in size and revenue can suggest that these organizations are visionary and on path V. However, where an organization that has been following paths II, III or IV merges with, or is taken over by, another organization, there is likely to be a change of strategy, culture and possibly leadership. The acquired business may therefore experience a path V change.

As well as sustained entrepreneurial behaviour, new entrepreneurs are required to start new businesses to replace the jobs which are lost when other companies collapse and certain industries decline, as have coal mining, steel making and shipbuilding, for example. Typically, a different type of business, with dissimilar labour requirements, will emerge. In general, the issue is not so much in stimulating business start-ups, but in encouraging them to grow. However, growth demands changes in structure and style and requires the owner–manager to relinquish some power and control. Growing too quickly often implies problems with cash flow and co-ordination. Minicase 12.3 features an interesting example of a visionary entrepreneur who grew a successful business, sold it and began afresh.

It is, therefore, important for us to understand the motivation of entrepreneurs and how they see and activate opportunities.

## Achievement and power motivation

McClelland and Winter (1971) have argued since the 1950s that all managers, in fact all workers, are influenced and motivated by three desires: the desire to achieve, the desire for power, and the desire for affiliation at work. The relative strength of each of these three desires or motives will vary from individual to individual, and what matters as far as management is concerned is to understand what does motivate people rather than to believe that all people can be motivated in the same way.

Entrepreneurial behaviour is characterized by high achievement motivation, supported by a power motive, and with affiliation very much third.

Achievement motivation is characterized by concern to do a job well, or better than others, with the accomplishment of something unusual or important, and with advancement. Such managers thrive where they have personal responsibility for finding answers to problems, and they tend to set moderate achievable goals and take calculated risks. If the targets are too modest, there is little challenge and little satisfaction, but if they are too high they are too risky.

# Minicase 12.3 David Bruce

David Bruce was in his late twenties when he opened his first pub-brewery in 1979. He had previously worked for a number of UK breweries, including Courage and Theakstons, and felt that there was a market opportunity for a pub that brewed its own beer on site. He bought the lease on a site at the Elephant and Castle in London, an existing pub which was being closed down, and renamed it the Goose and Firkin. The pub was completely remodelled with one large bar with wooden seats, bare floor boards and several decorations such as a stuffed goose. The aim was to re-create a traditional drinking house. Brewing took place in the cellar, which had a production capacity of 5000 pints per week. In addition, other real ales were sold. Lloyds Bank lent £10,000 for this new venture, but Bruce was turned down by others whom he approached. He had to take a second mortgage on his house to provide collateral for his overdraft and he borrowed some money from a friend of his wife.

Three types of real ale were brewed and sold, all with individual brand names and varying in strength. These were Bruce's Borough Bitter, Bruce's Dog Bolter and Bruce's Earth Stopper, which at o.g. 1075 was claimed to be the strongest draught beer in Britain. Traditional food of high quality supplemented the beer. Success came instantaneously and the turnover was into the thousands of pounds within weeks of opening. It quickly reached an annual quarter of a million pounds. A manager and a team of seven, including a brewer, were employed to run the pub.

A second outlet was opened in 1980; by 1985 there were seven, with the total reaching 11 in 1987. All 11 were in the Greater London area, and nine of them had in-house breweries. The last two were called the Fuzzock and Firkin and the Flamingo and Firkin. By the mid-1980s Bruce was the fifth largest operator of breweries in the UK. All of the pubs had Firkin in the name, and by this time a number of new real-ale brands had been introduced, including Spook, brewed exclusively in the Phantom and Firkin. Bruce had also developed a reputation for promotional slogans for each pub. The Flounder and Firkin was a 'plaice worth whiting home about' and at the Phantom and Firkin you could 'spectre good pint when you ghost to the Phantom'.

Sales in 1986–87, with eight outlets operating, were £4 million. Bruce had sold 10% of the equity to Investors in Industry for £120,000, and they also provided additional loan facilities. There had been difficulties, however. In 1982 Bruce had obtained a pub-brewery with additional warehouse capacity in Bristol. His aim was to distribute his real ales to West Country pubs. But the company was already experiencing problems from the rapid growth. Beer quality was inconsistent, there were cash-flow problems, and David Bruce's own role was unclear. A microbiologist and an accountant were brought into the business, which relieved the first two of these. However, Bruce still faced the problem that, while there were managers in every outlet, he was personally responsible for ensuring that his original success formula at the Goose and Firkin was implemented and maintained in all of the pubs and at the same time was seeking new opportunities for growth and development. Once the company spread outside London Bruce felt that he was no longer able to pay sufficient attention to detail throughout the organization. Essentially the problem was one of managing growth and at the same time retaining the 'personal touch', a key success factor for this type of service business. The Bristol site was sold.

Bruce had hoped to take the company to the Unlisted Securities Market in 1987, but this never happened. Further growth, he felt, was inhibited by a lack of equity capital and the problems of interest charges on loans. In March 1988 Midsummer Leisure, an expanding public house, snooker club and discotheque business with some 130 outlets, bought Bruce's Brewery, comprising 11 outlets and one site for development, from David Bruce for £6.6 million in cash. The business had a number of different owners in the 1990s, during which period it continued to expand to a chain of 179 pubs, not all of which brewed on site. It was sold again in 1999, this time by Allied Domecq to Punch Taverns, who plan to close some outlets and take on-site brewing out of all the others. Punch had little choice in this, because of legislation and their present mix of activities; but the brand will be preserved. Is it the end of an era?

After paying off loans and capital gains tax, Bruce was left with £1 million in 1989, part of which he used to establish a charitable trust to provide canal holidays for disabled people. In 1990 David Bruce started brewing again. Two pubs, both named The Hedgehog and Hogshead, and offering beers such as Hogbolter and Prickletickler, were opened in Hove and Southampton. The conditions of sale of Bruce's Brewery prevented Bruce from opening in Greater London. Key staff were recruited back from Midsummer Leisure, the sites were leased rather than freehold, and borrowing was kept to a minimum. Bruce personally invested £500,000. He later moved to other ventures before entering a joint venture with WH Brakspear in September 1999. Brakspear has brewed in Henley-on-Thames since 1779. One of his other ideas has been the Bertie Belcher brand, 'pubs that brew the beer you'll want to repeat'.

The name for the new venture is Honeypot Inns; David Bruce is chief executive. Brakspear has put seven managed pubs into the venture (six more will be added every year) and they will be retained as independent pubs which reflect the character of the building and their local communities. They will be a loose chain, linked by a common brand name but they will all be individual. The new additions will be unusual sites rather than typical high streets.

Brakspear believes that Bruce has 'tremendous skills for identifying opportunities for the development of retail operations that catch the imagination of consumers'. He is certainly a master of the weak pun. Bruce asserts that 'creating the right ambience is an innate skill – not something I can explain'. He fully intends to move on again when the venture is properly up-and-running . . .'I put my all into these ventures for up to 5 years and then I have to do something else'.

*Figure 12.10* Typology of the entrepreneur. Adapted from Ettinger, JC (1983) Some Belgian evidence on entrepreneurial personality. *European Small Business Journal*, 1(2). Reproduced with permission.

| | | Independence/power | |
|---|---|---|---|
| | | Dominant need for independence | Dominant need for power |
| Need to create | Weak | Marginal businesses Professional people | Company executives |
| | Strong | Independent entrepreneurs | Entrepreneurs – organization makers |

Actually achieving the goal is important. They also prefer constant feedback concerning progress. Achievement motivation is closely linked to the desire to create something.

Entrepreneurial behaviour also features a desire for power, influence and independence.

Ettinger (1983) has developed this thesis, and argues that there are two types of entrepreneur (Figure 12.10). Independent entrepreneurs are intent on creating and developing their own organization and retaining control, as they are more concerned with independence than power. Where power is stronger, organization makers are looking for growth opportunities, because growth and size yield power. Arguably, they will accept a loss of independence if they can build something important.

Some strategic leaders will exhibit more entrepreneurialism than others. The management style, the nature of objectives set and chased, and the type and magnitude of change within the organization will all be influenced.

Entrepreneurs need both creativity and confidence if they are to seek out and exploit new ideas; and they must be willing to take risks. While McClelland and Winter describe achievement-motivated people as those who take very measured risks, there are some entrepreneurs who thrive on uncertainty and are successful because they take chances and opportunities that others would and do reject. They will not always succeed, however.

In contrast with this analysis, one might expect to see people who aspire to be leaders to be driven more by a desire for power.

## Intrapreneurship

Entrepreneurial activity, innovation and growth are affected greatly by the ambition and style of the strategic leader, his or her values, and the culture that he or she creates, but arguably they should be spread throughout the organization. Intrapreneurship is the term given to the establishment and fostering of entrepreneurial activity within large organizations. Many new ideas for innovation, for product or service developments, can come from managers within organizations if the structure and climate encourage and allow them to contribute. There is a number of ways. Special task forces and development groups are one alternative. Allowing individual managers the opportunity, freedom and, if necessary, the capital to try new ideas is another. Success requires that change is perceived more as an opportunity than a threat, that the company is aware of market opportunities and is customer orientated, and that the financial implications are thought through.

The subject of intrapreneurship is explored in greater depth in Chapter 13.

## Seeing and activating opportunities

Stevenson and Gumpert (1985) argue that entrepreneurs are opportunity driven and that they constantly seek answers to a series of key questions.

- Where are the opportunities?
- How do I capitalize on them?
- What resources do I need?
- How do I gain control over them? It is generally acknowledged that entrepreneurs use networks and contacts to 'beg, steal or borrow' *suitable* resources which do not have to be the best available.
- What structure is best? – accepting that without this, renewal and growth are less likely to happen.

These points are combined in Figure 12.11. The entrepreneur is placed in the centre of the diagram, the orchestrator of the whole process. His or her contribution is to input a vision, realize where there is an *opportunity*, engage it and stimulate action. To develop and grow effectively, the organization needs to find a *strategic position* in the market where it can offer, and be seen to be offering, something that provides value for the customer. Either the product or service is different from everything else, and different in a meaningful way, or it offers 'better value', perhaps by being cheaper but not of inferior quality. The idea for the winning position can start with ideas from inside the organization, perhaps using new technologies to do new things, or it can be a response to issues raised by customers.

Where it starts is less relevant than the need to bring together the customers' needs and the resources required to satisfy them. Finding this position, then, is the theme of *strategy creation*. Planning will play an important role in the process, but it may well be the actual implementation of the idea that is planned rather than the idea itself, which might have been realized more opportunistically, largely reliant on the entrepreneur's attentiveness and insight into the market. Plans should be flexible rather than rigid as implementation is a learning process. Ideas are refined with experience. It is impossible to foresee all of the issues involved in activating the idea.

As one moves further with *strategy implementation*, team and organization building become increasingly significant. However, strong and winning strategic positions will have finite lives, which in today's world can be relatively short ones. Successful companies attract competitors, who are themselves looking for new, profitable opportunities. Success is maintained by innovation and *strategic change* which keeps an organization perpetually one step (or even more) ahead of its competitors. The path 1 loop in Figure 12.11 highlights how intrapreneurship

*Figure 12.11*   The entrepreneur: seeing and activating opportunities.

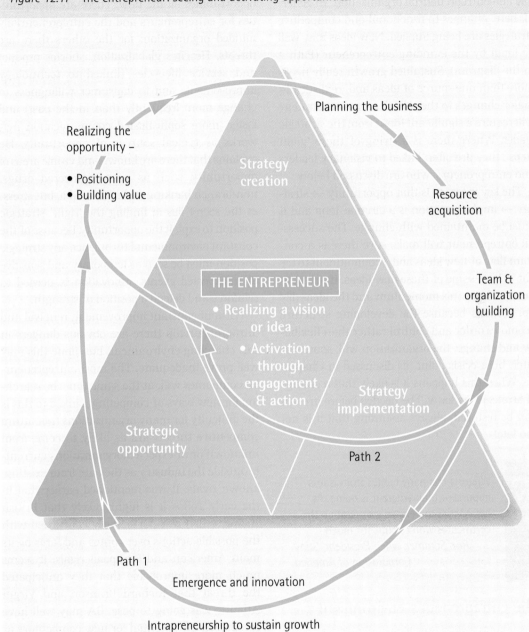

Path 1: Intrapreneurship/corporate entrepreneurship.
     A flow of ideas from inside the organization.

Path 2: Fresh ideas from an entrepreneurial strategic leadership.

can foster new ideas and improvements in a flexible and entrepreneurial organization. In general, here, changes to functional and competitive strategies are being implied. New ideas may well be input by the founding entrepreneur (Path 2 in the diagram). Sustained growth really needs more than one source of ideas and, realistically, major changes to the overall corporate strategy will require a significant input from the strategic leader. Where there is a string of these 'giant steps', they are often linked to visionary leaders and entrepreneurs, who are discussed below.

The key message is that opportunity → strategy → implementation is a circular loop and it must be maintained with change. The successful entrepreneur will make sure there is a constant flow of new ideas and a commitment to try out at least some of these new ideas. If an organization loses this momentum and the ideas dry up, perhaps because the developing structure promotes order and control rather than flexibility and change, the organization will, sooner or later, hit a crisis point, as discussed in Chapter 10. When this happens it is likely that a change of strategic leader will be needed before growth can be restored, always assuming that it is not too late!

Where a company comes from is less important than where it is going. As boundaries are erased, corporate birth certificates won't count for much.
*Ron Sommer, when President, Sony Corporation of America*

## The entrepreneur's environment

*The future was predictable – though very few predicted it!*

(Allen Kay, when Research Fellow, Apple Computers)

Hamel (1997) argues that a changing business (or external) environment opens up the possibili-ty for finding new business and competitive opportunities all the time. There are opportunities for entrepreneurs and the entrepreneurially minded organization; for the others there are threats. He cites globalization, shorter product and service lifecycles (linked to technology improvements and to consumer willingness to change more frequently than in the past) and faster, more sophisticated communication networks as typical sources of opportunity. He explains that there are known and visible areas of opportunity, such as gene-engineered drugs, non-branch banking and multimedia, but stresses the secret lies in finding the 'right' strategic position to exploit the opportunity. Because of the constant environmental turbulence any strategic position must be seen as temporary and sensitive to unexpected events; innovation is needed to reinforce and defend a position of strength.

Without constant improvement, renewal and intrapreneurship there are obvious dangers in this changing environment, but alone this may well prove inadequate. The most entrepreneurial companies will, at the same time, be searching for new ways of competing. Linked to this is the difficulty for many organizations that future competitive threats are as likely to come from unknown or unexpected organizations currently outside the industry as they are from existing, known rivals. It was mentioned earlier that in the early 1980s it is highly likely that British Airways (BA) was particularly concerned with the possible actions over routes and fares by its main American and European rivals; it seems much more improbable that they anticipated the threat that Richard Branson and Virgin Atlantic was going to pose. BA may well have recognized the potential for new competitors as deregulation changed the air-travel environment, but predicting the source was another matter. The outsider Direct Line had the same impact on the insurance industry.

Successful entrepreneurs find new products and new needs ahead of both their rivals and their customers. Market research can tap into issues that are important for customers, but it is unlikely to provide the answers. Creativity, insight and innovation stimulated within the organization are more likely to achieve this. Entrepreneurs and entrepreneurial organizations thus 'create proprietary foresight from public knowledge' by synthesizing information and environmental signals and creating new patterns and opportunities.

This intellectual foresight has a number of possible sources, according to Hamel and Prahalad (1994).

- It can be a personal restlessness with the existing status quo: the Schumpeter view. It is often concluded that many entrepreneurs are not content with their lot and this spurs them into action.
- It can be a natural curiosity, which the education system does not manage to stifle, which leads to creativity. Sometimes the entrepreneurs concerned have a childlike innocence in the questions they ask, and the process is stimulated by a wide network of contacts.
- It may be a willingness on the part of certain individuals to speculate and manage the risk of investigation. Invention has to precede learning.
- It is sometimes a desire to change things and 'leave footprints'.
- Often there is an empathy with the industry and market concerned, coupled with
- The ability to conceptualize what does not yet exist ... 'you can't create a future you can't imagine'.

## Visionary Leadership

Visionary leadership is often associated with an organization that might be described as entrepreneurial, and many visionary leaders are legitimately entrepreneurs, but not always.

Moreover, it is not a requirement that, to be effective, a strategic leader has to be personally visionary.

Mintzberg *et al.* (1998) contend that for a visionary strategic leader, strategy is a mental representation of the successful position or competitive paradigm inside his or her head. It could be thought through quite carefully or it could be largely intuitive. This representation or insight then serves as an inspirational driving force for the organization. The vision or idea alone is inadequate; the leader must persuade others – customers, partners, employees and suppliers – to see it, share it and support it. Flexibility will always be an inherent factor, and detail emerges through experience and learning.

For Mintzberg *et al.* (1998), visionary entrepreneurs often, but not always, conceptualize the winning strategic position as a result of immersion in the industry. They may simply have a genuine interest; equally they may have worked in the industry for some length of time. Their secret is an ability to learn and understand, making sense of their experiences and the signals they see. While some people would never be able to make sense of a pattern of strategic signals pertinent to an industry, others learn very quickly.

*There are two types of people in the world – reasonable and unreasonable. A reasonable man adapts himself to the world; the unreasonable man persists in trying to adapt the world to himself.*

George Bernard Shaw

This quotation from Shaw appears to reinforce the relative merits of two schools of thought concerning what entrepreneurs are actually doing: Schumpeter's (1949) belief that entrepreneurs disturb the existing market equilibrium and stability with innovation, contrasted with the Austrian contention that entrepreneurs actually create equilibrium and market stability by finding new, clear, positive strategic positions in a business environment characterised by chaos and turbulence. The Austrian perspective is that of the reasonable man who observes chaos and uncertainty and looks for an opportunity gap that others have missed. Schumpeter's innovators are unreasonable; they are trying to disturb the status quo, turn things upside down, find new strategic positions and make life hard for any existing competitors. Blanchard and Waghorn (1997) claim that Ted Turner (with CNN 24 hour network news) and Steve Jobs (Apple, a case discussed in Chapter 24) are unreasonable men who, like entrepreneurs in the mobile phones business, have been instrumental in changing the world we know.

Successful visionary, aspirational leaders and entrepreneurs are clearly not all 'from the same mould'. This author believes that there is a hypothetical 'well of talent' and as individuals we possess the potential most suitable for us to become either a leader, an entrepreneur, an intrapreneurial manager, an inventor, a 'follower' or whatever. We remain in the well until we are released. We can, of course, propel ourselves out with sheer determination; equally, if we are fortunate, we can be spotted, nurtured and encouraged. It is not inconceivable that our true talents will lie buried for many years. The point is that when people with entrepreneurial talents emerge from the so-called well, they follow different paths. In Figure 12.12, hard entrepreneurship represents the paradigm of the independent, pragmatic, opportunistic and competitive entrepreneur. These achievement-orientated people are the typical managed risk takers and natural networkers in search of a deal. Not every entrepreneur fits this pattern. Some present a softer image. They operate in a more informal manner; they are strong on communication and they sell their vision to engage and motivate others. The hard and soft approaches lead to quite different cultures.

Some visionary, adventurous entrepreneurs set out to change the world. These are people with a real ability to galvanize others; they work hard, play hard and operate at the leading edge. They have to have enormous energy and generally they would be described as 'having a presence'. Again, this approach is not, and need not, be ubiquitous. The fourth arm, innovation, still requires imagination, creativity, passion and a commitment to bring about change (see Lessem, 1986, 1998).

It may be suggested that Bill Gates (Minicase 12.4) is a typical hard adventurer – Microsoft has literally changed the world of computing – while James Dyson is a hard innovator. Steve Jobs (Apple), Richard Branson and Anita Roddick are certainly visionaries, whose products have again had a major impact on our lives, but they have all adopted a softer style and approach. Ricardo Semler (see Minicase 13.4) is a visionary as far as management style is concerned, but Semco's engineering products, including pumps and industrial dishwashers, are hardly revolutionary. He appears to typify the soft innovator.

There is, however, one final category: the designer–inventor who lacks the necessary business acumen or interest to build the business on his or her own, but who can, with help, be part of a successful and entrepreneurial business. Sir Clive Sinclair is a designer–inventor who has come up with a number of truly innovative ideas and products, but he has never found the right partner and built a winning business. Trevor Baylis also fits here. He did find the right partner and his BayGen radio has provided the foundation for a successful business. This story is also discussed in Chapter 13.

## Visionary leadership and strategy creation

Visionary leadership, then, implies a strategic leader with a personal vision for the future of

*Figure 12.12*   Four dimensions of entrepreneurship.

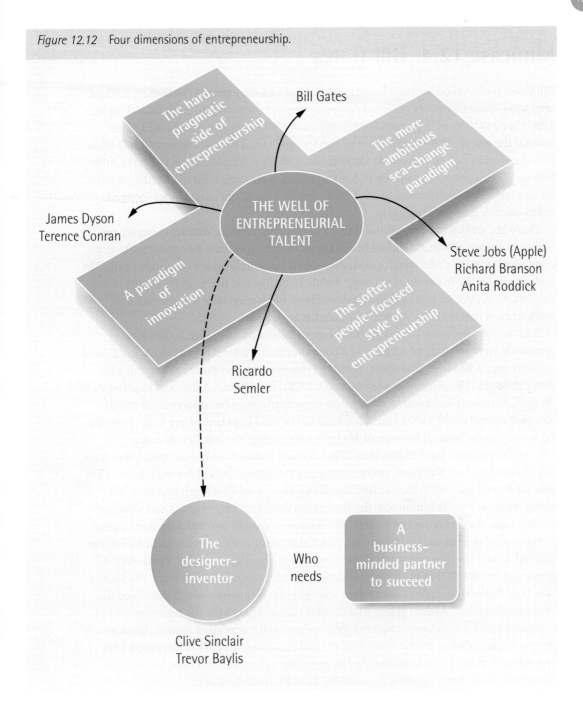

the organization and at least a broad idea of the strategies for pursuing the vision. Such leadership often appears to be based on intuition and possibly experience rather than detailed analysis, but truly visionary leaders possess strategic awareness and insight and do not require extensive analyses to understand key success factors and how the organization can use its abilities

# Minicase 12.4  Bill Gates

Bill Gates had a vision for transforming the lives of ordinary people, 'foreseeing a single operating system for every personal computer around the world' to complement Steve Jobs' (Apple) vision of 'a personal computer on every desk in every home and office around the world'. Dedicated pursuit of this focused vision through Microsoft has made him the world's richest person. At the beginning of 2000 Microsoft was valued at $600 billion; Gates' personal wealth exceeded $85 billion. Gates was born to wealthy parents; he was energetic and inspired to work 'ridiculously long hours', and he has inspired criticism and, inevitably, jealousy.

There are several reasons behind Gates' phenomenal success. Among them are his ability to absorb information quickly and his technical expertise – he can actually write computer code. He understands consumers and is uncannily aware of market needs. He has an 'eye for the main chance' coupled with an ability and will to make things happen. Moreover, he is an aggressive defender of his corner, which in the end may work against him with the American anti-trust authorities.

Born in 1955 in Seattle, Gates quickly became interested in science fiction and unusually went to a school which had a computer that students could use. A 'nerd' from an early age, it has been said Gates 'preferred playing with computers to playing with other children'. He nevertheless teamed up with his friend, Paul Allen, and together they 'begged, borrowed and bootlegged' time on the school computer, undertaking small software commissions. Gates and Allen went to Harvard together, where Gates proved to be an unpopular student because of his high self-opinion. Surreptitiously using Harvard's computer laboratories they began a small business on the campus. Gates later left Harvard to start Microsoft, never completing this formal part of his education. Allen was his formal partner in the venture, but Gates always held a majority control. Bill Gates' visionary contribution was the realization that operating systems and software (rather than the computer hardware) held the key to growth and industry domination.

Gates took risks in the early days but, assisted by some good luck, his gambles largely paid off. When the first commercial microcomputer (the Altair) needed a customized version of the BASIC programming language, Gates accepted the challenge. His package was later licensed to Apple, Commodore and IBM, the companies which developed the personal computer market. When IBM decided to attack seriously the personal computer market Gates was commissioned to develop the operating system. Innovatively improving an existing off-the-shelf package and renaming it MS-DOS (Microsoft Disk Operating System) Gates was now 'on his way'. Since then Windows has become the ubiquitous first-choice operating system for most PC manufacturers.

By-and-large, his success has depended on his ability to create 'standard products', the benchmark against which others are judged.

Gates hires the 'best and brightest' people and he has made many of them millionaires. He prefers a college-style working environment with a culture dedicated to learning, sharing and overcoming hurdles. Gates personally thrives on combat and confrontation. His colleagues have to be able to stand up to him, but it does generate creative energy. However, he is also seen as enormously charismatic, and employees desperately 'want to please him'. In his younger days he was branded a risk taker; stories are told of his love of fast cars and his tendency to leave late for meetings in order to provide him with an excuse for driving quickly.

After a two-year investigation by the American anti-trust authorities it was ruled (in 2000) that Microsoft should be split into two businesses – one for operating systems and one for applications, including the Internet – and should also be required to give away some of its coding. Gates and Microsoft had been found guilty of exercising monopoly power to the detriment of their competitors. Gates was incensed and at the time of writing the issue is with the American Supreme Court.

Since the ruling Gates has announced two key things. First, in the future Microsoft will focus its resources and energies on developing software that will be delivered as services via the Internet rather than loaded into individual PCs. Secondly, he was standing down as Chief Executive. He would continue as Chairman and adopt a new role as the company's top software architect. He was returning to his roots.

*I'm returning to what I love most – focusing on technology. These are dramatic times in our industry. We recognize that we must refocus and reallocate our resources and talents.*

The new CEO is Steve Ballmer, who had joined Gates during the Harvard days, where he was a fellow student. Having been a successful Vice President for sales, support and marketing he had later been appointed President. Ballmer is recognized as an aggressive hard-liner: Gates 'respects his ability to clearly discern key strategic issues'.

QUESTIONS: What are the strategic issues that confront Microsoft today? Does it make sense for Bill Gates to adopt his revised role?

(The new role also allows him more time to write and to work with his $17 billion Foundation, set up to support initiatives in health and learning.)

*Microsoft*   http://www.microsoft.com

and competencies to satisfy needs and expectations. There is a 'feel' for which strategies will be appropriate and feasible and for the potential of the opportunity.

When a visionary leader pursues new opportunities and introduces changes the detailed plans for implementing the new strategies are unlikely to be in place; instead, there will be a reliance on incremental learning, flexibility and adaptation. For the approach to succeed, the leader must be able to inspire others and persuade them of the logic and merits of the new strategies. This is true for all important strategic changes, but when new proposals have emerged from a more formal strategic planning system there will be substantive detail and analysis to justify the case instead of a strong reliance on vision and intuition.

Where major changes to the corporate strategy are being considered it may be necessary for the strategic leader to convince other members of the board of directors and, if new funding is needed, the institutional shareholders and bankers.

The strategy cannot be successful until it has been implemented and has brought the desired results and rewards. Such outcomes require the support and commitment of other managers, and consequently effective visionaries are often articulate, communicative and persuasive leaders.

In simple terms, then, visionary strategic leadership implies three steps: step one is the vision, step two is selling it to other stakeholders and managers; and step three is making sure it happens – aspects of vision, communication and pragmatism.

Richardson (1994) suggests that the following factors are typical of visionary leadership:

- 'covert' planning – planning is often cerebral rather than formal and systematic, such that planning *systems* are not a major aspect of strategy creation
- a passion about what they are doing and their business
- they are instrumental in creating and fostering a particular culture
- they are highly persuasive when encouraging others to implement their ideas and strategies
- they rely on charisma and personal power.

Although visionary leaders are sometimes entrepreneurs, and some entrepreneurs are visionary leaders, the two terms are not synonymous. In this book a visionary strategic leader is seen, typically, as someone who is a persuasive and charismatic agent of change, either starting a new, differentiated business which takes off, or changing the direction and corporate strategy of a business in order to maintain or improve its rate of growth. Major, discontinuous change is implied. The growth can be fuelled by astute acquisition. While entrepreneurship again implies growth, the growth need not always be visionary

or discontinuous. Equally, many entrepreneurs are not, and need not be, charismatic figures. The key element of visionary strategic leadership is a visionary impact on strategy creation.

Remember, however, that a strategic leader who succeeds in turning around a company in crisis and *restores growth* – a process sometimes called corporate entrepreneurship – can be a visionary. At the same time, it does not follow that visionary leadership is necessary for either new ventures or successful turnaround situations. When a company is in trouble, a good, analytical 'company doctor' who can restructure, rationalize and refocus the business can be very effective.

Individual managers, responsible for competitive and functional strategies, can act as internal entrepreneurs (intrapreneurs) and lead incremental or adaptive changes on a relatively small scale. Again, they are agents of change in a decentralized organization. They drive innovation, they make a difference, but they are not visionary leaders.

## Narcissistic leaders

Maccoby (2000) has highlighted how strategic leaders, especially those whom we would describe as visionary, are typically more visible today than they ever have been in the past. Some are excellent self-publicists to begin with, and the media are generally more interested in business stories, especially where they concern new industries. Partly as a result of this, Maccoby concludes that an increasing number of strategic leaders are 'narcissists', inspirational personalities who have a major impact upon culture and style, who enjoy the visibility and notoriety, and who often believe that they are 'something special'. Prior to his retirement (in 2001), Jack Welch, who we mentioned earlier and who we also talk about later in this chapter (see p. 446), negotiated an advance of several million dollars for his autobiography. Richard Branson published his own best-selling autobiography and

Bill Gates wrote a successful book on how digital processes can solve business problems.

What we have in these three cases are 'big-picture' visionaries who are associated with risks and who also come across as being charming personalities. They are typically entrepreneurial and competitive.

There is, however, a potential downside to the narcissist. He or she can be an unrealistic dreamer who has delusions of grandeur. He might also be a poor listener and a relatively isolated loner who is uncomfortable with challenge or criticism.

Richard Branson, for example has sued the author of an unauthorized biography which questions some of his strategies and claims.

> A lot of people want to be led – yet there are very few leaders in life. When people have a good leader who instils team spirit, and they work in an environment that demands excellence, energy, and the keeping of momentum in order to achieve a goal, then they want to stay . . . or, if they leave, they want to come back!
>
> *Linda J Wachner, when CEO, Warnaco (US)*

> To be effective, leadership has to be seen, and it is best seen in action. Leadership must be communicated in words, but even more importantly in deeds. Leaders must be seen to be up-front, up to their jobs and up early in the morning.
>
> *Lord Sieff of Brimpton, Chairman, Marks and Spencer, 1972–1984*

## Issues in Strategic Leadership

### A precarious position?

Chief executives of large UK businesses (ones in the top 100 in the Financial Times index) stay in post for an average of just four years, while their equivalents in the USA last, on average, a year longer. Simply, partly because of the visibility mentioned above, perceived poor performers are dismissed more readily than in the past. A price has to be paid for perceived failure.

Charan and Colvin (1999) suggest that these people are normally bright and experienced executives who can articulate a vision and strategy for their organization. This is not their failing. Instead, their shortcomings lie in an inability to implement strategy. This makes sense. In an age of visibility, visions and broad strategies soon become public property. Rivals can attempt to copy them if they wish. Hence, as was shown earlier (see, for example, Chapter 8, Figure 8.10) sustained competitive advantage lies not in ideas and strategic positions, but in the way strategies are executed.

Charan and Colvin specify a number of typical strategic leader misjudgements:

- underestimating the importance of people – a topic taken up in Chapter 13
- failing to put people in the right jobs – Buckingham and Coffman (1999) emphasize the importance of ascertaining people's individual strengths and natural behaviours and using these to judge where they are most likely to make their best contribution
- failing to deal with underperforming managers, especially if they are people they have appointed and who remain loyal
- not stretching people to the highest levels of performance that they can reach
- failing to put in effective decision-making processes – such that important decisions are either not made or not carried through. This relates to empowerment, another topic discussed in Chapter 13
- misjudging the balances between strategy and operations and between the external and internal focus of their efforts. Often this is linked to poor corporate governance, a topic taken up at the end of the chapter. The

outcome may well be that a good vision and broad strategy is neither implemented effectively nor updated in changing circumstances.

In the remainder of this section several of these points are taken up.

## Finite shelf lives?

All leaders, including the most successful, have finite shelf lives, periods of time when they can contribute effectively to an organization. Some know when to step down and either retire or move on, before they cease to be effective. Others stay too long and risk being remembered for their later shortcomings rather than their earlier successes. Churchill was at his peak at the end of World War II; Margaret Thatcher achieved her zenith once the main planks of Thatcherite reform were in place. When she stayed on, opposition to her later policies began to ferment, and the details of her downfall will be remembered at least as much as her achievements. Minicase 12.5 (Volvo) looks at another long-standing strategic leader who eventually lost the confidence of his board.

Kets de Vries (1994) argues that chief executives who fail to make a timely exit go through a three-phase lifecycle. As we progressed through the 1990s, the length of this lifecycle was shortening. The first stage is the entry of a new strategic leader into the organization, which is followed by experimentation with new strategies. Downsizing, acquisitions, re-engineering and a drive for improved service and quality are likely. The newcomers make their mark; results improve, certainly in the short term. This becomes the second stage of consolidation, when it is likely that the changes are cemented in a new culture. If an organization was in crisis, the risks are now perceived to have fallen back, and herein can lie the seeds of a new crisis. The third stage, then, is one of decline and a new crisis.

## The appropriate style

Visionary leadership is frequently associated with entrepreneurial strategies for companies enjoying prosperity in growth markets. As the organization continues to grow, a more formal structure, together with robust control systems, will be required. The leader must therefore be flexible, capable of adapting and willing to relinquish some personal control. Ideally, other managers will be empowered and encouraged to be entrepreneurial and visionary.

This will not always happen, as some visionary leaders tend to be inflexible. In such circumstances a change of leader would benefit the organization.

Similarly, companies in trouble, facing a strategic crisis or which need rationalizing require a leader who is skilled at managing detail and resources to generate productivity improvements – again different characteristics from the visionary. However, as highlighted earlier, once such an organization has been successfully rationalized, fresh growth requires vision, and here a more visionary leader can again prove ideal.

## Succeeding a visionary

Unless proper plans are made, succession can be a critical issue. Unfortunately, many visionary leaders are driven by personal ambition and a personal vision; they are difficult to work with and they do not share their 'game plan'. As a consequence, they fail to build a pipeline of managers ready for succession. This raises a number of possible problem scenarios:

- owner-managed businesses may need to be sold, but once an entrepreneurial leader has left, what is the true value of the remaining assets?
- on a visionary's retirement a complete outsider may be needed, implying major change

# Minicase 12.5  Volvo

Volvo was led from 1971 to 1993 by Pehr Gyllenhammar, a lawyer who was married to the daughter of the previous chief executive. Gyllenhammar has been credited as a visionary leader who failed to implement many critical strategic proposals.

In the early 1970s he realized Volvo was reliant on a limited product range (essentially large cars, trucks and buses) and constrained by Sweden not being a member of the European Union. He acquired Daf from the Dutch government; a prolonged period of learning curve was required before Volvo's subsequent range of small cars proved successful. He began to build the first foreign-owned car assembly plant in the USA, but production never started. He opened the revolutionary Kalmar assembly plant in Sweden in 1974, based on autonomous work groups rather than the traditional assembly line; the idea was successful, but not outstandingly so, and Kalmar was closed in 1993. In 1977 a proposed merger with Saab-Scania was abandoned when Saab had second thoughts. In 1978 Gyllenhammar agreed to sell 40% of Volvo to the Norwegian government in exchange for oil rights, but Volvo's shareholders revolted.

In the 1980s Volvo acquired the US White truck business and diversified into the food and drug industries in Sweden, but not without some friction with the Swedish government. Throughout this period Volvo's car subsidiary enjoyed continuing success, albeit with its relatively staid image and reputation.

In 1989 Volvo and Renault cemented a strategic alliance with the exchange of minority shareholdings, and in 1993 a full merger was proposed. Fearing the future role of the French government (Renault was nationalized but due for privatization), Volvo's shareholders again refused to back Gyllenhammar. After this defeat he resigned but has since been active in other business and civil-engineering ventures. Despite all the setbacks, Volvo proved to be robust and, under Gyllenhammar, grew into one of Sweden's leading businesses.

The diversification strategies had been focused on less cyclical industries to offset the uneven cash flow characteristics of car manufacturing, but a new corporate strategy was announced in April 1994. Non-vehicle interests would be divested systematically. Vehicle joint ventures with a series of companies worldwide would be sought.

Gyllenhammar's immediate successor as chief executive, Sören Gyll, appeared to be adopting a different style. He was more of a team player. The new strategy for cars became the responsibility of a new divisional head. In 1995 Volvo changed the marketing strategy for its cars, attempting to shift away from an image built wholly on safety, reliability and (more recently) environmental friendliness, to one of 'safe but sexy'. Advertisements claimed that (when accelerating in top gear) a Volvo 850 could outpace a Ferrari. The aim was to attract younger 'pre-family' and older 'post-family' buyers without losing the core 'family' customers and increase output by one-third.

In 1999 Volvo's car division was sold to Ford, which was concerned that 'Volvo had failed to attract younger buyers' and this needed addressing urgently. There would be further changes of management.

In 2000 Volvo bought Renault's truck businesses (which included the American Mack business) and became Europe's largest heavy truck maker. Some time earlier Volvo had been prevented by the European competition authorities from acquiring Swedish rival Scania.

QUESTIONS: Do you think that those who criticize Gyllenhammar for being an overambitious and individualistic strategic leader are being altogether fair? What do you think his strengths and his failings might have been?

*Volvo*    http://www.volvo.com

- the leader could have an accident or illness, leaving a yawning gap which cannot be filled in time to prevent a crisis.

The very successful diversified American conglomerate, General Electric (GE), is discussed at various points in this book. Comments from its visionary strategic leader, Jack Welch, also appear regularly. One apocryphal story of Welch concerns an alleged conversation with a New York yellow cab driver, who claimed he sells his GE shares every August and buys them back in September. 'Jack goes on holiday in August and who knows what might happen when he's away'.

When Welch gave GE advance notice that he would retire in April 2001, succession planning got underway. Three internal divisional heads, those for GE Medical Systems, GE Power Systems and GE Aircraft Engines, were identified as possible successors. They were all interviewed by GE main board members, as were the key staff who reported to them, to assess their style and suitability. To ensure that one of them could be moved up without leaving a gap at the top of their division, a new chief operating officer was appointed in each case, to provide for a second-stage orderly succession. 'Few large companies approach their succession planning with such care'. Of course, they do not always have as much notice!

In contrast, Minicase 12.6 looks at how succession issues have contributed to the declining fortunes at Sainsbury's.

When a new strategic leader is appointed, 'things may not be the same', strategically, culturally and stylistically. This can be good or bad. If real changes are required because the company has lost momentum or is in difficulty, then logically a new leader with a different style is being brought in to make changes. Where a company is successful, then 'change for the sake of change' may be a mistake. But it would not be unusual for a new leader to want to be seen to be his or her own person and to make an early mark. Returning to Figure 12.6, it is quite normal for any new leader to have a different preferred style.

## Leadership and corporate failure

Businesses 'fail' when they fail to meet the needs and expectations of their key stakeholders, or when decisions that they take lead to outcomes which are unacceptable to the stakeholders. These 'failings' may generate crises with which the business is able to deal, usually at a cost; they may also lead to the ultimate collapse of the organization. The outcomes can take a variety of different forms, but authors such as Slatter (1984) have clearly identified three main, direct causes of corporate failure and collapse:

# Minicase 12.6  Sainsbury's

Sainsbury's began in 1869 in London's Drury Lane, as a shop which sold dairy products – butter, milk and eggs. Expansion of the stores and the range of products really began in the London area in the 1880s. It was 50 years later when the company moved north into the Midlands. The company was floated in 1973. The first Savacentre (an extra large supermarket which sells non-food as well as food products) opened in 1977 and the first Homebase (DIY and gardening products) followed in 1981. Sainsbury's later acquired Shaw's, a relatively small supermarket chain located in the eastern states of the USA.

After the flotation the Sainsbury family still owned 39% of the shares, and a family member was Chairman of the Board from 1869 until 1998. Sainsbury's became grocery market leader in the 1980s and then lost its leadership to Tesco in the 1990s. At the beginning of the new millennium it is also under some threat from a revitalized ASDA, now owned by Wal-Mart. Profits are falling and its margins are lower than those of its rivals.

In 1998 the then Chairman David (Lord) Sainsbury stepped down to become a government Minister; one year later Sir Tim Sainsbury resigned as a director and for the first time ever there was no family member on the Sainsbury Board. The family then sold three-quarters of its 39% shareholding for £2 billion.

The current Chairman is Sir George Bull, recruited from Grand Metropolitan (now called Diageo), the spirits and foods group. Sir Peter Davis (ex-Prudential insurance) is the recently appointed Chief Executive.

One analyst's view is that 'Sainsbury's no longer appears to have a strategy to secure a place in the aggressive new world of grocery retailing'.

An opposing view suggests that 'Sainsbury's is still a strong brand and can be revived if it returns to its roots as a high quality grocer' . . . territory currently held by the considerably smaller Waitrose, a subsidiary of the John Lewis Partnership. This strategy might well require the divestment of Savacentre, Homebase and Shaw's.

Whichever view might prevail, there is a real challenge for the new strategic leadership.

What had gone wrong? A number of issues seems to have played a part.

- The patriarchal family culture, style and control, so valuable for so long, proved restricting when competition really intensified. Until the 1990s members of the family retained their own private entrance to the company's head office and were deferentially called Mr John, Mr David and so on.
- During the 1970s, 1980s and into the 1990s Lord John Sainsbury of Preston Candover was the strategic leader. A 'true grocer' he was very successful, but he left a huge gap to fill. He had, moreover, been very powerful and autocratic in style.
- By the late 1980s, under his leadership, the stores were trading profitably and to their full capacity and Sainsbury's was market leader but, with hindsight, the expansion

plans in place would prove inadequate for a market that was beginning to change. With a new strategic leader of its own, Ian MacLaurin, Tesco was setting new standards. It had seized the initiative for developing large out-of-town superstores with extensive parking, and when the government began to restrain planning permission for new sites, Tesco already owned a number of new sites that it could develop. Sainsbury's lost out by being reactive. Tesco was also developing new IT-based supply-chain initiatives to strengthen its links with its suppliers and distributors.

- The new Chairman (in 1992), David Sainsbury, who had been Finance Director, was not 'an instinctive retailer' like his predecessor. His style was more consensual and he was more cerebral. 'For the first time he began to ask managers to think for themselves'.

- In 1995 Tesco launched its Clubcard loyalty scheme. David Sainsbury dismissed it as a gimmick, a reaction that came back to haunt him when it proved successful and Sainsbury's had to follow it with their own scheme 15 months later. The press was rather unkind about the U-turn!

- Sainsbury's rivals were now proving to be more innovative in several ways, including 24 hour shopping, smaller specialist stores in the high street to complement the superstores and home shopping. Simply, Sainsbury had become a follower, whose stores and supply-chain infrastructure needed major investment.

- David Sainsbury's choice of chief executive, Dino Adriano from Homebase, failed to achieve the turnaround he was brought in to deliver.

QUESTIONS: Which of the two scenarios presented in the case – for the future of Sainsbury's – do you believe is more realistic?
Can you think of any other companies where a dominant family influence has finally left a huge gap?

*Sainsbury's*   http://www.sainsburys.com

Source of some of the material: Cope, N (2000) Checking out Sainsbury's, *Management Today*, February.

---

- weak or inappropriate strategic leadership
- marketing and competitive failings
- poor financial management and control.

It can be seen how these failings imply an *incongruency*, or lack of fit, between environment, values and resources, resulting from a lack of strategic awareness. Leadership issues also underpin the marketing and financial weaknesses.

Richardson *et al.* (1994) have identified a number of discrete failure crisis situations, against which we can consider strategic leadership.

A *niche becomes a tomb* when a small company, locked into a successful product or service, 'lives in the past' and fails to change. This is invariably a sign of poor leadership, and quite frequently it will be tied in to succession problems. When *markets are not understood* small companies will fail to establish a position in the market they have targeted and simply not take-off and grow. Sometimes this will be the result of attention being concentrated on the production aspects of the business, where the would-be entrepreneur may have expertise, at the expense of customer needs and expectations. Equally, sales may be achieved, but not in sufficient volume. In a similar way, larger companies can misjudge markets. The innovative Clive Sinclair, with his ill-fated C5 electric car, is an example of this point.

*Strategic drift* with larger organizations is the result of introversion and inertia in a changing environment. Complacency from past success, or a concentration on day-to-day reactive or crisis management, can lead to a failure situation. The company does not spot emerging threats until it is too late to deal with them easily. By the early 1980s the once very successful ICI was underperforming in markets threatened by new, strong competitors; the company was top heavy, inward looking and partially reliant on out-moded capacity. Sir John Harvey-Jones became chairman and proceeded to turn ICI around, but at the cost of lost capacity and lost jobs. Nevertheless, after Harvey-Jones retired, ICI was still vulnerable to threat. The acquisition of a block of shares by Hanson drew attention to the fact that ICI comprised two very different businesses with different cultures and key success factors, mature bulk chemicals and pharmaceuticals. The company was subsequently split in two: ICI and Zeneca.

*Overambition* can be seen in the guise of the failed entrepreneur and the failed conglomerate kingmaker. The former enjoys early success and rapid growth on the back of a good product or service, but the desire to maintain high growth encourages the entrepreneur to diversify into less profitable areas. A downward spiral begins. The conglomerate kingmaker wants to build a large and powerful corporation and is tempted to acquire businesses that cannot be justified financially. Specifically, they pay a price which either overvalues the assets or which cannot be

recouped from earnings, or they overestimate the potential for synergy with the existing businesses.

Good examples of this type of failure are provided by George Davies at Next and John Ashcroft at Coloroll; both businesses diversified, grew too rapidly in the 1980s and were financially embarrassed when trading conditions worsened. Both strategic leaders left. George Walker, founder of property development and leisure company Brent Walker, suffered a similar fate. Brent Walker acquired the William Hill chain of betting shops from Grand Metropolitan, a diversification demanding completely new skills which again overstretched the company financially.

Failures of this nature are frequently characterized by strong, powerful strategic leaders and inadequate attention to critical financial measures and controls. In some instances the result is inadequate governance. The business does not appear to be looking after the interests of all its stakeholders, but instead is driven by the strong, selfish and personal motives of the leader. Small business people will sometimes borrow money on the strength of the business and then milk it dry. Because they enjoy total control, their judgement is not questioned. Some leaders of large corporations, Robert Maxwell was an example, rule by fear and coercion, and as a result their actions are largely unchecked. Maxwell was driven by the desire to build a global empire and to receive recognition and acceptance.

Corporate failure is explored in more depth in Chapter 17.

## Disagreements with the City

Later in this chapter the topic of corporate governance is debated, where there is an argument that individual strategic leaders should not be allowed to become so powerful that there are no effective checks and balances on their activities. A similar argument is often made for the role of the stock market and, in particular, institutional block shareholders. Institutional shareholders own over two-thirds of all UK shares, with private shareholdings amounting to some 20%. In the early 1970s, the respective percentages were 39 and 54%. Institutions have their own shareholders, and consequently they pay close attention to the performance of the businesses in which they have invested.

As debated in Chapter 3, supporters of the stock market claim that institutional restrictions on management behaviour are a positive benefit for a company in terms of discipline and performance measurement. Critics suggest that the constant fluctuation in share prices, resulting from changes to both short-term performance and future expectations, is a deterrent to the long-term investment that is vital for future growth and success.

Although almost all of Britain's largest companies are quoted on the stock exchange, in large part due to their need for equity funding at certain stages of their development, some of the country's most dynamic entrepreneurs find this to be an uncomfortable state. They perceive the price of being a public company too high. Richard Branson (Virgin) and Andrew Lloyd Webber (The Really Useful Group) both bought back and reprivatized the successful companies that they had developed. Fortunes in the entertainment business can fluctuate upwards and downwards quickly and dramatically; consequently, some believe that the stock market will be tempted to underestimate the true long-term value of the business and mark down the share price accordingly. The company is then undervalued.

## Falls from grace

Institutional pressures, then, can ensure that the strategic leader is held accountable for his or her strategic decisions and the performance of the company. Three years after the stock market

crash of 1987, only one chief executive from the ten worst performing companies (measured by their share price movements) was still in the post. Visible 'losers' included Sir Ralph Halpern of Burton (Halpern had earlier been responsible for turning Burton around after a poor performance during the 1970s), George Davies, the creator of Next, and Tony Berry, who had built Blue Arrow into the world's largest employment agency. The lone survivor was Brian Beazer of Beazer (Construction), which was acquired by Hanson in 1991.

In the early 1990s David O'Brien, who had a 'strikingly unconventional style of management for a sector characterized by tradition', promoted a new, open, team-based, customer-focused empowered culture at the National & Provincial Building Society. Profits increased dramatically in a Society which had been struggling, but costs also rose and staff found some of the changes to be quite stressful. 'Consolidation of the achievement', and a slowing down of the pace of change, was required, but the institutional shareholders felt that this would be better achieved by the Society's financial director; O'Brien was forced out in 1994. Within a year it was announced that the National & Provincial was to be acquired by Abbey National.

Another colourful leader to lose shareholder support, and his job, was Gerald Ratner, who had been largely responsible for the rapid growth of the Ratner's jewellery chain after the acquisition of H Samuel. At an Institute of Directors conference in 1991 he claimed that this company was able to sell sherry decanters at really low prices because they were 'total crap'. The tabloid newspapers were very critical and the company's previously strong image was damaged. The group name has subsequently been changed to Signet.

Although sometimes described as 'losers', many such chief executives resign and receive generous golden handshakes. Interestingly, after Robert Ayling resigned as chief executive of BA in 2000, institutional shareholders demanded that the board review the generous payout that was being proposed. The real losers, of course, are the employees who also lose their jobs in the contraction, and sometimes the shareholders.

## Corporate Governance

The main responsibilities of the board of directors of an organization were summarized briefly at the beginning of this chapter. The execution of these responsibilities is normally through the appointment of a chief executive; but the board will also have a chairman to oversee decision making and operations. The chairman will additionally be responsible for ensuring that the structure and composition of the board is appropriate.

There are two contentious issues. First, should the roles of chairman and chief executive be separated or combined? This is debated in Box 12.2. Secondly, what contribution should be made by non-executive directors, i.e. members of the board who are not employed as executives within the firm? There are conflicting opinions on these issues, and no straightforward answers. The challenge is to ensure that there is effective leadership and control, and objectivity. This requires strong and capable leaders, but also opportunities for debate amongst the key executives who are responsible for both the creation and implementation of strategic change. Objectivity can often be improved by the appointment of outside non-executive directors with the ability to contribute particular skills and expertise. The Guinness affair in the mid-1980s, which concerned illegal share support operations during an acquisition, has been partially blamed on a board which was not properly informed and objective. Strong and independent non-executive directors might have alleviated the difficulties.

The importance of good governance was also highlighted in the early 1990s with a number of controversies surrounding the pay levels and share-option schemes for senior managers in the privatized utility companies.

A 1992 report by the Committee on Financial Aspects of Corporate Governance (chaired by Sir Adrian Cadbury) recommended that:

- board authority should be divided between a chairman and chief executive – but if boards chose to combine the roles they should ensure 'the presence of a strong independent element with an appointed leader'
- more decisions should be deferred to non-executive directors, who should also constitute an audit and remuneration committee
- more information should be given to shareholders.

Later reports, such as the one by a committee chaired by Sir Ronnie Hampel of ICI in 1998, reinforced the Cadbury recommendations and added further detail concerning company–auditor links and responsibilities, and remuneration packages for company directors.

The recommendations are supported by the Confederation of British Industry, the Stock Exchange and the Institutional Shareholders Committee, but they remain largely voluntary.

Corporate governance varies between countries, and it could impact increasingly on corporate strategies as companies become more global, and seek to acquire businesses, or set up joint ventures, more widely. Germany, for example, employs a two-tier board structure to introduce checks and balances and ensure that employees, as well as shareholders, are properly represented. This became an issue in 2000 when Vodafone successfully acquired Airtouch. In France and Italy executives wield significant power and are rarely challenged by shareholders. In Japan, shareholders again tend to be passive, and the board, essentially an extension of management, has no independent powers.

**The topic for debate: Should organizations separate the roles of chairman and chief executive, or combine them?**

If they are separated the chairman could be either executive (full-time) or non-executive (part-time). Typically, a non-executive chairman would act as a sounding board for the chief executive, manage board meetings and liaise with institutional shareholders. The chief executive would be in charge of both strategy and control. An executive chairman would accept responsibility for corporate strategy, with the chief executive controlling the business.

The majority of institutional shareholders in the UK favour a split in the roles for public companies, but not all large companies agree.

*The case for the combined role*
- Allows for clear, strong and accountable leadership.
- Part-time, non-executive, chairmen are unsuitable for large, complex, multinational businesses – the job is too demanding.
- A non-executive deputy chairman is an ideal compromise.
- The strength of the board as a whole, in terms of both executive and non-executive directors, is a more critical issue.

- The executive workload can be spread among all of the executive directors, allowing for greater cohesion.

However, it is important to ensure that the strategic leader does not become lonely and isolated.

*The case for splitting the roles*
- More likely to guarantee proper checks and balances.
- An ideal way of tightening control over strategic decision making without placing it in the hands of one person – large boards are not always going to agree.
- Allows for complementary skills, with each role requiring different expertise.
- Succession issues are likely to be less complicated.

However, it is critical that the two people involved generally agree with each other and can work together.

Clearly, no single answer is appropriate for all companies. Strategic demands vary and individual abilities differ. The challenge is to establish both clear leadership and objectivity.

Partial source: Morrison, R (1991) Two views on a split personality, *Financial Times*, 4 October.

## Styles of chairman

Corporate head-hunters CCG (1998) have identified four main styles, which, in descending order of preference for main board members in the UK, are as follows.

- The facilitator – who is relatively hands-off, enjoys a warm relationship with senior executives, and in particular with the chief executive and who adopts a trusting and supportive style of control.

- The thinker – who works through the chief executive but is someone who clearly understands the business and its markets and has strong opinions. He or she will make recommendations on key strategic issues. Where there is a good working relationship between this type of chairman and the chief executive they can be a formidable partnership.
- The driver – who is another forceful personality. He or she is unlikely to be a visionary himself, but instead is very focused on actions and

results. He sees himself very much as 'number one' and sees the chief executive as a subordinate rather than an equal partner. Inevitably, he is unpopular with chief executives!

- The integrator – whose talent lies in winning hearts and minds. He or she will generally be very strong on the 'big picture', intellectually brilliant and an excellent communicator. Moreover, he will be immersed in the business, but adopting an open, trusting, empowering style. Ideally, he will focus on strategy and free up the chief executive (who ideally will have complementary qualities) to manage operations. The integrator is the preferred style with non-executive directors.

All of the styles can work successfully. The issue lies with the company and its requirements and the comparable qualities of the chief executive who is in post.

## The contribution of non-executive directors

In thinking about the future direction of the organization, strategic leaders can, and will, seek advice and ideas from a variety of people, including fellow managers, outside contacts and non-executive directors.

Historically, there has been some tendency to regard non-executive directors as people who contribute little more than their actual presence at Board meetings. However, this may represent a wasted opportunity. It can prove useful, for example, to appoint an external director who understands the mood and mentality of the City, in addition to having contacts who might help with financing arrangements.

Smaller companies, who may not employ experts in every functional area, can obtain their expertise from non-executives. New businesses, run by young managers, can obtain experience by appointing older or even retired businessmen who understand their products, services and markets. Most companies, in fact, could benefit from fresh insights from people whose perspective is different from that of the executive directors and managers. However, it will be important for the strategic leader to make use of their expertise by keeping them informed and discussing matters with them, rather than simply inviting them along to board meetings.

Ideally, there will be only limited interference from non-executives when things are progressing well, but they will be there when they are needed. A final essential contribution that they can make is to stand aside and appraise the performance of the strategic leader and the other executive directors more objectively than they can do it themselves.

Finally, it is important to emphasize that while non-executive directors provide checks and balances on senior management teams, the performance of the non-executives should also be appraised.

## Summary

The *strategic leader* of an organization affects both strategy creation and strategy implementation. He or she is responsible for establishing the basic direction of the organization, the communications system and the structure. These influence the nature and style of decision making within the firm. In addition, decision making and change is affected by the personal ambitions of the strategic leader, his or her personal qualities such as entrepreneurialism and willingness to take risks, the style of management adopted and the management systems used. Power – how it has been obtained and how it is used – will also affect the style and approach of the strategic leader.

Strategic leaders come in 'all shapes and sizes'. Some are personally visionary, but this is not a prerequisite for effective leadership. It is, however, incumbent on the strategic leader to ensure that the organization has a vision and clear direction and that resources are committed towards its achievement.

Strategic leaders must perform four key tasks or, at least, ensure that they are performed by someone. They must ensure that the organization thinks strategically, that people are engaged and committed and that as a result there is positive action, and that the organization has an appropriate public face and visibility.

The leader can contribute by starting a new business or venture, by turning around a company in trouble, by transforming an already successful company or even by splitting up a company to exploit the true value of its subsidiary parts.

Six different *leadership styles* were identified, often related to past experiences. The leader's natural or preferred style will have a major impact upon the culture of the organization. The six are: analytical, aspirational, public relations, financial engineering, operational, and people-based.

Visionary leaders typically provide a strategic vision and rely less on formal planning systems. They are persuasive and charismatic and operate through the culture.

*Entrepreneurs* are similar in many respects, but they are different. Entrepreneurs build value around opportunities. Internal entrepreneurs (intrapreneurs) will be provided with opportuni-ty and encouragement in some organizations where they will drive emergent strategic change.

Clearly, some strong leaders are instrumental in the success and prosperity of organizations. On other occasions they are perceived to fail. In reality, the 'shelf-life' of many large company chief executives is relatively short. Where they are seen to fail it is often the result of poor implementation, which implies that leaders are more likely to know what they would like to achieve than how to do it. This has a further implication: it suggests that it is easy to think that success lies in a good idea, in a strategic position; but ideas and positions can be copied. Sustained competitive advantage lies in the ways in which things are done. Processes and behaviours are harder to replicate.

*Succession* is a crucial issue, particularly succession for someone who has been especially successful or charismatic. It would not be unusual for a newcomer to want to make changes, possibly for no other reason than to stamp his or her personality and preferences on the organization.

*Corporate governance* is another critical issue. Chief executives must be held accountable and a strong, possibly non-executive, chairman can be extremely valuable here. It is important to ensure that both strategic and operational issues are dealt with synergistically and sometimes two people at the head of the organization can make a powerful and balanced team.

# References

Bennis, W, Interview recorded in Crainer, S (1988) Doing the right thing, *The Director*, October.

Blanchard, K and Waghorn, T. (1997) *Mission Possible*, McGraw Hill.

Bolton, WK and Thompson, JL (2000) *Entrepreneurs: Talent, Temperament, Technique*, Butterworth-Heinemann.

Buckingham, M and Coffman, C (1999) *First, Break all the Rules*, Simon and Schuster.

CCG (1998) Research report summarized in Summers, D, Four styles of chairman, *Financial Times*, 24 September.

Charan, R and Colvin, G (1999) Why CEOs fail, *Fortune*, 21 June.

Derr, CB (1982) Living on adrenaline – the adventurer entrepreneur, *Human Resource Management*, Summer.

Ettinger, JC (1983) Some Belgian evidence on entrepreneurial personality, *European Small Business Journal*, 1(2).

Hamel, G (1997) Address to the Strategic Planning Society Conference, London, November.

Hamel, G (1999) Bringing Silicon Valley inside, *Harvard Business Review*, September–October.

Hamel, G and Prahalad, CK (1994) *Competing for the Future*, Harvard Business School Press.

Kets de Vries, MFR (1994) CEOs also have the blues, *European Journal of Management*, September.

Kets de Vries, M (1996) Leaders who make a difference, *European Management Journal*, 14, 5, October.

Kirzner, IM (1973) *Competition and Entrepreneurship*, Cambridge University Press.

Lessem, R (1986) *Enterprising Development*, Gower.

Lessem, R (1998) *Managing Development Through Cultural Diversity*, Routledge.

Maccoby, M (2000) Narcissistic leaders, *Harvard Business Review*, January–February.

McClelland, D and Winter, D (1971) *Motivating Economic Achievement*, Free Press.

Mintzberg, H (1973) Strategy making in three modes, *California Management Review*, 16(2), Winter.

Mintzberg, H, Ahlstrand, B and Lampel, J (1998) *Strategy Safari*, Prentice-Hall.

Richardson, B (1994) Towards a profile of the visionary leader, *Small Business Enterprise and Development*, 1, 1, Spring.

Richardson, B, Nwanko, S and Richardson, S (1994) Understanding the causes of business failure crises, *Management Decision*, 32, 4.

Schumpeter, J (1949) *The Theory of Economic Development*, Harvard University Press; original German edition, 1911

Slatter, S (1984) *Corporate Recovery: Successful Turnaround Strategies and their Implementation*, Penguin.

Stevenson, HH and Gumpert, DE (1985) The heart of entrepreneurship, *Harvard Business Review*, March–April.

Test your knowledge of this chapter with our online quiz at: http://www.thomsonlearning.co.uk

Explore Strategic Leadership and Entrepreneurship further at:
*Management Decision*   http://www.mcb.co.uk/md.htm

## Questions and Research Assignments

TEXT RELATED

1. Using the Volvo case (Minicase 12.5) as a background, discuss why effective leadership involves both strategy creation and strategy implementation. From your experience and reading, which other well-known strategic leaders do you believe are strong on
   (a) creation
   (b) implementation
   (c) both?

2. Minicase 12.3 (David Bruce).
   (a) Do you think David Bruce's approach to growth and change was appropriate for the business he first began? Do you see it as opportunistic or incremental or planned?
   (b) Why do you think Bruce's brewery ventures have been successful?
   (c) Do you think David Bruce's approach of starting off a venture and then leaving to start something else confirms that he is a habitual entrepreneur?

3. Where do the entrepreneur and the visionary leader overlap and where are they different?

4. Apply Figure 12.6 (alternative styles of leadership) to any strategic leader whom you are in a position to evaluate.

## Internet and Library Projects

1. What has happened to David Bruce recently?

2. Select at least one well-established large corporation which is quoted on the Stock Exchange, together with one of the companies privatized during the 1980s.
   (a) Examine the composition of the Board of Directors in terms of executive and non-executive members.
   (b) Determine whether the roles of chairman and chief executive are split or combined.
   (c) What conclusions might you draw concerning strategic leadership and corporate governance in these organizations?

*Stock Exchange UK*   http://www.londonstockexchange.com

3. The following facts relate to Sir Alan Sugar, founder of Amstrad, and one of Britain's richest businessmen.
   1947   Born Hackney, East London
   1963   Left school
   1966   Began selling car aerials from a van
   1968   Founded Amstrad to sell plastic covers for record players. Involvement in televisions, video receivers and CB radio led to
   1985   Launch of a low-cost word-processor and compact disc player

1986   Acquisition of the intellectual property rights of Sinclair computers from Clive Sinclair and launch of an IBM-compatible microcomputer

1988   Entered satellite dish market

1991   Entered laptop computer market.

Research the growth and success of Amstrad in the consumer electronics and microcomputers markets and assess what has happened to Alan Sugar in the past 10 years.

What can you conclude about his style of leadership? Is he an entrepreneur?

*Amstrad*   http://www.amstrad.com

4. How has the General Electric succession issue been resolved?

*General Electric*   http://www.ge.com

# 13

# Emergent Strategy and Intrapreneurship: The Contribution of People and Information

*Emergent strategy takes two forms: incremental changes as intended strategies are implemented, and new strategies as the organization adapts to opportunities and threats in a dynamic environment. The idea is that the organization stays flexible in order that it might get ahead and stay ahead of its rivals, and to accomplish this it needs to be innovative and intrapreneurial. Emergent strategy is clearly dependent upon decision-making processes in the organization: who makes the decisions, how, their quality, and their outcomes. In turn, this comes down to people and information.*

*Companies comprise physical, technical and human resources, and it is these resources that create new value. Arguably, people are the most precious resource. There is evidence that 'ordinary people can be inspired to produce extraordinary results' in particular circumstances. Where this happens in successful organizations, power has been handed over to people by the strategic leader, and they have been offered the appropriate support and encouragement. We can see where this has happened, but that does not mean that it is easily replicated by other organizations, and for this reason it is often the key to sustained competitive advantage. Communications, information and organizational knowledge provide the lubrication for the processes.*

*Simply, we cannot understand emergent strategy in an organization if we do not examine the relevant people and information strategies and achievements. Together with an examination of intrapreneurship and innovation, these themes provide the content of this chapter, which concludes with a short assessment of the impact of the Internet.*

# Minicase 13.1  Richer Sounds

Electrical goods retailers are not new. The dominant names in the UK are Comet and Curry's, but Richer Sounds is different, and very successful. Richer is more focused than its main rivals, specialising in hi-fi, especially separate units. According to the *Guinness Book of Records*, Richer achieves the highest sales per square foot of any retailer in the world. Sales per employee are also high. Stock is piled high to the ceilings in relatively small stores in typically low-rent locations. All the main brands can be found; the latest models feature alongside discontinued ones, these at very competitive prices. 'We just aren't that ambitious [to justify diversifying] . . . we feel that by staying with what we know best we can concentrate our effort and resources in one field and hopefully do it well'.

Julian Richer was born in 1959; his parents both worked for Marks and Spencer. He was just 19 when he opened his first shop at London Bridge: 'seventy thousand commuters passed the shop every day'. He now owns 39 stores in the UK and Eire and two more in The Netherlands. Apart from Christmas, Richer will not open on Sundays. His employees are known as colleagues and they are empowered to work 'The Richer Way'. He claims that his suggestion scheme has generated the highest number of suggestions per employee of any scheme anywhere in the world, and the best ideas are rewarded with trips on the Orient Express. The most successful employees (in terms of sales) can win free use of a holiday home; the most successful shops earn the free use of a Bentley or Jaguar for a month. Every employee is allowed £5 per month 'to go to the pub and brainstorm'. Julian Richer has advised ASDA (featured later in this chapter) on suggestion schemes, and ex-ASDA Chairman, Archie Norman, has said: 'Julian has gone to great lengths to create a system that works without him, but, to a great extent, his business is his personality'.

Richer has established a parallel consulting arm, with eight consultants who offer 'The Richer Way as a philosophy for delighting customers'. Consultancy is provided free to charities and good causes. Richer has also established a foundation to help selected good causes, and he owns a number of other small businesses. These include a retail recruitment agency, a property portfolio, and an award-winning tapas bar in Fulham. He has, however, 'one business and a number of hobbies'.

QUESTIONS: Is 'The Richer Way' a key to sustained competitive advantage? Why do you think it has been successful?

*Richer Sounds* http://www.richer-sounds.co.uk

The executives and employees who go to make up a total work force are the most important assets of the company. They always have been and always will be. The real issue is how to maximize the value from those assets and that is why all senior executives irrespective of function have an obligation to contribute to people development at every level.

*Unattributed quotation from a manufacturing company director. Taken from Coulson-Thomas and Brown (1989)*

In times of discontinuity and accelerated change, survival depends on flexibility, on our ability to learn to adapt. Organizations which learn fast will survive. Management must take the lead. We must mobilize our greatest asset, our people, invest in their training and orchestrate their talents, skills and expertise. Their commitment, dedication, quality and care will build the competitive advantage of a winning team. Only they can provide our customers with the best product and service in the industry. The management of change takes tenacity, time, talent and training.

*JFA de Soet, President, KLM Royal Dutch Airlines*

# Intrapreneurship

## Building the organization

Effective leaders possess a number of characteristics, they set direction and they inspire others. However, their strong leadership should not throttle flexibility and learning by a resistance to trusting other managers and involving them in key decisions. The most successful strategic leaders realize that they cannot do everything on their own and build a team to whom they can delegate important decisions and contributions. While some of these people will, by necessity, be specialists, professionals and technocrats, Horovitz (1997) stresses the importance of also recruiting or developing entrepreneurial managers to ensure the flow of innovation and change and prevent entropy. He argues that one of the reasons for Club Méditerranée losing momentum in the 1990s was the result of a failure to accomplish this back-filling effectively (see Minicase 5.4). Quinn (1980) also emphasizes the importance of innovation and ongoing learning by this team because not all of the issues and difficulties that will have to be faced can be foreseen.

*The aim in a global business is to get the best ideas from everywhere. [In General Electric] each team puts up its best ideas and processes – constantly. That raises the bar. Our culture is designed around making a hero out of those who translate ideas from one place to another, who get help from somebody else. They get an award, they get praised and promoted.*

(Jack Welch, Chief Executive, General Electric)

Horovitz (1997) contends that organizations should look for the problems before they even arise, by questioning what the (possibly very successful) organization is doing wrong. At times it is important to abandon products, services and strategies which have served the organization well in the past, as they are not the future. de Geus (1997) contends that businesses need to become 'living organizations' if they are to enjoy long and sustained success. This requires that the company:

- knows 'what it is about'
- understands where 'it fits in the world'
- values new ideas, new people, and fresh views and opinions
- manages its resources (especially financial resources) in a way which places it in a position to govern its own future; in other words, it is prudent and does not spend beyond a level it can earn.

These requirements are manifest in:

- clear direction and purpose (awareness of its identity)
- strategic positioning (its sensitivity to its environment)
- the management of change (its tolerance of new ideas) and
- the efficient use of its capital investment.

People, then, must been seen as key assets and managed accordingly; controls must have some element of looseness and flexibility; and constant learning must be possible.

Rosabeth Moss Kanter (1989) clearly supports this view when she argues that the whole organization holds the key to competitive advantage.

She suggests that five criteria are found in successful, entrepreneurial organizations:

- *focused* on essential core competencies and long-term values
- *flexible* – searching for new opportunities and new internal and external synergies with the belief that ever-increasing returns and results can be obtained from the same resources if they are developed properly and innovative
- *friendly* – recognizing the power of alliances in the search for new competencies
- *fast* and able to act at the right time to get ahead and stay ahead of competitors
- *fun* – creative and with a culture which features some irreverence in the search for ways to be different; people feel free to express themselves.

This argument is revisited in Chapter 22.

In her earlier work, Kanter (1983) warned about the potential for stifling innovation by:

- blocking ideas from lower down the organization, on the grounds that only senior or very experienced managers are in a position to spot new opportunities. On the contrary, she argues, younger people with fresh minds are in an excellent position to question and challenge the status quo
- building too many levels in the hierarchy so that decision making is slowed almost to a point of non-existence
- withholding praise from people who do offer good, innovative ideas, and instilling a culture of insecurity so that people feel too terrified even to question authority, policies or procedures
- being unwilling to innovate until someone else has tried out the idea – a fear of leading change.

Minicase 13.1, Richer Sounds, illustrates an organization that has benefited substantially from involving employees widely in new strategy creation.

While robust questioning and assumption-testing of new ideas is crucial, it is particularly important to remember that many people fear change, partly because of uncertainty about its impact on them personally. As a result, some people will seek to resist valuable change initiatives, and may even attempt to mount an active and orchestrated opposition. They are, in fact, enterprising and entrepreneurial, but they channel their energy in an unhelpful way. Their tactics may be aimed at preventing an idea ever taking off; equally, they may wait until it has taken root and is gaining some support and momentum. Managing change effectively, therefore, requires continuous effort and sometimes patience, reinforcing the significant contribution made by the project champion.

## The process of intrapreneurship

Bridge *et al.* (1998) highlight the importance of recruiting, spotting and using people with entrepreneurial talent who are motivated to use their abilities and initiative and do something on their own, but who may not want to start their own business. These internal entrepreneurs have been called *intrapreneurs* by Pinchot (1985). Intrapreneurship, then, is the term given to the establishment and fostering of entrepreneurial activity in large organizations which results in incremental improvements to existing products and services and occasionally to brand-new products.

Figure 13.1 shows that both entrepreneurship (creating outcomes which imply a real difference) and intrapreneurship (less ambitious changes which are more likely to be based around improvements than major changes of direction) are broadly similar. They both begin when someone has a personal vision from which an idea and a related opportunity emerge. The opportunity must then be engaged and resources acquired as prerequisites to action and implementation. Intrapreneurship

*Figure 13.1* Intrapreneurship and entrepreneurship.

happens as individual managers promote and sell their ideas inside the organization and build a team of supporters. They drive change.

This was illustrated in Chapter 8 (p. 282) with the example of 3M and Post-It Notes, but realistically this is an extreme case. The innovation is more likely to be a minor, but significant improvement to a product or service or process: anything that makes a valuable difference. Minicase 13.2 illustrates how Shell has attempted to foster intrapreneurship with a special programme.

Intrapreneurs, typically, are strategically aware, ideas-driven, creative, flexible, innovative, good networkers, individualistic but also able to work well in a team, persistent and courageous. If frustrated by a lack of freedom they will underachieve or possibly leave. But they are volunteers; intrapreneurship is not right for everyone.

# Minicase 13.2  Shell's GameChanger

Royal Dutch Shell, with revenues of around £85 billion and over 100,000 employees worldwide, is an industrial giant in an established industry: petroleum. Historically, access to capital has been carefully controlled and radical ideas from internal entrepreneurs have been rare. Managers switch between divisions and countries for experience and promotion, but they are generally disciplined and loyal to corporate policies and procedures. In 1996, Tim Warren, Director of Research and Technical Services in Exploration and Production (Shell's largest division), was determined to change this, and to free up ideas, talent and resources. He was concerned that competition was intense in the dynamic and turbulent oil industry and Shell was 'not inventing radically new businesses'. Moreover, he firmly believed that Shell possessed the talent to drive a different behaviour.

In November 1996 he secured the resources to launch *GameChanger* and £12.5 million was set aside to fund radically new ideas submitted by employees. A group of key people would evaluate the ideas put forward by their peers. Consultants were brought in to run a series of creativity laboratories for volunteers; 72 turned up to the first one.

The focus was on:

- identifying and challenging industry conventions
- identifying emerging discontinuities
- leveraging and exploiting existing competencies to create new competitive opportunities.

The ideas began to flow from the laboratories and their interactive sessions. Some of the money set aside was used to ensure that the ideas which passed the first selection and screening were put into action. The creativity laboratory was supplemented by further work on project management.

As the programme has developed, Shell's intranet has been used increasingly to move ideas around the organization. Initial funding has averaged some £60,000 per project selected, but it has been as high as £350,000. Employees are encouraged to stay involved. Once the concept is proven, further funding can be arranged. A number of important new Shell initiatives have emerged from *GameChanger*.

QUESTIONS: Why do you think many large organizations ignore the potential of initiatives such as this?

What are the dangers in their approach?

Source: Hamel, G (1999) Bringing Silicon Valley inside, *Harvard Business Review*, September–October.

*Shell (Royal Dutch Shell)*  http://www.countonshell.com

According to Pinchot (1985), the key lies in engaging people's efforts and energy for championing, capturing and exploiting new ideas and strategic changes. This must stretch beyond the most senior managers in the organization, who do not have a monopoly on good ideas. On the contrary, the potentially most valuable and lucrative ideas are likely to come from those people who are closest to the latest developments in technology or to customers. Suggestion schemes are linked in, but on their own do not constitute intrapreneurship. The ideas need to be taken forward, and they can only be developed if the potential intrapreneurs are able to obtain the necessary internal resources and, moreover, they are willing to do something. This in turn requires encouragement and appropriate rewards for success. People must feel involved in the process and comfortable that they are being supported. Intrapreneurship cannot work where people feel 'frozen out' or 'dumped on'. Churchill (1997) summarizes the philosophy as skills following opportunities. People in entrepreneurial businesses see the opportunities and set about acquiring the necessary resources. The whole process of change then becomes gradual and evolutionary. The momentum for change and improvement is never lost and the organization is less likely to be exposed and weakened by its competitors, resulting in it having to cross a 'bridge too far'.

Maitland (1999) has described how Bass developed new pub brands. In the early 1990s Bass' traditional customers (older people, and more working than middle class) were deserting pubs; young people became the new target. '[Bass] needed a radical "break-out" strategy of new product development and concept innovation'. Bass spotted the new It's A Scream format, conceived by entrepreneur David Lee and popular with students. Lee was a builder in Farnham who had been given a pub in lieu of an unpaid debt and had transformed it. Bass bought the pub and the concept and recruited Lee as a con-

sultant with a profit-share and a fixed fee for every new It's A Scream pub which opens. The All Bar One theme pubs, an up-market, well-lit, city-centre chain with large windows which attracts groups of young female drinkers, reflects a similar story. Other initiatives have been developed from ideas put forward by existing managers, who have been offered secondment to champion their project ideas. Bass recognized the importance of visible support and encouragement from the top, so this became an engineered and not a random process. Bass ensured that adequate financial resources were available and also utilized sophisticated computer mapping systems to help with location issues. The two parallel questions are: Where are the ideal places for siting a particular format? What would be the best format for a site they already own? The key variables are age, affluence and car ownership, linked to how far people are willing to travel to eat or drink out. In other words, Bass brought together ideas, talented intrapreneurs and the resources that they needed.

To summarize these points, Hurst (1995) likens entrepreneurial strategic leaders to gardeners. They prune. They clear out. They plant, by recruiting other entrepreneurial managers. They feed, by encouraging and rewarding managers for being creative and innovative. Simply, they nurture and manage the organization as they would a garden. Paradoxically, many good ideas begin in the same way that weeds emerge in a garden, i.e. randomly. They then need spotting and looking after – the equivalent of transfer to a hothouse?

## The intrapreneurial organization

Fradette and Michaud (1998) describe four main elements to an organization which succeeds with intrapreneurship. First, the strategic and structural environment is 'right'. The purpose and direction implies a realistic vision and it is widely understood and shared. Formal systems and controls do not stifle innovation and people are free to make limited changes. Inhibitive internal 'chimneys' are pulled down so that people can collaborate and share ideas readily. Secondly, an appropriate workforce has been built. Enterprising people have been recruited. They have been trained in key skills and there is an appropriate reward system. The organization's main heroes are the entrepreneurial ones. Thirdly, the workforce is backed by the necessary support systems. Teamworking is commonplace, people collaborate and network naturally, information is shared and learning is fostered. After all, several people in the organization may be thinking along the same lines at the same time concerning future possibilities. Fourthly, successes are visibly rewarded and mistakes are not sanctioned so harshly that people are dissuaded from further initiatives. These points are discussed further later in this chapter.

An intrapreneurial organization will often feature a relatively flat structure with few layers in the hierarchy; too many layers tend to slow decision making down. The culture and atmosphere will be one of collaboration and trust. The style of management will be more coaching than instructional, and mentoring will be in evidence. Ideally it will be an exciting place to work. The entrepreneur's enthusiasm will have spread to others. In other words, it will be decentralized.

The centralization–decentralization issue is debated in Chapter 21, but a brief summary of key issues is relevant here. Centralization of decision-making power with the strategic leadership allows for more straightforward controls: intended information flows are clear and it is not essential that information is shared widely through the organization. However, decision making can be relatively slow and potentially valuable information that individual managers have may well not be available. Intrapreneurship and individual innovation are restrained. While decentralization can overcome these

drawbacks, it demands a different form of control system, based on information *sharing* rather than instructions, if the organization is to stay cohesive and synergistic. To many strategic leaders decentralization will appear to imply a greater risk because centralization seems easier to operate.

Terazano (1999) also reminds us that effective intrapreneurship is not that easily achieved, and that many organizations set off down the road but fail to reap the anticipated rewards. Balancing control (to ensure that current activities and strategies are implemented efficiently) with flexibility (to foster and embrace changes to the same strategies) can imply different cultures, which are difficult to achieve without tension and conflict. Another difficulty frequently lies with finding the appropriate reward and remuneration systems to ensure fairness. It is a brave organization which only awards bonuses to the visibly entrepreneurial people. Managers in established companies often find it difficult to handle setbacks and disappointments when initiatives fail. But there always has to be the risk of failure, albeit temporary, when experimenting with new and unproven ideas. While intrapreneurs often have the security of large company employment, such that the penalty for failure is to some extent reduced, the rewards for real success are unlikely to equal those of the true entrepreneur. Nevertheless, 'increased competition in global markets and the pressure for innovation is forcing Britain's large companies to look for methods to stimulate ideas for new products'.

## Innovation

Innovation takes place when an organization makes a technical change, e.g. produces a product or service that is new to it, or uses a method or input that is new and original. If a direct competitor has already introduced the product or method then it is imitation, not innovation. However, introducing a practice from a different country or industry rather than a direct competitor would constitute innovation.

Innovation implies change and the introduction of something new. Creating the idea, or inventing something, is not innovation but a part of the total process. While at one level it can relate to new or novel products, it may also be related to production processes, approaches to marketing a product or service, or the way in which jobs are carried out within the organization. The aim is to add value for the consumer or customer by reducing costs or differentiating the product or total service in some sustainable way. In other words, innovation relates to the creation of competitive advantage; and, to summarize, there are four main forms of innovation:

- new products, which are either radically new or which extend the product lifecycle
- process innovation leading to reduced production costs, and affected partially by the learning and experience effect
- innovations within the umbrella of marketing, which increase differentiation
- organizational changes, which reduce costs or improve total quality.

Where the innovation reflects continuous improvement, product or service *enhancement*, and only minor changes in established patterns of consumer behaviour, the likelihood of success is greater than for those changes that demand new patterns of usage and consumption. Examples of the latter include personal computers and compact disc players. Discontinuous innovations such as these are more risky for manufacturers, but if they are successful the financial payoffs can be huge. By contrast, continuous improvements – which, realistically, are essential in a dynamic, competitive environment – have much lower revenue potential.

Innovation can come about in a variety of ways:

- Ideas can come out research and development departments, where people are employed to come up with new ideas or inventions. Some would argue that there is a risk that departments such as this are not in direct touch with customers; however, while customers may sense that a product or service has drawbacks, they may have no idea how it might be improved. This requires a technical expert.
- People from various parts of an organization working on special projects.
- Employees being given freedom and encouragement to work on ideas of their own, e.g. the 3M approach mentioned earlier.
- Everyday events as people interact and discuss problems and issues.

There is a mix of routine, structured events and unstructured activities.

Changes in the service provided to customers and the development of new products and services imply changes in operating systems and in the work of employees, and some of the proposed changes may well be the result of ideas generated internally. However, many of the ideas for innovations come from outside the organization, from changes in the environment. This emphasizes the crucial importance of linking together marketing and operations and harnessing the contribution of people. For example, Ford in the USA realized some years ago that a number of its engineers had a tendency to 'over-engineer' solutions to relatively simple problems. As a result, its costs were higher than those of its rivals, particularly Japanese and Korean companies, and its new product development times were considerably longer. Instead, the company needed 'creative engineers' with a fresh perspective and greater realization of customer expectations.

## Creativity, innovation and entrepreneurship

'There is a great myth about innovation – that it is all about an idea. But the idea is almost incidental – innovation is about making it work as a business'. There is a clear link between entrepreneurship and innovation; indeed, Drucker (1985) argues that innovation is the tool of entrepreneurs. In addition, both innovation and entrepreneurship demand creativity. The link between these terms is therefore in need of clarification.

*Creativity* implies conceptualizing, visualizing or bringing into being something that does not yet exist. It is about curiosity and observation. Creativity often seems to come 'out of the blue' triggered by a problem to be solved or an idea to be expressed. Its roots and origins are mysterious and unknown but its existence cannot be denied.

Entrepreneurs (and intrapreneurs) are familiar with ideas that suddenly come to mind and are not too concerned with their origins. This is the starting point of the entrepreneurial process. Creativity is seen as a talent, an innate ability, although we recognize that it can be developed and that there are techniques that promote creativity and problem solving. Creativity is also a function of how people feel. Some are more creative under pressure while others need complete relaxation. Some use divergent thinking in their creativity while others prefer convergent thinking.

One thing that seems common to all forms of creativity is joy. Einstein comments that the idea that 'the gravitational field has only a relative existence was the happiest thought of my life' (Pais, 1982). His creative genius had come up with the idea of relativity and it made him happy. There is an intense personal satisfaction in having come up with something new and novel.

This is one reason why many entrepreneurial people see their activities and contributions as fun. There is the joy of creativity all around them. For the entrepreneur creativity is both the starting point and the reason for continued success. It is the secret formula by which he or she overcomes obstacles and outsmarts the competition.

Arguably every one of us has the ability to be creative, but do we all use and exploit this ability? Many of us simply do not act creatively much of the time. Possibly we are not motivated and encouraged; maybe we do not believe in ourselves and the contribution and difference that we could make. There is certainly a skills and technique element to creativity; in a business context, for example, we can be taught creative thinking and behaviour in the context of decision making, but this is clearly only part of the explanation.

*Innovation* builds on creativity when something new, tangible and value-creating is developed from the ideas. Innovation is about seeing the creative new idea through to completion, to final application, but, of course, this will not necessarily be a business. It is the *entrepreneur* who builds a business around the idea and the innovation. Both can be difficult roads and require courage and perseverance as well as creativity and imagination. These are attributes that the entrepreneur brings and his or her role in innovation is crucial.

There are three basic approaches with innovation, which are not mutually exclusive. First, it is possible to have a problem and to be seeking a solution, or at least a resolution. Edwin Land invented the Polaroid camera because his young daughter could not understand why she had to wait for the pictures to be printed when he took her photograph. Secondly, we might have an idea – in effect a solution – and be searching for a problem to which it can be applied. 3M's Post-It Notes happened when a 3M employee created a glue with only loose sticking properties, and a colleague applied it to a need he had for marking pages in a manuscript (see p. 286). Thirdly, we might identify a need and design something which fits. James Dyson's innovatory dual cyclone cleaner came about because of his frustration with his existing machine, which was proving inadequate for cleaning up the dirt and dust generated when he converted an old property.

Generating opportunities from ideas requires us to attribute meaning to the ideas. Ideas form in our minds and at this stage they mean something to us, personally. Typically, they become a real opportunity when we expose the ideas and share them with other people, who may well have different perceptions, attribute different meanings and see something that we miss initially. This process of exploration is fundamental for determining where the opportunities for building new values are. In other words, innovation comes from the way in which we use our ideas. Crucially, the person with the initial idea may not be the one who realizes where the real opportunity lies. An inventor is not always an opportunity spotter, and often not a natural project champion who masterminds the implementation. Picasso claimed that 'great people steal ideas and create opportunities where others cannot see the potential'.

Minicase 13.3 shows how an inventor with a great idea needed a business partner to exploit the idea and build the value inherent in his idea.

The *Sony Walkman* provides an excellent illustration of these points. The idea came to Sony co-founder Akio Morita when he was questioning why he was finding it difficult to listen to music when he was in public places or walking round a golf course. The idea became an innovative new product, and a valuable opportunity, when Morita shared his idea with other colleagues in Sony, and existing technologies and competencies were used to develop the compact personal radio with adequate playing time from its batteries and individual head-phones. The project was championed, resourced and implemented. The original radio has systematically been joined by personal cassette and CD players. It was simply a great idea which rejuvenated Sony at the time it was conceived, and it has brought value and affected the lives of millions of people around the world.

## Disruptive technology

Christensen (1998) uses the term 'disruptive technology' to explain partially why it is often outsiders that succeed in changing the rules of competition in an industry. His arguments are illustrated in the case of James Dyson (Minicase 9.1).

When a new idea is very much at the embryo stage, and not particularly thought through, the conclusion could be that there 'might be something in it' but it is by no means certain. Whether the idea starts with their own people, or is offered to them by an outside inventor, large, established organizations may at this stage disregard the idea because it has no clear and outstanding advantages. A smaller, entrepreneurial company, in contrast, as long as it can somehow find the necessary resources, is much more likely to accept the risk associated with the idea and pursue it. Eventually the idea might well turn out to have real value – it is truly different and may offer a cost advantage as well. By the time the large company is in a position to respond it could well have lost market share.

Why does this happen? Paradoxically, according to Christensen, because large companies become very customer focused and avoid disruptive ideas or technologies that might put existing relationships and loyalties at risk. Of course, large companies can set up and resource smaller subsidiaries, and charge them with developing this form of disruption.

# Minicase 13.3 The Baygen Radio

The BayGen Radio was invented by English inventor Trevor Baylis in the early 1990s. Unlike other portable radios, the BayGen does not use batteries; it is powered by clockwork. Its main target market is the developing world, where the cost of batteries is often prohibitively expensive.

Baylis developed the idea after watching a television documentary on the spread of AIDS in Africa, where it was stated that important information was not being made available to people because they could not afford radios. Baylis felt there must be enough power in a spring to drive a small generator, and experimented until he had one which worked. He tried without success to interest the business community in his prototype.

His prototype radio was, however, featured on the BBC's *Tomorrow's World* programme, where it was seen by Christopher Staines, who at the time was a director of mergers and acquisitions with a leading accountancy firm. Staines was motivated to work through the night on a business plan proposal which he faxed to Baylis. Within 48 hours Staines had the worldwide development rights. Baylis realized that he needed external support to exploit the potential of his invention. The deal was that Baylis would retain ownership of the technology and the trademarks but grant Staines a licence in perpetuity. Staines and a partner then set up the BayGen Power Manufacturing Company to build and distribute the radios.

Staines raised £143,000 from the Overseas Development Agency and took the idea to South Africa, where he had family connections. He succeeded in raising start-up capital of £600,000, and the publicity generated brought endorsement from President Nelson Mandela. A new factory with a capacity to build 20,000 radios a month was ready in September 1995. The generator has been improved and refined to yield 40 minutes of listening from 20 seconds' winding. The secret lies in a special spring which releases energy at a constant rate; by contrast, the spring used for a toy train releases energy with a decreasing flow. Many of the employees are disabled, and early customers targeted by BayGen included the Red Cross and UNICEF.

The market failed to take off as quickly as Staines anticipated and he experienced early cash-flow problems. He was able to secure additional funding; Gordon and Anita Roddick (The Body Shop) made personal investments, for example.

The first radios were eventually sold to the aid agencies at a wholesale price of $30 (£19). The agencies are free to subsidize them and sell on at lower prices. The objective is to market the radio at a price lower than the cost of a normal radio and a one-year supply of batteries. Staines had intended to minimize his involvement in distribution, but he back-tracked on this idea and began to sell direct to the market.

In January 1996 the radio was also available in the UK by mail order at a price of £65. In 1997 General Electric of the US (GE) bought one-third of the business for the equivalent of £8 million. GE then introduced BayGen to a mail-order catalogue company in the USA in which it also owns a stake. The generator always had the potential to be adapted for use in other products and Baylis has since designed an improved radio and a torch. Baylis remains an active but independent inventor, and he is now a wealthy man.

QUESTIONS: Can you think of other inventions which have been similarly successful with the help of the appropriate business person?

Do you think that Britain should be doing more to help inventors to become to successful innovators?

*BayGen*  http://www.winduppower.com

## Human Resource Strategies

### The 'people contribution'

Successful organizations meet the needs and expectations of their customers more effectively than their competitors; at the same time, they generate acceptable financial returns. Achieving these outcomes requires competent and committed people. People, then, are critically important strategic resources. Successful companies will be able to attract, motivate, develop, reward and keep skilled and competent managers and other employees. They will be able to create and implement strategic changes in a supportive culture. People need to be used and stretched to get the best out of them but, correspondingly, they need to be looked after and rewarded. However, even successful companies have lean periods, and when these occur, they will again be able to retain their most important people. There is no 'one best way' of achieving this.

Everything that an organization does, in the end, depends on people. Although technology and information technology (IT) can make a major strategic impact, it is people who exploit their potential. Managers and employees are needed to implement strategies and to this end they must understand and share the values of the organization. They must be committed to

the organization and they must work together well. At the same time, where an organization is decentralized and operating in a turbulent environment, the strategic leader will rely on people to spot opportunities and threats, to adapt and create new strategies.

Consequently, it is people who ultimately determine whether or not competitive advantage is created and sustained. Adding new values with innovation, they can be an opportunity and a source of competitive advantage; equally, unenthusiastic, uncommitted, untrained employees can act as a constraint. People's capabilities are infinite and resourceful in the appropriate organizational climate. The basic test of their value concerns how much they – and their contribution – would be missed if they left or, possibly worse, left and joined a competitor. They could take customers with them and not be easily replaced.

Achieving the highest level of outcomes that people are capable of producing will therefore depend upon the human resource practices adopted by the organization. While the issues are clear and straightforward – they involve selection, training, rewards and work organization – there is no single 'best approach' to the challenge. A relatively formal, 'hard' approach can prove very successful in certain circumstances; other organizations will derive significant benefits from a 'softer', more empowered style. One issue here is whether the business is being driven by a small number of identifiable, key decision makers or by the employees collectively.

Minicase 13.4 tells the remarkable story of Ricardo Semler, who took over the family engineering business in Brazil and transformed its fortunes by releasing the abilities and energies of its people.

To bring out the best in people, they have to be managed well, and this requires leadership. A useful metaphor is that of an orchestra. Every member (manager/employee) is a specialist, with some making a unique contribution which, on occasions, can take the form of a solo performance. Nevertheless, all the contributions must be synthesized to create harmony (synergy), which is the role of the conductor (strategic leader). A single musician (weak link) can destroy a performance; a chain is only as strong as its weakest link.

A successful organization, therefore, needs people with appropriate skills and competencies who can work together effectively. People must be:

• committed (commitment can be improved)
• competent (competencies can be developed, and can bring improved product quality and productivity)
• cost-effective (ideally costs should be low and performance high, although this does not imply low rewards for success)
• in sympathy with the aims of the organization (are the values and expectations of all parties in agreement?)

Where people grow, profits grow.
*Dr Alex Krauer, when Chairman and Managing Director, Ciba-Geigy*

## Involving and empowering people

There are two recognized approaches to human resource management: the 'hard' approach and the 'soft' approach. The key tension or dilemma that is being addressed is the balance between centralization for control and decentralization for greater empowerment. The two approaches imply contrasting styles, but they can both be appropriate in certain circumstances. Moreover, companies can be hard on certain aspects and soft on others. In addition, the style may alter with the strategic demands placed on an organization. When times are difficult and a company must rationalize and downsize, a hard approach may prove to be appropriate for driving through the changes quickly. However, a softer, more empowered style may be required to rejuvenate the company and bring new sources of competitive advantage.

Hard human resource management assumes that:

• people are viewed as a resource and, like all resources, companies gain competitive advantage by using them efficiently and effectively
• the deployment and development of employees – who are essentially there to implement corporate and competitive strategies – is delegated to line managers who are responsible for groups of people
• scientific management principles and systems can be useful but should be used cautiously.

Soft human resource management assumes that:

• workers are most productive if they are committed to the company, informed about its mission, strategies and current levels of success, and
• involved in teams which collectively decide how things are to be done
• employees have to be trusted to take the right decisions rather than controlled at every stage by managers above them.

Soft human resource management argues that

# Minicase 13.4  Ricardo Semler and Semco

Ricardo Semler was just 21 years old when he took over as chief executive of his family's business, Semco. This Brazilian company manufactures pumps, food mixers, meat-slicing equipment and dishwashers. Brazil is a country characterized by high inflation and a massive relative wealth gap between the rich and the poor. His father believed that if he handed over the reins when Ricardo was still young, 'he could make his mistakes while he was still around to fix them!' His father had run the business along traditional and autocratic lines; Ricardo was to change everything, and the company has thrived and prospered.

Although he has an MBA from Harvard, Ricardo Semler's stated business philosophy is: 'follow your intuition'. He inherited a company where 'people did not want to come to work and managers watched everything and everybody constantly, trusting nobody', and transformed it into one which is 'ultimately democratic' and based on 'freedom, respect, trust and commitment'. Things did not happen instantaneously; many new approaches and experimental methods were tried and abandoned. However, in a ten-year period from the mid-1980s Semco achieved 900% growth.

There is no reception area, no secretaries and no offices. Managers walk around constantly to provide help and assistance when it is requested; the workers organize their own flexible working time arrangements. Employees work in small clusters, and they can also rearrange their working space and environment as they wish. Semco has come to believe that clusters of no more than ten are required if this approach is to work effectively. Twelve layers of a management and supervisory hierarchy have been reduced to three. The appointment of any manager has to be approved by the workforce, and managers are subjected to regular assessment by their subordinates and shopfloor employees. People talk openly and 'when someone says they'll do something, they do it'. Consequently, managers also feel that they can spend time away from the plant, with customers and suppliers.

Profit sharing is by consultation and negotiation – 23% of after-tax profits is available for the workforce – and all employees are trained to ensure that they can read the company accounts. There is no longer a formal chief executive post for Ricardo, who is now President. Instead, there is an informal board of six associates (the most senior managers) who elect a nominal chief executive for a six-month period. Ricardo sometimes attends their meetings as an adviser.

Ricardo has recently taken his ideas further, encouraging employees to consider starting up satellite supply companies and subcontracting for Semco. Those who have opted for this entrepreneurial route have been allowed to take Semco machines with them, leasing them on favourable terms. One advantage for Semco is the fact that it is no longer responsible for the maintenance and safety of the equipment. In addition, there is an opportunity for the machinery to be used more effectively as the satellite companies are free to work for other organizations; their efficiency gains can be passed through in the form of lower prices. If the venture fails, Semco takes back the equipment and the people. It is a relatively low and managed risk for all concerned.

Ricardo Semler has not been a man who has hidden his achievements! He has written the story of his role at Semco with the title *Maverick*. Like Julian Richer, he helps other companies as a consultant and he has become a recognized member of the management guru circuit around the world. He has also campaigned against corruption in Brazil, and he has exposed government officials who have been demanding bribes for domestic planning permission. As a result, he has generated hostility from certain prominent people in his country.

'Successful companies will be the ones that put quality of life first. Do this and the rest – quality of product, productivity of workers, profits for all – will follow'.

QUESTION: Is Ricardo Semler really a 'maverick'?

Source: Semler, R (1993) *Maverick*, Century.

people are different from other resources (and often more costly) but they can create added value and sustainable competitive advantage from the other resources. Therefore, soft human resource management places greater emphasis on control through review and evaluation of outcomes, such that employees are led rather than managed.

*Empowerment* is explored more fully in Box 13.1, which also describes the Wal-Mart approach and thus picks up on issues introduced in Minicase 12.1. United Airlines in the USA provides another but quite different example. In 1994, the employees of United Airlines, the largest airline in the world, agreed to accept paycuts in exchange for majority control of the company, which was experiencing financial difficulties. As an outcome, decision making was decentralized more. One example was the bringing together of 350 pilots, flight attendants, mechanics and other employees to plan the development of a new, low-cost, short-haul shuttle service on the West Coast. United had to achieve very high service levels and low prices to compete with SouthWest Airlines. The new

venture was established reportedly 'without a single flaw'.

In an instance such as this, people who normally deal with problems and 'fire-fight', with a tactical perspective, are being encouraged to think more operationally and strategically: designing a service and the necessary systems whereby, ideally, many of the problems with which they are familiar are eliminated at the design stage.

Many organizations, however, still prefer more rigid controls from the centre, even though they may have reduced the number of layers in the organizational hierarchy and widened managers' spans of control. This, they believe, is the way to achieve efficiency and managed costs. Tighter systems inevitably constrain innovation and employee development; but, they assume, new ideas and people can be bought in or recruited.

## Manager competency

Simply, some companies will seek to develop their employees and managers, invariably promoting from within. A strong culture and vision

KEY CONCEPT – Box 13.1
Empowerment

Empowerment means freeing employees from instructions and controls and allowing them to take decisions themselves. Total quality management implies constant improvement; to achieve this employees should be contributing to the best of their ability. Proponents argue that rules stifle innovation and that future success relies not on past results but on the continuing ability to manage change pressures. Managers must be free to make appropriate changes in a decentralized structure.

There are three main objectives of empowerment:

- to make organizations more responsive to external pressures
- to 'delayer' organizations in order to make them more cost effective. British Airways, for example, now has five layers of management between the chief executive and the front line who interface with customers. It used to be nine. Managers become responsible for more employees, who they are expected to coach and support rather than direct
- to create employee networks featuring teamworking, collaboration and horizontal communications. This implies changes in the ways in which decisions are made.

The important questions are why, how and when. The leading retailers, for example, benefited from increasing centralization throughout the 1980s. Information technology enabled cost savings and efficiencies from centrally controlled buying, store and shelf layouts, stocking policies and reordering. In the 1990s there was little support for changing this in any marked way and delegating these decisions to store level. In its early years, Waterstone's delegated book-buying responsibility to individual store managers, and this was regarded as exceptional. Once the company was acquired by WH Smith this decentralization was systematically removed. At the same time individual stores are judged in part on the quality of service provided to their customers; and it is in this area that there has always been considerable scope for empowering managers. However, in 2000, in an attempt to win back market share, Marks and Spencer has begun to decentralize purchasing and stock decisions and give store managers more opportunity to ensure that they stock ranges which best match local needs.

Since C&A announced it was closing all its stores it has allowed individual store managers the freedom to stock and sell what they think is appropriate locally. Both sales and profits have improved!

As empowerment is increased it is important that employees are adequately informed and knowledgeable, that they are motivated to exercise power, and that they are rewarded for successful outcomes. In flatter organization structures there are fewer opportunities for promotion.

There are, then, three basic empowerment options:

- Employees can be encouraged to contribute ideas. As seen in Minicase 2.1, several new product ideas for McDonald's have come from individual franchisees. In reality, however, this may represent only token empowerment.

- Employees work in teams which share and manage their own work, but within clearly defined policies and limits. This should increase both efficiency and job satisfaction.
- More extensive decentralization means that individuals are much freer to change certain parameters and strategies. Evaluating outcomes is seen as the important control mechanism rather than rules and guidelines. An important distinction here is between making people accountable for their individual actions and making them accountable for the overall result. Constructive accountability gives people freedom to make decisions and demands that they accept responsibility for the consequences. This requires strong leadership, a clear mission and effective communications, rewards and sanctions. Information must flow openly upwards and sideways as well as downwards. In many organizations there is a tendency for 'bad news' to be selectively hidden, with perhaps two-thirds not flowing up to the next layer. Many potential threats are thereby not shared within the company. This would be unacceptable in an empowered organization.

For many organizations empowerment implies that the core organization strategies are decided centrally, with individual managers delegated a discretionary layer around the core (as shown in Chart A).

It is crucial first to find the right balance between the core and discretionary elements, and secondly to ensure that managers support and own the core strategy.

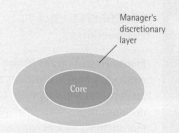

The deciding factors are:

- The competitive strategies and the relative importance of close linkages with customers in order to differentiate and provide high levels of service. When this becomes essential empowerment may imply an inverted pyramid structure. The structure exists to support front-line managers, as shown in Chart B.

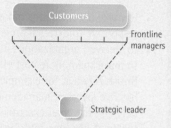

- Successful empowerment means putting the 'right' people in place and ensuring that they are able to do their job, which they understand and own. In this way they feel important.
- The extent to which the environment is turbulent and decisions are varied rather than routine.
- The expectations and preferences of managers and employees, and their ability and willingness to accept responsibility. Not everyone wants accountability and high visibility. If empowerment is mishandled it is possible that work will be simply pushed down a shorter hierarchy as managers seek to avoid responsibility.

Successful empowerment requires appropriate skills, which in turn frequently implies training. The appropriate style of management is coaching. Moreover, it is important to link in monitoring systems together with rewards and sanctions. Finally, empowerment must be taken seriously and not simply limited to non-essential decisions. Empowerment implies risk taking, and any mistakes, while not overlooked, must be handled carefully.

*Empowerment is a powerful motivator as long as it does not suddenly stop when the really important and interesting decisions have to be taken.*
Jeremy Soper, ex Retail Sales Director, WH Smith

**Wal-Mart's strategies for empowering people**

- Every project has a clear end-date.
- Everybody must experience success. Success can be built on success and people must never become complacent. People are therefore moved from clearly successful to less successful activities, so they can experience elements of both success and relative failure. In this way,

'winners' help others improve their standards and confidence; and people who are experiencing disappointment are moved into positions where morale is much higher. Linked to this,

- There is a 'no-blame' culture and no 'victims'.
- By moving around, people also become more multi-skilled and thereby grow personally.
- People are encouraged to become involved in several, small, improvemental projects – many of them driven by ideas from customers
- New ideas are tried out locally before being rolled-out more extensively.
- People are required to 'think, react and break-down barriers'.
- There is a philosophy that: *Track record + Empathy = Credibility*. Empathy develops as people 'get out', network and meet people so they can better understand their needs. It is credibility that 'gets things done'.
- To get ahead and stay ahead, speed is 'everything'.

Source for Wal-Mart material: Turner, K (1999) *The Wal-Mart Experience*, Presentation to a Retail Solutions International Conference, May.

should foster both commitment and continuous, emergent change. Necessary new competencies are *learned*. In such organizations, teamworking and networking are likely to be prominent. Other organizations prefer to search for the best people who might be available; they willingly recruit outsiders. They are seeking to *buy in* the new competencies that they require. People may feel less committed to such organizations in the long term, and consequently there will be a greater reliance on individualism and individual contributions.

The challenge for companies growing from within is that they need to become and stay very aware strategically if they are to remain ahead of their rivals; they will actively benchmark and look for new ideas that might be helpful. Companies securing new skills and competencies from outside face a different dilemma. If the competencies are available, and can be bought by any competitor, how can they ensure that they find the best ideas and people, and how can they generate some unique competency and competitive advantage?

Some companies will look to do both, finding, in the process, an appropriate balance. An analogy would be a leading football club which buys expensive, talented players in the transfer market while, at the same time, nurturing young players. There are many instances where highly skilled, experienced players do not fit in at a new club, certainly not at first; and when several arrive at once, it can be very disruptive until they are moulded into an effective team.

Capelli and Crocker-Hefter (1995) further distinguish between companies that seek to compete by moving quickly, perhaps by necessity, responding speedily to new opportunities, and those that have developed a more sustainable advantage in a long-standing market. They conclude that organizations competing on flexibility will typically find it more appropriate to recruit from outside. A reliance on developing new competencies internally may mean that they are too slow to gain early advantage from new opportunities. By contrast, organizations competing in established markets with long-standing relationships are more likely to rely on internally developed, organization-specific skills and strong internal and external architecture.

There are, inevitably, implications. In general, industries and markets are becoming more dynamic and turbulent, demanding that companies develop new product and market niche opportunities. This appears to imply an increasing reliance on recruiting strong, competent people from outside. In turn, this means that internal relationships and the culture may be under constant pressure to change. Companies are recruiting and rewarding individual experts; at the same time, synergistic opportunities demand strong internal architecture and co-operation. This is another organizational dilemma. Companies that succeed in establishing a strong, cohesive and motivating culture while developing new competencies flexibly and quickly are likely to be the future high performers.

Reinforcing points from earlier chapters, this demands effective strategic leadership and a shared, understood vision for the organization. The extent to which an organization can become a 'learning organization', discussed later in this chapter, is of great significance.

Figure 13.2 repackages the notion of manager competency in the form of five distinct mindsets. Managers, in different degrees, will and must possess all of these abilities. The issues concern the balance and the opportunity. Some managers will be extremely competent in certain areas, but their profile, approach and style may not be appropriate for the demands placed on them. In addition, and given the way in which managers work with constant interruptions, and performing a series of short, pragmatic tasks, it can be difficult for them to find time to think, reflect and challenge. Short-termism and 'more-of-the-same' can all too readily be the result.

Many books have been written, and continue to be written, describing the behaviour patterns and practices of successful organizations. While there is inevitably some element of idiosyncrasy and uniqueness, this approach is interesting and valuable. It can be a rich source of ideas. However, it is not the same as identifying those competencies which have been shown empirically to be associated with the creation of superior performance.

A *real manager* has to be a good leader in the sense that he has to embody an open-minded attitude of leadership in himself, in his fellow managers and even in the heads of each employee of his organization. *Leadership*, therefore, means to enable and help people to act as individual entrepreneurs within the frame of a commonly born vision of the business. A *bad manager*, on the other hand, is more an administrator who follows severe rules and customs within a stiff bureaucratical hierarchy.

*Dr Hugo M Sekyra, CEO and Chairman, Austrian Industries*

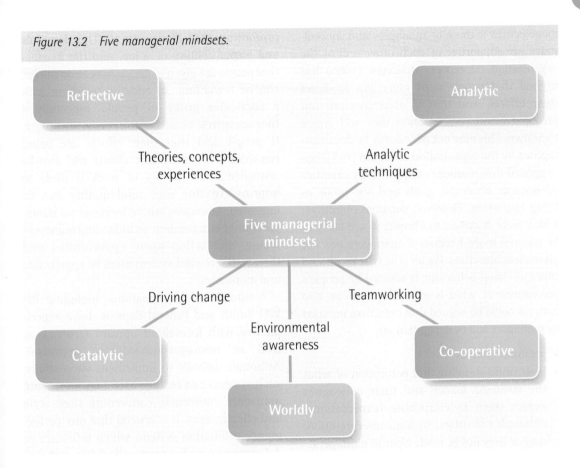

Figure 13.2    Five managerial mindsets.

It is because these questions are complex that some organizations will adopt and build human resource practices that help to create and sustain competitive advantage. They are peculiar to that organization's environmental matching challenge. Such organizations enjoy strong E–V–R (environment–values–resources) congruence. The competitive value of their competencies lies in the fact that while the general approach may be transferable, the specifics are not.

## Managing Human Resources

We need the 'right' people if we are to foster effective emergent strategy. Appropriate people with the required and desired competencies, and/or the potential for growth and development, need to be recruited. They require clear objectives to give them both direction and performance yardsticks, backed by training and development opportunities. Outcomes should be measured, and performance reviewed and rewarded as appropriate. Underperformance or failure should be sanctioned in some way. This section looks briefly at a number of these issues, and also considers the importance of motivating employees, team building and succession planning.

## Managers' objectives

Hersey and Blanchard (1982) contend that organizational success and performance are affected by the congruence between the objectives of managers and those of their subordinates. They argue that the organization can only accomplish its objectives if those of managers and subordinates are supportive of each other and of the organization. Moreover, McGregor (1960) has argued that people need objectives to direct their efforts, and that if objectives are not provided by the organization they will create their own. This may not necessarily be disadvantageous for the organization as Schein (1983) has suggested that managers are generally orientated towards economic goals and see profit as being important. However, personal objectives, which were discussed in Chapter 3, are likely to be allowed more freedom if managers are not given clear objectives. Porter *et al.* (1975) contend that individual behaviour is affected by people's perceptions of what is expected of them; and hence it could be argued that objectives pursued by managers will be dependent on:

- personal motives
- their understanding and perception of what the strategic leader and their colleagues expect them to contribute (expectations, although still subject to some interpretation, may or may not be made clear to managers)
- the culture of the organization.

Various systems and policies for setting and agreeing managers' objectives are available, but they are outside the scope of this book. Ideally, the resultant objectives will be 'SMART': specific, measurable, achievable, realistic and with a timescale.

While objective setting is important for dealing with tasks and priorities, it should never be forgotten that managing people effectively also involves communicating and interacting, and making sure there is always time and opportunity available for dealing with unexpected events.

## Rewards

Rewards are an important motivator, but it is important to appreciate that an individual may feel rewarded by things other than money or promotion (see Figure 13.3). The demands and responsibilities of a job, and the freedom that people are given to decide how to do things, can be rewarding. In addition, working with a particular group of people, especially if they are seen to be successful, can be rewarding. If people feel that their efforts are being rewarded and that future efforts will also be rewarded, their quality of work is likely to improve. In this way, total quality can be improved. Moreover, where incremental strategic change is dependent on individual managers seeing, and acting upon, opportunities and threats, the reward system must be appropriate and motivating.

A number of organizations, including BP, WH Smith and Federal Express, have experimented with formalized upward feedback as well as manager/subordinate appraisal. Although difficult to implement successfully, such systems can be very useful for increasing managers' awareness concerning their style and effectiveness. It is crucial that any performance evaluation systems which influence or determine rewards are open and fair, and perceived as such.

Rewards depend upon the success of the organization as a whole as well as individual contributions. Hence, individual motivation and the issues involved in building successful management teams are looked at next.

## Involving and motivating people

If people are to be committed to the organization, and to the achievement of key objectives, they must be involved. Employees at the so-called grass-roots level are likely to know the details of the business and what really happens better than their superiors and managers. If they are involved and encouraged to contribute their ideas for improvements, the result can be innovation or quality improvement.

Figure 13.3   Alternative rewards.

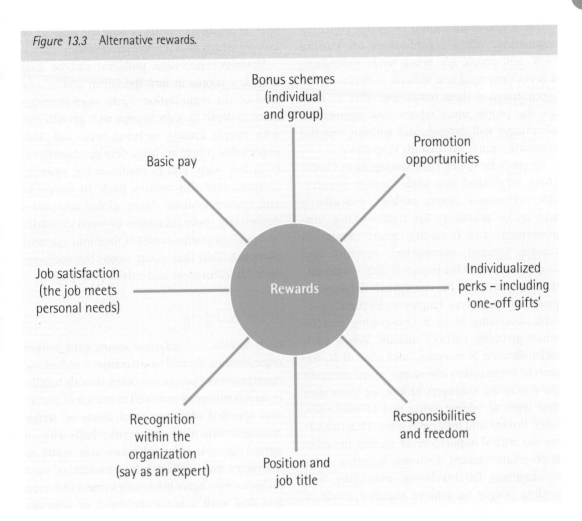

Moreover, if managers and other employees are to make effective strategic contributions it is important that they feel motivated. While money and position in the organization can motivate, there are other essential factors. Hertzberg (1968) emphasized the importance of the following:

- the potential to contribute and achieve through the job
- recognition for effort and success
- promotion opportunities
- interesting work
- responsibility.

David McClelland (McClelland and Winter, 1971) emphasizes the importance of knowing colleagues and subordinates and understanding what motivates them. He contends that people have three needs in varying proportions – achievement, power and affiliation – and individual profiles of the balance between these needs vary. He argues that managers should attempt to understand how much their subordinates desire power, look for opportunities where they can achieve, and want close or friendly working relationships, manifested, say, by not working in isolation. If managers then seek to meet these needs, subordinates can and will be motivated.

One major motivational challenge concerns downsizing. When organizations are cutting back, and people are being made redundant, it is both essential and difficult to maintain the commitment of those remaining. After all, they are the people upon whom new competitive advantages will depend, and without this the company cannot successfully rejuvenate.

Research by Roffey Park Management Centre (1995) established that while there is considerable enthusiasm among authors, consultants and senior managers for teamworking, empowerment and flexibility, many employees remain 'cynical, overworked, insecure and despondent' about the impact of flatter organization structures and the consequent reduction in promotion prospects. Employees frequently perceive delayering to be a cost-cutting exercise which actually reduces morale. When such rationalization is essential, and often it is, the real challenge comes afterwards, in encouraging the remaining managers to look for innovative new ways of adding value and to take risks, albeit limited and measured risks. This reinforces the critical importance of finding the most appropriate reward systems, together with mechanisms for involving, managing and leading people to achieve superior levels of performance.

## Succession issues

Succession problems can concern both strategic leadership and managerial positions throughout the organization. Small firms whose growth and success have been dependent upon one person, most probably the founder, often experience problems when he or she retires, especially where there has been a failure to develop a successor in readiness. Some very large organizations also experience problems when particularly charismatic and influential strategic leaders resign or retire. Although they may be replaced by other strong leaders there

may be changes to either or both the strategy or culture which do not prove successful.

However, succession problems can be seen with key people in any specialism and at any level of the organization. Firms need management in depth in order to cope with growth and with people leaving or being promoted. This implies that people are being developed constantly in line with, and in readiness for, strategic change; and this relates back to appraisal and reward systems. Many global companies deliberately move managers between countries and product groups as part of their management planning. This, they claim, opens the company up to 'different ideas and outside perceptions'.

## Team building

Both formal and informal teams exist within organizations. Formal teams comprise sections or departments of people who work directly together on a continuous basis and in pursuit of particular specified objectives, and teams of senior managers who meet on a regular basis with an agreed agenda. Informal teams can relate to managers from different departments, or even divisions, who agree informally to meet to discuss and deal with a particular issue, or who are charged with forming a temporary group to handle an organization-wide problem. In both cases relationships determine effectiveness. Ideally, all members will contribute and support each other, and synergy will result from their interactions. Simply putting a group of people together in a meeting, however, does not ensure that they will necessarily work well together and form an effective and successful team.

A successful team needs:

- shared and agreed objectives
- a working language, or effective communications
- the ability to manage both the tasks and the relationships.

Cummings (1981) contends that individual contributions to the overall team effort are determined by personal growth needs (for achievement and personal development) and social needs – perceived benefits from working with others to complete tasks, rather than working alone.

Within any team, therefore, there will be a variety of skills, abilities and commitments. Some people will be natural hard workers who need little supervision or external motivation; others, who may be diligent and committed, may need all aspects of their task spelt out clearly; the major contribution of particular members might be in terms of their creativity and ideas. Meredith Belbin (1981) argues that a good team of people will have compensating strengths and weaknesses, and that as a group they will be able to perform a series of necessary and related tasks. Belbin has identified a number of characteristics or contributions that individuals make to teams. They relate to the provision of ideas, leadership, the resolution of conflict, the gathering and analysing of data and information, carrying out certain detailed work which might be regarded as boring by certain members, organizing people to make their most useful contributions, and developing relationships within the group. Individuals will contribute in a number of areas, not just one or two, but they will often be particularly strong in some and weak in others. A balance is required if the team is to work well together and complete the task satisfactorily.

Whoever is responsible for leading the team – it might be the strategic leader and his or her team of senior managers, or department managers – should consider the various strengths and weaknesses of people and seek to develop them into an effective and cohesive team. If any essential areas of contribution are missing this should be dealt with, and any potential conflicts of strong personalities should be determined early.

## The 'learning organization'

When we think of building strong, cohesive and integrated teams, we generally, and quite rightly, think of small groups of employees. However, the same themes can be extended to the scale of the whole organization. Where all the parts can be integrated effectively, share with each other and learn from each other we have what Senge (1991) has called a 'learning organization' – which is explained in Box 13.2. Simply, as shown in Figure 13.4, the whole organization is able to think strategically and create synergy by sharing its knowledge and ideas and generating actions which contribute to the interests of the whole. The process is self-reinforcing as managers objectively review their progress.

Minicase 13.5 looks at the attributes of a learning organization in the context of Team New Zealand, the sailors who took the America's Cup from the USA. Clearly, the team was relatively small in size and it must be appreciated that creating a learning organization in a large company is no easy task. However, wherever it can be achieved to some creditable degree, there are likely to be substantial benefits.

*Figure 13.4* The learning organization – leadership and vision. Based on ideas of Charles Handy (1989).

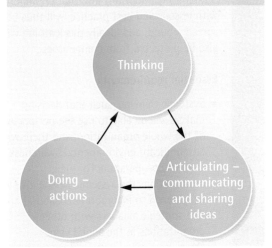

**KEY CONCEPT – Box 13.2**
**The Learning Organization**

The basic arguments are as follows:

- When quality, technology and product/service variety are all becoming widely available at relatively low cost, speed of change is essential for sustained competitive advantage.
- If an organization, therefore, fails to keep up with, or ahead of, the rate of change in its environment it will either be destroyed by stronger competitors, or lapse into sudden death or slow decline. The ideal is to be marginally ahead of competitors – opening up too wide a gap might unsettle customers.
- An organization can only adapt if it is first able to learn, and this learning must be cross-functional as well as specialist.

*Hence a learning organization encourages continuous learning and knowledge generation at all levels, has processes which can move knowledge around the organization easily to where it is needed, and can translate that knowledge quickly into changes in the way the organization acts, both internally and externally.*

Senge (1991)

Strategically important information, together with lessons and best practice, will thus be spread around; and ideally this learning will also be protected from competitors.

**Essential requirements**

- Systemic thinking, such that decision makers will be able to use the perspective of the whole organization; and there will be significant environmental awareness and internal co-operation. For many organizations the systemic perspective will be widened to incorporate collaboration and strategic alliances with other organizations in the added value chain.

- Management development and personal growth – to enable effective empowerment and leadership throughout the organization, and in turn allow managers to respond to perceived environmental changes and opportunities.
- A shared vision and clarity about both core competencies and key success factors. Changes should be consistent through strategic and operational levels.
- Appropriate values and corporate culture – to exploit fully core competencies and satisfy key success factors.
- A commitment to customer service, quality and continuous improvement.
- Kotter and Heskett (1992) argue that the appropriate culture is one which is capable of constant adaptation as the needs of customers, shareholders and employees change.
- Team learning within the organization through problem sharing and discussion.

These points have been used to develop the following matrix which draws together a number of points discussed in this chapter and relates them to key issues of change management.

| | | Effectiveness orientated | The learning organization |
|---|---|---|---|
| Employment and development | | Focus on problem-solving approach | Innovative intrapreneurial risk taking |
| | | Change accepted | Change initiated |
| Culture and values | | Concentration on resource efficiency | Supportive organization |
| Orientation towards efficiency and results | | Consistent and systematic | Cross-functional co-operation |
| | | Change resisted | Response to change pressures |
| | | Individuals and tasks | Teams and integration |
| | | | Structural focus |

# Minicase 13.5  Team New Zealand

The America's Cup series of yacht races, between the current holder and a preselected challenger, lasts over several weeks and requires considerable preparation and dedication. When New Zealand won in 1995 it was only the second time a team from outside America had won in 144 years, the first being Australia in 1983. Moreover, New Zealand won 41 races and lost just one, an incredible margin of victory. The team had 'continually expanded its ability to create its destiny'. There had been a driving vision throughout the preparation and the race series: 'to build, modify and sail the fastest boat on any given day'. This vision had brought together the (technical) designers with the users, the sailors, and created synergy where often there is conflict. Their respective perspectives are, quite simply, different.

Several factors, all characteristic of a successful learning organization, have been put forward as important contributors:

There was an *inspirational leader* in the form of Sir Peter Blake, who was an experienced sailor, but not the skipper of the actual crew. Nor was he an experienced boat designer. Blake convinced everyone that winning was possible, and he then made sure that happened.

There was a *strong sense of community* in the team. Blake was visible in driving this, leading from the front. He ensured that the designers were not allowed to drive the agenda without challenge from the sailors.

*Open communications* were sponsored, in the form of free-flowing ideas. No hidden or undeclared agendas were permitted. Resources had to be shared. Blake held meetings between the designers and sailors at regular intervals during the build-up period and ran them without ceremony or hierarchy. He encouraged people to be creative in their search for different and unusual answers to problems and issues. It was noted that the secretary at one meeting felt comfortable contributing an idea that turned out to be really valuable.

There was a *sustained record of improvement* in product design and racing skills right through to the end of the race series. Team New Zealand did not stop searching for improvements even when they were winning every race! They built on their successes to reinforce their advantage. There was a willingness by the sailors to accept design modifications if they made the boat go more quickly, even where it made their task of sailing it more difficult or uncomfortable. During the pre-race trials Team New Zealand sailed two identical boats, rather than two different designs in competition. Their choice of design had been made by simulation. Because the two boats began as identical, any successful modifications to the design of one could be copied by the team sailing the other. As a result, considerable emphasis was placed on improving sailing skills as well.

There was clear evidence of a very *strong commitment* by the individual team members, who were convinced that winning the America's Cup mattered immensely to the whole country, which was drawn behind the team in a positive and supportive way.

The *team* was *carefully selected* to ensure that they were people who would 'own' what they were taking on. They needed to have individual sailing skills and experience, but they had to be able to interact well with others. They also had to demonstrate they were able to handle disappointment and quickly put it behind them. Outstanding individuals who might be reluctant team players, however good they were personally, were rejected by Blake, who built his team around the tasks. (Interestingly, and in contrast, it sometimes appears that certain footballers are selected for the England football team because of their individual skills, and then asked to play out of position. Right-footed players play on the left of the field, for example, and then do not play to their potential).

QUESTIONS: Do you agree that Team New Zealand is a learning organization? Use the Internet to check their progress in the follow-up series of America's Cup races.

Source: Maani, K and Benton, C (1999) Rapid team learning – lessons from Team New Zealand's America's Cup campaign, *Organizational Dynamics*, Spring.

*Team New Zealand*   http://www.teamnz.org

## Information and Information Technology

### The strategic value of information

Information is the fuel used in decision making; it can also be an importance source of competitive advantage in certain circumstances. It must be stressed that IT, per se, is rarely a source of advantage, but information management can be. So, what exactly do we mean by 'information' and how might it be exploited?

Information has been defined as 'some tangible or intangible entity that reduces uncertainty about a state or event' (Lucas, 1976), which is a way of saying that information increases knowledge in a particular situation. When information is received, some degree of order can be imposed on a previously less well-ordered situation.

Information is needed for, and used in, decision making. Information, information systems and information technology are all aids to deci-

sion making. The more information managers and other employees have about what is happening in the organization, and in its environment, the more strategically aware they are likely to be. Information about other functional areas and business units can be particularly helpful in this respect.

Ackoff (1967), however, suggested that management information systems can easily be based on three erroneous assumptions:

- Managers are short of information. In many cases managers have too much irrelevant information.
- Managers know the information they require for a decision. However, when asked what information they might need, managers play safe and ask for everything which might be relevant, and thereby contribute to the overabundance of irrelevant information.
- If a manager is provided with the information required for a decision he or she will have no further problem in using it effectively. How information is used depends on perceptions of

the issues involved. Moreover, if any additional quantitative analysis or interpretation is required, many managers are weak in these skills.

Nevertheless, decisions and decision making do involve both facts and people. While the right information available at the right time can be extremely useful, the real value of information relates to how it is used by decision makers, particularly for generating and evaluating alternative possible courses of action. In designing and introducing IT and management information systems into organizations it is necessary to consider the likely reaction of people as well as the potential benefits that can accrue from having more up-to-date and accurate information available. Information gathering should never become an end in itself, for the expertise and experience in people's heads can be more useful than facts on paper.

Moreover, it is important to evaluate who actually needs the information, rather than who might find it useful for increasing awareness, and to ensure that those people receive it. Although information technology and information systems can be expensive to introduce, those organizations that receive information, analyse and distribute it to the appropriate decision makers more quickly than their competitors can achieve a competitive edge, particularly in a turbulent environment. Hence, the structure and culture of the organization should ensure that managers who need information receive it, and at the right time. However, while information can lead to more effective decision making, it remains a manifestation of power within the organization, and this aspect needs monitoring. If information that could prove useful is withheld from decision makers, negligently or deliberately by political managers pursuing personal objectives, the effectiveness of decision making is reduced.

Information is used through a filter of experience and judgement in decision making, and its relative value varies between one decision maker and another. In certain instances the available information will be accurate, reliable and up to date. In other circumstances the information provided may already be biased because it is the result of the interpretation of a situation by someone who may have introduced subjectivity. Some managers, perhaps those who are less experienced, will rely more heavily on specific information than others, for whom experience, general awareness and insight into the situation are more important.

To complicate matters further, Day (1996) argues that organizations do not know what they know. In other words, they are awash with data that do not get translated into valuable information and hence real organizational knowledge. Linked to this, it is clear that quite frequently they also fail to realize the value of some of the information that some people in the organization possess. This can be taken even further. If organizations do not know what they know, it must follow they do not know what they do not know. They remain unaware of certain opportunities that others will seize and that they would have found valuable if they knew of their existence. Correspondingly, they do not find out about certain threats until it is too late to act.

## Decision making and the interpretation of information

Spear (1980) argues that when information systems and the provision of information for managers are being considered it is important to bear in mind how people make decisions, interpret data and information, and give meaning to them. In decision making managers sometimes behave in a stereotyped way and follow past courses of action; sometimes they are relatively unconcerned with the particular decision and may behave inconsistently. In each case they may ignore information which is available and which if used objectively would lead to a different conclusion and decision. At other times information is used selectively and ignored if it conflicts with strongly held beliefs or views about certain things. In other words, information may be either misused or not used effectively.

Moreover, when considering a problem situation managers have to interpret the events that they are able to observe and draw certain conclusions about what they believe is happening. The question is: do managers perceive reality? Is there even such a thing as reality, or are there simply the meanings that we give to events? The following example will explain the point. Worker directors, popular in some other European countries, have always been a controversial issue among managers and trade union officials in the UK, with some of them supportive and others, in reality a majority, strongly opposed to their introduction. Managers who oppose them argue that they will reduce managerial power to run an organization; union opponents argue they would increase managerial power because the directors would be carefully selected or co-opted to include mainly those who were antagonistic to many of the aims of the union. These views represent meaning systems. The idea of worker directors, and what they are, is definite and agreed; their meaning and the implications of using them are subjective and interpretative.

A parallel situation would concern the interpretation of economic data. If, say, interest rates are rising, share prices are falling or the value of the pound is strengthening, do economic analysts agree or disagree on their meaning?

## Counterintuitive behaviour

A failure to think through the implications of certain decisions on other managers, departments or business units can have effects that are unwelcome. The same can happen if there is an inability to appreciate the consequences because of a lack of information, or if there is a misunderstanding resulting from the wrong interpretation of information. Such an event is known as counterintuitive behaviour, and it often creates a new set of problems that may be more serious than those that existed originally.

Jay Forrester, in his book *Urban Dynamics* (1969), discusses how a strategy of building low-cost housing by the US equivalent of a local authority in order to improve living conditions for low-income earners in inner city areas has done more harm than good. The new houses draw in more low-income people who need jobs, but at the same time they make the area less attractive for those employers who might create employment. General social conditions decline. The area becomes even more destitute, creating again more pressure for low-cost housing. 'The consequence is a downward spiral that draws in the low-income population, depresses their condition, prevents escape and reduces hope. All of this done with the best of intentions.'

A more recent and real example concerns horse racing. It has always been the case that flat racing is cheaper and easier to stage than National Hunt racing over hurdles. Generally, but not exclusively, and dictated by ground conditions, flat racing is focused on the summer with National Hunt in the winter months. Weather conditions are more likely to be adverse in the winter, and so artificial turf all-weather surfaces were put on trial to see test their value in overcoming the problem for horses of hard, frozen ground. The intention was to make National Hunt economically more attractive. Paradoxically, the all-weather surfaces proved too tough for chasers and hurdlers when they landed from jumping, but they proved ideal for flat racing. The outcome is that the flat racing season can be extended, giving it even more of a relative advantage over National Hunt.

Related problems occur with misinterpretation of information. Consider the example of a small independent retailer who finds that he is selling more of a particular item than normal and more than he expected to sell. Deliveries from his wholesaler or other suppliers require a waiting period. Does he simply replace his stock, or increase his stockholding levels? How does he forecast or interpret future demand? When he starts ordering and buying more, or buying more frequently, how do his suppliers, and ultimately the manufacturer, respond? On what do they base their stockholding and production decisions, given that there will be penalties for misunderstanding the situation? Such problems are made worse by time-lags or delays. The use of IT by major retail organizations has proved that the impact of this dilemma can be reduced.

Summarizing, the fact that information is available does not necessarily mean that more effective decisions will result.

Information technology is a solution looking for a problem.
*Donald Jones, CEO, ETSI (Consultants in call centre technology)*

## Information systems and information technology: a cautionary comment

IT can be regarded as 'the application of hardware (machinery) and software (systems and techniques) to methods of processing and presenting data into a meaningful form which helps reduce uncertainty and is of real perceived value in current or future decisions'.

A management information system collects, processes and distributes the information required for managers to make decisions. It should be designed to be cost-effective, in that the additional revenue or profits generated by more effective decisions exceed the cost of designing, introducing and running the system, or that the value of management time saved is greater than the cost of the system. In addition, the informa-

tion provided should be valid, reliable and up to date for the decisions concerned.

It should be realized that while computers and IT might be an essential feature of a management information system, the basic ideas behind an information system have little concern with computers. The terms are not synonymous.

Earl and Hopwood (1980) expressed a concern that there would be a tendency for the potential of IT to lead to an increasingly technological perspective on the way in which information is processed by managers. This would lead to increasingly formal systems and bureaucratic procedures which 'neither fit nor suit the realities of organizational activity'. On many occasions, informally exchanged information between managers who trust and respect each other is extremely important, and in some organizations political activity and power is important in certain decisions. In addition, organizations can become overloaded with information that they cannot utilize effectively.

In the mid-1990s Tesco introduced its customer loyalty card, Clubcard, and was later followed by Safeway (ABC card) and Sainsbury (Reward Card). Every time shoppers pass through a till their card is swiped to record their purchases. Customers build up points which can be used as a discount on future purchases either with the supermarket in question or with partner organizations. At the same time the computer records every item the customer has bought. The idea was that this could be used to profile people's habits and preferences so that special promotions could be targeted, instead of the more traditional 'blanket coverage' approach. Safeway invested £50 million a year for five years to run its system and then abandoned it. Customers had used the cards, but many possess more than one supermarket card in any case, reducing the value of the loyalty element. Safeway also admitted that it had underestimated the scope of the systems needed to handle, analyse and exploit the data it was collecting. In the end, Safeway concluded the £50 million per year would be better spent on reducing prices. ASDA, incidentally, had not gone down this route. A company survey of 5500 shoppers in 1999 was used to justify this decision: only five wanted a loyalty card, they said!

With the complexities discussed above as a backcloth, it is now important to examine the strategic information challenge facing organizations.

## The strategic information challenge

Why do some organizations, which are currently enjoying success and high profits, fail to realize when products, services or strategies are about to lose customer support? Why do they fail to anticipate competitor initiatives? Why are others able to be more proactive?

Being close to customers, and in touch with new developments in a dynamic and possibly chaotic marketplace, requires information, intelligence and learning. Successful organizations monitor the activities of their customers, suppliers and competitors; they ask questions and test out new ideas. They express a willingness to learn and to change both their perspective on competition – their mindset concerning which factors determine competitive success – and the things they actually do. Sophisticated analyses and models of past and current results and behaviour patterns make an important contribution but, as Day (1996) argues, it is also necessary to think through how a market might respond to actions designed to retain existing customers and win new business, while outflanking and outperforming competitors. One of the reasons for Canon's continued success has been its ability to spot new market opportunities for its advanced technologies and exploit them early. Canon is also adept at reducing its dependency on products/markets as competition intensifies and demand plateaus. In the 1970s, for example, Canon successfully and systemati-

cally switched emphasis away from cameras (while remaining active and innovatory in the market) to photocopiers, and then to computer printers and facsimile machines, always adopting the same focus principles.

In order to become and remain strategically successful, organizations must create and sustain competitive advantage. They must continue to enjoy E–V–R (environment–values–resources) congruence, frequently in a dynamic and turbulent environment. To achieve this, information must be gathered and shared, but this is not merely a question of designing a new information system.

Day (1996) contends that many organizations 'do not know what they know' either because data and signals are misinterpreted or because the flows are inadequate. Decision makers do not receive the information that they need, or they fail to learn about things that might prove useful. Organizations that prioritize vertical channels and ignore horizontal flows are the ones most likely to fail to learn. The important elements for strategic success are:

- tracking events in the market and the environment, choosing responses (both proactively and reactively) and monitoring the outcomes of the actions which follow. Competitor initiatives must be dealt with; benchmarking best practices and general awareness can suggest new ideas
- making sure that important information from the questioning and learning from these emergent changes is disseminated effectively
- reflecting upon outcomes in the context of E–V–R congruence to ensure that the organization can sustain an effective match with its environment
- where appropriate, adapting policies and procedures to better guide future decisions.

The implication is a constant willingness to be flexible and to change as necessary. Companies must work from the twin perspectives of opportunity and threat. First, a willingness to learn and grow and, secondly, a realization that without appropriate and timely change a company is likely to face a crisis. Gilbert (1995) further argues that strategically successful organizations leverage their innovative competitive ideas with speed and act quickly.

They obtain market feedback continuously and rapidly and adapt to the feedback ahead of their rivals. They exploit the potential of strategic as well as competitive and operating information systems.

## Three levels of information

- *Operating information systems* – Cost accounting systems, sales analyses and production schedules are essential for efficiency and control. Used creatively as, for example, is the case with airline reservation systems, they can create competitive advantage, but they are not designed to drive strategic change.
- *Competitive information systems* – Important elements of the various operating systems need to be integrated and synthesized to ensure that the organization is using its resources both efficiently and effectively. Specifically, it is meeting the needs and expectations of important external stakeholders. Competitive information systems, therefore, relate to competitive advantage and E–V–R congruence. They require managers to think and work across functional boundaries and consider the total service package provided to customers, encapsulating all the ways in which an organization can add value in a co-ordinated way.

  However, Gilbert (1995) argues that managers will not always be aware of the information they have used in arriving at a competitively successful formula. Where organizations do not fully understand why they are successful, that success may be fragile.

- *Strategic information systems* – While competitive information systems will typically focus on existing competition, organizations must also be able to learn about the business environment in order that they can anticipate change and design future strategies. Marchand (1995a) stresses that strategic information management should not be confined to the level of the strategic leader, but rather dispersed throughout the whole organization. This implies an innovative culture and an organization structure which facilitates the sharing of information – one essential element of a learning organization. A learning organization requires considerable decentralization and empowerment, which must not be at the expense of control. Centralized systems are often required for sound control and effective co-ordination, thus presenting organizations with the dilemma of how to obtain the speed and flexibility benefits of decentralization without sacrificing control.

  It is important to stress that appreciating the significance of particular events, and assessing the potential significance of opportunities and threats which have been spotted, often requires judgement, which will be discussed at greater length in Chapter 19.

Hence, as one moves up these three levels of decision making, the contribution of IT and information systems to decision making changes. Once operating systems are established, they can be used to make a number of decisions and drive the operations. By measuring performance, the systems can again make a valuable contribution and highlight when things are going wrong. For strategic decisions, however, IT is primarily an aid to decision making. Systems cannot realistically make the decisions, and consequently interpretation and meaning systems are particularly important. For such decisions the systems should be designed to provide information in a form that is useful to decision makers.

## Information uses

Expanding this point, Marchand (1995b) distinguishes among four important and distinct uses for information at the operating, competitive and strategic decision-making levels.

- *Command and control* – The formal gathering of information to allow centralized control and decentralized accountability. Budgeting and resource allocations will typically be included. Command and control is valuable for managing resources efficiently but, used in isolation, it does not drive rapid change. Many organizations use tight financial targeting and monitoring as an essential driver of their competitiveness. Command and control invariably requires an organization to be broken down into subunits, such as independent businesses, divisions or functional departments.
- *Improvement* – Here the emphasis is on integrating the functions to improve both efficiency and effectiveness through better all-round service. Processes that link the functions are often the focus of attention, and initiatives such as total quality management and business process improvement will be integral.
- *Opportunities for organizational synergy* – If complex multibusiness organizations can find new opportunities for internal synergy, sharing and interdependency, they can clearly benefit. Teamworking and special project teams are one way of doing this. This can be particularly important if the organization acquires another business which needs to be integrated.
- *Environmental opportunities* – Market intelligence, competitor monitoring and benchmarking best practice can generate new ideas and opportunities, as we have seen. This requires that managers are vigilant and enquiring. Critically, ideas spotted by one part of an organization, and of no discernible use

to that business, might be valuable for another business or division, and consequently the ability to share – based on an understanding of needs and a willingness to trust and co-operate – is essential.

Figure 13.5 illustrates that an organization must be able to manage all four information needs simultaneously and harmoniously if it is to benefit from improved efficiencies and manage change both continuously and discontinuously. Herein lies the real strategic information challenge. The deployment of organizational resources, the corresponding style of management and the cultural implications vary between the four information needs and the decision-making processes that they support. Command and control management requires the organization to be separated into functions, businesses and/or divisions for clarity; the others demand different forms of integration, both formal and informal, to share both information and learning.

Figure 13.6 illustrates how organizations need first, to develop a perspective on how they can add value and create competitive advantage. Through monitoring, measurement, continuous improvement and innovation they should seek to become increasingly efficient and effective. This continual process represents single-loop learning and it is essential if competitive advantage is to be sustained in a dynamic environment. This requires sound operating and competitive information systems. However, over time, on its own, this will not be enough. Organizations must always be looking for new competitive paradigms, really new ways of adding different values, ahead of competitors – both existing rivals and potential new entrants – looking for an opportunity to break into the market. Effective strategic information systems, relying on informality, networking and learning, are required for this double-loop learning.

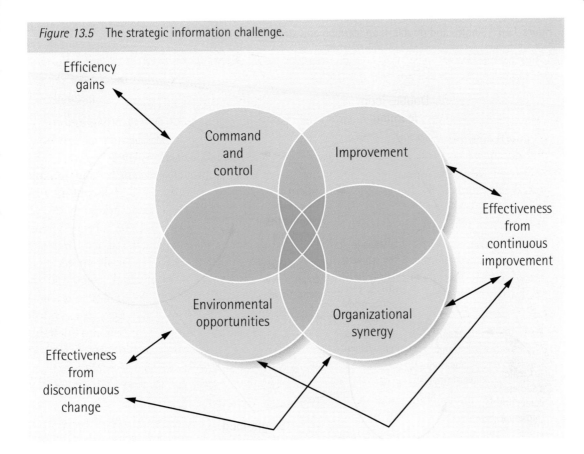

*Figure 13.5* The strategic information challenge.

Fostering a culture of improvement and single-loop learning in an organization is more straightforward than the challenge of double-loop learning. Organizations that invest in strategic planning, research and development and new product/service programmes are locked into the process, but the real benefits cannot be gained if these activities and the requisite learning are confined to head-office departments and specialist functions. They must permeate the whole organization and become embedded in the culture. This reflects a key organizational tension and dilemma – the paradox of stability and instability – which was introduced in Chapter 2. Stability concerns running existing businesses efficiently and effectively, exploiting strategic abilities and continually looking to create high-

er returns from the committed resources. Instability refers to the search for the new competitive high ground ahead of one's rivals.

Information, however, as well as being a vital element in decision making, can also be a source of competitive advantage, as shown in the next section.

## Information, Information Technology and Competitive Advantage

It is clear that IT offers many potential strategic opportunities which go beyond the notion of faster data processing, but that harnessing these

**Figure 13.6** Single- and double-loop learning and strategic change.

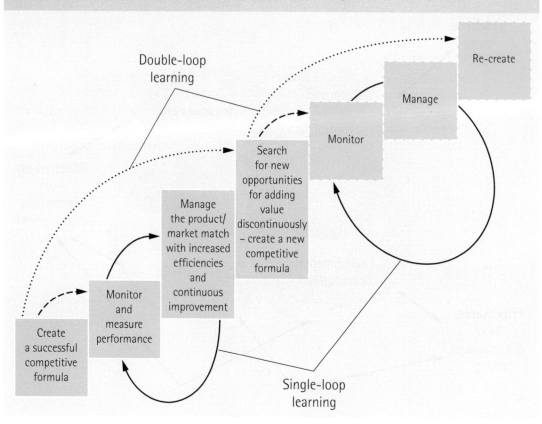

opportunities involves changes in attitude and culture among managers. McFarlan (1984) claims that IT strategies should relate to two criteria:

- How dependent is the organization on IT systems which are reliable 24 hours a day, seven days a week? International banks and stock and currency dealers who trade around the clock, and who use IT to monitor price movements and record their transactions, need their systems to be wholly reliable.
- Is IT crucial if the organization is to meet key success factors? If it is, there is an implication that companies can benefit from harnessing the latest technological developments. An obvious example is the airline industry.

Minicase 13.6 looks at IT in British Airways, but in fairness it reflects developments by all the leading airlines.

Rayport and Sviokla (1995) argue that competition is now based on two dimensions: the physical world of resources and a virtual world of information. Information clearly supports and enhances every activity in an organization, but it can itself be a source of added value and consequently competitive advantage as long as organizations are able to extract that value.

Michael Porter (1985) had earlier suggested that technological change, and in particular IT, is among the most prominent forces that can alter the rules of competition. This is because most activities in an organization create and

# Minicase 13.6  British Airways

British Airways has been investing some 5% of its gross revenue in IT during the 1990s. IT was first utilized over 30 years ago to streamline the reservations systems. Subsequently, it was used for aircraft scheduling, spares control and crew rostering. BA now obtains many of its supplies by Internet procurement. Improved efficiencies in these areas are critical as cargo and passenger volumes grow, and continue to grow.

Increasingly, IT has also been used to add value and to improve BA's overall service and effectiveness in a very competitive industry. A number of the applications is described below.

Computerized reservation systems now link travel agencies directly with the airlines and provide instantaneous information on availability, followed by reservations and tickets. There is a number of systems but the market is dominated by two, which carry up-to-date information on hundreds of airlines and their flight schedules. Sabre (begun by American Airlines) quickly became 'market leader' for the US market abut has a more limited presence in Europe; Galileo/Apollo (two merged systems, owned at one stage by United Airlines and BA together with nine other airlines) was market leader in Europe and second largest in America. Most airlines have sold their stakes in these systems: BA sold its holding in two separate tranches. These systems allow airlines to change prices and pricing policies frequently in their attempt to maximize their yield. In other words, fares for a particular flight can be adjusted in line with demand, and ticket prices can be discounted to try to fill the aeroplane if there are spare seats. The airlines want to sell seats at the highest prices they can obtain, but an empty seat means lost and irrecoverable revenue. This is complex as there are 30 different fares available on a typical trans-Atlantic flight on a Boeing 747.

Travel agents and specialist 'consolidators' (who buy blocks of discounted seats and sell them on either directly or via other travel agents), with access to substantial information, will often shop around for the lowest fares. In addition, computer reservation systems allow passengers to be allocated specific seats well in advance of their flight rather than when they check in at the airport. Clearly, both the airline and the passenger can benefit. The airlines further argue that these systems give them better control over their deliberate overbooking policies. An airline is often willing to sell more seats than they have available on a flight, assuming that some passengers with tickets will not travel, and balancing the cost of compensation and lost goodwill against the lost revenue from empty seats.

BA, like most major international airlines, has a frequent flyer programme with Air miles and various other benefits. Air miles are also available from organizations with whom BA has an alliance, including other airlines, car rental companies and leading hotel chains. Without IT to record the relevant flight and fare details, such programmes would not be feasible.

New ticketing machines at airports enable passengers on certain flights (in BA's case on shuttle services) to buy their ticket and obtain their printed boarding card in 40 seconds. The technology also exists for machines to scan a passenger's thumbprint (assuming that it has been previously verified), issue a ticket and debit that person's bank account. This is seen as more secure than the existing machines, which respond to credit and debit cards, and more likely to generate customer loyalty. Hand-held computers are available to speed up checking-in and reduce queuing.

ACARS (Aircraft Communications Addressing and Reporting System) allows fast transfer of information by radio waves between computers on the ground and computers on board aircraft. Data transmitted during a flight can help to plan routine and extra ground maintenance and boarding delays can be reduced. Some of the ground time between flights is spent analysing and responding to information on load and balance.

Personal video players, which are typically standard in first and business class, can be adapted to enable passengers to book hotels and cars during their flights and possibly use their credit cards for mail-order shopping. (Hertz already have touch-panel machines with visual prompt screens at airports to enable passengers to reserve cars at their destination just before they fly. A printed confirmation takes 6 seconds.)

BA has also harnessed IT to improve its response to complaints. Only three customers in 1000 complain about anything, but this still represents several hundred letters every day. Most people are only looking for an explanation and an apology, but they expect it quickly. If they receive a satisfactory response, they tend to stay loyal to BA, and customer retention is much less expensive than generating new business. Given that the customer's explanation must be checked carefully, it has proved beneficial to link the customer service system with BA's other information systems, such as bookings and flight information. New letters of complaint are scanned in and the relevant records checked quickly before a response is generated. Each letter is given a priority rating.

Prior to his resignation early in 2000, chief executive Robert Ayling committed BA to increasing the percentage of its tickets sold by the Internet from 1% to 50% in less than five years. His successor has reinforced the strategy but trimmed the target. EasyJet promotes itself as the 'Web's favourite airline' (as a spoof on BA's claim to be the 'World's favourite airline') and sells its tickets only via the Internet and its own telephone call centre.

QUESTION: Can you think of other opportunities where BA might seek to exploit IT for competitive advantage?

*British Airways*    http://www.britishairways.com

use information. Porter and Millar (1985) contend that IT could affect competition in three ways:

- IT can change the structure of an industry, and in so doing alter the rules of competition

- IT can be used to create sustainable competitive advantage by providing companies with new competitive weapons
- as a result of IT new businesses can be developed from within a company's existing activities.

These three themes are examined in greater detail below.

## Industry structure

As shown in Chapter 8, according to Porter (1980), the structure of an industry can be analysed in terms of five competitive forces: the threat of new entrants; the bargaining power of suppliers; the bargaining power of buyers; the threat of substitute products and services; and rivalry amongst existing competitors. Porter and Millar (1985) suggested that IT could influence the nature of these forces, and thereby change the attractiveness and profitability of an industry. This is particularly applicable where the industry has a high information content, such as airlines, and financial and distribution services. Moreover, firms that were either slow or reluctant to introduce IT might well be driven out of the industry, because they would be unable to offer a competitive service. Where the cost of the necessary IT, both hardware and software systems, is high it can increase the barriers to entry for potential new firms.

Minicase 13.7 builds on Minicase 13.6 and explains how holiday companies have made use of IT to lower costs and allow them to compete more aggressively on pricing. The result of the competitive activity has been an increase in concentration, with the largest companies gaining market share at the expense of smaller rivals, many of whom have left the industry.

Porter and Millar show that IT can both improve and reduce the attractiveness and profitability of an industry, and that as a consequence manufacturers should analyse the potential implications of change very carefully.

IT and the Internet – which is discussed below – have transformed such financial services as banking, enabling customers to carry out many of their financial transactions by telephone or personal computer without needing to queue for a cashier. However, there is the disadvantage that certain aspects of banking are being made more impersonal, and the personal service aspect is being reduced.

## The creation of competitive advantage

### Lower costs

If costs are reduced to a level below competitors' costs and this advantage is maintained, above-average profits and an increased market share can result. Porter and Millar suggest that while the impact of IT on lower costs has historically been confined to activities where repetitive information processing has been important, such restraints no longer apply. IT can lead to lower labour costs by reducing the need for certain production and clerical staff. As a result, there should be both lower direct production costs and reduced overheads. IT applied to production systems can improve scheduling, thereby increasing the utilization of assets and reducing stocks, and in turn lowering production costs.

### Enhancing differentiation

Differentiation can be created in a number of ways, including quality, design features, availability and special services that offer added value to the end consumer. McFarlan *et al.* (1983) contend that IT offers scope for differentiation where:

- IT is a significant cost component in the provision of the product or service, as in banking, insurance and credit-card operations
- IT is able to affect substantially the lead time for developing, producing or delivering the product (CAD/CAM systems play an important role in this)
- IT allows products or services to be specially customized to appeal to customers individually
- IT enables a visibly higher level of service to customers, say through regular and accurate

Minicase

# Minicase 13.7  The Holiday Travel Industry

Minicase 13.6 showed how airline tickets are increasingly available direct from airline call centres and via the Internet. In recent years holidays, especially last-minute bargains, have been advertised on teletext to encourage direct bookings, and the Internet is also becoming accepted as an appropriate channel for customers to use. Both of these imply that the high-street travel agent is bypassed. However, many people still prefer the personal help and advice provided by a travel agent, but travel agencies have increasingly made use of IT to provide a better, faster and cheaper service. A 1999 MORI survey concluded some 45% of people *would* book a holiday direct via the Internet, but so far only 1% had. Digital television will inevitably have a further impact.

## Thomson Holidays: pioneer of it for competitive advantage

The package tour holiday industry is extremely competitive, with pricing an important weapon. The leading holiday companies are vertically integrated and own high-street travel agency chains as well as their own airlines. Thomson, which became the market leader several years ago, believes that much of its early competitive advantage derives from its pioneering of IT-based booking systems, and that further developments with IT have helped it to retain market leadership.

In general, it is difficult to create and sustain competitive advantage in this industry. Package tour companies hire beds and airline seats, put them together, and by adding fringe services market them as a package holiday. Offering better service at airports or a wider range of tours in the various resorts can easily be copied by rivals, and so any competitive edge is quickly eroded. The same is true of different holiday 'packages' such as self-catering apartments as an alternative to a hotel.

Thomson first introduced computers in ten regional offices in 1976, allowing easier access for travel agents. Previously, agents had to telephone one location; now they had access to ten linked centres. The computer generated management information and invoices as well as providing availability data for agents, but the agents still relied on the telephone, backed up by paperwork for confirming bookings.

Thomson recognized that what was needed was a terminal in every travel agent's office, but appreciated that if the system were exclusively Thomson it might be less popular than one that also allowed access to rival organizations. In 1979 they began experimenting (with Prestel), and in 1982 introduced TOP or the Thomson Open-line Programme. Through TOP travel agents enjoyed instant access to Thomson holiday information on their terminal screens, but their terminals also accessed rival and, at the time, less sophisticated, systems. The problem of customers having to wait while telephone calls to check availability ring unanswered because the system is congested had been largely eliminated. This proved particularly valuable on busy Saturdays and enabled Thomson to save on staff costs. The computer could handle both options and confirmed bookings, and customers were encouraged to book because more and better information was being made available to them. The system has been continually improved, and the effect has been reduced booking costs for both Thomson and the travel agents. In addition, the role of the agent has been changed more towards selling than administration. Other operators have followed, but the time-lag clearly proved beneficial to Thomson.

Thomson has also been able to obtain more control and planning information for future capacity planning, and the gradual introduction of terminals linked to the UK in their offices abroad has improved the total service in other ways.

## More recent IT applications

IT has had a major impact on the marketing and selling of holidays because at the booking stage it is information that is being exchanged. Nevertheless, for certain elements of the service, IT has had only limited impact: travel shop windows are invariably filled with hand-written signs for late booking holidays and prices, for instance.

Tour operators move the prices of holidays several times a day when they are chasing last-minute bookings, based on the number of unsold holidays, the current levels of demand and, most importantly, competitor prices for the equivalent holiday. Sophisticated IT systems are essential to facilitate this flexibility. From the customers' position, both teletext and the Internet provide information on the availability of last-minute holidays, as pointed out above.

Some travel agencies provide self-service, touch-screen terminals which allow customers to access multimedia information about holidays and talk to sales people via a video-telephone link. Interactive televisions also offer information about hotels in audio, video and text forms. The Internet can be used to acquire information on airlines, resorts and hotels.

The leading travel agents, including Thomson and Airtours, the 'number two' in the market, have invested in Internet booking systems. In most cases they have bought out small, specialist companies that have been set up independently, rather than start their own.

Travel agencies can print airline tickets directly in their branches, rather than simply order them from the airline who would issue them at a later date. Commissions vary and represent more of a 'management fee' than a percentage commission at a standard rate.

In 2000 Airtours opened a 24-hour telephone call centre in Majorca to provide its customers with help and advice. This will clearly mean a reduction in the number of representatives who tour the various hotels and apartments on a routine basis.

Project: Use teletext to access and evaluate the holiday bargains that are available.

QUESTION: Can you see a real future for auctioning last-minute bargain holidays via the Internet?

*Thomson Holidays*   http://www.thomson-holidays.com

progress and delivery information, which might be charged for

- more and better product information can be provided to consumers.

Most insurance companies quote rates for insuring property and cars partially based on specified postcode districts. To achieve this they need accurate information on the risks involved in different areas and how these are changing. This in turn requires close liaison and information exchanges with brokers. The insurers, brokers and ultimately customers can all benefit as premiums more accurately reflect risks.

Supermarkets began to use hand-held computers several years ago, and these allowed staff to record the current stock levels each evening. Shelves could then be replenished overnight or the next day from regional warehouses. Sales representatives from, say, food manufacturers who sell extensively to small outlets were able to use similar hand-held computers for entering their orders. The computer could price the order immediately and a confirmation was then printed out. Further cost savings were possible where computer systems could be networked. Tesco also sought to establish closer linkages with its suppliers. Orders for immediate delivery were transmitted electronically, although projections based on the latest sales analyses would have been provided some weeks earlier. If supplier delivery notes were sent ahead of the actual delivery these were then used to check the accuracy of the shipment and a confirmation was returned. This represents a promissory note to pay by an agreed date, and no further invoicing is required. These linkages made use of electronic data interchange systems to exchange information. More recently, using the Internet, e-markets have begun to appear and these are discussed later (see p. 503). These developments clearly saved costs and allowed for lower prices, but they also streamlined the distribution network. Fast replenishment meant that customers

should not find that stores have run out of an item; moreover, fresh produce could easily be replenished daily. Overall, the level of service was improved.

## New competitive opportunities

IT has resulted in the creation of new businesses in three distinct ways.

- New businesses have been made technologically feasible. Telecommunications technology, for example, led to the development of facsimile services and organizations that provide fax services. In a similar way microelectronics developments made personal computing possible.
- IT created demand for new products such as high-speed data communications networks that were unavailable before IT caused the demand.
- New businesses have been created within established ones. Several organizations have diversified into software provision stemming from the development of packages for their own use.

There are numerous examples of how competitive advantage has been derived specifically from IT. Debit cards, such as Barclay's Connect, have replaced cash and cheques for many customers; similar to credit cards in format, they allow money to be debited immediately from a bank account. Because computers can store and process information very quickly, they allow the banks and building societies to offer rates of interest which increase and decrease directly in line with the size of a customer's deposit.

The US company McKesson, which supplies over-the-counter pharmaceuticals to retail chemists, used its salesforce to record on a computer the counter and shelf layouts of their customers. This allowed McKesson to pack orders in such a way that customers could unpack them and display them quickly and sequentially.

Most newspapers now enjoy cost and differentiation benefits from computerized typesetting, whereby type is set directly by a journalist typing at a keyboard. The files can now be transmitted electronically via the Internet so the journalist need not be located in the newspaper building. In the case of UK national daily newspapers, and against some trade union resistance, computerized typesetting was pioneered by Eddie Shah, when he established the *Today* newspaper which, after changes of ownership has now been closed down. For the *Financial Times*, IT supports all the share prices, charts and other information included every day.

Most large hotel chains, including Sheraton and Marriott, operate clubs or programmes for their regular visitors. Participants receive such benefits as free upgrades and free meals as well as the programme points which they can exchange later for free stays or air miles. It is quite normal for travellers to prioritize a particular chain because of the perceived benefits of programme membership. These hotel chains typically cover much of the world, and often include independent hotels in franchise arrangements. Loyalty programmes would simply not be feasible without IT.

The US retailer Wal-Mart issues pagers to customers waiting for prescriptions so that they can continue shopping rather than either wait in line or come back speculatively to check whether their package is ready.

In summary, implementing IT for competitive advantage requires:

- an awareness of customer and consumer needs, changing needs, and how IT can improve the product's performance or create new services
- an awareness of operational opportunities to reduce costs and improve quality through IT
- an appreciation of how the organization could be more effective with improved information provision, and how any changes might be implemented. The impact upon people is very significant.

The argument is that competitive advantage can stem from any area of the organization.

## The Impact of the Internet

The emergence and rapid growth of the Internet and the World Wide Web during the 1990s spawned a number of new and very entrepreneurial businesses. It is easy to be seduced by Internet possibilities and, supported by venture capital, many new Internet companies have grown rapidly. Few, however, have turned growing revenues into profits. At the same time, it has also demanded that every organization develop a strategy for harnessing its potential: it will 'not go away' and, for some, will completely transform their ways of operating and doing business. This section briefly explores some of these issues.

The Internet:

- provides information – which can make decision making much easier, but is potentially in quantities so great that it is hard to assimilate
- allows a company to advertise and promote itself and its products and services
- speeds up communication by replacing printed memos and telephone calls
- enables electronic trading. This again can take several forms. For consumer sales, information on a product (such as a book) can very readily be provided, along with reviews; moreover, in the case of a compact disc, sample tracks can be played. Virtual reality can be employed to move people around either a shopping mall or a supermarket.

Minicase 4.1 showed how certain organizations have been able to secure very large amounts of capital to pursue an apparent good idea for an e-commerce business. However, it also showed how volatile the traded shares of these businesses can be as they grow in size but fail to post any profits.

The fundamental principle behind many new *e-commerce businesses* is trading without either manufacture or long-term inventory. E-commerce cuts out the retail store element. New organizations dedicated to e-commerce are similar in principle yet distinctly different from the situation where established organizations (for example, Tesco and Waterstone's) sell via the web as well as through their own high-street outlets. The large retailers are increasingly moving in this direction because of the impact of the specialist e-commerce companies on customer buying habits. While the new businesses may own warehouses for collecting stock for onward transmission and holding limited numbers of fast-moving items, there will rarely be any need for them to employ either sales or production staff, and this element can be outsourced to specialists in logistics, leaving the e-commerce company to focus on creating and maintaining a successful website once the supply chain is set up. Simply, they are a virtual company.

The transaction begins when a potential customer uses a home computer to check out the website of the e-commerce business, selects an item and places an order electronically. Typically, credit-card information will be requested, and an instant credit check will be carried out by contacting the computer system of the relevant credit-card company. Once the payment details have been confirmed, an order is transmitted to the manufacturer of the product in question. If the e-commerce company is holding the product in stock, this would be replaced by an order to the company's own warehouse, who will later reorder from the manufacturer. Delivery to the customer can be direct from the manufacturer or via the e-commerce business who will receive bulk supplies and post out individual parcels.

Their fundamental advantage is their ability to reach a wide customer audience at low cost, as long as they can be attracted in the first place and then retained as a regular customer. Relatively specialist items can thus be made available to people who find it difficult to visit the shops that sell them directly. One key disadvantage is that the goods cannot be touched and inspected, which matters more for some customers and products than it does for others. The main infrastructure requirements for a successful e-commerce business are appropriate managerial and technical skills, venture capital to set up a sophisticated supply chain and secure payment systems. They also need customers who can and do access their site, recognize the convenience and benefits being offered, and believe that the payment systems are private and secure.

Every business needs an Internet strategy; it has to decide upon the extent to which it intends to use the Internet for promotion and for commercial transactions. For many organizations, it is far more important for business-to-business transactions than it is for direct sales to customers.

The ultimate popularity of Internet trading for consumer products remains difficult to predict for a number of reasons. More and more households are 'on-line' but the penetration is uneven. While all age groups are involved, younger people are more likely to use the Internet than older generations. Men seem more comfortable with the technology than women in many cases, and there is a greater incidence when people have enjoyed higher education and have above-average earnings. The geographical coverage in the UK is biased to the southern counties. But this is 'now'. Various predictions for future take-up have been offered and they are not all in accord. Some customers are keen to use the Internet for information gathering but stop short of buying electronically. This is partly linked to a reluctance to input credit-card details into a personal computer.

However, the potential of the Internet to link business with business is enormous and it offers both cost savings and service improvements.

*Figure 13.7* Using knowledge for competitive success.

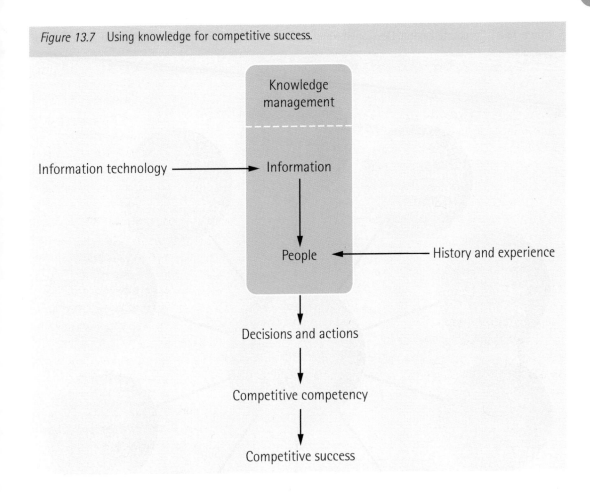

The term *e-markets* is normally used for this linkage. E-markets:

- link computers and databases
- constitute virtual and private networks where companies and their suppliers can share vital information
- allow easy and fast transfer of up-to-date information on current orders, contracts, prices, inventory, deliveries and so on – access can be controlled through passwords
- monitor and analyse activities
- have a facility for transactions
- enable cost reductions together with better information and a faster response time
- allow suppliers to auction any surplus stock, and

- allow buyers to ask for bidders against a special or an emergency need.

## Conclusion: Information, Knowledge and Corporate Capital

Information, then, is required to support the decision-making processes related to strategic change – both formally planned changes and emergent, adaptive, incremental change – at all levels of the organization. Figure 13.7 summarizes the key points. Information, itself supported by IT, is used by people to help them to make decisions. History and experience

*Figure 13.8* Corporate capital. Developed from ideas contained in the 1994 and 1995 Annual Reports of Skandia.

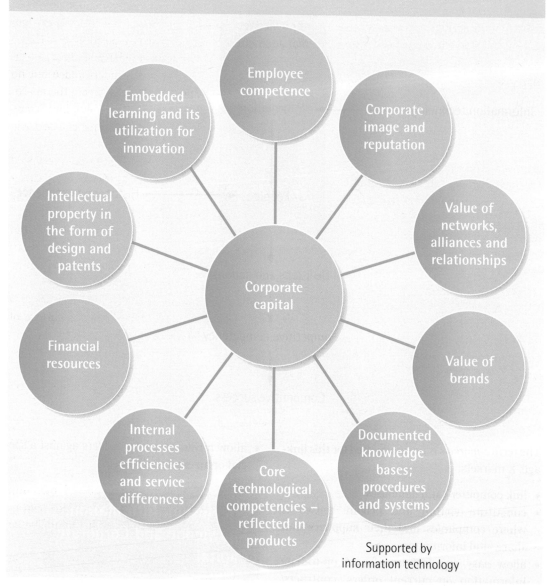

qualify the information and analysis. The information, and the way in which people use it, comprises the organization's knowledge.

Figure 13.8 attempts to draw together those elements and resources which comprise the organization's corporate capital. It is a summary

of many of the points and issues raised and discussed in Parts Two and Three. Part Two opened by distinguishing between opportunity-driven and resource-based strategy. Figure 13.8 is a comprehensive summary of all the resources that an organization possesses and which it should lever and exploit to create and sustain competitive advantage and strategic success. Logically, it can be argued that a company which aims to build and sustain competitiveness and success will audit these elements and use this analysis as a source of ideas for attention and improvement.

## Summary

*Emergent strategy* creation takes two forms. *Incremental* changes happen as intended strategies are implemented and managers learn from their ongoing experiences. *Adaptive* strategies happen when managers, with delegated authority, respond to opportunities and threats in the environment.

Emergent strategies are a reflection and an outcome of *decision making* in the organization. Who makes them? How? Decision making involves two key themes: people and information. Information matters, but it must be harnessed as knowledge.

Emergent strategies imply learning and change in a dynamic environment. Consequently, *innovation* is a fundamental element.

Innovation by managers who accept delegated responsibility represents *intrapreneurship*, with the relevant managers acting as internal entrepreneurs. Here power has been released from the centre and effective control is based on information gathering and synthesis rather than instruction.

Innovation can happen at the product, service or process level. They are all important and capable of improvement. Innovation happens when someone builds value from a creative idea.

However, ideas with potential may look relatively unproven at the outset. As a consequence some large organizations will see the idea as potentially disruptive and thereby open a gap for the smaller business, if it can find the resources to exploit the idea and the opportunity.

People who contribute as innovators and intrapreneurs must be in a position where they feel stretched and rewarded. For some organizations, *empowerment* is a wonderful idea but no more. They find it difficult to create the appropriate climate and culture; their employees may not wish to be empowered to some considerable degree.

Emergent strategy possibilities are enhanced where people work well together and collectively. There is a team spirit, sharing and learning. *Synergy* is the outcome. Extended to the level of the organization, this constitutes a learning organization. Like empowerment, this can seem attractive as a theoretical idea and ideal but be difficult to implement effectively.

The information that feeds the whole process of decision making comes from a variety of internal and external sources, both formal and informal. Formal information systems and *information technology* can both make a valuable input, but information is more than information technology.

However much information they have, managers are still not 'seeing reality', rather they are put in position where their perception of events can be more informed and hopefully more insightful. Because issues of meaning are crucial, it is possible that decisions lead to counterintuitive behaviour with unanticipated outcomes.

Nevertheless, as well as informing decision making, information and information technology can be a source of competitive advantage in its own right.

The emergence of the *Internet* has spawned a host of new businesses. It has also required every company to formulate a strategy for harnessing its potential effectively.

# References

Ackoff, RL (1967) Management misinformation systems, *Management Science* (14), December.

Belbin, RM (1981) *Management Teams: Why They Succeed or Fail*, Heinemann.

Bridge, S, O'Neill, K and Cromie, S (1998) *Understanding Enterprise, Entrepreneurship and Small Business*, Macmillan.

Capelli, P and Crocker-Hefter, A (1995) HRM: The key to competitive advantage, *Financial Times Mastering Management Series*, No 6, 1 December.

Christensen, CM (1998) *The Innovator's Dilemma*, Harvard Business School Press.

Churchill, NC (1997) Breaking down the wall, scaling the ladder. In *Mastering Enterprise* (eds S Birley and D Muzyka), Financial Times/Pitman.

Coulson-Thomas, C and Brown, R (1989) *The Responsive Organization. People Management: The Challenge of the 1990s*, British Institute of Management.

Cummings, TG (1981) Designing effective work groups. In *Handbook of Organizational Design* (eds PC Nystrom and WH Starbuck), Oxford University Press.

Day, G (1996) How to learn about markets, *Financial Times Mastering Management Series*, No. 12, 26 January.

de Geus, A (1997) The living company, *Harvard Business Review*, March–April.

Drucker, PF (1985) *Innovation and Entrepreneurship*, Heinemann.

Earl, MJ and Hopwood, AG (1980) From management information to information management. In *The Information Systems Environment* (eds HC Lucas, FF Land, JJ Lincoln and K Supper), North-Holland.

Forrester, J (1969) *Urban Dynamics*, MIT Press.

Fradette, M and Michaud, S (1998) *The Power of Corporate Kinetics – Create the Self-adapting, Self-renewing, Instant Action Enterprise*, Simon and Schuster.

Gilbert, X (1995) It's strategy that counts, *Financial Times Mastering Management Series*, No. 7, 8 December.

Handy, C (1989) *The Age of Unreason*, Hutchinson.

Hersey, P and Blanchard, K (1982) *The Management of Organisational Behaviour*, 4th edn, Prentice-Hall.

Hertzberg, F (1968) One more time how do you motivate employees? *Harvard Business Review*, January–February.

Horovitz, J (1997) Growth without losing the entrepreneurial spirit. In *Mastering Enterprise* (eds S Birley and D Muzyka), Financial Times/Pitman.

Hurst, DK (1995) *Crisis and Renewal – Meeting the Challenge of Organizational Change*, Harvard Business School Press.

Kanter, RM (1983) *The Change Masters – Innovation and Entrepreneurship in the American Corporation*, Simon and Schuster.

Kanter, RM (1989) *When Giants Learn to Dance*, Simon and Schuster.

Kotter, JP and Heskett, JL (1992) *Corporate Culture and Performance*, Free Press.

Lucas, H (1976) *The Analysis, Design and Implementation of Information Systems*, McGraw-Hill

Maitland, A (1999) Strategy for creativity, *Financial Times*, 11 November.

Marchand, DA (1995a) Managing strategic intelligence, *Financial Times Mastering Management Series*, No. 4, 17 November.

Marchand, DA (1995b) What is your company's information culture? *Financial Times Mastering Management Series*, No. 7, 8 December.

McClelland, D and Winter, D (1971) *Motivating Economic Achievement*, Free Press.

McFarlan, FW (1984) Information technology changes the way you compete, *Harvard Business Review*, May–June.

McFarlan, FW, McKenney, JL and Pyburn, P (1983) The information archipelago – plotting a course, *Harvard Business Review*, January–February.

McGregor, DM (1960) *The Human Side of Enterprise*, McGraw-Hill.

Pais, A (1982) *Subtle is the Lord – The Science and the Life of Albert Einstein*, Oxford University Press.

Pinchot, G III (1985) *Intrapreneuring*, Harper and Row.

Porter, LW, Lawler, EE and Hackman, JR (1975) *Behaviour in Organizations*, McGraw-Hill.

Porter, ME (1980) *Competitive Strategy: Techniques for Analysing Industries and Competition*, Free Press.

Porter, ME (1985) *Competitive Advantage: Creating and Sustaining Superior Performance*, Free Press.

Porter, ME and Millar, VE (1985) How information gives you a competitive advantage, *Harvard Business Review*, July–August.

Quinn, JB (1980) *Strategies for Change: Logical Incrementalism*, Irwin.

Rayport, JF and Sviokla, JJ (1995) Exploiting the virtual value chain, *Harvard Business Review*, November–December.

Roffey Park Management Centre (1995) *Career Development in Flatter Structures*, Research report.

Schein, EH (1983) The role of the founder in creating organizational culture, *Organisational Dynamics*, Summer.

Senge, P (1991) *The Fifth Discipline – The Art and Practice of the Learning Organization*, Doubleday.

Spear, R (1980) *Systems Organization: The Management of Complexity*, Unit 8, *Information*, The Open University, T243.

Terazano, E (1999) Fresh impetus from the need to innovate, *Financial Times*, 25 June.

## Additional material on the website.

In 1988 Peter Drucker wrote an insightful paper on the link between people and information in organizations. The reference is:

Drucker, PF (1988) The coming of the new organization, *Harvard Business Review*, January–February.

For those who do not want to read the complete paper, a short summary is included on the website.

Test your knowledge of this chapter with our online quiz at: http://www.thomsonlearning.co.uk

## Explore Emergent Strategy and Intrapreneurship further at:

*FT Mastering Management online*   http://www.ftmastering.com

*Management Science*   http://www.informs.org/Pubs/Mansci

## Questions and Research Assignments

### TEXT RELATED

1. Think of any example of an emergent strategy with which you have been involved and consider how people and information were contributory to the decision. What were the outcomes? What can you learn from this experience?

2. Consider how strategic changes in one retail sector, from an emphasis on hardware stores that specialize in personal service and expert advice to customers from all employees, to a predominance of do-it-yourself supermarkets and warehouses, might have affected issues of staff motivation, personal development needs and appropriate reward systems.

3. Albeit by rule of thumb, take a team of people with whom you associate closely and evaluate their behaviour characteristics. Where is the team strong? Weak? Do you believe that it is balanced? If not, what might be done to change things?

4. Consider how the increasing utilization of information technology in retailing has affected you as a customer. Do you feel that the major retail organizations which have introduced and benefited from the greater utilization of IT have attempted to ensure that the customer has also benefited and not suffered?

5. Consider why it is argued that the increasing utilization of IT by organizations is a cultural issue. How might managers be encouraged to make greater use of the available technology?

6. How do you personally use the Internet? Do you feel that you are exploiting its potential?

## Internet and Library Projects

1. Take an industry of your choice, ideally one with which you have some personal experience or insight, and determine the main innovations (product, service, process) in the last five years (ten years if you wish). How much of a difference has each major innovation made, and how? How and where did each one start?

2. For an organization of your choice ascertain the range of products and services offered and answer the following questions:
   - What are essential information needs from outside the organization (the environment) for managing these products and services both now and in the future?
   - Where are the limitations in availability?
   - What role might IT play in improving availability?

3. By visiting and talking to staff at an appropriate level and with several years' work experience in that environment, in both a travel agency and a retail store which makes extensive use of an EPOS (electronic point of sale) system, ascertain the effect that IT has had on their decision making. Do the staff feel that they are more aware strategically? If so, has this proved valuable?

# Strategic Alternatives and Strategy Selection

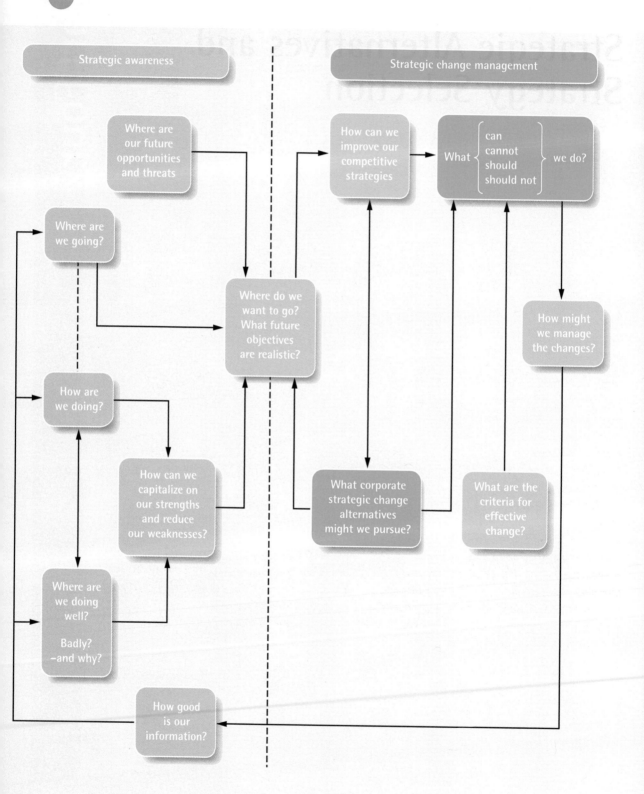

**Strategic awareness**

Where are our future opportunities and threats

Where are we going?

Where do we want to go? What future objectives are realistic?

How are we doing?

How can we capitalize on our strengths and reduce our weaknesses?

Where are we doing well?

Badly? –and why?

How good is our information?

**Strategic change management**

How can we improve our competitive strategies

What { can cannot should should not } we do?

How might we manage the changes?

What corporate strategic change alternatives might we pursue?

What are the criteria for effective change?

# Strategic Alternatives and Strategy Selection

*This part of the book is about choices.*

*Chapter 14 provides an outline of the whole range of strategic alternatives, together with the alternative means of implementing them, only some of which will be relevant for a particular organization at a particular time, although organizations often pursue different strategies at different times. This chapter also contains a section on international strategy. International strategy is deliberately incorporated into this chapter, rather than allocated a chapter of its own, to reinforce the fact that it is not a strategic alternative as such, but, instead, it is a different, and often more complex, dimension to strategies such as horizontal integration and diversification and means such as strategic alliances.*

*Chapters 15 and 16 concentrate on growth. Respectively, they discuss diversification and acquisition strategies and strategic alliances. Chapter 15 introduces the critical debate on focus or diversity, but this issue is expanded later when strategy implementation is discussed.*

*At times, of course, organizations need to retrench rather than grow – maybe, in fact, they have grown too quickly! This is the subject of Chapter 18.*

*Chapter 19 looks at how the actual choices might be made in an organization, taking in decision making and judgement, and offers a set of evaluation criteria.*

*Part Four also includes a short chapter – Chapter 17 – on business failure.*

# 14

# Strategic Alternatives and Market Entry Strategies

*This chapter outlines the various strategic alternatives that might be available to an organization in thinking and deciding where it wants to go, and for helping to close the planning gap. The attractiveness of particular alternatives will be affected by the objectives of the organization. While a whole range of options is discussed, it does not follow that they will all be available to an organization at the same time. Because of the costs or risks involved, particular alternatives might be quickly rejected. The appropriate strategy always matches the environment, values and resources congruently.*

*For many organizations the appropriate strategies will have a global dimension, and consequently a section on international issues is included in this chapter. As shown in Minicase 14.1, Diageo, organizations change their strategies over time, and the corporate profile takes a new shape.*

In their consideration of strategic alternatives, some organizations will be entrepreneurial and actively search for opportunities for change. Others will only consider change if circumstances dictate a need. Some organizations will already have sound and effective strategies that are producing results with which they are satisfied. Others may ignore the need to change. Some texts have quoted the example of the typewriter companies who knew instinctively that electric typewriters, let alone word processors, would never catch on.

Minicase

## Minicase 14.1   Diageo

By the early 1990s Grand Metropolitan (GM) had become the world's leading manufacturer and distributor of spirits, through its IDV (International Distillers and Vintners) subsidiary, and an important manufacturer of foods, particularly in the USA. GM owned Pillsbury, the Jolly Green Giant foods company. The strategic perspective had changed dramatically in the previous 25 years, influenced markedly by three strategic leaders, and it was about to change again!

In the early 1960s, led by Sir Maxwell Joseph, GM, then known as Grand Metropolitan Hotels, was a leading hotel company and was specialized. Through a series of acquisitions GM then diversified into restaurants, dairies and supermarkets, leisure activities, brewing and spirits. Additional hotel chains were also acquired. This external growth activity slowed down in the 1970s because GM had become highly geared and was affected by the international oil crisis and high interest rates. When Joseph retired in 1980 three strategic problems could be identified:

- GM was overreliant on the UK (90% of turnover)
- IDV was inadequately represented in the USA, a key market for spirits
- many hotels needed upgrading if they were to capitalize upon the increase in tourism, especially from the USA.

The new chief executive, Stanley Grinstead, sought mainly to consolidate and build, concentrating on the USA. GM acquired its US spirits distributor, Liggett and Myers, in 1980. Liggett also manufactured cigarettes but the tobacco interests were quickly sold off. GM bought Inter-Continental hotels from Pan American and adopted a strategy of repositioning its hotels. Lower grade properties were divested. GM concentrated on exploiting its major brand names and also bought Pearle Health Products in the USA. By the mid-1980s hotels contributed 19% of turnover and 6% of profits. The breweries were suffering as lager became more popular at the expense of bitter beers.

Sir Allen Sheppard, who took over in 1986, chose to focus on those businesses where GM could obtain world market strength and divest everything else. The major acquisitions were Heublein (1987), owners of Smirnoff Vodka, the world's second largest spirits brand, Pillsbury, whose main brands are Green Giant, Burger King and Häagen Dazs ice cream, and Pet, which includes Old El Paso Foods (USA) and Shippam pastes in the UK. Mexican food is an important growth sector in the USA. After divestments over half of GM's revenue was now being earned in the USA.

The true synergy potential of food and drinks was always debatable – while food is essentially a necessity, drinks are more aspirational – but both businesses feature strong, international brands. GM essentially had developed competencies in people, management and control systems, and operational effectiveness, and used these to add value to its businesses.

Sir Allen Sheppard retired as chief executive in 1996 and was replaced by George Bull, an internal promotion. One year later, Grand Met merged with Guinness, and the group was subsequently renamed Diageo. The name was a combination of the Latin *dia*, meaning day, and the Greek *geo*, meaning world. Diageo therefore symbolized 'everyday pleasure, everywhere'.

A number of important changes happened in 2000. Principally, Burger King (which had been acquired with Pillsbury) was floated off as an independent business, and the remaining food businesses (Pillsbury and Pet primarily) were sold to General Mills. It was then speculated that if a suitable joint venture partner could be found (as a way of overcoming potential resistance from the relevant competition authorities) Diageo would bid for the drinks businesses owned by the Canadian conglomerate Seagram. These included Chivas Regal brandy. In the event Diageo joined forces with Pernod of France to follow up this opportunity. The joint bid was successful, but Pernod acquired Chivas Regal – Diageo obtained Captain Morgan rum and several prominent American and Canadian whiskies.

Paul Walsh replaced George Bull as chief executive.

In essence, this left Diageo more focused as the world's leading spirits business together with additional interests in wine and brewing (Guinness). IDV's leading brands are: J&B and Bells (whisky), Smirnoff (vodka), Gilbey's (gin), Bailey's and Piat d'Or. The merger with Guinness added UDV (United Distillers and Vintners) and the following brands: Dewar's and Johnnie Walker (whisky) and Gordon's gin.

The following time-line traces the main acquisitions (normal case) and *disposals* (shown in italics).

1957  Origin of Grand Metropolitan in hotels

1966  Chef and Brewer (restaurants)

1969  Express Dairies (Eden Vale and Ski products)

1970  Berni Inns (restaurants)

Mecca (including William Hill) – leisure activities (bingo), casinos and betting shops

1971  Truman Hanbury Buxton (brewers)

1972  Watney Mann (brewing)

1973  IDV (spirits)

1980  Liggett and Myers (US) – tobacco plus spirits distribution

*Liggett and Myers tobacco interests*

1985 Pearle Health Care (US) – eye products
1987 Heublein (US spirits, including Smirnoff)
*Beginning of divestment of hotel portfolio*
1988 Pillsbury – including Green Giant foods, Häagen Dazs ice cream and Burger King
1989 Wimpey restaurants
*Mecca and William Hill*
1990 20% stake in Rémy Cointreau
*Pubs put into Inntrapreneur, a joint venture with Courage*
*Brewing interests sold*
*Wimpey restaurants*
*Berni Inns*
1992 Cinzano
*Express Dairies*
1993 Glen Ellen – US wineries
*Chef and Brewer*
1995 Pet (US foods, including Old El Paso and Shippam's pastes)
1996 *Pearle Health Care*
1997 MERGER WITH GUINNESS AND CREATION OF DIAGEO
1999 *Cinzano*
2000 *Burger king floated off*
*Pillsbury and Pet (to General Mills).*
*Spirit brands from Seagram*

QUESTIONS: Is a focused spirits business with brewing interests strategically more defensible than a diversified food and drinks business?
Was synergy between food and drinks – two consumer products sold through overlapping outlets – realistic or opportunistic?

*Diageo* http://www.diageo.com

## Introduction

Figure 14.1 provides a summary of the main strategic alternatives, which are separated into three clusters: limited growth, substantive growth and retrenchment. In addition, an organization can opt to do nothing; and on occasions the whole business will be sold or liquidated.

From origins in a single business concept, market penetration and product and market development are shown as limited growth strategies as they mainly affect competitive strategies rather than imply major corporate change. Invariably they involve innovation. The substantive growth strategies imply more ambitious and higher risk expansion which is likely to change the corporate perspective or strategy. These options, explained below, may involve either a strategic alliance or an acquisition, and these *strategic means* are discussed later in the chapter. It was established in Chapter 1 that it is important for organizations to seek competitive advantage for each business in the portfolio. Consequently, once an organization has diversified, it will be necessary to look for new competitive opportunities, or limited growth strategies, for the various individual businesses.

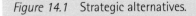

Figure 14.1 Strategic alternatives.

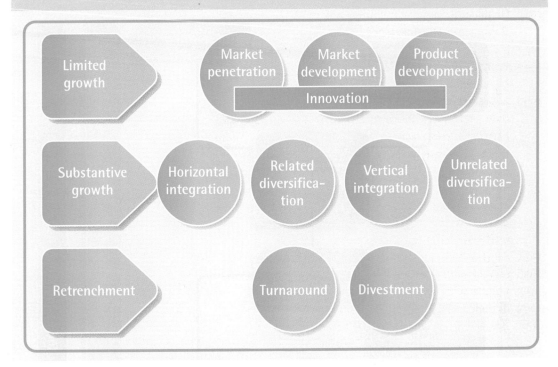

The bottom section of Figure 14.1 shows the main strategies for corporate reduction, namely turnaround and divestment.

Figure 14.2, market entry strategies, summarizes the various ways in which an organization might implement its chosen strategies. It should be appreciated that any strategic alternative can be international in scope, rather than focused on a single country or market, and that as we move from the top to the bottom of the chart the inherent scope, risk and potential benefits all increase.

The choice must take into account the risk that the strategic leader considers acceptable given any particular circumstances, and the ability of the organization to deal with the risk elements. Some organizations will not select the most challenging and exciting opportunities because they are too risky.

The options should not be thought of as being mutually exclusive – two or more may be com-bined into a composite strategy, and at any time a multiproduct organization is likely to be pursuing several different competitive strategies.

Table 14.1 combines the themes of this chap-ter. It provides examples of seven growth direc-tions related to three alternative means of pur-suing each of these strategic alternatives. Many of the examples included are discussed in greater detail throughout the book. The one strategy not discussed in detail here is inventing a new way of doing business. On relatively rare occasions a newcomer to an industry or market will have a disruptive influence through real innovation and, in effect, rewriting the rules of competition. They thus force other competitors into a defensive reaction. While the real signifi-cance of this possibility is recognized, and dis-cussed in other chapters, it is not realistically an alternative open to a normal organization.

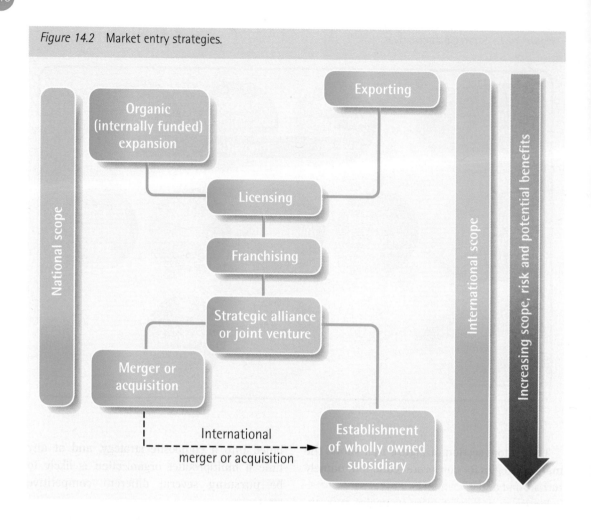

*Figure 14.2*   Market entry strategies.

## Limited Growth Strategies

### The do-nothing alternative

This do-nothing alternative is a continuation of the existing corporate and competitive strategies, whatever they might be, and however unsuccessful the company might be. The decision to do nothing might be highly appropriate and justified, and the result of very careful thought and evaluation. However, it can also be the result of managers lacking awareness, being lazy or complacent, or deluding themselves into believing that things are going well when in fact the company is in difficulties. Doing nothing when change is required is a dangerous strategy.

A company might appear to an outsider to be doing nothing when in reality it is very active. Some companies, for example, prefer not to be the first to launch new product developments, especially if they know that their competitors are innovating along similar lines. A product may be developed and ready to launch but be held back while another company introduces its version into the market. This allows the initial reaction of consumers to be monitored and evaluated, and competitive and functional

*Table 14.1* Examples of strategic growth and change

| | Direction of growth | | | | | | |
|---|---|---|---|---|---|---|---|
| | Inventing a new way of doing business | Market penetration/ development | Globalization | Vertical integration/ diversification | Related diversification | Unrelated diversification | Focus by divestment |
| **Organic/internal** | Southwest Air Amazon.com Hotmail | Toyota (with Lexus) | McDonald's Canon | Exxon (with refineries) Disney (with stores) | Sony Disney (with cruise ships) | Tata* (India) Virgin Atlantic Airways | Hanson Burton/ Debenhams |
| **Strategic alliance** | Benetton and IKEA (with their supply chains) | General Motors and Saab | Star Alliance+ Coca-Cola and its bottlers | MBNA/Co-op Bank credit cards | Nokia and 3 Com (internet mobile phones) | Siam Cement‡ (Thailand) | Yorkshire Water's onion outsourcing strategy |
| **Merger, acquisition take-over** | Royal Bank/ Direct Line | Ford with Jaguar, Land Rover, Volvo, Daewoo | Astra/Zeneca | Merck with Medco, a distributor | Disney/ABC Television Wal-Mart and ASDA | General Electric (GE) and NBC Television | ICI's sale of non-core businesses after splitting from Zeneca |

**Means of growth**

*Tata: construction machinery, engineering, locomotives; Tea (where it has global leadership).

+ Airline code sharing alliance: includes United Airlines, Air Canada, Air New Zealand, British Midland, Lufthansa, SAS.

‡ Siam Cement: also pulp and paper, construction materials, machinery and electrical products, marketing and trading.

strategies reviewed before eventual launch. Timing is the key to success with this strategy. A company will want sufficient time to be sure that its approach is likely to prove successful; at the same time it must react sufficiently quickly that it is not perceived to be copying a competitor when that competitor has become firmly established. In general, the rather more theoretical than realistic do-nothing alternative could conceivably be viable in the short term but is unlikely to prove beneficial or plausible in the long term as environmental factors change.

We next discuss internal growth strategies – market penetration, market development, product development (all of them dependent upon innovation) and combination strategies. It should be appreciated that the strategies described are typically organic in nature (namely, growth from within) and they are not fully discrete and independent of each other. The ideas behind them are closely linked, and it may be very difficult to classify a particular strategic change as one of these strategies rather than another. They can all be linked to the idea of the product lifecycle for they provide suitable means of extending the lifecycle once it reaches a stage of maturity and potential decline. It will also be appreciated that they are the key elements of the Ansoff grid introduced in the discussion of the planning gap in (Chapter 11). At the heart of all these competitive strategies are customers. It is essential that organizations develop strategies for:

- simply retaining existing customers, which may itself require innovation in a competitive market or industry
- expanding the relationship with existing customers by providing them with additional products or services. Direct Line began with car insurance, but soon realized that there was an opportunity to provide home and contents insurance for its existing client base.

Kwik Fit also realized that it had a valuable database of motorists and diversified into providing them with insurance as well as tyre and exhaust services. Sometimes the relationship can be expanded by providing more specialized product and service alternatives to target quite narrow niches

- winning new customers (and hence market share) from competitors.

Consequently, the important issue is the line of thought and the reasoning behind the strategy in question, and the objectives.

## Market penetration

This strategy can have one of two broad objectives. First, to seek assertively to increase market share; and secondly, and more defensively, to hang on to existing customers by concentrating, specializing and consolidating, which implies what Peters and Waterman (1982) designate 'sticking to the knitting' in their book *In Search of Excellence*, which was discussed in Chapter 3.

It involves concentrating on doing better what one is already doing well, and quite frequently involves an investment in brands and brand identity. Although it may seem similar to doing nothing, growth is an objective and there is an implicit search for ways of doing things more effectively. In this respect, and because market environments are invariably dynamic, it overlaps with the ideas of market and product development described below.

Resources are directed towards the continued and profitable growth of a 'single' product in a 'single' market, using a 'single' technology. This is accomplished by attracting new users or consumers, increasing the consumption rate of existing users and, wherever possible, stealing consumers and market share from competitors. The word 'single' needs careful interpretation, in the context of the limited growth strategies, as companies such as Kellogg (breakfast cereals) and Timex (watches) would be classified as organizations which have succeeded with specialization strategies based around a core brand identity. An extensive product line of differentiated brands designed to appeal to specific market segments would periodically have new additions and withdrawals.

At the same time, productivity and more effective cost management can make significant contributions. Sometimes this will be achieved by investing in new technology at the expense of labour.

The two main advantages are, first, that the strategy is based on known skills and capabilities and in this respect it is generally low risk. Secondly, because the organization's production and marketing skills are concentrated on specialized products and related consumers, and not diversified, these skills can be developed and improved to create competitive advantage. The company has the opportunity to be sensitive to consumer needs by being close to them, and may build a reputation for this.

Market penetration strategies generally have a high likelihood of success, greater in fact than most other alternatives. There are important limitations, however. Alone they may be inadequate for closing an identified planning gap.

Whilst market penetration is a growth strategy, the long-term growth is likely to be gradual rather than explosive. This should not be seen as a disadvantage, because steady growth can be more straightforward in managerial terms. Any firm pursuing this strategy is susceptible to changes in the growth rate or attractiveness of the industry in which it competes, and therefore the strategy can become high risk if the industry goes into recession. There is also a constant need to monitor competitors and ensure that any innovations do not constitute a major threat.

This strategic alternative is particularly applicable to small businesses which concentrate their efforts on specific market niches.

## Market development

Market development, together with product development which is considered next, is very closely related to a strategy of specialization. All of these strategies build on existing strengths, skills, competencies and capabilities. Market development is generally another relatively low-risk strategy; and the idea behind it is to market present products, with possible modifications and range increases, to customers in related market areas. This may imply broadening a product range to increase its attractiveness to different customers in different market segments or niches. Clearly, therefore, this strategy is about modifications to strategic positioning. Changes in distribution and advertising will also typically support this strategy.

In summary, the key themes are:

- modifications to increase attractiveness to new segments or niches
- new uses for a product or service
- appropriateness for different countries with particular tastes or requirements.

One example of a market development strategy, then, would be a firm which decided to modify its product in some minor way to make it attractive to selected export markets where tastes and preferences are different. This would be supported by advertising and require the opening of new channels of distribution.

Minicase 14.2, Charles Tyrwhitt Shirts, provides an example of how the Internet is opening up new market opportunities and allowing organizations to develop new services.

## Product development

Product development implies substantial modifications or additions to present products in order to increase their market penetration within existing customer groups. It is often linked to an attempt to extend or prolong the product life-

# Minicase 14.2  Charles Tyrwhitt Shirts

Charles Tyrwhitt shirts was begun in 1986 by ex-consultant Nick Wheeler. The business idea was mail-order shirts and ties for 'ABC1 men' (essentially upper- and middle-class men with so-called white-collar jobs) and it was built around telesales and a warehouse in West London. For each shirt design there were 48 alternatives, taking into account different collar sizes, sleeve lengths and cuff preferences. They were mainly made in Egypt, where cotton is abundant, but also in Portugal and Cyprus.

By 1999, with a small flagship store in London's Jermyn Street since the previous year, sales topped £15 million from 280,000 customers. The warehouse had 3000 lines in stock. The margins, however, were under 10%, relatively low for some retail businesses, as brochure costs represented some 35% of total revenue. Wheeler was publishing and distributing 14 brochures a year.

In 2000 Wheeler decided to switch the whole business from brochure-driven mail order to the Internet. His intention was to grow sales to £100 million by 2006 and to become more global. He also planned to open two additional boutiques in the City of London and in Canary Wharf.

QUESTIONS: Are shirts an ideal product for sales over the Internet? Does such a complete switch of distribution make strategic sense?

*Charles Tyrwhitt*  http://www.ctshirts.co.uk

---

cycle, and typical examples would include the second and revised edition of a successful textbook, or the relaunch of a range of cosmetics with built-in improvements which add value. As product lifecycles contract and time becomes an increasingly important competitive issue, this strategy becomes more significant. Minicase 14.3 looks at how Lego has built its success around constant product development.

This strategy is customer driven. Another example would be a retailer such as WH Smith which relatively frequently changes its product ranges and offerings to provide a suitable and profitable package for its regular customer base. As new retail competitors threaten the viability of certain products, making them less attractive for WH Smith, Smith's looks for other alternatives which will be relevant for its customers.

Toys are less prominent than in the past; in-store travel agencies have disappeared; stationery has been increased; and the ranges of books, music and video have been adapted. Sometimes, as we shall see later, these product line changes constitute a strategy of diversification, highlighting again the fact that these alternatives are not mutually exclusive and some changes are hard to categorize.

Operational issues cannot, however, be ignored. The example of Lesney products and Matchbox toys was mentioned earlier in the book (see Minicases 2.4 and 8.2). In its heyday Lesney withdrew and replaced two miniature car models every month to maintain an evolving range of 72 models. Had it increased the number in the range the production complexities would have threatened both controls and profits.

# Minicase 14.3  Lego

*In a volatile and competitive environment we have concentrated and used our strength to go deeper into what we know about.*

(Kjeld Kirk Kristiansen, President)

Lego, the brightly coloured plastic building bricks, was launched in 1949, and has always proved popular in an industry renowned for changing tastes and preferences and for innovation. On the strength of this one product Lego has become the world's fifth largest toy maker. Lego is Danish, family owned and historically has been relatively secretive, hiding its actual sales and profit figures. The company admits to sales of 10 billion Danish Kroner (£830 million) in 1999.

The basic strategy is one of product development, with Lego developing an enormous number of variations on its basic product theme. By the mid-1990s some 300 different kits (at a wide range of prices) were available worldwide. There were 1700 different parts, including bricks, shapes and miniature people, and children could use them to make almost anything from small cars to large, complex, working space stations with battery-operated space trains. Brick colours were selected to appeal to both boys and girls; and the more complex Lego Technic sets were branded and promoted specially to make them attractive to the young teenage market. Over 200 billion plastic bricks and pieces have been produced since Lego was introduced.

In a typical year Lego has replaced one-third of its product range, with many items having only a short lifespan. New ideas are developed over a two- to three-year period and backed by international consumer research and test marketing. Lego concentrates on global tastes and buying habits. The Pacific Rim was perceived to offer the highest growth potential during the 1990s. 'If you differentiate too much you start to make difficulties for yourself, especially in manufacturing.' Competition has forced Lego to act internationally and aggressively. One US company, Tyco, markets products that are almost indistinguishable from Lego. Lego has attempted unsuccessfully to sue for patent infringement and now views this competition as undesirable but stimulating. More recently new competition has come from another rival construction product, K'Nex, again American.

In the mid-1990s sales were being affected adversely by changing tastes and by the growing popularity of computer games. In 1997 Lego opted for a new range extension. A new kit, especially for girls, was launched – a doll's house series complete with miniature dolls and furniture. Lego also began to market construction kits with microchips and instructions on CD-ROMS. In 1998 the company introduced a new Mindstorms range, built around a brick powered by AA batteries, which could be incorporated into a variety of different models that could then be instructed to move with the aid of an infra-red transmitter and a typical personal computer. Lego had had the technology for some while but had been waiting until it could reduce costs to a realistic level. More recently,

Lego has ventured into the computer games market with CD-based products enabling users to 'build' train sets, vehicles, etc., on screen.

Lego manufactures in Switzerland, Germany, Brazil, South Korea and the USA as well as Denmark, making its own tools for the plastic injection moulding machines. Tool making could easily be concentrated in one plant, but takes place in three to engender competition and to emphasize quality. Lego deliberately maintains strong links with its machinery suppliers. In this and other respects Lego sees itself as being closer culturally to a Japanese company than a US one. Investments in production and improvements are thought to be in the region of at least £100 million per year.

Some years ago Lego diversified with a theme park, featuring rides and displays built with Lego bricks, in Denmark. This has been followed with a similar development on the site of the old Windsor Safari Park in the UK and followed by a third in San Diego, USA. In the late 1990s the UK park was attracting 1.5 million visitors every year.

QUESTION: Is Lego poised for further growth and prosperity with its focused strategy or is it still vulnerable to competitive threats?

*Lego*    http://www.lego.com

Moreover, research and development issues are critical as often new competencies have to be developed.

## Innovation

Innovation is linked to the three strategies described above but it often involves more significant changes to the product or service. As a strategy it can imply the replacement of existing products with ones which are really new, as opposed to modified, and which imply a new product lifecycle. The line which differentiates a really new product from a modification is extremely difficult to quantify. In the case of cars such as the Ford Escort or Ford Fiesta, for example, which appeared in new forms every few years, the changes for each new model were typically marked differences rather than essentially cosmetic. Each new model was very different from the existing model, simply the name was the same.

Similarly, it is important to consider which product lifecycle is being addressed. The Sony Walkman and similar personal cassette players have enjoyed their own successful lifecycle; at the same time they have extended the product lifecycle of cassette players in general. As shown in Table 14.1, innovation can be behind the invention of a new way of doing business.

It can be risky not to innovate in certain industries as a barrier against competition. Innovatory companies can stay ahead by introducing new products ahead of their rivals and concentrating on production and marketing to establish and consolidate a strong market position. All the time they will search for new opportunities to innovate and gain further advantage. Several food manufacturers have utilized innovation to consolidate their market positions as the major food-retail chains have increased in size and power. Not only were the retailers in an increasingly strong negotiating position concerning prices and trading arrangements, they

## Minicase 14.4  Flymo

Flymo was started in the 1960s in the North East of England by a Swedish inventor who adapted hovercraft technology for use in lawnmowers. Initially his Flymos were powered by petrol; the electric versions came later.

The company remained focused on lawnmowers for over 20 years before it added additional, but related, garden products. Trimmers came first, in 1988, designed to capture the grass around trees and along lawn edges more easily. In the 1990s Flymo introduced garden vacuum cleaners, using a design that had been brought to them by a British inventor. The company has, however, continually developed and improved its lawnmowers and has over 70 patents registered. One example of a valuable improvement is the mower that can compact grass cuttings tightly in a box so that the machine needs emptying less frequently. 'The innovation comes from focusing on customer needs, not product features'.

Flymo's design approach is based on teams which embrace research and development, marketing and manufacturing as well as their key suppliers.

QUESTION: Can you think of any sensible new product that Flymo might add to its range?

*Flymo*    http://www.flymo.com

were also beginning to market their own-brand alternatives at very competitive prices. Astute manufacturers have innovated and maintained a flow of new products to retain a competitive advantage by limiting the market potential for retailer own-brands.

Constant innovation is likely to prove expensive, and will require other products and strategies to be successful in order to provide the funding.

Minicase 14.4, Flymo, looks at innovation and product development by a discrete business within a more diversified conglomerate – Flymo is a subsidiary of Electrolux. This case emphasizes the importance of design for competitive advantage. Minicase 14.5, the Swiss watch industry case, might also be considered as a turnaround strategy because in the early 1980s the industry was in difficulty. However, innovation, and the appeal to new market segments

through repositioning the products, have proved extremely successful. Elements of market and product development are included.

## Combination strategies

A firm with a number of products or business units will typically pursue a number of different competitive strategies at any time. Product development, market development and innovation may all be taking place. Minicase 14.6, Honda, shows how three different, but related, divisions pursue different strategies because of different competitive circumstances.

The internal growth strategies discussed in this section are primarily concerned with improving competitive strategies for existing businesses. Such changes may not prove adequate for closing the planning gap, and conse-

# Minicase 14.5  Swiss Watches

In the early 1980s the Swiss watch industry was in deep trouble. Many firms had closed and numerous jobs had been lost. Only the select companies manufacturing expensive and high-quality watches were secure from competition from the Far East, particularly the low-labour-cost countries, and their digital electronic watches. The Swiss watch industry had effectively missed out on the early growth of electronic watches, although the first one was actually produced in Switzerland.

By the mid-1980s the situation had been transformed as a result of the Swatch and similar analogue electronic watches. They were low priced, plastic, reliable and fashion orientated. It has been estimated that in 1985 output from the Swiss watch industry accounted for 45% of world output in value terms from 10% of the volume. The corresponding figures for Japan were 35:35 and for the rest of Asia 14:50.

This required a change of culture in response to changes in consumer expectations. Although there are limited but highly profitable opportunities for expensive quality watches, in general watches are no longer expected to last a lifetime. They are now perceived as a fashion accessory, and consumers buy them more often and replace them periodically or when they go wrong. In the mid-1970s 274 watches were purchased for every 1000 Britons; ten years later the figure had risen to 370. In the USA the corresponding figures were 240 and 425.

Swatch watches, which have benefited from constant innovation and new designs, have become attractive to many new and different consumers. They are now so popular that at leading airports small concessionary units concentrate exclusively on them.

QUESTIONS: Did it make sense for the parent company of Swatch to join forces with Mercedes to design a new compact car?
Could this possibly have been a dangerous distraction?

*Swatch*    http://www.swatch.com

quently higher risk external growth strategies may also be considered. Such changes are likely to involve a new strategic perspective.

## Substantive Growth Strategies

While this section provides an overview of four substantive growth strategies – horizontal integration, vertical integration, related and unrelated diversification – many of the key issues are discussed in more detail in Chapters 15 and 16.

Substantive growth strategies are frequently implemented through acquisition, merger or joint venture rather than organic growth. Franchising can provide another means of generating external growth, but it is only likely to be applicable for certain types of business.

External growth can involve the purchase of, or an arrangement with, firms that are behind or ahead of a business in the added value chan-

# Minicase 14.6  Honda

In an era of cross-border mergers and alliances Honda has made a determined effort to remain independent. In fact, of the main Japanese car manufacturers, only Honda and Toyota are not allied in some significant way to an American or a European producer.

'Success is not related to size – it is about satisfying customers'.

Honda's strategy has focused on related high added-value products from a limited number of platforms. Traditionally they have earned above-average margins for their industries. They manufacture outside Japan, and have significant plants in both the UK and USA.

There are three main divisions:

- *Cars* – Honda currently concentrates on models which have a sporty image and high performance; as well as cars there is a range of people carriers. The strategic focus for cars is *innovation*.
- *Motorcycles* – although Honda has a comprehensive range it is probably more associated with smaller versions. The current focus is on *revitalization*.
- *Power products* – which include lawn mowers, marine engines and agricultural equipment. Honda is looking to *strengthen* its position in these markets.

Honda has developed core competencies in engine technology and power transmissions and has found it valuable (and synergistic) to transfer its learning and technology across the three divisions.

QUESTIONS: Might Honda be in danger of becoming a niche player with relatively high costs in the motor vehicle industry if it remains 'independent'?
Would this necessarily be a disadvantage in an industry plagued by overcapacity?

*Honda*  http://www.honda.com

nel, which spans raw material to ultimate consumption. Similarly, it can involve firms or activities that are indirectly related businesses or industries, those which are tangentially related through either technology or markets, and basically unrelated businesses. The key objectives are additional market share and the search for opportunities that can generate synergy. The outcome from this will be larger size and increased power, and ideally improved profitability from the synergy. In reality, as will be explored in greater depth in Chapter 15, the outcome is more likely to be increased size and power than improved profitability. Synergy often proves to be elusive.

Proposed acquisitions of organizations which would result in substantial market share, and possible domination may well be subject to reference to either the UK or European Competition Commission, or both, which, as discussed earlier (see p. 254), may act as a restraint on proposed corporate development. Certain avenues for growth may in effect be closed to an organization.

## Horizontal integration

Horizontal integration occurs when a firm acquires or merges with a major competitor, or at least another firm operating at the same stage in the added value chain. The two organizations may well appeal to different market segments rather than compete directly. Market share will increase, and pooled skills and capabilities should generate synergy. Horizontal integration is, therefore, concerned with issues of critical mass, which are discussed in Chapter 15.

Numerous examples exist. Rover Cars, recently part of BMW and previously known as Austin Rover, and before that British Leyland, was the result of a series of amalgamations over many years. Such brand names as Austin, Morris, MG, Wolsley, Standard, Triumph and Rover, which were all originally independent car producers, became combined. Jaguar was also included until it was refloated as an independent company in the mid-1980s and later bought by Ford. The new owners of Rover, a financial consortium, are anxious to resurrect some of the older brand names.

In 1998 Enso (Finland) merged with Stora (Sweden) to create the world's largest forest products (paper making) company. Interestingly, the company enjoyed only a 4% share of the global market, although holding strong positions in certain segments, particularly newsprint, fine paper and liquid-beverage packaging board. The aim was to provide a stronger base for expansion in South-East Asia where wood fibre is cheaper than it is in Europe.

In the financial services sector, the National Westminster Bank was created by the merger of the National Provincial Bank and Westminster Bank. In early 2000 NatWest was itself acquired by the Royal Bank of Scotland, but this was a hostile take-over in competition with the Bank of Scotland. NatWest had failed to implement a number of strategies over a period of years and had become vulnerable. Shareholders were promised cost savings and profit increases from the larger group, which would be in a position to close some branches and consolidate overlapping activities. The new group, although operating as independent banks at the moment, is second in the UK for current accounts, sixth for mortgages and the leading lender to small and large businesses. Similarly, a number of building society mergers has taken place. The Alliance and Leicester and Nationwide Anglia are typical examples.

Insurance has also been affected. In 1998 Commercial Union and General Accident merged; two years later the new CGU merged with the floated Norwich Union. In 1997 BAT (British American Tobacco) merged its insurance activities (Eagle Star and Allied Dunbar in the UK, Farmers in the USA) with Zurich of Switzerland. Two years later, BAT's residual tobacco interests were merged with Rothman's to create a company large enough to compete seriously with global market leader, Philip Morris. The larger company might also be in a stronger position to deal with the increasing litigation resulting from tobacco-related illnesses. Also in 1999, the French insurer, Axa (which already owned Sun Life) merged with Guardian Royal Exchange, itself an earlier merger.

Minicase 14.7, Electrolux, is an example of international horizontal integration and it shows how difficult it can be to pull everything together and achieve synergy, despite broadly similar competencies and products.

## Vertical integration

Vertical integration is the term used to describe the acquisition of a company which supplies a firm with inputs of raw materials or components, or serves as a customer for the firm's products or services (a distributor or assembler). If a shirt manufacturer acquired a cotton textile supplier this would be known as backward vertical integration; if the supplier bought the shirt

# Minicase 14.7 Electrolux

In 1970 Electrolux was a Swedish-based manufacturer of mainly vacuum cleaners, supported by refrigerators. A new chief executive introduced a strategy of horizontal integration and acquisition, and within 20 years Electrolux became the world's leading manufacturer of white goods: refrigerators, freezers, washing machines, tumble dryers and dishwashers. The company also owns Flymo (garden products) and Husqvarna (chain saws).

Major acquisitions included:

1984  Zanussi (Italy)
1986  White Consolidated (third largest US producer)
1987  Tricity (UK, from Thorn-EMI)
1988  Corbero/Domar (Spain)
1991  Lehel (largest producer of white goods in Hungary – providing a base for expansion in Eastern Europe)
1994  AEG.

Electrolux bought 400 companies over 20 years, with unrelated businesses and surplus assets often being sold off to recoup part of the purchase price.

Production has been rationalized, with many parts standardized, in an attempt to reduce costs, but Electrolux remains a global manufacturer. Wherever possible the best practices from new acquisitions are shared across frontiers, and clearly Electrolux has faced a series of challenges in integrating the new businesses with their distinctive, national cultures. The integration strategy is based upon speed and the immediate input of a small task force to search for synergy and divestment opportunities.

The ultimate success will depend upon the ability of Electrolux to integrate its marketing, particularly in Europe, which accounts for some two-thirds of the sales. Product differentiation is possible, but the fact that competing white goods invariably look alike in many respects adds difficulties. In addition, tastes and preferences concerning particular features vary from country to country.

In 1991 products carrying the Electrolux brand name were relaunched as a pan-European upper mass-market brand, with new design features and common advertising and promotion. A similar strategy, but with a more down-market image, was to follow for Zanussi-branded products. Local brands have also being retained, targeted at individual country preferences: for the UK this means Tricity and Bendix, and for the USA, Frigidaire. This dualistic strategy, involving up to four distinct brands in most countries, differs from that of Whirlpool, the US company which acquired Philips' white goods business, and is Electrolux's main rival. Whirlpool is more reluctant to differentiate between countries.

In June 1992 Electrolux agreed a joint venture with AEG, a smaller European competitor and a subsidiary of Daimler-Benz. Electrolux then acquired the whole AEG appliance business in 1994. The AEG brand is particularly strong in Germany, and this final acquisition gave Electrolux individual country shares of some 35% in France, Germany, Italy and the UK. The Electrolux brand is most popular in northern Europe and Zanussi in southern Europe.

However, the concentrated white goods industry has oversupply and fierce price competition; in 1997 Electrolux announced the closure of 25 plants around the world and a workforce reduction of 11%. Electrolux admitted that Whirlpool was enjoying higher operating efficiencies because it had fewer brands. One analyst commented that 'Electrolux has been good at acquiring companies but not so good at integrating them into one unit'. While the challenge seemed to be one of reducing the number of different brands, the trick is to find the right number. Whirlpool had attempted to design a 'world washing machine' to a single specification, and failed.

In 1999 Electrolux settled on a reduced number of global platforms. Ovens for much of Europe would be to a common size, but have special features for individual countries. Italians insist on a special pizza setting, for example. Similarly, in France refrigerators have special compartments for fish and shellfish. Figure 7.2 showed how design preferences for washing machines vary between European countries. There are to be fewer brands and the Electrolux name will be featured on every appliance.

QUESTIONS: Are the barriers to global products insurmountable in this industry? Are the preference differences too great to overcome? Has Electrolux found an ideal compromise? Can you see any parallels with motor cars? What impact might the new Dyson washing machine have? (See Minicase 9.1.)

*Electrolux* http://www.electrolux.com

manufacturer, its customer, this would constitute forward vertical integration.

At times firms will reduce the extent to which they are vertically integrated if they are failing to obtain the appropriate benefits and synergy from the fusion of two sets of skills and capabilities. Early in 1988, for example, the UK clothing retailer Burton Group sold the last of its suit-making factories in order to concentrate on retailing. At one time Burton had been one of the leading clothing manufacturers in Europe, but that was before made-to-measure suits were substantially replaced in popularity by ready-made suits.

Backward vertical integration aims to secure supplies at a lower cost than competitors, but

after the merger or acquisition it becomes crucial to keep pace with technological developments and innovation on the supply side, or competitive advantage may be lost.

In 1987 Rover divested its parts distribution business, Unipart – an example of vertical disintegration. Eight years later, after its acquisition by BMW, Rover sought unsuccessfully to buy Unipart back, arguing that it needed to control its parts distribution to support its increasingly international role.

Forward vertical integration secures customers or outlets and guarantees product preference, and it can give a firm much greater control over its total marketing effort. At the consumer end of the chain, retailers generally are free to decide at what final price they sell particular products or services, and their views may not always accord with those of the manufacturer. However, greater control over distribution might mean complacency and a loss of competitive edge through less effective marketing overall. In addition, manufacturing and retailing, if these are the two activities involved, require separate and different skills, and for this reason synergy may again prove elusive.

With vertical integration there will always be uncertainty as the system of relationships among a group of suppliers and manufacturers, or a group of manufacturers and distributors, is changed. It is generally argued that if there are only a few suppliers and several buyers vertical

integration can have significant effects. Figure 14.3 features a system comprising three suppliers, five manufacturers and four retailers, all of whom are independent. The lines joining the boxes show the trading relationships. If supplier C acquired, or was acquired by, manufacturer 5 (option 1) then a number of issues has to be resolved. Currently manufacturer 5 relies exclusively on supplier C. Does it make sense for this to continue, or might it be useful to establish a trading relationship with another supplier (also now a competitor) to hedge against future possible difficulties such as technological change and innovation? At the moment, also, competing manufacturers 2, 3 and 4 all buy some of their supplies from supplier C. Will they continue to

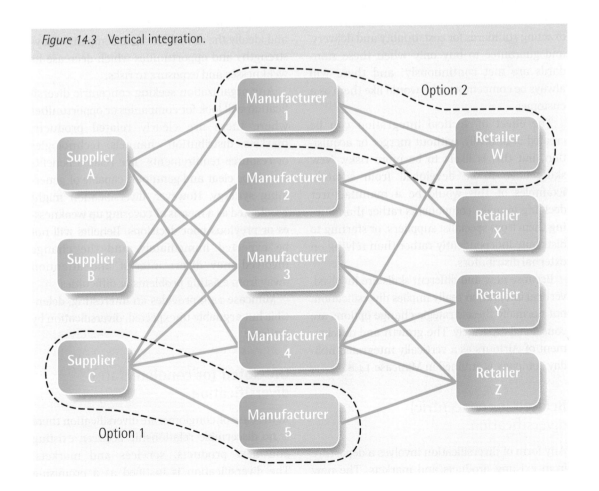

*Figure 14.3* Vertical integration.

do so? If not, supplier C is likely to have substantial spare capacity. Similar issues would be raised by option 2, integration between manufacturer I and retailer W.

Many of the benefits of vertical integration can be achieved without merger or acquisition. Joint ventures, discussed later, are one option. In addition, there may simply be agreements between companies who appreciate that there can be substantial gains from proper co-operation. Marks and Spencer (Minicase 1.2) provide an excellent example historically. Marks and Spencer have benefited from long-term agreements with their suppliers with whom they have worked closely. Many suppliers of a wide variety of products sold by Marks and Spencer rely very heavily upon them, as they are their major customer. At the same time Marks and Spencer set exacting standards for cost, quality and delivery, and guarantee to buy only when these standards are met continuously; and there will always be competitors who would like them as a customer.

The effect of vertical integration can be created organically, without merger or acquisition, but this is likely to be more risky. New skills have to be developed from scratch. Examples of this would be a manufacturer deciding to make components rather than buying them from specialist suppliers, or starting to distribute independently rather than relying on external distributors.

Because new and different skills are involved, vertical integration really implies diversification, but normally these strategic change options are considered separately. The growth and development of Airtours as a vertically integrated holiday company is outlined in Minicase 14.8.

## Related (or concentric) diversification

Any form of diversification involves a departure from existing products and markets. The new products or services involved may relate to existing products or services through either technology or marketing; where this is the case, the diversification is known as concentric rather than conglomerate. A specialist manufacturer of ski clothing who diversified into summer leisure wear to offset seasonal sales would be an example. Potential consumers may or may not be the same; distribution may or may not change; the existing production expertise should prove beneficial.

Similarly, when retailers such as WH Smith add new and different lines and products, they are seeking to exploit their resources and their retailing skills and expertise (core competencies) more effectively.

There is an assumption that synergy can be created from the two businesses or activities; and ideally the new, diversified, company enjoys strengths and opportunities which decrease its weaknesses and exposure to risks.

Any organization seeking concentric diversification will look for companies or opportunities where there are clearly related products, markets, distribution channels, technologies or resource requirements. The related benefits should be clear and genuinely capable of generating synergy. However, diversification might be adopted as a means of covering up weaknesses or previous poor decisions. Benefits will not be expected immediately, and the change involved may divert interest and attention away from existing problems or difficulties.

Minicase 14.9 provides an interesting, defensible but arguably unexpected, diversification by Unilever.

## Unrelated (or conglomerate) diversification

In the case of conglomerate diversification there is no discernible relationship between existing and new products, services and markets. The diversification is justified as a promising

# Minicase 14.8  Airtours

In 2000 Airtours was Europe's second largest tour operator, some way behind Germany's Preussag which had recently acquired the UK market leader, Thomson. Founded in 1972 by David Crossland, who remains Chairman and Chief Executive, Airtours could boast 900 customers in 1980. Today that number exceeds 15 million.

Ten years before, in 1990, Airtours was still a relatively small but fast-growing package tour operator. Based in Lancashire, it offered low-price holidays in cheaper resorts and for a while had a reputation for carrying rowdy youngsters. Most of its customers were based in the north, and Airtours benefited competitively when the impact of the recession was felt first in the south. When bookings fell dramatically before and during the Gulf War (in Airtours' case, by 40%), the company pulled out of selected markets, slowed down its planned move to new premises and froze capital expenditure on new information technology. Airtours was, however, building an airline, and was committed to taking delivery of five McDonnell Douglas aircraft (on lease) which would operate from Manchester (three planes), Birmingham and Stansted.

Airtours successfully predicted the collapse of International Leisure Group, which included Intasun, the second largest package tour operator. When ILG ceased trading in March 1991 Airtours had agents in place in targeted resorts (the Balearic and Canary Islands, Portugal and Greece) who were ready to buy up all of the released Intasun beds. Striking early, and with the Gulf War still an issue, Airtours obtained good price deals. Within just one week Airtours booked 90,000 new holidays and quickly became the third largest package tour operator. The company had no debt. In 1992 Airtours bought Pickfords, the third largest travel agency in the UK with 333 branches, using its own cash reserves.

In 1993 Airtours narrowly failed to acquire Owners Abroad, then marginally the second largest UK package tour operator ahead of Airtours. Together the two businesses would have been bigger than the existing market leader, Thomson. However, Airtours did buy the 214 Hogg Robinson travel agencies to add to Pickfords, giving it number two position in this sector of the market – the travel agency sector leader was Thomson subsidiary Lunn Poly. Pickfords and Hogg Robinson have subsequently been combined and renamed Going Places.

Further acquisitions of small UK tour operators soon gave Airtours second position in the package tour market; the company also expanded in Europe by buying the leisure activities of SAS (Scandinavian Airline Systems). At the time of acquisition, SAS Leisure owned or managed 14 resort hotels and also had a substantial interest in its own charter airline.

Airtours diversified into the cruise business in 1994 when it bought two cruise ships and began to provide its own holidays in the Mediterranean and Canaries. In 1996, Carnival, the leading US cruise company, set out to acquire a 29.6% stake in Airtours, firmly linking the two businesses. Together, as a joint venture, Airtours and Carnival bought the Italian cruise line Costa.

In 1997 Airtours bought Belgium's largest tour operator and continued to strengthen its presence throughout Europe. A year later it took a 30% stake in one of Germany's largest tour operators, for example. Also in 1998 were acquisitions in Ireland and America and of a Glasgow-based telephone sales business, Direct Holidays.

1999 saw a major setback. Airtours launched a hostile bid for First Choice, the fourth largest UK tour operator, but was thwarted by the European competition commissioner. At this time Airtours was credited with an 18% market share, Thomson had 23%, Thomas Cook/Carlson 16% and First Choice 15%.

However, in 2000 Airtours bought an American Internet travel company to complement its increasing Internet booking in Europe. The company has opted not to supply other competing Internet businesses: 'Airtours is only willing to work with agents who can bring something to the table'. The company is also opening a call centre in Majorca to deal with all of its customers and their needs and queries. The company's partial shareholding in Costa Cruises has been sold to its partner, Carnival. Difficulties in its German operations, however, have constrained its profits.

QUESTIONS: Given that for many customers a holiday essentially comprises the sale and provision of a 'package' of services, such as hotel beds, apartments, flights and resort services, how much of the supply chain does Airtours need to own?
Do you see resort-base call centres adding more or less value than the more traditional holiday representatives who tour the hotels and apartments?

*Airtours*   http://www.airtours.co.uk

investment opportunity. Financial benefits and profits should be available from the new investment, and any costs incurred will be more than offset. Financial synergy might be obtained in the form of greater borrowing capacity or acquired tax credits.

The strategy is regarded as high risk because the new technologies, new skills and new markets involved constitute unknowns and uncertainties. Moreover, because the change is uncertain and challenging, it can be tempting to switch resources and efforts away from existing businesses and areas of strength, and this compounds the element of risk involved.

Conglomerate diversification is often linked to portfolio analysis, and sometimes the search for businesses which might remedy any perceived strategic weaknesses. A company with reserves of cash to invest, because it has a number of cash cow businesses, might seek to buy businesses with growth potential in new industries. Some acquisitive and financially orientated companies diversify in this way with a view to rationalizing the businesses that they buy. Parts will be retained if they feel they can add value and benefit accordingly; other parts will be divested. In such cases, the critical issue should be the opportunity-cost of the money involved. In other words, the long-term return on capital employed should exceed alternative uses for the money, including simply keeping it banked! While some companies build up substantial capital reserves to ensure that they have the resources to manage during the recessionary stage of a business cycle – as was the case with

## Minicase 14.9  Unilever

While this case documents one incidence of related diversification, Minicase 11.1 earlier explained how Unilever has perceived a switch in customer demand from products to services.

Unilever, manufacturer of a vast range of household products, has decided to launch a new business, Myhome, a service company whose staff clean houses and wash and iron clothes. These businesses clearly already exist, but many of them are small and local in scope. The UK market is projected to grow to £1.3 billion a year and Unilever believes that a share of 20% can be obtained by targeting some 88 selected areas.

Unilever began by acquiring Mrs. McMopp, a London-based home cleaning service which it rebranded Myhome. This was followed by a laundry and dry-cleaning business in Fulham, London, which it rebranded Persil. The companies would obviously clean with Unilever products! New staff were recruited and a website was set up. Unilever remains comfortable that if targets are not reached it can see a return on its investment with a management buy-out.

QUESTIONS: Does this diversification make strategic sense?
If it is successful, how might Unilever develop it further?

*Unilever*  http://www.unilever.com

GEC under Arnold (Lord) Weinstock – others will use the cash to buy back equity. Shareholders will like to see a company enjoying sound financial health but may well feel that a 'cash mountain' should be used for something! It can be a difficult balance. Referring to points made earlier, where a company is anxious to grow, it might initially look for closely related acquisitions but find such routes blocked by competition authorities who feel that customers might be disadvantaged. When such companies opt for unrelated acquisitions they are very likely to argue that there is more relatedness than in reality there is!

Unrelated diversification became less popular in the 1990s (see p. 566). The real issue concerns whether the strategic leadership can deliver value for all key stakeholders from the diversification. Certain conglomerates such as Hanson (Minicase 22.2) were successful because they targeted underperforming companies and turned them around – linkages and synergies were not high on the agenda. Such strategies are only feasible when sleepy companies are there to be acquired, and this is less likely in a strong economy. Hanson, as a consequence, was ultimately split into five parts. At the same time General Electric (GE) remains a highly successful diversified conglomerate which achieves synergies across unrelated businesses through its ability to operate as a 'learning organization' which exchanges skills and ideas.

Some companies diversify to build a bigger business and thus reduce the likelihood of being acquired by an unwelcome outsider. The argument is, the bigger they become, the fewer companies can afford to buy them. Paradoxically, if they fail to achieve synergy, they may look attractive to an outside bidder who sees value in buying them to split them up.

Diversification and acquisition strategies and tests to establish whether or not a proposed diversification seems worthwhile will be considered further in Chapter 15.

After considering both internal and external growth strategies, the next section describes a number of consolidation and reductionist strategies, primarily for companies experiencing difficulties. Quite often the problems arise because previous growth, diversification and acquisition strategies have been either poorly conceived or poorly implemented.

## Disinvestment Strategies

The term 'disinvestment' is an umbrella term which encompasses retrenchment (consolidation), turnaround and divestment. It is used to represent strategic alternatives where money is not invested for growth purposes. However, the sale of assets or businesses may be involved and money raised from this may well be reinvested to develop or enhance competitive advantage and support those remaining areas of the business which are seen as essential. Where disinvestment strategies are successful, and businesses in difficulty are turned around, money may then be invested for future growth.

In 1990 ACT, at the time UK manufacturers of Apricot computers, were in financial difficulties. The hardware business was sold to Mitsubishi, leaving ACT to focus on their remaining core competence: computer services. Some of the money from the sale was used to acquire a related financial services software company. Rappaport and Halevi (1991) defended this strategy, arguing that at that time the best opportunities for adding value in computing lay in applications. Existing technology had created powerful machines whose potential consumers had yet to exploit.

Disinvestment strategies involve consolidation and repositioning strategies as well as the sale or closure of one or more parts of a business. They are applicable in certain circumstances, including:

- where a firm is overextended in a particular market
- where it experiences an economic reversal because of competitor or other pressures
- when demand declines
- where the opportunity cost of resources being used is such that better returns could be earned elsewhere
- when the synergy expected from an acquisition proves elusive.

Minicase 14.10 covers the demerger of ASDA and MFI in 1987. Although some years old, it is an excellent illustration of the last point. The two organizations had only merged in 1985 and used potential synergy as a justification. In the event the combined organizations were less successful than they had been individually before the merger, or have been since the demerger. This case also illustrates the search (by ASDA) for effective corporate and competitive strategies and links back to the SWOT (strengths, weaknesses, opportunities and threats) analysis of ASDA that we included earlier presented in Chapter 7, p. 266.

Disinvestment can be accomplished through retrenchment, turnaround, divestment or liquidation, and the choice from these particular alternatives determines whether the changes relate to functional, competitive or corporate strategies. Sometimes the term 'turnaround' is used to represent both the retrenchment and the turnaround strategies described in this section; and the expression 'recovery strategies' is also synonymous with both. Where part of a firm is sold to generate funds which can be channelled into areas or business units which are regarded as good future prospects, this too would be categorized as a recovery strategy.

# Minicase 14.10 The ASDA–MFI Merger and Demerger

ASDA, now owned by Wal-Mart, enjoys third position in the UK groceries market. Its real growth into one of the UK's largest food retail chains began in the mid-1960s when it first recognized the potential for out-of-town sites with large car parks. ASDA remain strongest in the north of England; the head office is in Leeds. Its other main retailing activity in the 1980s was carpets and furnishings. ASDA had tried unsuccessfully to divest Allied Carpets in the mid-1980s and instead boosted it by buying two-thirds of Waring & Gillow (furniture shops) and forming Allied Maples, again in 1989. Allied Maples was finally sold to Carpetland in 1993. ASDA's success has been attributed to low overheads, cost control, high sales per square foot and low-cost sites, but it has historically been less profitable than its main rivals, Sainsbury's and Tesco. This is no longer the case.

In 1985, with a welcome bid, ASDA acquired MFI, the nationwide retailer of self-assembly furniture. This represented concentric diversification as, although the products were different, the customer base was essentially the same. Synergy was expected between the food superstores and MFI rather than through the furniture links, as both were professional edge-of-town retailers in complementary businesses. Both were innovators and their management teams could learn from each other. There was an additional hidden motive. The chairman of ASDA, Sir Noel Stockdale, was approaching retirement and there was no natural successor. Derek Hunt of MFI was thought to be an ideal replacement. Hunt became chief executive of ASDA–MFI in 1986, but retained his working base in the south of England where MFI headquarters had been.

The expected benefits and synergy did not accrue. In 1984 the return on net assets of ASDA was 43% and of MFI 38%. In the three years that the companies were merged the relevant figures for the group dropped from 40% in 1985 to 27% in 1987.

In 1987 MFI was sold in a management buy-out to a consortium led by Derek Hunt, but ASDA retained a 25% interest. Since the demerger MFI has acquired its main supplier of furniture packs, Hygena, and this backward vertical integration quickly brought some tangible financial benefits. However, the improvement was temporary, and in the recession at the end of the 1980s/early 1990s MFI traded at a loss. Interest costs arising out of the buy-back and a reputation for poor quality compounded their trading difficulties.

At ASDA, John Hardman took over as chairman in 1987, but he resigned in 1991 when ASDA also started losing money. The losses continued in 1992. The company was trading profitably but exceptional charges were leading to pre-tax losses. ASDA had paid too much for 60 Gateway stores in 1989 and still owned 25% of the debt-ridden MFI. The MFI shares have since been sold, but the Gateway stores were valued in the balance sheet at just two-thirds of their acquisition price. Moreover, ASDA lacked an effective competitive identity and was perceived to be a less successful retailer than its main rivals, who were also proving more successful in obtaining the premium sites for new stores. ASDA had centralized its distribution into a limited number of regional warehouses, but had been a follower rather than a leader in this key strategic development. In 1990 ASDA formed a joint venture with George Davies (ex-Next) in an attempt to revive its non-food activities with a range of designer clothes.

The new chairman (Patrick Gillam) and youthful chief executive (Archie Norman, then aged 37) embarked on a three-year programme which 'would not produce significant results in the immediate future'. Their aim was to turn back the clock and return to 'meeting the weekly shopping needs of ordinary working people and their families'. ASDA saw itself positioned and differentiated as 'the store for ordinary working people who demand value'. The market was carefully segmented and prices made keener; they set out to be some 5–7% below Sainsbury and Tesco to drive higher volumes. Productivity has been improved and service quality stressed; supplier arrangements have been strengthened; and there is an increased emphasis on fresh foods and clothing, where ASDA believes it has a relative strength. There are also regional variations in stocking policy. Norman perceived the increasing success of the discount-price food retailers to be a threat as ASDA has retained a number of small stores in less affluent areas. ASDA decided to convert 65 such stores to a discount format, branded Dales, and to offer core food lines only. (This sector is already very competitive.) The remaining 140 stores would remain as multiproduct supermarkets, but their layouts have been redesigned. The intention is a 'market hall atmosphere' with fresh food, bakery and butchery departments, as well as George clothing areas. By continuing to stock a wide range of non-food items, ASDA continues to differ from Sainsbury's, Tesco and Safeway.

When Gillam and Norman took over, the *Financial Times* suggested that ASDA's institutional investors 'would be persistently whispering thoughts of mortality into the ears of Asda's new emperors'. In the event, ASDA has been successfully turned around. After exceptional charges the company recorded further pre-tax losses in 1992 and 1994, but it was healthy and profitable in 1995. Debts of £1 billion in 1991 have largely been eradicated and ASDA soon overtook Argyll's Safeway to capture third place in the market.

The culture has also changed. ASDA now has a huge open-plan head office and managers are asked to wear ASDA baseball caps at their desks if they do not want to be disturbed. In its attempt to strengthen its customer focus, ASDA has increasingly pushed head-office managers out into the stores. Internal communications have been fostered and a 'Tell Archie' [Norman] suggestion scheme has proved particularly successful. Archie Norman became non-executive chairman when he became a Conservative MP in 1997, but gave this up some time after the acquisition by Wal-Mart. His previous deputy, Allan Leighton, remained firmly in charge. However, in September 2000, Leighton announced that he was leaving ASDA. Was it coincidental that the renewed growth at ASDA had begun to slow down in this dynamic and competitive industry?

[The logic behind the MFI diversification is evaluated in a separate case in Chapter 15.]

QUESTIONS: Why and how was ASDA able to overcome a major strategic misjudgement? Since its demerger, has MFI also proved to be better-off?

ASDA http://www.asda.com
MFI http://www.mfi.co.uk

The causes and symptoms of decline, which determine the need for such strategies, are brought together in Chapter 17, and while this chapter outlines the alternatives, recovery and divestment strategies are discussed further in Chapter 18.

## Retrenchment

Remedial action is required when a company experiences declining profits as a result of economic recession, production inefficiency or competitor innovation. In such circumstances efforts should be concentrated on those activities and areas in which the company has distinctive competence or a superior competitive position. The assumption would be that the firm can survive.

In order to improve efficiency three aspects are involved, either individually or in combination:

- *cost reduction* through redundancies, leasing rather than buying new assets, not replacing machinery or reducing expenditure on such things as maintenance or training – the danger lies in cutting spending in areas where competitive advantage might be generated
- *asset reduction* – selling anything which is not essential
- *revenue generation* – by working on the debtor and stock turnover ratios.

Essentially, the aim is to reduce the scale of operations to a position where the company has a solid, consolidated and competitive base. The key issue concerns how much reduction is needed, whether it is minor or drastic, and how quickly the company must act. It is all too easy to cut back and slim down an organization to a size where is does not have the solid base required for later expansion. It has been downsized but not 'rightsized'. Where any changes are regarded as temporary, it is important to ensure that there is the necessary flexibility to allow for renewal and growth.

## Turnaround strategies

Turnaround strategies involve the adoption of a new strategic position for a product or service, and typically lead on from retrenchment. Resources that are freed up are re-allocated from one strategic thrust to another; particularly significant here is the re-allocation of managerial talent, which can lead to an input of fresh ideas. Revenue-generating strategies, such as product modifications, advertising or lower prices designed to generate sales, are often involved; and in addition products and services may well be refocused into the niches that are thought to be most lucrative or defensible.

Retrenchment, cutting back, is accomplished relatively easily as long as managers are willing to take the necessary steps. As suggested above, the three key issues are:

- cutting in the 'right' areas and not destroying important competencies
- cutting back to a carefully determined core, and then
- creating new competitive advantages to build upon this core and generate new growth.

In 1990 Tony O'Reilly, the Irish businessman and entrepreneur who was, at that time, chief executive of Heinz in the USA, formed a group of investors to buy the struggling Waterford Wedgwood crystal and ceramic products group. Three years of further losses in the early 1990s then preceded years of profit once the business was rationalized with the loss of 3000 jobs. In the mid-1990s O'Reilly felt that he was in a position to set ambitious targets for doubling the size of the reduced business in the next five years. Strategies, which were typical for a situation like this, put forward included:

- expanding core businesses by targeting new markets. Younger buyers, attracted by lower price points, were seen as one possible opportunity, and a new brand, Marquis, was developed to exploit it

- diversification into loosely related areas such as linen and leather products to exploit the company's competency in brand management
- developing the collectability of products such as Coalport figurines. This strategy opened international opportunities in the USA and the Far East
- increasing product availability through more specialist gift boutiques in large stores and mail order
- infill acquisitions such as the purchase of Stuart Crystal in 1995.

## Divestment

Divestment can be proactive, from a company that chooses to follow this route but is not under real pressure necessarily to do so. A successful company may decide that both it, as a parent, and the, possibly very successful, subsidiary would simply be better off if the subsidiary were sold to another company or to its managers. There is no synergy from the linkage.

It can also be more essential and reactive. Where retrenchment fails, or is not regarded as feasible, a part of the business may have to be sold. Basically the organization is hoping to create a more effective and profitable portfolio of products and services. The key problem is finding a buyer if the business in question is in difficulties, and particularly a buyer who is willing to pay a premium price for the assets. This can happen where a prospective buyer feels that he or she has the appropriate skills to manage the business more effectively, or where there is potential synergy with the activities already managed by the acquirer. Management buyouts relate to the first of these issues. Existing managers often feel that they could manage their business more profitably if they were freed from any constraints imposed by the parent organization and were completely free to try out their ideas for change.

Divestment often happens, then, when a company needs to raise money quickly, or when a business is seen as having a poor strategic fit with the rest of the portfolio and, as a result, is holding back the whole organization. Divestments of parts of a business often follow an acquisition. This could be the sale of parts that do not appear to fit strategically. However, it is sometimes a key requirement for the acquisition imposed after an investigation by the Competition Commission.

Where a business is not contributing strategically to a parent organization, but there is no urgent need for cash, it may be floated off as an independent company rather than sold. Existing shareholders are simply given separate shares in the newly formed company, which needs to be strong enough to survive on its own. Organizations adopting this strategy hope to see the market value of their shares improve as the more concentrated business is perceived to be stronger. Evidence of this was seen in Minicase 14.1, where Diageo floated its Burger King subsidiary rather than sold it.

Sometimes companies will swap assets with other organizations. In 1992 ICI swapped its fibres operations for the acrylics businesses of Du Pont, the US chemicals company. This was just one aspect of ICI's strategy of specializing in activities where it could achieve a strong global presence, and divesting others. Du Pont benefited by becoming the leading supplier of nylon in Europe, an area that they had targeted for expansion; ICI moved from third place to world leadership in acrylics, which are used, for example, in windows and bathroom furniture. The strategic changes at ICI in the 1990s are explored in greater detail in Minicase 22.1.

## Liquidation

Liquidation involves the sale of a complete business, either as a single going concern or piecemeal to different buyers, or sometimes by auctioning the assets. It is generally regarded as an unpopular choice as it appears to represent an admission of failure by the present management team, but it may well be in the best long-term interests of the stakeholders as a whole. However, there are also instances where a successful entrepreneur, whose business has grown to a size where he or she has obtained all the benefits that they sought, is seeking to sell out. This can be linked to a situation where there is no natural successor to the entrepreneur who simply wants to capitalize on his or her investment.

This section concludes by emphasizing that organizations change their strategies, either

*Figure 14.4* Changing strategies.

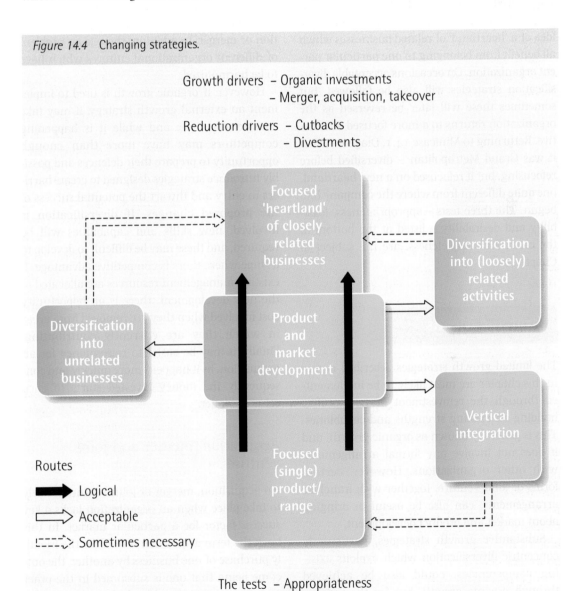

Growth drivers – Organic investments
– Merger, acquisition, takeover

Reduction drivers – Cutbacks
– Divestments

Focused 'heartland' of closely related businesses

Diversification into (loosely) related activities

Diversification into unrelated businesses

Product and market development

Vertical integration

Focused (single) product/range

Routes

➡ Logical

⟹ Acceptable

⇢ Sometimes necessary

The tests – Appropriateness
– Feasibility
– Desirability

regularly or occasionally, to pursue different alternatives at different times. Figure 14.4 tracks a range of possible moves. For many, the most logical strategic choices are built around relatedness and the consequent synergy. The central spine of the chart shows that product and market development are used to extend a single product range while retaining a clear focus. Chapter 22 looks in greater detail at the idea of a 'heartland' of related businesses which all benefit from belonging to one particular parent organization. On occasions acceptable diversification strategies will also be followed, but sometimes these will later be reversed as the organization returns to a more focused alternative. Returning to Minicase 14.1, Diageo – when it was Grand Metropolitan – diversified before refocusing, but it refocused on a new heartland, one quite different from where the company had begun. The three tests – appropriateness, feasibility and desirability – listed at the bottom of the chart for completeness, are the subject of Chapter 19.

## Strategic Means

The limited growth strategies described earlier in this chapter are most likely to be implemented through the reinvestment of past profits, building on existing strengths and capabilities. This is generally known as organic growth, and it does not involve any formal arrangements with other organizations. However, certain forms of joint venture, together with franchise arrangements, can also be useful in bringing about market and product development.

Substantive growth strategies, particularly concentric diversification which exploits existing competencies, could also be achieved through organic growth, but for the reasons outlined below, they are more likely to involve acquisition, merger or joint venture. These three

strategic means are mentioned briefly in this section and given a more detailed treatment in Chapters 15 and 16.

## Organic growth

Organic growth is an attractive option in that it can be controlled and the changes need not be sudden or traumatic as is typical of an acquisition or merger. In addition, there is no problem of different organizational cultures which have to be harmonized.

However, if organic growth is used to implement an external growth strategy, it may take considerable time; and while it is happening competitors may have more than enough opportunity to prepare their defences and possibly introduce strategies designed to create barriers to entry and thwart the potential success of the proposed changes. If diversification is involved, new skills and capabilities will be required, and these may be difficult to develop to a stage where there is competitive advantage. If existing management resources are allocated to the new development, there is an opportunity cost involved when they are removed from areas in which they are currently contributing. Finally, it may be easier to raise money for an acquisition, as it happens more quickly and consequently the money invested starts to earn returns sooner.

## Acquisition, merger and joint venture

An acquisition, merger or joint venture is likely to take place when an organization lacks a key success factor for a particular market. In this book the term acquisition is used for the friendly purchase of one business by another, the outcome being that one is subsumed in the other and over time its name largely disappears. When it was still a building society, the Halifax acquired the Leeds Permanent, and the name of the latter has disappeared from the high street. Where the two businesses in effect pool their assets and retain their individual identities afterwards, the term merger is used. Take-overs are when one company acquires another acrimoniously and often, as a result of resistance on the part of the business being bought, pays a premium price. Joint ventures (jointly owned independent companies set up by other organizations) and strategic alliances (partnerships) are particularly useful where there are strong reasons against a full merger or acquisition. Joint ventures and strategic alliances can take a number of forms. When a group of oil companies collaborated in the development of the Alaskan pipeline to transport oil from the wells in the north of Alaska to the unfrozen ports in the south, it amounted to joint ownership. The strategy was logical: the pipeline was prohibitively expensive for one company alone, and the appropriate capacity was far in excess of the demand from any single company involved. Agreements could concern collaboration on design or rights to manufacture products designed by other companies. These types of joint venture are particularly popular with companies in different countries. Finally, if a manufacturer acquired a minority shareholding in a supplier, this would also constitute a form of joint venture aimed at achieving the advantages of vertical integration without a full merger and the need to fuse two cultures and sets of skills.

Joint ventures with local companies are essential for strategic development and growth in many developing countries, which wish to limit foreign ownership, promote domestic employment and obtain some involvement in industries that operate multinationally.

Whatever the strategic means selected, there are likely to be problems in bringing together the interests, skills and managers of two companies and cultures. The managerial time required to make it work can compromise the value added

and reduce profitability, and divert attention away from other important issues within existing businesses.

## Franchising

Franchising again takes many forms, and it provides an opportunity for rapid growth for established businesses and a relatively low risk means of starting a small business. Service businesses are more common than manufacturing in franchising, and as the UK continues to switch from a manufacturing to a service economy they may become increasingly important. Tie Rack is one example of a retail organization which has concentrated on specific market segments and grown rapidly with franchising. Thornton's chocolate shops, Fastframe picture framing, Prontaprint printing and copying shops, The Body Shop and the British School of Motoring are other examples. Although McDonald's is franchised throughout the USA, many restaurants in Britain are owned by the company. Kentucky Fried Chicken, Burger King and Spud-U-Like, however, are franchised.

A company which chooses franchising as a means of strategic growth enters into contractual arrangements with a number of small businesses, usually one in each selected geographical area. In return for a lump sum initial investment and ongoing royalties, the typical franchiser provides exclusive rights to supply a product or service under the franchiser's name in a designated area, know-how, equipment, materials, training, advice and national support advertising. This allows the business in question to grow rapidly in a number of locations without the investment capital that would be required to fund organic growth of the same magnitude. Another advantage for the franchiser is the alleviation of some of the need for the development of the managers, skills and capabilities required to control a large, growing and dispersed organization. Instead, efforts can be concentrated on expanding market share. It is essential, though, to establish effective monitoring and control systems to ensure that franchisees are providing the necessary level of quality and service.

The small business franchisee needs sufficient capital to buy into the franchise, but the risk is lower than for most independent starts because the business is already established. As a result several small, independent businesses operate as part of a chain and can compete against larger organizations.

## Licensing

Licensing is an arrangement whereby a company is allowed to manufacture a product or service which has been designed by someone else and is protected by a patent. Companies in different countries are often involved. Pilkington, for example, patented float glass and then licensed its production throughout the world. Pilkington earned money from the arrangements and established world leadership; they would not have been able to afford to establish production plants around the world. In contrast, Mary Quant, designer of cosmetics, tights, footwear, beds and bed linen, never manufactured the products that she designed. They were all licensed; and some were marketed under the Quant name and some under the manufacturer's name (Myers beds and Dorma bed linen, for example). Licensing also provides an ideal opportunity for the owners of valuable intellectual capital (such as Disney with their characters) to earn revenues from their knowledge-based resource without having to invest in manufacturing. One argument in favour of this arrangement has been that production and labour relations problems are avoided, enabling the business to concentrate on the areas in which it has expertise and competitive advantage.

Globalization is now no longer an objective, but an imperative, as markets open and geographical barriers become increasingly blurred and even irrelevant. Corporate alliances, whether joint ventures or acquisitions, will increasingly be driven by competitive pressures and strategies rather than financial structuring.
*John F Welch, Chairman and CEO, General Electric, quoted in Fortune, 26 March 1990*

In future we will have local [retail] companies and global companies and not much in-between. Globalization pressures will lead to those who are not in the first division and those who are purely national to make alliances.
*David Bernard, Chairman, Carrefour (hypermarkets)*

## International Strategies

Internal growth, external growth and disinvestment strategies may all involve an international dimension with special complexities. Countries differ economically (variable growth rates), culturally (behaviours, tastes and preferences) and politically. National politics can dictate the appropriate strategy – some markets cannot be penetrated effectively without joint ventures with local companies.

Internal growth might involve exporting to new markets overseas and the development of special varieties of a product or service in order to target it to the specific needs and requirements of overseas customers. External growth can range from the creation of distribution or assembly bases abroad, to joint ventures and licensing agreements with foreign companies, to the establishment of a comprehensive global organization. The latter can be accomplished through both acquisition and strategic alliances.

Kay (1990) recommends that organizations should seek to determine the smallest area within which they can be a viable competitor. While a retail newsagent can still succeed by concentrating on a local catchment area, most car manufacturers, in common with many other industries and service businesses, now see their relevant market as a global one. Diageo (Minicase 14.1) is illustrative of a company which chose to concentrate on products or services where it was able to be an internationally strong competitor. Such companies are hoping to create synergy by specializing in core skills and competencies and exploiting these as widely as possible. The term 'multinational' is generally applied to any company that produces and distributes in two or more countries; a transnational, global, corporation is one that has a large proportion of its sales, assets and employees outside its home base. Using these criteria, Nestlé is the most global business in the world.

Organizations that develop their corporate strategy internationally have to consider in particular:

- marketing and financial strategies
- the structure of the organization
- cultural and people issues.

Before discussing these factors individually, Figure 14.5 endeavours to link them together and implicitly reinforce the notion of E–V–R (environment–values–resources) congruence. The situational factors have to be 'right' for an international strategy to make sense. Specifically, the returns must exceed the investment. This is illustrated in Figure 14.6.

Gupta and Govindarajan (1998) argue that the potential payoff can be assessed by addressing a number of obvious questions:

- Which product lines are (most) suitable for internationalization?

- Which markets should be targeted – and in what order of priority?
- What are the most appropriate ways of entering these target markets?
- How rapidly does it make sense to expand? Does a fast-track approach (such as Glaxo licensing Zantac for production in various countries simultaneously) make more sense than a slower approach (IKEA deliberately restricting the number of new branch openings every year to retain tight control)?

## Marketing

The issue of how global products and services can be made, and the extent to which they have to be tailored to appeal to different markets is critical. Markets vary from those termed multidomestic (where the competitive dynamics of each separate country market are distinctive and idiosyncratic) to global (where competitive strategies are transferable across frontiers). Coca-Cola, Levi jeans and the expensive perfumes and leather goods marketed by LVMH, Moët Hennessy Louis Vuitton attract a global consumer with identical tastes, but they are more exceptional than normal. The challenge to design the 'world car', for example, remains unresolved. Honda initially hoped to achieve this when it began redesigning its Accord range in the mid-1980s, but concluded that international performance expectations, and in turn components, are irreconcilable. In Japan the Accord is seen as a status-symbol car for congested roads where driving is restricted; in the USA it is a workaday vehicle for travelling long distances on open highways. Standardizing platforms and hidden components for different models and countries has provided a suitable compromise.

Different competitors in the same industry adopt a variety of competitive strategies. Some owners of premium and speciality beer and lager brands elect to control the brewing of their product and rely on local, individual country

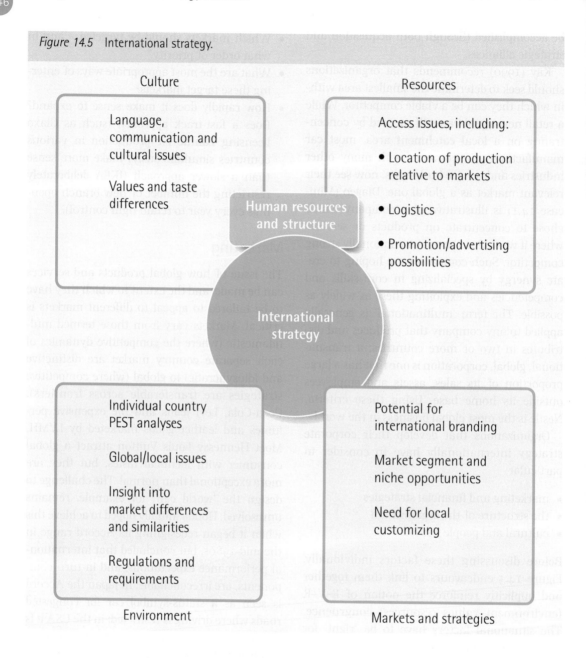

*Figure 14.5*   International strategy.

**Culture**

Language, communication and cultural issues

Values and taste differences

**Resources**

Access issues, including:

- Location of production relative to markets
- Logistics
- Promotion/advertising possibilities

**Human resources and structure**

**International strategy**

**Environment**

Individual country PEST analyses

Global/local issues

Insight into market differences and similarities

Regulations and requirements

**Markets and strategies**

Potential for international branding

Market segment and niche opportunities

Need for local customizing

brewers for distribution, whereas others license the actual brewing to these national companies. Grolsch, recognizable by its distinctive bottles with-metal frame tops, is brewed and bottled in The Netherlands and exported. Most UK premium beers which succeed in the USA are similarly exported to that country. Guinness is brewed in Dublin and exported for bottling in the USA, while Fosters and Budweiser are both brewed under licence in the UK.

There is a follow-up issue concerning the appropriate range of products or services. The framework illustrated as a 2 × 2 four-quadrant matrix in Figure 14.7, could be a useful starting

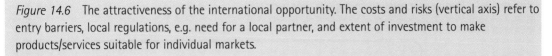

*Figure 14.6* The attractiveness of the international opportunity. The costs and risks (vertical axis) refer to entry barriers, local regulations, e.g. need for a local partner, and extent of investment to make products/services suitable for individual markets.

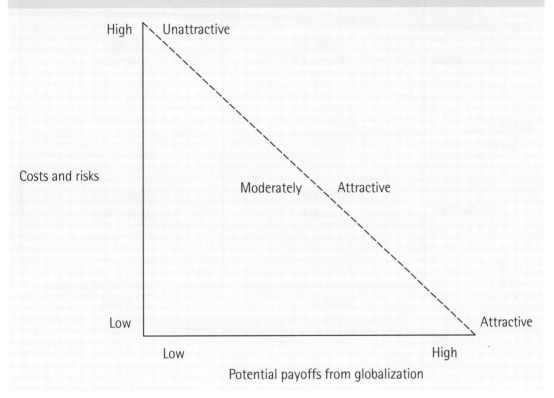

point for analysing both opportunities and competitor strategies:

Where organizations find it necessary to be located close to customers in order to provide the delivery and other services demanded, this can be achieved with strategic stockholding rather than manufacturing.

## Finance

The management of currency transfers and exchange rates adds complexity. Floating exchange rates imply uncertainty, although companies can, and do, reduce their risk by buying ahead. The European Exchange Rate Mechanism (superseded by the single European currency, the Euro) was originally designed to minimize currency fluctuations, but economic pressures still cause periodic devaluations. Predictable or fixed rates benefit, for example, a car manufacturer which produces engines and transmission systems in one country, transfers them to assembly plants in a second and third country, each specializing in different cars, and then finally sells them throughout Europe. Costs and estimated profits must be based on predicted currency movements, and any incorrect forecasting could result in either extra or lost profits.

Where such an organization structure is created, transfer pricing arrangements are required.

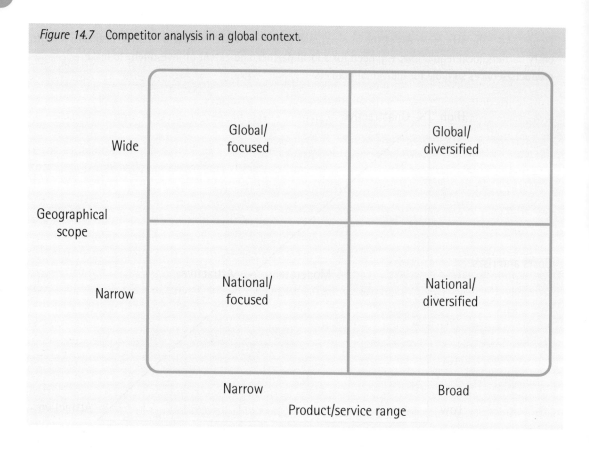

*Figure 14.7* Competitor analysis in a global context.

If managers of the various divisions or business units are motivated or measured by their profitability figures there will be some disagreement about transfer prices which affect their value-added figures. Equally, the organization may be seeking to manage transfer arrangements for tax purposes, seeking to show most profit where taxes are lowest.

Companies with a main base in a country whose currency is strong and appreciating may find their international competitiveness weakened. Exported products will become relatively expensive and competing imports cheaper. Such companies may be tempted to invest and relocate elsewhere. In 1995, for example, Toyota, which already had a number of manufacturing plants around the world, began seriously to consider closing down plants in Japan because of the high yen, an issue which is also incorporated in Minicase 14.11. Companies must also see financial markets as global, seeking to borrow where loans are cheapest, as long as the source is not too risky.

While both governments and companies would ideally like a strong local currency and to be able to export at high prices to earn substantial wealth internationally, this may not be practical. It certainly requires high added value and very clear differentiation.

## Structure, culture and people

The two key questions are:

1. Where to make the various products and services to obtain the necessary people and

other resources required, to be as close as appropriate to each defined geographical market, and to manage costs efficiently; and

2. How best to structure the organization in order to control it effectively but, at the same time, ensure that it is sufficiently responsive to changing environments. The speed and nature of change pressures may be uneven. IT increasingly offers opportunities for more effective control of globally dispersed businesses.

The alternatives are:

- a globally centralized organization, remote from markets, and relying on exporting. This is likely to prove cost-efficient but possibly out-of-touch
- manufacturing plants located close to markets in order to satisfy local needs and preferences. This structure, known as both international and multidomestic, could still be controlled centrally, or substantially decentralized into fully autonomous units, in which case the plants may be independent or co-operate in some way. This is a more expensive structure, but one that can offer higher levels of service. Unilever, which relies on localized manufacturing and marketing, is an example. While cement is an international commodity product, companies are structured in this way because there is no benefit to be gained from transporting cement across frontiers
- centralized manufacture of key components, possibly in a low-wage country, with final assembly or finishing nearer to markets. Caterpillar Tractor utilizes this strategy
- an integrated global structure with production locations chosen on resource or cost grounds. Finished goods will be transported to markets. In this structure the organization will have an international presence, but in say country X its sales could consist mainly of products imported from other locations, while most of country X's production is exported. Marketing, production control, purchasing and research and development will all be co-ordinated globally if they are not centralized
- A global network via strategic alliances.

Centres of excellence may be established where cultural values and behaviours are most appropriate. Philips chose to concentrate technology development in the Far East, where a long-term perspective is natural, whereas IBM has established R&D facilities in Italy, which it regards as suitably intuitive and innovative. However, if national preferences and requirements are markedly different, there is an argument in favour of establishing dedicated R&D facilities in several countries. ICI established a technical centre in Japan for developing special chemicals and materials in collaboration with the major car and electronics manufacturers. The intention was to sell their products to Japanese plants throughout the world. 'Japanese companies prefer to collaborate with chemicals suppliers which have scientists and engineers in Japan, and a factory to produce material locally.' General Motors strengthened its Opel technical development centre in Frankfurt to spearhead its expansion in all international markets outside the USA. Eastern Europe and the Pacific Rim are targets for growth in respect of both production and sales. Meanwhile, Ford has sought to integrate product development globally in its search for a range of world cars.

This alternative has many strategic advantages, but it can be complex to control and costly in overheads. Typical companies are Sony (featured in a long case at the end of the book) and Coca-Cola (Minicase 8.1). Coca-Cola, based in Atlanta, USA, commands 50% of the world's soft drinks market and 44% of the US domestic market. The key success factor is obtaining distribution and access to markets, and because

Coca-Cola is mostly water this is decentralized. Branding and marketing is global and centralized. The strategy is to sell concentrate or syrup to local bottlers, be they independent businesses or joint venture partners. Pricing is based on what can be afforded locally, and a variety of support mechanisms is offered. Coke is frequently promoted with local endorsements, but marketing and advertising also features sponsorship of international sporting events. The evolving international strategies of Matsushita and Canon are described in Minicase 14.11.

The international location decision is affected by a number of key issues, including:

- the existence of any national resources that influence competitive advantage in any significant way. Nike and Reebok have built factories in China, Thailand and the Philippines for labour-cost savings. A number of leading computer and semiconductor businesses is located in California's Silicon Valley because of the pool of skilled labour and acquired expertise to support research and development. Consumer electronics and pharmaceuticals are further examples of industries where the headquarters of the leading companies are concentrated in one or a few countries
- scale economies from key resources in, say, production or technology. Toyota, Honda and Nissan preferred to produce in Japan and export for many years, but the strong yen eventually encouraged them to locate abroad
- transport considerations
- the availability of a suitable supply chain
- political issues.

Whatever the structural format, a truly international business must develop a global mission and core values (such as consistent quality worldwide), and achieve integration through effective communications. The corporate strategy must be centralized even if the company has a number of independent sub-sidiaries and operates in several multidomestic markets. However, the organization must be able to embrace the different national cultural traits and behaviours, and this presents an important managerial challenge. Decisions have to be made concerning the balance of local managers and mobile 'international' managers who are easily transferable between divisions and countries.

Bartlett and Ghoshal (1989) summarized the above points as three potentially conflicting issues which must be reconciled. These are:

- the need for efficiency through global centralization
- the need to respond locally through decentralization
- the need to innovate and transfer learning internationally.

Bartlett and Ghoshal (1992) also reached the following conclusions.

- There can be no such thing as a 'universal international manager'. Large global companies will need functional specialists (such as production experts) and national managers (committed to one country and most familiar with that culture) as well as those executives who are able to switch readily between divisions and countries. International managers are responsible for corporate and competitive strategies within the organization, while national managers ensure that the needs of local customers, host governments and employees are satisfied effectively. The organizational challenge in respect of functional managers is to ensure that best practices are learned and spread throughout the organization.
- The attempts to integrate all of the global operations (products, plants and countries) should be concentrated towards the top of the organizational hierarchy. At lower levels managers should have clear, single-line,

# Minicase 14.11  Matsushita and Canon

MATSUSHITA, whose brands include Panasonic, National and Technics, is the world's largest consumer electronics company. JVC is a subsidiary business. The product range includes video and audio products, electronic components, batteries, home appliances and kitchen equipment.

In the early 1990s Matsushita operated 150 plants in 38 countries including Brazil, the USA, Austria, Tanzania, Malaysia and China. 'The sun never sets on its holdings.' Products are moved widely across frontiers, some even back to Japan, but 70% of Matsushita's employees still work in Japan.

Matsushita has become international for a variety of reasons, not least the strength of the yen, but its growth overseas has been measured and careful.

Initially a plant would be opened in a country to manufacture specifically for that market. The next stage during the 1980s was to move these plants away from merely replicating products designed and manufactured in Japan to the production of variants which had been adapted for local markets. Exporting from these overseas plants then followed. One example here was microwave ovens. European customers like their ovens to finish meat in different ways; the UK, for example, has a preference for crispy fat and consequently needs microwaves with extra strong heating elements. 'It is difficult for product engineers in Japan to understand all the differences and to respond accordingly.'

A further stage involved 'export centres' where all the design and development of a range of products is now based outside Japan, often using lower cost labour. Malaysia now produces 25% of all Matsushita's televisions, and 90% of that country's production is exported, mostly to other countries in South-East Asia and the Middle East. It is argued that Malaysian television plants outperform those back in Japan in terms of both quality and efficiency.

Typical of Japanese companies, Matsushita remains strongly centralized. Subsidiaries cannot deposit or borrow money locally; all financial transactions are handled through a central treasury in Japan. One reason for the caution has been the difficulty in transferring important Japanese values to certain other countries. China is said to be relatively poor on punctuality; the Chinese are not natural teamworkers and do not share their knowledge readily. Matsushita's US employees have very high technical skills, higher than their colleagues in Japan, but they are apparently less willing to take responsibility for changing things and to tinker with manufacturing processes.

Nevertheless, there have been problems and relative failures. Following the lead of Sony, which bought Columbia Pictures and CBS Records, Matsushita acquired MCA film studios and music interests. The deal did not prove successful because of the cultural differences and the real difficulty in trying to manage a business such as this, focused in Hollywood, from a base in Japan. MCA managers were refused investment money to buy either Virgin Records or a stake in NBC Television. The subsidiary was eventually sold to

Seagram. Sony too experienced problems with this type of diversification but was willing to decentralize more power and responsibility to local managers.

Schlender (1994) offers six lessons from the international approach and experience of Matsushita:

1. Be a good corporate citizen in every country; respect local cultures, customs and languages.
2. Export your best manufacturing technology to overseas subsidiaries, not second-hand equipment.
3. Minimize the number of expatriate managers and groom local talent to take over.
4. Allow plants to establish their own rules and procedures, finetuning the manufacturing processes to match the skills of the local workforce.
5. Invest in local R&D facilities to tailor products to markets.
6. Encourage competition between those plants located overseas and those back home.

*Matsushita*   http://www.panasonic.co.jp

CANON has adopted a different approach to globalization. Canon began after World War II, manufacturing cameras. Systematically it has used its technological competencies to move into related areas, each time seeking market leadership for its new product but never abandoning its previous interests as long as they are still relevant for the market. Canon invented the bubble-jet and laser printers for computers; it has also been successful with desk-size photocopiers.

Since the mid-1980s Canon has devolved more and more responsibility overseas. Manufacturing was migrating in any case, as Japan was becoming a relatively high-cost producer. Canon increased the numbers of foreign managers employed to a level higher than is normal for Japan and watered down some Japanese practices in favour of the 'best of the rest'. By the mid-1990s 30% of manufacturing was overseas, with the percentage rising every year. Of Canon's overseas staff only 20% were Japanese.

In 1995, again unusually, world responsibility for key research projects was shifted from Tokyo: research and development consumes some 7% of annual revenues, more than Canon spends on capital investment. The USA became the new base for software research, France for telecommunications, and the UK for automated language translation. Canon's was projecting that some years hence it would have a global set of Canon regional headquarters each with world responsibility for development, manufacturing and sales of particular products. 'Tokyo cannot know everything'. Instead, the role of the head office should be to:

- provide low-cost capital
- move top management around and
- come up with investment initiatives.

Previously, Canon had 'trawled the world' for ideas and then sought to develop them in Tokyo, an approach which was becoming more difficult as the USA in particular was more vigilant to the potential of good new ideas. Canon believes that 'Americans are more creative'.

QUESTION: In the end, do you think that this Canon approach (also favoured by Sony) is inevitable for any company seeking world domination in a particular industry?

*Canon* http://www.canon.com

## Reference

Schlender, BR (1994) Matsushita shows how to go global, *Fortune*, 11 July.

responsibilities and reporting relationships. (This structural issue is discussed further in Chapter 21.).

One benefit of adopting these recommendations is a limited requirement for international managers who, inevitably, are in short supply because of the qualities that they are required to have. Some industrialists would argue that this supply constraint is the deciding force, and that a successful global matrix structure would be preferable. One such structure is described in Minicase 21.4 on ABB, Asea Brown Boveri. ABB's managers are encouraged to 'think globally but act locally'. Their key measure is profitability and this can be enhanced if managers respond effectively to local employee and customer needs, seeking to satisfy different aspirations and requirements, while thinking globally about, say, sourcing and supply flexibility to take advantage of price and currency opportunities.

## Contrasting views on international strategy

Porter (1990) believes that global strategies essentially supplement the competitive advantage created in the home market. Firms must retain their national strengths when they cross over borders. Ohmae (1990) disagrees and argues that global firms should shake off their origins. Managers must take on an international perspective, avoiding the near-sightedness that often characterizes companies with centralized and powerful global headquarters. Markets, he says, are driven by the needs and desires of customers around the world, and managers must act as if they are equidistant from all of these customers, wherever they might be located.

Ohmae is perhaps presenting a futuristic vision of how he believes things will be as global forces strengthen. At the moment, while world leaders such as IBM, Sony and Nestlé are spread around the world, and substantially dependent on non-domestic customers, their underlying cultures and competitiveness remain rooted in the USA, Japan and Switzerland, respectively.

Chandler (1990) stresses the continuing importance of economies of scale (cost advantages with large-scale production) and economies of scope (the use of common materials and processes to make a variety of different products profitably). This implies carefully targeted investment in large-scale operations and a search for international marketing opportunities.

## The Selection of a Strategy

The issue of what constitutes a good strategic choice is the subject of Chapter 19, but it is important here to emphasize that the strategic choices described above may not be real options for an organization at any given time. Theoretically, they may exist as alternatives; realistically, they could not be implemented. Equally, certain alternatives may be forced on organizations.

While internal or external growth strategies might be preferred to fulfil objectives and fill the planning gap, disinvestment strategies may be required because of competitor or other environmental pressures. Strategies are only feasible if they can be implemented; a desire to grow through horizontal or vertical integration, concentric or conglomerate diversification may require a suitable acquisition to be available at a price the company can afford to pay. An inability to raise money for any reason can act as a constraint on a particular choice. If management skills are not available to manage a merger or acquisition it may prove sensible to avoid or delay such a choice, however desirable it might be. Penrose's (1959) argument that growth is limited by the organization's spare resources, particularly management, was discussed in Chapter 3. The ability to succeed with product or market development will be dependent on the firm's relative strength and power in relation to competition; there may be competitive barriers to successful implementation.

Whichever strategy is selected, issues of competitive advantage and implementation become paramount. Chances of success increase if there is an opportunity to create and sustain competitive advantage.

The influence and preference of the strategic leader will be a major determinant of the strategy selected. The strategic leader will also build the organization structure, and ideally the strategy and structure will mould together to generate synergy from the various activities. This in turn will depend upon the organization culture. Hence there is a relationship between strategy, structure, leadership and culture. When there is a change of leadership there may well be a change of strategy and in turn of structure and culture; when strategies fail to meet up to expectations, there may be a change of leadership. Minicase 14.1, Diageo, is an example of a company whose corporate strategies have undergone major changes of direction and focus. The developments can be linked to changes in strategic leadership.

## Summary

There is a range of strategic alternatives and strategic means that organizations might review and possibly choose at any time. Organizations will change their directions and strategies and they do not always pursue the same strategy in the same way. Normally, they will aim to be proactive and purposeful about this. Sometimes, however, they are constrained: an option that they would like to pursue is unrealistic. This would be the case if a proposed acquisition was blocked by the Competition Commission. Similarly, the Commission might insist on a particular divestment in return for permission to proceed with a merger.

Over time, the corporate portfolio migrates. It should be built around a defensible heartland of related businesses, accepting that at times there will be diversification into related and unrelated activities. We cannot finally judge the worthiness of a particular choice until we take account of the organization's ability to implement the strategy that it has chosen.

The key strategic alternatives are limited growth, substantive growth or retrenchment.

Limited growth:

- market penetration, either in a deliberate attempt to build market share or as a form of consolidation to protect a customer base
- market development – opening up new opportunities with different customers, possibly in overseas markets
- product development – extending the range in order to expand the level of business with existing customers.

Substantive growth:

- horizontal integration – generally merging with a direct or indirect competitor, again to increase market share
- vertical integration – linking with another company in the same supply chain
- related diversification – moving into an area where either marketing or technology issues are similar, often by acquisition, merger or strategic alliance
- unrelated diversification – the higher risk strategy involving new markets, new products and new technologies.

Retrenchment – beginning with ideas of consolidation either:

- as a basis for turnaround of a company experiencing difficulties, or
- linked to the divestment of non-core activities.

The key strategic means are:

- organic growth – internal investment to develop new competencies
- acquisition (friendly purchase), merger (two companies simply joining together) and take-over (hostile purchase)
- strategic alliances (partnerships, whatever the form) and joint ventures (alliances which involve a major financial investment by the parties concerned)
- franchising and licensing – two alternative forms for exploiting intellectual capital while minimizing the financial outlays.

Certain of these strategies can have an important international dimension, which brings its own special complexities and impacts upon the structure of the organization in conjunction with the strategy.

## References

Bartlett, C and Ghoshal, S (1989) *Managing Across Borders: The Transnational Solution*, Harvard Business School Press.

Bartlett, C and Ghoshal, S (1992) What is a global manager? *Harvard Business Review*, September–October.

Chandler, AD (1990) The enduring logic of industrial success, *Harvard Business Review*, March–April.

Gupta, A and Govindarajan, V (1998) How to build a global presence, *Financial Times Mastering Global Business*, No 1.

Kay, JA (1990) Identifying the strategic market, *Business Strategy Review*, Spring.

Ohmae, K (1990) *The Borderless World*, Harper.

Penrose, E (1959) *The Theory of the Growth of the Firm*, Blackwell.

Peters, TJ and Waterman, RH Jr (1982) *In Search of Excellence: Lessons from America's Best Run Companies*, Harper and Row.

Porter, ME (1990) *The Competitive Advantage of Nations*, Free Press.

Rappaport, AS and Halevi, S (1991) The computerless computer company, *Harvard Business Review*, July–August.

Test your knowledge of this chapter with our online quiz at: http://www.thomsonlearning.co.uk

Explore Strategic Alternatives and Strategy Selection further at:

*Business Strategy Review*    http://www.blackwellpublishers.co.uk/journals/BSR

## Questions and Research Assignments

### TEXT RELATED

1. For each of the following strategic alternatives, list why you think an organization might select this particular strategy, what they would expect to gain, and where the problems and limitations are. If you can, think of an example of each one from your own experience:

   - do nothing; no change
   - market penetration
   - market development
   - product development
   - innovation
   - horizontal integration
   - vertical integration
   - concentric diversification
   - conglomerate diversification
   - retrenchment
   - turnaround
   - divestment
   - liquidation.

2. What are the relative advantages and disadvantages of organic growth as opposed to external growth strategies?

## Internet and Library Projects

1. What has happened to ACT since Apricot Computers were divested? Was the argument that the future lay in specialist software a robust one?

2. What has happened to Waterford Wedgwood? Was the ambitious growth objective to double the size of the business between 1995 and 2000 realistic? Has it been achieved? What strategic changes – both corporate and competitive – have been employed?

*Waterford Wedgewood*   http://www.waterford-usa.com

3. (a)  What are the essential differences between an export, an international and a global organization?

   (b)  Consider the most appropriate strategy for a sizeable UK-based company with international ambitions in the following industries (assume that your choice could be implemented):
      - steel
      - pharmaceuticals
      - civil aircraft
      - ladies' cosmetics/fragrances.

4. For an organization of your choice, trace the changes of strategy and strategic direction over a period of time. Relate these changes to any changes in strategic leadership, structure and, wherever possible, culture.

5. Sony is renowned as an innovative company within the consumer electronics industry, and its success has depended substantially on televisions, videos and hi-fi equipment. In recent years Sony has followed a strategy of globalization and diversification, arguably in related product areas. The international strategy has been called global localization; Sony aims to be a global company presented locally, and this involves devolving authority away from Tokyo and expanding manufacturing and R&D around the world.

   How does Sony achieve this?

   *Sony*  http://www.sony.com

# 15

# Diversification and Acquisition Strategies

*This chapter looks at selected aspects of growth strategies, namely diversification, mergers and acquisitions. Most diversification by UK companies since the 1960s has been through acquisition and merger rather than the internal creation of new activity. Partly as a consequence of this link between a strategy and a means of carrying it out, it is difficult to separate the key issues and relate them to either diversification or acquisition. Consequently, diversification and acquisition are looked at together.*

*One of the highest risk strategies is diversification through acquisition. Companies who wish to avoid this level of risk can consider alternatives. One possibility is to stay relatively focused rather than to diversify, although this can leave an organization vulnerable; another option is diversification through organic growth, accepting that while this may seem safer it may be too slow to implement. A final alternative is to look for a suitable alliance partner, where the competencies of the two organizations can be combined for mutual benefit, and this is discussed in Chapter 16.*

*External growth strategies continue to be popular alternatives for many companies, particularly larger ones, but research suggests that* they often fail to meet expectations. *Growth strategies need careful, thorough and objective analysis before they are pursued, and care and attention in implementation.*

This chapter explores diversification and acquisition strategies by UK companies, and considers the major reasons why a number are regarded as failures. In addition, it considers how to manage these strategies effectively. The important debate on focus versus diversification in considered but a more exhaustive discussion is left to Chapter 22. Strategies can only be judged to be relatively successful or unsuccessful when implementation issues are also considered. In Chapter 22, therefore, corporate strategy is explored in the context of both the strategy and its implementation.

# Minicase 15.1  Granada

# GRANADA

## Granada's acquisition of Forte

Hostile take-overs had become relatively rare during the recession of the 1990s when Granada launched its unwelcome bid for Forte in November 1995. At this time Forte was the UK's largest hotel group, with a number of divisions and activities. The hotels included Exclusive hotels around the world, the Méridien chain (bought from Air France), the Heritage, Posthouse and Travelodge brands and White Hart hotels. Little Chef-type restaurants and airport catering were the other main activities. Forte's strategic leader was Sir Rocco Forte, son of the chain's founder. He had been chief executive since 1982 and chairman since 1992. The company had recently been growing at a slower rate than Granada and was underperforming against the FTSE index.

Granada was mainly diversified into Granada Television (based in the north-west of England and famous for its long-running *Coronation Street*), London Weekend TV, Granada Rentals and Sutcliffe contract catering. Granada also operated motorway service stations with linked lodge accommodations. The strategic leader was Gerry Robinson, an Irish-born accountant whose first job had been as a cost clerk with Lesney products. Robinson has been described as instinctive and impatient, and under his leadership Granada had outperformed the FTSE index. He was perceived as a success by Granada's institutional shareholders. Granada was run from a small, tight head office of 24 people; Forte's head office, by contrast, employed 290.

Granada stated that if the bid was successful it would seek buyers for a number of Forte businesses and that the intended retentions were Forte Posthouse hotels, Travelodges in the UK and the chain of Little Chef (364), Happy Eater (68) and Côte (30 in France) restaurants. This collection of assets was valued at £1.7 billion and it generated 80% of Forte's profits. Heritage and White Hart hotels might also be retained; a decision would be taken later. Forte's shareholding in the Savoy, a hotel that it wished to acquire but where it had so far been thwarted, would also be sold.

Forte's defence against the bid was comprehensive:

- Future profit forecasts were raised.
- The hotels were revalued at £3.35 billion – a figure higher than Granada's £3.26 billion bid.
- A share buy-back was proposed at a premium on the current price.
- A dividend increase of 20% for the next three years was promised.

Shortly after the bid, Forte also sold its wine and spirits distribution business, Lillywhite's sports retail store and 490 Travelodges in the USA. It sought buyers for its Savoy shares, the airport catering and White Hart hotels, and later agreed to sell the UK Travelodges and Little Chef-type restaurants to Whitbread if Forte's bid failed. Granada had applied to the UK Take-over Panel to restrain further asset sales during the period of the bid. Forte also announced Britain's largest ever share repurchase, again if the bid failed. Forte was looking to refocus on its core competency in hotels and retain the Exclusive, Méridien, Heritage and Posthouse brands. The company was credited with a creative and positive defence strategy, but maybe the divestments were coming too late.

Granada's initial bid was increased in January 1996 to a figure equivalent to a 35% premium on the share price prior to the initial bid. The offer was a mixture of shares and cash, fully underwritten by a cash alternative. The additional amount represented a special dividend to be paid out of Forte's own assets. The outcome depended upon the attitude of a number of City institutions, many of whom held shares in both organizations. A key player, and one of the last to announce its decision, was Mercury Asset Management (MAM), a shareholder in Granada which also owned 14% of Forte. MAM backed Granada and the bid succeeded.

Granada finally paid £3.9 billion to acquire Forte. Its new balance sheet showed £3.5 billion debt. Granada urgently needed to dispose of some Forte assets to raise cash and then to generate a positive cash flow from the businesses that it retained.

Sir Rocco Forte immediately announced that he was putting together a consortium to try and buy back Forte's Exclusive, Méridien and Heritage hotels; however, he later withdrew.

## Granada after the merger

In 1996 it was being speculated that Granada might be split into two separate businesses: television and media (with rentals a possible disposal), and hotels and catering. This was subsequently ruled out by Granada.

Granada abandoned the Forte structure of multiple business units for the hotels. It reduced a portfolio of 11 discrete units to three geographical divisions, based on London, the rest of the UK and the rest of the world. Granada did succeed in selling some of the hotels that it had targeted for disposal, but by no means all of them. It refocused on three brands: Posthouse, Travelodge and Le Méridien, into which it incorporated all of its four-star hotels. Heritage hotels were retained, as no buyer was found. In addition, this part of Granada included Little Chef, motorway services and Sutcliffe catering.

The remaining part of the group, Granada Media, acquired additional independent UK television franchises, namely Yorkshire, Tyne Tees and Border. It also sold its stake in BSkyB in order to establish a digital television joint venture with rival independent television broadcaster, Carlton Communications.

## Acquisitions and splitting up

In 2000 Granada announced that it was merging with Compass Catering, a company with a strong presence in canteen vending services and outsource catering for businesses. Compass also owned a number of restaurants. Gerry Robinson knew Compass – in the 1980s he had led a management buy-out of the business from Grand Metropolitan. Since this buy-out the company had expanded dramatically to become one of only two truly global catering businesses.

Shortly afterwards, Granada Media was spun off as a separate business, led by Charles Allen, previously deputy to Robinson. During summer 2000 the Department of Trade and Industry (DTI) relaxed its rules on the ownership of independent television franchises. It was willing to allow further acquisitions as long as at least two major players remained – this ruling recognized the increasing threat of cable and satellite broadcasters. However, an investigation between a proposed merger of the two other main players, Carlton and United News & Media, required the divestment of UNM's Meridian, the franchise for the south-east. The two abandoned their plans and Granada bid for UNM. This time the requirement would be the divestment of the strategically less important HTV, the franchise for Wales. Granada was basically acquiring Meridian and Anglia Television. The general assumption at the time was that the DTI rules would later be relaxed further and Granada would absorb Carlton as well.

Towards the end of the year, with its shares underperforming against the FTSE index, Granada Compass announced it was auctioning off all of its hotels with the exception of Travelodge. It hoped to raise £3.5 billion.

QUESTIONS: Assume that you are a hotel manager who began with Forte before the acquisition by Granada – how do feel your life might have changed?
Do you think you would better off or worse off?

*Forte*   http://www.forte-hotels.com
*Granada Food Services*   http://www.granadafoodservices.co.uk
*Granada Media*   http://www.granadamedia.com
*Granada Rental*   http://www.box-clever.com
*Granada Television*   http://www.g-wizz.net

## Introduction: To Diversify or Not – and How

The introduction to this topic begins by defining key terms and looking at diversification and acquisition in a wider context.

Figure 15.1 demonstrates that the growth challenge is to find opportunities for developing and deploying technologies, processes and competencies in ways that generate a more effective and beneficial match between the organization's products and services and its customers and markets. Some of the key themes are:

*Figure 15.1* The growth challenge.

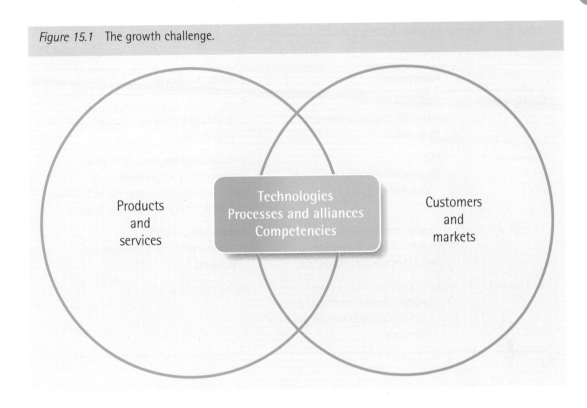

- the potential for synergy from internal and external linkages and alliances
- the diversification/focus dilemma
- opportunities for, and abilities in, transferring skills and competencies
- opportunities to benefit from the exploitation of a successful corporate brand name.

Table 15.1 provides a brief summary of the advantages and drawbacks of the main growth options, namely:

- organic growth — growth from within, utilizing the organization's own resources and developing new competencies as required
- acquisitions — an umbrella term to encompass the friendly purchase of one company by another, an unfriendly purchase (a take-over) and a straightforward merger of the assets of two or more organizations
- strategic alliances — some form of agreement between two or more companies
- joint ventures — alliances, but where there is the exchange of minority shareholdings between the companies involved or the establishment of an independent company, jointly owned by the organizations who start it.

A merger of two organizations will always be agreed mutually, and in some cases acquisition of one firm by another is friendly and agreed. In other cases proposed acquisitions are opposed and fought bitterly by managers in the

*Table 15.1* Alternative growth strategies

|  | Advantages | Possible drawbacks |
| --- | --- | --- |
| Organic growth | Lower risk<br>Allows for ongoing learning<br>More control | Slow<br>Lack of early knowledge – may be misjudgements |
| Acquisition | Fast<br>Buys presence, market share and expertise | Premium price may have to be paid<br>High risk if any misjudgement<br>Preferred organization may not be available<br>May be difficult to sell unwanted assets |
| Strategic alliance | Cheaper than take-over<br>Access to market knowledge<br>Useful if acquisition impractical | Possible lack of control<br>Potential managerial differences and problems |
| Joint venture | As for strategic alliance plus:<br>greater incentive and closer contact<br>can lock out other competitors more effectively | As for strategic alliance |

threatened firm who try to persuade their shareholders that the company would be better off remaining under their control. These are referred to as take-overs; and when the bid succeeds a premium price is often paid. Although not all acquisitions are aimed at bringing about diversification, the majority appears to represent some form of diversification, related or unrelated.

There is another important reason, a financial one, for differentiating between the types of acquisition. When a business is acquired by another, be it in a friendly or hostile manner, the assets of the acquired business are revalued before they are absorbed into the balance sheet of the acquirer. Any difference between the new valuation and the price paid to buy the business would be reflected in the value of goodwill. Because of this revaluation and possible price premium, the capital employed of the acquiring business may increase quite substantially, and in turn affect (detrimentally) its profitability

ratios and return on capital employed for a number of years into the future. In a merger situation, no price is paid and therefore the assets of the two businesses are simply pooled together. Wherever they can, businesses will seek to treat any form of acquisition as a merger for the balance sheet.

Many acquisitions and mergers lead to disappointing results: profitability is reduced and synergy does not emerge. It is difficult to predict success or failure in advance, as issues of both strategy creation and implementation are involved. Changes in corporate strategy are generally more unpredictable and risky than those that concentrate on improving competitive and functional strategies. However, growth opportunities for the present products and markets may be limited and insufficient to fill the planning gap. Few products and ideas cannot be copied and so a company must build and retain a superior competitive position. Experience, applied properly, is of great importance in this.

Nevertheless, well-executed acquisitions and diversifications can be sound and very good strategic moves. However, some organizations will turn to strategic alliances or joint ventures as an alternative approach in their attempt to achieve the potential benefits, but avoid some of the potential drawbacks, of acquisitions. In Chapter 16 it is shown that strategic alliances bring their own problems and challenges.

Minicase 15.1 brings out a number of these issues. The acquisition of Forte represented diversification; the approach was hostile but successful. The subsequent divestment of assets was less extensive than had been predicted and some analysts quickly began to suggest that the new Granada should be split up. The hotel and catering businesses have now been separated from Granada's media activities, which are being expanded with related acquisitions in a changing legislative and competitive environment.

## The increasing tendency to diversify

Some years ago, Channon (1983) analysed the extent to which the largest firms in the UK had become increasingly diversified over a 30 year period from the early 1950s. He used the *Times* Top 200 companies as his database and categorized them as follows:

- *single-product companies* – Not less than 95% of sales derived from one basic business
- *dominant-product companies* – More than 70%, but less than 95%, of sales from one major business
- *related-product companies* – Companies whose sales are distributed among a series of *related* businesses, where no single business accounts for 70% of sales. This would include companies who had pursued strategies of vertical or horizontal integration or concentric diversification
- *conglomerate/unrelated-product companies* – Companies whose sales are distributed amongst a series of *unrelated* businesses,

again where no single business accounts for 70% of sales.

Channon contends that typically a company would start life as a single-product enterprise and then graduate through the dominant-product stage to become a related business, before finally emerging into a conglomerate. However, he emphasizes that companies do not have to follow this particular growth pattern. Some will miss one or more of the natural stages; others will choose to stay in one form and not change.

Table 15.2 illustrates the changes in the structure of the largest UK enterprises between 1950 and 1980, and compares the structural patterns with those of the largest 500 US companies in 1970 and 1980. Utilizing data from Dyas and Thanheiser (1976), some historical comparisons with French and German companies in 1970 are also provided.

In 1950 only 25% of the top 200 companies in the UK had become diversified to the related or unrelated stage, and of these only 5% were classified as conglomerates. By 1980 the respective percentages had increased steadily to 65 and 17%. This compares with percentages of 78% and 24% for the largest 500 companies in the USA. Over the same period the number of concentrated single product companies had declined from 35 to 8%.

In contrast with 1970 UK figures of 60% (related and unrelated) and 11% (conglomerate/unrelated) the respective figures for France were 52 and 10%, and for Germany 56 and 18%.

During the late 1980s and 1990s conglomerate diversification has decreased in popularity, and instead companies have sought to grow in related areas where skills and competencies are more clearly transferable. Acquirers now typically seek to avoid diversifications that are unrelated to their basic businesses on more than one of the following dimensions: geography, technology, type of product/market or service/market, and the style of corporate parenting required (i.e. cultural and leadership issues).

*Table 15.2*    Diversification by UK and international companies

| | UK Percentage of top 200 companies | | | | International comparisons | | | |
|---|---|---|---|---|---|---|---|---|
| | | | | | France, percentage of top 100 | Germany, percentage of top 100 | USA percentage of top 500 | |
| | 1950 | 1960 | 1970 | 1980 | 1970 | 1970 | 1970 | 1980 |
| Single | 35 | 20 | 11 | 8 | 16 | 22 | 10 | 0 |
| Dominant | 40 | 43 | 29 | 27 | 32 | 22 | 41 | 22 |
| Related | 20 | 28 | 49 | 48 | 42 | 38 | 36 | 54 |
| Conglomerate/unrelated | 5 | 9 | 11 | 17 | 10 | 18 | 13 | 24 |

Sources: Channon, DF (1983) *Strategy and Structure in British Industry*, Macmillan; Dyas, GP and Thanheiser, HT (1976) *The Emerging European Enterprise: Strategy and Structure in French and German Industry*, Macmillan.

The minimum scale for effective survival is always rising. A niche can easily become a tomb.

*Lord Weinstock, when Chief Executive, GEC*

## Critical mass

As markets and industries become increasingly global a certain minimum size and market share is often thought to be necessary for competitive viability. This is known as critical mass and it is one explanation for the growing incidence of mergers and alliances between related and competing organizations. Critical mass is important to ensure that:

- there is sufficient investment in R&D to keep pace with the market leader
- the important cost benefits of the experience curve can be achieved
- marketing activities achieve visibility and a competitive presence. This might require a wide product range and good coverage globally.

Lloyds Bank has systematically acquired fellow organizations TSB, the Cheltenham and Gloucester (C&G) Building Society and Scottish Widows (life insurance) to give it a comprehensive geographical coverage in UK financial services; critical mass and cost-reduction opportunities were used to justify the acquisitions. The new company is one of the top three in all of the financial services sectors that it targets. Mortgages are now marketed through C&G; Lloyds was already strong in this segment. Lloyds is also a key player in the small business lending market and TSB is very popular with savers. TSB included an important insurance underwriting business to merge with Lloyds Abbey Life.

Box 15.1 discusses critical mass in greater detail and provides additional examples from the global oil industry.

As stated at the beginning of this chapter, much of the post-World War II growth and diversification by UK companies has been brought about by merger and acquisition. Some of this has been outside the UK, for a long time, mostly in the USA. Statistics from JP Mervis, London-based corporate finance advisers, suggest that,

## DISCUSSION – Box 15.1
## The Significance of Critical Mass

### The reality

The current trend is for horizontal and cross-border integrations:

- to establish critical mass and as
- industry rationalization to create global players.

*Examples:*

- Airbus (combining the relevant British, French and German interests to create a single business that can compete with Boeing)
- pharmaceuticals companies (as shown in Chapter 7 and prompted by high research costs)
- banking – NatWest's acquisition by the Royal Bank of Scotland for cost-saving potential
- Vodafone/Mannesmann – for European/world power and economies.

Industry concentration in the UK has, however, been stable since the 1970s.

### Points of debate

There is clear evidence that 'big can be best'.

Shell and Exxon (see later in the box) as well as Coca-Cola are long-term survivors. At the end of the 1990s, Lloyds TSB was the best performing British bank.

But do they always stay the best? Are they more vulnerable to the external rule changer?

After all, size is no protection against lost competitive advantage.

Glaxo grew from semiobscurity to become the top pharmaceuticals company in the world on the back of a single new drug, Zantac, but arguably the rules in this industry have changed since then. Governments are cutting back their spending; generic drugs are becoming more

popular all the time; and smaller, entrepreneurial biotechnology companies are having an impact on the industry giants.

However, privatization and splitting up of the utilities has improved efficiencies.

At the same time, many dominant industry leaders do falter and fail.

United Steel was once the world's largest company and is now 'nowhere in sight'.

Sometimes an industry declines, but sometimes large organizations become sluggish with power.

Others diversify and get it wrong strategically, and then get taken over and possibly split up.

### What, then, goes wrong?

- Lost control
- lack of co-ordination and communication
- lost momentum/motivation/hunger.

### The key issues

Big must think and behave small! Because:

- speed is critical as product lifecycles are getting shorter
- information can be dispersed quickly and, electronically
- do alliances make more sense?

### Consolidation and critical mass in the oil industry

During the latter years of the 1990s oil was one industry that has seen a new round of consolidation and merger activity. To a large extent the major players at the end of the twentieth century had dominated the industry from its very beginning.

| August 1998 | BP (British Petroleum) merges with Amoco |

| | | | |
|---|---|---|---|
| September 1998 | Royal Dutch Shell and Texaco discuss (but abandon) plans for a refining joint venture | March 2000 | BP/Amoco/Arco acquires Burmah Castrol to 'plug a gap in its portfolio', and later launches a completely new corporate logo |
| November 1998 | Exxon (already global leader) absorbs Mobil | September 2000 | Texaco and Chevron agree to merge. |
| December 1998 | Total (second largest French oil company) merges with Petrofina (Belgium) | | |
| July 1999 | TotalFina makes a hostile bid for Elf (number one in France) | | |
| Early 2000 | BP/Amoco merges with American Arco | | |

By mid-2000 the market positions were:

1. Exxon-Mobil
2. Royal Dutch Shell
3. BP/Amoco/Arco
4. TotalFina + Elf
5. Chevron } both some way behind the
6. Texaco } leading four companies.

of acquisitions by UK companies in Europe and the USA in the late 1980s, over 90% of the spending was in the USA. Acquisitions involved some well-known companies and brand names. Grand Metropolitan (now Diageo; Minicase 14.1), the leisure and hotels group, took over Pillsbury (the Jolly Green Giant foods group) after an acrimonious battle; and Marks and Spencer bought Brooks Brothers, an upmarket menswear retailer. Marks and Spencer have experienced implementation difficulties with this acquisition, and Pillsbury has recently been sold back to the American food business, General Mills.

During the 1990s links with European companies have inevitably grown in popularity. Because of both competitive requirements and regulatory and cultural issues many of these links are between existing competitors and they often take the form of joint ventures and strategic alliances rather than mergers or acquisitions. On occasions there will be clear arguments in favour of linking two organizations, but pressure from shareholders, managers or governments may mean that acquisition is not feasible.

## Introducing the diversification/ focus debate

Although their popularity has waned in the 1990s, research evidence confirms that *successful* diversified conglomerates can be very profitable at certain times and in certain circumstances. Hanson and BTR (whose histories are discussed in greater detail in Chapter 22) have been notable examples. They succeeded because they:

- carefully targeted their acquisitions
- avoided paying too much (normally)
- adopted an appropriately decentralized structure and control systems; and
- corporately added value.

Implementation is critical. These two conglomerates were structured as holding companies with very slim head offices; individual businesses enjoyed considerable autonomy; and tight financial control systems prevailed. Financial improvements took precedence over a search for skills transfer and synergies. Businesses were sometimes acquired (and divested) more on the logic of their financial contribution than on arguments concerning strategic fit.

Head-office capabilities and contributions for adding value included low-cost financing for the subsidiaries and skills in trading assets and improving operating efficiencies. In simple terms, these organizations developed a strategic expertise in running a diversified conglomerate, skills not matched by many organizations which choose this strategic alternative. During the late 1990s Hanson has been split into five parts and BTR has itself been acquired. Their particular strategies – which relied on finding acquisitions of a suitable size at a favourable price – became increasingly inappropriate as the British economy revived and weak, underperforming companies either became more productive or disappeared. However, as will be seen in cases in Chapters 22 and 24, the American General Electric (GE) has remained a very successful diversified conglomerate with a completely different style of management. GE does look to transfer ideas and skills to generate synergy between its businesses.

Goold *et al.* (1994) use the term *heartland* to describe a range of business activities to which a corporation can add value rather than destroy value by trying to manage a conglomerate which is too diverse. Key constituents are:

- common key success factors – often market driven
- related core competencies and strategic capabilities
- related technologies.

These issues are debated further in Chapter 22 but, as a final comment here it should not be forgotten that a strategy of focus is not immune from the risk of overdependency. Minicase 15.2 considers the different challenges faced by three focused organizations.

As soon as things go wrong, companies start talking about focus. Focus is the crutch of mediocre management ... If you are trained in the techniques of management ... you should be able to apply them across a range of companies. Diversified companies possess both defensive qualities in recession and a springboard for new ventures in more expansive times.

*A comment in defence of conglomerate diversification by Sir Owen Green, previously a successful Chairman of BTR; source Management Today, June 1994, p. 40*

## Causes and effects of diversification activity

Constable (1986) argues that the UK experienced the highest rate of diversification among the leading industrial nations between 1950 and 1985, and as a result developed the most concentrated economic structure. Coincidentally, this trend was accompanied by a trend to the weakest small company sector.

The process of diversification was achieved largely through acquisitions and mergers, which have taken place at a higher rate than that experienced in other countries, especially Japan where there are few large-scale acquisitions. Constable contends that Japan, the USA and Germany have concentrated more on product and market development and on adding value to current areas of activity, and that partly as a result of this they have enjoyed greater economic prosperity. Hilton (1987) has suggested that one reason behind this is that in Germany and Japan there is a greater emphasis on the respective banking systems providing funding, rather than shareholders, and this has influenced both the number of take-over bids and expectations of performance.

# Minicase 15.2  Rolls Royce, Kodak and Nokia – Three Focus Strategies

## Rolls Royce

Rolls Royce had to be rescued with an injection of government funding early in the 1970s; the company had become too dependent financially on the success of one engine project, the RB211. At the end of the 1990s the company was still focused on the design and manufacture of large, powerful aero engines. Rolls Royce's main two competitors are General Electric and Pratt and Whitney, both American and both more diverse. Not only is GE a diversified conglomerate, GE Finance controls GPA, the aircraft-leasing company based in Ireland.

Most development funds are committed to high-thrust engines whereby two engines can power large jets over increasingly long distances. Typically, engines are customized for particular aeroplanes, and airline customers normally specify their engine preference from the alternatives available. Rolls Royce's Trent 700, for example, has captured 40% of the engine orders for the Airbus A330, but it has so far been less successful with early orders for the Trent 800, designed specifically for the newest Boeing, the 777. Development work on the Trent 800 began in 1988, with an estimate of at least ten years' investment before any real payoff.

The competitive arena is now focused on the 'battle' between the proposed new giant Airbus (capable of carrying over 600 passengers on two levels) and a stretched version of the Boeing 747. Which aeroplane will dominate and which engine will dominate?

*Rolls Royce*   http://www.rolls-royce.com

## Kodak

Kodak's growth and success has been heavily dependent on photographic film and printing paper. During the 1980s Kodak realized that it faced a possible future threat from digital photography, which had the potential to make traditional film redundant. Half-hearted attempts to develop expertise in digital photography were relatively unsuccessful and consequently Kodak changed to a diversification strategy. In 1988 Kodak bought a pharmaceutical company, Sterling Drug.

Synergy was not forthcoming – the move was not seen as a success – and a new chief executive, George Fisher, was eventually recruited from the electronics company Motorola. Fisher divested peripheral businesses to focus on those related to *imaging*. He rationalized that even when digital cameras were successful and popular, people would still want hard copies of their photographs. Clearly, digital offered important new opportunities; customers could experiment alongside a technician who would be able visibly to enlarge and crop images before a final picture is printed. The technology has existed for a while; the challenge is making it affordable for typical consumers.

In 1998 Kodak acquired Picture Vision, a leading software company which specializes in digital photography. The intention was jointly to develop a strategy that would allow customers to drop their films off at a store and then the developed images would be posted on the Internet for them to download digitally. With this technology customers could then send their pictures electronically to friends and family for them to download as well.

*Kodak*   http://www.kodak.com

## Nokia

In the early 1990s Nokia of Finland decided to focus on the telecommunications industry. Four key strategic themes were identified: telecommunications orientation, globalization, focus, and value-added products.

Nokia grew rapidly and profitably during 1992–1994 by concentrating on becoming a major player in mobile telecommunications (where it achieved a 20% share of the world market, second only to Motorola) and digital cellular equipment, where it became second to Ericsson of Sweden. Other Nokia products included televisions, tyres and power, but telecommunications grew from 14% to 60% of the total. Nokia was very successful with its small, lightweight portable telephones; one range competed with Japanese phones by including Japanese numerical characters.

In 1996 there was a profits warning and a collapsing share price. The growth in demand for mobile phones had led to production bottlenecks, compounded by component supply issues. Nokia was experiencing problems in training its new recruits quickly enough. World prices for analogue phones were falling rapidly; even though market demand was growing healthily, new competitors such as Siemens and Alcatel (Germany and France) were causing supply to exceed demand. Nokia undertook drastic cost reduction programmes and sought to become even more focused on telecommunications. Television manufacture was just one divested activity. The target was for 90% of sales to relate to telecommunications.

By 2000 Nokia was focused on mobile phones together with (a much smaller) networks division. It was the world's leading manufacturer of mobile phones (with a 28% market share) – Motorola (16%) and Ericsson (12%) are some way behind. However, Nokia announced a delay with new models.

*Nokia*   http://www.nokia.com

QUESTIONS: Should all three companies remain focused?
Would any form of real diversification make sense for any one of them?
If so, why?

As a result of the diversification, merger and acquisition activity the UK has developed a number of large companies with sizeable asset bases and domestic market shares, but few which are dominant in their industries or sectors at a world or even a European level – points that were also discussed earlier in the book (see Chapter 7). Constable argues that the high level of strategic energy devoted to these strategies created an illusion of real growth, with an emphasis on the shorter-term financial aspects of strategic expertise as opposed to the operational and market-based aspects which, long term, are of great significance. Arguably, too much top management time and effort has been spent on seeking and implementing acquisitions, and avoiding being acquired.

Although the nature of investment funding and stock market expectations have been significant influences behind the diversification and acquisition activity in the UK, there are other explanations. If a company has growth objectives and there are finite limits to the potential in existing markets, as well as barriers to becoming more international in order to penetrate related markets abroad, diversification may be an attractive option. However, there may already be intense competition in domestic markets which the company considers entering, especially if the industries involved are attractive and profitable. The competition may be both UK producers and imported products and services and may be compounded by active rivalry for share and dominance. In such circumstances, direct entry may seem less appropriate than acquisition of an existing competitor.

As acquisitions and mergers increase industrial concentration and the power of certain large organizations, government policy on competition may act as a restraint on particular lines of development for certain companies. Large firms may be encouraged to diversify into

unrelated businesses where there is little apparent threat to the interests of consumers, rather than attempting horizontal integration which might be prevented by the intervention of the Competition Commission. Joint ventures offer another way round this constraint.

A contrasting argument suggests that a company which has grown large, successful and profitable in a particular industry is likely to seek diversification while it is strong and has the resources to move into new business areas effectively. The benefits of such a move are likely to seem more realizable by the acquisition of an existing organization than by the slower build-up of new internal activities. This type of growth requires finance, which generally has been available for successful companies.

When companies are acquired then both sales and absolute profits increase quickly, and sometimes markedly. But does profitability also increase? Are assets being utilized more effectively in the combined organization? Is synergy really being obtained? Or are the increased sales and profits merely an illusion of growth?

Finally, Constable offers two further arguments to explain the strategic activity in the UK. First, strategic leaders of large organizations are typically aggressive in nature, and acquisition is an expression of aggression. Secondly, there is a commonly held belief that the larger a company becomes the less likely it is to be a victim of a take-over bid. Hence, while diversification is essentially offensive and designed to bring about expansion and growth, it could be argued that on occasions it is a defensive strategy.

In choosing whether to diversify or not, Markides (1997) recommends that organizations should address five key questions:

1. What can we do better than our competitors? This, of course, is the area around which to focus and build.

2. What strategic resources are required in the possible new areas? What are the implications of this?

3. Can we 'beat the competition' and become a strong player?

4. Is there a downside risk? In particular, might existing businesses be affected in any detrimental way?

5. What learning potential is there? Can the new business enhance synergy and improve our existing businesses and the organization as a whole? This assumes, of course, that the organization is able to exploit the learning potential.

## Reasons for diversification and acquisition

There is then a number of sound and logical reasons why a firm might seek to diversify through acquisition. Some of these have been mentioned above; others are discussed below. Most are economic. The fact that diversification and acquisition strategies often prove less successful than the expectations for them is more likely to result from the choice of company to acquire and from issues and problems of implementation than the fact that the idea of diversification was misguided. This will be explored further later in the chapter.

Diversification may be chosen because the existing business is seen as being vulnerable in some way: growth potential may be limited; further investment in internal growth may not be justified; the business may be threatened by new technology. Some businesses are undervalued by the stock market, making them vulnerable to take-over if they do not diversify. Some products and businesses may currently be valuable cash generators, but with little prospect of future growth. In other words, they may be cash cows generating funds that need to be reinvested elsewhere to build a future for the company. Leading on from this, the company may have growth objectives that stretch beyond the potential of existing businesses.

Diversification may occur because a company has developed a particular strength or expertise and feels that it could benefit from transferring this asset into other, possibly unrelated, businesses. The strength might be financial (high cash reserves or borrowing capacity), marketing, technical or managerial. If genuine synergy potential exists, both the existing and newly acquired businesses can benefit from a merger or acquisition.

A company which has become stale or sleepy, or which has succession problems at the strategic leader level, may see an acquisition as a way of obtaining fresh ideas and new management, and this may seem more important than the extent to which the businesses are related.

Some diversification and acquisition decisions are concerned with reducing risk and establishing or restoring an acceptable balance of yesterday's, today's and tomorrow's products in a complex portfolio. This will be especially attractive where a company is relying currently on yesterday's products.

Some strategic changes in this category will result from the ego or the ambitions of the strategic leader, who may feel that he or she can run any type of business successfully, regardless of the degree of unrelatedness. Some may be very keen to grow quickly, possibly to avoid take-over, and acquisitions may happen because a company is available for purchase rather than as the outcome of a careful and detailed analysis.

It will be suggested later that the major beneficiaries of an acquisition are often the existing shareholders of the company being acquired. Consequently, it is sometimes argued that the self-interest of the City and large institutional shareholders might be behind certain mergers and acquisitions.

Figure 15.2 provides a useful summary of related and unrelated diversification opportunities. The top part of the diagram suggests that the degree of unrelatedness increases when:

- the resources involved, both tangible (plant and equipment) and intangible (brands) are different rather than similar, and
- the processes – the ways in which these resources are deployed and utilized – also changes.

The bottom part provides examples of each situation. It will be appreciated that the strategic risk increases as the extent of the newness and learning increases.

## Research into Diversification and Acquisition

### The relative success of diversification and acquisition

A number of research studies has been carried out in both the UK and the USA on the relative success of diversification and acquisition strategies. There are some general conclusions as well as specific findings, and the major ones are documented here. In the main, most of the findings are consistent.

It is important to emphasize, however, that this is a particularly difficult area to research because of problems with data availability. If, for example, one is attempting to study the change in a company's performance before and after an acquisition, then one needs several years of data to ensure that longer-term effects are studied once any teething problems of early implementation are overcome. However, company W may have acquired company X in, say, 1995 and as a result been included in a research study which began in the same year. Ideally, the performance of the combined WX would be compared with the previous performance of W and X as independent companies. If company W is naturally acquisitive it may divest some unattractive busi-

nesses from X during 1996 in order to raise money to help to finance the purchase of company Y in 1998 and company Z in 1999. An ongoing programme of this nature means that it is impossible to compare the long-term effects of one particular acquisition on an organization. The original sample continually reduces. In the same way, a comparison of the performance over a period of time of companies which might be classified as single, dominant, related and unrelated product will be affected by firms which change category as a result of the strategies they follow. The relevance of these points can be seen in Minicase 15.1, Granada.

General conclusions from the research suggest that no more than 50% of diversification through acquisition strategies are successful. Quite simply, the synergies that were considered to exist prior to acquisition are frequently not realized. There is also agreement that shareholders in a company which is taken over or acquired benefit from selling their shares to the bidder, who often pays an unwarranted premium. Shareholders who accept shares in the acquiring company instead of cash, together with the existing shareholders in that company, tend to be rewarded less in the longer term using share price appreciation as a measure. As mentioned earlier in the chapter, the research findings also support the contention that the profitability gains attributable to internal investments in companies are generally much greater than those accruing to acquisition investments.

Lorenz (1986) suggests that research in this field can be classified into four schools: accounting, economic, financial and managerial. The accounting school have concentrated on post-merger profitability in the 1970s, and their general conclusion, accepting sampling problems, is that few acquisitions resulted in increased profitability and for most the effect was neutral. Some had negative effects. Cowling *et al.*

*Figure 15.2* Diversification alternatives. Developed from Chiesa, V and Manzini, R (1997) Competence-based diversification. *Long Range Planning*, 30.2.

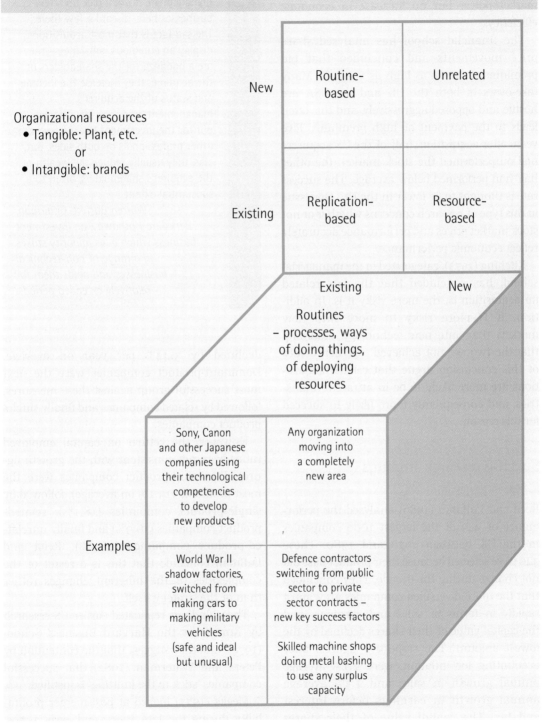

(1979), members of the economic school, concluded that there has been an increase in market power but no increase in economic efficiency.

The financial school has analysed share price movements and concluded that bid premiums are often as high as 20–40%. Many take-overs in both the UK and the USA are hostile and opposed aggressively, and this often leads to the payment of high premiums. Five years after acquisition, half of the US acquirers had outperformed the stock market; the other half had performed below average. The success rate is thought to be lower in the UK. One issue in this type of research concerns whether or not stock market prices and performance accurately reflect economic performance.

Kitching (1973), categorized in the managerial school, has concluded that the less related an acquisition is, the more risky it is. In addition, it is more risky to move into new markets than into new technology, assuming that the two are not achieved together. Critics of this conclusion argue that related acquisitions are more likely to be in attractive industries, and consequently more likely to succeed for this reason.

## Specific research findings

### British research

Reed and Luffman (1986) analysed the performance of 349 of the largest 1000 companies in the UK between 1970 and 1980. These 349 were selected because their product base did not change during the decade. They concluded that the more diversified companies grew most rapidly in terms of sales and earnings, and the capital value of their shares declined by the lowest amount. The respective figures, after accounting for inflation, were 2.1% average annual growth in sales and 1.3% average annual growth in earnings before interest and tax. The capital value of their shares

There is a 'gin rummy school of management' . . . you pick up a few businesses here, discard a few there. The sad fact is that most acquisitions display an egregious imbalance – they are a bonanza for the shareholders of the acquiree; they increase the income and status of the acquirer's management; and they are a honey pot for the investment bankers and the other professionals on both sides. But, alas, they usually reduce the wealth of the acquirer's shareholders, often to a substantial extent.

*Warren Buffett, Chairman, Berkshire Hathaway, an investment business which buys minority stakes in a range of non-technical businesses and holds them for relatively extended periods.*

declined by 3.44% per year on average. Dominant-product companies were the next most successful group against these measures, followed by related companies and finally single-product companies.

However, the return on capital employed ratios were not consistent with the growth figures. Dominant-product companies were the most profitable (19.1% on average), followed by single-product companies (18.1%), related-product companies (16.9%) and finally unrelated-product companies (16.7%). Reed and Luffman conclude that this is a result of the complexities of the inherent changes rather than of the strategy itself.

These findings replicated earlier US research by Rumelt at the Harvard Business School (1974), and they suggest that the contention by Peters and Waterman (1982) that successful companies 'stick to the knitting' is justified.

Meeks (1977) looked at post-merger profitability during the late 1960s and early 1970s.

He started with a sample of 213 firms, reducing the sample size annually as the organizations concerned changed their strategies again in some significant way. In four years the sample halved; and after seven years there were only 21 companies left from the original 213. Meeks looked at the percentage of remaining firms each year and considered whether their profitability had increased or decreased. In the first year after the merger 34% of the firms exhibited lower combined profitability than they had enjoyed previously as independent companies. This percentage increased during the first four years to a high of 66%, with half the original sample left. At the end of seven years of research, 62% of the remaining 21 companies were showing reduced profitability.

Meeks concluded that mergers which involved related businesses increased market power, but this was not the case for conglomerate mergers. All types experienced lower profitability and reflected reduced efficiency as a result of the merger activity. Greater size primarily yields higher salaries for executives, a generally more stable corporate performance and increased immunity from take-over.

Houlder (1997) reports on research from Warwick University which concludes that acquisitions are prone to fail where the acquirer neglects the new business after the acquisition. In such cases, the managers in the acquired business become frustrated and depressed – they feel that they have been left to 'operate in a vacuum'. Their subsequent underperformance increases the likelihood that the business will be sold again. Therefore, a careful balance needs to be struck between independence and 'arms-length freedom' and determined integration with the parent. The appropriate style will depend upon the extent and the nature of the fit between the two. The research also distinguishes between repeat acquirers, who have learned about integrating new businesses into a corporate whole and have developed key implementation skills, and occasional, even first-time, acquirers who are at the start of a learning curve.

## US research

Salter and Weinhold (1982) studied 36 widely diversified US companies between 1967 and 1977 and concluded that 'diversification strategies designed to raise performance actually brought return on equity down'. In 1967 the companies concerned were producing returns which were 20% above the *Fortune* 500 average, and consequently they could afford to diversify. In 1977 they were 18% below average.

Porter (1987) analysed the strategies and performance of 33 large US conglomerates during the 1970s, and based his general conclusions upon the pattern of later divestment of the acquisitions. Well over half his sample divested at least some of their acquisitions, and a typical retention period seemed to average five to six years. Companies which moved into related activities generally performed better than those which diversified into unrelated areas. From this research Porter suggested three tests for successful diversification, and these are discussed later in this chapter (see p. 586).

McKinsey, in research published in 1988, documented the performance of 116 large UK and US companies since 1972. Sixty per cent had failed to earn back the cost of capital on the funds invested in acquisitions, and this figure rose to 86% for large unrelated acquisitions.

Nesbitt and King (1989) examined the progress of 1800 US companies between 1978 and 1988 and concluded that corporate performance is dependent on strategy implementation rather than the strategy itself. The degree of diversification as opposed to specialization, taken in isolation, has little impact.

Burgman (1985) studied 600 US acquisitions which took place between 1974 and 1978 and concluded that:

- the higher the premium paid to acquire a company, the less likely it was to be successful
- prospects for success were greater where the acquirer had a functional appreciation of the business being acquired
- success depended upon the ability to retain key managers in the acquired company
- larger acquisitions were often more successful, possibly because the sheer size and financial commitment necessitated a thorough appraisal beforehand.

Further research, some of it more recent, confirms these key findings.

These research programmes and papers by Biggadike (1979) and Kitching (1967) suggest a number of reasons why acquisitions fail, and these are considered below.

## Why acquisitions fail

It has been mentioned previously that a key reason why acquisitions fail is that they do not generate the synergy that was anticipated or at least hoped for. This is particularly true for conglomerate rather than concentric diversification. Minicase 15.3 looks at the search for synergy by Daimler-Benz. In general, it is easier to gain synergy from production and operations than it is from marketing. It is difficult to gain real additional benefit from selling more than one product or service into one market.

Linked to this issue is the reality that in many cases the real weaknesses of the acquired company are hidden until after the acquisition, and consequently are underestimated. Also underestimated are the cultural and managerial problems of merging two companies and then running them as one. As a result insufficient managerial resources are devoted to the process of merging, and hence the hoped-for synergy remains elusive.

This problem typically arises because the acquiring company concludes that the skills which were to be transferred to the new acquisi-

tion in order to generate the synergy are in reality not available. They are already fully committed and in the end are not transferred.

Key managers who have been responsible for the past growth and success of the company being acquired may choose to leave rather than stay with the new conglomerate. Where this happens, and depending on the extent of the contribution of these managers, past successes may not be repeatable.

Further reasons concern the amount paid for the acquisition, and the extent of the premium. For a contested take-over in particular, the bidding company may become overenthusiastic and optimistic about the prospects, overstretch itself financially and then not be able to afford the necessary investment to generate benefits and growth in the new company. When a premium is paid the acquirer is likely to set high targets initially for the new company in order to try and recover the premium quickly. When these targets are missed, because they are unrealistic, enthusiasm is lost and feelings of hostility may develop. It can be argued that if synergy really is available, price is less significant as an issue, and a premium may well be justifiable. However, if an acquisition is fundamentally misconceived a low or a cheap price will not make it successful at the implementation stage.

Finally, the reaction of competitors may be misjudged.

The difficulties apply in service businesses as well as manufacturing, as the following examples illustrate. The long-established and family-owned Cadbury was persuaded by management consultants to believe that 'successful managers can manage anything' and diversified into Schweppes soft drinks (related distribution channels) and the unrelated Jeyes (disinfectants). Jeyes was quickly divested when it became clear that the core chocolate business was suffering as managers became preoccupied with the new activities. Interestingly, the same consultants also persuaded Cadbury to

# Minicase 15.3  Daimler–Benz

This case charts Daimler-Benz's search for synergy in its quest to create an integrated transport company.

Daimler-Benz has long been renowned for engineering excellence, product quality and marketing. At the beginning of the 1990s it was Europe's largest manufacturing group, and comprised:

| | |
|---|---|
| Mercedes-Benz | – commercial vehicles |
| | – passenger cars |
| AEG | – electrical and electronic products |
| Dasa | – aerospace |
| Debis | – financial information services. |

Vehicles were responsible for two-thirds of annual sales revenue; AEG and Dasa each generated approximately 15%.

The majority of the non-vehicle businesses had been acquired systematically during the 1980s; the intention had been to create an 'integrated technology' group. Daimler-Benz's stated objectives for the acquisitions were, first, to offset stagnating vehicle sales by expanding into high-technology growth markets, and secondly, to strengthen the automotive businesses by applying advanced technologies from the new acquisitions. The challenge was always to achieve this potential synergy; the time-scale to realize the benefits was set at ten years, and the important institutional shareholders allegedly pledged their support for the strategy.

Initially, vehicles had to subsidize the new businesses; but critics argued that the second of the two objectives did not require ownership and that in reality the synergy argument was being used as an afterthought to justify the diversification.

Daimler-Benz's strategic dilemma was that both AEG and Dasa required turning around at the same time that vehicles were under threat from Japanese car manufacturers, who were becoming increasingly competitive in the more up-market sectors. Mercedes needed new, more competitive models to prevent being squeezed into too small a niche. An alliance with Mitsubishi was mooted as one suitable way forward.

AEG, which Mercedes had rescued from near bankruptcy, was already diversified (it included white goods, typewriters and traffic-control systems) and was itself searching for synergies. Some AEG business areas were losing money, and in 1994 AEG's appliance business was sold to Electrolux (see Minicase 14.7). AEG's railway equipment division became a 50:50 joint venture with ABB, Asea Brown Boveri. Daimler-Benz actually had to pay ABB as AEG's division was currently losing money and its new partner was profitable. The two businesses complemented each other well: ABB focused on heavy locomotives, high-speed trains and signalling; AEG was concentrated on light and urban railways and airport transit systems.

Dasa (Deutsche Aerospace) comprised a number of separately acquired companies and there was some duplication of activities. Messerschmitt has always been a major supplier to the European Airbus project, but its contribution, rear fuselages, is technically less sophisticated than Aerospatiale's forward fuselages and flight decks and British Aerospace's wings. Further alliances with other members of the Airbus consortium, to develop commuter aircraft and helicopters, were discussed. In 1992 Daimler-Benz added to this division when it acquired a 78% shareholding in the Dutch aerospace company, Fokker. The Dutch government held the remaining shares but, again, the company was already in difficulty.

The promised synergies simply did not materialize as Germany suffered its deepest recession in manufacturing since 1945. Mercedes-Benz began to trade at a loss in 1993, and this led to job reductions and investment in plants outside Germany (to avoid the difficulties of high domestic wage rates and a strong Deutschmark). Development work on new four-wheel drive vehicles and a micro-car were already underway, the latter in conjunction with SMH of Switzerland, best known as the manufacturer of Swatch watches.

A new chairman was appointed in Summer 1995 and later that year Daimler-Benz announced a trading loss equivalent to £2.7 billion, 'the worst non-fraudulent result ever recorded by a German company'. A leading analyst commented that the company was 'so bogged down with aerospace and AEG it had missed important opportunities in the automotive arena'. Drastic action was anticipated.

In January 1996 further AEG divisions were sold to Alcatel Alsthom (France); the remainder were to be fully absorbed into Mercedes-Benz. Daimler-Benz also announced the withdrawal of further financial support for Fokker, making its collapse inevitable unless a new buyer came forward.

Daimler-Benz redefined itself as a 'transportation group' and restructured into 25 operating units in seven main divisions. All operating units had to fit the core strategy and achieve a target return of 12% return on equity. Failure to achieve would result in sale or closure. The future of Dornier (manufacturer of regional aircraft) and MTU (Daimler aero engines) thus looked particularly precarious unless alliance partners could be found to help.

In 1997 Daimler-Benz increased its already dominant presence in the global heavy trucks industry by acquiring Ford's activities. Also in that year Mercedes launched its first small car, the 'A' class hatchback. Almost immediately the car was withdrawn from sale when a motorist, admittedly driving in unusual and extreme conditions, had turned one over. The car was redesigned and relaunched. The launch of the Smart micro car was also delayed for safety reasons. As a consequence Mercedes bought out its partner in this venture to take total control.

In 1998 Daimler-Benz announced a merger with America's third largest, and most profitable car manufacturer, Chrysler. The new company would be called Daimler-Chrysler, but ownership was split 57:43. It would be the fifth largest in the world, after General Motors, Ford, Toyota and Volkswagen. There was no product overlap, as Chrysler's Dodge and Plymouth cars were less luxurious than Mercedes, which also had the monopoly on small cars. Chrysler was prominent in pick-up trucks and four-wheel drive vehicles (the Jeep brand), which were new to Mercedes. However, it was arguable that together the two companies would have too many platforms and some rationalization would be required. The intention was to retain separate brands, plants and dealerships. The synergy would come from administration, shared skills and (later) common platforms. Chrysler, however, was less global than Daimler-Benz and the cultures of the two companies were very different. Daimler-Chrysler has subsequently bought minority stakes in Mitsubishi and Hyundai. Towards the end of 2000 it was clear that there were significant implementation problems with the Daimler–Chrysler merger.

Meanwhile, Dasa has been merged with British Aerospace, its partner in the Airbus project.

QUESTION: Do you believe that the Daimler-Chrysler merger can eventually unlock the synergy which Daimler-Benz had earlier found elusive?

*Daimler-Chrysler*   http://www.daimlerchrysler.com

abandon its paternalistic style of management, manifested in the Bourneville village and community which the Quaker family had built for its workforce. General Accident acquired a related insurance business in New Zealand in 1988 and as part of the purchase inherited the NZI Bank. The loan book deteriorated in the worldwide recession and, lacking the necessary turnaround skills, General Accident decided to close the bank. The Prudential similarly chose to exit estate agencies after incurring huge losses. They had overpaid for their acquisitions and the anticipated learning and synergy was slow to materialize. Some would argue that the strategy of linking insurance with estate agencies was misjudged; others that the problems were really those of implementation. In particular, the Prudential attempted to exercise central control over a disparate group of acquisitions.

In reality, acquisition is an uncertain strategy. However sound the economic justification may appear to be, implementation or managerial issues ultimately determine success or failure. These issues are the subject of the next section.

## Issues in diversification and acquisition

Where two companies choose to merge there is the opportunity for a reasonably comprehensive assessment of relative strengths and weaknesses, although it does not follow that one or both will not choose to hide certain significant weaknesses. In the case of a contested take-over less information will be available. UK take-over law requires that once a company has built up a shareholding of a particular size in another company it must offer to buy the remaining shares,[1] at which stage, the targeted company must make certain information

[1]Since 1989 one company must inform another if it builds up a share of 3% or more. When the ownership reaches 10% a company has to declare its intent – preparation for a later bid or a mere investment. Companies will be held to this declaration. If one says that it is merely investing it will not then be able to launch a bid for at least one year. A company can own up to 29.9% without making a bid for the remainder, but once this figure is exceeded a bid for the rest must follow.

available through the process of due diligence. Crucially, however, the information that will affect the ease or difficulty of merging the two cultures and organizations, and implementing the changes, is less freely available than financial data. It is never easy to determine from outside an organization what the style of management is, its managers' attitude to risks, how decisions are made and whether managers are largely self-reliant. In the final analysis, the success of an acquisition or merger will be influenced markedly by the way the companies fit (or do not fit) together as well as by the logic used to justify the strategy (see Figure 15.3). As a result financial analysis may be used to justify the acquisition, but it will not answer questions relating to implementation. Table 15.3 highlights the significant information that is unlikely to be available until after the acquisition.

The following list of questions and issues indicates the key considerations which should be addressed by a company before it acquires another:

- how the acquiring company should restructure itself in order to absorb the new purchase, and what implications this will have for existing businesses and people
- what acceptable minimum and maximum sizes are for proposed diversifications in relation to present activities
- what degree of risk it is appropriate for the company to take
- how to value a proposed acquisition and how much to pay
- how to maintain good relationships with key managers during negotiations to try to ensure that they stay afterwards
- how to maintain momentum and interest in both companies after a successful offer
- how quickly to move in merging organizational parts and sorting out problems
- reporting relationships and the degree of independence allowed to the acquired

company, particularly where the business is unrelated
- whether and how to send in a new management team.

Some of these issues are considered in the next section where effective acquisition strategies are discussed, but many of them are taken up in later chapters which consider the implementation aspects of strategic change. Figure 15.3 illustrates that an effective strategy is one that is based upon good vision and sound implementation prospects. Vision is in relation to the organization's strengths and market opportunities, and an effective strategy will match these. In the context of diversification and acquisition, implementation relates to a consideration of how the two organizations will be merged together and the changes required to structures, cultures and systems in order to ensure that potential synergy is achieved. Poor vision and poor implementation will both cause strategic management to be less than effective. If the logic behind an acquisition is poor, then the merged corporation is likely to underperform, however well the two companies might be managed as one corporate whole. If the vision is good but implementation is weak, underperformance is again likely because synergy will not be created.

If companies develop by a series of acquisitions it is quite typical for several banks to become involved. These could be spread worldwide; their cultures and lending philosophies may differ; their levels of exposure will vary; the assets securing the loans will not be the same; and certain banks may see themselves as lenders to just one company rather than the whole organization. Problems are likely to arise if one of the banks gets into financial difficulties or if the company seeks to extend a loan or adjust the terms.

*Table 15.3* Information available before and after an acquisition

| Before | After |
|--------|-------|
| Organization charts | Inner philosophy and culture |
| Data on salaries of top management | Real quality of staff in decision roles |
| Reasonably detailed information on board | Salary and reward structures and systems |
| members and key executives – but only brief | Decision processes |
| details on middle management | Interrelationships, power bases, hidden conflicts and |
| Products | organizational politics |
| Plants | Individual objectives being pursued |
| Corporate identity, image and reputation | |
| Past record, especially financial | |

*Figure 15.3* Strategy creation and implementation. Based on a matrix devised by Booz, Allen and Hamilton.

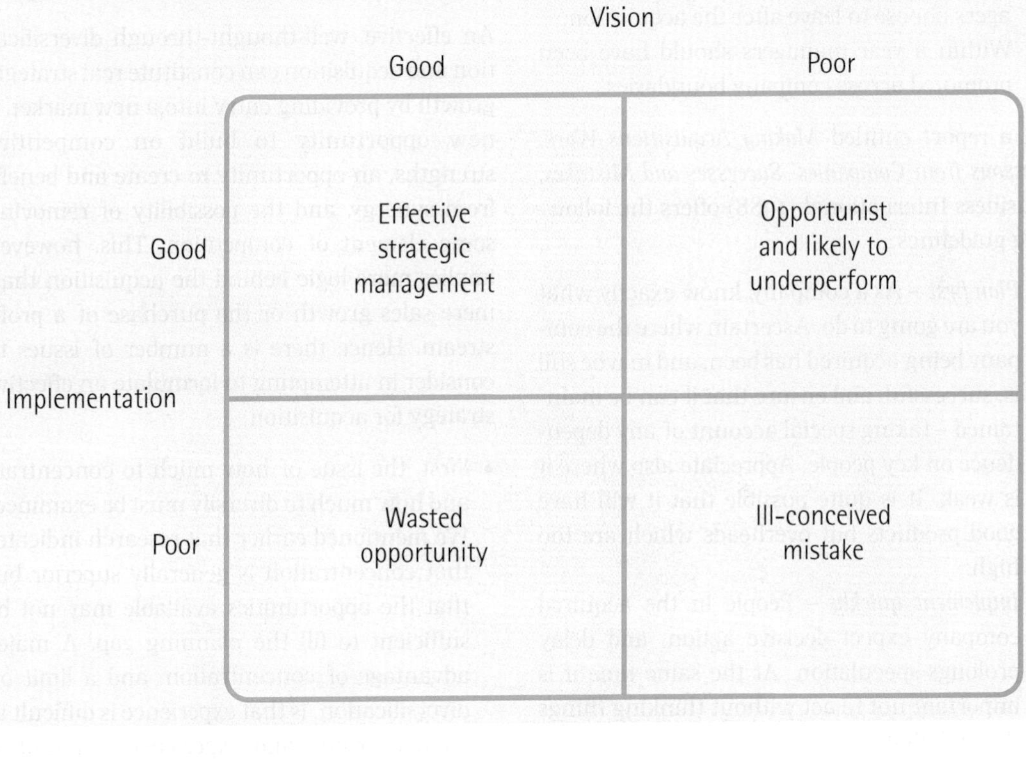

## Effective Acquisition Strategies

A number of authors have suggested ways of improving the effectiveness of acquisition strategies.

Drucker (1982), for example, argues that there are five rules for successful acquisitions.

1. It is essential for the acquiring company to determine exactly what contribution it can make to the acquired company. It must be more than money.
2. It is important to search for a company with a 'common core of unity', say in technology, markets or production processes.
3. The acquiring company should value the products, services and customers of the company that it is taking over.
4. Top management cover for the acquired company should be available in case key managers choose to leave after the acquisition.
5. Within a year managers should have been promoted across company boundaries.

In a report entitled *Making Acquisitions Work: Lessons from Companies' Successes and Mistakes*, Business International (1988) offers the following guidelines.

- *Plan first* – As a company, know exactly what you are going to do. Ascertain where the company being acquired has been, and maybe still is, successful, and ensure that it can be maintained – taking special account of any dependence on key people. Appreciate also where it is weak. It is quite possible that it will have good products but overheads which are too high.
- *Implement quickly* – People in the acquired company expect decisive action, and delay prolongs speculation. At the same time it is important not to act without thinking things through first.

- *Communicate frankly* – Explain the acquisition or merger, the expected benefits and the changes which will be required. In addition, it is useful to ensure that there is an understanding of the values and expectations of the acquiring company.
- *Act correctly*, particularly as far as redundancy is concerned.

Ramsay (1987) argues that effective acquisition strategies have four stages, which are illustrated in Figure 15.4:

- the need to formulate a clear strategy
- the search for possible acquisitions
- the acquisition
- the merger of the organizations following acquisition.

These four stages are now discussed in detail.

## The formulation of a clear strategy

An effective, well-thought-through diversification and acquisition can constitute real strategic growth by providing entry into a new market, a new opportunity to build on competitive strengths, an opportunity to create and benefit from synergy, and the possibility of removing some element of competition. This, however, implies more logic behind the acquisition than mere sales growth or the purchase of a profit stream. Hence there is a number of issues to consider in attempting to formulate an effective strategy for acquisition.

- First, the issue of how much to concentrate and how much to diversify must be examined. We mentioned earlier that research indicates that concentration is generally superior but that the opportunities available may not be sufficient to fill the planning gap. A major advantage of concentration, and a limit on diversification, is that experience is difficult to copy. Learning and experience can lead to

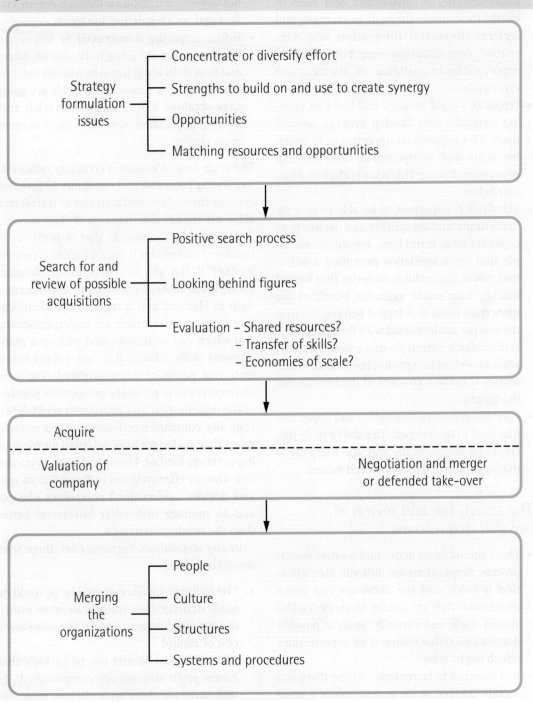

*Figure 15.4*   Effective acquisition strategies.

superior competitive positions through an understanding of customers and how to satisfy their needs through production and service. Horizontal integration and concentric diversification can both provide opportunities to capitalize on learning and experience.

- Secondly, a good strategy will build on existing strengths and develop synergy around them. This requires an opportunity to transfer skills and competencies and achieve economies of scale. This issue is discussed further below.

- Thirdly, it is important to be able to spot an opportunity and act quickly and decisively to capitalize on it. It has been argued, for example, that, once legislation permitted it in the mid-1980s, the building societies that moved quickly into estate agencies benefited far more than those that lagged behind, because the cost per site increased with the acquisition activity. Such a strategic move would be classified as vertical integration because an estate agency is really a channel of distribution for mortgages.

- Fourthly, resources (strengths) and opportunities need to be matched. The ability to do this effectively relates to the way the company is managed, and to the culture and values.

## The search for, and review of, possible acquisitions

- There should be an active and positive search process. Acquisitions are difficult, diversification is risky, and the decisions can prove expensive if they are wrong. Strategic leaders should track and carefully analyse possible acquisitions rather than rely on opportunities which might arise.

- It is essential to be realistic. Where there is a friendly merger, or the acquisition of a company in difficulties, it is possible that certain key weaknesses may be hidden; and in the case of a hostile bid situation it is important not to become unrealistic through determination and, as a result, pay too much.

- Before acquiring it is crucial to assess just how resources are going to be shared, where and how skills are going to be transferred, and where and how economies of scale are going to be obtained. If such an analysis is left until after an acquisition, synergy is likely to prove more elusive.

The price paid to acquire a company relative to its earning potential, and the ability to generate synergy through shared activities or transferred skills, are the key determinants of likely success.

Porter (1987) contends that a portfolio of unrelated companies is only a logical corporate strategy if the aim is restructuring. Restructuring is the strategy pursued by conglomerates such as Hanson, and it requires the identification of companies which are underperforming and which can be transformed with new management skills. Ideally, they are valued below their real potential when acquired. The new owner seeks to improve the competitive position of the organization and improve its profitability. Logically, companies or business units are sold when they no longer have potential for increasing earnings further. The opportunity to pursue this strategy effectively lies in the ability to spot and acquire undervalued companies cheaply and to manage unfamiliar businesses better than the existing managers.

In any acquisition, Porter argues, three tests should be passed.

1. The industry involved should be or could be made structurally attractive. In other words, the potential returns exceed the company's cost of capital.

2. The entry cost should not be so high that future profit streams are compromised. As well as the purchase price, the cost must also take account of professional fees involved in the merger or acquisition.

Granada incurred professional fees exceeding £100 million for its take-over of Forte. Forte's defence costs, post-acquisition divestment fees, together with other payments and provisions, built up an accumulated total of some £250 million. Granada paid £3.9 billion for Forte.

3. One of the companies should be able to gain competitive advantage, and the newly acquired business should be better off in the new corporation than elsewhere. In other words, the interrelationships, based on shared activities and transferred skills, must give added value which outweighs the costs incurred. These benefits are often not gained for two main reasons. The new, more diverse, more complex, organization is likely to be decentralized, but the business units may be independent in practice rather than interdependent. Managers may not be able to understand and implement the interrelationships.

Minicase 15.4 evaluates the ASDA-MFI merger against these three tests and argues that it did not pass them all. It was mentioned in Minicase 14.10, which described the merger and demerger, that the expected synergy was not achieved.

Van de Vliet (1997) reports on research from Mercer Consulting which confirms the switch during the 1990s from 'conglomeration' to mergers with a more defensible strategic logic, but also confirms a concurrent increase in hostile take-overs. The implication is that higher premiums are being paid. This seems to be a situation of gain against one test and deterioration against another!

Some commentators have also argued that a fourth test should be added to Porter's three: how much will have to be invested in the future, post-acquisition? The experience of BMW with Rover is testimony to the significance of this test. BMW underestimated the investment requirements and eventually sold the business 'for a song' to avoid further spending.

Figure 15.5 attempts to pull these points together diagrammatically.

Hence companies that are seeking to grow through acquisition and the consolidation of the acquired and existing businesses should ensure either that skills can be transferred or that activities can be shared, i.e. clear interrelationships can be identified. These can relate to any part of the value chain. The aims are greater economies of scale, lower costs or enhanced differentiation through sharing activities, know-how or customers, or transferring skills and know-how. The research findings quoted earlier suggest that these opportunities are more likely to be found in industries which are in some way related. Tobacco companies in both the UK and the USA, for example, when faced with declining demand and hostile pressure groups, realized that they would have to diversify if they were to avoid decline. They chose such industries as food, wine and brewing initially because they felt that they could transfer their skills and expertise in marketing consumer products.

Acquisitions are likely to prove disappointing if the opportunity for such synergy is not evaluated objectively in advance, or if the companies convince themselves that synergy must be possible without establishing where and how.

It is also vital to check carefully for any 'skeletons' prior to an acquisition. In 1990 ICI Explosives bought Atlas Powder in the USA. In the same year, a US rival of Atlas, Thermex Energy, was declared bankrupt, and when, some years later, Atlas was found guilty of conspiring to drive Thermex out of business, ICI was held responsible by the US courts. Substantial, but contested, damages were awarded against ICI.

One final point worth making is on timing. The ideal time to bid for a company is during the period between any 'dirty work' designed to turn it around or improve its competitiveness, and the outcome of these strategies being properly reflected in the company's value or share price.

# Minicase 15.4   The ASDA – MFI Merger II

The case considers whether the merger of ASDA and MFI, described earlier in Minicase 14.10, met the criteria for successful diversification suggested by Porter.

## The attractiveness of the kitchen furniture industry

In the case of kitchens supplied direct to individual customers (as opposed to sales to building contractors) the actual suppliers of kitchen furniture did not enjoy as strong a market profile as did MFI, and buyers individually had very little power. *En masse* they are influential. Any competitor wanting to enter the market on the MFI scale would require massive investment; substitute products were often units which were already assembled, such as those sold by Magnet Southern. Increases in disposable income might make these more attractive. There was intense rivalry for market share, however, as sales of kitchen furniture were flat in the 1980s.

On balance the industry was not unattractive, and MFI was a past 'winner'. Profits had grown 87% in real terms between 1980 and 1985.

## The cost of entry

MFI cost ASDA £570 million, which represented 5.5 times net assets and 14 times 1984 pre-tax profits. It was a 31% premium on the current market capitalization, and it measured MFI on a price-to-earnings ratio of 22 rather than the 18 that it had been before the bid. Debt and equity funding were both involved; and ASDA's gearing increased from little more than zero to 40%.

Both sets of shareholders were supportive, but with hindsight it seems a high price.

## Increased competitive advantage

There was no real benefit to be gained from common purchasing, no site sharing, and the two companies enjoyed different geographical concentrations. ASDA was northern and MFI national.

After the merger the companies were run autonomously with few activities shared. Prior to merging it had been argued that there would be intangible benefits from shared expertise. In the event, there was little cross-flow of managers, product innovation, marketing or operations skills. The cultures remained separate; and
Derek Hunt, who became chief executive, worked from London despite ASDA's northern base.

While ASDA did compete with Sainsbury's, who have a chain of Homebase DIY stores, this was not seen as a threat that MFI would address, and in any case MFI was very narrowly focused within the DIY sector.

While the industry was not unattractive the merger proved expensive for ASDA, and the potential synergy used to justify the merger to shareholders seemed not to be there in reality.

QUESTIONS: Do you agree with this final assessment?
Could this merger ever have been successful or was it always misguided strategically?

ASDA http://www.asda.com
MFI http://www.mfi.co.uk

*Figure 15.5* The effective acquisition.

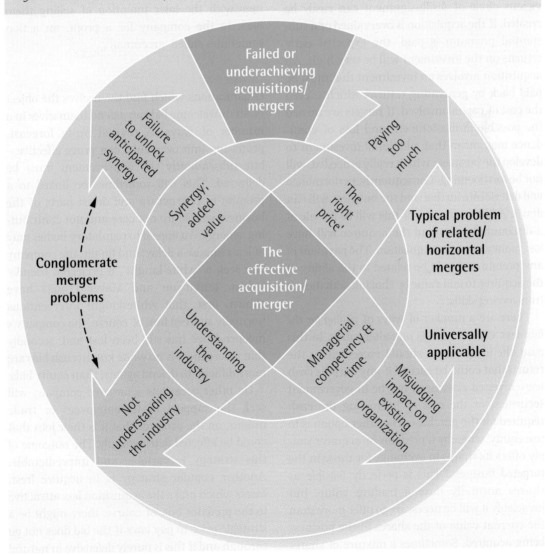

## Acquiring the company

The key issues involved in the acquisition itself have been discussed earlier; alternative ways of valuing a business – in order to determine an appropriate bid price – are described in Box 15.2. It was emphasized above that it is important to look for hidden weaknesses in friendly mergers and avoid paying too much in a contested take-over bid. It was also mentioned earlier that if too high a premium is paid the acquisition is less likely to be successful (Burgman, 1985), and a vicious circle of disillusionment can easily be created. If the acquisition is overvalued or a substantial premium is paid, the expected early returns on the investment will be very high. An acquisition involves an investment that must be paid back by generating returns which exceed the cost of capital involved. If targets are missed the possible disillusionment and loss of confidence may mean that additional investment to develop the business, which really is needed, will not be forthcoming. Consequently, performance will deteriorate further and the business will run down. A likely outcome of this will be its sale at a discounted price, and the acquirer will have lost money from the acquisition. The payment of any premium should be related to the ability of the acquirer to add value by sharing activities or transferring skills.

There are a number of ways of *paying for the business*. Clearly cash is one alternative. In this case, the likely return should exceed either the return that could be earned if any surplus cash were invested elsewhere, maybe in government securities, or the cost of borrowing the cash required for the purchase. The other option is to use equity, whereby a predator or acquirer simply offers its shares in exchange for those in the targeted business. This is perfectly feasible as shares normally have a trading value, but invariably it will be necessary to offer more than the current value of the shares in the business being acquired. Sometimes a mixture of shares

and cash will be chosen. The decision will be influenced by:

- whether there is surplus cash in the balance sheet
- the prevailing rate of interest
- the impact on the acquirer's debt ratio and gearing.

In the UK a company cannot use the assets of a targeted business as collateral for a loan, although this is permissible in the USA. It is also legal in the USA to buy shares in another business with the later intention of selling them back to the company for a profit, an action sometimes called 'greenmail'.

### Unwelcome bids

Organizations which find themselves the object of an unwelcome bid can defend themselves in a number of ways. A revised profit forecast, promising improvements, can prove effective – but subsequently the improvement must be delivered. This will sometimes be linked to a promise to restructure and divest parts of the business which are not core and not contributing synergy. An appeal to regulatory bodies may at least impose a delay; and finally, the company can seek a 'white-knight', a preferred friendly bidder. Jenkinson and Mayer (1994) have shown, first, that white-knight interventions normally succeed but, of course, the company's independence has still been lost and, secondly that where there is no white knight cash bids are more difficult to defend against than equity bids.

On other occasions a targeted company will seek the support of its employees or trade unions, on the grounds that it is their jobs that could be affected detrimentally. The outcome of this strategy is variable and unpredictable. Another popular strategy is to acquire fresh assets which make the acquisition less attractive to the predator but, of course, there might be a strategic price to pay later if the bid does not go through and if this is purely defensive in nature!

Acquisition of another company constitutes an investment, although one major strategic objective might be to avoid being taken over by another firm. Whatever the strategic reason, the current value of an organization is important. Assuming that we are not talking about a merger (of assets), a company will normally be acquired when another company buys an appropriate percentage of its shares. While the bid price will always be influenced substantially by their current market price in trading, the likely purchase price in both a hostile and a bidding situation (where more than one prospective buyer is in evidence) will reflect a premium. However, the market price at any time may or may not reflect the value of the organization.

## Alternative valuation methods

### Rule of thumb

A typical rule of thumb valuation of a company would be to multiply the most recent annual profits (or an average of the last few years) times an *x* factor. Relatively small *x*s will be selected for small companies (which have fewer customers and fewer key people) and service businesses, where it is easier for key people to be lost during or after the acquisition. The *x* factor might vary from 3 up to 13 for large, established manufacturing businesses.

### The balance-sheet valuation

The balance-sheet value of a company is normally taken from the value of the net assets. Divided by the number of ordinary shares issued, this yields the asset value behind every ordinary share, and it can therefore be useful in assessing what an appropriate bid price for the ordinary shares might be. However, caution is needed because the balance sheet traditionally records historical costs rather than present values, and this can be misleading in the case of property. In addition, although some companies do account for this, the value of such intangible assets as brand names is rarely reflected in the balance sheet.

### The market valuation

The market valuation of a company is the number of ordinary shares issued multiplied by their present price plus the inherited debt. This will reflect the likely lowest cost to a buyer, as any bid for shares at a price below their existing price is unlikely to succeed. In reality, the price of shares is likely to increase during the period between when current shareholders realize that a bid is likely, or when one is announced, and when control is finally achieved by the bidder.

The current share price and the asset value of shares should be looked at together.

### Earnings potential

Many contend that it is future earnings potential that determines how valuable a company is, not historical results – see, for example, Allen (1988). An analysis of past and current performance is therefore limited in its usefulness. In isolation, a high return on capital employed, for example, can hide the reality of an asset base which is declining in real terms. Therefore, one should estimate the future cash flows that the company is capable of generating and discount these by the cost of capital. The current value of the company is determined by this net present value calculation.

The decision to acquire a company, however, will not be based solely on the discounted future earnings, nor the purchase price, but both of these are very important. Future earnings potential for both the

KEY CONCEPT – Box 15.2
(Continued)

acquiring and the acquired companies could be improved with a merger if valuable synergy of some form is derived, and for this potential a premium price might be justified.

*A multifactor approach*

Consequently, Copeland *et al.* (1990) recommend a five-level valuation approach:

- The first level is the current market value, described above.
- The second level is the earnings potential, the value of the projected cash flow, discounted.
- The third level projects a value once internal improvements have been undertaken. New business processes, for example, could improve the cash flow.

- The fourth level is the value after restructuring, when non-core or poorly performing activities have been sold or divested.
- The fifth level combines level three and four benefits. Significantly, the improvements implied in these three levels may require a fresh management team and style.

References

Allen, D (1988) *Long Term Financial Health – A Structure for Strategic Financial Management*, Chartered Institute of Management Accountants (CIMA).

Copeland, T, Kotter, T and Murrin, J (1990) *Valuation: Measuring and Managing the Value of Companies*, John Wiley.

---

A number of defensive strategies by Forte is evident in its attempt to avoid take-over by Granada (Minicase 15.1).

These issues are explored further in Box 15.3.

## Abandoned discussions

There are occasions when merger talks fail and are abandoned. Walton and McBride (1998) provide a number of possible reasons for this, few of which relate to the actual strategic logic of the merger:

- There is a reluctance on the part of one company to accept that they are in reality 'number two' and that it is not a 'partnership of equals'.
- There is disagreement on future strategic leadership – who will run the new merged company. Egos get in the way. There was a delay in the merger between Glaxo Wellcome and SmithKline Beecham for exactly this reason (Minicase 7.1).

- There is inadequate consultation with key shareholders – typically institutions – who then intervene.
- There is an insistence on preserving too many elements from the past – often things related to a strategic leader who is reluctant to 'let them go'.
- Relationships and trust simply break down as negotiations proceed.

## Implementation issues

Ernst and Young (1995) argue that the nature of the post-acquisition challenge depends upon the type of acquisition and the objectives behind it. They identify four alternatives:

- *Financial acquisitions* are companies brought into a holding company, sometimes for the purpose of restructuring. The main objectives for the acquisition are the financial opportunities from cost (overhead) eradica-

## STRATEGY IN ACTION – Box 15.3
## Hostile Takeovers

In a research sample year (1989) in the UK there were 161 bids for publicly listed companies; 35 of these were hostile take-over attempts as distinct from agreed or friendly acquisition bids. In one sense the year was seen as typical: some 70% of the *largest* acquisitions/take-overs were hostile. Of these about half will normally succeed; in the other cases the target company will be able to mount an effective defence strategy.

By contrast, Germany had experienced just three hostile take-over bids since 1945. They are equally rare in France and almost unheard of in Japan. They remain popular in the USA, where a larger number of defence mechanisms are available than is the case in the UK.

### Alternative defence strategies
(Listed in order of popularity in the UK)

#### Financial responses

Companies will hope to be able to announce forthcoming profit improvements – they have been targeted because, although fundamentally competitive and sound, recent profits have been disappointing. They may also seek to revalue their assets to make the bid appear to be undervaluing the true worth of the business.

#### Legal and political tactics

Political lobbying and attempts to get a bid referred to the competition authorities, the latter to, at the very least, buy time and allow a company to mount a stronger defence.

#### Attempted white-knight bids

An alternative, preferred, outside bidder is sought.

#### Corporate restructuring

As seen in Minicase 15.1, disposals are announced. Bidders will claim that attempts to rationalize and downsize, while appropriate and desirable, have been provoked by the bid and are indicative of reactive senior management. Sometimes the strategic leadership will attempt to mount a management buy-out as an alternative to the outside bid.

#### Poison pills

This strategy, most popular in the USA, describes shareholder rights plans which effectively increase the price to the bidder. An example would be preferentially priced stock being available to existing shareholders, giving them a later right to new ordinary shares. Similarly, the term *golden parachutes* describes special departure terms for directors in the event of an unwelcome acquisition.

In 1999, for example, American Airlines (linked to Canadian Airlines and allied with British Airways in the Oneworld alliance) was interested in bidding for Air Canada, which was experiencing financial difficulties. However, Air Canada was part of the Star Alliance, dominated by American's main rival, United Airlines. A poison pill was in evidence – whoever might own Air Canada, it would remain a member of the Star Alliance for ten years or United and its partners would be entitled to huge damages. The presence of this arrangement was sufficient to deter American.

### Outcomes

In general a well-formulated and strategically logical bid for a poor performer should succeed; a strong performer will clearly be in

STRATEGY IN ACTION – Box 15.3
(Continued)

a stronger position to defend itself and its record. However, in isolation, a strong financial performance is not everything – simply, there may appear to be more strategic logic in the business being parented by the bidder instead of staying as it is.

Cash bids have the greatest likelihood of success. In 1989, 21% of the 161 bids were equity based and just 11% of these succeeded; 43% were cash only with a 56% success rate; the remaining 36% were mixed cash/equity bids and 53% of these succeeded.

Normally, the value of a hostile bid will be increased once the nature and robustness of the defence is revealed.

Cash bids are most likely to fail if an alternative *white-knight* bidder is found. The likelihood of the success of equity and mixed bids appears to depend upon the quality of the financial defence.

Source: Jenkinson, T and Mayer, C (1994) *Hostile Take-overs: Defence, Attack and Corporate Governance*, McGraw-Hill.

---

tion, cost reduction and improved efficiencies. Those parts of the business which do not offer these opportunities are likely to be offered for sale; and, in fact, any part of the business is likely to be available for sale to a buyer offering a premium price. The critical implementation issues concern timing and decisiveness.

- *Geographical acquisitions* are intended to expand the acquirer's core business across new frontiers. Merging different country cultures is the key challenge, but this is generally regarded as manageable as long as the strategic logic for the merger is sound. One dilemma concerns cuts and job losses in the acquired business; alleged 'national bias' may well cause resentment.

- *Symbiotic acquisitions* describe situations where newly acquired products and competencies are absorbed into the parent's business but the acquired company retains some independence. Abbey National's purchase of Scottish Mutual is an example. The establishment of an appropriate new structure, culture and communications system are the implementation issues.

- *Absorption acquisitions* imply that the two businesses are fully integrated, with one effectively losing its identity. Such acquisitions are particularly challenging to implement as really everything changes.

For any acquiring company to gain financially, sales must be increased and costs reduced to a level which compensates for any price premium paid. Researchers suggest that this is rarely less than 20%. Easy savings are rare, particularly in the case of many hostile bids, where the target is often a high, rather than a poor, performer. Too many companies, apparently, pursue the elusive synergistic opportunities and do not act on the cost base quickly and decisively. They also tend to postpone the difficult issues relating to culture and style. Successful acquisitive companies such as Hanson and BTR did act quickly, concentrating on cost eradication and reduction; they also imposed their own style of management on their new businesses, top–down from the centre.

Clearly, the type of acquisition and the rationale behind it must influence the appropriate implementation strategy; as noted already, Hanson and BTR were restructuring organizations. Where genuine synergy potential exists, a more participatory style is likely to prove appropriate and foster the necessary learning and skills transfer.

## Merging the two organizations

Merging two organizations involves decisions about the integration of strategic capabilities, in particular:

- operating resources – salesforces, production facilities
- functional skills – product development, R&D
- general management skills – strategy development, financial control, human resource strategies.

The speed and pattern of the integration will be dependent on the desired interdependency of the businesses, and the opportunities for synergy. It is essential that there is a strategy for the implementation, and ideally this will be developed after the merger or acquisition when fuller details are available. Moreover, important issues concerning people, culture, structure, systems and procedures must be thought through.

- *People* – It is accepted that many chief executives and other senior managers leave acquired companies either immediately or within one to two years after the acquisition, especially where the acquisition was contested. This may or may not be significant, depending on the strengths of the acquiring company. In some cases it will prove crucial, particularly where the managers have been the major source of competitive advantage. The managers in the two organizations being merged may well have different values, ethics and beliefs in quality and service, and these will somehow have to be reconciled.
- *Culture* – It is quite possible that the two organizations will have different cultures, which also must be reconciled. One may be a large company and the other small, with typical role and power cultures, respectively. Managers will be used to different levels of responsibility. One may be much more formal and procedural than the other. One may be entrepreneurial and risk orientated, and the other cost conscious and risk averse. These cultural issues should be considered when the post-acquisition structure is designed, and in the new systems and procedures.

- *Structure, systems and procedures* – While mentioned here, this issue is the subject of Chapter 21, and it concerns the degree of decentralization. As companies become larger and more complex they must be broken down into business units, and managers must be given some degree of independence – to motivate them and to ensure that functional and competitive strategies can be adapted in response to environmental changes. However, if activities are to be shared, or skills transferred, it is essential to ensure that independence does not inhibit, or even prohibit, the implementation of the necessary interdependencies.

McLean (1985) contends that six factors determine whether the integration of two or more companies is a success or a failure:

- first, active leadership by the strategic leader of the acquiring company in conveying objectives and expectations, and in redesigning the structure of the organizations
- secondly, the conscious development of shared values and a transfer of the important aspects of the culture of the acquiring firm
- thirdly, an appropriate interchange of managers between the firms, which can be one way of retaining valuable managers from the acquired company
- fourthly, proceeding with caution (although some changes may have to be implemented quickly, say to reduce costs in certain areas, others will be less urgent; this provides an opportunity to learn about the underlying

strengths of the new business which might be capitalized on)

- fifthly, relationships with customers must be protected until decisions about future products and market priorities are taken
- sixthly, rigid new systems, which might be inappropriate for the new business, should not be imposed too ruthlessly or too quickly. Where there are differences in, in particular, culture, technology and marketing needs, managers in the acquired company should be allowed the necessary freedom to manage the competitive and functional strategies and respond to market pressures.

To summarize this section, it could be argued that:

- the price paid for an acquisition should reflect the ability of the acquirer to add value, share resources and transfer skills
- the strategy for achieving this should be soundly based, and the potential synergy real rather than imagined
- post-acquisition management should recognize that, while changes will have to be made in order to add value, two cultures have to be integrated if the strategy is to be implemented effectively.

Finally, five factors for implementing acquisitions and mergers successfully can be identified:

- 'Tread warily' and carry out sufficient analysis – especially where there is a hostile reaction from the target.
- Evaluate any prospective partner fully, carrying out a culture and style assessment as well as a financial evaluation.
- Take on board the best practices from both (all) businesses to increase the prospects for synergy. It is highly unlikely that one partner will have a monopoly on good ideas.
- Communicate with those people affected to the maximum extent that is expedient.
- Ensure that key people are identified and stay.

## Summary

Periodically, organizations must make decisions about how focused and how diversified they wish to be. Horizontal integration, such as acquiring or merging with a competitor, will engender critical mass but may be restrained by the relevant competition authorities. Diversification can be into related or unrelated businesses, or vertically forwards or backwards in the supply chain.

Where a company does choose to diversify it is more likely to implement this strategy through acquisition (friendly purchase), merger (bringing together the assets of two businesses) or take-over (hostile purchase) than it is through organic growth.

Unrelated diversification is invariably high risk, but it may be justified or chosen for one of the following reasons:

- weakness of the present businesses
- existing businesses having strengths and competencies that could be exploited in other industries
- the ambitions of the strategic leader.

Research in both the UK and US consistently indicates that diversification through acquisition has only a 50% likelihood of success, specifically delivering the hoped-for benefits. The typical reasons for failure are:

- the synergy potential is overestimated
- managerial problems and issues are underestimated
- key managers leave after the acquisition
- hidden weaknesses are not spotted until it is too late
- too much money is paid and the premium cannot be recovered.

The companies that succeed with this strategy tend to follow a number of simple rules:

- they carefully target their acquisitions

- they learn from previous experiences and become 'professional acquirers'
- they avoid paying too high a premium

- they adopt an appropriate post-acquisition structure and style and ensure that the businesses are integrated effectively
- corporately, they add value.

## References

Biggadike, R (1979) The risky business of diversification, *Harvard Business Review*, May–June.

Burgman, R, Research findings quoted in McLean, RJ (1985) How to make acquisitions work, *Chief Executive*, April.

Business International (1988) *Making Acquisitions Work: Lessons from Companies' Successes and Mistakes*, Report published by Business International, Geneva.

Channon, DF (1983) *Strategy and Structure in British Industry*, Macmillan.

Constable, CJ (1986) Diversification as a factor in UK industrial strategy, *Long Range Planning*, 19(1).

Cowling, K, Stoneman, P and Cubbin, J (eds) (1979) *Mergers and Economic Performance*, Cambridge University Press.

Drucker, PF (1982) Quoted in Drucker: The dangers of spoonfeeding, *Financial Times*, 15 October.

Dyas, GP and Thanheiser, HT (1976) *The Emerging European Enterprise: Strategy and Structure in French and German Industry*, Macmillan.

Ernst and Young (1995) Key success factors in acquisition management, Research project with Warwick Business School, Ernst and Young, London.

Goold, M, Campbell, A and Alexander, M (1994) *Corporate Level Strategy*, John Wiley.

Hilton, A (1987) Presented at 'Growing Through Acquisition', Conference organized by Arthur Young, London, 31 March.

Houlder, V (1997) Neglect of the new addition, *Financial Times*, 5 February.

Jenkinson, T and Mayer, C (1994) *Hostile Take-overs: Defence, Attack and Corporate Governance*, McGraw-Hill.

Kitching, J (1967) Why do mergers miscarry? *Harvard Business Review*, November–December.

Kitching, J (1973) Acquisitions in Europe: causes of corporate successes and failures, Report published by Business International, Geneva.

Lorenz, C (1986) Take-overs. At best an each way bet, *Financial Times*, 6 January.

Markides, C (1997) To diversify or not to diversify, *Harvard Business Review*, November–December.

McLean, RJ (1985) How to make acquisitions work, *Chief Executive*, April.

Meeks, J (1977) *Disappointing Marriage: A Study of the Gains from Merger*, Cambridge University Press.

Nesbitt, SL and King, RR (1989) Business diversification – has it taken a bad rap? *Mergers and Acquisitions*, November–December.

Peters, TJ and Waterman, RH Jr (1982) *In Search of Excellence: Lessons from America's Best Run Companies*, Harper & Row.

Porter, ME (1987) From competitive advantage to corporate strategy, *Harvard Business Review*, May–June.

Ramsay, J (1987) The strategic focus: deciding your acquisition strategy, Paper presented at 'Growing Through Acquisition', Conference organized by Arthur Young, London, 31 March.

Reed, R and Luffman, G (1986) Diversification: the growing confusion, *Strategic Management Journal*, 7(1), 29–35.

Rumelt, RP (1974) *Strategy, Structure and Economic Performance*, Division of Research, Harvard Business School.

Salter, MS and Weinhold, WA (1982) *Merger Trends and Prospects for the 1980s*, Division of Research, Harvard Business School; quoted in Thackray, J (1982) The American take-over war, *Management Today*, September.

van de Vliet, A (1997) When mergers misfire, *Management Today*, June.

Walton, C and McBride, J (1998) Broken engagements, *Financial Times*, 26 February.

Test your knowledge of this chapter with our online quiz at: http://www.thomsonlearning.co.uk

Explore Diversification and Acquisition Strategies Further at:

*Chief Executive*   http://www.execmag.com

## Questions and Research Assignments

### TEXT RELATED

1. From the various points and issues discussed in this chapter list the possible advantages and disadvantages of diversification and acquisition strategies, and from your experience list one successful and one unsuccessful example of this strategy. Why have you selected these particular cases?

2. What are the key arguments for and against strategies of unrelated diversification and focus? Again, from your own experience, list examples of each.

## Internet and Library Projects

1. Do you think that Forte would have been better off if it had remained independent? Had Sir Rocco Forte been shocked to an extent that he would have adopted a different strategy and style? What has happened to Sir Rocco Forte since the acquisition?

*Forte*   http://www.forte-hotels.com

2. Obtain statistics on either a selection of large companies which interest you, or the largest 20 companies in the UK, and:
   (a) ascertain the extent to which they are diversified and classify them as either single, dominant, related or conglomerate product companies
   (b) determine their relative size in relation to their competitors in the USA, Japan and Europe.

3. Research the diversification and acquisition strategies of Trafalgar House plc – a property and construction conglomerate that diversified into shipping (Cunard), hotels and newspapers (the *Daily Express*). (A useful early summary can be found in Barber, L (1986) Bruised Trafalgar struggles to regain its political touch, *Financial Times*, 19 May.)
   (a) Trafalgar bid for the P&O shipping line in 1983, but it was referred to the then Monopolies and Mergers Commission. Although approval was granted, Trafalgar allowed the bid to lapse. Given that they already owned Cunard, was this an appropriate strategic move?
   (b) Trafalgar acquired the Scott Lithgow (1984) and John Brown (1986) shipyards from British Shipbuilders. Where do you think a land-based construction company thought it would be able to add value in this declining industry?

(c) Trafalgar bid unsuccessfully against Eurotunnel for the Channel tunnel, proposing a linked bridge and tunnel scheme. They were, however, successful with their bid to build a bridge across the Thames at Dartford to relieve congestion in the existing Dartford tunnel. Trafalgar built the bridge with private investment money which is being recouped by tolls on traffic. Do you believe that these developments could be justified strategically? Why? Why not?

(d) Should Trafalgar House have divested its interests in passenger shipping and hotels much earlier than it did?

(e) What has happened to the Trafalgar businesses since the acquisition of the company by Scandinavian shipbuilder, Kvaerner?

*Trafalgar House*   http://www.kvaerner.com/EandC

4. Why did Woolworth Holdings change its name to Kingfisher in 1989? What was the reaction of the City to this proposal?
How successful has Woolworth/Kingfisher been? Has its strategy of diversification been successful?

*Kingfisher Group*   http://www.kingfisher.co.uk

# 16

# Strategic Alliances and Joint Ventures

Introduction

Forms and Examples of Strategic Alliances and Joint Ventures

Key Issues in Joint Ventures and Strategic Alliances

*Acquisitions happen for a number of reasons, some strategic, others more personal to a strategic leader. There is a strongly held view that the strategic argument of synergy should only be used to justify an acquisition which implies real diversification if the companies concerned are somehow blocked from working together in some form of partnership, alliance or joint venture. Simply, there is an argument that alliances and joint ventures are often a better alternative than a full acquisition, merger or take-over for generating synergy and fuelling growth. Alliances and joint ventures are not, however, without risks and they can sometimes be problematical in the implementation stages. However, they will generally offer more flexibility. Their downside for many strategic leaders is that they do not create a larger and more powerful organization.*

*This relatively short chapter explores these issues by looking at different forms of partnering and the various reasons for doing so.*

# Minicase 16.1 British Airways

John King (later Lord King) was recruited from outside the industry to become Chairman of the then nationalized British Airways (BA) in 1981. Supported by Chief Executive, Sir Colin Marshall, he turned the ailing company around and, in 1987, BA was successfully privatized. By the early 1990s, BA was ranked seventh in the world in terms of revenue, but fifth in terms of passenger miles flown (behind the four leading American carriers with their huge domestic networks). Only Swire Pacific (of Hong Kong) and Singapore Airlines were more profitable. In fact, many of the world's largest airlines were being run at a loss, many of them subsidized by their governments.

By 2000, Lord King had retired. He had been succeeded by Marshall, who had in turn been replaced by Robert Ayling. Growth and prosperity had fluctuated in the intervening years. BA had been affected by the expansion of Virgin Atlantic and had 'lost the war of words' between these two rivals, fuelled originally by the tension in the relationship between Branson and King. Capacity globally had expanded to exceed demand, but airlines were still being propped up – as a result prices had fallen, in some cases to uneconomic levels. BA had changed many of its tailplanes, using designs from around the world to replace the Union Jack symbol. Popular outside the UK, unpopular at home, this was always controversial. An acrimonious strike by cabin crew, handled clumsily by BA, left Ayling's reputation tarnished. After BA's profits and profitability fell dramatically, Ayling resigned. The general consensus, nevertheless, was that BA's corporate and competitive strategies remained strong.

## The corporate strategy

Lord King always wanted BA to become the 'world's first truly global airline'. Progress has been made towards this vision, but it has not been achieved. Maybe it is not even achievable. In line with this, BA adopted the advertising slogan: 'The world's favourite airline'.

King and Marshall realized that BA needed to establish a strong presence in Europe, North America and Asia/Pacific if it was to be a global carrier. It endeavoured to achieve this with a series of acquisitions, alliances and franchise arrangements.

BA purchased 25% of US Air, America's fifth largest airline, which has hub bases in four eastern American cities: Pittsburgh, Philadelphia, Baltimore and Charlotte. BA crew then flew the existing scheduled US Air services between London Gatwick and these American cities; joint ticketing arrangements allowed BA's passengers to enjoy easier onward travel, albeit not across the whole of the USA. The benefits, therefore, were clear but limited. In 1996 BA began to talk with American Airlines, number two in the market, with a view to a much stronger and more beneficial arrangement.

Combined, the two would have enjoyed enormous power, and consequently the American and European competition authorities were interested. America wanted a more open-skies arrangement allowing more US airlines access to Heathrow as well as Gatwick; the European Competition Commissioner was insisting that BA give up slots at Heathrow. This discussion partly involved a debate over whether they could be sold or had to be given away. In the event the alliance that BA and American envisaged has never happened, but negotiations continue with varying levels of intensity.

However, BA has sold its shareholding in US Air, which objected to the ongoing discussions. In addition, in 1999, BA, American, Canadian Airlines, Cathay Pacific and Qantas formed the Oneworld alliance, and they have since been joined by Iberia (Spain) and Finnair. Arguably this alliance (like the rival Star Alliance) provides seamless global travel for passengers through interchangeable ticketing, shared air mile programmes and the use of each other's lounges. Passengers can reach a wide variety of destinations with what amounts to a single ticket.

In 1992, BA bought a 25% stake in the Australian national airline, Qantas, from the Australian government. Also in 1992 it acquired 49.9% of the French regional carrier, TAT. BA bought the remaining shares in 1997 and linked TAT with Air Liberté, which it had acquired in 1996. Again in 1992 BA purchased a German airline, Delta, which it rebranded Deutsche BA. A minority stake in Iberia followed in 1998.

By this time BA also owned a minority stake in Eurostar and it had divested both its in-flight catering business and its ground fleet services. These are now both bought in from the specialist alliance partners to whom it sold the businesses.

BA also opted to give up operating a number of short-haul domestic UK and European routes – to concentrate on major European cities and the long-haul routes to the rest of the world – and entered into franchising arrangements with other airlines who would fly the routes but retain BA flight numbers and use BA's livery on their aeroplanes. These arrangements included British Mediterranean Airways (who fly some London to Middle East routes), British Regional Airways (Scottish routes), Brymon (Channel Islands) and Comair (internal routes in South Africa). BA owns Brymon and CityFlyer Express, which flies to Europe from Gatwick and which Virgin was interested in acquiring.

In the late 1990s BA established Go as an independent, low-price, low-cost, no-frills airline which would fly within the UK and between the UK and Europe from Stansted, in competition with Ryanair and EasyJet. After two years of trading losses, Go is forecast to start breaking even. But BA is now looking to sell Go. Go carries some 2 million passengers a year between its 20 destination airports. This move arose hostility, especially from EasyJet, which believed Go would be unfairly subsidized by BA.

All-in-all, these strategic moves provide BA's international passengers with access to a very wide spectrum of routes and destinations.

## The competitive strategy

As well as opting to focus on major world cities, and cover the rest with a variety of different arrangements, BA wanted to increase its flight revenues on its major long-haul routes in particular.

In 1999 a decision was made to increase the number and quality of first- and business-class seats on each aeroplane, in particular business class: BA's 'Club class'. The intention was to reduce by 15% the number of heavily discounted economy tickets being sold. This was combined with a stated intent gradually to change the fleet and replace some larger Boeing 747s with smaller aircraft such as the new Boeing 777. In addition, a new class and cabin, World Traveller Plus (for full-fare economy passengers) would provide a higher level of economy service in a segregated and quieter area on the plane.

BA has also found an Internet booking partner in its quest to sell more tickets over the Internet and thereby reduce costs.

## The proposed merger with KLM

The new Chief Executive (in 2000), Rod Eddington, struck quickly. A merger with KLM (of The Netherlands) had been discussed and abandoned in 1992, but the idea was resurrected in a different market situation. Together they would be the third largest airline worldwide when measured by passenger miles. Clearly, there is some route overlap, and it was anticipated that the European Commission would, at the very least, require BA to divest Go and KLM its similar no-frills subsidiary, Buzz. Again, however, the merger has been abandoned partly because of reservations with the European Competition Commission.

QUESTIONS: Given national resistances, and the desire of many countries to have their own international airline, has BA developed as far as any airline might in the quest to become global?

Is a merger with KLM strategically logical even though it might never be implemented?

*British Airways*  http://www.britishairways.com

Photographer: Chris Sheldon

# Introduction

While some form of partnership can be one of the quickest and cheapest ways to grow or develop a new and maybe global strategy, it is also one of the toughest and most risky. Many alliances fail. The needs of both partners must be met, and consequently three important questions must be answered satisfactorily:

- *Why* use an alliance?
- *Who* to select as a partner?
- *How* to implement the agreement?

Garrette and Dussauge (1999) argue that many European companies have tended to think about alliances from a defensive perspective rather than as a proactive growth opportunity. All too often they are a fall-back when the competition authorities stand in the way of a merger or acquisition. Many of the examples referred to throughout this chapter indicate that many successful American and Japanese companies adopt a different perspective. In the late 1990s, for example, research into the largest 1000 American companies revealed that 20% of their revenues came directly from alliances.

Minicase 16.1 shows how British Airways (BA) has mixed mergers and alliances, together with both positive and reactive strategies for its alliances, in an attempt to create the world's first truly global airline. BA has not totally succeeded in its quest.

There is evidence of some disagreement amongst strategy authors concerning the meaning of the terms 'joint venture' and 'strategic alliance'. Here, 'strategic alliance' is used to encapsulate all forms of agreement between partners, and 'joint venture' for those agreements which involve either the establishment of a new, independent company owned jointly by the partners, or the minority ownership of the other party by one or both partners.

The term 'consortium' is also used in this context. One instance would be where companies in an industry generally collaborate or share, maybe through a trade association. The Japanese 'keiretsu' (or family of businesses) is another, but quite different, example. Here companies, often in a geographical cluster, own stakes in each other and share and collaborate wherever possible. This might take the form of intertrading; it might equally be by seconding staff to help with a particular problem or difficulty.

An alliance (or joint venture) could involve:

1. direct competitors, maybe sharing common skills, and with the objective of increased market share
2. less direct competitors with complementary skills – where the intention is more likely to be benchmarking and learning for mutual benefit, and the possible development of new ideas
3. related companies sharing different skills and competencies. Here organizations might well be linked in the same added-value chain (e.g. a manufacturer and either a supplier or a distributor). Such an alliance should generate synergy through co-operation, innovation and lower costs while allowing each partner to concentrate on its core competencies.

The intention will invariably be to increase competitive advantage without either merger or acquisition. As we move from an alliance to a joint venture and from 1 to 3 in the above hierarchy, the significance increases for the partners involved. Some companies will be involved in several alliances with different companies at the same time – this is not a one-off strategy for them. As an example, Toshiba (Japanese manufacturer of heavy electrical apparatus, electronic devices, information systems and consumer products such as televisions, videos, kitchen appliances and white goods) has created a global network of allies for different products and technologies, including GEC Alsthom, Siemens, Ericsson, General Electric, Motorola, Time Warner and Apple. Toshiba sees this 'circle of friends' as an opportunity for sharing ideas to obtain the latest technology and to gain competitive advantage through learning. Minicase 9.2 showed how Benetton has built strong partnership sourcing agreements and a network of retail franchisees who together yield economies, speed and competitive advantage. Here, the ability to manage a network of partners is a core strategic capability and source of competitive advantage. Minicase 16.2 describes how Yorkshire Water adopted an onion strategy to allow it to concentrate more on its core service competencies; as a result it had to form a network of partnerships.

## Reasons for joint ventures and strategic alliances

- The cost of acquisition may be too high.
- Legislation may prevent acquisition, but the larger size is required for critical mass.
- Political or cultural differences could mean that an alliance is more likely to facilitate integration than would a merger or acquisition.
- The increasing significance of a total customer service package suggests linkages through the added value chain – to secure supplies, customize distribution and control costs. At the same time individual organizations may prefer to specialize in those areas where they are most competent. An alliance provides a solution to this dilemma.
- The threat from Japanese competition has driven many competitors into closer collaboration, but they may not wish to merge. For example, American and European car manufacturers have taken stakes in Japanese businesses, where outright acquisition is unlikely.

- Covert protectionism in certain markets necessitates a joint venture with a local company. This has been particularly true in China, one of the world's fastest growing economies.

Developing these points, Minicase 16.3 contrasts the acquisition approach of Ford with the alliance strategy of General Motors as they have both become increasingly global in their endeavours to remain the world's largest car manufacturers.

## The likely outcomes

- In simple terms, increased competency, synergy and a stronger global presence are the potential outcomes targeted most frequently by alliance and joint venture partners.
- Greater innovation could well accrue from the pooling and sharing of ideas and competencies, which in turn enables greater focus (by each partner) combined with resource leverage.
- The partnership and sharing could also result in lower costs. A virtual circle of learning, where each partner learns new skills and competencies from the other, contributes to this.
- Finally, the linkage could provide access to new markets and technologies.
- Simply, an alliance is a means to an end. It is not necessarily going to be seen as a permanent arrangement, and it most probably can be changed as time goes on.

Developing these outline points, Connell (1988) contends that companies collaborate strategically for primarily three reasons:

1. *To gain access to new markets and technologies as markets become increasingly international.*

In 1989 Pilkington, the UK float glass manufacturer and world market leader, sold 20% of its

# Minicase 16.2 Yorkshire Water's Onion Strategy

Since being privatized in 1989 most of the ten water companies in the UK have pursued diversification strategies. The core business activities are water supply and the management of waste water (i.e. sewage treatment). Prices and quality standards are closely regulated, and consequently the diversification is aimed at offsetting the perceived risks and constraints inherent in regulated businesses. The most popular activity has been waste management, the collection and disposal of industrial and domestic waste. For example, Severn Trent Water acquired Biffa, and Wessex formed a joint venture with Waste Management of the USA, one of the world's largest companies in the industry.

Yorkshire Water (YW) created two separate, but linked, businesses: Yorkshire Water Services to control the core businesses, and Yorkshire Water Enterprises, later renamed Yorkshire Environmental Solutions, for other commercial ventures.

## Yorkshire Water enterprises

This business became active in the following areas:

- *Waste management* – Industrial effluents and clinical waste. This was sold in 1998 to Waste Recycling, but Yorkshire Water retained a 46% shareholding in the enlarged Waste Recycling business.
- *Engineering consultancy and support* – A joint venture with Babcock International. Since 1989 YW have been investing in treatment plants (mainly) and water-distribution networks, the latter to free up engineering resources which the joint venture would seek to deploy and exploit.
- *'Pipeline Products'* – The sale of existing stores items to external customers.
- *'Waterlink'* – A network of approved subcontractor plumbers. YW provides an arrangement service.
- *Laboratory services* – Providing analytical services to a range of businesses and agencies.
- *Management training* – Primarily exploiting existing markets and competencies.
- *Property development* – Representing 'real' diversification.

The Director General of OFWAT, the industry regulator, emphasized that he was not going to ignore these strategic developments. 'Customers of core services must not be affected adversely.' For example, the water companies were prevented from selling services from the associated businesses to the core at contrived prices which benefited shareholders at the expense of captive water customers. In addition, 'the required investment funds for the water supply services must not be put at risk'.

## Yorkshire Water services

YW stated quite early that it did not intend to build and then manage a diversified corporation. Once the appropriate business had been constructed, with YW's resources deployed effectively, the layers would be peeled away systematically – an onion focus strategy – until only the core business remains. The defined core activity is *water delivery*, which incorporates the removal of sewage and water treatment. The pursuit of this strategy entails divesting certain non-core or support activities into either wholly owned subsidiaries or independent contractors (in properly negotiated alliances), and possibly more joint ventures, but only where there are providers able to deliver the range and quality of services.

Four alternative implementation approaches for this strategy are illustrated in the figure overleaf. The services divested by YW are also highlighted. Where there were agreements with multiple outside contractors (alternatives 2 and 3), separate geographical regions were typically the predominant logic. For example, the pipework to sewage treatment works was divested to individual local authorities.

This corporate onion strategy aims to improve a company's competitiveness with the premise that non-core services can invariably be acquired more effectively from an experienced outside provider, selected because it already has competitive advantage. It is essential to define the core carefully and to establish the appropriate ongoing relationships in order to minimize risk. The order and timing of each divestment is also an important issue. The company benefits because it can concentrate on its core activities; it has access to a wider skill and resource base, which should promote best practice, enable greater service flexibility and lead to overall quality improvements. Resources should match needs more effectively. In addition, clearer accountability should foster cost reductions, and the introduction of controlled competition should enhance the quality of in-house service provision and act as a catalyst for change throughout the organization. To implement the strategy successfully the central organization must develop competency in network management. Effective partnership sourcing such as this requires unambiguous long-term agreements, clear performance measures and shared risk. It is most appropriate where the service is a core activity for the contracted supplier. The partners should engage in ongoing dialogue and maybe even exchange personnel periodically.

However, in the mid-1990s a summer drought caused Yorkshire Water considerable embarrassment. Public relations were clumsy; the Managing Director suggested people could easily wash with just a basin of water as opposed to having a bath, for example. The company ended up hiring road transporters to move water from north-east England to its own reservoirs, but supplies were never cut off. In the end the chairman and managing director both retired and, with a new strategic leader, the parent company was renamed Kelda.

**Strategy 1**

Examples: Stores
       Fleet service

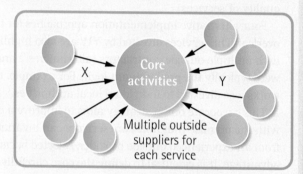

**Strategy 2**

Examples: Pipe manufacture,
       Electrical spares

Key success factor:
Partnership sourcing
establishing firm alliances
with each supplier

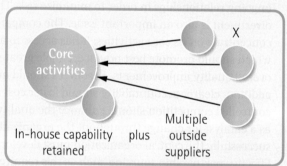

**Strategy 3**

Examples: Sewerage management
(pipework to the sewage
treatment works)

Objective: Develop the in-house
capability into a centre of
excellence

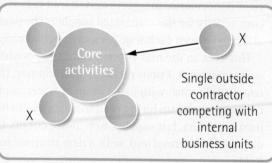

**Strategy 4**

Examples: Electrical and
mechanical maintenance

Objective: Form an alliance with
an outside expert and benchmark
to drive internal improvement

Four alternative onion-focus strategies applied in Yorkshire Water Services.

Option 3 in the figure, sewage management, has subsequently been taken back from local authority control, and the company has bought Aquarion, an American water company. But price regulation continued to bite, and profits and the shareholder value of Kelda have been hit.

In 2000 Kelda announced a radical proposal. It indicated an intent to sell all of its physical assets (pipes, sewage works and reservoirs) to a new mutual company, which would be owned by Kelda's customers and financed with debt capital. Kelda would simply lease back the assets and employ contractors. Other activities would also be sold to leave a water *services* company. Aquarion and the 46% of Waste Recycling would not be sold. Environmental groups, customers and the water regulator all opposed the plan, which was subsequently abandoned.

QUESTION: Can alliance-based networks such as the one developed (and proposed) by Yorkshire Water deliver the equivalent or even greater value to customers than a company which owns and manages all of its activities?

*Yorkshire Water*   http://www.yorkshirewater.com

US vehicle glass subsidiary to Nippon Sheet Glass of Japan. Pilkington had 17% of the world market for vehicle glass, Asahi of Japan 19%. Nippon already had 9% and manufactured float glass under licence from Pilkington. Nippon gained access to the US market; Pilkington was looking to build a customer base in Japan, arguing that as car manufacture becomes increasingly global they needed a presence in all major markets. Pilkington already supplied the Toyota plant in the USA.

*2. To share the costs and risks of increasingly expensive research and development.*

Nippon Steel (a related business) has another strategic alliance – designed to cut production costs – with Posco (South Korea's Pohang Iron and Steel). Nippon and Posco are the world's largest steelmakers (a joint market share of just 7%, nevertheless) and wish to retain their positions of leadership. When the South Korean government privatizes Posco, which is

imminent, Nippon is expected to buy a stake. Research and development resources are pooled but so far there is no collaboration on either production or marketing. Suppliers are concerned that the partners might use their alliance to drive down prices.

The past alliance between Rover and Honda provides another valuable example, and one that was affected by changes of ownership. The agreement was started with an initiative from Sir Michael Edwardes in 1978 when he was Chief Executive of the Rover Group, then called British Leyland (BL). Edwardes considered that the new models being developed by BL were inadequate, particularly in the middle car range. He chose Honda because they were not too big to be interested in a deal with BL and because their technology was regarded as being very good. The Triumph Acclaim was the first car to emerge from the collaboration. BL enjoyed exclusive production and marketing rights to a Honda design and bought the necessary tooling from

# Minicase 16.3  Ford and General Motors

General Motors (GM) is the world's largest car manufacturer; Ford is second. Their corporate headquarters are less than 10 miles apart in Detroit, America. These two companies have followed quite different strategies in their quest for globalization.

General Motors has formed a loose network of international partners. 'We can realize synergies faster than in a full buy-out situation – we get most of the gain and less of the pain'.

GM's joint ventures have included the following:

- GM owns 20% of Fiat Auto (Italy) with an option to buy the remaining 80% should it so wish in 2003 – a reflection of Europe's overcapacity. As part of the deal, GM helps Fiat to market its Alfa Romeo brand in America, but the expensive Ferrari and Maserati brands are excluded from the alliance.
- GM also owns 20% of Fuji Heavy Industries, which includes Subaru cars and major components businesses.
- GM has 10% of Suzuki and 49% of Isuzu (trucks as well as cars).

In all of these cases, GM gains access to technology and platforms that would be hugely expensive to develop in-house.

- GM has also bought the remaining 50% of Saab to give it total control – it had held the first 50% for over ten years.

GM's philosophy is one of accord and it is generally opposed to hostile take-overs, but GM is on a learning curve for yielding the potentially elusive synergistic benefits of these alliances.

*General Motors*  http://www.gm.com

Ford, meanwhile, after many years of fundamentally organic growth, has made a series of acquisitions in the late 1990s: Jaguar, Land Rover, Aston Martin and Volvo. In 2000 Ford was declared 'preferred bidder' for Daewoo (which GM wanted as an alliance partner). Ford also bought Kwik Fit, the tyre and exhaust replacement specialist.

Ford's strategy is to buy and own *strong brands*, which it can position and market as it likes to complement the complete Ford portfolio. Chief Executive, Jacques Nasser, claims that GM would also have bought brands like these if it had been able.

There is a number of parallel alliances. Ford is allied with Peugeot-Citroën for diesel engine development, and with Yahoo!, Oracle and Microsoft for Internet services of various forms. It also has joint ventures in China, India and Turkey.

An earlier alliance with Volkswagen to build people carriers on a common platform failed to deliver the anticipated results and was abandoned. In addition, Ford took a 33%

shareholding in Mazda (in 1996) and accepted a major role in the control and running of the Japanese company. Importing American techniques into Japan is difficult, and Mazda's fortunes have fluctuated. Ford's dilemma concerns whether the Mazda brand should stand apart or be integrated into the rest of the Ford portfolio.

*Ford Motor Company*   http://www.ford.com

QUESTIONS: Whose approach do you believe is the better one? Why?

Honda. The first Rover 200 series was also developed jointly, with the 213 model having a Japanese engine. Later the agreement included the assembly of each other's related models, specifically the Rover 800 series and the Honda Legend.

During 1989 further progress was made. In July that year, having been acquired from the UK government by British Aerospace, Rover bought 20% of Honda (UK), which was to build a manufacturing plant in Swindon, Wiltshire. In return Honda acquired 20% of the Rover shares. In October Honda agreed that Rover's Longbridge plant in Birmingham would be the sole European source of its new model, the Concerto. The updated Rover 200 series was a comparable car.

Following this, Honda agreed to help Rover to raise its efficiency and productivity to world-class levels during the 1990s. Honda would also buy most of the body panels required for its European factories from Rover, but develop its new Swindon plant to produce more than one car. Rover would then cease to assemble for Honda.

When British Aerospace wanted to sell Rover in the early 1990s Honda was reluctant to take it over, as it did not want an overseas subsidiary of this nature. In the event Rover was bought by BMW which underestimated the investment required. Rover's links with Honda disappeared systematically and it became more European in nature. When BMW decided (in 1999) that it had 'had enough' Rover was handed over to a financial consortium based in the UK, but with American finance securing the bid. Afterwards it became apparent that Rover needed another alliance partner to help it to develop new models.

*3. To manage innovation more effectively.*

This is important because of high R&D costs and greater globalization, which together often ensure that any competitive advantage gained from technology is relatively short-lived. Both the opportunities and threats require that companies are able to be flexible and change quickly.

In 1995 Motorola joined with IBM, Siemens and Toshiba (an existing alliance) to develop the next generation of advanced memory chips, which are highly complex and extremely costly to develop and make. There is arguably a fourth reason – an attempt to regain lost competitiveness in a marketplace. This is thought to be the cause of a series of agreements among European electronics manufacturers, and links between them and Japanese and US competitors.

While there is a number of reasons and justifications for such strategic alliances, they can again be difficult strategies to implement effectively, as shown later in the chapter.

## Forms and Examples of Strategic Alliances and Joint Ventures

Strategic alliances and joint ventures can take a number of forms. The six categories which follow should not be seen as mutually exclusive; some joint ventures will cover more than one.

### Component parts of two or more businesses might be merged

GEC Alsthom was a 50:50 joint venture company formed in 1988 when the power systems divisions of GEC (the UK General Electric Corporation) were merged with the Alsthom subsidiary of France's CGE. The company, the largest manufacturer of generating equipment in the EU, was created to allow GEC and CGE to compete more effectively with ABB, Asea Brown Boveri, the Swedish/Swiss multinational and the world's biggest electrical engineering group. The companies compete directly in a number of sectors, such as railway equipment and rolling stock. More recently an alliance between GEC Alshtom and Siemens was mooted, to develop the high-speed trains of the future. The intention here would have been to reduce risk in an industry bedevilled by political issues. Governments around the world are inevitably involved and projects are frequently delayed or even cancelled for both political and financial reasons. In the event, GEC Alsthom was floated off as an independent business when George Simpson replaced Lord Weinstock as Chief Executive of GEC.

### Companies might agree to join forces to develop a new project

Club Méditerranee and Carnival Cruise Lines (US) joined forces to provide cruise-based holiday packages for Europe and Asia.

Philips and Nintendo have jointly developed a new generation of video games on compact discs compatible with Philips' CD-i (compact disc-interactive) players which link up to high-definition televisions.

Airbus Industrie was formed because no partner alone could afford the development costs of large passenger aircraft, and because of pressure from European governments who wanted to reduce the predominance of the large US companies.

Psion, UK manufacturer of palm-size computers and electronic organizers, has joined forces with the world's largest mobile telecommunications companies, Nokia, Motorola and Ericsson, to develop Internet-linked mobile phones and other products which use WAP (wireless application protocol) technology. This alliance was seen as a means of counteracting the power of Microsoft in one of the fastest growing areas of the computing industry.

Sony has been an innovative company throughout its 50-plus years of existence. Using its competencies in miniaturization it has developed a vast range of home electronics products, including the Walkman (in its many variants) and the PlayStation games consoles, sales of which now exceed 75 million units worldwide. Sony has recently joined forces with Intel (manufacturers of sophisticated memory chips) to develop applications that can again be linked to the Internet. One example is the Memory Stick, which stores images, music and computer files and then allows them to be used in various electronic devices. Sony is also partnered with DoCoMo, another Japanese company which has 17 million subscribers and specializes in delivering computer games and other services directly over the Internet.

## Companies might agree to develop a new business jointly

Sony and Apple (computers) of the USA earlier formed a new multimedia company as a joint venture. The aim here was to produce a 'palm-size, wire-less personal communication device with digital audio and visual functions'.

Cereal Partners World-wide is a joint venture designed to strengthen market access for the two companies involved. General Mills, an American rival to Kellogg, had developed a number of popular products (particularly Cheerios), but was not geared up to distribute them outside America. Nestlé owned a formidable distribution network and could provide access to most of Europe. Nestlé had earlier tried to break into this industry without any marked success.

## There might be specific agreements between manufacturers and their suppliers

Some years ago a new chief executive was appointed at the American electronics company NCR. As well as making sure that he formed a personal relationship with all of the company's major business customers (a very typical approach) he set up a programme of visits to every major supplier, which is more unusual. As a result, relationships have been strengthened for mutual benefit. Typical outcomes have been extended contracts but a reduction in the number of suppliers. Learning about each other's needs has delivered both service differentiation and lower costs.

American Express (AMEX), like many other large corporations, had a travel department which organized the global travel arrangements for its managers. They developed a competency which they now provide as a service to other corporations who prefer to outsource this task when they can find someone with the appropriate expertise. AMEX developed this competency further and moved into consumer travel as well.

## A company might make a strategic investment in another firm

Several years ago Guinness and LVMH exchanged shareholdings and formed a whole series of distribution joint ventures around the world. There were efficiency savings and marketing advantages from combining, in particular, the spirits brands of the two companies. LVMH owns the world's leading cognac brand, Hennessy, as well as its leading champagnes; Guinness, through its United Distillers subsidiary, owned a portfolio which includes Johnnie Walker, the world's best-selling Scotch whisky, and Gordon's gin, another international best-seller. However, Guinness merged with Grand Metropolitan (Minicase 14.1) and this put enormous stress on the joint venture. In fact, LVMH was able to dictate certain terms of the merger agreement.

British Telecom (BT) sees minority stakes and joint ventures as its path to a global presence. It has used this strategy to become the second largest competitor in several European countries, namely Sweden, France, Germany, The Netherlands, Spain, Portugal and Italy. BT, which has the most extensive portfolio of assets in the European telecommunications industry, claims that acquisitions were 'never on the cards' but does not rule out increasing its stake in the partner organizations.

## Companies might form international trading partnerships

Fujitsu of Japan has owned 80% of ICL, the UK computer manufacturer, for many years, but runs it as an independent subsidiary.

However, they are allied in the form of joint retailing and servicing in North America and Australia.

Disney Corporation, McDonald's and Coca-Cola, owners of three of the most important brands in the world, have a loose partnership which varies from country to country, depending upon how local managers wish to exploit its potential. There are several aspects to the partnership:

- McDonald's is Coca-Cola's largest customer and buys its soft drinks exclusively from Coca-Cola
- McDonald's sponsors activities and exhibits at Disney attractions as well as running restaurants on site
- Disney collaborates with McDonald's on special worldwide promotions which feature Disney characters, especially when new movies are released
- Coca-Cola is also the sole supplier of soft drinks to Disney's theme parks.

## Key Issues in Joint Ventures and Strategic Alliances

This concluding section summarizes the views of a number of key authors who have examined the relative success of alliances and joint ventures.

Kanter (1990) offers the following criteria as key determinants of their success:

- The alliance or joint venture must be important strategically for both partners.
- Ideally they should bring complementary, rather than exactly the same, competencies to the arrangement.
- Information must be shared openly.
- There should be genuine integration to create linkages, even though this may be across divergent cultures. Trust becomes essential.

- The arrangements should become institutionalized into some framework which can demonstrate a clear identity and a position of importance.

Kanter reinforces the point that alliance management needs to become a key strategic capability.

Ohmae (1989) argues that the following issues are significant and help to determine whether the agreement is likely to prove effective:

- Successful collaboration requires commitment on both sides. Without sufficient management time, trust and respect the agreement is likely to fail. In reality, all the required resources must be committed. Either for managing linkages, or for managing a new joint venture company, capable managers must be transferred or seconded. The outcome of the alliance will depend upon both the commitment of the partners and the emergent power and influence they exert.
- There must be mutual benefits, the attainment of which may well involve sacrifices on both sides. Both partners should appreciate clearly what the other party wants from the agreement, and their objectives. If the commitment of each ally is uneven, the keener partner or the faster learner is likely to assume control. This might mean that the interests of the weaker partner are either bought out or simply taken over.
- If circumstances change during the period of the alliance, flexibility may be required as the objectives and priorities of either or both partners may change.
- Cultural differences, which might be either geographic or corporate in origin, will have to be reconciled.

In addition, it is sensible if alliance partners see their joint involvement as an opportunity to learn new skills and good practices. Partners are not simply there to plug gaps or weaknesses.

Analysts acknowledge that the Japanese have been very good at learning from their alliances, and that Western companies have been slower to exploit the learning opportunities.

Badaracco (1991) differentiates between

- migratory knowledge – easily transferred technical skills, and
- embedded knowledge about how a company does business, which is particularly useful for deepening insight into new markets.

Where companies do enter an alliance through weakness rather than strength, it is vital that they use the partnership for learning and development. In 1991 Ford formed an alliance with Yamaha to develop a new engine for its Fiesta and Escort ranges. While such high-performance engines as the Ford Cosworth are the outcome of past joint ventures, this was the first incidence of an alliance for mainstream car engines. Analysts have commented that Ford needed an agreement because they had become weak in a rapidly changing industry, stimulated by new materials, higher fuel consumption expectations and tighter emission standards. 'Ford must learn from the deal, and not subcontract their engine technology for the long term.' Ford prefers acquisition to alliances (see Minicase 16.3).

Acquisitions should be evaluated in terms of their ability to generate synergy. Joint ventures and strategic alliances should be regarded in the same light. Devlin and Bleackley (1988) argue that the key issues are the strategic wisdom behind the decision to form an alliance in the first place, the choice of partner, and the management of the alliance once it has been agreed. The position of both parties to the agreement should be improved from the alliance. If there is a real opportunity for synergy, joint benefits and mutual trust and commitment by both parties, joint ventures can be an effective means of implementing strategic change. However, although some of the inherent diffi-

culties of acquisition are avoided by this type of agreement, there will still be implementation issues. Unless these are tackled properly, the joint venture is likely to prove expensive and tie up resources which might otherwise be deployed more effectively.

Alliances can fail and/or be dismantled for a number of reasons and consequently the extent to which any organization is dependent upon its alliances should be carefully monitored.

## Summary

Strategic alliances and joint ventures (a stronger type of alliance where shares are exchanged or an independent company is set up) provide an alternative to an acquisition or merger. While they are designed to deliver synergy, cost savings and access to either technology or markets, they are not without their own implementation challenges.

It is generally acknowledged that the Japanese in particular have developed real capabilities in alliance management and that many Western companies have looked upon them from a more defensive perspective. For example, they are an alternative when an acquisition is not feasible for whatever reason.

There are three main reasons behind this strategy:

- to gain access to new markets and technologies
- to share expensive research and development costs
- to manage innovation more effectively.

Clearly these reasons overlap.

There are six particular, and again overlapping, forms of alliance and joint venture:

1. the merging of component parts of two or more businesses
2. companies joining forces to develop a new project

3. companies joining forces to develop a new business together
4. agreements between partners in the same supply chain
5. where companies purchase a stake in another business for strategic, rather than purely financial, reasons
6. international trading partnerships.

For alliances and joint ventures to work successfully, commitment from all parties is required. Everyone must appreciate that they can benefit and commit accordingly. Trust, sharing and collaboration become essential, even though different cultures and languages might be involved.

## References

Badaracco, JL (1991) *The Knowledge Link: How Firms Compete Through Strategic Alliances*, Harvard Business School Press.

Connell, DC (1988) Strategic partnering and competitive advantage, Presented at the 8th Annual Strategic Management Society Conference, Amsterdam, October.

Devlin, G and Bleackley, M (1988) Strategic alliances – guidelines for success, *Long Range Planning*, 21(5), October.

Garrette, B and Dussauge, P (1999) Strategic alliances – why Europe needs to catch up, *Financial Times Mastering Global Business*, No. 5.

Kanter, RM (1990) *Synergies, Alliances and New Ventures*, Harvard Business School video package.

Ohmae, K (1989) The global logic of strategic alliances, *Harvard Business Review*, March–April.

Test your knowledge of this chapter with our online quiz at: http://www.thomsonlearning.co.uk

Explore Strategic Alliances and Joint Ventures further at:

*Harvard Business Review*    http://www.hbsp.harvard.edu/products/hbr/index.html

*Long Range Planning*    http://www.lrp.ac

## Questions and Research Assignments

### TEXT RELATED

1. What exactly is the difference between a strategic alliance and a joint venture? Can you provide examples of each – in addition to those included in the text?

2. Do you agree with the view that, if they are established and managed carefully, strong alliances can provide all the benefits of an acquisition or merger without most of the drawbacks?

## Internet and Library Projects

1. Take any well-known Japanese manufacturer, such as Toshiba or Sony, and determine how many alliances and joint ventures they have and what they are designed to contribute strategically.

*Toshiba* http://www.toshiba.co.jp

*Sony* http://www.sony.com

2. Using actual examples as your base point, could the high-technology things we currently take for granted (such as mobile phones, personal computers and the Internet) have been developed to the stage they have if companies had worked in isolation? Has the co-operation approach been more sensible and realistic than a series of cross-border mergers?

# 17

# Business Failure

*Ultimate business failure implies closure or liquidation. The organization has failed to satisfy certain key stakeholders and it has ceased to be financially viable. It is beyond turning around by new management. This happens with many small businesses and it also happens from time to time with much larger and established organizations. However, the larger the organization the greater the general likelihood that at least some part can be rescued. Where the fortunes of a business have sunk to a crisis level and radical changes of strategy are required, this clearly also represents failure – even if with sound retrenchment and turnaround strategies (the subject of Chapter 18) the business can be rescued. It is a failure of strategic management because mistakes have been made, in the form of either poor decisions or relative inactivity in the face of a need to change. If a business, or a part of a business, is sold because it is unprofitable, this may well represent failure by the current management team. The assumption is that the business has a stronger future 'in different hands'. However, one should not assume that all divestments of this nature imply failure – they may simply represent poor strategic fit and maybe a past misjudgement. Hence the study of failure here concerns why the performance of a business can sink to a crisis level which demands either drastic remedial action, sale or closure.*

Poor strategic leadership, insufficient control of the essential aspects of financial management and the failure to be competitive are the key issues behind corporate decline and failure. All of them are manifested in the opening case on Laker Airways.

A number of the references used here are some years old, which implies that the realities of business failure have been known about for several years and that any more recent research has tended merely to confirm previous work.

# Minicase 17.1  Laker Airways

Freddie Laker, who became Sir Freddie in 1978, was an entrepreneur and a pioneer in the
competitive international air transport industry. He was a well-quoted self-publicist whose
commercial exploits brought him fame and recognition. He introduced cheap trans-
Atlantic air travel, providing travel opportunities for many people who previously had not
been able to afford the fares, but his business collapsed in the early 1980s. At the time he
blamed others for his demise and, while there is substance in his argument, the fact
remains that he had personally sown the seeds of his downfall with a flawed strategy.
However, he would later bounce back again.

Laker was born in 1922 in Canterbury. His trigger for a life in aviation was a sight of the
*Hindenberg* and a Handley-Page biplane flying over his house when he was still a boy. He
subsequently learned to fly and served with the Air Transport Auxiliary in World War II.
In 1953 he began his first business, Channel Air Bridge Ltd, to sell air transportation of
vehicles, passengers and cargo (including live animals) on the same aircraft. He was
involved in the design and development of Gatwick Airport, before he helped to develop
and run British United Airways in 1960. At this time BUA was the largest aircraft company
in the private sector. His next venture, Laker Airways in 1966, was a small independent
company 'operated on a shoestring' which offered inclusive package holidays and provided
charter flights for organizations who could book all the seats on a plane and flights for tour
companies who did not own their own airline. He was the first all-jet carrier in the UK.
Laker's stated intention was to stay small: 'If we get any bigger than six planes you can
kick my arse.' From a marketing perspective, Laker was always pioneering new ideas.

In the 1970s his ambitions changed and he became determined to 'try a new market and
offer transport to a lot more people'. At this time the only cheap air fares across the
Atlantic were charter flights, whereby travellers had to be a member of some sponsoring
organization for at least six months before flying. The international carriers operated a

price-fixing cartel organized by the International Air Transport Association (IATA) with the connivance of all governments concerned. Charter flight regulations tended to be abused, and consequently the major carriers fought for stricter monitoring which brought about a decline. Laker conceived Skytrain, a 'no booking, no frills' operation with prices significantly below those offered by the major airlines, who naturally opposed his idea.

Laker applied to the Civil Aviation Authority (CAA) for a licence first in 1971 and was refused. In late 1972 he was given permission as long as he flew out of London's Stansted airport, although his base was on the other side of London at Gatwick. Delaying tactics involving British and US airlines, the UK Labour government, the US government and the American equivalent of the CAA meant that the first flight did not take place until September 1977, when Skytrain was launched with enormous publicity, this time from Gatwick. In this period oil prices had increased dramatically and Skytrain, although still under £100 for a single fare, was double the price estimated in 1971. In turn, the Skytrain fare was well under half the cost of the cheapest fare offered by IATA carriers, who subsequently had to reduce their fares in the face of this new competition.

Although they claimed that they did this reluctantly, it had a devastating impact on Laker, who accused them of adopting a predatory pricing strategy purely to try and drive him out of business. Skytrain's competitive strategy, and apparent advantage, was its low price resulting from its low cost base, but its service package was clearly inferior to that of the major carriers. When the price gap was narrowed, Skytrain became less attractive to customers and its early competitive advantage was not sustainable.

Skytrain made £2 million profits in its first year of operation, but difficulties experienced when it was extended to Los Angeles in 1978 effectively wiped out the profitability. In 1979 Laker became a fully licensed trans-Atlantic carrier and for the first time was able to pre-sell reserved seats. Laker's confidence grew, and anticipating that he would be given permission to fly more routes around the world he ordered ten Airbus A-300s and five McDonnell Douglas DC10s at a total cost of £300 million. Eventually this was to bring about his downfall. Laker was already using DC10s for Skytrain and when the US government grounded all DC10s for checks in 1979 Laker lost £13 million in revenue. In 1980 he failed to win licences to fly Skytrain in Europe and to Hong Kong, although he did begin services from Prestwick and Manchester and to Miami.

Profits of £2.2 million were reported for 1980–81, but significantly three-quarters of this came from favourable currency movements. By 1981 the pound was falling against the dollar, demand was declining, revenue was down, but the debt interest payments, mostly in dollars, were rising. There were, in effect, too many planes and not enough passengers flying the Atlantic. The major airlines wanted fares to rise, but Skytrain remained the force that kept them low. Laker managed to renegotiate some interest payments and a cash injection from McDonnell Douglas, but he also had to increase fares and sell his Airbuses. He was left with a break-even level of virtually all the seats on every Skytrain, but was able to fill only one-third of them. When the receiver was called in (February 1982) Laker had debts of some £270 million.

Laker had pioneered cheap trans-Atlantic air fares, which have stayed in different guises since his collapse, but he made the mistake of becoming overconfident. The man who originally intended to stay small went for growth. At the same time he was determined to retain total control of his company and therefore raised loan capital against very limited assets rather than seeking outside equity funding. The interest payments brought him down, particularly as he raised most of the money in dollars without adequate cover against currency fluctuations. Finally, as something of a buccaneering character described by one airline executive as a man who 'a few hundred years ago would have brass ear-rings, a beard and a cutlass', he underestimated the power of the vested interests who opposed him. Had their opposition not delayed the introduction of Skytrain by six years, maybe things would have turned out differently.

A bitter Sir Freddie moved to Florida, and by the early 1990s he was back. In 1992 he began regular flights to and from the Bahamas from his new hub; and then, in 1996, he returned to the UK with return charter flights to Gatwick from Orlando. This time he intended to compete on service as well as discounted prices – he had learned a hard lesson. He negotiated convenient take-off and landing times and offered above-normal baggage allowances. His drinks (in crystal glasses) and food (served on china with stainless steel cutlery) were to be superior to most other charter flights. Would the package prove sufficiently different and would he be able to fly his small fleet of DC10s reliably? Yet again, all would not go smoothly.

QUESTION: How much of Freddie Laker's downfall was the result of his own misjudgements and how much was it external forces?
Project: Use the Internet to assess the significance of the last comment: 'again, all would not go smoothly'.

Photograph: City 2000 Plc (www.city2000.com)

## Introduction: Failure in Context

In broad terms it could be argued that a company is failing if it does not meet the objectives set for it by its stakeholders, or if it produces outputs that are considered undesirable by those associated with it. The outcome may not be ultimate failure, closure or liquidation, however. When the 'failure' or the decline reaches a certain level, or continues for a certain length of time, this should act as a trigger for remedial action. Such action might be spurned, of course, or prove inadequate, such that the business deteriorates and is finally liquidated.

A company which polluted or harmed the natural environment in some way would be classified as unsuccessful – and maybe even perceived as a failure – by certain stakeholders, but it would not necessarily fail financially and go out of business. Companies sometimes develop and launch new products that fail because very few people buy them – the Ford Edsel car and Strand cigarettes are well-quoted examples. In this respect the companies are unsuccessful with particular competitive strategies, but again they may not necessarily experience corporate failure as a result.

Corporate failure, liquidation and the lack of success should not then be seen as synonymous terms. A private-sector, profit-seeking organization would certainly be classified as a failure if it ended up in liquidation and was closed down with its assets sold off piecemeal. A similar company might be unsuccessful and in decline, but able to avoid liquidation. Appropriate strategic action that addresses the causes of the decline may generate recovery. For example, the major shareholders might insist upon the appointment of a new strategic leader, or the financial or competitive weaknesses might be acted upon. Such a company might also be acquired by another, and this may be because the shareholders are happy to sell their shares or because the company has been placed in receivership and the receiver has arranged the sale of the business as a going concern. Receivership occurs when a business is unable to pay its creditors, for example its suppliers or bank-loan interest. The receiver is normally a professional accountant and is charged with saving the business if it is possible to do so.

In a similar way a non-profit-seeking organization could be closed down or provided with new leadership and direction on the insistence of its major financial stakeholders or trustees.

A company might be relatively unsuccessful compared with its competitors for a prolonged period if the key stakeholders allow it, but it is never perceived to be failing. For example, a small private company whose shares are not quoted on the stock exchange might be making only very limited profits and growing at a rate slower than its industry, but its owners may be happy for it to stay in existence as long as it is solvent. This could be because the owners are drawing substantial earnings and not reinvesting to build a future – for them the business exists to provide them with a lavish lifestyle. In the English football league a large number of clubs, particularly outside the Premier League, fail to make any profit on their footballing activities because their crowds are too low, but other commercial activities, sponsorship, sales of players – and particularly benevolent directors – keep them in business. However, such a lack of

success consistently will weaken the company, cause it to exhibit symptoms of decline (discussed below) and may ultimately lead to failure.

The forthcoming sections look at what factors typically lead to corporate decline and failure and at how managers might realize that their company is heading for failure unless remedial action is taken. Turnaround strategies for companies in trouble will be considered in detail in Chapter 18.

## Symptoms of Decline

Symptoms of decline are not the causes of failure but indicators that a company might be heading for failure. They will show when a company is performing unsuccessfully relative to what might be expected by an objective outsider or analyst. As mentioned above they will indicate the outcome of poor strategic leadership, inadequate financial management or a lack of competitiveness. Slatter (1984), building on the earlier work of Argenti (1976), analysed 40 UK companies in decline situations which either have been turned around or have failed. He concluded that there are ten major symptoms. In the same way that relative success can be evaluated from financial analysis, several of these symptoms of decline are finance based:

- falling profitability
- reduced dividends, because the firm is reinvesting a greater percentage of profits
- falling sales, measured by volume or revenue after accounting for inflation
- increasing debt
- decreasing liquidity
- delays in publishing financial results, a typical indicator that something is wrong
- declining market share
- high turnover of managers
- top management fear, such that essential tasks and pressing problems are ignored

- lack of planning or strategic thinking, reflecting a lack of clear direction.

If any of these symptoms are perceived it will be necessary to identify the underlying causes before any remedial action might be attempted. Slatter concluded that a number of causal factors recurred on several occasions in the companies that he studied, and these are summarized below, but categorized in terms of issues of leadership, finance and competitiveness.

While Slatter's work is over ten years old, more recent research by the Society of Practitioners of Insolvency (1995) reaffirms his arguments. An investigation of 1000 insolvencies in 1994 determined that the greatest single cause of business failure was loss of market, which was responsible for 29% of the insolvencies. Inadequate cash flow accounted for a further 25% and leadership failings 16%. Earlier analyses by the SPI placed greater emphasis on inadequacies in the financial structure of organizations.

## Signals of weak strategic leadership

This list of warning signals has been largely derived from Heller (1998) and Oates (1990) and it relates mainly, but not exclusively, to smaller organizations.

1. *The existence of (too many) 'would-bes'* – Something critical is missing. Possibly the interested people have a will to do something different but lack a good new idea; some key competence is missing, making implementation difficult; or there is a lack of true commitment to an idea, opportunity or venture.
2. *The single-dimension paradox* – The start-up stage for a small business has progressed well, but there is a lack of ability or opportunity to grow the business beyond the initial stages. The idea might only be viable in the short term; there may be inadequate funding; the entrepreneur may be unwilling to let go at the critical time; the initiative could

simply run out of steam. The paradox is that the clear focus and individual drive that get the initiative moving in the first place can be what brings it down, through a lack of necessary flexibility.

3. *The business is a 'half-way house'* – In other words it is a franchise or co-operative (or something conceptually similar) and critically dependent upon the continued support and engagement of others who may be outside the business.
4. *The business is 'impoverished'* – Specifically, it fails to achieve, or it loses, a winning strategic position – it is not sufficiently different. Funding is difficult or mismanaged and the business is undercapitalized. Insufficient attention is given to getting the quality right to 'delight' customers. The management team has not developed in the appropriate way, or it has been weakened by people leaving, such that key skills are missing. The business cannot cope when succession becomes an issue.
5. *The business is blinkered* – There is too much self-belief, perhaps driven by an orientation to production rather than customers – the 'we know best' syndrome. The strategic leader is unwilling to accept outside views and advice.
6. *The business is technology shy* – There is a tension here – the business needs capital and technology, but it all costs money. The key questions are just when do you invest and how much do you spend?
7. *The business has become smothered* – Specifically, it has become too bureaucratic, either because of government or even European legislation/rules and regulations, or because it has become bigger and more structured and has lost its creative spark. This latter issue is debated in greater depth in Chapter 24.
8. *The business is (now) run by a crisis manager* – a manager who relies too much on an ability

to deal (or not deal!) with setbacks and crises as they arise, often implying the wrong trade-off between reactive and proactive strategies.

9. *The business has started making (too many) mistakes* – Possibly it has become too ambitious, say with misjudged diversification or acquisition. Maybe it has ignored warning signs such as a cash shortage. Maybe it is simply too greedy.

The next section discusses how these signals are often the prelude to decline and failure.

## Causes of Decline

### Inadequate strategic leadership

#### Poor management

It was shown in Chapter 12 how inadequate strategic leadership can be manifested in a number of ways, which in turn cause key strategic issues to be neglected or ignored. The company could be controlled or dominated by one person whose pursuit of particular personal objectives or style of leadership might create problems or lead to inadequate performance.

The organization might fail to develop new corporate or competitive strategies such that previous levels of performance and success are not maintained when particular products, services or strategies go into decline. This issue can be compounded or alleviated by weak or strong managers, respectively, supporting the strategic leader, and by the quality of non-executive directors on the board.

Poor strategic leadership in terms of building an appropriate organization might mean that key issues or key success factors are ignored or are not given the attention they deserve. A company that is dominated by accountants or engineers might, for example, fail to pay sufficient attention to changing customer requirements and competition. Equally, a company without adequate financial management might ignore aspects of cost and cash-flow management – a factor which will be explored next. Similarly, a company that is undergoing rapid change and possibly diversification might concentrate its resources in the areas of development and neglect the core businesses which should be providing strong foundations for the growth.

#### Acquisitions which fail to match expectations

As shown in Chapter 15, companies seeking growth or diversification may acquire or take over other companies, or merge with them. Research consistently confirms that in many cases the profits and successes anticipated from the acquisition fail to materialize. This can be the result of a poor choice by the strategic leader, who overestimates the potential, or an inability to manage the larger organization effectively because the problems are underestimated. It is not unusual for companies which fail to have sought fast growth, often following strategies involving major acquisitions.

#### Mismanagement of big projects

This is related to the previous point, but incorporates a number of other possible strategic decisions. By big projects is meant any really new venture for an organization, including developing new and different products and entering new markets, possibly abroad. It is essential to forecast potential revenues without being unrealistically optimistic, and to control expenditures and costs, but this does not always happen. It seems that companies often:

- underestimate the capital requirements – through poor planning, design changes once the project is underway, and inaccurate estimations of the development time that will be required

- experience unforeseen start-up difficulties – sometimes resulting from lack of foresight and sometimes from misfortune
- misjudge the costs of market entry because of customer hostility or hesitation, or the actions of competitors.

Companies should be careful not to stretch their financial and managerial resources with big projects as they can cause other healthier parts of the business to suffer.

## Dishonesty

There is no doubt that some strategic leaders and businesses take chances and risks which amount to 'sharp practice' and rely on not being found out. However, if there is real dishonesty, and it is found out, then ultimately the business may find survival difficult. The story of the collapse of Robert Maxwell's business empire, after his untimely death by drowning, is well known – he had been using funds from the Mirror Group pension fund to shore up other businesses which needed cash. Once the real extent of the funding needs became known, the whole empire was in danger. A very astute businessman had become too greedy and then turned to desperate measures.

# Poor financial management

## Poor financial control

This can manifest itself in a number of ways. Particularly important are the failure to manage cash flow and the incidence of temporary illiquidity as a result of overtrading. Inadequate costing systems can mean that companies are not properly aware of the costs of the different products and services that they produce, and as a result they can move from profit to loss if the mix of products that they produce and sell is changed.

If an organization invests in expensive equipment for potentially lower costs or product differentiation, then it automatically increases its fixed costs or overheads. This will increase the break-even point and consequently make the company more volume sensitive. Investments of this nature should not be undertaken lightly and without a thorough and objective assessment of market potential; but some companies do invest without adequate analysis and create financial problems for themselves.

Finally, some companies in decline situations appear not to budget properly. Budgets are short-term financial plans which forecast potential demand and sales revenue, the costs that will be incurred in meeting this demand, and the flow of cash in and out of the business. If budgeted targets are not being met it is essential to investigate why and take any steps necessary to improve the situation. Without proper budgeting companies cannot estimate profits and cash needs adequately and can therefore experience unexpected financial difficulties.

## Cost disadvantages

In addition to the problem of breaking even and covering overheads, described above, companies can experience other cost disadvantages which result in decline.

Companies without scale economies can be at a cost disadvantage relative to larger competitors and suffer in terms of low profit or a failure to win orders because their prices are higher.

Other companies which are vertically integrated and able to exercise control over their supplies, or which are located in areas where labour or service costs are relatively low, can enjoy an absolute cost advantage over their rivals and thereby put pressure on them.

Company structure can yield both cost advantages and cost disadvantages. Large multi-product companies can subsidize the cost of certain products and again put pressure on their rivals; or conversely they can find that their costs are higher than their smaller competitors because of the overhead costs of the organization structure, say through an expensive head office.

Finally, poor operating management can mean low productivity and higher costs than ought to be incurred, and thereby cause decline. These cost problems all affect competitiveness and they are therefore linked to the additional competition factors discussed below.

## Other issues

The debt ratio should be controlled so that companies do not risk embarrassment through not being able to pay interest charges because of low profits. Companies which rely on loan capital may find that in years of low profits they are unable to invest sufficiently and this may lead to decline. Conversely, other companies may decline because they have not invested as a result of conservatism rather than financial inability. This reflects another weakness of strategic leadership.

## Competitive forces

Porter's model of the forces that determine industry profitability was discussed in Chapter 8. While all the relevant forces can be managed to create competitive advantage, each of them could cause a weak competitor to be in a decline situation.

### The effect of competitive changes

Primarily, companies can find themselves in decline situations if their products or services cease to be competitive. Their effective life and attractiveness to customers might be ending; or their competitors might have improved their product or introduced something new, thereby strengthening their product differentiation and competitive edge and inevitably causing demand for other products to fall. In other words, decline can result from a loss of clear differentia-

tion and in turn a failure to maintain competitive advantage.

If costs increase, say because of increased labour costs which competitors manage to avoid, then pressure will be put on prices or profit margins, and it may no longer be worthwhile manufacturing the product or service.

### Resource problems

It was mentioned above that increased labour costs can render a company uncompetitive; other resources controlled by strong suppliers can have a similar effect. In addition, a company can experience cost problems as a result of currency fluctuations if it fails to buy forward appropriately to offset any risk, and with property rents if leases expire and need renegotiating during a period of inflation.

### Inadequate or badly directed marketing

This factor relates to issues of rivalry between competitors. Companies whose competitive strategies rely on differentiation must ensure that customers recognize and value the source of the differentiation. This requires creative and effective advertising and promotion targeted to the appropriate segments and can be very expensive, especially if the industry is characterized by high advertising budgets. Companies who fail to market their products or services effectively may decline because they are failing to achieve adequate sales.

Minicase 17.1, Laker Airways, illustrates a number of the above points. Freddie Laker, when he launched his Skytrain, undercut the prices of the major airlines and appealed to a distinct sector of the market, but he was overconfident and committed too many resources to his new venture and to possible growth which did not materialize. His financial arrangements constituted his downfall. The case also illustrates the importance of understanding and not underestimating the environmental forces that influence the organization.

Minicase

# Minicase 17.2  de Lorean

The case of John de Lorean goes back some 20 years, but provides an ideal example of a high profile business failure.

In 1978 the UK (Labour) government was completely behind de Lorean's ambitious plan to build a radical new car in Northern Ireland. While de Lorean was ultimately the architect of his own downfall, the appointed receiver to the business later commented that 'a more robust project could have succeeded'. Anxious to secure the car plant for the troubled Belfast region, the government was pushed into acting quickly, arguably too hastily, and failed to investigate all of de Lorean's past business experiences. They were persuaded by his public image and salesmanship. In the event, £80 million of public money and 2600 newly-created jobs were lost.

John de Lorean was born in 1925, the eldest son of a Detroit foundry worker. He obtained degrees in music, industrial engineering and business administration; his first employer was General Motors, where he rose through the ranks. By 1970 he was general manager of GM's Chevrolet division and he was being tipped by some as a future GM president. Tall, elegant, stylish and charismatic he was 'unparalleled as a salesman' and hugely popular with the company's extensive and powerful dealer network. While his career progressed rapidly and was seemingly trouble free, his high-profile personal life was different. In 1969 he was divorced from his first wife and quickly remarried to the 19-year-old daughter of a football star. Two years later he was divorced again and dating film stars from Hollywood. He had been attracted by the glamour of the movie industry and his position in General Motors allowed him to socialize accordingly. His third wife was a New York fashion model. At this time he grew his hair and took to dressing in trendy clothes, which was seen as unusual for a prominent corporate executive. His whole lifestyle was 'expensive and flamboyant'.

Nevertheless, he was incredibly focused and worked long hours and, partly for this reason, other 'skeletons in his cupboard' were largely ignored. Over a period of years he had made substantial personal investments in businesses which had all folded with acrimony and litigation. These activities, which included motor racing circuit franchising and car radiator manufacture, were related to automobiles. In 1973 he resigned from GM and announced his vision for an innovative and radical new car built in a state-of-the-art production facility. He blamed 'restrictive management controls' in GM for his move. There had been a number of signals and indicators that de Lorean might be a high-risk investment for the UK government, but they were largely overlooked.

The dream car would be built of stainless steel and feature distinctive gull-wing doors, hinged at the top. There were 'innovations to improve safety and driveability . . . an emphasis on style and quality . . . all at a reasonable price'. Part of its ultimate fame would come from its starring role as a time machine in the three *Back to the Future* films. John de Lorean was able to secure $175 million to finance the venture and finally chose Belfast in preference to Detroit, Puerto Rico and the Republic of Ireland, influenced by grants and a speedy decision. His outline concept was translated into a production model by Group Lotus under a subcontract arrangement. Both John de Lorean and Colin Chapman of Lotus agreed to handle the financial arrangements through a Swiss-based third party organization. It later transpired that this company was in reality also a convenient vehicle for siphoning UK government funds and moving them back to the US to cover personal loans to de Lorean himself.

The deal was struck in 1978, and within two years cars were coming off the line. A 72 acre field, with two rivers running through it, had been transformed into an advanced production facility. A dealer network was in place across the key market of North America, for where most of the cars were destined, and various personalities were signed up for endorsement advertising. De Lorean made things happen, but the controls were inadequate. Costs were escalating, production difficulties were emerging, and de Lorean began to talk about prices 20% above the original estimate. He needed more money than he had forecast, and he began to seek funds from every source he could identify. Attempting to hide the severity of the problems, he continued to insist that the funding stream was secure. Flying across the Atlantic on Concorde on at least a weekly basis and maintaining his expensive lifestyle, de Lorean successfully covered up the precarious state of his personal and business finances. The extra funding was never in place and the company went into receivership in 1982. The plant ultimately closed; the dream was over. Nevertheless, 8000 cars had been made and sold. In 1999 some 6000 of these were still on the road. Judged on the sales record after its launch, the car was clearly a success. Customers liked it and bought it. John de Lorean understood his market.

However, to compound matters further in 1982, de Lorean was charged with attempting to broker a $24 million cocaine deal in an endeavour to raise money. While he was acquitted on the grounds of federal entrapment, his credibility was finally shattered. It seems an ultimate irony that de Lorean described his factory as 'the world's first ethical car company' and chastised GM managers as 'men of sound personal morality, but all too capable, as a group, of reaching business decisions which were irresponsible and of dubious morality'.

QUESTIONS: Why do you think the receiver to de Lorean commented that 'a more robust project could have succeeded'?
What are the lessons concerning success and failure in this case?

*De Lorean* http://www.delorean.com

Minicase 17.2, de Lorean, tells the story of another product which customers liked and which, this time, had real competitive advantage. The failure here came down to inadequate controls and then apparent dishonesty in an attempt to cover up and deal with the difficulties.

In a decline situation a number of the factors above may be present and interlinked, and it may not be easy to distinguish between cause and effect. For example, a company may be losing market share or sales and experiencing a decline in profits because its product or service is no longer competitive. It may have a cost disadvantage or its competitors may have more effective sources of differentiation. Is the cause of this situation poor management internally which has failed to contain costs or create and sustain competitive advantage, or the result of external competitive forces to some extent outside the control of the organization? If the company is to be turned around, then both the symptoms of decline and the underlying causes need to be acted upon.

In simple terms, when a company is in real trouble the strategic leader, who may be new and brought in specially, might be expected to perform one of a number of alternative roles. He or she may have to act as first an undertaker and liquidate the company, secondly a pathologist, carrying out major surgery such as divesting poorly performing parts of the business or cutting their size, or thirdly a health clinic doctor, restoring the company's fortunes. Prices might be increased to generate more revenue or improve the gross margin. Variable costs, and if possible fixed costs, might well be reduced, again to improve margins and also to reduce the need for working capital. Divestment is one way of reducing assets and generating revenue. Attempts are also likely to be made to improve stock and debtor turnover in order to improve the cash flow. The alternative strategies will be explored in detail in Chapter 18.

It should be emphasized that the strategic leader who is an expert at consolidating a company experiencing difficulties may or may not be the ideal person to rebuild new competitive advantages.

## Predicting a Failure

KEY CONCEPT – Box 17.1
Z-scores

The original Z-score of Altman (1968) is:

$$Z = 1.2 \times X^1 + 1.4 \times X^2 + 3.3 \times X^3 + 0.6 \times X^4 + 1.0 \times X^5$$

Where

$X^1$ = working capital divided by total assets

$X^2$ = retained earnings divided by total assets

$X^3$ = earnings before interest and tax divided by total assets

$X^4$ = market value of equity divided by book value of total debt

$X^5$ = sales divided by total assets

and

• working capital is current assets less current liabilities
• total assets is fixed assets plus all current assets
• retained earnings is accumulated profits in the business
• market value of equity is the number of ordinary shares × their current market price + the value of preference shares
• book value of total debt is long-, medium- and short-term debt, including overdraft.

For US companies. Altman argued that if *Z* is less than 1.8 they are 'certain to go bust' and if it exceeds 3.0 they are 'almost certain not to'. Argenti (1976) suggests that the appropriate UK figures are more of the order of 1.5 and 2.0, respectively.

Companies with a strong asset base will tend to have a high *Z*-score under the Altman formula, but such businesses do fail, generally then being sold as going concerns.

Taffler (1977) has devised an alternative formula which places greater emphasis on liquidity:

$$Z = 0.53 \times X^1 + 0.13 \times X^2 + 0.18 \times X^3 + 0.16 \times X^4$$

Where

$X^1$ = profit before tax divided by current liabilities (incorporating profitability)

$X^2$ = current assets divided by total debts (working capital)

$X^3$ = current liabilities divided by total assets (financial risk)

$X^4$ = the no credit interval (liquidity)

and the 'no credit interval' is defined as:

$$\frac{\text{Immediate assets} - \text{current liabilities}}{\text{Operating costs} - \text{depreciation}}$$

Using Taffler's formula a score in excess of 0.2, and certainly 0.3, indicates a company with good long-term prospects; below 0.2, and definitely below 0.0, is a score characteristic of companies which have failed in the past.

*Sources*: Altman, El (1968) Financial ratios, discriminant analysis, and the prediction of corporate bankruptcy, *Journal of Finance*, **23**(4), September. Argenti, J (1976) *Corporate Collapse*, McGraw Hill. Taffer RJ (1977) Going, going, gone, *Accountancy*, March.

Financial databases, such as Datastream, typically provide an index known as a Z-score, which was originally devised by Edward Altman (1968) and which purports to predict potential corporate failure as a result of insolvency. Altman's research in the USA in the 1960s found the Z-score to be a good indicator of potential bankruptcy, but further research in the UK by Argenti (1976) and others suggests that the index should be used cautiously. The Z-score, which is explained in Box 17.1, is thought to be more appropriate in the last two years before bankruptcy when it could be argued that a good financial analyst should be able to see clearly that a company is experiencing difficulties and is in decline. Box 17.1 also includes details of a refined version developed by Taffler (1977). The attractiveness and potential value of these indicators remain, despite their limitations, and Urry (1999) reports a more recent framework, an *H*-score, from Company Watch, which increases the number of ratios to 7. The *H*-score again relies on profits in relation to current liabilities, liquidity and the adequacy of the long-term capital base.

Argenti argues that managers rarely look for symptoms of decline, and consequently the Z-score can be a useful indicator of when such an analysis might be appropriate. If a company appears to be in decline and the trend is identified soon enough, then recovery strategies can be initiated.

## Summary

Ultimate business failure happens when a business is liquidated or sold. Its managers have made strategic errors or misjudgements; maybe they simply avoided the need to change in a dynamic environment. However, a business can similarly fail to meet the needs and expectations of key stakeholders, experience financial difficulties but be 'saved'. In this latter case, one or more factors might be involved. A new strategic leader might be appointed who succeeds in turning the company around. Part, or all, of the business might be sold.

There are several signals of a company in difficulty – these constitute symptoms of the failing situation. These should normally be easily discerned by vigilant managers who are tracking a company's performance although, on occasions, circumstances can change quickly. It is the actions which follow that are critical, as shown in Chapter 18. At the end of this chapter a summary of Z-scores was included; these are sometimes used as a predictor of failure.

Companies fail for a variety of reasons, and normally more than one factor is in evidence. The main ones are:

- *Poor management* – either at strategic leader level, or through the heart of the organization. The latter is also indicative of weak leadership.

- *Poor financial control* – weak budgeting and cost management; an inability to cover overheads.
- *Competition* – the company has become relatively weak in comparison to its competitors.
- *Decline in profits* – meaning that there is inadequate funding to meet the business' commitments (suppliers' bills and interest on loans, for example), let alone reinvest in the business. This can be the outcome of lost competitiveness or poor financial management.
- *Decline in demand for the product or service* – which implies a need to change and suggests an inadequate response by the company's managers.

These last three factors all imply *poor marketing*.

- *Misjudged acquisitions or other changes in corporate strategy* – implying that the company's resources have been overstretched and attention has been diverted away from the needs of existing products and services.

## References

Altman, EI (1968) Financial ratios, discriminant analysis and the prediction of corporate bankruptcy, *Journal of Finance*, 23(4), September. The Z-score is explored further in Altman, EI (1971) *Corporate Bankruptcy in America*, Heath.

Argenti, J (1976) *Corporate Collapse*, McGraw-Hill.

Heller, R (1998) *Goldfinger – How Entrepreneurs Get Rich by Starting Small*, Harper Collins.

Oates, D (1990) *The Complete Entrepreneur*, Mercury.

Slatter, S (1984) *Corporate Recovery: Successful Turnaround Strategies and their Implementation*, Penguin.

Society of Practitioners in Insolvency (1995) *Personal Insolvency in the UK*, SPI, London.

Taffler, RJ (1977) Going, going, gone, *Accountancy*, March.

Urry, M (1999) Early warning signals, *Financial Times*, 3 October.

Test your knowledge of this chapter with our online quiz at: http://www.thomsonlearning.co.uk

Explore Business failure further at:

*Accountancy*   http://www.accountancymag.co.uk

*Financial Times*   http://news.ft.com

*Journal of Finance*   http://www.afajof.org/jofihome.shtml

## Questions and Research Assignments

### TEXT RELATED

1. Do the causes discussed in this chapter provide an adequate explanation for any corporate failure with which you are familiar?

## Internet and Library Projects

1. In the 1980s, Z-scores provided by Datastream suggested that the following companies (amongst others) were in decline:

- Rover Group (then British Leyland)
- British Aluminium
- Renold (chainmakers)
- Acrow (cranemakers)
- Dunlop
- Lucas
- Tube Investments.

A number of other companies (including those listed below) was considered vulnerable to acquisition because their share prices were low in comparison with the book value of their assets:

- Lonrho
- P&O
- House of Fraser
- Debenhams
- Tootal Group
- Coats Patons
- British Aerospace
- Vickers.

Ascertain what has happened to these companies in the past 15 years, and based on your findings, decide how valuable you believe the Z-score might be.

You will realize that several of these organizations are used as examples in different parts of the book.

*Datastream*   http://www.dstm.com

# 18 Strategies for Consolidation and Recovery

The Feasibility of Recovery

Retrenchment Strategies

Turnaround Strategies

Divestment Strategies

Managing in A Recession

Strategies for Declining Industries

Implementing Recovery Strategies

*At any given time certain industries will provide attractive growth prospects for those companies who already compete in them, and for potential newcomers. At the same time, however, other industries will be in terminal decline. This might be taking place slowly or rapidly. In the case of slow decline, profitable opportunities may still exist for those companies that can relate best to changing market needs. Where decline is rapid, prospects are likely to be very limited. A third group of industries might be undergoing significant change, and the companies that can adapt effectively will be able to survive and grow.*

*Japan and South Korea now lead the world with 'run-of-the-mill' tankers and container ships. Western Europe cannot compete and has seen its shipbuilding yards decline. Some yards, however, have survived by focusing on high added-value vessels such as gas and chemical carriers, ferries and modern cruise ships which, together in any one year, amount to 10% of the global tonnage but represent 33% of total value.*

*The causes and symptoms of decline were discussed in Chapter 17. Developing the points discussed there, any recovery from a difficult situation will be related to, first, improved marketing effectiveness, competitiveness and revenue, and secondly, managing the organization more efficiently in order to reduce costs. Where these changes in functional and competitive strategies prove inadequate, something more drastic will be required.*

*Retrenchment strategies aim to increase revenue and reduce costs by concentrating and consolidating – these involve changes in functional strategies. Turnaround strategies relate to changes in competitive strategies and frequently feature repositioning for competitive advantage. Retrenchment and turnaround strategies are often collectively called recovery strategies. Divestment occurs when part of an organization is sold, normally because it is diverting resources which could be used more effectively, but sometimes just to raise money. These result in changes to the company's corporate strategy.*

*This chapter explores recovery and divestment strategies in greater detail, considering first the overall feasibility of recovery and different recovery situations. These issues are of primary concern to companies that are already experiencing difficulties and showing symptoms of decline. The last section looks at strategic alternatives for declining industries, which is relevant for companies that may be currently successful or unsuccessful in a situation of change. The opening case emphasizes just how difficult sustained turnaround can be.*

# Minicase 18.1  Arcadia

Arcadia was previously known as the Burton Group of retail outlets.

## Origins and diversification

The Burton Group became a retailer of fashionable clothing for men and women through a number of branded outlets. The company was started as a single shop in 1901 by Montague Burton, who had built the company into a vertically integrated organization of factories and some 600 stores when he died in 1952. The main product area had been made-to-measure suits for men.

In the late 1960s the company had problems of management succession and it was basically stagnant with underutilized assets. Burton was also experiencing a number of specific problems:

- The menswear market was switching in preference from made-to-measure to ready-made suits.
- The company had a large manufacturing base in relation to the falling demand for its products. Moreover, the factories were inefficient and insufficiently capital intensive.
- There was growing competition from such stores as Marks and Spencer.
- The company had an old-fashioned image, made worse by stores which were not designed or fitted for the growing market for ready-made clothes.

A new management team was appointed and their strategy was one of diversification. In the early 1970s Burton acquired five new businesses:

- Evans – outsize fashions for women with fuller figures
- Ryman's – office supplies
- St Remy – clothing stores in France
- Green's – cameras and hi-fi equipment
- Trumps – an employment agency.

Burton also opened a chain of womenswear shops with the Top Shop brand name.

## Divestment and turnaround; the acquisition of Debenhams

The diversification strategy failed in overall terms, although parts did prove successful, and divestment began in the mid-1970s.

In addition:

- Branches were modernized and some were enlarged. The aim was to make Burton stores more appealing to younger buyers. Some stores, though, were closed.

- A new chain of Top Man stores was opened to complement Top Shop.
- There was greater emphasis on the womenswear market, with more Top Shops and the acquisition of Dorothy Perkins.
- The Principles chain was developed.
- Manufacturing was pruned and the final factory was disposed of in 1988.

Between 1976 and 1979 the number of employees was reduced from 21,400 to 11,000.

These changes were led by Ralph Halpern, who became chief executive in 1977 (and executive chairman in 1981), and the result was revitalization, new growth and profitability. The Burton Group built up a 12.5% share of the UK clothing market, second only to Marks and Spencer. Halpern was fêted as a retailer of genius, and rewarded with a million pound salary, a knighthood and celebrity status. However, when this expansion required consolidation in the 1980s, a number of strategic misjudgements was made.

- In 1985 Burton took over Debenhams after a fierce and very acrimonious battle. The new department stores required expensive revamping and the payback was slower than anticipated. Moreover, different retailing skills were involved.
- Burton diversified into shopping-centre development, and was financially exposed when property prices fell.
- The growth led to overexpansion and the acquisition of new sites with very high rent and lease charges. These proved too expensive in the retail recession of the late 1980s.

Profits and the share price collapsed and Halpern departed in November 1990, to be replaced as chief executive by his deputy, Lawrence Cooklin. In mid-1991 Burton sought to raise money in a 'desperate rights issue', imposed a pay freeze and looked to rationalize by reducing both the number of stores and head-office administration.

The company traded at a loss during 1991–1992; a new, experimental, out-of-town discount format, branded IS, was introduced and the flagship Harvey Nichols London department store was sold for £51 million in August 1991. (Harvey Nichols was floated on the stock exchange in 1996 with a valuation of £150 million.) Analysts commented that Burton was still searching for a retail format suitable for the 1990s and estimated the odds of a second successful recovery to be no better than 50:50. Cooklin was replaced in February 1992 by American John Hoerner from Debenhams.

## A second turnaround

Hoerner was determined to tackle two key strategic issues:

1. The Burton brands/businesses saw themselves in competition with each other; they frequently targeted the same customers
2. The company was too willing to discount its prices when trading levels were disappointing.

Three years later Burton was profitable again. What had happened? Initially:

- Hoerner initiated a cross-formats review of target markets, design, merchandising, pricing strategies, visual marketing and buying.
- The formats were then refocused, some more than others, and new strategies trialled. Top Shop, for example, targeted 16–19-year-olds by experimenting with a 'funky, grungey' look. Those targeted loved the new image; unfortunately Top Shop's other customers did not, and they voted with their feet. Top Shop switched to a less radical look which had appeal for all ages up to 30.
- Locations were reviewed from a corporate perspective. Some sites were closed and replaced with new ones, although not as many. In addition, some formats were exchanged for other Burton brands to try and achieve the most appropriate location for each one.
- The new but unprofitable IS format was abandoned in 1994.
- The head office was reduced in size and numbers. In the branches there was a programme of switching employees from full-time contracts to flexible part-time hours.

Hoerner then turned his attention to supplier relationships and to the links and interdependencies between the Burton formats. The future strategy was to be based on building the strength of the various brand names.

During 1996 mail order (or home shopping) began to play a more prominent role in Burton. Two acquisitions: first, the Innovations (unusual and inventive household and leisure products) and secondly, the Racing Green (smart casual clothes) catalogues were added to Hawkshead and McCord which Burton already owned.

## Demerger

In July 1997 Burton Group announced that it was to demerge the department store chain Debenhams into an independent business. It was generally acknowledged that it has not been able to prosper in a Burton Group beset with other high-street problems. In recent months Debenhams had been growing much more quickly than Burton's other brands. Burton's menswear sales in particular were being affected by the increasing success of specialist designer menswear brands and branded sportswear companies.

John Hoerner would remain as chief executive of Burton – which was to be renamed Arcadia – and which now comprised the Burton, Dorothy Perkins, Evans, Principles, Top Shop and Top Man high-street stores, together with Burton Home Shopping. The new chief executive of Debenhams was to be Terry Green, who was currently in charge within Burton's. Shareholders should benefit from identified cost savings amounting to £30 million. There would be job losses as the operating and administration systems for all the Burton stores would now be amalgamated and centralized. Each store chain would retain its independence for product sourcing, range building, supplier development and customer relations.

It is invariably possible to reduce costs after a strategic change such as this. The real challenge lies in finding new opportunities for adding value and differentiating to give fresh life to the brands and stores concerned. The prediction was that both Burton Group and Debenhams could benefit and grow after this split. Time would tell.

An argument was put forward that department stores such as Debenhams could prove to be the new retail force for 'thirty-something and forty-something' shoppers as they would be able to offer designer brands (concessions), smart cafés, baby changing rooms and affordable own-label products in a single store, and thus provide convenience for the whole family.

In 1999 Burton extended its women's wear chains by buying Wallis, Warehouse and Evans (again) from Sears.

## Arcadia/Burton in 2000

In April 2000 Arcadia announced that 400 shops would be closed and 3500 jobs lost. Casualties included all of the Principles for Men and Top Shop branches and some Miss Selfridge and women's Principles stores. In addition, Burton stores would be paired with Dorothy Perkins rather than remain as stand-alones. The reason was intense discounting in the clothing sector in late 1999. Arcadia was trading at a loss and could no longer afford the rents and rates that it was paying.

Customer comments reinforced Arcadia's difficulties: it was often difficult to differentiate between the product ranges in the various high-street chain stores. Cut-price warehouses (such as Matalan) were also making real inroads into the market.

QUESTIONS: Given the announcement in June 2000 that rival C&A was also closing all of its high-street stores, what is the future for specialist clothing retailers such as Arcadia?

If you were John Hoerner, what would you do to try and secure Arcadia's future?

*Arcadia (Burton Group)*  http://www.arcadia.co.uk

# The Feasibility of Recovery

When sales or profits are declining because a company is uncompetitive or because an industry is in decline, recovery may or may not be possible. If a company is a single-product firm, or heavily reliant on the industry in question, then it may be in real difficulties and in danger of liquidation unless it can diversify successfully. If profits are declining, such a strategy may be difficult to fund. Where the situation applies to one business unit in an already diversified company, the company as a whole may be less threatened. However, a change of strategy will be required, and the issue concerns whether or not a successful recovery can be brought about and sustained.

The likelihood of a possible recovery improves where:

- the causes of the decline in the firm's sales and profits can be tackled and the problems overcome – this depends upon how serious and deep-rooted they are
- the industry as a whole, or particular segments of the industry which might be targeted, remains attractive
- there is potential for creating or enhancing competitive advantage.

## Recovery situations

Slatter (1984) has postulated that there are essentially four types of recovery situation, and these are illustrated in Figure 18.1(a). Once the profits of the firm or business unit have declined to a crisis stage, then a change in strategy is essential. However, the industry and competitive factors might be such that recovery simply is not feasible. Insolvency is inevitable, whatever alternative strategies might be tried. Successful retrenchment strategies might be implemented and profits improved to a non-crisis level again.

However, unless the industry remains in some way attractive and potentially profitable, or the firm retains its competitive advantage, the retrenchment might subsequently fail. A third alternative is a successful turnaround but no real growth and sustained recovery. Possibly in a low-profit industry insufficient funds are generated to finance investment for further growth and diversification. A sustained recovery implies real growth, and possibly further changes in functional, competitive and corporate strategies.

Weitzel and Johnson (1989) drew attention to the issue of timing and highlighted that the later an organization leaves it before it attempts to recover itself from a downward trend, the more difficult the task. Figure 18.1(b) shows that sustained survival or sustained recovery is a much steeper challenge (with less likelihood of success) when remedial action is delayed. There is a point in time – shown as a 'crisis zone' – when recovery is unrealistic.

### Non-recoverable situations

Slatter argues that in situations where there is little chance of survival and the likelihood that both retrenchment and turnaround strategies will fail, a number of characteristics is likely to be present.

- The company is not competitive and the potential for improvement is low. This might be the result of a cost disadvantage that cannot be remedied. Certain businesses and industries that have declined in the face of foreign competition, especially from countries with low wage costs, are testament to this.
- The company is not diversified and lacks both the resources and access to resources to remedy this weakness.
- Demand for the basic product or service involved is in terminal decline.

### Temporary recovery

Where a retrenchment strategy is implemented successfully it may or may not be sustained. If

Figure 18.1 The feasibility of recovery. (a) Adapted from Slatter, S (1984) *Corporate Recovery*, Penguin. (b) Adapted from Weitzel, W and Johnson, E (1989) Decline in organizations – a literature integration and extension. *Administrative Science Quarterly*, 34(1), March.

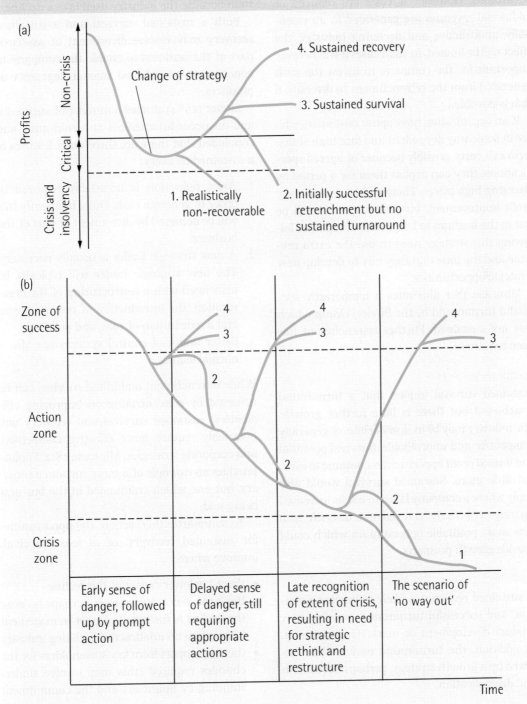

new forms of competitive advantage are found and sustained, or the product or service is effectively repositioned, subsequent insolvency may be avoided. However, if costs are reduced or additional revenues are generated in an essentially unattractive and declining industry, the effect will be limited. In such cases it will become important for the company to invest the cash generated from the retrenchment to diversify, if that is possible.

If an organization has captive customers who are in some way dependent and face high short-term exit costs, possibly because of agreed specifications, they can exploit them for a period by charging high prices. There will be a temporary profit improvement, but the customers will be lost in the medium to long term. Companies following this strategy need to use the extra revenue and the time that they buy to develop new strategic opportunities.

Minicase 18.1 illustrates a temporarily successful turnaround by the Burton Group which was not sustained. Further retrenchment has been required.

### Sustained survival

Sustained survival implies that a turnaround is achieved but there is little further growth. The industry may be in slow decline, or generally competitive and unprofitable. Survival potential and limited profit opportunities continue to exist, but little more. Sustained survival would also apply where a company failed to use its increased earnings effectively and did not diversify into new more profitable opportunities which could provide growth prospects.

### Sustained recovery

A sustained recovery is likely to involve a genuine and successful turnaround, possibly new product development or market repositioning. In addition, the turnaround may well be followed by a growth strategy, perhaps acquisition and diversification.

The recovery is helped if the industry is strong and attractive and the company's decline has been caused by poor management rather than because the industry itself is in a decline.

Both a sustained survival and a sustained recovery may involve divestment of assets or part of the business to enable the company to concentrate on selected market segments or products.

Slatter (1984) studied a number of successful and unsuccessful attempts at turnaround, and concluded that there are three main features of a sustained recovery:

1. Asset reduction is invariably required in order to generate cash. Quite frequently this will be achieved by divestment of part of the business.
2. A new strategic leader is usually necessary. The new strategic leader will typically be associated with a restructuring of the organization, the introduction of new strategies and a redefinition of roles and policies.
3. Better financial control systems are also a normal feature.

While retrenchment and initial survival can be achieved by concentrating on improving efficiencies, sustained survival and recovery will invariably require more effective competitive and corporate strategies. Minicase 18.2, Filofax, provides an example of a more sustained recovery, but one which culminated in the business being sold.

To summarize this section, the opportunities for sustained recovery, or at least survival, improve where:

- there are fewer causes of the decline
- the crisis is not deep-rooted, perhaps because the decline is the result of poor management rather than an unattractive declining industry
- there is support from key stakeholders for the changes required (this may involve understanding by financiers and the commitment

# Minicase 18.2  Filofax

Although it has been in existence for many years, Filofax became prominent and grew rapidly in the early 1980s; its success was based on its range of personal organizers. Growth was maintained throughout the 1980s by extending the product lifecycle for organizers. A number of distinct price points brought in new users, additional page sets facilitated new uses by adding extra value and a Deskfax business organizer was pioneered. In 1988 turnover was just under £15 million, with pre-tax profits of £2.75 million. The company was afraid to advertise for fear of generating demand in excess of its ability to supply.

Filofax's success, however, attracted competition, most notably from lower-priced alternatives such as WH Smith's own-label range. WH Smith was also one of Filofax's main retail outlets. Filofax products began to look overpriced, and the distribution network was seen as weak and fragmented. By 1990 the company was losing money. At the end of the decade, Robin Field, a management consultant who had been helping the company, became the new chief executive.

Filofax was immediately rationalized. Jobs were lost, prices were cut and marketing expenditure was reduced. The most popular organizer within the range was now selling at just half its 1985 price. If growth and prosperity were to be restored, however, new competitive advantages had to be found.

Filofax segmented and targeted its potential customers. Products were improved to appeal particularly to those people who have to organize their own lives without the assistance of a secretary; the armed forces and members of the clergy were always keen buyers. The emphasis stayed with domestic users, as distinct from business customers, to minimize the impact of electronic organizers, which have grown in popularity in the late 1990s; and a new budget range has been introduced. Thirty-thousand organizers were sold in 1987; 80,000 in 1994. Much of the sales revenue comes from refills.

In addition, Field looked to acquire suitable distributors and manufacturers of related products. In 1992 Filofax bought Lefax, a US manufacturer of luxury organizers, and a French distributor. This was followed in 1993 by Drakes, which has a 90% share of the UK market for duplicate message books, and distribution businesses in Germany and Sweden. In 1994 Henry Ling was acquired. Ling produces greeting cards, a high-growth product which sells through the same outlets as organizers. In 1995 Filofax bought Topps, a UK manufacturer of leather and simulated leather goods; Topps already owned Microfile, a competitor of Filofax.

At this time organizers still accounted for 75% of revenue and the company was still dependent on them. However, sales were growing rapidly again as new markets overseas were being opened up. Unfortunately, a year later, UK sales fell back as WH Smith reduced its stocks. Field announced the launch of 90 new versions in an attempt to reinvigorate sales.

In 1998 Day Runner, market leader for paper-based organizers in the USA (with over 50% of the market) launched a hostile bid for Filofax. Day Runner summed up Filofax as:

- an underperforming company that lacks direction
- a brand that had lost its edge, but was still a good brand
- a company which had tried to diversify, but which had failed to do so effectively.

Day Runner believed that it had the skills and competencies to turn the company around once again, particularly as there was no geographical overlap of any consequence in the markets for the two businesses.

In the event Filofax was bought for £50 million, some 1.2 times its current annual revenues. Trading profits were £4.3 million.

QUESTIONS: Do you agree with Day Runner's strategic assessment of Filofax? How difficult is it to extend the product lifecycle of a product such as paper-based organizers?

*Filofax*   http://www.filofax.com

of managers and other employees to the necessary changes)

- strategic opportunities exist to differentiate, refocus and create competitive advantage
- the company has the ability to reduce costs.

Rescue, to provide a platform for recovery, could well take 12–18 months and the key theme is making the business cash rich by: selling assets, obtaining a new injection of funding and restructuring debt; and tightening operations by: strengthening margins, better cost control, better working capital management and better information.

True renewal and recovery could then require a further 3–5 years.

The skills required for the rescue and recovery stages are different. There may be a requirement or a logic in changing the strategic leader to find the most appropriate person at any time.

It is worth remembering that a vision for recovery is of little use until the business has been rescued and consolidated; equally, consolidation without a future vision is likely to show only limited and short-term benefits.

Van de Vliet (1998) provides the following list of useful questions for attempting to assess the situation and the recovery potential:

1. Is there some part of the business worth rescuing?
2. What are the key core activities in the business?
3. Does the organization have the people it is going to need, people who truly understand the business at an operational level?
4. Do these managers have the freedom to manage?
5. Are there ways in which the product(s) and/or service(s) could be improved?
6. Can the necessary resources (other than people) that are going to be required be secured?

Minicase 18.3 illustrates how a company can appear stronger than in reality it is, and that an unexpected event can precipitate a major crisis. Ratner's was not regarded as a company in any real trouble until Gerald Ratner described some of its products as 'total crap'. Once the media

# Minicase 18.3  Ratner's

Gerald Ratner was born in 1949 and became joint managing director of the family business (jewellery retailers) in 1978. By 1984 he was sole managing director, and chairman in 1986. He saw a real opportunity in critical mass and in product standardization across a range of stores for low-cost, lower quality fashion jewellery. He realized that some people, with some products, will treat jewellery as discardable rather than a lifelong investment. A major competitor, H. Samuel, was acquired to yield the critical mass. To ensure standardization everything was sourced centrally. Staff at head office experimented with window designs and layouts, and when they were satisfied they took photographs which were sent to every branch. The exact same layout, down to the position of an individual ring on a tray, must be replicated in every branch. The business invested in advertising and promotion. Later, Ratner's bought other retail outlets including, in 1988, Zales (jewellers) and Salisbury's (principally leather goods) which were acquired from Next. Ratner was very aggressive. 'I was a complete megalomaniac, very ambitious, very competitive. If another jeweller opened, I'd do anything to put him out of business'. The strategy worked, but it was always replicable. His rivals could follow – and some did, even if they were smaller and less profitable. He was never a major threat to the expensive and exclusive specialist.

Speaking at an Institute of Directors' Conference in 1991 Gerald Ratner claimed that his company was able to sell sherry decanters at really low prices because they were 'total crap'. Ratner's continued success relied on its reputation for slickness and efficiency; denigrating his company's products in this way would prove a 'bridge too far'. The tabloid newspapers seized on the comment, were very critical, and the company's previously strong image was damaged. The group name has subsequently been changed to Signet, and although the company still trades profitably, the name Ratner's has disappeared from the high street.

Gerald was forced to resign, devastated by the reaction to what he saw as a light-hearted, throw-away comment. After a numbers of years 'recovering from the shock' Ratner has started a new business, a health club in Henley-on-Thames.

QUESTIONS: How robust would a business have to be to survive a self-imposed setback such as this?
Do you think that the adverse publicity would have affected the business as much as it did Gerald Ratner himself?
Would the change of name be the main strategy required?

*Signet Group*  http://www.hsamuel.co.uk/hr/companyinfo.htm

picked up on this comment the fragility of the company's competitive advantage was exposed, but recovery was possible because there was a sound resource base to build on.

Having considered the background feasibility of recovery, the actual recovery strategies are now examined in greater detail.

## Retrenchment Strategies

In this section organizational and financial changes, cost and asset reduction, and strategies aimed at generating revenue are considered. Retrenchment strategies are essentially functional, rather than competitive or corporate, and are aimed at making the company more productive and profitable while retaining essentially the same products and services, although there might be some rationalization. By concentrating on financial issues, they often address major causes of the company's decline.

## Organizational changes

It was emphasized above that a change in strategic leadership is frequently involved in recovery strategies. In addition, there might be a need to strengthen the management team in other areas. The fact that there are personnel changes is not the important issue. The subsequent changes to strategies, structure and policies, and the effect on the existing staff and their motivation, are what matter. Reorganizations are likely to take place, involving new definitions of roles and responsibilities. Policies and management and control systems may also be changed to give managers new opportunities to achieve, and to convince them that recovery prospects are real.

## Financial changes

Poor financial control systems, say a badly managed cash flow, are often a feature of companies in difficulties. In addition, overheads may have been allowed to become too high in relation to direct production costs, and the company may not know the actual costs of producing particular products and services or be able to explain all expenditures. The establishment of an effective costing system, and greater control over the cash flow, can improve profitability and generate revenue.

Another retrenchment strategy is the restructuring of debt to reduce the financial burden of the company. Possibly repayment dates can be extended, or loan capital converted into preference shares or equity, thereby allowing the company more freedom through less pressure to pay interest. Eurotunnel provides an excellent example of this: loans were rescheduled and some were transferred into equity to reduce the interest burden as the company struggled to generate enough revenue to cover its costs. Operationally, Eurotunnel is now a success. Passenger and freight traffic, supported by income from Eurostar, delivers a trading profit – but the cost of its debt, required for the enormous construction project over several years, drastically reduces this.

## Cost-reduction strategies

When the acquisition strategies of such companies as Hanson and BTR were discussed briefly in Chapter 15, p. 567, it was emphasized that they looked for companies with high gross margins and relatively low after-tax profitability. These are indications of overheads which have been allowed to grow too much, thereby providing opportunities for improving profits by reducing organizational slack and waste.

Companies can address the overheads issue for themselves, without being acquired, if they recognize the extent of the problem and are determined to reduce their costs in order to improve their competitiveness and profitability. This happened increasingly in the late 1980s and 1990s, reducing the number of attractively priced acquisition targets. By-and-large those companies that could not reduce their costs were liquidated as the economy tightened.

In terms of reducing costs, the normal starting place is labour costs. In many cases opportunities will exist to reduce labour costs and improve productivity, but if the reductions are too harsh there can be a real threat to the quality of both the product and the overall service offered to customers. One opportunity is to examine working patterns and attempt to manage overtime, part-time arrangements and extra shifts both to meet demand and to contain costs. Companies can slip easily into situations where overtime and week-end working are creating costs which cannot be recovered in competitive prices.

Redundancies may be required to reduce costs and bring capacity more into line with demand. Again this can be implemented well or poorly. In most cases the issue is not losing particular numbers of people and thereby saving on wages, but losing non-essential staff or those who fail to make an effective contribution. There is always the danger in a voluntary redundancy programme that good people will choose to leave or take early retirement.

Costs can be reduced anywhere and every-where in the value chain. Better supply arrangements and terms can reduce costs; products can be redesigned to cost less without any loss in areas significant to customers; and certain activities, such as public relations, training, advertising, and research and development (R&D) might be cut. The argument here is that these activities are non-essential, and this might be perfectly plausible in the short term. It may not be the case for the longer term, and there-fore they would need to be reinstated when extra revenues had been regenerated.

## Asset-reduction strategies

*Divestment* of a business unit, or part of the business, is an asset-reduction strategy but is considered in greater detail later. It is really more of a corporate than a functional strategy, and the decision should not be made on financial grounds alone. While the sale of a business can raise money, this gain may be more than off-set if there is existing synergy with other parts of the company which suffer in some way from the divestment.

*Internal divestment or rationalization* can take a number of forms. Plants might be closed and production concentrated in fewer places; production might be rescheduled to generate increased economies of scale. The idea is to reduce both overheads and direct costs.

*Assets might be sold and leased back* – As far as the balance sheet is concerned, assets have been reduced and in turn cash has been generated. The scope and capacity of the business may be unaffected; the changes are exclusively financial.

## Revenue-generating strategies

The marketing strategies considered in the next section on turnarounds are essentially revenue-generating strategies, and they frequently involve changes in competitive strategies. How-ever, revenue can also be generated by improving certain management control systems. If stocks are reduced by better stock management or by a review of the whole production system and a move towards just-in-time, cash is freed. In the same way, if debtors can be persuaded to settle accounts more speedily, cash flow can be improved.

## Turnaround Strategies

Retrenchment strategies will usually have short time horizons and they will be designed to yield

We weren't making money at SAS [Scandinavian Airlines System] when I came here. We were in a desperate situation, and that's the worst time to focus on preventing mistakes and controlling costs. First, we had to increase revenues. We had to decide what business we were going to do – before you can start managing effectively you must know who is your customer and what is your product – and go to work on the revenue side. Then we could think about cutting costs, because only then would we know which costs could be cut without losing competitiveness.

*Jan Carlzon, when President and Chief Executive Officer, Scandinavian Airlines System*

immediate results. Turnaround strategies are likely to address those areas which must be developed if there is to be a sustained recovery. They involve changes in the overall marketing effort, including the repositioning or refocusing of existing products and services, together with the development of new ones. They are designed to bring quick results and at the same time contribute towards longer-term growth. They overlap with the internal limited growth strategies outlined in Chapter 14, and they may also be a stepping stone to growth through diversification.

Retrenchment strategies do not affect customers directly, but the following turnaround strategies are designed to improve the effectiveness of the company's marketing. Consequently, they are addressing customers and consumers directly, and for this reason some degree of caution is required in implementing the changes involved.

## Changing prices

Prices can be changed at very short notice, and price increases or decreases can result in increased revenue. Price rises can increase revenue as long as the elasticity of demand ensures that sales do not decline unacceptably with the price increase. Price decreases can improve demand and hence revenue, again depending on the elasticity of demand. Hence, it is important to have an insight into the demand elasticity for individual products and services, although forecasting the effect of price changes will be subject to some uncertainty. In general, the opportunity to increase prices is related to the extent of existing differentiation, and the opportunity to differentiate further and create new competitive advantage.

It is important to remember that unless particular products and services are regarded as underpriced by customers in relation to their competition, a price rise should be accompanied by advertising support and possibly minor changes and improvements in the product or packaging. The price change must be justified.

It is also important to consider the likely reaction of competitors, which in turn will be influenced by the structure of the industry and the degree and type of competitive rivalry. Markets with an oligopoly structure, an essential feature of UK industry, were introduced in Chapter 3, when it was emphasized that oligopoly competitors tend to follow price decreases but not price rises.

In relation to the concept of price changes, discount structures might be altered to favour certain groups of customers at the expense of others. Such a strategic move can both raise revenue and improve the attractiveness of a company to certain market segments. Any negative effect on other customer groups should be monitored carefully.

## Refocusing

The idea behind refocusing is to concentrate effort on specific customers and specific products, relating the two closely together. The strategy requires careful thought and attention in relation to why people buy and opportunities for differentiation, segmentation and competitive advantage. The selection of particular product/market and service/market niches for concentrating effort will depend upon revenue and growth potential, gross margins, the extent and type of competition for the segment or niche, and the potential to create a response to marketing activity, such as advertising.

In the short term products or services that sell quickly and generate cash quickly may be attractive opportunities even if their gross margin is small; and there may well be a group of customers for whom an appropriate package can be created.

## New product development

The replacement of existing products with new ones may be required to effect a turnaround if a company has been losing competitiveness in an attractive industry by falling behind competitors in terms of innovation and product improvement. Equally, product improvements, designed to prolong the product lifecycle, can be extremely useful in low-growth or declining industries. They can be used to help a company to concentrate on the particular segments of the market that are remaining relatively strong.

## Rationalizing the product line

Variety reduction can similarly be useful for concentrating efforts on the stronger market segments and opportunities, particularly where the industry overall is losing attractiveness. Such a strategy needs a proper understanding of costs, and which individual products and services are most and least profitable. In a multiproduct organization, with interdependencies between the business units, for example, transfer price arrangements can distort prof-

itabilities. As mentioned earlier, certain products and services can be vital contributors to overall synergy, but individually not very profitable, and care needs to be taken with these.

## Emphasis on selling and advertising

An emphasis on selling and advertising might take the form of selected additional expenditure in order to generate greater revenue, or the examination of all current marketing expenditure in order to try and ascertain the best potential returns from the spending.

Expenditure on advertising, below-the-line promotions and the salesforce is used to promote products and services in order to generate sales revenue. However, all of these activities are investments, and their potential returns should be considered. The increased revenue expected from any increased spending should certainly exceed the additional costs incurred, and there is an argument that the opportunity cost of the investment funds should also be assessed.

While five alternative approaches to improving marketing effectiveness have been considered in this section, a number of them may be used in conjunction at any time. Moreover, these turnaround strategies may also be combined with the retrenchment strategies discussed earlier, the aim being both to reduce costs and to improve revenue at the same time.

Minicase 18.4 shows how marketing strategies were used to engineer a turnaround at LTS Rail.

It has already been explained that the divestment of products or business units can be useful for reducing assets in retrenchment strategies. Divestments can also be used to rationalize the product line, as discussed above.

## Rejuvenating mature businesses

Pulling these points together, Baden-Fuller and Stopford (1992) define a mature business as 'one

# Minicase 18.4  LTS Rail – The Misery Line

When British Rail was privatized in 1996, the line between London Fenchurch Street, Tilbury and Southend was taken over by LTS Rail. The line is extremely busy, with almost 350 train services every day. Many of the trains, which typically stop at several stations on route, are full. But LTS inherited a service plagued by a reputation for failure and regular delays and one which had been starved of investment. Many of the actual trains had been in service for 40 years and the stations were in need of refurbishment. Hence its nickname – 'the misery line'.

Railtrack was committed to new signalling and track improvements to help to improve running times and reduce delays.

Ken Bird took over as chief executive of the new company in 1996. Under his leadership there have been several changes and an acknowledged improvement in the service:

- Several of the stations have been upgraded.
- New, large information displays keep passengers fully informed of train times and any delays, which have been reduced
- The driver cost base has been reduced in conjunction with more efficient scheduling – basic salaries have increased but overtime requirements have come down
- A new call centre was opened in 1997 in Southend. Companies are encouraged to use the centre to take out attractively priced block bookings for their staff to save them from queuing individually for season tickets every few weeks.
- There are special price reductions for people who opt to travel before 7.00 am to ease rush-hour congestion and, at the same time, win back passengers from rival coach services.
- Smart cards can be used by passengers – pre-paid, the credit balance is reduced every time the card is slotted into a barrier.
- New trains began to arrive in 1999.

QUESTION: Can you think of other turnaround strategies that Bird might have adopted?

LTS Rail (part of Prism Rail plc)   http://www/prism.rail.plc.uk

whose managers believe themselves to be imprisoned by their environment and unable to succeed'. As a consequence they are invariably giving poor service to their customers and achieving financial returns that are barely adequate. Often, with a more creative, entrepreneurial, innovative approach, they can be rejuvenated. The challenge, simply, is to become a stronger competitor. This transformation is likely to require a number of developmental steps over an extended period, rather than be achieved with a one-off major project; it implies a change of culture and style. Success will not be instantaneous; it will need building. Baden-Fuller and Stopford have developed a four-stage model for rejuvenation, which is summarized in Figure 18.2.

1. *Galvanization* comes when there is a clear recognition of the true state of the business and the establishment of an able management team which is committed to dealing with the problem. This may only need a change of strategic leader; on other occasions the changes will be more extensive. If those managers who are responsible for bringing about the crisis, through poor decisions and judgement, or negligently allowing the situation to deteriorate, stay, they will need to change.

   Progress then requires resources. Independent businesses are likely to require fresh capital and possibly new owners. Subsidiaries of larger organizations will have to justify new, corporate investment.

2. *Simplification* follows, implying a clearer focus and the concentration of scarce resources on a smaller agenda to build a strong and sustainable core. Strategies, structures and styles may all have to change.

This level of change is sometimes termed strategic regeneration, and the demands and implications are looked at further in Chapter 24. The business must next

3. *Build* new competencies and competitive advantages. Because of resource pressures this is again likely to take time and prove highly challenging. Finally, true rejuvenation requires it to

4. *Exert leverage* to extend its new competencies and capabilities into new products, services, markets and opportunities.

Total quality management initiatives and business process re-engineering programmes can make a major contribution, but alone they will not make an organization more innovatory. The whole enterprise must become more customer focused, committed to efficiency and improvement, and responsive to environmental demands.

It would be useful at this point to return to Figure 13.6. Through double-loop learning an uncompetitive firm has found new opportunities for adding value and creating advantages; it has then used single-loop learning initially to leverage this new advantage.

## Turnaround themes

To round off this section, van de Vliet (1998) suggests that the following themes determine the likelihood of turnaround success:

- the existence of some 'fat to live off'. An organization which has reached a certain size, perhaps a turnover of some £10 million, and has a strong customer base, will have a more realistic chance than a much smaller organization without an equivalent customer base
- some identifiable potential, such as market leadership in a niche or segment
- the consistency or focus in the portfolio – and the potential for synergy. If there has been a

*Figure 18.2* Rejuvenating the mature business. Adapted from Baden-Fuller, C and Stopford, J (1992) *Rejuvenating the Mature Business*, Routledge.

series of non-synergistic acquisitions, divestments should be straightforward

- the opportunity for a fresh perspective from a new strategic leader
- the existence of a strong management team, or one with potential, even if they are currently underperforming
- the existence of a clear structure and communications
- the ability to eradicate quickly any overtrading to strengthen the cash position.

## Divestment Strategies

Divestment can be essentially *internal*, the closure of a plant as part of a rationalization programme, or *external*, the sale of part of the business. The justification will be similar for each, and any resources saved or generated should be re-allocated.

Davis (1974) argues that divestments are often sudden decisions rather than decisions reached as part of a continual evaluation process which reviews all of the products and services in the firm's portfolio periodically. Companies that utilize portfolio analysis as part of their planning will be in a position to identify which parts of the business are the poorest performers and possible candidates for divestment. However, Devlin (1989) contends that effective divestment is a skill that few strategic leaders actually possess. This, he suggests, is a critical strategic issue, given that many acquisitions fail to achieve their expected returns. While divestment may suggest an admission of failure, it can be used positively, as Minicase 18.5, Boots, shows.

There will be an obvious reluctance to sell a business unit to another company, especially a competitor, who might succeed and transform the business into an effective performer. This will be particularly important if such success could pose a future threat to business units that

have been retained. For these reasons divestments are often associated with a change of strategic leader, as an outsider is less likely to feel any loyalty to past decisions.

## Issues in selecting a divestment candidate

A number of possible considerations might be relevant in selecting a product, service or business unit for divestment. Both financial and strategic aspects are important:

- the current position in the product lifecycle, and the likely future potential for further growth and profitability
- the current market position, and opportunities for competitive advantage
- taking these two points further and considering portfolio analyses, the future potential for cash generation and future investment requirements in order to remain competitive (linked to this is the opportunity cost of the resources being utilized)
- identified alternative uses for the resources which could be freed up, and in certain cases the extent of the need to free up resources for relocation
- the ability to find a suitable buyer willing to pay an acceptable price.

In Minicase 15.3 we saw how Daimler-Benz decided to withdraw funding from its Fokker aircraft subsidiary. Realistically, a new owner was required for Fokker. One possibility was Bombardier, the Canadian company which had already rescued Shorts (Belfast, and a major subcontractor to Fokker), de Havilland and Learjet. Bombardier's post-acquisition strategy is to invest heavily to restructure, modernize and extend the product line. It weighs the turnaround chances carefully, looking for good management and stable employee relations, sound technologies, products with competitive advantage and long-term growth potential,

## Minicase 18.5  Boots

Boots is well known as a high-street chemists, but many of the large stores sell a much wider range of household products and there are also the specialist opticians' stores. In recent years Boots has faced competition from Superdrug, owned by Kingfisher, the Woolworth's chain. Up to a few years ago, Boots also manufactured many of its own-label pharmaceutical products, but this activity was sold to BASF.

In 1989 Boots paid £900 million to buy unrelated retail group Ward White. The stated aim was to 'provide an entry into new, large consumer markets with growth prospects' and the price paid was high. Ward White owned most of the property where it traded and 1989 was the height of a boom in property prices. The portfolio included:

- Stanley, which had a chain of home-improvement stores trading as FADS and Homestyle. When the housing market slumped in the early 1990s these businesses fell back dramatically. A.G. Stanley was sold in 1997.
- Payless, a DIY (do-it-yourself) chain with no effective market position in an increasingly competitive sector. Boots was again in competition with Kingfisher, who own market leader B&Q. Payless was joined with Do It All, owned by WH Smith, as a joint venture. Do It All struggled against stronger rivals and eventually WH Smith paid Boots £50 million for Boots to take over control of the joint venture. In 1998 the business was sold to Focus.
- Halfords, which at the time sold car parts and accessories and bicycles. Since then Halfords has diversified into car servicing and tyre and exhaust replacement. Again this is an extremely competitive sector.

QUESTION: Does it make strategic sense for Boots to retain Halfords as long as it is profitable, or should it too be divested?

*Boots*   http://www.boots.co.uk

component orders to offset cyclical downturns and tight cost management. In the event, Bombardier decided that Fokker was not an appropriate purchase.

- *In addition to these points*: the strategic potential to divest some business or activity which is profitable in order to raise money to invest in something which is likely to be even more profitable (implicit in this might be a desire to limit the strategic perspective and scope of diversification, or a desire to contain borrowing)

- the issue of whether it is cheaper to close a business or plant or keep it running despite low returns, i.e. exit costs and barriers
- the contribution to existing synergy, and the overall value to the organization (certain businesses may be making a loss but be valuable to the organization because of their contribution to other activities, their past reputation, their significance to certain customers who are important to the organization and their general value as a competitive weapon)

- the opportunity to satisfy existing customers, which the organization would wish to retain, with alternative products and services
- the tangible and intangible benefits from specializing and reducing the extent to which the organization is diversified.

## Issues in the divestment

Once the decision to divest has been taken, there is a number of further considerations.

First, there is the issue of how active and how secretive the search for a buyer should be. It can be argued that there should be an active search for an acceptable buyer who is willing to pay an appropriate premium, on the grounds that it is all too easy to sell a business cheaply. A low price might be expected where the sale is hurried, perhaps because there is a pressing need to raise money or where a first offer is accepted without an exploration of other options. There is also an argument in favour of secrecy and speed as opposed to prolonged and publicized negotiations. Employees may leave if they feel that their company is no longer wanted by its existing parent, and relationships with important suppliers and customers may also be affected.

In addition, simply offering a business for sale may not be productive. Sales must be negotiated and potential buyers must be vetted. The terms of the sale should be financially acceptable, and the buyer should not be an organization that can use the newly acquired business to create a competitive threat to retained activities.

Devlin (1989) suggests that, in general speed is of the essence. Long delays are likely to mean lost confidence. However, some businesses may be difficult to sell.

Secondly, buyers can be categorized into different types, and the potential of the business for them needs careful consideration during negotiations:

- *Sphere-of-influence buyers* might expect immediate synergy from the acquisition. These would include competitors for whom it would be horizontal integration, and buyers and suppliers for whom it would imply vertical integration. These are the buyers who are most likely to pose future threats unless the divestment removes any involvement in the industry in question.
- *Related industry companies* – these might not be current competitors but companies for whom it might be possible to share activities and transfer skills.
- *Management buy-outs* – discussed in Box 18.1 and supported by additional material on the website.

> **STRATEGY IN ACTION – Box 18.1**
> **Management Buy-outs in the UK**
>
> *Management buy-outs* involve the purchase of a business from its existing owners by the current managers in conjunction with one or more financial institutions.
>
> In Europe the proposal to purchase a business from its existing owners has typically come from the managers; in the USA, where the investment banks play a more aggressive role, the idea has often originated with the financial institutions. In the USA the sales have often been associated with a need to reduce borrowing; in the UK this has been less of a necessity. Sales have been aimed at generating greater focus and concentration and divesting businesses which are not producing acceptable financial returns or generating synergy. Some buy-outs occur because family owners have no organized succession and a sale to the existing managers is seen as more desirable than sale to an unknown outsider.

*Management buy-ins* occur when a group of outside managers is brought in to run a company which is sold to them and their backers rather than to existing managers. The disadvantage is the loss of continuity and the lack of insight and experience in the particular company; a possible advantage in certain circumstances is the influx of fresh ideas.

*Management buy-outs generally involve three parties:*

1. *Managers* acquire control of their own business, often with a substantial equity stake while investing only a small proportion of the total funding involved.
2. *Vendors* divest businesses which may be performing poorly or failing to create synergy with their other activities, and they frequently accomplish this amicably and profitably.
3. *Financiers* are attracted to management buy-outs because they offer the potential to earn higher financial returns than investing in large companies and lower failure rates than traditional start-up businesses.

## Objectives and key success factors

While there are important issues of managers wanting to own their own businesses, and possibly preserve their jobs when their company is in difficulties, management buy-outs are characterized by important financial objectives and constraints. Buy-outs typically have unusual financial structures and high gearing, and the financial institutions which back them have financial targets and expectations. Management buy-outs are expected to prove to be profitable for their shareholders and other backers by earning out the debt assumed when the company is bought out and by improving the company's performance in comparison with the results achieved by the previous owners. The banks will normally agree to a higher percentage of debt in relation to equity (gearing) or in relation to total capital employed (the debt ratio) than is conventional, and will look for a cash flow that can both pay the interest and repay the debt after an agreed number of years.

It is important that managers are able to make the business more competitive and overcome the constraints imposed by the high debt burden. In addition, they must be able to generate a positive cash flow.

## Advantages to the vendor

- The cash is from a willing buyer who has knowledge of the business. If the price is acceptable, the cash is neither better nor worse than cash from elsewhere, but such a sale is good for the corporate image.
- It can reduce borrowings, divest a loss-making activity, or enable specialization and concentration.
- Because of the existing knowledge of the buyers, the negotiations will concentrate on the financial package rather than any possible hidden truths about the business.
- If there are any interrelationships or interdependencies with activities which are being retained, continuity should be maintained.

## Advantages to the managers

- There is continuity of employment, and also continuity of both management and trading relationships for suppliers and customers.
- There is commitment to the business because of personal financial involvement, providing real incentives to

succeed. This is often used to justify the high gearing allowed by financiers.

- They know the problems, and probably how to improve productivity and reduce overheads. The latter is often crucial for transforming a marginal business into a profitable operation.
- It could lead to real substantial long-term gains if a flotation results.

## Three issues

- A company or business unit which a vendor is willing to sell at a particular price may be seen as incapable of being turned round sufficiently to meet the needs of potential financiers.
- The vendor has the problem of ensuring that he or she obtains a good deal, if not the best deal, for existing shareholders, and at the same time takes appropriate account of other stakeholders. The managers may not be the only bidders.
- A company is possibly unwilling to sell a business to its existing managers and then watch them improve performance and thereby expose the previous failings. This is regarded as less of an issue than it used to be.

## Success and failure

The success rate tends to be relatively high. Many end up being floated or sold on for a substantial premium. Where this happens the key managers tend to become very rich people.

There are cases of failure, though. The main funders accept that they will back a mixture of winners and losers and balance their portfolio accordingly. A buy-out is not guaranteed to succeed.

## Exit routes

One important consideration for all parties investing in a buy-out is their ability to withdraw their money at any time. Exit routes are particularly important for financiers, who are likely to want some flexibility.

The main exit routes are:

- liquidation
- sale to another business
- flotation
- earn out – the managers buy out their financiers.

## Notable examples

- Charles Letts (diaries)
- Dolland and Aitchison (opticians)
- Hornby Hobbies, the long-established toy company
- Levington (horticultural products)
- Parker Pen
- Premier Brands, the foods and confectionery arm of Cadbury Schweppes which produces Cadbury's drinking chocolate, biscuits and Smash instant mashed potato
- Shepperton Film Studios
- Standard Fireworks
- Sweater Shop
- Tetley tea (see Minicase 18.6)
- Typhoo tea and Chivers and Hartley's products.

Virgin and Andrew Lloyd Webber's Really Useful Group were management buy-backs of publicly quoted companies.

Thirdly, there is an argument that the cash raised from the sale should be deployed effectively and without undue delay. If a company is decreasing in size, building up reserves of cash, and can find no suitable investment opportunities, it might become vulnerable to acquisition. Ideally, a use for the cash will be determined before the sale, but implementation of a combined sale and investment may prove difficult. Devlin argues that where these changes can be managed effectively, divestment can provide a source of new competitive advantage.

Having explored retrenchment, turnaround and divestment strategies, these strategies are discussed specifically in the context of an economic recession, and this chapter concludes by considering alternative strategies for declining industries and how the most appropriate strategy might be selected.

We have used the recession as a time to bring new products out. It shows you're not demoralized, and its something new to go to customers with.

Being private has enabled us to plough our own furrow through the good and the bad times and not be swallowed up. All our capital investment would be looked at in a different way if we were a public company.

*Sir Anthony Bamford, Chairman,*
*JC Bamford (JCB Excavators),*
*quoted in the Financial Times,*
*2 June 1993*

## Managing in a Recession

The early 1990s was characterized by an economic recession. The latter years of the decade provided clear evidence of an economic recovery in the UK, but the real beneficiaries were service businesses rather than the manufacturing sector, which was affected by the high value of the pound sterling. This recession was global and it affected most countries, industries and businesses, regardless of size or sector. It is highly likely that another recession will occur at some stage in the future, but the unpredictable issue is its possible extent.

In a recession, retrenchment strategies are frequently required as demand falls and costs need containing; at the same time, there is a need, wherever practical, to invest and prepare the organization to benefit from the recovery when it comes.

Recession alone will not necessarily put a company into a crisis or turnaround situation; rather, it highlights existing weaknesses either created in, or hidden in, boom conditions. The organizations that are best prepared to cope with a recession are those with relatively low borrowings. Highly geared companies may be forced to divest assets in order to raise cash to cover their interest and repayment needs.

Clifford (1977) has suggested that companies that survive a recession most successfully are characterized by superior management which emphasizes the protection of margins, the efficient use of capital, and a concentration on markets or segments where distinctive competitive advantage is possible. Such competitive advantage will result from more effective cost control, innovative differentiation, a focus on service and quality and speedy reaction and change in a dynamic environment. An economic recession will typically force organizations to be creative in their search for cost reductions, especially if productivity drives have already eliminated many operational inefficiencies. Information technology (IT) has provided some valuable opportunities in recent years. Cost savings must then be controlled to ensure that they do not creep up again. The focus of the cost cutting is critical. Training and R&D, for example, should not be sacrificed unnecessarily because new ideas and service quality are increasingly important for adding value, helping customers to find new competitive opportunities themselves and persuading consumers to buy when their spending power is limited. R&D, then, should be managed better rather than cut, and directed more towards short-term improvements. However, the long-term needs should not be wholly ignored. In particular, the development time for new products and services should be speeded up.

Dividend payments and investment funding may have to be traded off against each other. Some organizations will reduce dividends when profits fall to conserve their resources; others will maintain them to appease shareholders.

Moreover, increasing global competition has forced companies to target markets and niches more effectively and, in many cases, increase their marketing rather than cut expenditure. The emphasis has typically focused on efficiencies and savings rather than luxury – consumers with less discretionary purchasing power have been more selective.

Whittingham (1991) reinforces points made earlier in the book and contends that innovation and product and service improvement is a more effective use of scarce resources in a recession than is diversification, and that cutting back too much leaves companies exposed and under capacity for the recovery. Ideally, organizations will consult and involve employees, looking to, say, negotiate pay freezes and reduce hours rather than make staff redundant. This provides greater flexibility to grow. Nevertheless, many firms will not have sufficient resources to pursue their preferred option.

When companies emerge from a recession and attempt to satisfy increasing demand there is a fresh challenge: the need to control events, monitor the cash flow and guard against overtrading.

Paradoxically, a recession can be an ideal time to invest for the future, to ensure that the organization is in a state of readiness to capitalize fully when the economic recovery begins. This could imply investing in new plant and equipment, in R&D or in new IT at a time when the company is struggling. The secret is money. If a company builds up a 'cash mountain' when its revenues and profits are high, there is a real likelihood that it will be criticized for not finding opportunities to spend it. It may even come under pressure to return some of it to shareholders. It might also be persuaded to diversify or acquire unnecessarily. It is such a cash mountain that helps to pay staff when future revenues and profits are restrained. This can allow an organization to hang on to the people whom it does not want to lose rather than face enforced redundancy programmes. It can also be used for investments when the timing is most appropriate.

Table 18.1 provides a useful summary of these and other points.

Finally, in a recession it is quite normal for individual company strategies to bring about industry restructuring. Tarmac, for example, once the UK's leading housebuilder, refocused on aggregates and contracting during the recession of the early 1990s. In 1993 Tarmac swapped its roof tiles business for Marley's bricks, which it later sold to Ibstock. In 1996 Tarmac then swapped its housebuilding interests for Wimpey's quarries and contracting businesses. Tarmac, which has since merged with Minorco, built up a 28% share of the aggregates sector – in other words, it is now the largest producer of crushed rock, sand and gravel. In addition, Tarmac/Minorco is the second largest producer of ready-mix cement, with a 21% market share. Tarmac/Minorco was then sold to Anglo American at the beginning of 2000.

This made sense as the key success factors for housebuilding (finding and buying good building land at the right time at the right price, design and marketing) are clearly different from

| *Table 18.1*  Managing in a recession |
|---|

*In a recession, companies should:*
- Determine and clarify strategic priorities
- Be willing to act rather than procrastinate with some tough decisions
- Stay fully informed about trends and changes in relevant industries, making use of IT for this and other potential benefits
- Monitor gross profits and cash flow very carefully
- Identify where there is any overcapacity
- Spend carefully
- Seek to extend payment times to creditors
- Look for possibilities to reduce overheads or fixed costs
- Cut back on borrowings if at all possible
- Monitor currency fluctuations if the company trades in foreign currencies, buying forward where appropriate
- Recognize that high prices may be unsustainable and act sooner rather than later
- Keep staff informed of the situation, taking as positive a stance as is realistic
- Tighten staffing levels where appropriate, but not by losing key people
- Make any necessary redundancies all at once
- Invest in training for those who remain and look to retain morale
- Stay in close contact with customers and look for opportunities where both parties can help each other
- Seek out relevant marketing opportunities at home and abroad – recessions are uneven in their impact
- Accept that flexibility and innovation are crucial

aggregates (plant and equipment management, cost controls for price stability and service to large contractors).

## Strategies for Declining Industries

Rarely is an industry unattractive for every company competing in it; mature and declining industries can be made attractive for individual competitors if they can find appropriate and feasible opportunities for adding value and creating competitive advantage. Although tea is a more popular drink than coffee in the UK, consumption is declining. Tetley became the market leader in the 1990s and Minicase 18.6 shows how it has set about retaining its leadership.

Some firms experiencing decline in a mature industry will be the cause of their own demise, through their persistence with dated, inappropriate competitive strategies; and in some cases, an innovatory new strategy by one competitor can rejuvenate the whole industry.

When an industry has reached maturity or begun to decline, a number of issues must be faced. Generally:

- while demand overall is declining, the pattern can vary markedly – some sectors or segments may be static or expanding
- consumers will be knowledgeable because the product or service has been around for a while
- many customers will become increasingly price conscious and prices will tend to fall in real terms
- the 'commodity' perception of products will increase

# Minicase 18.6  Tetley Tea

In 1970 British adults on average drank 4.5 cups of tea every day. By 1995 this had fallen by one-third to 3 cups a day. By this time, tea bags were the normal and convenient way of making tea, and the day of fresh leaves had largely passed. The resultant gap had been filled by coffee and soft drinks. However, over the same period coffee consumption increased from an average of just 1 cup to 1.5 cups. Although tea consumption is in decline, it is still well ahead of coffee, despite the success of Starbucks and similar niche specialists.

Tetley replaced Brooke Bond (owned by Unilever and known for its PG Tips brand and the infamous television advertisements with chimpanzees) as UK market leader in the early 1990s. Tetley promoted itself intensely, spending some 20% of sales revenue on advertising. Its television advertisements claimed that 'Tetley make tea bags make tea'. However, Tetley is neither a focused nor an exclusively UK business. It is diversified into fresh coffee beans and it earns 40% of its revenue in the USA. It also manufactures a number of own-label products. Tetley was a management buy-out from Allied Domecq in 1995. At this stage it was valued at £200 million. Three years later it was floated with a valuation of £400 million.

Tetley has pursued a number of strategies in its endeavours to stay profitable and retain market leadership:

- It has diversified into flavoured (hot) teas but chosen not to manufacture iced tea, which is very popular in the USA.
- Production has been rationalized in fewer plants.
- Marketing has attempted to switch some consumers from standard teas to higher priced premium flavours such as Earl Grey and Lapsong.
- There have been a number of innovations. Tetley invented round tea bags, and Brooke Bond responded with pyramid bags which have not proved as successful. More recently, Tetley launched tea bags with drawstrings which eradicate dripping when the bag is taken out of the cup.
- Exports have been increased – China, Russia and Poland have been targeted and are big tea-drinking markets. This strategy has been a strategic alliance with Tata (of India), the world's leading tea-maker. Tata has the basic product; Tetley has the bagging technology. The alliance was necessary to help to secure distribution channels. The partners have opted to trade at break-even initially in order to build up a strong market presence.

Between 1995 and 1998 profits quadrupled.

QUESTIONS: Do you see tea as a declining industry?
Do people generally think of coffee as a more 'sexy' product? If the answer to this is yes, is it of any real consequence for Tetley?

*Tetley Tea*  http://www.teafolk.com

- distribution is likely to become more concentrated.

Companies will again be attempting to find new ways of adding value and differentiating, but as time goes on the opportunities become increasingly limited. Paradoxically, they will often find it harder to justify both R&D spending (to develop new variations) and marketing expenditure to inform and persuade customers of the differentiation. However, as the decline continues and overcapacity emerges, there will be a tendency for the weakest or least profitable producers to withdraw from the industry. This relieves some of the pressure on those who remain.

Harrigan (1980) draws upon the themes outlined when portfolio analysis was discussed in Chapter 11 and considers whether retrenchment, turnaround or divestment is the most appropriate strategy for an individual competitor in a declining industry. Strategies of leadership and niche marketing (turnaround), exploiting or harvesting (retrenchment) and divestment are considered in the light of the overall attractiveness of the industry while it is declining and the opportunities for an individual competitor to create and sustain competitive advantage. These are illustrated and defined in Figure 18.3.

Harrigan contends that the most appropriate strategy is dependent on four factors:

- the nature of the decline, and the causes – the speed at which decline is taking place, and whether specific segments are still surviving and offering differentiation and niche marketing opportunities for companies who can create and sustain competitive advantage. These factors affect the attractiveness of the industry
- the ability of a company to target these market segments effectively and create consumer preference. This is affected by company strengths and weaknesses

- the exit costs for all competitors. Exit costs influence the degree of urgency that companies feel towards finding a way of remaining competitive rather than simply withdrawing. Exit costs relate to:
  - the inability to find a buyer for the business, and the cost of closure
  - the strategic significance for the company as a whole, particularly if vertical integration strategies are affected
  - the possible effect upon key stakeholders, such as shareholders, managers and the strategic leader, especially if they have had a long-term commitment to the product service or business unit.
- linked to all these, the opportunities or threats which exist as a result of competitor activities, what they choose to do and why. If the product is strategically significant, certain competitors may choose not to withdraw, accepting very low profits or even no profits, and thereby making it more difficult for others.

Figure 18.3 encapsulates the first two points above; the decision will also involve the last two points.

Competitive advantage is likely to be attained by those companies who are aware early of the decline, and the opportunities present during the decline, and who seek to create the most advantageous positions ahead of their competitors. Companies who react when things have started to go wrong are less likely to succeed in creating an effective strategy.

## Implementing Recovery Strategies

In Chapter 16 it was stressed that organizational issues and difficulties often result in failure of the diversification and acquisition strategies to yield the desired results. Organizational issues

*Figure 18.3*  Strategies for declining industries. The asterisks indicate the terms that are used in the directional policy matrix discussed in Chapter 11 (Figure 11.7). Developed from: Harrigan, KR (1980) *Strategies for Declining Businesses*; Heath, Harrigan KR and Porter, ME (1983) End-game strategies for declining industries. *Harvard Business Review*, July–August.

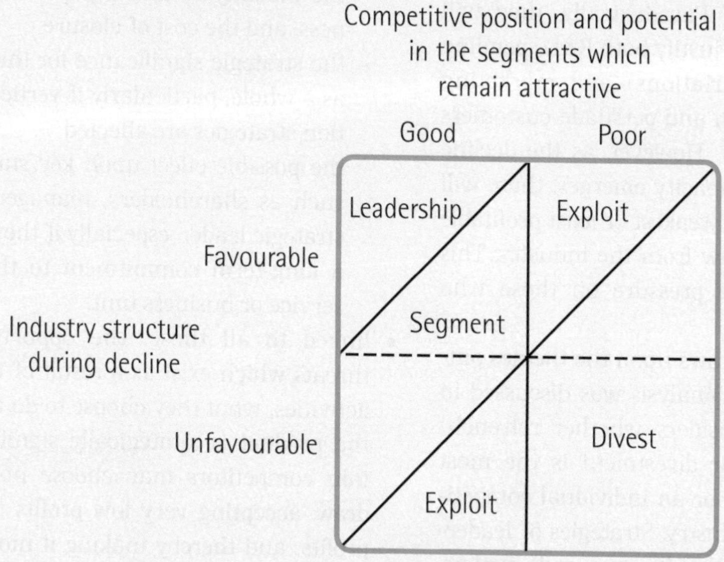

Competitive position and potential
in the segments which
remain attractive

|  | Good | Poor |
|---|---|---|
| Favourable | Leadership / Segment | Exploit |
| Unfavourable | Exploit | Divest |

Industry structure
during decline

Leadership | Selective investment*; turnaround
Invest as appropriate to give real competitive advantage
Idea: Become one of the strongest competitors in the declining industry with either the lowest costs or clear differentiation

Segment or niche | Selective investment*; turnaround
Identify one or more attractive segments, those with greatest potential for longer-term survival or short-term returns, and seek a strong position while divesting in other segments

Exploit or harvest | Phased withdrawal*; retrenchment
Controlled disinvestment, reducing product alternatives, advertising and so on in order to cut costs
Problem: losing the confidence of suppliers and buyers as they witness the obvious reduction in commitment
Must lead eventually to divestment or liquidation

Quick divestment | Immediate sale or liquidation

will again be important in the case of recovery strategies. Time is likely to be limited and proposed changes will have to be implemented quickly. The support and co-operation of managers and other employees will be essential, particularly where redundancies, changes in organization structures or changes in working practices are required. Quite possibly changes in attitudes – an issue of organizational culture – will be involved. Although the gravity of the situation may be visible, and the dangers of failing to change clearly understood, the changes will need managing properly if they are to prove effective. The issues involved in managing change are discussed in Chapter 24.

## Summary

At any time certain industries will be declining and others will be relatively unattractive as far as particular companies are concerned, generally because of intense competition. Individual companies might be performing poorly and in need of either a recovery strategy or an appropriate divestment.

When this is the case, the feasibility of recovery will vary from situation to situation, and the four possible outcomes of a change in strategy are:

- a failure to recover
- temporary recovery
- sustained survival, and
- sustained recovery.

The likely outcome is inevitably affected by the timing of the intervention. If a company realizes the gravity of a pending situation at an early stage, it will be better placed to deal with it. Recovery will be more difficult to achieve it the organization waits until it facing a real crisis.

In simple terms, *retrenchment* – to create a platform for possible expansion later on – concerns stronger cash management and tighter operations. Renewal brings in marketing and the search for new opportunities for adding value and differentiating. It is about building new forms of competitive advantage.

*Divestment* can be an important theme in retrenchment and consolidation. Management buy-outs are sometimes used as a convenient means of divesting a business which has the potential to grow but which is no longer core to its existing parent.

A four-stage model of the process can be summarized as:

1. galvanization – engaging the problem
2. simplifying the situation so it can be dealt with
3. building new competencies
4. exerting leverage to develop and sustain new competitive advantages.

From time to time economies move from 'boom' conditions into recessions, the depth and length of which vary markedly. In a recession company revenues and profits will fall and a number of the issues and strategies discussed in relation to retrenchment and consolidation become relevant. Paradoxically, an economic recession is often an ideal time for a company to invest if it has the appropriate resources. If it can afford to hold on to its staff, the chances are that they will have time to deal with the implied changes. New plant, equipment and technology could then be in place in time for when the economy turns around – placing the organization in a strong position.

There are several possible strategies for individual competitors in mature and declining industries. Some companies will withdraw from the industry. Others will find attractive niches. The fact that an industry is in decline does not make it automatically unattractive for everyone.

## References

Baden-Fuller, C and Stopford, J (1992) *Rejuvenating the Mature Business: The Competitive Challenge*, Routledge.

Clifford, DK (1977) Thriving in a recession, *Harvard Business Review*, July–August.

Davis, JV (1974) The strategic divestment decision, *Long Range Planning*, February.

Devlin, G (1989) Selling off not out, *Management Today*, April.

Harrigan, KR (1980) *Strategies for Declining Businesses*, Heath.

Slatter, S (1984) *Corporate Recovery: Successful Turnaround Strategies and Their Implementation*, Penguin.

Van de Vliet, A (1998) Back from the brink, *Management Today*, January.

Weitzel, W and Johnson, E (1989) Decline in organizations – a literature extension and integration, *Administration Science Quarterly*, 34(1) March.

Whittingham, R (1991) Recession strategies and top management change, *Journal of General Management*, 16(3), Spring.

## Additional material on the website

The web pages contain additional material on management buy-outs.

Test your knowledge of this chapter with our online quiz at: http://www.thomsonlearning.co.uk

Explore Strategies for Consolidation and Recovery further at:

*Administrative Science Quarterly*    http://www.gsm.cornell.edu/ASQ/asq.html

*Management Today*    http://www.managementtoday.haynet.com/magazines/mantod

## Questions and Research Assignments

### TEXT RELATED

1. Why might a company wish to remain a competitor in an industry despite low or declining profitability?

   Classify your reasons as objective or subjective. Can the subjective reasons be justified?

2. What factors do you feel would be most significant to all parties involved in a proposed buy-out during the negotiations? Where are the major areas of potential conflict?

## Internet and Library Projects

1. Update Minicase 18.1 to ascertain what has happened to Debenhams since its split from Burton.

*Debenhams*   http://www.debenhams.com

2. What has happened to the retail group Signet since Gerald Ratner was forced to resign? In the event, were his comments a 'minor blip' or a much more serious strategic issue that needed careful handling if a recovery were to be engineered?

*Signet Group*   http://www/hsamuel.co.uk/he/companyinfo.htm

3. Reed Elsevier's origins are not in publishing, where they now concentrate, but in paper and packaging. They became a force in publishing when they acquired IPC (International Printers Ltd) in the early 1970s.

- Why has Reed chosen to divest all non-publishing activities in recent years?
- What is Reed's current position in the publishing industry? How strong are they?
- What growth strategies in publishing do you feel would be appropriate? You may wish to include opportunities in electronic publishing.

*Reed Elsevier*   http://www.r-e.com

4. Hornby is one of the few survivors in the UK toy industry, but it has experienced some dramatic changes in strategy and ownership. Hornby was acquired by Lines in 1964; in 1971 Lines was in liquidation. Dunbee-Combex-Marx then bought Hornby, but DCM itself collapsed in 1981. At this stage Hornby was bought out by its managers. Its main products are still electric train sets and Scalextric, but production in the UK has been replaced by foreign sourcing.

- What has happened to the company since 1982?
- How successful has the MBO been?
- What are Hornby's current products and strategies?

*Hornby Hobbies*   http://www/hornby.co.uk

# 19

# Strategy Evaluation and Decision Making

*We might like to think that strategic decisions would be taken objectively rather than subjectively. After all, there is a host of useful techniques available to decision makers – if only they always had the time to use them! Then again, it does not follow that using a selection of these techniques would provide consistent answers or priorities, leaving the manager(s) concerned to exercise judgement.*

*Some of the relevant issues have been discussed in earlier chapters. The issue of 'who' chooses was discussed in the chapters on leadership (Chapter 12) and intrapreneurship (Chapter 13). It was noted that some strategic leaders are particularly concerned with the size of the organization, together with the power and status that size can bring, and that individual managers sometimes have personal agendas that can conflict with the objectives of other people and the organization as a whole. Several techniques were described which are useful for strategic analysis and which contribute to the 'what' element of strategic choices.*

*This chapter pulls together the strands of the 'what' element and provides a comprehensive evaluation framework for strategic decisions. The* 'how' element is looked at in detail by considering strategic decision making in practice and discussing judgement.

A sound choice will always address four issues:

1. competitiveness and competitive advantage
2. strategic logic and synergy
3. the financial returns, which should normally exceed the cost of capital
4. the ability to implement.

The opening case on Walt Disney considers issues 1, 2 and 4.

# Minicase 19.1  Walt Disney Company

Walt Disney's fame and initial success was based substantially upon films, books and comics featuring cartoon characters such as Mickey Mouse and Donald Duck. Walt Disney was an entrepreneur and cartoonist who eventually found his fortune in the moving picture industry of the 1930s. He was not, however an 'overnight' success. To utilize these characters further, which Disney saw as resources, and to capitalize upon increased leisure spending (a window of opportunity) the first Disneyland theme park was later opened in 1955 in Anaheim, California. Within one year Disneyland contributed 30% of the company's revenue. The success of the theme-park strategy must be attributed to Walt personally, as others in the corporation, including his brother, Roy, were against the development.

Although Walt Disney died in 1966 his strategies were continued. The Magic Kingdom Park was opened in Florida in 1971, followed 11 years later by Epcot. These have proved immensely successful, but were not seen as 'really new'. In the 1980s the environment for leisure businesses was perceived to be changing dramatically, but Disney was no longer regarded as a trendsetter. Revenues, profits and stock prices all fell.

Disney Corporation appointed a new strategic leader, Michael Eisner, in 1984, and he successfully opened several new windows of opportunity for the corporation. He introduced more aggressive marketing (together with price increases) at the theme parks, and throughout the 1980s the numbers of visitors, including foreigners, grew steadily. Additional attractions, including the Disney-MGM studios in 1989, were added, together with a support infrastructure including Disney resort hotels. Eisner found hundreds of cartoons not previously syndicated to television. New marketing and licensing opportunities for Disney characters have always been sought. Disney established a new film company, Touchstone Pictures, to enable it to make movies with more adult themes for restricted audiences without affecting the Disney name and family image. They also invested in videos and satellite television. One key theme pervades most of the developments – the hidden wealth of the Disney name and characters. Disney has been a successful, growing, profitable company, partially thanks to recent films such as Aladdin, The Lion King, Pocahontas, Toy Story and Hercules.

Simply, Disney had developed distinctive competencies in storytelling and 'set' management and continually sought, and found, new ways of exploiting these competencies. Of course, over time it also strengthened its competency in these key areas.

## Five strategic developments

In 1992 Disney opened EuroDisney, its new theme park outside Paris – the concept had already been moved successfully to Japan. However, the initial visitor, revenue and profit targets had to be revised downwards after the first trading year. Drastic refinancing of the project was required. While attendance levels were disappointing, the key problem was that visitors, affected by the recession, were not spending liberally. The recession was also affecting Disney's ability to sell associated properties in the theme park; the projected cash flows needed this extra income. High French interest rates then compounded the difficulties. However, it was also apparent that European employees were initially unable to replicate the enthusiasm of their US counterparts, and the overall service package was not the same. EuroDisney [now Disneyland Paris Resort] has since established itself and become profitable, but there was a steep learning curve, which involved the need to bring in outside partners to help to finance overseas developments of this magnitude. In 1999 Disney announced that it would build a second park outside Paris – Disney Studios should open in 2002.

In 1994, environmentalist opponents forced Disney to abandon plans for a new park in Virginia (near Washington DC) which would have celebrated the main events in US history. Disney concluded it had 'lost the perception game'. Arguably, Disney perceived itself as a 'guardian of wholesome American values', but to its opponents it came over as an 'outsize entertainment company with a penchant for sugar-coating'. Disney has not confirmed that the idea has been shelved permanently!

One year later, in 1995, and following a gradual downward trend in theme-park attendances in Florida, Disney began to construct a new attraction – Disney's Animal Kingdom, its biggest so far – which it billed as 'a celebration of all animals that ever or never existed'. The live animals would (unusually) be presented in 'true-life adventure stories of mystery, danger and humour' rather than in zoo or safari park settings. Mechanical, mythical animals will be featured alongside the live ones.

Also in 1995 Disney paid the equivalent of £12 billion to acquire Capital Cities/ABC, owner of ABC Television in America, to create the world's largest entertainment company. A major *content* company, Disney, was merging with a leading *distribution* company. The deal was justified with two arguments. One, Disney's valuable intellectual property would enjoy enhanced media access – ABC owned eight television stations, ESPN cable TV and an extensive radio network. ABC also published newspapers, books and magazines. Two, Disney's existing distribution network was ideally placed to exploit and syndicate ABC's programmes. However, having mainly concentrated on content and intellectual property, Disney was now diversifying into a new area with new strategic demands. It was moving away from direct competition with focused companies such as Viacom to rival communications giants such as Time Warner.

In 1998 Disney launched its first cruise ships, named *Disney Magic* and *Disney Wonder*. These identical ships can carry 1750 passengers and they sail on short cruises between Florida and the Bahamas all through the year. They are designed for families, but adults who wish to be kept apart from children can achieve this aim. The lounges are, inevitably, Disney themed, and the shows are 'unlike any other in the cruise industry'. Disney invested in 1000 seat theatres with state-of-the-art acoustics. Naturally, there are also cinemas on board the ships. Externally, the ships look like other cruise liners, but internally they incorporate the latest in technology.

QUESTION: How would you evaluate these five strategic developments?

*Walt Disney Company*    http://disney.go.com

# Introducing Strategy Evaluation

There is no single evaluation technique or framework as such that will provide a definite answer to which strategy or strategies a company should select or follow at any given time. Particular techniques will prove helpful in particular circumstances. Several frameworks and techniques which are often classified as means of evaluating strategy have been discussed in earlier chapters and are listed in Box 19.1, together with a number of additional financial considerations which are explained and discussed in the Finance in Action supplement.

Certain essential criteria, however, should be considered in assessing the merits and viability of existing strategies and alternatives for future change. This chapter considers how one might assess whether or not a corporate, competitive or functional strategy is effective or likely to be effective. The issues concern *appropriateness, feasibility*

> **STRATEGY IN ACTION – Box 19.1**
> **Strategy Evaluation Techniques**
>
> SWOT analysis
>
> E–V–R congruence
> Planning gap analysis
> Porter's industry analysis and competitive advantage frameworks
> Break-even analysis
> Sensitivity analysis
> Portfolio analyses
> Scenario modelling
> Simulations of future possibilities using PIMS
>
> Investment appraisal techniques using discounted cash flows
> Net present value
> Internal rate of return
> Payback
> Cash-flow implications
> (The public sector often also uses cost–benefit analysis)

and *desirability*. Some of the considerations are likely to conflict with each other, and consequently an element of judgement is required in making a choice. The most appropriate or feasible option for the firm may not be the one that its managers regard as most desirable, for example.

In many respects the key aspects of any proposed changes concern the *strategic logic*, basically the subject of this book so far, and the *ability to implement*. Implementation and change are the subject of the final chapters.

Strategic logic relates to:

- the relationship and fit between the strategies and the mission or purpose of the organization; and the current appropriateness of the mission, objectives and the strategies being pursued (synergy is an important concept in this)
- the ability of the organization to match and influence changes in the environment
- competitive advantage and distinctiveness
- the availability of the necessary resources.

Figure 19.1, which recrafts the earlier model of E–V–R (environment–values–resources) congruence, shows that organizations must seek and exploit opportunities for adding value in ways that are attractive to customers. This can be at both the corporate and competitive strategy levels. At the corporate level, the organization is looking to establish a heartland of related businesses and activities; at the competitive level, the challenge is to create and sustain competitive advantage. Resources must be deployed to exploit the new opportunities, and this is driven or, in some cases, frustrated by strategic leadership and the culture of the organization.

Implementation concerns the management of the resources to satisfy the needs of the organization's stakeholders. Implicit in this is the ability to satisfy customers better than competitors are able to do. Matching resources and environmental needs involves the culture and values of the organization, and decisions about future changes involve an assessment of risk. Relevant to both implementation and strategic logic is the role and preference of the strategic leader and other key decision makers in the organization.

This chapter addresses the following questions:

- What constitutes a good strategic choice?
- What can the organization do and what can it not do?
- What should the organization seek to do and what should it not seek to do?

The last question should not be treated lightly. There will always be options available which are not appropriate for the organization as a whole, even though they might be attractive to some managers and could be readily implemented. This point is brought out in Minicase 19.2 on Peugeot-Citroën.

When evaluating any corporate, competitive or functional strategy it is worth considering ten strategic principles, all of which are discussed in detail elsewhere in the book. Where

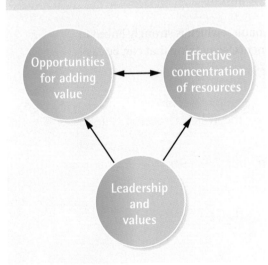

*Figure 19.1*    E–V–R congruence restated.

Minicase

# Minicase 19.2  Peugeot–Citroën

Jean-Martin Folz, the new president, appointed in 1998, inherited what he saw as three weaknesses in this well-known and largely focused French car manufacturer which competes in a European car industry plagued by overcapacity:

- a lack of volume
- a lack of innovation, and
- a lack of profitability.

One key dilemma was the extent to which the merged Peugeot and Citroën businesses should be kept separate. They compete in the same segments of the market. Their designs may be different but technologies are shared. In many respects this is a potential advantage. Research confirms that 75% of car buyers think they will be able to find what they are looking for in most models of a particular car size just by opening the door. It is the looks and feel – the aesthetics, which are often associated closely with the actual brand name – that determine the perception of difference.

As an immediate strategic change, Folz established a corporate Innovation Directorate to collect a library of ideas upon which everyone in the corporation could draw.

Shortly afterwards he decided upon a number of strategies that Peugeot-Citroën would *not* contemplate in the immediate future. Folz opted not to:

- build a plant in Eastern Europe – where other competitors have 'gone before'. When these countries ultimately join the European Union, these plants will simply add to the existing overcapacity
- build a plant in America, where, again, others have 'gone before'. The USA would be too expensive and the domestic market is very mature
- develop a 'world-car' as the various markets are too different
- acquire any specialist, niche company
- merge with France's largest car manufacturer, Renault – which is strongly linked to Nissan. The only real savings would be on components, something that can be easily acquired with a strategic alliance or a joint venture.

QUESTION: Referring back to the alternative strategic approaches of Ford and General Motors (Minicase 16.3), what would you do if you were the strategic leader of Peugeot-Citroën?

*PSA Peugeot-Citroën*   http://www.psa-peugeot-citroen.com

these principles, which are listed in Box 19.2, are evident, and particularly where they are strong and powerful forces, the likelihood of strategic success and effectiveness is enhanced. In addition, the financial returns should always exceed the costs involved, unless there is a defensible strategic reason for cross-subsidization.

## Corporate strategy evaluation

Rumelt (1980) argues that corporate strategy evaluation at the widest level involves seeking answers to three questions:

- Are the current objectives of the organization appropriate?
- Are the strategies created previously, and which are currently being implemented to achieve these objectives, still appropriate?
- Do current results confirm or refute previous assumptions about the feasibility of achieving the objectives and the ability of the chosen strategies to achieve the desired results?

It is therefore important to look back and evaluate the outcomes and relative success of previous decisions, and also to look ahead at future opportunities and threats. In both cases strategies should be evaluated in relation to the objectives that they are designed to achieve. A quantitative chart along the lines of Table 19.1 could be devised to facilitate this. In this illustration, and in order to evaluate current and possible future strategies and help to select alternatives for the future, the objectives are listed at the top of a series of columns. It will be appreciated from the sample objectives provided that some can have clear and objective measurement criteria while others are more subjective in nature. The alternatives, listed down the left-hand side, could be ranked in order of first to last preference in each column, or given a numerical score. In making a final decision based on the rankings or aggregate marks it may well prove appropriate to weight the objectives in the light of their relative importance. This table could simply be used as a framework for discussion without any scoring or ranking, if this approach is preferred.

In terms of assessing the suitability of strategic alternatives in particular circumstances Thompson and Strickland (1980) suggest that market growth and competitive position are important elements. Table 19.2 summarizes their argument. Concentration, for example, is seen as an appropriate strategy where market growth is high and the existing

*Table 19.1*    Evaluating strategies in terms of objectives

| Strategic alternative | Objectives* | | | | |
| --- | --- | --- | --- | --- | --- |
| | Ability to achieve specific revenue or growth targets | Ability to return specific profitability targets | Ability to create and sustain competitive advantage | Synergy potential – relationship with other activities | Ability to utilize existing (spare) resources and skills    and so on |
| Existing competitive strategies for products, services, business units | Score out of say 10 | | | | |
| and | or | | | | |
| Possible changes to corporate and competitive strategies | rank in order of preference | | | | |

*For evaluation purposes, each objective could be given a relative weighting.

*Table 19.2*    Strategic alternatives: their appropriateness in terms of market growth and competitive position

| Strategy | Market growth | Competitive position |
| --- | --- | --- |
| Concentration | High | Strong |
| Horizontal integration | High | Weak |
| Vertical integration | High | Strong |
| Concentric diversification | Not material | Not material |
| Conglomerate diversification | Low | Not material |
| Joint ventures into new areas | Low | Not material |
| Retrenchment | Low | Weak |
| Turnaround | High | Weak |
| Divestment | Not material | Weak |
| Liquidation | Not material | Weak |

Developed from ideas in Thompson, AA and Strickland, AJ (1980) *Strategy Formulation and Implementation*, Irwin.

competitive position is strong. By contrast, where market growth is slow and the competitive position is weak, retrenchment is likely to be the most suitable strategy for the organization.

Where 'not material' is listed in a column, the contention is that the strategy is appropriate for either high or low growth or strong or weak competitive positions.

## Criteria for Effective Strategies

When assessing current strategies, and evaluating possible changes, it is important to emphasize that there is no such thing as a right or wrong strategy or choice in absolute terms. However, certain factors will influence the effectiveness of strategies and the wisdom of following certain courses of action. A number of authors, including Tilles (1963) and Hofer and Schendel (1978), have discussed the factors that determine the current and future possible effectiveness of particular strategies.

The factors that they suggest, and others, are considered in this chapter in three sections: appropriateness, feasibility and desirability. This categorization has been selected for convenience, and it will be appreciated that there is some overlap between the sections.

The major issues are summarized in Figure 19.2 and are discussed below.

### Appropriateness

In reviewing current strategies, assessing the impact of adaptive incremental changes that have taken place and considering strategic alternatives for the future it is important to check that strategies are consistent with the needs of the environment, the resources and values of the organization, and its current mission. These general points are elaborated below. For the rest of this section the term 'the strategy' is used to refer to each particular strategy being considered, be it a current one or a proposed change or addition.

#### Mission and objectives

Does the strategy fit the current mission and objectives of the organization? Is it acceptable to the strategic leader and other influential stakeholders? (This issue is developed further in the Desirability section below.)

#### Effect on the strategic perspective

Does the strategy proposed have the potential for improving the strategic perspective and general competitive position of the organization? In other words, will the individual business not only have a strong competitive position (possibly drawing upon strengths and competencies from elsewhere in the organization) but also be able to make a positive and synergistic contribution to the whole organization?

The company, then, must be responsive to changes in the environment and it may wish to be proactive and influence its market and industry. All the time it should seek to become and remain an effective competitor.

#### SWOT; current strategic position

Is the strategy appropriate for the current economic and competitive environment?

Is the strategy able to capitalize and build on current strengths, competencies and opportunities, and avoid weaknesses and potential threats?

To what extent is the strategy able to take advantage of emerging trends in the environment, the market and the industry?

#### Skills, competencies and resources: available and needed

Are the strategies being pursued and considered sufficiently consistent that skills, competencies and resources are not spread or stretched in any disadvantageous way?

Does any new proposal exploit key organizational competencies? For current businesses and strategies: can the organization effectively add value, or would a divestment strategy be more appropriate?

It will be appreciated that this consideration embraces both the opportunity-driven and resource-based perspectives on strategy.

*Figure 19.2* Criteria for effective strategies.

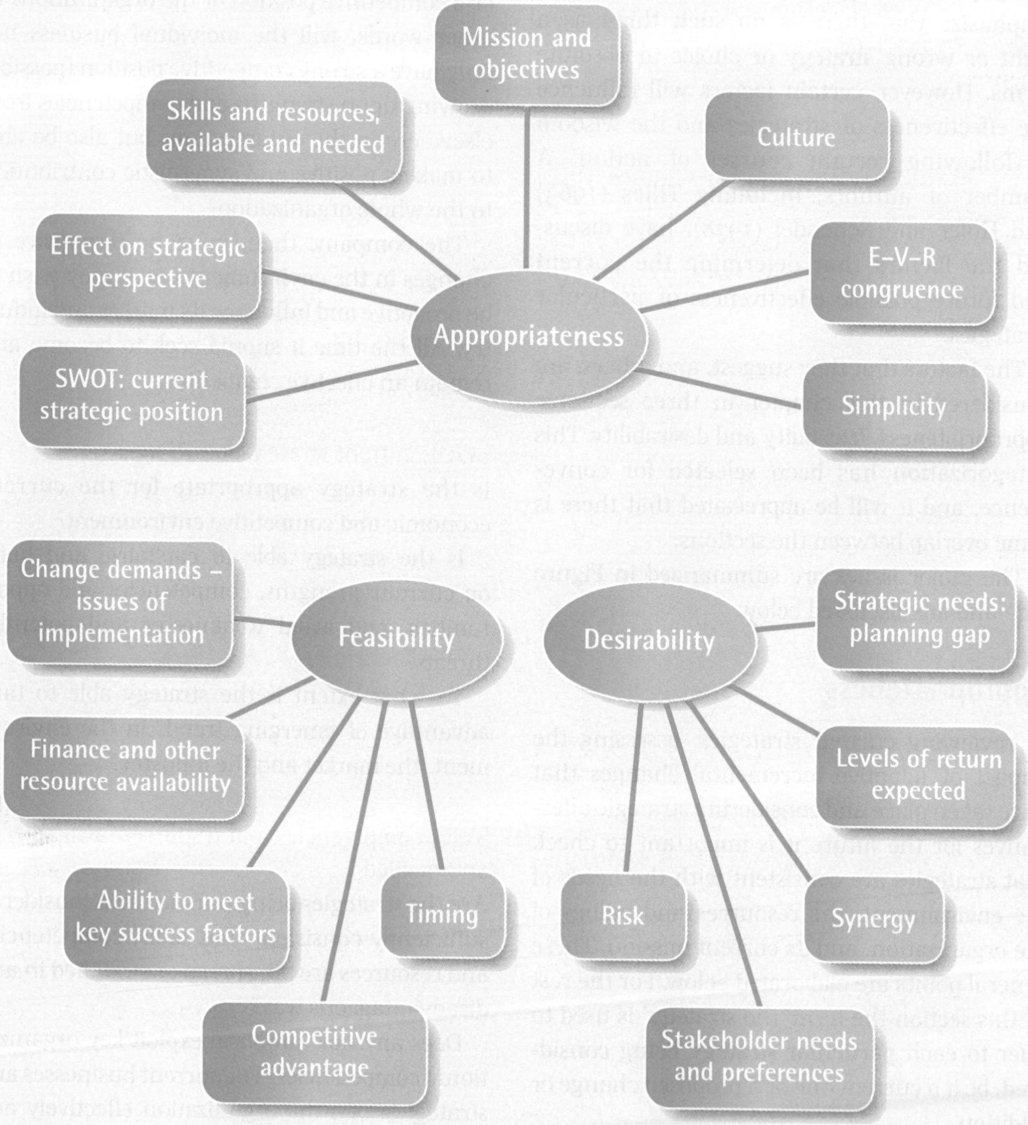

- Mission and objectives
- Skills and resources, available and needed
- Culture
- Effect on strategic perspective
- E–V–R congruence
- SWOT: current strategic position
- **Appropriateness**
- Simplicity

- Change demands – issues of implementation
- **Feasibility**
- **Desirability**
- Strategic needs: planning gap
- Finance and other resource availability
- Levels of return expected
- Ability to meet key success factors
- Timing
- Risk
- Synergy
- Competitive advantage
- Stakeholder needs and preferences

## Culture

Does the strategy fit the culture and values of the organization? If not, what are the implications of going ahead?

## E–V–R congruence

Summarizing the above points, is there congruence between the environment, values and resources?

## Simplicity

Is the strategy simple and understandable? Is the strategy one which could be communicated easily, and about which people are likely to be enthusiastic? These factors are also aspects of desirability.

# Feasibility

## Change demands – issues of implementation

Is the strategy feasible in resource terms? Can it be implemented effectively? Is it capable of achieving the objectives that it addresses?

Can the organization cope with the extent and challenge of the change implied by the option?

## Finance and other resource availability

A lack of any key resource can place a constraint on certain possible developments. The cost of capital is explained in the Finance in Action supplement at the end of this chapter.

## The ability to meet key success factors

A strategic alternative is not feasible if the key success factors dictated by the industry and customer demand, such as quality, price and service level, cannot be met.

## Competitive advantage

The effectiveness of a strategy will be influenced by the ability of the organization to create and sustain competitive advantage. When formulating a strategy it is important to consider the like-

ly response of existing competitors in order to ensure that the necessary flexibility is incorporated into the implementation plans. A company which breaks into a currently stable industry or market may well threaten the market shares and profitability of other companies and force them to respond with, say, price cuts, product improvements or aggressive promotion campaigns. The new entrant should be prepared for this and ready to counter it.

## Timing

Timing is related to opportunity on the one hand and risk and vulnerability on the other. It may be important for an organization to act quickly and decisively once an opening window of opportunity is spotted. Competitors may attempt to seize the same opportunity.

At the same time managers should make sure that they allow themselves enough time to consider the implications of their actions and organize their resources properly. Adaptive incremental change in the implementation of strategy can be valuable here. An organization may look to pursue a new strategy, learn by experience and improve by modification once they have gone ahead.

Strategic leadership and the structure, culture and values of the organization are therefore important.

Timing is also an implementation issue; Minicase 19.3 provides one illustration of its significance. This case shows how Next introduced a number of successful strategic changes which resulted in growth and increased profitability, but then overstretched themselves by pursuing strategies for which they had insufficient resources at the time. This theme relates to the theory of growth and the existence of the receding managerial limit suggested by Edith Penrose (1959), which was discussed in Chapter 3.

Minicase 19.3 also addresses an important paradox of resource management. Resources

**Minicase**

# Minicase 19.3  Next

At the end of 1988 George Davies lost the chairmanship of Next, the retail company that he had built which had experienced rapid growth and success during the 1980s. Recent strategic changes had failed to provide the desired level of success. Arguably, the speed of the growth and the extent of the diversification had been too great for Next's resources, and profits had fallen as a result.

Over four years and with a series of strategic moves, Davies had transformed the relatively dowdy menswear retailers J Hepworth into Next, a group which was innovative, design led and fashion orientated. Next segmented the retail market, selling fashionable clothing to younger men and women, as well as jewellery and furniture. However, alone a strategy of targeting new segments is not a source of sustained advantage. Rivals will soon see the new opportunity and seek to move in. In addition, Next had diversified into general mail order by the acquisition of Grattan, one of the largest catalogue retail operations.

The moves which proved problematical occurred in 1987 and 1988. In 1987 Next took over Combined English Stores (CES), a large and already diversified retail group which included Biba (the West German fashion retailer), Zales (jewellery), Salisbury's (luggage, handbags and the like), a chain of chemist's shops, a carpet business and a holiday company. This gave Next a substantial high-street presence, together with the problem and expense of converting a large number of stores to the fashionable Next image and format, which was regarded as a key factor in their record of success. Critics argued that Next had acquired too many stores, however, and Zales and Salisbury's were sold to Ratner's in autumn 1988. This reduced the extent of Next's diversification, and helped to reduce the gearing from 125%.

In January 1988 the Next Directory, an exclusive mail-order catalogue, was launched and *sold* to potential customers through advertising and direct mail. At this time catalogues were normally free. The product range in the Directory was designed to appeal to upmarket buyers, not the traditional mail-order customers, who could specify when they wanted their goods delivered. The launch and the new concept proved less successful than forecasts and expectations. Moreover, in 1988 there was growing friction between Next and Grattan. Grattan disagreed with Next's plans to redevelop their product line. Davies has claimed that in October 1988 there were serious discussions about splitting Next and Grattan, as happened with ASDA and MFI.

At the end of 1988 Next's profitability had declined, its strategy was not co-ordinated, and there were concerns about a fall in demand in 1989 as a result of increased interest charges and inflation.

QUESTION: Had the diversification into mail order and the acquisition of Combined English Stores been appropriate and feasible?

Next was unable to provide all of the necessary resources at the time they were required; and George Davies was quoted in the *Financial Times* on 5 December 1988 as saying, 'The lesson that I've learnt this year is that you must stick to the markets you know'.

Next, also, was a highly innovative company, yet Davies was seen as an autocratic strategic leader who had failed to develop an appropriately supportive team of managers and an organization that was sufficiently decentralized.

After Davies' departure Next concentrated on two principal businesses:

- retailing ladies', men's and children's clothing, accessories and home furnishings – the remaining retail businesses were divested
- the Next Directory – Grattan was sold to Otto Versand, the German mail-order company.

George Davies, whose collaborative alliance with ASDA has been successful, was replaced as chief executive by David Jones, who had joined Next when it acquired Grattan. Jones has been described as a cautious, conservative accountant.

> *I probably gamble a little more than people think, but only when I have the information to ensure it is a safe bet.*
>
> (David Jones)

Jones' strategies for rationalizing and consolidating the business proved very successful and by the end of 1995 Next had been turned around.

| | Index of sales revenue (1986 = 100) | Trading costs as a % of turnover | Return on capital employed |
| --- | --- | --- | --- |
| 1986 | 100 | 88 | 11.4 |
| 1989 | 500 | 97 | 6.7 |
| 1992 | 255 | 93 | 19.2 |
| 1994 | 344 | 86 | 33.6 |

The figures show how quickly sales revenue rose during the 1980s with the acquisitions and the more aggressive retailing style, but costs were also rising and profitability was falling. With divestments sales then fell, before rising again. Under Jones the return on capital advanced steadily. In 1995 Next was not only profitable, it had accrued cash reserves of £150 million.

QUESTION: What strategies would be appropriate, desirable and feasible for utilizing these resources effectively?

In the event, there was some international expansion but no major acquisitions.

Paradoxically, once there were no major crises to deal with, some complacency set in. Next sales fell back during 1998, the first reduction during the 1990s.

- There had been operational misjudgements – resulting in inadequate stocks of the best-selling lines of women's and children's wear.
- By switching its range emphasis to provide a stronger appeal to 'higher fashion' customers Next had partially taken its eye of its core customers.
- The problems were compounded by complacency over issues at the store level. After the run of success Next management had turned its attention more to improving its warehousing and logistics.

Jones commented: 'We do not have a divine right to be successful'.

The real danger was that some customers might have been lost permanently to rival high-street retailers.

QUESTION: David Jones has clearly been successful – and he remains as strategic leader. But: could a case be made for ensuring that he had a 'partner' with a greater willingness to take risks and who would deliberately seek to stretch the organization more?

*Next*    http://www.next.co.uk

must be stretched if they are to achieve their full potential, but if the targets set for them imply a 'bridge too far' there is a real danger of both underachievement and damage to the rest of the organization. Here, resources might have to be redeployed, which will have consequences for the business from which they are taken. The reputation of the organization might easily be tarnished. Clearly, the decisions reached will reflect the risk perspective of the managers concerned.

## Desirability

### Strategic needs; the planning gap

The ability of the strategy to satisfy the objectives of the organization and help to close any identified planning gap are important considerations. Timing may again be an important issue. The ability of the strategy to produce results in either the short term or the longer term should

be assessed in the light of the needs and priorities of the firm.

### The level of returns expected

Decisions concerning where a company's financial resources should be allocated are known as investment or capital budgeting decisions. The decision might concern the purchase of new technology or new plant, the acquisition of another company, or financing the development and launch of a new product.

Competitive advantage and corporate strategic change are both relevant issues.

The ability to raise money, and the cost involved, are key influences, and should be considered alongside two other strategic issues:

- Does the proposed investment make sense strategically, given present objectives and strategies?

- Will the investment provide an adequate financial return?

The latter question is partly answered by the company's cost of capital and the whole topic of investment decisions is explored in the Appendix to this chapter. Strategic fit is a broad issue and is addressed in the main part of the chapter.

## Synergy

Effective synergy should lead ideally to a superior concentration of resources in relation to competitors. The prospects for synergy should be evaluated alongside the implications for the firm's strategic perspective and culture, which were included in the section on Appropriateness. These factors in combination affect the strategic fit of the proposal and its ability to complement existing strategies and bring an all-round improvement to the organization. Diversification into products and markets with which the organization has no experience, and which may require different skills, may fit poorly alongside existing strategies and fail to provide synergy.

## Risk

It has already been pointed out that risk, vulnerability, opportunity and timing are linked. Where organizations, having spotted an opportunity, act quickly, there is always a danger that some important consideration will be overlooked. The risk lies in these other factors, many of which are discussed elsewhere, which need careful attention in strategy formulation:

- the likely effect on competition
- the technology and production risks, linked to skills and key success factors. Can the organization cope with the production demands and meet market requirements profitably? Innovation often implies higher risks in this area, but offers higher rewards for success
- the product/market diversification risk – the risk involved in overstretching resources

through diversification has been considered earlier in this chapter
- the financial risk – the cash flow and the firm's borrowing requirements are sensitive to the ability of the firm to forecast demand accurately and predict competitor responses
- managerial ability and competence – the risk here involves issues of whether skills can be transferred from one business to another when a firm diversifies, and whether key people stay or go after a take-over
- environmental risks – it is also important to ensure that possible adverse effects or hostile public opinion are evaluated.

Many of these issues are qualitative rather than finite, and judgement will be required. The ability of the organization to harness and evaluate the appropriate information is crucial, but again there is a trade-off. The longer the time that the organization spends in considering the implications and assessing the risks, the greater the chance it has of reducing and controlling the risks. However, if managers take too long, the opportunity or the initiative may be lost to a competitor who is more willing to accept the risk. The subject of risk is revisited in Chapter 23.

In my experience those who manage change most successfully are those who welcome it in their own lives and see it as an opportunity for stimulation and learning new things. Implicit is the willingness to take risks, including making intelligent mistakes. I am much more interested in important failures that prepare the way for future success than I am in cautious competence and maintaining the status quo.

*Robert Fitzpatrick, when President Directeur Général, Euro Disneyland SA*

### Stakeholder needs and preferences

This relates to the expectations and hopes of key stakeholders, the ability of the organization to implement the strategy and achieve the desired results, and the willingness of stakeholders to accept the inherent risks in a particular strategy.

Strategic changes may affect existing resources and the strategies to which they are committed, gearing, liquidity and organization structures, including management roles, functions and systems. Shareholders, bankers, managers, employees and customers can all be affected; and their relative power and influence will prove significant. The willingness of each party to accept particular risks may vary. Trade-offs may be required. The power and influence of the strategic leader will be very important in the choice of major strategic changes, and his or her ability to convince other stakeholders will be crucial.

## Using the evaluation criteria

The criteria can be used in a number of ways in the search for an appropriate balance and trade-off; it is rare that one strategic option will be the most appropriate, most desirable and completely feasible. For example:

- A company might well discern just which option or options are highly appropriate and desirable and then evaluate or test their feasibility.
- An objective review of internal resources and relative strengths and competencies could flag options which are appropriate and internally feasible. These can then be evaluated for external feasibility and desirability. Is there a real market opportunity? Does it accord with the ambitions and preferences of the strategic leader?
- Environmental scanning can be used to highlight opportunities which would be

appropriate and externally feasible. These then need testing for internal feasibility and desirability, taking into account the risk element.

Sometimes a new window of opportunity will be spotted and all of the criteria will need to be applied, possibly quite quickly. The final choices and prioritization may be difficult. There might be two feasible alternatives, one of which is highly desirable to certain stakeholders but logically less appropriate than the other for the organization's overall strategy. Some organizations, particularly small companies and ones dominated by powerful, idiosyncratic leaders, may be tempted to place desirability first. A strategic leader may have personal ambitions to develop the organization in particular directions and in terms of growth targets. If the preferred strategy is implemented successfully, it will later be rationalized as highly appropriate.

Conversely, a risk-averse company may have an acquisition opportunity which is strategically appropriate and feasible, but for cultural reasons is seen as undesirable.

It is important to stress again that a strategy must be implemented before it can be considered effective. The formulation may be both analytical and creative, and the strategy may seem excellent on paper, but the organization must then activate it. The value of commitment and support from the strategic leader, managers and other employees should not be underestimated.

It would be appropriate at this stage to return to Minicase 19.1 and reconsider the relative merits of the five strategies which are described.

While evaluation techniques can assist in strategic decision making, individual subjectivity and judgement will also be involved. Consequently, we now need to look in more detail at decision making in practice.

## Decision Making

It has already been emphasized that strategies can form or emerge as well as be formulated or prescribed. Strategic change results from decisions taken and implemented in response to perceived opportunities or threats. The management of change therefore requires strategic awareness and strategic learning, which implies the ability to recognize and interpret signals from the environment. Signals from the environment come into the organization all the time and in numerous ways. It is essential that they are monitored and filtered in such a way that the important messages reach decision makers. If strategic change is to some degree dependent on a planning system, then that planning system must gather the appropriate data. Equally, if there is greater reliance on strategic change emerging from decisions taken within the organization by managers who are close to the market, their suppliers and so on, these managers must feel that they have the authority to make change decisions. In both cases appropriate strategic leadership is required to direct activity.

This section looks at decision making in practice, at how decisions are taken and might be taken, and at why some bad decisions are made.

### Decision making and problem solving

Decision making is a process related to the existence of a problem, and it is often talked about in terms of problem solving. A problem, in simple terms, exists when an undesirable situation has arisen which requires action to change it. In other words, a problem exists for someone if the situation that they perceive exists is unsatisfactory for them. They would like to see something different or better happening and achieving different results.

However, in many instances the problem situation is very complex and can only be partially understood or controlled, and therefore decisions are not so much designed to find ideal or perfect answers but to improve the problem situation. In other instances, managers may find themselves with so many problems at any time that they can at best reduce the intensity of the problem rather than systematically search for a so-called right answer.

Russell Ackoff (1978) distinguishes between solving, resolving, dissolving and absolving problems. A *solution* is the optimum answer, the best choice or alternative, and rational decision making (developed below) is an attempt to find it. A *resolution* is a satisfactory answer or choice, not necessarily the best available, but one that is contingent upon circumstances, such as time limitations, or lack of real significance of the problem. This will again be developed below. A *dissolution* occurs when objectives are changed in such a way that the problem no longer seems to be a problem. Feelings about what should be happening are changed to bring them in line with what is happening; current realities are accepted. Typically managers accept new, weaker objectives which allow them to feel that there is no longer a problem. For example, achieving a target revenue growth of 5% in a static market might be proving difficult; a revised (downwards) figure of 2% would be much more achievable! *Absolution* happens when problems are simply ignored in the hope that they will rectify themselves. Some people tend to treat minor illnesses in this way.

While there will always be an objective element in a strategic decision, other more subjective influences will also play a part. Figure 19.3 shows that the ultimate decision will have been affected by three elements:

- the results of whatever analyses have been used to evaluate the data available

*Figure 19.3*  Decision making.

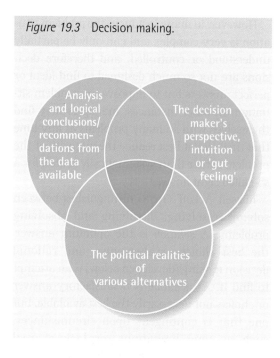

Figure 19.4 presents these themes in a different way by illustrating the four key issues in any decision:

1. the nature of the actual intervention. The idea of 'meaning systems' was mentioned in Chapter 13. The person or people involved will be involved for a reason. Maybe it is their direct responsibility. Perhaps they have been asked to advise and help. Possibly they have been brought in because those whose responsibility the problem is are simply not coping. Regardless, they bring their own perspective, interpretation and objectives to the situation. Naturally this will have an important bearing on

2. the relevant political issues and political realities

3. the quality and reliability of the information available

4. cultural issues, in particular norms, values and key roles. The decision taken should never ignore the likelihood of it being implemented successfully. If people oppose the changes or strategy proposed, for whatever reason (again discussed in Chapter 24), they may be minded to try and block its implementation. Where the change complements existing values and practices it should be more acceptable than if it implies a change of culture and behaviour. Radical change is sometimes essential, and should not be avoided simply because it is likely to attract opposition. However, it must be realized that it will take longer to implement.

- the intuition and perspective of the person or people involved. Past experiences and their willingness to trust the reliability and validity of the information that they have will both be influential issues. Some managers and strategic leaders, particularly those whom we would describe as entrepreneurial, often have an uncanny and difficult-to-explain understanding of a market or industry and of which strategy would work. They do not appear to carry out any formal analysis or use any of the techniques described here. But such managers are a minority and others are well advised to use formal analysis!

- the political realities of the various alternatives. The contingent decision is the one that people believe can be implemented. It is not necessarily the alternative that 'on paper' promises the highest rewards. To be effective, all managers must be able to handle the relevant political issues, as discussed in Chapter 24.

## 'Good' and 'bad' decisions

Decision making, then, involves both information and people. While the strategic leader must develop an appropriate information system, he or she must also ensure that a good team of

*Figure 19.4*  Key issues in decision making.

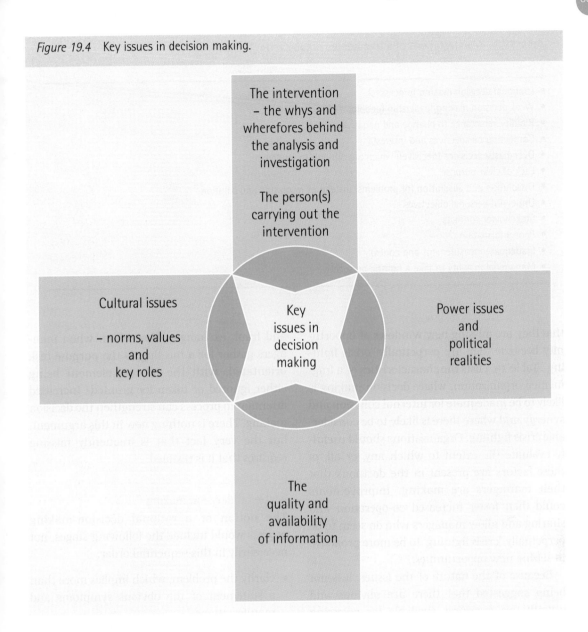

people has been gathered and manage them well.

*The conductor is only as good as his orchestra.*
(André Previn)

Considerable research has been carried out into group behaviour and it is not within the scope of this book to examine it in detail. But no leader-

ship style is universally better than the others. Much depends on the personality, power and charisma of the leader.

In just the same way that we might like to see evidence of more objectivity in some decisions, we would also like to see organizations being proactive as well as reactive in their decision making. In the latter case, there is a real risk

*Table 19.3*    Manifestations of a fragmented organization

- Irrational decision making (processes)
- Weak decision making/leadership (people)
- Rigidity, reluctance to change and negative politics
- Conflicting perspectives and interests
- Over-hasty decisions (decisive!) which are difficult to implement
- Lack of clear purpose
- Dissolution and absolution (of problems) instead of resolution and solution
- Unhelpful personal objectives
- Stakeholder conflicts
- Poor information
- Inadequate measurement and control
- Managerial inability to take a holistic perspective

that they are missing new windows of opportunity because they are perpetually 'crisis fighting'. Table 19.3 lists the characteristics of a fragmented organization, where decision making is likely to be inadequate for internal cohesion and synergy and where there is likely to be considerable crisis fighting. Organizations should usefully evaluate the extent to which any, or all, of these factors are present in the decisions that their managers are making. Improvements could then foster increased co-operation and sharing and allow managers who do seem to be perpetually 'crisis fighting' to be more proactive in seizing new opportunities.

Because of the nature of the issues, it is not being suggested that there are obvious and quantitative measures available for assessing them. Rather, managers should be encouraged to confront and discuss the ways in which they behave, make decisions, carry out the decisions they make and, in the process, help or hinder their colleagues and other stakeholders. Hopefully, this will persuade people to reflect on the inherent style weaknesses without the process being either hostile or confrontational. While a personal self-audit is possible, the process is enhanced with groups of managers

and frank exchanges. How often, when managers gather for a meeting, is the purpose task orientated, with the process element being either ignored or taken for granted? Increased attention to process can strengthen the decision making. There is nothing new in this argument, but the very fact that is frequently missing requires that it is restated.

### Irrational decision making

The notion of a rational decision-making process would include the following stages, not necessarily in this sequential order:

- clarify the problem, which implies more than a statement of the obvious symptoms and manifestations
- establish clear objectives for the desired outcome
- generate possible alternative courses of action
- assess the probable outcomes for each alternative
- select a course of action, by considering likely outcomes and desired objectives
- implement this choice and
- monitor and evaluate progress.

It is clear that most decisions and managerial actions do not follow a sequence such as this, or incorporate all of these stages. Short-cuts are taken, often because of a lack of time or a lack of information, and sometimes through laziness. A number of explanations for this is available. Simon (1976) offers the idea of 'satisficing', the acceptance of a satisfactory course of action (not necessarily the best solution) which at least deals with the problem. Lindblom (1959) and later Quinn (1980) offer alternative theories based around the concept of trial and error in incremental, learning stages as distinct from a more hands-off decision. Etzioni (1967) argues that managers make a judgement on the relative importance and priority of an issue or problem, and then base the time and attention that they give to the issue on this judgement. All of these are logical and defensible. The issue concerns the extent to which managers are avoiding – consciously or unconsciously – the elements of the rational approach, especially in the case of major, serious problems and, in the end, making poor decisions which fail to deal adequately with the problem.

## Weak decision making

Here we are looking for managers to realize and discuss the extent of their:

- tunnel vision, leading to a lack of internal synergy
- information flows and communications which prevent the right information reaching the people who need it when they can make best use of it
- personal objectives and agendas which lead to subjectivity, selfishness and internal tensions
- willingness to ignore the potential downside impact of their actions on other managers and other parts of the organization
- unwillingness to compromise to reach an accommodation with other managers.

Many of these issues are always likely to be present. Are they being ignored – causing frustration and maybe even despair – or dealt with? It is important here to stress the idea of *accommodation* among managers, as distinct from consensus, where multiple objectives and perspectives are present.

## Resistance to change

Heirs and Farrell (1987) identify three 'destructive minds', the impact of which organizations must minimize if they are to manage change effectively:

- the rigid mind which stifles originality and creativity and ignores the need to change
- the ego mind which fosters subjectivity and makes collaboration very difficult
- the machiavellian mind which uses political activity to achieve personal objectives at the expense of others.

All effective managers will be political; they will use their power and influence to bring about decisions and actions which serve the needs and interests of the organization. Negative politics occurs when this power and influence is used against the best interests of the organization.

How many of these minds are evident in a crisis fighting organization that is largely reactive to events?

## Over-hasty decisions

Crisis fighters are typically pragmatic and decisive. Sometimes, though, decisions taken in haste prove difficult to implement, as valuable time is spent trying to justify the decision. Taking time initially to search for support and agreement, involving a range of people and opinions in the process, can be hard to justify when time pressures are tight. However, if decisions enjoy people's support because they have been consulted and understand the background, implementation can be smoother, actually saving time in the end. We can learn a great deal from the Japanese here – but in many organizations, are managers listening and learning?

### Stakeholder conflicts – the need for a holistic perspective

It is unlikely that all the preferences of every internal and external stakeholder can be met in full and, as we saw earlier, accommodation is necessary. The issue here concerns the ability of managers to appreciate and accept that different people have different perspectives, and they do not see problems and issues in the same way. There is a saying: 'the way we see the problem is the problem'. Too narrow a perspective leads to a poor decision with adverse impacts on others. Taking account of different perspectives demands dialogue and sharing.

## Implementing decisions

The implementation aspects of the decision are of vital importance. Simply, a decision can only be effective if it is implemented successfully and yields desirable or acceptable results. It may prove very sensible to spend time arriving at a decision by, say, involving the people who must implement it, aiming to generate a commitment at this stage even though it may be time consuming. Such a decision is likely to be implemented smoothly. One alternative to this, the speedy decisive approach, may prove to be less effective. If it is not supported, the alternative chosen may result in controversy and reluctance on the part of others to implement it. Vroom and Yetton (1973) have developed a model of five alternative ways of decision making.

### Vroom and Yetton's model

A short summary of the five approaches is as follows.

- The leader solves the problem or makes the decision him or herself using information available at the time.

- The leader obtains necessary information from subordinates and then decides on the solution to the problem him or herself. Subordinates are not involved in generating or evaluating alternative solutions.
- The leader shares the problem with relevant subordinates individually, obtaining their ideas and suggestions without bringing them together as a group. Then the leader makes the decision, which may or may not reflect the influence of subordinates.
- The leader shares the problem with the subordinates as a group, collectively obtaining their ideas and suggestions. Then he or she makes the decision, which again may or may not reflect their influence.
- The leader shares the problem with the subordinates as a group, and together the leader and subordinates generate and evaluate alternatives and attempt to reach an agreement on a solution.

(Vroom and Yetton use the expression 'solve' throughout.)

Vroom and Yetton contend that the choice of style should relate to the particular problem faced, and their model includes a series of questions which can be used diagnostically to select the most appropriate style. While the model is useful for highlighting the different styles and emphasizing that a single style will not always prove to be the most appropriate, it is essentially a normative theory ('this is what you should do') and in this respect should be treated with caution.

**The judgement dilemma**
Judgement, per se, cannot be taught or learned; instead it comes from experience. Experience is gained by making mistakes, which, of course, are the result of poor judgement! Managers exercise poor judgement because it cannot be taught or learned.

# Judgement

Strategic changes can be selected by an individual manager, often the strategic leader, or a team of managers, and Vickers (1965) stresses that three contextual aspects have a critical impact on the decision:

- the decision makers' skills and values together with aspects of their personality (*personal factors*)
- their authority and accountability within the organization (*structural factors*)
- their understanding and awareness (*environmental factors*).

Related to these, the decisions taken by managers are affected by their personal judgemental abilities, and understanding judgement can, therefore, help us to explain why some managers appear to 'get things right' while others 'get things wrong'.

Vickers suggests that there are three types of judgement:

1. *reality judgements* – Strategic awareness of the organization and its environment and which is based upon interpretation and meaning systems.
2. *action judgements* – What to do about perceived strategic issues.
3. *value judgements* – Concerning expected and desired results and outcomes from the decision.

Figure 19.5 shows how these are interconnected. Decision makers need to understand 'what is' (*reality*), 'what matters' (*values*) and 'what to do about it' (*action*). Their choice will be based upon a conceptualization of what might or what should be a better alternative to the current situation. Ideally, it will incorporate a holistic perspective, implying either an understanding or a personal interpretation of the organization's purpose or mission, and it also requires an

appreciation that what matters is a function of urgency and time horizons. A company with cash difficulties, for example, might need a strategy based upon immediate rationalization or consolidation; a liquid company evaluating growth options has greater flexibility. The choice will also be affected by managers' relative power and influence, their perception of the risks involved, and their willingness to pursue certain courses of action.

To conclude this chapter, Figure 19.6 draws together key points from the sections on decision making and judgement. The top part of the diagram explains that managers have to assess any problematical situation and determine the extent to which it is normal or unusual. This is their reality judgement of the situation. Where they perceive that there is a real degree of normality to the events, the likelihood is that they will continue to rely on traditional routines and approaches. However, where the situation is seen as more unusual a decision has to be made about how to deal with it. This choice reflects action judgement, and there are six (and possibly more) alternatives to choose from:

- Continue to rely on approaches which have worked well in the past.
- From a position of leadership, take decisive action – reflecting an entrepreneurial style.
- Involve others in formal analysis, discussion and planning.
- Possibly involving others, adopt a trial-and-error approach to craft a new strategy adaptively or incrementally.
- Seek input from an expert, maybe an external consultant.
- Establish that there is a change project underway and follow a 'textbook' approach – along the lines of the one explained in Chapter 24.

The outcomes are going to be dependent upon the people who become engaged and involved, their relative positions, power and competency and the time and resources allocated to the

*Figure 19.5*   Judgement and strategic decision making.

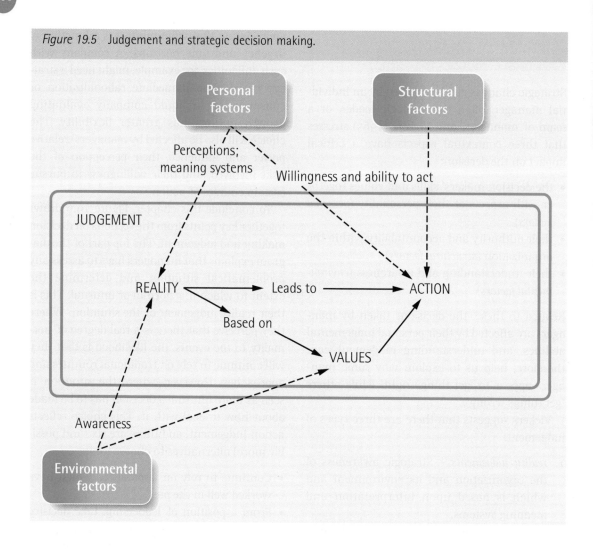

decision taking and implementation. This final part is the relevant value judgement.

Having considered a number of possible frameworks through which organizations might formulate their strategies and changes in strategies (Part Three) and a variety of strategic alternatives in Chapters 14, 15, 16 and 18, this chapter has considered the criteria which determine the effectiveness of strategies. It has been emphasized that effective strategies take account of both formulation and implementation issues. Implementation is therefore the subject of the remaining chapters of the book.

## Summary

It is important for organizations to address the following questions:

- What constitutes a good strategic choice?
- What can the organization do and what can it not do?
- What should the organization seek to do and what should it not seek to do?

An effective strategy is one that meets the needs and preferences of the organization, its key deci-

**Figure 19.6** Judgement and strategic decision making.

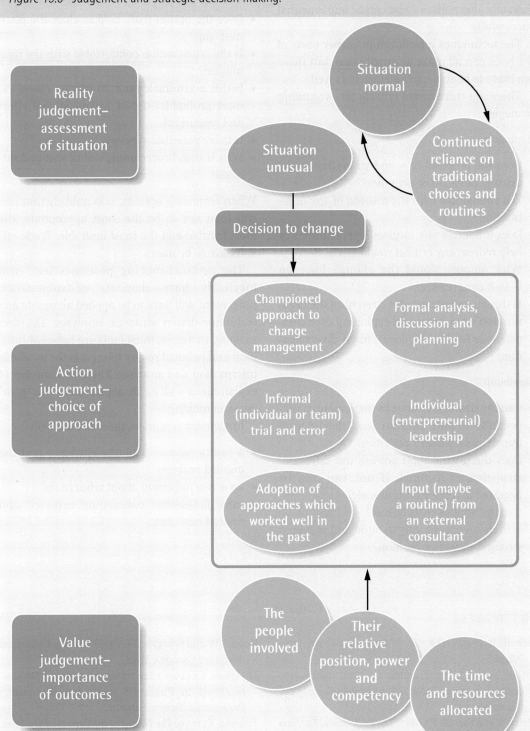

sion makers and influencers – ideally better than any alternatives – and can be implemented successfully.

The techniques introduced in earlier parts of the book can all make a contribution, but there are likely to be subjective elements as well.

There are three broad criteria for evaluating strategies:

*Appropriateness*

- Does the proposal fit – and strengthen – the existing portfolio of activities?
- Is it compatible with the mission of the organization?
- Does it address any targeted opportunities or help redress any critical weaknesses?
- What impact would the change have on E–V–R congruence?
- Is this an opportunity for stretching the organization's resources and exploiting core competencies further? Or does it imply diversification?

*Feasibility*

- Can the strategic change be implemented successfully – and without any detrimental impact upon present activities?
- Does the organization possess the skills and competencies required? If not, can they be acquired in a relevant timescale?
- Can the implied costs be met?
- Is there an opportunity to build and sustain a strong competitive position?

*Desirability*

- Does the option truly help to close the planning gap?
- Is the organization comfortable with the risks implied?
- Is this a justifiable (and, in certain cases, the most profitable) use of organizational effort and resources?
- Is there potential synergy?
- Which stakeholder needs will be met and satisfied?

When reviewing options, it is unlikely that one will turn out to be the most appropriate, the most feasible and the most desirable. Trade-offs will have to be made.

The decision-making processes used will inevitably have elements of subjectivity. Judgement will have to be applied alongside any technique-driven strategic analyses. Decision making, therefore, must embrace issues of intuition and political reality alongside the available information and analyses. There is a number of explanations – all easily appreciated – for 'poor' decision making.

Judgement comprises three key elements:

- a *reality judgement* of the situation and the implied problem
- an *action judgement* about what to do.
- *value judgements* concerning expected and desired outcomes.

## References

Ackoff, R (1978) *The Art of Problem Solving*, John Wiley.

Etzioni, A (1967) Mixed scanning: a third approach to decision making, *Public Administration Review*, 27, December.

Heirs, B and Farrell, P (1987) *The Professional Decision Thinker*, Sidgwick and Jackson.

Hofer, CW and Schendel, D (1978) *Strategy Evaluation: Analytical Concepts*, West.

Lindblom, CE (1959) *The Science of Muddling Through*, reprinted in Pugh, DS (ed.) 2nd edn (1987) *Organization Theory*, Penguin.

Penrose, E (1959) *The Theory of the Growth of the Firm*, Blackwell.

Quinn, JB (1980) *Strategies for Change: Logical Incrementalism*, Richard D Irwin.

Rumelt, R (1980) The evaluation of business strategy. In *Business Policy and Strategic Management* (ed. WF Glueck), McGraw-Hill.

Simon, HA (1976) *Administrative Behavior: A Study of Decision Making Processes in Administrative Organizations*, 3rd edn, Free Press.

Thompson, AA and Strickland, AJ (1980) *Strategy Formulation and Implementation*, Richard D Irwin.

Tilles, S (1963) How to evaluate corporate strategy, *Harvard Business Review*, July–August.

Vickers, G (1965) *The Art of Judgement: A Study of Policy Making*, Chapman & Hall.

Vroom, V and Yetton, P (1973) *Leadership and Decision Making*, University of Pittsburgh Press.

## Additional material on the website

The following article will supplement the section on decision making included in this chapter:

Thompson, JL (1998) Strategic crisis aversion – the value of a 'style audit' *Learning Organization Journal*, **5**(1).

Test your knowledge of this chapter with our online quiz at: http://www.thomsonlearning.co.uk

## Explore Strategy Evaluation and Decision Making further at:

*Learning Organization Journal*   http://www.mcb.co.uk/tlo.html

*Public Administration Review*   http://par.csuohio.edu

## Questions and Research Assignments

### TEXT RELATED

1. Which of the evaluation techniques listed at the beginning of the chapter (Box 19.1) do you feel are most useful? Why? How would you use them? What are their limitations?

2. From your experience and reading, which evaluation criteria do you think are most significant in determining the effectiveness of strategies?

List examples of cases where the absence of these factors, or the wrong assessment of their importance, has led to problems.

## Internet and Library Projects

1. In 1996 Walt Disney Corporation was thought by analysts to be a prospective buyer for EMI Music after its split from the Thorn Rentals part of Thorn-EMI. Would 'music' have been an appropriate and desirable addition to the Disney portfolio? Do you think that the acquisition of an essentially British company would have been difficult for Disney to absorb?

   What in fact has happened with EMI Music? Was the actual outcome more appropriate, feasible and desirable for EMI?

   *Walt Disney Company*   http://www.disney.go.com

   *EMI Group*   http://www.emigroup.com

2. In 1983 Tottenham Hotspur became the first English football club to be listed on the Stock Exchange. Subsequently, the club diversified, acquiring a number of related leisure companies. The intention was to subsidize the football club with profits from the new businesses. Initially this happened, but in the recession of the late 1980s football had to prop up the other activities. Businesses were closed or divested, and the ownership of Tottenham Hotspur changed hands in 1991. Research the various changes and evaluate the strategies. Was it appropriate and desirable for Tottenham to become a public limited company?

   How different was the approach taken some years later by Manchester United? What strategies have made Manchester United the richest football club in the world?

   *Tottenham Hotspur plc*   http://www.spurs.co.uk/corporatenew/index.html

   *Manchester United FC*   http://www.manutd.com

# Finance in Action

# Financial Management

## Sources of funds

Most funds used by established UK organizations are normally generated internally through retained profits, but from time to time it is necessary to raise funds externally. This conclusion applies to both the public and the private sectors. In general, loan capital or borrowing has been used more extensively than equity, which might take the form of new equity issued openly or rights issues to existing shareholders.

At present in the UK and USA, equity funding is proving more significant than borrowing; the reverse is the case for Germany, France and Japan, partially the result of different regulations. In the 1990s some UK companies used new equity to compensate for reduced cash flows and retained earnings, and US companies bought back shares and returned funds to their shareholders. This strategy is a form of defence against possible unwelcome bids. Regulations reduce the likelihood of German, French and Japanese companies being acquired by unwelcome predators.

Investment funding, then, is available through borrowing or increased equity, but assets can be increased without investing to the same extent. This is accomplished by leasing them rather than purchasing them.

### Equity capital

In general, equity capital would be increased by a rights issue of ordinary shares to existing shareholders. As an example, holders of ordinary shares might be offered one new share for every two or three that they already own, at a price equal to or below the current market price. At a higher price people would be unlikely to purchase. If all shareholders take up the offer then the percentage breakdown of the shareholders' register will remain the same; if they are not taken up by existing shareholders they will be offered to the market by the institutional underwriters, and the share register profile may change. Blocks of shares could be built up quite readily, and at a price below the current market price; and depending upon who was buying them threats to the organization from powerful shareholders could emerge.

Rights issues will not be successful without the support of institutional shareholders. This requires investor confidence in the company's strategy and strategic leadership.

Although many shareholders buy and retain shares with a view to a long-term capital gain, resulting from their sale at a price higher than the one at which they were bought, dividend policy is important. Dividends represent a rate of return on shareholders' investments. Although dividends are not fixed and can theoretically be raised or lowered freely and in relation to increases or decreases in profits, and to any changing need for retained earnings for investment, companies generally seek stability.

### Loan capital

There are various forms of loan capital, but they all have one essential characteristic. They do not carry ownership, which ordinary shares do. Loans might well be for a definite period, after which they are repayable, and with a fixed rate of interest for each year of the loan. Hence, interest payments come out of profits, but they cannot be reduced if profits decline through unfavourable trading conditions. Overdrafts provide flexible short-term funding up to an agreed limit, and their cost will vary both up and down as the prevailing market rate of interest changes. Loans are invariably secured against assets, which reduces the risk for the lender. If interest payments are not met, the bank, or whoever has loaned the money, is free to appoint a receiver and effectively take over day-to-day control of the company. Interest is paid out of profits before they are assessed for taxation, and they can thereby reduce the company's tax burden; dividends for ordinary shareholders are paid after tax.

Generalizing, the cost of borrowing can be expected to rise as the degree of risk for the lender increases. Lenders will expect higher returns from higher risk investments. Government securities are considered very safe, for example, and consequently the anticipated rate of return will typically be lower than for other investments. Secured loans are safer than ordinary shares, as mentioned above, and therefore borrowing should normally prove cheaper than equity.

The ability to obtain either – and the cost – are likely to be dependent on how well the company has been performing, and how well it has been perceived by the market to have been performing. Opportunity, ability and cost are therefore essential criteria in deciding upon a preference between equity and loan funding, but this decision should be related to the decision concerning whether to invest at all. Investments, which are discussed later in this Appendix, should be analysed by comparing their returns, discounted for the period they are earned, with the cost of financing them, or the opportunity cost of the money being used. The viability of an investment is therefore dependent upon the cost of the capital used. The cheaper the cost of capital, the more likely it is that an investment is viable and profitable. Hence if the cost of obtaining investment funding is high, opportunities might be lost.

Moreover, the capital structure of the company determines the impact of profit fluctuations on the money available after tax for paying dividends and for reinvestment. Large loans and high interest payments absorb profits, and this can be crucial if profits fluctuate significantly for any reason. The more is paid out in dividends, the less is available for reinvesting, and vice versa. In turn, dividend payments are likely to affect the view held by shareholders and the market of the company's performance, and this will affect their willingness to lend more.

## Leasing

In many cases organizations are more concerned with using assets than actually owning them. Leasing assets is one way of acquiring them without paying their full price at any one time; the popularity of leasing has grown since the late 1970s.

When an asset is leased there will normally be an agreed annual charge for a fixed number of years, and possibly there will be an arrangement whereby the company obtains ownership of the asset for a residual price at the end of the period of the lease. In aggregate terms leasing is unlikely to be cheap, but it can have a significant effect on cash flow. In addition, there have been advantageous tax regulations. Leasing is generally low risk for the lessor, who retains legal ownership of the asset and can reclaim it if the lease payments are not met.

Leasing has offered strategic opportunities, as well as financial benefits, for certain organizations. Some companies have chosen to sell and lease back property that they owned, for example, finding willing partners in property companies and institutional investors. The funds released have then been available for other investments.

# The cost of capital

## The optimal capital structure

In theory there is an *optimal capital structure* (OCS) in terms of debt and equity for any firm, and it will depend on:

- the amount of risk in the industry
- the riskiness of the company's corporate and competitive strategies, and their potential impact on profits
- the typical capital structure for the industry, and what competitors are doing – the cost of funding can provide competitive advantage
- management's ability to pay interest without too serious an impact on dividends and future investment
- both the owners' and the strategic leader's preference for risk, or aversion to it.

## The weighted average cost of capital

In considering, or attempting to decide, the OCS it is important to evaluate the *weighted average cost of capital* (WACC). The WACC, again in theory, is the average rate of return that investors expect the company to earn. In practice it is the average cost of raising additional investment funding. If a company used only loan funding the WACC would be the after-tax cost of borrowing more; but most organizations have a complex structure of debt and equity, each of which carries a different cost. The WACC is therefore an attempt to approximate what more funding would cost if it were raised proportionately to the percentages of debt and equity in the OCS. In practice it will relate to the current capital structure.

## Determining the weighted average cost of capital

The formula is:

WACC = (Percentage of long-term debt in the OCS × After-tax cost of debt)

*plus*

(Percentage of ordinary shares in the OCS × After-tax cost of equity)

As mentioned above, the WACC will normally be calculated in terms of the firm's current capital structure rather than the theoretical OCS.

The *cost of long-term debt* is the weighted average of the various interest rates incurred on existing loans, after accounting for tax. Hence, for a company which pays 10% interest on 40% of its loans, 12% on the other 60% and tax at an effective rate of 30%, the cost of long-term debt is:

$$((10\% \times 40) + (12\% \times 60)) \times (1 - 0.3) = 7.84\%$$

The *cost of equity* is more difficult to calculate. One popular model for estimating it is the capital asset pricing model (CAPM), which is described here only in outline.

## The capital asset pricing model

In theory the cost of equity for an individual company should equal the rate of return that shareholders expect to gain from investing in that company. This is based on their perception of the amount of risk involved. The CAPM attempts to capture this. The formula is:

$$R = F + \text{beta}(M - F)$$

$R$ is the expected earnings or return on a particular share and $F$ represents the risk-free rate of return expected from the most secure investments such as government securities, where the likelihood of default is considered negligible. The expected risk-free rate is determined by the current interest rate on these securities and expected inflation. $M$ is the average rate of return expected from all securities traded in the market and beta is a measure of risk based on the volatility of an individual company's shares compared with the market as a whole. A beta of 1.6 (empirically high) means that a company's share price fluctuates by 1.6 times the market

| Source of funding | Total £ million | Percentage of total | Cost % | Weighted cost |
|---|---|---|---|---|
| Equity | 1.2 | 60 | 16 | 9.6 |
| Loans | 0.8 | 40 | 8 | 3.2 |

average. In other words, if the market average rises or falls by 10%, the company's share price increases or decreases by 16%. A low beta might be 0.3. Low beta shares in a portfolio reduce risk, but in general high beta shares do little to reduce risk.

Research at London Business School yielded the following betas in the mid-1990s:

| | |
|---|---|
| Hong Kong and Shanghai Bank (includes Midland Bank) | 1.6 |
| J. Sainsbury | 0.6 |
| Manchester United Football Club | 0.4. |

As an example, assume that the risk-free rate is 10%, the market as a whole is returning 18% and a company's beta is 1.2:

$$R = 10 + 1.2(18 - 10) = 19.6\%$$

In other words, the market would be expecting the company to achieve 19.6% earnings on shareholders' funds. This is earnings after interest and tax divided by total shareholders' funds, including reserves.

By contrast, if a company's beta was 0.5:

$$R = 10 + 0.5(18 - 10) = 14\%$$

The CAPM is useful for estimating the cost of equity but there are certain problems in implementing it. Primarily, all of the data will be adjusted and extrapolated historical data, when really it is realistic forecasts of future earnings and returns that matter. $F$ and $M$ theoretically represent expected future returns, and beta should be based on expected future fluctuations, but normally historical data will be used in the model on the assumption that trends continue. The prevailing and predicted rates of interest in

the economy will be used to increase or decrease past return figures.

The WACC can now be calculated – see top of the page. Assume that a company has £1.2 million equity funding and £800,000 in long-term debt, and that the relative costs of each are 16% and 8%, respectively:
Thus WACC = 12.8%.

Of course, retained earnings that can be reinvested in the company could alternatively be paid out as dividends, which shareholders could themselves invest wherever they chose. Consequently, the return on such reinvestments in the company should be at least the same as that which investors expect from their existing shares. Given that all shareholders' funds are incorporated in the CAPM, this is taken into account.

This whole area is extremely complex, but nevertheless the cost of capital is an important consideration alongside availability. The cost of capital can affect the viability of a proposed investment, and it can affect the overall costs of producing a product or service and thereby influence competitive advantage. Investments, and how they might be evaluated, are the subject of the next section.

## Investments and Capital Budgeting

In simple terms, an investment represents the commitment of money now for gains or returns in the future. The financial returns are therefore measured over an appropriate period. Estimating these returns relies substantially on forecasts of demand in terms of both amount and timing; and generating the returns further relies upon the ability of managers to manage resources in such a way that the forecasts are met. Uncertainty is therefore an issue.

In general, any investment should be evaluated financially on at least the following two criteria:

- Individually, is it worth proceeding with?
- Is it the best alternative from the options the company has, or if money is reasonably freely available to the company, how does the proposal rank alongside other possibilities?

In the financial evaluation of a proposed investment which produces a cash flow over a period of time, it is necessary to incorporate some qualification for the fact that inflation and other factors generally ensure that a 'pound tomorrow' is worth less than its current value. This is achieved by discounting the cash flow.

## Analysing proposed investments

### The background to discounted cash flows

If the prevailing rate of interest on bank deposit or building society accounts is 10% an individual or organization with money to invest could save and earn compound interest with relatively little risk. If the rate stayed constant, £100 today would be worth £110 next year and £121 the year after if the interest was not withdrawn annually. To calculate future values simply multiply by $1 + r$ each year, where $r$ is the rate of interest. Therefore, in ten years' time £100 is worth $£100(1 + r)^{10}$.

Reversing the process enables a consideration of what money earned in the future is worth in today's terms. In other words, if a company invests now, at today's value of the pound, it is important to analyse the returns from the investment also in today's terms, although most if not all of the returns from the investment will be earned in the future when the value of the pound has fallen. This is known as *discounting future values*. So £100 earned next year is worth $£100/(1 + r)$ today, i.e. £90.90.

Similarly, £100 earned ten years' hence would be worth in today's terms $£100/(1 + r)^{10}$. This is known as *net present value*.

In discounting cash flows and calculating net present value discount tables are used for simplicity.

### An example

Assume that a company invests £1 million today and in return earns £250,000 each year for five years, starting next year. Earnings in total amount to £1.25 million, but they are spread over five years. The company's estimated cost of capital is 10%:

| Year | Cash-flow receipts £ thousand | Discount factor at 10% | Net present value £ thousand |
|------|------|------|------|
| 1 | 250 | 0.909 | 227 |
| 2 | 250 | 0.826 | 206 |
| 3 | 250 | 0.751 | 188 |
| 4 | 250 | 0.683 | 171 |
| 5 | 250 | 0.621 | 153 |
|   |     |       | 945 |

Hence £1 million is invested to earn £945,000 in today's terms – a loss of £55,000. Logically, a positive figure is sought; and if the investment is required to show a return which is higher than the cost of capital, this target return rather than the cost of capital should be used as the discount rate and a positive net present value should be sought at this level.

Financially, this investment would only be viable with a lower cost of capital. Logically, all projects look increasingly viable with lower capital costs. The calculation which follows is of the cost of capital at which this particular project becomes viable.

## The internal rate of return

The next step would be to discount at a lower rate, say 5%:

| Year | Cash-flow receipts £ thousand | Discount factor at 5% | Net present value £ thousand |
|------|------|------|------|
| 1 | 250 | 0.952 | 238 |
| 2 | 250 | 0.907 | 227 |
| 3 | 250 | 0.864 | 216 |
| 4 | 250 | 0.823 | 206 |
| 5 | 250 | 0.784 | 196 |
| | | | 1083 |

This time a positive net present value of £83,000 is obtained.

The following formula is used to calculate the internal rate of return:

$$\frac{83,000}{138,000} \times \frac{5}{100} = 3\%$$

(£83,000 is the positive net present value at a 5% cost of capital, £138,000 is the difference in net present value between the 5% and 10% rates, and the 5/100 represents the percentage difference between the 5 and 10).

This 3% is added to the 5% to give 8%, which is the yield or internal rate of return from this investment.

Check:

| Year | Cash-flow receipts £ thousand | Discount factor at 8% | Net present value £ thousand |
|------|------|------|------|
| 1 | 250 | 0.926 | 232 |
| 2 | 250 | 0.857 | 214 |
| 3 | 250 | 0.794 | 198 |
| 4 | 250 | 0.735 | 184 |
| 5 | 250 | 0.681 | 170 |
| | | | 998 |

In other words, this investment gives a yield of 8%. This is also known as the internal rate of return, the discount rate which makes the net present value of the receipts exactly equal to the cost of the investment. In the same way that one might look for a positive net present value, one would be looking for an internal rate of return that exceeded the cost of capital.

## Payback

Payback is simply the length of time it takes to earn back the outlay; and obviously one can look at either absolute or discounted cash flows, normally the former. In the example above the payback is four years exactly. The outlay was £1 million, and the receipts amounted to £250,000 each year.

Payback is quite useful. For one thing it is relatively simple. For another it takes some account of the timing of returns, for returns can be reinvested in some way as soon as they are to hand.

## Evaluating proposed investments

If an organization wishes to be thorough and objective, investments could usefully be analysed against the six criteria listed below. The first three of these are essentially quantitative; the second three incorporate qualitative issues. Sometimes the strategic importance of a particular proposal may mean that, first, the most financially rewarding option is not selected or that, secondly, an investment is not necessarily timed for when the cost of capital would be lowest. As an example of the first point consider a firm in a growing industry which feels that it has to invest in order not to lose market share, although the current cost of capital may mean that the returns from the investment are less than it would wish for or that it could earn with a strategically less important option. An example of the second point would be a firm whose industry is in recession but predicted to grow, and where investment in capital in readiness for the upturn might result in future competitive advantage. At the moment the cost of capital might be relatively high, but the strategic significance of the investment might outweigh this.

The six criteria for evaluating a proposed investment are as follows:

- the discounted present value of all returns through the productive life of the investment
- the expected rate of return, which should exceed both the cost of capital (the cost of financing the investment) and the opportunity cost for the money (returns that might otherwise be earned with an alternative proposal)
- payback – the payout period and the investment's expected productive life – which is a very popular measure as it is relatively easily calculated
- the risk involved in not making the investment or deferring it
- the cost and risk if it fails
- the opportunity cost – specifically, the potential gains from alternative uses of the money.

Discounting techniques are theoretically attractive and used in many organizations, although more in the USA than Europe, and particularly where the proposal is capital intensive. However, the technique must involve uncertainty if the cash flows cannot be forecast accurately, as is often the case. In addition, the net present value is dependent on the discount rate used, and this should relate to the weighted average cost of capital, which again may be uncertain.

There will always be some important element of managerial judgement, and one might argue that this managerial intuition will be preferred in some smaller firms which place less emphasis on planning than do larger firms and in those companies that are more entrepreneurial and risk orientated. However, if the decision maker really understands the market and the strategic implications of the proposed investment, this may not be detrimental.

Large organizations evaluating possible investments for different divisions or business units should consider the estimated rate of return from each proposal, the current returns being obtained in each division and the company's average cost of capital, as well as any strategic issues. Take the following two possibilities:

|  | Division A | Division B |
|---|---|---|
| Rate of return on proposal | 20% | 13% |
| Current returns | 25% | 9% |

Division A's proposal could seem unattractive as it offers a lower return than existing projects, while B's investment offers an improvement to current returns. If the company's cost of capital is 15%, A's proposal is profitable and B's proposal is not.

## Questions

1. Calculate the weighted average cost of capital given the following information:
   Optimal capital structure 50:50
   Debt funding: half is at 10% interest, half at 12%
   Effective tax rate 30%
   Risk-free rate 8%
   Return expected in the stock market 12%
   Company's beta 1.2.

2. A firm has two investment opportunities, each costing £100,000 and each having the expected net cash flows shown in the table below. While the cost of each project is certain, the cash-flow projections for project B are more uncertain than those for A because of additional inherent risks. Those shown in both cases can be assumed to be maxima. It has therefore been suggested that while the company's cost of capital is of the order of 10%, B might usefully be discounted at 15%.
   (a) For each alternative calculate the net present value, the internal rate of return and the payback.
   (b) On the data available what would you advise the firm to do?
   (c) How limited do you feel this analysis is?

| | Expected cash flows | |
| | Project A (£) | Project B (£) |
| --- | --- | --- |
| Year 1 | 50,000 | 20,000 |
| Year 2 | 40,000 | 40,000 |
| Year 3 | 30,000 | 50,000 |
| Year 4 | 10,000 | 60,000 |

# Strategy Implementation and Strategic Management: Managing and Changing the Corporation

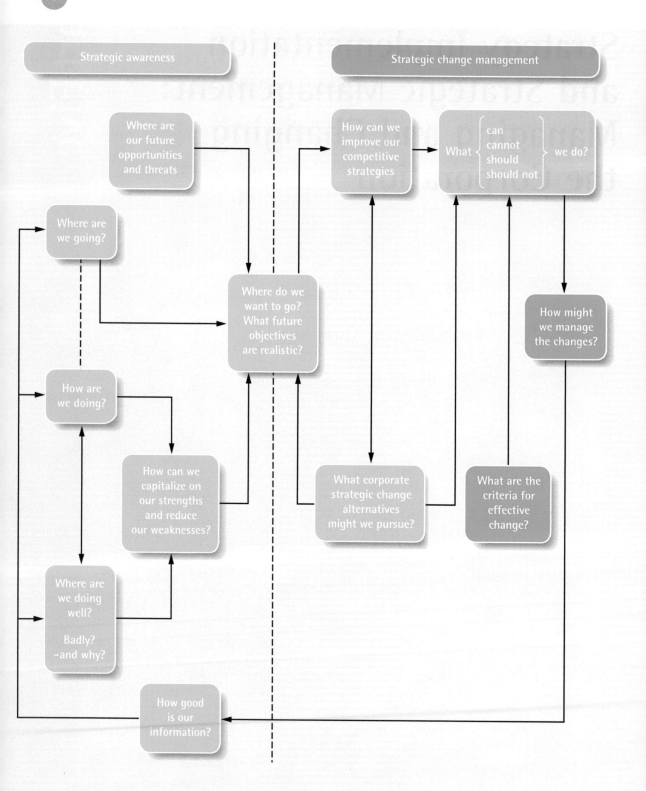

# Strategy Implementation and Strategic Management: Managing and Changing the Corporation

*Parts One and Three – an introduction to strategy and a consideration of strategy creation – have addressed a number of important 'how' questions, in particular, how strategies are created, while Parts Two and Four have been more focused on 'what' and 'where' issues. This final part of the book addresses a number of additional 'how' questions regarding the management of strategy and strategic change.*

*In particular, the following questions are asked:*

- *How are intended strategies implemented? (Chapter 20)*
- *How does emergent strategy actually happen? (Chapter 20)*
- *How should the organization be structured and designed to ensure that both happen? (Chapter 21)*
- *How should resources be deployed and managed? (Chapter 23)*
- *How can the organization manage risk and avoid and manage crises? (Chapter 23)*
- *How can the strategic leader manage both the organization structure and resources to achieve corporate-level synergy? Are the various functions, activities and businesses co-ordinated and contributing towards clearly understood objectives? (Chapter 22)*
- *How should the organization seek to deal with the pressures and demands of change, appreciating that cultural and behavioural changes may be required? (Chapter 24)*

# 20

# An Introduction to Strategy Implementation

Strategy → Structure or Structure → Strategy?

Implementation and Change

Problems of Successful Implementation

Successful Implementation

*It was emphasized in Chapter 19 that to be considered effective a chosen, intended strategy must be implemented successfully. The prospects for effective implementation are clearly dependent upon the appropriateness, feasibility and desirability of the strategy. Some strategies are not capable of implementation. At the same time, competency in implementation – the ability to translate ideas into actions and generate positive outcomes – can itself be a source of competitive advantage. Internal processes can add value by creating high levels of customer service and/or saving on costs by, say, removing any unnecessary delays or duplication of activities. In this last section of the book therefore we consider issues of strategy implementation and control. Reed and Buckley (1988) suggest that new strategies are selected because they offer opportunities and potential benefits, but that their implementation, because it involves change, implies risk. Implementation strategies should seek to maximize benefits and minimize risks. How might this be accomplished?*

*This short introduction to these issues considers a number of general aspects of strategy implementation.*

# Minicase 20.1  Amstrad

Amstrad, the UK-based producer of personal computers and other electrical and electronic products, has been run since 1968 by its founder, entrepreneurial businessman Sir Alan Sugar, who, until 2001, was also the chairman and leading shareholder of Tottenham Hotspur football club. Amstrad was floated in 1980 but, when Sugar tried to buy it back in 1992 – offering investors a lower price per share than they had paid originally – he was frustrated by the company's institutional shareholders. Corporate and competitive strategies have changed creatively over the years, but Amstrad has experienced a number of implementation difficulties.

Amstrad's real success began when Sugar identified new electronics products with mass market potential, and designed cheaper models than his main rivals were producing. Manufacturing was to be by low-cost suppliers, mainly in the Far East, supported by aggressive marketing in the West. Expenditure on high-profile marketing was possible because little or no capital was tied up in plant and machinery. Central overheads were kept low and potential suppliers were 'played off against each other in order to reduce direct costs'.

Sugar does not have a background in engineering, and when he bought Sir Clive Sinclair's computer business in 1986 he is reported to have said: 'For God's sake, Clive, I don't care if they have rubber bands in them as long as they work'. Instead, Sugar has a flair for understanding the *external* design requirements of electronic products and the price points that will attract large numbers of customers.

In 1988 the flexibility that Amstrad had built into this strategy turned from a strength to a weakness. There were five main reasons for this:

- In 1987 there was a worldwide shortage of memory chips, essential components for Amstrad. Some chip prices were doubled and others trebled, and in order to maintain production Amstrad had to pay whatever suppliers asked. The production of certain products was cut back deliberately.
- The launch of a new personal computer was delayed because a sophisticated chip, designed by Amstrad, failed to work when full production began.
- Labour shortages in Taiwan led to a reduced supply of audio products.
- A joint venture with Funai of Japan for the production of videos in the UK took off more slowly than anticipated. Previously all Amstrad's videos had been manufactured for them in Japan, by Funai.
- Amstrad established its own distribution network in West Germany, replacing an existing agreement with a third party. However, the previous distributor was left with surplus, unwanted, stock which it sold off cheaply, undercutting Amstrad's own price.

## Changing strategies

As a consequence Sugar began to move production to higher cost locations in Europe and Amstrad became a manufacturer. However, the recession of the early 1990s affected Amstrad's sales and the company traded at a loss for the first time in 1991–92; it was to record three consecutive years of losses. Sales of personal computers suffered when manufacturers of higher quality and more expensive machines, including IBM and Compaq, slashed their prices to try and stimulate demand and Amstrad's competitive edge (its price advantage) was lost. Alan Sugar's dilemma was that if he withdrew from the market he had nothing really new to replace PCs.

Amstrad had earlier withdrawn from computer games, unable to compete successfully with the aggressive Nintendo. Satellite dishes (introduced in 1988), however, seemed safer with continental sales buoyant; and the increasing involvement of BSkyB in major sporting activities (exclusive coverage of the cricket world cup and live football from the Premier League) augured well for the 1990s. Amstrad's word processors and fax machines (introduced in 1989) were continuing to sell satisfactorily; and although demand for video cassette recorders (VCRs) had fallen, Amstrad had successfully innovated a new double-decker machine which allows users to edit their own tapes and to record from two television channels at the same time. The company had launched a new lap-top computer in 1991.

Sugar's initial reaction was to consolidate and to minimize inventories in order to strengthen Amstrad's balance sheet. He commented: ' . . . no intention of moving into technology-led businesses or the high end of the market. Our vocation is always in the lower end of the market'.

The appropriateness of the strategy for the 1990s was questionable. Although new electronics products were in the development pipeline, Amstrad's basic problem was that the markets in which it competed were already crowded. It needed to find new market niches with real growth potential. It was at this stage, and faced with these issues, that Sugar attempted unsuccessfully to reprivatize Amstrad.

Late in 1993 Amstrad acquired Viglen, a rival manufacturer of personal computers, but a company which focused on direct sales and corporate customers. Within a year Amstrad had reduced its high-street sales by withdrawing its products from Dixons, whose margins, it claimed, were too low. To compensate, Amstrad began a direct-selling operation, using the expertise that it acquired with Viglen.

Amstrad bought two other businesses. First, it acquired the loss-making Danish manufacturer of cellular telephones, DanCall, and entered this fast-growth market. DanCall was a high-technology business; Amstrad could offer complementary skills in mass production. Second was a controlling interest in Betacom, another telephone equipment company.

## Restructuring

Also in 1994, Sugar recruited David Rogers from Philips to be his new chief executive and to take over some of the strategic leadership responsibilities. Rogers was mainly responsible for the new businesses, but his brief was to:

- help to introduce more robust management systems
- integrate the new acquisitions to achieve synergies
- help determine new growth areas, and
- foster new strategic alliances that would reduce Amstrad's dependency on personal computers. One alliance was with an IBM subsidiary that manufactured ink-jet printers, and which Amstrad later bought.

Amstrad was restructured into three divisions: ACE (Amstrad Consumer Electronics), personal computers and telecommunications. By early 1995 Amstrad was again profitable, but ACE was making losses. ACE was then split into two divisions, one which would focus on buying-in and trading low-price products, mainly from South-East Asia, and one whose main role was to spot and develop new opportunities. ACE was cut back at the beginning of 1996 with a number of job losses.

Late in 1995, history also repeated itself in one respect – new DanCall products were delayed. At this time, after just 18 months with the company, Rogers resigned.

In June 1996 it was reported that Amstrad had been having discussions with Psion, and that Psion was likely to launch an acquisition bid. Psion, founded in 1980 by an academic turned entrepreneur, David Potter, is best known for its palm-size computer diary/organizer. Psion's products are typically high added value and high margin, and the real synergy was thought to be between Psion's data management competencies and DanCall's competencies in mobile telephone technology. New opportunities for combining data and voice technologies were believed to exist. Commentators assumed that Viglen would be retained as a stand-alone subsidiary but that ACE would be divested. David Potter commented: 'Psion has no interest in the consumer electronics side'.

The proposed acquisition of Amstrad by Psion foundered when Alan Sugar refused to accept a price below 'that which he believed Amstrad was worth'. Psion was offering 200 pence per share.

## Corporate split

In April 1997 Amstrad sold Dancall, the Danish mobile telephone business that it had acquired in 1993, to the German company Robert Bosch. Just one month earlier, Dancall had announced the launch of a typical Amstrad product. Its new and innovative mobile phone could be used interchangeably in Europe and America; previously, separate handsets had been required to cope with different transmission systems.

Two months later, in June, Alan Sugar announced that Amstrad would be split up during the summer and two separate companies formed. Viglen Technology would be focused on personal computers; Betacom (which had already absorbed the limited remains of Amstrad's consumer electronics activities, its original business), and which was now built around telecommunications, would comprise the new Amstrad.

Shareholders would be given:

1. one Viglen share for every existing Amstrad share. Because Viglen has no direct competitor in the UK it is a difficult business to value. Analysts' preliminary predictions varied between a value of 50 pence and 110 pence per share. When they opened in August 1997 the early price was around 70 pence

2. a pro-rata distribution reflecting Amstrad's 70% shareholding in Betacom. Assumed value: 28 pence per existing Amstrad share

3. loan notes, convertible for cash in June 1998, worth 163 pence per share

4. 'litigation vouchers' which would entitle holders to a proportion of any court awards arising from outstanding cases against two suppliers. The estimated worth at this time was 110 pence per Amstrad share, but the eventual settlement was 43 pence per share. The litigation concerned two suppliers of disc drives; Amstrad blamed faulty parts for the demise of its PC business at the end of the 1980s.

The value of this combined package clearly exceeded the value of Psion's offer. Interestingly, when Alan Sugar tried unsuccessfully to buy Amstrad back from its shareholders in 1992, he was offering just 30 pence per share.

Alan Sugar would remain as chairman of Amstrad but become a non-executive director of Viglen, which had been managed independently ever since its acquisition. Sugar retained a 34% shareholding in Viglen and he personally received over £100 million from the break-up.

## The new Amstrad

From the beginning, the new Amstrad seemed to have a logical growth path – digital television decoder boxes, a natural extension from satellite dishes. But in February 1999 Amstrad launched a new generation of consumer products. Its 'Phone Book Databank' was a telephone with a QWERTY (computer) keypad – up top 500 numbers could be input and stored. The phone also had an integral palm-size organizer. It was priced at under £100.

A year later Amstrad followed this with a new e-mail business, called e-m@iler. The business was built around telephones with e-mail access, courtesy of an integrated screen and keypad. Dixon's bought a 20% stake in this new business. Alan Sugar's earlier disagreement with the retailer over prices and margins was no longer an issue. The phones were sold below their cost price – Amstrad had an agreement with British Telecom, through which it received a share of the call revenues.

In 2000 Amstrad opted to re-enter the mobile phone market with a range of pay-as-you-go telephones, which it would sell to just one network operator in any one country. Amstrad had sold its previous mobile phone business to Bosch in 1997, when it signed an agreement to stay out of the market for three years. However a supply delay meant the lucrative Christmas 2000 sales opportunity was missed.

## Viglen Technology

Viglen, meanwhile, was also progressing. In October 1997 an agreement was reached with Microsoft for jointly branded PCs to be sold through Dixons. This represented a first for both organizations. It was the first time that Microsoft had allowed its name to be linked with a particular PC, and it was the first time Viglen had used independent distribution rather than sold direct.

In December 1998 Alan Sugar made a bid for the remaining Viglen shares and he ended up with a 72% shareholding and control. In January 2000 Viglen announced the launch of an investment fund to support embryo start-up proposals for products directly linked to Viglen's business interests.

QUESTIONS: How might you judge the relative success of Amstrad's strategy – both ideas and implementation – over its 30 plus years of life?
Is Viglen's new venture capital fund an ideal way of sourcing new technologies and ideas?

*Amstrad* http://www.amstrad.com
*Viglen* http://www.viglen.co.uk

## Strategy → Structure or Structure → Strategy?

The structure of an organization is designed to break down the work to be carried out, the tasks, into discrete components, which might comprise individual businesses, divisions and functional departments. People work within these divisions and functions, and their actions take place within a defined framework of objectives, plans and policies which are designed to direct and control their efforts. In designing the structure and making it operational it is important to consider the key aspects of empowerment, employee motivation and reward. Information and communication systems within the organization should ensure that efforts are co-ordinated to the appropriate and desired extent and that the strategic leader and other senior managers are aware of progress and results.

It has already been established that in a competitively chaotic environment one essential contribution of the strategic leader is to provide and share a clear vision, direction and purpose for the organization (see Figure 20.1). From this, and taking into account the various ways in which strategies might be created (incorporating the themes of vision, planning and emergence), actions and action plans need to be formalized – the middle column in the figure. These strategies and proposals for change cannot be divorced from the implementation implications, which are shown in the right-hand column. Is the structure capable of implementing the ideas? Are resources deployed effectively? Are managers suitably empowered? Do organizational policies support the strategies? If the answers to these questions contain negatives, then either the strategic ideas themselves, the structure, organizational policies or aspects of resource management will need to be reviewed and rethought. The final decisions will either be determined or

Figure 20.1    Strategy implementation.

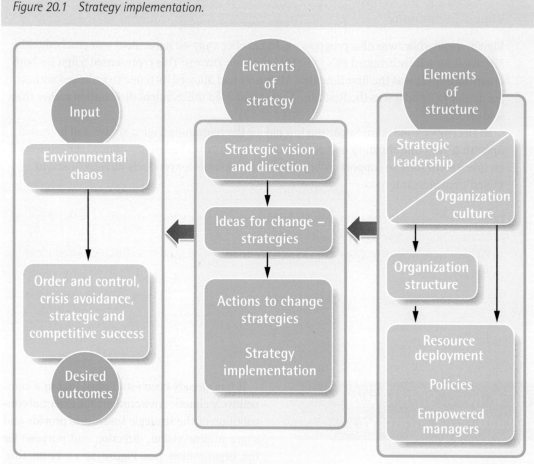

strongly influenced by the strategic leader, and affected by the culture of the organization. Minicase 20.1 describes a number of strategic, structural and managerial changes at Amstrad; Amstrad has always been a strategically creative company but it has sometimes been constrained by implementation difficulties. The case documents a number of changes of fortune and potential crises and describes how Amstrad has managed these various challenges.

If appropriate, feasible and desirable strategies that *are* capable of effective implementation are selected and pursued, the organization should be able to establish some order and control in the environmental chaos and avoid major crises

– the left-hand column of Figure 20.1. This still requires that strategies, products and services are managed efficiently and effectively at the operational level. Responsibility for operations will normally be delegated, and consequently, to ensure that performance and outcomes are satisfactory, sound monitoring and control systems are essential.

It is important to appreciate that while structures are designed initially – and probably changed later at various times – to ensure that *determined or intended* strategies can be implemented, it is the day-to-day decisions, actions and behaviours of people within the structure which lead to important *emergent* strategies.

There is, therefore, a continual circular process in operation:

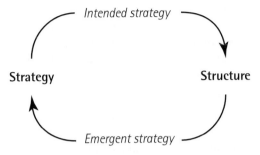

Consequently, while issues of structure and implementation are being considered at the end of this book, they should not be thought of as the end-point in the strategy process. They may be the source of strategic change.

Figure 20.2 explains the implementation of intended strategies in more detail. The strategic leader is charged with ensuring that there are appropriate targets and milestones, establishing a suitable organization structure and securing and allocating the relevant strategic resources such as people and money. People then use the other strategic resources, working within the

*Figure 20.2* Intended strategy implementation.

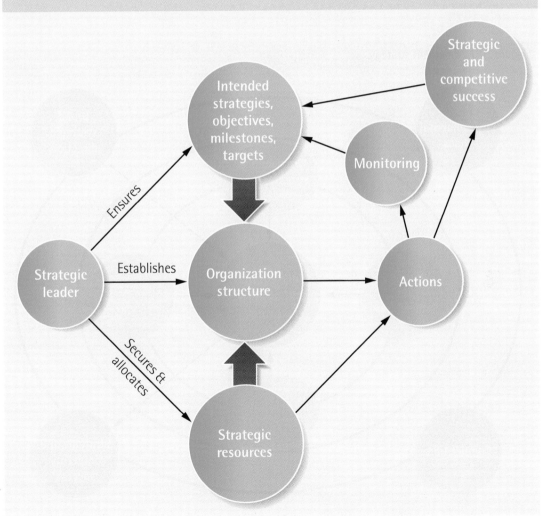

structure, to carry out the tasks that they have been allocated, and their actions should be monitored and evaluated to check that the targets and objectives are being achieved.

Figure 20.3 summarizes the emergent strategy process which, clearly, is less prescriptive. The strategic leader this time provides a broad strategic direction. Empowered managers work within a decentralized structure, but they are constrained by any relevant rules, policies and procedures. The strategies that emerge are affected by the constraints, the extent to which managers accept empowerment and the accumulation, sharing and exploitation of organizational knowledge. The outcome of the strategies is related to the extent to which they deal with the competitive and environmental pressures with which the organization must deal.

To summarize, the outcome, in terms of strategic management and organizational success, is dependent on:

- the direction provided by the strategic leader
- the culture of the organization
- the extent to which managers throughout the organization understand, support and *own* the mission and corporate strategy, and appreciate the significance of their individual contribution

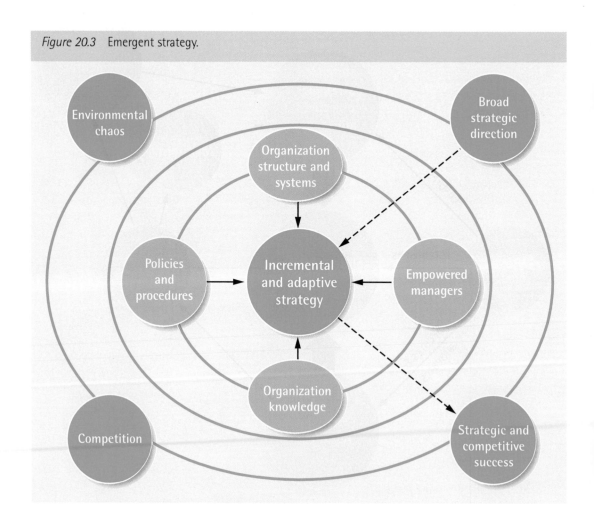

*Figure 20.3*    Emergent strategy.

- the willingness and ability of suitably empowered managers to be innovative, add value and take measured risks to deal with environmental opportunities and competitive surprises
- the effectiveness of the information sharing, monitoring and control systems.

## Implementation and Change

Implementation incorporates a number of aspects, some of which can be changed directly and some of which can only be changed indirectly. The latter aspects are more difficult for the strategic leadership to control and change. The success of the strategic leader in managing both the direct and indirect aspects influences the effectiveness of:

- the implementation of strategies and strategic changes which are determined through the planning and visionary modes of strategy creation, and
- the ability of the organization, and its managers, to respond to changes in the environment and adapt in line with perceived opportunities and threats.

### Aspects of implementation that can be changed directly

- The organization structure (the actual, defined structure, not necessarily the way in which people behave within the structure)
- management systems
- policies and procedures
- action plans and short-term budgets
- management information systems.

### Aspects of implementation that are changed indirectly

#### Communication systems
While the management information system can affect formal information flows, the network of informal communications truly determines awareness. Such communications are affected by, and influence, the degree and spirit of co-operation between managers, functions and divisions.

#### Managing and developing quality and excellence
Attention to detail, production on time and to the appropriate quality, and the personal development of managers and other employees are all factors in this. As well as developing managers' skills and capabilities generally, it is important to consider the quality of management in particular areas and the cover for managers who leave or who are absent. The organization structure should provide opportunities for managers to grow and be promoted.

#### Manifested values and the organization culture
This involves the way in which things are done: standards and attitudes which are held and practised.

#### The fostering of innovation
The willingness of people to search for improvements and better ways of doing things. Their encouragement and reward is very much influenced by the strategic leader, with leadership by example often proving significant.

Those aspects that can be changed directly generally imply physical changes in the way in which resources are allocated. Behavioural aspects, which imply changes in beliefs and attitudes, can only be modified indirectly. Both are considered in the forthcoming chapters.

## Problems of Successful Implementation

Owen (1982) contends that in practice there are four problem areas associated with the successful implementation of strategies.

1. At any time strategy and structure need to be matched and supportive of each other. Products and services need to be managed independently, or in linked groups or business units, if they are to be matched closely and effectively with their environments. There may be good reasons for having a structure that does not separate the products, services and business units in this way. The strategic leader might prefer a centralized structure without delegated responsibilities, for example. The organization might possess certain key skills and enjoy a reputation for strength in a particular area, and this might be influential in the design of the structure. Equally, certain skills might be absent and have to be compensated for. Related to this might be the willingness or reluctance of managers to change jobs or location within the structure. Structures cannot be created and activated independently of the people involved; their individual skills may provide either opportunities or constraints. Changing attitudes and developing new skills is accomplished indirectly, as pointed out above, and takes time.

   It is also possible that related products may be produced in various plants nationally or internationally, when a geography-orientated structure, which keeps the plants separate, is favoured for other sound reasons. In addition, it may not prove feasible to change the structure markedly every time there is a change in corporate strategy and, instead, acceptable modifications to the existing structure are preferred to more significant changes.

2. The information and communications systems are inadequate for reporting back and evaluating the adaptive changes that are taking place, and hence the strategic leader is not fully aware of what is happening. Hence the performance of the existing structure is not monitored properly, and as a result control mechanisms may be ineffective.

3. Implementing strategy involves change, which in turn involves uncertainty and risk. New skills may have to be developed, for example. While managers may agree in meetings to make changes, they may be more reluctant in practice to implement them. Motivating managers to make changes is therefore a key determinant.

4. Management systems, such as compensation schemes, management development and communications systems, which operate within the structural framework will have been developed to meet the needs of past strategies. They may not be ideal for the changes that are taking place currently, and again it is difficult to modify them continually.

Alexander (1985) argues that additional factors are also significant, especially:

- the failure to predict the time and problems that implementation will involve, such as the time required for a new business or venture to take off, which is invariably underestimated. This may not seem critical, but it can be. In the early months of a new business, more cash is typically spent than revenue is earned. The accumulating debt is a so-called 'valley of death' that the business must come through and out of before it can start earning real money and (eventually and hopefully) enter the 'land of plenty'.

- other activities and commitments that distract attention and possibly cause resources to be diverted. Paradoxically, one way of coping with the likelihood of disruptive and distracting events is to ensure that the organization has spare resources in readiness for such emergencies; but slack of this sort can appear to imply inefficiency and underutilized resources, and it can be expensive

- the bases on which the strategy was formulated changed, or were forecast poorly, and insufficient flexibility to deal with the change pressures has been built in.

All of these problems presuppose that the formulated strategic change is sound and logical. A poorly thought-out strategy will create its own implementation problems.

## Successful Implementation

To counter these problems Owen suggests the following:

- Clear responsibility for the successful outcome of planned strategic change should be allocated.
- The number of strategies and changes being pursued at any time should be limited. The ability of the necessary resources to cope with the changes should be seen as a key determinant of strategy and should not be overlooked.
- Necessary actions to implement strategies should be identified and planned, and again responsibility should be allocated.
- 'Milestones', or progress measurement points, should be established.
- Measures of performance should be established, as well as appropriate monitoring and control mechanisms.

These, Owen argues, can all be achieved without necessarily changing the structural framework but rather changing the way in which people operate within it.

In addition, Alexander contends that the involvement and support of people who will be affected by the changes in strategy must be considered, and that the implications of the new strategies and changes should be communicated widely, awareness created, and commitment and involvement sought. Incentives and reward systems underpin this.

In the same way that no single evaluation technique can select a best strategy, there is no best way of implementing strategic change. There are no right answers, as such. A number of lessons, considerations and arguments, however, can be incorporated into the thinking and planning; and these are the themes of the next four chapters.

Three final points need to be mentioned to conclude this introduction. First, although there are no right answers to either strategy formulation or strategy implementation, the two must be consistent if the organization is to be effective. Arguably, how the organization does things, and manages both strategy and change, is more important than the actual strategy or change proposed.

Secondly, the style of strategic leadership will be very influential. It was argued in the previous chapter that the preference of the strategic leader affects the desirability of particular strategic alternatives. The structure of the organization, the delegation of responsibilities, the freedom of managers to act, their willingness to exercise initiative, and the incentive and reward systems will all be determined and influenced by the strategic leader. These in turn determine the effectiveness of implementation. The strategic leader's choices and freedom to act, however, may be constrained by any resource limitations and certain environmental forces.

Thirdly, the timing of when to act and make changes will also be important. In this context, for example, Mitchell (1988) points out that timing is particularly crucial in the implementation decisions and actions that follow acquisitions. Employees anticipate changes in the organization, especially at senior management level, and inaction, say beyond three months, causes uncertainty and fear. As a result, there is greater hostility to change when it does occur. The dangers of hasty action, such as destroying strengths before appreciating that they are strengths, are offset. Mitchell concludes that it is more important to be decisive than to be right, and then learn and adapt incrementally.

The forthcoming chapters examine issues of structure, considering both the design of the framework and the management and control of the activities that operate within the framework. This is followed by an assessment of action plans, policies and control mechanisms, and finally an assessment of the issues involved in change and the management of change.

## References

Alexander, LD (1985) Successfully implementing strategic decisions, *Long Range Planning*, 18(3).

Mitchell, D (1988) *Making Acquisitions Work: Lessons from Companies' Successes and Mistakes*, Report published by Business International, Geneva.

Owen, AA (1982) How to implement strategy, *Management Today*, July.

Reed, R and Buckley MR (1988) Strategy in action – techniques for implementing strategy, *Long Range Planning*, 21(3).

Explore Strategy Implementation further at:

*Long Range Planning*    http://www.lrp.ac

# Issues in Organizational Structure

*It was established in Chapter 20 that the organization structure provides the framework through which intended strategies are implemented – or not, as the case may be. However, at the same time, the structure also provides a foundation for emergent strategy creation. By dividing up tasks, the structure places people in certain roles with certain expectations. The accompanying systems, which in part are designed to co-ordinate all of these tasks into a meaningful whole and thus create synergy, help to determine the freedom that individual managers have to change things. It is the style of management, largely dictated by the strategic leader, which finally determines how co-ordinated the efforts are, how co-operative managers, functions and businesses are with each other, and how willing managers are to accept empowerment and make changes.*

*This chapter looks at the linkages between strategy and structure by examining a number of alternative structural forms and by considering the key issues of centralization and decentralization. The forces that influence and determine the structure are discussed. The structural challenges of global and small, entrepreneurial businesses, manufacturing and service companies and organizations in the public sector are covered.*

Minicase

## Minicase 21.1 Nantucket Nectars

**ALL NATURAL NANTUCKET NECTARS ®**

Nantucket Nectars is an unusual but very successful business which was started by two friends. When Tom First and Tom Scott graduated from Brown University in Rhode Island they decided they wanted to live on Nantucket Island, off the New England coast, and find some way of earning a living. In the summer of 1989 they started a small business for servicing the yachts belonging to visitors to the island. This was always going to be seasonal. They travelled around the harbour in a distinctive red boat, delivering newspapers, muffins, coffee, laundry and any other supplies for which there was a demand. They also washed boats, emptied sewage and shampooed dogs. This seemed to lead naturally to them later opening the Nantucket Allserve general store, which still exists. They used the following promotional slogan in the early days: 'Ain't nothing those boys won't do'.

Once the summer was over, demand for their services fell as the yachts disappeared. They decided to experiment with fruit juices, mixed in a household blender. They first sought to replicate a peach-based nectar that they had sampled in Spain. During the following summer they sold their bottled juices from their red boat. They always produced distinctive flavours from the best quality ingredients. By investing their joint savings they were able to hire a bottler to produce 1400 cases. Overall, though, the business merely struggled on for a couple of years, until one wealthy yacht owner offered them a $500,000 loan to develop the business. They seized the opportunity. Nantucket Nectars then expanded quickly to cover a number of states on the American east coast. Initially they did their own bottling, but this is now subcontracted.

*If I were on the outside looking in, I'd say Nantucket Nectars was an overnight success. Being on the inside, it's been a long, long time. We almost went out of business a thousand times.*

(Tom Scott)

The company now employs over 100 people and sells in over 30 US states and a number of selected export markets. Values are a key element, the partners remain determined to 'create the best quality product in the juice market', and yet the company remains enigmatic. The bottle labels state: 'We're juice guys. We don't wear ties to work'; folksy radio commercials are utilized extensively in America; but the new head office is in an old Men's Club near Harvard University. It is furnished with antiques and managers have private offices instead of the open-plan arrangement which is increasingly popular in many informal organizations. First and Scott typically take their dogs into work. Each week every head-office manager focuses on talking personally with one of their salespeople in the field, staff who would otherwise have little contact with head office.

The founders claim that the company has always been run on gut instinct and trial and error. Few people have any formal business qualifications. In 1997 Nantucket Nectars was awarded a contract to provide juice for Starbucks, and later that year Ocean Spray – leading manufacturer of cranberry juices and other products – acquired a 50% stake. The companies believed that they could make extensive savings on supplies if they joined forces. First and Scott continue to run the business that they founded.

QUESTIONS: How easy will it be for First and Scott to maintain their informal style and culture as Nantucket Nectars grows further?
Will more formality be required?
TASK: Apply the three Figures from Chapter 20 to this case.
How are strategy and structure linked? What is the balance between intended and emergent strategy?

*Nantucket Nectars*   http://www.juicegnys.com

## Introduction – Four Structural Alternatives

Lawrence and Lorsch (1967) have argued that the organization should be structured in such a way that it can respond to pressures for change from its environment and pursue any appropriate opportunities which are spotted. Given that strategies are concerned with relating the organization's resources and values with the environment, it follows that strategy and structure are linked. Structure in fact, is the *means* by which the organization seeks to achieve its strategic objectives and implement strategies and strategic changes. Strategies are formulated and implemented by managers operating within the current structure. Thompson and Strickland (1980) comment that while strategy formulation requires the abilities to conceptualize, analyse and judge, implementation involves working with and through other people and instituting change. Implementation poses the tougher management challenge.

The essential criteria underpinning the design of the organization structure are first, the extent to which decision making is *decentralized*, as opposed to centralized, and secondly, the extent to which policies and procedures are *formalized*. Decentralization to some degree is required if incremental and adaptive strategic change is to take place; and the issue of centralization/ decentralization is explored early in this chapter,

## DISCUSSION – Box 21.1
### Centralization and Decentralization

Centralization and decentralization relate to the degree to which the authority, power and responsibility for decision making is devolved through the organization. There are several options, including the following.

- All major strategic decisions are taken centrally, at head office, by the strategic leader or a group of senior strategists. The size of any team will depend upon the preference of the overall strategic leader together with the size, complexity and diversity of the organization. Strictly enforced policies and procedures will constrain the freedom of other managers responsible for business units, products, services and functional areas to change competitive and functional strategies. This is centralization.
- Changes in the strategic perspective are decided centrally, but then the organization is structured to enable managers to change competitive and functional strategies in line with perceived opportunities and threats.
- The organization is truly decentralized such that independent business units have general managers who are free to change their respective strategic perspectives. In effect they run a series of independent businesses with some co-ordination from the parent headquarters.

The role of general managers in charge of divisions and business units is explored in Chapter 22.

The extent to which true decentralization exists may be visible from the organization's charted structure. It is useful to examine the membership of the group and divisional/business unit boards, regardless of the number and delineation of divisions. The organization is likely to tend towards decentralization where there is a main board and a series of subsidiary boards, each chaired by a member of the main board. The chief executive/strategic leader, who is responsible for the performance of each subsidiary, will not necessarily have a seat on the main board. The organization will tend towards greater centralization where the main board comprises the chairmen/chief executives of certain subsidiaries, generally the largest ones, together with staff specialists. Hence decentralization and divisionalization are *not* synonymous terms.

*The ten main determinants*

- the size of the organization
- geographical locations, together with the
  - homogeneity/heterogeneity of the products and services
  - technology of the tasks involved
  - interdependencies
- the relative importance and stability of the external environment, and the possible need to react quickly
- generally, how quickly decisions need to be made
- the workload on decision makers
- issues of motivation via delegation, together with the abilities and willingness of managers to make decisions and accept responsibility
- the location of competence and expertise in the organization. Are the managerial strengths in the divisions or at headquarters?
- the costs involved in making any changes

- the significance and impact of competitive and functional decisions and changes
- the status of the firm's planning, control and information systems.

*Advantages and disadvantages*

There are no right or wrong answers concerning the appropriate amount of centralization/decentralization. It is a question of balancing the potential advantages and disadvantages of each as they affect particular firms.

It has been suggested that companies which achieve and maintain high growth tend to be more decentralized, and those which are more concerned with profits than growth are more centralized. The highest performers in terms of both growth and profits tend to retain high degrees of central control as far as the overall strategic perspective is concerned. Child (1977) contends that the most essential issue is the degree of internal consistency.

*Advantages of centralization*

- Consistency of strategy
- easier to co-ordinate activities (and handle the interdependencies) and control changes
- changes in the strategic perspective are more easily facilitated.

*Disadvantages of centralization*

- May be slow to respond to changes which affect subsidiaries individually rather than the organization as a whole, depending upon the remoteness of head office

- easy to create an expensive head office that relies on management information systems and becomes detached from customers, and for which there are too many diverse interests and complexities
- general managers with real strategic ability are not developed within the organization. Instead the organization is dependent on specialists and as a result the various functions may not be properly co-ordinated. Does this achieve a fit between the organization and its environment?

*Advantages of decentralization*

- Ability to change competitive and functional strategies more quickly
- improved motivation
- can develop better overall strategic awareness in a very complex organization which is too diverse for a head office to control effectively.

*Disadvantages of decentralization*

- May be problems in clarifying the role of head-office central services which aim to co-ordinate the various divisions and business units and achieve certain economies through, and the centralization of, selected activities
- problems of linking the power that general managers need and the responsibility that goes with the power. General managers must have the freedom to make decisions without referrals back.

in Box 21.1. Formality is linked to the extent to which tasks and jobs are specialized and defined, and their rigidity, i.e. the period over which jobs have remained roughly the same. The longer the period is, arguably, the greater will be the resistance to changing them. Clearly, communications and formality are linked. In a formal organization there will be a reliance on vertical communications, with instructions passing downwards and information on results passing upwards. In some organizations, there is a tendency for 'good news' to flow upwards quickly and readily and for 'bad news' to be covered up. The greater the informality, the greater the likelihood of strong and effective horizontal communications as people across the organization are encouraged to talk and share.

The challenge for most organizations, then, is to find the appropriate degrees of decentralization and informality to enable them to maintain control while innovating and managing change in a dynamic and turbulent environment. In turn, this requires that managers are *empowered*. (Empowerment was explained in Chapter 13.)

Centralization and formality in the structure yield economies but at the same time remove initiative from managers who are most closely in touch with the organization's customers and competitors. This is likely to affect motivation and slow down the firm's sensitivity to changes in the environment. Decentralization therefore allows decisions to be made by the people who must implement the changes, and informality allows these managers to use their own initiative and change things in a dynamic turbulent environment.

Where power is centralized, control is dependent upon objectives, targets and milestones set centrally at the top of the organization. The theoretical information flows are clear. It is a drawback, but not a fundamental problem, if people throughout the organization do not share and wholly support the purpose and direction of the firm. Where power is decentralized, the importance of a shared direction, to which people commit, is much more important. Here information is the means of control, and the information systems must be good enough to capture all of the decisions and changes that happen as empowered managers make and take decisions.

Decentralization, therefore, carries more risk and uncertainty – but it can be essential for coping with environmental demands. Centralization should be easier to operate but it is more rigid and less flexible. What we often find are periodic changes of emphasis. If an organization is finding that it is struggling to cope with the change demands of a dynamic environment, it may well switch from centralization of power to decentralization. If it later finds that with the devolution of power its information system is inadequate and the strategic leader feels that he or she is no longer in effective control, there will be a tendency to recentralize, at the expense of flexibility and responsiveness. Once control has be reasserted at the top, there will be a search for opportunities to decentralize again.

These criteria create four extreme types of structure. First, those which are *centralized and formal*, which tend to be bureaucratic, slow to change and efficient in stable circumstances. Companies which are *centralized and informal* tend to be small, with power concentrated in the hands of one central figure. *Decentralized formal organizations* are typically large businesses divided up into divisions and business units. Power is devolved to allow adaptive change, but formal communication systems and performance measures are required for co-ordination. Finally, *decentralized and informal organizations* tend to be groups or teams of people who are put together for a specific purpose and then abandoned once the task is accomplished. Film crews would be an example, as would special project groups within large firms.

It would not be unusual for an organization to be centralized and informal when it first starts up. Afterwards, as limited power and responsibility is devolved to identifiable managers, the structure becomes more formalized, but the central power of the strategic leader remains strong. As the organization grows beyond a stage where one person can really remain in effective control, the switch is to decentralized with formal controls through policies, procedures and reporting relationships. It is not difficult to imagine how the need for a formal structure developed and became urgent as Nantucket Nectars (Minicase 21.1) grew in size.

These structural types, then, will be evidenced in the organization frameworks and structural designs which are explored in detail in the next section of this chapter. It is important to appreciate that structure involves more than the organization chart or framework which is used for illustrative purposes and to explain where businesses, products, services and people fit in relation to each other. Charts are static; structures are dynamic and involve behaviour patterns.

## Structural Forms

A number of discrete structural forms can be adapted by an organization when attempts are made to design an appropriate structure to satisfy its particular needs. The following are described in this section:

- the entrepreneurial structure
- the functional structure
- the divisional structure
- the holding company structure
- the matrix structure.

This is not an exhaustive coverage in the sense that personalized varieties of each of these alternatives can easily be developed.

Chandler (1962) and subsequent authors such as Salter (1970) have suggested that as firms grow from being a small business with a simple entrepreneurial structure, a more formal

In my experience, the key to growth is to pick good managers, involve them at the outset of discussions on strategy and objectives, and then devolve as much responsibility as they will accept. That's the only way you know if they are any good.
*Michael Grade, when Chief Executive, Channel Four Television*

Autonomy is what you take, not what you are given.
*Roy Watts, Chairman, Thames Water*

Organisational flexibility is essential. Rates of change have speeded up. The hierarchical organization is slow to respond. Decisions taken at the centre are too far away from the coal face. While the centre seeks local and relevant understanding, delays in decision making result.

In today's turbulent business environment speed of decision making is critically important . . . decisions should be pushed down the organization and as close to the customers as possible.
*Sir John Harvey-Jones MBE, quoted in* The Responsive Organisation, *BIM, 1989*

functional structure evolves to allow managers to cope with the increasing complexity and the demands of decision making. As the organization becomes diversified, with a multiplicity of products, services or operating bases, a different structure is again required, and initially this is likely to be based on simple divisionalization. In other words, there are stages of structural development which evolve as strategies change and organizations grow. Chandler contends, however, that while strategy and structure develop together through a particular sequence, structures are not adapted until pressures force a change. The pressures tend to relate to growing inefficiency resulting from an inability to handle the increasing demands of decision making. Matrix organizations have been designed to cope with the complexities of multiproduct, multinational organizations with interdependencies which must be accommodated if synergy is to be achieved. However, matrix organizations are difficult to manage and control. Large organizations in particular change their structures (at least in part) quite frequently as they search for one that allows effective implementation of intended strategies while permitting emergent strategy creation to a desired level.

It has been emphasized earlier (see Chapter 15) that many organizations fail to achieve the anticipated synergy from strategies of diversification and acquisition, and as a result divest the businesses to which they cannot add value. Implementation difficulties are often linked to a failure to absorb the new acquisition into the existing organization, and this is likely to involve changes in the structure.

It is important to appreciate that the structural forms described in this section are only a framework, and that the behavioural processes within the structure, the way in which resources are managed and co-ordinated, really determines effectiveness. In turn, this is related to the way in which authority, power and responsibility are devolved throughout the organization, and whether generally the firm is centralized or decentralized. These themes were explored in Box 21.1, where it is emphasized that decentralization and divisionalization are not synonymous. The establishment of a divisionalized structure does not necessarily imply that authority to adapt competitive and functional strategies is freely delegated; the firm could remain centralized.

## The entrepreneurial structure

The entrepreneurial structure, built around the owner–manager and typically utilized by small companies in the early stages of their development, is illustrated in Figure 21.1. The structure

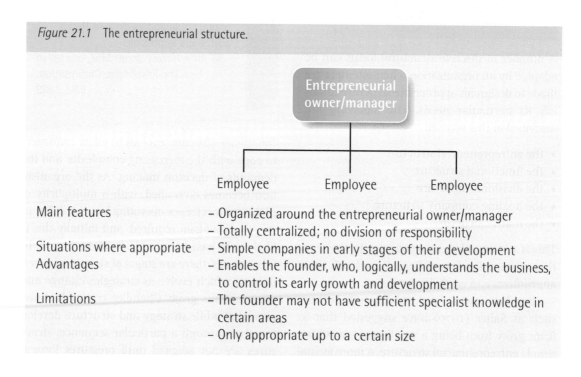

*Figure 21.1*   The entrepreneurial structure.

|  |  |
|---|---|
| Main features | – Organized around the entrepreneurial owner/manager |
|  | – Totally centralized; no division of responsibility |
| Situations where appropriate | – Simple companies in early stages of their development |
| Advantages | – Enables the founder, who, logically, understands the business, to control its early growth and development |
| Limitations | – The founder may not have sufficient specialist knowledge in certain areas |
|  | – Only appropriate up to a certain size |

is totally centralized. All key decisions are made by the strategic leader, and employees refer everything significant back to him or her. It is particularly useful for new businesses as it enables the founder, who normally will have some expertise with the product or service and whose investment is at risk, to control the growth and development.

There is an argument that this is not really a formal structure as all responsibility, power and authority lie with one person. However, in some small companies of this nature, selected employees will specialize and be given job titles and some limited responsibility for such activities as production, sales or accounting. In this respect the structure could be redrawn to appear more like the functional organization discussed below. The functional form only really emerges when *managers* are established with genuine delegated authority and responsibility for the functions and activities that they control.

New firms with entrepreneurial structures are likely to be established because the owner–manager has contacts and expertise in a particular line of business and, for whatever reason, wishes to establish his or her own business. While the entrepreneur will want to control the early stages of growth, it does not follow that he or she will have expertise in all aspects of the business. Many start-ups occur because the founder understands the technology and production or operational aspects of the business. Marketing, sales and financial control may well be areas of potential weakness with a consequent reliance on other people together with an element of learning as the business develops. This need can prove to be a limitation of the entrepreneurial structure.

Another limitation relates to growth. At some stage, dependent on both the business and the founder, the demands of decision making, both day-to-day problem decisions and longer-term planning decisions, will become too complex for one person, and there will be pressure to estab-

lish a more formal functional organization. The owner/manager relinquishes some responsibility for short-term decisions and has greater opportunity to concentrate on the more strategic aspects of the business. This can prove to be a dilemma for some entrepreneurs, however, particularly those who started their own business because they wanted total control over something, or because they were frustrated with the greater formality of larger companies.

## The functional structure

The functional structure, illustrated in Figure 21.2, is commonplace in small firms that have outgrown the entrepreneurial structure and in larger firms that produce only a limited range of related products and services. It is also the typical internal structure of the divisions and business units that comprise larger diversified organizations. It is more suitable in a stable environment than a turbulent one as it is generally centralized with corporate and competitive strategies again being controlled substantially by the strategic leader.

The structure is built around the tasks to be carried out, which tend to be split into specialist functional areas. Managers are placed in charge of departments which are responsible for these functions, and they may well have delegated authority to change functional strategies. Consequently, the effectiveness of this structure is very dependent on the ability of these specialist managers to work together as a team and support each other and on the ability of the strategic leader to co-ordinate their efforts.

The functional structure can be highly efficient with low overheads in comparison with divisional structures, which have to address the issue of functions duplicated in the business units and at head office. Functional managers will develop valuable specialist expertise which can be used as a basis for the creation of competitive advantage, and the relatively simple

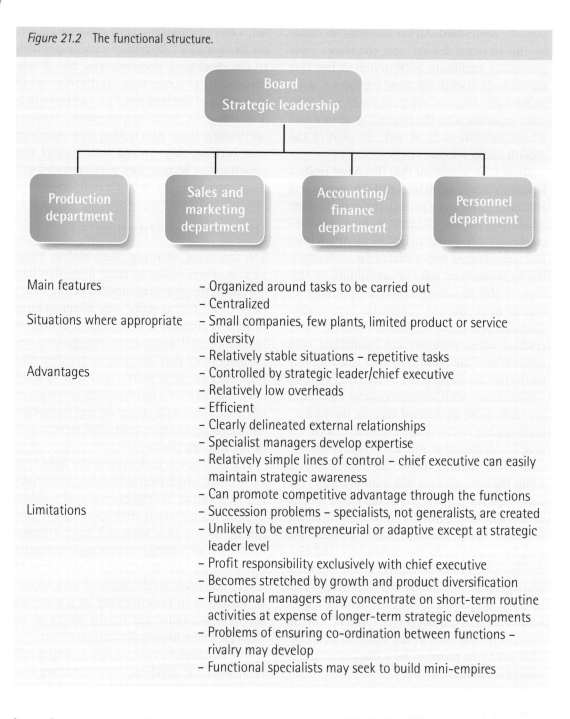

*Figure 21.2* The functional structure.

| Main features | – Organized around tasks to be carried out |
| | – Centralized |
| Situations where appropriate | – Small companies, few plants, limited product or service diversity |
| | – Relatively stable situations – repetitive tasks |
| Advantages | – Controlled by strategic leader/chief executive |
| | – Relatively low overheads |
| | – Efficient |
| | – Clearly delineated external relationships |
| | – Specialist managers develop expertise |
| | – Relatively simple lines of control – chief executive can easily maintain strategic awareness |
| | – Can promote competitive advantage through the functions |
| Limitations | – Succession problems – specialists, not generalists, are created |
| | – Unlikely to be entrepreneurial or adaptive except at strategic leader level |
| | – Profit responsibility exclusively with chief executive |
| | – Becomes stretched by growth and product diversification |
| | – Functional managers may concentrate on short-term routine activities at expense of longer-term strategic developments |
| | – Problems of ensuring co-ordination between functions – rivalry may develop |
| | – Functional specialists may seek to build mini-empires |

lines of communication between these specialists and the strategic leader can facilitate a high degree of strategic awareness at the top of the organization.

There are some limitations, however. The concentration on the functions tends to lead to managers with greater specialist expertise rather than a more corporate perspective.

General managers who can embrace all of the functions are not developed, and consequently any internal successor to the chief executive is likely to have a particular specialist viewpoint, which may involve cultural change. This might conceivably mean a change from a financial orientation to a customer-led organization, for example, or vice versa.

Functional organizations are less likely to be entrepreneurial throughout the company than is the case in more decentralized forms, although the strategic leader could be personally dynamic and entrepreneurial. Because corporate and competitive strategy changes are generally the responsibility of the strategic leader, functional managers may concentrate on short-term issues at the expense of longer-term strategic needs. The tendency for profit responsibility to lie primarily with the strategic leader compounds this. Functional managers may seek to build mini-empires around their specialism, and this can lead to rivalry between departments for resources and status and make the task of co-ordination and team-building more difficult.

The structure is stretched and becomes more inefficient with growth and product or service diversification. As the firm grows from a limited range of related products to unrelated ones, co-ordination proves increasingly difficult. Hence, a need grows for some form of division-alization, together with a revised role for the strategic leader. The strategic leader is now responsible for co-ordinating the strategies of a series of business units or divisions, each with a general manager at their head, rather than co-ordinating specialist functional managers into a cohesive and supportive team. Financial management skills become increasingly necessary. Adaptive changes in competitive strategies are now likely to be delegated.

Once organizations reach the functional stage, their choice of future corporate growth strategy will have a major bearing upon the structural developments. Figure 21.3 shows the structures discussed in this section linked to relevant growth strategies. These linkages must be seen as indicative; it does not follow that organizations must follow these routes. Figure 21.3 additionally includes the global structure which was discussed in Chapter 14 and, for this reason only, is excluded from this chapter.

## The divisional structure

One example of a divisional structure is illustrated in Figure 21.4, using product groups as the means of divisionalizing. Geographical regions are another means that are frequently used, and sometimes both geography and product groups are used in conjunction. Vertically integrated organizations might divisionalize into manufacturing, assembly and distribution activities.

The primary features are as follows:

- a set of divisions or business units which themselves are likely to contain a functional structure, and which can be regarded as profit centres
- each division will be headed by a general manager who is responsible for strategy implementation and to some extent strategy formulation within the division
- decentralization of limited power, authority and responsibility.

Divisional structures are found when complexity and diversity increase and where turbulent environmental conditions make it appropriate to decentralize some responsibility for making sure that the organization is responsive and possibly proactive towards external forces in a variety of different industries. They are also useful where there are major differences in needs and tastes in the company's markets around the world.

The major advantage of this structure is that it can facilitate the ability of the organization to manage the strategies of a number of disparate

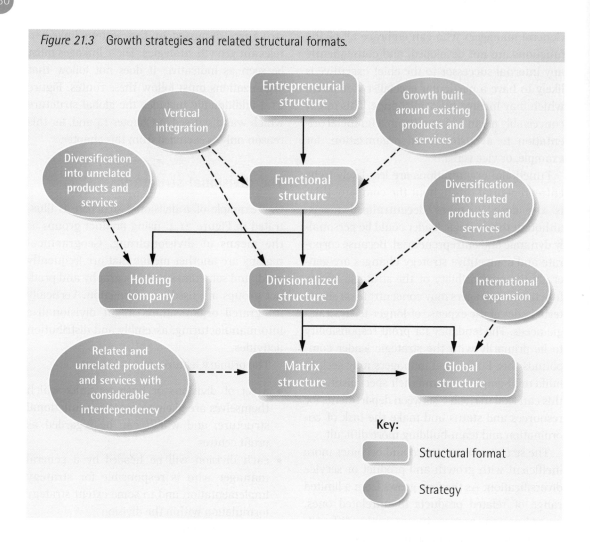

*Figure 21.3*   Growth strategies and related structural formats.

products and markets effectively. The major difficulty lies in designing the most appropriate structure.

There is no one best way of dividing a business into divisions, especially if the composition of the whole corporation changes with acquisitions, divestments and closures. Large companies will change their structures periodically in an attempt to improve both efficiency and effectiveness. Structural changes of this nature imply changes in the power structure, the relative amount of decentralization and managers' jobs, and for these reasons they may prove disruptive. Minicase 21.1 charts how Tube

Investments has increased the number of its operating divisions in an attempt to engineer more effective decentralization.

Other advantages of divisional structures are that profit responsibilities are spread between the divisions or business units. This helps to motivate managers who can be given authority and responsibility for profit, and enables an evaluation of the contribution of each activity to the organization as a whole. Responsibility for changes in competitive and functional strategies can be delegated to the general managers in charge of each division or business unit; and it is feasible for these managers also to have

*Figure 21.4* The divisional structure. A product divisional structure is illustrated. Geographical divisions, or a mixture of the two, are also used.

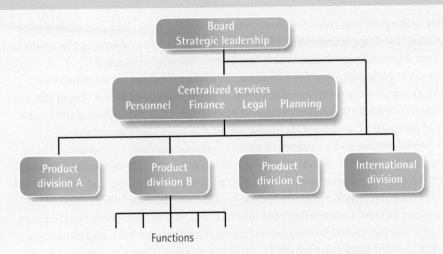

|  |  |
|---|---|
| Main features | – Divisions are likely to be profit centres and may be seen as strategic business units for planning and control purposes |
|  | – Divisions/business units are headed by general managers who enjoy responsibility for their own resources |
|  | – Decentralized |
| Situations where appropriate | – Growing size and complexity |
|  | – Appropriate divisional/business unit splits exist |
|  | – Organizations growing through merger and acquisition |
|  | – Turbulent environments |
|  | – Product/market divisions/business units most appropriate where there is a diverse range of products |
|  | – Geographic divisions are common where there are cultural distinctions between the company's markets – especially if distances are great |
|  | – Divisionalization may also be a mix of products and geography or based on different production processes |
| Advantages | – Spreads profit responsibility |
|  | – Enables evaluation of contribution of various activities |
|  | – Motivates managers and facilitates the development of both specialist and general managers |
|  | – Enables adaptive change |
|  | – Chief executive can stay away from routine decisions and concentrate on corporate strategy |
|  | – Growth through acquisition more readily implemented |
|  | – Can be entrepreneurial throughout the organization |
|  | – Divestment can also be handled relatively easily |
| Limitations | – Conflict between divisions, say for resources |
|  | – Possible confusion over locus of responsibility (head office and divisions) and duplication of efforts and resources |
|  | – Divisions may tend to think short term and concentrate on profits |
|  | – Divisions may be of different sizes and some may grow very large – evaluation of relative performances may be difficult |
|  | – Co-ordinating interdependent divisions and establishing transfer prices between them |

# Minicase 21.2  Tube Investments*

Christopher Lewington was recruited in 1986 to become the new chief executive and he quickly decided that Tube Investments (TI) needed a clear vision and strategy, in contrast with previous acquisition strategies which had been relatively haphazard.

It was stated in early 1987 that 'TI's strategic thrust is to become an international engineering group concentrating on specialized engineering businesses and operating in selected niches (particularly automotives) on a global basis. Key businesses must be able to command positions of sustained technological and market share leadership'.

In 1986 Raleigh cycles and a number of varied domestic appliance products constituted 42% of TI sales revenue, 30% of pre-tax profits and 45% of capital employed. These were the areas for divestment. Cycles, with their low technology, had been affected by foreign competition which compounded the problems caused by falls in demand in parts of Western Europe. Because different markets required specific product differences, and because of the emergence of defined niches such as those for BMX and mountain bikes, Raleigh 'needed marketing which TI could not provide'. Domestic appliances was an international industry and multinationals such as Philips and Electrolux were very powerful competitors. TI was too small.

Lewington felt that TI had neither the financial resources nor the breadth of management to run a company diversified across specialist engineering and consumer products and markets. Specialist engineering was where TI could add most value and gain the greatest benefit.

In 1987–88 TI sold Raleigh to Derby International, a specially formed foreign-backed consortium who more recently acquired Royal Worcester pottery. Glow Worm and Parkray central heating systems were sold to Hepworth Ceramics; Creda and New World domestic appliances to GEC and Birmid Qualcast, respectively; and Russell Hobbs kitchen equipment to Polly Peck. Machine tool interests and some welded tube products were also divested.

At the same time TI acquired companies, especially in the USA, including Bundy, the largest US manufacturer of small diameter tube for use in cars and refrigerators, and John Crane, a manufacturer of mechanical seals.

TI then specialized in a range of engineering products including aircraft piston rings, industrial furnaces, and tubes for specific market segments. For the automotive industry, silencers, suspension systems, car seats and seat slide mechanisms are manufactured.

In 1992 TI launched a successful but hostile bid for the Dowty Group. Dowty gave TI polymer engineering products, which link with Crane, and related aerospace businesses in landing gear and propellers. These latter activities became a joint venture with Snecma of France in 1993. The remaining Dowty businesses (modems, terminals and electronic systems) were quickly divested.

For five years after the Dowty acquisition, until 1997, the corporate structure remained largely unaltered. TI, instead, sought growth from the better exploitation of the knowledge and service aspects of its businesses and from a stronger focus on anticipating and meeting customers' needs – competitive strategies.

Sales of £1.5 billion in 1995 were double those when Lewington arrived; profits increased fivefold in the same period. 'Newcomers' Bundy and Crane were contributing some 80% of sales revenue; 40% of TI's business was in the USA.

In 1997, the TI structure was changed from three operating divisions to seven distinct businesses, each with its own managing director. The businesses would have operational independence, but the TI head office would retain responsibility for the overall corporate strategy. In the list below the three divisions are shown on the left, and the seven businesses on the right.

| | | |
|---|---|---|
| Seals | – | General mechanical seals (for process plants) |
| | | Marine equipment |
| | | Polymer-based sealing systems (for the industrial, automotive and aerospace markets) |
| | | |
| Fluid equipment (fuel storage systems) | – | For cars |
| | | For refrigerators |
| | | |
| Aerospace | – | Landing gear (joint with Snecma) |
| | | General aerospace systems. |

QUESTIONS: What do you think are the advantages of changing from three divisions to seven businesses?
Is one potential drawback the issue that interdependencies and interbusiness trading might be harder to manage?
How might this be overcome?

*Towards the end of 2000 Smith's Industries (Minicase 22.6) made a bid for Tube Investments.

*Tube Investments*  http://www.tiindia.com

responsibility for changes in the corporate strategy of their divisions. In this way the strategic leader of the corporation can concentrate substantially on corporate strategy and avoid involvement in routine decisions. Acquisitions and divestments can be handled so that only parts of the firm are affected directly. Finally, this structure facilitates innovation and intrapreneurialship throughout the corporation if there is encouragement for this by the strategic leader.

In addition to the difficulty of designing an appropriate structure, there are problems of implementation. It was highlighted above that divisions are normally seen as profit centres, and consequently their profit targets will be used as a basis for assessing performance and effectiveness. There may be problems in establishing profit targets which are seen as equitable, given that divisions (a) may well be of uneven sizes, (b) are likely to be operating in markets which differ in their attractiveness, (c) may have strong or weak relative market shares, (d) may be interdependent upon each other, and (e) have to compete with each other for scarce corporate resources. Where there are interdependencies the corporate policy on transfer prices will favour certain divisions at the expense of others, which again can cause conflict. Wherever profits are a key measure, buying divisions will look for discounts and favourable treatment from within the corporation; selling divisions will expect other parts of the company to pay the going market price, or they will prefer to sell outside. Such profit orientation may also encourage divisions to think in terms of short-term financial measures rather than address more strategic issues.

Where an organization has a variety of different products, all of which depend on core skills and technologies, the challenge is to harness and improve the skills (which are, in effect, corporate resources) while ensuring competitiveness and operating efficiency for each product range. Minicase 14.11 showed how Canon has developed a range of discrete products (cameras, copiers, printers, etc.) around three core competencies: precision mechanics, fibre optics and microelectronics.

Finally, each division is likely to contain a functional structure, and there is also likely to be functional support from headquarters. The corporation as a whole may be able to negotiate better borrowing terms than an individual division could; personnel policies may need to be consistent throughout the firm; and head-office planners may provide support to divisional planners. Reconciling any conflicts between these divisional and head-office groups, together with the need to minimize the potential waste from duplicate resources, can be a limitation of this structural form. The problem can be more difficult to resolve where there are layers of divisions, as discussed below.

Where organizations grow very large, complex and diversified it may be necessary to estab-lish a number of layers of divisions or business units within larger divisions. Each business unit or subdivision may also be a profit centre with its own general manager.

The top part of Table 21.1 shows how WH Smith chose to structure its various businesses in 1995. While it would have been possible to have several more divisions, instead of just four main ones, they would be of significantly different sizes. There were other alternatives to the chosen structural groupings: Waterstone's could have been organized as a single worldwide business, for example. In addition, the retailing and distribution activities involve basically the same products. A few years earlier, when WH Smith owned travel agencies and specialist stationery stores, its structural challenge had been more complex. Since 1995 there have been a number of changes to the corporate strategy, coincident with the appointment of a new chief executive, Richard Handover, in 1997. The bottom part of Table 21.1 describes the basic structure in 1999, after the portfolio had been simplified. The appropriate support and co-ordination roles for both head-office and divisional staff will depend on the structure that is preferred. For example, the purchasing of books, records and stationery for wholesale and retail could usefully be centralized, and the same electronic point-of-sale (EPOS) system could be relevant for all the retail activities. There is no one right answer to the WH Smith structure problem.

As organizations develop globally the structural issues are compounded. It was shown in Chapter 14 that Porter (1990) and Ohmae (1990) disagree about how a company should transform itself into a successful global firm. Ohmae argues that it should shake off its origins, whereas Porter thinks they must be preserved. Should all of the high added value activities (such as design, development and engineering) be centralized at a global company's home base or spread around the world? Ohmae advocates decomposing the central head office into a number of regional

*Table 21.1* WH Smith: group structure, 1995 and 1999

**1995**

1. Retailing: UK and Europe

| | |
|---|---|
| WH Smith Retail | High-street stores – books, sounds, stationery |
| | Airports and stations |
| | Specialist Playhouse video stores |
| Virgin Our Price (75% holding) | Virgin Megastores – *divested 1998* |
| Waterstone's | Specialist booksellers – large towns and cities – *divested 1998* |

2. Retailing: USA

| | |
|---|---|
| WH Smith Inc. | Gift shops, typically in hotels and airports |
| The Wall Inc. | Specialist bookselling in major cities and airports – *divested 1998* |

3. Distribution: UK and Europe

| | |
|---|---|
| WH Smith news and books | Newspaper and magazine wholesaling and distribution |
| | Book distribution to retailers, schools and libraries |
| WH Smith business supplies | Five acquired suppliers of commercial stationery and office products amalgamated under the Nice Day brand – *sold in 1996 to Guilbert of France* |

4. Do It All — DIY retailers, at this time a 50:50 joint venture with Boots– *sold to Boots in 1996.*

**1999**

| | |
|---|---|
| WH Smith High Street | 545 stores – books, sounds, stationery, in the main |
| WH Smith Europe Travel Retail | 183 station and airport stores |
| WH Smith USA Travel Retail | 412 'gift shops', mainly in hotels and airports |
| WH Smith Asia Travel Retail | Hong Kong, Singapore and Sydney airports |
| WH Smith Direct | Internet retailing, with terminal access in selected stores |
| Hodder Headline | Consumer books publisher – with an 8.5% share of the relevant market segment |
| WH Smith News Distribution | 51 depots, making WHS the UK's leading wholesaler of newspapers and magazines |

(The High Street and Europe Travel Retail included the rebranded John Menzies stores acquired by WH Smith in 1998)

*WH Smith*   http://www.whsmith.co.uk

headquarters, with the control of different functions (marketing, production, etc.) being dispersed to different extents and to different locations. The approaches of Ford and Nestlé are featured in Minicase 21.3; later, Minicase 21.4 discusses ABB, a company which has deliberately followed a strategy of devolution.

The traditional divisionalized structure may prove inadequate for coping with the complexities of diversity and globalization. While the holding company and matrix structures provide alternatives (the choice depending on interdependencies and synergy needs), some organizations will eventually choose to split up into

# Minicase 21.3  Ford and Nestlé – Decentralization in Two Global Businesses

The challenge for these multiproduct, multinational businesses is to design and implement a structure which enables them to be sensitive to different customer requirements while containing costs. The successful competitors, especially in a recession, are those that can deliver high service and quality at low cost.

## Ford

In 1995 Ford decided to change from being a 'multi-national organized by geography, with regional profit centres, into a global car manufacturing business organized by product line'. Ford is smaller than General Motors and was less profitable than Chrysler, its two main US rivals; it needed to be more efficient and more effective.

Ford elected to integrate operationally its previously separate North American and European operations – it intended to incorporate its businesses in Asia-Pacific, South America and Africa at a later stage – to create a single global profit centre for all vehicle operations. The main aim was to remove duplication of the 'basic' elements of its various cars, including chassis, engines and transmissions. Even with these combined, Ford argued, the design and feel of a car can readily be customized to suit local tastes around the world. Cars which are essentially global should also emerge from the restructuring, together with speedier new product development processes.

The new structure would feature three distinct levels and responsibilities:

- a single product development organization, incorporating design and engineering, based in the USA and responsible for all Ford vehicles
- within this single product development umbrella, five 'vehicle centres' (four located in the USA, one split between the UK and Germany), each of which would have responsibility for the worldwide development of a particular range of vehicles. The European centre would cover small and medium front-wheel drive cars such as the Fiesta, Escort and Mondeo and their equivalents. The other US centres were: large front-wheel drive cars; rear-wheel drives, including Jaguar; personal use trucks; and commercial trucks

- production plants, which must work together but still retain independence. They are located all round the world. At the time of this restructuring it was planned that the next generation Escort, designed and specified by the small car vehicle centre, and due in either 1998 or 1999, would be produced in several plants in several countries – including the UK, Germany, the USA, Mexico, Brazil, Argentina and a plant somewhere in Asia – and this would require co-ordination. Under the surface the car would be identical everywhere, but externally it would be customized for local markets. Some of the plants produce more than one car
- cross-centre teams would co-ordinate functional knowledge and development across the five vehicle centres in functions such as purchasing, manufacturing and marketing. Individual managers would be seen as functional specialists but transferable between vehicle centres.

Once implemented, the structure proved complex to operate. In addition, Ford already owned car rental company Hertz, and it also acquired Kwik Fit in the UK. The acquisitions of Volvo and Land Rover would follow, but only after further restructuring.

In 1998 the four US vehicle centres were combined into just one large car and truck division. In January 1999 Jacques Nasser, a 'lifelong' Ford employee with over 30 years' service, took over as chief executive. Nasser was determined to 'make Ford more customer oriented' while accepting that it was fundamentally in a 'design, engineering, manufacturing and distribution business'. He was attracted by geographical business units with consumer-defined divisions. He appointed the following vice presidents:

- Global Business Development
- Global Purchasing plus South America
- Global Manufacturing
- Global Product Development
- Premier Automobiles (the specialist brands)
- Global Consumer Services plus North America
- Marketing, Sales and Service, Europe.

*Ford Motor Company*  http://www.ford.com

## Nestlé

Nestle began in the 1860s as a condensed milk factory in Switzerland, where it still has its global headquarters. Having developed largely by acquisition (followed by organic growth), Nestlé now produces in 500 factories in 60 countries and sells in over 100 countries, many of which have strong local preferences. Only 2% of its sales now originate in Switzerland. It aims to be number one or number two in all of the markets that it targets, and consequently invests in branding. The main products and brands are as follows:

- Beverages – coffee (its Nescafé brand is ubiquitous around the world), mineral water (Perrier was acquired in 1992 to add to Vittel) and fruit juices
- milk products – based on its original brand name, Carnation but also including Libby's
- ice cream, chocolate (Rowntree and Kit Kat, for example, both acquired in 1988) and confectionery (Smarties)
- prepared dishes (Crosse and Blackwell), frozen foods (Findus), sauces and condiments (including Maggi and Buitoni)
- Pet foods – Spillers was acquired in 1998 to supplement the existing business.

Nestlé also owns a substantial stake of French cosmetics business, L'Oréal.

Its corporate headquarters was slimmed down in the early 1990s in an attempt to be more innovative and more customer focused. There are now seven strategic business units (including coffee and beverages; foods, etc.) which have worldwide *strategic* responsibility. Operations in the various countries are co-ordinated through a regional network. Six business unit head offices are colocated at corporate headquarters in Switzerland; Nestlé's mineral water interests, including Perrier, are run from Paris. There were plans to locate the global confectionery business in York (where the Rowntree business was built and based) but these were abandoned because of the travel implications.

Each strategic business unit is free to operate in the most appropriate way – there is no longer a 'central way of doing things'. The style and approach appears to vary with the degree of novelty/maturity of the business, its market share and technological intensity, and the need to be localized. The intention is to establish the most appropriate cost structure and decision-making procedures. The requirements for E–V–R congruence vary between the divisions. There are, however, in-built mechanisms to try and spread best practices and to overcome a past tendency to resist adopting ideas developed in other countries.

*Nestlé*   http://www.nestle.com

QUESTIONS: How different are these two alternative structures?
Do they both make sense for the scope and diversity of the businesses concerned?
Given Jacques Nasser's two new thrusts at Ford, how much might he have to change the structure again?

smaller, less diverse parts. Courtaulds was split into its separate textiles and chemicals businesses in 1990; both companies competed in the same industry, but at different stages of the supply chain. ICI and Zeneca were formed out of the original ICI in 1993. Both cases are explored in detail in Chapter 22.

The arguments for such splits are:

- the whole is worth less than the sum of the parts – the complexity is preventing individual businesses from achieving their true potential; and
- being part of a large organization prevents or delays important decisions.

## The holding company structure

The holding company structure, illustrated in Figure 21.5, is ideal for diversified conglomerates where there are few interdependencies between the businesses. The small head office acts largely as an investment company, acquiring and selling businesses and investing money as appropriate. The subsidiaries, which may or may not be wholly owned, are very independent, and their general managers are likely to have full responsibility for corporate strategy within any financial constraints or targets set by headquarters. It is quite common to find that the subsidiaries trade under individual names rather than the name of the parent organization, especially where they are acquisitions who may at any time be sold again.

The holding company structure is particularly appropriate for companies pursuing restructuring strategies, buying, rationalizing and then selling businesses when they can no longer add further value. Some examples are presented in the discussion on diversified conglomerate organizations in Chapter 22.

The advantages of this structural form are that it implies low central overheads and considerable decentralization but enables the head office to finance the subsidiaries at a favourable cost of capital. In fact, low-cost finance can reduce the total costs for a business and thus help to provide competitive advantage. In addition, risks are spread across a wide portfolio, and cross-subsidization is possible between the most and least profitable businesses. This again raises the issue of ascertaining a fair reward structure for the general managers.

The limitations relate, first, to the vulnerability that general managers may feel if they suspect that their business may always be for sale at the right price. There are fewer centralized skills and resources supporting the businesses, little co-ordination and therefore few opportunities for synergy. In addition, there may be no group identity among the business units and a lack of coherence in the corporate strategy. The potential benefit to headquarters lies in their ability to earn revenue and profits from the businesses, ideally in excess of pre-acquisition earnings, and being able to sell for a real capital gain.

The constituent companies [in LVMH, Moët Hennessy, Louis Vuitton] have asked for the following: simplified structures, autonomy for the operational units and a method of administration in keeping with their particular culture.

I am convinced that the success of our group and its subsidiaries is due to the fact that we trust the operational teams to carry out their own quest for quality.

We keep these companies autonomous at middle management level so that they can have the advantages of medium size companies as well as the advantage of belonging to a powerful group that can fund their development.

*Bernard Arnault, Group Chairman, LVMH, Moët Hennessy, Louis Vuitton*

**Figure 21.5** The holding company structure.

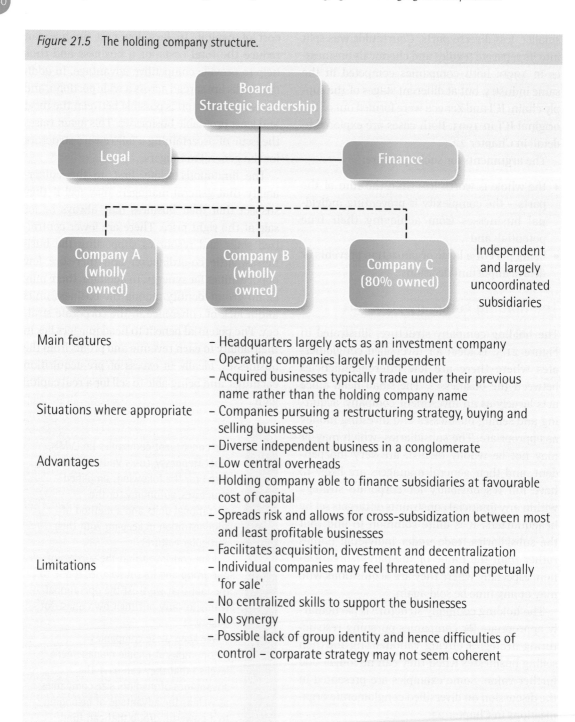

| | |
|---|---|
| Main features | – Headquarters largely acts as an investment company<br>– Operating companies largely independent<br>– Acquired businesses typically trade under their previous name rather than the holding company name |
| Situations where appropriate | – Companies pursuing a restructuring strategy, buying and selling businesses<br>– Diverse independent business in a conglomerate |
| Advantages | – Low central overheads<br>– Holding company able to finance subsidiaries at favourable cost of capital<br>– Spreads risk and allows for cross-subsidization between most and least profitable businesses<br>– Facilitates acquisition, divestment and decentralization |
| Limitations | – Individual companies may feel threatened and perpetually 'for sale'<br>– No centralized skills to support the businesses<br>– No synergy<br>– Possible lack of group identity and hence difficulties of control – corparate strategy may not seem coherent |

Several control issues which face head offices of divisionalized and holding company structures have been mentioned in the above sections, and these will be explored in greater detail later in the chapter.

## The matrix structure

Matrix structures are an attempt to combine the benefits of *decentralization* (motivation of identifiable management teams; closeness to the market; speedy decision making and implementation) with those of *co-ordination* (achieving economies and synergy across all the business units, territories and products). They require dual reporting by managers to, say, a mix of functional and business unit heads or geographical territory and business unit general managers.

The matrix structure is found typically in large multiproduct, multinational organizations where there are significant inter-relationships and interdependencies, as illustrated in Figure 21.6 and Minicase 21.4, and in small sophisticated service businesses such as a business school. The matrix structure in Figure 21.6 illustrates an organization which is split into a series of divisions, based on both products and geographical territories. The product groups would be responsible for co-ordinating the production and marketing of their particular products in a series of plants which might be based anywhere in the world. The geographical divisions would have responsibility for co-ordinating the sales, marketing and distribution of all of the corporation's products, regardless of where they are manufactured, within their territorial area. The operating units would be the production plants, who were members of one or more product groups, depending upon the range of products manufactured in the plant, and whose products are marketed in more than one territory or geographical region. Consequently, the general

manager in charge of each operating unit is responsible in some way to a series of product and territory chiefs (four in the illustration), all of whom will have profit responsibility. The matrix is designed to co-ordinate resources and effort throughout the organization. Structures such as this evolved in the 1960s and 1970s because of the need to establish priorities in multiproduct, multinational organizations. Should the resources and efforts be concentrated on the product groups or in the geographical territories? The ideal answer is both.

Figure 21.8 (p. 746) is a more straightforward illustration of how the staff in a business school might be organized. It is assumed that all of the academic staff would have a specialization which would fit into one of the six columns shown, and that expertise and development in their subject specialism would be important to the staff. At the same time the business school would offer a series of 'products' or services, which are shown as four rows. Staff from each subject group would be allocated to each of these areas. Each product group, and possibly each course within the group, would have a leader with responsibility for delivering a quality product and earning revenue; each subject group would also have a leader responsible for allocating resources and ensuring that staff develop academically.

The potential advantages of a matrix are that responsibility and authority are delegated and spread throughout a complex organization and the stifling tendencies of a bureaucracy are avoided. Because of the flows of information, and the establishment of priorities, decisions are informed and quick. Conflicts between the various groups are reconciled within the structure by the establishment of the priorities and objectives. In addition there are numerous specialist and generalist development opportunities for managers.

Also, in theory, changes in priorities should be readily accommodated. A typical large

Figure 21.6   The matrix structure.

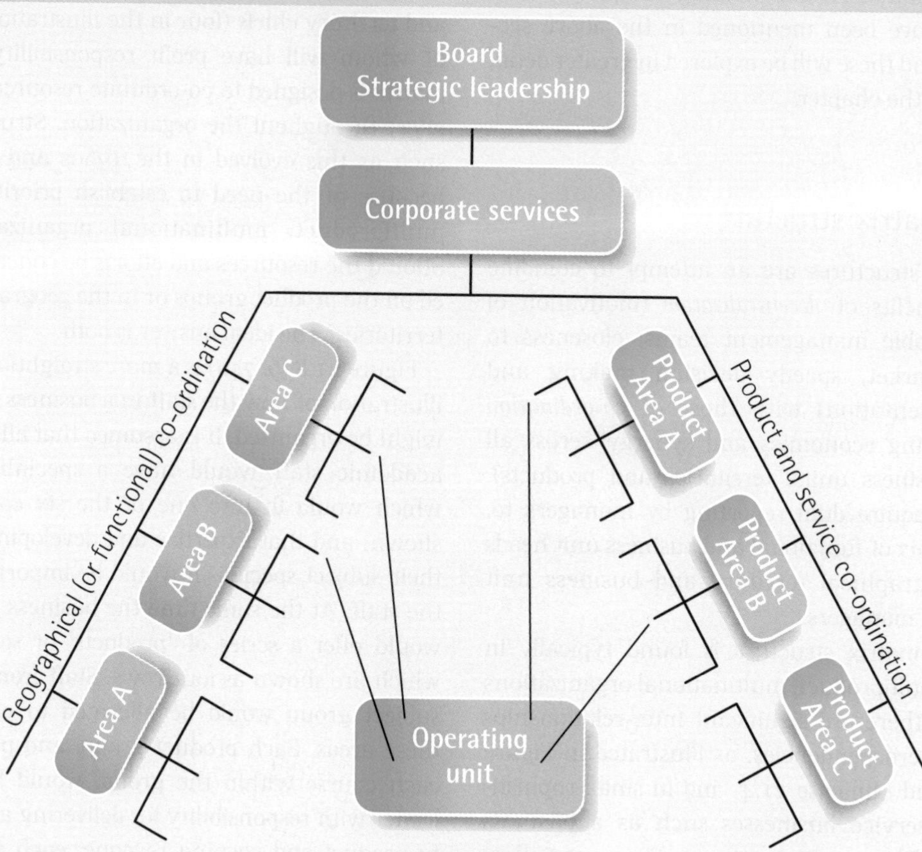

| Main features | – Double definition of profit centres<br>– Permanent and full dual control of operating units – although one wing will generally be more powerful than the other<br>– Authority and accountability defined in terms of particular decisions |
|---|---|
| Situations where appropriate | – Large multiproduct, multinational companies with significant interrelationships and interdependencies<br>– Small sophisticated service companies |
| Advantages | – Decisions can be taken locally, decentralized within a large corporation, which might otherwise be bureaucratic<br>– Optimum use of skills and resources – and high-quality informed decisions, reconciling conflicts within the organization<br>– Enables control of growth and increasing complexity<br>– Opportunities for manager development |
| Limitations | – Difficult to implement<br>– Dual responsibilities can cause confusion<br>– Accounting and control difficulties<br>– Potential conflict between the two wings, with one generally more powerful<br>– High overhead costs<br>– Decision making can be slow |

# Minicase 21.4 ABB (Asea Brown Boveri)

ABB was formed in 1988 when the Swedish company ASEA merged with Brown Boveri of Switzerland to create a global electrical engineering giant. At the time this was the largest cross-border merger in modern history. ABB has since acquired over 100 additional, but smaller, businesses in Europe and America, all of which have needed integrating effectively. The chief executive who masterminded the merger and consequent restructuring was Percy Barnevik (of ASEA), who realized that he had a major challenge if he was to maintain both drive and dynamism during the integration. He became committed to an individualized matrix structure and his aim was to make ABB the global low-cost competitor. His creation has been declared 'the ultimate global organization' – a decentralized structure with centralized control over information and knowledge development. Simply, ABB has become a 'multi-national without a national identity'.

Barnevik is Swedish and he has been described as soft spoken, intense and philosophical. He was noticeably strong on information technology (IT) and he was very committed to the economic development of Eastern Europe and to the fostering of 'clean' energy and transportation.

Under Barnevik ABB was divided up into 1300 identifiable companies and 5000 profit centres. These were aggregated into eight business segments and 59 business areas. There were over 200,000 employees worldwide.

The eight segments were:

- power plants, further subdivided into
  - gas turbine plants
  - utility steam plants
  - industrial steam plants
  - hydro power plants
  - nuclear power plants
  - power plant controls
- power transmission
- power distribution
- electrical equipment
- transportation (such as high-speed trains)
- environmental controls
- financial services
- other activities.

The segments were responsible for organizing manufacture around the world and for product development. Horizontally, ABB was divided up into a mix of countries and regions. Figure 21.7 summarizes the basics of the matrix. There was a 12 member executive board representing products, regions and corporate operations, and a slim head office (under 200 employees) in Zurich. It is not seen as essential that the divisional headquarters for the eight business segments are located in Zurich. Some years earlier

ASEA had had a head office staff complement of 2000; Brown Boveri employed 4000 in its head office.

Zurich essentially retained control over:

- acquisitions
- shifting production to Asia and Eastern Europe
- raising and managing corporate finance.

Financial reporting and evaluation is on a monthly basis.

The basic structure, therefore, was based on small units (of 50 people each on average) supported by good communications and IT. Although ABB comprises distinct businesses, both technology and products are exchanged. Under Barnevik, every employee had a country manager and a business sector manager. Dual responsibilities such as this are often key issues in matrix structures which fail. However, Barnevik insisted that ABB's version is 'loose and decentralized' and that it was easily recognized that the two bosses are rarely of equal status.

Barnevik was obsessed with the idea of creating a small-company and entrepreneurial climate within his large corporation. Extra costs and some fragmentation in the structure were seen as 'a small price to pay for speed and flexibility, with employees staying close to customers and understanding the importance of their own individual efforts for the success of their profit centre'. He also believed that if a large company is to manage internal communications effectively it must develop a 'horizontal integration process'.

The front-line managers, the heads of the 1300 businesses, were no longer implementers of decisions from the strategic leader; instead they were initiators of entrepreneurial action, creating and chasing new opportunities. The role of middle managers – in this flatter structure – concerned coaching and technology and skill transfer. Strategic leadership was about creating purpose, challenging the status quo and setting stretching, demanding targets for front-line managers; it was not simply, as historically it was, to allocate corporate resources and resolve internal conflicts.

Barnevik also commented that the biggest problem has been 'motivating middle and lower level managers and entrenching corporate values – particularly a customer and quality focus'. He believed that his executives should see the business as their number one priority and assumed that highfliers would spend up to 30 hours a week (in addition to their regular tasks) travelling, attending conferences and evening seminars and lectures.

*It is the responsibility of every manager to network within the family of companies, developing informal relationships and looking for synergistic opportunities.*

(Barnevik)

In 1997 Barnevik gave up the chief executive role and became non-executive Chairman of ABB. His successor was Göran Lindahl, perceived as more of a detail and less a concept person. Under Lindahl the process of transferring manufacturing to Asia and Eastern Europe from America and Western Europe accelerated. He also reduced the importance of those executives with geographical responsibilities to focus more emphasis

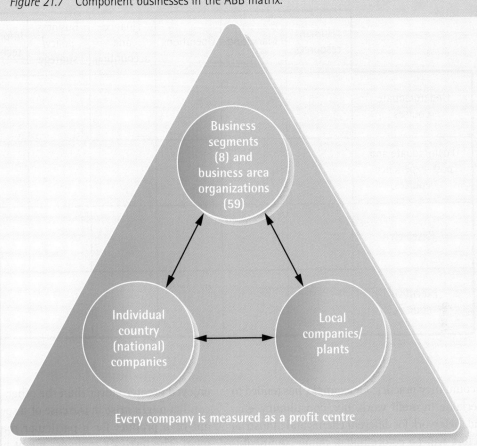

*Figure 21.7*   Component businesses in the ABB matrix.

Business segments (8) and business area organizations (59)

Individual country (national) companies

Local companies/ plants

Every company is measured as a profit centre

on manufacturing and to iron out some of the complex, dual-reporting issues. The learning style and the concentration on small units did not alter, however.

Lindahl resigned in 2000 after initiating some changes of strategic direction. His successor, Jörgen Centerman has restructured ABB around four consumer segments – utilities; process industries; manufacturing and consumer industries; oil, gas and petrochemicals – and two product segments – power technology and automation technology. In recent years, sales growth has fallen back and Centerman believed ABB must focus more on its customers.

QUESTIONS: While the idea of a matrix structure is very attractive, it is inherently complex. Why do you think Barnevik's structure has been described as the 'ultimate global organization'?

How do you think it would feel to work within a structure such as this?

*ABB (Asea Brown Boveri)*   http://www.abb.com

*Figure 21.8*   Possible matrix structure for a business school.

|  | Human resources | Marketing | Operations | Finance and accounting | Business policy/ strategy | Information technology |
|---|---|---|---|---|---|---|
| Undergraduate courses |  |  |  |  |  |  |
| Postgraduate and post-experience courses |  |  |  |  |  |  |
| Research |  |  |  |  |  |  |
| Executive courses |  |  |  |  |  |  |

accountancy practice, for example, has tended to specialize in audit work, tax, consultancy, etc., and their work for different clients and industrial sectors will be co-ordinated. Some commentators believe that in the future 'clients must come first' and any internal, parochial boundaries built around specialisms must be destroyed. To this end, some have even chosen to separate financial services from consultancy as discrete businesses.

The limitations have tended to ensure that the potential advantages have rarely been achieved. Dual responsibilities are difficult to handle; conflicts are not very easily reconciled; and as a result decision making can be slow. In addition, the overhead costs can be quite high. It is also very difficult to establish the appropriate objectives and targets for the general managers, and to get priorities agreed. As a result it has often been the case that one wing of the matrix has enjoyed greater power than the other. A typical conflict might arise in the case of a special variant of a product for a particular market segment. The territory manager might be keen to market this product in order to offer a comprehensive range and support other, possibly completely different, products from other product groups within the corporation. The product chief, responsible for production of the product, might feel that the volume in question was too small and insignificant and that the product should not be produced. The locus of power within the matrix, together with any political activity by the managers concerned, would determine the decision reached.

## Temporary matrices

As an alternative to the full matrix, and in an attempt to gain some of the benefits and avoid the drawbacks, some organizations make use of temporary project teams. In such cases groups or teams of managers are brought together from various parts of the organization to work on a particular project for a period of time before returning to their normal jobs. Such groups are very useful for the management of change, and they can be superimposed on any basic structure. Peters and Waterman (1982), in *In Search of Excellence*, pointed out that such teams are frequently in evidence in the most successful large corporations. They also provide excellent training and development opportunities for managers. The major advantage of these groups is that they are less costly than the complete matrix form, with its high overheads, but there are again limitations. There might be a tendency to seek to use the best managers quite frequently; and in such instances conflicts will be created within the organization when they are taken away from their other responsibilities.

Where there is a rigid hierarchy, specialization and narrow functional perspectives which prevent managers taking a holistic approach, the structure will inhibit managers from pursuing the organization's purpose effectively. Crises are likely to result. A typical response would be a task force to deal with the problem. As a result strong informal relationships will be formed, and these networks are likely to survive after the project team is disbanded and be used to overcome structural rigidities.

### Alternatives to the matrix

In many cases, then, the matrix has proved to be too complicated to be effective. The primary reason has been the inability to deal with the issues of dual responsibility. Henri Fayol (1916) established a number of basic management principles, one of which was 'unity of command', the need to be responsible to only one manager; and the matrix has challenged this premise. Fayol's contention, however, has not been overturned. Decisions have been stifled by confusion, complexity and delay because managers have not

been sufficiently sophisticated to operate effectively within this theoretically ideal structure. The need for a structural form which offers the potential advantages of the matrix to large complex multiproduct, multinational organizations, and which can be implemented, remains. If an organization is unable to design and operate a structure that enables the effective linking of a diverse range of related interests to achieve synergy, and at the same time permits the various business units to be responsive to environmental change, the organization may need to be split up.

Hunsicker (1982) quotes Philips, Ciba-Geigy and Texas Instruments as examples of multinationals that introduced and then retreated from the pure matrix structure. ABB (Minicase 21.4) has changed its matrix to adjust the balance of power. Hunsicker argues that matrices were designed to co-ordinate activities, and that the real strategic need has now become the development of new initiatives. This suggests a greater emphasis on temporary project teams, and the development and encouragement of managers within the organization so that they are more innovative and intrapreneurial. This implies that attention is focused more on changes in behaviour than on changes in the structural framework.

Pitts and Daniels (1984) list the following opportunities for obtaining the benefits of a matrix-type structure within more unitary forms:

- Strengthen corporate staffs to look after corporate strategic developments. They might, for example, search for new opportunities that existing business units could exploit.
- Rotate managers between functions, business units and locations. This increases their awareness and provides inputs of fresh ideas.
- Locate those executives responsible for product co-ordination in geographical territories

physically closer to those managers responsible for production of the key products. Quite often such territory managers are based in their territories, close to their customers and somewhat divorced from manufacturing.

- Create some form of liaison groups which meet periodically and whose brief is to co-ordinate related issues. Such a group might attempt to co-ordinate the global strategies of a number of related products in a search for synergy and mutual benefits.
- Build the notion of agreed contributions between business units into both the management by objectives systems and the compensation schemes.
- Periodically review and amend the constitution of the divisions without restructuring the whole organization.

These suggestions again concentrate more on the processes within the structure than on the framework itself. Therefore, a number of basic structural forms has been considered and it is now appropriate to look in greater detail at the needs and considerations underpinning the design of a structure which are appropriate for both the strategies and the people who must implement these strategies.

## Structure: Determinants and Design

This section draws together the key points concerning the determination and design of effective organization structures. Many of the points have been incorporated in the discussion of structural forms.

## Determinants of structure

There are four main determinants of the design and effectiveness of an organization structure: size, tasks, environment and ideology.

### Size

The previous section on alternative structural forms illustrated that, as the organization grows larger and becomes increasingly complex and diverse, the structure needs to change to allow for effective communication and co-ordination.

### Tasks

The need for co-ordination is linked to the complexity, diversity and interdependence of the tasks that the organization must carry out. Where the businesses are unrelated, for example, the holding company structure can be appropriate. Where the business units are interdependent and particularly where there is considerable trading activity within the organization between the various activities, a divisional or matrix structure will be needed. The structure must take account of the information needs and exchanges required for effective decision making.

### Environment

The key environmental issues concern the nature of the pressures for change and the speed at which the organization must be able to respond and act. These in turn relate to the nature of the industry, competition, and the general sensitivity of demand to environmental forces and changes. The extent of centralization/decentralization is therefore important in dealing with this issue, together with the readiness and willingness of managers to accept and implement change.

### Ideology

Ideology can be either a driving force or a limiting force with regard to certain structural alternatives. It could be argued that the longer an existing structure has existed, the more difficult it will be to make changes because people will be used to particular jobs and responsibilities. The preference of the strategic leader to retain a particular structure, or experiment with new forms, and his or her views on the appropriate amount of decentralization will also have a significant bearing.

The basic logic behind the design of the structure is to make the complexity manageable so that the organization can perform effectively with existing strategies and deal with the formulation and implementation of strategic change. Organization structures should be designed with this in mind, and the above four factors should be taken into consideration. It will not be possible, however, to predict whether a particular structural change will be more or less effective than the present structure. Much depends upon the reaction of managers and other employees to the changes implied, and their ability to deal with the communication and decision-making needs.

## Structural design

Lorsch and Allen (1972), building on earlier work by Lawrence and Lorsch (1967), contend that the design of the structure must accommodate two requirements:

- the need to *differentiate* and separate the various groups that comprise the organization, and
- the need to *integrate* their respective contributions.

The need for differentiation is influenced by the different attitudes, values and behaviour of the various groups. While total quality and consumer satisfaction are important considerations for all managers, the objectives of a production department, a sales department and the finance department could be expected to differ. Production might be concerned with simplifying the demands on production control and reducing costs through efficiency. Their flexibility would be increased if they were allowed to hold high levels of raw material and components stock, but this would increase costs and possibly cause

conflicts with the accountants. A sales department might prefer to choose which customers and orders should receive priority, regardless of production costs, and suggest high levels of finished goods stock to allow instant deliveries. In a similar way, the various product groups might operate in environments that place quite different pressures on them. The values and styles of management appropriate in each case might lead to inconsistencies of style within the organization as a whole.

Integration – the 'internal architecture' of the organization – is concerned with the collaboration and co-ordination between the various activities, and conflict reduction. The various functions within a business unit must be integrated so that their differences are reconciled and objectives and priorities are agreed. The need for integration between business units will relate to interdependencies.

### Dividing and separating tasks

The division of work is normally achieved in two ways: first, by the way in which the tasks are separated and grouped into functions or divisions – the basic structural forms described earlier in this chapter – and, secondly, by the shape of the departmental and divisional structures within the organization. Shape is concerned with the number of levels in the management hierarchy and the span of control of each manager. In general, as the number of levels increases the span of control decreases, and vice versa. These points are illustrated in Figure 21.9. The tall pyramid on the left could represent an organization with a number of divisional layers or a department with several levels of management. This shape can lead to delays and increasing formality as there is a greater separation of the top and bottom levels. However, it does offer an increased number of promotional opportunities for managers. The flatter shape on the right illustrates fewer layers of management, but greater demands on individual managers as

*Figure 21.9*  Alternative structural shapes.

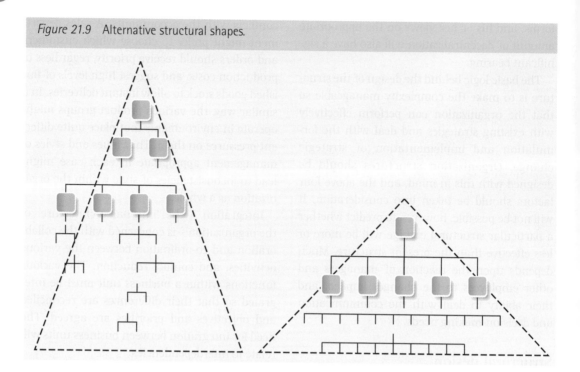

their span of control, the numbers of people reporting directly to them, increases. Communications are likely to be easier and more informal, but there will be fewer promotional opportunities. In general, there has been a tendency for structures to become flatter, and as this happens individual jobs and roles are having to change.

The management style of the future is the flattened pyramid. It's not a trick, but a fantastic invention: you don't order people from the top, you lead them. You give them vision and help. You must let the manager do his own thing. If you do not, the company cannot run fast enough.

*Jean-Marie Descarpentries, President,*
*CMB Packaging*

## Co-ordinating and integrating work

Communications are again an essential issue, together with the relationships between people, functions and businesses. Ideally, team-working and cross-fertilization will strengthen the external architecture and generate synergy. A selection of alternative approaches is listed below:

- linking related profit centres into appropriate strategic business units
- partial centralization
- clearly defined policies
- special task forces and liaison groups
- management by objectives and performance management
- team briefing
- manager rotation
- communicated mission and core values.

Some managers are by nature outgoing and intrapreneurial; they will establish and nurture their own networks which share information and support organizational learning. The actual physical location of managers, functions and businesses can be an important element in achieving this. Where people are located close together, maybe in open-plan cross-functional offices, such networking is much easier. Where businesses are geographically separated, integration is inevitably more difficult, despite the opportunities provided by the latest developments in information technology (IT).

Minicase 21.5 summarizes aspects of the approach utilized by General Electric in the USA.

## Business process re-engineering

In relation to cross-functional integration, business process re-engineering (BPR) became very popular for a while in the 1990s. Books on the subject were best-sellers and courses were very popular. BPR is about restructuring in order to manage processes more efficiently and thus create and add value more effectively. It turned out to be something of a 'fad' because if was often implemented clumsily; nevertheless the issues that it addresses remain.

To be successful organizations must add value for their customers and other stakeholders in some distinctive way. Strategic capabilities are the means and *processes* through which value is added, as distinct from the products and services themselves and their competitive positioning. When managers are delegated responsibility for changing and improving the ways in which tasks are carried out it is these processes that are being changed incrementally and adapted.

Typical processes include:

- supply-chain management – to fulfil orders, but also including administrative procedures for dealing with enquiries and orders
- developing new products and services
- providing service to customers
- managing people – including, for example, developing people
- managing finances – especially the cash flow.

These processes clearly cut across individual functions and, as processes, they are replicated in different divisions and businesses, albeit with specific variations. Successful innovation in these internal processes can:

- lead to greater efficiency
- improve quality and service
- save time
- create or enhance differentiation, and thus
- *add value for customers.*

Sometimes this gradual change may not be enough in a competitive environment. The existing processes – and their outcomes – may simply be inadequate or even unacceptable. Consequently, a more radical review is necessary if the organization is to become or remain a leading competitor in an industry. Managers must systematically benchmark and evaluate best practice, using competitors and any other relevant organizations, and consider the extent to which the processes need redesigning. This objective appraisal, and the changes that result from it, can take the form of BPR, which is really another example of planned change. BPR implies that an organization completely rethinks how certain tasks are carried out, and searches for new ways through which performance can be improved.

US Air, when it was British Airways' American partner, reviewed the process by which aeroplanes flying domestic routes are emptied and cleaned, and the passengers and luggage loaded for the next flight. The outcome was a time reduction from 45 to 25 minutes for selected flights. As a result, operating efficiencies were increased – the planes are in the air longer and on the ground less – without passengers being inconvenienced.

It was, however, often found that radical process re-engineering requires the reduction or breaking down of functional and individual job boundaries as the new processes do not have to coincide with the existing departmental structure. People and departments were now expected

# Minicase 21.5  General Electric

General Electric (GE) is diversified into aircraft engines, medical systems, plastics engineering, defence electronics and household consumer goods. GE also provides financial services (through the specialist GE Capital subsidiary) and owns NBC Television in the USA. It has annual revenues in excess of $100 billion and profits of $10 billion.

John F (Jack) Welch has been Chief Executive for some 20 years, in which time there have been 1000 acquisitions. The latest major acquisition of Honeywell (computing, avionics and industrial controls) has caused Welch to postpone retirement, which was scheduled for Spring 2001. He is determined to implement the merger of the two organizations. His successor  has, however, already been named.

The company is decentralized and employees are encouraged to speak out and pursue ideas. External contacts and sources are constantly monitored for new leads and opportunities. 'We'll go anywhere for an idea'. Welch, always believed 'the winners of the 1990s would be those who could develop a culture that allowed them to move faster, communicate more clearly, and involve everyone in a focused effort to serve ever more demanding customers'. GE has its own 'university' and brings managers of various levels in all the businesses together regularly to explain what they are doing and to share new ideas.

> *We have this incredible intellect in GE . . . we are exposed to so many industries that when we [senior managers] all get together we have the opportunity to maximize our intellect. That's the advantage of a multi-business company . . . we can share ideas.*
>
> (Welch)

*Fortune* magazine declared Welch to be the 'manager of the century' for his achievement in turning a 'slumbering dinosaur' into a 'lean and dynamic company with a paradigm of a new management style'. Whereas Percy Barnevik (Minicase 21.4) redesigned the ABB structure, Welch transformed GE through management style. They both believed that 'small is beautiful' and that innovation and intrapreneurship are critical. The decentralization at GE aims to 'inject down the line the attitudes of a small fast-moving entrepreneurial business and thereby improve productivity continuously'. Integration strategies promote the sharing of ideas and best practices.

There is a developed strategy of moving managers between businesses and countries to transfer ideas and create internal synergy, together with a reliance on employee training. It has been said that 'if you sit next to any GE executive on a 'plane they will all tell the same story about where the company is going'. There is a shared and understood direction and philosophy, despite the diversity.

Welch regularly attends training courses to collect opinion and feedback. 'My job is to listen to, search for, think of and spread ideas, to expose people to good ideas and role models.' GE's '*work out*' programme involves senior managers presenting GE's vision and ideas to other managers and employees, and then later reconvening to obtain responses and feedback on perceived issues and difficulties. All employees in a unit, regardless of level, are thus provided with an opportunity to review and comment upon existing systems and procedures. The check is always based on whether they add value. External advisers (such as university academics) monitor the programme to ensure that communications are genuinely two-way.

Managers are actively encouraged to work closely with suppliers and customers, and they have '360 degree evaluations', with inputs from superiors, peers and subordinates. 'People hear things about themselves they have never heard before.' Products and businesses should be number one or number two in a market, and if they are not achieving this, their managers are expected to ask for the resources required to get there.

Welch summarizes his philosophy as follows:

*If we are to get the reflexes and speed we need, we've got to simplify and delegate more – simply trust more. We have to undo a 100-year-old concept and convince our managers that their role is not to control people and stay on top of things, but rather to guide, energize and excite. But with all this must come the intellectual tools, which will mean continuous education of every individual at every level of the company.*

QUESTIONS: Do you think Welch's management style could be easily copied by both his successor and other organizations? Why? Why not?

*General Electric*   http://www.ge.com

There are further cases on GE in Chapters 22 and 24.

to be more supportive of each other and share information and best practices. These linkages and the greater flexibility in turn imply empowerment and learning. BPR undoubtedly enjoyed a period of popularity as organizations, sometimes using consultants, initiated restructuring programmes. Invariably, these have involved job losses and downsizing. Unfortunately, with hindsight, some organizations realized that they had lost important skills and competencies in the exercise and also caused demoralization among those employees who stayed. The downsizing did not result in the organization establishing the efficient and effective 'right size' from which new opportunities for adding value can be generated. Not unexpectedly, therefore, BPR has been widely criticized, but defended by its proponents who argue that too many organizations do not appreciate how to apply it properly.

## Mintzberg's co-ordinating mechanisms

Mintzberg (1979) also considers that it is necessary for an organization to divide the whole task into smaller subtasks in order to achieve the benefits of specialization and division of labour. In order to accomplish the total task Mintzberg agrees that the subtasks must then be co-ordinated and integrated, and argues that there are five main co-ordinating mechanisms:

- *mutual adjustment* – essentially informal communication systems
- *direct supervision* whereby managers take responsibility for the work of others, controlling and monitoring activity
- *standardized work processes* – the content of tasks is specified clearly, say through detailed job instructions

- *standardized outputs* – expected results are specified and manager performance is evaluated against these targets (this is a performance-orientated mechanism)
- *standardized skills* where the training and experience required to do jobs effectively are specified.

Standardized skills incorporate the notion of specific qualifications being required for particular specialist positions. Co-ordination is achieved through workers and managers understanding what is expected of each other and making effective contributions naturally. An anaesthetist and a surgeon, for example, appreciate each other's roles and contributions.

In addition, there is a sixth mechanism which results from mutual adjustment and adaptive changes in strategy. Mintzberg refers to this as the *standardization of norms*, where employees share a set of common beliefs. This is a cultural issue which evolves as mutual adjustment and informal communications lead to adaptive changes and the establishment of new norms of behaviour. The evolution of a road through a forest from a well-trodden path would constitute an analogy.

Mintzberg argues that small entrepreneurial firms rely mainly on direct supervision by the owner–manager, and that as the organization grows and becomes more complex standardized work processes, outputs and skills become increasingly popular in a sequential and ascending order. Mutual adjustment is the favoured mechanism in what Mintzberg terms adhocracies, and which are discussed later in this section. Each structural type and style of management has a most appropriate co-ordinating mechanism, and this is explored below.

Mintzberg's contribution to our appreciation of structure is particularly useful for helping us to understand strategic management in large, public-sector corporations.

## Mintzberg's structural configurations

Mintzberg (1983) has also described five structural configurations, each of which is suitable for organizations at certain stages of development and in particular environmental circumstances. Each structural configuration achieves co-ordination and E–V–R (environment–values–resources) congruence in different ways. Moreover, while each configuration comprises five basic parts or sets of resources, as outlined below, the relative size and importance of these parts varies between the configurations.

### The five constituent parts of the organization

Mintzberg's five parts are illustrated in Figure 21.10 and are as follows.

- The *operating core* – those employees who carry out the various tasks involved in the primary activities of the value chain, which include securing inputs, transforming the inputs into

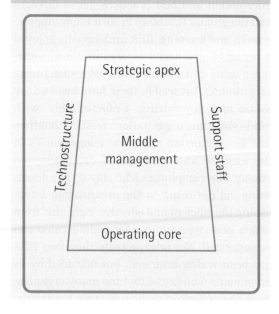

*Figure 21.10* The basic parts of the organization. Developed from Mintzberg, H (1983) *Structure in Fives*, Prentice-Hall.

outputs by adding value and then distributing the outputs.

- The *strategic apex* – the strategic leader and his or her colleagues who are responsible for developing the corporate strategy, managing relations with the environment, designing the structure and allocating resources.
- The *middle management* – middle managers, with authority, link the strategic apex with the operating core. They manage the tasks carried out by the operating core, applying any policies and systems established by the strategic apex, and feed information up and down the organization.
- *Support staff* – support activities occur at various levels in the hierarchy and provide assistance to both middle managers and the operating core. Such activities would include research and development, public relations and certain aspects of the personnel function such as running the payroll.
- The *technostructure* comprises analysts who affect the work of others, such as work study analysts, planners and the training and recruitment staff in personnel. Galbraith (1969) uses the expression 'technocrats' to describe the experts and specialists who control much of the activity in large, powerful and growth-orientated corporations.

## The five configurations

Mintzberg's five configurations are discussed below, and the salient points are compared in Table 21.2. These configurations do not match completely with the structural forms outlined earlier, but they are clearly related.

*The simple structure* – Mintzberg's first configuration relates very closely to the entrepreneurial structure. It is typically small, and has no technostructure and little formal planning. Decision making is centralized with the chief executive or owner–manager, and performance is very dependent on the strategic leader.

*The machine bureaucracy* – Machine bureaucracies are generally found where the work is routine, with standardized production processes. Jobs are tightly defined and regulated, and there is a powerful technostructure to search for efficiencies and cost-control opportunities. This configuration is typical of mass-production assembly systems.

Some power is decentralized to the specialist functional managers, but strategic change decisions are largely centralized. As the specialists implement the proposed changes, strategy formulation and implementation are separated. The machine bureaucracy is relatively slow to change, and therefore more suitable for stable environmental conditions. In a number of respects it is similar to the functional structure.

*The professional bureaucracy* – The professional bureaucracy is typically found in organizations which rely heavily on administrators and administration systems, such as hospitals and universities. It is bureaucratic but not centralized, and power lies with specialist professionals and professional managers. Where professionals are in evidence they are likely to hold formal qualifications, and standardized skills will be the main co-ordinating mechanism. Support administrators are unlikely to be as well qualified as the professionals. However, in the 1980s and 1990s there has been an increasing tendency for administrators in some of these organizations to study for high-level management qualifications.

The old polytechnics in the UK were examples of professional bureaucracies which had to change their structures. Until 1989 their administrative systems provided a link between the powerful academic structure, comprising highly qualified academics and heads of department, and the respective local authorities who controlled their financial affairs. When the polytechnics were in effect privatized in April 1989, and they became independent higher education corporations with plc status, new administrative

*Table 21.2* Selected elements of Mintzberg's five configurations

| | Simple structure | Machine bureaucracy | Professional bureaucracy | Divisionalized form | Adhocracy |
|---|---|---|---|---|---|
| Key co-ordinating mechanism | Direct supervision | Standardization of work | Standardization of skills | Standardization of outputs | Mutual adjustments |
| Key part of organization (resource concentration) | Strategic apex | Technostructure | Operating core | Middle management | Support staff |
| Roles of strategic apex/ leadership in addition to responsibility for corporate strategy | All administration | Co-ordination and conflict resolution | External liaison and conflict resolution | Strategic perspective and control of performance | External liaison, conflict resolution and project monitoring |
| Centralization/decentralization | Centralized | Limited horizontal decentralization | Decentralized | Decentralized vertically | Decentralized |
| Environment | Simple and dynamic | Simple and stable | Complex and stable | Relatively simple and stable but diverse | Complex and dynamic |
| Power and values | Controlled by strategic leader – possibly owner – manager | Technocratic and sometimes external control | Professional manager control | Middle management control, i.e. general managers | Expert control |
| Typical examples | Small firms Young organizations | Processing companies Assembly companies | Hospital University | Diversified or multi- product organization | Management consultants |

and financial structures were introduced with additional layers of management. Because new funding arrangements have also been introduced, commercial considerations and market orientation increased in significance. The polytechnics became 'new universities' in 1992, when it was necessary for them to review their distinctive mission and market niche.

Does this structural configuration encourage or inhibit change? Adaptive change is likely to be evident and influenced significantly by external professional organizations. Committee structures will restrict the freedom of the professionals to change things, but the changes will still prove difficult to co-ordinate in many instances. More substantial strategic changes are difficult to implement as the structure tends to be inflexible. Performance measures relating to effectiveness, rather than to the efficient utilization of resources, are difficult to establish and monitor because of the nature of the service.

*The divisionalized structure* – This configuration represents any structure based on autonomous divisions or business units co-ordinated by a central administrative structure. It typically develops out of a machine bureaucracy when there is diversification. Power and responsibility is devolved to the divisions, creating a key strategic role for the general managers who head the divisions. These general managers, who comprise Mintzberg's middle line in this configuration, are responsible for changes in competitive strategies; but the extent of the decentralization in the organization as a whole may be restrained. General managers, for example, may centralize the power within their divisions.

Divisions will be expected to agree objectives and targets with the strategic leader; and measures of effective performance related to these will be used for monitoring and control purposes. Hence, the standardization of outputs is the most appropriate co-ordination mechanism.

Recapping on points made previously, the overall strategic leader in a divisionalized structure is responsible for managing and co-ordinating a portfolio of businesses. General managers at lower levels in the hierarchy are responsible for portfolios of business units or product/markets. If they are to accomplish this effectively they must be able to reach informed decisions concerning resource allocation, especially finance. The technocracy therefore provides an important support function.

*The adhocracy* – An adhocracy is an informal and innovative organization which features teams of specialists and decentralized power. An advertising agency or a management consultancy group would be a typical example. Liaison between groups of experts is very important, and some variant of the matrix structure, such as temporary project teams or liaison groups, is likely to be evident. Expertise lies throughout the organization, with the operating core and support staff being particularly important.

Adaptive strategic changes, originating anywhere within the organization, are likely to be commonplace and encouraged as this configuration is attempting to deal with a complex and dynamic environment. The pursuit of personal objectives and organizational politics (considered in greater detail in Chapter 24) is facilitated and must be monitored and controlled. Decision making may be slowed down where people are very active politically. Linked to these issues, conflict will also be present, and resolving this will be a key role for the strategic leader.

It is quite possible to find more than one configuration present in an organization where diverse interests mean that E–V–R congruence cannot be achieved effectively with only one style of management. A newspaper, for example, may have an adhocracy for dealing with editorial aspects and a machine bureaucracy for printing. A university overall is likely to be a professional bureaucracy, but the business school within it may well be more of an adhocracy and built around a matrix, as described earlier (see p. 741).

To conclude this chapter, it is worth recapping an earlier argument. Drucker (1988) suggested that the organization of the future would have fewer managers and fewer layers in the management hierarchy. He believed that IT would lead to more autonomy for individual managers and more informed decision making when specialists have decentralized responsibility for key activities within the organization. Strategy co-ordination would still constitute a major challenge, however. We are now in a position to judge his prediction. Virtually every manager has access to a personal computer, an organizational intranet and the Internet. For many, letters, memos and phone calls have been replaced by e-mails.

## Summary

To be successful a strategy must be implemented. This requires that the organization's strategic resources are developed, deployed and controlled appropriately. This is accomplished through the organization structure.

Organization structures are designed to ensure that intended strategies can be implemented effectively. The processes within the structure also affect and facilitate emergent strategy. Particularly significant for ensuring that both happen is the location of power, responsibility and authority in the organization and the extent to which these are centralized and decentralized. In large organizations the relationship between the head office and the various subsidiaries (businesses or divisions) relates to this issue.

*Centralization* yields consistency and control, but it can result in an organization being slow to respond to the pressures for change in its external environment. In addition, entrepreneurial managers may feel constrained. *Decentralization* enables flexibility, but control is more difficult. It is dependent upon an effective information system which can gather together the various changes that are taking place as empowered managers make and take decisions.

Centralization/decentralization and formality/informality (the nature of control mechanisms and communications) determine the broad structural type.

There are five main structural forms:

- The *entrepreneurial structure* is found in the typical small business where everything is centred around a key person, often the owner–manager.
- The *functional structure* emerges as departments and managers are created to deal with the increasing number of tasks.
- The *divisionalized structure* is a popular structure for organizations with several products or services which may or may not be related.
- The *holding company* is adopted by a diversified business with largely unrelated activities or businesses which can advantageously be kept separate for control purposes.
- The *matrix structure* – or some variant of it – is most frequently used where there is a need to co-ordinate both products and countries in a business which manufacturers and markets worldwide. Because of its inherent complexities alternative forms of integration might be sought.

Organizations change their structures as they grow. They may also be changed in line with alterations to the corporate portfolio to try and keep the two in balance.

The main determinants of structure are: size, tasks to be carried out, environment and ideology.

The basic structure divides up the tasks but, of course, the structure is merely a framework for allocating tasks and roles and positioning people. The real follow-up challenge is one of integration.

Our understanding of structure – and particularly the structural challenges of large public-sector organizations – is aided by Henry Mintzberg's identification of five co-ordinating mechanisms and five structural configurations: the simple structure, the machine bureaucracy, the professional bureaucracy, the divisionalized form and the adhocracy.

## References

Chandler, AD (1962) *Strategy and Structure: Chapters in the History of the American Industrial Enterprise*, MIT Press.

Child, JA (1977) *Organization: A Guide to Problems and Practice*, Harper & Row. (A more recent edition is now available.)

Drucker, PF (1988) The coming of the new organization, *Harvard Business Review*, January–February.

Fayol, H (1916) *General and Industrial Administration*, Pitman, 1949 (translation of French original).

Galbraith, JK (1969) *The New Industrial State*, Penguin.

Hunsicker, JQ (1982) The matrix in retreat, *Financial Times*, 25 October.

Lawrence, PR and Lorsch, JW (1967) *Organization and Environment*, Richard D Irwin.

Lorsch, JW and Allen, SA (1972) *Managing Diversity and Interdependence*, Division of Research, Harvard Business School.

Mintzberg H (1979) *The Structuring of Organizations*, Prentice-Hall.

Mintzberg, H (1983) *Structure in Fives: Designing Effective Organizations*, Prentice-Hall.

Ohmae, K (1990) *The Borderless World*, Harper.

Peters, TJ and Waterman, RH Jr (1982) *In Search of Excellence: Lessons from America's Best Run Companies*, Harper & Row.

Pitts, RA and Daniels, JD (1984) Aftermath of the matrix mania, *Columbia Journal of World Business*, Summer.

Porter, ME (1990) *The Competitive Advantage of Nations*, Free Press.

Salter, MS (1970) Stages in corporate development, *Journal of Business Policy*, Spring.

Thompson, AA and Strickland, AJ (1980) *Strategy Formulation and Implementation*, Richard D Irwin.

Test your knowledge of this chapter with our online quiz at: http://www.thomsonlearning.co.uk

## Questions and Research Assignments

### TEXT RELATED

1. It was stated in the text that decentralization and divisionalization are not synonymous. What factors determine the degree of decentralization in a divisionalized organization?

2. For an organization with which you are familiar, obtain or draft the organization structure. How does it accord with the structural forms described in the text? Given your knowledge of the company's strategies and people, is the structure appropriate? Why? Why not? If not, in what way would you change it?

3. 'Sophisticated innovation requires a configuration that is able to fuse experts drawn from different disciplines into smoothly *ad hoc* project teams' (Henry Mintzberg discussing adhocracies).

    Do you agree? Can innovation not be incorporated into the alternative structures? Do you believe that the adhocracy approach will overcome the perceived drawbacks of the matrix structure?

4. How uncertain and traumatic might it be to work in a middle or senior management position in a large organization which changes its structure relatively frequently? Despite this, is change inevitable?

## Internet and Library Projects

1. Obtain an up-to-date organization chart for the WH Smith Group, and consider how the various businesses featured in Table 21.1 are integrated. Do you feel that this is the most suitable structure? Do you think that WH Smith might try and co-ordinate these activities to try and achieve the inherent synergy potential?

   *WH Smith*   http:www.whsmith.co.uk

2. Evaluate the divisionalized or holding company structure of a large, diverse, multiproduct multinational, considering the main board status of the key general managers. Does this suggest centralization or decentralization? If you are familiar with the company, do your findings accord with your knowledge of management styles within the organization?

3. How is Ford currently managing its global structure? On balance, and to what extent, do you think structure is following strategy and strategy is following structure?

   *Ford Motor Company*   http://www.ford.com

# Corporate Strategy and Style

*Growth is often an important objective for organizations. Frequently this growth has involved diversification and acquisitions in either related or unrelated areas. In recent years the strategic logic of large, diversified conglomerates has been questioned as many organizations have instead chosen to focus on related businesses, technologies or core competencies, where they can more readily add value across the businesses and generate synergy. Whatever the strategic choice, though, it must be implemented successfully. The opening case looks at how ICI, once one of the UK's leading manufacturers, has been split into two and then transformed into a different business. However, conglomerate, diversified businesses cannot be automatically dismissed; they can be both successful and profitable if they can find new, suitable businesses to acquire, opportunities for growth with their subsidiary businesses and if their strategic control system is appropriate. Simply, the strategy can still be justified if it can be implemented successfully. This chapter explores alternative approaches to strategic control and applies these issues to diversified conglomerates. The relationship between the corporate centre and individual subsidiary businesses is examined, and a discussion is presented on the role and contribution of corporate head offices which, generally, in recent years, have been slimmed down as organizations have become more decentralized.*

*The particular role of general managers is examined and the chapter concludes with some short comments on organizations at the beginning of this new millennium.*

*This is a chapter of debates, opinions and interpretations, but few clear-cut answers. Simply, both the strategy and the structure need to change but stay complementary as the business environment changes. If accomplishing this was straightforward and clear-cut many organizations would be more successful than they actually are.*

# Minicase 22.1 ICl and Zeneca

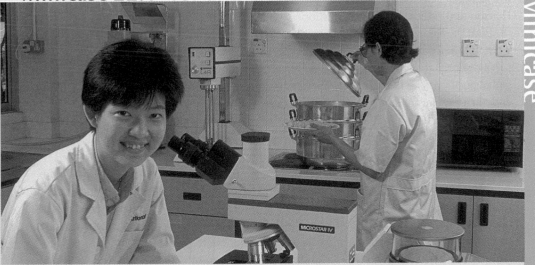

The range and diversity of ICI's products created strategic and structural problems for the organization. These products ranged from bulk chemicals, including chlorine and petrochemicals (plastics from oil and gas), to more sophisticated products such as pharmaceuticals and pesticides. The prospects for bulk chemicals are traditionally dependent on the world economic cycle, and consequently profits vary dramatically from year to year. Drugs are classically immune from the economic cycle, and they are also cash generative. ICI's dilemma concerned the utilization of its profits for research and development and capital investment, and whether to cross-subsidize or treat the businesses separately. During the boom years of the mid-1980s chemicals and related products were very profitable; but in the recession of 1991 they contributed just 30% of ICI's profits from 70% of the turnover. Between 1980 and 1985, chaired by Sir Maurice Hodgson and later Sir John Harvey-Jones, ICI reduced its global workforce from 225,000 to 175,000 and purged its costs. The early 1980s were also recession years. ICI's competitive position strengthened. The company was also restructured into seven global product divisions co-ordinated through nine regional territories. Financial responsibilities were split among the divisions and the regions. UK inflation later in the 1980s meant that ICI's costs started to rise again, and more rapidly than those of its main competitors. The workforce was further reduced (to 132,000 in 1990) and productivity improved, but it was still not enough.

In 1990 ICI was restructured again in an attempt to place greater emphasis on the global nature of its businesses, increase the financial accountability of the divisional business managers, and focus greater attention on improving shareholders' wealth. The head office was slimmed down, and the number of regional chairmen was reduced to three. The regions lost any managerial responsibility over individual businesses. The product division heads became autonomous, and they could spend up to £10 million without reference to the main board. When Hanson acquired 2.8% of ICI's shares in spring 1991, and raised the threat of a hostile take-over bid, the company was encouraged to evaluate again both its strategy and structure. No actual bid ever materialized, but Hanson and external analysts questioned whether ICI was effectively exploiting its assets. In the end, the Hanson view that ICI would be better split up was defensible, but arguably what followed came too late.

ICI declared that it would now concentrate on businesses where it could achieve a strong global position. The fibres operations were swapped for the acrylics businesses of Du Pont early in 1992, for instance.

In July 1992 ICI's board announced plans to split the company into two separate businesses in 1993 – ICI and ICI Bio, later renamed Zeneca. Shareholders in ICI would be given an equivalent shareholding in the new company. ICI would retain industrial chemicals, paints and explosives, it would have 88,000 employees worldwide and be the seventh largest chemical company in the world (relegated from fifth). These businesses are all high volume and capital intensive. Zeneca, geared more towards differentiated, high added value products, would comprise the drugs and agrochemicals businesses and be the ninth largest pharmaceutical company in the world. There would be 35,500 employees. It was assumed that most of ICI's cash reserves would remain with the bulk chemicals when it was announced that Zeneca would have an early rights issue. The opportunities for synergy really lay within the two product clusters, not between them.

Moreover, each business had different strategic needs. A successful split would enable the necessary further rationalization at ICI and foster new product investment in Zeneca. Both companies should now become better protected from hostile take-over. ICI might appear to be relatively unattractive; Zeneca would probably be very expensive as long as it remained successful and profitable. Immediately after the split Zeneca shares performed well compared with those of other international drugs companies; ICI shares, by contrast, were poor performers in the international chemicals industry.

ICI reached an agreement with Union Carbide of the USA to exchange information for benchmarking purposes; ICI realized that it was overstaffed and that its costs were still relatively high and had to be reduced further. In 1995 ICI appointed a new chief executive, a recruit from Unilever, Charles Miller-Smith. He found 'a traumatized organization of survivors from one of the world's most comprehensive management delayerings'. After extensive deliberation, Miller-Smith decided that ICI needed to focus on intermediate (acrylic and polyester film products) and consumer-orientated products (including Dulux paints) and not bulk chemicals. In addition, ICI's future would be more dependent on investment and development in the USA and Asia than in Europe.

In May 1997 it was formally announced that ICI was looking to sell off 60% of its businesses (mainly bulk chemicals and worth approximately £3 billion) to help to fund its acquisition of Unilever's speciality chemicals businesses, which would then constitute 70% of a 'new' ICI, which was more focused on consumer markets. This was a reverse take-over in everything but name. The purchase price was £4.9 billion. Charles Miller-Smith had joined ICI from Unilever Chemicals; he knew the businesses involved. He also realized that the cultures were different. ICI was currently focused more on production, Unilever on marketing. The Unilever businesses had typically enjoyed steady growth, while those of ICI had been far more cyclical, with the attached cash management difficulties. ICI's head office would now receive an infusion of 'tough American and gritty Dutch' managers.

Four Unilever businesses were included in the purchase:

- *National Starch* – industrial adhesives as well as starches. Brought real opportunities for business with Procter and Gamble, previously prohibited as P&G are established rivals of Unilever. The relevant adhesives are used in disposable nappies; Procter's Pampers product is the leading global brand
- *Quest* – food flavours and fragrances
- *Unichema* – chemicals from natural fats
- *Crosfield* – detergent ingredients; a business that ICI planned to divest.

One month later, and to help to fund the Unilever acquisition, a majority share of ICI's business in Australia was sold for £1 billion; and in July ICI agreed to sell a number of its industrial chemicals businesses to Du Pont for £1.8 billion. This proposed sale included ICI's polyester and titanium dioxide plants which produce raw materials for paints and plastics. ICI was aiming to become less vertically integrated. Du Pont specializes in bulk chemicals and this acquisition would consolidate its position as the largest American chemicals company. For this reason it was subject to ratification by the US competition authorities. The deal was eventually stopped in January 1999, and the delay had a severe impact on ICI's cash position.

The fertilizer business was sold to an American buyer in November 1997; a month later ICI's explosives division was sold. In 1998 ICI acquired a cluster of home-improvements businesses from Williams, including Polyfilla. A possible sale of Crosfield fell through. However, concurrent with these strategic changes, profits were declining as part of the inbuilt economic cycle and ICI was finding it difficult to deal with its accumulated debt burden of £4 billion. The disposals were going to have to be more dramatic than Miller-Smith had originally planned.

In 1999 ICI sold all of its petrochemicals businesses, including polyester and titanium dioxide, to Huntsman of America for £12.7 billion. Acrylics (ingredients for paints and adhesives, bathtubs and sinks) were divested to a management buy-out. ICI had basically become a 'holding company for specialist assets'. Of the old – and once huge – ICI, only paints remained.

Zeneca merged with Astra of Sweden in 1999 and continues to grow successfully.

In the end the UK has lost a major bulk chemicals business, one on which many other industries depend. Arguably the necessary research and development did not take place during the 1960s – a time when the UK was not a member of the European Community and when, as a consequence, some market opportunities were unavailable to companies such as ICI. In addition, costs had been allowed to escalate and the issue was not tackled as early as it needed to be. This was one issue to which Hanson drew attention. Some analysts argue that bulk chemicals is so tied in to the global oil industry that survival demands some form of strategic alliance, something that ICI did not have.

QUESTIONS: Assume that the 'unthinkable' happened and ICI was acquired by Hanson in 1991 and then split up as part of a restructuring process. Do you think that more of the original business might have been retained in the UK?

However undesirable at the time for many shareholders and managers of ICI, would an acquisition by Hanson have, overall, been a better alternative to what actually did happen?

*ICI*   http://www.ici.com

*Astra Zeneca*   http://www.astrazeneca.com

Photograph: National starch and chemical food laboratory, Singapore.

## Introduction: Strategy and Implementation

There is a number of key themes to a synergistic, successful and profitable portfolio:

- related competencies and capabilities, which can be transferred between businesses and between each of these businesses and the corporate headquarters, or the overall strategic leader
- the ability to create and build value, both individually and collectively, by the businesses and the corporate headquarters
- the ability to implement strategies and strategic ideas to achieve their potential. This contribution is again individual (in, say, the form of profit streams because of a strong competitive position) and collective, through learning, sharing and the transfer of skills and resources.

In this chapter, therefore, two key themes are brought together.

First, the relatedness of the actual businesses in the portfolio. Where technologies or markets are similar or even the same, there must be relatedness. However, some diversified conglomerates have shown that they can relate unlike businesses to create value. This relates to issues of style and culture, rather than basic strategic logic.

Secondly, the management of the portfolio of activities to ensure that strategies are implemented effectively. As a result, the overall organization should be demonstrably 'better off' from the existence of the businesses and strategies involved. Its is clearly possible for a problematical business to be a distraction which draws resources (people, money and time in particular) away from potentially more lucrative opportunities.

Figure 22.1 shows how strategy and implementation must work together harmoniously for competitive, strategic and (where relevant) financial success. Where the strategy is 'stretched' or particularly demanding for the resources possessed by the organization, there is still likely to be underachievement even where there is sound implementation. If the accompanying implementation is also weak, the organization is likely to seem fragmented and fragile. A basically sound strategy, poorly implemented, would typically suggest structural and stylistic flaws.

The basic dilemma for many organizations is understanding why, when something is wrong. If performance is below expectations, is it the strategy or the implementation which is mainly to blame? The reaction of many businesses to the very competitive and increasingly global business environment of the 1990s has been to work on both. Strategies have typically become more focused and structures less hierarchical.

*Figure 22.1* Strategy and implementation.

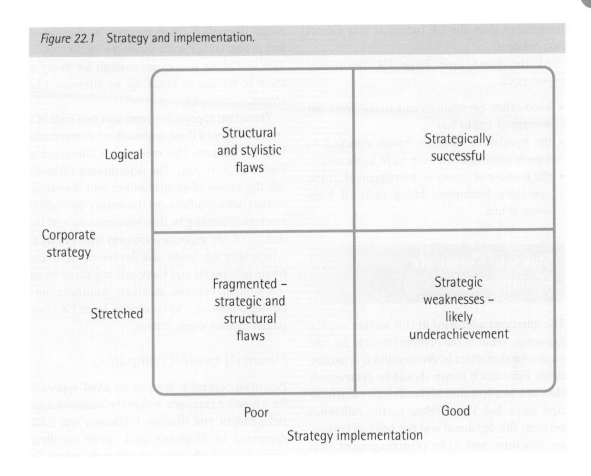

Richter and Owen (1997) show how there has been:

- refocusing – organizations have reduced the number of industries in which they compete, and
- simpler structures – characterized by smaller head offices and fewer layers of management.

In the end we are left to question whether there has been too much reaction and an over aggressive response, partly the result of pressure from institutional investors and the financial markets, which have tended to be intolerant of diversity. Yet the most valuable and respected business in the world, General Electric, remains a very diversified conglomerate. We have tended to assume that diversified conglomerates are

strategically illogical, and yet it could be that many managers have simply been unable to manage them in the 1990s when a radically different approach was required from that which succeeded with diversified conglomerates in the 1980s.

Richter and Owen (at the London School of Economics and Public Science) used primary research and secondary data to track the strategic progress of large UK and German companies between 1986 and 1996. They found that over this decade 75% of British companies became more focused compared with only 50% in Germany. The figure for the USA was even lower. Only 16% of acquisitions (32% for Germany) were in unrelated businesses. Germany experienced more vertical integration than the UK, where it was almost non-existent.

At the same time large UK businesses experienced:

- head-office personnel reductions, from an average of 175 to 100
- the number of business heads reporting to Boards coming down from eight to six and
- the number of layers of management in the operating businesses being reduced from seven to five.

## Styles of Corporate Management

The questions addressed in this section are the following. What is the appropriate role for corporate headquarters in divisionalized organizations? How much power should be centralized? How independent should the divisions and business units be? These relate to the difference between the divisional and the holding company structures and styles of management, and the themes of integration and behavioural processes within the structural framework are explored further.

In relation to these issues Goold and Campbell (1988) have contrasted the views of Sir Hector Laing, ex-chairman of United Biscuits, with those of Lord Hanson. Laing contended that it takes a number of years to build a business, and that during this period corporate headquarters should help the general managers of business units to develop their strategies. Hanson argued that it is more appropriate for head office to remain detached from operations, and instead of involvement to set strict financial targets. All Hanson businesses were reputedly for sale at any time. Both approaches have been shown to work, but with different levels of overall performance and strategic growth patterns. The Hanson approach typified that of

many diversified conglomerates in the 1980s, but it lost favour with investors in the 1990s. This fact alone was cause enough for many of them to refocus or break up, as Minicase 22.2 shows.

These two approaches represent two ends of a spectrum, and a third approach is a compromise between the two. This spectrum is illustrated in Figure 22.2 (p. 774). The determining variables are the extent of centralization and decentralization (which influences the nature and role of strategic planning in the organization) and the nature of key reporting systems (the extent to which they are loose and flexible or tight and financial). Goold and Campbell use three terms – financial control, strategic planning and strategic control – to categorize large UK companies against these criteria.

### Financial control companies

Financial control is seen as an ideal approach for a holding company where the businesses are independent and unrelated. Hanson and BTR, discussed in Minicase 22.2, were excellent examples and advocates of this style, which for many years under the leadership of Lord (Arnold) Weinstock was also preferred by the more focused GEC.

- Strategy creation is heavily decentralized to business unit managers. Within their agreed financial targets they are free to develop and change their competitive and functional strategies.
- Budgets and targets – and their achievement – are critically important control mechanisms.
- The small head office monitors financial returns closely and regularly, intervening when targets are missed – head office is a 'controller'.
- Head office also acts as a corporate investment banker for investment capital.
- Achievement is rewarded, and units are encouraged to put forward and chase ambitious

# Minicase 22.2  Four diversified conglomerates: BTR, Hanson, Tomkins and Williams Holdings

This case tracks the strategic development of four leading acquisitive UK diversified conglomerates. At different times in the 1980s and early 1990s, all four companies were very successful, typically using a 'hit squad' approach by a small team of turnaround specialists who were expert in evaluating recent acquisitions, setting demanding (financial) targets, rewarding success and dismissing managers who could not perform. In the second half of the 1990s, BTR was merged with another conglomerate, Hanson was broken up, and Tomkins and Williams have pursued more focused strategies. In every case two major challenges were:

- the ability to find and fund a suitable acquisition at the appropriate time and stage of corporate development, and then
- finding opportunities to add value.

Here there is evidence of a concentration on mature industries where the right competitive strategy could bring high rewards but where there was only limited growth potential.

## BTR

BTR grew strongly in the 1970s and 1980s under the strategic leadership of Sir Owen Green. By the early 1990s the company was diversified into control systems, polymers (including factories in Taiwan), electrical products (Hawker Siddeley motors as well as Newey and Eyre), construction (Tilcon*, Graham Builders Merchants*, Pilkington Tiles* and aggregate businesses in the USA), transportation (railway equipment), packaging (Rockware Glass), paper technology and consumer products (Dunlop Slazenger* and Pretty Polly lingerie).

Alan Jackson succeeded Sir Owen Green as chief executive in 1991 (Green remained as chairman for some time afterwards) and instituted a strategy of withdrawal from non-manufacturing interests. The companies marked with an asterisk were sold to other parents or to their existing managers. At the same time Jackson made a number of acquisitions, including Varta, the German battery manufacturer and Gencorp, a US company which produces vibration controls. Hawker Siddeley (1991) was the last *major* acquisition by BTR.

Goold *et al.* (1994) examined the parenting style of BTR. They concluded that the company's underlying belief or paradigm was that businesses can benefit from pressure on costs and productivity; focused, mature, businesses which are pushed to increase prices and margins (at the expense of market share and growth) can be made more profitable. BTR's parenting skills were intensive profit planning, the ability to manage a decentralized business with multiple profit centres, low central overheads, and skills in acquiring and turning around acquisitions. This last point includes the ability to introduce the BTR culture into the new business.

BTR's heartland was based on manufacturing businesses, industrial customers, low to moderate technology and capital intensity, relatively stable environments with only limited impact from economic cycles and niche markets. Critics of BTR claimed that the strategy was uncoordinated and based on cost-cutting and price rises during periods of inflation. The prospects for both of these strategies largely disappeared in the 1990s.

Jackson's successor in 1996, Ian Strachan, continued with the strategy that he inherited, declaring that BTR was to be focused on four core activities: automotive components, power drives, control systems and other specialist engineering products. Several remaining businesses were targeted for divestment, but there were to be accompanying acquisitions of related businesses and new joint ventures overseas. Strachan advised institutional shareholders that 'BTR's day as an acquisitive conglomerate is over' and that organic growth around its core strengths was to be a priority. In the past BTR had not invested heavily in organic growth.

At this time BTR still comprised over 1000 business units worldwide. Turnover approached £10 billion, although at the peak of it success revenues had reached £14 billion. The style of corporate management was changed from financial control to strategic control in order to encourage business managers to take a longer-term and more strategic view. Instead of annual profit planning being the key focus, growth priorities for up to five years were sought.

As disposal followed disposal, Jackson, now retired and living in Australia, expressed his belief that BTR was being reduced to too tight a core. Whoever was correct in his belief, the share price continued to fall through 1997 and 1998.

In November 1998 BTR was merged with fellow engineering conglomerate, Siebe, and the new business eventually renamed Invensys. The Chief Executive of Siebe, Allen Yurko, was to be the strategic leader and Strachan his deputy. Based on share distribution, Siebe comprised 55% of Invensys and BTR 45%. There were now five broad and complementary divisions: intelligent automation, controls, power systems, industrial drives and equipment and automotive components. The combined revenues were around £9 billion. In portfolio terms, both BTR and Siebe contributed 'cash cows' but BTR had more of the 'dogs' and Siebe more 'stars'. Some BTR businesses were still for sale.

*BTR (now Invensys)*   http://www.invensys.com

## Hanson

The development of Hanson, essentially a company which pursued a restructuring strategy, is discussed in detail in the full case study at the back of the book. Hanson was based in the UK and USA and led by partners Lord (James) Hanson and Lord (Gordon) White. Over a period of some 20 years Hanson was involved in 35 agreed acquisitions, six hostile take-overs and 15 unsuccessful bids. Following the 41 acquisitions there were 40 business disposals. Hanson also bought sizeable stakes in 22 other companies. On a number of occasions (in particular the acquisitions of SCM and Imperial Group) Hanson raised more money from business disposals than it paid to acquire the companies in the first place, and in each case it was left with a valuable core business – SCM Chemicals and Imperial Tobacco, respectively.

This 'Hansonizing' strategy was based on three essential principles:

- The key objective is to maximize shareholder value.
- Many companies do not do this and are therefore run badly.
- Such companies are good buys because their assets can be made to create more value for shareholders.

James Hanson always argued the strategy could be applied successfully in any industry, and consequently Hanson diversified into a number of unrelated areas including construction, bricks, textiles, animal foods and meat processing, pulp, coal, gold, tobacco and chemicals. Hanson did not always stay in an industry, and instead divested companies and business units when appropriate for its basic strategy.

Typically, businesses in competitive industries, and which required investment, were sold, and mature, slow-growth companies retained. Cyclical businesses were also attractive targets for Hanson. In the early 1990s some 90% of Hanson's profits were from mature industries. Despite the lack of growth potential in these businesses the Hanson restructuring strategies generated a high and consistent growth in group profits. Hanson believed that earnings per share were maximized when business units achieved the highest possible sustainable return on capital employed. Earnings per share could be improved by increasing returns from existing capital or by reducing capital and maintaining earnings. The latter theme encapsulates divestments.

Although it does not always happen, it could be argued that in an organization such as this, which is not primarily concerned with staying in particular industries, business units should be sold when their earnings cannot be increased further and should be replaced by others with greater potential. Shareholders who support such organizations expect the increased returns to be generated quickly, and consequently Hanson was not thought to be interested in companies that could not be improved within three to four years. Although earnings per share could be improved by investing and using debt financing, rather than equity, Hanson was basically risk averse and sought to constrain its gearing. The companies in the group also benefited from low-cost finance and astute tax management, which helped to lower their total costs.

Business units were decentralized and given strict targets to achieve, but all capital investments were carefully scrutinized at board level. Profits from the businesses were returned to the parent, who decided how they would be used and spent. General managers in charge of businesses could not spend over £500 without the approval of James Hanson (in the UK) or Gordon White (in the USA). Within these financial constraints businesses could adapt their competitive and functional strategies as they wished.

For many years Hanson was acknowledged to be a very successful company from which many other organizations could learn some important lessons. Up to the mid-1980s

Hanson consistently outperformed the stock market. However, once the acquisition trail became more difficult, with a series of well-publicized hostile bids failing to result in take-overs, the strategy was questioned. When Lord Hanson's partner, Lord White, died, Hanson himself was over 70 years old and succession became a real issue of concern.

In 1995 it was announced that the American businesses were to be floated off as US Industries, and the remaining activities split into four separate businesses. Existing shareholders would receive stock in each of the new, more focused, companies. The four were:

- Millennium Chemicals (based around SCM and Quantum in America)
- The Energy Group (Peabody Coal and Suburban Propane (US) and Eastern Electricity (UK))
- Imperial Tobacco
- Hanson (based on bricks and aggregates in the UK and USA).

*Hanson* http://www.hanson.com

## Tomkins

This conglomerate grew out of a buckle-manufacturing business based in Walsall, UK; acquired businesses included Smith and Wesson handguns, Hayter lawnmowers, Murray bicycles (in the USA) and a range of different industrial products. The chief executive until 2000, Greg Hutchings, was ex-Hanson.

In 1992 Tomkins acquired Rank Hovis McDougall (the milling and baking business which owns the Bisto, Paxo and Mr Kipling brands), beating off a rival bid from Hanson. Four years later, after successfully absorbing RHM, Tomkins bought the US company Gates Rubber, the world's largest manufacturer of power transmission belts and industrial hoses. RHM cost £93.5 million; Gates was roughly the same. In 1997 Tomkins added a US manufacturer of windscreen wipers (Stant) to bolt on to Gates. At this time Tomkins was building up a cash pile which it used to buy back shares – it was not finding suitable new acquisitions and there were few investment opportunities in the businesses that it owned.

In 1998 Tomkins opted to dispose of its distribution businesses to focus on manufacturing. Tomkins bought a US tyre-valve manufacturer and sold the original buckle company. In the same year it was a loser in the auction for Dalgety Foods, which was bought by the Kerry Group of Ireland. However, Kerry sold Dalgety's Spillers flour mills to Tomkins. This provoked an investigation by the UK competition authorities who demanded that Tomkins sell four of the six Spillers mills that it had bought.

In 1999 Tomkins bought Aquatic, a Texas-based manufacturer of whirlpools, but opted to divest all of its baking and foods businesses to concentrate on automotive and building products. This was completed in summer 2000.

*Tomkins* http://www.tomkins.co.uk

## Williams Holdings

Built by accountants Nigel Rudd (a deal-maker) and Brian McGowan (acknowledged to be good at handling City institutions), Williams grew during the 1980s from an English Midlands base in foundries. McGowan left in 1993; Rudd remained as strategic leader. The acquisition strategy in the 1980s was based largely on good opportunities for restructuring, but Williams quickly realized the value of established brand names and concentrated on businesses where it could exploit its brand management skills.

Through the 1980s and early 1990s the acquisitions included: Fairey Engineering, Rawlplug, Polycell, Crown Berger paints, Smallbone (kitchen units), Amdega (conservatories), Dreamland (electric blankets), Kidde (from Hanson – aerospace and fire extinguishers), Yale (locks) and Valor (locks and heating). Several of these were then sold as Williams chose to focus on three business areas: building products (including DIY), fire protection and security (locks). Other UK fire-equipment companies were added to the portfolio: Angus, Rockwell and a Thorn-EMI subsidiary. These were followed by related fire and locks acquisitions in Italy and the USA, and in 1996 Williams bought Sicli and Siddes, the largest fire-protection company in France. At £175 million, Sicli was its largest purchase for five years.

At this stage in its development Williams claimed to be Britain's first 'focused conglomerate' but some critics argued that focus requires more than the structural 'bundling of a number of businesses into separate divisions'. The fire and security businesses helped to offset the economic cycles of the construction and building industries, and Williams (with 12% of the world market) offered a wider range of fire-protection products than any of its rivals. As fire-regulations were tightened around the world, this industry was enjoying a high growth potential; it had yet to reach the maturity stage.

> *(Tomkins, Hanson, BTR and Williams) . . . all started in the same place; buy what you can, sort it out and move on. Now our aspirations are to build businesses internationally.*
>
> Roger Carr, Chief Executive, Williams, in 1996

In 1997 Williams acquired Chubb Security (alarms and locks) on its second attempt and in 1998 it began to divest its home-improvements businesses, a move that it completed in late 1999. Now it was focused on fire and security. In 2000 the company was split into two: Chubb Security Services and Kidde Fire Protection. Yale was sold to a Swedish company.

*Kidde International*  http://www.kidde.co.uk
*Kidde Safety*  http://www.kiddesafety.com
*Chubb Security Systems*  http://www.chubbsecurity.com

QUESTION: Track the share price movements of these businesses during the 1990s and check their progress against the all-share index. Why exactly did the conglomerate diversification strategy of these businesses lose favour with shareholders?

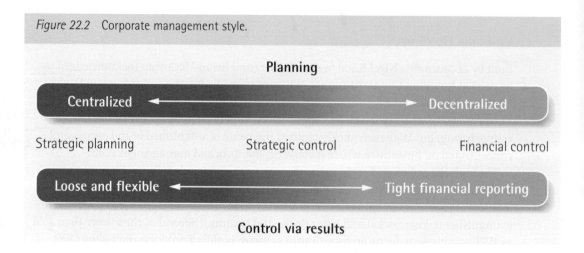

*Figure 22.2*    Corporate management style.

targets. Underperforming managers are likely to be removed.

- The head office adds value by acquiring and improving underperforming businesses; if additional value cannot be added it may well sell off businesses.
- There will, typically, be few interdependencies and links between the businesses.
- Growth is more likely to be by acquisition than organic investment, with many financial control companies taking a short-term view of each business and being reluctant to invest in speculative research and the development of longer-term strategies.

Owen Green, Chief Executive and architect of BTR, had the following philosophy:

1. Never pursue extra sales at the expense of profit margins.
2. Raise prices whenever there is an opportunity.
3. Investment should never exceed the amount written off in depreciation.

The result was high profit margins but a lack of capital investment; growth was mainly by acquisition rather than by investing in the existing businesses. Herein lay the ultimate limitations.

## Strategic planning companies

Strategic planning tends to be adopted in organizations which focus on only a few, and preferably related, core businesses. Examples include Cadbury Schweppes, United Biscuits and BP. Historically it has been the favoured approach for most public-sector organizations.

- Strategic plans are developed jointly by head office and the business units, with head office retaining the final say. Strategic planning is centralized.
- Day-to-day operations only are wholly decentralized.
- Head office sets priorities and co-ordinates strategies throughout the organization, possibly initiating cross-business strategies, and thereby acts as an 'orchestrator'.
- A long-term perspective is realistic, and the search for opportunities for linkages and sharing resources and best practice can be prioritized. This normally requires central control. Individually the businesses would tend to operate more independently; organization-wide synergies may involve sacrifices by individual businesses.
- Goold and Campbell conclude that there are co-ordination problems if this approach is used in truly diversified organizations.

- Budgets are again used for measuring performance.
- The tight central control can become bureaucratic and demotivate managers, who may not feel *ownership* of their strategies.

Other dangers are that thinking may become too focused at the centre, with the potential contributions of divisional managers underutilized; and that the organization may be slow to change in response to competitive pressures. Value can be added successfully if corporate managers stay aware and expert in the core businesses and if the competitive environment allows this style to work.

## Strategic control companies

Financial control and strategic planning are appropriate for particular types of organization, but both styles, while having very positive advantages, also feature drawbacks. The strategic control style is an attempt to obtain the major benefits of the other two styles for organizations that are clearly diversified but with linkages and interdependencies. Value is added by balancing strategic and financial controls.

- Strategy creation involves decentralization to the business units, although head office still controls the overall *corporate* strategy.
- The role of head office is to review divisional and business plans, and approve strategic objectives and financial targets, accepting that they may need to be changed in a competitive environment. Performing a 'coaching' role, head office encourages businesses to achieve their potential by active involvement and by fostering the spreading of learning and good practice through the organization.
- Strategy creation and budgetary control can be separated, allowing for more creative performance measurement. Sometimes competitive pressures and misjudgements mean strategies have to be changed, and hoped-for

financial targets may be missed. A strategic control style can recognize this and deal with the implications.
- Head office does, however, monitor and control financial performance and success against strategic milestones and objectives.

Although decentralization is a feature, head office still requires considerable detail about the various businesses if it is to ensure that the synergy potential is achieved and very short-term thinking is avoided. Political activity will be prevalent as individual businesses compete with each other for scarce corporate resources.

It was mentioned earlier that GEC, under Lord Weinstock – who was in charge for 32 years – adopted a financial control style. When he retired (in 1996) and was replaced by Lord (George) Simpson the style was quickly changed to strategic control. Simpson inherited a GEC that was diversified and financially sound, but it was risk averse and experiencing relatively low growth. It was also in possession of a legendary cash mountain of £2.5 billion. Simpson created a new agenda for growth. With divestments and acquisitions the portfolio was changed. The style also changed. There was to be more focus on customers and people and less on cost control. There was greater decentralization, accompanied by robust reporting systems. It is not unusual to see changes of strategy, structure and style accompanying a change of leadership, especially if a company is in difficulty or the predecessor has been in place for a long time.

Two leading organizations that utilized the strategic control style – ICI and Courtaulds – both concluded that they were overdiversified. This belief was strongly reinforced by institutional investor pressure. The attitude of the stock market and their shareholders meant that their share prices were underperforming against the 'index', the average of the UK's largest companies. There were numerous businesses in each organization, although some were clearly interlinked. At the same time these 'clusters' had little in common and featured different strategic needs and cultures. Because of these differences, and the inevitable complexity, corporate headquarters could not add value with a single entity. Both companies split into two distinct parts to enable a stronger focus on core competencies and strategic capabilities. Minicase 22.1 explained the ICI story. Minicase 22.3 discusses Courtaulds, which has now been completely absorbed by other companies, despite the split.

## Levels of success

Goold and Campbell studied 16 large UK compa- nies, including those given as examples above, and concluded that each style has both advantages and disadvantages and that no one style is outstandingly the most successful.

*Strategic planning companies* proved to be consistently profitable during the 1980s, mainly through organic growth. Head-office corporate staff tended to be a quite large group and differences of opinion with general managers sometimes caused frustration within the divisions and business units. *Financial control companies* exhibited the best financial performance. In a number of cases, particularly BTR and Hanson, this resulted from acquisition and divestment rather than organic growth. Short-

---

## Minicase 22.3  Courtaulds

Begun in 1849, Courtaulds became one of the UK's most prominent and profitable manufacturers. By 1990 it was based on textiles and chemicals, where it was the third largest UK manufacturer of artificial fibres. The industry links were relatively loose as the two were at different stages of the same supply chain. In that year these two businesses became separate companies.

In February 1998 Courtaulds Chemicals announced that it was planning to split again, this time into three separate businesses: polymers (the smallest and one which it expected would be bought by a competitor), fibres (which was struggling to deliver profits in a cost-driven global industry and was holding back the other activities, despite its exciting new Tencel product), and coatings and sealants. However, in April 1998 Akzo Nobel (coatings) successfully bid for the whole business.

In February 2000 the American conglomerate Sara Lee made a hostile bid for Courtaulds Textiles. The valuation was just one-third of the company's value two years earlier. Sara Lee was interested in Courtaulds' hosiery brands – Gossard, Berlei and Aristoc – and its supply agreements with Marks and Spencer (who buy 40% of its turnover). Sara Lee already owned Playtex and Pretty Polly. It was also diversified into foods and coffee, sun-tan lotions and Kiwi shoe-care products. The acquisition went through.

QUESTION: Given the apparent fragmentation of the businesses in 1990, do you think that Courtaulds had a 'heartland'?

*Courtaulds*  http://www.courtaulds-textiles.com

term financial targets were felt to reduce the willingness of general managers to take risks. There were few trade-offs whereby short-term financial targets were sacrificed for long-term growth. A general manager, for example, might consider a programme of variety reduction and product rationalization with a view to developing a more consistent and effective portfolio. In the short term this would result in reduced revenue and profits before new orders and products improved overall profitability. This temporary fall might be unacceptable in the face of short-term financial targets. *Strategic control companies* also performed satisfactorily but experienced difficulties in establishing the appropriate mix of strategic and financial targets for general managers. Financial targets, being the more specific and measurable ones, were generally given priority.

Goold and Campbell concluded that while the style of management adopted within the structure determines the strategic changes that take place, the overall corporate strategy of the company very much influences the choice of style. Large diverse organizations, for example, will find it difficult to adopt a strategic planning approach. Equally, where the environment is turbulent and competitive, increasing the need for adaptive strategic change, the financial planning approach is less appropriate. Not unexpectedly, Hanson's main acquisitions were of companies in mature, slow-growth sectors.

While companies may appreciate that there is a mismatch between their corporate strategy and style, changing the style can be difficult. Moreover, many organizations will not be able to implement a new style as effectively as the one that they are used to.

Goold *et al.* (1993) revisited the organizations and their research five years later, partly stimulated by the change in fortunes in some of the companies involved. This review reinforced the conclusion that financial control is ideally suited to a group of autonomous businesses in a conglomerate, but it is less suitable for a portfolio of core businesses or ones seeking to compete globally. In 1988 Goold and Campbell had argued that the adoption of a hands-off, financial control style by GEC and other electronics companies in the UK had hindered their development as globally competitive businesses. Global development demands synergy between a number of national businesses. BTR and Hanson had already begun to focus more on selected core businesses, and their relative performance was deteriorating.

Strategic planning continued to add value as long as corporate managers had close knowledge and experience of their core businesses. Where their portfolio was arguably too diverse – although not so diverse that they could be classified as diversified conglomerates – strategic control companies were experiencing difficulties. The researchers poured scorn on the idea that a decentralized structure, supported by a modern budgeting and planning system, would enable a competent management team to add value to almost any new business. Strategic control can only work with an effective mix of tight financial control and devolved authority to instigate emergent strategic changes; to achieve this successfully, head offices again need to appreciate the detail of competitive strategies in the subsidiaries.

Appreciating the specific problems and opportunities faced by subsidiary businesses is particularly important for establishing fair reward systems.

Reward systems are likely to be based on specific performance targets, but these could relate to growth in revenue, absolute profits or profitability ratios. Stonich (1982) has suggested that business units might be categorized as having high, medium or low growth potential. Four factors could be used in evaluating their relative performances: return on assets; cash flow; strategic development programmes; and increases in market share. The relative weighting attributed to each of these four factors would be changed to reflect their specific objectives and whether they were of high, medium or low-growth potential. Return on assets and cash flow would be critical for low growth business units, and market share and strategic development programmes most important for those with high growth potential. The factors would be weighted equally for medium growth. This approach would be particularly relevant where general managers were changed around to reflect their particular styles of management and the current requirements of the business unit.

One question left unanswered concerns the extent to which the conclusions of Goold and Campbell are a result of British management strengths, weaknesses and preferences. Certain Japanese companies appear to grow organically at impressive rates while maintaining strict financial controls and directing corporate strategic change from the centre. This tendency, however, is affected by legislation which restricts the ability of Japanese companies to grow by acquisition and merger. Without this control Japanese firms may have followed different strategies.

Minicase 22.4 shows how a particular approach to style, championed by an exceptionally charismatic strategic leader, has allowed General Electric of the US (GE) to succeed as a diversified conglomerate. GE's strategy concentrates on segment leadership and growth, which makes it very different from the approach and philosophy of conglomerates such as Hanson and BTR. Hence, in GE there is a style that works for a contemporary diversified conglomerate. In Hanson and BTR there was a style that became increasingly inappropriate for the global environment emerging in the 1990s.

The next section endeavours to pull together the lessons from this and other research and the cases quoted herein.

## Diversification or Focus: A Key Corporate Dilemma

It is now appropriate to look in greater detail at corporate strategic trends in the UK. The emphasis seems to be on 'divest unrelated activities; acquire related ones'. Restructuring to take out costs has been emphasized, but many organizations have simply downsized; they have not *rightsized* to create an organization with the necessary competencies and motivation to stimulate renewal and new growth. In addition, a more recent trend has been share buy-backs, as company after company changes its gearing to make it less vulnerable to shareholder pressure. Really, this is an admission that they cannot find desirable growth opportunities where any accumulated cash might be deployed and used for long-term growth and effectiveness.

As seen in Chapter 15, acquisition and diversification strategies are frequently linked together. Acquisitions (agreed corporate purchases), take-overs (hostile buys) and mergers (the joining of two organizations) fuel organizational growth and, quite often, the necessary capital is available from the City if the organization does not have sufficient reserves. With such strategies, organizations are likely to be able to grow much more quickly than by investing in organic growth to build existing activities and businesses. While organic growth is always going to be important, there is often a dearth of inspirational ideas.

The downside of acquisitions is that often two (or even more) cultures need to be integrated. Growth in size happens, but it may not be accompanied by increased profitability and the synergy required to generate real growth. There is also a paradox of timing and opportunity. An acquisition will use up any spare cash, managerial expertise and managerial time – all scarce resources. Until the businesses have been integrated, resources are stretched and the

# Minicase 22.4 General Electric

America's General Electric (GE), as already explained (Minicase 21.5), is the world's most admired and valuable company (it is worth $500 billion) and yet it remains a very diversified conglomerate. The company is truly global – it sells more in Europe than British Aerospace, one of the UK's leading manufacturers and a direct competitor. GE, under chief executive Jack Welch, has proved that a business does not have to be 'focused on one or two related activities' to be successful and profitable. Welch has:

- changed the culture
- 'turned people on' and
- delivered results through carefully crafted incentives.

Unlike the companies featured in Minicase 22.2, GE has sought to gain 'maximum' value from its disparate activities by investing to provide a platform for growth. GE wants to be number one or number two in every market segment in which it competes. It seeks to exploit the breadth and diversity of its portfolio to find new ways for adding value and new customers.

> *Being a conglomerate makes no sense unless you can leverage the size and diversity of the company and spread learning and best practices across the company.*
>
> Larry Johnston, GE Executive

The strength of GE's culture is built on its 'social architecture' and its operating systems. Its social architecture exploits the potential of individuals by removing barriers to the transfer of intellectual capital between businesses and countries. 'GE is an ideas laboratory not a conglomerate'. The operating systems aim to turn ideas into company-wide initiatives which can be run by the 'best people' through appropriate incentives and rewards. Managers freely help colleagues in other businesses with their marketing, both physically and with advice. Promotion is normally given to those managers who can prove they are 'boundary-less'.

Much of this is facilitated through Management Councils, comprising people from different businesses and divisions, who meet quarterly. Every member of a council must bring to every meeting at least one idea from which other managers could learn something valuable or useful. One notable example was the idea of 'reverse mentoring' to deal with the demands of e-commerce. Older managers were encouraged to use younger and more aware managers as their mentors, even though they might be lower in the current hierarchy.

QUESTIONS: Just how different is the GE approach from that adopted by BTR and Hanson? Where does GE fit in our framework of corporate management styles?

*General Electric* http://www.ge.com

organization would find it difficult to deal with a further acquisition. Do the best opportunities occur when the organization is ideally prepared or ill prepared?

Diversification implies new products, services and markets. The extent of the differences implies that the diversification is either related in some way, or unrelated. Where new technologies, new skills, new resources, new distribution channels and new markets are all implied, the learning challenge is considerable, together with the inherent uncertainty. However, related diversification, perhaps by the acquisition of an existing competitor, can provoke interest from the competition authorities in individual countries or the European Commission, which can result in its being stopped. Whatever the strategy, in the end its relative success or failure depends upon the ability of the managers involved to generate greater returns from the assets, possibly implying restructuring and some asset sales, and certainly requiring that any anticipated synergy is delivered. This in turn demands that too high a price is not paid for the acquisition in the first place.

At different times, different strategies and approaches enjoy greater or lesser favour. Strategies that are popular today may be unfashionable next year; when this happens those pursuing unfashionable strategies are subjected to considerable scrutiny from the media and from analysts.

The systematic cross-border acquisitions of Rowntree and Perrier by Nestlé have contributed to the growth of a successful international foods business. There are some links between the products, with opportunities for sharing and learning. This strategic approach continues to be fashionable. More recently, for example, the Zurich Group (Swiss financial services) has merged with BAT (originally British American Tobacco, which had already diversified into insurance and other financial services). The tobacco interests were quickly divested. Similarly, Reed Elsevier (joint UK and Netherlands) has merged with the Dutch company Wolters Kluwer to create the world's largest scientific and professional publishing business. Other similar examples are:

- Glaxo Wellcome's merger with SmithKline Beecham
- the acquisition of Mannesmann by Vodafone – unusual as it is rare for German companies to be acquired by non-German predators.

In contrast, in the mid-late 1990s, conglomerate diversification – building a corporation with unrelated acquisitions – became much less fashionable than it was a decade ago. There are strong arguments in favour of this change of popularity but, nevertheless, it can still be a successful strategy if it is supported with appropriate implementation skills, and it may well become more fashionable again in the future.

As seen earlier, the outstanding example of a successful diversified conglomerate in recent years is General Electric. On the whole, however, GE is not acquisitive on a regular basis; there are frequent bolt-on acquisitions and very occasional major purchases which imply further diversification. Its success comes largely from its ability to foster sharing and learning among its disparate businesses and, most significantly, leverage its existing resources to create new forms of competitive advantage.

*Our intellectual capital is not US-based . . . we aim to get the best ideas from everywhere. Each team puts up its best ideas and processes – constantly. That raises the bar. Our culture is designed around making a hero out of those who translate ideas from one place to another, who help somebody else. They get an award, they get praised and promoted.*

(Jack Welch, Chief Executive, GE)

This philosophy is in stark contrast to the finance-driven holding company style of Hanson and BTR (in the past), an approach which saw each business as a very independent activity and shunned major investment. The GE philosophy has also been seen to be successful at other diversified American conglomerates. Another example is United Technologies, which comprises Otis, Carrier and Sikorski – respectively, the world leaders for elevators, air conditioners and helicopters – Pratt and Whitney (jet engines), aerospace and automotive components. Here again, there is emphasis on segment leadership.

*If one of the companies needs some new ideas, they should go and grab them from wherever is appropriate.*

(George David, President and CEO, United Technologies)

One diversified UK conglomerate, Wassall, adopted a different approach. In 1994 Wassall bought the US company General Cable for £150 million. This company manufactured copper wire and cable products which were not essential for Wassall's long-term product interests. After successfully turning around an underperforming business, Wassall floated off General Cable as an independent company worth £340 million. Wassall then chose to return the original purchase price directly to its shareholders and retain just £190 million for further acquisitions with which it hoped to repeat the approach. With this strategy Wassall aimed not to become dependent on finding ever-larger companies that it could buy to turn around. Wassall was, in reality, acting as a venture capitalist, so it seems hardly surprising that it was acquired by US venture capitalists in 2000.

Focus, then, is unquestionably fashionable. Caulkin (1996) argues that if you have relatively poor management, focus makes absolute sense as focused companies are easier to manage. Unfortunately focus, per se, is unlikely to create new value. The dilemma with diversification lies in establishing clearly whether it is the corporate logic of the diversification strategy

itself which is in question, or the inability of many companies to add value to a disparate range of activities and sustain real growth in some way. Sadtler *et al.* (1997) defend the case for a clear focus, built around a defensible core of related activities, arguing that focus is now a more popular corporate strategy for a number of important reasons:

- It allows greater control. Diversified conglomerates must decentralize to allow flexibility and this can imply a trade-off with central control unless the organization can truly share information and learn.
- Divesting unrelated businesses can provide the finance necessary to strengthen the core.
- It often builds shareholder confidence, supporting the share price and making the organization less vulnerable to take-over.
- In increasingly competitive markets and industries poor performance is harder to hide. Focus can ensure that the weakest companies are divested and stronger businesses not held back because of the need to cross-subsidise.

For Sadtler the activity core is built around similar critical success factors (what the businesses have to be good at) and similar improvement opportunities (what they are going to have to do in the future). A corporate centre must be able to add value to every constituent business; every business in the portfolio should add value by contributing to the success of the whole organization.

Detailed criteria can be readily and sensibly established to justify what should and what should not be in the core. The factors embrace financial performance over a number of years, the company's stated mission, the relatedness of tasks and technologies, customer requirements and the opportunities for internal sharing and trading. These points are taken up later.

From their objective analysis based on these criteria, Sadtler *et al.* produced a list of American organizations which they believed were candidates for breaking up. Featured prominently on the list were:

- Ford and General Motors, which as shown in Minicase 16.3 have adopted different growth strategies in recent years
- PepsiCo, which has divested its fast-food restaurants to concentrate on snack foods and soft drinks
- Exxon, Amoco and Chevron, competitors in the global oil industry, which has been characterized by horizontal integration and consolidation
- Berkshire Hathaway, the investment company run by Warren Buffett which invests long term in other businesses. In recent years its performance has deteriorated but its shareholders remain very loyal and supportive.

In contrast, strategic leaders who have grown successful diversified businesses continue to disagree. Harold Geneen (1997), who died in 1997, is often credited as the founder of truly diversified conglomerates. Geneen's ITT at one time included telecommunications, hotels, baking, cosmetics and lightbulbs, book publishing and Avis Rent-a-Car. ITT has been comprehensively broken up – although Geneen's tight financial control style worked, when he retired there was no natural succession. However, Geneen continued to claim:

*To succeed in business it is essential to take risks. But they must be smart risks – researched, understood, survivable. The conglomerate is a good vehicle for identifying and exploiting them . . . but . . . running a conglomerate requires working harder than most people want to work and taking more risks than most people want to take.*

Sir Owen Green (1994), ex-BTR, has defended conglomerates even more strongly:

*As soon as things go wrong, companies start talking about focus. Focus is the crutch of mediocre management . . . if you are trained in the techniques of management . . . you should be able to apply them across a range of companies. Diversified companies possess both defensive qualities in a recession and a springboard for new ventures in more expansive times.*

This argument is further borne out by the success of the US conglomerate, Textron, which has outperformed the Wall Street stock index by 50% during the 1990s. Textron manufactures light aircraft (Cessna), helicopters (Bell), machine tools, automotive components, lawnmowers, watch straps and Shaeffer pens, as well as owning a consumer finance business. The company argues that its balanced diversity (not being overdependent on any one product) allows it consistently to improve its overall earnings through economic cycles. This case has always been used as an argument to defend diversity, while recognizing that with the wrong approach it can become dangerously short-termist. To succeed it needs a particular management style.

Summarizing this section of the chapter, most strategies can be made to work effectively and efficiently, but the ultimate success of any strategy lies in its implementation. Decisions concerning the implementation issues of structure and management style, as well as those affecting the competitiveness of each product or service in the portfolio, provide additional dilemmas which need to be investigated further.

It should not be forgotten that concentrating the debate on this manifestation of corporate strategy can draw attention away from the real strategic issue, which is creating new values. With Hanson and BTR, once businesses had been turned around and profitability restored, little new value was being added, and so there was an argument that the individual businesses might be better off on their own or with a new parent. Is this an argument for focus or for a different style of corporate management? Reinforcing earlier points, Hamel and Prahalad (1994) contend that today there is too much strategic convergence. High-performance organizations reinvent industries and regenerate core strategies. They innovate around the theme of positioning.

> If the past couple of years have taught anything about corporate structure, it is that broad generalizations about integration versus specialization, or conglomeration versus focus, are worthless. Everything depends on the pressures affecting individual industries: and within them, the different circumstances of the companies themselves.
>
> *Jackson, T (1995) Giant bows to a colossal pressure, Financial Times, 22 September*

## Managing the Corporate Portfolio

Porter (1987) argues that corporate strategy is that which makes the corporate whole add up to more than the sum of its parts, but further contends that the corporate strategies of too many companies dissipate rather than create shareholder value. He comments:

*Moving from competitive strategy to corporate strategy is the business equivalent of passing through the Bermuda Triangle. The failure of corporate strategy reflects the fact that most diversified companies have failed to think in terms of how they really add value.*

Porter's arguments are as follows. Corporate strategy involves two key questions or issues. First, what businesses should the company choose to compete in. Secondly, how strategically distinct businesses should be managed at the corporate level.

When the debate on corporate strategy opened in Part Four of this book, synergy was held out as the justification for strategic changes, especially if they involved diversification. The ideas behind synergy are defensible, but synergy *potential* alone cannot justify change. Implementation matters and, being realistic, synergy is frequently based on intangibles and possibilities rather than definites. When we look back on acquisitions that fail to deliver the promised synergies, we can never be sure how much the problem was the strategic logic and how much was implementation. For these reasons, portfolio management, backed by the analytical techniques discussed in Chapter 11, was attractive when it was developed by management consultants.

### Portfolio management

The basic premise of portfolio management is that competition occurs at the business level and this is where competitive advantages are developed. Businesses should compete for centralized corporate investment resources, and they should be divested if there are no further opportunities for developing new values. To facilitate this, a cost-effective organization structure should enable cross-fertilization between the businesses while maintaining overall control. The role of the corporate headquarters was to seek and acquire attractive (potentially highly profitable) businesses, fit them in to the organization, assess their requirements and allocate strategic resources according to their position in the relevant matrix. Of course, in reality, many low-performing businesses were retained, diluting the earnings potential and, as a consequence, shareholders sometimes became sceptical. Their belief was that they could diversify their own portfolio of investments as a hedge against risk – they did not need the businesses to do this on their behalf.

In addition:

- 'undervalued' companies were not always easily acquired – they were simply not available

- all too often excessive premiums were paid when businesses were acquired
- professional management and capital resources alone do not build value and yield competitive advantage
- businesses are often interdependent for all sorts of reasons and therefore strategies cannot be 'ring-fenced' and set in isolation
- some businesses (and their managers) are defeated by the complexity and diversity of the portfolio.

However, one variant of portfolio management, restructuring, does have its logic and attraction.

## Restructuring

Restructuring requires the identification of industries and companies with the potential for restructuring and transformation with new technologies, new people and/or consolidation. There is no need for them to be related to the existing businesses in the portfolio. The new parent intervenes to turn around the business: first, by cost cutting and increased efficiency, and secondly, by adding new values to build a stronger competitive base and position. Once there are no further opportunities to add value the business should be sold to raise money for further acquisitions. Restructuring is not about 'hoarding businesses to build an empire' and never divesting anything which, clearly, some strategic leaders have been prone to do.

Clear elements of restructuring can be seen in the Hanson approach. Certainly, efficiencies were increased as businesses were slimmed down, and businesses were always for sale at the right price. However, Hanson did not invest substantially to build new competitive advantages.

Restructuring works well when the strategic leadership can spot and acquire undervalued companies and then turn them around with sound management skills, even though they might be in unfamiliar industries. In a sense,

there is an underlying, belief that good managers can manage anything, and to a degree there is some truth in this assertion. The issue is whether they manage the renewal as well as the consolidation. The appropriate structure and style of corporate management are clearly critical. Naturally, if suitable undervalued businesses cannot be found – which is typically the case when a country's economy has been tightened and weak competitors have already disappeared as closures or acquisitions – restructuring has no basis.

## Sharing activities and transferring skills

Porter's three tests for a successful acquisition were explained in Chapter 15. He argues that they are most likely to be met where there is some interrelationship between the existing and new businesses. The basis for this might be tangible or intangible and therefore it is easy to be deluded into thinking that there are similarities when in reality there are differences. Minicase 22.5 looks at this issue in relation to the recent acquisitions of the UK's three leading roadside-assistance businesses: the AA, RAC and Green Flag.

Interrelationships are defined as 'connections among distinct businesses that lead to competitive advantage from being in both'. Hanson found a connection in low-cost capital and astute tax-avoidance strategies, but it would be more typical to see them in marketing or technology. The search for these synergies begins with an analysis of the value chains and the objective is to find opportunities for lowering costs and creating or enhancing differentiation. Activities, know-how, customers, distributors and competitors can all be shared. The benefits must outweigh the costs involved, for while there are always opportunities to share they may not lead to any competitive advantage. The outcome of sharing can be clearly tangible (such as better capacity utilization) or more

# Minicase 22.5 The AA, RAC and Green Flag – Changes of Ownership

These three organizations dominate the roadside-assistance industry in the UK. In 1999 they had the following numbers of members:

AA            9.4 million
RAC           5.5 million
Green Flag     2.3 million.

In 1998 and 1999 they all experienced a change of ownership. Would their new parents be able to share resources or transfer skills to improve their performance?

The first to be acquired was Green Flag, once known as National Breakdown. Unlike the AA and RAC, which employ their own staff and repair fleets, Green Flag is really a central marketing agency for local, independent roadside-assistance specialists. Along with Capital Logistics (an airport coach business) Green Flag was already owned by National Parking Corporation, known as NCP, which runs 500 town and city car parks in the UK. Recently, NCP had been struggling to find good new sites through which to expand. NCP was bought by the American company Cendant in 1998. Through a series of acquisitions Cendant had grown into the world's largest provider of consumer services, embracing hotels (Ramada and Howard Johnson), car rental (Avis) and real-estate agencies. Its strategic logic was to 'provide its marketing machinery with new products to sell to its existing customers'.

In 1998 Cendant was also believed to be a possible bidder for the RAC – the Royal Automobile Club. At the time the RAC was 'owned' by the existing members of the RAC. A bid was prevented by government intervention, on the grounds that prices would probably rise and quality and innovation reduce if the industry was dominated by just two competitors. In the end the RAC was sold to Lex Service, a group focused on vehicle distribution and contract hire. Lex is a decentralized service operation. Its business 'units' are relatively small and operate in local markets with considerable autonomy. The parent provides central services and systems. Some years previously Lex had believed that this style of management lent itself to hotels and acquired eight up-market hotels, four in the UK and four in the USA. Lex found it difficult to acquire additional suitable properties for its portfolio, failed to reach what it believed was critical mass, and systematically divested every property. Again, Lex was looking for opportunities in consumer service, businesses.

By 1999 the AA (the Automobile Association) had divested its previous retailing and travel businesses but it still provided insurance services. Like other organizations such as Kwik Fit and Virgin, the AA was simply exploiting its brand and its customer database. The AA does not underwrite insurance, it merely sells policies. Other specialist insurers are the real providers of the actual insurance. The business was acquired by Centrica, the trading arm of British Gas. Centrica sells gas to 15 million customers, and installs and maintains central-heating systems. Centrica also offers a Goldfish credit card and markets insurance. Centrica believed that it was widening its product offering for its huge customer database and could exploit shared support services, especially centralized call centres and billing systems.

QUESTION: Which of these three new parents – Cendant, Lex and Centrica – has the best opportunity for sharing resources and transferring skills to a roadside-assistance business?

*AA (Automobile Association)*    http://www.theaa.co.uk
*Green Flag*    http://www.greenflag.co.uk
*RAC (Royal Automobile Club)*    http://www.rac.co.uk

intangible where it comes through learning and intelligence.

There is invariably a difficult balancing act involved. A shared salesforce is often a possibility, for example. Where this happens, higher calibre people can sometimes be recruited as there are more promotion prospects, buyers can be more easily accessed as more products are being sold at any one time, and less time is spent travelling between calls. However, different selling skills may be required for different products – some are sold on price, others on performance differences – and the attention given to certain ones may be inadequate.

The greatest returns should normally be found where activities are actually shared, but where this is not feasible, transferring skills can also be beneficial. The thinking here begins with a clear appreciation of strategic capabilities and the search for 'related' industries in which these skills and capabilities could be usefully applied – again for savings or differentiation. The businesses must be sufficiently similar that sharing expertise is meaningful, and the potential advantage will always be greater if the capabilities involved are fresh to the new industry.

Where activities are to be shared and/or skills transferred, the corporate structure must be one that encourages it to happen and actively

encourages managers to search out for opportunities. Many are actually structured in ways that erect barriers to sharing.

Finally, one key challenge in organizations that are heavily diversified and decentralized is to ensure that there is a shared corporate identity, which goes beyond the structural framework and comes down to the style of leadership and management. Porter concludes that diversification, decentralization and sharing can be complementary, although they may appear contradictory. They simply demand a sophisticated approach to the management of diversity.

## Corporate Parenting

Goold *et al.* (1994) reinforce Porter's arguments when they contend that acquisitions can be justified where the corporation can add value to the business, generating either synergy or valuable emergent properties. Any business must add value to its parent corporation; in turn, the corporation must add value to the subsidiary. The company is better off with its existing parent than it would be with another parent or on its own. Parenting skills, therefore, relate to the ability of a head office and strategic leadership to manage a portfolio of businesses efficiently and effectively and to change the portfolio as and when it is necessary. It is quite conceivable for head offices to destroy value if a subsidiary simply does not fit with the rest of the portfolio and is consequently held back.

Parenting skills vary between countries and cultures. In Japan, for example, the most successful companies are skilled at:

- securing and sustaining access to government, power and influence
- accessing investment capital, and
- retaining skilled managers.

Much of this is facilitated by the *keiretsu*, families of companies interlinked by share ownership and characterized by intertrading, regular meetings of senior executives and sometimes geographical proximity in a single 'corporate village'. Interestingly, and significantly, these companies are interwoven but there are no corporate headquarters.

Figure 22.3 builds on the arguments of Goold *et al.* and draws these points together. On one axis is strategic logic, the link between products, services, competencies and key success factors across the corporate portfolio. On the other axis

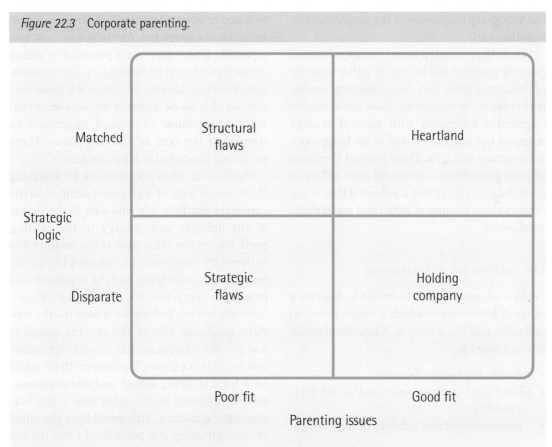

*Figure 22.3*   Corporate parenting.

**Strategic logic** – Link between products, services, competencies and key success factors across the portfolio

**Parenting issues** – The fit between the needs of individual businesses and the capabilities of the parent

are the parenting issues, the fit between the needs of individual businesses and the corresponding capabilities of the parent organization. Where they fit together well, there is a *'heartland'* of related businesses, which is explained below. Where there is no natural synergy between the businesses, the organization can be successful to some degree if the parent company uses a *holding company* structure. This implies strong individual companies that could survive elsewhere, but which are managed in a 'hands-off' way. In this respect it is interesting that both Lord Hanson and Lord Weinstock had a reputation for rarely visiting the subsidiary businesses in the conglomerates that they ran.

Where the parenting issues are not addressed properly evidence will be seen of either strategic or structural flaws and the consequent under-performance. Here, *strategic flaws* again implies fragmented businesses with no real synergy potential but this time linked to an inappropriate structure and style. There is a real likelihood of poor performance. *Structural flaws* reflects a potential for synergy but a potential that is not being realized because of structural and stylistic weaknesses.

## The notion of a 'heartland'

Goold *et al.* use the term *heartland* to describe a range of businesses to which a corporation can add value and not destroy it. A heartland might be constituted by:

- common key success factors
- related core competencies and/or strategic capabilities
- a common or related industry or technology.

The assumption being made is that any individual business within the heartland should be able to achieve levels of success that it would not be able to achieve as an independent business or with another parent. At the same time,

the parent organization should benefit both financially and strategically – in other words, other businesses in the portfolio benefit from the presence of the 'one under the spotlight'. This implies a 'win–win' situation, whereas it can easily be a 'win–lose' or even a 'lose–lose' where the fit is so poor that there is a real resource distraction.

The relative success of conglomerate diversification is, therefore, largely an issue of strategy implementation, specifically the parenting skills of the acquirer, and the ability to add value for both the subsidiary and the parent. The basic argument is that the corporate portfolio should be based around a heartland of businesses that are in some way related. Any which are not, and especially where they are a potential or actual distraction, should be divested. As an organization divests in this way to refocus it is quite normal for this to be followed by, or concurrent with, acquisitions of related businesses to strengthen the core of the new focus. These points are illustrated in Minicase 22.6.

Figure 22.4 offers a framework for assessing the strategic logic of a proposed addition to the corporate portfolio. On one axis is the extent of the linkages and synergy in the existing portfolio; on the other axis is the relationship between the competencies required to run the new business effectively and the organization's existing competencies and capabilities. Logically, we are looking for a match – the top-right quadrant. Where the existing match is low but the newcomer has similar competencies to certain existing businesses, there could be a logic in going ahead and divesting non-related activities at the same time – the bottom-right quadrant. This could have the effect of strengthening the portfolio. In the top-left quadrant there is the potential for an unrelated business to dilute value and synergy. An unrelated business added to a non-synergistic portfolio would merely enhance the strategic problems.

# Minicase 22.6 BBA and Smith's Industries – Developing New 'Heartlands'

In 1993 Roberto Quarta, an Italian–American, was appointed as the new chief executive of BBA. BBA stands for British Belting and Asbestos, which helps to explain the company's origins. By the early 1990s BBA was an engineering business which manufactured a wide range of industrial belting products and vehicle components, especially friction products for brake pads.

Quarta stated his intention to transform BBA into a 'service-based business'. Acquisitions and divestments have allowed eight different divisions to be reduced to two business areas – aerospace engineering and services, and materials technology – both of which have growth potential.

BBA has disposed of its fire protection, automotive components, electrical components and industrial rubber products. It has acquired aerospace interests in aircraft refuelling, engine overhaul and pilot training. It also manufactures high-technology textiles, such as non-wovens for hygiene and industrial uses. It has money remaining from its disposals for further bolt-on acquisitions.

*BBA*   http://www.bbagroup.com

Smith's Industries owns an 'apparently widespread portfolio of engineering businesses' but argues that there is a related heartland. The Stock Exchange categorizes Smith's as an aerospace business, but it comprises:

- aerospace components
- telecommunications products
- flexible hoses for vacuum cleaners
- medical products
- electrical instruments for cars.

Structurally, there are three divisions:

- aerospace – civil, military and after-sales service
- medical – equipment and consumables
- industrial.

The chief executive, Keith Butler-Wheelhouse, was recruited from Saab and he argues the company is about 'clever engineering'. Between 1996 and summer 2000, under his leadership, there were 26 acquisitions, mainly bolt-on related businesses. The company has delivered 'above average returns and profit growth from some unpromising sectors' and its share price performance has been better than most engineering companies.

Butler-Wheelhouse argues that Smith's is:

- focused on niche markets and relatively small businesses
- spread across eight distinct markets such that no single business can make or break the whole organization
- able to generate a cash flow which can fund both organic growth and further acquisitions.

*Smiths Industries plc*   http://www.smiths-industries.com

QUESTIONS: How would you summarize the 'heartlands' of BBA and Smith's Industries? If Smith's Industries does acquire Tube Investments (see Minicase 21.2) do you think that this will strengthen or compromise Smith's 'heartland'?

Figure 22.4   Changing the corporate portfolio.

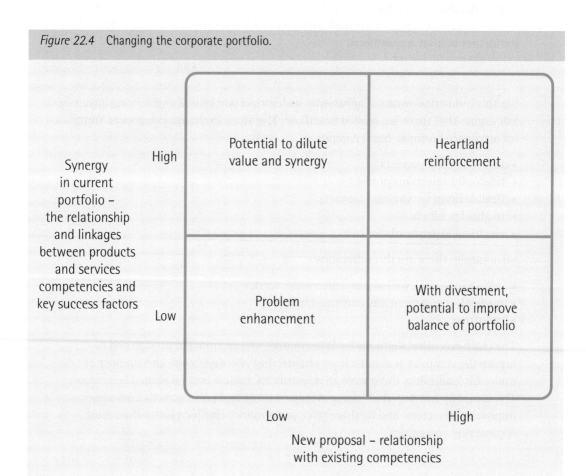

## Determining the heartland

The issues concern:

- first, whether the parent is able to provide – and is actually providing – the services and support the individual businesses need, and
- secondly, whether the businesses have the people and competencies to fulfil the expectations of the parent.

Goold *et al.* offer the following framework as a starting point for assessing the existence of, or potential for, a heartland.

1. Mental maps (or philosophies) of the parent, incorporating issues of culture and values and broad policies for dealing with events and opportunities.
2. Issues of structure, systems and processes – incorporating the style of corporate management. This would include: procedures for appointing, promoting and rewarding people; the relative significance of budgeting and financial reporting; strategic planning systems; and capital allocation procedures.
3. Central services and resources – what is provided centrally and what is devolved.
4. Key people throughout the organization; key functions; key skills and competencies.
5. The nature of any decentralization 'contracts' and expectations – linked to issues of power, responsibility and accountability; reward and sanction systems; and the expectations that subsidiaries can have for the support they receive from corporate headquarters.

## The role and contribution of corporate headquarters

This section draws together many of the above issues by considering the role and contribution of company head offices. Typically, these will be larger and grander in centralized organizations; but historically powerful centres have generally been reduced in size, and their work distributed to subsidiaries, as corporations have become more decentralized and adopted flatter organization structures.

There are two fundamental purposes of corporate headquarters:

- serving the global legal and financial needs of the business, and
- supporting strategy making.

In general, this means that they:

- add and subtract businesses from the corporate portfolio
- create linkages to drive synergy throughout the organization – This can include rules for intercompany trading, opportunities for exchanging knowledge and ideas, and facilitating the sharing and transfer of assets
- design, support and maintain the organization structure – This will incorporate communications, the extent of the decentralization, the formality of systems and procedures, and systems for feedback and reward.
- provide certain key services – At a minimum this will be a treasury and corporate secretarial service, but others can be added as well.

However, many head offices have historically provided a more extensive range of services to their constituent businesses, including for example:

- marketing
- management development and personnel
- property management
- centralized research and development
- corporate public relations
- industrial relations.

There is a clear need for head offices to add value to the corporation and not simply to 'spend the money earned by the businesses'. With the recent trend for organizations to slim down the size and scope of head offices, in many cases only corporate strategy, financial reporting and control and secretarial/legal services remain centralized. Some head offices retain a responsibility for *policies* but not the activities.

Summarizing points made earlier, large, centralized head offices where all the key business heads are located in one place – Unilever has been a good example until recently – can control the corporation *efficiently*, but strategies can easily become top–down and slow to change. Decentralized organizations such as ABB (Minicase 21.4) push profit responsibility down to the businesses and empower managers. The head office provides more of a support role with few discrete functions. The new challenge is one of co-ordination.

In considering how head offices can best add value to the business as a whole, four broad issues must be addressed:

- how to control and co-ordinate the constituent businesses – issues of structure, corporate leadership and internal communications and synergy
- how to advise the strategic leader and keep him or her strategically aware
- driving performance and improvement through effective reward systems
- deciding which activities should be
  - provided from head office – for which a fee should be levied
  - devolved to the individual businesses
  - bought in from outside specialists.

The alternative approaches include the stand-alone holding company, financial control approach; centralizing specific functions and services; controlling strategic change at the corporate level; and fostering linkages, learning and sharing good practices.

Head offices can destroy value if they:

- become established as *the* perceived centre for expertise in the corporation – they cannot understand all of the important detail about competitiveness in their constituent businesses, whose managers will become demoralized

if their potential contribution is not acknowledged

- assume that potential linkages and synergy will happen automatically
- duplicate effort and costs unnecessarily
- buy and sell businesses at the wrong prices
- create or perpetuate a culture where internal competition takes precedence over the need to compete with external rivals.

Here at head office, we don't go very deep into much of anything, but we have a smell of everything. Our job is capital allocation – both intellectual and financial capital. We smell, feel, touch, listen, then allocate.

*John F Welch, Chief Executive Officer,*
*General Electric*

## The Role of General Managers

Basically, general managers co-ordinate the work of subordinate specialist managers; they are responsible for the management of strategy implementation and, in certain cases, strategy formulation. The chief executive or managing director of the company, the overall strategic leader, is a general manager. So too are the heads of divisions and business units, and the heads of operating units in a matrix structure. Their task is to match effectively the resources they control with their particular environment and to achieve E–V–R congruence.

Divisionalized organizations were examined in Chapter 21, where it was shown that the degree of decentralization and the power, authority and responsibility enjoyed by general managers will be affected by their relationship with head office and headquarters corporate staff. Whatever the extent of the decentralization from head office to business units, the business units themselves might be highly centralized. This depends on the style of management adopted by the particular general manager in charge.

Each division or business unit is part of a larger organization and corporate structure, and consequently it is not fully autonomous. While the organization as a whole has an external environment comprising customers, suppliers, competitors and shareholders among other influences, each division will have corporate headquarters as part of its environment. Business units may have both divisional headquarters and corporate head office in their environment. General managers in divisions and business units therefore do not have full responsibility for strategy creation and implementation. They can be pressurized by corporate headquarters, and they can turn to head office in their search for additional finance and other resources. The provision of finance within the organization may operate differently from the external market, but justification should still be required.

The relationship between general managers and head office will determine whether they are free to change their portfolios of business units and products or just adapt competitive and functional strategies. Performance measures and expectations will also affect this. Where specific short-term objectives and targets are set, and monitored strictly, general managers are less likely to focus on corporate changes and instead will concentrate on more immediate changes which can yield faster results. Their flexibility to make changes will increase as their targets become more vague and directional and less specific. Even though the general managers of

business units may not be responsible for the formulation of changes in the corporate strategy which will affect their sphere of influence, they will invariably be responsible for the implementation of the changes.

## General management skills and values

It has been established, then, that effective strategic management concerns issues of formulation and implementation. Strategic choices concern:

- the nature and orientation of the organization – the strategic perspective
- the deployment of its resources, ideally to achieve and sustain competitive advantage.

The strategic choice is implemented by the strategic leader, either the chief executive, the owner – manager in the case of a small business, or a general manager. It was pointed out in Chapter 12 that different strategic leaders (a) exhibit different patterns of behaviour and styles of management, and (b) will have different technical skills and biases as a result of their background. Arguably, alternative general managers would seek to implement basically the same strategy in different ways. The views of a number of authors concerning the relationship between general manager skills and particular strategies are discussed below.

Herbert and Deresky (1987) have examined the issue of match between the general manager and the strategy, concluding that the orientations and styles given below were important for particular strategies:

| Strategy | Styles and qualities required |
| --- | --- |
| *Development* (start-up and growth) | Aggressive, competitive, innovative, creative and entrepreneurial |
| *Stabilizing* (maintaining competitive position) | Conservative, careful and analytical |
| *Turnaround* | Autonomous, risk and challenge oriented and entrepreneurial |

Herbert and Deresky contend that financial skills are important for all strategies, with marketing skills being particularly important at the development stage and production and engineering skills invaluable for stabilizing strategies. This raises three issues. (1) Which specialist functional managers might be most appropriate for promotion to general management in particular circumstances? More recent research in the USA confirms that the most typical background for large company chief executives is finance; the same pattern applies in the UK. Marketing, technical and manufacturing specialisms also feature but it is rare for a manager with a human resources background to become the strategic leader. (2) Is a change of general manager appropriate as products and businesses grow and decline and need changes in their strategies? (3) As strategies evolve and change should general managers adapt their styles of management accordingly?

Dixon (1989) suggests that *innovatory general management skills* are most required in the early and late stages of the life of a business or product in its present form. These skills are required to establish or re-create competitive advantage and, in the case of terminal decline, to find an alternative product, service or business. These changes are often best accomplished by outsiders with fresh ideas. Correspondingly, the constant search for efficiencies and improvements while an established product or business is maturing is normally best carried out by specialists.

A major problem with this type of innovation lies in the fact that changes in senior management, structure or values may be involved. The outlook and styles of general managers are likely to be different, and their responses to different sets of expectations and performance targets will vary. Again, this raises the issue of which managers are most appropriate for managing particular strategies.

There are similarities and differences in these various conclusions, reflecting again that there is no one best answer. The issue of match between general manager and strategy is important, and consequently one might expect that changes in one will lead to changes in the other.

Clearly, as organizations become flatter and more decentralized skills in synthesis and integration are critically important.

## Organizations at the End of the 1990s

### Kanter's view

Developing these arguments further, Rosabeth Moss Kanter (1989) has researched the general management skills required to run businesses effectively in the competitive environment of the late 1980s and the 1990s. Large companies, she contended, must be able to match corporate discipline with entrepreneurial creativity in order to become 'leaner' and more efficient whilst being committed to both quality and innovation.

Three strategies are particularly important:

- restructuring to improve synergy from diverse businesses
- the development of joint ventures and strategic alliances to input new ideas
- the encouragement of intrapreneurship within organizations.

These points are explained in greater detail in Box 22.1.

Kanter's main conclusion is that *process is more important than structure*. She suggests that:

- general managers must be able to balance maintenance and entrepreneurial skills
- internal competition (typically fostered in organizations which are divided into discrete divisions and business units) can be harmful and impede synergy
- incentive and reward schemes should reflect the need for co-operation and support between business units

## DISCUSSION – Box 22.1
### Competitiveness

Future success lies in the capability to change and to accomplish key tasks by using resources more efficiently and more effectively. Organizations must be innovative and, at the same time, control their costs. Sustainable competitive advantage, however, does not come from either low costs, or differentiation, or innovation alone. It needs the whole organization to be *focused, fast, flexible and friendly*.

Being *focused* requires investment in core skills and competencies, together with a search for new opportunities for applying the skills. Intrapreneurship should be fostered to improve the skills constantly; and managers throughout the organization should be strategically aware and innovative. They should own the organization's mission, which, by necessity, must be communicated widely and understood.

*Fast* companies move at the right time, and are not caught out by competitors. New ideas and opportunities from the environment will be seized first. Ideally, they will be innovating constantly to open up and sustain a competitive gap, because gradual improvements are likely to be more popular with customers than are radical changes. However, 'instant success takes time' – the organization culture must be appropriate.

*Flexibility* concerns the search for continual improvement. The implication is a 'learning organization' where ideas are shared and collaboration between functions and divisions generates internal synergy. This, in turn, suggests that performance and effectiveness measures, and rewards, concentrate on outcomes.

Internal synergy can be achieved with cross-functional teams and special projects, and by moving people around the organization in order to spread the best practices. General Motors allows components and assembly workers, who work in separate plants in different locations, to contact each other by telephone to sort out problems and faults without relying on either written communications or messages which go 'up, across and down again'. These workers see each other as 'colleagues in the *whole* organization'. It is important that internal constraints (imposed by other functions and divisions) and which restrain performance are highlighted and confronted. To be effective this requires a clear and shared vision and purpose for the organization, decentralization and empowerment.

*Friendly* organizations are closely linked to their suppliers and customers to generate synergy through the added value chain. Such external collaboration may be in the form of strategic alliances.

Summarized from: Kanter, RM (1989) *When Giants Learn To Dance*, Simon and Schuster, but the points remain pertinent and relevant over ten years on.

- the increasing incidence of joint ventures, which requires the forging of closer links with other external businesses, suggests that structures may need revision if the potential and desired synergy is to be achieved.

## Handy's view

Charles Handy (1994, 1995) contends that in order for companies to remain competitive internationally they have had to rethink their basic structures. 'Fewer key people at the heart of the organization, paid very well, producing far more value.' Handy acknowledges that it is quite feasible that corporations will continue to grow, either organically or through acquisition, but believes that either physically or behaviourally they need to be in small units, focused and closely networked to their suppliers and customers. More activities and components will be bought in from specialists than is the case at the moment; internally, they will also comprise networks characterized by subsidiarity, with the 'centre' (as distinct from a traditional head office) doing only what the parts cannot do themselves. The real power will switch from the top of the organization to the businesses, and consequently a co-ordinating mission and purpose will be essential. Handy favours 'federalism' or reverse delegation – the centre acts on the bidding of, and on agreement with, the parts. Basically, Handy is supporting the decentralization trend, but going much further.

Supported by sophisticated information technology and systems, people will become recognized as the most important strategic resource and, because their expertise and intelligence is an intangible asset, largely unquantifiable, it will become harder to value the *real* assets of a business. Consequently, the appropriate measures of performance must be carefully evaluated, and reward systems will have to be derived which motivate and keep those managers who are potentially the most mobile. The valuable managers will not all be at the most senior levels. Disagreeing with many strategic leaders of global organizations, Handy believes that switching jobs regularly and moving people between different parts of the organization, perhaps to other countries, can be dysfunctional. Simply, they will not be in place long enough to become known and, in the future, trust will be an essential element in management, strategic change and strategy implementation.

> *We have designed organizations based on distrust. We have designed organizations so that people will not make mistakes. And, of course, we now encourage people to make mistakes because that is how they learn.*
>
> (Handy)

Handy's arguments imply major changes to strategies, structures and styles of management for many organizations. Where these changes are simultaneous – amounting to *strategic regeneration* in effect – the changes are dramatic, painful and often difficult to carry through. This is discussed further in Chapter 24.

## Summary

Strategies must be implemented if they are to be judged successful and effective. This is accomplished through the structural framework, as we have seen earlier. There are two key variables:

- First, the logic of the *corporate portfolio*. Is synergy a realistic possibility? Is the range too diverse? Is the portfolio built around activities and businesses with overlapping or similar competencies?
- Secondly, are the *structure and style* of management appropriate for the actual portfolio and its diversity? Does the style of managing the corporation ensure that the potential synergies are achieved?

Evidence confirms that in the 1990s companies became less diverse and less centralized. The urge to be more focused was encouraged by pressure from shareholders who concluded that conglomerate diversification was not an appropriate strategy for the time. Shares in diversified conglomerates underperformed against the all-share index. While the logic of their argument is defensible, one cannot ignore the fact that the most valuable and admired company in the world, General Electric, is a diversified conglomerate – but one that invests in its businesses in an attempt to be number one or number two in every industry in which it competes.

Goold and Campbell have described three broad styles of corporate management. The *financial control style* is akin to a holding company, where the head office adopts a very decentralized approach to manage a portfolio where there is (normally) little natural interdependency between the businesses. The *strategic planning style* is based on centralization – the strategic leader believes that he or she is in the best position to dictate strategy for all the businesses in the portfolio. The *strategic control style* is a sort of 'half-way house' that attempts to build on the strengths of the other two.

Defining corporate strategy as the overall strategy for a diversified firm, Michael Porter described four approaches to managing a corporate portfolio. *Portfolio management* is the approach whereby each business is looked at independently to assess its worth to the firm. The assessment is based on industry attractiveness and competitive strengths. Investment should be targeted at priority businesses. *Restructuring* is the attempt to make both an industry and a business more attractive by improving competitiveness – when an organization can no longer add any further value, the business should be divested. *Sharing assets* offers the best opportunity for creating and exploiting synergy across a range of businesses, but *transferring skills* can also prove valuable.

Goold *et al.* have highlighted the importance of *corporate parenting* – essentially the fit between a head office and the subsidiary businesses in an organization and the opportunities for two-way benefits. Where each business can benefit from being part of an organization, and at the same time make a positive contribution to the whole organization, we have what Goold *et al.* call *a heartland* of related businesses. Businesses should be acquired and divested to strengthen the heartland.

The *corporate headquarters* drives the strategy of the business and provides the structural framework. The range of services which remain centralized is a reflection of the adopted style of corporate management. Head offices should add value and not merely spend money earned by the subsidiaries. In recent years, head offices have been slimmed down.

In conjunction with decentralization, an appropriate role must be found for the general managers in charge of each subsidiary business.

To cope with the pressures and demands of contemporary business environments Rosabeth Moss Kanter argues that the organization must be *focused, fast, flexible and friendly*. She argues that competitive advantage comes from the way in which everything is integrated and works together.

Charles Handy puts forward a more radical thesis and argues for *federal organizations*, where head offices are merely there to serve the needs of subsidiaries.

## References

Caulkin, S (1996) Focus is for wimps, *Management Today*, December.

Dixon, M (1989) The very model of a mythical manager, *Financial Times*, 10 May.

Geneen, H (1997) *The Synergy Myth*, St. Martin's Press.

Goold, M and Campbell, A (1988) *Strategies and Styles*, Blackwell.

Goold, M, Campbell, A and Luchs, K (1993) Strategies and styles revisited: strategic planning and financial control, *Long Range Planning*, 26, 5; Strategies and styles revisited: strategic control – is it tenable? *Long Range Planning*, 26, 6.

Goold, M, Campbell, A and Alexander, M (1994) *Corporate Level Strategy*, John Wiley.

Green, O (1994) Quoted in *Management Today*, June, p. 40.

Hamel, G and Prahalad, CK (1994) *Competing for the Future*, Harvard Business School Press.

Handy, C (1994) *The Empty Raincoat*, Hutchinson.

Handy, C (1995) *Beyond Certainty: The Changing Worlds of Organizations*, Hutchinson.

Herbert, TT and Deresky, H (1987) Should general managers match their business strategies, *Organizational Dynamics*, 15(3), 40–51.

Kanter, RM (1989) *When Giants Learn to Dance*, Simon & Schuster.

Porter, ME (1987) From competitive advantage to corporate strategy, *Harvard Business Review*, May–June.

Richter, A and Owen, G (1997) The UK cut down to size, *Financial Times*, 10 March.

Sadtler, D, Campbell, A and Koch, R (1997) *Break Up! When Large Companies are Worth More Dead Than Alive*, Capstone.

Stonich, PJ (1982) *Implementing Strategy*, Ballinger.

Test your knowledge of this chapter with our online quiz at: http://www.thomsonlearning.co.uk

Explore Corporate Strategy and Style further at:

*Long Range Planning*   http://www.lrp.ac

*Management Today*   http://www.managementtoday.haynet.com/magazines/mantod

## Questions and Research Assignments

### TEXT RELATED

1. For which (general) corporate strategies are the financial control, strategic planning and strategic control styles of corporate management most appropriate?

2. How do you think the need for general managers might have changed as organization structures have generally been flattened and delayered?

## Internet and Library Projects

1. Update the material on any or all the four conglomerate businesses discussed in Minicase 22.2.

Using this and details of the corporate strategies pursued by other large companies with which you are familiar, which of the following two statements do you most agree with?

'Conglomerate diversification has now given way to focus strategies – focus is here to stay'.

'Focus strategies cannot generate sufficient growth long-term to satisfy shareholders – diversification will make a comeback'

2. Take any large organization with which you are familiar. How have its head-office structure and roles changed in recent years?

3. Investigate the role of:
   (a) general managers in the health service
   (b) the heads of financial services (whatever they might be called) in universities.

   How has their role changed and developed in the last five years? How is their performance assessed, and how might it be? What are the most appropriate measures of effectiveness, and why? Are they rewarded in line with measures of performance?

4. Investigate the changes made by Lord Simpson at GEC since he replaced Lord Weinstock. What is GEC's new heartland? What has happened with joint ventures and strategic alliances?

*GEC (now Marconi)*   http://www.marconi.com

# 23

# Strategic Resources, Risk and Crisis Management

Strategic Resource Management

Policies, Procedures, Plans and Budgets

Risk Management

Crisis Avoidance and Management

*The implementation of intended strategies, and the ability of the organization to be responsive in a dynamic, competitive environment, require the organization's strategic resources to be deployed and managed both efficiently and effectively. It is also vital for the organization, on the one hand, to seek to be crisis averse rather than crisis prone and, on the other hand, to be able to deal with crises if and when they do occur. All of these issues are a reflection of the organization's ability to appreciate and manage risk and they are the subject of this chapter.*

*The key elements in risk are the potential upside and downside from future events and the likelihood of certain things happening. Although forecasting and scenario planning are uncertain, they are still important as managers exercise judgement in the decisions that they take. The greater their awareness, insight and understanding of emerging trends and opportunities, the more informed their decisions should be. Decisions and risk are linked irrevocably as the strategic decisions made by organizations and managers reflect their management of the risks they face. When organizations are managing risks effectively they will be less crisis prone and in a stronger position to deal with potential crises and unexpected events when they do occur.*

*The opening case shows how two airlines, Air France and British Airways, reacted differently to the Air France Concorde crash in July 2000. There is always uncertainty following a disaster such as this, but BA believed that its safety preparations were robust and it kept its Concordes in the air. Air France opted to ground its planes until it had more knowledge. Both airlines were fully aware of the interest of the world's media but they had different perceptions of the risk.*

# Minicase 23.1 Air France, British Airways and the Concorde Disaster

To understand the impact of a major accident with Concorde a number of background factors must be remembered.

- Concorde has become a symbol of pride for Britain and France.
- Technologically it is a triumph.
- People make efforts to see it, let alone want to fly in it.
- The project helped to cement Anglo-French relations when the UK was wanting to be seen to be European.
- It proved that two countries could work together and challenge American dominance of the aerospace industry. In this respect it was a forerunner to the Airbus consortium.
- The project ran late and was heavily over budget.
- The plane was barred from flying overland at supersonic speeds because of the noise factor.
- Only two airlines ever flew it – when it began both were nationalized. British Airways (BA) has since been privatized.
- The BA Concorde services pay their way operationally, but all of the development costs were absorbed by the British and French governments – in today's money some £9 billion was absorbed.
- The services are mainly London and Paris to New York, but there are some UK to West Indies flights and a wide range of charter opportunities.
- In 1999 BA earned £140 million in revenues and Air France £70 million from Concorde – BA's services were marginally profitable; Air France lost money.

The first crash of a Concorde plane happened on the last Tuesday of July 2000. The passengers on the Air France flight from Paris to New York were German tourists flying out to meet a cruise ship. The plane was seen to be on fire before it even left the ground at Charles de Gaulle airport, but once Concorde has reached a certain speed on the runway take-off cannot be aborted. Two minutes later it had crashed onto a hotel on the outskirts of Paris. Altogether 113 people, the bulk of them passengers and air crew, died. The whole sequence of events was filmed by two amateur video-makers and so the disaster was very high profile.

Immediate speculation blamed an engine fire. There are two engines slung under each wing and those on one side had been clearly on fire. Moreover, the flight had been delayed in Paris while one of these engines was repaired. However, the landing gear was still down: in the little time he had available the pilot had reported that the hydraulics had also failed. Why?

In the event it was to transpire that a rogue strip of metal on the runway had punctured a tyre, and then tyre debris had punctured a fuel tank incorporated in the wing. It later became apparent that the metal strip had probably been jettisoned from a Continental Airlines DC10 a few minutes earlier. The escaping fuel was ignited by the heat of the adjacent engines. The engines, and in turn the engineers who had repaired one of them, were not to blame.

## The Air France response

- The chairman went to the crash site immediately, signalling a personal involvement.
- All five remaining Concordes were grounded immediately, communicating that safety was the first priority.
- Later, the chairman attended a number of the family funerals and was available to talk to families of the victims.
- Air France provided free flights for relatives to and from Germany.
- Interim compensation payments were offered.

## British Airways

BA opted to keep its seven Concordes flying, although flights were suspended for the first 24 hours. This determination continued even when one had to make an emergency landing in Newfoundland after passengers complained that there was a smell of smoke in the cabin.

BA's pilots were happy about this – they had no fears for the aircraft's safety. Their representatives, together with retired pilots, were all happy to be interviewed by television reporters to confirm this view. Passengers were generally undeterred as well.

It transpired that in 24 years of flying there had been 70 previous incidents where tyres had burst, but never with catastrophic consequences. As a result of this BA had made certain modifications to the wheels which Air France had not copied. In addition, BA used new tyres (Air France used remoulds) which it changed regularly, after a fixed (and limited) number of take-offs or landings.

On 15 August, some three weeks after the crash, BA announced that it was grounding its Concordes. This pre-empted the withdrawal of its Certificate of Air Worthiness by the Civil Aviation Authority (CAA) on 16 August. Air France commented that it was surprised that it had taken as long as it had.

Senior BA pilots demanded an immediate reprieve and suggested that it could be a ploy by France to end Concorde flights altogether because they were afraid of the cost of possible modifications that might be necessary.

## The UK Civil Aviation Authority

The CAA duly withdrew the Certificate of Air Worthiness, in reality a very rare event. The only time this had happened before as the result of a civil accident was when McDonnell Douglas DC10s were grounded temporarily in 1979. As shown in Minicase 17.1, this contributed to the failure of Laker Airways.

The CAA was asked why it had not acted earlier. The reply was that there had been speculation but no concrete evidence. Only now was the cause of the accident clear. The CAA emphasized its belief that Concorde remained a safe aircraft but that (as yet unspecified) modifications would be required. There was, however, a real concern that a tyre burst had been able to trigger the catastrophic chain of events that followed. Some commentators believed that the reluctance of Air France to restore Concorde services implied that there was an unacceptable risk with the plane.

QUESTIONS: Regardless of the actual facts and motives, whose reputation do you think might be most enhanced (or at least protected) by its reaction and behaviour?
Did BA do the right thing in the circumstances or should it have reacted differently?

*Air france*   http://www.airfrance.com
*British Airways*   http://www.britishairways.com

Photograph: Tony Rogers (aero@btinternet.com)

---

Perhaps the most apposite definition of strategy for me is drawn from the world of chess. Strategy is knowing what to do when there is nothing to do; tactics is knowing what to do when there *is* something to do.

*Sir Trevor Holdsworth, ex-Chairman, GKN, quoted in the Strategic Planning Society News, 1991*

On 25 June 1876 General George Armstrong Custer was informed that a significant number of Indians were gathering at Little Big Horn. Without further intelligence or analysis, he decided he would ride out with his 250 men to 'surround the Indians'. It is difficult for 250 soldiers to surround 3000 Indians – Custer made a serious error of judgement.

## Strategic Resource Management

Figure 23.1 recapitulates how the corporate mission and purpose provide the basis from which corporate and competitive strategies are derived. The corporate portfolio provides a number of ways for the organization to pursue its mission – but each business in the portfolio will require different levels of attention and resourcing. These decisions relate to priorities linked to the potential of, and desired outcomes from, each business. The achievement of competitive advantage and success comes down, in the end, to individual contributions, and to guide and manage these, objectives, targets and milestones will be set. The early part of this

*Figure 23.1*  Strategy implementation and resource management.

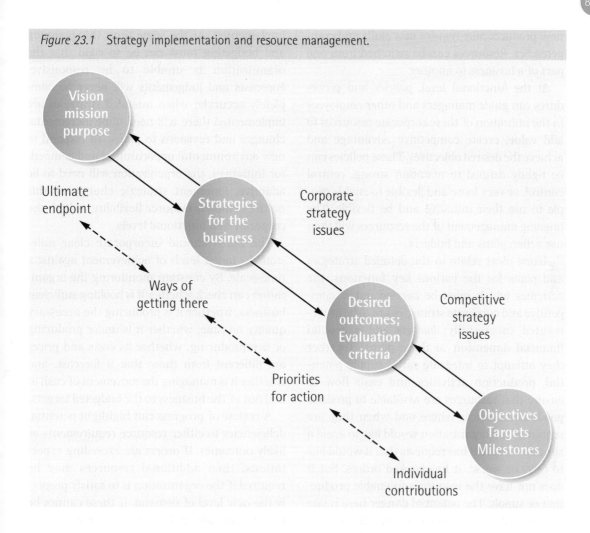

chapter discusses the framework through which this process happens.

Once intended strategies have been determined, either in broad outline or in greater detail, the organization must plan their implementation. This means, first, that the resources required for implementation – including capital equipment, people and finance – are available where and when they are needed. Resources need to be *allocated* to different managers, functions and businesses, and then *co-ordinated* to generate synergy. Secondly, the managers responsible for implementation must understand what is expected of them and be empow-

ered and motivated to take the necessary decisions and actions. In addition, *monitoring and control* systems are required.

At the corporate strategy level, organizations might establish priorities for different divisions and businesses using portfolio analysis, and evaluate the strategic and financial implications of alternative investments. Decisions may be taken within the constraints of existing capital, financial and human resources; if they demand new resources, then these must be obtained in an appropriate time-scale. Proposed acquisitions may require an organization to raise funding externally; organic development of new products may require new skills and competencies. Resources can be switched from one part of a business to another.

At the functional level, *policies* and procedures can guide managers and other employees in the utilization of these corporate resources to add value, create competitive advantage and achieve the desired objectives. These policies can be tightly defined to maintain strong, central control, or very loose and flexible to enable people to use their initiative and be flexible. The ongoing management of the resources will then use action plans and budgets.

*Action plans* relate to the detailed strategies and plans for the various key functions, the activities which must be carried out if competitive and corporate strategies are to be implemented successfully; *budgets* add a crucial financial dimension to these plans. Together they attempt to integrate sales, supply potential, production activities and cash flow to ensure that resources are available to produce goods and services where and when they are required. The organization would like to avoid a situation where it has requests that it would like to take, or worse, it has booked orders, but it does not have the resources to enable production or supply. The potential danger here is one of overtrading and overcommitment. Both its bank and its customers can easily end up disappointed. It would also wish to avoid situations where it has idle capacity and no orders, or instances where it is producing for stock rather than for customers. This dilemma is a key issue in the story of the Optica in the long cases at the end of the book. It is one faced all the time by many small businesses, and in it we can see an endeavour to balance the resource-based perspective of strategy with the opportunity-driven approach.

This planning process then provides a useful check that the corporate and competitive strategies that have been formulated are both appropriate and feasible in the sense that they can be implemented. At the same time, this planning and budgeting must not be so rigid that the organization is unable to be responsive. Forecasts and judgements will never be completely accurate; when intended strategies are implemented there will need to be incremental changes and revisions to plans. To respond to new environmental opportunities and competitor initiatives, the organization will need to be adaptive. Emergent strategic change of this nature demands resource flexibility, at both the corporate and functional levels.

The plans should incorporate clear milestones – target levels of achievement against a time-scale. By constant monitoring the organization can check whether it is booking sufficient business, whether it is producing the necessary quality on time, whether it is under producing or overproducing, whether its costs and prices are different from those that it forecast, and whether it is managing the movement of cash in and out of the business to the budgeted targets.

A review of progress can highlight potential deficiencies to either resource requirements or likely outcomes. If orders are exceeding expectations, then additional resources may be required if the organization is to satisfy properly the new level of demand. If these cannot be found, schedules will need to be changed and maybe future supplies rationed. If orders are below expectations, then either new business opportunities will need targeting at short notice, possibly implying very competitive prices and low margins, or end-of-year targets revised downwards. Vigilance and pragmatism here can help to ensure that the organization does not face unexpected crises. Effective communications and management information systems are essential for planning, monitoring and control.

Figure 23.2 explains the role of information feedback and the importance of measuring the most critical variables. Ideally, the organization will continuously measure customers' perceptions of the level of service that they are receiving, highlighting both the need and opportunities for improvement. Speedy action can then follow. Satisfied customers will help the organization to achieve its other objectives, such as high and sustained profits. This is the top half of the diagram.

The bottom half illustrates the danger of relying on other performance measures which, although essential yardsticks, are inappropriate for stimulating action at the right time. Poor service, relative to that provided by competitors, will lead to systematic reductions in sales, market share and profits. If the organization waits for these indicators, bearing in mind that there

will be a delay before the information is fed back and analysed, it may be too late to recover the lost market share. Accurately measuring customers' perceptions of service is more difficult than measuring sales and profits.

## Corporate resource planning

Corporate resource planning relates to the allocation of resources between the various parts of the organization together with corporate investment decisions concerning the acquisition of additional resources. If investment funds are limited their allocation will be based on the strategic importance of the various spending

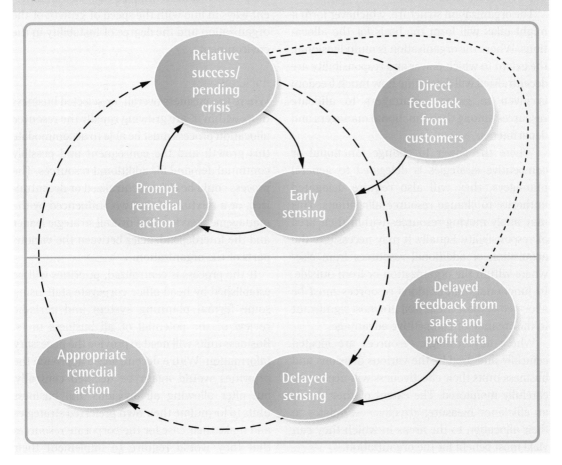

*Figure 23.2*   Early and late sensing.

opportunities as well as financial evaluations of the viability of each project. If funds are not available and need to be borrowed to finance possible projects, the return on the investment should exceed the cost of capital.

Organizations should seek the best possible returns from investments because, as Seed (1983) suggests, they can be seen as an undesirable but necessary freezing of corporate funds. However, some general and functional managers, especially if they have a technical background, may see investments in new plant and equipment as a reflection of status, preferring the best and most modern technology. Where this happens there could be a suboptimal allocation of corporate resources. This argument can also be applied to the purchase of large, luxurious city-centre head offices.

The organization structure, whichever form it might take, will form the basis for the allocations. Where the organization is multidivisional, the extent to which power and responsibility are decentralized will determine how much freedom is given to general managers to allocate resources among their functional managers and departments.

Where the power to change functional or competitive strategies is delegated to general managers, they will also require delegated authority to change resource allocations. This may imply moving resources within their area of responsibility. Equally, it may necessitate the acquisition of additional resources from elsewhere within the organization or from outside. In functional organizations resources must be allocated to those areas that are most significant in the creation of competitive advantage.

Where any strategic resources are located centrally and used by the various divisions and business units their effectiveness will need to be carefully monitored. The extent of their use is an efficiency measure; effectiveness relates to their allocation to the areas in which they can yield most benefit for the organization.

The allocation of resources at a corporate level is closely tied in to the planning system through which priorities must be established. Portfolio analyses such as the directional policy matrix may well be used to help to determine which products and business units should receive priority for investment funding; and any new developments that are proposed will require resources. An acquisition, for example, will need to be financed, but the integration of the new business after the purchase may also involve the transfer of managers and other resources.

## Corporate resource planning and organization growth

Corporate resources may be allocated in different ways in line with the speed of growth of the organization and the degree of instability in the environment.

### Rapid growth

Where the business overall, or selected business units within it, are growing rapidly the resource allocation process must be able to accommodate this growth and the consequent and possibly continual demand for additional resources. The process could be either centralized or decentralized, or a mixture of the two, influenced by the management style of the overall strategic leader and the interdependencies between the various parts of the organization.

If the process is centralized, priorities will be established by head office corporate staff using some formal planning system and periodic review of the potential of all business units. Business units will need to provide the necessary information. With a decentralized approach the priorities would again be decided centrally, but after allowing all divisions and business units to formulate their own preferred strategies and make their case for the corporate resources that they would require to implement their preferences. A mixed approach would involve resources for continuing activities being allocated through centralized mechanisms and incremental additions funded through a bidding process.

In all cases the decisions should balance the potential financial gains with the strategic logic implied. While divisions or business units may be making individual requests for resources to support certain programmes, the opportunities for synergy, sharing activities and transferring skills across activities should be assessed. In addition, the desirability of the implications of the various proposals for the overall strategic perspective of the organization should be considered.

## Limited change and stability

Where businesses are growing more steadily and in a relatively stable environment, resource allocation for continuing programmes could be a straightforward extrapolation of previous budgets, incorporating an allowance for inflation. However, a mere continuation of present strategies without evaluation and proper review may lead to ineffectiveness.

Established policies, such as fixing advertising budgets at an agreed percentage of projected sales revenue or maintaining particular levels of stocks, are likely to be a key feature of this approach.

## Decline situations

Where businesses or business units are in decline some quite tough decisions often have to be taken. Where the organization as a whole is in difficulty the strategic leader must search for new opportunities for redeploying resources. In the case of selected business units that are experiencing decline, unless there are opportunities for turnaround, resources should be transferred to activities with better growth and profit potential. In both cases the decisions are likely to be centralized, particularly as there

may have to be structural changes to accommodate the rationalization, divestment or other strategic changes.

Once resources are allocated to divisions, business units and functions there will be further allocations to individual managers within each area; and this to a greater or lesser extent will be delegated to the general manager or functional manager in charge of each one. This is known as functional or operational resource planning; in the process it is important not to overlook any interdependencies between the budget holders.

## Functional resource planning

When resources are allocated to functions, and to particular activities within functions, there is a number of essential considerations.

1. It is important to consider the relative importance of each function; the concept of the value chain, explained in Chapter 9, could prove helpful in establishing this.
2. Competitive advantage is established within functional activities; consequently, an appreciation of key success factors and competitive opportunities is crucial if the resource allocation is to lead to strategic effectiveness.
3. The important linkages between functions, which are the sources of potential synergy, should be considered. Any appropriate sharing of resources should be encouraged. To this end, activities should be complementary and supportive.
4. Where there are sequential dependencies, the whole resource allocation process must take account of these. For example, if activity Z is dependent upon activity X which precedes it, then it is both inefficient and ineffective to allocate resources to Z unless adequate resources are also given to X. An obvious application of this would be production activities which must be built around

any bottlenecks. Similarly, the capacity of hospital operating theatres should be consistent with the number of beds available for recuperation.

The marketing department of a large high-street retail chain ran a series of promotions in the mid-1990s, whereby customers who spent a designated amount of money (on any goods) could then buy a particular item for a substantially reduced price. Success was dependent upon the company's buyers making sure that there was sufficient stock of the promoted item in all of its branches on the appropriate days. This did not always happen, and qualifying customers had to be given vouchers which they could redeem once stocks were received.

Certain techniques, such as network analysis, can be very useful in planning a project and establishing the resource needs. The whole project should be managed for efficiency, with time and resources being saved wherever appropriate. Nevertheless, as Robert Burns said, 'The best laid schemes o' mice an' men . . . gang aft a-gley'. In the early 1960s it was decided to introduce into the UK a successful American car wax. The decision was made to launch the product initially within the Granada television region, using limited television advertising and concentrating distribution only in selected garages. The commercials were scheduled in the middle of a late-night magazine programme with a relatively small audience. However, in the event an important European football match featuring Manchester United was reprogrammed at short notice and the car wax advertisements filled the half-time commercial break. A demand for the car wax was generated which the importers simply could not supply. The situation was made worse by people asking for the product in outlets other than garages.

Minicase 23.2 looks at the particular resource and co-ordination problems of Standard Fire-

works, a company which manufactures fireworks for ten months of the year but delivers virtually all of its production during a one-month period.

## Efficiency and effectiveness in resource allocation and management

It is important to consider both efficiency and effectiveness measures in relation to the allocation and deployment of resources. An examination of the way in which resources are employed and managed in the production and marketing of existing products and services can be used to search for improvements. Savings in time and costs (without threatening quality) lead to higher productivity, higher profits and the freeing up of resources which can be deployed elsewhere. This is essentially a search for greater efficiency.

At the same time, it is also useful to consider whether resources are being allocated to those products, services and activities which are most important for the organization as a whole and for the achievement of its objectives. This analysis is applicable at organizational, divisional and business unit level – wherever there is an opportunity cost of the resources in question. If resources are finite and limited to the extent that choices have to be made concerning which products to concentrate resources on and which to give low priority to, then the opportunity cost of the resources should be considered. If growth or profitability or both are important objectives, the resources should be allocated to those products and services which can best fulfil the objectives. This is an assessment of effectiveness. However, as discussed above, it is important to ensure that sufficient resources are allocated to development programmes that will lead to growth and profits in the future.

If decisions are made to alter resource allocations and concentrate them in different areas, issues of managing change arise; these are

# Minicase 23.2  Standard Fireworks

Standard began manufacturing fireworks in the UK in the 1890s. By the 1960s the number of UK producers had declined to 11, and Standard was one of the largest. In the mid-1990s, with factories in Huddersfield and Doncaster – as well as a joint venture in China – it was the only UK *manufacturer*. Standard (with its subsidiary, Brock) had some two-thirds of the UK market; imported brands such as Astra and Black Cat, mostly from China, but with some from Hong Kong, constitute the remainder. Europe has tighter regulatory standards than the Far East, where labour costs are also lower. Simply, UK manufacture is less profitable than production in China, but if offers more political stability. The quality of UK production is higher in the case of the more sophisticated fireworks; for lower-price items quality differences are not an issue. Quality control is always important.

Standard has 17,000 customers in the UK, many of them small, independent retailers, who buy over 80 million fireworks (worth £18 million to Standard in 1996) each year. The UK's biggest demand for fireworks is on 'bonfire night', 5 November each year, which marks the anniversary of Guy Fawkes' ill-fated attempt to blow up the Houses of Parliament. Although Standard's team of eight salesmen collects provisional, indicative orders all through the year, confirmed orders tend to be placed during October for immediate delivery. Virtually all deliveries are made in the three to four weeks which precede bonfire night; all payments are due in late November. The company was profitable, with pre-tax profits of £3.5 million in the mid-1990s.

The company was controlled by its founding family for over 90 years before it was acquired by the mini-conglomerate Scottish Heritable Trust in 1986. SHT's other businesses included hospital beds, golf clubs, sock manufacture and gravel pits. Standard acquired its competitor, Brock, in 1987, and chose to utilize the Brock brand for the fireworks that it manufactured in China. Standard was bought out by its managers in 1992 but then sold to its Hong Kong-based rival, Black Cat, in 1997. Black Cat already had a UK base in Burton-on-Trent which it set about consolidating on to Standard's Huddersfield site.

Historically, Standard decided what it would make in any one year, and essentially told its retail customers what they could have. This is no longer the case. Production takes place mainly between January and September; Standard does not manufacture any fireworks in November and December, the last two months of its financial year. The product mix, and the numbers of each firework, are initially based on the previous year's delivery pattern, and then adjusted in line with the indicative orders received. Production is constant, rather than loaded at the end of the period, and there are no night shifts. Safety considerations rule out a last-minute rush. It is a 'one-shot' business, with little opportunity to alter the product mix at the end of the cycle if forecasting has been poor.

Fireworks are not produced in a 'typical' factory, again for safety reasons. Teams of one to three employees work in small huts which are geographically separated on the site. If there is an explosion, the hut roof blows upwards and the sides outwards; only a limited number of people is at risk. Gunpowder is delivered in small quantities to each hut on a regular basis, and finished products are taken away for storage elsewhere. Transport is by rubber-wheeled hand carts; there are no petrol-driven vehicles within the confines of the production area. The amount of gunpowder and fireworks that can be stored in any one building and on any one site is regulated and restricted. Standard hires secondary storage facilities near Gretna Green and in Staffordshire.

Standard cannot physically distribute all of its fireworks itself during October. It has to hire capacity from independent carriers. Standard delivers large loads to the carriers who then take the fireworks (in small packages) to the retailers. Co-ordinating this network is critical for success. A few years ago, for example, there were problems with one carrier who was simply unable to deliver the packages on time; given the tight deadlines, this constituted a crisis for Standard.

Managing the cash flow is also critical. The bulk of Standard's inward cash flow is in November; by February the cash reserves have been spent and the overdraft then grows steadily and remorselessly until the following November. There is some limited flexibility in that low-cost fireworks can be manufactured early in the cycle, leaving the most expensive ones until the end.

Looking ahead, it is not inconceivable that resins could replace gunpowder in fireworks, in which case many of the current production constraints would disappear. Production in factory units could be more mechanized. An interesting opportunity concerned the demand for fireworks for the new millennium celebrations, New Year 1999/2000. When should Standard manufacture – and what should it produce?

QUESTIONS: What would you have done about the new millennium demand? Given that most European manufacturers focus almost exclusively on high added value (and premium price) display fireworks, what is the future for Standard?

*Standard Fireworks (now Jubilee Fireworks)*   http://www.jubilee-fireworks.ltd.uk

considered in Chapter 24. It should be appreciated that particular business units, products and services are likely to have their champions within the organization. Resource reductions in favour of alternative products may be resisted by certain managers. Their ability and willingness to resist change pressures from higher management will be related to their power bases and their ability to influence decisions. These issues also are considered in Chapter 24.

It is now appropriate to consider in more detail how resources are allocated to managers and how policies influence the way in which resources are used. Put simplistically, managers are allowed certain resources, which represent costs to the organization, and are then expected to use them to generate revenues and profits. The budgeting process determines how many of which resources managers are allocated. Their agreed objectives and targets concerning particular products and services determine how the resources are further deployed, and established policies influence the way in which they are deployed and managed.

Too many businesses spend money they have yet to earn to buy things they don't need to impress people they don't even like.

## Policies, Procedures, Plans and Budgets

### Policies

Policies are designed to guide the behaviour of managers in relation to the pursuit and achievement of strategies and objectives. They can guide either thoughts or actions, or both, by indicating what is expected in certain decision areas. Over time they establish the way in which certain tasks should normally be carried out, and place constraints upon the decision-making freedom that managers have. In this respect they imply that the implementation of strategies formulated by strategic leaders is a planned activity, and recognize that managers may at times wish to make changes and pursue objectives which are personally important to them. Policies, therefore, should be related to stated objectives and strategies and assist in their implementation; at the same time they should not restrict managers to the extent that they are unable to make incremental and adaptive changes when these are appropriate or necessary. Managers should be offered sufficient inducements to comply with organizational policies, and sanctioned when they fail to comply without justification.

Policies need not be written down or even formulated consciously. They may emerge as certain behaviour patterns become established in the organization and are regarded as a facet of values and culture. A policy can exist simply because it is the perceived way that something has always been done. Policies are particularly significant in the case of recurring problems or decisions as they establish a routine and consistent approach.

Policies can be either advisory, leaving decision makers with some flexibility, or mandatory, whereby managers have no discretion. Koontz and O'Donnell (1968) suggest that mandatory policies should be regarded as 'rules' rather than policies. They argue that mandatory policies tend to stop managers and other employees thinking about the most efficient and effective ways in which to carry out tasks and searching for improvements. Policies should guide rather than remove discretion.

Koontz and O'Donnell further argue that advisory policies should normally be preferred because it is frequently essential to allow managers some flexibility to respond and adapt to changes in both the organization and the environment. Moreover, mandatory policies are unlikely to motivate managers, while advisory guides can prompt innovation.

### The creation and use of policies

It has already been mentioned that policies may be created both consciously and unconsciously.

The main stated policies are those that the managers of the company draw up in relation to their areas of discretionary responsibility. Certain key policies will be established by the overall strategic leader and will be filtered down the organization. It is important that when general managers create policies for their divisions and business units, and functional managers for their departments, there is some consistency between them.

Some policies will be forced on the company by external stakeholders. Government legislation upon contracts of employment, redundancy terms and health and safety at work all affect human resource policies, for example. The design of certain products will have to meet strict criteria for safety and pollution. The fabric used for airline seats in the UK must be fire resistant, and there are similar restrictions upon the type of foams that can be used in furniture. Car engines must be designed to meet certain emission regulations. In some cases financial policies can be dictated by powerful shareholders or bankers.

It is useful, then, if the major functional areas of the business are covered by explicit policies which are known to all employees who will be affected by them. Where they exist in this form they provide a clear framework in which decisions can be made; and they also allow people to understand the behaviour patterns that are expected of them in particular circumstances. However, the policies should not be too rigid and prevent managers making important change decisions. Changes in strategies may require changes of policy if they are to be implemented successfully.

## Examples of functional policies

Policies can exist for any functional task undertaken by the organization, and consequently the following examples are merely indicative.

In *finance* the dividend policy constitutes one example. It is typical for dividends to be held constant or increased gradually even though annual profits may be moving upwards and downwards quite significantly. This is meant to convey confidence when profits are falling and prudence when they are rising. Similarly, there may be policies for assessing the viability of proposed investments and ranking a set of alternatives. Where the firm has a financial strategy of investing cash balances on a short-term basis there may well be policies and criteria for evaluating appropriate opportunities.

*Human resource* policies would include the following:

- the type and qualification of employees for particular jobs
- the recruitment activities and procedures that will take place
- the training and development of particular skills and competencies in relation to specified jobs

- communicating to employees how well (or poorly) the company is performing
- policies concerning overtime and bonuses.

Policies with regard to quality and meeting delivery dates are examples from the *operations* function. Policies may also establish who has the authority to change production schedules; and in a retail organization there are likely to be policies concerning the reordering of stock, the refilling of shelves, and the ways in which merchandise should be displayed both in-store and in the windows.

*Marketing* policies are related to the four components of the marketing mix: product, price, promotion and distribution. One product policy of a car manufacturer might establish which models are made in anticipation of sale and displayed in distributor showrooms and which ones are only made when orders have been placed for them. A pricing policy of certain retailers is to reduce prices to the level of their competitors when customers highlight the differential. A preference for advertising in certain magazines or the use of a particular layout would constitute examples of promotional policies. The willingness of Marks and Spencer to exchange goods on demand, regardless of whether they are faulty, is a merchandising policy.

## Procedures

A procedure is a type of plan designed to establish the steps that managers and other employees should follow in carrying out certain, normally routine, tasks, such as a formal disciplinary procedure. If a customer complains, there could be an established procedure for gathering the required information and dealing with the complaint. Where products fail inspection there may be procedures for establishing the cause. Algorithms, whereby a series of questions is posed and the answer to one question determines the next question asked, can be used to provide an appropriate framework for diagnosing faults.

These again would constitute a formalized procedure. This approach is particularly useful for some call-centre employees, such as those who help customers who are experiencing problems with their electrical goods, and those nurses who answer patient queries for the NHS (National Health Service) Direct service.

In the same way that policies help to clarify expectations, a well-conceived and straightforward procedure can ensure that the necessary action in certain circumstances is clear to everyone. In addition, procedures can provide a useful control mechanism.

## Functional and single-use plans

When strategic planning was discussed in general terms in Chapter 11 and alternative approaches were considered, it was pointed out that the thinking process was often more important than the production of a definite rigid plan. The activities to be carried out by certain divisions, business units and functional managers must be clarified through a planning process if the resources required for their implementation are to be allocated efficiently. Certain functional activities, however, lend themselves to detailed planning and specific plans. The scheduling of production, of operator hours and of the receipt of supplies under a just-in-time (JIT) system are examples.

In addition, there are single-use plans which are self-explanatory, designed to meet specific contingencies and generally detailed. The plan for the launch and development of a new product, the plans for the installation of a new piece of equipment, and the change-over plans linked to the implementation of a new organization structure are all examples of single-use plans. The value of single-use plans lies in forcing managers to set down the steps required to accomplish specific tasks and at the same time to examine the impact on all of the people who are in some way affected. Techniques such

as network analysis and Gantt charts (activity flow charts) can prove helpful in single-use planning.

## Budgets

Budgets, quite simply, are plans expressed in numerical terms, usually in financial terms. They will indicate how much should be spent, by which departments, when, and for what purpose.

Pearce and Robinson (1985) distinguish between three types of budget. *Capital budgets* concern the allocation of resources for investment in buildings, plant and equipment. These new resources will be used to generate future revenues. *Sales budgets* reflect the anticipated flow of funds into the organization based on forecast sales; and *revenue or expense budgets* concern the operating costs that will be incurred in producing these products and services. Because of such factors as seasonal demand, the need to hold stock, and the fact that the final payment for goods and services is likely to occur after all operating expenses have been paid, the flows of cash in and out of the business need to be controlled through these budgets.

Budgeting the direct costs of producing certain products and services requires an estimate of the raw materials, components, labour and machine hours that are likely to be needed. Standard costing techniques usually form the basis of this, with analyses of any variances being used to measure both performance and the reliability of the standard costs.

People are a crucial strategic resource, and their physical contribution in terms of hours of work can be budgeted. Work study and other techniques will be used to establish the standard times required to complete particular tasks, which can then be costed. Lilliput Lane cottages were discussed in Chapter 8 – there is also a long case at the end – when the importance of the individual hand-painting element was pointed out. Expert painters practise painting new cottages in different ways until they have a 'fast time'. This constitutes the benchmark against which individual painters will be measured. Although all of the painters are shown how the expert does it, they are quite free to paint the cottages in any way they wish, as long as the quality of their work is high and the colours are right. Their wages are partially dependent upon their speed.

While such standards, and the wage rates which are used to determine the payment for these inputs, are likely to be common throughout the organization, and in many cases agreed centrally, the selection and training of the people in question are likely to be decentralized. While the skills and capabilities of staff should be considered when the budgets are quantified, the process of budgeting can be useful for highlighting weaknesses and deficiencies.

Developing from this, another expense that needs to be budgeted is training and management development programmes. This involves the utilization of funds which are currently available to improve the long-term contribution and value of people. Training and development should therefore be seen as an investment. However, the anticipated returns will be difficult to quantify, and as a result the investment techniques considered earlier may be of only limited use. Moreover, the contribution of people will also depend upon their commitment to the organization, which in turn will be influenced by the overall reward and incentives packages which are offered and the ability of the organization structure to harness and co-ordinate their various contributions.

## The budgeting process

All managers who spend money, and whose departments consume resources, should ideally be given a budget. These budgets should repre-sent agreed targets that relate closely to the manager's objectives, again agreed with his or her superior. In the same way that individual manager objectives contribute towards the objectives for departments, business units, divisions and ultimately the organization as a whole, individual budgets will be part of a master budget. Activities that constrain other activities, because they involve scarce resources for which demand exceeds supply capability, should be budgeted early.

Budgets and objectives are clearly related, and consequently resources should be allocated to those areas and activities in the organization that are seen as priorities. If important objectives are to be achieved, and priority strategies implemented, resources must be provided. Where growth and profits are important organizational objectives, those business units and products that are best able to contribute to their achievement should be funded accordingly. This approach suggests that the strategies being implemented have been formulated to satisfy corporate objectives, and personal objectives have been contained. However, the process of budgeting can facilitate the ability of managers to pursue personal objectives. Moreover, budgeting can be perceived as a technique for short-term financial management rather than a key aspect of strategy implementation. These contentions are expanded below.

Where resources are available and new developments are being considered, the previous record and contribution of managers is likely to have an influence. Rather than select strategies on merit and then allocate the most appropriate managers to implement them, the strategies championed by successful managers may be preferred.

Furthermore, the ability of certain managers to exercise power and influence over resource allocations within the organization, issues discussed in the next chapter, may result in allocations to areas and activities that potentially are not the most beneficial to the organization as a whole. Bower (1970) points out that where the objectives of the organization are difficult to agree and quantify, as is the case in many not-for-profit organizations, the political ability of managers to defend existing allocations and bid for additional resources grows in importance. Wherever this is evident, the resource allocation process becomes a determinant of the objectives and strategies pursued by organizations.

## Flexibility with budgets

The budgeting process will normally take place on an annual basis, but as the targets will be utilized for regular performance reviews there should be scope to adjust budgets either upwards or downwards. While sales and revenue budgets are by nature short term, capital budgets have long-term implications. Investments may be paid for in instalments, and their returns are likely to stretch over several years. The budgets are interrelated. Once capital investment decisions have been taken there are immediate implications for revenue to support them.

The allocation of resources to managers is dependent upon the strategies that the organization has decided to continue and develop, but adaptive changes require flexibility which must be accounted for. Where resources are limited and finite, strategic opportunities may be constrained. New alternatives may only be feasible if other activities are divested. Flexed budgets are designed to allow for changes in the level of activity, which might result from adaptive changes in functional and competitive strategies. Managers would realize that, if they were able to sell in excess of their targets, then resources would be found to facilitate increased production. The assumption would be that more sales equals more profit, which may well be true. However, if the implication is that resources would be diverted from other activities, issues of

opportunity cost are again relevant; and the resources should only be diverted from activities which are either less profitable or strategically less important to the organization in the long term.

## Zero-base budgeting

Where a traditional approach to budgeting is adopted, once the continued production of a product or service has been assumed or decided, demand prospects are forecast. Against these are set expense budgets based on standard costs. Overhead contributions are most probably adjusted for volume changes and inflation. Previous experiences are therefore carried forward and used as a base. With zero-base budgeting no previous experience is assumed, and every proposed activity must be justified afresh.

It was suggested earlier that many local authorities have, historically, sought to continue with existing service provisions, supplemented by new and additional services when resources could be found to fund them. Local authorities who make use of zero-base techniques start with the assumption that all services must be justified and priorities established on merit. Existing services might well be replaced rather than continued simply because they already exist, or better ways of providing the services might be found.

Under traditional budgeting methods it is easy to carry forward past inefficiencies which result in overspending. Zero-base budgeting should prevent this and offer opportunities for reducing expenses by searching for improved efficiencies. Moreover, the establishment of priorities on merit can result in greater effectiveness, depending on the assessment criteria selected for evaluation.

Zero-based budgeting is conceptually very attractive as it distinguishes between high- and low-priority areas and constrains the pursuit of personal objectives by managers. Its implementation presents a number of difficulties, however, which often result in traditional budgeting being preferred. The most serious problems concern the administration, paperwork and time required to implement it effectively and establish priorities objectively. In large, complex organizations the decision-making burden concerning low-level priorities, which individually may not be very significant, can draw senior management attention away from the overall strategic needs of the organization. Finally, zero-based budgeting implies that any job might be declared redundant at any time, and this causes both uncertainty and increased political activity.

## Measurement and control systems

The need to measure and evaluate performance, and to make changes when necessary, applies at all levels of the organization. Budgets establish quantitative targets for individual managers, departments, business units and divisions. Progress against these targets can be measured through the information system; and the feedback should be both fast and accurate to enable any corrective actions to take place quickly. The ability of all of these budget holders to achieve their targets will be useful when reviewing their futures.

When establishing budgets and performance targets it is, however, important to ensure that the attention of managers is not focused too narrowly on only their areas of responsibility. Their contributions to other managers and their commitment to the overall interests of the organization are the sources of synergy. While these measures of individual performances are crucial, the effectiveness of all functional, competitive and corporate strategies and their abilities to achieve corporate objectives are the ultimate measures.

The effectiveness of the contribution of such activities as research and development is difficult to assess, but this is no excuse for not trying.

*Figure 23.3*  Monitoring and control.

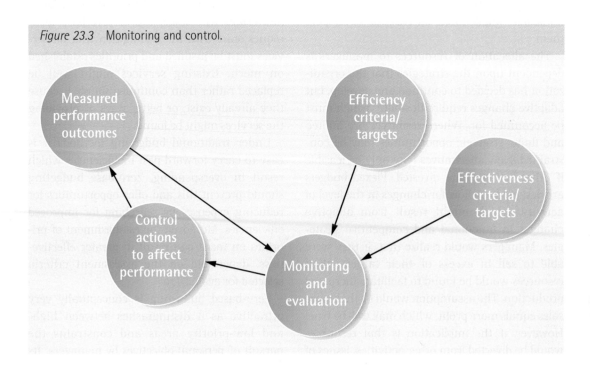

*Figure 23.4* Some possible measures of performance.

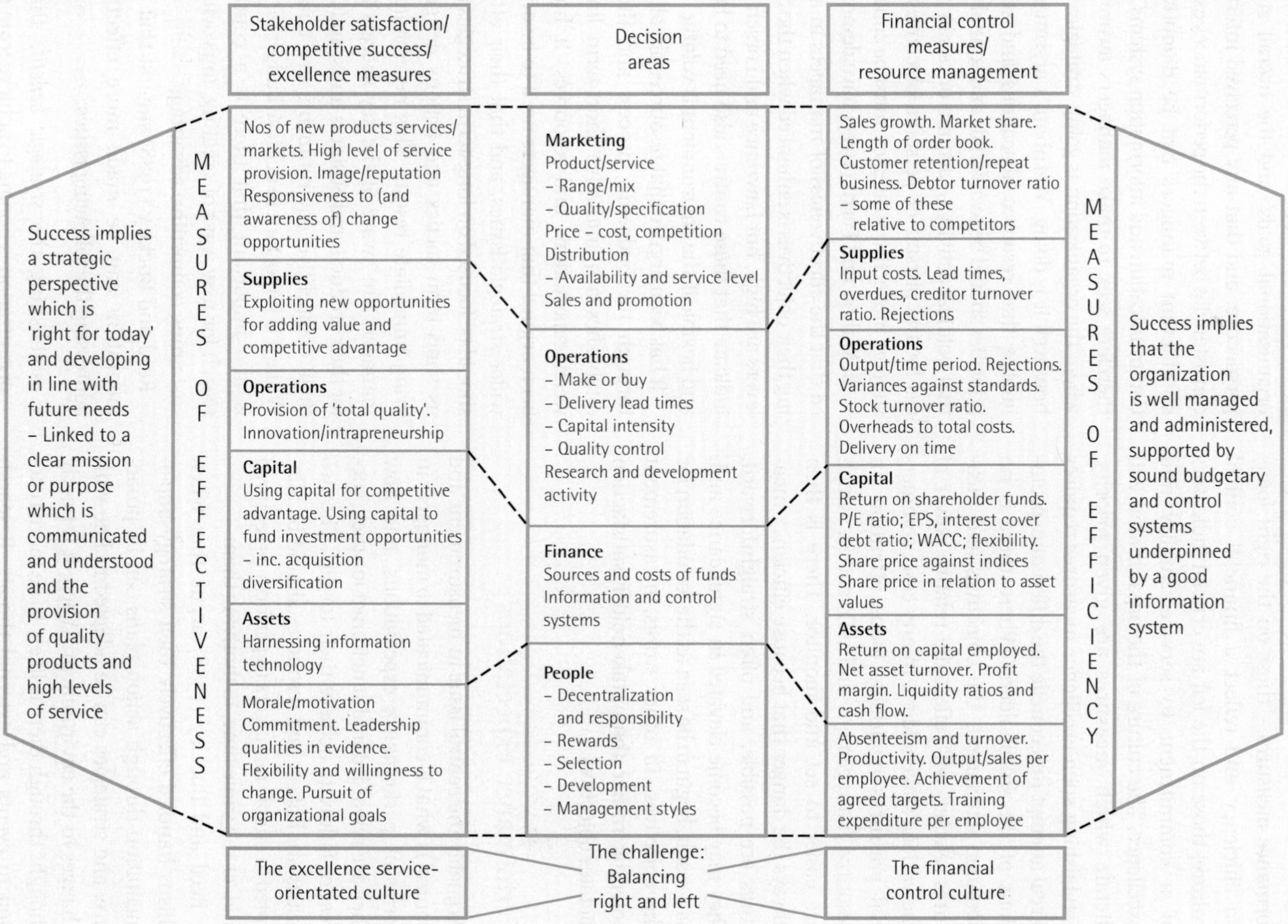

**Stakeholder satisfaction/competitive success/excellence measures**

Nos of new products services/markets. High level of service provision. Image/reputation. Responsiveness to (and awareness of) change opportunities

**Supplies**
Exploiting new opportunities for adding value and competitive advantage

**Operations**
Provision of 'total quality'. Innovation/intrapreneurship

**Capital**
Using capital for competitive advantage. Using capital to fund investment opportunities – inc. acquisition diversification

**Assets**
Harnessing information technology
Morale/motivation. Commitment. Leadership qualities in evidence. Flexibility and willingness to change. Pursuit of organizational goals

MEASURES OF EFFECTIVENESS

Success implies a strategic perspective which is 'right for today' and developing in line with future needs – Linked to a clear mission or purpose which is communicated and understood and the provision of quality products and high levels of service

**Decision areas**

**Marketing**
Product/service
– Range/mix
– Quality/specification
Price – cost, competition
Distribution
– Availability and service level
Sales and promotion

**Operations**
– Make or buy
– Delivery lead times
– Capital intensity
– Quality control
Research and development activity

**Finance**
Sources and costs of funds
Information and control systems

**People**
– Decentralization and responsibility
– Rewards
– Selection
– Development
– Management styles

**Financial control measures/resource management**

Sales growth. Market share. Length of order book. Customer retention/repeat business. Debtor turnover ratio – some of these relative to competitors

**Supplies**
Input costs. Lead times, overdues, creditor turnover ratio. Rejections

**Operations**
Output/time period. Rejections. Variances against standards. Stock turnover ratio. Overheads to total costs. Delivery on time

**Capital**
Return on shareholder funds. P/E ratio; EPS, interest cover debt ratio; WACC; flexibility. Share price against indices. Share price in relation to asset values

**Assets**
Return on capital employed. Net asset turnover. Profit margin. Liquidity ratios and cash flow. Absenteeism and turnover. Productivity. Output/sales per employee. Achievement of agreed targets. Training expenditure per employee

MEASURES OF EFFICIENCY

Success implies that the organization is well managed and administered, supported by sound budgetary and control systems underpinned by a good information system

The excellence service-orientated culture | The challenge: Balancing right and left | The financial control culture

Figure 23.3 summarizes these ideas and Figure 23.4 charts a number of possible performance measures – those on the right focus on efficiency and reflect a financial control culture; those on the left are crucial indicators of a commitment to service, quality and excellence. The culture of the organization will dictate which measures are given priority. Establishing such excellence measures requires a real attempt to reconcile the different expectations of the stakeholders. Where there is no common agreement, the objectives and measures selected will reflect the relative power of the various stakeholders. In any case, commercial pressures invariably focus attention on resource management and efficiencies, which are easier to set and monitor. There is then always the danger that because efficiency measures are possible, and often straightforward, they may become elevated in significance and, as a result, begin to be seen as the foundation for the objectives. In other words, measurement potential rather than stakeholder satisfaction dictates objectives.

## Performance expectations

Arguably the central issue in measurement and control is what is communicated to managers in terms of performance expectations, and how they are rewarded and sanctioned for their success or failure to achieve their targets. The two issues are linked, and resources should be allocated to enable managers to perform as required and, at the same time, to motivate them.

Reed and Buckley (1988) argue that when this is handled effectively then strategy implementation through action plans can be proactive, and strategies can be adapted in line with changes in the environment. Where it is poorly thought through there is likely to be more reaction to events and external threats. Research indicates that this aspect of implementation is difficult to achieve, however.

Wernham (1984) contends that managers benefit from an appreciation of 'superordinate organizational goals' and the overall strategic perspective, and that any perceived internal inconsistencies between the performances expected of different managers can be demotivating. Communication and information systems should therefore seek to make managers aware about where the organization is going strategically and how well it is doing. Wernham's argument also implies that resource allocations and strategic priorities should be seen as fair and equitable, and that political activity to acquire or retain resources for the pursuit of personal objectives, or to support ineffective strategies, must be contained.

McMahon and Perrit (1973) have demonstrated that the effectiveness of managers in achieving their objectives is enhanced when the control levers are high, but Lawrence and Lorsch (1967) indicate that these controls also need to be loose and flexible if the environment is volatile.

It has been argued that resources are allocated through the budgeting process and that this establishes a quantitative short-term link between expectations and resources. It has also been argued that managers need to be aware of wider strategic issues, and that their attention should be focused on long-term strategies as well as short-term tactics and actions designed to bring immediate results. This necessitates that managers are aware of the key success factors for their products and business units, and of how their competitive environments are changing. While it is important to achieve budget targets, it is also important that there is a continuing search for new ways of creating, improving and sustaining competitive advantage.

Reed and Buckley (1988) suggest that implementation can be made more effective by addressing the following issues:

- establishing the *strategic benefits* that the organization is hoping to achieve from particular strategic options – both immediate and long-term benefits

- clarifying the managerial actions that will be required if these benefits are to be attained, and using these as a basis for action plans
- incorporating the matching of resources with key success factors, and the development of sustainable competitive advantage, in the objectives and targets that are agreed with managers
- appraising and rewarding the ability of managers to contribute to the development of sustainable competitive advantage and not merely their ability to meet short-term budget targets
- ensuring that sufficient flexibility is built in.

These arguments emphasize that, while budgeting is essential for allocating resources on a short-term basis and progress against budget targets is a vital efficiency measure, organizational effectiveness also depends on longer-term flexibility. New developments and strategies, and improved ways of doing things, must also be considered. These may well involve changes in structures and policies as well as in the status of individual business units and managers. Issues in the implementation and management of change are the subject of Chapter 24.

## Risk Management

### Strategic risks

Risk can be best understood as an uncertain prediction about future behaviour in a market or industry, with a chance that the outcome of this behaviour could be detrimental to an organization. Clearly, an organization must try to manage these risks to reduce both the likelihood of a particular event and the extent of any possible downside. In turn, this demands a clear understanding of the inherent risks in decisions and situations.

Minicase 23.3 highlights the wide range of uncertainties that a company faces as it grows.

Opportunities and strategies that involve new customers, new markets, new countries and/or new competencies all imply risk – an element of chance that something can go wrong. The greater the potential impact (the downside) of what could go wrong, the greater the risk. This reinforces the value of a 'heartland' of related businesses, which in turn should reduce the number of risk variables. When a company moves away from 'what it knows' it increases its risk because there are more unknown factors. At the same time, not changing in a dynamic environment can also be very risky! Futures, simply, are uncertain.

Companies, then, must make strategic choices – and sometimes they 'get it wrong'. Sometimes what appears to be a poorly judged choice can be turned around with appropriate changes during the implementation phase. It follows, therefore, that risk is best managed in an organization that has a culture of flexibility and innovation and is successful at getting its people involved and committed.

Certain business environments involve higher risks than others. High-technology industries, where there is constant innovation and technological change, involve high levels of risk. In pharmaceuticals it takes a number of years to develop and test a new drug before it can be introduced on to the market, and for much of this time there will be a real possibility that the new drug may never become a commercial success. Again, therefore, there is a high level of risk, as shown in Minicase 23.4. A third example is oil exploration. Oil companies have to invest several million pounds in the hope of finding oil. While they can reduce their risk with sophisticated geological surveys before full exploration is embarked upon, there is always a risk of failure and loss of investment.

Summarizing the points so far, risk occurs whenever anyone must make a choice and the potential outcomes involve uncertainty. If a manager is faced with a decision and the

# Minicase 23.3 Jollibee

Jollibee, based in the Philippines, is the most rapidly expanding fast-food chain in Asia. It was established in 1978 by five Chinese–Filipino brothers, the Tan Caktiong family, since when it has acquired 55% of the fast-food market in the Philippines and 75% of the hamburger chain market. In the late 1990s there were over 200 branches, of which one-third are in Manila. McDonald's had 84 outlets; Wendy's and Kentucky Fried are also active competitors.

Boosted by a relaxation of laws concerning the extent of foreign investment in Filipino companies, Jollibee has expanded abroad. An Australian, Tony Kitchener, was appointed to spearhead international developments. The early concentration has been in South-East Asia and the Arab Gulf states, targeting especially Filipinos living in Indonesia, Malaysia, Brunei and Bahrain. The number of overseas branches then began to expand at a rate of 30 each year, with Hong Kong, China, Los Angeles and Rome high on the list of priorities. Vietnam was to follow. Increasingly, non-Filipinos are being attracted by the chain's individual products, which have been designed for low- to middle-income families with a sweet tooth, and for children's parties.

The main product is an Asian-style hamburger, distinctive because it is cooked *with* the spices rather than them being placed on top afterwards – McDonald's has countered this with its local McDough brand. In addition, there are Spaghetti Fiesta (a Chinese-type mixed chow), salads and mango pie (a locally popular dish). While the hamburger tends to be ubiquitous, different countries have separate menus. Chicken masala is the most popular product in Malaysia and the Gulf.

Jollibee is waiting for critical mass before announcing that 'its burgers are THE Asian fast food'. The company has also diversified, beginning with the acquisition of a pizza chain in the Philippines in 1993.

Expansion is now with joint ventures and franchising such that capital for growth is not a big problem. It also takes some account of the fact that Jollibee's first independent overseas development in Taiwan (in 1988) was not altogether successful. The chosen location was wrong.

In 1997 Jollibee had to overcome one interesting setback. After the company opened a branch in Port Moresby in Papua New Guinea someone, possibly a competitor, placed the following advertisement in a newspaper: 'Wanted urgently, dogs and cats, any breed. Will pay 40 toea (equivalent to 24 US cents) per kilo live weight. Apply to the Jollibee . . .'. The company described this as a criminal attempt to try and sabotage their business, but failed to track down the instigator.

In 1998 and 1999 Jollibee, like many Asian businesses, had to deal with a far bigger potential crisis – the uncertainty caused by high domestic inflation and drastic falls in the value of local currencies.

QUESTIONS: Can anything sensible be done to *prevent* an incident such as the rogue advertisement, or does it always come down to effective reaction?
Do you think this amounts to anything more than 'bad luck'?

*Jollibee*   http://www.jollibee.com.ph

# Minicase 24.4  Celltech and British Biotechnology

Celltech and British Biotechnology are two competitors in the growing biotechnology segment of the pharmaceuticals industry. The main pharmaceuticals manufacturers are large, global companies and they will typically be developing a whole string of new drugs at the same time. Many will never make it to market launch – the attempt is to use the successes to fund the inevitable failures. The biotechnology firms are smaller and more specialist, and they are often the most creative and innovative. Because they will only be developing a few drugs at any one time they have a different exposure to risk and their relative success or failure is clearly visible.

Developing a new drug requires: investigating an idea; developing a new (possible) product or treatment for an illness; testing it at length and robustly; launching and marketing it (if it passes all the tests); and growing a more substantial business. Most new drugs take at least ten years to pass through the development and testing phases and the majority is abandoned at some stage. While a real breakthrough can be 'worth billions' a number of things can go wrong:

- trial results are disappointing
- trials take longer than expected and have a severe impact on the cash flow
- certification is withheld for some reason
- competitors find a way to circumvent a patent
- something happens to a rival, affecting market and public confidence in the whole sector.

Companies have to strike a delicate balance. While it is essential to talk very positively about the prospects for a new drug, in order to raise investment funds, promising too much and then not delivering can have dramatic consequences.

In 1997 Celltech announced that it was abandoning trials of its new post-surgery blood-poisoning treatment. Early results had been disappointing. In 1996 its share price had reached 680 pence but it was down at 630 pence just before this announcement. It immediately fell to 340 pence, almost halving the value of the company. Other shares in the sector were also marked down, as were the shares in Bayer, with whom Celltech had a strategic alliance. Fortunately, Celltech was working on other new developments, in particular one for pancreatitis. By 2000 the price had risen and was over 1400 pence, illustrating the volatility of the sector. The price began to fall marginally when it was reported that rival PowderJect was interested in acquiring Celltech's vaccine businesses.

In 1999 trials of an anticancer agent by British Biotechnology failed. Three years earlier British Biotech's share price had been at 330 pence, but it had been falling steadily since its clinical research director resigned in 1998. He had left after commenting that the company was giving out overoptimistic progress reports. His intervention had merely increased the uncertainty although, inevitably, the company denounced his view. After the failed trial the share price was marked down to just 21 pence and the chief executive resigned. A year later the price was hardly changed. Investors believed that they had been misled, and the company was seen as a 'victim of its own hype'.

QUESTION: We clearly need biotechnology companies which are small and innovative, but can they be protected more effectively from the downside risk in their activities?

*Celltech*  http://www.celltech.co.uk
*British Biotech*  http://www.britishbiotech.co.uk

alternative choices involve estimated potential gains and losses which are not certainties, the situation involves risk. The outcome of a typical decision will be dependent on a number of factors, such as customer reaction, levels of demand and competitor responses. Some managers will understand the situation better than others might, and partly for this reason be happier to accept the risk involved in a particular choice. Personality also affects the willingness to accept and take a particular risk. It is important that there is compatibility between the strategic leader's attitude towards risk and the demands of the industry. A risk-averse strategic leader in a high-risk industry may miss valuable opportunities.

Risk increases as the amount of potential loss increases. As a simple example, a person might be offered a ticket in a raffle which costs £1.00, and the chance of winning the first prize of £150 might be 1 in 200. Another person might be offered the opportunity to invest £100 with a similar 1 in 200 chance of winning £15,000. Although the odds of winning and losing are identical, the risk involved in each situation is different. The potential loss in the second case is 100 times greater than in the first, and it consequently involves greater risk. The key issues are the uncertainty (the odds of certain eventualities, and which may or may not be predictable) and the amount that could be lost.

The following four criteria are important in the decision:

- the attractiveness of each option to the decision maker
- the extent to which he or she is prepared to accept the potential loss in each alternative
- the estimated probabilities of success and failure
- the degree to which the decision maker is likely to affect the success or failure.

## Risk, entrepreneurship and decision making

In considering risk in an organization a number of factors is worth investigating. It may well have an effect if the strategic leader is a significant shareholder rather than a minor one. Similarly, in the case of managers throughout the organization who are involved in strategic decisions in various ways, the culture and values of the organization with regard to reward for success and sanction for failure will be important. Here we are returning to the subject of entrepreneurs and intrapreneurs.

Entrepreneurs are often described as risk takers. Indeed, they do take risks, including a personal risk – it is their business, often their money and sometimes their reputation that is at stake. This personal risk can increase as the business becomes more successful and visible. The rewards for entrepreneurial success can be very high; the social stigma of a major failure can be traumatic.

The issue of entrepreneurs and risk is a complex one. There is an argument that risk awareness and opportunity awareness should be separated. Risk then concerns that which can be quantified, and opportunity that which is much more judgemental. A 'professional manager', trained in a business school, may well seek to measure and evaluate the risk in the decisions that he or she has to take. Where there is an uncertain opportunity he may well perceive the risk to be too great. There is a potential downside that he is anxious to avoid. Entrepreneurs are aware of both but are attracted by the opportunity.

In chasing an uncertain opportunity, then, the entrepreneur is taking a risk. Sometimes entrepreneurs have a feel for, or an insight into, a situation and an opportunity. This may be the outcome of learning from previous experiences. Basically, though, they know what they are doing; and in many instances they do not see themselves taking major risks; in which case,

they are really *managing* the risks, even though they may not be able to quantify them. They are accepting and retaining the inherent risk and going ahead. Other people, whose understanding of the situation, and perception of the inherent risk, is different, may be unwilling to take the same risk. They do not pursue the opportunity.

Some successful entrepreneurs also recognize when an opportunity is beginning to disappear and they time their exit carefully, and focus their endeavours on a new opportunity. This is an excellent illustration of risk management for they are seeking to avoid future risks.

A case can also be made that entrepreneurs have a lack of risk awareness. In other words, they either elect not to quantify the risks, or they simply 'turn a blind eye' to them. Their philosophy is one of 'take things as they come'. They accept that things will not proceed straightforwardly or 'go according to plan', and so they brace themselves to deal with the setbacks and challenges as they occur. They have a great faith in their courage and their ability to deal with these setbacks – and in many instances this is good judgement on their part. They are creative and innovative and they do overcome the difficulties, often turning a potential threat into a new opportunity.

Their perception of risk will change over time and with experience. Once an entrepreneur has grown one venture successfully he or she is likely to develop confidence alongside their experience. The canny entrepreneur will accumulate a 'pot of capital' that can be reinvested in a way that does not imply bankruptcy if something goes wrong. Some entrepreneurs, however, start with a failure. Kets de Vries (1997) articulates a view that many entrepreneurs do indeed start in this way but are then determined to start all over again with a fresh risk. They are convinced that the world is against them – there is a resentment of people who succeed – and so failure can be expected. Their challenge is to have another go, but this time to succeed. 'The b*******s won't get me a second time'.

Attitudes towards risk affect the way in which all managers make decisions. Dunnette and Taylor (1975), whose research involved industrial managers, concluded: 'high risk takers tended to make more rapid decisions, based on less information than low risk takers, but they tended to process each piece of information more slowly . . . although risk-prone decision makers reach rapid decisions by the expedient of restricting their information search, they give careful attention to the information they acquire.'

Environmental factors may prove significant. The availability and cost of finance, forecasts of market opportunities and market buoyancy, and feelings about the strengths and suitability of internal resources will all be important. For other managers within the organization the overall culture and styles of leadership and the reward systems will influence their risk taking.

## Managing risk

The term 'risk management' is often associated with the idea of insurance and, indeed, insurance is relevant, but it is too narrow a perspective.

Organizations will often pursue strategies that seek to manage or minimize risk. Hanson (Minicase 22.2), for example, always investigated 'the downside' in any strategy or proposed deal. Lord Hanson said of his late partner, Lord White: 'We would actually have done a lot more deals if Gordon did not have so many worries. He is constantly looking for the potential trouble in a deal'. The whole Hanson strategy was based on spreading risk. The small corporate headquarters retained the overall financial risk for the organization; all of the market risks were delegated to the individual businesses. When Richard Branson started Virgin Atlantic Airways, clearly a high-risk venture, he was cautious and spread his risk in a different way. He began with just one Boeing plane on sale or return for one year.

The first main step in risk management is clarifying the risks involved. There are four elements:

- personal risk
- opportunity risk
- (business) environmental risks, and
- resource-based risks.

Table 23.1 provides a framework for evaluating the environmental and business risks.

The second step is deciding what to do about the various risks, selecting from a number of alternatives:

- *retain* the risk and prepare for possible eventualities – Some risks have to be taken or an opportunity or a venture would have to be abandoned
- *transfer* the risk – This could be achieved by switching it to someone else (divesting a business), diluting it (through a joint venture or strategic alliance) or insuring against it
- *regulate* the risk, perhaps by investing to reduce it.

If you make a mistake in the UK you have had it . . . consequently we have a low expectation of achievement and too many people try and survive by not making a screw-up. In America they don't consider you're a businessman until you've screwed something up, because by definition you are not pushing at the frontiers. Almost everything done in the UK, by banks as well as companies, is an endeavour not to make a mistake – and when this happens we are never in front.

*Sir John Harvey-Jones,*
*ex-Chairman, ICI*

Silicon Valley is a graveyard . . . failure is Silicon Valley's greatest asset.

*Table 23.1*    Assessing business risks

| Type of risk | Example |
| --- | --- |
| **External environmental risks** | |
| Supply risks | Overdependency on a supplier |
| | Outsourcing something which is strategically critical |
| Market/demand risks | Customer preference changes |
| Stakeholder risks | Misjudged priorities |
| Social responsibility and ethical issues | Failure to deal effectively with a chemical spill or a major incident |
| Politico-economic risks | Turbulence in an overseas market |
| Innovation risks | Misjudging market acceptance for a new idea |
| Competitive risks | Existing competitors 'out-innovate' the business |
| | Price competition |
| | Powerful new rivals enter the industry |
| **Resource-based risks** | |
| Materials risks | Need to handle/transport dangerous materials |
| Process risks | 'Corner-cutting' to save time and money |
| Managerial risks | People's ability to cope with the dynamics of change in the organization |
| People risks | Inadequate or inappropriate training |
| Commitment risks | Individuals do not 'pull their weight', especially in a crisis |
| Structural risks | Inappropriate balance between centralization (for control) and decentralization (for flexibility) |
| | Internal barriers to co-operation |
| Complexity | The spread of activities is too complex and leads to fragmentation and internal conflict |
| Financial risks | Undercapitalization |
| | Cash-flow problems |
| Technology risks | Inadequate information systems |

There is a belief that in some instances organizations do not take certain risks sufficiently seriously. They place people's lives in danger – either by not appreciating the existence of a risk, or by ignoring the dangers. With some Health and Safety regulations it is clearly cheaper to ignore and pay a fine if caught out rather than invest to regulate the risk in the first place. In 2000 UK civil servants began drafting a new bill to revise the law on corporate manslaughter. The proposal is that where a company can be shown to have been negligent, and lives have been lost, individual senior managers could be held accountable and sentenced to imprisonment. The intention is to circumvent the 'collective failure' defence.

Clarke and Varma (1999) argue that changes in the external business environment mean that satisfying stakeholders effectively is more risky and uncertain for organizations than it was in the past. Risk management has really become a strategic issue but too many organizations still treat it tactically and piecemeal. As a consequence they are more crisis prone than ideally they should be. This is the subject of the next section.

## The risk-taking organization

Drawing together a number of points discussed earlier in the book, Birch and Clegg (1996) list a number of characteristics that will restrict risk taking by individual managers and employees:

- centralized and/or committee decision making
- adherence to formal systems and budgets
- reliance on performance rewards based on preset (and inflexible) plans
- early evaluation of new ideas and proposals
- mistakes being sanctioned too readily (arguably making the same mistake more than once should be punished, of course!)
- management by fear
- a culture of caution.

Risk taking can be encouraged by:

- decentralization and informality
- initiatives and projects which cut across organizations
- rewarding managers and employees for new initiatives which have succeeded
- providing resources to develop new ideas
- limited adherence to 'badges of office' and job titles
- encouraging and respecting learning
- trusting people and encouraging them to enjoy what they do – a culture with an element of fun.

Remember chaos in time of order. Watch out for danger and chaos while they are still formless.
*Sun Tzu, some 2000 years ago*

## Crisis Avoidance and Management

Crisis management concerns the management of certain risks and future uncertainties. Organizations should be ready to deal with both opportunities and surprises, and resources should be managed to cope with unexpected and unlikely events in the organization's environment: E–V–R (environment–values–resources) congruence again. It is important strategically because failure to deal effectively with crises can lead to losses of confidence, competitiveness, profits and market share.

Crisis management involves elements of planning and management. Planning constitutes crisis prevention or avoidance – the search for potential areas of risk, and decisions about reducing the risks. Management is being able to deal with crises if and when they occur. The way in which organizations do deal with crises can either enhance or damage their reputation. After all, there is always going to be an economic cost and there is little logic in trying to avoid it. Minicase 23.5 looks at how Swissair and TWA reacted to two separate air crashes, with different outcomes for each airline.

Simplified, there are three decision areas in determining the crisis strategy:

1. Decisions concerning what can go wrong, the probability of it happening, and the impact it will have if it does happen.
2. Crisis planning – Decisions about investing in prevention in order to reduce or minimize the risk. Invariably this implies cost increases; and for this and other reasons less is often done than conceivably could be done.
3. Mechanisms for contingency management.

The decisions involve trade-offs between costs and risks in an attempt to find the best balance between 2 and 3. The successful management of crisis situations involves both awareness and the ability to deal effectively with unexpected change pressures.

# Minicase 23.5  TWA and Swissair – Two different responses to a crash

In 1996 a TWA jet en route from New York to Europe came down off Long Island shortly after take-off. TWA was accused of incompetence and insensitivity for the way in which it responded to queries from families of the victims. The Mayor of New York and the media were both critical of TWA. Lasting damage was done to the airline's reputation. What had happened?

- Publication of the passenger list was delayed until every victim's family had been contacted.
- A special toll-free number was set up but calls went unanswered.
- Only limited help was provided for families of the victims who wanted to travel to the crash scene.

In reality, TWA was not a wealthy airline and it had only limited resources with which to respond to an incident of this nature. Moreover, there was immediate speculation that the crash might be the work of terrorists and, consequently, government agencies intervened and banned relatives from the crash site.

Four years after the crash there is still uncertainty as to its cause. Terrorism has been ruled out and an electrical fault is thought to be the most likely explanation.

Two years later, in September 1998, a SWISSAIR flight out of New York plunged into the sea off the coast of Nova Scotia. Swissair was praised for its efficiency and compassion; public confidence in the airline remained intact. This time the Mayor of New York was full of praise.

- The passenger manifest was published within hours.
- Families were provided with quick access to crisis counsellors.
- Flights from Switzerland to the crash site were organized, and families were provided with expenses for the trip.

Swissair was provided with support from its code-share partner, Delta Airlines, which immediately seconded its full crisis team. Moreover, the response was affected by new legislation which had been enacted after the TWA crash.

The issues from the two contrasting incidents are:

1. The speed of response in the first 24 hours is critical. This is the 'make-or-break' period. If confidence is not built with the affected families in this time then conflict will follow.
2. Rehearsal really helps.
3. Money has to be found and spent to do what is necessary. This is clouded by a cultural issue in America, where there is a fear that providing financial assistance for travel and accommodation could merely provoke additional litigation as it implies an admission of guilt.

Source: Tomkins, R (1998) Moments that build or destroy reputations, *Financial Times*, 29 September.

QUESTIONS: What are the key lessons for all organizations from the alternative reactions illustrated here?
Are there any comparisons or contrasts with the situation described in Minicase 23.1, the Concorde crash?

*TWA*   http://www.twa.com
*Swissair*   http://www.swissair.com

Fire provides a useful example of these points. Fires are caused by such events as smoking, overheating machinery and electrical faults. All of these are predictable. The likelihood of a fire happening will differ from situation to situation, and the potential damage will similarly vary. Smoking can be banned and all conceivable safety measures can be invested in, if necessary, in order to minimize the risks. However, these may not always be practical or affordable, and consequently detectors, sprinklers and fire doors to isolate areas are used as contingency measures. Nuclear power generation and airlines are examples of businesses which invest substantially in safety and prevention, often led by legislation. Situations are, however, frequently unclear. In 1991, following research after the 1985 fire on board a Boeing 737 at Manchester Airport, the Civil Aviation Authority (CAA) ruled out the use of passenger smoke hoods on aircraft. The CAA argued that they delayed the time required to evacuate an aircraft and thereby risked causing more deaths. The Consumers' Association is one group who disagreed, saying that it was 'outraged' at the decision.

## Defining crises

The word *crisis* covers a number of different issues and events, and it includes a mixture of technical and managerial elements. Some inci-

dents are clearly 'thinkable' and efforts can be made to avoid them or reduce their potential impact. Others remain more 'unthinkable'. Fires, fraud and computer failure are typical crises that might affect any organization almost any time. Poisoning scares or contamination with food products, and oil or chemical spillages, are foreseeable crises for particular companies. Major transport accidents, when they happen, are crises for the railway, shipping company or airline involved. Sometimes, but not always, the accident will prove to have been preventable. In relation to these there is an obvious logic in making contingency plans and being prepared. In addition, organizations can sometimes be affected by natural disasters, events outside their control.

Shrivastava *et al.* (1988) provide us with a valuable definition for a major crisis: 'Organizationally-based disasters which cause extensive damage and social disruption, involve multiple stakeholders, and unfold through complex technological, organizational and social processes'.

Figure 23.5 provides a framework for categorizing different incidents. On one axis is the issue of 'thinkability', while the horizontal axis separates the planned from the unplanned response. Here the terms 'crisis management' and 'disaster management' are used as a convenient form of separating the planned and unplanned response to a major event.

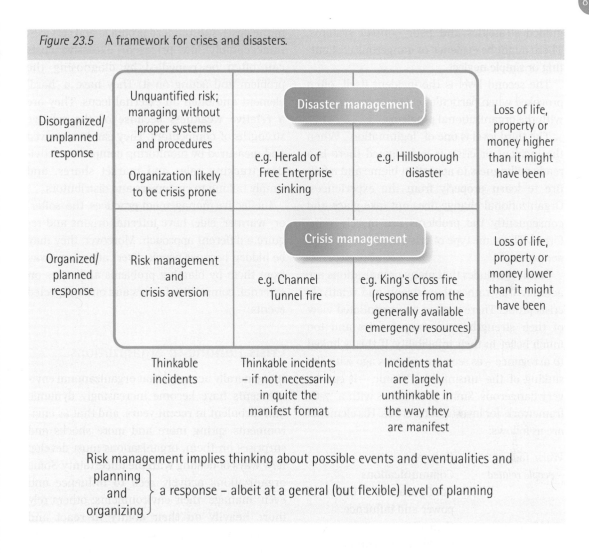

*Figure 23.5* A framework for crises and disasters.

Knight (2000) reports on research at Oxford University which confirms that catastrophes – defined as man-made, rather than natural, crises or disasters – invariably have an immediate negative effect on share prices. Over time, the share prices either recover or stay depressed. The long-term impact is rarely neutral.

In a quite different way, strategic changes can also lead to crises of confidence, particularly amongst employees. Rumours that a firm might be taken over often imply redundancies; falling sales and profits suggest possible cutbacks or closure. Good internal communica-

tions and openness are required to minimize the potential damage, especially as competitors might see these situations as competitive opportunities.

## Understanding crises

Smith (1990) identifies three 'levels' that help to explain why some crises happen when they might have been avoided.

The first level is a set of organizational problems which make the organization crisis prone. These relate to issues of culture and power, misguided strategies and poor control systems. There might be evidence of dangerous cost cutting or simple neglect.

The second level is the incident itself, often provoked when particular external events clash with the organizational problems.

The third level is one of 'legitimation'. When the incident or crisis is investigated there is a ready willingness to apportion blame and a failure to learn properly from the experiences. Organizational change does not take place and consequently the problems are merely reinforced. The same type of crisis could easily happen again.

Smith concludes that many organizations are actually frail rather than strong and relatively crisis prone. There is often an overinflated view of their strengths and competencies and too much belief in their infallibility. If this is linked to arrogance – as seen many years ago with the sinking of the 'unsinkable' Titanic – it can be very dangerous. Smith provides us with a '7-Cs framework' for investigating crises. His elements are as follows:

| | | |
|---|---|---|
| *Warm* factors | – | Culture |
| *– people related* | | Communications |
| | | Configuration – issues of power and influence |
| *Cold* factors | – | Control |
| *– technocratic* | | Coupling and complexity – the nature of the event itself |
| | | Costs |
| | | Contingency planning. |

He argues that we tend to focus our interest on the 'cold' factors and by ignoring the 'warm' ones we make the organization more crisis prone.

Box 23.1 applies these points to the Millennium Dome in Greenwich, London.

Organizational difficulties and crises, then, occur in several ways and take many forms. Weak strategies (which may have been strong in the past), substandard products and services, unacceptably low prices or excessive costs can often be remedied by diagnosing the problem and acting on it. They have a 'hard' element and often an external focus. They are a relative weakness because of the relative strengths of competitors. They can be observed and measured by monitoring competitor activities, tracking sales and market shares, and simply talking to customers and distributors.

Ineffective management practices, the 'softer' or 'warmer' side, have internal origins and require a different approach. Moreover, they may be hidden because people divert attention away from them by blaming problems and crises on external, competitive factors and on unexpected events.

## Crisis fighting in organizations

It is generally accepted that organizational environments have become increasingly dynamic and turbulent in recent years, and that as environments spring more and more shocks and surprises on them, organizations must develop new ways of dealing with the uncertainty. Some organizations actively seek to influence and even 'manage' their environments; others rely more heavily on their ability to react and respond quickly. These latter organizations, in particular, may well make a virtue out of their ability to 'crisis fight'. After all, crisis situations often bring out the best in people who call on their reserves of inner strengths. However, extensive crisis fighting carries a downside risk. It is time-consuming, reducing the time and space available for wider strategic thinking, and consequently real growth opportunities may well be missed.

It is unrealistic to think that a 'perfect' organization which is successful, seen as successful, and unaffected by crises, can be created. But most organizations could manage their resources more efficiently and more effectively

STRATEGY IN ACTION – Box 23.1
The Millennium Dome – an Application of the Crisis Management Framework

**The intention** with the Millennium Dome was to build a lasting structure in Greenwich, London, funded with a mixture of government funding, lottery money and private sponsorship. It would be opened on the evening of 31 December 1999 to celebrate the new millennium and then used for one year as a special exhibition with individual zones designed and funded by the sponsors. It was not to be a theme park, but it was to be a signal to the world that Britain could manage a major and ambitious celebratory project 'as well, if not better, than anyone else in the world'. After 2000 the Dome would be sold to a private company for a use to be determined later. The whole project was tied in to public-transport developments, notably the Jubilee Line Extension of the London Underground, – for parking at the Dome was to be severely limited.

**The outcomes**

- The Dome was opened on time.
- However, many of the guests for the special opening night ceremonies had not received their tickets and had to queue for them at an underground station.
- There was hostile media criticism from the moment the Dome was opened. Many visitors commented on the lack of any 'wow' factor. Ironically, the London Eye the viewing wheel built by British Airways), which experienced technical difficulties and a delayed start, received a better reaction and has proved very popular and lucrative.
- It quickly transpired that the sales and revenue projections were overoptimistic and were never going to be met. They have been revised downwards more than

once.
- Additional money from the National Lottery has been provided on more than one occasion to prevent bankruptcy.
- The person appointed as chief executive of the New Millennium Experience Company (which managed the whole project), Jennie Page, was forced to resign, as was the non-executive chairman of the board, Robert Ayling of British Airways. Jennie Page was replaced by Pierre-Yves Gerbeau from Euro-Disney; Ayling by David Quarmby, chairman of the British Tourist Authority. After just a few weeks in the post, Quarmby returned to his original non-executive role on the board. David James, an experienced 'company doctor', was recruited to rescue a rapidly deteriorating situation. James took over some of Gerbeau's responsibilities.
- After just one day in the post James commented publicly that he was 'appalled' at the financial systems that he had inherited. Controls were inadequate and there was no proper register of assets. Visitor projections (already reduced substantially) were still unrealistic and yet more lottery funding was required if the Dome was to remain open until the end of 2000.
- The Conservative (opposition) party called for the Dome to be closed early and for political resignations. Both demands appeared to 'fall on deaf ears', although Prime Minister Blair acknowledged that mistakes had been made. It was also commented that the Dome 'had always been a regeneration project and not a visitor attraction'.
- Nomura (the Japanese Bank) initially agreed to buy the building, to develop

theme park activities in 2001, but pulled out of negotiations when it was unable to gain access to the financial information that it needed for its planning.

**Applying the crisis management framework**

*Culture*

- Arrogant assumptions about what people (paying customers) would want.
- Arrogance about British achievements – in the event France's lighting of the Eiffel Tower received more praise.
- There was a clear culture of blame.
- There was a failure to synthesize the political agenda of the government and private sector project management.

*Communications*

- Clearly fragmented.
- Lack of cohesion amongst the stakeholders.
- Some 'truths' were kept hidden.
- Arguably, the general public was never fully clear about the project and what it stood for.
- What was to be a 'triumph' has become an embarrassment linked to 'face saving' and damage limitation.
- The media generally became hostile towards the project.

*Configuration*

- There was a clear political agenda, driven by the early leadership of Peter Mandelson. The project had to be seen as a success.
- There was also a secondary agenda – it was to be linked with public-transport developments. The Jubilee Line itself was fraught with problems and was

handed over to American contractors to complete.

*Control*

- There was a lack of clear governance and responsibility – who actually 'owned' the project?
- Financial controls were inadequate.
- The immovable completion deadline added a new dimension with extra pressures.

*Coupling and complexity*

- There were too many perspectives and expectations.
- This was exacerbated by the underlying desire to demonstrate creativity, innovation and 'great achievement'.

*Costs*

- Poor forecasting – especially concerning paying visitors – meant that the costs and break-even projections were never realistic.
- There was a very visible need to 'beg' for more subsidy which reinforced a perception of mismanagement.

*Contingency planning*

- An early closure was never a realistic option for the government.
- This made cost overruns more likely and sponsorship more difficult.
- Revenue shortfalls would be allowed, but only in a culture of blame.

*Millennium Dome*
http://www.dome2000.co.uk

and, as a result, be less prone to crises. Sometimes an externally generated crisis occurs; on other occasions, the organization actually creates the crisis. As shown above, the long-term situation is made worse when an organization, having somehow dealt with a crisis, fails to learn and make itself less crisis prone for the future.

Crisis aversion demands both single-loop and double-loop learning. Programmed responses to perceived events, the acceptance of current operating practices, norms and policies, can be speedy and efficient. They can reflect the organization's ability to share and learn and to benefit from its experiences. However, there is an important distinction between 20 years of accumulated learning and one year's experiences repeated 20 times over. The danger signals are present when 'we've seen it all before; this is the way we do it here' is utilized too readily and without checking the current circumstances. Double-loop learning demands that managers question why things are done in a particular way, paying attention to environmental changes whose impact will require more than a programmed response.

It is both significant and salutary to emphasize that managerial competency in crisis fighting will often be perceived as a strength and a virtue. People complain about stress levels but paradoxically enjoy the challenge of a crisis. Dealing with the problem quickly and pragmatically gives people satisfaction and a sense of achievement. Even laid-back people can find new motivation and strength. It is human nature. We have all seen television programmes which report how 'passers-by' willingly help in an emergency situation, sometimes improvising on the spot, and frequently with only limited regard for their own safety, until expert help can be called in. In turn, those with expertise also have to improvise on many occasions; instructions and procedures cannot predict every eventuality. At the Hillsborough football stadium disaster in 1989, traumatized people who had just escaped the crush themselves returned to the terraces to help other victims.

People prove themselves to be naturally inventive in particular circumstances. Yet how difficult might it be to persuade many of the same people to be more innovative and intrapreneurial on a day-to-day basis, and to try and move away from the crisis-fighting paradigm?

Crisis fighting in organizations takes up time. Managers are pragmatic but often not thoughtful beyond the confines of their immediate span of responsibility. Internal rivalry may well be reinforced such that people's competitive energy is focused on beating other parts of the organization (who are perceived as rivals rather than colleagues) instead of the real external competitors.

It forces a short-term time horizon on many issues and decisions. People then become frustrated and lose confidence in their organization because they seem to be operating in an 'organizational darkness' where, metaphorically, the right hand does not know what the left hand is doing. It was mentioned earlier that one major retailer recently ran a special promotion where people who spent a certain amount on anything could buy an extra item at a very substantial discount. Unfortunately, the supply chain let the stores down; there were insufficient stocks of the discounted item. A disillusioned staff simply gave out vouchers for use when stocks were renewed.

Ironically, though, crisis fighting can be very customer orientated as managers react to customer pressures and requests. Consequently, the long-term damage to the organization, which it is fostering through a failure to learn properly, can be hidden behind short-term successes. This is further reinforced by people using the short-term successes to hide and ignore the deeper problems.

In contrast, trying to eliminate the regular and ubiquitous crisis fighting and replace it with a more harmonious culture where people share information and trust and help each other may seem positively boring. However, success with this frees up time and can foster valuable innovation. It goes further than opening up new windows of opportunity for an organization; it can elevate it to a new level of opportunity which previously it could not access. In this respect it is like promotion from the First Division in English football to the Premier League. Here, promotion opens the door to millions of pounds of television and sponsorship money which hopefully will be invested sensibly to strengthen both the team and ground facilities. It is a world inhabited by only the privileged clubs, who will work hard to maintain their status and position. Over time, the gap between the Premier League and the other divisions widens and the poorest clubs inevitably become more crisis prone.

Organizations must invest in people if they are to prevent a competitive gap, let alone a chasm, developing between them and the industry leaders internationally. While organized programmes such as *Total Quality Management* and *Investors in People* have a relevance, the emphasis must be on cultural rather than procedural change. Scenario building, contingency planning and crisis management strategies can all help with unexpected events, which to some large extent are often foreseeable but not necessarily avoidable. Well-managed innovation and new product and service developments can strengthen an organization's competitiveness and reduce its crisis proneness. Internal crises generated by complacency with current good fortune, a reluctance to change, poor decisions and weak management demand a change in culture and style. Understanding, trust and commitment must be fostered.

## Crisis proneness and crisis aversion

There are, then, several characteristics which indicate crisis proneness in an organization, and these are listed in Table 23.2. Organizations need to determine the extent to which they are manifest.

Managers often believe that they are better at knowing what needs to be changed than in actually managing and implementing the changes. However, this may well be based too much on personal opinion and judgement. Without openness, trust, sharing and learning it is highly likely that organizations will not realize what they already know; consequently, they will not be able to leverage and exploit a critical strategic resource, their knowledge. Moreover, they will not realize what they do not know – they will not fully appreciate the opportunities available to the privileged competitors in an industry.

Figures 23.6 and 23.7 summarize the important themes of this section and highlight the demands on an organization. A fragmented organization with a focus on the short term will spend too much time and waste resources in crisis fighting. If it fails to manage the soft issues involved in establishing trust and co-operation it is likely to underachieve as it develops longer-term strategies. If, however, it can manage the people issues more effectively it can single-loop learn and foster innovative improvements with existing products and services. Now as it develops longer-term strategies it will be better placed to take a more holistic view and improve its overall effectiveness.

*It's not going to be one heroic act or gesture by me that's going to make the real difference; it's going to be thousands and thousands of separate actions by people in the company, every hour of the day, that will make the difference. Add all these up and the combined power is enormous.*
(Beverley Hodson, Retail Managing Director, WH Smith, after her appointment, quoted in the company's internal magazine, Newslink, June 1997)

*Table 23.2*   The crisis-prone organization

Specialist functions that cannot or do not think and act holistically

A tendency to look inwards at the expense of looking outwards – internal-competition not external-competition focus

A strong, rigid belief in present (even past) competitive paradigms

A reluctance or inability to embrace properly the demands of a changing environment

Inadequate communications – e.g. vertical but not horizontal; horizontal at discrete levels but only vertical downwards

An inability correctly to interpret triggers and signals.

Willingness of individuals readily to break rules and procedures for short-term results – and hide the details!

*Figure 23.6*   Strategy implementation and crises.

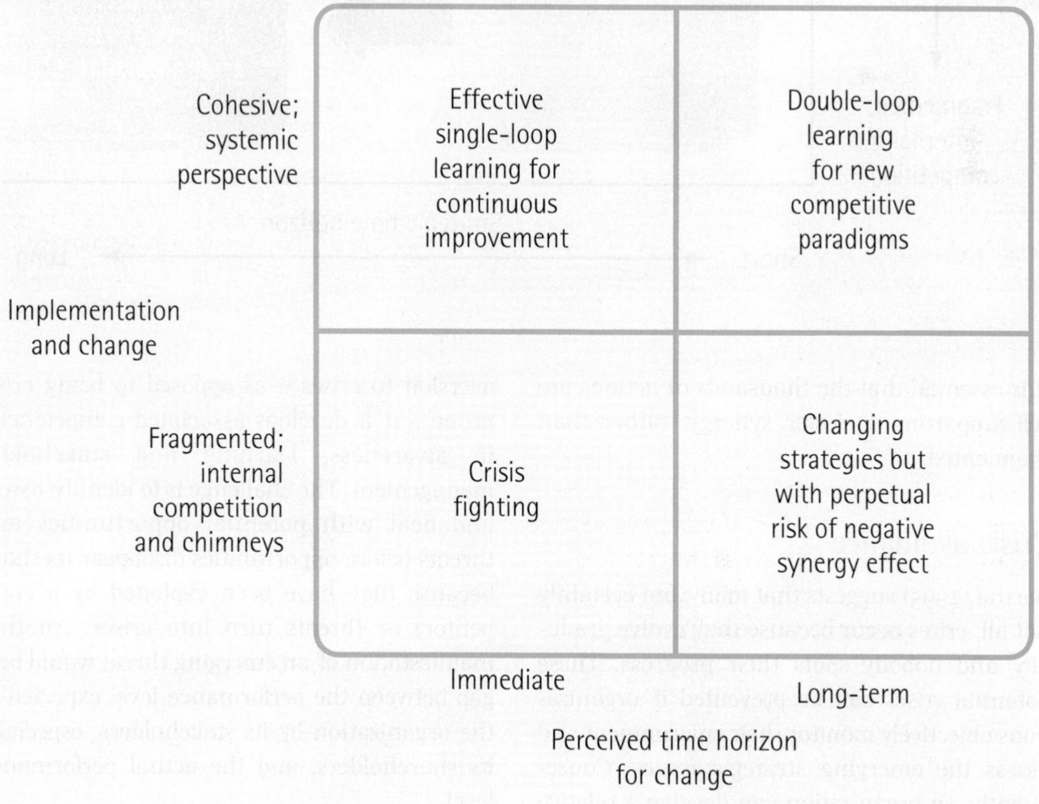

| | | |
|---|---|---|
| Cohesive; systemic perspective | Effective single-loop learning for continuous improvement | Double-loop learning for new competitive paradigms |
| Fragmented; internal competition and chimneys | Crisis fighting | Changing strategies but with perpetual risk of negative synergy effect |

Implementation and change

Immediate          Long-term

Perceived time horizon
for change

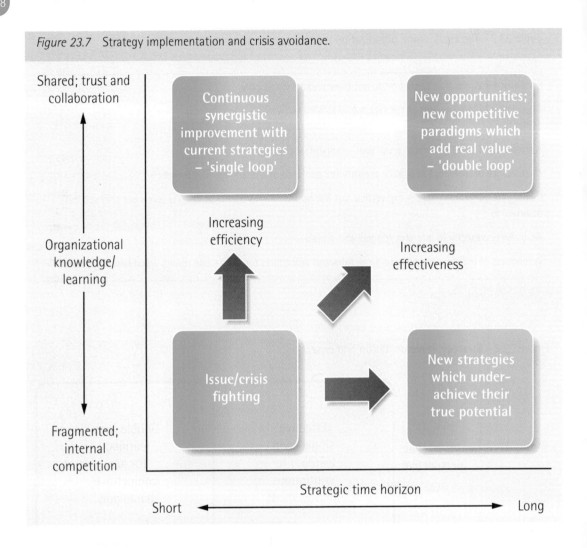

*Figure 23.7*   Strategy implementation and crisis avoidance.

It is essential that the thousands of actions are self-supporting to foster synergy, rather than fragmented.

## Crisis avoidance

Bartha (1995) suggests that many, but certainly not all, crises occur because they evolve gradually and nobody spots their progress. These potential crises can be prevented if organizations objectively monitor their environment and assess the emerging strategic issues. Consequently, an organization can develop a relative aversion to crises – as opposed to being crisis prone – if it develops associated competencies in awareness, learning and stakeholder management. The challenge is to identify, assess and deal with potential opportunities and threats before opportunities disappear (perhaps because they have been exploited by a competitor) or threats turn into crises. Another manifestation of an emerging threat would be a gap between the performance level expected of the organization by its stakeholders, especially its shareholders, and the actual performance level.

A number of elements is involved in *scanning the environment*. Competitor activity should be monitored as far as possible; while their most recent actions and changes will be visible, the challenge is to determine future strategic changes before they are implemented. There should be constant contact with key stakeholders, such as customers, distributors and suppliers; and the organization should be aware of pending government legislation and pressure group developments. The media can be a valuable source of information.

However, the strategic challenge is not one of obtaining information, but rather discerning the important messages and separating out the key issues. Quite often it is necessary to synthesize snippets of information to create a meaningful pattern. The significance of the issue then needs determining and appropriate action plans need to be initiated. Managerial judgement will be an important element.

Opportunities will emerge where the organization can build upon its strengths or tactically outmanoeuvre a rival; the crisis might occur if the opportunity is missed by the organization but picked up by a competitor. A potential threat can be present in a number of ways: new legislative restrictions, a disappearing market, financial difficulties for an important supplier or distributor. Information and triggers can be received anywhere in the organization at any time; making sure that their significance is appreciated and that they are channelled to those people, functions and businesses who could benefit is the next critical step. Communication systems are crucial, together with the ability of individual managers to take an organization-wide, or holistic, perspective.

The ability of managers to act upon the information will, in turn, depend upon organizational policies and the extent of their empowerment; their willingness to act will be affected by their personality, their competencies, their motivation and the reward/sanction system practised by the organization.

## Crisis management

There is a number of identifiable steps in attempting to manage crises effectively:

- Initially it is necessary to identify the most obvious areas of risk.
- Following on from this firms should establish procedures and policies for ensuring that risks do not become crises. Discussing possible scenarios, training sessions and actual rehearsals can all contribute, in addition to the investment in physical prevention.
- A crisis management team should be identified in advance, trained and prepared to step aside from all normal activities in the event of a crisis occurring. Experience suggests that the expertise required will be primarily communications and public relations, financial and legal. Clear leadership of the team by the strategic leader will be expected; and personnel, operations and marketing skills can be added as required. Secretarial support is sometimes overlooked.
- Building the team is one aspect of a planning process which should also cover how to get hold of key people over weekends and during holidays, how to restore critical facilities that might go down, and how to gain fast access to important regulatory bodies.
- Stakeholder analysis is another crucial aspect of the planning. It is vital to clarify which stakeholders are most likely to be affected by particular crises – and how. After a crisis

> The fact you may get knocked down is not the issue – what matters is whether you get up again.
> *Based on a quote from a US football coach*
>
> If you think education is expensive, think what ignorance might cost you.

customers either exhibit loyalty or switch to competitors; the confidence of distributors and the banks may also prove important. The media often play a significant role and their stance is likely to influence the confidence of other stakeholders. Where stakeholder perspectives and expectations differ it may be necessary to deal with each group on an individual basis.

In 1991 the insurance brokers Sedgewick showed that while 75% of Britain's largest companies claimed to have contingency plans for dealing with sudden crises when they occur, few had plans to cover the follow-up implications. Plans should also be in hand for relaunching products that might have to be withdrawn and for dealing with investors and possible litigation. 'Most companies only find out about the cost of a crisis once it's over'. Infoplan International (1997) state that 84% of the UK's leading 500 companies then saw crisis management as a senior management responsibility, up from 58% in 1995. Seventy-five per cent had experienced a crisis and put their strategies into action.

- Finally, a clear communications strategy is essential. Ethical issues may be involved, and the company will be expected to be co-operative, open, honest, knowledgeable and consistent. They must be seen to be in control and not attempting to cover up. The media will want to know what has happened, why, and what the company intends to do about the situation. 'No comment' may well be interpreted as defensive or incompetent. An effective information system will be required for gathering and disseminating the salient facts.

Regester and Larkin (1997) offer the following advice to organizations:

1. Be prepared.
2. Demonstrate human concern when something happens.
3. Consider the worst possible outcomes.
4. Communicate at all times, at all levels.

5. Avoid obsequious people as spokesmen or women.
6. Do not believe procedure manuals prevent incidents.
7. Do believe 'there is a first time for everything'.

## Strategies and examples

The most proactive strategy for crisis management can be compared with the notion of total quality management. The organization is looking for a culture where all employees think about the implications and risks in everything they do.

Reactions when a crisis has happened can prove to be effective or ineffective. Effective management is likely to mean that confidence is maintained and that there is no long-term loss of customers, market share or share price. Booth (1990) quotes research which indicates that this is more likely to happen in an open, flexible structure than it is in one which is bureaucratic.

Sandoz, the Swiss chemical company, was perceived as handling a crisis in 1986 ineffectively. Water used to fight a fire in a warehouse, possibly caused by arson, drained into the River Rhine because the local 'catch basins' were too small for the volume of water involved. The river was polluted. When pressed by the media Sandoz did not have important details readily available; and the company, the local authority and the Swiss government put out contradictory statements. Considerable ill-feeling was manifested against the company, and it has been suggested that the incident led to a medium-term loss of confidence in both Sandoz and the Swiss chemical industry.

Kabak and Siomkos (1990) offer a spectrum of four reactive approaches. At one extreme (and normally ineffective) is *denial of responsibility*, arguing the company is an innocent victim or that no harm has been done. Similarly, some organizations will attempt to pin the blame on identified individuals (who possibly did make mistakes), or argue that the general public must share the risks. Where individual errors do lead to crises there may well be a lack of effective organizational control systems; and equally the public can only be expected to share the risk if they have available all the information required for decision making. Much of this is likely to be exclusive to the company, and quite possibly buried away in files.

A better, but still ineffective, approach is *involuntary regulatory compliance*. Exxon's reluctant acceptance of responsibility after their tanker *Exxon Valdez* ran aground and spilled oil off North Alaska in 1989 is given as an example. The incident was the result of human error rather than poor systems, but the company is still held accountable. Bad weather prevented Exxon's chief executive from reaching the site, and consequently a local manager stood in for him. Whatever the reason, unfortunately the wrong message was conveyed, and Exxon's reputation was damaged.

Kabak and Siomkos offer Perrier as an excellent example of the third strategy, *voluntary compliance*. Here there is a positive company response towards meeting its responsibilities (see Minicase 23.6). The incident highlights that even though companies may have crisis management strategies unforeseen difficulties are likely to be encountered.

The other extreme strategy is the *super effort*, whereby the company does everything it can, openly and honestly, and stays in constant touch will all affected stakeholders. In 1982 an extortionist succeeded in introducing cyanide to packs of Tylenol in America. Tylenol is manufactured by Johnson and Johnson and at the time it was the country's leading painkiller with a 35% market share. Six people died.

All stocks were recalled immediately 'to contain the crisis and demonstrate responsibility'. The media were provided with constant up-to-date information. The product was relaunched in tamperproof containers and the associated heavy advertising featured the new containers rather than simply claiming that the product was safe. The incident was costly, but market share was quickly regained. Some had suggested that Johnson and Johnson should drop the Tylenol brand name, but this was resisted. Interestingly, the name *Townsend Thoresen* has been dropped by its parent company, P&O, after the ferry *Herald of Free Enterprise* capsized off Zeebrugge in 1987.

While there is little argument against the logic of planning ahead of a crisis, some organizations are cautious about the extent to which one should attempt to plan.

*The scale of the Bhopal [Union Carbide chemical plant in India] disaster [gas leak in 1984] was unimaginable. There is simply no way anyone could have anticipated it.*
(Union Carbide Director of Corporate Communications, quoted in Nash (1990)).

While the extent and magnitude of a disaster may be unexpected, events such as Bhopal are predictable, often because there have been similar incidents in the past. Union Carbide argued that they tried to be as honest as they could, but they were limited by the lack of hard facts from a remote area of India. Nash comments that the organization appreciated the need to act quickly and develop effective communications but, after the event, remained sceptical about establishing rigid guidelines, arguing that one can never be certain in advance about the actual nature and detail of any crisis.

## A crisis management framework

Companies succeed if they meet the needs and expectations of their stakeholders; companies which fail to meet these needs and expectations, long term, must be in trouble and they may collapse. Perception of relative success and failure is critical. Companies that are succeeding need

# Minicase 23.6 Perrier

In 1989 Perrier was the world leader in the fast-growing market for bottled water. In the UK, for example, the Perrier brand accounted for over one-third of the market for sparkling water, which represented 20% of the whole market. Perrier also owns Buxton, which is second to Evian in the still water segment. The name 'Perrier' had become synonymous with bottled water.

In February 1990 minute traces of benzene were discovered in a sample during routine tests in North Carolina, America. The trace, six parts per billion, did not represent any discernible health risk. Within one week every Perrier brand worldwide had been withdrawn from sale. This amounted to 160 million bottles in 110 countries.

> *Even if it is madness, we decided to take Perrier off the market everywhere in the world. I don't want the least doubt, however small, to tarnish our product's image of quality and purity.*
>
> (Gustave Leven, then Chairman, Perrier)

(Leven, 77 years old in 1990, had built Perrier from a run-down business to world leadership over 40 years. He retired later in 1990.)

> *Perrier had created crisis management strategies some years earlier . . . 'Everyone knew what they were supposed to do . . . in spite of this we never, ever, imagined a world-wide withdrawal. We'd never dreamed of a problem of such magnitude'. Only Tylenol had previously been withdrawn on such a scale; and in that crisis people had died.*

## Actions in the UK

Local tests were arranged as soon as news spread from the USA. The tests took a normal 48 hours, and benzene was again found in the sample. Unfortunately, during this period a Perrier spokesman in Paris speculated prematurely that a greasy rag might have introduced the wrong cleaning fluid onto bottling equipment. Moreover, when the worldwide withdrawal was announced to the world's press in Paris – rather than local press conferences – the room was too small for the press and television crews attending.

On the following day advertisements appeared around the world, explaining the situation, and clarifying what people, including retailers, should do. The 24-hour emergency telephone network in the UK 'received mostly friendly calls'.

A major problem in the UK concerned the disposal of all the water and the further disposal or recycling of the bottles. A large proportion of the stocks was in the distinctive Perrier green glass which, recycled, has few alternative uses.

The source of the contamination was quickly traced to a filter at the bottling plant in France, a filter used to purify carbon dioxide being added to the water. This revelation suggested that Perrier is not 100% naturally carbonated, although the label on the bottles stated 'naturally carbonated natural mineral water'. It transpired that the gas used is collected underground with the water and added back after purification. Only the gas, not the water, is purified. Nevertheless the publicity caused Sainsbury's to refuse to stock Perrier for a period after it was re-launched in April 1990.

One month after the re-launch Perrier was already selling at half its previous volume; and market leadership was quickly regained. The world-wide cost was estimated to be £125 million.

Competitors had not attempted to exploit the situation, possibly believing they might spread a scare by association and affect the market for all bottled water.

It has been suggested that the very popularity of Perrier had caused the problem. Demand world-wide had put pressure on the supply side. Some years earlier, and before the increased consumer awareness and concern with health issues, the problem would probably have been contained on a smaller scale.

The balance of opinion seems to be that Perrier got the big decisions right. It adopted a worst case scenario, acted fast, and spoke out honestly.

Shortly after the crisis Perrier was bought by Nestlé, which already owned the Vittel brand and the top US bottled water, Poland Spring.

Sources: Butler, D (1990) Perrier's painful period, Management Today, August; Caulkin, S (1990) Dangerous exposure, Best of Business International, Autumn.

*Perrier* http://www.perrier.com

QUESTION: Do you agree that Perrier 'got the big decisions right'?

to be recognized for this. Companies that are not succeeding will want to cover up their weaknesses if they can.

The simple matrix illustrated in Figure 23.8 is based on these premises. Companies that satisfy their stakeholders, and are seen to do so, are classified as crisis avoiders. Crisis-prone organizations fail on both counts. Companies with a strong reputation they do not wholly deserve are termed 'thin high profile' as the situation is likely to be very fragile and fluid. The fourth quadrant contains 'unsung heroes', companies whose reputation does not do justice to their real achievements.

It is worth considering in which quadrant the following three companies should be placed.

The *Body Shop* has seen its share price and price to earnings ratio fall in recent years as it has faced increasing competition internationally. In 1996, disillusioned with City investors, the

Body Shop looked at the viability of reprivatization, but concluded that it would not be an appropriate strategy to follow. Nevertheless, its customers and employees remain loyal and supportive, and the company's reputation as an environmentally concerned organization also remains strong.

In 1995 *Shell*, one of Europe's most successful and respected companies, was forced to change an important strategic decision following a high-profile campaign by a leading pressure group. Shell had chosen to sink its redundant Brent Spar oil platform in deep seas some 150 miles west of Scotland. It had reached an agreement with the UK government that, scientifically, this was the most appropriate means of disposal for the platform. Greenpeace objected and protesters boarded the platform, claiming that it still contained 5000 tonnes of oil which would eventually be released to

*Figure 23.8*    A crisis-management framework.

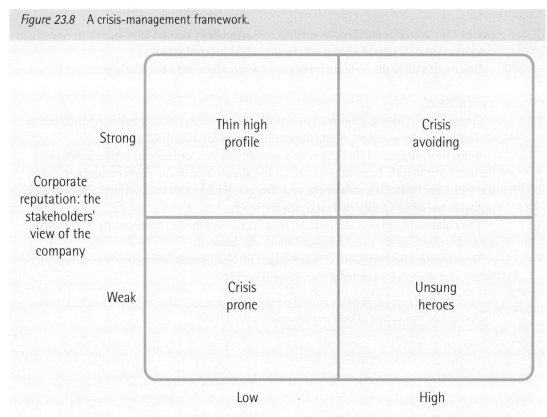

pollute the sea. The ensuing and professionally orchestrated publicity fuelled public opinion, and there were protests in a number of European countries, including attacks on petrol stations in Germany. Shell backed down and agreed to investigate other possibilities for disposal. The UK government expressed both anger and disappointment with this decision. Independent inspectors later proved that Greenpeace's claims were gross exaggerations – the residual oil was much, much less than 5000 tonnes. The press concluded: 'Shell went wrong in spending too much time convincing government of the case for sea-bed dumping,

but not attaching enough importance to consulting other stakeholder groups'. Shell had been made to appear socially irresponsible, even though the ethics of the Greenpeace campaign are questionable.

Again in 1995, *Yorkshire Water* was criticized on a number of occasions by its customers, provoked by the threat of rota cuts and a very visible road-tankering operation to bring water into areas of the county threatened by drought. Essential though it was, given the genuine and severe drought experienced, this operation upset residents who were affected by the noise of the lorries. There were definite technical issues such as the amount of water leaking from the infrastructure, combined with the past failure of the company to remedy this problem, and concerns over environmental damage as water was diverted out of rivers. However, many of the difficulties faced by the company were the result of poor public relations. The company's request to companies to restrict water use (and thus restrict manufacturing) was not well received. The statement by the managing director that he had not bathed in several weeks, subsequently proven not to be wholly accurate, was really another PR disaster. Similarly, positive statements that £50 million was being committed for new infrastructure investment were overshadowed in just two days by the announcement of strong profits and a 10% increase in dividend. The company's share price, however, held up throughout the crisis, perhaps explaining why the company was accused of placing its shareholders ahead of its customers.

## Summary

Successful strategy implementation requires that strategic resources are allocated and controlled efficiently and effectively. In reality, the availability and suitability of resources is a determinant of the feasibility of a particular strategic option. Of course, the existence of resources does not, in itself, guarantee effective implementation – they have to be managed. In addition, resources should be flexible to allow adaptive and incremental change.

We can think of *resource allocation* at two key levels:

- The allocation of *corporate* resources to particular businesses or divisions, based on perceived needs and priorities, and often linked to the growth of the business or industry in question

- The allocation of *functional* resources to build and add value in order to create and sustain competitive advantage.

*Policies* are designed to guide the use of resources by managers.

*Budgets* are used to allocate resources for particular activities and tasks. Budgets, however, are often short term in scope and the measurement of performance against budget targets may be more an evaluation of efficiency in the use of resources than of longer-term strategic effectiveness.

*Resource allocation and management* – and the inherent decisions – reflect the way in which the organization and its managers are dealing with the risks that they face. The key dimensions of risk are:

- the likelihood of certain eventualities – some of which could imply a detrimental impact for the organization, and
- the extent of the downside (perhaps a loss of orders, revenues or confidence) if the particular incident in question does occur.

While there is always a personal risk for entrepreneurs and strategic leaders in corporate strategy changes, a useful framework for clarifying and analysing risks is based on external (environmental) and internal (resource-based) factors.

Risks can be retained, transferred or regulated.

The relative success or relative failure of an organization to deal with the risks that it faces determines the extent to which it is crisis prone or crisis averse.

Crises can be major or minor, 'thinkable' in advance or more realistically unforeseeable. Consequently, organizations need strategies for avoiding crises in the first place and then for dealing with those crises that do occur. Handled well, a crisis can enhance the reputation of an organization. Handled badly, the impact can be substantial and prolonged.

Crises and disasters contain a mixture of 'cold' (technocratic) and 'warm' (people-related) elements. All too often organizations focus their attention on the cold elements when it is the warm ones that hold the key. By not learning lessons and by apportioning blame too readily organizations can 'legitimate' crises and simply increase the likelihood of them happening again.

It remains a paradox that many managers are proud of their ability to 'crisis fight' and deal with problems as they arise. This merely reinforces a reactive attitude and a short-term perspective, and it can be short-sighted.

## References

Bartha, P (1995) Preventing a high-cost crisis, *Business Quarterly*, Winter.

Birch, P and Clegg, B (1996) *Imagination Engineering*, Pitman.

Booth, S (1990) Dux at the crux, *Management Today*, May.

Bower, JL (1970) *Managing the Resource Allocation Process: A Study of Corporate Planning and Investment*, Division of Research, Harvard Business School.

Clarke, CJ and Varma, S (1999) Strategic risk management – the new competitive edge, *Long Range Planning*, 32(4).

Dunnette, MD and Taylor, RN (1975) Influence of dogmatism, risk taking propensity and intelligence on decision making strategy for a sample of industrial managers, *Journal of Applied Psychology*, 59(4).

Infoplan International (1997) *Review of Crisis and Risk Management*, London.

Kabak, IW and Siomkos, GJ (1990) How can an industrial crisis be managed effectively? *Industrial Engineering*, June.

Kets de Vries, M (1997) Creative rebels with a cause, in Birley, S and Muzyka, D, *Mastering Enterprise*, Financial Times/Pitman.

Knight, RF (2000) Recovering well from tragedy, *Financial Times*, 3 August.

Koontz, H and O'Donnell, C (1968) *Principles of Management*, 4th edn, McGraw-Hill.

Lawrence, PR and Lorsch, JW (1967) *Organization and Environment*, Richard D Irwin.

McMahon, JT and Perrit, GW (1973) Toward a contingency theory of organizational control, *Academy of Management Journal*, 16.

Nash, T (1990) Tales of the unexpected, *The Director*, March.

Pearce, JA and Robinson, RB (1985) *Strategic Management*, 2nd edn, Richard D Irwin.

Reed, R and Buckley, MR (1988) Strategy and action: techniques for implementing strategy, *Long Range Planning*, 21(3).

Regester, M and Larkin, J (1997) *Risk Issues and Crisis Management*, Institute of Public Relations.

Sedgewick (1991) Research quoted in de Jonquières, G (1991) Taking the drama out of a crisis, *Financial Times*, 14 November.

Seed, AH (1983) New approaches to asset management, *Journal of Business Strategy*, Winter.

Shrivastava, P, Mitroff, I, Miller, D and Miglani, M (1988) Understanding industrial crises, *Journal of Management Studies*, 25(4).

Smith, D (1990) Beyond contingency planning – towards a model of crisis management, *Industrial Crisis Quarterly*, 4(4).

Wernham, R (1984) Bridging the awful gap between strategy and action, *Long Range Planning*, 17.

Test your knowledge of this chapter with our online quiz at: http://www.thomsonlearning.co.uk

Explore Strategic Resources, Risk and Crisis Management further at:

*Academy of Management Journal*   http://www.com.pace.edu/amj

*Journal of Applied Psychology*   http://www.apa.org/journals/apl.html

*Journal of Business Strategy*   http://www.faulknergray.com/busstrat/jbs.htm

## Questions and Research Assignments

### TEXT RELATED

1. Should top management policies be essentially broad and general, and lower level policies narrow, explicit and rigid? Why? Why not?

2. What are the contributions and limitations of budgeting and the measurement of performance against budgets in the implementation of strategy and the monitoring of strategic effectiveness?

3. Are you personally risk averse or perceived as a risk taker? On what evidence are you drawing this conclusion?

## Internet and Library Projects

1. For an organization with which you are familiar, ascertain the main stated policies for finance, production, personnel and marketing.

   How are these policies used? How were they created? How do they rate in terms of the principles of good policies discussed in the text?

2. Ascertain the budgeted resources and targets allocated to one manager whom you are able to interview.

   What measures of performance are utilized? What feedback is provided? What does the manager do with the feedback?

   What do you believe is the personal impact of the budget and measures of performance on the manager? Is he or she motivated? Rewarded or sanctioned for success or failure?

3. Either by contacting a local councillor or using the Internet, ascertain how planning and budgeting are managed in your local authority. What have been the priority areas in the past? What are the current priorities? How have the changes in priority been decided?

4. In 1999 Coca-Cola withdrew its product from shelves in Belgium. What caused the incident and how well did Coca-Cola deal with it? To what extent do you think it contributed to the early retirement of chief executive Douglas Ivester at the end of the year?

*Coca-Cola*   http://www.coca-cola.com

5. In August 2000 the Russian nuclear submarine Kursk sank in the Barents Sea after an internal explosion. The whole crew was lost and the Russian government was criticized for not calling on foreign help and expertise as quickly as it might have done. What are the lessons in risk and crisis management from this incident?

6. Use the Internet to assess the possible long-term damage to Ford Motors when it was discovered (in 2000) that the Bridgestone/Firestone tyres used on its Explorer four-wheel drive vehicles were potentially dangerous and had been the cause of a number of accidents over a period of time. How do you think both Ford and Bridgestone handled the crisis – effectively or ineffectively?

# Strategic Change Management

*Organizations and managers face change on a continuous basis, especially in volatile environments. Some changes are reactions to external threats; others are proactive attempts to seize opportunities and manage the environment. Organizations should seek to obtain and maintain a congruence between their environment, values and resources, making changes when there are pressures from either the environment or their resources. It is crucial that organizations seek to create and sustain competitive advantage, and wherever possible innovate to improve their competitive position. This implies a readiness to change within the organization and the ability to implement the proposed changes. At times there will be a perceived need to try and change values and culture. Towards the end of the twentieth century the pressures for change in a wide cross-section of businesses were clearly visible. Food manufacturers and distributors were affected by changing consumer attitudes to their diets and by the public reaction and concern to the growing awareness of incidences of food poisoning. Building societies and banks were responding to changes in the competitive regulations that directly affect them, generally seeing the changes as opportunities. The water authorities and electricity industries have followed a number of other corporations into privatization, which has forced major changes of strategy, resource management and culture. Organizations within the umbrella of the National Health Service have been responding to new proposals and legislation on controls and performance measures. Some National Health Service employees see the changes as threats; others as opportunities.*

*This chapter looks at various issues and problems in the management of change. Organizations must be reactive to external change pressures and proactive in seeking to take advantage of opportunities and shape their environment if they are to be effective strategically. Cultural and power considerations are important variables in the management of change. It is particularly useful at this point to refer back to the earlier discussions of intrapreneurship, empowerment and learning organizations.*

*The opening case looks at a series of strategic, structural and leadership changes at Apple Computers. The case charts the story of Apple over some 20 years and shows how the company has enjoyed mixed fortunes. Sometimes highly innovative and successful, Apple has also been affected by competitor initiatives which have changed the personal computer industry in dramatic ways. Some of the changes documented were therefore reactive while others were more proactive.*

# Minicase 24.1 Apple Computers

Apple was started in 1976 by a young entrepreneur, Steven Jobs, and his partner, computer nerd Stephen Wozniak. They began by making personal computers (PCs) in a garage. In 1983 the company's turnover, from essentially one model – the distinctive Apple computer – was approaching $1 billion. At this stage in the company's development Wozniak had already left and Jobs had been quoted as saying that he was no longer able to do what he most enjoyed, working with a small group of talented designers to create new innovative products. To overcome his frustration with an increasingly bureaucratic organization Jobs had formed a new team of designers and set about developing the company's second major product, the Apple Macintosh, away from corporate headquarters and the production plant. The Macintosh was regarded as very user friendly and featured an illustrated screen menu and a hand-held mouse unit for giving instructions. It was launched in 1984 and sold immediately. However, it was launched at a premium price, which remained high as sales took off. This niche-marketing approach left a wide-open gap which was ultimately filled by Microsoft.

Jobs had actually seen the first graphic-user interface being demonstrated at Xerox PARC (Palo Alto Research Center) where it had been developed by a Xerox scientist in the 1970s. At this stage, Xerox failed to appreciate the value of the idea they had; Jobs immediately saw the potential of this new technology and set about developing a PC which used it. Jobs used Bill Gates to help with some of the development work – and this was the birth of *Windows*. Had Xerox executives been more visionary, they would probably have driven the PC industry instead of Microsoft.

John Sculley, previously CEO of PepsiCo, was recruited by Jobs to be Apple president in 1983 and he took over executive control. Sculley reports that Jobs challenged him: 'Do you want to spend the rest of your life selling sugared water or do you want a chance to change the world?' His initial priorities were to co-ordinate product development activities, which he felt were fragmented, and to integrate these developments with existing programmes. To achieve this, power was centralized more than it had been in the past and was supported by formalized reporting procedures and new financial control systems.

Sculley was regarded as being more marketing orientated than Jobs, and their business philosophies clashed. Jobs resigned in 1985, together with a number of other key employees, deciding to concentrate his efforts on the development of sophisticated PCs for university students in a small, entrepreneurial organization environment.

Despite the increased business discipline, Sculley attempted to preserve important aspects of the original Apple culture. Informal dress codes, a 'fun working environment' and elaborate celebrations when targeted milestones are reached were all considered important. Apple retained a structure with few layers of management, few perks and few status-carrying job titles.

Sculley's challenge was to move the company away from an informal and entrepreneurial management style to a more functional and later (1988) a divisionalized structure, while retaining the important aspects of the culture. In addition, Sculley felt that Apple needed to be repositioned in the market in order to overcome the competitive threats from the Far East.

With new versions of the Macintosh, Apple moved from an education and home computer base into a business computer company which also sold to schools and universities. Apple was a major innovator in desk-top publishing, pioneering the market in advance of competition from IBM and Xerox.

Apple prospered in the late 1980s, but its strategy began to appear inappropriate for the recession and the 1990s. Apple had concentrated on, and succeeded with, high-margin products which were substantially differentiated. However, Sculley claimed that Apple's ideas were being copied and used in cheaper rival products – Apple began a legal action against Microsoft, alleging that its Windows software used ideas from the Macintosh. Moreover, PCs have become more of a commodity product in a maturing market. Although Apple had sold 22 million Macintosh computers at this time, the continued success of Microsoft has been very damaging to the company.

In 1991 Apple agreed a series of strategic alliances, mostly with IBM, historically its main rival. The alliances concentrated on areas where Apple lacked either development skills or the ability to fund the research and development independently. New PC technology and operating systems software were key areas. Cultural and other differences between Apple and IBM have led to their alliances being relatively unsuccessful.

Coincidental with its agreements with the global IBM Apple's culture had actually been changing. Empowerment, flexibility and freedom remained important, but 'there had to be more discipline. Our cost structure was out of line. We did not know how to meet schedules. We were a benevolent company that sponsored people to work on things they were interested in' (Sculley).

Apple reduced the prices of its existing products, hoping for higher volumes which would more than compensate for the lower margins, and introduced a range of cheaper, lower-performance Macintosh computers. In terms of new products Apple was arguably two years late with its lap-top computer. Other new products concentrated on personal electronics devices and included electronic books and a notebook computer. In 1993 Apple launched

*Newton*, a $7 \times 4\frac{1}{2}$ inches black box with a $5 \times 3$ inches screen; users could jot down ideas on the screen and draw sketches as they talked and thought, and record notes and appointments. The machine could translate the images, store and organize. In addition, electronic data, such as a map, could be input. Sales of the Newton were disappointing and it failed to live up to Apple's early expectations.

As market shares and gross margins fell during the early 1990s, Apple's pre-tax profits and share price were both erratic. Sculley, the Newton product champion, was accused of neglecting the main hardware products to push the new idea, and his position was threatened. Sculley was in fact replaced by Michael Spindler in 1993, an internal promotion but, three years later, Spindler also left. Another new strategic leader, Gil Amelio, joined Apple from National Semiconductor in 1996. After his own departure Sculley commented: 'I don't think anyone can manage Apple'.

Amelio decided to halve the Macintosh product range (responsible for 80% of Apple's revenue) in order to reduce costs and help to restore profitability. This controversial cut radically affected Apple's strategy of market segmentation. In addition, six varieties of its software operating system were consolidated into one, which Apple would also seek to license to other manufacturers. Allied with Adobe – which could put on to a laser printer what was appearing on a screen – Apple pioneered desk-top publishing. The Macintosh has always been the preferred machine for designers.

The company was also restructured into seven profit-centre divisions: four for different hardware products, plus software, service and Internet – the Macintosh has always been an ideal machine for creating Internet products.

Amelio recognized that cultural change was again an issue – he believed from one where 'employees felt free to question, and even defy, management decisions' to a more conventional style. Product managers would no longer be 'free to veto the strategic leader'.

Apple's core competency was still its ability to make technology easy to use and Amelio argued that it needed to exploit this in ways that allowed it to move further away from the cut-throat PC market and capitalize upon the new opportunities that were emerging as more and more people worldwide gained access to computers. Currently just 9% of the world's population had access.

Apple's new Macintosh operating system, called Copland, and due around the end of 1996, was being predicted 'to make Windows 95 seem as quaint and feeble as DOS' because of its radical new ability to organize, track and retrieve stored data and files. However, in 1996 Steve Jobs stated:

> 'If I were running Apple I would milk the Macintosh for all its worth – and get busy on the next great thing. The PC wars are over. Done. Microsoft won a long time ago'.

Declining sales and falling profits were a feature of 1996, and Amelio had to shoulder some of the blame. The new Macintosh operating system, Copland, was not launched on time; the development team had been depleted too much by redundancies and resignations. However, in December 1996, Apple attempted to help rectify these weaknesses by acquiring NeXT Software, the company formed by Apple cofounder Steven Jobs after he was ousted by John Sculley in 1985. The assumption was that Apple should now get the new technology it required for updating the Macintosh. In addition, though, it would obtain the part-time consultancy services of Steven Jobs, who would advise on product strategy.

Jobs commented: 'For the past ten years the PC industry has been slowly copying the Mac's revolutionary graphical user interface. Now the time has come for new innovation . . .'. The key relationships lay with other software developers who typically produced a Windows version first, and only released Macintosh versions some months later.

NeXT's software had generally been highly acclaimed, but it had enjoyed only limited commercial success. Jobs meanwhile had been more successful with his other company venture, Pixar. Pixar is the film animation company which worked with Disney on *Toy Story* and had a ten-year partnership deal with the Walt Disney Corporation. Jobs quickly began to make an impact. Executives from NeXT took over senior positions at Apple and a close colleague of Amelio was demoted. Jobs' cofounder at Apple, Steven Wozniak, was also brought back as a consultant. Costs and employees continued to be cut back, however. The workforce of 13,000 was reduced to between 10,000 and 11,000. Product development, sales and marketing were streamlined. It was quickly speculated that the Apple Newton would be floated off as a separate business.

Once Amelio had left it was also speculated that Jobs would take over full-time, although he continually denied any interest in the challenge, emphasizing his commitment to Pixar. While some assumed that he would be able to rejuvenate Apple with his renowned entrepreneurial flair, one analyst was sceptical: 'The idea that they are going to go back to the past to hit a big home run to beat Microsoft is delusional'. In addition, there were fresh rumours that the NeXT software was after all proving to be inappropriate for Macintosh.

So, two questions arose. One, where did Apple currently fit in the PC industry? And two, could it continue to survive in its present form? Sales of Macintosh had declined to a level where Apple had less than a 5% share of the US PC market; just two years ago it had an 11% share. The odds on Apple being taken over began to shorten. After all, IBM had already made two unsuccessful offers (in 1994 and 1995) and Sun Microsystems one (in 1996).

Early in August 1997 Steve Jobs announced that Microsoft was to invest $150 million in Apple and the two companies were forming a partnership. The key terms of the agreement were as follows:

- Microsoft would develop and distribute office applications for the Apple Macintosh
- Apple would bundle Microsoft's Internet browser software, Internet Explorer, in future Macintosh products.

For Apple, the alliance clearly provided a positive new lease of life. For Bill Gates and Microsoft, it was more of a defensive strategy. If Apple collapsed, Microsoft would be a monopoly supplier – between them, Apple and Microsoft accounted for virtually all the sales of PC operating systems software around the world – and this might raise issues for the US anti-trust authorities. Moreover, Microsoft's real competitive threat at this time did not come from Apple's software and PCs, but rather from Netscape's rival Internet browser and Oracle's network computer which could grow at the expense of independent PCs. Consequently, this deal was designed to strengthen its overall position.

Early in 1998 Apple became profitable again. A new range of PCs was beating sales forecasts – the latest G3 version of the Mac was faster and cheaper than equivalent Windows-based PCs, a very different situation from the earlier years. Jobs, now firmly in control again, took the credit. Newton was abandoned. One lingering concern, though, was that sales were still to committed Mac users, who were updating, rather than to new buyers.

In May 1998 Apple announced its radical new iMac, an integrated computer and monitor in a single unit and in a bright, translucent housing. A keyboard and mouse could be attached in an instant. The keyboard was also translucent and the mouse lit up. At its launch in August it 'flew off the shelves'. In 1999 Apple launched a new range of notebook computers in a similar style and packaging to the iMac. Jobs appeared to have tapped into a new market segment – 'the Generation Y buyer that likes individuality'.

QUESTIONS: Do you think Apple's latest turnaround might be real and sustainable? What would be required for sustainability?
In the context of Apple, do you agree with the view that 'the right strategy depends upon personal vision, and personal vision depends upon having the right person'?

*Apple computers*   http://www.apple.com

There is nothing more difficult to take in hand, more perilous to conduct, or more uncertain in its success than to take the lead in the introduction of a new order of things.

*Machiavelli*

In this race . . . you run the first four laps as fast as you can – and then you gradually increase the speed.

*William Weiss, when CEO, Ameritech*

## Introducing Strategic Change

Figure 24.1 illustrates the strategic change process. The process is driven by the strategic leader and is affected markedly by the organizational culture. The organization is attempting to both manage in (reactively) and manage (proactively) its external environment. The structure,

objectives and the related performance measures are determined by the mission and direction and they, in turn, guide the decisions, actions and outcomes. These outcomes can then be compared with performance expectations. The timing of change is critical. If things are not changed at the appropriate time the organization is likely to be reactive and may well end up perpetually crisis fighting.

Effective organizations must be able to *manage change*, with managers and employees supportive rather than resistant or hostile. When strategies change, there are often accompanying changes in structures and responsibilities, and people are clearly affected. Kotter and Schlesinger (1979) and Waterman (1987) have suggested that most companies or divisions need to make moderate organizational changes at least every year, with major changes every four or five years.

While organizational changes can be reactive and forced by external change, effective strategic management really requires *learning*.

*Figure 24.1*   The strategic change process.

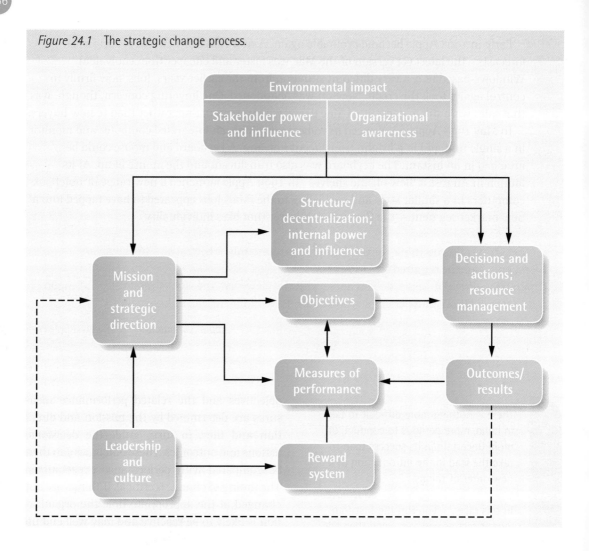

Managers must be aware of their environment, assessing trends and deciding in advance what should be done about perceived opportunities and threats. Planning activities and systems should ensure that the future is considered, and the resultant plans should encompass the implementation aspects of any proposed changes and the need to be flexible to accommodate unexpected changes. Moreover, innovation should be possible within the organization. Managers should be constantly looking for ways of being more effective and able to proceed with appropriate changes.

Ideally, the organization will seek to develop a culture where people do not feel threatened when they are constantly asked to question and challenge existing behaviours and acknowledged ways of doing things, and change them – a culture that sees innovation and change as normal; a culture that is ideal for dealing with the competitive chaos that characterizes many industries and markets; a culture where people do not automatically ask: 'Who is already doing this?' when someone proposes an innovative change. This cannot happen without strong strategic leadership which fosters, encourages and rewards intrapreneurial and innovative contributions from managers and other employees throughout the organization.

A culture such as this will frequently be based around a working atmosphere of creativity and fun; people must enjoy doing things differently and originally, actively looking for new competitive opportunities, instead of simply copying others.

A change culture is highly desirable for many organizations but very difficult to achieve.

Hence, the implementation of change requires:

- *a perceived need for change* – this can originate with either the strategic leader or managers throughout the company who are aware of the possibilities
- *the necessary resources* – this involves aspects of competency as well as physical resources, and the ways in which managers use power to influence the allocation and utilization of resources
- *commitment* – the culture of the organization will influence the extent to which managers are responsive and innovative.

Figure 24.2 takes the concept of E–V–R (environment–values–resources) congruence and restates the idea from the perspective of effective change management. The *environment* provides opportunities for organizations to benefit from innovation and continuous improvement; on other occasions the environment will encourage more dramatic, discontinuous change. This pressure can take the form of a threat (major environmental disturbance) or an opportunity (whereby the organization, 'seeing the future' ahead of its rivals, can shape its environment). The relative strength of the organization's *resources* is reflected in the success of existing strategies; *values* dictate the ability of the organization to manage change effectively. Strategic effectiveness demands congruency. The bottom bars confirm that an organization

which enjoys E–V–R congruence is likely to be enterprising and relatively crisis averse, whereas strategic drift and lost congruence are matched with crisis proneness and a relative lack of enterprise.

## The cycle of growth

Figure 24.3 is based around four stages of organizational development and growth: creativity, nurturing, 'doing' and control. Organizations must be able to accomplish all four elements: if any one is relatively overabundant or underachieved, there will be a weakness.

The model is iterative and systematic. Originally it begins with creativity – new ideas in a somewhat chaotic environment. This active stage should be followed by more passive reflection and nurturing when the idea is crafted into a real opportunity. Often this is where a new business idea springs up. While many organizations and entrepreneurs spend insufficient time carrying out this essential strategic thinking, it is equally possible to become 'bogged down' in planning and not move on to action. Generally, it is this action or 'doing' phase that brings about success and growth, demanding proper organization and structure in order that there can be management and control. The danger is that this control can stifle innovation through stasis and a loss of entrepreneurial drive. To ensure that the organization can continue to grow, fresh ideas – renewed creativity – are needed once more. Some strategic leaders deliberately engineer a (perceived) crisis before a real one takes hold in order to drive the change process.

Ideally, an organization will progress from one stage to another and continue around the cycle. However, many people have ideas which never become opportunities, for example. Some opportunities are never enacted, and some entrepreneurial organizations are so involved in the 'doing' stage that they only put in the prop-

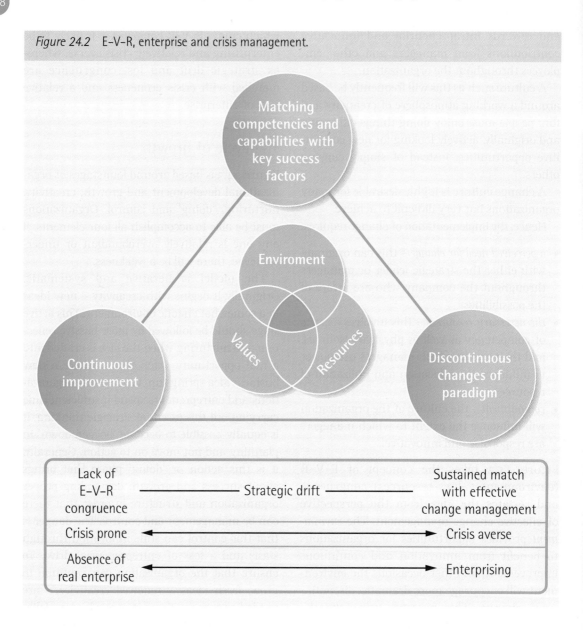

*Figure 24.2*    E–V–R, enterprise and crisis management.

er structure when it becomes essential. Once systems, rules and control procedures begin to take hold, fresh creativity can easily be stifled. Naturally creative people may not seem to fit in with the more disciplined approach that the organization has adopted. Most of us are capable of being creative, but we need to be working in an appropriate organization culture which encourages us to be creative. Consequently, this

progression is unlikely to just happen – movement is likely to require triggers and some clear manifestation of need.

In addition, there are sub-loops in the cycle. Creating and developing an opportunity is often an iterative loop in itself. Strategic thinking and action can be the same. Strategy and structure are also linked. Intrapreneurship in large and established organizations is represented by a

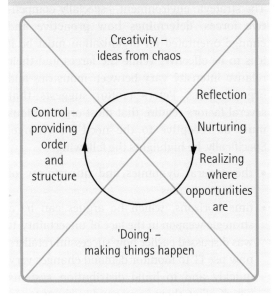

*Figure 24.3* The cycle of growth.

creativity–reflection–doing sub-loop within an appropriate structure.

As individuals, we are likely to feel comfortable in one or two of these four roles and less comfortable in the others. Hence, entrepreneurs and strategic leaders must build management teams to make sure that they secure the help they need to overcome their naturally weaker areas.

## Issues in the Management of Change

It was mentioned earlier that organizations face change pressures from the environment, and the significance, regularity and impact of these pressures will be determined by the complexity and volatility of the environment (see Chapter 7). At the same time managers may see opportunities and wish to adapt existing strategies. There are therefore several forces which encourage change, and a variety of different change situations. Change, though, affects people, their

jobs and responsibilities and their existing behaviour patterns. It can also lead to changes in the underlying culture of the organization. For these reasons people may be wary or even hostile. This is increasingly likely if they fail to understand the reasoning behind the proposed changes and if they personally feel that they are losing rather than gaining from the changes. The various forces for change, the reasons why people resist change, and an outline framework for the effective management of change are considered in this section.

## Forces for change

Five major forces for change are as follows.

- *Technical obsolescence and technical improvements* – Technical change pressures can stem from outside the organization in the form of new developments by competitors and the availability of new technologies which the organization might wish to harness. Internal research and development and innovatory ideas from managers can generate technical change internally. In high-technology companies and industries, and particularly where product lifecycles are becoming shorter, this can be a very significant issue. Some organizations follow product strategies built around short lifecycles, product obsolescence (both physical and design) and persuading customers to replace the product regularly. A number of service businesses also find this a useful strategy.

- *Political and social events* – Many of these change pressures will be outside the control of the firm, but companies will be forced to respond. In the mid-to-late 1980s there was considerable pressure on companies not to trade with South Africa, and in the late 1980s increased public awareness of environmental issues began to place pressure on certain firms. Government encouragement for the use of lead-free petrol, in the form of both media coverage and price advantages from lower taxation, forced car manufacturers to respond. New cars were capable of running on both leaded and lead-free petrol; conversion kits for older cars have had to be developed.

- *The tendency for large organizations and markets to become increasingly global* – While this again has provided opportunities and new directions of growth for many organizations, others have been forced to respond to changing competitive conditions. The growing incidence of joint ventures and strategic alliances, discussed in Chapter 16, is a feature of this.

- *Increases in the size, complexity and specialization of organizations* – The growth of organizations, linked to internal changes of structure, creates pressure for further changes. Large complex specialist organizations have made increasing use of information technology (IT) in their operations, introducing automation and just-in-time (JIT) systems. These create a need for greater specialist expertise from both managers and other employees, possibly necessitating training and changes in their jobs. Effective use of these technological opportunities also requires greater co-operation and co-ordination between functions and managers.

- *The greater strategic awareness and skills of managers and employees* – Able and ambitious managers, and employees who want job satisfaction and personal challenges, need opportunities for growth within the organization. These can be promotion opportunities or changes in the scope of jobs. Such changes require both strategic development and growth by the company, and appropriate styles of non-autocratic leadership.

## The current dynamics of change

The strategic environment, especially competitive forces, determines how proactive and change orientated an organization must be if it is to be effective. While the forces and their relative intensity vary between industries and organizations, Peters (1989) suggests that several factors require that most organizations must be receptive to the need for change. Specifically, he highlights the following:

- the general dynamics and uncertainty of world economies
- time horizons, which he argues can be a strategic weapon in the face of uncertainty. It was discussed earlier how successful retailers now use IT to monitor demand changes very quickly and to build distribution systems which allow them to respond to changes. As product lifecycles shorten, the development time for new products must also be cut
- organization structures must be designed to enable decisions to be made quickly
- quality, design and service – which must be responsive to customer perceptions and competitor activities – are essential for competitive advantage.

## Levels of change

Change decisions can be categorized in terms of their significance to the organization and the appropriate level of intervention (Table 24.1). The six levels form a vertical hierarchy, and it is crucial to clarify and tackle needs and problems appropriately. If the problem is one of operating efficiencies, then the intervention should be at functional strategy level, but this alone would be inadequate for dealing with higher order needs. As one ascends the hierarchy the challenges and difficulties increase – as shown in Chapter 5, changing the culture of the organization can be slow and problematical. Structural changes can sometimes be difficult to implement as well,

*Table 24.1* Levels of change

| Need | Level of change | Approaches/tactics |
|---|---|---|
| New mission; different 'ways of doing things' | Values; culture, styles of management | Organizational development |
| New corporate perspective/strategy | Objectives; corporate strategy | Strategic planning |
|  | Organization structure | New organization design |
| Improved competitive effectiveness (existing products and services) | Competitive strategies; strategic positioning; systems and management roles | Empowerment; management by objectives; performance management; job descriptions; policies |
|  | Business processes | Business process re-engineering |
| Improved efficiencies | Functional strategies; activities; organization of tasks | Method study; job enrichment |

particularly where individuals perceive themselves to be losing rather than benefiting.

In recent years the recession-hit high-street banks have introduced major changes in an attempt to protect and consolidate their profits, and these have systematically moved up to the highest level. A variety of approaches has been used to improve productivity and reduce costs, but this alone was inadequate. The services provided to customers have been reviewed, resulting, for example, in new branch interiors and the introduction of personal bankers and specialist advisers. These changes have been linked to restructuring, the closure of some small branches, job losses and increased market segmentation of business clients. More recently the banks have rethought their corporate strategies, having pursued growth through diversification and overseas expansion during the early 1980s. Concentration on core activities is now preferred. During the 1990s the cultural focus has seen a reduced emphasis on image and marketing and a return to the more productive utilization of assets, harnessing IT, in order to improve margins.

Minicase 24.2 describes a number of high-level strategic changes at the Halifax. These have been accompanied by the lower-level strategies described above.

## Types of change

Summarizing these points, Daft (1983) specifies four basic types of change which affect organizations:

- technology – production processes
- the product or service – the output of the business

# Minicase 24.2 Halifax plc

Several years after the Abbey National Building society had successfully demutualized and become both a bank and a public company, the UK's leading building society, the Halifax, did the same and set about becoming one of the largest financial services providers in the country. When the Abbey floated, the Halifax commented that it saw no need for it to demutualize – but circumstances were to change.

Three key forces have brought about the changes described in this short case:

- Deregulation — Discussed below.
- Technological innovation — IT in particular had reduced entry barriers in financial services, fostering such changes as telephone banking, telephone insurance and banking services at the leading supermarket chains.
- Competition — The above changes had introduced new competitors and new forms of competition.

Building societies originally began to grow in the industrial areas of the UK around the middle of the nineteenth century to help to provide houses for the working families who were then benefiting from the industrial revolution. These mutual societies (owned by their members for the benefit of their members, somewhat along the lines of the Co-operative movement), were increasingly regulated in the twentieth century. Exchange controls prevented competition from foreign banks, but their activities were limited to savings and property mortgages.

Things began to change after the election of a Conservative government in 1971. The liquidity ratio for high-street banks was eased and they were consequently free to lend out more money, if they could attract savers. Although there was some retightening when the economy 'boomed' the banks had already begun to introduce more attractive, higher interest accounts, thus reducing the gap between themselves and the mutual building societies, which had previously always been perceived as a better alternative for savers. When exchange controls were abolished in 1979–80 the banks additionally became real competitors in the mortgage market; and, to balance things out, the 1986 Building Societies Act widened their range of permitted activities.

The Abbey National was the first leading building society to convert to a plc (in 1988–89), since when it has (in turn) prospered as a bank, an estate agency and a diversified financial services organization. At this time, Halifax was adamant that it intended to retain its mutual status. Views changed, however, and Halifax merged with (and absorbed) the Leeds Permanent Building Society in 1995 as a prelude to a conversion in 1997.

## For and against conversion

The main argument in defence of mutual status is that it allows for higher interest rates for savers and lower charges for mortgage customers; there are no shareholders demanding dividends. However, conversion to a public company brings greater freedom to diversify into more activities. While there is an assumption that diversification into a financial services business is a superior strategy to that of the focused building society, there is also an argument that the focused building society will become less and less viable in the face of intensifying competition. Conversion raises new capital which can be invested in acquisition and expansion.

## The new Halifax

The key to the new organization is the power and potential of the Halifax brand, which can be applied to a range of related activities.
These activities now comprise:

- mortgages (the UK market leader)
- liquid savings
- long-term protected savings
- retail banking and consumer credit (i.e. loans)
- credit cards – focused on affinity cards for charities and other organizations
- personal and life insurance services
- estate agency services
- treasury activities.

Halifax used acquisitions to help its diversification into insurance and estate agencies. It systematically acquired Clerical Medical Insurance (1996), the Birmingham Midshires Building Society (1998 for £750 million) and the UK credit-card arm of America's Bank One (2000). The activities are distributed to customers in a variety of ways: Halifax branches, independent agents and distributors, independent financial advisers, estate agency branches, automatic teller machines, and direct telephone sales and services.

## A change of leader

In 1998 Mike Blackburn, who had successfully led the Halifax through its conversion, opted for early retirement and was replaced by James Crosby, an internal candidate. The bank had been criticized for:

- lacking ideas for spending the £3 billion plus surplus capital created when it floated. Some analysts believed that this should be used to reduce the Halifax's dependency on mortgages and savings, two very competitive segments. Some of the money had been spent on the acquisitions, and some on a share buy-back, but by no means all of it

- not articulating clear priorities for its future direction
- losing market share in mortgages
- persisting with a complacent culture.

A merger with another leading bank seemed a quite plausible alternative.

## The planned transformation

Several changes and intentions have been proposed by the new strategic leader:

- *strategic changes* – to exploit new technologies to improve the distribution of services. Telephone banking, Internet banking and interactive television all offer real opportunities
- *structure* – To help to reduce costs, Halifax anticipates employing fewer and younger people. Responsibilities must increase with greater decentralization.
- *style* – Crosby wants the Halifax to become more creative, innovative, fast-moving and flexible. Without this it seems unlikely that it will be able to take advantage of all the new opportunities which are arising. Halifax recognizes that it needs to attract fresh talent and, on occasions, buy in expertise. Peter Wood, founder of Direct Line, has joined to help to develop the insurance business. In conjunction with this, Halifax has adopted a smart casual dress style for its back-office staff.
- *image and reputation* – Brands are critical, and brand value must be delivered.

## An early setback

In May 2000 Halifax announced that it was trying to patent the account design and software for its new Internet bank – known as IF (Intelligent Finance) – which it planned to launch in July. Commentators were immediately sceptical about how different it might be, doubting that the Halifax was about to 'turn the banking industry upside down'. The idea with IF is that customers will be able to set off savings against borrowings, to achieve the best overall interest rate, without having to combine their accounts into a 'single pot', as is the case with rivals who offer a similar benefit.

The July launch was delayed because of a computer bug. One month later the attractiveness of Internet banking was dimmed when Abbey National's Cahoot product was also experiencing technical difficulties and computer fraud was discovered with the Prudential's on-line bank, Egg.

QUESTION: To what extent do you think the Halifax has proactively driven its change agenda, and to what extent do you think it has been responding to external forces and pressures?

*Halifax*    http://www.halifax.co.uk

- administrative changes – structure; policies; budgets; reward systems
- people attitudes – expectations; behaviour.

Invariably, a change in one of these factors will place demands for change on one or more of the others.

When an organization decides to launch a new product it may also need to invest in new technology, modify its existing production plant and either acquire people with, or train existing employees in, the new skills required.

Major changes in the strategic perspective, say the acquisition of a similar sized firm, will force changes in the organization structure, which in turn necessitates changes in jobs and behaviour patterns.

However necessary the changes may be, and however ready the organization might be to implement them, the outcomes will not necessarily be positive for everyone affected.

## The change process

Change frequently disrupts normality. Job security seems threatened; existing behaviour patterns and values are questioned; people are required to be more flexible and to take more risks. While the organization may be facing strong external pressures it is unrealistic to expect managers and other employees not to query or resist the need to change. This is particularly true if individuals feel threatened, or perceive themselves to be losing out rather than benefiting or not being rewarded in some way for co-operating.

It is important to encourage people to recognize the need for change, the benefits, and the external threats from not changing. This can involve the engineered crisis. Managed change should be planned and evolutionary, although some organizations have attempted to become more flexible such that people not only accept change, but constantly seek new opportunities for change and improvement. Although change can be speedy and dynamic – normally when it is forced by powerful external influences – managing change positively in a growth situation, taking advantage of opportunities rather than responding to threats, requires that the process begins gradually and on a limited scale, and then spreads. Advancement needs consolidation and learning. The innovation stage, which can easily go wrong, requires that the change agents (who will not always be the strategic leader) find powerful and influential allies and supporters. Time and effort must be invested in explaining, justifying and persuading. Trial and error leads to incremental learning. Early supporters should be visibly rewarded for their commitment, and this will encourage others and begin to consolidate the changes. Conservative people are inevitably going to be late joiners; and some older people, together with those who are very set in their ways, are likely to be laggards.

Remember, it is not always the man on the shopfloor who opposes change. It can be the second or third tier of management who are the most reactionary.
*Sir Peter Gibbings, ex-Chairman, Anglia Television*

No positive changes will occur within a company unless the Chief Executive realizes that people are basically opposed to change. A climate for change must be created in people's minds.

Changes need to be planned and everyone must be reassured that these changes will be for the betterment of the company, its employees, customers and shareholders.

Changes have therefore to be managed against a set of objectives and to a timetable.
*Jacques G. Margry, when Group Chief Executive, Parker Pen Ltd*

Because changes can be slow to take off they often appear to be failing once the process is well under way. This will renew opposition and resistance. During the process it is important to continue to monitor the environment. The programme may need amendment if circumstances alter.

## Resistance to change

There are several reasons why change pressures might be resisted, and certain circumstances where the implementation of change will have to be planned carefully and the needs of people considered.

- Some resistance can be expected where people have worked out ways of doing things which are beneficial to them in terms of *their* objectives and preferences. They may see change as a threat. Similarly, when people have mastered tasks and feel in control of their jobs and responsibilities, they are likely to feel relatively safe and secure personally. Again, change may be perceived as a threat to their security, although the aim might be to ensure the security of the organization as a whole.
- Resistance to 'sideways change' (expanding certain activities while contracting elsewhere) is likely unless the people affected are fully aware of the reasons and implications.
- Where particular policies, behaviour patterns and ways of doing things have been established and accepted for a long time and in effect have become part of the culture of the organization, change will require careful implementation. The need for change may not be accepted readily.
- It is not unusual for people to have some fear of the unknown and to feel comfortable with situations, policies and procedures that they know. Awareness and understanding is therefore an important aspect of change.
- The organization itself, or particular managers, may resist external pressures if the change involves considerable expense, investment in new equipment and the associated risks. This issue can be exacerbated where there has previously been substantial investment in plant and equipment which technically is still satisfactory. Although demand may be falling there may be a reluctance to sell or close.
- Resistance is likely to be forthcoming where there are perceived flaws or weaknesses in the proposal. Change decisions may be made by the strategic leader and then delegated for implementation. Managers who are closer to the market may have some justified reservations if they have not been consulted during the formulation process.

The opposition may be to the change itself, or to the proposed means of implementation. Both can and must be overcome if changes are to be implemented successfully.

Casualties are, however, possible and sometimes inevitable. Some people will leave because they are uncomfortable with the changes.

Kotter and Schlesinger (1979) have identified six ways of overcoming resistance to change, and these are described in Box 24.1. They suggest that each method has both advantages and disadvantages and can be appropriate in particular circumstances. Issues raised by some of these alternatives are developed further in this chapter. Organizational development is considered as an approach to gaining support through active participation by managers on a continuous basis; manipulative approaches are discussed as a 'machiavellian' use of power and influence. The next section considers a number of general aspects in the management of change before specific strategies are discussed in more detail.

## Implementing change: a general overview

Effective change occurs when managers and employees modify their behaviour in a desired or desirable way, and when the important changes are lasting rather than temporary.

### Education and communication

Education and communication should help people to understand the logic and the need for change. A major drawback can be the inherent time delays and logistics when a lot of people are involved. It also requires mutual trust.

### Participation and involvement

The contention is that people will be more supportive of the changes if they are involved in the formulation and design. Again, it can be time-consuming; and if groups are asked to deliberate and make decisions there is a risk that some decisions will be compromises leading to suboptimization.

### Facilitation and support

This can involve either training or counselling but there is no guarantee that any resistance will be overcome.

### Negotiation and agreement

Negotiation and agreement are normally linked to incentives and rewards. Where the resistance stems from a perceived loss as a result of the proposed change, this can be useful, particularly where the resisting force is powerful. However, offering rewards every time changes in behaviour are desired is likely to prove impractical.

### Manipulation and co-optation

This encompasses covert attempts to influence people, for example by the selective use of information and conscious structuring of events. Co-optation involves 'buying off' informal leaders by personal reward or status. These methods are ethically questionable, and they may well cause grievances to be stored for the future.

### Explicit and implicit coercion

The use of threats can work in the short run but is unlikely to result in long-term commitment.

Source: Kotter, JP and Schlesinger, LA (1979) Choosing strategies for change, *Harvard Business Review*, March–April.

Lewin (1947) contends that permanent changes in behaviour involve three aspects: unfreezing previous behaviour, changing, and then refreezing the new patterns. These three stages are crucial if changes in culture are required.

*Unfreezing* is the readiness to acquire or learn new behaviour. People are willing to accept that existing strategies and ways of doing things could be improved and made more effective. Normally this needs a trigger such as declining sales or profits, or the threat of closure or acquisition.

*Change* occurs when people who perceive the need for change try out new ideas. The changes could be introduced gradually or they may be more dramatic. Choosing the appropriate change strategy once the need is clarified may involve the selection of one from a number of alternatives, and consequently there are opportunities for involving the people who are most likely to be affected. Power structures are likely to be altered and consequently resistance might be evident from certain people.

Particularly where the pressures for change are significant, and the likely impact of the changes will be dramatic and felt widely throughout the organization, the change strategy will need a champion. Organizations in difficulty quite often appoint a new strategic leader to introduce fresh ideas and implement the changes. Newcomers are unlikely to be associated with the strategies which now need changing. Similarly, general managers might be moved to different business units when strategic changes are necessary .

*Refreezing* takes place when the new behaviour patterns are accepted and followed willingly. People are supportive and convinced of the wisdom of the changes; ideally, the new approaches become established within the culture. Rewards are often influential in ensuring that refreezing does take place.

While this simple model provides an excellent outline of the basic stages in a managed change process, if we want to foster a culture which embraces perpetual change we need to be careful about 'refreezing' new behaviours.

Throughout the change process it is important that people are *aware* of why changes are being proposed and are taking place, and that they *understand* the reasons. The key issues are participation, involvement and commitment.

Margerison and Smith (1989) suggest that the management of change exhibits four key features:

- *dissatisfaction* with the present strategies and styles
- *vision* of the better alternative – a clear picture of the desired state which can be communicated and explained to others (this again emphasizes the need for a champion of the change)
- a *strategy* for implementing the change and attaining the desired state
- *resistance* to the proposals at some stage.

## Force-field analysis

Lewin (1951) has proposed that changes result from the impact of a set of driving forces upon

A nursing team in a geriatric hospital wanted the seats of the toilets raised for the comfort of their patients. Hospital management was silent to their pleas. The team re-presented their request and argued that the change would reduce the amount of laundry and in turn the laundry bills. The proposal was approved and implemented.

*Anecdote told by Christine Hancock, General Secretary, Royal College of Nursing*

restraining forces. Figure 24.4 illustrates Lewin's theme of a state of equilibrium which is always under some pressure to change. The extent to which it does change will depend upon whether the driving forces or the restraining forces prove to be stronger. The driving forces, which may be external or internal in origin, are likely to have economic aspects. There may be a need to increase sales, to improve profitability, to improve production efficiencies or to generate new forms of competitive advantage. Corporate, competitive and functional strategies may appear in need of change, but existing strategies

*Figure 24.4* Force field analysis. Derived from Lewin, K (1951) *Field Theory in Social Sciences*, Harper & Row.

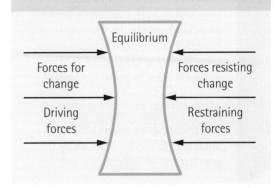

may have people who are loyal and committed to them. People will be affected and may feel concerned. Any resistance will constitute a restraining force, seeking to abandon or modify the change proposals.

Although the driving forces will be concerned with improving organizational efficiency and effectiveness, the opposition is more likely to stem from personal concerns than from disagreement that improved efficiency and effectiveness are desirable. Lewin suggests that the driving forces are based more on logic and the restraining forces on emotion. However, people who are aware of the situation may seek to argue their opposing case in relation to the relative ability of the change proposal to achieve the required improvements. As a result, the ensuing debate concentrates on these issues. The opponents may choose not to be honest and open about their personal fears, feeling that their arguments must concentrate on the economic issues. When this happens the decision, whatev-

er it might be, has not encompassed important underlying behavioural issues.

Effective managers of change situations will be clearly aware of both the driving forces and the real restraining forces. They will seek to strengthen the justifications by communication and explanation and diffuse opposition by exploring the likely impact with the people affected. Box 24.2 summarizes a number of important issues for the effective management of change.

This section has looked generally at the issues which affect and underpin the management of change. Lewin's force-field analysis is particularly helpful for establishing a holistic view of the change situation in terms of cause and likely effect. From this a clearer strategy for implementing the change can emerge. A number of strategies is explored in the following section. Where the extent of the change is substantial, and changes in culture are involved, it is important to ensure that the new behaviour patterns are permanent rather than temporary.

---

## DISCUSSION – Box 24.2
### Issues in Effective Change Management

- Change programmes must be championed.
- There needs to be a clear purpose to which people can subscribe . . . which can be justified and defended.
- The change proposals will not be backed by everyone.
- Managers must decide how much to communicate and when – there are dangers in both inadequate information provision and in being too open and candid.
- Senior managers must take responsibility; while empowerment is important, people still need effective leadership.
- Effective change management frequently involves well-led teams and may require process or even structural change.

- Creating and broadcasting early successes speeds up the process, especially as programmes often lose momentum part-way through.
- Setbacks must be anticipated and managed, and the momentum maintained.
- It is dangerous to 'claim victory' too quickly; the changes must become anchored in the culture.
- The feelings of people who might be hurt by the changes must not be overlooked.

Sources: Eccles, T (1994) *Succeeding With Change*, McGraw-Hill, and Kotter, JP (1995) Why transformation efforts fail, *Harvard Business Review*, March–April.

> To many, uncertainty is a shadow of the unknown, to be avoided; far better, as we are stuck with an uncertain world, is to look upon it as the spice of life.
>
> *Sir Peter Holmes, when Chairman, Shell UK*

> Teach people that change is inevitable and, if embraced, can be fun.
>
> *Leslie Hill, when Chairman and Chief Executive, Central Independent Television plc*

## Strategies for Implementation and Change

It is possible to view implementation as an activity which follows strategy formulation – structures and systems are changed to accommodate changes in strategy. However, implementation, instead of following formulation, may be considered in depth at the same time as the proposed strategy is thought through and before final decisions are made. This is more likely to happen where several managers, especially those who will be involved in implementation, are consulted when the strategy is evaluated. Strategies may evolve from the operation of the organization structure. Where managers are encouraged to be innovatory and make incremental changes, elements of trial and error and small change decisions are often found. Implementation and formulation operate simultaneously; the changes are contained rather than dramatic and resistance may similarly be contained. Innovatory organizations can develop change orientation as part of the culture. People expect things to change regularly and accept changes.

Bourgeois and Brodwin (1984) have identified five distinct basic approaches to strategy implementation and strategic change.

- The strategic leader, possibly using expert planners or enlisting planning techniques, defines changes of strategy and then hands over to senior managers for implementation. The strategic leader is primarily a thinker/planner rather than a doer.
- The strategic leader again decides major changes of strategy and then considers the appropriate changes in structure, personnel, and information and reward systems if the strategy is to be implemented effectively. Quinn (1988) contends that the strategic leader may reveal the strategy gradually and incrementally as he or she seeks to gather support during implementation. This theme is developed later in this section.

  In both these cases the strategic leader needs to be powerful as both involve top–down strategic change.

- The strategic leader and his or her senior managers (divisional heads, business unit general managers or senior functional managers) meet for lengthy discussions with a view to formulating proposed strategic changes. All of the managers are briefed and knowledgeable, and the aim is to reach decisions to which they will all be committed. Strategies agreed at the meetings are then implemented by the managers who have been instrumental in their formulation. While this approach involves several managers it is still primarily centralized.

- The strategic leader concentrates on establishing and communicating a clear mission and purpose for the organization. He or she seeks to pursue this through a decentralized structure by developing an appropriate organization culture and establishing an organization-wide unity of purpose. While the strategic leader will retain responsibility for changes in the strategic perspective, decisions concerning competitive and functional strategy changes are decentralized to general and functional managers who are constrained by the mission, culture, policies and financial resources established by the strategic leader.

- Managers throughout the organization are widely encouraged to be innovative and come up with new ideas for change. The strategic leader establishes a framework for evaluating these proposals – recognizing that those which are accepted and resourced result in increased status for the managers concerned.

Johne and Davies (1999) have investigated major change programmes in large, mature insurance companies and they have noted a number of points which separate the successful from the less successful. The success stories generally began where the chief executive created an internal perception of a crisis. Attention was focused on external, market forces which were demanding change. These tough-minded leaders then promoted the development of new skills for dealing with the changing market forces, fostering a new appreciation and understanding which helped managers to recognize the inevitability of change. This was followed up with a decentralized approach, designed, first, to encourage ownership of both the problem and the change initiatives, and second, to develop initiatives based on collaboration and experimentation. The strategic leaders had started with a belief that structures were crippling their organization's ability to harness future opportunities; strategic change eventually came out of transformed structures. Where the process remained more centralized, however strong the strategic leader, the change – and the organization – was less successful.

In this context, Ghoshal and Caulkin (1998) express a concern that major and dramatic change is often associated with charismatic and tough strategic leaders who attract and reward ambitious 'high-flying' managers who, like them, are willing to subscribe to a 'dehumanizing' style of management to drive through the

changes. There is 'a lot of change, a lot of stress and a lot of fear'. Instead, they argue, organizations need either people who can exercise power robustly but with wisdom, passion and constraint or checks to ensure that people are not forgotten in the drive for change.

Ideas for change, of course, can start at the bottom of the organization rather than always at the top; and change can be seen as both a clearly managed process and the incremental outcome of the decisions taken in an innovative, change-orientated organization where managers are empowered.

These basic approaches highlight a number of general themes and ideas, which are considered below.

## Top–down strategic change

A number of approaches can be involved in drawing up the strategic plans for the organization, but here changes in strategy are ultimately centralized decisions. This approach can be both popular and viable as long as the strategies that are selected can be implemented effectively. It was mentioned earlier that resistance can be expected if managers who are charged with carrying out changes in strategy feel that there are flaws in the proposals. It is important to ensure that the appropriate level of consultation takes place during formulation.

Capable managers are needed throughout the organization to deal with operational issues, and the quality of the information systems which underpin the planning is a crucial issue. The approach is attractive to strategic leaders who are inclined more towards the analytical aspects of strategy than they are towards behavioural issues.

## Quinn's incremental model

While Quinn's model is another primarily top–down approach it suggests a high degree of political skill on the part of the strategic leader, who appreciates the difficulties involved in implementing change. These skills are discussed in detail towards the end of the chapter.

Quinn (1988) argues that the hardest part of strategic management is implementation as transition and change impact structures and systems, organization culture and power relationships. The strategic leader is critical in the process because he or she is either personally or ultimately responsible for the proposed changes in strategy, and for establishing the structure and processes within the organization.

Quinn's approach is as follows:

- The strategic leader will develop his or her own informal information and communication channels, both within and external to the organization, and will draw on this as much as using the formal systems.
- The strategic leader must generate *awareness* of the desired change with the appropriate managers within the organization. This involves communication and cultural issues.
- The strategic leader will seek to legitimize the new approach or strategy, lending it authority, if not, at this stage, credibility.
- He or she will then seek to gather key supporters for the approach or strategy.
- The new strategy may be floated as a minor tactical change to minimize resistance, and possibly keep the ultimate aim unclear. Alternatively, the strategy may be floated as a trial or experiment.
- Opposition will be removed by, for example, ensuring that supporters chair key committees, and that stubborn opponents are moved to other parts of the organization.
- The strategy will be flexible so that incremental changes can be made in the light of the trials. There will be a strong element of learning by doing, so that any unexpected resource limitations, such as a shortage of key skills, will be highlighted.

- Support for the change will harden.
- The proposals will be crystallized and focused.
- Finally, the proposed changes will be formalized and ideally accepted within the organization. This should involve honest evaluation and attempts to improve upon the original ideas. It is particularly important to look ahead and consider how the new strategy might be developed further in the future.

Quinn's approach incorporates an appreciation of the likely impact upon people and the culture, and pragmatically searches for a better way of doing things once the decision to change has been made.

## Empowerment and change

To sustain a culture of change, employees must be empowered but, as shown in Chapter 13, not everyone is comfortable with added responsibilities and accountability. They are risk averse, and again, resistance can be expected. It would seem inevitable that change-focused organizations will be happy to see such people leave, for while they stay they constitute barriers to change. They actively seek to prevent changes which may be essential for the future of the business. Unfortunately, many of these people are likely to be very experienced and knowledgeable, and their underlying expertise is valuable. Their expertise might also be useful – at least temporarily – to a competitor, and for this reason there may be a reluctance to release them.

Empowerment cannot succeed without an appropriate reward system to support it. Financial rewards will remain important, but they are not the complete answer. People must not be rewarded simply because they are holding down a particular job or position; part of their pay must be based on their measured contribution. Outstanding performers must be rewarded for their continuing efforts, and as organizations are increasingly 'flattened', with fewer layers in the hierarchy, a series of promotions no longer provides the answer.

Empowered middle managers are critically important for the effective management of strategic change, but all too often they are hostile because of fear and uncertainty in a culture of blame. Mistakes are not tolerated, and people are reluctant to take risks. Such managers are portrayed as villains, when really it is the organizational climate which is making them victims. Change and empowerment will only happen when managers are not afraid to 'unfreeze and learn'.

Organizations can benefit from developing people, building their abilities and self-confidence and then providing them with greater stimulation and challenge. Success will yield the opportunity to take on more responsibility. Initially the organization motivates them but they become increasingly self-motivated. Part of their reward package is their enhanced reputation in a successful business, together with increased informal power and influence. They develop the ability to foster and champion innovation and change – strategic changes which they *own*.

A culture of innovation and gradual but continuous change will impact mainly on competitive and functional strategies – the lowest two levels of the hierarchy featured in Table 24.1 earlier. Clearly, they also support corporate strategic changes which may themselves be emergent in nature or the outcome of either a visionary or a planning mode of strategy creation.

## Discontinuous change and strategic regeneration

Powerful environmental issues such as deregulation, globalization, lower trade barriers and economic recessions have combined in the 1990s to place enormous change pressures on companies. The individual significance of these issues will vary from year to year but, in aggregate terms, the outcome is an increasingly turbulent and uncertain business environment for most organizations, private and public sector, manufacturing and service, large and small, profit-seeking and not-for-profit.

Companies have responded. Many have sought to manage their assets and strategic resources more efficiently and effectively – again the lowest two levels of the change hierarchy. Some have restructured; others have radically changed their processes through business process re-engineering.

However, continuous improvement to an organization's *competitive* capabilities, essential as it is, will not always be sufficient to meet these pressures.

Tom Peters (1992) argues that for some companies the challenge is 'not just about a *programme* of change . . . strategies and structures need to change perpetually'. Peter Drucker (1993) agrees and contends that 'every organization must prepare to abandon everything it does'. Both authors are implying wholesale corporate renewal or reinvention, which were termed strategic regeneration earlier in this book.

Successful regeneration requires both an external and an internal focus. Externally, organizations must search for new product, new service and new market opportunities, working with suppliers, distributors and customers to redefine markets and industries. Internally, structures, management styles and cultures must be capable of creating and delivering these products and services. Innovation is dependent on processes and people. Strategic awareness, information management and change are critically important if the organization is to outperform its competitors.

Achieving this position may require *simultaneous* changes to corporate strategies and perspectives, organization structures and styles of management. In order to implement strategic regeneration, Goss *et al.* (1993) insist that companies must be able to change their *context* – 'the underlying assumptions and invisible premises on which their decisions and actions are based'. Their 'inner nature or being' must be altered. Managers must learn how to think strategically, and be open to new paradigms and perspectives. The requirement is that they change 'what the company is' and not simply the things that it does. Companies are being challenged with changing all the levels of the change hierarchy simultaneously, a huge and complex task for any organization.

As shown in Minicase 24.2 earlier, high-street banks have been forced to adopt a new paradigm. They have recognized that they are not simply a home for secure savings and current accounts, but diversified financial services institutions. The changes – visible to all of us who are bank customers – have clearly involved strategies, structure and culture, and they have proved painful.

Incremental change at the competitive and functional level, trying harder and searching for improvements, must appear to offer an easier, less painful route. The fundamental question is: alone, is it enough to meet the strategic demands of the contemporary business environment?

Some of the international companies featured in this book have clearly attempted to tackle these important challenges. British Airways (BA) realized in the 1980s that, contrary to much popular opinion at the time, airline customers are willing to pay extra for service. The challenge lies in defining that service and differentiating successfully. BA consequently changed its strategies, structure and culture and became one of the most profitable airlines in the world. The changes at British Airways have proved successful, but that success has been inconsistent and the changes are not yet complete. General Electric (GE) of the USA is another example. The regeneration philosophy and programme at GE

is described in Minicase 24.3. GE has successfully reduced waste and improved efficiencies and competitive strategies. The first step was one of basically maintaining output levels while reducing assets (thus improving return on capital employed); the next challenge lay in regenerating the company and creating new growth from the reduced size. This subtle change of emphasis required new values. The culture has become one of challenging the frontiers of technology and competition – discontinuous changes to create new futures ahead of competitors. It is different from a culture of benchmarking, productivity gains, process re-engineering and continuous improvement.

In 1995, NBC, a General Electric subsidiary, was anxious to win the television rights for the Sydney Olympic Games in the year 2000.

Pre-empting its competitors, NBC:

- bid jointly for the Sydney games and the next Winter Olympics in Salt Lake City
- presented the International Olympic Committee (IOC) with take-it-or-leave-it figure before any bids had been invited
- included both cable and network television in its bid.

When the ideas (and the huge sum of money involved) were put to CEO Jack Welch, he took just half an hour to back the proposal. NBC executives spent the next 48 hours flying around the world to place their proposals before key IOC members; a deal was agreed and signed, all within a week.

The IOC commented that the reaction of NBC's rivals afterwards was one of 'disappointment but a reluctant admiration for the initiative NBC took'.

# Minicase 24.3  Strategic Regeneration at General Electric

John F (Jack) Welch became Chief Executive Officer at General Electric (GE) in 1981. His structural vision was summarized earlier, in Minicases 21.5 and 22.4. This case describes 'one of the most far-reaching programmes of innovation in business history'.

The programme involves three stages:

1. *awakening* – the realization of the need for change
2. *envisioning* – establishing a new vision and harnessing resources
3. *re-architecting* – the design and construction of a new organization.

Although Welch is the identified strategic leader, several committed senior managers worked together to drive through the cultural changes.

GE has been restructured, and clear progress has been made, but the process of change continues. The implementation of the programme is not yet complete.

## GE in the early 1980s – the need for change

The company had sound assets, reflected in a strong balance sheet, but it was seen as bureaucratic and heavily focused on the USA. It was not 'technologically advanced' and it clearly needed a more international perspective.

Specific problems were diagnosed:

- Revenue growth was slow. GE's core business (electrical equipment) was particularly slow.
- As a result, expensive investments were creating cash-flow problems.
- Poor productivity was causing low profit margins.
- Innovation was limited.
- Decision making was slow.
- Negative internal politics was rife.

## The transformation process

### Awakening

Welch realized that his first challenge was to determine which managers offered the greatest potential as 'transformational leaders', agents of discontinuous change.

He then sought to clarify and articulate the extent of the need for change, focusing on the above weaknesses. Resistance took three forms:

- Technical – A reliance on existing bureaucratic systems and a fear of the unknown; a distrust of international expansion.
- Political – A desire to protect existing power bases, especially where the strategic value of the particular business was declining.

- Cultural – an unwillingness to accept competitive weaknesses – overconfidence from past successes.

*Changes*

- Welch forced people to benchmark competitors' performance standards and achievements, rather than rely only on internal measures and budgets.
- He also took control of external corporate communications, and
- Radically changed GE's approach to management training and development. Rigid rules and procedures about how things should be done were abolished.

*Envisioning*

A new vision was developed gradually during the mid- to late 1980s, and it finally became encapsulated in a matrix. Highlights of the new vision are featured in Table 24.2.

*Table 24.2*   Highlights of GE's corporate vision

|  | Strategy | Structure | Management style |
|---|---|---|---|
| **Technical** | Focus on market (segments) where the company can be no. 1 or no. 2 | Decentralized | Different reward systems for different businesses, dependent on needs |
|  |  | Foster the sharing of best practices and |  |
|  |  | Pull down internal boundaries | Continuous training and development |
|  | Prioritize high-growth industries |  |  |
| **Political** | Foster internal and external alliances to harness synergy potential | Flatter, open structure to remove power bases | Flexible reward systems |
|  |  | Cross-function and cross-business development teams | '360 degree evaluations' from superiors, peers and subordinates |
|  |  | Empowerment to lowest levels of management |  |
| **Cultural** | Speedy change to strategies | Corporate values but individual business cultures and styles | Track attitudes and values – commitment to customers and quality – and to outperforming competitors |
|  | Intrapreneurial, innovative, incremental and adaptive change – as a result of – learning from upward, downward and lateral communications |  |  |

Welch saw the technical, political and cultural systems as three strands of a rope which must be changed and realigned together.

### Re-architecting

At the heart of the vision is an 'organization without boundaries' and with an emphasis on internal and external linkages and architecture. Information must flow freely. People must be in a position – and willing – to act quickly. 'A large organization with the speed, flexibility and self-confidence of a small one.'

A number of boundaries had to be removed as part of the implementation process:

- vertical/hierarchical – management layers were removed. Welch introduced performance incentives for many more managers and employees; in the past GE had focused on only senior executives
- horizontal/internal walls – cross-functional project teams were created
- external – there was a new emphasis on the whole supply or added value chain; alliances were forged with suppliers; customer satisfaction levels were tracked.

Removing these boundaries clearly required radical changes to the ways in which people worked together, made decisions and carried out tasks. Welch believed that the changes must be inspired from the top and that any senior managers who resisted the new style 'would have to go'.

Adapted from: Tichy, NM (1993) Revolutionize your company, *Fortune*, 13 December.

QUESTIONS: This case has described a major programme of change and transformation, championed by an exceptional strategic leader, Jack Welch. While it has been reported extensively, and 'the world' knows what Welch has set out to do and what he has achieved, few organizations have been able to replicate his achievement. So: how valuable might our insight really be?

Why would a programme of this scale and ambition be difficult to replicate?

*General Electric*   http://www.ge.com

Pascale *et al.* (1997) argue that for effective regeneration it is critically important that people understand the organization and its businesses – the 'big picture'. Robust straight-talking should be encouraged to tease out the existing weaknesses in the organization as well as ideas for new opportunities. Transformation then involves 'managing from the future'. A shared purpose and direction sets the agenda. Setbacks must be harnessed in true entrepre-neurial fashion. People must accept accountability but, linked to proper rewards, this should be done in an inventive way that ensures that people are engaged in the process. 'There has to be a relentless discomfort with the status quo'.

Hamel (1994) contends strategic regeneration needs vision and perseverance. Companies must invest resources in an attempt to set the new 'competitive high ground' first by changing the key success factors. This inevitably implies time and risk, and it must be a managed and understood process. Speculative investment in the long term must be risky because *spending precedes understanding*; companies are heading into unknown territory. However, companies which choose to avoid the risk, and rely instead on monitoring and copying competitors (such that *understanding precedes spending*) may be caught out.

Hamel cites three important barriers to effective strategic regeneration. First, too many senior managers in an industry have related, often industry-specific, backgrounds, and this inhibits their creative thinking. Secondly, there are political pressures to maintain the status quo from managers who feel threatened personally, an issue that is looked at next. Thirdly there is the sheer difficulty of creating new competitive strategies in industries that are changing dynamically, continuously and chaotically.

The essential pre-requisite for an effective change of direction is to create a climate throughout the organization where change is regarded positively. Professor Hague, when he was at Manchester Business School, made the following remark which I have always remembered: 'The successful manager will expect and understand change; the outstanding manager will anticipate and create it.'

Once the right climate exists, change must be preceded and accompanied by effective and honest communication, meaningful consultation and sound decision making. It is not easy and requires genuine top management commitment.

*Tom W Cain, ex-Director,*
*Human Resources,*
*The Channel Tunnel Group Ltd*

However, Abrahamson (2000) implies that major change could be going out of fashion, unless, of course, it becomes essential. Companies that periodically reinvent themselves often face resistance, distress, disaffection and upheaval. All too often the desired or planned changes are not implemented effectively, prompting another programme of change. Abrahamson therefore recommends '*dynamic stability*' – continuous tinkering with existing businesses, alternating occasional major changes with several incremental ones. His research suggests that:

- First, copying can prove very rewarding – there is no need always to be first. This point, though, needs careful interpretation. It is true that major leaps forward can be uncomfortable and disruptive for both customers and employees, and the competitors who follow when the situation has settled down again can enjoy the benefits without incurring the risk of the pioneer. However, sustained competitive advantage often comes from staying just ahead of rivals with constant innovation and leadership. It is a matter of degree.
- Secondly, home-grown processes are invariably more acceptable culturally than those imported from another country with an 'alien' culture.

Clearly, organizations need to ensure that they change in accordance with real external pressures and to recognize that good ideas can always be found by monitoring the world's best performers. They need to acquire and use this knowledge to craft something that can work for them.

## Organizational development and innovation

The basic underlying theme of organizational development (OD) is that developing an appropriate organizational culture will generate desirable changes in strategy.

Beckhard (1969) defined OD as effort which is 'planned, organization-wide, and managed from the top, designed to increase organizational effectiveness and health through planned interventions in the organization's processes, using behavioural science knowledge'.

OD is, in essence, planned cultural change. The model which has been used to provide the structure for this book shows strategic leadership and culture as being central to both strategic awareness and decision making. The appreciation by managers of the effectiveness of the current match between resources and the environment, their ability and willingness to make adaptive changes to capitalize on environmental changes, and the formulation and implementation of major changes in corporate strategy are all influenced by the culture of the organization and the style of strategic leadership. Hence, it is crucial for the strategic leader to develop the appropriate culture for the mission and purpose that he or she wishes to pursue. OD helps to develop a co-operative and innovative culture.

The aim of OD is to establish mechanisms that encourage managers to be more open, participative and co-operative when dealing with problems and making decisions. Specifically, the objectives are:

- improved organizational effectiveness and, as a result
- higher profits and better customer service (in its widest context)
- more effective decision making
- the ability to make and manage changes more smoothly
- increased innovation
- reduced conflict and destructive political activity
- greater trust and collaboration between managers and business units.

Organized OD programmes involve activities such as team building and collaborative decision making, bringing managers together and encouraging them to share and discuss problems and issues. The thinking is that when managers learn more about the problems facing the organization as a whole, and about other managers who may have different technical or functional perspectives, they become more aware of the impact of the decisions that they make. In addition, if they collaborate and share responsibilities, they are more likely to feel committed to joint decisions.

While one aim is to change the attitudes and behaviour of people in organizations, OD can also allow and encourage the same people to initiate and implement changes through their discussions. Establishing the programmes is likely to involve outside experts who can be seen as objective. OD programmes are not normally a response to specific problems but rather a general approach to the management of change in the longer term.

Given that one idea behind OD is collaboration and collective responsibility, a key theme is the reduction of conflict between managers, functions, business units or divisions within the organization. A reduction in the use of manipulative styles of management, or dysfunctional political activity, whereby managers pursue personal goals in preference to the wider needs of the organization, is also implied. Functional and dysfunctional political activity is explored in the last section of this chapter, which looks at the bases and uses of power by managers.

## Power and influence: introductory comments

The management of change requires that managers have the requisite power to implement decisions and that they are able to exert influence. There are several bases of power, both organizational and individual, which constitute resources for managers. The processes that they adopt for utilizing these power bases, their styles of management, determine their success in influencing others. The ability of managers to exert power and influence is manifested in a number of ways, including:

- budgets
- rewards
- organization structure and positions
- promotions and management development
- information systems
- symbols of power and status.

The greatest leader is the one who enables people to say: 'We did it ourselves.'
*Chinese proverb attributed to Lao-Tsu*

A leader can stop an organization in its tracks but he can't turn it around on his own. In a year you can change things on at a superficial level, using the charismatic model, but you need five to change the culture.
*Morpeth Headmaster, Alasdair Macdonald, discussing change in secondary schools*

## Power and Politics

Managers who regularly attempt to get things done, both with and through other people, and introduce changes, have the problem of generating agreement, consent or at least compliance with what should be done, how and when. Typically, opinions and perspectives will differ. Disagreements may or may not be significant, and can range from the polite and friendly to those involving threats and coercion. Each side, quite simply, is attempting to influence the conduct of the other. In this section we consider the power resources that managers are able to use and how they might use them.

Checkland (1986) defines organizational politics as the process by which differing interests reach 'accommodation' – a word that he chooses deliberately and in preference to consensus. These accommodations relate to the dispositions and use of power and influence, and behaviour which is not prescribed by the policies established within the organization. It will be shown later that political activity by managers in order to influence others, and ensure that their decisions and strategies are carried out, is essential. Politics can be legitimate and positive, although it can also be more negative and illegitimate. In the latter case managers are seeking to influence others in order to achieve their personal goals. This is often described as 'machiavellianism' and is discussed at the end of this section.

## The relative power of the organization

The need for change is affected by the relative power and influence of external stakeholders in relation to the organization. Powerful customers, powerful suppliers and changes in government legislation would all represent potential threats and demands for change. In turn, the management and implementation of change is affected by the relative power of the organization. Some proposed strategies can be implemented because the organization possesses the appropriate power to acquire the resources which are needed and to generate consumer demand. Others may not be feasible.

At the same time the decisions taken within organizations concerning changes of corporate, competitive and functional strategies are influenced by the disposition of relative power between functions, business units or divisions, and the ways in which managers seek to use power and influence.

## DISCUSSION – Box 24.3
## Internal and External Sources of Power

Mintzberg (1983) contends that it is essential to consider both internal and external sources of power, and their relative significance, when assessing the demands for, and feasibility of, certain strategic changes.

The organization's stakeholders will vary in terms of their relative power and the ways in which they exert influence. The interests of the owners of the firm, for example, are legally represented by the board of directors. While large institutional shareholders may exert considerable influence over certain decisions, many private shareholders will take no active part. Employees may be represented by external trade unions, who again may or may not exert influence.

The power relationships between the firm and its stakeholders are determined by the importance and scarcity of the resource in question. The more essential and limited the supply of the resource, the greater the power the resource provider has over the firm. According to Mintzberg these external power groups may be focused and their interests pulled together by a dominant power, or they may be fragmented.

Where there are very strong external influences, the organization may seek to establish close co-operation or mutual dependence, or attempt to reduce its dependence on the power source. The relationship between Marks and Spencer and many of its suppliers is a good example of mutual dependence of this nature. Marks and Spencer encouraged many of their clothing suppliers to invest in the latest technology for design and manufacturing in order that they can both succeed against international competition. Marks and Spencer are typically the largest customer of their suppliers, buying substantial quantities as long as both demand and quality are maintained. However, it is important that their suppliers are aware of

fashion changes because they bear the risk of overproduction and changes in taste.

Internal power is linked to the structure and configuration of the organization. Following from the issues discussed in Chapter 21, it is clear that the relative power of the strategic apex, middle management, operators, technocrats and support staff needs to be assessed.

Internal power is manifested in four ways:

* the personal control system of the strategic leadership
* rules, policies and procedures
* political activities external to these two factors
* cultural ideologies that influence decision makers.

External and internal power sources combine to determine a dominant source of power at any time, and Mintzberg suggests six possibilities:

* *a key external source,* such as a bank or supplier, or possibly the government as, say, a key buyer of defence equipment – the objectives of the source would normally be clearly stated and understood
* *the operation of the organization structure,* and the strategies and activities of general and functional managers who are allocated the scarce resources: the relative power of business units is influenced by the market demand for their products and services, but generally external sources exert indirect rather than direct influence; functional managers can enjoy power if they are specialists and their skills are in short supply
* *strong central leadership*
* *ideologies* – certain organizations, such as charities or volunteer organizations, are often dominated by the underlying ideologies related to helping others

- *professional constraints* – accountants' and solicitors' practices, for example, have established codes of professional practice which dictate and influence behaviour. On occasions this can raise interesting issues for decision makers. A frequently used example is the television journalist or news editor working for the BBC or ITN and able to influence reporting strategies and policies. When assessing sensitive issues does the person see himself or herself as a BBC or ITN employee or as a professional journalist, and do the two perspectives coincide or conflict?

- *active conflict* between power sources seeking dominance: while this can involve either or both internal and external sources it is likely to be temporary, as organizations cannot normally survive prolonged conflict.

The dominant source of power becomes a key feature of the organizational culture, and a major influence on manager behaviour and decision making.

Source of the basic arguments: Mintzberg, H (1983) *Power In and Around Organizations*, Prentice-Hall.

Internal and external sources of power are discussed further in Box 24.3, based on the work of Mintzberg (1983).

## Political activity

Farrell and Petersen (1982) classify political activity in terms of three dimensions:

- legitimate or illegitimate
- vertical or lateral
- internal or external to the organization.

For example, a complaint or suggestion by an employee directly to a senior manager, bypassing an immediate superior, would be classified as legitimate, vertical and internal. Discussions with fellow managers from other companies within an industry would be legitimate, lateral and external, unless they involved any illegal activities such as price fixing. Informal communications and agreements between managers are again legitimate, while threats or attempts at sabotage are clearly illegitimate.

Power and politics are key aspects of strategy implementation because they can enable managers to be proactive and to influence their envi-

ronment rather than being dominated and manipulated by external events. The issues affect managers at all levels of the organization and decisions concerning both internal and external changes.

## The bases of power

Seven bases of manager power were introduced and described in Chapter 5: reward, coercive, legitimate, personal, expert, information, and connection. The extent to which managers and other employees in organizations use each of these sources of power is a major determinant of corporate culture.

*Reward and coercive power* (the ability to sanction and punish) are two major determinants of employee motivation, and both can be very significant strategically. Thompson and Strickland (1981) argue that motivation is brought about primarily by the reward and punishment systems in the organization; and Blanchard and Johnson (1982) suggest that effective management involves three key aspects: establishing clear objectives for employees, and rewarding and sanctioning performance against objectives appropriately. Strategic leaders who dominate their organizations and coerce their senior managers can be effective, particularly when the organization is experiencing decline and major changes in strategy are urgently required.

*Legitimate power* is determined primarily by the organization structure, and consequently changes is structure will affect the power, influence and significance of different business units, functions and individual managers.

*Personal power*, which can lead to the commitment of others to the power holder, can be very important in incremental changes. Managers who are supported and trusted by their colleagues and subordinates will find it easier to introduce and implement changes.

*Expert power* can also be useful in persuading others that proposed changes in strategy are feasible and desirable. While expert power may not be real, and instead be power gained from reputation, it is unlikely that managers who genuinely lack expertise can be successful without other power bases. Moreover, expertise is job related. An expert specialized accountant, for example, may lose expert power temporarily if he or she is promoted to general manager. Consequently, an important tactic in the management of change is to ensure that those managers who are perceived to be expert in the activity or function concerned are supportive of the proposed changes.

*Information* and related *connection power* are becoming increasingly significant as IT grows in importance.

These seven power bases are all visible sources. There is, in addition, *invisible power*. One source of invisible power is the way in which an issue or proposal is presented, which can influence the way it is dealt with. Managers who appreciate the objectives, perspectives and concerns of their colleagues will present their ideas in ways that are likely to generate their support rather than opposition. Membership of informal, but influential, coalitions or groups of managers can be a second source of power, par-

ticularly if the people involved feel dependent on each other. Thirdly, information that would create opposition to a decision or change proposal might be withheld. In the same way that access to key information can be a positive power source, the ability to prevent other people obtaining information can be either a positive or a negative source of power.

Lukes (1974) has identified three further important aspects of power, namely:

- the ability to prevent a decision, or not make one
- the ability to control the issues on which decisions are to be made
- the ability to ensure that certain issues are kept off agendas.

The use of such power by individuals can inhibit changes which might be in the long-term best interests of the organization.

## Political effectiveness

Hayes (1984) contends that effective managers appreciate clearly what support they will need from other people if proposed changes are to be carried through, and what they will have to offer in return. In such cases they reach agreements (or accommodations) which provide mutual advantages. It is important for the organization as a whole that general and functional managers are effective and politically competent if personal objectives are to be restrained and undesirable changes, championed by individual managers, prevented. Problems can occur where some managers are politically effective and able to implement change, and others are relatively ineffective and reach agreements with other managers whereby their personal interests, and the interests of the organization, are adversely affected.

Allen *et al.* (1979) and Dixon (1982) point out that certain sources of personal power are essential for managers who are effective politically and able to influence others. In addition, they suggest certain tactics for managing change. These are featured in Table 24.3. It is important that managers are perceived by others to have expertise and ability, and it is useful if they have a reputation built on past successes. Depending on the relative power of outside stakeholders, such as suppliers or customers, external credibility can also prove valuable. It is essential to have access to information and to other powerful individuals and groups of managers.

It can be a disadvantage for a manager to be perceived as a radical agent of change, as this can arouse fear and uncertainty, possibly leading to opposition, in others. As discussed earlier, it can sometimes be valuable to implement a change of strategy gradually and incrementally, allowing people to make adaptive changes as the learning experience develops. At the same time it is important to ensure that opposition is manifested and brought out into the open rather than being allowed to develop without other people being aware.

Managers who are effective and successful politically, and able to implement their decisions and proposed changes, will generally appreciate and understand organizational processes and be sensitive to the needs of others. It is extremely useful if the strategic leader is an able politician. The type and incidence of incremental changes in strategies throughout the organization will also be affected by the political ability of managers. Those with ability will be instrumental in introducing changes. Where the strategic leader wishes to encourage managers to be adaptive and innovative it is important to consider the political ability of the managers concerned. Political ability relates to the use of power and influence in the most appropriate way in particular circumstances. This is the subject of the next section.

## Uses of power and influence

MacMillan (1978) argues that introducing and implementing change frequently requires the use of power and influence, which he examines in terms of the control of situations and the ability to change people's intentions. Where a person wishes to exercise control over the behaviour of other people, either within the organization or external to it, he or she has two basic options. First, he can *structure the situation* so that others comply with his wishes; secondly, by communicating with other people, he can seek to change their perceptions so that they see things differently and decide to do as he suggests. In other words he succeeds in *changing their intentions*. Both of these approaches are categorized as strategies of manipulation.

Where a manager is concentrating on structuring the situation he or she is using certain power bases as enabling resources; where he or she is attempting to change intentions he or she is seeking to use influence. Power, in particular personal power, is again important as a source of influence.

The outcome from both the situational and intentional approaches can be either positive or negative. When the effect is positive the other people feel that they are better off as a result of the changes; the effect is negative if they feel worse off.

MacMillan identifies four tactics in relation to these points:

- *Inducement* – This implies an ability to control the situation, and the outcome is perceived as beneficial by others involved. A large retail organization with several stores might require managers to be mobile as a condition of their employment, and reward them with improved status, salary increases and relocation expenses every time they move. The situation is controlled; ideally the managers concerned feel positive about the moves.
- *Coercion* – The situation is again controlled, but the outcome is perceived negatively. In the

*Table 24.3*  Political power bases and tactics

**Bases of personal power**

| | |
|---|---|
| Expertise | Particularly significant where the skill is in scarce supply |
| | It is possible to use mobility, and the threat of leaving, to gain support for certain changes of strategy – again dependent upon the manager's personal importance to the firm |
| Assessed stature | A reputation for being a 'winner' or a manager who can obtain results. Recent successes are most relevant |
| Credibility | Particularly credibility with external power sources, such as suppliers or customers |
| Political access | Being well known around the organization and able to influence key groups of managers |
| Control over information | Internal and external sources |
| | Information can be used openly and honestly or withheld and used selectively – consequently, it is crucial to know the reliability of the source |
| Group support | In managing and implementing change it is essential to have the support of colleagues and fellow managers |

**Political tactics to obtain results**

| | |
|---|---|
| Develop liaisons | As mentioned above, it is important to develop and maintain both formal and informal contacts with other managers, functions and divisions |
| | Again, it is important to include those managers who are most powerful |
| Present a conservative image | It can be disadvantageous to be seen as too radical an agent of change |
| Diffuse opposition | Conflicts need to be brought out into the open and differences of opinion aired rather than kept hidden. Divide and rule can be a useful strategy |
| Trade-off and compromise | In any proposal or suggestion for change it is important to consider the needs of other people whose support is required |
| 'Strike while the iron is hot' | Successful managers should build on successes and reputation quickly |
| Research | Information is always vital to justify and support proposals |
| Use a neutral cover | Radical changes, or those that other people might perceive as a threat to them, can sometimes be usefully disguised and initiated as minor changes. This is linked to the next point |
| Limit communication | A useful tactic can be to unravel change gradually in order to contain possible opposition |
| Withdraw strategically | If things are going wrong, and especially if the changes are not crucial, it can be a wise tactic on occasions to withdraw, at least temporarily |

- Politically successful managers understand organizational processes and they are sensitive to the needs of others.
- Effective political action brings about desirable and successful changes in organizations – it is functional.
- Negative political action is dysfunctional, and can enable manipulative managers to pursue their personal objectives against the better interests of the organization.
- The strategic leader needs to be an effective politician.

Source: Allen, RW, Madison, DL, Porter, LW, Renwick, PA and Mayes, BT (1979) Organisational politics: tactics and characteristics of its actors. *California Management Review*, 22, Fall; Dixon, M (1982) The world of office politics, *Financial Times*, 10 November.

above situation the same managers might be threatened with no further promotions unless they agreed to certain moves within the company.

- *Persuasion* – The manager does not try to control or change the situation but argues that the other people can or will benefit by behaving in certain ways. The desired outcome is positive. People might be persuaded to agree to a change which is not immediately desirable by suggestions that future rewards will be forthcoming.
- *Obligation* – This is another intentional tactic, but the outcome is negative. People are persuaded to behave in a certain way by being made to feel that they have an obligation. It might be suggested that people
  - owe the company something for the money that has been invested in their previous training, or
  - owe particular managers a favour for something that has happened in the past, or
  - are obligated to the group of people that they have been working with for some years and should not let them down.

In particular cases, individual managers may or may not have a number of alternative tactics to select from. Tactics that have positive outcomes must normally be preferable to those that cause negative feelings if both are available and likely to yield the desired results. At times managers whose power bases are limited and who need speedy results may have little option but to coerce or obligate people. Kanter (1983) emphasizes that successful managers of change situations are able to keep their power invisible both during and after the change. Participation in the change is then perceived to stem from commitment or conviction rather than from power being exercised over people. Kanter contends that it is very important for middle managers in organizations to be skilful in managing change as they implement the

detailed strategies, and that it is important for strategic leaders to ensure that they have support from their middle managers for the overall corporate strategy.

## Organizational politics and culture

Culture broadly encapsulates manifest actions and behaviours and underlying beliefs, and effective cultural change must include both (see Chapter 5). Where this happens, there will be willing support for, and compliance with, the change. Without a change in beliefs, compliance will be reluctant. Strong, political managers who oppose the changes will show either covert or even overt non-compliance, their choice reflecting their style and power.

Bartlett and Ghoshal (1995) argue that the radical and forced downsizing of the early 1990s has left many companies with a context of 'compliance, control, contract and constraint'. Behaviours have changed, but not beliefs; elements of the old culture remain to create confusion. The challenge for these companies is one of creativity and innovation; they must find ways of adding new values for competitive advantage, which will require a context of support, trust and liberation, and a willingness to accept stretching objectives, alongside appropriate control disciplines.

## Organizational politics and ethics

It is clear that managers can use political behaviour both for and against the best interests of the organization; at the same time, they can also behave either ethically or unethically. Positive and ethical behaviour is required to satisfy all the stakeholders effectively; negative politics, while ethical, implies that internal stakeholders (maybe even individual managers and functions) receive priority over external stakeholders. Positive politicking which is unethical may well appear successful in the short term, but possibly with a long-term downside risk. Where negative politics combine with unethical behaviour, there is likely to be corruption.

## 'Machiavellianism'

'Machiavellianism' is the term often used to describe coercive management tactics. Marriott (1908), translating Machiavelli's book *The Prince* written in the sixteenth century, uses the expression to cover 'the ruthless use of power, particularly coercive power, and manipulation to attain personal goals'. While coercive power can be used effectively by managers it may not always be easy to justify, especially if other alternatives are available. Coercion may not be practical on a repeat basis, and any fear of threats not carried out quickly recedes.

Jay (1967), however, contends that Machiavelli also offers much useful advice for ethical managers. Basing his arguments on Machiavelli's views on strategies and tactics for annexing and ruling nations, Jay argues that chief executive strategic leaders should concentrate their efforts outside the organization, developing and strengthening the strategic perspective. In order for them to feel able to do this, the internal structure and systems must be sound and effective, and managers must be supportive of proposals from the top. General and functional managers should be free to operate and feel able to make certain changes, but their overall power should be contained. They should exercise leadership, which is based on power. This power yields the freedom to decide how things should be done. Managers, though, should be afraid to pursue personal goals against the interest of the organization as a whole. Achieving this requires a clear awareness of what is happening throughout the organization and the appropriate punishment of offenders. Successful managers should be rewarded.

Pearce and DeNisi (1983) stress that most organizations are managed partially by informal coalitions or groupings of managers superimposed on the formal structure. It is particularly important that managers in key positions in the organization, those in charge of important resources or responsible for products upon which the profits or reputation of the organization depend, are known to be committed and loyal to the strategic leader. Moreover, any informal and powerful coalitions that develop should also be supportive. To achieve both of these it may be appropriate for the strategic leader to remove or switch senior managers occasionally as a reminder of his or her overall power. This is particularly likely to happen after an acquisition, during a restructuring exercise, or on the appointment of a new strategic leader.

Strategic coalitions can be a major force behind strategy formation, especially where the overall strategic leader is relatively weak. An effective leader will therefore seek to use coalitions that already exist, and encourage the formation of other loyal ones.

In considering the feasibility of changes and how to implement them, it is very important to examine the underlying political abilities and behaviour within the firm: who has power, how it is manifested and how it is used. Without taking these factors into account, implementation is likely to prove hazardous.

## Summary

Most organizations must compete or operate in dynamic environments where change is inevitable. Some of this will always be reactive, but the most effective organizations manage, as well as manage in, their environments. Much comes down to the strategic leader and the organization culture, which realistically drive the whole change process.

Machiavelli recommended that vanquished foes should be eliminated, but counselled that quite often only the King or Chief needs to be sacrificed; those spared will soon fall into line through fear.

Research into hostile take-overs and acquisitions in the UK between 1990 and 1994 shows that within one year of the take-over 70% of the chairmen of the acquired businesses had left; 57% of the chief executives left within two years.

Effective *change management* requires:

- a clear perception of need – dissatisfaction with the existing status quo
- a way forward – a new direction or perceived opportunity
- the capability to change – the necessary resources
- commitment – change needs managing.

A four-stage cycle of change can be identified: beginning with a creative idea, an opportunity is nurtured before an action stage grows the business. Structure follows to provide control. At this time it is important to find new ideas to maintain the cycle of growth.

There is a number of *levels* of change:

- the corporate culture
- the organizational mission
- corporate strategies
- organization structures, systems and processes
- competitive strategies
- operational tasks and activities.

As we ascend this hierarchy the complexity and the difficulty of the challenge increases.

A simple model of change *management* would have three stages:

- unfreezing existing behaviours
- changing behaviour

- refreezing the new behaviour as common practice.

However, there is an argument that organizations should have a culture that accepts and embraces constant change and consequently we need to be careful about the implications of refreezing.

There are forces for and against change. There is always likely to be resistance to change – after all, people's jobs are affected and some will perceive themselves to be losing out.

Change can be *continuous*, *innovatory* and *improvemental* – on occasions it will be discontinuous and imply simultaneous changes to strategy, structure and style. Sometimes this is essential, but it can be very disruptive and unsettling for people.

Change management cannot be separated from *power*. Power and influence are required to engineer and effect change – they may also be used in an attempt to stop it. There are two key dimensions: the relative power of the organization in respect of its external environment; and the relative power of different businesses, divisions, departments and individuals within the organization itself.

There are seven key *power bases*: reward, coercive, legitimate, personal, expert, information and connection.

The way that individuals use power and influence is a manifestation of their political abilities. *Organizational politics* can be positive if it is used to carry through and implement decisions that are clearly in the interests of the organization. Negative politics is the tool of 'machiavellian' managers who are minded to pursue self-interest at the expense of other colleagues and maybe at the expense of the whole organization.

## References

Abrahamson, E (2000) Dynamic stability, *Harvard Business Review*, January–February.

Allen, RW, Madison, DL, Porter, LW, Renwick PA and Mayes, BT (1979) Organisational politics: tactics and characteristics of its actors, *California Management Review*, 22, Fall.

Bartlett, C and Ghoshal, S (1995) Rebuilding behavioural context: turn process re-engineering into people rejuvenation, *Sloan Management Review*, Autumn.

Beckhard, R (1969) *Organisation Development: Strategies and Models*, Addison-Wesley.

Blanchard, K and Johnson, S (1982) *The One Minute Manager*, Morrow.

Bourgeois, LJ and Brodwin, DR (1984) Strategic implementation: five approaches to an elusive phenomenon, *Strategic Management Journal*, 5.

Checkland, PB (1986) The politics of practice. Paper presented at the IIASA International Round-table 'The Art and Science of Systems Practice', November.

Daft, RL (1983) *Organisation Theory and Design*, West.

Dixon, M (1982) The world of office politics, *Financial Times*, 10 November.

Drucker, P (1993) *Managing in Turbulent Times*, Butterworth-Heinemann.

Eccles, T (1994) *Succeeding With Change*, McGraw-Hill.

Farrell, D and Petersen, JC (1982) Patterns of political behaviour in organizations, *Academy of Management Review*, 7(3), July.

Ghoshal, S and Caulkin, S (1998) An escape route from ruthlessness, *Financial Times*, 18 November.

Goss, T, Pascale, R and Athos, A (1993) The Reinvention roller coaster: risking the present for a powerful future, *Harvard Business Review*, November–December.

Hamel, G (1994) Competing for the Future, Economist Conference, London (June).

Hayes, J (1984) The politically competent manager, *Journal of General Management*, 10(1), Autumn.

Jay, A (1967) *Management and Machiavelli*, Holt, Rinehart & Winston.

Johne, A and Davies, R (1999) Approaches to stimulating change in mature insurance companies, *British Academy of Management Journal*, 10, September.

Kanter, RM (1983) The middle manager as innovator. *In Strategic Management* (ed. RG Hamermesch), John Wiley.

Kotter, JP (1995) Why transformation efforts fail, *Harvard Business Review*, March–April.

Kotter, JP and Schlesinger, LA (1979) Choosing strategies for change, *Harvard Business Review*, March–April.

Lewin, K (1947) Frontiers in group dynamics: concept, method and reality in social science, *Human Relations*, 1.

Lewin, K (1951) *Field Theory in Social Sciences*, Harper & Row.

Lukes, S (1974) *Power: A Radical View*, Macmillan.

MacMillan, IC (1978) *Strategy Formulation: Political Concepts*, West.

Margerison, C and Smith, B (1989) Shakespeare and management: managing change, *Management Decision*, 27(2).

Marriott, WK (1908) Translation into English of *The Prince* written by N Machiavelli in the 1500s.

Mintzberg, H (1983) *Power In and Around Organisations*, Prentice-Hall.

Pascale, R, Millemann, M and Gioja, L (1997) Changing the way we change, *Harvard Business Review*, November–December.

Pearce, JA and DeNisi, AS (1983) Attribution theory and strategic decision making: an application to coalition formation, *Academy of Management Journal*, 26, March.

Peters, T (1989) Tomorrow's companies: new products, new markets, new competition, new thinking, *The Economist*, 4 March.

Peters, T (1992) *Liberation Management – Necessary Disorganization for the Nanosecond Nineties*, Macmillan.

Quinn, JB (1988) Managing strategies incrementally. In *The Strategy Process: Concepts, Contexts and Cases* (eds JB Quinn, H Mintzberg and RM James), Prentice-Hall.

Thompson, AA and Strickland, AJ (1981) *Strategy and Policy: Concept and Cases*, Business Publications.

Waterman, RH Jr (1987) *The Renewal Factor*, Bantam.

Explore Strategic Change Management further at:

*Academy of Management Journal*   http://www.aom.pace.edu/amj

*California Management Review*   http://www.haas.berkeley.edu/News/cmr/index.html

*Harvard Business Review*   http://www.hbsp.harvard.edu/products/hbr/index.html

*Management Decision*   http://www.mcb.co.uk/md.htm

*Sloan Management Review*   http://mitsloan.mit.edu/smr/main.html

*Strategic Management Journal*   http://www.smsweb.org/about/SMJ/SMJ.html

## Questions and Research Assignments

### TEXT RELATED

1. Describe an event where you have personally experienced forces for change, and discuss any forces that were used to resist the change. What tactics were adopted on both sides?

2. Describe a strategic leader (any level in an organization of your choice) whom you consider to be a powerful person. What types of power does he or she possess?

3. Describe a manager whom you believe is successful at using organizational politics. On what observations and experiences are you basing your decision? How might you measure political effectiveness and the elements within it?

4. As a manager, what are your personal power bases? How politically effective are you? How could you increase your overall power and improve your effectiveness?

## Internet and Library Projects

1. Select an industry or company and ascertain the forces that have brought about changes in the last ten years. How proactive/reactive have the companies been, and with what levels of success?

2. Analyse the news broadcasts of two rival TV networks, such as the BBC and ITN, and evaluate whether their reporting of industrial and business news is similar or dissimilar. Are they reporting to inform or to persuade about, say, the merits or demerits of government policy? To what extent are they constrained by government?

*BBC News*   http://www.bbc.co.uk
*ITN*   http://www.itn.co.uk

3. Research and update the Apple Computers case. How would you evaluate:
   (a) The contribution of Steve Jobs?
   (b) Jobs as a strategic leader?
   (c) Are Apple now less crisis prone than they were and more in control of the change agenda?

*Apple Computers*   http://www.apple.com

# Final Thoughts: What is Strategy?

*Success is never final.*
Winston Churchill

*Things may come to those who wait – but only the things left by those who hustle.*
Abraham Lincoln

## Introduction

In these last few pages the main ideas from this book are synthesized in order to reinforce the key ideas and address the question: 'What is strategy?'

Many organizations are now operating or competing in dynamic, turbulent, uncertain, 'chaotic' environments. This is partly the result of industries and markets becoming ever more global; it is also driven by continual improvements in technology which, among other things, causes product, service and strategic lifecycles to shorten. In turn this means that organizations must act, react and change more quickly. Some of these changes will be continuous and emergent, as vigilant, responsive organizations seize opportunities and innovate ahead of their rivals.

Other changes will be discontinuous and imply changes in competitive paradigms. Technology can both create and destroy industries, markets and windows of opportunity; breakpoints – or switches to new competitive rules and agendas – happen increasingly frequently. Organizations cannot ignore this reality and the pressures that they bring, however disruptive the changes might be.

Selected organizations, such as Coca-Cola and Walt Disney, continue to survive these breakpoints – sometimes actually creating them – and, as a result, they thrive, grow and prosper. They are recognized around the world and they exploit their competencies and their reputation. They create E–V–R (environment–values–resources) congruency and sustain it with carefully managed change. These organizations are truly entrepreneurial, but they are exceptional. We can learn from their actions, strategies and behaviours, although it will remain difficult to explain fully all of the reasons for their success. Simply attempting to copy their behaviour is not an adequate answer to the challenges facing organizations.

Other companies grow more steadily and uncertainly; they never seem to have the same command over their environment. Nonetheless, they do survive, partly with innovation, partly with contingent reaction. Others survive for some period of time, but then decline as they lose E–V–R congruency. Some organizations only survive with a change of leadership, style and culture. However, some businesses disappear every year, some to take-over, others to liquidation. It is, therefore, all too easy for currently successful firms to lose their edge and their competitive advantage. Miles and Snow (1994) argue that there are four main reasons for this:

- a lack of awareness and a failure to be alert to new opportunities and threats
- retaining a belief in a successful competitive paradigm for too long. Market leaders seem particularly prone to do this; they tend to rely on *continuous* change to retain their leadership
- an unwillingness to accept the need for structural or cultural change, and
- poor judgement, causing a company to make poor, inappropriate decisions.

There are also important lessons to be learnt from their relative demise.

In looking at strategic effectiveness and success, we can take two related, but distinct, perspectives. The first concerns success: what reasons lie behind the relative prosperity of our most successful organizations, those which continue to add value for their customers, differentiate their products and services, and control their costs? The second perspective concerns survival and environmental management: what factors distinguish a crisis-averse from a crisis-prone organization? The latter will typically lurch from problem to problem, difficulty to difficulty, crisis to crisis, never really managing its environment. It is fashionable, in the author's opinion, to talk about competitiveness, competitive advantage and success; it is less fashionable, but equally important – and in many cases, more relevant – to explore the issues behind crisis aversion. Too many organizations hover on the narrow line which separates survival from failure.

Organizations are systems that comprise people who are trying to act purposefully rather than thrash around without any real purpose (Checkland, 1981). However, people differ in their perspective and perceptions. They use their personal meaning systems to interpret events, actions, opportunities and threats and to decide upon responses. While their personal strengths must be captured and exploited, organizational information systems should ensure that they work within the parameters of the corporate purpose, vision and policies, and that their initiatives and contributions are shared and understood.

The new technological revolution and the increase in globalization have forced change on organizations everywhere, regardless of their type, size and sector. Few are unscathed. Some have embraced change positively and willingly; others more reluctantly. Those who have failed to change have probably been sold or liquidated. One outcome is a more flexible, but slimmed-down workforce.

On the positive side, many managers and employees are better educated. They are information technology (IT) literate, knowledge workers in a knowledge based society. Some of them possess scarce skills. In some organizations people have become less constrained and more empowered, willing to be creative and show initiative in a more open, less hierarchical firm. Finally, information often flows more horizontally and freely, enriching and speeding up decision making.

But this, clearly, is not the case everywhere.

Many workers are now part-time and 'peripheral', as opposed to 'core'. When re-engineering their processes and changing their structures too many companies have gone too far. They have downsized but not 'rightsized'. Important skills and competencies have been lost. Linked to this, strategies of focusing on core activities and competencies, and divesting those which are non-core, have created an increasing incidence of strategic alliances and networks. Managing these networks effectively demands new capabilities, which many organizations have yet to develop fully. People feel under greater pressure and stress; there is more fear and insecurity. 'Hard' as distinct from 'soft' human resource strategies are practised in many companies, and many employees, instead of committing themselves to a single company, look to switch organizations and industries as they take more control of their working lives, and this despite the widespread managerial unemployment and insecurity.

Sadly, many large organizations, composed of very intelligent people, are still slow to respond to change pressures and, when they do, their behaviour is often ponderous. Individuals can, and often do, act dynamically and entrepreneurially; yet many organizations have still to work out how to capture the intelligence and learning in order to facilitate the change process. This is the paradox of the large organization learning how to behave like the archetypal small business.

The challenge of embracing both the hard and soft elements of strategic management in order to increase strategic awareness and manage strategic change more effectively remains a major challenge for many organizations. It is a challenge that is more likely to intensify than to disappear.

This final chapter, therefore:

- identifies ten key elements of strategy
- discusses the idea of strategic competency
- revisits the strategic paradoxes introduced in Chapter 2 and which have been debated throughout the book
- presents a model of the crisis-averse organization, and
- finally, offers a view on what strategy is.

## Ten Key Elements of Strategy

Figure 25.1 shows ten elements of strategy that have been discussed at various points in the book. The first six are interdependent and if they are interwoven effectively the organization should be more crisis averse than crisis prone. The remaining four impact upon the whole process of strategy creation and implementation.

## 1. Perspectives of strategy

Strategy can be about the past (emergent patterns from previous decisions), the present (strategic positions) and the future (strategic plans). It can also be treated at the levels of broad purpose and narrow tactical ploys. All of these perspectives are relevant to the debate about what strategy is. The relevance of strategy will also vary for different people. The main perspective for the strategic leader is the overall

*Figure 25.1*    Ten key elements of strategy.

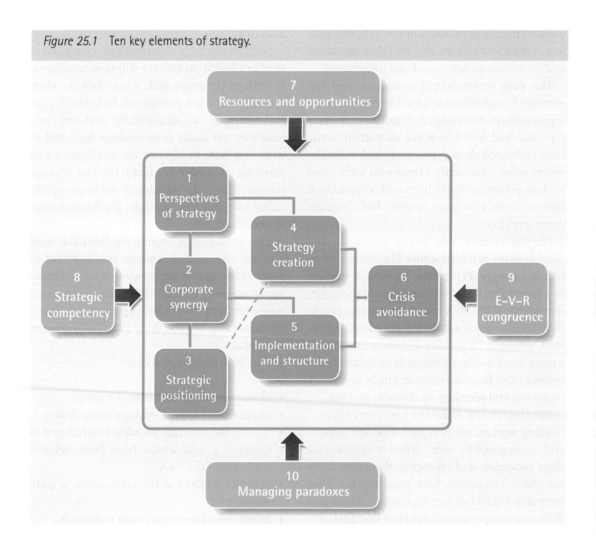

corporate strategy for the whole organization, although the other levels are clearly relevant. Other senior managers will be focused on competitive positions and the competitive strategies which determine whether or not the organization enjoys competitive advantage. The activities and functional strategies are perhaps most important to lower-level middle and junior managers but, at the same time, it is vital they understand the wider picture and the contribution that they make.

## 2. Corporate strategy and synergy

The issue here, which was discussed towards the end of the book, is whether or not there is a logical and defensible 'heartland' of related businesses comprising the corporate portfolio. Ideally, each business will be competitive and successful in its own right and, at the same time, contribute synergistically to the corporate parent and to other businesses in the portfolio. The parent organization should equally be able to contribute value to each business.

## 3. Strategic positioning and competitive advantage

To be successful, each business or activity will need to establish – and sustain with change – a clear and strong competitive position. Where this position delivers either a cost advantage (when compared with rivals in the market) or a differentiated position which customers perceive as relevant and valuable, or both, then competitive advantage is a real possibility. The advantage does not come from the position itself, but from the activities – competencies and capabilities – which create and sustain the position of advantage.

## 4. Strategy creation

Strategy creation is about change. Consequently,

the approach that the organization takes to strategy creation is dictated by the strategic leader and influenced, and possibly constrained, by the culture of the organization. Three broad approaches were identified. First, visionary or entrepreneurial strategy creation, itself a reflection of strong strategic leadership. Secondly, planned strategy, possibly the outcome of a planning system. Together, these reflect intended strategies. Thirdly, emergent strategy creation, which takes two forms: incremental changes to intended strategies during the implementation phase, and adaptive strategy creation in a dynamic and turbulent environment. Organizations need to find an effective blend of the three, all of which are likely to be present to some degree.

## 5. Strategy implementation and structure

Strategies must be implemented before they can be deemed successful. While organization structures are designed to ensure that intended strategies can be implemented effectively, the very operation of the structure is the foundation for emergent strategy creation. This issue is naturally tied in to the relative significance of centralization and decentralization, and the extent to which managers are empowered.

## 6. Crisis avoiding

If these first five points are being dealt with effectively the organization should be relatively crisis averse in a dynamic environment. Where there are significant weaknesses, the organization is likely to be more crisis prone.

## 7. Resources and opportunities

There are two approaches to the management of strategy. While they are different, it is a mistake to adopt one approach at the expense of the other. The two approaches are complementary and should be pursued together. The opportunity-driven approach begins with a scan of the external business environment in a search for new opportunities that the organization might be able to exploit. The resource-based approach builds on the organization's core competencies and strategic capabilities. In essence, the successful organization will address two questions simultaneously. (1) What new windows of opportunities are opening up that we might wish to follow because we possess, or can obtain, the necessary strategic resources? (2) What are our distinctive competencies and capabilities and where are there untapped possibilities for exploiting them further?

## 8.  Strategic competency

This is developed in the next section. It should, at this point, be pointed out that 'strategic competency' goes beyond the idea of core (technological) competencies and strategic capabilities discussed above.

## 9.  E–V–R congruence

Successful organizations create and sustain congruency between the external environment (the source of fresh opportunities and threats), their resources (competencies, capabilities and strengths) and their values. It is these values that dictate the ability of the organization to change both continuously (incrementally) and discontinuously (occasionally to new competitive paradigms).

## 10.  Strategic paradoxes

Again, this is discussed later in the chapter. Simply, the organization must work out a stance for dealing with a whole series of issues and challenges for which there are no clear-cut answers.

## Strategic Competencies

The author believes that strategists should view their organizations as portfolios of strategic competencies which need to be continually reviewed, deployed and developed in ways that enhance the organization's competitive position. Strategic effectiveness, strategic and competitive success in a dynamic and competitive environment, is dependent upon three groups of competencies: the *content* of the actual strategies, strategic *change* competencies, and strategic *learning* competencies.

Strong and appropriate *content* competencies will enable the organization to add value, innovate and exploit both its internal and external architecture to gain benefit from its core (technological) competencies and strategic (process) capabilities. From these should come distinct product and service advantages (in the form of differentiation) and controlled costs. In turn, these are the foundations of competitive advantage.

However, the organization must be able to manage both continuous and discontinuous *change* in a dynamic environment, which in turn demands that it understands its environment. This understanding and insight comes from *learning*. The organization can learn from all its stakeholders, including its external suppliers, distributors and customers, as well as from its own employees and from the tactics and strategies of its competitors.

Figure 25.2 draws together these layers of strategic competency as an interdependent and circular process. Organizations must be able to understand the complexity and trends of the changing environment. Some of the changes will be the result of external forces, maybe competitor actions. Others will be the outcomes of actions taken by the organization itself as it adopts a proactive approach to managing its environment. Using this understanding and

Figure 25.2  Interdependent competencies – I.

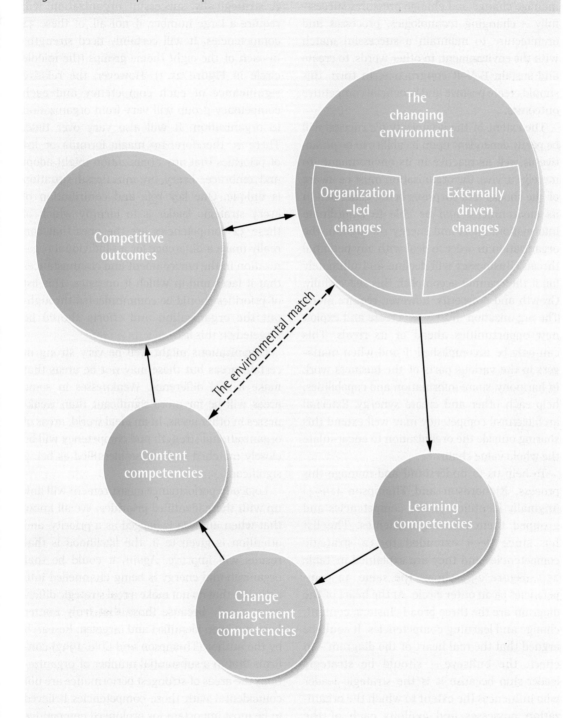

learning, the organization must be able to manage change and change pressures successfully – changing technologies, processes and architecture to maintain a successful match with the environment; in other words, to create and sustain E–V–R congruence. In turn, this should create positive and beneficial competitive outcomes.

The extent of the organization's success will be partly dependent upon its ability to be proactive as well as reactive in its environment. To merely survive, the organization must be aware of the shocks and surprises being generated in its environment, and be able to co-ordinate information, effort and energy throughout the organization in order to deal with any potential threats. Businesses will decline and ultimately fail if they cannot accomplish this successfully. Growth and prosperity, however, require more. The organization must spot, create and exploit new opportunities ahead of its rivals. This can only be accomplished if and when managers in the various parts of the business work in harmony, share information and capabilities, help each other and create synergy. External architectural competency may well extend this sharing outside the organization to encapsulate the whole value chain.

To help us to understand and manage this process, Richardson and Thompson (1994) originally identified 30 key competencies and grouped them into eight themes. The list has since been extended to 32 strategic competencies and they are explained in Table 25.1. Figure 25.3 shows the same 32 competencies as an outer circle. At the heart of the diagram are the three broad clusters: content, change and learning competencies. It could be argued that the real heart of the diagram – in effect, the bullseye – should be strategic leader-ship because it is the strategic leader who influences the extent to which the organization possesses and exploits each of the competencies.

The fundamental argument is as follows. A strategically successful organization will require a large number, if not all, of these 32 competencies. It will certainly need strengths in each of the eight theme groups (the middle circle in Figure 25.3). However, the relative significance of each competency and each competency group will vary from organization to organization. It will also vary over time. There is, therefore, no magic formula or list of priorities that any organization might adopt and embrace. Every organizational situation is unique. One key role and contribution of every strategic leader is to identify which of these 32 competencies are the ones that can really make a difference for an individual organization in the environment and circumstances that it faces and in which it operates. This list of priorities should be communicated throughout the organization and efforts should be targeted on this list.

Organizations might well be very strong in certain areas but these may not be areas that make a real difference. Weaknesses in some areas will be far more significant than weaknesses in other areas. In an ideal world, areas of organizational strength and competency will be closely matched with those identified as being significant.

Logically, performance measurement will link up with these identified priorities. We all know that when an area is flagged as a priority, and attention is given to it, the likelihood is that results will improve. Again, it could be that organizational energy is being channelled into activities that do not make a real strategic difference, simply because those that truly matter have not been identified and targeted. Research by the author (Thompson and Cole, 1997) confirms that in a substantial number of organizations the areas of strongest performance are not coincidental with those competencies believed to be most important for prolonged competitive success.

*Table 25.1*  Thirty-two generic competencies

**Strategic awareness abilities**
1. Think strategically and holistically, encapsulating issues of past, present and future
2. Maintain an awareness of environmental changes and their implications
3. Design and operationalise a 'fitting' organization, the structure and systems of which match its environment(s) and stay matched in times of change and turbulence
4. Avoid the trap of self-enacted reality (whereby an organization would drift into problems because it retains an unrealistic view of its true position) and instead reach more objective, informed and environmentally aware decisions

**Stakeholder satisfaction abilities**
5. Understand the needs and expectations of stakeholders and manage the organization to meet those which must be prioritized
6. Appreciate key success factors (for satisfying stakeholders) and match these with organizational competencies and capabilities, taking into account new opportunities and potential threats

**Competitive strategic abilities**
7. Understand the competitive environment, choose where and how to compete, design effective, 'winning' competitive paradigms and improve these continuously
8. Get and stay close to customers – to understand, attract and satisfy them more effectively than competitors with differentiated, high added-value products and services

**Strategic implementation and change abilities**
9. Establish appropriate objectives, plans and targets and achieve these, while always appreciating the need for flexibility, adaptation and change
10. Implement intended strategies throughout the organization, making (the right) things happen
11. Create, share and implement a winning vision or paradigm
12. Empower people and motivate them towards continuous organizational improvement
13. Foster internal cross-functional and cross-business synergies through co-operation and sharing
14. Co-operate in external strategic alliances for competitive advantage
15. Move to new competitive paradigms discontinuously at timely intervals

**Quality and customer case**
16. Provide excellent quality – as perceived and recognized by customers
17. Continuously improve productivity and cost reductions without ever sacrificing key aspects of quality
18. Invoke a creative, innovative and self-organizing climate in the organization

**Functional competencies**
19. Acquire new, relevant technologies and utilise R&D to help to create a future for the business
20. Develop and launch new products and services both effectively and in the appropriate time-scale
21. Develop and introduce new processes for cost savings and speedier decision making
22. Attract, develop, reward and retain people with appropriate skills and competencies
23. Reach and satisfy customers with effective distribution systems, both nationally and internationally
24. Harness the potential of information technology in design and for fast, efficient and effective information harnessing and sharing
25. Maintain strong financial controls and be able to access capital for future investment programmes

**Table 25.1**    *(Continued)*

**Failure and crisis avoidance**

26. Avoid business failures by becoming and staying crisis averse
27. Plan for when things do go wrong, and
28. Manage any crises (business and sociotechnical) effectively
29. Turn around a business when there are critical financial, competitive or leadership difficulties

**Ethics and social responsibility**

30. Manage 'green' issues, either to avoid crises or to create competitive advantage
31. Manage socially responsibly
32. Become more ethically aware and manage with an ethical underpinning

**Figure 25.3**    Interdependent competencies – II.

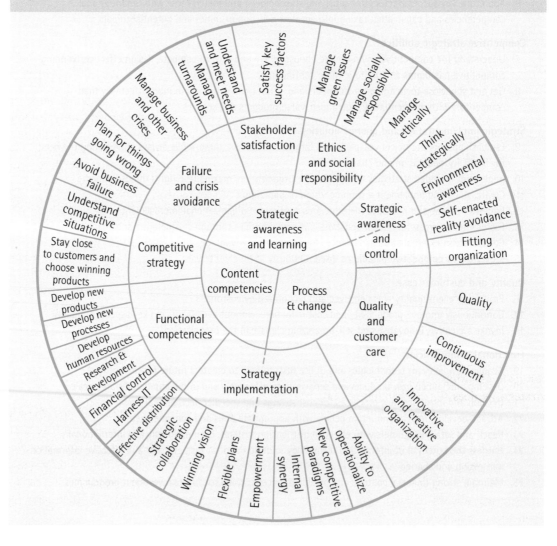

## Strategic Paradoxes

In Chapter 2 a number of strategic issues, challenges or paradoxes were listed, about each of which the organization has to make decisions. Again, the answers are not clear-cut. Rather, the choices that the organization makes – and the relatedness of the decisions that it takes on each of the issues – will have a marked impact upon its strategic effectiveness.

This section recaps the main ones – readers will appreciate how every one of these has been debated at some stage in the book.

### Paradox 1: Past and future

All organizations build on the past. Sometimes they learn from their successes; on other occasions they learn from their mistakes. Normally, developments from the past will imply continuous improvement around the same competitive paradigm. Sometimes, however, the future requires more dramatic and discontinuous change which implies that past and current competitive paradigms are abandoned. It is a mistake to persist with 'yesterday's' and 'today's' products if their lifecycle is heading for decline but, equally, 'change for the sake of change' can be unnecessarily disruptive and threaten control and quality. The challenge, then, is one of balance.

### Paradox 2: Intended and emergent strategy

Strategic planning plays an important role in strategy, as does the contribution of a strong and charismatic entrepreneurial leader. However, plans must be seen as flexible and there is an inherent danger in being reliant on just one main source of ideas. In a dynamic and competitive environment, learning and emergent strategy will always be vital. The challenge is again one of balance.

### Paradox 3: Reactive or proactive?

Simply, organizations must be able both to manage in and to manage their environments. They must respond to the unexpected events and surprises; they must at times lead the change agenda.

### Paradox 4: Resource based or opportunity driven?

This point was explained earlier in this chapter, when it was highlighted that both need adopting simultaneously. The chances are that one or the other will take priority – but which, and with what emphasis?

### Paradox 5: Cost or differentiation?

Again, the answer is both! Organizations, in their search for competitive advantage, can never ignore costs. There is, however, a distinction between striving to be the cost leader (with lower costs than one's main rivals for the same product or service) and effective cost management. Organizations that look to add new values and differentiate their products and services in distinctive ways must invest (and increase their costs) to create this difference – at the same time, there is no benefit in adding costs and benefits that are of little consequence to customers. The secret lies in understanding and managing the key cost drivers.

### Paradox 6: Focus or diversify?

Contemporary strategic logic says focus. The era of the diversified conglomerate is over, at least for the moment. However, a very tight focus can restrain growth, and consequently most organizations that are seeking to grow will diversify in justifiably related areas. The link might be technology or markets.

## Paradox 7: How big?

The focus/diversify dilemma is related to growth ambitions. The large organization may be able to claim critical mass, perhaps important in its industry, especially where it has ambitions to be a global competitor. Some very successful organizations deliberately set out to be number one or number two in every market segment in which they compete. Their challenge is to retain the flexibility and the innovation of the small, entrepreneurial business as they grow, to ensure that they do not reach a position of stasis in the cycle of growth and maybe have to engineer a crisis to address the need for renewed creativity. Even the largest, global organizations need to be relevant locally around the world.

## Paradox 8: Centralize or decentralize?

Centralization certainly retains control at the top of the organization and allows for hands-on leadership from the strategic leader. Unfortunately, it can make the organization slow to respond in a dynamic environment. Decentralization and empowerment can increase flexibility, in conjunction with a hands-off leadership style, but now control has to be achieved through a carefully crafted information system. It seems impossible to balance the two in a totally satisfactory manner and so organizations continually swing from one to the other. Sometimes the adjustments are minor; on other occasions there are major structural changes.

## The Crisis-averse Organization

Figure 25.4 highlights that an organization must meet the needs and expectations of all its stakeholders if it is to survive. It is vital to retain customers; new customers then bring new business rather than merely replace others who have been lost or neglected. Employee support and commitment is essential for delivering the competitive quality and service that customers demand. To achieve this, employees must be motivated and rewarded. In addition, financial targets must be met to ensure shareholder loyalty.

Achieving these outcomes is dependent upon aspects of both strategy and structure, which in turn depend upon effective strategic leadership. A sound, appropriate, communicated and shared purpose and vision should be manifested in appropriate, feasible and desirable corporate and competitive strategies. These must be:

- implemented with a high level of customer service
- improved continuously, and
- changed to new corporate and competitive paradigms at appropriate times and opportunities.

This demands environmental awareness and the ability of the organization to respond to change pressures and to external strategic disturbances. While we talk about an organization-wide response, the real challenge lies with individual managers and employees, who are closest to customers, suppliers and distributors. Innovative people drive functional-level improvements which can strengthen competitiveness; but they must be empowered and committed – issues of structure, style and implementation. The 'hard' aspects of strategy – leadership, vision and ideas – must be supported by the 'soft' people aspects.

People and process issues determine whether managers and other employees support and facilitate change, or inhibit the strategic changes that are necessary for survival. Egan (1993) adopts the term 'shadow side' of organizations to embrace issues of culture, complexity, politics, power, personal objectives and the ability of the organization to deal with the range of strategic issues and paradoxes discussed above.

*Figure 25.4*   The crisis-averse organization.

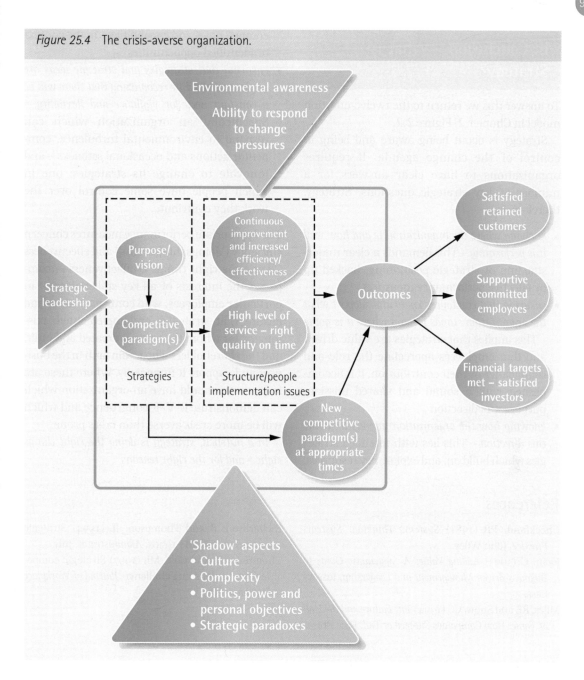

They can be positive or negative influences. Where they are negative, the organization is likely to be more crisis prone; for the organization to be crisis averse, they must be largely positive. Organizations must find ways of empowering their employees, harnessing their commitment and promoting organizational learning if the 'shadow side' is to make a positive contribution to strategic management and change.

## In Conclusion – What is Strategy?

To answer this we return to the twelve-question model in Chapter 2, Figure 2.2.

Strategy is about being aware and being in control of the change agenda. It requires organizations to have clear answers for a number of key strategic questions. Strategy, therefore, is:

- *knowing where the organization is and how well it is performing* – This demands a clear understanding of strategic positioning, backed up by effective performance measures
- *ensuring that employees know and support what the organization stands for and where it is going* – This implies that strategies are value driven and that employees appreciate the role and significance of their contribution. It is accomplished with a sound and shared mission, purpose and direction
- *knowing how the organization intends to follow this direction* – This lies with intended strategies which build on, and exploit, key resources, competencies and capabilities – in the context of identified opportunities
- *ensuring that strategies and strategic ideas are implemented, while recognizing that there will be a constant need for vigilance and flexibility* – Specifically, an organization which can respond to environmental turbulence, competitor actions and occasional setbacks – and innovate to change its strategies; one in which people have some control over the work they contribute.

The appropriate performance measures concern efficiency ('doings things right') and effectiveness ('doing the right things'). Effectiveness encompasses the interests of all key stakeholders – in particular employees, who contribute ideas and ensure that strategies are implemented, customers, for whom the value is created and built, and the shareholders who retain faith in the business and support it financially. Where these are in place we should have an organization which can demonstrate E–V–R congruence and which will be more crisis averse than crisis prone.

*In a nutshell, strategy is doing the right things right – and for the right reasons.*

## References

Checkland, PB (1981) *Systems Thinking, Systems Practice*, John Wiley.

Egan, G (1993) *Adding Value: A Systematic Guide to Business-driven Management and Leadership*, Jossey-Bass.

Miles, RE and Snow, CC (1994) *Fit, Failure and the Hall of Fame: How Companies Succeed or Fail*, Free Press.

Richardson, B and Thompson, JL (1994) Strategic competency in the 1990s, *Administrator*, July.

Thompson, JL and Cole, ME (1997) Strategic competency – the learning challenge, *Journal of Workplace Learning*, 9(5).

## Support material on the website

Thompson, JL and Richardson, B (1996) Strategic and competitive success – towards a model of the comprehensively competent organization, *Management Decision*, 34(1).

Thompson, JL (1998) Competency and strategic paradox, *Management Decision*, 36(4).

# An Introduction to the Case Studies

The main text featured over 100 short cases and examples which have generally been written to illustrate specific points and strategic issues. The 17 full-length case studies which follow will provide readers with an opportunity to develop a deeper insight into strategic awareness and strategic change management in manufacturing and service businesses, large conglomerates and small, entrepreneurial companies, the profit-seeking and not-for-profit sectors. To a large extent they feature instantly recognizable organizations with which students should feel comfortable. Every case covers a range of issues, but each one has a central theme. The accompanying chart lists these issues and shows how the cases link to the chapters of this book. The first case, the National Trust, is designed to be used very early in a course as it covers basic strategic principles and issues at a straightforward level. Virgin, included in the middle, could be used alongside Thorn EMI partway through a course, as Virgin Music was eventually sold to Thorn EMI. It could also be used towards the end as it covers a wide range of strategic issues. The case on Scottish and Newcastle Breweries focuses on the defence strategy against a hostile take-over bid and is ideal for analysing and discussing acquisition strategies. As the bid was referred to the (then) Monopolies and Mergers Commission (discussed in Chapter 7) it could also be included earlier. The Sony PlayStation is included immediately after the larger Sony case; the three Hanson cases are included together at the end. There is also a follow-up to the Lilliput Lane case on the accompanying website. They address different, albeit related, issues in the three organizations. It is not necessary for the Sony, Hanson and Lilliput Lane cases to all be used at the same time, although they can be.

It is, therefore, not essential that the cases are read or studied in the order in which they are presented in the book; it is also clearly possible for strategy teachers to substitute or supplement any of the cases with ones that they have written or prefer. While market

and financial data are included wherever it is seen as appropriate, the cases have been written to illustrate strategic issues and provoke discussion of these issues rather than as a vehicle for extensive quantitative analyses. A set of indicative questions is included at the end; they are not necessarily the only appropriate questions. Equally, lecturers may well prefer to focus on only selected aspects of the case.

Most of the cases have been produced with the support and encouragement of the organizations involved; in many instances they cover a range of topics but they are not fully comprehensive of all the strategic issues faced by the company concerned. They have all been written to foster discussion; they should not be taken as representative of either good or bad management practice.

## Analysing cases

There is no doubt that the greater the effort you put into case preparation and subsequent classroom discussions, the greater will be your personal benefit. Cases are designed to help you to develop your analytical skills and your powers of reasoning and persuasion. This cannot be achieved if you rely on others to do the preparation and talking.

There is no single best way of tackling case preparation. It can, however, be useful to read the case through once very quickly – to gain an overview of its scope and issues – before studying it in more detail. The questions at the end can be read before you start as a guide to the issues that the case writer thinks are worthy of debate. While the questions will draw your attention to relevant frameworks and lines of thought, they may not explain the complexities and the underlying problem issues faced by the company.

Cases have several uses. One is to provide real 'stories' of strategy in action to help you to make sense of strategic ideas and concepts. The class discussion should then help to make these strategic theories and concepts more meaningful to you. Another is to present you with a problem that the company had to deal with – and maybe a description of what its managers chose to do – and invite you to analyse the problem situation for yourself and to come up with your own recommendations. Managers may not – and here you have the benefit of hindsight – have made the 'best' decision. But in such cases, please do not expect to find correct and tidy 'solutions' to the issues raised in the case studies. There are never 'right' and 'wrong' answers as such. We could never substantiate that a different strategy would have delivered better results. After all, apparently good strategic ideas can fail during implementation. There are, however, certain recommendations which can be justified as more appropriate, feasible and desirable than others. While many case writers try to convey important issues of culture and style, these are always issues of interpretation – and most of the time you will be an external analyst making assumptions about certain of these very important issues.

When preparing the case for the class it is useful to focus on the questions at the end as these will often explain the approach taken by the class teacher; but you should always look at:

1. the nature of the problem (or problems) and the underlying strategic issues
2. the alternative courses of action – where relevant, critiquing the choice that the organization made
3. which course of action – or alternative strategy/strategies – you would have recommended
4. the implementation implications of your choice.

It is useful to use simple frameworks such as SWOT (strengths, weaknesses, opportunities and threats) and E–V–R (environment–values–resources) congruence to synthesize the information. Figure 9.1 also provides an ideal framework for situation analysis, by encouraging you to look at aspects of the organization and its environment which impact upon the situation and:

- its competitive environment
- company resources
- stakeholder expectations
- culture and values,

and a number of relevant factors and specific functional activities and strategies through which changes are likely to have been driven:

- the structure of the organization
- human resources
- marketing strategies
- manufacturing (or operations) strategies
- financial strategies
- research and development.

It is always useful to share your ideas with other students before the class discussion. Once in class, the case teacher can be pressed for an opinion, but he or she should not be pressed for a specific answer. His or her role is to make you think about the situation, the issues, possible alternative courses of action and maybe a possible way forward. In the process of doing this you may find that your class colleagues do not agree with your point of view.

Some case writers on some occasions explain the problems and issues in detail; at other times you will find that the most important issues have been obscured. This is deliberate as, after all, most managers see symptoms of problems and have to learn diagnostic skills to penetrate beneath the surface and reveal the true problem. You might usefully consider the following:

1. How important is this issue? What will happen if it is not addressed?
2. How urgent is it? How quickly must it be dealt with?
3. To what extent is it a result of other issues and problems?
4. Realistically, can anything be done about it – either at all, or in the relevant time-scale?

Detailed information is sometimes provided in the form of market statistics and financial results. This should always be questioned to determine the extent to which it is reliable and, more particularly, sufficiently comprehensive. This point should not be taken as an invitation to set about using the Internet and other sources to find as much additional data and information as you can possibly lay your hands on. Sometimes it can be useful to update a case study, but invariably you are provided with the information that you need to analyse and debate the issues with which the writer is concerned. It is all too easy to allow a surfeit of data and information to hide or obscure the real issues, and it is the issues that you are attempting to clarify and discuss. Intuition, imagination, creative thought and judgement are just as important as analytical skills when dealing with management problems and management case studies. Quantitative analysis, however, should always be used to back your recommendations, when it is available and possible; a failure to use the information available must weaken your argument.

## Case study reports

In the real world of organizations written management reports are important. Quite often they are too long and wordy and, once again, the real issues can be obscured. Often short, pithy and readable reports which clarify the issues, the arguments and a recommended (or possible) way forward are very valuable. Sometimes it is inevitable that they have to be long and detailed, but then an attached short summary can be invaluable. Writing good management reports is a skill not possessed by every manager. The same logic and arguments can be applied to case study reports. This section does not set out to provide you with a comprehensive guide to report writing, but rather to draw your attention to a number of key issues.

It is always important to think who your report is being written for and what their expectations are. How much time will they have to read it? What is their relationship to you? How much relevant knowledge do they already have?

While there may be an initial 'executive summary' the report itself is meant to show how a set of recommendations has been reached through analysis, argument and justification. Consequently, the following framework might be useful, although it should not be taken to be prescriptive for every report that you might write:

- Title page – including reasons and purpose
- Executive summary – of the problem, the issues and the recommendations

- Introduction – to the problems and purposes – and including any necessary background detail that needs to be included
- Analysis – of the situation, the issues and the problems
- Statement and evaluation of alternatives
- Recommendations – including implementation implications
- Exhibits and appendices – which should always be cross-referenced in the main body of the report.

You will see that you are presenting your conclusions first and then giving the detailed reasoning. In this respect, it is not a novel where you might have to wait until the last page for the hidden explanation or final twist.

You will rarely find your first draft is your final version. Think everything through first, write down outline notes and ideas, complete your quantitative analyses, write the main body of the report, then add your executive summary and possibly final conclusions. Then take a break before revising and improving – and proof-reading as well as running a spell-check.

## The cases

1. The National Trust
2. Amazon.com
3. Lilliput Lane
4. P&O, Princess and the International Passenger Cruise Industry
5. Tesco
6. Kwik Fit Financial Services
7. Virgin
8. Thorn EMI
9. The Sony Corporation
10. The Sony PlayStation
11. Scottish and Newcastle Breweries plc
12. The Optica
13. C&J Clark
14. Polly Peck International
15. Hanson (A)
16. Hanson (B)
17. Hanson (C)

**Strategic Management Case Studies**

KEY
- √√√ Central theme
- √ Issue in the case
- (√) Peripheral, Support issue

| Ch. | CHAPTER | The National Trust | Amazon.com | Lilliput Lane | P&O, Princess and the International Passenger Cruise Industry | Tesco | Kwik-Fit Financial Services | Virgin | Thorn-EMI | The Sony Corporation | The Sony PlayStation | Scottish and Newcastle Breweries | The Optica | C & J Clark | Polly Peack | Hanson (A) | Hanson (B) | Hanson (C) |
|---|---|---|---|---|---|---|---|---|---|---|---|---|---|---|---|---|---|---|
| 1–2 | Strategic Management Principles | √√√ | √ | √ | | | √ | | | | | | | | | | | |
| 3 | Organizational Mission and Objectives | √ | √ | √ | | | | √ | | | | | | √ | | √ | | |
| 3 | Measuring Success | √ | √√√ | | | | | | √ | | | | | √ | | | | |
| 4 | Culture and Values | √ | | | | | √ | √ | | √ | | | | √ | | | (√) | |
| 5 | Strategic thinking and synergy | √ | √ | | | | √ | √ | √ | √ | √ | √ | | | | | | |
| 6 | Environmental analysis | | √ | | √ | | √ | | √ | | | √√√ | | √ | | √ | | |
| 7 | Dynamics of competition | | √ | √√√ | √√√ | √√√ | √ | √ | √ | √ | √ | | | √ | √ | | | |
| 8 | Strategic resoures | | √ | √√√ | √ | | √√√ | | | √ | √√√ | | | √ | | | | |
| 9 | Strategy creation | | √ | | | | √√√ | | | √ | | | | | √ | | | |
| 10 | Strategic planning | | | | √ | | | | | | | | √ | | | | | |
| 11 | Strategic leadership and entrepreneurship | | √ | √ | | | | √ | (√) | √ | | | | √ | √ | √ | √ | √ |
| 12 | Emergent strategy | | √ | | √ | | | | | | √ | √ | | √ | | | | |
| 14 | Strategic alternatives | | | | √ | | | | √√√ | √ | | | | | | | | |
| 15 | Diversification and acquisition | | √ | √ | | | √ | | | √√√ | | | | | √ | √ | | √ |
| 16 | Strategic alliances and joint ventures | | √ | | | | √ | √ | √ | | | √√√ | | | | | | |
| 17 | Business failure | | (√) | | | | | | | | | | √√√ | | | √√√ | | |
| 18 | Consolidation and recovery | | | √ | | | | √ | √ | | | | | √ | √√√ | √ | | |
| 19 | Strategy evaluation | | | | | | | √ | √ | | | | | | | | √ | |
| 20 | Strategy implementation | | | | | | | √ | √ | | √ | | | √ | | | | |
| 21 | Organizational structure | | | | | | | √ | √ | √ | | | | | √ | √ | √ | |
| 22 | Corporate strategy and style | | | | | | | √ | | | | | | | √ | √√√ | | √√√ |
| 23 | Strategic resources, risk and crisis management | | | | | | | | | √ | | | √ | | √ | √ | | |
| 24 | Strategic change management | | | | | | | √ | | | | | | | | | √√√ | √ |

# The National Trust

This case study is a longer version of Minicase 2.3 in the main text. It explains the work, the objectives and the performance of the National Trust, and concludes with an examination of the Trust in terms of E–V–R (environment–values–resources) congruence.

This version of the case was written by John L Thompson in 2000 with the earlier co-operation of the National Trust. It is for classroom discussion and should not be taken to reflect either effective or ineffective management.

## Introduction

*As we move into the twenty-first century, it will become increasingly important to safeguard the country's heritage, enabling us to understand and enjoy it, and passing it on to future generations.*
(Prime Minister John Major, 1995)

The National Trust, in essence, holds countryside and buildings in England, Wales and Northern Ireland 'for the benefit of us all'. Trust properties include woodlands, coastal paths, nature reserves and country parks; sites of archaeological interest; castles and country houses, some associated with famous people such as Sir Winston Churchill and Rudyard Kipling; abbeys and priories; lighthouses; and even whole villages and hamlets. In 2000 these amounted to some 250,000 hectares, over 600 miles (970 kilometres) of coastline, 164 historic houses, 19 castles, 160 gardens, 47 industrial monuments, 49 churches and chapels, nine ancient sites, 73 landscaped parks and 1000 designated ancient monuments, many of which are open to the public. Some 250 properties charge an entry fee. In 1997/98 a record 11.7 million visitors were recorded at properties where admission fees are charged, but this fell to 11.1 million in 1999/2000. Millions more visit the other properties and the open countryside free of charge. The most popular property, measured by the number of visitors, was Fountains Abbey and Studley Royal in North Yorkshire.

The National Trust, which is independent of government despite the 'national' in the name, is now over 100 years old. Founded in 1895 by three Victorian philanthropists concerned with conserva-

tion and preservation of the countryside and important buildings, the National Trust now boasts 2.64 million members. The two million figure was reached in October 1990. The growth of membership was particularly dramatic during the 1980s. The first thousand was reached in 1926, increasing to 10,000 in 1946, 100,000 in 1961 and one million in 1981. The growth rate is now slower than in recent years. Members pay an annual subscription in return for free entrance to Trust properties and a variety of support publications. Initially the Trust concentrated on looking after land and ancient buildings; country houses have been included since 1934. The Trust is also heavily dependent on the annual contribution of 38,000 people who work voluntarily in a number of ways. Their contribution is estimated at 2.25 million hours of work. Her Majesty Queen Elizabeth the Queen Mother is President of the National Trust; HRH The Prince of Wales is Vice President.

To celebrate its centenary in 1995, the Trust launched Project Minerva, a lifelong learning programme linked to conservation for both adults and children. Minerva includes discovery days, study bases and environmental activity centres, and it reflects the Trust's increasing emphasis on learning in recent years.

The Trust was formally incorporated by an Act of Parliament in 1907. It has a constitution and legislation enables it to acquire property and hold it is as either 'inalienable' or 'alienable'. That part which the Trust formally declares 'inalienable', usually the important core of an estate, cannot by law be sold. For this reason it is not valued in the Trust's balance sheet. It has been estimated that the current market value, hypothetically, would exceed £2 billion. Land, however, can, and frequently is, leased to farmers in return for an annual rent. In fact, the National Trust has 1100 tenant farmers on its land. Consequently, the recent difficulties faced by UK farmers has been a problem that the Trust has had to share. Strategies have been developed to help tenant farmers to sustain a living and diversify their activities.

The National Trust is also involved in a number of environmental projects, including soil management, waste conservation, genetically modified crops, specific restoration programmes and the protection of endangered species of wildlife.

## The mission and objectives

In simple terms, the purpose of the National Trust is the preservation of historic houses and beauty spots in England, Wales and Northern Ireland, keeping them open for the nation.

The 1907 Act of incorporation states:

*promoting the permanent preservation, for the benefit of the Nation, of lands and tenements (including buildings) of beauty or historic interest, and as regards lands, for the preservation (so far as is practicable) of their natural aspect features and animal and plant life.*

Given this mission and the 'inalienable property' constraint the time-scale is clearly infinite, and the planning period for certain gardens is 100 years.

Conservation and preservation, however, cost money; revenues must be generated. The primary sources are members' subscriptions and the fees paid by non-member visitors, in addition to rents (see Appendix for details). This implies accessibility, which could result in damage if there are too many visitors. Light, humidity and the passage of time are all enemies to old properties and their furnishings; so too (are curious fingers and thundering feet). *Hence there is an important potential conflict between conservation and access.*

During the late 1980s and 1990s, for example, gardens have been more popular with visitors than country houses. While the Trust is generally happy to see more visitors at its various properties – enjoying

them and at the same time contributing to their upkeep – occasionally a certain stage is reached where it is felt that more visitors would conflict with the preservation needs of the property 'and the brakes need to be applied'. To prevent overuse and damage the Trust has selectively introduced policies to restrict entry, but these are exceptional rather than general practice. They have taken the form of direct controls (fixed numbers at any one time, say a half-hour period) and indirect influence such as reduced marketing, higher admission prices and limited car parking availability. These restrictions have taken precedence over the thought of investing more resources to make the most popular properties even more enjoyable in order to attract increasing numbers of visitors and generate additional revenues. In general, the commercialism of many privately owned estates and houses is avoided by the National Trust. There are no safari or theme parks in the grounds. Activities such as practising farmyards, mainly for children, are as far as the Trust is happy to go.

Instead attention has focused on the revenue potential of shops, restaurants and holiday cottages (National Trust Enterprises) and publications. In 1994–95 National Trust Enterprises made a financial contribution of £6.2 million from a turnover of £38.8 million (16%); a further £2.9 million was provided through additional advertising and sponsorship. Five years later, in 1999/2000, turnover had increased to £46.9 million and the contribution to £7.5 million (again 16%). Advertising and sponsorship added £4.2 million. Donations and investment income are other significant sources of funds. These are discussed in greater detail later in the case.

In the main, the National Trust takes over properties where no-one else can or will, mainly the latter, responding to need, rather than specifically seeking to acquire identified houses and gardens. The objectives are, therefore, more concerned with the preservation and improvement of properties already owned rather than the acquisition of new ones. There is, though, a clear long-term objective of acquiring some 900 miles (1450 kilometres) of 'threatened' British coastline. This is almost half of the total of 2000 miles (3200 kilometres) of coastline; and the project, Enterprise Neptune, which has been running for 30 years, is over half way to its target. The rate of coastline acquisition depends on the success of the support fund raising.

## Administration

The Trust has a head-office executive staff comprising the new Director-General, Fiona Reynolds, successor to Martin Drury (who retired at the end of 2000), the Deputy Director-General and Directorates for Estates, Finance, The Regions, Historic Buildings, Marketing and Communications, Legal Affairs, Public Affairs, National Trust Enterprises and Personnel. The previous Director-General, Sir Angus Stirling, retired in 1995 after 12 years in office; he had presided over the important surge in membership. In addition there are 16 regional offices which are directly responsible for the properties in their regions. This executive operates within, and reports to, an elaborate committee structure of honorary non-executives.

The ruling committee is the Council, which is made up of 52 members, half of these nominated by organizations interested in, and appropriate to, the Trust's activities, such as the Victoria and Albert Museum, the National Gallery, the Council for British Archaeology, the Royal Agricultural and Royal Horticultural Societies, the Ramblers' Association and various other protection and conservation agencies. The other half are elected by the members and come from all parts of the country. The Council has an Executive Committee which appoints, among others, a Finance and a Properties Committee and 16 regional committees. The Executive Committee 'reviews and carries out policies required to pursue the principles laid down by Council'. The Council, incidentally, is not bound by decisions taken at the Annual General Meeting of National Trust members. This was evidenced at the end of the 1980s when the Council did not adopt an AGM decision in favour of banning hunting on National Trust lands. In fairness, only a small minority of members actually voted, either for or against. However, in 1997, the Trust opted to ban deer hunting on its lands. The issue of fox hunting

remains unresolved, with the Trust waiting for publication of the Burns Report and any subsequent legislation before it makes a decision.

Since the mid-1980s the senior executives of the Trust have operated with a management board which meets fortnightly. Prior to this, control was more directly hierarchical. These senior managers are responsible to all main committees of non-executives.

Staff in regional offices, guided and constrained by head-office staff, put forward proposals and plans to the various committees for approval. In general, the Properties Committee considers property management issues in terms of policy, and issues papers on such subjects as the care of historic buildings, forestry and archaeology, whereas the Finance Committee approves the annual budget and accounts. When an acquisition is recommended by regional staff, the Properties Committee will evaluate the merit of the proposal and the Finance Committee the financial implications. Both pass their recommendations to the Executive Committee for the final decision.

While the National Trust amends some of its strategies on a continuous basis, this is underpinned by a formal three-year planning cycle. In 1999, and for the first time, the Trust invited all of its members to participate in the strategic planning process.

## Regional offices

The 16 regional offices are directly responsible for the maintenance and improvement of existing properties, and they will also be involved in potential new acquisitions. Each property has a managing agent who is charged with drawing up an annual plan or budget for repairs, maintenance and possible investments in say a larger car park or better sales kiosk facilities. Revenues from admission charges for non-members and all associated sales of publications and so on are estimated to arrive at a subsidy figure. In the main this subsidy will be provided from general funds, made up of such things as members' subscriptions and profits from retail activities.

A head-office committee of senior staff reviews the management and finances of individual properties, roughly every five years on a continuing cycle. If any growing deficit or subsidy requirement is seen as being in need of close examination, then a number of options will be considered, such as:

- the potential (if desirable) for attracting more visitors, say by working through tourist authorities
- additional marketing activity by the Trust to target the property at defined market segments or niches
- new uses for the property, such as rallies, wedding receptions and outdoor concerts
- higher entry fees, and
- lower staff costs.

The constraint of not threatening conservation by commercialism is ever-present in discussions, but is, apparently, rarely a real issue because of the culture and values held by the Trust's employees both nationally and regionally.

## New projects

New projects, such as new exhibition material, better presentations or better visitor facilities can be financed from a special fund introduced a few years ago by the Trust's finance director. Regions can apply for investment funding if they can demonstrate that the projected return on the capital is likely to exceed a particular target. This fund is seen as a revolving fund, on the grounds that moneys should be repaid within a relatively short space of time. While the objective of the investment should primarily be to improve quality in the form of enjoyment from the visit, the financial return is utilized as a constraint.

## Finance

A more detailed summary of income and expenditure in 1999/2000 is appended to this case, but the following table provides a breakdown of the percentages of the various contributions – excluding grants – to the Trust's income.

| | 2000 % | 1995 % | 1990 % |
|---|---|---|---|
| Subscriptions | 46 | 44 | 40 |
| Rents (farms, etc.) | 17 | 15 | 16 |
| Admission fees | 7 | 7 | 11 |
| Investment income | 20 | 21 | 22 |
| Profit from Enterprises | 9 | 10 | 7 |
| Produce sales | 1 | 2 | 2 |
| Gifts | 0 | 1 | 2 |

Two points are worth noting: first, the increasing significance of members' subscriptions, balanced by the corresponding reduction in admission fees; and secondly, the growing contribution from National Trust Enterprises.

In addition, the Trust receives grants from government departments, conservation agencies and individuals, together with legacies, appeal proceeds and the sale of leases. The magnitude of these varies every year, often quite substantially. Ordinary income does not cover ongoing expenditures; grants and legacies are critical.

The National Trust is Britain's leading charity in terms of both total incomes and total voluntary contributions. Its scope is so wide that it can appeal to all five National Lottery distributors.

## Investments

The National Trust holds and invests substantial funds, the majority of which have been donated over the years to support the upkeep of particular properties. In 2000 over £700 million was invested, comprising:

- the Capital Endowment Funds, endowments tied to specific properties, and required before the properties were acquired by the Trust. This is discussed below. Only the interest, not the capital, from this fund can be spent
- the Defined Purpose Funds, gifts and donations tied to specific repair and maintenance projects and/or specified properties. Both the interest and the capital can be spent

- the General Fund, cash which can be used as the Trust chooses. As highlighted earlier, this is typically the annual subsidizing of those properties (in reality, most of them) that cannot be self-funded.

Wherever possible, investment policies are linked to relevant time horizons. Funds designated for repairs are often earning short-term returns; capital endowment funds are invested for the optimum long-term benefits.

## The acquisition of new properties

The National Trust only agrees to take on new properties if an endowment (calculated by a formula) to cover maintenance for the next 50 years is in place. Present owners, conservation agencies and the government, through the Department of the Environment and the National Heritage Memorial Fund, are the traditional sources of endowment funds.

The National Trust accepts that sometimes it underestimates the funding which will be required, and consequently the endowment covers only a percentage of the 50 years. Wage inflation has proved difficult to forecast over 50 years; depreciation is unpredictable, although not markedly relevant; most significant has been the march of scientific knowledge which results in ever higher standards being set by the state, and expected by the public, in hygiene, security and accommodation. Higher targets for maintenance and improvement often prove expensive.

When the National Trust acquires a property it seeks to decorate and furnish it as closely as possible to the way that Trust employees believe the original owners would have had it. This requires extensive knowledge of period preferences and tastes, and it can also again prove difficult and expensive. Where the most recent owners have views on the way in which the property should be presented these are encapsulated into a 'Memorandum of Wishes', but this is not legally binding.

Funds are also boosted continually by donations and legacies, and by fund raising, usually tied to specific appeals. Enterprise Neptune, to cover the cost of acquiring and looking after threatened coastline, has been ongoing for 30 years. As additional funds are raised more can be accomplished in this long-term project. There was a successful Trees and Gardens Storm Disaster Appeal following storm damage in 1990. The Lake District Appeal is another long-term venture to cover the cost of improving paths and preserving facilities, often utilizing volunteer labour. These are just a sample of many special appeals.

## Measuring success

Measuring the success of the National Trust is a complex issue, and the various stakeholders and interest groups are likely to have differing views on the most appropriate measures, and on priorities.

- The Trust would argue that the main measure of success is the standard of preservation achieved, although this is clearly and inevitably subjective.

  Other measures support the achievement of preservation standards:
- the number of members, including those who renew their subscriptions and those who join for the first time. The growth figures would suggest that the Trust is successful, and this is logically linked to
- the ability to meet public expectations. The National Trust believes that its members and visitors are, in the main, seeking period authenticity – the property presented as it would have been lived in originally – rather than 'museum collections' say covering several generations, or activities for children. Resources are committed to achieving this type of presentation.

Clearly there is support for the way in which the National Trust markets its properties. Were it to change its policies in any significant way it may well lose existing supporters but at the same time appeal to different market segments;

- the number, and particularly the substance, of complaints. The Trust argues that it treats all complaints seriously

- the ability to generate new funds and endowments to enable them to take on additional properties where necessary.

In addition, the National Trust has to measure the extent of any damage and decay at properties and react accordingly. There is, as highlighted earlier, a penalty for attracting too many visitors.

The Trust also has a number of key financial yardsticks which are measured on a monthly basis. Where figures fall below trigger thresholds remedial actions are implemented.

## Environment–values–resources

The major environmental influences (the Trust's stakeholders), the National Trust's core skills and competencies and the manifest values of the Trust and its employees are listed below.

### Stakeholders and interested parties

These include:

- members and visitors – 'represented' at the AGM and by Committee members
- donors of properties – many are motivated by genuine altruism, a wish to spread the enjoyment of their inheritance. Their wishes are sought and often followed; and visitors often find that their interest in a property is enhanced if they know that the donor or a descendant, frequently related to the family that may have owned the property for centuries, is still resident
- conservation agencies
- ramblers' associations
- government – government provides some financial support and legislates about certain requirements. Increasingly the National Trust may be affected by European legislation
- financial benefactors – although in some cases it must be debatable whether the financial support is directed at the specific properties rather than the work of the National Trust as a whole
- employees – whose values and orientations, as well as their expertise, are likely to be an important issue when they are appointed
- the nation itself (as opposed to the state).

### Core competencies and capabilities

The National Trust recognizes that to be successful it must develop and preserve expertise in a number of areas:

- property management – as well as the general maintenance and upkeep of properties the land resources must be managed effectively, and this includes the commercial lease arrangements with farmers and so on
- expertise in arts, furnishings and in the ways in which people historically have lived and kept their properties. Many National Trust members are themselves experts and connoisseurs
- public relations and marketing – attracting the most appropriate visitors and providing them with an enjoyable, satisfying visit; in addition, running the National Trust shops both profitably and in keeping with the desired image of the Trust. Generally high-quality merchandise is sold at premium prices
- financial skills, including the management of a sizeable investment portfolio, together with an understanding of the fundamentals of economics. Yields do rise and fall, but the National Trust is substantially dependent on the returns from its various investments.

### Values

- The National Trust feels that a high moral tone is appropriate for all of its activities.
- The themes of preservation and improvement are dominant, but financial accountability and responsibility cannot be overlooked.
- The Trust also seeks to be educational where it is appropriate. Involving children is seen as important, but it is encouraged mostly at specific sites selected for their location, intrinsic interest and the 'resilience of the fabric'.
- In general, Trust staff also share an 'ethos' which combines the feeling of working for a good cause, a degree of identification with its purpose and principles, and a certain readiness (typically shared by people who work for other charities) to accept rewards which may be less than employees

of many manufacturing and service businesses would normally receive.

## The future

While the National Trust can cover its ongoing expenses and acquire those new properties which both the Committees and staff feel it should take over, then its policies, which have emerged incrementally over a long period through a democratic, if potentially bureaucratic organizational structure, need not change dramatically.

The dilemma comes when the National Trust cannot meet its expenses from current activities, supplemented by external grants, appeal proceeds and legacies. Membership fees could be increased substantially, but members are under no obligation to pay them. Other than in their first or early years of membership, members frequently and happily regard a proportion of their annual fee as a subsidy. They could save money by paying at individual properties when they visited, but of course they would not receive the Trust's directory, magazines and details of new properties and developments.

Admission charges could be raised, but this is likely to deter visitors and, in fact, is more likely to be used when a property is too popular and conservation needs are threatened.

Support commercial activities, shops, restaurants, publications and holiday cottages are all capable of growth as long as they do not conflict with the values and culture of the Trust. However, these activities remain small in relation to the Trust's total income.

*The National Trust*
http://www.nationaltrust.org.uk/

## Questions

1. What are the objectives of the National Trust?
   What are the inherent conflicts?
   How do you feel the objectives would be prioritized by the major stakeholders?

2. Do you think the performance measures used by the National Trust are wholly appropriate?
   If not: what measures should be adopted either instead of, or in addition to, those used?

3. Assess the National Trust in respect of E–V–R congruence. What, if any, changes are required if the National Trust is to enjoy congruence in the early years of the new millennium?

4. What opportunities for change are available to the Trust?
   What would constitute appropriate change?
   Do other charities pose any threats?
   Where are the main constraints to change?

Appendix: The National Trust–outline income and expenditure

| | 1999/2000 | | 1994/1995 | | Comparative figures for 1986 |
|---|---|---|---|---|---|
| | £m | £m | £m | £m | £m |
| **Ordinary income** | | | | | |
| Membership fees | 60.0 | | 41.8 | | 16.8 |
| Rents from land leases, etc. | 21.5 | | 14.5 | | |
| Admission fees | 8.5 | | 7.4 | | 14.0 |
| Other property income, e.g. produce sales | 1.8 | | 1.7 | | |
| Investment income | 26.4 | | 20.2 | | 8.3 |
| Profit from National Trust Enterprises | 11.7 | | 9.1 | | N/A |
| Gifts (not tied) | | | 1.2 | | |
| | 129.9 | | 95.9 | | |
| **Capital receipts** | | | | | |
| Appeals and tied gifts | 8.6 | | 3.0 | | 3.7 |
| Grants and contributions | 14.5 | | 16.6 | | |
| Legacies | 36.4 | | 24.5 | | 8.7 |
| Sales of leases | 2.8 | | 1.6 | | |
| Others | | | 1.0 | | |
| | 62.3 | 192.2 | 46.7 | 142.6 | |
| **Ongoing property expenditure** | | | | | |
| Property maintenance | 69.5 | | 45.7 | | |
| Property management | 20.2 | | 13.9 | | |
| Conservation and advisory services | 4.9 | | 4.5 | | |
| Membership and recruitment | | | 6.9 | | |
| Publicity and fund raising | 18.9 | | 6.7 | | |
| Administration | 1.9 | | 4.6 | | |
| | 115.4 | | 82.3 | | |
| **Capital works and projects** | | | | | |
| Capital works and projects | 43.1 | | 38.5 | | |
| New acquisitions | 12.5 | | 6.8 | | |
| | 55.6 | | 45.3 | | |
| Total expenditure | | 171.0 | | 127.6 | |
| Comprising total expenditure on property | 148.5 | | 109.4 | | 55.8 |
| Non-property expenditure | 22.5 | | 18.2 | | |
| Total income less total expenditure | | 21.2 | | 15.0 | |
| Represented by: | | | | | |
| retentions in tied funds | 14.0 | | 10.0 | | |
| retentions for future expenditure | 7.2 | | 5.0 | | |

Note: where total expenditure exceeds ordinary income, capital funding is required.

# Amazon.com

Amazon.com is the story of an amazing company, led by a true entrepreneur, at the forefront of e-commerce and online retailing. Its growth rate has been astounding but it has yet to make a profit. This case study looks at the growth of Amazon.com and its impact on bookselling, the business where it began, and at its further expansion and diversification. Several key strategic issues in e-commerce are discussed.

This version of the case was written by John L Thompson in 2000. It is for classroom discussion and should not be taken to reflect either effective or ineffective management.

An alternative version appears in Bolton, WK and Thompson, JL (2000) *Entrepreneurs: Talent, Temperament, Technique*, Butterworth-Heinemann.

## Introduction

Amazon.com, the 'Earth's largest bookstore', pioneered bookselling via the Internet and, in the process, changed consumer buying habits and forced the existing major booksellers to react and also offer electronic sales and postal deliveries. It has also become the world's largest, and probably the best-known, online retailer. Paradoxically, this has happened in an environment where – and in parallel – 'good bookstores have become the community centres of the late twentieth century' by providing comfortable seats, staying open late and incorporating good coffee bars.

The Amazon site allows bibliophiles to exchange views and reviews as well as place orders – and some browsers apparently spend hours searching through the catalogues for titles that they think will interest them. Amazon.com can never replace the hands-on element of a physical bookshop, nor engage authors for meet-the-customer signing sessions, but it can, and does, offer a far wider choice. The number of people around the world who are connected to the Internet – and buying goods electronically – is now growing rapidly. And the number of people who buy at least one book a year is huge. Many of them are willing to buy on the strength of an author's reputation or a good review of the content and style, sacrificing an insistence to inspect the book beforehand. Because of the different time zones around the world, Amazon.com can sell 24 hours every day.

However, Amazon.com is now far more than an online bookstore, having diversified into a much wider and diverse range of products and activities.

Its premise or 'business model' relies on a difficult balance between short- and long-term issues. Internet retailers such as Amazon.com must grow quickly to claim a substantial slice of a developing market, and for this they have to be able to raise funds for continued investment. However, they are unlikely to be profitable in their early years and argue that short-term profits do not matter as long as the company is growing and establishing a strong reputation. Inevitably, this is an uncertain world and adverse publicity can be one factor behind the associated volatility in the trading prices of any shares in these businesses. Not unexpectedly, their book value tends to rise and fall very steeply.

## Bookselling

Books are bought and read all round the world and they are published in various languages. The UK market is worth some £2 billion per year, but the American market is about ten times this size. Sales of best-selling paperback fiction titles can be huge, but other more specialized books may only sell a few hundred copies during the time they are in print. While many people buy books regularly, others rely more on libraries. The industry risk lies with the publishers, who pay royalties to their authors on confirmed sales and who accept unsold books back from their wholesalers and retailers. Publishers can reprint books which sell consistently well, but generally they will always carry surplus stock because of time lags. Final returns of 30% are not exceptional, but the average is something below 20%.

Distribution is fragmented and comprises the following channels:

- specialist book 'superstores', which often also sell music. The largest chains are Barnes & Noble and Borders, American-based businesses which are now expanding into the UK. Waterstone's/ Dillons is the market leader in the UK. All of these are still growing in size and opening new stores. WH Smith has the second largest market share in the UK and is the leading travel (airports and railway stations) bookstore

- smaller independent bookshops, both single outlets and small chains. These are generally served by wholesalers as well as directly by publishers

- supermarkets, who typically sell only a limited range at discounted prices

- book clubs

- supplies to libraries, sometimes via specialist library wholesalers

- sales through university bookshops and to schools. In the UK, Waterstone's is a leading university campus retailer

- virtual bookstores. As well as Amazon.com, Barnes & Noble, Borders, Waterstone's and WH Smith all sell electronically via the web, and there are several other specialist e-commerce booksellers.

Since the abolition of the NBA (the net book agreement, which allowed publishers to set prices and reduced the incidence of discounting) in the UK in the mid-1990s, price discounting has been a major feature of the industry, as it is in the USA. The scope for this is significant as full retail prices are often twice the amount that the publisher receives. This latter amount typically breaks down as follows:

| | |
|---|---|
| Direct manufacturing costs | 20% |
| Overheads (including marketing) | 30% |
| Returns and allowances | 25% |
| Author royalties | 10–20% |
| Operating profit | 5–15%. |

The market overall grew throughout the 1990s, but some forecasters predict that it will be more stagnant in the early years of the new millennium.

## Jeff Bezos – the entrepreneur

Amazon.com was founded in 1994 by Jeff Bezos. The son of a Cuban immigrant, Bezos once dreamt of being an astronaut and consequently went on to graduate in electrical engineering and computer science from Princeton. While a teenager, a paper he wrote on the effect of zero gravity on the common housefly won him a trip to the Marshall Space Flight Center in Alabama. After Princeton he became a successful investment banker on Wall Street. He was the youngest senior vice president ever at D.E. Shaw, which he joined from Bankers Trust. Intrigued by the speed of growth of the Internet in the early 1990s, he decided to 'seize the moment'. He had experienced his trigger and he left the bank with the straightforward intention of starting an e-commerce business.

At this stage he had no specific product or service in mind, and so he began by drawing up a list of possible activities. He narrowed down his first list of 20 to two – music and books – before choosing books. In both cases, the range of titles available was far in excess of the number that any physical store could realistically stock. In 1994 there were 1.5 million English-language books in print, and another 1.5 million in other languages, yet the largest bookstore carried only 175,000 titles. Moreover, Bezos appreciated that the distribution was fragmented. He believed that there was scope to offer books at discounted prices and wafer-thin margins to seize sales from existing retailers, while also boosting the overall size of the market.

His second decision was location. He quickly narrowed the field to Boulder, Portland and Seattle before selecting Seattle. In theory, he could have picked anywhere, but he believed that a number of important criteria had to be met. A ready supply of people with technical ability was essential, and other key members of his management team would need to find it an attractive place to live and work. As the firm has grown, several experienced people have been recruited from nearby Microsoft. In addition, it had to be a relatively small state. Bezos would have to charge a relevant sales tax to residents of any state where Amazon.com had a physical presence, but others would be exempt.

He rented a house and started in the garage, using the coffee shop in the nearby Barnes and Noble bookstore to interview potential staff. He personally made the first desks they used from old, recycled doors. After raising several million dollars from venture capitalists and private investors whom he knew, he moved into a 400 square foot (40 square metre) office and began trading on the Internet in July 1995. Bezos is adamant that he warned his investors of the inherent risks in his ambitious venture. Sales began immediately, and within six weeks he moved to a 2000 square foot (200 square metre) warehouse. Six months later he moved again. This time he set up Amazon's headquarters in a 12-storey former hospital.

Within its first year, Amazon.com earned revenues of $5 million, equivalent to a large Barnes and Noble superstore. Sales have since grown dramatically as the company has expanded rapidly, but so too have the costs. After five years the company is still trading at a loss, and profits are not in the forecast time horizon. The company went public in May 1997. Not unexpectedly, its share price and market valuation are very volatile, but Amazon has been valued at $27 billion, some $2 billion more than Wal-Mart. Bezos remains infectiously enthusiastic. He is noted for two personal quirks: his loud and frequent laugh and his tendency to always have to hand a small camera. His closest colleagues confirm that he is 'sometimes goofy'. Bezos is married to a novelist who has occasionally been involved in his business. She was, for example, instrumental in negotiating his first freight contract.

## The virtual bookstore

There are four value propositions to Amazon.com: convenience, selection, service and price.

Clearly, there are no books to touch, open and read. All communications are through the world wide website pages or via e-mail. The website allows customers to search the extensive (one million plus titles) book catalogue by topic and author, to read explanations and summaries from authors as well as reviews from other readers, specialist reviewers and Amazon's own staff, and to order with a credit card.

Those who prefer can reserve books via the web and then telephone Amazon with their credit card details. Orders are processed immediately. Amazon holds limited stocks of its best-selling titles, which it can post out immediately when it receives an on-line order from a customer and credit card details have been confirmed. Otherwise, the customer order triggers an order to the relevant publisher or a specialist wholesaler. These books are redespatched very quickly after Amazon receives them into stock. Delivery to the customer of a non-bestseller, therefore, is normally around a week, with more unusual titles taking longer.

The site can also provide information on any books which are similar to any title a customer nominates, and Amazon.com will also keep customers up to date with new publications from selected authors. Readers are encouraged to post their own book reviews and, if they wish, they can communicate electronically with any other readers looking at the same book or topic at the same time. This allows an instantaneous exchange of views and opinions.

All books are discounted: bestsellers typically by 30% and others by at least 10% of the jacket price. For special promotions, and to compete with the websites of Barnes and Noble and Borders, bestselling titles have occasionally been discounted by as much as 50%. Amazon.com can do this because a book is held in stock for just two days; a high-street bookseller is holding the equivalent of at least three months sales in stock at any time. Increased marketing expenditure (mostly on the Internet) for a virtual bookstore partially offsets this relative cost advantage. Moreover, the price gap is narrowed again when packing, postage and administrative charges are added back to the discounted price. These vary and depend on the point of delivery. There are no salespeople. The 'store' is open 24 hours every day and is accessible from anywhere in the world.

The combination of price and service is instrumental in attempting to persuade customers to return to the website and to Amazon.com. After all, the most committed bookbuyers buy several titles at different times through the year. Finally, there is an element of fun and irreverence. Every week Amazon makes an award for the most amusing and obscure book on order at the time. Past winners include *Training Goldfish Using Dolphin Training Techniques* and *How to Start Your Own Country*. Bezos, however, maintains that:

> *people don't understand how hard it is to be an electronic merchant . . . most correspondence is by e-mail . . . some people do nothing but answer customer e-mails . . . we have to develop our own technologies . . . no-one sells software for managing e-mail centres. There are lots of barriers to entry.*

## Behind the success

> *We always wanted to build something the world has never seen.*

Bezos is allegedly obsessed by customers and service. 'The Internet is this big, huge hurricane . . . the only constant in that storm is the customers'. Bezos was not the first Internet bookseller, but he was always determined to be the most customer friendly. When interviewed, he talks about his customers constantly; they have clearly been a major focus for the business. In many respects, this view contradicts a belief held by many that there is no customer loyalty on the Internet. His efforts have paid off: 70% of Amazon shoppers are regular customers.

In reality, Amazon.com should not be seen as a bookselling operation but as an 'e-commerce customer relationship business' because it has successfully used its website, its image and reputation and its network to expand into other areas such as electronic greeting cards, music, videos, pharmaceuticals and pet supplies. Amazon.com also hosts Internet auctions. Some of this diversification has been achieved by the acquisition and absorption of other e-commerce businesses. Amazon's core competencies are in generating site traffic and potential customers, persuading them to order and then satisfying them with excellent service. An innovative and robust website, and a distinctive brand, have always been critical elements of the Amazon strategy. The company has been at the forefront in a number of ways, many of which have been copied by other Internet businesses. It pioneered

numbered steps in the purchasing operation, proactive order confirmations, credit cards sales and the single-click transaction. In the case of the single-click transaction Amazon obtained a temporary injunction against Barnes and Noble for copyright infringement.

Bezos clearly understands web technology and knew the type of people to recruit to build a strong central team. As an organization, Amazon.com is structured into five divisions: marketing, operations (order processing and warehousing), business expansion (new products and services), development (software innovations) and editorial (website design and content). He was willing to offer generous stock options. There are five vice presidents (VPs) who report directly to Bezos. The marketing VP was recruited from Cinnabon World Famous Cinnamon Rolls, and prior to this he had several years' experience in a variety of fast-moving consumer goods businesses and an MBA degree. The operations VP came from Black and Decker. The business expansion VP was experienced in book retailing. Originally the founder of a software business, Omni Information systems, he was working for Barnes and Noble before he joined Amazon. The development VP was a mathematics graduate with over 20 years' experience in designing both hardware and software systems. The executive editor, the fifth VP, was a PhD graduate who had had a similar post at PC Magazine, which he had also launched on the web. Clearly, Bezos wanted a team that was both intellectually strong and experienced in areas which would be critical for the success of the business. The team remained intact until summer 2000 when the operations VP resigned. His resignation prompted analysts to query the real value of stock options when share prices are extremely volatile.

Bezos always recognized the importance of the supply chain. His second and third warehouses in Delaware and Nevada were again located to reduce the impact of sales tax on purchases. At the end of 1999 there were five warehouses in the USA and one in the UK. Specialist websites in the UK (Amazon.co.uk) and Germany supplement the main website.

## Growth and success

Without question, Amazon.com has grown dramatically to become the world's third largest bookseller through constant change and innovation. But with 12 million customer accounts and a brand name recognized by 118 million adults in America (1999) it is far more than a bookseller. Bezos maintains that he now offers 'the earth's biggest selection of goods'.

Sales began by doubling in size every ten weeks. In 1996, revenues amounted to $16 million, by 1997 they had increased to $150 million, and in 1998 they almost quadrupled again. The 1999 figures were $1.64 billion sales and $390 million losses. In comparison, the leading players in bookselling, Barnes & Noble and Borders, earn approximately $3 billion and $2.5 billion, respectively. Tables 1 and 2 use indices to illustrate the costs, profits and losses as a percentage of sales revenue for Amazon over a period of five years and for Amazon compared with its two main competitors in 1997. When it was launched, it was thought that Amazon.com could

be profitable within five years, but this milestone has been abandoned. Towards the end of the 1990s Bezos commented: 'If we are profitable anytime in the short term it will just be an accident'.

The total Amazon.com trading volume and revenues in the first six months of 2000 were recorded as almost double those for the comparable first half of 1999. However, two points were worthy of mention. First, the second quarter (April–June) was no higher than the first quarter, implying some flattening, when a year earlier there had been growth over the same period. Secondly, although overall sales were up nearly 100%, sales of the core books, music and video had increased by 38%. Analysts wondered whether the current Internet market for these products might be nearing saturation, and that the rate of growth enjoyed in the past would require a substantial increase in Internet shoppers.

Throughout the 1990s Jeff Bezos was able to raise the investment funding he needed to fuel the company's rapid growth. The public offering of shares in May 1997 was followed by three separate

**Table 1** Amazon profitability shown as an index of revenues

| | 1995 Part-year | 1996 | 1997 | 1998 | 1999 |
|---|---|---|---|---|---|
| *Indices for* | | | | | |
| Revenue | 100.0 | 100.0 | 100.0 | 100.0 | 100.0 |
| Cost of goods sold | 80.4 | 77.8 | 80.5 | 77.1 | 79.0 |
| Gross margin | 19.6 | 22.2 | 19.5 | 22.9 | 21.0 |
| Overheads | 80.4 | 59.9 | 39.3 | 40.3 | 45.0* |
| Loss as % | (60.8) | (37.7) | (19.8) | (17.4) | (24) |

* Increasing because of new developments requiring additional investments.

**Table 2** Amazon compared with Borders and Barnes & Noble, 1997

| | Amazon.com | Borders | Barnes & Noble |
|---|---|---|---|
| Revenue | 100.0 | 100.0 | 100.0 |
| Cost of goods sold | 80.5 | 72.1 | 72.2 |
| Gross margin % | 19.5 | 27.9 | 27.8 |
| Overheads* | 39.3 | 24.3 | 22.0 |
| Profit/(Loss) % | (19.8) | 3.6 | 5.8 |

* Mainly marketing and product development.

bond issues, two of which were convertible bonds. These are exchangeable for stock at a prescribed later date. The Appendix tracks how Amazon was financed until 1999. However, in summer 2000 the shares were trading at a price which represented a 70% discount on the all-time high and which was lower than the initial offer price in 1997. Bonds could be bought at 60% of their original price and the convertibility element did not look attractive. Could Bezos continue to raise funding and grow, and ignore the need to bring Amazon.com into profits, or would the business model have to change?

The shares had fallen by 20% in June 2000 when a report from Lehman Brothers suggested that Amazon.com was indeed running out of cash – something that Bezos quickly denied. The report also implied that cost cutting was not a realistic option for Amazon.com and that aspects of the strategy needed rethinking.

## Strategic developments

The key people at Amazon realized some years ago that the Internet would generate a proliferation of new enterprises, many of them small and specialist, and that a network would offer enhanced distribution and selling opportunities. Consequently, in 1996 Amazon.com pioneered the idea of strategic alliances with other websites. Visitors to the sites of any Amazon Associate company can hyperlink and buy relevant books from the Amazon catalogue. There are now over 60,000 Associate companies. Typical examples would include a food-orientated site linked to cookery books, and a horticulture site and gardening books, and an outdoor clothing site and guide books. Amazon pays a referral fee of between 5 and 15% of sales revenues for the introduction and sales. The Amazon site is set up to provide a unique, customized collection of relevant titles for each Associate.

Music and video were added to books on the website after Amazon bought Junglee Corporation in 1998, a company which had developed innovative comparison shopping technologies. Consumer electronics, games, toys and pharmaceuticals – a market six times as big as books – have followed at various times. Simply, Amazon.com became increasingly concerned with lucrative electronic sales of almost anything to a vast number of customers rather than specializing as a bookseller. It is a brand.

The next step from this was almost inevitable. Late in 1999 Amazon opened its site and customers to products being sold by other companies, for whom it essentially provides an electronic shopfront. Amazon charges a small monthly fee and a percentage of sales revenue, in the region of 2–5%. Beauty products, pet foods, branded sports wear and antiquarian books were early subscribers to this opportunity. Amazon bought equity stakes in most of these partner businesses to strengthen the alliance. In 1999 Amazon also entered the electronic auction market, another area of rapid growth, in a further attempt to exploit its customer base. Simply, it provides access to its site for companies who want to auction goods over the Internet. To support these strategic developments, Amazon earlier (1998) bought PlanetAll, a business that had built a site which allows people to maintain their personal calendars and web directories. The intention was to use it to develop a reminder service to prompt people to buy birthday and other presents.

In August 2000 Amazon.com announced a ten-year strategic alliance with Toys R Us, the world's largest toy-store chain. Amazon would link its toy business with the on-line subsidiary of Toys R Us. Toys are a very seasonal product with the bulk of the year's sales coming in the run up to Christmas. In this period in 1999 Amazon.com had been left with considerable unsold merchandise – it had bought in too many items which simply did not sell. In contrast, Toys R Us had been unable to fill all the orders it had received as its distribution network was inadequate. Clearly there was an opportunity to generate synergy from an alliance.

Amazon.com would provide:

- the electronic shop window for the combined businesses
- the distribution network – including the warehousing of the inventory
- customer service

and Toys R Us would contribute the merchandising – the selection, purchasing and management of the inventory. Toys R Us will finance the stock in Amazon's warehouses and collect the revenues from sales and then pay Amazon a fee.

Later the same month another alliance with Microsoft was announced. With this agreement, Microsoft's Reader software would be used by Amazon.com to distribute electronic books, which people could download onto their personal computers or hand-held devices. Reader enables large amounts of text to be read easily on a computer screen. At this time the market for electronic books was uncertain and still emerging. Interestingly, Stephen King, popular author of bestselling horror stories, had begun to put his latest novel on the Internet, releasing it chapter by chapter. Readers can access the material completely free but are asked to contribute $1 for each chapter they read. The next chapter is only released when King has received a level of contributions with which he is happy.

## Challenges and risks

Amazon.com is a pioneer and 'the quintessential Internet company'. Its customer base and its range of products continue to grow and diversify. But each new development appears to require additional investment. In the end, Amazon may be profitable, but it might also be a disaster waiting to happen.

There is no shortage of direct competition to its main business from other Internet book retailers, which keeps margins very low. Establishing an efficient, effective supply chain is a barrier to entry, but setting up a website is relatively easy. As the range of activities becomes more extensive, and the company's site becomes more diverse, it is conceivable that the more serious book buyers will select a more focused competitor such as Barnes & Noble, Borders, Waterstone's or WH Smith, all recognized brands with an e-commerce presence. This switching could even be encouraged if Amazon is too aggressive at targeting its promotions of non-book products and services at customers whose buying profile has been tracked and analysed, or if it allows other partner companies access to this information. After all, Jeff Bezos has said: 'customers are loyal right up to the point somebody offers them a better service'. Although books are a reducing proportion of Amazon's business, they are where the company started and they are the product upon which its reputation has been built.

Although Amazon invests considerably in developing and improving its site, it is not inconceivable in this dynamic and turbulent industry that some form of technological breakthrough by a rival could make Amazon appear much less attractive and innovative.

*Amazon.com*   http://www.amazon.com

## Questions

1. How would you define and justify the Amazon.com 'business model'?

2. How significant is reputation for Amazon.com – in relation to both customers and potential investors? Is there a link between reputation and the share price volatility? How might Amazon.com attempt to reduce this volatility?

3. How might the alliance with Toys R Us affect both the business model and Amazon's reputation?

4. Does Amazon.com have a distinctive competitive advantage? If so, what is it – and how might it be sustained? If not, how might it achieve one?

5. Evaluate the challenges listed at the end of the case. Can you think of additional issues?

6. What is the contribution of Jeff Bezos to Amazon.com and to e-commerce generally?

Appendix: Financing of Amazon.com (1994–1999)

| Dates | Share price | Source of funds |
| --- | --- | --- |
| 1994: July to Nov. | $0.0010 | Founder: Jeff Bezos starts Amazon.com with $10,000; borrows $44,000 |
| 1995: Feb. to July | $0.1717 | Founder's family: Bezos' father and mother invest $245,000 |
| 1995: Aug. to Dec. | $0.1287–0.333 | Business angels: 2 angels invest $54,400 |
| 1995/96: Dec. to May | $0.3333 | Business angels: 20 angels invest $937,000 |
| 1996: May | $0.3333 | Founder's family: Bezos' siblings invest $20,000 |
| 1996: June | $2.3417 | Venture capitalists: 2 venture capital funds invest $8 m |
| 1997: May | $18.00 | Flotation: 3 m shares issued raising $49.1 m |
| 1997/98: Dec. to May | $52.11 | Bond issue: $326 m bond issue |

Source: Van Osnabrugge, M and Robinson, R (2000) *Angel Investing: Matching Start-Up Funds with Start-Up Companies*, Jossey Bass.

# Lilliput Lane

Lilliput Lane, based on the edge of the English Lake District, manufactures a range of miniature plaster cottages which are marketed to customers throughout the world, many of whom are committed collectors.

This case study traces the early growth of the company in the 1980s, its subsequent setbacks, a successful turnaround, followed by a flotation and sale in the 1990s.

It focuses on the issues of strategic leadership, stakeholder expectations, core competencies, adding value, diversification and focus strategies.

A follow-up case (Lilliput Lane – B) – available on the accompanying website – outlines further strategic developments after Lilliput Lane was acquired by ENESCO in 1994 and discusses issues of synergy in the enlarged group.

This case was written by John L Thompson. It is for classroom discussion and should not be taken to reflect either effective or ineffective management. Lilliput Lane was reproduced in *Small Business and Enterprise Development*, Vol. 2, No. 2, 1995, John Wiley.

## Introduction

At the beginning of September 1994 it was announced that the Lilliput Group was to be sold to an American company, Stanhome, which markets and distributes consumer products, giftware and collectibles. Stanhome's best-known range of collectibles is the Precious Moments series. The bid valued Lilliput at £37.2 million; in November 1993 the company had been floated with a value of £31.4 million.

Lilliput, based at Skirsgill, near Penrith, on the edge of the English Lake District, is one of the UK's leading manufacturers of collectibles. Its main product is a range of some 180 high quality, hand-painted miniature cottages and other buildings – one is illustrated at the end of the case. Following early growth in the 1980s – the company was founded in 1982 – Lilliput enjoyed mixed fortunes. During the 1990s, however, and following the disposal of non-core activities, rationalization, recapitalization and the appointment of a new strategic leader, profits have grown significantly.

The cottages are marketed through 2400 retail outlets in the UK and exported to 44 countries. There is an important and active Collectors' Club with over 75,000 members worldwide.

The following extract, taken from company promotional literature, summarizes the philosophy on which the success has been built:

*A cottage is a home, but to some it is a living thing which breathes and grows. It has a personality and character all of its own. Like every living thing the cottage needs to be nurtured, protected, loved and respected and every generation leaves its mark, however small, on the life of the building.*

*Many factors determine the character and personality of a cottage, the style of architecture, the materials used in its construction, the dictates of its environment, old age and decay, but mostly the area of the country from which it originates. As you travel around Great Britain you will notice many old buildings with similar features and overall appearance which have evolved a quite different look and character to cottages only a few miles away.*

*Each cottage was originally built to meet the needs of the family who were to occupy it and as the family grew, so did the cottage. The cottage was built and designed by the people who were to live in it, country folk who used their skills and crafts together with materials which were close at hand. This has given Britain an architectural heritage which is amongst the most varied and beautiful in the world.*

*Communities built using methods proved and improved by generations of their own craftsmen. Where stone was found that was used – flint, rubble, Cotswold or dressed stone. Wood is used in some form on almost every building, but in the once densely wooded areas of England and the Welsh borders it produced the spectacular timber framed buildings which we marvel at today. Clay was used in many different ways, in cob walls, wattle and daub panels or shaped into bricks and tiles and then fired. Roofs were covered in a number of different local materials, thatch, slate, stone flags, pantiles, claytiles or even heather.*

*The cottages which we at Lilliput Lane have chosen for our collection, are hidden away in the countryside behind high hedgerows, down farm tracks, in valleys or woods or high in the hills; the twentieth century has passed them by. Only after months of research do our sculptors discover these sometimes long forgotten homes. They will then take up to a hundred photographs before they are ready to magically create, in wax to minute scale, a three-dimensional cottage; every brick, tile and leaf faithfully captured as a true reflection of the original building.*

*The cottage then embarks on a long painstaking journey through the workshops and studios at Lilliput Lane. Complex moulds are made, then many painted samples are produced by our master-painters before we decide upon exactly the right colour combination for each miniature masterpiece. Finally every sculpture is exquisitely painted in Lilliput Lane's studios by one of our team of talented artists to the very highest standard. We do not compromise on quality. Every piece is rigorously inspected many times which assures our collectors that they are receiving a model perfect in every way.*

Over 15 million pieces have been sold since the company was started. The founder, David Tate, has suggested that many people 'see their ideal home, or their ideal retirement home, in many of the models'.

## The early years

Lilliput Lane Ltd was founded in 1982 by the families of Yorkshireman David Tate and Anthony Barnes to manufacture and market hard plaster cast (gypsum amorphite), hand-painted miniature cottage models 'unsurpassed in quality of workmanship and design'. Barnes left the organization in 1985. Tate had had to re-mortgage his house and sell most of his possessions to raise his share of the capital. Although both partners originally 'invested everything they had', the company was substantially dependent on long-term loans from their bankers and Lazard Ventures.

David Tate left school at 16 'with no qualifications', and subsequently spent 13 years in the Army – half of this in public relations work – and seven years in the fibreglass industry. For a short while he was also a self-employed sculptor and mould maker. He was 37 years old in 1982. His interest in cottages had begun much earlier, when, as a boy, he spent his school holidays with family relations in Bedfordshire. The Army taught him the technicalities of glass-fibre moulding and other skills which he later used to develop a revolutionary new system for enabling small, intricate objects to be moulded in one piece.

The company began at Skirsgill with 12 people in low-cost premises when Tate was offered the lease on a privately owned but semi-derelict group of red sandstone buildings sited on a disused eighteenth-century farm. Tate was introduced to the owner by Penrith Council, anxious to promote industrial development. Neighbours on the emerging industrial site included a horsebox manufacturer and a builder of wooden houses. The company's headquarters today are on the same estate, where cows still graze just over the boundary wall and the view takes in the nearby Pennine Hills. The site has both the look and feel of a true cottage industry.

For the first six months, David Tate, his wife and two daughters 'lived in a rented damp cottage and slept on the floor. The whole family worked 18 hours a day, 7 days a week' on the original range of 14 models. The business enjoyed some early success with small sales through gift shops, and it has subsequently grown into Penrith's largest employer. It was first profitable in 1983–84.

Between 1984 and 1987, and following a favourable reception at an important trade fair, sales grew rapidly from £318,000 to £4.1 million (see Exhibit 1). Two further production sites, again in Cumbria, were opened. The fast, demand-driven growth, reinforced by the ever-present need to recruit and quickly train new people – by late 1986 the number of employees had risen to 350 (see Exhibit 2) – led to some slack cost management. Profit before interest and tax, 13.5% of sales in 1985, fell back to 6.9% in

**Exhibit 1**  Lilliput Lane
Profit and loss account highlights.

| | Lilliput Lane | Turnover | Lilliput Group | | Profit/loss before |
| | | | Continued | Discontinued | |
| | | Total | activities | activities | interest and tax |
|---|---|---|---|---|---|
| | £'000 | £'000 | £'000 | £'000 | £'000 |
| 12 months to | | | | | |
| 30.9.1983 | 123 | | | | (4) |
| 30.9.1984 | 318 | | | | 24 |
| 30.9.1985 | 793 | | | | 107 |
| 30.9.1986 | 2138 | | | | 133 |
| 30.9.1987 | 4124 | | | | 285 |
| 30.9.1988 | | 6450 | 5898 | 552 | 413 |
| 30.9.1989 | | 9109 | 8294 | 815 | (421) |
| 30.9.1990 | | 12,145 | 11,080 | 1065 | (367) |
| 15 months to 5.1.1992 | | 15,162 | 15,162 | | 1427 |
| 12 months to 3.1.1993 | | 13,581 | | | 2129 |
| 31.12.1993 | | 16,506 | | | 3075 |

**Exhibit 2**  Lilliput Lane

| | Number of employees |
|---|---|
| 30.9.1983 | 24 |
| 30.9.1984 | 47 |
| 30.9.1985 | 86 |
| 30.9.1986 | 229 |
| 30.9.1987 | 453 |
| 30.9.1988 | 483 |
| 30.9.1989 | 641 |
| 30.9.1990 | 663 |
| 5.1.1992 | 577 |
| 3.1.1993 | 472 |
| 31.3.1994 | c. 600 |

1987. Cash-flow difficulties, realized as early as the 1983–84 trading year, intensified.

At the end of 1984, the company's auditor, William Dodd, agreed to invest a substantial sum of money in the business – and at the same time he became company chairman. 'It was time to match artistic impression with more formalized business organization'. Output continued to grow rapidly.

## Diversification strategies

Dodd was ambitious for Lilliput Lane to grow and sometime later the company decided to diversify, partly by acquisition, in order to expand its product range. It has been said, with hindsight, that this decision represents the time when the company 'stopped thinking about what its business was about, and what market it was in'.

In June 1987, a new company, Lilliput Group, was incorporated and it acquired the shares of Lilliput Lane. Later the same year Lilliput formed three new subsidiaries.

First, Land of Legend, to manufacture resin demons and fantasy models. A new production process was implied. Considerable learning was needed to catch up and match the quality of the leading resin manufacturers such as Border Fine

Arts, which is also located on the edge of Cumbria, but specializes in animals and birds.

The second subsidiary, Lilliput Creations, was established to acquire, in January 1988, the Albany Fine China Company Ltd. with borrowed cash. Albany manufactured large and expensive fine bone china pieces. 'The finest bone china studies available world-wide', ranging from a lady in period costume at £300 to large animals at £16,000. Again this was another new production process and a niche business which was difficult to expand. The resin business was based in Stoke-on-Trent; Albany's factory was in Worcester.

Lilliput Lane began to change its behaviour, style and culture from that of a small company. Some managers left, the company was restructured and overheads grew. The two new subsidiaries were never profitable, with the following recorded losses:

| Trading year | Trading loss |
| --- | --- |
| 1987–88 | £64,000 |
| 1988–89 | £635,000 |
| 1989–90 | £677,000 |

These trading losses, and the extra borrowing they had created, proved costly to Lilliput Group. A very high debt ratio meant recapitalization and rationalization were essential. In the event Albany was sold for cash in July 1990, and in August 1990, Lilliput's interests in Land of Legend were wholly demerged.

William Dodd left the company to concentrate on Land of Legend which has prospered on its own.

## The core business

Meanwhile, throughout the 1980s, the core miniature cottage business prospered. With constant innovation in production methods, the quality and aesthetic appearance of the models improved. Overseas sales and markets were developed – see Exhibit 3 – and the third subsidiary to be formed in 1987 was Lilliput Inc., an American distribution network based in Columbia, Maryland. Special ranges were developed for the American market and for selected European countries. New plants were opened in the Lake District and by the early 1990s Lilliput operated two sites in Penrith, one for production and one for warehousing and distribution, supported by factories in Workington and later Carlisle.

In 1988 Lilliput received the Queen's Award for Export, and in both 1987 and 1988 the company was a shortlisted finalist in the CBI Business Enterprise Awards. The 1987 winner was Body Shop International, and fellow-finalists in 1988 included Amstrad, Sock Shop and Iceland Frozen Foods. Also in 1988 David Tate was awarded the MBE for his contribution to local employment in Cumbria.

## Refinancing and turnaround

By 1989, due substantially to the fast growth and the losses of the two diversified subsidiaries, Lilliput's debt ratio had risen to 75% – see Exhibit 4. At its

**Exhibit 3**  Lilliput Lane
Worldwide sales (continuing operations)

|  | 12 months to | | | 15 months to | 12 months to |
| --- | --- | --- | --- | --- | --- |
|  | 30.9.88 | 30.9.89 | 30.9.90 | 5.1.92 | 3.1.93 |
|  | £'000 | £'000 | £'000 | £'000 | £'000 |
| Sales | 5898 | 8294 | 11,080 | 15,162 | 13,581 |
| Of which: |  |  |  |  |  |
| UK | 4910 | 5901 | 7519 | 10,250 | 8132 |
| USA | 564 | 1836 | 2680 | 3694 | 4043 |
| Cont'l Europe | 230 | 286 | 543 | 888 | 906 |
| Rest of world | 194 | 271 | 338 | 330 | 500 |

**Exhibit 4**   Lilliput Lane
Balance-sheet highlights

| | At 30.9.88 £'000 | At 30.9.89 £'000 | At 30.9.90 £'000 | At 5.1.92 £'000 | At 3.1.93 £'000 | At 31.12.93 £'000 |
|---|---|---|---|---|---|---|
| Total fixed assets | 1388 | 2409 | 2009 | 1843 | 1862 | 1801 |
| Net current assets* | 1179 | 68 | 656 | 833 | 1149 | 3585 |
| Provisions | (31) | | (17) | (26) | (8) | |
| | | | | | | |
| Creditors falling due after 1 year | 1189 | 1885 | 2000 | 1465 | 664 | 662 |
| Shareholders' funds† | 1347 | 592 | 648 | 1185 | 2339 | 4724 |
| | | | | | | |
| *Current assets and liabilities | | | | | | |
| Stocks | 1174 | 1554 | 1692 | 716 | 416 | 858 |
| Debtors | 1694 | 2202 | 2393 | 1734 | 2020 | 2145 |
| Cash | 105 | 25 | 47 | 803 | 1244 | 4021 |
| Short-term creditors | 1794 | 3713 | 3476 | 2420 | 2531 | 3439 |
| | | | | | | |
| †Shareholders' funds | | | | | | |
| Share capital | 524 | 524 | 1700 | 1700 | 1700 | 1163 |
| Share premium account | 226 | 226 | 140 | 140 | 140 | 2286 |
| Reserves (i.e. profit & loss account) | 597 | (158) | (1192) | (655) | 499 | 1275 |

height the company's total indebtedness amounted to £5 million. The company turned to Lazard Ventures and other investment groups for help. The North of England Venture Fund (NEV) and Lazards agreed to invest £1.2 million in new equity – but there were strings. First the divestments described above. Second the appointment of new directors, some non-executive, but particularly John Russell as Chairman and chief executive. Although William Dodd left, David Tate remained committed and he had a particular expertise to offer. He took the title of technical director with responsibility for research into new manufacturing techniques and the development of new models.

Although Tate has always retained an interest in product design, his most significant contribution over the years has been in technical innovation and production methods. A series of creative ideas has improved both the products and productivity. In addition, he has continued to travel widely and internationally, speaking frequently at Collectors'

Club promotional events. Tate is an extrovert who has rationalized his new role and who enjoys the adoration and respect he receives from collectors all round the world. Lilliput's collectors still see Tate as the organization and, for example, queue willingly for his personal signature on one of their pieces. His public relations contribution is of enormous value.

John Russell is a chartered accountant who had worked in consultancy and for the Burton Group (14 years) and Courtaulds (10 years). The new strategic leader sought to:

- reduce the level of working capital required by more efficient stock control and cash collection
- improve production, productivity and production planning systems
- invest in new information technology to improve decision making. A total investment of £500,000 was made, and this has contributed substantially to reductions in production lead times and inventories

- overhaul internal communications, and
- cultivate and extend Lilliput's Collectors' Club – the real reason why the turnaround has been sustained.

Effective control of the Collectors' Club has also been dependent on the new information technology (IT).

Commenting upon the IT, John Russell said he saw it as 'simply spending on necessities, like pencil and paper used to be . . . most small companies are terrified of the idea of spending on IT. If being in big business has taught me one thing, it is that the biggest problem affecting small businesses is that they think small'.

In 1991, after two loss-making years, Lilliput was again trading profitably. Growth and success continued.

Most of the production and administrative staff at Lilliput are young; many of them are teenagers. The management team is also relatively a young one; Russell and Tate are the elder statesmen. There are five other executive directors, all aged between 35 and 40 in 1994. Four of them worked for the company prior to the recapitalization. The average age of the 11 senior (non-director level) managers was 39 in 1994; five had been appointed since 1990.

## The Lilliput products

### The product range

The majority of Lilliput's products are models of vernacular architecture, indigenous to clearly identifiable countries and regions. Many models are copies of actual buildings; others are 'summaries of a style'. The English Collection, with individual regional subsets, is the largest of the ten discrete product groups. The full set is listed in Table 1.

The English Collection represents 70% of total UK sales, and also sells well in Europe and America. The Dutch, French, German and American Collections are marketed primarily in their respective countries as a means of market entry, but they can be obtained by special order through UK retailers.

The majority of pieces are produced in unlimited numbers in response to demand in the form of firm orders. However, to reinforce the collectability of Lilliput cottages:

**Table 1** The Lilliput Lane collections

| Collection | Description |
|---|---|
| English | A diverse collection of cottages and other buildings, subdivided into four geographical regions, to reflect different architectural styles |
| Classics | Relatively new small-scale miniatures |
| Scottish | Scottish cottages and castles |
| Welsh | Distinctive Welsh houses |
| Irish | Typical Irish buildings |
| American Landmarks | Typical rural American buildings. Unlike all the other collections these are sculpted in America by a local artist, but manufactured solely in the UK |
| Dutch | Amsterdam street scenes |
| French | French regional pieces |
| German | Again regional pieces, with an emphasis on castles (schlosses) |
| Christmas | Selected pieces given a snow effect |

- there is an ongoing programme of introductions and retirements
- certain large, high-price models are produced with a finite maximum, and
- there is an annual Collectors' piece available only to members during the relevant year.

As a result there is a free secondary market where pieces which have been retired trade at premium prices.

The products fit into a number of clear price bands, and Lilliput's policies for new product launches and for retirements are designed to maintain these bands. Some 50 pieces, for example, are priced below £20.00 in the UK, and a further 50 are priced between £20.00 and £30.00.

New products are normally launched in February and July; retirements are announced six months in advance, which normally creates a surge in demand for the threatened pieces. Secondhand prices tend to rise almost immediately after a product is withdrawn.

## Customers

People generally buy Lilliput pieces either as gifts or as collectibles. Gift purchases are often made on impulse by individuals buying either for themselves or buying presents for others. Clearly this market is very competitive with a wide variety of often quite different products available at comparable prices. Success depends on allotted retail space, retailer support and point-of-sale material.

The collectibles market embraces people who prefer collecting new products to antiques. Moreover, Lilliput pieces are generally more readily available than most antiques, they are likely to be cheaper and the amateur enthusiast is not worried about being 'ripped off' with fakes. This market, which is far more developed in the USA than the UK, is served by the Collectors' Club. Lilliput aims, not unexpectedly, to persuade gift buyers to become collectors, who tend to buy more pieces – and to purchase the more expensive ones in the range.

Because the UK is more reliant on the gift market, sales are most buoyant in the pre-Christmas period. It is quite normal for the company to have to close its order book for the calendar year at around the end of September.

## Distribution

In the UK, Lilliput's products are sold through around 2400 outlets, most of which are china and glass specialists, gift shops, department stores or jewellers. H. Samuel, Lawley's (the retail division of Royal Doulton), House of Fraser and John Lewis Partnership together account for a quarter of the sales in the UK. The number of outlets in any individual town or city is carefully regulated.

Few stores stock the whole range, or even the majority of it, concentrating on the most popular pieces. Lilliput's own sales force targets the stores which are most likely to assist in building the number of collectors. Members of the Collectors' Club receive regular information bulletins from the company, including information on launches and retirements, but they buy the majority of their pieces from high-street retailers, either off-the-shelf or by special order. Lilliput has a gift shop on-site in Skirsgill, where it displays an example of every model ever produced, but sells only those which are currently available in stores elsewhere. There is no direct distribution to individual customers and no mail-order system. The store really caters for members of the Collectors' Club who come from around the world to visit the company's headquarters. There are organized tours on a daily basis, which allow collectors to meet the people who make the cottages, especially the artists who provide the finishing touches. Developments are underway on the Skirsgill site to create a proper 'Lilliput area' and thus augment the visitors' experience. A Collectors' Club cottage is being built using a traditional frame structure and thatch.

In the USA over 40% of the sales are achieved through specialist collectibles stores.

## The Collectors' Club

An organized club is now both typical and essential for products which are marketed as collectibles. Lladro porcelain and Caithness paperweights – both more expensive products – and David Winter Cottages, Lilliput's main direct rival, for example, all have clubs. Members are 'really committed; they are like train spotters'.

The Lilliput Collectors' Club was formed in 1986, and during 1993 it grew rapidly from 58,000 to 68,500. In 1994 it has been growing at a rate of 1000 a month. Some 40,000 of the members live in the UK with another 20,000 plus in America. The remainder are mostly in Canada, New Zealand, Australia and Continental Europe. The Club has active branches in the UK, USA, Canada and New Zealand. Members, who pay an annual fee, receive a free piece when they join, the right to buy an annual Collectors' piece, a quarterly magazine called 'Gulliver's World' and a catalogue of special merchandise available only to them. The magazine contains features on the company, its products and the actual cottages from which the models have been developed.

The Club costs Lilliput over £1 million in administration and carefully targeted promotions every year, but it is entirely self-financing. The Club organizes regional evening events and an annual trade fair where, for example, members can buy plaster blanks, fresh from the mould, receive help and tuition and paint their own cottage. In addition, retired pieces are auctioned privately. Typically the annual fairs are held in the grounds of a stately home and they attract up to 15,000 collectors. Medieval jousts and similar events provide the entertainment and David Tate invariably attends. Members from the USA also come to the UK for organized tours which take them to the actual cottages which have been sculpted.

Although there is an active secondary market for Lilliput cottages, particularly in the US, both the company and the Collectors' Club remain detached. The record sale so far appears to be a model of an old Cornish Tin Mine – a very early piece which retailed at under £10 before its retirement – which was sold for £1600 at the 1993 Collectors' Fair.

It is estimated that purchases made by Club members amount to 65% of Lilliput's total sales revenue each year. Members own, on average, 21 pieces, and typically they will buy three new pieces every year and receive two more as gifts.

## International Sales

Some 40% of sales are now outside the UK. The company's international strategy has been to, first, open an American subsidiary, Lilliput Lane Inc., which is based in Maryland but also has an outlet in Chicago. Lilliput Lane (UK) sells products to Lilliput Lane Inc. on an arm's length basis; prices in the USA are generally higher than those prevailing in the UK partly because the collectibles market is more established. While Lilliput has been successful in America, William Dodd's entry strategy of high price/exclusive image has inhibited growth. The company has found it difficult to reposition itself with lower prices in order to replicate the market position it enjoys in the UK.

Second, Lilliput has appointed dedicated distributors in countries with large populations of British expatriates, namely Canada, Australia and New Zealand, who 'enjoy rural reminders'. There are also well-established distributors in Italy and Japan. Elsewhere a mix of distributors and agents is used. In the 1990s Continental Europe has shown growth potential, with sales growing by 40% in 1992–93, and it is believed to offer exciting future prospects.

## Competition

*On the face of it, barriers to entry are not very great. You get a mould, pour plaster in and paint it!*

*But what we have is a strong brand and market awareness. Our research suggests that people think our business is ten times as big as it is.*

(John Russell)

There are estimated to be some 130 competing manufacturers of miniature model cottages, but of course many of these will be one-person businesses with substantially localized demand. Lilliput's most visible rival is David Winter Cottages, which is the trading name for The Studios and Workshops of John Hine, and whose turnover is 50% greater. Winter has 50,000 American members in its Collectors' Guild, and half of these are known to be active speculators in the secondary market. The company was started two years before Lilliput, and its product range features more limited editions and generally higher prices. On occasions Winter is known to have withdrawn existing models from sale and destroyed all stock pieces and the moulds in order to encourage the collectability. Like Lilliput it has no direct role in the secondary market. One piece, the only known surviving copy of a Provençal cottage, launched and withdrawn in 1981, has sold at auction for $42,000. Its original price was £7.50. In 1992 the complete collection of past and present models, a total of 146 pieces – half are still freely available – was estimated to be worth upwards of $200,000.

David Winter Cottages are reputed to be the third most popular collectible in America, behind Lladro porcelain (Spanish) and the Precious Moments collection of whimsical cherub-like creatures distributed by Stanhome's Enesco subsidiary.

Like Lilliput, David Winter pays considerable attention to detail, but the cottages feature a different style and range of colours. There are also certain different specialist ranges, including, for example, a set of Dickensian buildings. David Winter is based in Hampshire, and again it is housed in a true 'cottage-industry' setting. The company began with few full-time employees and relied on some 2000 home workers for painting; later 100 full-timers were employed.

## Research and development

Active research and development is seen as an important aspect of Lilliput's competitive strength and distinctiveness. The company, for example, has designed all its own tooling for producing thin one-piece moulds for manufacturing the most detailed models. Some pieces include intricate features such as small archways, which present particular problems for this type of modelling.

Research and new product development encompasses the sculpting of proposed new models. Prior to this, as highlighted earlier, numerous photographs and illustrations of actual buildings are used to finalize a design which is then built out of wax. Normally a number of alternatives will be built; each individual prototype can take up to three weeks to sculpt. A Kentish oasthouse, now discontinued, contained 7500 identifiable roof slates. Aesthetic appeal, accuracy and the need for simplicity in order to minimize production difficulties are all seen as critical variables. Before production begins a number of colour combinations will also be tested and a 'production master' selected. The company strives very hard to replicate accurately the original style, materials and colouring, and consequently the whole design process can easily absorb six months, start to finish.

## Production

The vertically integrated production process includes a number of distinct phases.

### Mould making

The finally selected wax sculpture is used to produce a number of identical masters, traditionally from resin, each of which is subsequently used to produce a number of rubber moulds. Moulds have finite lives, dependent on the size of the piece, its detail and complexity and the relative ease with which plaster casts can be removed. Lilliput Lane's mould making is innovative and new materials such as polyurethane and softer rubber compounds are constantly tried out. The quality of the mould affects productivity, rejection rates and the final aesthetic appearance of the model; it is a competency which the company believes gives it a competitive advantage. Once a model is retired all the relevant tooling is destroyed.

### Casting

A specialist liquid plaster is poured into the moulds – a number of identical moulds will be fitted into a special tray – and allowed to set. The small team of casters is substantially empowered and rewarded well for high quality and high throughput. Their work is repetitive; and the continuous removal of the models from their rubber moulds in an undamaged state can be tiring. Models are rejected for a blemish the size of a pin-prick.

### Fettling

After demoulding the plaster cast is inspected for any faults or discrepancies, and any rough surfaces and edges are fettled smooth.

### Dipping

The next stage, another Tate innovation, is to immerse the model in a paint tank containing a basic background colour, which also acts as a seal. The shade selected for each model will be the most predominant of its finished colours in terms of surface coverage. Certain models are dipped twice; the finish of the plaster, smooth or stippled, on different parts of the model affects colour retention and can be used in conjunction with multiple dipping to bring out different shades of stone colours.

At this stage in the process the *direct* costs incurred will generally be less than £1.00. Lilliput's most expensive model – which retails at £450.00 – has cost approximately £5.00 at this stage. The real value – and costs – is added in painting. Because of the relatively low direct costs incurred, Lilliput holds a predetermined level of stocks of most of the models in this semi-finished state.

All these processes are centred on the company's main site in Penrith. For most of the year orders will be satisfied with a delivery time of no more than 28 days. Lilliput does not hold stocks of finished goods in any quantity, although clearly some are held to support the on-site shop.

## Painting

The dipped models out of stock are finished when retail orders are received and batched into an appropriate quantity. Painting takes place at all of the company's sites – Penrith, Workington and Carlisle. In the past Lilliput has also utilized a number of experienced home workers, but this practice has recently been discontinued. Reasons include the added costs and potential delays involved in delivering and collecting.

Most of the painters, who comprise over half the total workforce, are female and relatively young. They need 'a good eye and a steady hand' and they sit in small groups, sometimes facing each other across tables, painting up to ten models of the same cottage at any one time. The painting rooms are well-lit and exhibit a friendly atmosphere. The painters can talk to each other and they are encouraged to respond to visitors. Collectors who visit the Penrith site are shown round the painting rooms and they inevitably want to talk directly with the artists.

Painters copy the production master, but they are free to put on the colours in any order they wish. Typically they will paint one colour onto several pieces, allowing them to dry properly before applying the next colour. Each painter has a personal style, and each finished piece, while appearing basically the same as the others, will in some small, subtle way be unique.

Speed, accuracy and efficiency are critical. The simplest models can be finished by an experienced painter in just a few minutes, with perhaps only 30 seconds of actual painting time involved; the most complex pieces take several hours. Product planning and development always takes account of the likely painting time, which is related directly to the total cost and the eventual price band. A vicarage, which retails at £14.00, takes seven-and-a-half minutes to paint; a Welsh Lodge priced at £50.00 requires thirty-three-and-a-half minutes.

Training can take up to six months to complete, and productivity-based bonus schemes, linked to both quality and quantity, are used extensively. A painter's workload and remuneration is determined by her current efficiency rating – how long it takes her to paint particular pieces in relation to the predetermined standard times. Experienced painters enjoy efficiencies comfortably over 100%; the average at Penrith is just over 90%. The bonus schemes are undoubtedly successful, but the organization is beginning to question whether they are the most appropriate reward system for a workforce that they would like to see being highly flexible. The company would, for example, like its casters also to do the fettling, and for painters to put on the baize bases and pack the finished models. These changes would reduce unpopular wage differentials between departments and help to reduce the risk of repetitive strain injury for the painters.

## Finishing and packing

The completed models are inspected visually and a piece of baize and an identification label are fixed to the base. Lilliput inspects its products but relies more on a culture of 'right first time' rather than post-production inspection. Every cottage is sandwiched between two small 'bean bags' or pillows filled with polystyrene chips (an invention of Lilliput Lane for which the company is seeking a patent) and individually packed in its own box. A small certificate, replicating a set of title deeds, accompanies every model.

To reinforce the idea of collectability it is normal for a small booklet illustrating all of the pieces in a particular range also to be packed in the box.

## People

The relative importance of the workforce in the production of Lilliput cottages can be seen in the following breakdown of costs for 1992–93:

|  | £ '000 |
|---|---|
| Turnover | 13,581 |
| Less: Cost of sales | 6960 |
| Including: Wages and salaries | 5372* |
| Distribution costs | 2576 |
| Administration costs | 1916 |
| Leaving: Profit before interest and tax | 2129 |

*Representing an average of 434 manufacturing employees, 38 in management and office administration and 23 in the USA.

The painters comprise the majority of the production employees. In 1994 the following figures applied:

| Site | Number of painters | Current painting capacity | |
|---|---|---|---|
| Skirsgill | 55 | 75 | } Supported by |
| Carlisle | 45 | 65 | } 20 casters |
| Workington | 160 | 180 | |

If the company needed to expand quickly, a number of options is open to it. It could, for example, readily acquire a suitable location on the eastern side of Penrith; Skirsgill is on the west. The young employees typically live locally.

Its main people issues are:

- flexibility
- the ease with which productivity-based wage differentials can widen and cause resentment, giving rise to
- the risk of absenteeism
- constant natural wastage and the need to balance demand with a supply of *trained* labour. It was highlighted earlier that painters in particular require up to six months' training; they have to be recruited in advance of the need for their skills. Demand is seasonal and Lilliput Lane tries to minimize its stocks of finished cottages.

## The flotation

In 1993, with the company solvent and profitable, a flotation was announced. Lilliput had been turned around successfully and could boast a number of strengths:

- the active and growing Collectors' Club
- the quality of the products – authentic reproduction, colouring and finishing
- strong promotional material and high levels of customer service
- the range covered a wide variety of price points, from around £10.00, for a simple cottage, to £450.00 for the most expensive piece, a hamlet based on two Suffolk villages
- the brand name and its worldwide level of recognition
- a set of clear objectives and accompanying strategies:
  - to sustain the collectability of the products worldwide, and build the Lilliput Lane brand
  - to concentrate marketing around the Collectors' Club, and
  - to develop the product range and provide marketing support to retailers in order to maintain a competitive advantage.

*(Float prospectus)*

Europe was seen to offer important opportunities, and future acquisitions were 'not ruled out' if and when they are appropriate.

The time seemed appropriate for the main backers, NEV and Lazard Ventures, to realize their investment. In 1993 NEV and Lazards held 50% of the issued ordinary shares; David Tate and his family retained 29.9%; Tate's fellow directors held a further 14%. The total share capital was split as follows:

|  | £'000 | |
|---|---|---|
| 9.8 million ordinary shares | | } split as |
| 5 pence ordinary shares | 229 | } detailed |
| 0.05 pence deferred ordinaries | 2 | } above |
| | | |
| Deferred shares | 319 | } mostly NEV |
| Redeemable preference shares | 1150 | } and Lazards |
| Total issued share capital | 1700 | |

The flotation would take place in late November 1993, when 2,222,214 new ordinary shares would be issued to supplement the existing 9,814,823 ordinaries and deferred ordinaries.

A proportion (51.7%) of the enlarged equity would then be offered for sale at 135 pence per share.

Afterwards, and assuming the sale was successful, the existing leading investors would retain the following shareholdings:

| | |
|---|---|
| David Tate and family | 16.5% of the equity |
| Other directors | 6.3% |
| NEV | 12.7% |
| Lazard Ventures | 10.5% |
| Total | 46.0% |

The company was being valued at £31.4 million; £16.5 million of new money was being raised. It was estimated that the major shareholders, in particular NEV, Lazards and David Tate, would receive £13.5 million. Tate would personally receive some £5 million.

The 2.22 million new shares would generate exactly £3 million for the company, of which £1.47 million would be used to buy out the deferred and redeemable preference shares issued in 1990. After accounting for dealer costs, approximately £1 million would remain as investment capital for Lilliput Lane.

Initial enquiries indicated a strong interest from members of the Collectors' Club, who could now own part of the company behind their hobby. As many as 4.2 million of the 12 million ordinary shares could be held back for priority investors, namely Lilliput retailers and employees. In the event their interest in investing was overestimated, and only 1 million shares needed to be clawed back.

At the time of the flotation Lilliput was estimating pre-tax profits of £3 million for the trading year to the end of December 1993. Earnings per share were forecast at 9.3 pence, showing a P/E ratio of 14.5. The *Investors Chronicle* regarded the issue as 'worth considering for a medium-term investment'.

When the results were finally announced in March 1994, profits slightly exceeded £3 million; sales had grown to £16.5 million. UK sales, comprising 60% of total revenue, had increased by 25%; in the USA (representing 27% of turnover) sales growth had been a more modest 10%.

Cash reserves in early 1994 stood at £4 million, and John Russell, still the Chairman and Chief Executive, commented: 'Lilliput was looking for an acquisition where it could use its skills in marketing collectible products'. The lines, however, 'must be complementary and not imply diversification'.

Lilliput Lane began to discuss a possible merger with Border Fine Arts, whose products [mainly wildlife figures] were already distributed in the USA by Lilliput Lane Inc. Border Fine Arts was also involved in discussions with Enesco, the collectibles and giftware subsidiary of the US company, Stanhome. Stanhome specializes in marketing and distributing a range of consumer products; Enesco's best-known product is Precious Moments, the second most popular collectible in the USA.

Meanwhile, the share price fluctuated:

| | |
|---|---|
| December 1993 | 115 pence |
| February 1994 | 140 pence |
| March 1994 | 130 pence (results announced) |
| July 1994 | 90 pence |
| Early September 1994 | 90 pence. |

It has been argued that the stock market did not fully understand the nature of Lilliput's business.

In September 1994 it was announced that Stanhome was making a recommended cash offer of 160 pence per share for the Lilliput Group. Following the acquisition, Lilliput would stand alone within Stanhome's Enesco subsidiary. Lilliput was now being valued at £37.2 million. Russell would receive £1 million for his shareholding, and Tate a further £6 million. The company's venture capitalists could bow out with a handsome profit, a solid reward for their continued support over several years of mixed fortunes.

Enesco imports most of its products from the Far East, especially China, where Precious Moments are made. Another Enesco range, growing quickly in popularity in the 1990s, is Cherished Teddies, a range of small plaster teddy bears, also manufactured in China.

The fact that Lilliput actually manufactures in the UK is seen as important by Stanhome, especially for building sales in the Far East. Another benefit from the acquisition for the American company is a foothold in Europe, which would be strengthened further if Enesco also acquires Border Fine Arts. In the past Lilliput has relied on outside carriers to distribute its products from the Penrith warehouse. Distribution represents another large slice of its costs and Enesco is reviewing the distribution strategy for all of its products throughout Europe. Should Lilliput Lane now think to invest in its own distribution system? Lilliput would also benefit from reduced distribution costs in America; the Chief Executive of Lilliput Lane Inc. had resigned earlier in 1994 and he had not been replaced when the bid was announced.

What of David Tate? Tate had remained loyal to the company he founded 12 years earlier, accepting a new role when John Russell took over the strategic leadership, and he was now a rich man. He has vowed to continue working for the company. 'I've made a lot of money . . . but what would I do if I retired now? I'd go mad sitting at home.'

*Lilliput Lane*   http://www.lilliputlane.co.uk

## Questions

1. In what ways does Lilliput Lane *add value* for its customers?
   Identify the most significant core competencies and strategic capabilities involved.
   Use Porter's 5-Force industry model to assess the company's competitive position.

2. Identify and prioritize the company's main stakeholders. How have they been rewarded for their support of the organization? How do you feel the interests of the key stakeholders might be best served in the future?

3. Critically evaluate the strategy of diversification pursued in the 1980s. In your opinion, do you believe the strategy failed because it was poorly conceived or poorly implemented?
   What are the lessons for the future?

4. Would you describe David Tate as an *entrepreneur*?
   Is Lilliput Lane *entrepreneurial*?
   How dependent do you feel Lilliput Lane still is on the continued involvement of David Tate?

# P&O, Princess and the International Passenger Cruise Industry

Mike Moulin was distracted as he looked out over the calm, blue Caribbean waters. He was soon to go home on leave – but afterwards he would not be returning to this ship. His employer, Princess Cruises, had invited him to be the first Captain of *Grand Princess*, the largest cruise ship in the world and due for her maiden voyage in Summer 1998. *Grand Princess* would split her cruising year between the Caribbean and Mediterranean – her choice of destinations limited by her sheer size. Captain Moulin knew just how dependent a cruise ship is on its staff and wondered whether the issues would be any different on the first Princess ship to require a crew of over 1000 people.

This case looks at the nature of competition in the growing passenger cruise industry.

The author is indebted to the UK Passenger Shipping Association and, in particular, the US Cruise Lines International Association for permission to reproduce statistical data. Most of the tables in the case are derived from information supplied by the PSA and the CLIA; a limited amount has been abstracted from a Euromonitor report. This case is Copyright, John L Thompson, University of Huddersfield, 1998. It is for classroom discussion and should not be taken to reflect either effective or ineffective management.

## Introduction

Cruise holidays are no longer confined to the wealthy and elderly – a popular misconception for many people – but these groups continue to be important customers. Younger, more energetic tourists are now providing the revenue streams to build state-of-the-art luxury liners and develop new itineraries and destinations around the world. The industry is enjoying rapid growth. In 1997 North American cruise passengers (the largest segment) increased by 8.6% to 4,860,000. This is almost a tenfold increase since 1970, when just half a million Americans cruised. Also in 1997, UK passengers increased by 25% to 521,500; more British people cruise than from any other European country. However, Germany experienced a 12.3% increase to 401,000. The UK forecast for 1998 is 600,000. Overall, American cruise liners sail with 90% occupancy rates, but some lines enjoy figures well in excess of this. The growth of cruising has brought new prosperity to shipyards in Italy, Germany and Finland, which have been able to specialize in these high added-value vessels and compete again with Asian yards.

Cruising is popular for a variety of reasons. For most people it represents fun; it can be highly entertaining and, for some, romantic. It allows people to travel widely without constant packing and unpacking. It provides luxury at increasingly affordable prices. The holiday can be extensively organized for those who want it that way, freer for more independent travellers. In general it is a 'safe' way to see the world, minimizing the likelihood of illness from strange climates, foods and water. The market is dominated by large, specialist competitors, mainly American based, and particularly Carnival Group, Royal Caribbean Cruise Lines (RCCL) and Norwegian Cruise Line as well as P&O/Princess, but newcomers such as Airtours, Saga and Disney are opening up new segments and opportunities, particularly with short-duration and more informal cruises.

The established cruise operators are investing in ever-larger vessels. Princess Cruises' *Grand Princess*, launched in 1998, is the largest in the world. She registers 109,000 tons (111,000 tonnes) and offers 1296 cabins to (normally) 2600 passengers. Costing $385 million to build, she sails with a crew of over 1100. The smaller *Carnival Destiny* takes more passengers; but 1999 saw the first of three new 130,000 ton (132,000 tonnes) (3100 passengers) liners on order by Royal Caribbean. Each of these costs some half a billion dollars and the first has both a TV studio and an ice-skating rink. These new, large megaliners are critical for the future of the industry and, to build, they cost roughly $150,000 to $160,000 per berth. Every new ship implies a step increase in capacity, unless it is matched by a withdrawal, but a failure to order new ships several years ahead can mean a missed opportunity. P&O and Princess are adding capacity equivalent to 12% per year, for example. One constraint with the newest large ships is their inability to sail through the Panama Canal, itself a popular cruise destination, but the key transit route between the Caribbean and Pacific Oceans. The largest cruise liners, therefore, can offer holidays in the Caribbean and Mediterranean, but Alaska, Hawaii and the South Pacific are effectively prohibited.

P&O/Princess is the third largest of the international cruise line groups, and the largest with UK ownership. It is part of the P&O Group. Princess is a leader in Alaska and the Panama Canal, but these are by no means the most popular destinations for passengers. Equally, Princess has an important position in the dominant Caribbean and Mediterranean markets, where P&O mainly concentrates. P&O and Princess operate as separate companies, based in London and Los Angeles, respectively. They are distinct brands and appeal to different passengers.

New ships, new itineraries and new standards reflect innovation and continuous improvement, but is there an opportunity for a radical new offering? Disney has recently entered the industry with a theme-park-style ship offering lavish entertainment for families. One London designer has conceptualized a 240,000 tons (244,000 tonnes) floating resort, incorporating a 120,000 seat arena, and supported by two 130,000 tons (132,000 tonnes) satellite ships which would provide cruise holidays and, at the same time, ferry people to the resort for short-stay holidays and special concerts and sporting events. This higher risk proposal 'requires a backer who relishes innovation'.

The potential seems enormous. Cruising is still under 2% of the American vacation market, way behind Orlando and Las Vegas, which both command a 10% share. Just over half the people cruising in any year are repeat customers; the other 45% are trying it for the first time, but many of these will choose to cruise again – if they enjoy the experience.

## The emergence of the modern cruise holiday

European explorers sailed the oceans to discover the world and open up new trading routes. Later, people migrated to other countries by sea. Fast, convenient, affordable air travel is a relatively recent phenomenon. It was, however, in 1840 that Samuel Cunard began the first regular passenger trans-Atlantic steamship service. These early ships were not renowned for their passenger comfort, and up to World War I migrants were the target market. The White Star Line was the first to incorporate an indoor swimming pool, in 1910, but White Star's *Titanic*, launched in 1912, set new standards with superior, luxury accommodation for her most wealthy passengers. *Titanic* personified elegance. The 1920s have been termed the 'golden age' for steamship travel; during the American prohibition years the ships were not required to sail dry! New standards of lounges, accommodation and entertainment were introduced. However, it was the 1950s before the top deck was transformed into a centre for sports and outdoor activities, a feature which is ubiquitous today. When jet airliners began regular trans-Atlantic services in 1958, the market for five-day crossings by sea was hit dramatically.

The modern cruise holiday began properly in 1966 when the Norwegian Caribbean Line (now the Norwegian Cruise Line) began three and four day cruises to the Bahamas from Miami. One general feature of the modern cruise, present from the beginning, is the absence of different classes of travel. Cabins or staterooms certainly vary in size and facilities, but passengers mingle freely and eat together. Generally passengers pay more for staterooms on the higher decks, where all the suites and cabins with balconies are located. Separated first, second and third classes were important features of trans-Atlantic crossings, and something similar is still available today on the QE2, which has 22 different grades of cabin and restaurants dedicated to certain cabin grades.

The industry grew more dramatically once the first fly/cruise packages were introduced in the

1970s. Ships could now be moved readily around parts of the world to exploit seasonal differences. In 1980 Norwegian Cruises was responsible for another key innovation; it converted an existing ship into one with a large theatre and a promenade of shops. Other new ideas followed quickly. The *Royal Princess*, launched in 1984, has, for example, no inside cabins. The *QE2* pioneered the daily newspaper by satellite in 1986. Windstar cruises traded on nostalgia with luxury sailing ships featuring computerized sails. RCCL introduced the five-deck atrium.

Perhaps paradoxically, the popularity of the movie *Titanic* in 1998 has boosted the industry. Research indicates that passengers have been tempted by the perception of romance and, of course, safety considerations are not the same as they used to be.

Passengers can now choose between large and small ships and luxury and less luxurious accommodation – all major lines offer high standards as a minimum. Ships with 2000 or more passengers are classified as megaliners. Superliners hold between 1000 and 2000; midsize from 400 up to 1000; small are under 400; and the term 'boutique' is attributed to exceptionally high-quality ships below 300 passengers. The industry is extremely competitive, with considerable discounts available for regular and loyal cruisers and people who book early. The major lines all have loyalty organizations of some form, designed to encourage people to return. The 12 key cruise destination areas are listed below and Table 1 summarizes the relative popularity of selected destinations in 1997. In addition, Appendix 1 provides details of the world's leading ports of embarkation and disembarkation in 1998.

The 12 key destination areas are:

- Eastern Caribbean – the area incorporating the US and UK Virgin Islands, Martinique, Grenada, Barbados and Trinidad
- Western Caribbean – originally the Bahamas, but now including Jamaica and the East coast resorts of Mexico. San Juan (Puerto Rico) is a leading cruise port which tends to divide the Caribbean into East and West; both Eastern and Western Caribbean cruises will sometimes be linked to partial or complete transits of the Panama Canal

**Table 1**  Cruise destinations (1997)

| Destination | % of US total | % of UK total |
|---|---|---|
| Eastern Caribbean | 26.5 | } 23.4 |
| Western Caribbean | 22.0 | |
| Mediterranean | 8.4 | 44.8 |
| Rest of Europe | 7.2 | 14.6 |
| Alaska | 9.2 | 1.8 |
| Panama Canal | 7.2 | 1.0 (est.) |
| World/trans-Atlantic | 2.9 | 2.4 |
| Other destinations | 16.6 | 12.0 |

NOTES:
- The market each year is 5 million American cruise passengers, 1.2 million Europeans and 1 million Asians.
- The US market (the number of Americans cruising) is 9.3 times bigger than that of the UK, itself the largest in Europe; as a result,
- for every one UK passenger cruising in the Mediterranean, there are two Americans.
- The US:UK ratio for the Caribbean is 20:1; the Alaskan ratio is almost 50:1.
- In the 1990s, the key growth destinations have been:

|   | US passengers | UK passengers |
|---|---|---|
| 1 | Mediterranean | Mediterranean |
| 2 | Western Caribbean | Caribbean |
| 3 | Panama Canal | Rest of Europe |

- The beginning of this new millennium is perceived by many to offer a wonderful opportunity for those cruise lines which can offer something special and distinctive.

- Eastern Mediterranean – Italy east to Turkey, Israel and Egypt
- Western Mediterranean – North Africa, Spain, Portugal, France and Italy – stretching to the Canary Islands. Some Mediterranean cruises will blend ports from both regions
- Scandinavia and northern Europe – including the Baltic ports and St Petersburg
- Alaska (north from Vancouver)
- Mexico's Pacific Coast (including Acapulco)
- South America – incorporating a trip around Cape Horn for those with a strong stomach!
- Australasia – and stretching to the South Pacific islands
- The Orient – China, Japan and the Philippines
- The Indian Ocean – the east coast of Africa, India and Malaysia

- South-east Asia – Malaysia, Indonesia, Singapore and the Philippines.

(Clearly there is some overlap with these designated regions.)

These different regions enjoy seasonal popularity, linked to changing weather and sea conditions. Cruises in the Mediterranean and Eastern Caribbean tend to be the most port-intensive ones available. The Caribbean is seen as an all-year-round destination despite the unpredictable hurricane season in the autumn. Relative prices vary, based on several issues: popularity and competition, the distances that people have to travel to join the cruise and the potential for supplementary on-board earnings. These are reputedly highest in the Caribbean, where cruises tend to be cheaper than in Alaska and the Mediterranean.

## The market for US passengers

The US passenger cruise industry has enjoyed an average growth of 7.6% per year since the beginning of the 1980s; this is faster than the leisure market overall. Some 67 million people have taken a cruise lasting for longer than two days since 1970, almost 70% of this total in the past 10 years and 40% in the past five years. Of those passengers who have cruised in the past five years, one cruise every two years is typical. Throughout the period of research, the average length of a cruise has remained between six and seven days. Research for the New York-based Cruise Lines International Association (CLIA) projects that the market will rise from 5 million passengers per year to 7 million by the year 2000. CLIA argues that taking a cruise is a dream for 60% of US adults – especially those born in the baby-boom years after World War II – but to date only 10% of the population has ever cruised. One-third of the adults surveyed indicated an interest in taking a cruise within the next five years. While the features designed into the new megaliners and the new destinations and itineraries are the result of extensive passenger and potential passenger research, the key challenge lies in translating this interest into real bookings.

Recent American cruisers have been categorized as follows:

|  | % of market | % who are first-time cruisers |
|---|---|---|
| Restless baby boomers | 33 | 59 |
| Enthusiastic baby boomers | 20 | 46 |
| Consummate shoppers | 16 | 20 |
| Luxury seekers | 14 | 30 |
| Explorers | 11 | 20 |
| Ship buffs | 6 | 13 |

Restless baby boomers are seen as people who have tried and enjoyed cruising, but who have not necessarily committed themselves to a follow-up; they are interested in trying other vacation packages. Enthusiastic boomers are more committed. Typically they lead intense, stressful lives and prioritize their vacations. Consummate shoppers are those looking for 'best value for money' in their holidays; again they are frequently committed, believing that cruising meets their needs. Luxury seekers are those who will choose the boutique ships and the up-market lines which offer luxury – at a price. Explorers are those seeking new experiences and new destinations, while ship buffs are the regular, seasoned cruisers.

Seventy-five per cent of cruisers are married and 54% take children with them. 47% are male, 53% female, and their average age is 49. The age ranges 25–40, 40–59 and over 60 are roughly evenly represented.

In order of priority, the following five prospect segments have been identified and will be used to direct marketing and promotional strategies designed to persuade people to cruise for the first time.

First, families, who are not looking for adventurous holidays and for whom expenditure is critical. Sightseeing, shopping and swimming are high on the agenda. Secondly, comfortable spenders, who are less constrained financially. Typically sports orientated and physically active, they take more vacations than the average household and frequently travel abroad. Thirdly, want-it-alls, who aspire but have yet to achieve the status and income they desire. Because they work hard, there is an element of escapism in their holiday choice. Expectations are very high, and there is a fear that the cruise may be a disappointment. Cautious travellers are fourth. Content with the simpler things in life, they are neither trendy nor fashion conscious. They are not physically active or sporty; instead they are attracted by sightseeing and shopping opportunities. The fifth target group, adventurers, are experimenters. Confident and independent, they tend to be experienced travellers who are willing to spend money to access unusual and exotic destinations. This group would include those interested in unusual wildlife and archaeology. Appendix 2 provides a more detailed summary of this research.

## The market for UK passengers

The UK market has been transformed in the 1990s as Airtours and Thomson Holidays have both entered what was previously perceived to be a more up-market sector of the holiday industry. Growth in the cruise holiday industry is in double figures for all leading Western European countries, but UK passengers exceed those from any other country. Germany is second, but Italy and France account for under 200,000 each. In the early 1990s, and before the impact of Airtours, some 80% of UK cruisers were couples; 10% were single and the other 10% families. Targeting families with limited-length cruises on medium-quality ships has proved very successful in persuading people to cruise for the first time. In its first full year, 1995, Airtours took over 20% of the market. At this time P&O/Princess led with a 35% share and Cunard (18%) was pushed into fourth place. World market leader, the Carnival Group, had 24%.

Relative to the overall holiday industry, cruising is small, but growing, with the real potential in fly/cruise holidays as distinct from those which start in either Dover or Southampton. Cruises to the Mediterranean from the UK imply extra days at sea, instead of ports of call, and require a journey through the highly unpredictable, and frequently rough, Bay of Biscay. In 1996, 49% of UK cruisers were first-timers, but for fly/cruise holidays this proportion rises to 60%.

Averaging 56 years in 1996, UK cruisers tend to be slightly older than Americans on average, although those journeying to the Caribbean to cruise are younger. A substantial number here is under 40. UK passengers typically take longer cruises than their American counterparts, with those lasting between eight and 14 days being the most popular. The average duration exceeds seven days, unlike in America. The average is falling all the time, however, with the impact of the industry's newcomers. In 1996 some 6% of UK cruisers were persuaded to book over 12 months in advance – both to take advantage of early-booking discounts and to secure their first choice of cabin. Forty-seven per cent booked over six months ahead. This proportion increased during the 1990s.

The UK Passenger Shipping Authority believes that of those UK people who can afford to cruise, just 1% do. Forecasts for growth in the UK market postulate annual increases of around 20% such that the annual total will surpass 1 million people early this century. The value of the market should exceed £1 billion in the year 2000. The perpetual growth in capacity is tending to hold prices constant in real terms; and consequently, as operating costs continue to grow and new vessels have to be financed, it becomes increasingly imperative to 'part people from their money' more and more while they are on board ship. This requires more and better shopping opportunities and imaginative, exciting trips ashore for which cruisers are willing to pay.

## Competition

The main bases for a competitive strategy are as follows:

- overall size and facilities available
- the grades and size of cabins/staterooms – including facilities, furnishings and balconies
- restaurants and cuisine – quality, variety and flexibility (fixed or variable dining times)
- service and tipping – some lines adopt a strictly no-tipping policy; others encourage certain amounts

- on-board entertainment – clearly the largest ships have larger theatres and more scope. Big shows will be interspersed with specialist individual acts
- sports facilities, indoor and outdoor
- on-board, duty-free, shopping alternatives
- itineraries – numbers of days at sea and in port; actual ports of call; busyness of ports (some feature maybe six cruise ships on the same day!); length of stay at each port (it is typical for ships to sail at night and stay in port all day)
- shore excursions – emphases on shopping, sightseeing, activity (snorkelling, scuba-diving, rafting, biking) and adventure (helicopter and seaplane rides)
- facilities for children – and the opportunity for parents to enjoy activities on their own.

The leading cruise lines adopt different approaches in their search for distinctiveness and real competitive advantage, and these are described later in the case. Table 2 shows the capacities of the leading lines; Table 3 compares passenger:crew ratios for selected ships.

Ships and cruise lines certainly look and feel different, but clearly there are common elements which constitute 'the modern cruise experience'. Lines such as Celebrity deliberately target the 45–65 age group, but the facilities are sufficiently extensive that younger people can enjoy the experience and fit in. Carnival concentrate on 'fun', but most Carnival ships are large enough that people who want simply to relax can do so.

Food is often a major talking point for both cruisers and non-cruisers, who have probably heard that

**Table 2**

Capacities of the four major cruise lines (figures are based on numbers of berths)

| Group/line | Passenger capacity, end 1997 | Projected capacity at end of 2001, based on new orders and planned withdrawals |
|---|---|---|
| Carnival Group | 41,681 | 53,839 |
| Including Carnival Line | 20,103 | |
| Holland America | 10,302 | |
| Costa* | 7533 | |
| Cunard | 3131 | |
| Seabourn† | 612 | |
| Royal Caribbean Cruise Line | 21,726 | 32,312 |
| Celebrity | 8218 | 8218 |
| P&O Group | 14,744 | 28,244 |
| Including P&O | 3984 | 5784 |
| Princess | 10,760 | 22,460 |
| Norwegian Cruise Line | 10,612 | 22,644 |
| Totals | 96,981 | 149,807 |

These four cruise lines represent some 80% of the current global cruising capacity – which is targeted at the key American market. Cruise lines also operate from countries in eastern Europe and the Far East where English is less likely to be the first-choice language. There is a small presence in the Pacific. Guides normally feature 32 mainstream lines with 131 ships; there are perhaps another 30 or so lines operating, none of them large in size.
*Costa Cruises is a 50:50 joint venture between Carnival of the USA and Airtours (UK). Carnival, however, also owns 29% of the shares in Airtours.
†Seabourn is another 50:50 joint venture involving Carnival and a Norwegian entrepreneur. Carnival merged Cunard and Seabourn, its two prestige brands, in 1998.

**Table 3**

Selected passenger:crew ratios

| Ship | Passenger numbers | Crew numbers |
|---|---|---|
| Carnival Destiny | 2640 | 1070 |
| Veendam (Holland America) | 1627 | 571 |
| Wind Star (Carnival) | 168 | 91 |
| QE2 (Cunard/Carnival) | 1500 | 1015 |
| Sea Goddess (Cunard) | 116 | 89 |
| Costa Victoria | 2250 | 800 |
| Splendour of the Seas (RCCL) | 2440 | 760 |
| Oriana (P&O) | 1975 | 760 |
| Royal Princess | 1200 | 520 |
| Dawn Princess | 1950 | 900 |
| Grand Princess | 2600 | 1150 |
| Norwegian Majesty | 1509 | 500 |
| Celebrity Galaxy | 1870 | 909 |

it is relatively easy to put weight on! Meals throughout the typical day can be 'sit-down' or self-service, as people prefer, but in the evening most people will dine in the restaurant. Some evenings will be casual and informal; on other occasions passengers are required to dress more formally. Nobody should ever go hungry. All cruise liners have pools and exercise facilities of various forms, theatres, discos and shops. Bingo can be a popular way to gamble, but normally there is a casino with tables and slot machines. When the ship is sailing all day, a whole range of activities will be organized for the fit and the unfit or lazy. Shore activities will offer sightseeing, shopping and activity, the latter depending on location. White-water rafting can be offered in Alaska; snorkelling and scuba diving in the Caribbean, for example.

## Cruise staff

The cruise liner will be staffed by a mix of career officers supported by both long-service crew members and others who do not intend to stay for very long. In charge of the ship is the Captain. The other members of the key support team are the staff captain, the chief engineer, the purser and the cruise direc-

tor. The purser is responsible for all financial, immigration and on-shore tour issues, and may also be responsible for the 'hotel'; if not there will be a hotel manager who will manage the restaurants and kitchens. The cruise director controls the recreation and entertainment and recruits his or her own staff. These are critical roles because the passengers' *feel-good factor* is extremely dependent on the food and entertainment. Officers come from various parts of the world, but it is quite typical to have a mainly British team (say on P&O) or a mainly Italian team. Cruise directors are most likely to be American or British.

Basically the staff fit into clusters. Some run the ship as a form of transport. Some look after the hotel and catering aspects while others are there to entertain the passengers and look after their well-being. A fourth cluster provide retail and other services.

All staff work for a number of months, say four or six, and then have an extended break. Career staff will be paid during their leave; the others are not – although they will be flown home. Crew members on temporary contracts may or may not be invited back. Again they can come from almost anywhere in the world. Their basic wages are likely to be lower than the prevailing American rates for on-shore work, but for many they are extremely high compared with wages in their home countries. Some cruise lines pay more than others and treat their staff better. Many will manage to avoid paying income tax – and many also rely heavily on (undeclared) tips from passengers. On some lines, tipping is (in theory, at least) forbidden; on others it is positively encouraged. It is also quite typical for high-ranking staff to tip lower-status crew members occasionally.

Training programmes attempt to ensure passenger service, as a large number of the crew actually meets passengers at some point on the voyage. This, however, is unlikely to be in passenger lounges and areas if they are not on-duty. Crew who work for concession holders (perhaps the photographers or retail staff) may have more freedom to mingle, but it remains a dismissible offence if a crew member is found in a passenger cabin (unless they are working in it, of course) or if a passenger is found in the crew member's quarters. Rules on drugs are also typically very tight.

The cruise lines have interesting arrangements with the countries that they visit. Staff passports are held by the purser throughout the period of the contract; the moment a contract is finished the crew member resorts to immigrant status.

Everyone works hard; there is really no escape from this. Staff will be on duty at some time during every day of a voyage; there are no days off as such, as there is little delay when one complement of passengers is disembarked to be replaced by another a few hours later. It would be unusual if a ship were ever empty overnight, except when it is laid off in dry-dock for cleaning and refitting. The exterior is often repainted and woodwork revarnished while the ship is at sea. The workload and pattern will vary between days at sea and days in port, when some staff are free of any duties and allowed onshore. Nevertheless, food is available somewhere on the ship 24 hours a day. The cabin staff typically work during the mornings (cleaning and tidying) and again in the evenings (tidying the rooms again while passengers have their evening meals. They have a break during the afternoons.

Staff all receive free accommodation and meals. Many will be required to share cabins, and these will typically be those that would be least popular with passengers – inside with no windows or down in the bowels of the ship. Although allocated berths, staff will inevitably make informal arrangements and move around. Depending on the line, their food may or may not be the passenger menu. On the face of it, the high-quality passenger menu might seem like a bonus – but the same menus run week after week after week! A selected number of the officers is expected to eat in the passenger dining rooms, at least once during the voyage. The actual number of times is likely to depend on the passengers with whom they end up sitting!

## On-board services and revenues

Although transport to and from the cruise liner, together with all accommodation and food, is pro-

vided in the holiday price, on many lines passengers also have to pay separately for drinks, hairdressing and beauty services and shore excursions. In addition, the retail shops, on-board photography and the casino are money-earners. These constitute between 20 and 30% of the revenues of the cruise line. Many of the services will be provided by the cruise line itself, but some may be concessions. On Royal Caribbean, for example, photography is a concession but they run their own shops. On Carnival, the reverse is the case. The casino is invariably a concession. In such cases the concession holder employs and deploys the staff in return for a fee; their people are provided with food and accommodation on-board by arrangement.

## A profile of a new superliner

When *Sun Princess* was launched in 1995 she was the largest cruise ship ever built. 856 feet long and 83 feet wide (261 by 25 metres), she will sail comfortably through the Panama Canal. A crew of 900 serves 1950 passengers. She was joined in 1997 by her sister ship, *Dawn Princess*, and two more sisters, *Ocean Princess* and *Sea Princess*, in 1999. But she is dwarfed by *Grand Princess* which joined the fleet in 1998. At 935 feet long and 118 feet wide (285 by 36 metres) she is bigger than three football pitches. Her crew of 1150 serves 2600 passengers. She is the first Princess ship not able to pass through the Panama Canal. The appended illustration (Appendix 3) highlights her main features.

Some 70% of her 710 outside cabins have verandas, giving her the largest number of private balconies on any cruise ship. In general, the cabins are spacious. There are three show-lounges and three dining rooms, supported by nine other food venues, including a pizzeria and 24 hour bistro. There are five swimming pools and some lifts are glass walled. The golf club boasts a putting green and full-scale simulator; and another unusual feature is a virtual-reality arcade. *Grand Princess* also provides 'Grand Class Gold' butler service in its suites and minisuites. This has normally only been available on the most expensive luxury liners. Quite typically, money has not been spared on the interior decorations – paintings, sculptures, tiles and glass work and furnishings.

*Grand Princess* sails the Caribbean from October to May. The weekly cruises go from and to Port Lauderdale (north of Miami) and call at St. Thomas (the US Virgin Island renowned for duty-free shopping), St. Maarten and Princess Cays (a private beach ideal for water-sports in the Bahamas). Three days are spent at sea and three on-shore.

Her summer months offer cruises from Barcelona to Istanbul and from Istanbul to Barcelona. There are nine port days and two full days at sea but, because of flights the actual holiday period is some 13 days. The ports of call take passengers to Monte Carlo, Florence, Pompeii, Venice, Athens and Ephesus.

Interestingly, 40% of UK cruise holidays last for between five and seven days and 43% last for eight to 14 days. For Americans, 36% last for just two to five days, 53% for five to seven days and 11% between eight and 14 days.

## The leading competitors

This section describes and compares the four leading cruise groups identified in Table 2 earlier. These profiles could be used to try and identify which lines are best placed to exploit the predicted growth in the market. In addition to the lines considered, there is a number of important and successful niche operators. Crystal and Silversea Cruises, for instance, and like Cunard and Seabourn, offer exceptionally high-quality, luxurious cruises on smaller ships for those passengers willing to pay a premium price. Other lines specialize in river cruises on, say, the Mississippi, the Nile or the Rhine. Windstar and Clipper offer cruises on distinctive (and still luxurious) sailing yachts.

Generally, Celebrity, Holland America, Princess and Costa are acknowledged as premium cruise lines, with Carnival, Norwegian and Royal Caribbean 'contemporary' and not quite as up-market.

Carnival (as an organization, and including all associated lines) has the lowest cost structure and strongest balance sheet in the industry. Its net income (profit before interest and tax) in 1997 was $666 million from a turnover of $2.5 billion. P&O/Princess showed corresponding figures of $280 million and $1.65 billion. Royal Caribbean lagged behind with $175 million income from revenues of $1.9 billion. The cruise lines, not unexpectedly, enjoy tax and regulation concessions from being registered in places such as Panama and Liberia, but the downside of this is that their ships cannot sail from one American port to another without first calling into an international port.

### Carnival

Carnival provides casual, contemporary, mass-market fun ships. They are generally perceived to offer exceptionally good value for money in the lower price ranges, and they are very strong on entertainment and recreation – Las Vegas on the water. The average age of passengers is early 40s; 70% are first-time cruisers. Carnival is seen as ideal for couples and for families with children, rather than, say, singles or groups.

Carnival was started in 1972 by Ted Arison, then a cruise holiday executive based in Florida, who joined forces with a Boston-based travel company to acquire the Empress of Canada, which had run aground off Miami. Carnival lost money for the first three years, but has since grown to become the world leader, and run by second-generation Micky Arison. Carnival became a public company in 1987.

The *Empress of Canada* was renamed the *Mardi Gras* and, after the early period of disappointment, the idea of 'the fun ship' was conceived. Arison's declared aim was to 'take the stuffiness out of cruising and abandon the elitist image on which classic ocean liners had thrived'. He targeted 'middle America', who had previously 'never dreamed of a holiday at sea'. His new and innovative marketing strategy implied making the ship itself the most important element in the holiday experience – with casinos, gymnasiums, cocktail lounges, bingo, Las Vegas-style shows, etc., as well as all the food people could eat. 'We took an approach of positioning ourselves in the vacation business, not just the cruise business.'

The 1970s and 1980s saw the addition of new ships and new itineraries, focusing increasingly on families but maintaining an emphasis on the Caribbean. When the 101,000 ton *Carnival Destiny* was launched in 1996, she was the largest cruise ship in the world, accommodating 2640 passengers. She was also the first liner to be too wide for the Panama Canal.

Carnival deliberately sets its prices below those of its main competitors, but enjoys scale economies which enable it not to sacrifice high levels of service. The emphasis remains on three, four and seven day cruises – the alternate and different three and four day cruises can be doubled up into a seven day cruise as well – from San Juan and Florida, and these run throughout the year. There were 11 ships in the fleet at the end of 1997, with two more in 1998 and a further one in 1999. Of these 14, ten can take over 2000 passengers.

In 1989 Carnival acquired the more up-market Holland America and Windstar Lines and formed the Seabourn joint venture. Carnival's partial ownership of Airtours (1996), its half ownership of Costa Cruises (1997) and the acquisition of Cunard (1998) have made it a dominant force in world cruising. The lines are run as separate businesses with different images, customers and target markets.

## Holland America

Holland America has eight cruise liners, with two more launched in 1999. The emphasis is on superliners and cruises for more mature travellers who value consistency, quality and high standards of service. It is positioned more up-market than Carnival; its passengers average mid-50s in age during the winter, but are younger in summer. Around half the total are holidaying with a tour group of some sort. While the passenger profiles might be different, Holland America and Princess tend to concentrate on similar itineraries and ports of call. It is typical for a white Princess liner to be moored alongside a navy Holland America ship in a port.

Originally a classic steamship company, Holland America was another pioneer of the modern cruise holiday, acquiring Windstar before being acquired itself by Carnival. Windstar offers cruises for younger professionals in four de-luxe sailing yachts. Holland America had also bought Westours, the Seattle-based travel company which pioneered land-based tours to Alaska. A recent joint venture with Tauck Tours has linked trips through inland Alaska with those to the Canadian Rockies to supplement a cruise along the Alaskan coast.

Holland America has always been kept separate from its parent but provided with the investment capital it has needed to expand its fleet.

## Cunard

This old-established English line was acquired by the diversified conglomerate Trafalgar House in 1971. Trafalgar slimmed the fleet in the 25 years it owned the line and then was acquired itself by the Scandinavian company Kvaerner which, as a shipbuilder, had only a passing interest in operating a cruise line.

In 1998, Carnival acquired a business with an up-market profile, a reputation for service and outstanding itineraries, but just five ships. The flagship is the *QE2*, last in a long line of famous Queens. She had been launched in the late 1960s as the epitome of style and elegance and refitted in 1987 to make her one of the most luxurious ships afloat. A more recent refit in Germany brought adverse publicity when she had to leave the yard with the work unfinished and the workmen still on board. *QE2* takes 1500 passengers and operates a form of class separation by linking cabin grades and restaurants. Five-day trans-Atlantic crossings are a speciality, linked for many with a return flight on Concorde. In addition, the *QE2* sails round the world every year, a voyage lasting for some three months. Passengers can sail for the whole or just part of these world cruises. The other Cunard ships are the *Royal Viking Sun* and *Vistafjord*, both 740 passengers, and *Sea Goddess I* and *Sea Goddess II*, both just 116 passengers.

These five liners have joined forces with *Seabourn's* three ultra-luxurious, 204 passenger ships, whose service is reputed to be among the best afloat and which roam the world with a wide variety of itineraries.

## Costa Cruises

Together with the UK travel company Airtours, Carnival owns Costa, a maritime company which has been based in Genoa for over 100 years and which has been providing cruise holidays in the Mediterranean for 40 years. In the 1980s Costa adopted the phrase 'cruising Italian style' but, although the staff are predominantly Italian, the appeal is broadly European for the mass market. In the winter Costa ships sail in the Caribbean with some 80% American passengers and an average age of 45 plus. In the summer, in the Mediterranean, 80% of the passengers come from Italy, France and Spain. The cruises typically exceed seven days, and consequently the passengers tend to be reasonably affluent.

## Airtours

Airtours is number two to Thomson Holidays in the UK for air-inclusive travel packages. It operates its own airline and the Going Places travel-agency chain. In April 1994 Airtours bought its first ship, a 800 passenger liner which it refitted and renamed *Seawing*. This ship sailed at full capacity throughout 1995, selling its capacity very quickly. She was soon joined by the 1962 passenger *Carousel*, which had been previously named *Nordic Prince* and operated by Royal Caribbean. Airtours later added *Sundream*, which carries over 1000 passengers. All of these are classed as three-star, whereas most of the major ships are four- or five-star. A four-star ship is planned. Airtours' aim has always been to offer cruises which their typical package holidaymaker can afford.

The initial strategy was short breaks in the Mediterranean with a strong family focus at affordable prices, and often linked to a resort stopover. Throughout the summer all three ships provide seven day cruises in the Mediterranean (from a Mediterranean base port), and offer alternate weeklong routes, allowing people to enjoy 14 nights and different ports if they so choose. In the winter *Seawing* offers alternate three and four day cruises in and around the Canaries on a similar basis; the others sail the Caribbean.

Its main travel company rival, Thomson, operates on a smaller scale with just one 660-berth ship which it charters and sails on five different Mediterranean routes in the summer.

## Royal Caribbean Cruise Line

RCCL provides the 'big ship experience' and is extremely popular with active, fun-seeking couples and families. Some 90% are American with an average age of early 40s. Although it offers destinations around the world, its speciality is year-round Caribbean cruising. RCCL was formed in 1969 when three Norwegian shipping companies merged. Admiral Line, which specialized in short cruise holiday breaks, joined the group in 1995; and in 1997, RCCL merged with Celebrity, which Carnival had been eying. Recently, RCCL has been enjoying very high occupancy rates.

When RCCL launched the *Sovereign of the Seas* in 1988, she was the largest cruise ship then afloat. Reports say that land traffic ground to a halt when she first arrived in her home port of Miami. When *Legend of the Seas* joined in 1995 she was the first ship to boast an 18-hole miniature golf course.

RCCL currently has 13 ships, of which nine carry over 1800 passengers and five are classed as megaliners. The company's shares are traded publicly on the New York Stock Exchange but the original founders remain the majority shareholders. These families also have a controlling interest in Hyatt Hotels. It is quite normal for passengers to add on extra days at the ports of embarkation and disembarkation.

## Celebrity Cruises

Celebrity's reputation is built around good value for money in the mid-price categories. Cruises on Celebrity's five superliners are moderately priced, but there is still an emphasis on quality for a relatively affluent clientele. Some two-thirds of the cruises sail from the east coast, with trips between New York and Bermuda a speciality. Typically, the ships sail from Florida into the Caribbean for seven days; they all offer a wide range of entertainment and are designed without the popular but space-consuming atriums. Michel Roux acts as a consultant to Celebrity's chefs.

Celebrity is a young cruise line; it was started in 1989 by the owners of Chandris Cruises (long-established in the budget cruise industry) to 'provide deluxe cruises for experienced travellers at affordable prices'. Some industry experts were sceptical of this strategy, but it has worked.

The *Celebrity Galaxy* was the subject of a regular documentary programme on BBC Television in 1998, a series which generated considerable publicity for the ship and some of its crew. A factual programme such as this will entice some people to try a cruise holiday while putting others off.

## Norwegian Cruise Line

The 'line for everyman', Norwegian provides highly acclaimed entertainment and (especially) sports facilities. Originally Norwegian Caribbean Line, and begun in 1966, Norwegian was the first line to offer mass-market cruising. There are currently nine ships including one megaliner. Over the years the company's fortunes have risen and fallen and, consequently it has been overtaken by its rivals in the industry. There have been no new ships since 1993, but some existing ones have been refitted and stretched to create additional berths. However, six new ships are on order, two each due in 1999, 2000 and 2001.

## P&O Cruises

P&O is a leading operator of high-quality cruises, designed for and marketed to the UK market; it operates alongside, but separate from, Princess in the P&O Group. P&O stands for the Peninsular and Oriental Steam Navigation Company, which was founded in 1737 to provide, essentially, mail services which linked England with India, China and Australia – the eastern routes which pre-dated the Panama Canal. The current P&O flag is blue, white, red and gold – the Royal colours of Portugal (blue and white) and Spain (red and gold) which the company has been allowed to use in recognition of its 'support for legitimate causes' in the civil wars of the 1830s. The *Canberra*, a cruise-ship leg-

end for 36 years until it was retired and scrapped in 1997, also enjoyed active service in the Falklands War.

P&O's first passenger cruise was one from Southampton to Constantinople (now Istanbul) in 1844; it lasted for six weeks. The real expansion came after World War II when new routes were opened in America and the Pacific. P&O merged with Orient Lines in 1960, but this name was abolished, and now an American cruise line operates with this brand. Cruising (both the P&O and Princess brands) provides some 15% of P&O's total revenue and 30% of the operating profit. Before recent corporate changes, the other businesses were ferries (P&O merged with Stena in 1998), container ships (the largest revenue contributor), bulk shipping, property and construction (Bovis). P&O also manages Earls Court and Olympia, which are both used for exhibitions and major events.

P&O has just three ships: *Oriana*, which carries 1800 passengers, and which is due to be joined by a new sister ship in the year 2000; the 1470-passenger *Arcadia*; and the 714 passenger *Victoria*. *Arcadia* was transferred (after a refit) from Princess Cruises – she had previously been the *Star Princess* – to replace the slightly larger *Canberra*. *Victoria* is a compact and informal ship; her suites are smaller than the designated mini-suites on *Arcadia*, for example. For the three-month period December 1999 to February 2000 she was leased to Union Castle Lines, which will re-badge her for special millennium cruises.

There is a strongly European flavour to the cruise programme, with many starting in Southampton. There is a substantial proportion of the market which prefers not to fly before joining the cruise; this option is also ideal for organized groups which can travel by coach at the beginning and end of their holiday. Because of P&O's colonial origins, world cruises remain popular, and both *Arcadia* and *Oriana* sail round the world each year between January and March. In a typical year, P&O carries 75,000 short-break passengers and 9000 on its round-the-world voyages. The programme is normally along the following lines:

|  | *Arcadia* | *Oriana* | *Victoria* |
|---|---|---|---|
| January–March | Round-the-World | | Caribbean |
| April–October | Europe | Europe | Europe |
| November– | | | |
| December | Europe | Caribbean | Caribbean |

Some P&O advertising features exotic locations but with the important qualification: 'Everywhere you go you'll find England in the little things'. The ships have British officers, feature British cooking, present British television and radio programmes, and 'run their activities with precise timing'. 'Many of the passengers do not like change, so not much has changed aboard the line's ships in many years'. It is a carefully designed product for an identified and discerning segment and it works. Regular passengers are members of the POSH club, for which there is an annual subscription and various discount and other entitlements.

An example of a P&O advertisement is appended (Appendix 4), together with a typical one for Princess, which adopts a quite different style and approach and provides far more detail about the cruise itself.

P&O in London also operate the Swan Hellenic Line, which has just one small ship, the *Minerva* which specializes in cruises for people interested in archaeology and culture. P&O Australia has one cruise ship, *Fair Princess*, which sails in the South Pacific.

## Princess

In 1997 some 450,000 passengers sailed with Princess, many of them attracted by its reputation for shore excursions. The line is 'moderately up-market' and describes its all-white ships as 'Love Boats'.

Princess began as an independent company in 1965, with just one ship sailing to Mexico and Alaska from Los Angeles. A casual and relaxed atmosphere was a feature from the very beginning. Princess acquired more ships, including the *Island Venture*, before P&O bought the line in 1974. The *Island Princess* was the *Venture's* new name; and in 1975 her sister ship *Pacific Princess* was added. Carrying 640 passengers each, they still remain as the two 'baby' ships of the fleet. *Pacific Princess* became the 'Love Boat' when an American television producer raised the finances to make a series based on a cruise ship. The ship was distinctively white and different passenger characters (and their stories) were featured every week. For nine consecutive years the programme received high ratings in America; overall it has been translated into 29 languages and exported to 93 countries. The distinctive Princess seawitch logo has remained synonymous with cruising ever since. The programme had an incalculable impact on modern cruising for Americans, dispelling the elitist image and opening up new markets.

When the *Royal Princess* was christened by Diana, Princess of Wales, in 1994 she was described as the 'most stylish and elegant ship of her day'. She remains British in character with British officers – Princess normally uses Italian offices.

Princess acquired Sitmar cruises, an Italian cruise line, in 1988, and thereby added three more ships. *Star Princess* is now *Arcadia* but *Crown* and *Regal Princess* remain. These two Italian ships have a very distinctive dolphin-inspired shape and interior design; their cabins and public areas are relatively spacious and the ships carry fewer passengers than others of a similar size. Critics say that they are more like hotels than ships. The outcome is an unusual fleet of quite different ships, many of which have passengers loyal to the ship rather than the cruise line – as was the case with *Canberra*. This is being remedied to a degree. *Dawn, Sun, Ocean* and *Sea Princesses* are all sisters; and sisters are planned for *Grand Princess*. The full fleet is summarized in Table 4, while Table 5 summarizes their annual schedules.

Princess attracts experienced cruisers, and in 1997 the average age fell below 50 for the first time. The New England coastal voyages from New York to Montreal, an annual and extremely popular feature of *Royal Princess'* schedule in September and October, for example, attract older passengers. The Caribbean passengers generally tend to be younger. Princess has an established link with PADI (the Professional Association of Diving Instructors)

**Table 4**

The Princess fleet

| Ship | Launch date | Passengers |
|------|-------------|------------|
| Crown Princess | 1990 | 1590 |
| Dawn Princess | 1997 | 1950 |
| Grand Princess | 1998 | 2600 |
| Island Princess | 1971 | 640 |
| Pacific Princess | 1972 | 640 |
| Regal Princess | 1991 | 1590 |
| Royal Princess | 1984 | 1200 |
| Sky Princess | 1984 | 1200 |
| Sun Princess | 1995 | 1950 |
| | | |
| (on order) | | |
| Ocean Princess | 1999 | 1950 |
| Sea Princess | 1999 | 1950 |
| xxxx Princess | 2001 | 2600 |
| xxxx Princess | 2001 | 2600 |

The older ships are typically refitted every six to eight years.

which allows passengers the opportunity to become fully certified divers while on a cruise.

With six ships on regular summer duty in Alaska and seven sailing through the Panama Canal, Princess is a major player in these two key destinations. To support one of the most extensive shore excursion packages available anywhere, Princess has invested in developing a holiday infrastructure in Alaska. Table 6 shows the percentage growth of passengers to these destinations from 1987 to 1997. The new, larger megaliners should boost its share of the key Caribbean market in the future.

Princess' loyalty club is called the Captain's Circle. Membership is free, and there are a number of concessions and members' only cruises. Passengers automatically join after their first cruise. After two they become First Officers; after four, Captains; and after nine, Commodores. They are given distinctive pins if they are minded to wear them. An all-ship occupancy rate of 98.4% in 1997 was a slight reduction on the 1996 figure.

Princess advertises and promotes its cruises widely. Expensive and glossy brochures are supported by extensive media advertising. Princess Cruises is run from Los Angeles, with a second office in Seattle for the Alaskan holidays. There is also an office in London, but the main market is America. American holidaymakers join most of the cruises with domestic flights; UK passengers with international ones. To a great extent, the package is the same. But there is certainly one key difference. Americans can cancel without penalty up to 60 days before the ship sails; British passengers would normally lose their deposit

**Table 5**

The Princess fleet schedule

| Ship | January/March | April/September | October/December |
|------|---------------|-----------------|------------------|
| Island | Far East | Mediterranean & Baltic | Holy Land |
| Pacific | Africa | Mediterranean & Baltic | Holy Land |
| Sky | Australasia/ South Pacific | Alaska | Far East |
| Royal | South America | Mediterranean & Baltic New England | New England South America |
| Crown | Mexico | Alaska | South Pacific |
| Regal | Caribbean/Panama Canal | Alaska | Caribbean |
| Sun & Dawn | Caribbean/Panama Canal | Alaska | Caribbean/Panama Canal |
| Grand | Caribbean | Mediterranean | Caribbean |

Where required, there are additional one-off trans-Atlantic and Panama Canal repositioning cruises.

**Table 6**

Percentage changes in cruise passengers to Alaska and the Panama Canal (1987–1997)

| Year | US passengers | UK passengers |
| --- | --- | --- |
| Alaska: | | |
| 1989 from 1987 | (7) | NA |
| 1991 from 1989 | 23 | NA |
| 1993 from 1991 | 14 | NA |
| 1995 from 1993 | 34 | NA |
| 1996 from 1995 | NA | 19 |
| 1997 from 1995 | 20 | NA |
| 1997 from 1996 | NA | (28) |
| 1998 from 1997 (projected) | | 16 |
| | | |
| Panama Canal: | | |
| 1989 from 1987 | 1 | |
| 1991 from 1989 | 11 | |
| 1993 from 1991 | 50 | 62 |
| 1995 from 1993 | 40 | (28) |
| 1996 from 1995 | NA | 6 |
| 1997 from 1995 | 1 | |

NA: not applicable.

unless covered by insurance. Prices are competitive and reflect seasonal variations; there are special discounts for early bookings. These can be reinforced by travel agents' cruise discounts. Most reservations come via travel agents, but some cruise wholesalers buy blocks of non-returnable tickets at special prices to sell independently, often via teletext or the Internet. There are some late-booking 'distress prices' available but people may not be able to obtain their preferred cruise or cabin if they wait in anticipation.

Some 40% of UK passengers book at least six-months ahead, with 75% booking three months ahead. The American pattern is similar.

Some cruise lines feature special event cruises as part of their itineraries. Wine tasting, music of a particular style (say big band or country) and eclipses of the sun are typical.

The last sections of the case now examine (briefly) cruising through the Panama Canal and (more extensively) up and down the Alaskan coast. The development here of a holiday infrastructure by Princess, in particular, and Holland America has been critical for supporting growth. The cruise experience has to be enhanced with carefully selected itineraries and shore excursions.

## Cruises through the Panama Canal

For some passengers, a trip through the Panama Canal is a 'must', more for the experience than the scenery. The Canal is 50 miles long and runs from the north-west to the south-east across the state of Panama to link the Atlantic (Caribbean) and Pacific oceans, and shave a mere 7873 miles (12,670 km) off the journey! Unlike the other major transit canal, the Suez, there are locks at both ends. They are all double locks, handling two large ships side by side separately. In three stages (three locks) a ship is raised 84 feet (26 metres) and then lowered the same amount at the other end. In between is a large lake, Gatun Lake, fed naturally by rivers in one of the wettest places on earth, and the Gaillard Cut, which slices through a steep tropical forest. Some cruise liners go up the locks at Gatun (the Caribbean end) and then turn round in Gatun Lake before returning to the Caribbean.

Ships are held firm in the locks by towing locomotives, known as mules, which each weigh 56 tonnes and cost several million dollars. Rather than actually tow the ships, with lines on either side the mules simply hold them straight. It takes approximately eight hours for a ship to complete its transit.

The first survey of Panama was conducted as early as 1534, under instructions from Charles I of Spain, but it was the French (who also built the Suez Canal) who first began construction. Having worked for 20 years between 1880 and 1900 they abandoned their attempt at a huge cut, beaten by disease, finance and engineering problems. In 1903 Columbia granted independence to Panama, which quickly signed a treaty with America, granting the USA the right to build the canal and control its operations until the end of the twentieth century. The USA financed everything and paid Panama $10 million. Costing $387 million, the Panama Canal opened in 1914.

The locks are all 1000 feet long and 110 feet wide (305 by 36 metres). The largest passenger ship ever to sail through is the *QE2* at 963 feet long and 105 feet wide (294 by 32 metres). The longest ship ever through is 973 feet and the widest had a beam of 108 feet.

The *Sun* and *Dawn Princesses* are both 856 feet long and 83 feet wide, but the *Grand Princess* is too wide. The other Princess regulars, *Crown* and *Regal Princess*, are 811 feet long and 105 feet wide (247 by 32 metres). Based on size, the cost of a single transit for either of these ships was $164,000 in 1998. Cruises which include the Panama Canal are likely to start in Florida, San Juan or Acapulco, they are unlikely to be round trips and they will normally be for at least ten days. This makes them a relatively expensive cruise.

The Panama Canal is floodlit and operates 24 hours a day. It is permanently busy with shipping, and the Gaillard Cut is currently being widened to allow two large ships to be able to pass each other. At the moment, for wide vessels, a constraint of a single ship at any one time applies. For these reasons advance booking is essential. After all, a cruise liner operates to a timetable which demands that it enters and exits the Canal at a particular time or otherwise its whole programme is thrown out. There is little scope to make up much lost time. Transits are booked years ahead, not months or weeks ahead. This replicates the need for detailed planning for the whole voyage well before a season begins. Popular ports of call also tend to be very busy, with ships from several lines often in port on the same day. Some obtain the good or best berths; others have to anchor offshore and tender passengers in. Some berths, of course, are only suitable for smaller ships. Again, with embarkation and disembarkation ports such as Port Lauderdale, Miami, San Juan and Vancouver, several ships can be turning round on the same day. To maximize occupancy it is typical for a cruise ship to disembark its passengers during a morning and then set sail on the same evening with a whole new set of passengers. At this time, the ship tends to take on all the food it will require for the voyage.

## Alaska

While Alaska is an American state, it is not adjacent to any other state of the union: Canada separates Alaska from Washington State. The attraction, fundamentally, is the glaciers, which are more easily seen and appreciated from the sea – the Inside Passage – than from the land. Distances are long in Alaska and no road hugs the coastline. It is necessary to keep travelling inland and then returning to the coastal towns. In addition, the cruise ships now sail very close to the 500 foot (150 metre) high glaciers and the shore, allowing people on the higher decks to appreciate their mass – and also to hear the dramatic noises as large masses of ice break off and float away. Seaplane and helicopter tours from the various ports of call allow closer viewing and, for some, an opportunity to land and walk about. Consequently, Alaskan cruising saw a 140% growth during the 1990s.

Wildlife provides an added bonus. Whales swim south for the winter but return to Alaska for the summer months; different varieties, such as grey, killer and humpback whales, can often be seen quite close to the ships. Porpoises, sea otters and particularly sea lions are also clearly visible at times. Generally, the sea will be calm through most of the summer months; the ships rarely sail far from the coastline. The weather varies, but the bitter cold of winter gives way to comfortable temperatures. There can be rain; Ketchikan is the wettest place in North America.

The appended map (Appendix 5) shows where the cruise lines, in particular Princess and Holland America, have designed extensive programmes of pre- and post-cruise tours in Alaska and Canada to enhance the holiday experience. Inland Alaska, for example, includes Mt. McKinley, at 20,320 feet (6195 metres) the tallest mountain on the continent; the Canadian Rockies are also easily accessible for both coach and rail tours. Most Alaskan cruise holidays will begin with people being flown into either Seattle or Vancouver. From there they can easily be transported to Anchorage (to begin a southbound cruise), Calgary or Banff in Canada, or Fairbanks to begin a tour.

Alaska also has a history for the tour guides to exploit. One hundred years ago, the Gold Rush was in full swing; the first discovery had been made in 1861. Prospectors came up the coast to towns such as Skagway and Haines and then ventured inland, which was only possible at certain times of the year and on steep and dangerous trails, such as the legendary 33-mile (53-kilometre) Chilkoot trail into the Klondike. The nineteenth-century buildings still stand, largely unaltered, in some of the towns; and there are other remains, such as narrow gauge railways which cling to mountain sides.

The most popular add-on involves a trip between Anchorage and Fairbanks, in the heart of Alaska, where visitors can visit a gold mine and cruise down a river on a paddle steamer. Demonstrations of dog mushing highlight the relative inaccessibility of much of the country during the winter months. The journey from Anchorage to Fairbanks is by train. Princess owns eight Ultra Dome double-decker, high-visibility railcars for the 'Midnight Sun' route. Princess' coaches have the widest domed windows ever built for a rail car and provide panoramic views of the mountain scenery. The journey is broken in Denali National Park, where visitors are only allowed if they use park transport. Wildlife trips to spot moose, caribou, Dallsheep and grizzly bears are provided.

Princess has built two luxury lodges in Denali Park. Open for five months of the year, these lodges contain 440 rooms between them and employ 260 people. Visitors can extend their stays to make use of a wide range of organized sporting activities such as kayaking, salmon fishing and river rafting. Princess has a third lodge, on the Kenai Peninsular close to Seward, the port which serves Anchorage. This lodge is open for ten months a year and provides 77 jobs. Again it is designed to provide short breaks for those who enjoy the 'great outdoors'. The other areas of Alaska can be incorporated, including Prudhoe Bay, famous for two things: it is the base for the Alaskan oil industry, and one end of the Alaskan oil pipeline, which runs above the land to Valdez, east of Seward on the southern coast. To protect the tundra (permanently frozen ground) and not inhib-

it wildlife movement the pipeline is on raised mounts. It is also visible near Fairbanks.

Holland America also offers rail trips in panoramic coaches. Dedicated Princess and Holland America coaches are coupled together on the same train. Both companies own fleets of luxury coaches, Holland America also owning the Gray Line coach concession in Alaska. In addition, this leading rival owns the 15 Westmark hotels in Alaska.

Table 7 lists the ships offering Alaskan cruises in 1998. Princess has some 30% of the market. Cruises are offered for a minimum of 18 and a maximum of 20 weeks between May and September each year; there is capacity for some 30,000 passengers each week.

The main Princess ships are *Regal Princess*, which provides seven-day cruises from and to Vancouver, and *Crown*, *Dawn* and *Sun Princess*, which sail from Vancouver to Seward (seven days) and back again all through the summer. By staggering the changeover days, Princess can fully exploit its rail and lodge capacities. *Sky Princess* includes 11 day round trips from San Francisco in its itinerary.

The impact of the cruise industry on the Alaskan economy has clearly been significant. In 1995, Princess alone contributed an estimated $120 million. This is made up of supplies bought in, wages, and spending by passengers and ships' crews while on-shore. Jobs have been created; the capital investment in lodges, hotels and trains has opened up the market for other tourists, independent of the cruise industry. Princess, like the other cruise lines, recognizes the critical importance of waste management and environmental protection in Alaska and in other ports of call around the world. When several cruise lines disembark thousands of passengers every day in a small town on the isolated Alaskan coastline or a small island in the Caribbean, the potential for them to damage the environment and infrastructure clearly exists, but they introduce real relative wealth. They are invariably welcome visitors!

## Some final issues

New hull technology and innovations in propulsion

**Table 7**  Ships cruising the Alaskan coastline in 1998

| Line | Ship | Capacity | |
|---|---|---|---|
| Carnival | *Jubilee* | 1486 | |
| Celebrity | *Century* | 1740 | |
| | *Mercury* | 1870 | } 4984 |
| | *Zenith* | 1374 | |
| Clipper | *Yankee Clipper Yorktown* | 138 | |
| | *Yorktown* | 1214 | |
| Crystal | *Harmony* | 940 | |
| Holland America | *Maasdam* | 1266 | |
| | *Nieuw Amsterdam* | 1214 | |
| | *Noordam* | 1214 | |
| | *Ryndam* | 1266 | } 7720 |
| | *Statendam* | 1266 | |
| | *Westerdam* | 1494 | |
| Norwegian | *Norwegian Wind* | 1758 | } 2510 |
| | *Norwegian Dynasty* | 752 | |
| Princess | *Crown Princess* | 1590 | |
| | *Dawn Princess* | 1950 | |
| | *Island Princess* | 640 | |
| | *Regal Princess* | 1590 | } 8920 |
| | *Sky Princess* | 1200 | |
| | *Sun Princess* | 1950 | |
| Royal Caribbean | *Legend of the Seas* | 1808 | } 3808 |
| | *Rhapsody of the Seas* | 2000 | |

systems are allowing the newest ships to travel more rapidly through the water without any additional passenger discomfort. Not only does this offer potential cost reductions, it means that the balance between time at sea and time in port is changed. Cruise durations could be shortened; the potential for earning more revenue from passengers could be increased.

But are there any constraints to the growth possibilities?

The large, new, modern ships are clearly popular with passengers, and arguably essential to drive future growth in the industry. The largest ones are too large not only for the Panama Canal, but also for many ports. Across the Caribbean, piers are being extended to accommodate them. Other destinations around the world, anxious to attract the cruise liners and the revenue that they bring, will need to invest in infrastructures. Moreover, as cruising becomes more popular, the congestion at the most popular ports of call must increase. Some destinations can only cope with a certain number of people in any one day; after all, the cruise boats all want to disernbark people early in the morning and have everyone back on board for an evening sail. Similarly, the roads can become very congested as people travel around. Bermuda, where visitors cannot hire cars, is transformed around Easter when the cruise ships start coming from New York, and it stays very busy all through the summer as each ship tends to stay for three days or so and provide what amounts to floating hotel accommodation.

Because major US shipyards are subsidized if they produce vessels for the military, only four shipyards, all of them in Europe, are experienced in building luxury cruise liners. The largest is Fincantieri at Monfalcone in Italy, which is contracted to build for Carnival, Princess and Disney. Kvaerner Masa-Yards (Turku, Finland) is building the new and very large Royal Caribbean ships; Chantiers de l'Atlantique (St. Nazaire, France) is committed to Celebrity. The other is Meyer Werft at Papenburg in Germany. The capacity of all four is fully booked for the next three years. One might wonder why no British yards build these ships.

One final question: where is the next area of the world to benefit from an infusion of cruise passengers? Cuba is talked about, but there is an American embargo. The Indian Ocean is by-and-large undeveloped. Greece and her islands must be a possibility: until recently, only Greek-registered vessels have been allowed to offer round trips in Greek waters. There are cruises around the South American coast, but the seas can be very inhospitable at certain times of the year. Australia and New Zealand are relatively unexploited, but the long flights to and from the ship can be a major deterrent.

## Additional references

Egger, BD and Smith, JR (1998)
*Cruise Lines: Cruisin' into the 21st Century*
(An equity research report), Donaldson, Lufkin and Jenrette.

Farley, RM and Davis, EQ (1998)
*Size Does Matter: An Investment Overview of the Cruise Industry*, BT Alex Brown (September).

See also the websites of the major cruise lines.

## Appendices

Appendix 1.  Activity at the leading ports of embarkation and disembarkation (1998)
Appendix 2.  Profiles of US cruise passengers

Reproduced with permission from publications of the Cruise Lines Industry Association, New York.

Appendix 3.  Grand Princess
Appendix 4.  Examples of advertisements for P&O and Princess Cruises
Appendix 5.  A cruise map of Alaska

Reproduced with permission from publications of P&O and Princess Cruises.

*P&O Group*    http://www. p-and-o.com
*Princess Cruises*
http//www. poprincesscruises.com

## Questions

1. What are the key strategic issues involved in the international passenger cruise industry?

2. How competitive is the passenger cruise industry? What opportunities are there for creating and sustaining competitive advantage?

3. What are the competitive strategies of P&O and Princess and how successful/well placed are they?

4. What do you think are the key human resource issues – given that this is a distinctive people-driven service business?

5. What do you feel that P&O Group's future strategy for the two cruise lines (brands) should be?

Appendix 1    1998 CLIA destination analysis summary report – all cruises

| Port of embarkation | Number of cruises | Berths available | Days in market | Total bed-days | Average per diem | Total market potential | % of total berths available |
|---|---|---|---|---|---|---|---|
| Acapulco | 43 | 62,612 | 443 | 641,604 | 334 | 214,551,324 | 0.96% |
| Amsterdam | 29 | 14,851 | 307 | 166,866 | 375 | 62,568,790 | 0.23% |
| Anchorage | 5 | 4750 | 50 | 47,500 | 453 | 21,517,500 | 0.07% |
| Athens (Piraeus) | 329 | 170,860 | 2155 | 1,077,017 | 335 | 360,359,379 | 2.63% |
| Auckland | 12 | 8489 | 155 | 107,777 | 503 | 54,200,480 | 0.13% |
| Bali | 7 | 1248 | 72 | 12,752 | 607 | 7,735,672 | 0.02% |
| Bangkok | 17 | 4816 | 146 | 57,440 | 371 | 21,283,936 | 0.07% |
| Barbados | 43 | 10,424 | 340 | 90,520 | 479 | 43,389,024 | 0.16% |
| Barcelona | 93 | 104,699 | 742 | 929,549 | 360 | 334,666,846 | 1.61% |
| Bombay | 9 | 3269 | 131 | 50,449 | 429 | 21,659,817 | 0.05% |
| Boston | 60 | 65,072 | 437 | 482,896 | 294 | 141,841,296 | 1.00% |
| Buenos Aires | 21 | 16,010 | 280 | 225,792 | 418 | 94,277,540 | 0.25% |
| Cairns | 5 | 1764 | 64 | 23,536 | 651 | 15,328,028 | 0.03% |
| Cannes | 17 | 3402 | 119 | 23,814 | 320 | 7,619,150 | 0.05% |
| Charleston, SC | 5 | 510 | 35 | 3570 | 387 | 1,381,590 | 0.01% |
| Civitavecchia (Rome) | 78 | 43,687 | 737 | 512,813 | 395 | 202,594,563 | 0.67% |
| Copenhagen | 46 | 23,626 | 452 | 235,174 | 483 | 113,476,626 | 0.36% |
| Genoa | 108 | 106,516 | 952 | 905,934 | 254 | 229,749,090 | 1.64% |
| Hamburg | 16 | 1792 | 112 | 12,544 | 259 | 3,248,896 | 0.03% |
| Hong Kong | 10 | 7159 | 133 | 99,583 | 464 | 46,162,052 | 0.11% |
| Honolulu | 68 | 66,940 | 540 | 554,228 | 318 | 176,463,926 | 1.03% |
| Istanbul | 96 | 43,898 | 897 | 453,284 | 433 | 196,265,686 | 0.68% |
| Lisbon | 32 | 11,377 | 405 | 137,794 | 527 | 72,598,522 | 0.17% |
| London | 52 | 60,778 | 643 | 746,752 | 418 | 312,317,504 | 0.93% |
| Los Angeles | 305 | 502,520 | 1721 | 2,716,462 | 236 | 639,955,239 | 7.73% |
| Manaus | 5 | 2766 | 73 | 38,756 | 411 | 15,913,688 | 0.04% |
| Miami | 752 | 1,392,744 | 4348 | 8,047,488 | 239 | 1,923,191,816 | 21.42% |
| Mombasa | 6 | 3034 | 99 | 45,746 | 500 | 22,855,470 | 0.05% |

Appendix 1   1998 CLIA destination analysis summary report – all cruises

| Port of embarkation | Number of cruises | Berths available | Days in market | Total bed-days | Average per diem | Total market potential | % of total berths available |
|---|---|---|---|---|---|---|---|
| Monte Carlo | 31 | 9244 | 270 | 94,952 | 564 | 53,507,680 | 0.14% |
| Montreal | 5 | 4080 | 50 | 40,800 | 470 | 19,167,920 | 0.06% |
| New Orleans | 107 | 78,489 | 774 | 554,987 | 202 | 112,331,014 | 1.21% |
| New York | 151 | 177,200 | 1141 | 1,398,326 | 347 | 485,042,192 | 2.72% |
| Nice | 27 | 7716 | 203 | 57,364 | 666 | 38,180,616 | 0.12% |
| Osaka | 1 | 1214 | 14 | 16,996 | 374 | 6,356,504 | 0.02% |
| Papeete | 48 | 10,194 | 360 | 87,856 | 763 | 67,026,920 | 0.16% |
| Port Canaveral | 310 | 699,546 | 1127 | 2,593,416 | 239 | 620,836,472 | 10.76% |
| Port Everglades/Ft. Laud. | 341 | 513,600 | 2916 | 4,185,940 | 307 | 1,286,069,712 | 7.90% |
| Quebec | 6 | 578 | 71 | 6834 | 218 | 1,486,650 | 0.01% |
| Rio De Janeiro | 18 | 13,480 | 236 | 183,318 | 273 | 50,095,232 | 0.21% |
| San Diego | 9 | 15,686 | 100 | 174,754 | 258 | 45,106,204 | 0.24% |
| San Francisco | 5 | 5018 | 219 | 177,840 | 499 | 88,703,650 | 0.08% |
| San Juan | 473 | 751,822 | 3213 | 5,136,910 | 250 | 1,282,731,742 | 11.56% |
| Seward | 75 | 106,768 | 543 | 757,528 | 394 | 298,182,452 | 1.64% |
| Singapore | 31 | 9709 | 356 | 125,247 | 515 | 64,554,267 | 0.15% |
| Southampton | 18 | 32,350 | 140 | 255,200 | 505 | 128,949,600 | 0.50% |
| St. Thomas | 44 | 5608 | 316 | 40,288 | 510 | 20,560,076 | 0.09% |
| Stockholm | 13 | 2210 | 108 | 19,384 | 554 | 10,737,476 | 0.03% |
| Sydney | 10 | 9259 | 143 | 132,979 | 450 | 59,780,629 | 0.14% |
| Tampa | 131 | 127,518 | 809 | 786,090 | 221 | 173,339,037 | 1.96% |
| Tokyo | 1 | 184 | 15 | 2760 | 568 | 1,567,680 | 0.00% |
| Vancouver | 296 | 446,312 | 2176 | 3,243,918 | 399 | 1,294,509,720 | 6.86% |
| Venice | 117 | 126,540 | 908 | 945,842 | 343 | 324,289,226 | 1.95% |
| X – Misc. Asian Port | 14 | 6892 | 165 | 92,910 | 526 | 48,880,856 | 0.11% |
| X – Misc.Caribbean Port | 201 | 136,664 | 1490 | 973,228 | 223 | 217,405,526 | 2.10% |
| X – Misc. European Port | 609 | 257,434 | 6489 | 2,892,463 | 204 | 590,830,337 | 3.96% |
| X – Misc. Mediterranean Port | 26 | 4260 | 180 | 29,588 | 392 | 11,606,828 | 0.07% |

Appendix 1   1998 CLIA destination analysis summary report – all cruises

| Port of embarkation | Number of cruises | Berths available | Days in market | Total bed-days | Average per diem | Total market potential | % of total berths available |
|---|---|---|---|---|---|---|---|
| X – Misc. Mexican Port | 6 | 5704 | 55 | 62,574 | 261 | 16,347,210 | 0.09% |
| X – Misc. Port | 154 | 64,245 | 1599 | 613,992 | 459 | 281,644,862 | 0.99% |
| X – Misc. US Port | 301 | 134,202 | 2204 | 914,404 | 291 | 266,120,968 | 2.06% |
| Grand total | 5848 | 6,503,339 | 44,978 | 45,046,328 | 296 | 13,323,122,708 | |

Appendix 2    Profile of cruise prospect segments

| | Family folks | Want-it-alls | Adventurers | Comfortable spenders | Cautious travellers |
|---|---|---|---|---|---|
| Demographics | 40 years old | 42 years old | 44 years old | 44 years old | 50 years old |
| | 38% college grad | 37% college grad | 65% college grad | 56% college grad | 49% college grad |
| | 89% married | 70% married | 60% married | 76% married | 66% married |
| | $48K avg income | $53K avg income | $56K avg income | $64K avg income | $40K avg income |
| Psychographics | Family orientated | On the way up | Independent | Physically active | Cautious |
| | Practical | Workaholic | minded | Successful | Not physically |
| | Down-to-earth | Fashionable | Ready to try new | Sports-orientated | active |
| | Budget conscious | Trendy | things | Well-travelled | Happier with |
| | Satisfaction | | Willing to take | Cultured | simpler things |
| | w/ basics | | risks | Fashionable | |
| | Cautious | | Well-travelled | | |
| | Happier with | | Intellectual | | |
| | simpler things | | Cultured | | |
| Vacations in past 3 years | Avg Number = 3 | Avg Number = 3 | Avg Number = 4 | Avg Number = 5 | Avg Number = 3 |
| | Avg Days = 6 | Avg Days = 9 | Avg Days = 8 | Avg Days = 7 | Avg Days = 7 |
| | Avg per diem = $115 | Avg per diem = $157 | Avg per diem = $140 | Avg per diem = $154 | Avg per diem = $130 |
| | 5% took int'l vacation | 21% took int'l vacation | 24% took int'l vacation | 23% took int'l vacation | 8% took int'l vacation |
| | 43% stayed at resorts | 49% stayed at resorts | 42% stayed at resorts | 59% stayed at resorts | 42% stayed at resorts |
| | 67% trvl w/ children | 38% trvl w/ children | 25% trvl w/ children | 45% trvl w/ children | 29% trvl w/ children |
| Vacation activities | Swimming | Shopping | Cultural activities | Dining in fine restaurants | Fewest activities |
| | **Less interested in:** | Dining in fine restaurants | Hiking | Sunbathing | |
| | – dining in fine restaurants | Nightlife | **Less interested in:** | Nightlife | |
| | – cultural activities | **Less interested in:** | – Gambling | Gambling | |
| | – gambling | – hiking | – Golfing | Golfing | |
| | – nightlife | | | Skiing | |
| | | | | Tennis | |
| Intent to cruise | 35% likely/next 5 yrs | 46% likely/next 5 yrs | 33% likely/next 5 yrs | 39% likely/next 5 yrs | 19% likely/next 5 yrs |
| | 26% hot prospects | 37% hot prospects | 24% hot prospects | 30% hot prospects | 14% hot prospects |
| Perceived barriers to cruising | Expense Not for children | Not highest quality | Lack of freedom Not enough to do | No major barriers | Unfamiliar experience |

This chart is based on statistically significant differences from the norm for all cruise prospects.

| | Total | Family folks | Want-it-alls | Adventurers | Comfortable spenders | Cautious travellers |
|---|---|---|---|---|---|---|
| **Age** | | | | | | |
| 25–39 | 46% | 57% | 49% | 42% | 46% | 25% |
| 40–59 | 41% | 39% | 41% | 45% | 37% | 49% |
| 60 or older | 13% | 4% | 10% | 13% | 17% | 27% |
| Average | 43 | 40 | 42 | 44 | 44 | 50 |
| Median | 41 | 38 | 40 | 42 | 41 | 48 |
| **Marital status** | | | | | | |
| Married | 75% | 89% | 70% | 60% | 76% | 66% |
| Not married | 25% | 11% | 30% | 40% | 24% | 34% |
| **Household composition** | | | | | | |
| Have children under 18 | 47% | 70% | 38% | 31% | 41% | 25% |
| Adults only | 53% | 30% | 62% | 69% | 59% | 75% |
| Average | 3 | 4 | 3 | 3 | 3 | 2 |
| Median | 3 | 4 | 2 | 2 | 2 | 2 |
| **Education** | | | | | | |
| Some college or less | 51% | 62% | 63% | 35% | 44% | 51% |
| College graduate or more | 49% | 38% | 37% | 65% | 56% | 49% |

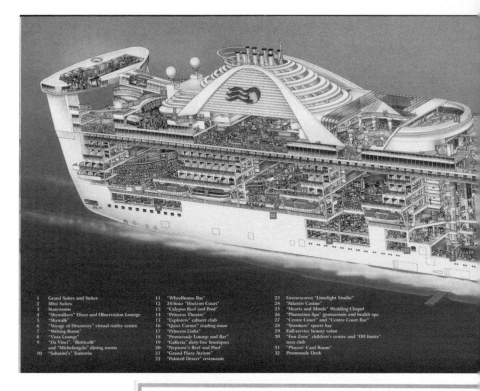

| | | | | | | |
|---|---|---|---|---|---|---|
| 1 | Grand Suites and Suites | 11 | "Wheelhouse Bar" | 23 | Green-screen "Limelight Studio" |
| 2 | Mini Suites | 12 | 24-hour "Horizon Court" | 24 | "Atlantis Casino" |
| 3 | Staterooms | 13 | "Calypso Reef and Pool" | 25 | "Hearts and Minds" Wedding Chapel |
| 4 | "Skywalkers" Disco and Observation Lounge | 14 | "Princess Theatre" | 26 | "Plantation Spa" gymnasium and health spa |
| 5 | "Skywalk" | 15 | "Explorers" cabaret club | 27 | "Centre Court" and "Centre Court Bar" |
| 6 | "Voyage of Discovery" virtual reality centre | 16 | "Quiet Corner" reading room | 28 | "Snookers" sports bar |
| 7 | "Writing Room" | 17 | "Princess Links" | 29 | Full-service beauty salon |
| 8 | "Vista Lounge" | 18 | "Promenade Lounge and Bar" | 30 | "Fun Zone" children's centre and "Off limits" teen club |
| 9 | "Da Vinci", "Botticelli" and "Michelangelo" dining rooms | 19 | "Galleria" duty-free boutiques | 31 | "Players' Card Room" |
| 10 | "Sabatini's" Trattoria | 20 | "Neptune's Reef and Pool" | 32 | Promenade Deck |
| | | 21 | "Grand Plaza Atrium" | | |
| | | 22 | "Painted Desert" restaurant | | |

A vast expanse of nothingness stretching to the horizon. (And that's just De

ORIANA *fro*

&O CRUISES

# Tesco

Leading UK supermarket group, Tesco, can serve some 2 million Internet customers with home deliveries from 100 of its stores. In doing this it is not alone – its main rival, Sainsbury's, also offers home deliveries driven by orders over the Internet. Tesco also runs an on-line bookshop. These are recent developments which have been facilitated by the power and potential of information technology (IT).

Price cutting, an important competitive strategy in retailing, does not truly distinguish one food retailer from another, as price cuts can be followed by rivals, although creative advertising can suggest a price differential when one really does not exist. Supply-chain cost savings, also facilitated by IT, however, can be an important source of advantage and improved profitability.

This case looks at how Tesco exploited IT in the early 1990s to drive competitive advantage.

Since the case was written in 1996 events have moved on, but the basic strategic issues raised here remain pertinent and relevant. Tesco, for example, now shares live sales information with its suppliers and, by embracing IT themselves, more and more suppliers are linked electronically to Tesco. Again using the power of the Internet, e-markets allow any retailer to post up 'confidential' information but limit access to it through password-driven 'firewalls'. Going beyond the advantages discussed in this case, the Internet allows retailers to invite suppliers to engage in bids or auctions when either the retailer has a specific shortage or a supplier has excess inventory.

This case has two themes:

- the use of information technology by Tesco to strengthen its competitiveness, and
- the role of information technology in forging strategic linkages between Tesco and its distributors and suppliers.

Information technology has both reduced costs and strengthened Tesco's competitiveness by improving its overall level of customer service.

The case is designed to be used in conjunction with Chapters 9 and 13.

This version of the case was written in 1996 by John L. Thompson with the co-operation of Tesco. It is for classroom discussion and should not be taken to reflect either effective or ineffective management.

## Introduction

In the mid-1990s Tesco overtook Sainsbury's to become the market share leader for UK groceries. By the 1960s Tesco had become successful with a policy of 'pile it high, sell it cheap', the philosophy of the founder, John Cohen. Tesco concentrated at that time on relatively small supermarkets close to town centres. The shops offered only a basic level of comfort and service. In the 1970s it became apparent that future growth and prosperity required a new strategy. Tesco appeared to have too many small stores, poor warehousing and stock control and weak administration systems. The strong concentration on price was limiting the total service, and strategically implied a focus, rather than a broad appeal. Desiring a strong market presence, Tesco sought to reposition itself. The new strategy would be based on quality and service in a pleasant shopping environment, together with competitive prices.

In the 1970s Tesco had some 600 stores. This number was systematically reduced to 337 in 1987 through a series of closures and new openings of single-storey units with car parking. Redesigned new superstores have been built in carefully selected locations and a further 57 stores were acquired in 1994 when Tesco bought the Scotland-based Wm. Low Group. In 1995 Tesco had 519 stores in the UK plus 105 Catteau stores in France and 44 Global stores in Hungary. The UK stores comprise:

- superstores
- compact stores – smaller supermarkets
- metros – town centre stores designed to serve specific local needs, and
- express stores – convenience stores adjacent to a petrol forecourt.

The total product range of some 17,000 food and non-food items is available in only the largest stores; the smaller ones carry just 3000 lines. Products are sourced from around the world, although British goods are used whenever it is possible and appropriate. Three of Tesco's eight stated objectives relate specifically to the stores and product range:

Tesco is committed to:

- offering customers the best value for money and the most competitive prices
- improving profitability through investment in efficient stores and distribution depots, in productivity improvements and in new technology
- working closely with suppliers to build long-term business relationships based on strict quality and price criteria.

The early Tesco stores (the company was founded in the 1930s) concentrated on canned and processed foods – fresh foods were added in the late 1970s. In addition, Tesco has invested in scanning technology and distribution systems. The aim was to be at the forefront of retail technology, and use information technology (IT) for competitive advantage as well as cost savings. Tesco looks to have sufficient product on the shelves to cover a maximum day's sales without needing substantial on-site warehousing. It is both cheaper and easier to restock shelves outside peak shopping hours. Implementation of the IT strategy has required close co-operation with suppliers.

*Every opportunity must be taken for retailers, suppliers and manufacturers to work closer together. We must move further away from the old retailer-versus-supplier arguments and accept that, if we are to grow, we can only do this together and on the basis of co-operation and mutual understanding.*

(Lord MacLaurin, Chairman since 1985)

Before discussing the utilization of information technology by Tesco, an introduction to the key success factors for supermarket retailing and supply-chain management in the 1990s is provided as background information.

## Key success factors for supermarket retailing

Successful supermarket chains must satisfy certain key success factors:

- The location of the stores is critical. Easy access for cars, and sufficient parking places, is essential.

In addition, new out-of-town shopping developments provide important opportunities.
- The product range. Larger stores, quite simply, offer wider ranges.
- Product availability. Shelves must be stocked and quickly replenished. However, large stocks in stores are costly, and in-store 'warehousing' must inevitably be at the expense of selling space.
- Competitive prices – which in turn depend in part on controlling costs.

If customers visit the store regularly, and buy more items, then the retailer's turnover and profits will both increase.

The cost of distributing grocery products from the point of manufacture to the retail outlet accounts for between 12 and 20% of their value. These costs can be reduced by investment in IT, which may be used to reduce both transport and inventory costs. Seizing this opportunity requires close co-operation between the manufacturers and the retailer and, quite often, a linked contribution from specialist distributors. IT has also allowed retailers to offer additional services, such as 'cashpoint banking' when switch cards are being used for payment. More recently, Tesco has been a pioneer of loyalty or frequent-purchase cards. Tesco's Clubcard has a magnetic strip which records a customer's purchases and awards a credit for use with future purchases.

The increasing predominance of retailer own-brand food products has increased the need for close co-operation between the store chain and its suppliers, and an expectancy that the retailer would develop expertise in *food* technology. Food legislation makes the retailer responsible for the composition and quality of products marketed under its brand name. Tesco was a late starter with own-brand products, but it has since developed one of the largest food-technology departments in the country and been a pioneer of ethical product labelling.

## The importance of distribution

Effective distribution can reduce costs while improving the overall level of service. The distribution or supply chain encapsulates the storage, handling and movement of goods from the point of manufacture to the point of sale. This distribution can be direct from the manufacturer to the individual retail stores, and in the early 1980s some 90% of grocery products were moved this way. A large Tesco store would see between 50 and 60 different lorries every day, each dropping off just a portion of its load. Now 90% of products are distributed via intermediate warehouses, and a store will be fully supplied every day by three large container lorries. Depots, though, must be able to give the stores a fast response time if the system is to be effective. This changeover has led to enormous savings and benefits, but it has only been possible through harnessing the potential of IT.

The intermediate warehouse may be run by the retailer; it is more likely that it will be run for the retail chain by a specialist distribution company. Distribution to the warehouse is known as *primary distribution*; the movement on to the retail stores is designated *secondary distribution*. Primary distribution is still normally provided by manufacturers.

Tesco utilizes 18 regional warehouses for the secondary distribution of all of its products in the UK. These comprise:

- eight multi-temperature food warehouses for frozen, chilled and ambient short-life foods
- five dry grocery centres for canned and long-life foodstuffs
- one national centre for Home 'n' Wear
- two bonded centres for wines and spirits
- two centres for slow-moving items.

Multi-temperature composite warehouses (described in detail later in the case and an invention of Tesco) require very specialized skills, and consequently Tesco utilizes the services of expert distributors to run seven out of its eight. The whole of the north of England, from a line drawn westwards from The Wash, together with Scotland, is served by three warehouses, all run by Glass Glover. The sites, all near motorway junctions, are at Doncaster, Middleton (in Lancashire) and Livingston, which is between Glasgow and Edinburgh. Glass Glover specializes in food warehousing, and Tesco's business constitutes over 40% of its revenue. Although it also provides similar facilities for Littlewoods, ASDA, Leo and Safeway, Tesco is substantially its major customer. However, Tesco's other

warehouses are run by National Freight Corporation (2), Hunter Distribution and Hays Distribution, and in these cases, Tesco is only a relatively small client.

There is a number of advantages to using such specialists:

- The skills required are different from those needed to run a successful retail chain.
- The retailer is better able to focus on its core skills and competencies.
- Cost savings – it is likely that there will be improved efficiencies and productivity. In addition, the capital investment in the facilities and the trucks is provided by the distributor.
- The stores, quite frequently located in expensive, prime sites, are not required to carry any unnecessary stocks.

The contractor's purpose is clear and unequivocal – to provide a cost-effective, high service level, distribution system. Success requires close co-operation (utilizing IT), mutual understanding and trust. Given this, distribution, stock control and replenishment become a single, integrated system.

## Key success factors for supply-chain management

There are five critical factors:

- Automated data capture in stores using electronic point-of-sale (EPOS) – examined in detail in the next section.
- Electronic data interchange (EDI) for the rapid transmission of sales and stock data, order confirmations and delivery schedules. EDI requires that the computer systems of the retail chain and its suppliers are linked directly. EDI is also described in greater detail later.
- Pre-planning with suppliers. This implies that basic schedules are agreed in advance but that arrangements are sufficiently flexible to take account of demand changes which were not forecast.
- Decision support systems to help forecasting, planning and inventory management.
- Streamlined distribution to utilize these links and the improved information to achieve high levels of service cost effectively.

All the technology to achieve this is available; the challenge is one of implementation and achieving the potential. The systems require substantial investment; the benefits will only be achieved if retailers are able to establish network arrangements with their suppliers. In addition, and very significantly, the impacts upon people must be tackled.

IT on this scale implies that decisions concerning product ranges for stores, shelf layouts and stock levels, and replenishment orders are centralized. Store managers and staff may be empowered in respect of the *customer care and service* that they provide, but they will not control the product and stock decisions. In addition, the multi-temperature warehouses with large frozen sections have been described as the 'coal mines of the 1990s'.

## Electronic point-of-sale

EPOS systems rely on products being bar coded at source, which again requires co-operation with suppliers. Check-out systems scan the bar code. This provides an instant record of sales and stock movements out of the store, data which can be used for several purposes:

- stock replenishment from the warehouse
- analysing actual against forecast sales to monitor and modify orders with suppliers
- evaluating profitability. The central computer will contain information on the margin and relative profitability of every item, and this can be added to the sales data. Sales may be increasing, for example, but these additional sales may be of the company's least profitable products (*this cost and margin information is not normally made available to individual store managers*)
- making decisions concerning which products to boost and promote and which ones to drop. Every time a new product is added to a store's range, something has to give way for it.

Another benefit of bar coding and EPOS is the elimination of the need to price every single product. The price can be displayed where the products are shelved; the EPOS system inputs the price once the bar code is read. This means that products can be put out onto shelves very quickly after they are received into the store. (This benefit is clearly available to Tesco and the other food supermarkets. For retailer such as Boots and WH Smith it is available only for certain products. In the case of cassettes and compact discs with their ranges of different prices, for example, every individual item has to be priced separately). In addition, price changes can be implemented rapidly. By the end of 1992 every Tesco store had up-to-date scanning technology.

## IT and the supply chain key success factors

IT can be utilized to strengthen the link between the retail chains and their customers in a number of ways. Sophisticated models have been developed to predict demand patterns for individual stores (and possible new locations) by capturing data on the size and dispersion of the local population, age groupings, incomes, socioeconomic groupings and car ownership. Clubcard purchasing information is captured at the point of sale and stored in a database for tracking exactly what individual, identifiable customers are buying. This information and forecasting can be used to target particular customer groups and to provide the 'right' range of products. This in turn provides a high level of customer service, and at the same time it should improve the retailer's profitability. Forecasts can be updated and modified with EPOS information.

It was stated earlier that IT offers the potential both to speed up stock replenishment and to reduce the costs of distributing the products. If costs are to be reduced throughout the supply chain, the information must be shared and suppliers kept informed of changing trends. If a retailer used sales information purely to generate orders to its suppliers – and over a period of time demand fluctuated – the suppliers would only be able to meet demand quickly if they held high levels of stock. For short-life products this is often impractical. Moreover, they would be required to interpret the changing orders that they were receiving from the retailers to try and clarify any changing trends. Their interpretation may well be different from that of the retail buyers, and this could be a recipe for waste or lost opportunity. The suppliers could either overestimate or underestimate demand changes and change their production schedules accordingly. If the retailers share their forecasting and interpretations the total system can be run more effectively. EDI enables suppliers and retailers to be in constant contact. Initial forecasts can be provided together with an anticipated schedule of orders. This can be updated on a constant basis. Suppliers should then be able to meet demand without undue waste.

IT can also be used to minimize duplication. The fewer times that actual deliveries and the support documentation need to be checked, the speedier and cheaper is the system.

Finally IT systems can also monitor warehouse efficiencies – space and vehicle utilization, delivery times linked to route planning, etc.

## The Tesco supply chain
### Electronic data interchange

Tesco supplies its 500 stores mostly from 18 regional warehouses. These depots handle some 17,000 food lines together with household, health and beauty products and wines and spirits. These are sourced from 2500 different suppliers. In the past, linking 2500 suppliers and 500 stores has implied a large volume of paper orders and paper invoices. The switch to linked computer systems began in the early 1980s, when most deliveries were still direct to the stores. The changeover began with the centralization of Tesco's purchasing from its major suppliers. Sales representatives were no longer required to call on stores and collect their orders. In 1986 Tesco first began to transmit orders electronically via Tradanet.

Tradanet is an EDI service operated by International Network Services Ltd, and it requires that Tesco's suppliers join Tesco in subscribing to the system. Each user has an electronic computer link into the system, and within the system each has both a 'post box' and a 'mail box'. In other words, a user can transmit information (such as an order or an invoice) into the system via its post box. This is then instantaneously switched to the mail box of the intended recipient. Information is received by periodically checking the mailbox and it can again be integrated into the recipient's internal information system for immediate action. Over a period of time

both Tesco and its suppliers are in a position to learn how to maximize the benefits offered by such a system of fast and reliable information transfer.

The initial suppliers who pioneered the system with Tesco were Birds Eye (Unilever), Coca-Cola, Colman's, Nestlé, Schweppes and Spillers Foods. By the early 1990s three quarters of Tesco's long-life products and over half of their short-life products were handled via the Tradanet system. The vast majority of Tesco's purchase orders is now dealt with centrally.

### Composite distribution

EDI has been developed in parallel with composite, multi-temperature food warehouses and trucks, which can accommodate the need for storing and transporting different food products at different temperatures. Frozen foods need to be kept at approximately −20°C; cold chilled fresh meat and fish is handled at 0°C; fresh produce and provisions should be retained between +5 and +10°C. Grocery products such as biscuits, breakfast cereals, cakes and crisps should be kept at ambient temperature. Historically this has required five different types of truck.

Exhibit 1 illustrates a typical Tesco composite distribution warehouse. The total size is in the order of 25,000 square feet (2300 square metres), and each section can be managed individually to take account of the different handling and operating procedures that are necessary. Tesco pioneered these warehouses, opening the first one in 1988. Each of the eight existing warehouses serves about 50 stores in a defined region using specialized vehicles. A composite distribution trailer contains flexible bulkhead partitions and can be utilized as one, two or three sections at different temperatures. The coolest compartment would be at −20°C, the middle at 0°C and the third would be at +10°C.

### The Tesco system
See Exhibit 2.

Tesco's central buying division negotiates supply terms and prices with suppliers, and agrees a target schedule. In reality they are selling shelf space, and Tesco will generally look to stock a brand leader, their own-label variant and possibly one other alternative. For long-life products a 13-week rolling fore-

*Exhibit 1*   Layout of a composite distribution centre.

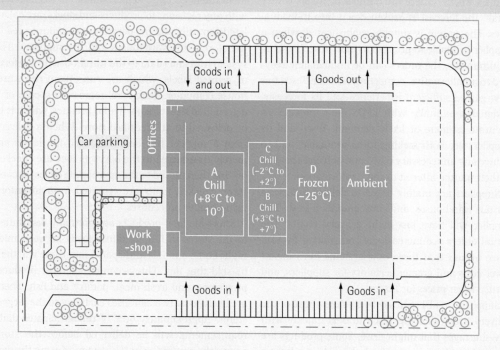

*Exhibit 2*   Tesco's supply chain.

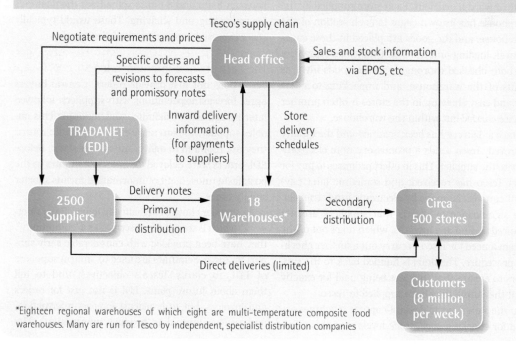

*Eighteen regional warehouses of which eight are multi-temperature composite food warehouses. Many are run for Tesco by independent, specialist distribution companies

cast is provided; for fresh goods it varies between one and six weeks. Where the number of weeks is very small, the forecast is broken down into individual days. The system is suitably sophisticated: when a supplier is unable to promise to meet Tesco's asking requirements, the orders can be immediately recycled to an alternative, competing supplier. Tesco has now gained sufficient experience and its forecasts, updated continually with EPOS data, provide an accurate estimate of likely demand. Tesco and its suppliers are both seeking to be profitable, and to reduce any unnecessary costs, and perceive that it is in their mutual interest to share information.

Suppliers are mainly asked to deliver to Tesco's various warehouses, and consequently a fresh-food supplier will have just eight delivery points. The actual orders are increasingly transmitted by EDI. Tesco argues that these new systems have meant lower costs and greater certainty for suppliers, and in turn lower prices for Tesco.

Suppliers on EDI send a delivery note ahead of the delivery itself, allowing Tesco to deal quickly with any shortages that might arise. Some products are received into warehouses for holding in stock for a limited period; other deliveries are sorted for immediate onward movement. Each store supplied by the warehouse has its own cages in each section of the warehouse, and the goods are placed in these cages to await loading and transfer. Quality and quantity are both checked thoroughly at the goods inwards points of the warehouse; and unpacking to allow fast and easy shelving in the stores is often another service carried out within the warehouse.

Once a delivery has been scanned and the quality approved, Tesco sends a promissory note electronically to the supplier. This in effect promises to pay for what Tesco has received; and sometime later payment can also be made by electronic funds transfer. The significance of this is that suppliers are not required to send any invoices, which takes out of the system a need for Tesco to carry out a further checking procedure. The onus is handed back to the suppliers to ensure that they are being paid for exactly what they think they have supplied to Tesco.

In the stores, portable data-capture machines are used for checking shelf stock levels, and this infor-

mation is transmitted back to head office to supplement the EPOS data. Replenishment needs, together with any revisions to products and stocks, are calculated centrally and the details are communicated to the stores, the warehouses and the suppliers. The system transmits data to the warehouses in the form of printed labels, which are run off on the warehouse computer. Each label represents a case of a determined size, of a particular product, which is to be delivered to an identified store. When a delivery from a supplier has been unloaded the labels are merely transferred to the boxes as they are checked off and then moved to the appropriate cages for each store. Stocked items are removed from inventory using similar procedures.

Short-life food products are normally distributed to the stores in full container loads between midnight and 8 am. It is anticipated that these will then be sold that day. This accounts for most produce, provisions, and fresh meat, poultry and fish. There are likely to be two deliveries each day to the largest stores. Approximately 60% of the anticipated daily requirements will be delivered before the store opens; the remaining 40% sometime during the day. Long shelf-life products are delivered separately between 8 am and 8 pm to spread out the demands for unloading and shelving. These would typically cover expected demand on the following day.

## The network and interdependency

Tesco does not just provide orders. Central buyers agree forecast expectations with suppliers, followed later by call-offs or definite confirmations. This enables suppliers to plan more effectively, but in return they are required to deliver quickly ex-stock. Before EDI, orders were delayed for at least 24 hours in the post; faster movement of information means shorter supply times.

As suppliers have systematically joined Tesco's network, which is sometimes described as a 'community', they have been provided with considerable early support by Tesco. Seminars are used to 'inform suppliers of EDI, to clarify Tesco's objectives, and to tell them about future plans. EDI is not just for orders and invoices, but to broadcast forecast information, and receive up-to-date product information'. The emphasis is on sharing. 'Retailers and suppliers need to work closely together to achieve their common aim of providing an excellent service to customers . . . suppliers are no longer dependent purely on their own forecasting. There are fewer surprises, and both partners develop a better understanding of each other's business.'

The system can only work effectively when there is common agreement about such factors as case sizes, volumes and weights, and no deviation in practice. Suppliers must deliver in an agreed format, and essentially exactly as Tesco expects their supplies. Cases and individual products must all be correctly bar-coded. Tesco is dependent upon this at the point of check-out in the stores.

*If Tesco can be more effective in communicating with suppliers than our competitors, then our business partnerships are strengthened and we get a better service, the benefits of which we pass on to our customers.*

## A summary of the benefits

There is a number of benefits from Tesco's supply chain, arising from the utilization of IT and collaboration with their suppliers. The main ones are as follows:

- It facilitates the achievement of the 'right' good at the 'right' place, at the 'right' time, and at the 'right' price.
- Daily deliveries to reduce stockholding in stores
    In 1994, for example, Tesco was able to add 35,000 square feet (3250 square metres) of sales space to existing stores by cutting out in-store stockrooms.
- In turn this enables a wider overall product range.
- It is easier for Tesco to deal with a large number of suppliers, including those based overseas.
- Products should reach the stores in better condition than in the past.
- Own-label products can be easily integrated into the system, which is in the interests of Tesco, the suppliers who manufacture for them, and customers.
- The likelihood of stock-outs and the consequent loss of sales is minimized.

- The wastage rates for short shelf-life products are reduced.
- The improved efficiencies and productivity generate a stronger cash flow and improved profits for both Tesco and their suppliers. Some of these benefits will be passed on to customers in the form of lower prices.

Clearly Tesco, in common with many other leading retailers, has become increasingly dependent on IT. Exhibit 3 features the McFarlan grid, which considers the relative significance of IT for a company's current and future competitiveness; it is appropriate at this stage to decide where Tesco would currently fit.

The full potential of networked supply-chain management has not yet been achieved by any retailer, and future opportunities and challenges await the leaders.

In the USA in the 1990s, Efficient Customer Response (ECR) captured retailers' attention. ECR fosters stronger links between supermarkets, their suppliers and their suppliers' suppliers because the purchase of a particular item at a supermarket checkout automatically triggers a replenishment decision at the supplier's warehouse together with orders for fresh ingredients, cans, bottles and labels further up the line. The outcome is a reduction in inventory plus the reduced likelihood of a stock-out. Information management (concerning what customers are actually buying) enables changing trends to be spotted quickly. Retailers are essentially handing over the responsibility for stock replenishment to their suppliers. While Tesco and other leading UK retailers have expressed interest in ECR, their inventory management systems were already far superior to those of the US supermarket groups. Moreover, because of the high incidence of own-label goods in the UK, Tesco is also its own supplier for many of its products. 'ECR is now being carefully examined for the further benefits that it might bestow.'

*Tesco*   http://www.tesco.com

*Exhibit 3*    The strategic importance of Information technology (developed from McFarlan, FW (1984) Information technology changes the way you compete, *Harvard Business Review*, May/June.

|  | Low | High |
|---|---|---|
| **High** | IT systems vital for the ongoing operations of the business. Certain activities have become dependent upon IT | Current operations are dependent on IT. Future IT developments can and will be harnessed to both improve efficiency and provide (greater) competitive advantage. It may well alter the competitive strategy |
| **Low** | IT systems useful for cost savings and efficiency. The organization is not using IT for competitive advantage | The organization is not dependent on IT but uses it for efficiency and effectiveness. Future development could be important in the formulation of new strategies |

Operational dependency on information technology

Strategic importance of developments in information technology

## Questions

1. How does EDI impact upon the retailing industry structure?

   (Michael Porter's industry analysis [See Chapter 8] provides an ideal framework for tackling this question.)

2. Using the McFarlan grid: to what extent has the grocery retailing industry become strategically dependent upon information technology?

   (McFarlan's analysis was briefly covered in Chapter 13, The original 'McFarlan grid' was introduced in: McFarlan, FW (1984) Information technology changes the way you compete, *Harvard Business Review*, May/June.

   The grid has been revised and refined by McFarlan in later works, but the original ideas are perfectly satisfactory for the purposes of this exercise.)

3. Does Tesco appear to have taken the appropriate steps to forge effective alliances within the supply chain?

4. How might Tesco utilize IT and its supplier network to strengthen its competitiveness further in the future?

# Kwik-Fit Financial Services

This case study discusses how Kwik-Fit, the tyres and exhaust business, diversified into financial services in 1995, making use of its valuable and extensive customer database. The company focused on direct sales via the telephone, entering that segment of the market opened up by Direct Line some years earlier.

This long case builds on issues outlined in Minicase 12.2.

This case was written by Dr Jim Gallagher with the co-operation of Kwik-Fit and Sir Tom Farmer. It is for classroom discussion and should not be taken to reflect either effective or ineffective management.

Copyright JG Gallagher, Napier University, Edinburgh.

## Recent developments in the industry

The arrival of Direct Line in 1985 heralded the start of the sale of financial services over the phone in the UK. Direct Line began, initially, by selling policies to customers of the Royal Bank of Scotland, its parent company. Characterized by out-of-town locations with low overheads, efficient and fast technology for speedy service and open seven days a week, telesales offered the potential for high returns on investment, Direct Line grew more rapidly than any other insurance company in the U.K.

The strategy underpinning Direct Line was a direct marketing one, which drove the whole organization. The focus of attention at every level of the organization was the customer. Consequently, product offerings were based on customer wants, i.e. competitive prices and a no-hassle claims department. Delivery of the product was 100% direct.

Direct Line obtained its customers through TV and press advertising. Prospective customers were chased through direct mail that was timed to coincide with the prospect's renewal date. Once a sale was made, all details were completed using 'direct distribution'. Direct Line has no broker network, nor is any high-street outlet used. If the customer had a query, he or she rang Direct Line, and everything was handled over the phone.

The result was that Direct Line captured about two million policies, some 10% of all private motor insurance sales in a market where the cyclical movement of prices had all but disappeared.

Other companies, such as Royal Insurance and General Accident, followed suit, with both launching into the direct market in 1989 with Insurance Services and General Accident Direct, respectively. These early adopters were themselves closely shadowed by such insurers as Admiral, Churchill, Guardian and Eagle Star. The cumulative effect of these 'me-too' entrants was an attack on Direct Line's market share and profits.

Motor is the most common policy sold over the phone, but household insurance, mortgage protection, critical illness and personal finance may also be bought in this way.

In 1994, industry average premiums fell by around 13%, even though the insurance companies had to absorb the cost of the Government's new 2.5% Insurance Premium Tax.

The Automobile Associations' AA Insurance had been in business for over 30 years and was the UK's largest broking network with over 1.7 million home and motor policies. But as the market for direct insurance became cut-throat, established suppliers such as AA Insurance found their traditional distribution of insurance services threatened by the boom in direct sales.

The response, in the case of AA Insurance, was a restructuring programme based on direct selling which saw its workforce cut from over 3000 to fewer than 2000; a delayering of its management and the introduction in 1995 of an almost completely new management team. The estimated cost of this restructuring was £19 million. AA had recognized that over the long term people would pay less for their insurance because of the efficiency of the direct sell.

In January 1995 Virgin announced a tie-up with Norwich Union to sell financial services under the Virgin banner. Richard Branson of Virgin commented (*Money Programme*, BBC1, 5 July 1998) that Virgin's strategy was based on:

*using the credibility of the brand to challenge the dominant players in a range of industries where we believe the consumer is not getting value for money.*

At the same time, January 1995, Direct Line announced that it would be progressing further from its highly successful move from motor insurance into house insurance with a further move into life assurance.

Thus, by the mid-1990s many companies using good stock-market performances had followed Direct Line into telemarketing, thereby creating a market which was oversupplied. This resulted in under-priced products and a scrabble for market share with the inevitable result that commission rates were being driven down at a time when volumes were falling dramatically.

The growth in call centres in the UK had been phenomenal, and it is now an area where Britain leads the field. Mitial, a Wrexham-based call-centre consultancy, conducted a census in November 1997 of all major call centre locations in Western Europe and the Republic of Ireland. (A call centre is defined as a dedicated operation handling inward and outward bound calls and having at least 20 seats).

The survey showed that of the 1800 call centres identified 1400 were in the UK. Moreover, it indicated that a further 350 call centres were expected to be set up in the UK during 1998. It also estimated that a quarter of a million people were employed in call centres and about a million more were expected to join them by the end of the decade.

The benefits associated with using the call centre, according to Ewan Gowrie, chairman of the Call Centre Association (CCA) are that:

*You save 30–40 per cent commission straight away by selling direct. On top of that you are making efficiency savings . . . Then you are saving in terms of location. You no longer need to be in a city centre.*

The downside is the quality and training of staff. Some organizations in particular the utilities, lose most of their call centre staff each year, with nearly 100% turnover.

Richard Branson made the comment (*Money Programme*, BBC1, 5 July 1998) that:

*A company is only as good as its people. If you know how to motivate and deal with people it does not matter if you are taking on the airline industry, soft drinks industry or the film industry. The same rules apply. You should never go into an industry just with a purpose of making money. One has to passionately believe that it is possible to change the industry, to turn it on its head, to make sure it will never be the same again. With the right people and that conviction anything is possible.*

Both Mori Financial Services, which estimated that motor insurance telesales in 1998 had a 35% penetration of the motor market, and the Association of British Insurers believed that by the year 2000 over half of the population of the UK would be buying its motor insurance over the phone.

The telesales industry, however, has not escaped criticism, particularly with regard to motor insurance. It has been accused of 'cherry-picking' by targeting only the lowest risk drivers, such as women. A driver of a fast car and aged under 25, would probably have to approach a broker for cover through more traditional channels. Even Peter Wood, Direct Line's chief executive (1984–June 1997) had to concede that some premiums would have to rise for motorists outside chosen areas where a 'good' postcode indicated a low risk.

As Sir Tom Farmer (chairman and chief executive, Kwik-Fit Holdings) put it:

*Insurance is part of life, something we know we have to buy. But the industry itself is bureaucratic and inefficient. It needs a good shake-up.*

On 17 August 1998 Barclays Bank threw down the gauntlet to other car insurers by guaranteeing for 12 months to beat any renewal premium. By June 1999 it had secured over 34,000 policies and 90,000 leads to policy renewals.

Barclays' offer is open to all except their current client base of 6000 motorists and drivers currently uninsured or not in receipt of a renewal notice. It offers fully comprehensive, third-party fire and theft, and third-party cover. A premier package, including uninsured loss recovery, breakdown cover and continental cover, can be added to any policy. In the event of an accident claimants are allocated a personal supervisor responsible for looking after their claim. A courtesy car is also available to claimants.

This car-insurance offer is backed by Privilege Insurance, the non-standard UK motor and home insurer. Run by Peter Wood and jointly founded by him and the Royal Bank of Scotland, Privilege is now wholly owned by the Royal Bank of Scotland, holding some 264,000 home and motor policies.

## Kwik-Fit Insurance Services: set-up

When announcing the annual results of Kwik-Fit Holdings plc in March 1995, Tom Farmer said that Kwik-Fit had been approached by several insurers to set up a phone-based insurance service by licensing the Kwik-Fit name to front a new direct insurance business. However, Kwik-Fit preferred to go it alone and would treat insurance the same way as it treated tyre manufacturers. Kwik-Fit had established strong (partnership) relations with major tyre suppliers built on trust, reliability and co-operation. It therefore sought to extend that relationship to its insurance companies. It would buy and sell, but not get into 'manufacturing'. 'We would work on an income basis', said Farmer, adding that insurance would fit well with the group's other products and loyal customer base. Kwik-Fit would earn commission by selling motor policies, underwritten by insurers, by telephone using its database of four million tyre and exhaust customers.

Farmer is further reported as saying:

*It's not a big diversification. You know, we are already the marketing arm for Dunlop and Pirelli. They make it, we sell it, and the commission is just the difference between what we pay for it and what we get from the customer. Insurance is the same thing. They make the policies, we sell them.*

By 1995 people were more proactive, shopping around for insurance. On average they were paying approximately £300 per policy, an expenditure which, by law, cannot be avoided (see Exhibit 1). However, insurance companies were selective about the risk that they were willing to underwrite. John Houston, Group Director of Strategy and Development, Kwik-Fit Holdings comments:

*What we set out to do was to be able to quote a good price for every customer which other underwriters would not be willing to do. We did this through creating a panel of insurers to complement each other thereby ensuring that a reasonable price is quoted to every interested Kwik-Fit customer.*

To this end, Kwik-Fit teamed up with one of the world's largest insurance brokers, Alexander & Alexander (now Aon Insurance) and a panel of 20 insurers to launch its phone-based Kwik-Fit Insurance Services (KFIS) from a call centre based in Lanarkshire, Scotland.

## The launch of KFIS

After its initial testing from 24 May in Scotland, in July 1995 Kwik-Fit launched its insurance services throughout the UK. It supported this with a £5 million advertising and marketing campaign based on competitive rates and promotional offers including parts discounts and free mobile telephones, and promising discounts of up to 20% for selected motorists.

Every day in 1995 8000–9000 customers went into a Kwik-Fit automobile repair centre somewhere, for a cash transaction. As part of its Customer Care Programme as many as possible of these customers are telephoned the next day or within 72 hours. During these customer research calls, if the service received by the customer was at a level which satisfied, Customer Care suggests a free motor insurance quote at the time when the customer's insurance renewal will be due and agree to call the customer at that time. For Kwik-Fit, customer care was not an empty gesture – it was, and is, the raison d'être of corporate life. Kwik-Fit people, in every aspect of the organization, are inculcated to be proactive about customer perception; customer satisfaction should be received and seen as a primary objective. The move into insurance was a means of providing additional value and service to the Kwik-Fit customer.

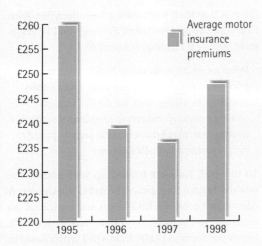

Exhibit 1   Average motor insurance premiums.

The Customer Care Unit provided between 2000 and 3000 leads each day in 1995. These leads were passed on, to be followed up by an insurance enquiry within a further 24 hours. Thus, by extending into insurance Kwik-Fit had discovered an engine for generating leads to cover the costs of its Customer Care Programme. Moreover, it found that if the average customer goes to a Kwik-Fit centre once a year its advertising at any time is relevant to 8% of motorists. The move to telesales allowed direct contact with customers, up to four times a year, through the insurance process plus any claim arising. By extending into insurance, Kwik-Fit increased its brand recognition with little fear of brand stretching.

At KFIS's new Tannochside headquarters some 280 full-time and part-time staff were employed, of whom some 60–80 staff were employed in the Customer Care Unit.

Within four months of its inception KFIS had acquired more than 30,000 customers and set its sights on catching the more established industry competitors. Given Kwik-Fit's market share of over 20% of the fast-fit services market, it aimed to achieve a significant market share (in excess of 5%) for KFIS.

KFIS managing director Laurence Law commented:

*we are making our own room in the market. Our conversion rate, the inquiries converting into business, is in the upper twenties, which is phenomenal.*

Kwik-Fit did not intend to spend fortunes on television and press advertising for its insurance arm. Other than that spent at the launch of KFIS and general group advertising (Yellow Pages, etc.) it was decided that the operation would depend on its Customer Care Unit.

## Building customer loyalty

### 1996

*We don't see ourselves as an insurance business; we are here to add value to the existing Kwik-Fit customers who use our auto centre. . . We want to make things as easy and pleasant as possible for them.*

(Ron Hewitt)

By 26 February 1996 Kwik-Fit had announced, in its year-end accounts, that 12,000 vehicles a day were providing 4000 leads which gave valuable feedback through its Customer Care Unit, thereby allowing it to identify where improvements were necessary.

The company saw its existing 'buy now – pay later' interest-free credit scheme, Autocharge Card, which by 1998 had a approximately 500,000 cardholders, as an important customer loyalty programme. This loyalty programme was enhanced by the new AutoSave card, which gave KFIS policyholders free membership of the Kwik-Fit AutoSave Club. Membership of the AutoSave Club entitled the holder to 10% discount on purchases at all Kwik-Fit centres in the UK, The Netherlands, Belgium and Eire, as well as all Apples Car Clinics. Together, they offered Kwik-Fit customers both an alternative way to pay their motoring expenses and a means of reducing the initial purchase price.

By the end of its first year of operation KFIS had performed beyond expectation and had moved into the black. It cost £900,000 in its first six months but by August it had moved into profit and by the end of the year KFIS had registered over £1 million profits.

Moreover, it was announced in the 1997 Accounts that the development costs of £5.1 million, which were scheduled to be written off over the first three years of operation, had been fully written off.

Part of the reason for KFIS's success was the conversion rates achieved by the Customer Care Unit, where 80% of the customers contacted agreed to take a quotation in the future when their policy renewal date was approaching. Initial experience was that about 30% of these quotations were taken up – about twice the insurance industry average. In all, an estimated 60,000 motorists switched to KFIS in its first year of operation.

*That definitely gives us an edge . . . The way this business is going you have to have a strong brand name.*

(Laurence Law, managing director)

These rapid improvements prompted plans to double the number of KFIS people in the telemarketing and customer survey centre, aiming to bring the total workforce up to 1000 by 1998. (Kwik-Fit does not talk or think in terms of workforce or employees; 'Kwik-Fit People' is preferred.)

KFIS, however, did not have it all its own way. The industry was facing saturation in terms of the number of telesales providers. More directly, KFIS faced increased competition with the launch of an equally successful offshoot of the Royal Bank of Scotland's Direct Line, Privilege, which saw the Scottish market as highly attractive.

Privilege, which specializes in quoting for the high-risk customers who make up a quarter of drivers on Britain's roads, signed up 52,000 customers in its first full year. It had advertised heavily in Northern Ireland and the south of England, and was then planning an advertising campaign in Scotland.

### The call centre: sales and technology

KFIS is split into sections, New Claims, New Business and Customer Care, and each section is split into teams, the members of which choose their own team names, e.g. Bulls, Ferrari, Seahawks, Tigers or Porsche.

With the installation of new telephone technology, which allowed it to target potential customers more scientifically, KFIS anticipated an increase in business volume. The initial automatic call distribution (ACD) equipment was designed to handle incoming calls and pass them on to a desk. This was augmented by the introduction of a predictive dialler. Essentially, the system is a queuing one, which automatically takes into account answering machines. For every 500 numbers called by the predictive dialler 100 calls are passed to the sales consultants on the basis of which operator it predicts will be free.

These sales consultants have a selection of prices on policies offered by the underwriters. From these they select the best deal possible for the customer. Any difficult cases can be passed to their team leader to be settled.

A team comprises about 12 members who operate in a competitive environment. Whenever a 'one-call sale' of a policy is made by a team member that member hits a button on the desk. This action registers the sale on a running total bar chart on an electronic scoreboard. The bar chart also shows how current team performance is doing against target. At the same time the team's musical signature is played to the whole room. In addition, the staff introduced a basketball hoop to take a shot at scoring a basket after the registration of a 'one-call sale'. If they score a basket they receive a small prize – a couple of tickets to the cinema, for example.

Clearly, there is a lot of background noise, but this noise is not filtered out for the customer as it is hoped that this background 'buzz' adds to the customers' perception of a busy business. In addition, sales consultants are encouraged to 'converse' with the customer and not stick purely to the questions required.

However, such was the growth of KFIS that it soon faced the problem of finding qualified people to staff the phones. It was especially difficult to recruit sales consultants in the evening, a time when an increasing amount of business was being done. Laurence Law commented:

*It is not so much a skill shortage. The people are there, it is just a question of finding the right way of getting to them.*

A further factor exacerbated the situation in that the 40,000 square foot (3700 square metre) site in Tannochside was almost bursting at the seams. By February 1997 KFIS was employing about 600 people.

The solution lay in acquiring an adjoining site at Tannochside. This almost doubled the size of the operation.

## Training

In November 1997 Kwik-Fit announced that it would be setting up Scotland's first ever telesales training academy at a cost of £600,000 at its original Tannochside site.

At the end of January 1998 the training academy was opened. KFIS's initial objective was to recruit a further 200 telesales staff to be put through their paces in the academy and then to be employed at KFIS's call centre. Prior to the opening of the academy KFIS's telesales operators were trained externally. The objective now is to give all staff members three weeks' training per year, except those in claims, who receive four weeks' training. The academy can handle approximately 100 people per day.

Ron Hewitt, Managing Director, Kwik-Fit Insurance Services, said:

*We need to invest more in the training of our people to ensure our own growth and success. By creating our own dedicated telesales centre of excellence, we will be able to guarantee a top-class service to our customers.*

The training centre features a state-of-the-art, self-learning multimedia centre, fully equipped with the latest Internet and personal computer facilities. It also has a lecture theatre, a training hall and two office training suites. It is open until 9 pm and staff can be booked in by their team leader if it is felt that they have to brush up on their skills or employees may use it for their own purposes, such as learning a new language.

The academy is also used for the auto centre side of the organization, with the emphasis being placed firmly on self-development.

Most of the current activity in the academy relates to the training of new recruits, but several

Leadership and Customer Care courses have been run for existing employees.

In its first four months 400 people used the academy's resources. This did not include the usage made by the local community when the facilities were not being used by KFIS.

## Recruitment: 'can-do' people

Six top qualities are required to work for Kwik-Fit's call centre in Uddingston:

1. Dedication – Each insurance consultant must work to ensure 100% customer delight at all times.
2. Willingness to learn – The job isn't just about answering customers' queries. Consultants must grasp a basic grounding of the insurance industry.
3. Friendly disposition – Staff must be polite towards customers, even the difficult ones!
4. Competitiveness – More than 20 Kwik-Fit teams daily pit their wits against each other to see which does best.
5. Flexibility – Working hours vary as the centre is open seven days a week from 8 am until midnight. There are shifts to suit most lifestyles.
6. Honesty – Kwik-Fit claim that there are no hidden extras in their insurance policies. This is reinforced when, after the policies are issued, quality surveys are undertaken.

'When we recruit we are looking for the "sparklies",' said Ron Hewitt, 'enthusiastic individuals who genuinely care about other people'. The emphasis here is on teamwork, which is fostered and supported by the organization. Furthermore,

*The people we take on don't need huge amounts of training in customer care – they are open and willing to help.*

KFIS had been disappointed in candidates who had backgrounds in insurance and financial services.

*We found that they are likely to have come from a bureaucratic environment which is overly concerned with the terms and conditions of the contract. They tend not to have been empowered in their jobs, whereas we want people who will take ownership of a situation and be prepared to see how they can help the customer. We are on the side of the customer, looking after their interests whilst ensuring at the same time that the insurance companies, which support us, are also catered for.*

Recruitment is aided by a large number of internal referrals with, for example, three generations of the one family working at Tannochside. Although staff are mainly local some commute from as far away as Edinburgh.

## Performance rewards

Ron Hewitt is quick to mention that every staff member at KFIS is rewarded for performance, but he is even quicker to highlight that KFIS's emphasis is on customer satisfaction, not sales per se. Unlike other companies, where business transacted by phone is done in as short a period as possible, the call length at KFIS is driven by the customer, in an attempt to enrich the customer's experience.

Sales staff are organized in teams, and performance rewards are made to both the individual and the team. Targets are set for each individual, but there are is no punitive action if these are not met; rather, corrective action is encouraged, by accessing the training facilities. Because the work is high pressure KFIS also provides a 'stress-busting line' which staff can utilize.

The salary package, which KFIS thinks is one of the best in the industry, comprises a basic salary of £10,000–12,000, which can be more than doubled by bonus payments. In addition, performance rewards for 'Quarterly Quality Awards' in the form of breaks to Paris, Nice, New York or Toronto have been made along with team night outs and the award of a car-parking space in front of the building as 'Quality Award Winner of the Month'. One 'Quality Award Winner' won a trip to Paris to see Scotland play Brazil in the opening match of the World Cup.

KFIS has no 'staff turnover'; rather, it has 'leavers' at about 25% which is made up, almost totally, of staff moving on to other jobs within KFIS, e.g. from sales consultant to Customer Care.

By June 1998 over 1000 people were employed, with an expectation of this rising to 1500 by the end of 1999/2000, handling some 40,000 calls a day. The average age is 24.

## Costs

The KFIS business is a low-cost one where the company only acts as a broker selling to its customers the terms negotiated from its insurers. In this way it avoids any insurance risk. Therefore, it offers not only a quality service but also competitive quotes to customers based on good 'policy purchases' from its list of insurers.

At one point they dealt with 24 insurers but this was felt to be too unwieldy. Furthermore, some of the smaller ones could not give the service required. The number of insurers was subsequently reduced to 14.

Payment of these insurers is on a 60 day basis, while over 70% of payments from KFIS customers are made by direct debit.

When Ron Hewitt joined KFIS he found that copies of driving licences, no-claims bonuses, etc. were being asked for and then stored. For him, this was wasteful as they took up both time and space and were rarely looked at. Consequently, he put an end to this practice. KFIS now asks for proof of no-claims bonus but in 90% of the cases do not chase this up; the remaining 10% are sought to ensure that there is control and integrity. Instead, KFIS issues a 'statement of insurance' saying that this is the information that the customer has provided to KFIS. In the event of a claim the relevant documentation to support the customer's claim must be produced, if requested by the insurer.

Everything is done by phone there are no claims forms to fill in. In the event of an accident and the customer's car being off the road all comprehensive policyholders are entitled to a courtesy car. At this point KFIS has tailored its service to achieve its desire of 100% customer delight.

Whenever a replacement car is offered KFIS will try to offer one that is better than the one which is 'off the road'. Kwik-Fit uses its purchasing power to do this, but the customer is not obliged to take it.

The phone is the lifeline of KFIS but it is also a cost. To minimize this both Scottish Telecom and

British Telecom lines have been installed, which allows the company to seek the lowest cost provider on a weekly or monthly basis.

It is estimated that each lead generation may cost a company in the industry up to £50 per new customer. In the case of KFIS the cost per lead generation is about £1 and the cost per sale about £5. By 1999 KFIS was approaching half a million customers generated from the customer base of the auto centre side of the business. In addition, other than the initial advertising budget at the launch of the operation KFIS does not advertise. It simply contacts customers whom it knows will be interested in its product.

## The future

In May 1998 KFIS introduced a household insurance policy which by July 1998 was achieving a 58% conversion rate. Also introduced was a personal protection policy, which rapidly achieved sales of 16,000 per month.

KFIS already manages claims for the companies on its underwriting panel. However, it is piloting a scheme that channels repairs through its own approved network of body shops instead of those used by insurers.

Joining these developments will be an MOT policy, costing approximately £50, which will conditionally insure the customer against the unexpected costs of a failed MOT.

April 1998 saw the launch of KFIS travel insurance, when all KFIS policyholders were sent a card wishing them a 'cracking good Easter', which outlined the different types of travel insurance available, ranging from coverage for a single trip or a whole year's travel.

Travel insurance not only augments KFIS's product portfolio but also was developed further when it was launched through the world wide web in late 1999. This allows the customer to specify on-screen his or her destination, make payment, receive a reference number and be covered immediately without documentation.

A snapshot of Kwik-Fit Financial Services in 1999 is provided in Exhibit 2.

In June 1998, in response to the pressures of growth, a new £6 million, 50,000 square foot (4650 square metre) call centre development at Tannochside was opened. Some 300 employees, made up of the Customer Care and Claims departments as well as some information services people, were initially accommodated there. There are also computer/ telephony rooms housing state-of-the-art technology to service the building. However, the building will not become fully operational until the new information technology systems are thoroughly integrated.

The Customer Care and Claims departments were relaunched, aiming to provide customers with a 'one-call close' to their queries or problems.

To do this KFIS launched a programme of events for service providers, team leaders and managers, designed to define and continue to deliver customer delight.

The programme aims to create the right environment for customers, provide service recovery when things go wrong, and encourage KFIS people to take ownership and responsibility for customers:

*In every interaction, customers judge whether we've made doing business with Kwik-Fit Insurance Services easy and a pleasure.*

*We have the opportunity to delight every time. But to do so, we have to take responsibility for each and every customer and, as service providers, take ownership of each customer until we know they are pleased with the outcome and promises are delivered.*

(Lawrence Fenley)

Working practices such as one consultant dealing with the customer throughout their claim are supported by the Kwik-Fit code of conduct, which ensures that contact with the customer is made at least once every three days, until the claim has been settled.

## Kwik-Fit Holdings plc

In August 1998 Kwik-Fit Holdings announced the strengthening of its group management by the appointment of Mr Graeme Bissett (40), a senior partner in Arthur Andersen, as group director of

| Kwit-Fit Financial Services  SNAPSHOT 1999 | | |
|---|---|---|

*Main businesses:*  Direct Motor Insurance

*Chairman:*  John M. Houston
(also Group Director)

*Managing Director:*  Ron Hewitt

*Industry*

Total Market  21m (cars)
Industry Value  £7bn

*Turnover and profits:*

| | 1997 £m | 1998 £m | 1999 £m |
|---|---|---|---|
| Sales | – | 32.7 | 36.3 +11% |
| Profits | 1.3 | 7.6 | 7.1 –7% |

| *Group Investments:* | £m |
|---|---|
| Development of Customer Care and Telemarketing facilities | 11 |

*Origin:*  Kwit-Fit Car Aftercare Service
Brand Extension

*Where is it going?:*  Major player in the insurance
retail market

*Market share:*  2% (National) 9% (Scotland)
in three years of operation

*Strategy:*  Quality product, value for money,
customer enhancement

| *Competitors:* | Market Share % |
|---|---|
| Direct Line | 10.1 |
| Royal Sun Alliance | 10.0 |
| AA | 5.2 |
| Liverpool Victoria | 3.2 |
| Kwik-Fit Financial Services | 2.0 |
| Privilege | 1.2 |

*Exhibit 2*  Kwik-Fit Financial Services – snapshot 1999.

finance and Tony Lochery as group director of operations as a result of the major expansion into Europe of the group fast-fit business.

In September 1998 Kwik-Fit acquired Speedy Europe, the tyre and exhaust chain, from SMK, Canada. Speedy Europe comprised some 574 outlets across Europe, including 376 in France, and cost £105 million.

As a result of this acquisition, Kwik-Fit increased the number of trading outlets which it operated from 1264 to 1907, with 774 in continental Europe

and 1085 in the UK and Republic of Ireland. This provided Kwik-Fit with a strong platform for the implementation of its emergent strategy of developing the Kwik-Fit business and reputation for customer service throughout continental Europe (Exhibit 3).

A snapshot of Kwik-Fit Holdings in 1999 is provided in Exhibit 4, and a detailed summary is presented in the next section.

On 12 April 1999 it was announced that the Ford Motor Company had acquired Kwik-Fit Holdings in an agreed bid of £1 billion.

| 1983 | 234 | | 1992 | 599 |
| 1984 | 264 | | 1993 | 626 |
| 1985 | 290 | | 1994 | 715 |
| 1986 | 318 | | 1995 | 770 |
| 1987 | 339 | | 1996 | 910 |
| 1988 | 392 | | 1997 | 1012 |
| 1989 | 518 | | 1998 | 1097 |
| 1990 | 609 | | 1999 | 1907 (includes 574 outlets from purchase |
| 1991 | 586 | | | of Speedy Europe) |

Exhibit 3   Kwik-Fit Holdings plc – number of trading outlets.

Kwit-Fit Holdings plc  SNAPSHOT 1999

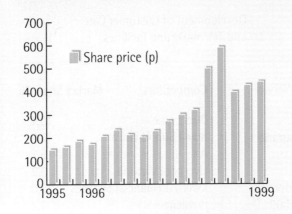

Turnover and profits:

| | 1998 £m | 1999 £m | |
|---|---|---|---|
| Sales | 472.8 | 515.9 | +9% |
| Profits | 58.4 | 58.7 | +1% |
| | | | |
| Operating Margin (%) | 12.4 | 11.4 | |
| EPS (p) | 22.3 | 26.0 | +15% |
| Gearing | Nil | 45.8% | |

| | |
|---|---|
| Chairman | Sir Tom Farmer |
| Chief Executive | Sir Tom Farmer |
| Origin | Tyre/exhaust replacement business |
| Where is it going? | Dominant company in industry |
| Market share | 23% |
| Strategy | Growth: organic, aquisition, diversification |

Group turnover by product 1999

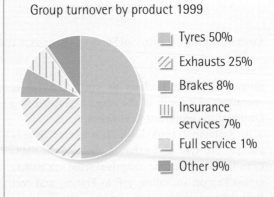

Tyres 50%

Exhausts 25%

Brakes 8%

Insurance services 7%

Full service 1%

Other 9%

Exhibit 4   Kwik-Fit Holdings plc – snapshot 1999.

## Details summary: Kwik-Fit Holdings plc – parent company

| | |
|---|---|
| Company name | Kwik-Fit Holdings |
| Registration number | 362333 |
| Date incorporated | 1974 |
| Issued capital (actual) | |
| Company type | Public Limited Company with share capital |
| Registration status | Scottish Company registered under Part I of the Co.'s Act |
| Quoted company type | Full London International Stock Exchange listing |
| Ownership status | An ultimate holding company |
| Turnover (GBP £m) | 1994: £260.10; 1995: £297.60; 1996: £365.40; 1997: £426.90; 1998: £472.80; 1999: £515.90 |
| Pre-tax profit (GBP £m) | 1994: £25.40; 1995: £29.30; 1996: £36.30; 1997: £43.30; 1998: £55.10; 1999: £64.90 |
| Number of Employees (1999) | 9500 |
| Estimated market share (1997) | Around 20% of the total automotive parts, repair and replacement market. |

Trading address
17 Corstorphine Road
Murrayfield
Edinburgh EH12 6DD
UK

Registered Address
St James's Court
Brown Street
Manchester M2 2JF
UK

| | |
|---|---|
| Telephone number | +44(0)131-337-9200 |
| Fax number | +44(0)131-337-0062 |

**Management structure**

Executive:

| | |
|---|---|
| Sir Tom Farmer CBE KCSG | Chairman and Chief Executive Officer |
| Graeme Bissett | Group Director of Finance |
| P Holmes | Group Director of Marketing |
| JM Houston | Group Director of Strategy and Development |

Non-executive:
N Hood
E Landau
I McIntosh
JR Padget

| | |
|---|---|
| K McGill | Company Secretary |

**Business classifications**

**Business description**

A group engaged in the operation of tyre, exhaust and automotive repair centres.

**Advisers**

| | |
|---|---|
| Auditor's name | Arthur Andersen 18 Charlotte Square Edinburgh EH2 4DF UK |
| Brokers | Panmure Gordon & Co. Ltd 9 Moorfields Highwalk London EC2Y 9DS UK |
| | UBS Philips & Drew 100 Liverpool Street London WC2M 2RH UK |
| Principal bankers | Midland Bank plc Bank of Scotland |

Group turnover by product (figures in £ millions)

| | 1999 | 1998 | % increase |
|---|---|---|---|
| Tyres | 256.3 | 241.4 | +6 |
| Exhausts | 130.1 | 121.2 | +7 |
| Brakes | 43.3 | 36.0 | +20 |
| Insurance services | 36.3 | 32.7 | +11 |
| Full service | 4.2 | | |
| Other | 45.7 | 41.5 | +10 |
| Total | 515.9 | 472.8 | +9 |

*Kwik-Fit*   http://www.kwik-fit.com

## Questions

1. What were the characteristics of the telesales insurance industry in the mid-1990s? Was it an attractive industry for a newcomer?

2. Discuss the fit between the industry key success factors and the skills, competencies and capabilities possessed by Kwik-Fit.

3. What strategies did Kwik-Fit use to enable it to penetrate the telesales insurance market as effectively as it did? Did it achieve competitive advantage?

4. Should Kwik-Fit diversify further into financial services and if so, where and how?

# Virgin

This case highlights how Virgin grew into and then expanded from a music company to become an international leisure business which later diversified into air travel by starting its own airline, Virgin Atlantic. The case then traces how music and retailing were largely divested leaving Virgin a much more focused business, which then diversified again as it exploited the potential of the Virgin brand. It also discusses how Virgin was launched on the stock exchange and later reprivatized.

It is the study of the growth of an entrepreneurial company and how the need for cash to fund expansion affected the strategic development.

Virgin cannot be separated from its founder and chairman, Richard Branson. Consequently, it is also the study of the motivation and style of a charismatic entrepreneur and strategic leader and his impact upon the culture and strategy of an organization.

Virgin can usefully be studied alongside the Thorn EMI case.

Minicase 1.4 in the main text provides an introduction to Virgin Atlantic and Minicase 2.2 is a shorter, edited version of this long case.

This version of the case was written in 2000 by John L Thompson. It is for classroom discussion and should not be taken to reflect either effective or ineffective management.

## History and development

Richard Branson was born in 1950. His father was a barrister and his grandfather a High Court judge. He attended public school, at Stowe; and it was here, at the age of 16, that he started the business that would eventually become Virgin.

Branson's first commercial venture was the *Student* magazine, designed for students worldwide, and with the aim of 'putting the world to rights'. Sales of 100,000 were claimed. The magazine, and the advertising on which it depended, were initially sold from a public telephone kiosk at Stowe school.

The magazine's success was patchy, and to generate a stronger cash flow Branson started selling popular records by mail order, using the *Student* to promote the venture. Certain records were normally sold only in selected London stores, and Branson saw an opportunity in making these more freely available to young people throughout the UK. Cash was required with every order, and the records were bought from wholesalers once a suitable size batch (for discounted prices) could be purchased. However, a number of record companies became suspicious of the venture and Branson had to change tactics and buy only through selected small record shops. The

business was named Virgin because Branson saw himself as 'commercially innocent'.

The business expanded after Branson left school, but the prolonged postal strike in the early 1970s threatened its viability. In 1971 Richard Branson, together with his school friend and *Student* partner, Nick Powell, decided to take the lease on a small shop unit in Oxford Street, London, and sell records direct to the public. The partners were joined by a distant cousin of Branson's, Simon Draper, who had come to England from South Africa. Draper started as the record buyer for Virgin, but eventually became Branson's number two and the initial strength behind the enormously successful music business.

The profits from the first store, supplemented by a loan from one of his aunts, allowed Branson to diversify and start a small recording studio in a country house.

Real growth took place after a young musician, Mike Oldfield, approached Branson. Oldfield was an instrumentalist who had been experimenting in the search for a new sound, but whose demonstration tapes had been rejected by several well-known record companies. Branson and Draper saw an opportunity and decided to take the risk. They released Oldfield's music under the title *Tubular Bells*. The first record eventually sold 10 million copies and provided Virgin with its first real cash flow.

Expansion continued steadily through the mid-1970s as new artistes were signed and new stores opened. The company was growing at some 20% per year. In May 1977 Virgin signed the controversial punk rock band, the Sex Pistols, and their immediate success provided another growth surge. Virgin signed the Sex Pistols after they had had two previous contracts with EMI and A&M cancelled within a six-month period. Advertisements for their records were refused by the television companies.

In 1978 Draper became managing director of Virgin Records (as the music division was then called) and Branson ceased to have a day-to-day operational involvement.

The period from the late 1970s to the early 1980s was a difficult one for Virgin, which found its earlier growth hard to sustain. Virgin needed new artistes with true success potential, and this problem was compounded when the whole industry experienced a recession in 1980. Virgin had attempted to penetrate the significant and lucrative American market, but failed. For several other countries Virgin simply licensed its artistes to other companies, but knew this would not be appropriate for establishing a real presence in America. Initially it attempted to run its own US operation to push UK artistes with seconded British personnel.

There were now 16 record stores which were reported to be trading at a loss because of inadequate management control. Retailing demands an attention to detail as well as creative flair and risk taking, which were Branson's main strengths. An attempt to start a new London magazine to rival *Time Out* proved unsuccessful and was closed down. Branson's long-standing partner, Nick Powell, left the organization in 1981. Virgin's image was deteriorating.

Consultants recommended that Virgin should develop complementary activities and Branson determined that the company should become more professional with a clearer strategy and supportive

structure. Related music and retailing activities, together with selected parts of the communications industry, were targeted because of the clear potential for synergy. Unrelated small enterprises and Virgin Atlantic Airways (begun in 1984) carried a different level of risk. The airline increasingly became Branson's main interest.

In 1982 Virgin signed Boy George and Culture Club and a third growth surge was provided for the music business. Branson recruited Don Cruickshank as managing director of Virgin (the central holding company) in 1984. Cruickshank, an accountant with an MBA who had previously been general manager of the *Sunday Times*, represented a more professional management style than had been previously associated with Virgin.

In 1983 Virgin was offered the opportunity to buy Our Price Records for £1 million, but was unable to raise sufficient cash. The company was sold to retail rival WH Smith instead.

However, by 1985 Virgin had become the 15th largest private company in the UK, with a turnover of £150 million and pre-tax profits of £12 million. For many years Virgin had been restricted by its bank to an overdraft limit of £3 million, but was now able to borrow £25 million from City institutions (in the form of convertible preference stock) to fund further growth. Fundamentally, Branson believed in organic growth rather than acquisition.

The continuing need for additional funding persuaded Branson that the time was right for Virgin to become a public company.

## Flotation and re-privatization

Prior to the flotation in November 1986 Branson, Draper and a third director, Ken Berry, who was deputy to Simon Draper at Virgin Music, purchased certain Virgin assets and formed a new private company, Voyager, which provided an umbrella for amalgamating Virgin Atlantic Airways, the related holiday business and a variety of small enterprises. A new managing director, again with an MBA and experience in the travel industry, was appointed. These activities, which were essentially unrelated to the mainstream Virgin entertainment businesses, were regarded as too volatile to be floated as part of Virgin.

The Virgin shares were sold by tender, with prospective investors invited to offer to buy a particular maximum number at a certain price. The price was struck at 140 pence, which valued the company at £240 million. Branson, Draper and Berry had retained 63% of the shares, and control. Some 60,000 small shareholders bought in to Virgin but the institutions were less enthusiastic. After expenses the flotation raised £55 million, half of which was injected immediately into Virgin. The remainder went to the directors, with Branson investing most of his £20 million share into Voyager.

Some of the money invested in Virgin was directed towards securing the elusive US presence. The company had learnt from its previous failure and now sought to establish a more permanent business with both US artists and locally recruited executives. Branson made no secret of the fact that he expected it would take a number of years before the venture turned in its first profits. The investment in the USA, and Virgin's increasing dependency on revenues from the USA, provoked Cruickshank into joking that Branson would have to moor his houseboat in mid-Atlantic. (For many years Branson ran Virgin's head office from a houseboat moored on a canal in West London.) Branson recognized the value of the back catalogue owned by EMI Music, a subsidiary of Thorn EMI, and contemplated how he might acquire the company to establish Virgin properly among the largest companies in the industry. It was rumoured in Autumn 1987 that Virgin would bid for the whole of Thorn EMI and divest the non-related businesses. However, the stock-market crash in October 1987 saw Virgin's share price marked down from 160 to 83 pence almost overnight, and Branson's opportunity to acquire EMI had vanished.

Meanwhile, Branson caused unease in the City when his first attempt to cross the Atlantic by balloon ended with an emergency landing. (Branson has set world records for trans-Atlantic crossings by both hot-air balloon and power boat.) Institutional investors were concerned with succession in the company if anything went seriously wrong. In a number of other ways Virgin settled uncomfortably as a public company. Branson, together with most of his colleagues, enjoyed an informal style of management; for example, they tended to dress casually rather than formally. They also claimed that they found it difficult to explain the uncertainties of the pop music business to City analysts. In reality, the links with the institutions were mainly forged by Cruickshank (who arguably did feel at ease), but inevitably Branson and Draper had to involve themselves.

Virgin felt that its real value was not being recognized by the City and that this was reflected in a low share price. It had introduced more robust management controls and was concerned to demonstrate that they were genuinely committed to 'the bottom line' and the interests of shareholders. Initially Virgin's shares had traded above the offer price, but once they fell below it they underperformed against the FT All-Share index.

*Being public is incredibly time consuming . . . every single thing has to be vetted by lawyers. You are tied up in tape. Around 50% of our time was spent worrying about going to stockbrokers' meetings, analysts' meetings, institutional meetings . . . and worrying about the next quarter's results . . . rather than planning for the long term. We thought: 'Let's try to get out of this'.*

(Richard Branson, quotation summarized from material included in: *Richard Branson and the Virgin Group*, Manfred Kets de Vries, Insead-cedep, 1989)

Virgin announced a fall in profits of 22% when it declared half-year results early in 1988, and this drove the share price down further.

*If anything goes wrong in a public company, it goes wrong very publicly and happens very quickly – and everybody panics and pulls the rug out.*

(Richard Branson, quotation taken from *Richard Branson and the Virgin Group*, op cit.)

The US music business was losing some £2–3 million on a turnover of £16 million, and Branson, who was perhaps too honest about the situation, commented that it would take another two years to move into profits. Branson also announced that the directors would buy back the 37% of the shares they did not have at the offer price of 140 pence.

The buy-back was completed in July 1988, and required a £182 million syndicated loan. One positive benefit to emerge from the period when Virgin was a quoted company was that the City insisted on sound control systems. They expected, for example, that Virgin would know the weekly turnover of each of its stores. These systems had been strengthened, and Virgin was therefore a sounder business when it was re-privatized.

Branson's problem now, though, would be funding the continued expansion of Virgin. Prior to going public he had often experienced difficulty in extending his overdraft facility.

Some time later Don Cruickshank left Virgin and he has since held a number of senior public-sector appointments, including Director-General of OFTEL, the telecommunications regulatory authority.

Exhibits 1 and 2 summarize the financial results for Virgin for the mid-1980s, and provide a comparison of Virgin's performance with that of the total leisure industry in 1988.

**Exhibit 2** Comparison of Virgin management with the total leisure industry

| | Leisure industry co. average | Virgin |
|---|---|---|
| | 12 months to 30.6.1988 | 12 months to 31.7.1988 |
| Return on net assets (%) | 16.5 | 9.3 |
| Return on equity (%) | 13.8 | 1.4 |
| Stock-days | 42 | 40 |
| Debtor days | 51 | 125 |
| Creditor days | 56 | 70 |
| Interest cover – times | 2.7 | 1.7 |
| Sales/employee – £'000 | 68.4 | 153.6 |

## Joint ventures

As one source of money Branson has entered a series of joint ventures and sold minority interests in several of his subsidiary businesses.

The Virgin group of companies, which remained separate from Voyager, was split into three distinct divisions: music, retail and communications. Voyager

**Exhibit 1** Virgin management – financial analysis for the five years before reprivatization (figures in £ millions)

| | 12 months to 31.1.1984 | 12 months to 31.1.1985 | 18 months to 31.7.1986 | 12 months to 31.7.1987 | 12 months to 31.7.1988 |
|---|---|---|---|---|---|
| Turnover | 99.6 | 152.8 | 312.2 | 299.7 | 377.0 |
| Profit before Interest and tax | 11.2 | 14.2 | 23.1 | 34.5 | 17.7 |
| Interest | 1.1 | 2.2 | 6.2 | 3.5 | 8.5 |
| Earnings | 4.1 | 6.6 | 9.3 | 16.9 | 1.0 |
| Profit after extraordinary items | 4.1 | 5.2 | 7.5 | 21.5 | (3.9) |
| Fixed assets | 14.5 | 45.4 | 78.8 | 55.8 | 74.4 |
| Current assets | 37.7 | 51.2 | 100.4 | 167.6 | 194.0 |
| Current liabilities | 35.8 | 50.4 | 67.7 | 68.5 | 78.6 |
| Net assets | 16.4 | 46.2 | 111.5 | 154.9 | 189.8 |
| Equity | 5.3 | 10.8 | 33.3 | 74.9 | 70.8 |
| Loan capital | 11.1 | 35.4 | 78.2 | 80.0 | 119.0 |

still encapsulated the airline, the holiday company and a variety of other enterprises. Each division comprised a series of small, autonomous businesses. More recently, Voyager has been renamed Virgin Travel Group.

At the end of the 1980s, Virgin consisted of some 200 subsidiaries. Each time a company expanded beyond a staff level of 80 Branson split it up and separated the people, perhaps into different premises. He believes that this prevents impersonality and maintains motivation.

In October 1989 Fujisankei of Japan bought 25% of Virgin Music for £96 million. Virgin as a whole (including retailing and communications as well as music) had been valued at £248 million when it was reprivatized in 1988.

In December 1989 Virgin formed a joint venture with Telfos Holdings for the manufacture of computer disks, videos and cassettes which would be sold under the Virgin label.

A joint venture with Marui of Japan followed in April 1990. Marui is a leading Japanese department store which caters mainly for young people. Virgin and Marui would jointly open a Megastore (multiple-products Virgin shop) in Tokyo in September the same year.

May 1990 brought Branson's third alliance with a Japanese partner. Seibu Saison, owner of Inter-Continental Hotels, paid Branson £36 million for 10% of Virgin Atlantic Airways. Branson's commitment to people and the quality of their working life meant that he felt comfortable doing business with the Japanese.

However, Branson bought back the Seibu Saison shareholding in November 1993, at which time he invested more of his own personal fortune in Virgin Atlantic.

Exhibit 3 summarizes the situation of Virgin and Virgin Atlantic in 1991. The joint ventures alone, however, were not going to see Branson through the recession. Divestment and further strategic alliances would follow.

## Virgin Music

Virgin Music mainly comprised the record label, recording studios and music publishing (finding opportunities for composers in recording, television,

**Exhibit 3**  The Virgin group – situation summary for 1990/91

|  | Virgin Music | Virgin Retail | Voyager Travel Holdings | Virgin Communications |
|---|---|---|---|---|
| Activities | Recording (80%) Music Publishing (18%) Studios (2%) | Megastores and Gamestores Europe and Japan | Virgin Atlantic (80%) Virgin Holidays (17%) Aviation Services (3%) | Computer games TV post-production Publishing and distribution |
| Turnover (£ million) | 350 | 175 | 383 | 140 |
| Pre-tax profit/(loss) (£ million) | 18 | (1*) | 6.2 | 14 |
| Outside shareholders | Fujisankei (25%) | UK: WH Smith (50%) Japan: Marui (50%) Europe: Consortium (20%) | Virgin Atlantic: Seibu Saison (10%) Voyager Hotels: John Laing (50%) | – |

*Profits in UK and Japan subsidizing expansion into Europe.

Source: *Financial Times*, 21 February 1992.

films and advertising). In addition, Virgin held merchandizing rights to sell a variety of products and publications at selected concert venues.

Virgin grew to become the 'largest second division' record company, smaller than the four majors (Warner, Sony, Polygram and EMI) and substantially bigger than most of the independent labels. Virgin's UK market share maximized at around 10% for singles, and 8% for LPs, cassettes and CDs. Over the years Virgin developed a reputation for picking 'winners', artists whose recordings would prove successful; and during the late 1970s and 1980s it obtained contractual rights for the music of Genesis, Phil Collins, Human League, Simple Minds, UB40 and many others in certain territories worldwide.

A record company contracts with an artist to exploit his or her talent in exchange for royalty payments. Normally a fixed number of albums and a number of years are agreed. The most successful companies are able to spot artists whose popularity will last for several albums (together with linked singles) and several years, and balance 'yesterday's winners' with future potential in a varied and extensive portfolio. Virgin had around 100 contracted artists on its various labels. In addition, Virgin enjoyed considerable success from a joint venture with EMI for a series of compilation albums in the series 'Now That's What I Call Music'. In the early 1980s Virgin acquired a number of small, independent record companies.

Virgin's early expansion abroad was through licensing agreements. After its initial failure in the USA the company realized that it would be increasingly profitable if it exercised greater control over marketing and promotion, and systematically it switched over to controlled subsidiaries. The USA was, however, always the prime target, and by the late 1980s Virgin was trading profitably with a wholly owned subsidiary employing experienced US staff. Ironically, the company became profitable earlier than Branson had anticipated.

## The sale of Virgin Music

By 1990 the total Virgin Group was experiencing cash problems again. This became more critical when the Gulf War hit airline revenues, and throughout 1991 it was speculated that Branson might be willing to sell all Virgin's music interests in order to support the retailing, communications and airline businesses.

During 1991 Sony, Polygram and Walt Disney all expressed interest before withdrawing from any negotiations. Bertelsmann (Arista and RCA labels) was also a serious contender. Since Branson's failed attempt to acquire EMI Music, Thorn EMI's chief executive, Sir Colin Southgate, had more than once tentatively approached Branson. EMI had already bought Chrysalis Records, and the acquisition of Virgin would elevate it to a position alongside the world leaders. The early overtures had been rejected, and throughout 1991 Branson remained undecided about whether he would actually sell. Early in 1992 Branson was seriously interested in a deal. Negotiations with Southgate finally took six weeks, and Thorn EMI agreed to buy Virgin Music for £560 million in cash. Southgate had wanted a deal involving both cash and shares, but Branson had demanded future compensation if Thorn's share price were to fall. The £560 million bought £3 million tangible assets, £507 million intangible assets (back catalogue material) and goodwill, and £50 million debt. The figure represented 1000 times Virgin's after-tax earnings in 1991.

Fujisankei received £120 million, Draper and Berry £70 million jointly and Branson £320 million. This allowed Branson to pay off all Virgin's remaining debt (£119 million) and support his airline further.

Perhaps not unexpectedly, Simon Draper subsequently left the more formal and culturally different Thorn EMI, but Ken Berry stayed and was instrumental as Thorn EMI proved that it could extract additional synergy from linking Virgin Music with EMI and Chrysalis. (The relative success of Virgin Music after the acquisition is discussed in the Thorn EMI case.)

Branson had obtained cash to support that business activity which he now cared most about, and although Virgin had sold the business for which it was best known the company was still a diversified leisure group with strong businesses.

In 1997 Virgin returned to the music industry when it set up a new, small, independent label, V2.

## Virgin Retail

Branson's challenge from retailing was to succeed with his preferred style of informal, empowered management as the number of stores increased and in an industry characterized by detail and normally making extensive use of control systems backed by information technology. Virgin developed with three different retail formats: specialist record stores, megastores and department store concessions. In 1984 all of the stores were redesigned by Conran to try and give them greater distinctiveness, promote additional business and strengthen the profit flow.

The single-product store format (mostly music plus some specialist games centres) was systematically extended to towns and cities throughout Britain. While they made an impact in terms of market share their returns were perceived as inadequate. In 1988 Virgin agreed to sell 74 specialist record shops to WH Smith's Our Price Music.

Virgin's megastores sell popular and classical music, back catalogue records and tapes, blank tapes, videos, T-shirts, posters, hi-fi equipment, computer games, books and stationery. They have a much greater selling area than the original single-product music stores and they have been concentrated in major cities in Britain, continental Europe, Australia and the Far East. By 1992 there were 14 stores in continental Europe and Australia.

In September 1991 Virgin and WH Smith formed a 50:50 partnership to manage and develop Virgin's UK chain of 12 megastores and seven games centres. WH Smith was providing both finance and retail expertise.

In November 1992 Branson announced his latest joint venture with Blockbuster Video, a Florida-based video-rental company. The purpose was to extend the Virgin megastore format to every large city in the USA as well as further sites in Europe and Australia. Consequently, this deal excluded Britain and Japan.

In simple terms Blockbuster bought an interest for an unnamed sum, and it was assumed that the two companies would jointly fund further expansion. Virgin and Blockbuster would jointly own the European stores and the one in Los Angeles (the first in the USA) on a 50:50 basis, but the new US units were to be 75% owned by Blockbuster. Virgin was to manage every megastore, and video rentals were to be added to the product range.

One year later the Virgin/WH Smith joint venture for megastores and games sold the games outlets, and in March 1994 the joint venture was absorbed into WH Smith's Our Price subsidiary. At this time there were 24 stores in the UK and Ireland. While the two brands remained separated on the high street, management was integrated. WH Smith now owned 75% of the joint venture, Virgin the remainder. No money changed hands and the overseas megastores were not affected. Simon Burke, managing director of Virgin Retail, took over the strategic leadership of the combined operation. (The fortunes of WH Smith deteriorated in the mid-1990s and a new strategic leader was appointed. At this time the main WH Smith retail branches were underperforming but Our Price and the Waterstone's specialist bookstores were profitable.)

At the same time Virgin established another joint venture with a Hong Kong trading company, Wheelock, and it was speculated that a Hong Kong megastore would be opened. In the event, Virgin decided that rents were too high and instead looked to Taiwan and China for expansion.

In 1998 Virgin bought the 75% shareholding held by WH Smith, initially taking out a loan to cover the £145 million price. The group now comprised 88 Megastores and 229 Our Price stores. Almost immediately it was rumoured there might be either a sale, a management buy-out or a management buy-in. None of these has so far happened and the Megastores have been deliberately repositioned to appeal to people in their twenties, thus reducing the early dependency on teenagers.

In 1996 Virgin first developed an Internet portal, Virgin.net; and this was followed in 1997 by on-line sales of CDs, books, financial products and train tickets. In 2000 Virgin followed up with a joint venture on-line wine-distribution business, where the classification was by taste instead of either grape variety or region of origin – 'to make things easier for consumers'.

## Virgin Communications

From 1981 Virgin diversified into a series of related communications activities. Branson felt that they offered new opportunities and synergy for his existing businesses.

He began with the distribution of filmed entertainment, arranging, for example, with major film studios to manufacture and distribute video copies of their old and new feature films. A subsequent dalliance with film making was discontinued in 1986. Virgin also provided services such as editing to the television and video industries, and acquired a company which produced television commercials. The film-distribution business was internationalized before being sold in 1989 for £50 million.

Virgin bought MGM Cinemas for £190 million in 1995; Branson believed that he could find new and distinctive opportunities for adding value and differentiating. Branson tested out a Virgin retail outlet in foyers and a premium-service cinema (as part of a multiple) with a personalized cloakroom, special snacks and waitresses serving drinks. Virgin only kept the largest MGM cinemas, including all of the multiplexes, and sold the others for £83 million, some of which it invested in new cinema complexes. The number of Virgin multiplex cinemas in the UK and overseas continued to grow, but the UK and Irish cinemas were all sold in 1999, and the money was used to repay the loans taken out to buy back Virgin Our Price.

Virgin entered broadcasting through an involvement in satellite television, and in November 1988 formed a partnership with the Italian television company Videomusic. The aim was to strengthen its European satellite business which at the time was failing to generate sufficient advertising revenue. In 1991 Virgin was part of a consortium which bid for (but failed to win) the franchise for a regional independent television channel.

Virgin Radio began broadcasting in the UK on medium wave in April 1993. This was an independent national radio station with a brief to provide 'popular music from the last 25 years'. It was a joint venture between Virgin and TVam, previously the provider of breakfast television for the ITV network. There was a lengthy delay before Virgin was able to acquire a national FM radio wavelength. After disc jockey Chris Evans left BBC Radio 1 he joined Virgin Radio, where he dramatically – but sometimes controversially – increased the morning audience figures. Later, when he realized that Branson was willing to relinquish control, he bought an 80% shareholding. Branson retained 20%.

The fourth arm of Virgin Communications was publishing. Virgin acquired WH Allen, and was also active in the manufacture and distribution of computer software games, many through its own stores. Virgin offered computer versions of Monopoly and Scrabble and, since 1989, had an agreement to distribute Japanese Sega games in the UK until the launch of Sony Playstation. Sega was number two to the then world leader Nintendo.

In 1994 Branson sold a 19.9% shareholding in Virgin Interactive Entertainment (VIE) to Blockbuster, in exchange for Blockbuster shares. VIE develops games software for, among others, Sega and Nintendo and has a lucrative licensing deal with Walt Disney for producing games which feature Disney film characters. Some time earlier 15% of VIE had been sold to Hasbro, the US toy company, and commentators began to speculate that VIE would eventually be floated as a separate company in the USA.

One major benefit for VIE was the 1993 merger between Blockbuster and Viacom, the US cable television company, which was developing rapidly in the field of multimedia. Six months later Branson (together with other smaller shareholders) sold a further 55% of VIE to Blockbuster; Virgin received $125 million and retained a 10% stake in VIE.

## Virgin Enterprises

This division was originally part of Voyager and embraced those entrepreneurial activities which could not be fitted elsewhere. If employees or out-siders attract Branson's interest with a new good idea that is likely to prove profitable he has generally been willing to provide venture capital and establish new small companies within the Virgin group. Those with the ideas are normally given shares in the new business, but not in Virgin overall. Early successful examples included a traditional pub, night clubs and a business set up to develop an elec-tronic synthesizer controller.

In September 1994 Virgin finalized an agreement with ICL (itself majority owned by Fujitsu) whereby ICL would manufacture Virgin-branded desktop, notebook and games computers for marketing through Virgin megastores and mail order.

Earlier that year Branson was part of a consor-tium which bid unsuccessfully against Camelot for the right to run the UK National Lottery. A second bid was again unsuccessful in 1989.

In September 1994 Virgin launched a new range of externally sourced consumer goods branded with the Virgin name. A new business, *Virgin Retail Brands*, was established. Typically these develop-ments have involved joint venture partners from the outset and, quite frequently, Virgin owns under 50% of the business. The first product was Virgin Vodka, a joint venture with William Grant, soon fol-lowed by Virgin Cola. Virgin Cola is mixed and canned by various companies from a concentrate produced by the Canadian company Cott (another joint venture arrangement), which also produces the concentrate for Sainsbury's Classic Cola. The timing seemed good; the cola market was expand-ing. Distribution through Tesco and a range of petrol forecourts was quickly secured; and Virgin used its own fleet of vans to collect supplies from cash and carry warehouses and deliver them to independent retailers. Virgin Cola was marketed as a quality product at a low price; Coca-Cola and Pepsi prices have always been higher, partly because of the money that they spend to promote the brand. Herein lay a problem: Virgin realized that it needed to undercut Coca-Cola and Pepsi but it still had to spend substantially on brand promo-tion. It did not enjoy the inherent benefits of a supermarket own-label product. Branson's declared aim was worldwide coverage using independent dis-tributors who would invest most of the funding required. Coca-Cola was sceptical about this new form of consumer goods network, commenting that Branson was 'either very brave or uninformed'. Virgin Cola made an immediate impact and its mar-ket share reached 5% at one stage. However, its ini-tial success has not been maintained and its share is now between 2 and 3%. The alliance with Cott was not successful and Virgin took over control of the business.

1995 saw Virgin enter the financial services mar-ket with a 50:50 joint venture with Norwich Union. The first product was a personal equity plan sold direct over the phone; personal pension schemes and insurance plans would follow later. Characteris-tically, Virgin planned to 'undercut competitors and remove the jargon and gimmicks from the products'.

In 1997 Virgin took a small shareholding in a floated company, Victory, set up by a ballooning friend of Branson. In turn, Victory owned two Virgin-branded businesses: Virgin Vie (not to be con-fused with VIE, Virgin Interactive Entertainments), which marketed a range of Virgin cosmetics, and Virgin Clothing, which began with jeans but later moved more up-market. Later the same year Virgin increased its stake to 46%, and thus became the largest shareholder.

In 1999 the Virgin brand was added to mobile phones with a 50:50 joint venture with One-2-One. The phones were an ideal product for Virgin Megastores and its other retail outlets. There were some operational hitches at the beginning but things settled down. In 2000 Virgin announced that it was entering into another joint venture to distrib-ute mobile phones in Australia.

## Virgin Atlantic Airways

Branson's business interest in a cut-price trans-Atlantic airline was triggered by a US lawyer, Randolph Fields, although his enthusiasm had earli-er been stimulated by his mother, an ex-air stew-ardess. Simon Draper was sceptical. Fields originally hoped to operate a Boeing 747 service from London to New York which was exclusively business class, but he was refused a licence. Branson typically set out to gather the information that he needed to reach a decision, and within a matter of weeks he had committed himself.

A major aspect of Branson's approach was an assessment of Freddie Laker's Skytrain – why Laker had failed, and what lessons could be learned. (The demise of Laker Airways is described in Minicase 17.1 in the main text.) Branson agreed with many other analysts that Laker had attempted to grow too quickly, and determined that his airline would stay relatively small. He also felt that Laker had made a mistake with his choice of aeroplane. Laker had flown DC10s, which are smaller than Boeing 747 jumbo jets, and Branson believed that in a tight price competition the airlines with the most seats available would have an advantage. Laker's competitive advantage was based wholly on his low prices, which he was able to offer by providing only the most basic of services. When the major carriers retaliated by discounting, Laker's initial advantage was unsustainable. Learning from this, Branson has ensured that Virgin Atlantic offers a high quality of service as well as competitive prices.

Branson quickly agreed the lease for a Boeing 747-200, and in summer 1984 he began flights from London Gatwick to Newark, New Jersey (which services New York). He added a second plane to the fleet and introduced flights to Orlando and Miami in 1986. In 1988 he received permission for a daily flight from Gatwick to Tokyo. British Airways (BA) had two flights every day from the preferred Heathrow airport. In 1991, after lengthy campaigning, Virgin was also allowed flight slots at Heathrow, competing directly with BA on several of its most profitable routes. Fields had parted company with Branson in 1985, arguing that the rate of expansion was too slow.

Virgin Atlantic now flies from Heathrow and Gatwick to several destinations in North America, and there are also regular scheduled flights to South Africa (Cape Town and Johannesburg) and Asia (including Tokyo, Shanghai and Hong Kong). A sea-sonal Manchester–Orlando route was inaugurated in 1996; and in partnership with CityJet Virgin also flies from London City airport to Dublin and Brussels.

Virgin launched three code-sharing partnership agreements (for through ticketing) in 1995: with Delta Airlines of the USA, Malaysia Airlines and British Midland.

Virgin's aircraft fleet is now based around Boeing 747s, some of these being the newest 747-400 series, which offers a higher payload and lower fuel consumption per nautical mile than the earlier versions. In addition, there is a number of Airbus A340s, the largest plane built by Airbus. All Virgin's aircraft are four-engined.

Virgin Atlantic was first profitable in 1986–87 after early teething problems, but this did not last. When Branson had just two aircraft (from 1986 to 1990) he had no spare capacity and, for example, any need for prolonged maintenance inevitably meant long delays for passengers.

Exhibit 4 provides a financial summary for the period 1987 to 1995. The figures for Virgin Travel (the renamed Voyager Group) include both the airline and the associated Virgin Holidays activities; the holiday business has typically been the more profitable activity. However, the airline has been profitable again since 1995. Exhibit 4 also includes data on passenger numbers and market-share achievements in the early 1990s. Exhibit 5 compares Virgin with BA and the complete transport industry sector in 1991. Care should be taken when comparing Virgin's ratios with those of BA, as the latter company is so much bigger and has an extensive portfolio of profitable and less profitable routes around the world. In 1989 Branson recruited BA's head of central marketing as an executive director, but he left after five days, commenting on a 'lack of systems and structure'.

During 1991 and 1992 the airline industry worldwide was hit hard by the economic recession following on from the business lost during the period of the Gulf War. For a period Branson became increasingly dependent on Virgin Travel's non-airline activities, and throughout much of 1992 Branson was reported to be seeking a partner willing to buy a 10–25%

**Exhibit 4** Virgin Travel Group (renamed from Voyager Travel Holdings) financial results (figures in £ millions)

| | 12 months to 31.7.1988 | 12 months to 31.7.1989 | 12 months to 31.7.1990 | 15 months to 31.10.1991 | 12 months to 31.10.1992 | 12 months to 31.10.1993 | 12 months to 31.10.1994 | 10 months to 31.8.1995 |
|---|---|---|---|---|---|---|---|---|
| Turnover | 84.7 | 106.8 | 208.9 | 382.9 | 356.9 | 401.0 | 503.4 | 507 |
| Profit before interest and tax (including non-trading income) | 12.5 | 11.6 | 13.5 | 12.6 | (10.3) | 5.5 | 1.05 | 38.1 |
| Operating profit | 12.0 | 8.9 | 10.0 | 10.7 | (9.4) | 8.4 | 1.9 | 38.7 |
| Interest | 2.0 | 3.2 | 4.9 | 5.6 | 4.0 | 5.0 | 4.0 | 2.76 |
| Profit before tax | 10.5 | 8.4 | 8.7 | 6.2 | (14.5) | 0.4 | (2.98) | 36.5 |
| Fixed assets | 46.6 | 64.0 | 89.6 | 92.1 | 95.1 | 97.5 | 93.5 | 91.2 |
| Current assets | 29.4 | 68.3 | 74.4 | 104.8 | 110.8 | 128 | 137.2 | 213.4 |
| Current liabilities | 29.0 | 48.5 | 75.9 | 99.5 | 125.6 | 146.5 | 145.1 | 181.8 |
| Net assets | 47.0 | 83.8 | 88.1 | 97.4 | 80.3 | 79.0 | 85.5 | 122.8 |
| Equity | 16.4 | 24.2 | 30.4 | 36.1 | 21.9 | 34.7 | 30.3 | 57.4 |
| Loan capital | 30.6 | 59.6 | 57.7 | 61.3 | 58.4 | 44.3 | 55.2 | 65.4 |
| | | | | **Virgin Atlantic Airways contribution** | | | | |
| Turnover | 75.39 | 92.29 | 180.54 | 336.7 | 303.4 | 346.6 | 444 | 448 |
| Exports (included) | 30.58 | 30.75 | 88.16 | 146.4 | 127.4 | N/A | 200 | 219.5 |
| Profit before tax | 10.14 | 7.19 | 7.57 | 0.7 | (21.0) | (6.0) | (9.8) | 31.6 |

Source: Company records.

**Exhibit 4**    (*Continued*)

| Total passengers carried | |
|---|---|
| 1990 | 906,199 |
| 1991 | 1,088,517 |
| 1992 | 1,232,983 |
| 1993 | 1,399,077 |
| 1994 | 1,694,871 |

Source: *CAA Annual and Monthly Operating & Traffic Statistics.*

| | Market share (%) | | | |
|---|---|---|---|---|
| | 1991 | 1992 | 1993 | 1994 |
| Route | – | – | – | – |
| New York (JFK & Newark) | 18 | 17.4 | 19.9 | 19.2 |
| Florida (Miami & Orlando) | 25.2 | 30.6 | 34.5 | 41.1 |
| Los Angeles | 25.8 | 22.3 | 23.8 | 24.1 |
| Tokyo | 16 | 17.3 | 18.3 | 16.6 |
| Boston | 15.3 | 19.7 | 23 | 24.6 |
| San Francisco | – | – | – | 15.2 |

Source: *CAA Nett and Mutual Exchange Statistics.*

**Exhibit 5**    Comparison of Voyager Travel Holdings with British Airways and the total transport and freight industry

| | Transport and freight industry company average | British Airways | Voyager |
|---|---|---|---|
| | 12 months to 30.06.1991 | 12 months to 31.03.1991 | 15 months to 31.10.1991 |
| Return on net assets (%) | 7.0 | 8.0 | 11.0 |
| Return on equity (%) | 4.4 | 9.9 | 13.7 |
| Stock – days | 22 | 3 | 5 |
| Debtor days | 67 | 58 | 38 |
| Creditor days | 88 | 100 | 48 |
| Interest cover – times | 1.8 | 1.8 | 2.0 |
| Sales/employee – £'000 | 53.3 | 90.7 | 126.3 |

stake in Virgin Atlantic in order to help to buy new aircraft and open up new routes. Nevertheless the expansion has continued.

The airline has provided excellent publicity opportunities, and self-publicity is a key feature of Branson's style of management.

From the beginning Branson decided to offer just two classes of travel, Business and Economy. He speculated that they should be named Upper Class and Riff Raff, but was talked out of the latter. His aim was 'the highest quality of travel at the lowest cost for all grades of passenger'. Branson's strategy has always been to discount trans-Atlantic fares, but recently this has been in an environment of low-price special fares offered by BA and all of the major US carriers. Virgin has less freedom for low prices on the Tokyo route. Virgin, however, has a different fare structure, providing its own equivalent of other airlines' first-class seats and service at traditional business-class prices. Virgin calls this its Upper Class service; and it also provides free limousine transport to and from airports for these particular customers, who are also provided with lounges to very high standards at most airports. Economy passengers who pay full fare rather than a specially discounted rate have a separate cabin. Legroom tends to be more generous on Virgin than on most other planes, and Branson has used his expertise in music and communications to pioneer new forms of in-flight entertainment, such as personal videos with a selection of films. The airline has won several awards for the quality of its services.

Branson has been involved in an acrimonious and protracted dispute with BA, whom he accused of discounting fares to uneconomic levels in order to force out any smaller competitors. He also alleged that BA poached his passengers and spread untrue stories about Virgin. In January 1993 BA 'apologized unreservedly' and agreed an out-of-court settlement of £610,000 plus costs. Branson had in turn provoked BA and its then chairman, Lord King, who once described him as a pirate. In response to this, Branson, with the media fully informed, dressed himself as a pirate and draped the Virgin logo over BA's model of Concorde, which is on public display at Heathrow.

Branson's long-term risk has always been that prolonged fare wars on the busy North Atlantic routes could make Virgin Atlantic's profits unsustainable. Flying in and out of Heathrow also brings Virgin into direct competition with the leading US carriers, who are also quite happy to offer special price promotions in order to increase their load factors. In 1999 Virgin was forced to cut its UK/US prices in the face of intense competition and excess supply. Later that year Branson negotiated the sale of 49% of the airline to Singapore Airlines for £600 million. Some of the money was invested in the airline but the bulk was to be used to expand Virgin's new Internet and mobile phone interests. The deal improved Singapore Airlines' access to the important US market.

Virgin has so far expressed no interest in following the hub-and-spoke strategies (several flights into and out of an important centre) of the major carriers. In December 1992 Virgin expanded in Florida, with a new holiday airline, Virgin Vintage Air Tours. Branson uses restored DC3 Dakotas to fly from Orlando to Key West, and saw opportunities for expanding the service to include flights from Key West to Havana, and between Orlando and Miami and Los Angeles and Palm Springs.

Through an acquisition in Belgium (in 1996) Virgin also entered the no-frills, low-price sector of the European market with Virgin Express, flying out of a base in Brussels. Only marginally profitable, Branson has commented that with hindsight he would have been better to have set up from scratch rather than take over an airline with problems. In 2000 Virgin began to set up a similar no-frills business in Australia.

## Virgin Railways

When the railways in the UK were privatized in 1992, Virgin bid for a number of operating franchises. It was successful in winning two major (and fixed period) franchises comprising 15% of the UK rail network. Its Cross Country network runs from Scotland through the north-east of England and Birmingham to Cornwall. The primary service on the West Country mainline is Glasgow to London Euston. However, there are also regular services from Liverpool and Manchester to London and some from the north of England to Brighton. The London–Birmingham–Shrewsbury route completes the picture.

Virgin has struggled to run its trains on time and has developed a reputation for unpunctuality. The truth is that the service is variable and sometimes very good. Part of the problem was that Virgin inherited some outdated rolling stock and routes where new track and signalling – in part Railtrack's responsibility – was urgently required. Massive investment is required and the picture will remain uncertain until the next round of franchises are announced. Virgin Rail was first profitable in 1998. During this year a 49% stake was sold to Stagecoach for £158 million. Stagecoach, managed by the well-known entrepreneur Brian Souter, already had a small rail franchise but it had grown through the acquisition of regional bus companies after this industry was also privatized.

## Richard Branson

It is impossible to assess the development, strategy and success of Virgin without examining the style and contribution of Sir Richard Branson. Branson began the company some 30 years ago and he still dominates every major move. Although perceived to be unconventional he is clearly astute, and he has become one of Britain's richest businessmen.

Branson is quietly spoken and informal, and he rarely wears a business suit. When Virgin was a public company it was commented that Branson was not very articulate when confronted by a room full of City analysts – a situation in which he clearly felt uncomfortable. His record of success has caused some outsiders to fear that he was always looking to increase his own wealth and reputation rather than develop Virgin in the best interests of the shareholders. Branson is entrepreneurial and a risk taker – arguably it was the City's inability to relate to the risks he took, and to understand properly the risks inherent in the music business, that caused the rift between them to develop.

Yet, despite his quiet manner, Branson is an insatiable self-publicist. His exploits in crossing the Atlantic by hot-air balloon and power boat are testimony to both his risk taking and his publicity seeking. When Virgin Atlantic was launched he invited the press to photograph him in his bath playing with a model aeroplane. He has also taken a personal interest in ventures unrelated to Virgin's businesses, launching, for example, Mates low-price condoms to help in the fight against AIDS.

The publicity has had a major impact. Branson is well known and easily recognized. Mrs Thatcher selected him to chair an independent committee to examine ways of clearing up the environment, on the grounds that he was a role model for young people. Branson has at the same time been able to direct the publicity for the benefit of Virgin. Before Virgin started flights to Tokyo Branson capitalized on his public image and gave numerous interviews in Japan.

Branson personally owns, among other things, an island in the British Virgin Islands (which people can rent from him), a South African game reserve, a castle in Morocco and 50% of the Storm modelling agency. He was very anxious to win the franchise for the UK National Lottery, putting forward proposals for a non-profit lottery – the People's Lottery.

### Branson's management style

For many years Branson ran Virgin's head office with very few staff from a houseboat moored on a canal in West London. The various divisions and businesses operated from offices all over London. Virgin is genuinely decentralized, with each division comprising several autonomous small businesses. The atmosphere everywhere is casual, and pop music is normally being played. Branson's aim is to ensure that people relate to the business in which they work, and feel part of something tangible and handleable. Virgin Atlantic is something of an exception and it is run from a more modern and formal office block near Gatwick airport.

Information flows and management are frequently informal (although there are effective control systems in place), and it tends to work. Branson scribbles endlessly in small notebooks. He is renowned for travelling frequently on Virgin Atlantic, talking to passengers about their expectations and levels of satisfaction with Virgin's service, and making notes of his conversations. Many Virgin employees are given Branson's work and home telephone numbers and encouraged to ring with problems and queries. There is considerable delegation and empowerment.

*If the staff are happy the business will prosper . . .*
  *You should never really criticize your staff. You*
  *should always be praising. If you praise somebody*
  *they are going to blossom.*

(Richard Branson, from
*Richard Branson and the Virgin Group*, op cit.)

Branson gives away shares in new venture companies within the Virgin group, arguing that this actually costs nothing to do but it acts as a powerful motivator for creating growth and success. He has stated that he believes that successful businesses are created and sustained with:

- quality products and services
- value for money
- innovation and
- an element of fun.

## An assessment

It is tempting to argue that Branson has been lucky. For example, he made his first fortune after Mike Oldfield turned up with *Tubular Bells*. However, Branson backed a project that other major record companies had already rejected. His success has been dependent upon his ability and willingness to seize opportunities which are offered to him. Randolph Fields provided the idea for Virgin Atlantic – Branson raised the money and took the risk. Branson's skill lies in taking other people's ideas and really developing them. He seems very astute at judging the implicit risks.

Initially, Virgin's development was haphazard and directionless, with no clear strategy. Joint ventures, partial sales and divestments have been utilized to fund new initiatives, and at times the decisions have

seemed inconsistent. The mail-order business was initially seen as a means of raising money to support his *Student* magazine. The record label and recording studio hardly seemed a natural progression from a record shop. However, Branson has later proved very successful at developing one business out of another, and seeing linkages. This has fitted well with his desire to run Virgin as a conglomerate of small entrepreneurial businesses, one which has been described as a 'branded venture capital company'.

Branson has proved himself to be a ruthless negotiator of a good deal, belying the media image of the happy-go-lucky entrepreneur or, as he was once described, a 'hippy capitalist'. But he remains more a deal maker than a detail man. This ability has been extremely valuable in establishing the series of strategic alliances and joint ventures which have enabled Virgin to continue expanding in recent years.

In the end one must question whether the Virgin group's diversification, and pursuit of ideas which interested Richard Branson, such as the airline, inhibited the development of the core Virgin company and ultimately necessitated the sale of Virgin Music. When Virgin became a public company the launch prospectus had stated: 'The Directors aim to develop Virgin into the leading British international media and entertainment group. Virgin will continue to expand those activities in which it has proven skills, knowledge and depth management'. But if this was never achieved, did it really matter? Is business about growth and power, or about pursuing interesting challenges?

*I never let accountants get in the way of ideas. You*
*only live once, and you might as well have a fun time*
*while you're living.*

(Richard Branson, from: Austin, T (1992)
Return ticket, *Sunday Times Magazine*,
6 December)

In the final analysis, Virgin remains a highly complex organization: it is difficult for an interested outsider to obtain accurate financial information as Virgin's finances are controlled through offshore

**Exhibit 6**  Virgin: selected financial results, 1997

| Activity | Revenues £m | Profit/loss before tax £m |
|---|---|---|
| Airlines | 678.5 | 45.2 |
| Total for Virgin Travel Group | 886.6 | 67.5 |
| Virgin Retail (UK) | 28.5 | −7.5 |
| Virgin Retail (overseas) | 300.0 | na |
| Virgin Entertainment | 30.6 | −7.6 |
| Virgin Direct | 315.7 | −19.7 |
| Virgin Cola | 19.3 | −2.3 |
| Virgin Spirits | 1.9 | −2.2 |
| Virgin Cinemas | 84.4 | −4.7 |
| Virgin Railways | 423.5 | 4.3 |
| Total for Virgin Group (excluding Virgin Travel) | 1228.0 | −65.3 |

Source: *The Economist*, 21 February 1998 (p. 83).

trusts and hidden shareholdings. Clearly (as shown in Exhibit 6) most of the profits now come from the airline, the business that once needed substantial investment. Profitable from the mid-1990s it is now subsidizing many of the other businesses. Stung by criticism, Richard Branson insists that Virgin has a positive cash balance which it can use whenever it needs funds.

*Virgin*   http://www.virgin.com

## Questions

1. What are the major strategic issues raised by the Virgin case?

2. What do you believe have been Richard Branson's objectives for his business interests?
   Are the objectives consistent?
   What strategies has he followed?
   What difficulties has he encountered?

3. Do you believe that Virgin Group (excluding Virgin Travel) and Virgin Atlantic are efficient and effective?

4. Apply the E–V–R (environment–values–resources) model to Virgin during the period when it was a public company and to the main Virgin businesses (Virgin Group and Virgin Atlantic) at the end of the 1990s.

# Thorn EMI

The Thorn EMI case (written mainly in 1995) tracks the development of the company until 1996, when it was split into two separate businesses, music (including music retailing) and rentals. The case shows how the company had been systematically transformed from a diverse manufacturing business to a somewhat more focused service business.

The case encourages debate on the interrelatedness of certain knowledge-based businesses and on whether recording, music publishing and music retailing form a strong 'heartland'. The case invites readers/students to consider whether a sale of the business (had there been a suitable buyer) would have been a long-term better alternative to a corporate split. While it is true that (a) EMI Music and Time Warner proposed to merge (in 2000) and began serious negotiations with Competition Authorities in both America and Europea, and (b) Thorn Rentals has been acquired by the Japanese bank, Nomura, these facts do not negate the value of discussing and evaluating the relative merits of the possible strategic alternatives under review in 1995.

The case examines the relative success and the key success factors for the company's two core businesses, music and rentals. The role of the company's strategic leadership is also examined.

The case opens a discussion on what might happen to Thorn EMI in the future.

This case was written by John L Thompson in 1995 from a variety of published sources and Thorn EMI Annual Reports. It is for classroom discussion and should not be taken to reflect either effective or ineffective management.

## Introduction

In 1995 Thorn EMI was an international company with a turnover exceeding £4 billion. Appendix 1 provides a five-year financial summary. It concentrates on carefully selected consumer-orientated *service* businesses where it enjoys both global scope and a strong market position. Its recent strategy has been to build world-class competitive strengths, partially achieved through appropriate cost cutting, while dramatically rationalizing its portfolio of activities. Historically Thorn EMI has competed as a manufacturer, most notably in the lighting and defence industries, but it has systematically divested most of these interests.

Thorn EMI is one of the world's leading music companies, along with *Polygram* (majority-owned by Philips of The Netherlands and focused on music and filmed entertainment), the US *Time Warner*, the world's largest media and entertainment company, *Sony* of Japan (the electronics giant which absorbed CBS and Columbia Pictures), *Bertelsmann/RCA* of Germany (publishing company, owner of Doubleday

and active in record and book clubs) and *MCA Music*, until recently a subsidiary (along with Universal Pictures) of Matsushita/JVC, another Japanese electronics giant. In the UK music industry, Thorn EMI and Polygram vie for market leadership. Their annual market shares are in the 20–25% range, varying with the relative success of album releases by their major artists, whose fortunes can often rise and fall. Warner and Sony Music enjoy shares of around 10% each. In music publishing in the UK, Thorn EMI leads jointly with Warner Chappell. Both have 20% market shares; Polygram Music has 11%. For 1994–95, Soundscan (US) estimated EMI's US market share at 9%, placing it sixth. Time Warner leads with 23%. The vital US market is three times the size of the UK market and the largest in the world (Japan, 50% bigger than the UK, is the second largest with the UK third, closely followed by Germany and France). Recent estimates for the $33 billion global music market give Time Warner leadership with a 14% share. EMI, Polygram, Sony and Bertelsmann all have some 10–11%; MCA has 6%. Music is now Thorn EMI's largest business (see

Appendix 2). It is profitable and premium rated, but by nature it is a risky industry.

The second-largest business is specialist equipment rentals (consumer household electrical products in the main) and associated activities. Thorn EMI has been described as the only worldwide specialist in this field, with again a 15% share of the global market. This business is less profitable than music, but it is perceived as 'solid' and less risky. The third key business is retailing. Thorn EMI is a leading retailer of music-based products in the UK; its HMV shops are also to be found in the USA, Canada, Australia, Japan, Hong Kong and Ireland. In March 1995 Thorn acquired the Dillons chain of specialist bookshops from the receiver of Pentos, its parent company. A fourth division encompassing security and electronics products was largely divested in early 1995.

In 1995 the company faced a number of key strategic issues. One concerned how the music business might be expanded further, possibly implying related diversification – book publishing was being suggested as an option worth considering even before the acquisition of Dillons. A second concerned the structure of the organization as a whole. Music is run from headquarters in New York; the rest of the businesses are controlled from London. At the Annual General Meeting in July 1995 it was announced that Thorn EMI was investigating ways of splitting the company into two separate businesses; HMV would stay with Music. Given its recent growth in profitability, an inevitable third issue is the potential for take-over bids.

## The development of Thorn EMI

The music interests developed around the original HMV (His Master's Voice) label, owned by EMI – the initials stood for Electric and Musical Industries. HMV has been a major player in the recorded music business from its very beginnings. EMI grew and diversified but in the 1970s it came close to financial collapse. The company had invented the world-beating EMI brain scanner but seriously underestimated the extent of the resources required to market such an innovative product. In 1979 EMI was merged with Thorn, a well-known manufacturer in the lighting and electrical industries. The subsequent history of Thorn EMI can be split into a number of stages.

Between 1979 and 1983 Sir Richard Cave (the chairman) set about integrating the two businesses into a cohesive whole; his declared aim was to create a leading company in selected industry sectors, information technology, entertainment and leisure. In 1983 Thorn EMI bought Software Sciences. This specialist company had been founded in 1970 by Colin Southgate, who had begun his working life as an actuary, and he now joined Thorn EMI.

Sir Richard Cave retired and was succeeded as chairman and chief executive by Thorn EMI's managing director, Peter Laister. The new strategic leader saw Thorn EMI's future as a global high-technology company, and in 1984 he agreed the purchase of Inmos.

Inmos had been set up in 1978 with funding from the then Labour government's National Enterprise Board. The intention was to give the UK a valuable presence in the fiercely competitive world semiconductor industry. Inmos was to design and manufacture high added-value memory chips. Initially the company was reliant on American expertise and it invested in state-of-the-art production facilities. The revolutionary transputer chip was invented but the company was unable to raise the development capital required. Thorn EMI, heavily dependent on consumer-orientated businesses, agreed to buy Inmos from Mrs Thatcher's government for £125 million in September 1984. In that year Inmos enjoyed a small trading profit, but it was losing money by the first quarter of 1985 and it was not profitable again until 1988. The main problems came from defective chips, which had been delivered to customers before the acquisition by Thorn EMI, and worldwide oversupply, which was driving down prices. Inmos was eventually sold in December 1988 to Thomson-SGS, the French microelectronics group, for £108 million. Thorn EMI had invested some £300 million in Inmos in four years and now retained a 10% share.

Meanwhile, in 1985, Laister had been replaced after a boardroom coup. Colin Southgate (later Sir Colin), who had joined the Thorn EMI main board in 1984, became managing director (1985) and later chief executive (1987) and chairman (1989). He remains the strategic leader in 1995 as executive chairman. He is supported by a strong board of directors, which includes the heads of the two main divisions, EMI Music and the rentals business, and several strong non-executives.

In 1985, Thorn EMI, labelled a 'lumbering giant' by some commentators, was a diversified conglomerate which comprised the following activities:

- consumer electronics – television manufacture (Ferguson brand)
- domestic appliances and heating products (including such brands as Kenwood kitchen appliances)
- rental and retail of consumer products (DER, Radio Rentals, Rumbelows, and so on)
- music
- film-making and screen entertainment
- lighting
- electronics, information technology and telecommunications
- semiconductors (Inmos).

Southgate has been reported as believing that 'Thorn had tried to be all things to all men in all areas'. He felt that it needed stronger focus.

## Strategic problems and changes in the mid- to late 1980s

Southgate, then, felt that Thorn EMI faced two critical strategic dilemmas. First, there was a lack of focus on the perceived core businesses; secondly, the company was not big enough in most of its markets to gain all the potential economies of scale. Southgate feared that without drastic changes Thorn EMI's growth would slow down, earnings would fall and the business could well become an acquisition (and break-up) target.

The company was competing in too many marketplaces and as a result the corporation was not able to add sufficient value in all of the subsidiary businesses. Many of Thorn EMI's markets were

becoming increasingly global in scope; the perspective of a UK-based company which exported, rather than a global organization, was inappropriate.

Southgate was instrumental in initiating a strategy of greater focus, and he started a major divestment programme which involved the sale of over 60 subsidiary companies in three years, 1985–88, with another 20 following in the next 5 years. These included such diverse businesses as property, telecommunications, instruments, film and video production and distribution (Elstree Studios), EMI cinemas and television manufacturing. Ferguson was sold to Thomson in 1987 for £90 million; simply 90% of its sales were in the UK whilst its major competitors were more international in scope. The sales ran parallel to an acquisition programme aimed at bolstering the selected core businesses. The number of companies bought is much lower than the number sold, but some of the acquisitions have been strategically very significant.

Sir Colin Southgate has therefore concentrated on acting as a *corporate* strategic leader and relied heavily on support and strong leadership from the heads of the remaining divisions.

*Thorn EMI was concentrating on businesses where it believed it could achieve an important world market share.*

Appendix 3 charts the response of the stock market to the varying, but generally improving, fortunes of Thorn EMI.

By 1988 Thorn EMI had been consolidated into four groups:

- *Rental and retail* – Radio Rentals, DER, Rumbelows and the HMV Music shops in the UK, together with related interests abroad.
- *Technology* – primarily software and security systems.
- *Consumer and commercial* – based on lighting and Kenwood appliances.
- *Music.*

Thorn EMI spent £371 million in 1987 to acquire the US rental specialist, Rent-A-Center, a national chain of owned and franchised outlets, and began to invest to increase the number of branches. Having bought a Swedish rental business from leading rival Granada in 1986, Thorn EMI bought five more continental electronic rental companies from Granada in 1987. The total investment was some £60 million. Vallances, a Yorkshire-based electrical goods distributor, was bought to supplement the Rumbelows high-street stores.

The technology division operated in three areas: software, security and electronics. Notably these businesses were primarily targeted at niche markets, mostly but not exclusively in the UK. Software Sciences was involved in various activities, including retail EPOS (electronic point-of-sale) systems; Marks and Spencer was an important customer. Security included building security and fire protection. Electronics had an important base in defence, but had expanded into ticketing systems for such customers as British Rail and London Underground.

Lighting spanned the automotive, industrial and consumer markets (the Mazda brand) and it was retained as a core activity in the 1980s because it fitted the requirements of a business which was profitable and in which Thorn EMI believed it could build a global presence. By early 1989, and following a number of acquisitions, Thorn EMI owned lighting companies in West Germany, Sweden, France and Italy (joint venture). A major acquisition in the USA had been sought. One important buy was the French company, Holophane, which manufactures pressed glass products for automobile lighting together with light fittings. However, Europe does not have standard voltages and light fittings, with the UK particularly out of alignment, leading to some fragmentation.

The kitchen appliances business, Kenwood, was divested in 1989. A management buy-out realized £55 million, with Thorn EMI retaining an 8% stake.

Throughout the 1960s and 1970s EMI had consistently been the UK market leader for popular music albums and singles, with a market share of around 20%. Artists such as Cliff Richard and The Beatles had ensured growth and prosperity. EMI was linked with the American Capitol label and consequently distributed the music of artists such as The Beach Boys in the UK. Stronger competition, particularly from Polygram, and a failure to maintain the relative

strength of the artist roster saw album market share fall to around 13% in 1987 – at this time EMI's share of the now less important singles market was some 8%. A determination to regain clear UK market leadership and become a force in the world music industry resulted in a number of key strategic acquisitions which are discussed later.

### The strategy from 1989

In 1989 Southgate clarified that lighting, music and the rental of electronic and white goods would be Thorn EMI's three core businesses for the future. All had international potential.

A year later *lighting* was made a candidate for divestment. Southgate explained that the underlying strategy of focus and international presence was consistent; simply the company no longer believed it could become a global player in lighting, the original Thorn business founded by Sir Jules Thorn in 1928. Thorn was strong in the provision of light *fittings*, but weak in light *sources* – the bulbs and tubes which go in the fittings. Moreover, the light source business was again too heavily dependent on the UK.

In November 1990 the first part of lighting (the loss-making lamp bulbs and tubes company) was sold to General Electric of America for £69 million. The remainder of lighting (fittings) was disposed of through a management buy-out in 1993. This raised £162 million, with Thorn retaining a 10% share.

The fittings arm of Thorn Lighting competed on quality products, high levels of service, innovation and new product development. Efficient cost management and productivity were critical in a competitive market. To succeed the company had to win tenders for major industrial, commercial and public amenity lighting schemes, such as new airports and the Channel Tunnel, and the associated new terminals.

Table 1 shows the relative profitability of the Lighting division in its last five years.

The software business was sold in 1991, and in 1992 the Rumbelows shops were partially converted from retail to rental. Thorn EMI's retail activities were now being focused more on the HMV music and video shops.

**Table 1**   Thorn Lighting, 1988–1993

| Year | Turnover £m | Operating profit £m |
|---|---|---|
| 1988/89 | 440.4 | 39.4 |
| 1989/90 | 537.8 | 32.7 |
| 1990/91 | 478.0 | (1.9) |
| 1991/92 | 343.7 | 12.6 |
| 1992/93 | 346.7 | 15.2 |

Thorn EMI had obtained a substantial minority shareholding in Thames Television, which it was rumoured to have offered for sale in early 1990. However, in February 1991, Thames shares owned by BET were bought by Thorn EMI at a 'very favourable price', and Thorn was now in overall control with a 59% stake. Shortly afterwards Thames lost its regional commercial television franchise in the government's new bidding system; Thorn EMI sold its shareholding to Pearson in 1993.

## Thorn EMI in 1995

Thorn EMI consists of four businesses or divisions.

*EMI Music*, based in New York, comprises 65 record companies and 23 music publishing companies with operations in 37 countries. EMI Music is vertically integrated, the implications of which are discussed in a later section of this case study, and includes:

- artist and repertoire (A&R) development – the acquisition and development of future talent
- studio recording
- production facilities, primarily compact disc pressing in the UK, the USA, The Netherlands, Australia and South Africa
- marketing and distribution – direct to HMV and other outlets
- promotional and music videos
- the 'ownership, management and exploitation of copyrights in songs and other compositions' – including the management of royalty earnings from EMI-owned music being for films and television programmes and commercials. EMI's extensive back catalogue of recorded music is particularly valuable here.

At the heart of the Thorn Group are the rentals businesses. The philosophy of this division is one of providing access to a range of household products to those customers who cannot afford, or choose not, to buy outright. These products now include televisions, videos and stereos, white goods (washing machines, refrigerators, etc.), furniture, jewellery (US only), computers, portable telephones and pagers. A variety of formats is targeted at selected niches worldwide, and customer options include long- and short-term hire, rent-to-own, rental with a purchase option and hire purchase. Thorn is also active in interactive in-room guest services and television systems for hotels. This is a business which requires heavy investment but, managed well, delivers a strong cash flow.

HMV is a specialist retailer of recorded music and associated products. A few years ago the chain consisted of 40 UK-based stores; now there are 200, based in the UK, the USA, Japan, Australia, Canada, Hong Kong and Ireland. Fifty per cent of sales are generated outside the UK. Dillons comprised 149 shops when it went into receivership in 1995; on the announcement of the acquisition, analysts predicted that Thorn EMI would 'cherry pick' and not keep open those stores with high rents or poor locations. In the end, 100 stores were retained, with the rest reverting to the receiver. Dillons is the second largest specialist bookseller in the UK; Waterstones, owned by WH Smith, is market leader.

TSE – Thorn Security and Electronics – was formed in 1992 to co-ordinate a number of technology-related businesses. Historically, the division exploited specialist competencies originally developed in defence-related industries, later transferred to civilian applications. The division as a whole, or the businesses individually, was available for sale at the right price since 1989. Many businesses, accounting for the major part of TSE's turnover, have been divested; in 1994–95, for example, ones manufacturing electron tubes, automation engineering products, defence electronics and fire detection systems were sold. Two of the three remaining in 1995 respectively produce and market transactions (ticketing) systems and credit/bank card security

**Table 2** Thorn EMI businesses

| Division | % of turnover | |
| --- | --- | --- |
| | 1986 | 1995 |
| EMI Music | 15 | 49 |
| Thorn Group | 26 | 35 |
| HMV | 2 | 11 |
| Other activities (TSE and discontinued) | 57 | 5 |

**Table 3** Breakdown of the price of a compact discs

| | £ |
| --- | --- |
| Manufacturing | 1.05* |
| Artist royalties | 0.88 |
| Publisher's royalties | 0.44* |
| Recording producer | 0.44* |
| Distribution/promotion | 4.66* |
| Retail margin | 3.25* |
| Tax | 2.27 |
| Total | 12.99 |

*Denotes EMI involvement in the operation.
Source: *Financial Times.*

systems (based on patented magnetic 'watermark' technology); the third, the Central Research Laboratories, has recently invented an electronic fingerprint identification system.

During the divestment process, some negotiations have failed. Southgate has a reputation for holding on for the right deal; his strategy for TSE has always been 'to work our way out over time' and continue investing in the businesses to make sure that operational improvements are achieved. Some analysts, however, believed that Thorn's failure to divest all of the businesses quickly reflected a weakness in the strategy.

The relative importance (in terms of turnover) of each business is shown in Table 2 and compared with the situation in 1986.

## The music business

Figure 1 illustrates the value of linking the recording and marketing of music with music publishing. EMI records, presses, distributes and retails popular and classical music in a vertically integrated supply chain; the company is also a world leader in music publishing, enabling the long-term exploitation of the performing rights associated with compositions and recordings. Table 3 illustrates the breakdown of the costs and margins involved in a compact disc and highlights that EMI 'owns' every part of the added value chain except the artist, who would normally be tied to the company by contract. On occasions these contracts will be geographically specific, rather than globally exclusive, and maybe cover the whole world except for North America; another company would hold the American rights.

The marketing of new music, even from established artists, is inevitably risky. Performers, particularly if they write their own songs, may well be late delivering their new material, and success with a previous album is no guarantee that a new album will sell. However, both back catalogue and compilations, and music publishing, provide a more stable and dependable source of revenue and earnings. Their relative importance for Thorn EMI is illustrat-

**Table 4** EMI Music Revenues, 1992

| | Percentage of sales | Return on sales (%) |
| --- | --- | --- |
| *Recorded music* comprising | 86 | |
| New releases | 52 | 5 |
| Back catalogue | 34 | 10 |
| *Music publishing* comprising | 14 | 36 |
| Mechanical | 8 | |
| Performance | 4 | |
| Synchronization | 2 | |

Classical music represents some 20%, popular music 80%

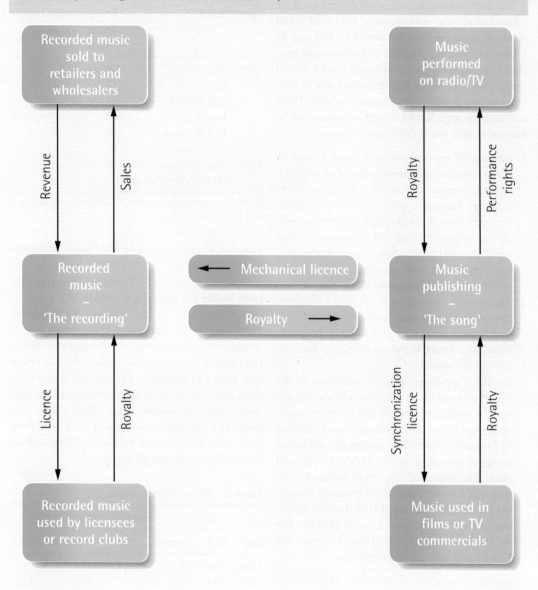

*Figure 1* Revenue flow in EMI music. The principle revenue streams in, and between, recorded music and music publishing. Source: Thorn EMI Annual Report.

ed in Table 4. Re-released back catalogue records also carry lower royalties to the artists.

The stability arises from two factors: first, multiple sources of income; and secondly, the breadth and depth of catalogue material owned by EMI and its major rival, Warner Chappell. It is additionally beneficial that these copyrights generally last for several years, with some songs and recordings able to earn reproduction royalties over several decades. There are three key ways in which song copyrights can be licensed to yield music publishing revenues.

1. Mechanical royalties are paid when a song or composition is reproduced and sold as a record, cassette, compact disc or video. This is an international business, with collection agencies around the world. Mechanical royalties account for the largest share of EMI's music-publishing revenues, and they are clearly boosted whenever EMI contracts a new recording artist or song writer who becomes successful.

2. Performance royalties arise when the composition or song is performed anywhere in public, say in a theatre or as part of a radio or television broadcast. Again, there are collection agencies around the world.

3. Income is generated from the utilization of the material as part of say a film soundtrack or a cinema or television commercial. In recent years music has played an increasingly important role in films and commercials, making this the fastest growing source of music royalties. Classical music has been used in a whole range of commercials, a factor linked to its generally increasing popularity. When music is used in film soundtracks, there is additional revenue from the sale of the associated album. These revenues are known as synchronization royalties.

Following a number of strategic acquisitions, described below, EMI Music Publishing controls over 800,000 musical compositions and songs and covers all types and ages of music.

## EMI Music in the 1980s

In the 1980s EMI's main star artists were waning in

**Table 5**  The relative success of EMI's main artists, 1989 and 1990

| Year | Artist | Best position(s) in the UK top 100 album charts |
|------|--------|-------------------------------------------------|
| 1989 | Tina Turner | 8 |
|      | Queen | 17 |
|      | Cliff Richard | 38 and 86 |
|      | Kate Bush | 39 |
|      | Paul McCartney | 56 |
|      | Duran Duran | 65 |
| 1990 | Nigel Kennedy (*Vivaldi's Four Seasons*) | 12 |

In 1989 EMI's top single was *Something's Gotten Hold of My Heart* by Marc Almond and Gene Pitney.

popularity and they had not been effectively replaced (Table 5).

In addition, while EMI's market share was relatively stable, the company's position of UK market leader was taken by the fast-growing Polygram. WEA, owned by Time Warner, was beginning to threaten the number two slot. During this decade the value of the UK singles market, at trade prices, rose from £50 million to £80 million; at the same time, partly the result of the emergence of compact discs around the middle of the 1980s, album sales (vinyl LPs, cassettes and compact discs combined) grew from £200 million to £600 million. Album market share was critical. See Table 6.

**Table 6**  Album market shares, UK

| Year | EMI | Chrysalis | Virgin | Polygram | WEA |
|------|-----|-----------|--------|----------|-----|
| 1984 | 14.6 | 2.9 | 7.0 | 12.5 | 9.2 |
| 1985 | 13.4 | 3.3 | 8.0 | 14.5 | 12.2 |
| 1986 | 13.8 | 2.9 | 7.3 | 14.8 | 13.2 |
| 1987 | 13.2 | 2.2 | 7.1 | 15.2 | 12.8 |
| 1988 | 12.6 | 2.8 | 7.7 | 16.1 | 12.6 |
| 1989 | 12.7 | 2.5 | 8.2 | 16.1 | 14.8 |
| 1990 | 15.3 | 2.9 | 7.7 | 23.2 | 12.8 |

Source: BPI.

Comparable market-share figures for singles were: Polygram 20% in 1990 (14% in 1984); EMI 13% (9%), Chrysalis 4% (3%), Virgin 7% (7%) and WEA 10% (11%). While the singles market is much smaller than albums, singles can be vitally important for supporting new albums and for launching new artists.

Throughout the 1980s EMI Music's chief executive (Bhaskar Menon) and the finance director were based in Los Angeles; the managing director and the worldwide administrative centre were in London. Menon was a deliberate man who liked details. He had a deep and profound understanding of the business, but he was a conservative decision maker. EMI had become sluggish and reactive, values inappropriate for a fickle and fashion-orientated industry. The division was big, but its profitability was disappointing. Margins overall were in the region of 5%, and the company was losing money in America, a critically important but notoriously difficult market for UK music companies to conquer. Bhaskar Menon retired in 1989, to be replaced by Jim Fifield, who had joined the company a year earlier. Fifield declared that he would double the profit margin in three years. His ambitions were pursued through a programme of rationalization, restructuring and strategic acquisitions in both music publishing and record production.

## The new Chief Executive

Colin Southgate head-hunted Jim Fifield to EMI Music. Fifield, an American, had built his early career in General Mills, where he had focused on their retail operations, but from 1985 to 1988 he was president and chief executive officer of CBS/Fox Video. In his first year he received a total remuneration package of some £13 million, which included a substantial 'signing-on fee'. In 1994 his basic salary was £2 million, supplemented by a cash and shares bonus of £5 million, making him 'the highest paid man in the music business'. By contrast in 1994, Sir Colin Southgate received a remuneration package of less than £1 million. Under Fifield the headquarters of EMI Music, including all corporate administration, was switched to New York.

After declaring that he would double EMI Music's

profit margin from 5 to 10% within three years Fifield later set himself a target of 13% for the business.

Jim Fifield is extremely energetic and pragmatic, a marked contrast to his predecessor. He wears 'exotic ties and trendy glasses'. Commentators have pointed out that in the last few years Sir Colin Southgate has also switched from horn-rimmed spectacles to contact lenses and they have mused about a culture change driven down from the very top of the organization. More conservative values, of course, remain far more appropriate for the less fashionable rentals business.

A new 'attitude and focus' in EMI Music has been attributed to Fifield, who has championed substantial investments in information technology and management information systems. Declaring 'I will only work for something that is fun', he has set about transforming the company's repertoire, its stable of artists and an acknowledged key success factor, partially by restructuring and decentralization and partly through acquisitions.

Fifield, who has been described as an 'archetypal numbers man', claims to work with six key managerial principles:

- never settle for anything but the best
- focus on the future not the past
- take risks
- succeed as a team
- build on strengths, and
- speak out – 'silence is not golden'.

## Strategic acquisitions

In 1989 Thorn EMI bought SBK Entertainment for $337 million, primarily to obtain its music publishing business. The deal was begun when SBK approached EMI with a view to buying EMI's music publishing arm. SBK had acquired its song collection by buying 250,000 song copyrights at a price of $130 million from CBS in 1986; these rights were earning annual royalties of $37 million worldwide. CBS had obtained the copyrights from a variety of different film studios and they included such titles as *Singin' in the Rain* and *Somewhere Over the Rainbow*. EMI already held the copyright to over 300,000 songs and compositions, and this acquisition put them alongside Warner Chappell as joint global market leaders. They each held 12% of the world market, measured by revenues. EMI's portfolio included compositions from David Bowie, Chris de Burgh, Kate Bush, Dire Straits, Carole King, Barry Manilow, Paul McCartney and Queen, some of whom, but not all, also recorded for EMI.

SBK had been founded by two American entrepreneurs, Martin Bandier and Charles Koppelman, who also discovered the folk rock singer Tracy Chapman, whose first album, released in 1988, sold 7 million copies. SBK held the rights to her songs but, because they did not own a recording business, she recorded for WEA. As a result of her success Bandier and Koppelman had the ambition of owning a record company, and this they now set up in a joint venture with EMI Music. This 50:50 arrangement was immediately successful; in its first year four albums out of 20 released reached the coveted number 1 slot in the charts.

This 50:50 joint venture format in America was repeated with alliances between EMI and Enigma, a heavy metal label, and IRS, a rock label. The Enigma agreement was later discontinued as it failed to work smoothly. Fifield's belief was that alliances of this nature preserved the entrepreneurial spirit of individual, repertoire-focused labels, each of which had a separate image and identity which made them uniquely attractive to particular artists. EMI's contribution is the vitally important international production and distribution network that small, independent labels need access to, but cannot afford to own.

In addition, and in accordance with the alliance objectives, EMI Music in America was split into three separate businesses, based on labels: Manhattan, EMI-America and Capitol. In the UK the company divided itself into EMI and Parlophone. The decentralized businesses/labels were all profit accountable and charged with attracting new talent. EMI companies quickly signed new artists such as the rap singer MC Hammer and country star Garth Brooks. EMI has subsequently bought the remaining 50% of SBK Records and absorbed the label into EMI-America; there were some redundancies. The challenge is finding a structure which permits devolution,

empowerment and entrepreneurialism – attractive to the company's recording artists – with cost control in a competitive and uncertain industry. Koppelman is now head of EMI Music Group, North America; Bandier is head of EMI Music Publishing.

There were, though, disappointments. Fifield sought to acquire Geffen Records, founded by David Geffen and holding an 8% share of the US market, but he was beaten by MCA. In 1990 EMI Music Publishing added Filmtrax, which was bought for $93 million. Filmtrax owned the copyright to some 140,000 titles yielding annual royalties of $9.5 million.

## Acquiring Chrysalis

Chrysalis, like Virgin, had grown into one of the UK's best-known independent record companies. Chrysalis, growing with the success of such artists as Jethro Tull, Blondie and Spandau Ballet, had expanded into studio recording, music publishing and television programming and had diversified more significantly when it acquired MAM in 1985. MAM's core activity was the management of international artists, but it had diversified differently into hotel management, juke boxes and amusement machines. The merger was successful, but Chrysalis hit financial difficulties when it tried to establish a serious presence in the US record industry. The US investment demanded more cash injections than had been initially budgeted. Chris Wright, Chrysalis' chairman (and one of the two original founders of the business), concluded with hindsight that Chrysalis had sought to create an organizational infrastructure in the USA, when what was crucially required was chart successes. Could the latter be achieved without the former?

In 1989 Chrysalis needed a cash injection which, although the company was now quoted, was not readily forthcoming. It was rumoured that 50% of Chrysalis Records would be sold to Bertelsmann, with whom Chrysalis already had distribution agreements. In the event EMI Music bought 50% for £46 million, with an option to buy the remainder by 1999. The second half was bought for a further £31 million three years later; Chrysalis still needed cash.

Fifield acquired a number of currently successful artists, in particular Sinead O'Connor and Billy Idol and a very valuable back catalogue. Chrysalis retained its independence as a label, but its operations and administration were absorbed. There were several redundancies.

## The big acquisition: Virgin

If Chrysalis could provide EMI with a useful new repertoire and back catalogue, Virgin could provide an invaluable supplement. Virgin Music, again a vertically integrated company, was bigger than Chrysalis. Unlike its smaller rival it had remained profitable while successfully also penetrating America. However, it was still too small to be classified as 'first division' in the global music industry. During the very late 1980s and early 1990s most independent labels the size of Chrysalis and Virgin had been absorbed by one of the leading global players. Virgin's artists included Genesis, Phil Collins, Janet Jackson, UB40, Simple Minds, Meat Loaf and The Rolling Stones, and there were 25,000 song copyrights. Virgin Music had grown and prospered with the 'visionary' Richard Branson at the forefront, backed by his cousin Simon Draper, Virgin's respected and key A&R person, and Ken Berry, 'the strategist'. Berry had been with Virgin for some 20 years, and he had been credited as their 'first person to handle accounts and bookkeeping'. He was popular with artists because he was 'willing to market and develop acts, not on quarterly statements, but based on their long-term career'. By the early 1990s Branson had lost interest in the music industry; his passion now was his airline. Draper felt stale. Branson was willing to sell at the right price; a deal would provide investment capital for Virgin Atlantic Airways. In the past, Branson had approached EMI with a view to buying its music business.

Branson negotiated with a number of the leading international music companies, but finally, and after 14 months of protracted negotiations, he agreed to sell to Sir Colin Southgate for £510 million, financed by a rights issue. This was in 1992. Virgin had tangible assets of just £3 million – Virgin did not own any manufacturing or distribution – and the figure represented 1000 times Virgin Music's recent after-tax earnings. Commentators queried the wisdom of such a high price for a number of key managers and a well-known repertoire. EMI, though, believed that there was enormous synergy potential from blending its global structure with Virgin's repertoire. Moreover, Fifield had a reputation as a shrewd cost-cutter and he would be able to achieve savings. This he duly delivered, implementing at Virgin a strategy that he had pursued already at EMI. Artists who were not contributing or who had passed their peak were dropped. Eighty jobs went in the UK and a further 80 in the USA in two tranches. The merging of the two businesses was assisted by Ken Berry agreeing to stay on and run Virgin within EMI. Richard Branson has also retained the title 'President for Life' of Virgin Music.

Towards the end of 1994 Berry took on additional responsibilities for the whole of EMI Music's International interests. He was seen to have an 'iron grip on the business along with the intuitive understanding needed to deal effectively with artists'.

## EMI Music in 1994

Thorn EMI's Annual Report for 1993–94 declared 'record results for the sixth consecutive year' in respect of EMI Music. Fifteen albums worldwide had each sold in excess of 2 million copies; EMI Records in the UK had received the Queen's Award for Export Achievement. Virgin Music had contributed £90 million out of a total of £246 million operating profits, and was the UK's top record label with six number one albums. 'The performance [of Virgin] continues to exceed expectations'. £90 million was £10 million higher than EMI's target expectations for Virgin, itself a figure described as 'optimistic' by analysts; a year earlier Virgin had achieved just £21 million operating profit.

EMI believed that the integration of the two companies had succeeded in preserving the cultural and artistic independence of Virgin while enabling its artists to benefit from EMI's stronger international structure and network. With hindsight, the acquisition of Virgin is generally acknowledged to be a major coup for Thorn EMI.

During this year EMI Music agreed to collaborate with Warner Music, Sony and Polygram in the development of a new music television channel, and invested in a digital cable radio venture in order 'to capitalize on the pace of change in the industry'. The company also acquired the largest independent German recorded music company.

EMI Music's artist roster now includes an array of 'yesterday's stars' with their valuable back catalogue recordings [including The Beatles, The Rolling Stones, The Beach Boys, Cliff Richard, Tina Turner and Diana Ross], artists still capable of chart-topping releases, such as Garth Brooks and Phil Collins, and new talent such as Blind Melon and Smashing Pumpkins. *The Beatles Live at the BBC* album was particularly successful late in 1994. In addition, EMI recorded Frank Sinatra, who made a successful comeback in the 1990s with his duet albums, easy listening music from artists such as Brian May and orchestral classics conducted by Simon Rattle and other renowned musicians. It is noticeable that the repertoire includes several leading American artists instead of being focused heavily on the UK.

EMI also owns a number of Christian music labels.

## Retailing

Music Retailing in the UK can be classified in four main categories:

- specialist multiples – EMI's HMV Music stores and those branded Our Price and Virgin but controlled by the WH Smith Group
- non-specialist multiples – Boots, Woolworths, WH Smith
- independents
- mail order and record clubs.

Smith's in total accounts for some 30% of the market, followed by Woolworth's (15%) and HMV with a 13.5% market share. HMV sells recorded music, videos and other related entertainment products; the basic strategy is one of mixing superstores with a range of smaller satellite stores in defined geographical regions in order to provide an appropriately comprehensive coverage. The superstores feature appearances by leading artists and they champion special regional promotions.

The competitive strategies of the major retailers are built around:

- competitive (or low) prices – a feature of WH Smith stores and Woolworth's
- a wide range of stock – Virgin and HMV, whose largest superstores are reputed to offer the widest and deepest range in the UK
- service – again a feature of HMV, who are clearly not alone with this
- location
- the ambience of the stores.

EMI Music owns a strong distribution network for its products within the UK, covering all important wholesalers and retailers. HMV imports directly from the USA and relies on several independent wholesalers for products from other key record companies and countries.

In 1993 HMV attempted to purchase the third largest US record retailer, Camelot, but failed.

## The acquisition of Dillons

The retail chain Pentos had grown rapidly in the 1980s under the leadership of Terry Maher, its founder, chairman and chief executive. In the late 1980s/early 1990s, Pentos (now comprising Dillons, Rymans [stationery and office equipment] and Athena [posters, cards, and so on]) followed an aggressive expansion strategy. Pentos entered into a number of 'reverse premium' agreements with landlords, accepting cash advances for taking on long-term leases at high rents. The slow pick-up after the recession left the group unable to generate enough cash to meet its overheads. Maher was ousted by institutional shareholders in late 1993. Some time later Thorn EMI enquired about the possibility of acquiring Dillons, but was rebuffed. When Pentos went into receivership Sir Colin Southgate struck decisively and a deal was agreed within days. Thorn agreed to pay £36 million for the Dillons stores it wanted; up to another £20 million would be required to settle outstanding debts with suppliers. Maher, who would have liked to buy back Dillons himself, was infuriated and claimed that the price was too low. The underlying strength and *competitive strategy* of Dillons had never been questioned when Pentos went into receivership; the group's problems with Athena and Rymans had been more worrying.

Dillons would be absorbed by HMV. After all, there are some similarities between music and book retailing. Both feature bestsellers which, at least for a number of months, sell in large numbers. At the same time stores need to stock huge numbers of slow movers which can turn over at the rate of just one a month or even less. Effective IT systems are needed to control such stocks.

## The Thorn Group – the rentals business

Mike Metcalf has been chief executive of the Thorn Group since 1991; he is also a member of the main Thorn EMI Board. In his early forties, he is ten years plus younger than both Sir Colin Southgate and Jim Fifield. He is an ex-finance director, and he has been described as more sober than Southgate and Fifield.

In 1991 the rentals business had a number of strategic problems.

- Rent-A-Center, the important American acquisition of the 1980s, was under Federal investigation; the company had been accused of strong-arm debt collection using 'guns and gangs of Hell's Angels'.

    Rent-A-Center was exonerated in 1993 but there was still some risk that the bad publicity would stick.
- Radio Rentals, Thorn's main UK high-street rental chain and the market leader, was being outperformed by its key rival, Granada.
- The rentals business was, in effect, triple branded, with Radio Rentals, DER and Multibroadcast all offering essentially the same service. Thorn had not used its acquisitions to establish clearly differentiated brands and consequently its overheads were unnecessarily high.

    DER and Multibroadcast have since been replaced as brands and the stores relaunched.
- Rumbelows, which sold rather than rented, household appliances and electrical goods, had no real

competitive advantage; it was too small a chain and it was being outperformed by market leader Dixons. Dixons had a 12% market share; Rumbelows just 2%. Rumbelows had traditionally concentrated on high-street sites while many of its rivals had also developed out of town. Rumbelows had lost £50 million in the last three years.

In 1992 the 450 Rumbelows stores were partially switched to a rental format, concentrating on low-cost rentals such as the re-rental of appliances which a previous customer had returned. Eight-hundred jobs were lost and over 150 stores closed. In 1986, Rumbelows' television rental accounts had been transferred to Radio Rentals with the loss then of 650 jobs.

In February 1995 Thorn announced that the remaining 285 Rumbelows stores were to be closed within the next three months with the loss of a further 2500 jobs. Losses had continued at £12 million per year. Sir Colin Southgate commented: 'electrical retailing is a mayhem market in which no-one makes any money either in or out of town'.

A month later, Escom, Germany's second largest PC manufacturer and retailer, agreed to take on the leases of 231 ex-Rumbelows stores. Rumbelows' employees were encouraged to apply for jobs. Escom's computers were already sold through Rumbelows outlets; the deal would elevate the German company to the position of the UK's largest specialist high-street PC retailer.

In the UK, Metcalf has also established a single administration and distribution centre for the whole business, inaugurated a warehouse sales operation for ex-rental equipment [a strategy copied from Granada], and introduced a rent-to-own format in the UK. Rent-to-own is the traditional format in the USA, whereas historically the UK has been mainly rent-to-rent. With rent-to-own, as with conventional hire purchase and credit sales, a customer rents an article and, after paying a certain number of instalments, becomes the owner. Unlike hire purchase, however, there is no down-payment and the customer can cancel the agreement or exchange the product for a different one at any time and without penalty. In addition, customers enjoy free repair services for the duration of the contract. In the USA the industry has been accused of charging 'unsophisticated customers'' two or three times the usual retail price for rent-to-own contracts.

As part of his strategy to create multiple brands targeted at distinct market segments, Metcalf introduced Fona (cash sales and rent-to-own and based on Thorn's successful Danish chain, where it is market leader in electrical retailing) and Crazy George's, radical format stores, piloted in Birmingham, which offer credit sales without traditional credit checks.

However, again in 1995, Thorn abandoned its UK experiment with Fona; the 36 stores were closed. While electrical *retailing* has been problematic, rental business in late 1994/early 1995 was buoyant.

In 1992 Thorn also acquired Remco for $55 million. Remco could add 64 stores in Houston, Dallas, Chicago and North Carolina to the growing Rent-A-Center chain which then boasted 1100 outlets and a 25% US market share. Thorn is now market leader in both the UK and USA, and it enjoys a market share of somewhere between 25 and 60% in each of the 19 countries [including 12 in Europe] in which it competes.

Service in the rentals industry is based on three key factors:

- the product range
- access options
- service support.

Table 7 illustrates the Thorn product/country/access matrix and Table 8 features a selection of the service options.

## Key success factors

- Flexibility – of access formats and rental systems, together with the flexibility to change from one system to another or upgrade the product or model. Some customers, for example, see rental as an ideal opportunity for trying out a new product (such as a high-definition television or CD-ROM system) before making a purchase commitment.

   In the UK Thorn has pioneered purchase options within rental agreements.
- To accomplish this flexibility, strong linkages with product manufacturers/suppliers are essential.

**Table 7**  The Thorn Group product/country/access matrix

| Product | Country |
|---|---|
| Televisions | |
| Videos | |
| Hi-fi equipment | UK, Europe Asia |
| White goods | Pacific, USA |
| Telephones | |
| Personal computers | |
| Furniture | USA, UK, France, Australia, New Zealand |
| Jewellery | USA only |

| Access format | Country |
|---|---|
| Credit sales | UK and Europe |
| Rent-to-own | Global; the only access format offered in the USA |
| Rent-to-rent | The world other than |
| Rent with purchase option* | the USA |

*The rent with purchase option includes a wide variety of access opportunities, each tailor-made to suit individual countries and market niches.

- High levels of service, with minimum financial commitment, supported with advice on products and options. After-rental servicing is vital as word-of-mouth is a critical aspect of marketing.

In the mid-1990s the prospects for the Thorn Group have been described as 'modest', but this is a relatively safe and stable business as long as a company succeeds with the key success factors. Other important strategic issues for Thorn are the extent of the capital tied up at any time and the lack of any real synergy with EMI Music.

## The future

Analysts have calculated that the value of Thorn EMI split into two separate and independent busi-

**Table 8** Selected access options

| Outlet | Selected access option |
|---|---|
| Radio Rentals | Option-2-Own – a premium rental charge provides for eventual ownership |
| Fona, Denmark | Easyown – similar; a credit sale leading to ownership |
| Crazy George's | New Buy Scheme – for customers disbarred from normal credit. A conditional sale agreement, no deposit, no credit checks. Weekly payments |
| Rent-A-Center | Rental purchase – weekly payments and free servicing |
| Remco | Customer's Choice – monthly payments; targeted at more affluent customers who elect to pay large monthly slices and who can terminate the rental in favour of buying the product at any time for an overall lower charge |
| Radio Rentals Australia | Rental-Try-Buy – payments reduce the equity that customers eventually need to buy the product outright, which they are free to do at any time. |

nesses would be in the order of £6.5 billion, £2 billion higher than the value of the group in 1994. In September 1995, when the shares stood at over 1500 pence each, Thorn EMI was valued at £6.55 billion. However, there must always be some value in size and diversity.

For a period Thorn EMI suggested that a split was unlikely and, if the right acquisition could be found, a move into book publishing, to complement Dillons, was more realistic. However, at the 1995 Annual General Meeting Sir Colin Southgate commented:

*We have concluded that demerger, if it can be achieved in an acceptable way, is in the best long-term interests both of the businesses that currently constitute Thorn EMI and the shareholders. Demerger would permit the management of each group to develop its individual strengths and pursue opportunities which each judges appropriate to its future growth. Furthermore, by demerging, the value of these businesses would be more fully recognized.*

*We are, therefore, considering proposals which, if implemented, would lead to the demerger of the Group . . . at present we believe that any demerger would separate the Rental business from the rest of the Group. There would then be two publicly quoted companies.*

Demerger requires the consent of 22 different national tax regimes.

There must, though, continue to be questions concerning the future of the music business. Most of the world's important independent record labels have now been absorbed by the majors; acquiring new repertoire is always going to be uncertain; once cost cutting and rationalization has been achieved, organic growth becomes vital for expanding the business.

One major boost for the record industry in the UK was provided in 1994 when the Monopolies and Mergers Commission ruled that compact discs [relatively more expensive than in other key markets in the world] were not being priced at exorbitant levels. However, throughout the 1980s and early 1990s many music buyers have systematically replaced their vinyl record collections with CDs, readily buying up 'greatest hits' albums based on back catalogue material. Has this opportunity peaked? Mini compact discs (minidiscs) and digital compact cassettes (DCCs), rival new formats, wait in the wings, but will either have the impact that the launch of CDs had? At the same time, though, there must be considerable potential for exploiting EMI Music's back catalogue in multimedia products such as CD-ROM.

Sir Colin Southgate has commented (in an interview for the *Daily Telegraph*, November 1993) that, with hindsight, he would have:

- speeded up the disposals programme, and
- attempted to cut back dividends to provide more cash for investment.

He also reflected that he had not been as hard on certain managers as perhaps he should have been.

He remains unconvinced about any need to link hardware and software in the entertainments industry. Sony (with Columbia Pictures and CBS Records) and Matsushita (Universal Pictures and MCA) have tracked a different route. Time Warner appears to side with Thorn EMI on this issue; Polygram are 75% owned by Philips. Southgate argues that consumer electronics companies must gain the support of the whole music industry for any new formats and that film companies will license the music *they want to use* regardless of who owns the copyright. Time Warner 'unites content and distribution' to take their intellectual property and copyright material direct to their audiences. Thorn EMI, meanwhile, has deliberately chosen not to enter into videos, video games and computer games software and, having come out of film making and cinemas, declared that it has no intention of returning.

What of the possibility of a take-over bid for Thorn EMI?

> *Thorn's management has spent 10 years cleaning up the group and [1995] results prove they've done a good job,* comments one leisure analyst. *But they've also made it more attractive to predators.*

Possible names which have been suggested include entertainment groups such as Disney and Viacom, which owns MTV, the global music video channel. Both corporations could usefully add music to their existing interests in films and television, and thereby become a more direct competitor for Time Warner. Other names to appear as possibly interested bidders are News Corporation, Microsoft and Seagram, which bought MCA from Matsushita in 1995. Given the ownerships of the large music companies, Thorn EMI is realistically seen as the only possible acquisition. Were a company such as Disney to bid successfully, it seems likely that the rentals business and Dillons would be seen as peripheral and Thorn EMI broken up.

The last section of this case study provides a brief picture of Thorn EMI's two main rivals in the music industry: Polygram and Time Warner.

## Two leading competitors

### Polygram

Polygram was formed in 1972 when the Dutch company Philips merged its record interests with those of the German company Siemens, following a successful ten-year alliance. Siemens contributed Deutsche Grammophon, a leading classical music label, and Polydor; Philips contributed the Philips, Fontana and Mercury labels. The new Polygram quickly added to these by acquiring Decca and London to create additional synergy and savings. In 1989 Philips bought out the Siemens' shareholding; equity sales, partly to finance acquisitions, have resulted in Philips' shareholding being subsequently reduced to 75%.

Key independents acquired more recently are: Island in 1989, A & M in 1990, and Motown in 1993, this after a two-year distribution arrangement. Polygram entered music publishing in 1986 and film, video and television production in 1987. There were some moderately successful releases, but the real breakthrough came with *Four Weddings and a Funeral* in 1994, the leading UK box office earner of all time. The film cost $5 million to make; it has so far grossed over $250 million at the box office. Polygram manufactures compact discs but not hardware, relying on the Philips link. Thirty per cent of Andrew Lloyd Webber's Really Useful Group was purchased in 1991, and Polygram also owns Britannia Music, the leading music mail-order company which alone accounts for 8% of recorded music sales in the UK.

Leading artists include: INXS, Abba, Bon Jovi, Bryan Adams, The Cure, Elton John, Sting, U2 and Chris de Burgh, together with the Motown back catalogue of Diana Ross, Lionel Richie, The Four Tops, Smokey Robinson and Stevie Wonder.

Polygram provides over 50% of the world's karaoke software and enjoys a substantial presence in the Far East, especially Japan and Hong Kong. As well as being a major market for karaoke, Japan is the world's largest classical music market. Polygram

**Table 9**  Polygram revenues, 1993

| | |
|---|---|
| Popular music | 69% |
| Classical music | 12% |
| Films and videos | 9% |
| Music publishing; licence fees | 10% |
| | |
| Europe | 52% |
| North America | 23% |
| Far East, including Japan | 20% |
| Rest of the world | 5% |

has subsidiaries in 30 countries and, like Thorn EMI, believes that a world-wide distribution network is essential for success. Table 9 provides a breakdown of Polygram revenues in 1993.

Polygram is now aiming to 'transform itself into a global entertainment company, to take advantage of the opportunities in multi-media'. Music and film production and distribution will remain at the heart of the business.

Film distribution is a targeted growth area; Polygram may have a strong presence in certain countries, including the UK, but it is thin elsewhere.

In January 1995 Polygram acquired – for £100 million – ITC Entertainment, formed in 1984 by Lord Grade. ITC owns the rights to some 350 feature films together with vintage television series such as The Prisoner and Thunderbirds, both of which enjoyed successful repeat showings in the UK in 1994. ITC thus provides valuable back catalogue material and access into US television syndication.

## Time Warner

Time Warner is the world's largest media and entertainment company, and it is focused on software. With music, plus videos, magazines and books, it is the biggest holder of copyrights in the world. It is diversified, mainly in related businesses, with music contributing some 25% of global revenues (1994–95). The company was created in 1990 when Time Inc. merged with Warner Communications; the vast majority of its earnings comes from the USA.

Time Warner is the world leader in television *programming*; in addition, it owns the HBO (Home Box Office) network, which is accessed both domestically and through hotel television sets, and important cable TV interests. Recent investments have given Time Warner the 'finest collection of cable properties anywhere in the world'. The company is a major film producer through Warner Brothers and Lorimar, controlling all the distribution of its own films. Time Warner owns movie theatres. With titles such as *Fortune*, *Time* and *Life*, Time Warner is a leading publisher; it also markets Time-Life books and owns the US Book-of-the-Month Club mail-order network.

The acquisition by Time Warner of the smaller but innovatory Turner Broadcasting (announced in September 1995) dramatically enhanced its already strong programming interests. Turner owns Cable News Network, best known for CNN Headline News, and cable entertainment businesses in Latin America, Europe, Asia and the Caribbean. It also owns a baseball team, the Atlanta Braves. Among other related interests being brought together, ownership of Yogi Bear and Flintstones programmes (Turner) will be added to Warner's Bugs Bunny!

The key music labels are Warner, Elektra and Atlantic, consolidated as WEA. Warner Chappell is a joint world leader, with EMI Music Publishing, owning 900,000 copyrights, including songs from Prince, Madonna and Elton John. Major recording artists are Simply Red, Madonna, Chris Rea, Enya, Rod Stewart, Prince and Eric Clapton. Madonna has been used as a springboard to exploit the potential synergies from linking book and music publishing.

*Content* is seen as a much lower risk industry than cable television, which is operating at the leading edge of the emerging multimedia technology – and it is subject to government regulation. Time Warner and Thorn EMI have different views on the long-term feasibility of separating content and distribution. Time Warner's chairman, Gerald Levin, has commented: 'creative material is not created in isolation from its audience, nor from the question of whether it will make money. The value to creative content comes when it is going through the largest number of channels world-wide. The money is made on the distribution side, not the content'. In contrast to Thorn EMI, Levin also believes that owning distribution brings an entertainment company closer to its ultimate customers and consequently acts as an important driver back down the value chain.

Time Warner, finally, has sizeable shareholdings in Atari (computer games) and the Six Flags Corporation, which runs a number of entertainment theme parks in the USA.

*EMI Group*   http://www.emigroup.com
*Thorn Rentals*   http://www.thorn-uk.com

**Appendix 1**   Thorn EMI five-year summary, 1991–1995

| For the years to 31 March | 1995 £m | 1994 £m | 1993 £m | 1992 £m | 1991 £m |
|---|---|---|---|---|---|
| **Results** | | | | | |
| Turnover | | | | | |
| Continuing operations | 4329.0 | 3829.0 | 3643.0 | 3198.7 | 2974.8 |
| Discontinued operations | 178.3 | 462.2 | 809.3 | 755.7 | 685.5 |
| | 4507.3 | 4292.1 | 4452.3 | 3954.4 | 3660.3 |
| Operating profit | | | | | |
| Cont. operations – normal | 458.5 | 385.9 | 314.0 | 221.8 | 223.5 |
| Cont. operations – exceptional | (126.9) | | | | |
| | 331.6 | 385.9 | 314.0 | 221.8 | 223.5 |
| Discontinued. operations | (3.1) | (3.4) | 65.3 | 59.3 | 72.2 |
| | 328.5 | 382.5 | 379.3 | 281.1 | 295.7 |
| Exceptional items | | | | | |
| Profits (losses) on businesses disposed or terminated | (35.3) | (14.5) | (30.3) | (15.3) | (78.1) |
| Cost of fundamental reorganizations and restructuring | – | – | (23.4) | (91.9) | – |
| Profits (losses) on disposal of fixed assets | 9.7 | (3.2) | 1.8 | 19.1 | 10.1 |
| Profit before finance charges | 302.9 | 364.8 | 327.4 | 193.0 | 227.7 |
| Finance charges | (31.8) | (38.3) | (53.9) | (62.3) | (67.4) |
| Profit on ordinary activities before taxation | 271.1 | 326.5 | 273.5 | 130.7 | 160.3 |
| Taxation on profit on ordinary activities | (157.6) | (121.6) | (107.8) | (70.2) | (75.1) |
| Profit on ordinary activities after taxation | 113.5 | 204.9 | 165.7 | 60.5 | 85.2 |
| Minority interests | (6.8) | (3.1) | 5.9 | 7.3 | (1.5) |
| Profit attributable to members of the holding company | 106.7 | 201.8 | 171.6 | 67.8 | 83.7 |
| **Key statistics** | | | | | |
| Net cash flow from operating activities | 938.8 | 740.7 | 678.6 | 620.5 | 661.1 |
| Capital expenditure: | | | | | |
| property, plant, equipment and vehicles | 214.3 | 150.4 | 143.7 | 140.1 | 160.0 |
| Rental equipment | 437.9 | 370.1 | 311.8 | 292.5 | 330.0 |
| Total capital expenditure | 652.2 | 520.5 | 455.5 | 432.6 | 490.0 |

| For the years to 31 March | 1995 £m | 1994 £m | 1993 £m | 1992 £m | 1991 £m |
|---|---|---|---|---|---|
| Basic earnings per ordinary share | 25.0p | 48.2p | 43.6p | 20.5p | 27.2p |
| Adjusted fully diluted earnings per ordinary share | 61.9p | 52.5p | 50.8p | 40.1p | 46.9p |
| Dividends per ordinary share | 36.5p | 34.0p | 32.0p | 30.1p | 29.3p |
| International proportion of operating profit before operating exceptional items | 76.1% | 74.5% | 62.2% | 64.5% | 70.5% |
| Return on sales (continuing operations) | 10.6% | 10.1% | 9.3% | 7.6% | 8.5% |
| Debt: shareholders' funds (inc. minority interests) | 55.2% | 57.2% | 154.9% | 109.5% | 98.6% |
| Debt: capital employed | 35.6% | 36.4% | 60.8% | 52.3% | 49.6% |
| **Employment of capital** | | | | | |
| Music publishing copyrights | 379.5 | 400.6 | 392.2 | 273.0 | 269.7 |
| Property, plant, equipment and vehicles | 709.6 | 502.6 | 558.5 | 502.9 | 501.7 |
| Rental equipment | 691.6 | 656.2 | 664.3 | 655.2 | 659.6 |
| Fixed asset investments | 52.3 | 131.8 | 142.1 | 122.5 | 119.6 |
| Stocks and debtors, excluding taxation and interest | 1017.1 | 1062.7 | 1192.6 | 1107.0 | 1129.9 |
| Investments: own shares | 38.8 | 18.2 | – | – | – |
| Creditors and provisions, excluding borrowings, taxation and dividends and interest payable | (1683.5) | (1475.6) | (1627.1) | (1422.6) | (1285.1) |
| Operating assets | 1205.4 | 1296.5 | 1322.6 | 1238.0 | 1395.4 |
| Deferred taxation | (17.2) | (18.9) | (22.1) | (22.7) | (36.6) |
| Corporate taxation | (53.8) | (8.4) | (29.1) | (33.8) | (39.9) |
| Dividends and net interest payable | (113.2) | (110.4) | (100.4) | (93.6) | (84.5) |
| | 1021.2 | 1158.8 | 1171.0 | 1087.9 | 1234.4 |
| **Capital employed** | | | | | |
| Share capital | 106.9 | 106.6 | 102.2 | 81.4 | 77.5 |
| Share premium account | 899.8 | 894.5 | 755.0 | 250.1 | 159.8 |
| Profit and loss account | 469.6 | 532.8 | 479.5 | 446.1 | 477.2 |
| Other reserves | 625.0 | 574.1 | 574.1 | 574.1 | 596.1 |
| Goodwill | (1517.5) | (1372.9) | (1458.2) | (847.5) | (710.6) |
| Convertible unsecured loan stock | – | – | – | 211.5 | – |
| Shareholders' funds | 583.3 | 735.1 | 452.6 | 715.7 | 600.0 |
| Minority interests | 74.1 | 2.1 | 6.8 | 15.0 | 21.6 |
| Net borrowings | 363.3 | 403.4 | 711.6 | 357.2 | 612.8 |
| | 1021.2 | 1158.8 | 1171.0 | 1087.9 | 1234.4 |

Source: Thorn EMI Annual Reports.

**Appendix 2**   Thorn EMI – turnover and profit by division, 1991–1995

| | Turnover (£m to 31 March) | | | | |
|---|---|---|---|---|---|
| | **1995** | **1994** | **1993** | **1992** | **1991** |
| Music | 2189.0 | 1760.5 | 1507.3 | 1128.6 | 1016.2 |
| Rental | 1589.4 | 1484.2 | 1387.5 | 1371.8 | 1255.9 |
| HMV · | 503.2 | 403.9 | 323.2 | 261.8 | 207.4 |
| TSE | 47.4 | 407.7 | 425.0 | 436.5 | 495.3 |
| Discontinued operations | 178.3 | 208.4 | | | |
| UK | 1371.3 | 1562.2 | 1903.7 | 1918.0 | |
| USA | 1293.0 | 1237.3 | 1051.7 | 818.5 | |
| Rest of Europe | 1207.0 | 1153.0 | 1200.3 | 931.1 | |
| Asia Pacific | 525.0 | 252.8 | 226.2 | 205.7 | |
| Rest of world | 111.0 | 86.8 | 70.4 | 81.1 | |
| Operating profit (£'m to 31 March) | | | | | |
| Music | 294.9 | 246.1 | 196.9 | 125.1 | 102.7 |
| Rental | 152.4 | 129.2 | 115.3 | 105.9 | 119.4 |
| HMV | 14.0 | 6.1 | 2.6 | 1.3 | 4.1 |
| TSE | (2.8) | (11.6) | 1.5 | 13.2 | 62.5 |
| Discontinued operations | *(3.1) | 11.7 | | | |

*These operating profit figures are before an extraordinary charge of £126.9 million.

Sources: Thorn EMI Annual Reports and the *Financial Times*.

**Appendix 3**   Thorn EMI share prices, 28 January 1985 to 30 January 1995

|      | High value | 1134.00p | | 28.04.1994 | Low value | 312.8p | | 26.07.1985 |
|------|------|------|------|------|------|------|------|------|
| 1985 | Jan. | 416.44 | Feb. | 430.84 | Mar. | 382.86 | Apr. | 402.05 |
|      | May | 450.03 | Jun. | 342.56 | Jul. | 312.81 | Aug. | 368.17 |
|      | Sep. | 342.56 | Oct. | 352.15 | Nov. | 404.93 | Dec. | 382.86 |
| 1986 | Jan. | 373.26 | Feb. | 428.92 | Mar. | 478.81 | Apr. | 480.73 |
|      | May | 454.83 | Jun. | 445.23 | Jul. | 428.92 | Aug. | 467.30 |
|      | Sep. | 438.51 | Oct. | 431.80 | Nov. | 453.87 | Dec. | 449.07 |
| 1987 | Jan. | 546.94 | Feb. | 584.36 | Mar. | 599.72 | Apr. | 663.05 |
|      | May | 677.44 | Jun. | 729.26 | Jul. | 728.30 | Aug. | 635.22 |
|      | Sep. | 670.72 | Oct. | 422.20 | Nov. | 518.16 | Dec. | 542.14 |
| 1988 | Jan. | 550.78 | Feb. | 540.23 | Mar. | 564.69 | Apr. | 602.60 |
|      | May | 604.51 | Jun. | 610.75 | Jul. | 622.75 | Aug. | 608.35 |
|      | Sep. | 605.47 | Oct. | 633.30 | Nov. | 617.95 | Dec. | 597.80 |
| 1989 | Jan. | 677.44 | Feb. | 672.64 | Mar. | 671.68 | Apr. | 660.17 |
|      | May | 675.52 | Jun. | 737.89 | Jul. | 806.02 | Aug. | 820.41 |
|      | Sep. | 780.11 | Oct. | 684.16 | Nov. | 714.86 | Dec. | 735.01 |
| 1990 | Jan. | 733.09 | Feb. | 668.80 | Mar. | 652.49 | Apr. | 620.83 |
|      | May | 691.83 | Jun. | 740.77 | Jul. | 690.87 | Aug. | 630.42 |
|      | Sep. | 563.25 | Oct. | 596.84 | Nov. | 624.67 | Dec. | 649.61 |
| 1991 | Jan. | 612.19 | Feb. | 672.64 | Mar. | 688.00 | Apr. | 688.96 |
|      | May | 678.40 | Jun. | 711.02 | Jul. | 723.50 | Aug. | 764.76 |
|      | Sep. | 762.84 | Oct. | 769.56 | Nov. | 745.57 | Dec. | 712.94 |
| 1992 | Jan. | 791.63 | Feb. | 776.27 | Mar. | 730.00 | Apr. | 843.00 |
|      | May | 835.00 | Jun. | 830.00 | Jul. | 732.00 | Aug. | 666.00 |
|      | Sep. | 789.00 | Oct. | 819.00 | Nov. | 833.00 | Dec. | 852.00 |
| 1993 | Jan. | 815.00 | Feb. | 842.00 | Mar. | 888.00 | Apr. | 849.00 |
|      | May | 874.00 | Jun. | 915.00 | Jul. | 952.00 | Aug. | 1006.00 |
|      | Sep. | 941.00 | Oct. | 938.00 | Nov. | 923.00 | Dec. | 1009.00 |
| 1994 | Jan. | 1091.00 | Feb. | 1093.00 | Mar. | 1053.00 | Apr. | 1134.00 |
|      | May | 1025.00 | Jun. | 1020.00 | Jul. | 1040.00 | Aug. | 1041.00 |
|      | Sep. | 1007.00 | Oct. | 978.00 | Nov. | 979.00 | Dec. | 1032.00 |
| 1995 | Jan. | 1018.00 | | | | | | |

The relative success of Thorn EMI's shares changed markedly during 1995. By September the traded price exceeded 1500 pence for the first time ever.

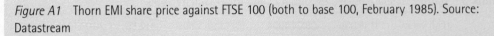

*Figure A1* Thorn EMI share price against FTSE 100 (both to base 100, February 1985). Source: Datastream

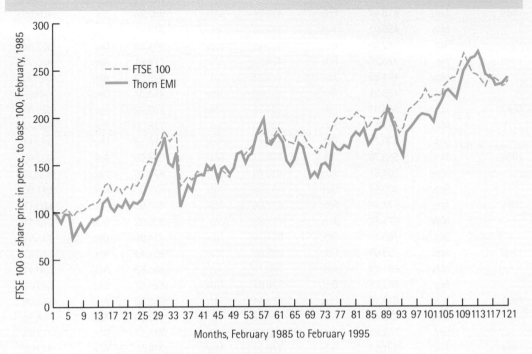

## Questions

1. Evaluate Sir Colin Southgate's declared focus strategy for Thorn EMI. Do you believe that this was the correct path for the company to follow? How and why has the strategy been changed during implementation?

2. How successful has the strategy been? What criteria are you using to evaluate this success? Evaluate the strategic position of Thorn EMI in 1995.

3. Review Thorn EMI's three main businesses in respect of
   - key success factors:
   - related core competencies
   - strategic issues facing the company in 1995.

4. In your opinion, which corporate strategic options were most appropriate, desirable and feasible for Thorn EMI at the end of 1995?
   (The issues raised by this question must take account of Thorn EMI's declared intentions, but an objective evaluation of the alternatives is nevertheless possible.)

# The Sony Corporation

Sony, 50 years old in 1996, became renowned throughout the world as an innovatory, pioneering company with an international presence and reputation in the consumer electronics industry. Sony is now an acknowledged leader in a number of very competitive and dynamic industries where no single company enjoys a dominant market share.

Sony has always sought to develop unique products rather than copy other companies. Although profitable, profitability per se has not been the driving objective. Sony has invested in research and development at a rate above the average both for its industry and for Japan. Technologists are seen as a critically important resource and allowed freedom to work within relatively open-ended briefs.

However, the company has come under enormous pressure as it has struggled to remain a leader in the changing world of consumer electronics and, as a result, there have been major changes in its strategies and structure in the 1990s.

This case study traces the growth, development, successes and setbacks of The Sony Corporation. It encapsulates issues of corporate and competitive strategies, structural evolution and the Japanese style of management. Sony's recent strategy of diversification into the American entertainment industry is examined in detail.

This version of the case was written by John L Thompson in 1996. It is for classroom discussion and should not be taken to reflect either effective or ineffective management.

## Introduction

Sony was at a critical point in its development as a global corporation as it celebrated its fiftieth birthday in 1996. The success of recent strategic changes is likely to have a major impact upon whether Sony restores its lost prosperity or declines to become a business legend.

The increasing significance of computers and communications equipment in consumer electronics, reinforced by the continuing convergence of computing, telecommunications and electronic entertainment in a range of new multimedia products, has forced consumer electronics companies such as Sony to focus their thinking and research on emerging technologies rather than concentrating on the innovatory development of new product variants. The conventional audiovisual products which have been at the heart of Sony's growth and development are now overshadowed by the latest developments in multimedia technology. To compete effectively in the late 1990s, Sony realized that it had to transform itself from a company which was dependent on the analogue technologies of conventional audiovisual products to one with competencies in digital technology which it could use to develop a range of new products for the multimedia age.

## History and product developments*

### Humble beginnings

Sony Corporation, begun in Japan after the end of World War II, is much younger than its major Japanese rivals. In 50 years it has become established as a market leader in the production of specialist electronic products in an environment of rapid technological change, economic growth and a global willingness to accept new technology.

Sony's corporate history has been built around core competencies in technological innovation and miniaturization and the development of quality products and quality systems which have led to high levels of differentiation. Early growth was organic and initially competition was limited. Today's competitors have typically followed Sony into the markets it pioneered. The successful targeting of innovators and early adopters generated healthy profit margins which were reinvested in the company, especially in research and development (R&D).

*This section on the early history of Sony has been developed in part from The Sony Corporation case study (1986) in Quinn, JB, Mintzberg, H and James, RM (1988) *The Strategy Process: Concepts, Contexts and Cases*, Prentice-Hall. Other material has been obtained from a variety of newspaper and journal articles.

The founder of Sony was Masaru Ibuka, who gathered together a group of engineers 'to develop some sort of electronics laboratory or enterprise'. He had previously owned and managed a factory supplying electronic instruments for the war effort, and he was now keen 'to do something that no other company had done before'. In the 1940s and 1950s Japanese companies were not perceived to be innovators or leaders in technology, but rather businesses which were very skilled at copying Western technology. From these humble beginnings, a truly innovatory company with a worldwide reputation and presence has emerged.

The new enterprise had little capital, a limited track record and no definite ideas. Essentially, the managers just had aspirations to apply the knowledge of the founder in the development of consumer products. Ibuka's first invention for the consumer market was an electric rice cooker manufactured from aluminium. It failed to sell. The electric element burnt the rice at the bottom of the pot while failing to cook the rice at the top.

To generate a stronger cash flow to fund further developments the company started repairing and modifying wartime radio sets. The company was already earning revenue from electronic instruments such as voltmeters which were still being manufactured and sold to the new peacetime markets.

From the beginning Sony developed as an independent company; it was not a member of a Japanese keiretsu or business network. Shortly after the company was started Ibuka was joined by a close wartime friend, Akio Morita, who initially combined a part-time post at the Tokyo Institute of Technology with his time at the company. Unlike Ibuka, Morita was a member of a leading Japanese Samurai family. Morita was expected to forge his career in the family business, which was brewing sake. He had been trained in business skills from an early age. However, at university, he had proved himself to be a very talented electronics engineer. While Ibuka was passionate about inventing, Morita was a more realistic businessman who understood finance and marketing. The two friends proved to have valuable, complementary skills.

In 1946 Ibuka successfully persuaded Morita's father to allow Akio to join his business on a full-time basis. Morita Snr actually invested in the business and eventually became the company's largest shareholder. The company was formally incorporated as Tokyo Telecommunications Engineering Company (TTK) in May 1946, and valued at ¥198,000, which approximated to US$500. TTK's next inventions were an electrically heated cushion and a resonating sound generator (for sending and receiving Morse code) which offered superior audio facilities to competing machines. The quality was high, and the American Occupation Forces were among the early customers. Although the products were relatively sophisticated the production facilities were housed in run-down, leaky premises. TTK also succeeded in obtaining contracts to convert and modernize all the equipment belonging to the Japanese Broadcasting Network. Noticeably, there were still no breakthroughs with products for the theoretically targeted consumer market. Ibuka then saw an early American reel-to-reel tape recorder in one of the offices belonging to the Occupation Forces.

### Tape recorders – the first consumer product

Ibuka realized the potential of the machine and purchased the Japanese patent rights immediately. He was convinced that TTK had the requisite skills to design and produce a good-quality tape recorder. One major stumbling block proved to be a shortage of plastic in Japan, from which TTK could manufacture the reel-to-reel tapes. Import regulations prohibited the acquisition of plastic from abroad. TTK tried cellophane, rice paper and finally a specially calendered paper with a smooth surface and which could be coated with magnetic powder. They overcame the inherent drawbacks in the paper tape by building superior quality into the circuitry, recording head and amplification system. Although it needed both patience and money TTK became the first company in the world to manufacture the complete range of tapes and recorders, including the component parts. Altogether, this implied 12 different basic technologies.

Their first recorder, weighing 100 lb (45 kg), was introduced into the market in 1949. Several months passed though before the first unit was actually sold – to the Japanese equivalent of a pub. Realistically, the device was too heavy, too bulky, too complex and too expensive. Once they realized why the market was slow and hesitant, Ibuka and his colleagues concentrated on reducing both the size and weight, and sought ways of halving the cost. Their main competition was from 3M, which was already a well-established and successful American corporation. 3M's magnetic tape, branded with the Scotch name, was a superior product which TTK sought to franchise. 3M were only willing to grant the franchise if TTK stopped manufacturing the hardware.

## Transistor radios

Ibuka went to America in 1952 in search of new market opportunities for his smaller, cheaper tape recorder. It was on this visit that he began to realize the future potential for transistors, an invention patented by Western Electric of the USA. He returned home and told his engineers that they were going to use transistors to build radios – radios that would not need electricity for power and which were small enough for individuals to carry around easily. Current 'portable' models were the size of a typical briefcase, weighed over 10 lb (4.5 kg) and needed the batteries changed every few hours. Ibuka conceptualized a pocket-sized model and took up the challenge of developing the technology.

TTK had to license the patent from Western Electric at a cost of $25,000. Protracted negotiations with the Japanese Ministry of International Trade and Industry (MITI) for the release of this amount of foreign currency imposed a nine-month delay. The transistor patent was granted in 1954.

Increasing sales of their lighter, cheaper tape recorders enabled TTK to invest in a research programme for transistors. Their aim was to achieve satisfactory yields of the high-frequency transistors which were needed if radios were to be manufactured at a commercial cost. Early transistors were utilized in such products as hearing aids, which operated at much lower frequencies. Nevertheless, TTK were beaten by Texas Instruments in the race to be first with a portable radio utilizing high-frequen-

cy transistors. However, in August 1955 TTK were also able to display a small portable radio. Its size was $8'' \times 4'' \times 1.5''$ ($20 \times 10 \times 3$ cm). The production target for the first year was 10,000, and they actually achieved 8000.

Ibuka's team concentrated on making an even smaller model, despite critics who argued that any further reduction in size would have to be at the expense of sound quality. TTK's greatest challenge lay in convincing their component suppliers that size reductions were achievable. TTK formed research alliances with a number of their suppliers and offered them technical help and expertise. Existing components were often straight copies of Western technology, a typical Japanese strategy at that time. Perseverance was rewarded in March 1957 when TTK was first to market with a pocket radio. The radio was marginally bigger than a normal shirt pocket, and consequently TTK started producing and marketing shirts with slightly larger pockets!

The company was renamed Sony at around this time. The new name had been derived from the Latin *sonis*, meaning sound. Ibuka and Morita believed the name to be simple, recognizable and easily pronounced in most languages. The name Sony quickly became a generic for transistor radios, and Sony enjoyed an early technology lead of between two and three years. Later product developments included transistorized short-wave and FM receivers.

## Consolidation and growth

Sony was growing into a very sound company, diversified into a number of related areas and with markets around the world as well as in Japan. Its reliance on the Japanese government (for aid) and banking system was minimal. Ibuka and Morita were firmly in control and able to make quick decisions. Rapid expansion drove Sony to poach senior managers from other Japanese companies, an unusual practice in that country, and one which was frowned upon. But Sony was clearly not a typical Japanese business.

A new director of research was recruited from MITI, where he had previously worked for over 25 years. A printing company manager was appointed and given a totally free hand to turn around a struggling semiconductor factory. An ex-jet pilot and talented opera baritone, Norio Ohga, was employed firstly as a music consultant. After his retirement from active stage work he became head of the tape recorder business and some years later he succeeded Akio Morita as chief executive of the whole Sony Corporation. It was Ohga who championed Sony's entry into the music and entertainments industries in the 1980s. One executive remarked: 'I never knew what hidden abilities I had until I came to Sony'.

Sony's workforce grew tenfold in the 1950s and fourfold in the 1960s. In the mid-1990s Sony employed 138,000 people around the world (see Exhibit 5). The business was controlled through firm budgeting and production control systems – but within these constraints employees were given considerable freedom and empowerment. Creativity was encouraged. Workers were provided with homes by the company, a normal Japanese practice. These homes, though, were small, prefabricated houses, whereas most large Japanese companies would house their workers in dormitories. Also unusually, Sony employees were given responsibility for their own residences.

## Working practices

Production was organized in small cells, each a specialized unit with full control over its own work and with responsibility for monitoring its own output. Internal co-operation between cells was encouraged and fostered. The cells formed an interconnected and interdependent network. Each cell had a second cell as its main supplier and a third cell as its main customer. The role of management was to assist the cells, helping them to solve problems, setting overall goals and praising superior performances.

New employees, regardless of their background, education and intended functional role, would spend several months on a production line. Ibuka and Morita believed that it was important that all employees should understand the company's products, working practices and culture. It was also typical for Sony to switch people between jobs every few years. Frequently, workers would move from an engineering to a production role, and vice versa. Rewards and bonuses were given to groups of workers rather than to individuals.

Employees were encouraged to be innovative 'in the interests of the company' and not to be afraid to make mistakes – as long as they did not make the same mistake twice. Young employees were deliberately given heavy workloads and considerable responsibility. New managers all had corporate mentors.

*Sony motivates executives not with special compensation systems, but by giving them joy in achievement, challenge, pride and a sense of recognition.*

## Television – an important new product

Sony began to use transistors in new consumer products, introducing the world's first transistorized television in 1959, the world's first transistorized video tape recorder in 1961, and the world's first micro-television in 1962.

In 1960 Sony established a subsidiary in the USA, and Akio Morita moved with his family to New York. Sony's managers felt that they needed to know the US market by intuition and not be reliant on published statistics. Sony Corporation of America was subsequently developed into one of US's highest quality companies, renowned for both its products and after-sales service.

By the mid-1960s colour television was becoming established in the USA. The standard technology, which had been pioneered by RCA, was known as the 'shadow mask' system. A triangle of three electron guns created a grid of colour dots to produce the colour image. Sony did not want to copy this widely licensed US invention, and sought to develop a system based on a line (rather than a triangle) of electron guns in the television tube. Early trials were not successful, and not for the first time Sony appeared to some to be investing in a dream. Morita commented: 'If we wait and develop a unique product, we may start several years later, but we will be stronger than all the others in ten years'.

After several setbacks, and considerable frustration, Sony's new 'Trinitron' system was ready in

1967. Trinitron was a unique concept, using a single gun and a three striped beam system. Its competitive advantage was that the colour reproduction was superior to the RCA system. By spring 1968 the new Sony televisions were in the shops, priced competitively, and within a year Trinitron dominated the small-screen (12″) market in Japan. Success in America, and systematically the rest of the world, followed almost automatically and inevitably. Production of Trinitron colour sets began in America in 1972 and in Britain in 1975.

Later, in the 1980s, Sony was the first company to develop a high-definition television standard. This innovation prompted a defensive competitive reaction in Europe. The European Commission founded an industrial consortium to develop a rival standard.

## Video recorders

Video tape recorders had been in existence since the mid-1950s, but they were used primarily by the professional broadcasters. A number of Japanese companies, together with leading American electronics corporations, produced models. Philips (of The Netherlands) dominated the market in Europe. Sony made a deliberate decision not to enter the professional video market. Instead, Ibuka decided that Sony should manufacture less expensive commercial video recorders. Some time later he also decided that Sony should seek to develop videos for use in the home.

It was his vision and innovatory zeal that led to Sony's early predominance in the home video tape recorder market, but it was not a lead that they were able to sustain.

Sony's high-quality commercial system, the U-Matic format, was launched in 1972. U-Matic machines and tapes were both bigger than the VHS systems that are commonplace today, but much smaller than the existing professional systems. U-Matic machines used a single recording head and tapes enclosed in cassettes – professional machines normally had four heads and used reel-to-reel tapes. Because of its high quality, U-Matic survived for a number of years after smaller systems were available.

Sony pioneered home video with the Betamax format in 1976. Betamax cassettes were also larger

than the VHS format which was developed by Japan Victor Corporation (JVC), a subsidiary of Matsushita, under a patent agreement with Sony. Sony had invited Matsushita to join them with the Betamax format, but their suggestion had been declined. The early VHS tapes offered twice the recording time of Betamax, but Sony stuck with Betamax because of its superior reproduction quality. They believed that this advantage would guarantee success and consumer preference. They misjudged the market and their competitors. Most Japanese and American consumers preferred the smaller and cheaper VHS system.

Although relatively slow to take off, the video tape recorder reached a penetration level of 25% of households by the mid-1980s. Sony gave up on Betamax for the domestic market and instead produced VHS recorders and tapes, but never achieved a substantial market position. In 1990, for example, Sony had a 1% UK market share for video recorders and a 6% share of the blank tapes market. Betamax was always a more popular format in the broadcasting sector of the market, where Sony still enjoys an 80% market share.

There was a number of lessons for Sony. Not only had they failed to understand the needs and preferences of their customers, they had failed to promote their system effectively. JVC, in contrast, had been willing to share their technology and had entered alliances with owners of software – namely the studios who owned the rights to feature and television films which could be released on video. These lessons were instrumental in strategic decisions made by Sony in the 1980s.

## The Sony Walkman

The Walkman is probably Sony's best-known product, and its launch in 1979 heralded the restoration of Sony's reputation and innovatory leadership. The Walkman introduced a new dimension to the way people listened to the radio and to pre-recorded music and 'changed the lifestyle of a generation'. The original Walkman was a compact cassette player with small earphones to enable highly portable listening without annoying or inconveniencing other people. Over 50 million sets were sold within the first ten years. It is useful when walking and jogging and on trains and aeroplanes. The concept was later extended to a variety of different models, including waterproof and sandproof sets, radio receivers, special versions for children, compact disc players and, in 1988, video playback systems using Sony's new 8 mm video cassettes.

The idea for the Walkman had come from Ibuka and Morita. Morita knew that young people liked to listen to music constantly, often wanting to play it at a loud volume, and that their tastes and preferences were frequently very personalized. He also played golf fanatically and believed that an individual cassette player would appeal to a whole range of sportsmen and women. His assumptions were correct this time. The Walkman was successful from the day it was launched.

## Other products and competition

Sony launched its Mavica all-electronic still picture camera in Japan in 1981. Marketing in America and Europe followed some years later. Mavica records the images on small magnetic discs, rather than film, and they can be viewed on home television screens instead of using slides or photographs. Hard-copy printing systems are available for people who also want a physical photograph.

These systems have so far failed to make major inroads into the popularity of film cameras, despite the dramatic success of hand-held video camera-recorders. These cameras became increasingly compact during the 1980s, making use of 8-mm video cassettes which can be transferred onto VHS format for viewing on domestic televisions. This market is very lucrative but very competitive and increasingly dynamic, with several major Japanese electronics companies involved.

Sony launched the first miniaturized camcorder in June 1989. It weighed just 1.5 lb (680 g), and it was one-quarter the size of existing camcorders. Within six months both Matsushita and its JVC subsidiary had introduced lighter models. Within a further six months there was additional competition from Canon, Sanyo, Ricoh and Hitachi. Sony intro-

duced two new models in Summer 1990. One was the lightest then available; the other had superior technical features.

Japanese competitors such as Matsushita (which also incorporates Panasonic branded products), Hitachi and Toshiba are all older and larger than Sony. Although their product ranges are not identical they are all diversified and active internationally. A number of these Japanese companies has, for example, diversified into consumer white goods (washing machines, refrigerators, and so on), which Sony has deliberately ignored. There are, in addition, many other smaller Japanese competitors. Sony also experiences competition from a variety of US and European producers, with certain companies successful in particular markets but perhaps less successful across the spectrum of the global consumer electronics industry. The major European competitors are AEG, Bosch, GEC, Philips and Thomson SA, which acquired Ferguson in the UK from Thorn EMI. Amstrad is a competitor for certain products only. No single competitor enjoys wide market dominance, although there are market leaders for different products. The dynamism of the market, with short product lifecycles and constant innovation, means that positions of leadership may well prove transient. Sony has always marketed its products creatively around the world, sometimes appearing more like a home producer than a Japanese company. Exhibit 1, which features examples of the humorous copy used in a number of radio and television advertisements in the UK, is included to illustrate that Sony is not a typical Japanese company. The advertisements all featured the instantly recognizable voice of John Cleese and date back to the late 1970s and early 1980s. It has also been claimed that many Americans actually believe that Sony is an American company.

In the early 1980s Sony formed an alliance with Philips to develop and launch compact disc players and CDs. At that time Philips had a substantial shareholding in Polygram, one of the leading recording companies, but not the controlling interest which it has today. Initially, the record companies in America and Europe were cautious about releasing their music on the new format; and this hostility

**Exhibit 1**  Sony radio and television advertisements featuring John Cleese used in the UK in the late 1970s and early 1980s

Good Evening.

Good Evening Sir.

I'd like to buy a Sony Trinitron Family Size Colour Television set please.

Well, this is an off-licence Sir.

I see. Well do you have anything else that would give me really bright, clear, colourful pictures?

How about a gallon of creme de menthe? That'd put you on the way.

But would the pictures be really sharp?

Hmm – not really!

And is it reliable?

Well, you don't get the pictures immediately and there's always the danger your head'll fall off.

Oh, I think the Sony'll be better then. I'll try a TV shop.

Well, why did you come here in the first place?

I wanted to annoy you.

(Shop door bell)

Ring

Good afternoon.

Good afternoon Sir. Can I help you?

Yes, I'm looking for a colour television – what about this one?

Ah, the Sony Trinitron 1810.

Now, does it give a nice fuzzy picture and break down a lot?

No, no, the Trinitron system means a very sharp, reliable …

Oh well, are the colours muddy and nasty?

No Sir, they're very bright. It's a feature …

It's for my wife you see.

Oh – doesn't she like television?

Oh yes, but I don't like her.

Ah well, now, this little Ruritanian set's a real shocker.

Really, really. I still like the look of this Sony Trinitron you know.

Oh.

Yes, I'll take it.

But I must warn you … it's not really right for you.

I know, but it's all right. I'll smash it up a bit. Do you sell mallets?

Sony the electronics people have asked me to tell you that they've just opened a fish and chip shop in Regent Street where you can wander in and play with the fish to your heart's content.

Sorry, sorry, that's quite wrong. I got confused – er – it's not a fish and chip shop, its a TV, Stereos and Radio showroom – sorry – I got a bit muddled there – I'm doing an ad for some fish and chip shops next – sorry – er.

Sony have a magnificent showroom and not a fish and chip shop in Reggent Street – sorry Regent Street – so if you want to go in and examine and operate stereo equipment, but not Halibut and Rock Salmon or anything fishy like that, go to 134 Regent Street. Sorry about the muddle.

Look I am frightfully sorry to bother you but some awfully nice people called Sony have agreed to pay me some money if I'll tell you they've a terribly nice showroom in Regent Street where you can just wander in and play with all the Sony Stereo and TV and Radio equipment and listen to the quadraphonic demonstration without being pestered by anyone, just to see if you like anything, you see.

It's at 134 Regent Street.

There, I've told you.

I've told them.

(Cash register)

Thank you.

had a formative effect on Sony's future diversification strategies. Sony and Philips still earn royalties for every CD that is sold.

Sony also competes in sectors of the global computer industry, which again involves several leading Japanese players such as Hitachi and Fujitsu, and many American and European businesses. The American competitors range from the giant IBM through a number of medium-sized businesses to several small and very entrepreneurial hardware and software companies. Sony has targeted particular niches and focused carefully.

Sony pioneered the 3.5″ floppy disc, which quickly proved more robust and popular than its 5.25″ predecessor. The disc, launched in 1980, was far more successful for Sony than its early word-processor, for which it was designed. This floppy has become the industry standard, and in the 1990s Sony retains 25% of the world market. Until the early 1980s Sony manufactured semi-conductors for incorporation in its own consumer products, and then, realizing the potential for sharing its technology, sold them externally. Sony has been a pioneer and market leader for several specialized components and has also introduced a successful range of high-powered workstations.

Exhibit 2 provides a summary of Sony's product range in 1996. Exhibit 3 analyses the breakdown of Sony's sales by product and geography for the period 1973 to 1996. In the tables the category 'other products' mainly comprises computers and computing equipment together with Sony's chemicals activities. These businesses are essentially suppliers of necessary materials and represent vertical integration.

## Lean manufacturing

Sony have seen lean manufacturing as another competitive weapon, and as both a supplement to, and partial replacement for, continuous innovation and new product developments. The improvements are still being sought, and are still happening, but for a number of products the speed of change has slowed down.

Lean manufacturing was necessary because the consumer electronics industry has become increasingly mature. At the same time it is this maturity, and the ability to slow down the rate at which new products and major product improvements are

---

**Exhibit 2** The Sony corporation. 1996 product range

| Percentage breakdown of sales in 1996 | | |
|---|---|---|
| 15% | Video equipment | – A leading manufacturer for broadcast and professional use. Domestic VCRs, digital camcorders, 8 mm camcorders, video disc players, laserdisc players, still image video cameras and tapes. Video tape |
| 20% | Audio equipment | – CD players, hi-fi and mini systems, radio cassette players and radios, personal stereos (Walkman series). DAT systems and car stereos. Audio tape |
| 17% | Television sets | – Including HD TB and giant monitors |
| 29% | Other products | – Semiconductors. Electronic components. Computers and associated equipment (including games machines, PCs, laptops, disc drives and floppy discs). Cellular telephones |
| 19% { | Music and entertainment | – Sony Music Entertainment – CD and cassette software |
| | Filmed entertainment | – Columbia Pictures |
| | | Tri-Star Pictures |

**Exhibit 3** The Sony Corporation
**Analysis of turnover by sector**

| | (Financial years) | | |
| --- | --- | --- | --- |
| Product sales (%) | 1973 | 1977 | 1981 |
| Video equipment | 6 | 14 | 27 |
| Audio equipment* | 12 | 12 | 7 |
| Televisions | 41 | 33 | 23 |
| Tape recorders and radio* | 27 | 20 | 17 |
| Other products | 14 | 21 | 26 |

*From 1982 these categories were consolidated.

| | (Financial years) | | | | | |
| --- | --- | --- | --- | --- | --- | --- |
| Product sales (%) | 1982 | 1987 | 1988 | 1989 | 1990 | 1991 |
| Video equipment | 43 | 31 | 29 | 27 | 26 | 25 |
| Audio equipment | 23 | 31 | 31 | 26 | 25 | 24 |
| Televisions | 23 | 21 | 20 | 16 | 15 | 16 |
| Other products | 11 | 17 | 17 | 15 | 15 | 15 |
| Music and filmed entertainment | | | 3 | 16 | 19 | 20 |

| | (Financial years) | | | | |
| --- | --- | --- | --- | --- | --- |
| Product sales (%) | 1992 | 1993 | 1994 | 1995 | 1996 |
| Video equipment | 23 | 24 | 18 | 18 | 15 |
| Audio equipment | 25 | 24 | 23 | 23 | 20 |
| Televisions | 16 | 16 | 17 | 18 | 17 |
| Other products | 18 | 20 | 22 | 23 | 29 |
| Music and filmed entertainment | 18 | 19 | 20 | 18 | 19 |

**Analysis of turnover by geography (selected years only)**

| | 1973 | 1977 | 1981 | 1987 | 1991 |
| --- | --- | --- | --- | --- | --- |
| Japan | 53 | 39 | 29 | 34 | 26 |
| USA | 26 | 30 | 27 | 27 | 29 |
| Europe | 11 | 15 | 20 | 24 | 28 |
| Rest of world | 10 | 16 | 24 | 15 | 17 |

launched, that has facilitated lean manufacturing. Lean manufacturing systems imply some inflexibility, and are therefore preferable when products are not being constantly changed and updated.

Lean manufacturing describes manufacturing systems which are designed to reduce lead times and costs. They are likely to require investment in information technology but not necessarily the most advanced manufacturing technology. 'Lean' implies simpler systems, often based on just-in-time principles, and greater reliance on a network of interdependent suppliers. It is these arrangements which reduce the flexibility. In 1992, for example, Sony reduced the lead-time for manufacturing a video recorder by two-thirds.

Typically parts are ordered firmly just 48 hours before they are needed. This is only practical if suppliers are integrated into Sony's value chain and if product cycles are relatively long. Although relatively inflexible for substantive product changes, such systems can be made very flexible for responding to changing consumer demand patterns. Face-lifts, such as new housings, which are still changed frequently, can be accommodated without undue difficulty.

### Overseas subsidiaries

Sony developed an extensive international business for three main reasons:

1. Sony lacked the domestic sales and distribution networks of its leading Japanese competitors and therefore looked to establish both production plants and sales networks around the world and close to its important markets
2. Sony wanted to be an innovatory pioneer for consumer electronics products and realized early in its history that it would be important to enjoy close proximity to its markets in order to understand and satisfy their disparate needs
3. The strength of the Japanese yen. When Sony was first incorporated the exchange rate was over 350 yen to the US dollar; in mid-1996 the rate was 108 yen to $1. When Sony built its UK plant in South Wales in 1974 £1.00 exchanged for 650 yen. In 1996 the rate was in the order of 170 yen to £1.00.

Sony's first production plant outside Japan was built in Taiwan in 1967. In 1972 Sony began manufacturing in San Diego, California. Europe followed in 1973 with a plant in Spain. Sony began producing televisions at Bridgend in south Wales in 1974, and this remains its only British manufacturing plant. The extent of Sony's operations in each European country tends to be focused. For example, audio equipment is manufactured in France, magnetic tape in Italy and CD equipment in Austria. Countries such as Malaysia (colour televisions, audio and video

equipment) and Thailand (semi-conductors and magnetic tape) have more than one plant and a more diverse range of products.

Sony now has plants in America and in all major European and Far Eastern countries. Altogether, there are over 600 subsidiaries, and over 70% of Sony's sales are outside Japan. In comparison, the overseas sales percentages for three of Sony's main Japanese rivals are: Matsushita, 45%; Toshiba, 31%; and Hitachi, 24%.

The following sections chart how the innovative, successful and influential Sony began to lose its way.

### Diversification into music and entertainments

Sony's diversification into the American music and entertainments industries was based on the following premise. To 'guarantee', or at least consolidate, the future potential for the permanently changing and improving consumer electronics hardware and gadgetry, Sony must be confident that the major entertainment companies would release their films and music in suitable formats. Sony therefore chose to integrate vertically and, by acquisition, secure a substantial presence in the entertainment software business.

In January 1988 Sony paid US$2.2 billion to buy CBS Records. This was followed in November 1989 with the purchase of Columbia Pictures (Columbia and Tri-Star studios) from Coca-Cola. See Exhibit 4 for a summary of the previous acquisition of Columbia by Coca-Cola. This acquisition cost $3.4 billion but Sony took on an additional $1.6 billion in debts. At the time, this constituted the largest ever overseas take-over by a Japanese company. CBS became Sony Music and Columbia was renamed Sony Pictures Entertainment. There was some cross-synergy potential with the increasingly important pop music videos and the release of film music albums.

Table 1 shows how the hardware–software linkages were to be created.

Sony was followed into America by Matsushita, which acquired MCA, owners of a recording business and Universal Studios, for $6.1 billion. Toshiba

**Exhibit 4** Coca-Cola's acquisition of Columbia Pictures

In March 1982 the managements of the Coca-Cola Company and Columbia Pictures Industries Inc. agreed that Columbia should become a subsidiary of Coca-Cola. The news was greeted with mixed feelings and the *New York Times* summarized many commentators' opinions: '... may be a mistake. To make a conglomerate of a company that has succeeded because it has stayed with its speciality is a dubious strategy'. At the time the Coca-Cola drink held a 25% share of the American soft drinks market, and it represented some 70% of the corporation's sales. The company had developed additional products for existing and related markets, namely Tab (sugar-free Coke, 1963) and Fanta (fizzy orange juice, 1960); and it manufactured and distributed tea, coffee, wine and natural fruit juices. Products were sold in 135 countries around the world, including China and the USSR.

Coca-Cola had been looking for possible acquisitions in the food, health care and entertainment industries to enable it to grow more quickly than inflation. Any acquisition must not involve high technology (no experience) or require heavy capital investment in plant. While looking for suitable companies Coca-Cola concluded that health care was becoming too high tech and that food companies did not offer a profit margin as good as its existing business. Columbia proved attractive because it was involved in home entertainments (cable TV and video), growth of which should be good for the Coca-Cola drink. In addition it had a reputation for successful films (*Kramer versus Kramer*, *The China Syndrome* and *Close Encounters* in the recent past), and it had an extensive film library of past productions which were undervalued in the balance sheet given their home movie potential.

Coca-Cola argued that potential synergy existed because both companies were experienced in mass consumer markets and worldwide operations, and both appealed significantly to young people. But were these sufficient grounds for synergy?

In 1986 David Puttnam, British producer of *Chariots of Fire* and *The Killing Fields*, joined Columbia, but left the following year. He departed two months after Coca-Cola signed an agreement with Tri-Star Pictures, another film and TV company in which they had built a 33% stake, whereby the entertainment interests of both organizations were formed into a separate independent company, 80% owned by Coca-Cola and managed by Tri-Star executives.

Commentators contended that one reason behind this move was the reality that Wall Street was increasingly favouring pure rather than conglomerate businesses. In truth, Columbia had always been profitable through the 1980s, but the key success factors for soft drinks and motion pictures were significantly different, and synergy proved elusive. Soft drinks, whatever their brand name, have certain similarities, and the emphasis must be upon effective marketing to build and maintain a market image. Films and often very different from each other.

By mid-1989 the film company was called Columbia Pictures Entertainment, and Coca-Cola held 49% of the equity. When Sony of Japan offered to buy Columbia Pictures, Coca-Cola was said to be 'demanding a high price for its shares'.

bought a stake in Time-Warner. Some critics argue that the Japanese 'have been mugged' and paid over the odds. Others have commented that Sony has been allowed to buy 'a significant part of America's soul'. Matsushita did not keep MCA for very long and re-sold it to Seagram, the Canadian drinks manufacturer. Matsushita tried unsuccessfully to run MCA

from Japan; it was less willing than Sony has been to devolve significant power to foreign managers. The Toshiba/Time-Warner link has proved lucrative for the development of digital video technology.

Sony's gamble concerns the future and its ability to derive the potential synergy it claims is there. There is certainly no universal agreement that the

**Table 1**    The synergy between Sony's hardware and new software products

| | |
|---|---|
| Film and recording studios | Cameras, broadcasting and recording equipment all provided by Sony |
| | Sony also manufacture all the blank recording tape and films required |
| Film and music production | Sony would determine the films and music which would be produced – and, critically, control the release formats |
| | Sony also gained control over 12 television stations and the Columbia libraries, including 300 film titles and 20,000 recorded television shows. These TV shows alone provide Sony with an annual income of $100 million |
| Consumer hardware | At the time Sony manufactured: high-definition televisions; video recorders; the range of Walkman products covering audio cassettes, CDs and videos (8 mm format); CD and hi-fi equipment |
| Consumer software | Sony manufacture the film, video tape, compact discs and cassettes upon which the software will be released |
| | There are, quite simply, several outlets for a single piece of recorded material |
| | Additional opportunities for Sony lie in computer games based upon their movies and designed for high-definition television and the Sony PlayStation; and in the future in digital video discs which are seen as the replacement for video tape. |

synergy is anything other than imaginary. The hardware and software businesses are, quite simply, different. It is a question of technology versus creativity; and the key success factors are not the same. Some analysts, who disagree with the change of direction, have argued that the money would have been better invested in information technology.

### The inherent risks

There were three areas of risk for Sony.

The management risk concerned Sony's ability to manage an American acquisition. Sony was innovatory but managed by engineers. CBS and Columbia are 'people businesses'. Rather than try and manage the acquisitions from Tokyo, Sony decided early on to decentralize the business and recruit experienced Americans to control the companies. The entertainments businesses were controlled wholly from Hollywood until 1995. Although Akio Morita's brother was chairman of Sony America, American-born Mickey Schulhof was the chief executive until he resigned in 1995. When he left, Schulhof had worked for Sony for 21 years; unusually for a foreigner, he had been appointed to the main Sony board in 1989. Producers Peter Guber and Jon Peters, who had recently made the box-office suc-

cesses *Batman* and *Rain Man*, were brought in by Schulhof at a cost to Sony of $200 million.

As it has become an increasingly global corporation, Sony has recruited more European and American managers to support the Japanese leadership. The integration of the different cultures is not perceived to be a problem. 'Sony's culture is heterogeneous and is strengthened by a continuous injection of new people and ideas.'

In reality, the Japanese have accepted that the Americans must be given a free hand with the entertainments businesses, and that they must be given sufficient capital. Although it cannot have been easy for Sony to delegate such authority and responsibility, they have nevertheless done it. As a consequence the hardware and software businesses have so far been run as separate, independent businesses.

The second risk was the political risk. Would there be a hostile reaction from the US public? Sony was well established and well known in the USA, thanks to the past efforts of Morita, and consequently this has not proved to be a major concern.

Third was the significant and still unresolved strategic risk. Did Sony need to go into the software business? Did it pay too high a price, and could it recoup its investment? Is the synergy potential real or imagined? Could Sony succeed where Coca-Cola had failed?

Peter Guber has commented that Sony in Tokyo did not use the expression synergy, but nevertheless expected that Sony Entertainments would find ways of marrying the technology resources of the electronics businesses with entertainments. In this respect a new film should ideally be accompanied by a soundtrack produced by Sony Music. Cinemas will use Sony's digital sound equipment, which is said to be superior to Dolby systems. Depending on the film Sony will manufacture related video games based on the movie's characters.

Two main arguments against the synergy between hardware and software have been put forward. First, Sony must still make its hardware freely available to all software producers. Secondly, the decision by retailers to stock particular software formats, and the decision of consumers to buy, can only be influenced and not controlled by Sony.

## The outcome – so far

### Filmed entertainment

Sony acquired a film studio which had previously been very successful with such films as *Lawrence of Arabia* and *Bridge Over the River Kwai*. Sony also inherited *Hook*, directed by Stephen Spielberg at a cost of $62 million. It recouped $250 million at the box office. Sony allowed Columbia an annual film budget of $700 million, which was above average for the industry and brought immediate criticisms of overspending.

In December 1992 Sony concluded an exclusive long-term deal with Barbara Streisand to cover her music and film work. Streisand already recorded on CBS. This followed a similar deal with Michael Jackson in 1991, mainly covering music.

Sony have brought out a number of major box office (and consequentially, financial) successes, including *Bugsy* (Warren Beatty), *Prince of Tides* (Barbara Streisand), *My Girl*, *A League of their Own* (Madonna), *Little Women*, *Legends of the Fall*, *Philadelphia* (Tom Hanks), *Jumanji* (Robin Williams), *The American President* (Michael Douglas) and *Sense*

*and Sensibility* (Emma Thompson). There has been one major disaster and box office failure: *Last Action Hero* with Arnold Schwarzenegger. Sony's films accounted for 15% of US cinema box office receipts in 1990, achieving an even higher proportion for a short period of time, but by 1994 they had fallen below 10%. At this time Sony was earning an average revenue of $18 million per film; Paramount Studios was averaging $55 million. Nevertheless, high-budget films continued to be made, leading to accusations that they were driving up the already high production costs. These comments caused Jon Peters to resign.

His departure was followed by that of Peter Guber in October 1994. One month later Sony wrote 265 billion yen (£1.67 billion) off the value of Sony Pictures Entertainment, commenting: 'the business has not provided adequate returns. Additional funding will be needed to attain acceptable levels of profitability'. It has been estimated that Sony had at this stage already invested $4.6 billion on top of the $3.4 billion it paid to acquire Columbia Pictures.

A Morgan Stanley analyst in London commented in 1994:

> If there is a moral to this story, it is that Japanese electronics groups do not make good parents for Hollywood movie studios.

Television films began to take priority over high-budget feature films, less attention was placed on finding elusive synergies and the relative success of the movie studios improved in 1995. Nevertheless, Schulhof left Sony at the end of the year and he was not replaced. His number two would continue with the same responsibilities but now report to the new strategic leaders, Nobuyuki Idei and Norio Ohga in Japan (the succession of Norio Ohga and Nobuyuki Idei to the senior positions in Sony is described later in the case). Wall Street interpreted this to mean that Sony would be willing to sell at the right price.

### Music

The music business was generally more stable and profitable than the movie studios; Sony's leading artists, in particular Michael Bolton, Mariah Carey, Oasis and Bruce Springsteen, continued to deliver successful albums. However, Michael Jackson's popularity fell back when he was accused of being involved with a minor, and Sony lost George Michael when he demanded to be released from his contract.

## Product disappointments: the mini-disc and DCC

These two new formats for recorded music were both launched towards the end of 1992. By this time vinyl records were almost forgotten and, in certain countries including the UK, CDs were outselling audio cassettes.

Mini-disc is a small (2.5″) compact disc which sells for roughly the same price as a conventional CD. It was invented by Sony, as were the new mini-disc players. Mini-discs are not compatible with existing CD equipment. There is no loss of quality, there is random access (instant track selection) and blank discs can be bought for home recording. These blanks cost 40% of the pre-recorded disc price. They are ideal for Walkman-sized players.

Digital compact cassettes (DCC) were developed jointly by Philips and Matsushita. Philips designed the hardware, Matsushita the software. DCC offers CD-quality sound reproduction (a marked improvement on standard audio cassettes) at the same price as a standard CD. DCCs contain a spare track for recording additional data, such as biographical details of the artists, which can be viewed on both special LCD and normal TV screens. The new DCC players will also play standard cassettes, as the two formats are the same size, but DCCs cannot be played on existing audio equipment. Philips and Matsushita saw this as a major advantage as the average person owns some 60 audio cassettes. Blanks are available. The major disadvantage was the existing drawback of standard cassettes – random access and track selection is not possible. In addition, the fear of piracy was greater for DCCs than for mini-disc.

Nevertheless, the six leading record companies worldwide (including Sony Music) all agreed to release music on DCC. Initially only Sony and EMI Music were willing to support mini-disc, with the others looking to protect their existing CD sales for the time-being. It seemed unlikely that they would not support mini-disc if consumers were enthusiastic about the new format. After all, mini-disc players were cheaper than DCC players, and Sony was able to offer a combined CD/mini-disc player in 1994.

Initially consumers were reluctant to commit themselves to either product until there were clear indications of leadership. Could both formats succeed, or must there be a winner? Technical superiority alone would not guarantee success. In the event, both have failed to really take off. Some 750,000 mini-disc players have been sold, but most of these are in Japan; it continues as a niche market product. DCC was less successful.

## Changes in strategic leadership

Globalization was always a personal crusade of Akio Morita.* In 1996 he was over seventy and retained only a peripheral involvement from his home in Hawaii, but he still exerted influence. Morita retired as chief executive officer in 1989 (he was succeeded by Norio Ohga, who had been chief operating officer since 1982) but stayed active with the title of chairman. Partially paralysed by a stroke in 1993, he relinquished this last position in 1995. Morita spoke perfect English and was highly Westernized. He was the public face of Sony, especially in America. He believed that Sony should be a good and ethical corporate citizen everywhere it operates, and he, like Ibuka, believed that the pursuit of profit is not the principal objective. Sony's plants have always been designed to fit into their local communities. In Alsace, for example, Sony inherited a vineyard with a piece of land that they bought. They continued to make wine, labelled Chateau Sony!

Morita frequently incorporated a strong element of intuition in his decision making. Ibuka was the same. Their executive successor, Norio Ohga, had a more considered style. According to Sony, however, his accession would have no effect on the basic culture. Sony would continue to 'operate rapidly and efficiently whilst placing strong emphasis on the long-term development of people and technology'.

*Akio Morita died in October 1999.

Morita believed that Sony's commitment to innovation was deeply embedded in the culture of the organization worldwide. He argued that there were three essential features:

| | |
|---|---|
| Creativity in technology | Sony is committed to high standards for the technical engineering within its products |
| Creativity in product planning | This technology must be harnessed to design useful, attractive and user-friendly products |
| Creativity in marketing | The organization must commit resources to ensure that customers are persuaded to buy Sony's products. |

Interestingly, Sony's Betamax video was characterized by the first two of these – but Sony failed to persuade the market that it was superior to the VHS format. The Walkman was a supremely successful example of effective product planning and marketing, but it was still harnessing 'old' technology.

Ohga was 65 years old in 1994; he had undergone a coronary bypass operation three years earlier. In 1995 he elected to step back and nominated Nobuyuki Idei to succeed him. Idei was currently the chief operating officer but, unlike Ibuka, Morita and Ohga, his background was not in engineering. He was essentially a marketing person who had worked for Sony for over 30 years. Typically he is perceived to be 'un-Japanese' and he speaks fluent English and French. Idei was determined to implement change in the once-mighty Sony whose performance had recently been deteriorating. In the year ended March 1995 Sony made a pre-tax loss for the first time in its history.

He stated that his main role would be to 'turn Sony into a company which can identify with a new generation of consumer electronics users – the digital dream kids'. There was to be an increased research and development emphasis on software, networks and information technology and new products relevant for the digital age.

The *Financial Times* (19 July 1996) commented that 'Sony, a young maverick company up to the 1980s, had become the sprawling, bureaucratic organization from which its founders sought to dif- fer'. Idei was also determined to continue with the structural changes he had begun in 1994.

## New products in the mid–1990s

### Digital video

Similar to the way in which the CD replaced the vinyl record, digital video is predicted to replace the video cassette players and tapes which prospered in the 1980s. Digital video discs (DVD) and players (DVP) play digitized images onto a screen and are seen as an ideal format for computer-linked interactive video, the multimedia dream. As was the case with video, authorship of the technical standard is seen as critical as it will bring lifelong royalties, marketing advantages, power and influence. For digital video, the hardware/software challenge demands that the hardware and data formats meet the needs of the so-called information superhighway, including music and film makers, and the personal computer, telecommunications, cable television and satellite broadcasting industries. For Sony this represents a philosophical shift. The last major Sony breakthroughs, the Walkman and the compact disc, were driven largely by the needs and preferences of customers; digital video will be producer driven because of the complex array of interested parties.

Sony chose to develop digital video with its CD partner, Philips. By 1993 it was clear that Sony-Philips was in competition with an alliance between Toshiba and Time-Warner. Sony's DVD was single sided and could store over 2 hours of video. Toshiba's super-density disc was double-sided and offered greater storage capacity, equivalent to seven and a half normal CDs. Sony was convinced that its costs and prices would be lower and that these issues would outweigh the capacity issue. However, by early 1995 Sony and Philips were largely isolated, supported in the main by Mitsumi, Ricoh and Teac, who all manufacture floppy disc drives. Hitachi, Pioneer, Mitsubishi, Thomson and, most critically, Matsushita/JVC supported the rival alliance. Initially Sony and Philips were determined to carry on with their own DVD, but in September they 'accepted the inevitable' and adopted the rival format.

## The PlayStation

Sony's PlayStation is one of a new generation of 32-bit computer games systems, which are far faster and more graphic than their predecessors, the 16-bit systems. Sony, which was already active in games software, entered the hardware market in September 1995 with a high-quality but competitively priced product and immediately took market share away from the two industry leaders, Sega and Nintendo. Sony's strategy was to price low to seize share and use this to boost sales of its more profitable and highly innovative games. The Sony PlayStation achieved sales of 3.2 million units in its first year, two million of these in trend-setting Japan.

The Sony PlayStation in explored further in the next case study.

## Personal computers

The case described earlier how Sony became a major player in the computer floppy disc industry; it also manufactured several other computer components. In November 1995 Idei announced a new strategic alliance with Intel to develop a new range of personal computers and associated software. Intel, the world leader for semiconductor products, would provide the main circuit boards for a computer which would offer exceptionally high-quality sound and graphics, ideal for multimedia applications.

Idei saw this as an essential development for Sony to exploit digital video. The PC industry is still growing and, although it is very crowded and competitive, there are real opportunities for truly distinctive new products. The Sony PCs were to be launched first in the discerning American market, with Japan and Europe following on later.

## Structural changes

In the 1980s Sony's international strategy was one of 'global localization'. Sony aimed to be a global company presented locally, and this involved devolving authority away from Tokyo and expanding manufacturing and R&D around the world. The typical large Japanese company had established both production and distribution networks around the world but had sought to remain centralized, with power firmly located in Japan.

Sony, however, divided the world into four – Europe, America, Asia and Japan – and created four organizations which *should* be virtually self-sufficient, and ultimately locally financed, independent businesses. In this respect Sony was seeking to become 'Japan's first truly global company'. The plan involved the systematic transfer abroad of all the functions required to 'perform the entire life cycle' of its products, namely design and development, engineering, production, marketing and sales. Sony already owned its own chains of retail outlets for consumer products in selected major markets. Sony was looking to devolve investment decisions, R&D, product planning and marketing. 'Changes can be implemented quicker when everything is on the spot.'

Sony created seven business groups in 1983 (this was later extended to 23) to co-ordinate the production and marketing of particular products around the world. With the exception of entertainments activities, the co-ordinating power remained in Tokyo. Structurally, Sony companies in the UK, France, Spain, etc., theoretically reported to Sony Europe, based in Cologne, and with a Swiss chairman.

With the exception of entertainment the structure was designed to work as follows. Strategic decisions were all to be made centrally in Tokyo; operational decisions, concerning such issues as pricing and production, would be devolved to regional managers. R&D at the basic development level remained centralized in Tokyo; local centres would concentrate on adaptations for local needs. Staff would be transferred between countries.

In theory, then, only corporate strategic issues should be referred back to Tokyo. These included requests for capital for investment to build a new factory and permission to alter the structure. In practice, managers bypassed the regional layers and contacted Tokyo for advice and guidance on operational matters. The actual practice and culture lagged behind the theory, and Sony became overburdened by administration, rather than an organization that was quickly responsive. It had 'drifted from a paragon of creativity and entrepreneurial spirit to a bloated bureaucracy'.

When the strategic leaders decided that a different form of decentralization was required to deal with the global/local issues, they acted quickly and decisively.

In spring 1994 Sony, with the exclusion of the American entertainments businesses, was divided up into eight separate divisions; these were not of equal size. They were to be called companies and they would enjoy considerable autonomy and power. Each would have its own president and would be responsible for design, manufacturing and marketing. The three largest companies were: consumer audiovisual products; components; and recording media and energy (batteries). The other five were: broadcast products (equipment); business and industrial systems (work stations); telecommunications (including mobile phones); mobile electronics (for cars); and semiconductors.

The changes proved to be successful but Sony decided to modify the structure further in spring 1996 to reflect its changing strategic emphasis. Eight companies became ten. A new one was formed to cover personal computers and information technology. The large audiovisual company was split into three. Telecommunications and mobile electronics were combined into a single company. Four new R&D laboratories would support information technology and semiconductors. In addition, Sony created a new executive board to oversee corporate strategy, to integrate the companies effectively, and to foster learning and sharing.

## Financial outcomes

Exhibits 5 and 6 provide summaries of key information from Sony's profit and loss accounts (1973 to 1996) and balance sheets (1986 to 1995). The data show that Sony has never been hugely profitable

(some, but not all, of its major Japanese rivals have been more profitable), and that until the 1990s it has experienced steady growth. The impact of the American acquisitions in the late 1980s is clearly illustrated in the 1994 and 1995 figures. Sony's once-high R&D expenditure was reduced to approximately 6%, which is actually typical for Japanese electronics companies. The figures should, however, be treated cautiously. The published figures will incorporate adjustments for profits and losses on currency fluctuations and therefore not reflect pure trading successes. The figures are in Japanese yen and, given the continual revaluations of the exchange value of the yen, were the accounts to be restated in the currencies of the countries in which Sony traded, the company's growth would have been more marked. A proportion of the stated long-term debt is in the form of Japanese bonds carrying a 1% rate of interest.

The first major setback was in the 1991/92 trading year when the parent company in Japan reportedly lost money and relied upon Sony's international businesses. Considerable income falls were experienced in chemicals and magnetic tapes; electronic parts and products held up satisfactorily in the global recession. Sony's music and entertainments businesses also performed relatively well in that year. Sales of consumer electronics reflected the effect of the recession in the 1992/93 results, when rising debt forced a reduction in capital expenditures. Sales began to pick up in 1993/94 but profits slumped after the film studio write-offs in the USA. New strategies and products brought about a restoration in sales revenue for 1995/96 but profits remained below those of earlier years.

Have Sony's fortunes been turned around with the strategic and structural changes introduced by the new strategic leader? How much more change will be required to sustain the renewed growth and prosperity?

*Sony Corporation*   http://www.world.sony.com

## Exhibit 5
Sony Corporation profit and loss summary, 1972–1996 (m¥)

| | 12 months to 31.10. | | | 12 months to 31.10.86 | 17 months to 31.3.88 | Year ended 31.3. | | | | | | | |
|---|---|---|---|---|---|---|---|---|---|---|---|---|---|
| | 1973 | 1978 | 1982 | | | 1989 | 1990 | 1991 | 1992 | 1993 | 1994 | 1995 | 1996 |
| Turnover | 314,000 | 534,900 | 1,114,000 | 1,325,000 | 1,431,000 | 2,145,329 | 2,879,856 | 3,616,517 | 3,822,000 | 3,879,000 | 3,610,000 | 3,827,000 | 4,593,000 |
| Profit before tax | 49,159 | 52,378 | 85,542 | 76,405 | 73,497 | 165,516 | 227,429 | 264,591 | 197,177 | 92,561 | 102,162 | (220,900) | 138,200 |
| Profit after interest and tax | 24,503 | 22,991 | 39,671 | 35,368 | 33,536 | 70,340 | 100,453 | 112,193 | 120,121 | 36,260 | 15,298 | (293,000) | N/A |
| Expenditure on R&D | N/A | N/A | N/A | N/A | N/A | N/A | 180,000 | 142,000 | 165,000 | 206,000 | N/A | N/A | N/A |
| Average number of employees | 20,600 | 27,112 | 43,126 | 47,600 | 60,500 | 78,900 | 95,600 | 112,900 | N/A | N/A | N/A | 130,000 | 138,000 |

## Exhibit 6
Sony Corporation balance sheet summary 1985–1995 (m¥)

| | 12 months To 31.10.1986 | 17 months To 31.3.1988 | Year ended 31.3. | | | | | | |
|---|---|---|---|---|---|---|---|---|---|
| | | | 1989 | 1990 | 1991 | 1992 | 1993 | 1994 | 1995 |
| Total fixed assets and investments | 476,014 | 789,856 | 931,000 | 2,168,000 | 2,369,000 | 2,589,000 | 2,411,00 | 2,246,000 | 2,077,000 |
| Total current assets | 974,130 | 1,077,000 | 1,434,000 | 2,202,000 | 2,234,000 | 2,358,000 | 2,110,000 | 2,024,000 | 2,147,000 |
| Total current liabilities | 628,294 | 944,271 | 1,119,000 | 1,996,000 | 2,105,000 | 2,052,000 | 1,734,000 | 1,408,000 | 1,609,000 |
| Net assets | 821,850 | 922,585 | 1,246,000 | 2,374,000 | 2,498,000 | 2,895,000 | 2,787,000 | 2,862,000 | 2,615,000 |
| Equity capital and reserves | 606,392 | 650,346 | 911,800 | 1,430,000 | 1,476,000 | 1,537,000 | 1,428,000 | 1,330,000 | 1,008,000 |
| Long-term loans | 144,000 | 196,000 | 221,000 | 646,000 | 695,000 | 885,000 | 880,000 | 984,000 | 906,000 |
| Long-term provisions | 71,458 | 76,239 | 113,200 | 298,000 | 327,000 | 473,000 | 479,000 | 548,000 | 701,000 |
| Total capital employed | 821,850 | 922,585 | 1,246,000 | 2,374,000 | 2,498,000 | 2,895,000 | 2,787,000 | 2,862,000 | 2,615,000 |

## Questions

1. Describe and evaluate the early strategies which made Sony a successful and innovative company.
   Can the recent changes to the corporate strategy and structure be justified strategically?

2. How would you evaluate Sony's track record as an innovative company?

3. Provide a strategic audit of Sony in the early 1990s.
   How do you think Sony will now develop during the mid/late 1990s?

4. How does Sony compare and contrast with the typical Japanese corporation?

# The Sony PlayStation

This short case supplements The Sony Corporation case. It discusses the rapid growth of Sony's first video games machine in the mid–late 1990s – and which quickly became a major contributor to Sony's profits – and the later supply-chain problems which hindered the launch of the successor PlayStation 2 in 2000.

This case was written by John L Thompson in 2001. It is for classroom discussion and should not be taken to reflect either effective or ineffective management.

## Introduction

Late in 2000 Sony was unable to satisfy the early demand in both the USA and Europe for its new PlayStation 2 video games console. It was experiencing internal supply problems of critical components, a real setback in the run-up to Christmas, the peak sales period. One rival, Sega, seized the opportunity thus created to promote its newest model. The other main competitor, Nintendo, planned a new model launch in 2001. Microsoft was also planning to enter this market for the first time in 2001.

In 1994 Sony had been a 'non-entity' in the video games market, but by 1996 it was the world leader of this fast growth market. At the end of this year Sony's accumulated sales of 12 million games consoles was well in excess of rivals Sega (7 million) and Nintendo (4 million). Later in the 1990s the PlayStation – together with sales of the complementary games software – was contributing 40% of The Sony Corporation's operating profits. It was estimated that the delay with PlayStation 2 could halve the Sony Corporation's profits in 2000/2001.

## The first PlayStation

When the market was opened up by Sega and Nintendo (both Japanese electronics companies) Sony expressed no manifest interest in following them. This was changed by chance. Shigeo Maruyama, a vice president of Sony Musical Entertainment (SME), the division which controlled the movie and music businesses, won a Nintendo Super Famicon games machine at a party. He started playing with it and became hooked. The short-term outcome was a division in SME – Sony Computer Entertainment, SCE – dedicated to pro-ducing games software for Nintendo. At this time Sony's consumer electronics division was also supplying Nintendo with sound semiconductor chips. Nintendo's Super Famicon depended upon games cartridges, and Sony's engineers mused about the possibility of a superior CD-ROM alternative. It was this interest that provoked the first cartridge-based PlayStation, or PlayStation 1 as it ultimately became known.

Sony realized that, for once, it would be entering an established market and knew that its product would have to offer some new value, something clearly different. The PlayStation was a 32-bit machine, faster than its predecessor 16-bit rivals which had opened up the market. It was backed by a number of high-quality games. Interestingly, Sony opted to play down the Sony corporation name and emphasize the PlayStation brand. Its consoles would be sold not through Sony's normal consumer electronics retailers but at discount stores and video games outlets, where the typical customers would expect to find them. Not surprisingly, Sony's existing retailers were incensed, but executives at SME were determined and stood firm on this issue.

The PlayStation 'package' comprised the basic games console, a number of dedicated Sony games and several licensed games designed for Sony by specialist games software companies. Eidos, for example, supplied Sony with the hugely popular *Tomb Raider*, a game in which heroine Lara Croft is hired to recover pieces of an ancient artefact and must overcome a series of traps and challenges from wolves and dinosaurs.

The basic price of the console (at its launch) was $300 in the USA, £300 in the UK and this equivalent in the rest of Europe. The cost of each game was around £40 minimum. The console prices soon came down as the market grew – Sony, like its competitors, knew that the real profits came from subsequent software sales and was happy to cross-subsidize a relatively low-priced console. Of course, Sony was also enjoying cost savings through the experience (or learning) curve effect and was happy to pass these on to consumers.

The success of The PlayStation 'exceeded all Sony's expectations', for a number of reasons:

- Sony was able to derive synergy from its competencies in both hardware and software. Its knowledge in electronics technology had been developed over many years; through Sony Music Entertainment it had developed valuable know-how in the marketing of software.
- Sony timed the launch carefully and entered the market just one month after Sega launched its new Saturn console, the first 32-bit machine. This suggested that the real competition lay between Sony and Sega, rather than with Nintendo as well.
- Its pricing strategy for consoles was competitive.
- A number of attractive licensing deals helped it to build up a strong portfolio of games from the outset. Several key games software companies were persuaded to switch their allegiance to Sony.

## The growth of PlayStation 1

The first PlayStation was launched in Japan in December 1994 and within six months sales of the console had exceeded 1 million.

By September 1995 the console was available in the USA (at $299.99) and Europe (at £299.99). In May 1996 these prices were reduced by $100 and £100, respectively. When, late in 1996, cumulative sales reached 10 million consoles, 4.2 million had been sold in Japan, 3.45 million in the USA and 2.35 million in Europe.

In March 1997, prices were reduced again – to £129.99 in Europe. At this time some 100 million PlayStation games had been sold worldwide. This number had reached 200 million by the beginning of 1998. Nintendo launched the first 64-bit console in 1997.

In August 1998 prices were reduced yet again – to £99.99 in Europe. At the end of the year some 50 million consoles had been sold. The price fell to £79.99 in September 1999.

PlayStation 2 was launched in Japan in March 2000, followed with launches in the USA and Canada in October, and Europe, the Middle East, Africa and Australasia in November. A portable version of PlayStation 1 (PS One) was launched in Japan in July 2000 and the rest of the world in the autumn.

By summer 2000 PlayStation 1 console sales topped 75 million, with 630 million units of games software.

## PlayStation 2

PlayStation 2 is a 128-bit machine, but it was not the first 128-bit machine on the market. Sega's Dreamcast was launched in 1999. Dreamcast sales were initially strong but by 2000 were sluggish. Arguably, customers were aware that PlayStation 2 was imminent and were prepared to wait.

The graphics on PlayStation 2 are of 'cinematic quality' and the console has a DVD (digital versatile disc) reader which can run movies. Because DVD players are more expensive in Japan than in the USA and UK, some people were thought to be buying PlayStations just to run DVD movies. Some 30 new games were being made available for the American launch, more than would normally accompany a new console. Some designers commented that PlayStation 2 was not an easy machine to work with. Dreamcast was not offered with a DVD player but it did have a modem connection. PlayStation's hard drive would later be able to accommodate an Internet connection.

Launched initially in Japan in March 2000, PlayStation 2 sales had reached 3.5 million by the summer. Sony was hoping to achieve worldwide sales of 10 million by March 2001.

When the PlayStation 2 console was launched in America just 500,000 were available. The intended number had been 1 million units. However, the half million was still five times as many as had been available when the first PlayStation was launched. Sony's 20,000 retailers had to be rationed. The hope was that 100,000 more units would be available every week in the run up to Christmas, when 50% of the year's sales take place. On-line sales were postponed.

Sony owns one dedicated PlayStation outlet in San Francisco, and here the queues began to form some 24 hours before the launch time. Many incidents were reported as people became desperate to get hold of a console. Outside one independent retailer, for example, two men attacked a mother and her child with baseball bats before stealing the one that they had just bought. In the UK a special pre-ordering system (with a paid deposit) was set up for the 20,000 consoles that would be available in November and December. Demand was estimated to be two to three times the likely supply. Sony was experiencing a real marketing dilemma – how actively should it promote the new model? Some excess demand can be healthy and add value to a product, but truly frustrated customers are a potential disaster. The price in the USA was $299 and in the UK £299. A secondary market soon opened up on e-Bay with prices in excess of $400. UK 'black market' prices of £1500 were reported.

The problem was a shortage of key components. Sony were reticent to provide comprehensive information, but the speculation was production yield problems with the critical graphics synthesizer.

## Sony's dilemma

Sony was anxious to achieve a strong position in the market by spring 2001, in order to consolidate its position as world leader in an uncertain competitive environment. Sony accepted that it might have to consider early price reductions after Christmas to try and maintain the growth momentum. Even if this meant selling at an initial loss, this may not be a major headache as most of the future profits would come from games rather than the actual consoles.

Sony knew that Nintendo was planning to launch its new GameCube console in 2001. It was, however, more concerned with the uncertainty surrounding the entry of Microsoft into the video games market. Microsoft was planning to launch its X-Box with a promotional budget of $500 million. The X-Box was known to be a powerful machine (three times as fast as PlayStation 2) and one that was popular with games developers because it used the familiar Microsoft PC architecture and offered superior graphics. However, the X-Box is not a games console that is directly competitive with Sony, Sega and Nintendo. It runs through a domestic television and its impact could be to stimulate the whole video games market. X-Box is due to be launched in the US and Japan in autumn 2001. Europe must wait until 2002.

At the same time, Sega had seen a window of opportunity open up. Marketing of the Dreamcast was changed to try and capitalize on Sony's problems. A DVD player was added to the package and the price aligned with that of PlayStation 2. Advertisements included the comment: 'Our deepest condolences to Sony on their PS2 shipping difficulties'. There was no availability problem and retailers were happy to build up their stocks. They believed that there was a real chance that some customers would switch to a Dreamcast if their intended first-choice PlayStation was not available.

However, in January 2001, it was reported that Sega, pioneer of this industry, planned to come out of games consoles and focus on games software. At the same time Eidos (Tomb Raider) announced its profits were being affected by the delay with PlayStation 2.

*Sony PlayStation*   http://www.playstation.com

## Questions

1. Why was Sony's PlayStation such a successful new product for the company?

2. Evaluate Sony's marketing strategy for the PlayStation console and the accompanying games.

3. Given the changing nature of competition in the video games market, do you think the launch problems with PlayStation 2 could do lasting damage to Sony's position in the market?

# Scottish and Newcastle Breweries plc

Defence Against a Hostile Take-over Attack

This case discusses the hostile take-over bid for Scottish and Newcastle Breweries by the Australian Elders IXL (brewers of Foster's lager) in 1988, the subsequent defence strategy of S&N and the intervention of the (then) Monopolies and Mergers Commission.

The case can be usefully cross-referenced to Minicase 7.3 (on deregulation and the brewing industry).

The case was written by Dr Jim Gallagher with the co-operation of Scottish and Newcastle. It is for classroom discussion and should not be taken to reflect either effective or ineffective management.

Dr JG Gallagher, Napier University, Edinburgh.

## Origins

In 1749 William Younger established a brewery in the coastal town of Leith just outside the city of Edinburgh. Younger's sons subsequently moved the brewery to the Edinburgh city boundary in order to take advantage of the waters at Holyrood, which had long been used by the monks of Holyrood Abbey to brew their own ales. In addition, this helped to avoid the city tax which was imposed within the city walls while at the same time allowing the closest proximity to their primary market.

A century later another brewer, William McEwan, set up a brewery on the opposite side of the city, in the village of Fountainbridge. His trademark soon became the familiar cavalier established after the British troops abroad found the brew to their liking. But it was not until the twentieth century that the two companies were to combine. In 1931 they merged to form Scottish Brewers Ltd, but continued to trade in competition to each other until 1959 when Robert Younger, T&J Bernard and J&T Morrison Ltd joined the group.

In the north of England a parallel concentration was likewise taking place. In 1770 John Barras and Company of Gateshead was founded. By 1890 several small breweries joined Barras to form The Newcastle Breweries Ltd. The 1950s saw further additions when Robert Deuchar Ltd and John Powell & Sons Ltd joined the group.

1960 saw the amalgamation of the two groups to form Scottish and Newcastle Breweries Ltd. By 1988 the annual accounts were showing S&N's structure as follows.

## Structure 1988

The principal company, Scottish & Newcastle Breweries plc, owns the breweries, warehouses and other properties which relate to the production and packaging of beer and wines and spirits, and owns licensed and other properties and fittings relating to the Group's hotels, managed public houses and tenancies. The company sells its beers under the brand names McEwan's, Younger's, Newcastle, Home, Matthew Brown and Theakston (see Exhibit 1).

The company is incorporated in Great Britain and registered in Scotland, as are all its subsidiaries except where stated otherwise. The principal country of operation of the company and its subsidiaries is the UK.

S&N was the fifth largest brewing group in the UK, employing approximately 24,000 people in over 30 locations. About one-third of the employees are based in Scotland. Many of those employed are employed in S&N subsidiary companies. The basic distribution of these companies is as follows:

- *Scottish Brewers Ltd* covers Scotland and Northern Ireland with its headquarters in Edinburgh, its regional offices in Edinburgh and Glasgow, and branches in Inverness, Aberdeen, Dundee, Kirkcaldy and Belfast, with depots at Hellington, Belshill, Ayr, Galashiels and Dumfries. Scottish Brewers also includes the Inns Division of the group – Welcome Inn.
- *Newcastle Breweries Ltd*, covers the north-east of England with its headquarters at Newcastle and regional offices in North Tyne, South Tyne and Cleveland.

**Exhibit 1** Structure of S&N in 1988

| Thistle Hotels Limited | Waverley Vinters Limited |
|---|---|
| Responsible for controlling the company's principal hotels in most major cities in the United Kingdom | Responsible for the wholesaling of wines and spirits throughout the United Kingdom |

| Scottish Brewers Limited | The Newcastle Breweries Limited | McEwan-Younger Limited | Matthew Brown PLC | Home Brewery PLC | William Younger and Company Limited |
|---|---|---|---|---|---|
| Scotland. | North-east of England. | Cumbria, North-west England, Yorkshire and North Wales. | Lancashire, North-west England and North Yorkshire. | The Midlands. | Southern England, South Wales. |

| Canongate Technology Limited | Scottish & Newcastle Breweries (sales) Limited | Scottish & Newcastle Beer Production Limited | Moray Firth Maltings PLC | Scottish & Newcastle Breweries (services) Limited |
|---|---|---|---|---|
| Responsible for the exploitation of the company's industrial property rights and technology. | Sales of packaged beers to the take-home trade in the United Kingdom. | Operation of breweries and other packaging and distribution facilities. | Responsible for the production and selling of malt and agricultural merchanting. | The provision of certain central functions. |

- *William Younger Ltd*, comprises McEwan-Younger Ltd, covering Cumbria, north-west England, north Wales and Yorkshire, with the head office at Chorley and branches in Cumbria (Carlisle) and Carnforth. It also includes William Younger & Company Ltd, which covers the midlands, south Wales and south England with its head office at St Albans, and branches at Birmingham, Leicester, Caerphilly, Norwich, Acton, Aylesford, Dunstable, Southampton and Bristol.
- *Thistle Hotels Ltd* was formed in 1965 to operate the groups premiere hotels, some 30 plus, throughout Scotland and Wales.
- *Waverley Vintners Ltd* handles all of the group's wines and spirits.

All of the subsidiary companies shown are wholly owned, non-trading and have been appointed by the Company as its agents.

The distribution of beer products and the operation of managed public houses and tenancies is the responsibility of the Regional Companies: Scottish Brewers Ltd, The Newcastle Breweries Ltd, McEwan-Younger Ltd, Matthew Brown plc, Home Brewery plc and William Younger and Company Ltd.

## Other subsidiaries

In addition to the subsidiaries shown the company owns 75% of the ordinary share capital of Coronation Inns Ltd, a company which owns and operates public houses in Scotland. Other subsidiary companies that do not affect significantly the assets or results of the group are not listed.

## Pre-attack development

Over the previous decade there had been many changes in the drinks industry, not the least of which had been a decline in beer sales (see Exhibit 2). Accompanying this decline was a reduction in the number of brewers as regional brewers either collapsed or had been acquired by larger brewing concerns.

Although by 1989 overall UK beer consumption was one-tenth below the 1979 industry peak of 41

*Exhibit 2* Beer sales (million barrels, 1979–1989)

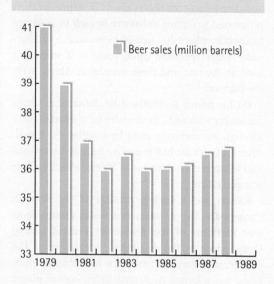

million barrels, over the same period lager consumption had risen by 50% and accounted for almost half of all beer drunk.

S&N's response to the hard times of the early 1980s was to move into more efficient production allied to the acquisition of regional brewers such as Matthew Brown as well as building up a 34-strong chain of hotels.

1982 was the low point in S&N's history, with profits of only £32.2 million. This was partly due to the lower margin associated with its sales, some 80%, through the free trade which is highly competitive. In addition, there appeared to be a heavy dependence on the depressed Scottish and northern England markets.

Sir David Nickson was appointed as chairman in 1983, a post that he agreed to hold until his sixtieth birthday when he would hand over to the deputy chairman, Alick Rankin. Rankin had been with the company since 1960, joining the board in 1973, becoming group managing director in 1983 and chief executive in 1986.

At the time of the take-over bid by Elders IXL, in October 1988, Alick Rankin had been with S&N for

28 years. His route to the higher levels of management was rather unconventional. Educated at Eton and then joining the Scots Guards for a time, he then progressed to Oxford university but left to emigrate to Canada where he aspired to become a lumberjack, before spending three years in a merchant bank in Toronto and three months in Alaska with the Eskimos.

On his return to Scotland he obtained a job as stocktaker with S&N, from where he worked his way through the company until he reached the board. After six years as chief executive he had determined that whatever the outcome of Elders' attack he was going to retire.

Rankin was a leading member of the Scottish Conservative Party's business advisory group. Elliott was President of the Australian Federal Liberal Party, which is the Australian equivalent of the Conservative Party, but there the resemblance ends. Elliott was a former Australian Rules football player who embodied the antipodean way of doing business: 'knock 'em down and drag 'em out'. Rankin, by contrast, typifies Britain's conservative 'beerage'.

The perceived structural weaknesses recognized by Rankin were attacked when he addressed them by pursuing a policy of rationalization and acquisition. Some 7000 jobs were cut, more tied pubs were sought. The over-centralized bureaucracy was reduced and a stronger portfolio of brands looked for.

But this policy did not prove easy to follow. S&N's £44 million bid for J Cameron, the Hartlepool brewer of Strongarm bitter, was referred to the Monopolies and Mergers Commission (MCC). Then came the three-year fight to acquire Matthew Brown, the Blackburn brewer and owner of 500 pubs and of the Old Peculiar and Theakston brands which was finally, along with Langdale, acquired in 1987 for £185 million.

This latter acquisition, in conjunction with the agreed purchase of the Nottingham-based Home Brewery for £120 million, added some 900 public houses and a variety of brands to S&N's portfolio. Furthermore, it also expanded its Thistle Hotels division to some 31 units, which included nine in London.

Promotion also proved a powerful tool in Rankin's arsenal, with large sums being spent as a direct attack on Tennent's Lager, one of the UK's bestsellers, through the promotion of McEwan's Lager. In addition, a £1 million sponsorship deal with Glasgow Rangers FC was signed which provided three years of high-profile publicity right in the heart of the lager-drinking west of Scotland.

## The attack

As early as spring 1987 John Elliott, chief executive of Australian company Elders IXL, had suggested to Rankin that their brewing interests should merge. This offer was rejected.

It was probably, therefore, no great surprise to Rankin that in February 1988, after intense City speculation, it came to light that the suspicious nominee names on S&N's share register referred to Elders, who had acquired a 2% shareholding. The result was that S&N's share price was driven up by 18 pence.

Over the next few months Elders increased their stake and finally asked for a meeting with S&N. On 15 March 1988 Elliott and Sir David Nickson, S&N's chairman, met in secret in London, where Elliott outlined his plans. He wanted to create one of the world's largest brewing concerns by amalgamating Elders' interests – Courage, Carlton United Brewers in Australia and Carling O'Keefe in Canada – with S&N.

The proposition was that S&N should acquire Elders' brewing interests through a share issue. With this agreed merger Elders would have simply 'reversed into' S&N. Elders would then take effective control of the enlarged group by topping up its S&N shareholding in the market. Again this was rejected.

*It was simply a way for Elders to buy us without paying a bid premium. It was totally against the interest of S&N's shareholders ... Australian businessmen feel they've got to demonstrate how big and brave they are. It's very sad. I'm told Australia is being raped by a couple of dozen men who have learned to play the modern highwayman.*

(Alick Rankin)

In July 1988 Elliott bought the S&N shares held by the Australian corporate raider Sir Ron Brierley, some 5%, thereby clearly signalling his intent. Once again Rankin and Elliott met and once again Elliott was rebuffed. On 17 October 1989 S&N became the target of a hostile £1.6 billion take-over bid from the Australian company Elders IXL. From February 1988 Elders had built up a 9.65% stake in S&N. Its purchase of a further 1.25 million shares at the offer price of £4 per share precipitated the bid. On the same day S&N arranged its purchase of a 50% stake in Pontins, the holiday company, for £42.5 million. This was then added to Langdale, its property time-share business on 21 October. Elders immediately criticized the Pontins' deal as being a large and expensive commitment for S&N in an area where it had no experience, describing it as bad for S&N on 'Financial operational and commercial grounds'. The deal committed S&N to acquire the rest of Pontins' at a price which valued the holiday business at £100 million should the brewer be taken over. In response S&N said that the acquisition was a logical business extension, 'This is a natural area for us to develop. We are not running scared and doing things that are illogical.'

Bass, the brewer, had sold Pontins in March 1987 to the company's former management.

S&N, which sells its beers in Pontins' outlets, provided part of the loan capital for the buy-out.

The initial 50 per cent stake was acquired by:

- conversion of S&N's existing convertible loan of £2.75 million into 16% of Pontins' equity
- the sale of Langdale to Pontins at a value of £14.6 million, £7.8 million of which would be satisfied by the issue to S&N of new shares in Pontins, and
- the issue of the 6.8 million S&N shares.

The main criticism that Elders levelled at S&N was that as a regional brewer, it had failed to export its lagers in any quantity. It suggested that it would have enormous difficulty competing with the European superbrewers, such as Heineken and Carlsberg, in the enlarged European market after 1992.

Elders saw the enlarged group of S&N and Elders' Courage as providing an effective springboard to attack the markets in southern Europe which, it was assumed, were poised to take off in a new era of economic prosperity. Furthermore, the amalgamation would prove an effective competitor to Bass, the UK market leader.

Elders started out as a food processor in Australia and only moved into beer in 1983 with the purchase of Carlton and United Breweries, which included Foster's among its brands.

The Australian beer market is dominated by Elders and its arch-rival Bond, which brews both Castlemaine XXXX and Swan. Elders is the world's seventh largest brewer and its chief executive John Elliott had made no secret of his desire to build a global brewing business spearheaded by Elders' Foster's Lager.

The UK beer market is the second largest in Europe, with the fragmented German one being the largest. Elliott clearly wanted to take advantage of the growing popularity of lager in the UK as well as the boom in lager throughout Europe. Elliott's antipodean rival Bond had just acquired an 11% stake in Allied, Lyons, Britain's second biggest brewer, a company that Elders had tried to acquire through a highly leveraged £1.8 billion bid in 1985. The bid for Allied, however, was referred to the MMC – not on market-share grounds but because of the highly leveraged nature of the bid. By the time the MMC had given clearance Allied had become too expensive and Elliott had in any event turned his attention to another target, Courage.

In 1986, after its acquisition of Imperial Group, Hanson Trust decided to auction off its brewing interest, Courage. Both Elders and S&N registered their interest. However, S&N's valuation was £200 million lower than the £1.4 billion that Elders paid for Courage, thereby giving Elliott his first UK brewing acquisition.

S&N were initially attracted by exactly the same commercial opportunities which Elders was putting forward as part of its rationale for its acquisition of S&N. Indeed, as early as 1971 a merger between Courage and S&N had been discussed. The fit between the companies appeared to be excellent. S&N's markets are predominantly in the north of

England and Scotland, whereas Courage pubs are mostly in the south. Furthermore, S&N's strength is in ale, especially its McEwans Export label, while Courage offers a strong selection of lagers, including Foster's Millar Lite. In addition, S&N said it was thought that S&N could save £40 million a year from the combined companies by eliminating overlapping depots and excess production capacity.

It was felt by Elders that acquisition of S&N would at a stroke lift Elders' stake in the UK beer market from 10% to 21% second only to the market leader Bass which has 22%, and overtaking Allied Lyon's 13.5%. What is more, Elders would gain S&N's experience in the free trade, which could be of even greater importance if the MMC, which was investigating the UK brewing industry, sought to loosen the tie – the system through which most British brewers sell their beer.

Rankin's rationale for opposing this latest proposed amalgamation with Courage was presented by Rankin as:

> I wouldn't make an issue of the geography. But the company we wanted to buy in 1986 (and for which Elders overpaid enormously) is nothing like the same now. We were interested in it for its breadth, it had a host of things which they've got rid of.

It was expected that should Elders win then Elliott's first move would be to weld together S&N and Courage, with Mike Foster managing director of Courage and other directors moving to Edinburgh.

Foster, it was expected, would replace Alick Rankin.

At the Caledonian Hotel in Edinburgh,* Michael Foster launched the formal offer document for shareholders, which spelt out four major points:

- He claimed that the offer was 79% higher than S&N's previous share price.
- S&N's business suffered from fundamental structural weaknesses which take-over would solve.

*It is likely that some of those present at this meeting felt a touch of déjà vu as it was from this same room that Ernest Saunders announced the Distillers bid.

- S&N was 'strategically at a loss', having been unable to become a truly national or international brewer.
- The proposed merger was based on expansion, which was in the interests of shareholders, the company and Scotland.

Foster also commented that S&N was facing a difficult future on its own, whereas Elders would bring to Scotland a major new international business. S&N had only a small tied estate of some 2300 pubs, compared with 7300 for Bass and 5000 for Courage. S&N had no national lager brand of importance, and lager was only one-third of their sales, compared with about a half for other major brewers. Furthermore, S&N was too dependent on the free house and carry-out trades.

The document also attacked S&N's recent purchase of S&N's 50% stake in Pontins, claiming that it smacked of defensiveness. It also claimed that S&N was doing exactly what it had criticized Matthew Brown's management for doing in the previous year when it acquired Langdale, which according to S&N was an 'illogical, expensive and defensive' move.

Finally, the document summed up Elders' aims as follows:

- There would be no job losses in Scotland.
- They would set up the headquarters of their UK and European brewing empire in Edinburgh.
- Central management of the Elders Brewing Group would come to Scotland after the group was listed on the UK Stock Exchange.

What would happen to S&N's non-brewing interests was left rather vague.

Elders was Australia's second largest company by market value. In only 15 years Elliott had transformed his original company, Elders, a sheep-shearing company which through a reverse take-over acquired Henry Jones IXL, from a sleepy jam company worth £18.5 million into a £2.2 billion brewing, finance and agricultural business. The primary step in this process came with the acquisition of the 100-year-old Elder Smith Goldsborough Mort company in 1981.

The strategy followed by Elliott was one of prosperity through acquisition, reasoning that a debt-free company was not optimizing returns on shareholders' funds. The cornerstone of the strategy was a brewing cash cow spanning three continents. Clearly, S&N now held the key to his ambitions. With brewing accounting for 65% of Elders' business the acquisition of S&N was essential. To this end Elliott's asset management leaves little room for sentiment. If a target's assets have no place in Elders' portfolio they are sold or suspended off the balance sheet.

Elders was a pioneer in non-resource financing in Australia. While some of its early off-balance-sheet mechanisms stretched the concept to its limits, its largest non-resource investments today have at least a logical underpinning. Perhaps of greatest concern, in British terms, was the Courage Pubs Company joint venture, in which Elders owns 50% of both the ordinary and preference capital as well as underwriting attractive entry terms for its partner, Hudson Conway. This deal took £875 million of debt off Elders' balance sheet.

Nevertheless, Elliott's plan to reduce the need for endless take-over activity and financial engineering to sustain growth by putting the group on a sounder footing by floating off its four divisions – brewing, agri-businesses, investment and resources – separately around the world was stopped by the stock-exchange crash of 1987. Had he succeeded, Elliott and the other Elders' executives would have retained control of the business through their own private company.

## The defence: 'We don't need Foster parents'
It quickly became apparent that S&N's defensive campaign would be rooted in its improved performance record. Rankin noted that:

*Elders had spun off [Courage's] pubs and sold its hotels, restaurants, wine and spirits operations and off-licences all that remains is brewing, beer distribution and its great god, Foster's. . . . our earlier restructuring and rationalisation demonstrated our clear strategy for the development of S&N. But they*

*also mean there are no benefits to be had from a link with an emasculated Courage.*

On 1 November 1988 the City stockbroker Kitcat Aitken declared that it was recommending its clients not to sell for anything less than 625 pence a share, accusing Elders of trying to get S&N on the cheap. They valued S&N at £2.6 billion. Elders was offering £4 per share, which to analysts appeared to be a very poor exit multiple.

The drinks analyst Martin Hawkins added his weight by saying that

*Elders' bid for Scottish & Newcastle is driven by need, rather than a true conviction that it can manage S&N's business better.*

While S&N ranks only fifth among Britain's brewers, its position as Scotland's largest publicly quoted industrial company ensured that it was strongly supported by Scotland's and Edinburgh's political establishment.

Rankin tried to enlist employee support by sending letters to all the groups staff telling them that 'a large number of jobs in all areas of the company would be at risk' if Elders' bid was successful.

Elders would sell or rationalize much of the company's activities, leaving 'a business concentrated only on the production and selling of beer and particularly of Foster's lager, which we already know is not a popular brand in the north of Britain.'

Elliott's claim that 'a lot of previous mergers in the brewing business have been about rationalising capacity. We are running short of capacity at Courage' and could enhance S&N's weak lager portfolio by putting Foster's into S&N's 2300 pubs was questioned. Courage was only using 80% of its own capacity, while Elders could not take immediate advantage of S&N's take-home trade because Watney's (part of Grand Metropolitan) controlled the rights to sell Foster's in cans until 1996.

City analysts, moreover, tended to think that the bid would be referred to the MMC.

S&N argued that despite Elders' promises that it would locate the international headquarters of its brewing operations in Edinburgh, the business would be run from Australia. Elders had already given assurances to its Australian Carlton United Breweries that control over it would not be exercised from outside that country.

Support for S&N came from various sources. Mr Jim Sillars, the then SNP candidate in the forthcoming Glasgow Govan by-election, said 'Scottish and Newcastle are being bought and sold with Aussie gold'. The Shadow Scottish Secretary Mr Donald Dewar said that he was 'appalled and very sad that the Royal Bank of Scotland was apparently prepared to put up a major share of the cash Elders needed in their bid for Scottish and Newcastle'. Other critics in Scotland said that they had heard it all before and referred to the 1986 Guinness affair. The Secretary of State for Scotland also put his weight behind S&N's defence.

## The Royal Bank of Scotland

On 23 October 1988 Mr Gordon Wilson, leader of the Scottish Nationalist Party, said that he regarded the Royal Bank of Scotland's action in participating in the £1 billion loan facility to finance Elders' hostile bid for S&N as financial cannibalism. The bank was 'enabling the take-over of one of the few remaining autonomous sectors of Scottish industry for short-term profit', he said.

Protest letters and telephone calls soon began to arrive at the bank's headquarters, with a spokesman commenting 'reaction has been much more intense than the board would have anticipated'. The bank, after all, was only providing £100 million of the £1 billion syndicated loan to Elders. In addition, the bank was faced with widespread threats of customers taking their business elsewhere.

The bank sent a circular to all branch managers with guidance on how to answer customer complaints about the Royal Bank's role in the Elders' loan. In it, the chief executive of the Royal Bank, Mr Bob Maiden, described Elders as a valued customer, stating that the bank's policy was one of not refusing to finance a customer bidding for a company simply because the target company was also a customer.

Mr Maiden told BBC radio:

*We were acting merely as bankers. Elders happen to bank with us for facilities, we looked at it on a credit-worthiness point of view and we acceded on that behalf.*

It was noted at the time by some writers that the National Westminster Bank, which handles some of S&N's business, decided not to participate in the loan syndicate, because of the risk of a similar conflict of interest.

Mr Dewar commented that the Royal Bank's defence on commercial grounds failed to reflect the support that Scottish institutions had given when the bank itself was under threat of take-over by Standard Chartered and the Hong Kong and Shanghai banks seven years earlier.

On 2 November Bob Maiden wrote to all of the bank's customers who had complained about its decision to finance part of Elders' take-over bid (see Exhibit 3).

Support for the bank's position came directly and indirectly from many sources. Professor Jack Shaw, director of Scottish Financial Enterprise, which represents the Scottish financial community and which called for the bid to be referred to the MMC, said:

*Scottish financial institutions have some special responsibility to encourage businesses on their doorstep, but not to the extent of cutting themselves off from international business.*

*An international financial community cannot be expected to act as a custodian of regional policy.*

Furthermore, S&N is a Scottish company in the sense that it had its origins there. It is not a Scottish company in the sense that a large private company might be, in which the shareholding capital was lodged in Scottish hands. The ownership of S&N has long been international, with only 12% of S&N's shares in Scottish hands. In addition, only one of S&N's breweries is north of the border. By 10 November Elders held 13.6% of S&N shares.

The majority of shares is held by the financial institutions whose first duty is to their clients, and

*Exhibit 3*  The Royal Bank letter in full

---

Involvement in Consortium to Fund Elders IXL Limited Bid

'Thank you for taking the trouble to let me know your reaction to our Bank's involvement in the above matter and at the same time to give me the opportunity to reply and to explain the reason for our stance.

I would emphasise that this principle of equal treatment for all customers is not some vague theoretical matter it is something, which is applied throughout our branches on a regular basis.

If you were to come to us, for example, for finance for a home expansion it is not for us to judge the reactions of our good customers living next door to you. If you were to come for backing to open up an hotel we could not as bankers consider whether or not this would offend another hotel customer we have in the same area.

In applying our principle we have to dissociate any personal opinions from our position as bankers. Any professional person should understand this position. The surgeon does not question the politics of the patient, the solicitor does not have to agree with the lifestyle of his client before providing him with a service, the chartered accountant does not have to endorse the principles of the company whose books he audits.

If Scottish & Newcastle had made a bid for Elders, or another company, we would have agreed to provide finance if asked to do so. I doubt if this would have raised such comment from public figures and customers.

There seems to be a perception that the Bank by making a banking decision, has made Scottish & Newcastle more vulnerable to a take-over. This is not correct, we neither have such power nor wish to have it. The decision makers will be the Monopolies and Mergers Commission or the Scottish & Newcastle shareholders. The bank has no shares, no vote and thus no influence in such decisions.

In the normal course of business apparent contradictions are happily accommodated without any glare of publicity and without charges of hypocrisy or betrayal. It is unfortunate that our helping to provide funding for Elders who have banking links with us not only in the UK but also in our branches in Singapore and New York is not being viewed in this same light.

In the bank we have been very upset by the unfair criticism of our banking decision. For over 260 years we have contributed immeasurably to the Scottish economy. We have helped customers not only in the creation of thousands of jobs but in assisting many of them through difficult trading periods, we have been instrumental in saving thousands of jobs.

Only two weeks ago we demonstrated our increasing commitment to Scotland when we announced some of our plans for expansion, which would provide 850 additional jobs in Scotland. Apart from being unjust, the comments about the bank being disloyal have been particularly hurtful.

I appreciate your concern for the outcome of this matter and it is always sad when a member of the public, customer or not, appears bitterly critical about any action taken by our bank. I hope this letter will help you understand our position more clearly.

---

who will shift funds to serve those clients. Some clients are Scottish, but many others who have substantial holdings in S&N are not Scottish. There is no real sense in which S&N can therefore be described as a Scottish-owned company.

S&N called on GJW, one of the best-known and well-connected political lobbyists to help fight their case. Elders had called on Dewe Rogerson, one of whose senior executives Anna McCurley is the former Tory MP for Renfrew West and Inverclyde. More controversially, Elders also appointed the late Sir Alex Fletcher, the former Scottish Office Minister and MP for Edinburgh Central who, like McCurley, was ousted at the General Election of 1987.

Sir Alex's appointment embarrassed Scottish Tory MPs, who were in the main backing S&N, and enraged Scottish Labour MPs, who put down a Commons move condemning his involvement. Mike Reynolds, public affairs director for Courage, said that Sir Alex was appointed not as a political lobbyist but primarily for his business and commercial advice, but he admitted that he had also been able to open a few doors.

Irrespective of this Elliott, assisted by Sir Alex, had been skilfully wooing leading members of the commercial community at private dinners in Edinburgh and Glasgow. A skilful communicator with considerable personal charisma, Elliott found more acceptance for his plans in those unpublicized encounters than would appear at first sight from the public utterances.

## The defence document

The long-awaited defence document of S&N hit directly at the financial weaknesses of Elders, contrasting it with its own record of continuous profits growth and financing. The document had the dual purpose of persuading shareholders to support S&N's continuing independence and indicated to the Office of Fair Trading that the state of Elders' finance and borrowings was suspect.

Essentially, Sir David Nickson accused Elders of exaggerating both its financial strength and the business potential of its UK brewing company, Courage.

*In our view, Elders is already overgeared and can have little or no financial capacity to develop Scottish and Newcastle businesses. [He accused Courage of] trying to buy the success that it would find hard to achieve through organic growth.*

He further accused Elders of attempting to buy S&N on the cheap. Stripping S&N of its pubs and hotels would, he said, raise £1.5 billion; £600 million from the sale of S&N's Thistle Hotels, and up to £900 million by floating off S&N's pubs into a separate company, and leave Elders paying only £100 million; or what he called 'the paltry sum of 25p per share' for the core brewing business.

Mike Foster criticized Alick Rankin for suggesting that 3000–4000 jobs would be lost, saying that the figure was excessive.

The crux of the document lay in the financial analysis prepared for S&N by the chartered accountants Arthur Young of the Elders' group's finance, structure and control. It suggested that Elders' indebtedness was almost seven times greater than the figure stated in its audited accounts. Elders stated that its debts amounted to only 32% of its share capital but the S&N analysis claimed that the true ratio was 210%. Were the bid to proceed then the debt burden would exceed 313% of total equity.

It was claimed that Elders had only achieved its low ratio by treating its convertible bonds as equity rather than debt. Likewise, the debts of Elders' finance subsidiaries were omitted while the debt of Courage's public houses were also shunted off. S&N claimed that without these financial manoeuvres Elders' debts would rise from Aus$1.33 billion to Aus$7.61 billion.

Elders' profit record was also attacked on the basis that the 1988 figure had little to do with the success of its main businesses. It was, rather, due to earnings – 31% of profit – arising from abnormal items.

S&N further claimed that when profits retained by associates were excluded Elders' profits barely covered the cost of dividends, and concluded that S&N was needed for its financial strength and growth potential.

In its analysis of its own operations, S&N pointed out that, since 1983, profits had grown by 175% while in the same period profits from the Thistle Hotels subsidiary had grown from £2.9 million to £19.1 million.

Mr Peter Bartels, chief executive of Elders' Brewing, described the S&N attack as 'a load of bloody crap'. None of the banks backing Elders had queried its financing.

It was also noted that Elders' penetration of the European market with its Fosters brand was a speculative venture with little evidence of any displacement of established brands such as Carlsberg, Kronenberg or Stella Artois.

## Finance

With the announcement of the bid S&N commissioned a three-month international investigation by Arthur Young into Elders' structure, control and financing. The investigation was understood to have highlighted three principal areas of concern.

1. Elders' unconventional structure involved a trail of cross-linking shareholdings between a network of subsidiaries and associated companies, many of them run by close friends of John Elliott.

2. One of these associated companies, the Monaco-registered Harlin Holdings in which Elliott and friends had a large stake would be, if options were exercised, the largest single shareholder in Elders.

3. Elders' financing which, in particular, used deals effectively to place large chunks of debt incurred in take-overs off the group's balance sheet. While the group debt-equity ratio was not out of line with many other industrial companies, once such off-balance sheet transactions were included the ratio was said to soar to as much as 400–500%.

*Figure 1*  Elders' structure.

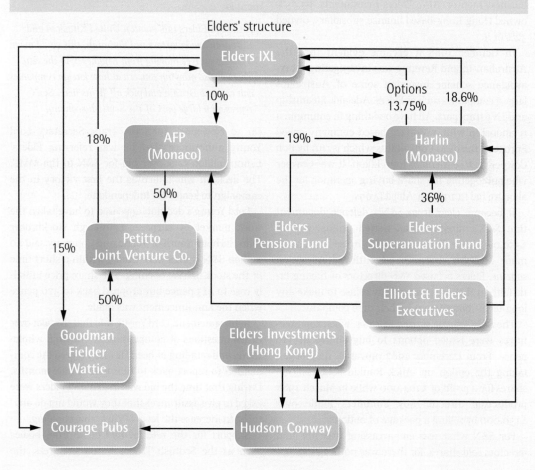

Elders' structure

For an international company with four main operating areas, Elders had a remarkably complex structure of ownership and control. Most of the companies were linked through cross-shareholdings between Elders and its subsidiaries (see Figure 1).

For example, the Monaco-based investment company AFP had 19% of Harlin Holdings (also Monaco based), which in turn had almost 32% of Elders. It had as a director Peter Scanlon, who also sat on Elders' board and who was generally acclaimed as the financial brain behind Elders' complex deals.

As well as shareholding deals involving friends, Elliott did business deals with them. The Courage pubs joint venture with Hudson Conway had as a key figure in it Sir Roderick Carnegie, Elliott's early business mentor. Also, Elders Investments, its 75% owned Hong Kong-based finance subsidiary, owned 32% of it.

In October 1988 it became evident that the Australian Inland Revenue was investigating a tax-avoidance scheme involving some of Australia's largest companies such as Elders, Adelaide Steamship and TNT transport. All have one thing in common, a relationship with a Monaco-based company called European Business Consultants which is run by Bob Cowper, a close friend of John Elliott. It was Cowper who put together the share-buying operation for the abortive bid in 1985 for Allied Lyons.

It became clear from S&N's defence document that S&N's directors had netted profits of over £550,000 since December 1987, by selling shares made available under an executive share-option scheme. Elders accused S&N directors of having little faith in their company: 'they refuse to make any long-term commitment to their own company'.

The S&N scheme started in 1984, when top executives were issued options to buy shares at 110 pence. From December 1987 onwards, they began taking the option up. Alick Rankin sold 100,000 shares for a profit of £104,000 while in March 1988 production director Roy Summers made over £130,000 by selling a package of options.

For S&N what was embarrassing was not that directors sold shares, for there was nothing improp-

er in this, but rather that they sold at a time when take-over speculation was increasing.

## The referral

The future of Elders' bid lay with the Office of Fair Trading, which would rule whether the bid should be investigated by the MMC. Sir Gordon Borrie had made it clear that he wanted to make a quick decision on the referral to the MMC. Arguments for a referral had concentrated on four issues:

- competition
- uncertainty over what Elders were offering
- loss of decision making from Edinburgh, and
- public interest

As Alastair Darling, MP for Edinburgh Central, commented:

*Although Elders talk about a United Kingdom and European headquarters in Edinburgh, this could mean a few executives moving from Middlesex to the city. There is also growing concern at how foreign companies can come to Britain and pick off firms here. S&N represent a large part of the Scottish economy.*

On 10 November 1988 the Trade Secretary Lord Young announced that he was referring Elders' £1600 million take-over bid for S&N to the MMC. The decision was hailed as the first victory in the campaign to keep S&N independent.

Lord Young's decision appeared to have taken the stock market by surprise. Edinburgh stockbroker John Barbour-Smith of Torrie and Company said 40 million S&N shares were traded within a short time of the stock market opening. The share price initially rose to 415 pence but dropped back to 376 pence when the announcement was made.

In his statement, Lord Young said that the take-over raised questions of competition in brewing, wholesaling and retailing of beer. He also ordered the commission to report back to him within four months. During that time the bid was frozen and Elders were asked to give assurances that they would not do anything to increase the level of their shareholding.

Support for the referral had come from bodies such as the Scottish Trades Union Congress, the

Scottish Development Agency, the Scottish Council Development and Industry, and the Confederation of British Industry Scotland, as well as a public petition with over 2 million names. The final decision on the bid lay with Lord Young, who did not have to accept the findings of the Commission.

A spokesman for S&N said:

> Our delight at the decision is measured. The battle will now intensify as we go into phase two of the campaign to beat Elders.

The intensity of the battle did indeed hot up. Elders forced S&N to climb down over remarks that they had attributed to John Elliott. They further claimed to have demolished the central plank of the S&N defence.

S&N's advisers Kleinwort Benson were forced to admit that figures published as a table showing the break-up value of S&N, and used to justify claims that Elliott wanted S&N on the cheap, had not been attributed to him directly. The figures themselves were not challenged directly by Elders.

Foster said that:

> the table is not Elders' arithmetic it is S&N's arithmetic and it is wrong. The effect of these wholly avoidable errors is to demolish S&N's arithmetic and conclusions.

On the day of the referral Elders took their holding in S&N up to more than 87 million shares some 23.6% of S&N. S&N pressed for Elders to sell nearly 10%, some 35.2 million shares acquired minutes after the referral was announced. Lord Young had no powers to force Elders to divest and came out on the side of non-intervention. Elders had simply gone against accepted practice.

Earlier, Elliott had hit out at what he called the 'Scottish Mafia', whom he blamed for the referral. He told reporters in Adelaide:

> We were very surprised that it was referred. I think there is a Scottish mafia up there, people associated with S&N who did everything they could to get a reference because they saw it as the best defence.

Elliott's remarks drew immediate response. Alastair Darling described them as deeply offensive:

> Elders has raised two fingers to the DTI. Elders' conduct and offensive remarks ought to send alarm bells and spur everyone to action.

Elliott nevertheless insisted that his take-over plans would continue and would mean more competition not less,

> Britain has the most fragmented beer production business of almost any western country other than Germany. . . . Our view is that we will increase competition particularly against Bass in Scotland. Bass has just got ahead of Scottish & Newcastle in Scotland. They don't have the lager brands to compete with Bass.

In early March 1989 Mr Nicholas Winterton, Tory MP for Macclesfield, warned that Mr Elliott 'brags in the Australian Press, to the boys back home of his easy access to No. 10 and the Secretary of State of Trade and Industry'. Mr Elliott, he said, must not be allowed to use his 'easy access' to the Prime Minister to win approval for his bid for S&N. He also attacked Lord Young for only describing as 'merely regrettable' the way in which Elders broke a City 'gentleman's agreement' not to buy any new shares after the Government announced that it was to investigate the bid.

## The MMC

The thrust of S&N's case lay not only on competition, but also on its investigation of Elders' ownership and financial structure – a gamble that it could discredit Elders to such an extent that the commission would rule against them, on the grounds that Elders was unfit to own a major UK-listed company. The indications were that the commission was not impressed by S&N's attack. Nevertheless, S&N continued its attack, pointing out to the MMC a statement by Mr Elliott made on radio:

> Now we've got 23.6 per cent of the stock, so we're in a strong position to command the direction of S&N, no matter what happens.

By mid-March 1989 the MMC had announced its decision to block Elders from renewing its hostile take-over bid. The commission reported that the acquisition would unacceptably reduce competition and would be against the public interest. The findings were:

- It would create a second big beer group.
- Consumer choice and competition would be reduced greatly, increasing the scope of the control of a single brewer that was seeking to expand sales of its Foster's lager.
- It would reduce competition for the supply of beer to the free trade.
- It would restrict competition in Scotland, reinforce the duopoly enjoyed by Bass and S&N and remove the possibility of Courage entering the market on its own.
- It would reduce competition in the supply of beers to off-licences where Elders' Hofmeister, for example, competes with S&N's Kestrel.

Lord Young, following its recommendations, also announced that Elders would be forced to reduce its holding in S&N to 9.9% within 12 months, later extended to 1 July 1990. Moreover, voting rights were restricted to this figure.

The commission's main objection to the proposed acquisition centred on a combined group with 20–21% of the total UK beer market. The result on S&N shares was a sharp fall of some 89 pence, which was estimated to have cost Elders a loss of £11.4 million on the shares that it would be forced to sell. Nevertheless, S&N still looked a tempting target.

March also saw the announcement of the MMC's investigations into the brewing industry, which had begun in August 1986. The main points of recommendation were:

- no brewer to own more than 2000 on-licensed premises, including pubs and restaurants
- tied tenants to be allowed to sell 'guest' draught beers brewed by companies other than the pub's owners
- tied tenants also to be free to buy low-alcohol beers, spirits, wines, cider and soft drinks from the most competitive supplier
- no new loan ties, which oblige owners of 'freehouses' to sell only one brewer's products. It is

common practice for brewers to offer low-interest loans provided owners agreed to stock their drinks
- protection and security of tenure for tied tenants under the Landlord and Tenant Act
- brewers to publish and adhere to wholesale price lists.

The immediate effect was that more than a quarter of Britain's 80,000 pubs would have to be sold over the next three years (see Exhibit 4).

In response to the finding, the Brewer's Society called it 'a charter for chaos', which would destroy the traditional British pub. The brewing industry alone accounts for some £16 billion a year or 25% of Britain's total leisure market, estimated to be worth about £65 billion.

A compulsory reduction in the tied houses, it was argued, would create an enormous increase in advertising spending, as brewers responded by promoting brands that would have to survive in a freer market than before. Losing the potential for vertical integration could increase the market share of the big brewers, who would no longer have their products restricted to certain pubs (see Exhibit 5).

In S&N's Annual Report 1989, Rankin put forward the view that it was:

*the Government's intention to reshape the recommendation in such a way as to minimise political risk. Thus local and regional brewers will get almost full protection while the major companies with substantial pub holdings, will feel the impact of heavy restrictions.*

*Exhibit 4* Pub and restaurant ownership

| Brewer | No. of properties | No. to be divested |
|---|---|---|
| Allied | 6600 | 4600 |
| Bass | 7300 | 5300 |
| Courage | 5100 | 3100 |
| Grand Metropolitan | 6100 | 4100 |
| S&N | 2300 | 300 |
| Whitbread | 6500 | 4500 |
| Total | 33,900 | 21,900 |

Source: MMC.

*Exhibit 5*  UK beer market estimated market share (%)

| | Courage | S&N | Merged group | Bass |
|---|---|---|---|---|
| Beer | 9.4 | 10.7 | 20.1 | 22.0 |
| Ale | 8.9 | 13.4 | 22.3 | 19.2 |
| Lager | 9.9 | 7.7 | 17.6 | 25.2 |
| Tied trade | 10.8 | 6.4 | 17.2 | 22.9 |
| Free trade | 7.0 | 14.7 | 21.7 | 24.6 |
| Take-home trade | 11.1 | 12.9 | 24.0 | 14.0 |

Source: Courage.

He felt that S&N, with its reliance on the free-trade sector and with its comparatively small number of public houses, should therefore be categorized as a regional brewer.

## S&N's new strategy

One outcome of Elders' attack was that it forced Rankin to make a total re-evaluation of S&N, its strategy, its assets and its relationships with the outside world.

*We have learned more about ourselves, people have told us more about ourselves, and we have to learn the lessons of what you are told. So every asset we have is being examined. Whether we are skilled enough as retailers with our 2,300 pubs will be carefully examined.*

By 30 April 1989 the group's hotels, licensed properties and certain other properties were revalued on the basis of market value for existing use. The valuation led to a total surplus of £490 million over net book value. Of this, £398 million were incorporated into the accounts. (See Appendices.)

Rankin and his management team were, moreover, concerned with the lack of appreciation of S&N's strengths and strategy that was uncovered by the bid, especially in relation to S&N's communications with the City and media. Rankin has spent more time trying to redress this situation and commented:

*I accept that we have not been good communicators in the past, but it is a difficult exercise and there are*

*some people who are naturally brilliant and cheerful communicators. But it is not given to every manager to be all things to all men, and some of us quite like to get on and spend time with our people in the field.*

In July S&N had announced its intention to sell its hotel chain in order to realize the value of Thistle's assets and concentrate on its brewing and leisure interests. At the same time S&N acquired a 65% stake in Center Parcs for £218.5 million in cash and the assumptions of the group's £300 million of debt. Center Parcs N.V. operates 13 quality holiday complexes in The Netherlands, Belgium, France and England. The remaining 50% in Pontins was also acquired for the equivalent of £60 million. The Thistle chain was being sold to realize a large capital gain on an asset that was giving an unacceptably low yield of 4%.

It was argued by Rankin that the switch into higher yielding strategic investments in brewing or leisure would benefit the shareholders.

*We are obviously a very major candidate for a strong expansion in brewing.*

On 28 September 1989, at the peak of the market, S&N sold its Thistle Hotel chain to Mount Charlotte Investments, Britain's second largest hotelier, for £645 million.

In the same month the management of Elders took a further step on the road to making Elders a private company by launching a management buyout which they asked their shareholders not to reject. The aim was to tighten the grip of Elders' chief executive. However, Goldman Sachs had valued Elders at Aus$5 per share while Harlin was only offering Aus$3, and they therefore recommended rejection. An earlier scheme had to be dropped after strong criticism from shareholders who suspected that Elliott was trying to take the company private at their expense.

In response, the board said that the purpose was to dismantle the pyramid, which had been a considerable source of suspicion about the company, and the cross-shareholdings between Elders and Goodman, Fielder and Wattie. The deal was then approved by the shareholders.

Perhaps the chief concern facing Rankin after the MMC's decision was the worry over what Elders was going to do with its stake. In declining Rankin's offer to help in finding a suitable buyer Elders fuelled fears that they might be looking towards brewers such as Anheuser Busch and Heineken who might want to buy into the UK.

Speculation in S&N soared once again in November 1989 when it was rumoured that Elders was about to dump its stake in S&N. It was thought that this was the prelude to another take-over campaign. S&N responded by saying:

*Once again, we have awoken to speculation about Elders' holding in the company and we are viewing it quite simply as that.*

Elliott was forced to contradict one of his senior aides, Ken Jarrett, for starting the rumour by announcing that a sale was imminent when, at the company's annual meeting in Adelaide, he said:

*No sale of our Scottish & Newcastle stock is imminent.*

In December 1989 it was announced that nearly 250 S&N public houses were going on sale. These pubs were not being offered to tenants but being sold off in lots of 20 to 30 to other companies. This move was taken, said Rankin, to 'ensure we are classified as a regional while having the market share of a national'. S&N would therefore qualify to get its guest beers into other brewers' pubs without having to offer the same facilities to its competitors.

On 11 December 1989 S&N announced a 21% profits increase and a 42% increase in interim dividend. The company had numerous approaches to sell from companies around the world to which Elders had been trying to offload its stake, but as Rankin said:

*The truth is, it is becoming increasingly unlikely a sale will happen . . . People know we would be unsupportive of the idea.*

On 2 March 1990, after failing to find a corporate buyer, Elders placed its shares in S&N in the London institutional market at an estimated cost of some £100 m. By late May, after attempts to restructure the group, Elliott resigned as chief executive of Elders IXL, but remained chairman of the group. This followed Mr Nicholas Ridley's referral to the MMC of a £366 m pubs for breweries swap between Elders and Grand Metropolitan which would, if successful, have confirmed Elders' position as one of the UK's leading brewers.

In late July 1990 shares in Elders IXL were selling on the Australian Stock Exchange for Aus$1.58, their lowest value since the world stock-market crash of 1987. This fall reflected the growing concern over the future of Harlin Holdings, the privately owned company that owned 56% of Elders. It was believed that Harlin had a negative net worth as a result of the falling value of its stake in Elders, its only asset; an asset, moreover, on which Harlin was dependent to service the reputed Aus$3.6 bn debt that it acquired to finance the purchase of this controlling stake in Elders.

By late September 1990, Elders announced a loss of Aus$1.3 bn (£575 m) for the year to June 1990, Australia's biggest corporate loss. Nevertheless, the directors of Elders decided to press ahead with their plans to dispose of non-core assets in order to restructure the group around its brewing interests, to be renamed Foster's Brewing Group. This was shortly followed by the announcement that Japan's second largest brewer, Asahi Breweries, had bought almost a 20% stake in Elders from Harlin.

After eight years as chief executive of S&N at the end of April 1991, Rankin stood down in favour of

Brian Stewart, previously group finance director. This accorded with his view that managerial effectiveness can decline after a certain number of years in particular jobs, and that in a company the size of S&N it is better that the role of chairman and chief executive be divided between two people.

In the Queen's birthday honours of June 1992 Rankin received a knighthood for his services to industry.

*Scottish and Newcastle Breweries*
http://www.scottish-newcastle.com

## Questions

1. Had Scottish and Newcastle made itself vulnerable to a take-over bid with the strategies it had been following?

2. How would you evaluate S&N strategically in 1988, before the bid was made?

3. How would you assess the bid by Elders and the strategic changes the company was proposing?

4. How would you assess S&N's defence?

5. Should the bid have been referred to the Monopolies and Mergers Commission and do you agree with the outcome of the investigation?

6. In the light of the changing industry environment, what should S&N do next?

Scottish and Newcastle Breweries plc

Appendix 1   Group profit and loss account (52 weeks ended 30 April 1989)

| | Notes | 1989 £m | 1989 £m | 1988 £m | 1988 £m |
|---|---|---|---|---|---|
| **Turnover** | 1 | | 1028.0 | | 911.5 |
| Deduct | | | | | |
| Change in stocks of finished goods and work in progress | | 0.2 | | (3.2) | |
| Own work capitalized | | (1.5) | | (1.2) | |
| Raw materials and consumables | | 267.1 | | 240.9 | |
| Customs and excise duties | | 234.0 | | 210.8 | |
| | | 499.8 | | 447.3 | |
| Staff costs | 2 | 182.7 | | 161.5 | |
| Depreciation | | 37.4 | | 32.4 | |
| Other operating charges | | 150.0 | | 142.9 | |
| | | | 869.9 | | 784.1 |
| | | | 158.1 | | 127.4 |
| Share of profit of associated company | | | 1.7 | | – |
| **Operating profit** | 3 | | 159.8 | | 127.4 |
| Income from investments | 4 | | 4.7 | | 5.5 |
| Interest receivable | | | 0.8 | | 0.7 |
| | | | 165.3 | | 133.6 |
| Interest payable | 5 | | 27.1 | | 20.5 |
| **Profit on ordinary activities before taxation** | 1 | | 138.2 | | 113.1 |
| Taxation on profit on ordinary activities | 6 | | 43.2 | | 36.0 |
| **Profit on ordinary activities after taxation** | | | 95.0 | | |
| Deduct | | | | | |
| Attributable to minority interests | | | 0.3 | | 0.2 |
| Extraordinary items after taxation | 7 | | 4.8 | | 2.8 |
| Allocation to profit-sharing scheme after taxation | 8 | | 3.4 | | 2.8 |
| | | | 86.5 | | 76.9 |
| Preference dividends | | | 5.3 | | 5.3 |
| **Profit attributable to ordinary shareholders** | | | 81.2 | | |
| Ordinary dividends | 9 | | 40.3 | | |
| **Profit retained** | 10 | | 40.9 | | 38.5 |
| **Earnings per ordinary share before extraordinary items** | 11 | | 23.4p | | 20.6p |

*Appendix 2* Group and company balance sheets (at 30 April 1989)

| | Notes | Group 1989 £m | Group 1988 £m | Company 1989 £m | Company 1988 £m |
|---|---|---|---|---|---|
| **Fixed assets** | | | | | |
| Tangible assets | 13 | 1299.3 | 847.5 | 1278.3 | 825.6 |
| Investments | 14 | 142.9 | 113.4 | 337.4 | 321.8 |
| | | 1442.2 | 960.9 | 1615.7 | 1147.4 |
| **Current assets** | | | | | |
| Stocks | 15 | 82.4 | 87.8 | 81.5 | 81.1 |
| Debtors | 16 | 144.1 | 130.7 | 144.1 | 129.1 |
| Cash and short-term deposits | | 11.3 | 6.6 | 11.0 | 3.8 |
| | | 237.8 | 225.1 | 236.6 | 214.0 |
| **Creditors**: amounts falling due within one year | 17 | 372.4 | 345.4 | 568.6 | 537.4 |
| **Net current liabilities** | | 134.6 | 120.3 | 332.0 | 323.4 |
| | | | | | |
| **Total assets less current liabilities** | | 1307.6 | 840.6 | 1283.7 | 824.0 |
| Less: | | | | | |
| **Creditors**: amounts falling due after more than one year | 18/19 | 143.7 | 149.8 | 136.1 | 140.3 |
| **Provisions for liabilities and charges** | | | | | |
| Deferred taxation | 20 | 0.9 | (0.4) | 1.0 | (0.5) |
| **Minority interests** | | 3.2 | 2.7 | – | – |
| | | 1159.8 | 688.5 | 1146.6 | 684.2 |
| **Capital and reserves** | | | | | |
| Called up share capital | 21 | 152.9 | 151.1 | 152.9 | 151.1 |
| Share premium account | 22 | 60.8 | 33.3 | 60.8 | 33.3 |
| Revaluation reserve | 23 | 529.4 | 133.1 | 527.6 | 133.1 |
| Other reserves | 24 | 89.0 | 84.2 | 94.7 | 94.7 |
| Profit and loss account | 25 | 327.7 | 286.8 | 310.6 | 272.0 |
| | | 1159.8 | 688.5 | 1146.6 | 684.2 |

### Appendix 3 Group statement of source and application of funds (52 weeks ended 30 April 1989)

| | Notes | 1989 £m | 1989 £m | 1988 £m | 1988 £m |
|---|---|---|---|---|---|
| **Funds generated** | | | | | |
| Profit on ordinary activities before taxation | | | 138.2 | | 113.1 |
| *Adjustment for items not involving the movement of funds:* | | | | | |
| Depreciation | | | 37.4 | | 32.4 |
| Share of profit of associated company | | | (1.7) | | – |
| *Funds from other sources:* | | | | | |
| Shares issued | | | 29.3 | | 100.0 |
| Disposal of tangible assets and investment | | | 57.4 | | 44.5 |
| | 26 | | 15.0 | | – |
| | | | 275.6 | | 290.0 |
| **Funds applied** | | | | | |
| Purchase of tangible assets and investments | | | 183.1 | | 122.4 |
| Acquisition of subsidiaries | 26 | | – | | 133.6 |
| Dividends | | | 40.1 | | 32.4 |
| Taxation | | | 36.7 | | 28.3 |
| Minorities | | | 0.3 | | – |
| Bid defence costs before taxation | | | 6.8 | | – |
| Allocation to profit-sharing scheme before taxation | | | 5.2 | | 4.3 |
| Working capital requirements | | | | | |
| Stocks | | 0.1 | | 7.8 | |
| Debtors | | 15.5 | | 1.3 | |
| Creditors (excluding dividends, corporate taxes and borrowings) | | | 5.6 | | 11.0 |
| | | | 21.2 | | (1.9) |
| | | | 293.4 | | 319.1 |
| **Net increase in borrowings** | | | | | |
| Increase in overdrafts and short-term borrowings net of cash and short-term deposits | | | 22.9 | | 47.4 |
| Decrease in loan capital (1988 increase) | | | (6.2) | | 0.9 |
| | | | 16.7 | | 48.3 |
| *Add*: Relating to disposal of subsidiary 1988 – less acquisition of subsidiaries | 26 | | 1.1 | | 19.2 |
| | | | 17.8 | | 29.1 |

# The Optica

The Optica is a revolutionary 'bug-eyed' spotter aeroplane. It history and development is a remarkable story of a small company which experienced a fatal crash, bankruptcy, financial rescue and arson.

The case describes the company's struggle to build a viable business to exploit a world-beating design. It is useful for addressing the following issues: strategies for small business, entrepreneurship and innovation, and company failure.

This case was written by John L Thompson. It is for classroom discussion and should not be taken to reflect either effective or ineffective management.

## The aircraft and its creator

The Optica was designed and developed in the 1970s to compete with small helicopters on patrol, inspection and policing duties. It is substantially cheaper to purchase and can be operated for about one-tenth of the cost of a helicopter.

The designer was John Edgley, who acknowledged that 'the idea was a gut feeling' and never formally supported by market research. A huge Perspex bubble at the front gives equivalent visibility to a helicopter, but the Optica is also quiet, easy to fly and relatively free of vibration – an advantage which makes it ideal for aerial photography (see Figure 1).

The 'bug-eyed' design is unusual and distinctive with a three-seater cockpit at the front. The propeller is encased in a cowling behind the engine, which itself is behind the pilot. The aircraft is not designed with a complete fuselage, as can be seen from Figure 2. It can loiter safely at speeds as slow as 50 knots, and turn within 55 metres.

*Figure 1*   The Optica.

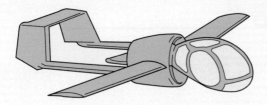

John Edgley was thirty years old in 1974 when he formed the Scenic Aeroplane Company 'to carry out research into the development of a tourist aircraft and the building of a prototype'. He was a civil engineering graduate who, basically disillusioned after working mainly for architects, had returned to university (Imperial College) and studied aeronautical engineering. Not a cautious man by nature, it is said he 'wanted to build an aircraft factory'.

He started building his aeroplane in a house in Islington, next door to where he lived. 'We did metal degreasing in the bathroom; the garden was our press-shop'.

Scenic Aeroplane started with £200 issued share capital, equally split between Edgley and his wife Fiona, i.e. 100 £1 shares each. Civil Servant EJRF Hood was a third director. With two separate directors (each investing £33) Edgley also started Scenic Flying Ltd for the 'prosecution of patent applications relative to light observation aircraft'.

In 1976 the company was renamed Edgley Aircraft, but with the same directors and the same shareholdings. Principally the business was being financed by loans from the directors: 'interest free, secured by a fixed charge over fixed assets and a floating charge over other assets'. Table 1 shows how the company grew through the 1970s. The asset value grew as development work was capitalized, to be eventually amortized against sales. The Optica had a successful maiden flight in 1979, having been taken in pieces to Cranfield Institute of Technology where it was assembled and tested in a wind tunnel.

*The Optica*

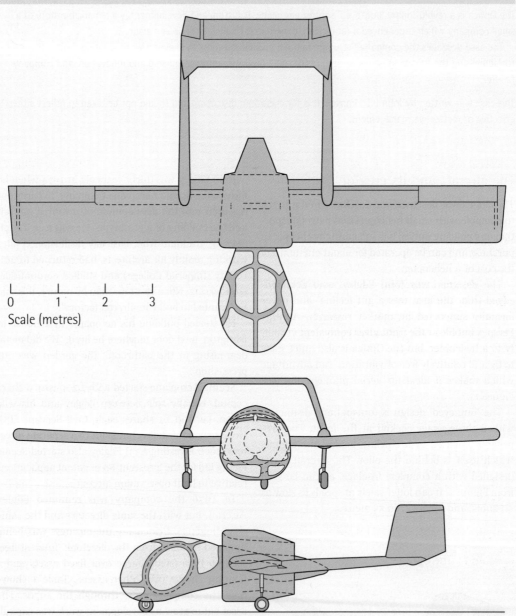

*Figure 2* Optical general arrangement – three views.

Scale (metres)

*Table 1*  Edgley Aircraft Ltd – summary balance sheets 1975–1981

| | 12 months to 30 November | | | | | | |
| | 1975 £ | 1976 £ | 1977 £ | 1978 £ | 1979 £ | 1980 £ | 1981 £ |
|---|---|---|---|---|---|---|---|
| Fixed assets (i.e. buildings, equipment, cars, tools) | 960 | 1657 | 1645 | 3434 | 4466 | 5909 | 5190 |
| Current assets | 683 | 3892 | 11,871 | 24,368 | 40,383 | 56,367 | 61,186 |
| incl. work-in-progress* | 553 | 3646 | 11,606 | 23,920 | 39,885 | 54,381 | 59,200 |
| Less: Bank loan | | | | 29,080 | | | |
| Overdraft[†] | | 183 | 603 | 661 | 11,208 | | 12,597 |
| Total net assets | 1671 | 5231 | 12,614 | (3338) | 30,337 | 59,137 | 16,924 |
| Financed by: | | | | | | | |
| Share capital | 200 | 200 | 200 | 200 | 200 | 200 | 200 |
| Directors' loans | 2694 | 8334 | 17,580 | 4717 | 44,784 | 86,347 | 90,347 |
| Accumulating loss[†] | (1223) | (3303) | (5166) | (8255) | (14,647) | (27,410) | (73,623) |
| | 1671 | 5231 | 12,614 | (3338) | 30,337 | 59,137 | 16,924 |

* Capitalized R&D for eventual amortization, and comprising the direct cost of labour and materials used in the construction of the prototype.

[†] The other current liabilities have been excluded from this summary. Essentially they are creditors, which were an insignificant amount for a number of years, but amounting to £35,000 in 1981.

[†] Ultimately chargeable against taxation.

## Company growth

In March 1980 Hood resigned as a director. However, at this time Bill Fraser, Fiona Edgley's brother and a management consultant, was becoming increasingly involved. At the Farnborough Air Show in 1980 the Optica was described as a 'bright yellow crowd stopper'. It was also well received a year later at a similar show at Le Bourget. Mrs Thatcher sat inside the Optica at Farnborough and claimed that it was a 'triumph of British enterprise and technology'. She did not go up for a test flight, but her journalist daughter did.

The company evaluated possible strategies of subcontracting and licensing and rejected both, on the grounds that letting someone else build it would take away control over production and pricing. British Aerospace, Shorts and Westland were all considered. They implied 'high overheads and high subcontract costs, and potentially threatened the development of future projects'. Significantly, Edgley decided that he wanted to sell his aircraft when he had installed proper production facilities, and this came to mean sophisticated computer-controlled machine tools.

1981 was spent searching for a suitable location to build this facility, and negotiating funding arrangements to enable full-scale production to commence. Old Sarum Airfield was found by chance, when one of Edgley's directors drove past and saw that it was for sale. Old Sarum was the original home of the Royal Flying Corps and the hangars dated back to World War I. A mortgage was arranged with Lloyds Bank in Salisbury and the two hangars and related buildings (some 60,000 square feet or 5500 square metres) plus the airstrip were due to be ready early in 1982.

In spring 1982 substantial external funding was arranged. Edgley Aircraft had 1000 £1 shares authorized, but only 200 had ever been issued. The shares were therefore divided into 10,000 shares of 10 pence, such that the Edgleys had 2000; and 4000 more were allocated to the directors and others. Bill Fraser was now a director.

These 6000 were designated A ordinary shares and partially allocated as follows:

| | |
|---|---|
| John Edgley | 2650 |
| Fiona Edgley | 2650 |
| Bill Fraser | 500 |

The other 4000, designated B shares, were sold to outside shareholders for £1,390,000. During the next three years more shares were issued, some designated C and D, and all carrying one vote. However, the composition of the board of directors was controlled. Originally it was to be eight maximum with up to five of these being nominated by the A shareholders, and the remaining three (maximum) by the B, C and D shareholders. The figures were later adjusted to ten, six and four, respectively. Directors nominated by B, C and D shareholders must also have approval from the As.

The board ultimately became eight-strong, as follows:

*'A' nominees*
John Edgley
Fiona Edgley
Bill Fraser
William Purbrick          (sales and marketing
                                    director, appointed 1983)
John William Edge      (manufacturing director,
                                    appointed 1983)
*'B' nominees*
Micheal Gwinnell        (merchant banker)
AF Atkin                       (Guernsey businessman)
Christopher John Kirman

When Edgley Aircraft moved to Old Sarum in June 1982, the total new funding amounted to £2.3 million. The company had received a £250,000 Government grant for machine tools under SEFIS (small engineering firms' investment scheme). However, Edgley and Fraser were biter that they had spent 'some considerable time' negotiating a DTI grant but with no success. Lynton McLain, writing in the *Financial Times*, recorded the following comments from Bill Fraser: 'We wasted an incredible amount of management time failing to persuade the Department of Trade and Industry to provide launch aid, repayable from orders. We proved to the DTI, as they requested, that we needed launch aid, for production tooling and for the jigs to build the aircraft'.

Then, according to the company, a Catch 22 situation ensued: 'Because the company had proved that it needed launch aid, the DTI said that it was clear that the project did not have sufficient funds and was not financially viable. Government funds are only available for financially viable projects'.

McLain followed this up and reported that the DTI confirmed that it only gave launch aid to large projects such as the A-320 Airbus. It appeared that there was some real concern as to where all the other development money would come from.

## Hope and success

As can be seen from Tables 2 and 3, more development money was spent on the Optica and by 1984 the company had reported accumulated losses in excess of £1 million. Accounting practice concerning this development expenditure was changed in 1982. All capitalized R&D up to 30 November 1981 was to be written off over five years commencing 1 December 1983. All new expenditure would be charged against the current profit and loss account and written off as it arose.

During 1983 the computer-assisted manufacturing facilities were completed at Old Sarum, and the first deliveries of the aircraft were scheduled for 1984. In addition, 'a worldwide sales and distribution network (excluding North America) was largely completed'.

During the 1982̶83 financial year the number of employees rose from nine to 102, approximately half being direct factory employees and the other half evenly split between indirect factory employees and drawing office, administration and marketing staff. In the following year the labour force increased to 176 in roughly the same proportions.

*Table 2* Edgley Aircraft Ltd – balance sheet at 30 November 1982–1984

| | 1982 £'000 | 1983 £'000 | 1984 £'000 |
|---|---|---|---|
| **Fixed assets** | | | |
| Intangible (production proving) | | 251 | 648 |
| Tangible | | 1389 | 2301 |
| Total fixed assets | 866 | 1640 | 2949 |
| **Current assets** | 899 | 933 | 543 |
| Less: | | | |
| Creditors (due within 12 months) | (88) | (310) | (746) |
| Other creditors | (522) | (575) | (1502) |
| **Net assets** | 1155 | 1688 | 1244 |
| | | | |
| **Financed by**: | | | |
| Called up share capital | 1 | 1.17 | 1.27 |
| Share premium account | 1390 | 2251 | 2873 |
| Other reserves | | 68 | 68 |
| Profit and loss account | (236) | (632) | (1698) |
| | 1155 | 1688 | 1244 |

*Table 3* Edgley Aircraft Ltd – recorded losses on zero turnover

| Trading year ended 30 November | £ |
|---|---|
| 1975 | 1223 |
| 1976 | 1937 |
| 1977 | 1863 |
| 1978 | 3089 |
| 1979 | 6392 |
| 1980 | 12,673 |
| 1981 | 46,123 |
| 1982 | 161,657 |
| 1983 | 396,416* |
| 1984 | 1,066,346 |
| | 1,697,809 |

*Originally stated as £769,769.

The first production aircraft was duly completed and demonstrated in 1984, and 'the flight performance exceeded projected figures in almost every respect'.

External observers commented that the workforce was unusually enthusiastic and wholly committed to the project. Overtime without pay was common.

Edgley Aircraft announced an order book in excess of 80 aeroplanes, 90% for export, and worth £11.6 million. This was 'in spite of the worst recession ever known in the general aviation industry', but no actual customer details were given. The price was £139,250, half the price of a small helicopter. Operating costs were estimated at one-tenth of those of the helicopter competitors.

It later transpired that costs had been allowed to grow without effective controls. There was unnecessary spending on non-essential items. The focus had been on making sure that the engineering aspects were satisfactory; instead, the focus should have included production systems. None of the active directors had any previous experience of building up a new *business* from scratch. In addition, the time required to establish the manufacturing facility properly was underestimated.

More shares were sold in 1984, the share premium account now reaching £2,873,000. Among the institutional backers were Norwich Union, National Provident, the Esso Pension Trust, Schroder UK Equity Fund and Schroder Investments. By April 1985 this had further increased to £3,500,000. Accounting practice was again changed. The prototype Optica, once proven, was reclassified as a fixed asset (from an intangible) and was being depreciated. New production for proving the aircraft was to be capitalized as an intangible fixed asset. Eventually the City would invest £8 million, an amount which was never budgeted for properly. Each time Edgley went back for extra money he felt obliged to make increasingly bullish promises. Although some would argue that this implied deceit, it was more probably self-delusion resulting from overconfidence in the aircraft.

A certificate of air worthiness was granted in February 1985, allowing customer deliveries to commence. A year earlier the Optica had won the annual Design Council award. The first production aircraft was consequently delivered in April 1985 to Air Foyle, a charter company based at Luton, to be used for observation by Hampshire Police.

A confident John Edgley was forecasting sales of 2000 Opticas in the next ten years; 5000 if it was adapted for military as well as civil use. 'The military market will have to wait. We cannot cope with demand from the civil market', where the Optica would be used for border and oil pipeline patrols as well as police observation duties. Deliveries were being quoted as 12 months minimum, which Edgley acknowledged was 'too long'. Capacity was targeted at 88 aircraft for 1986 and 176 for 1988. Marketing in America should commence in 1986, and if all went well the company would be floated around 1990.

## Setback

On 15 May 1985, on its first day of observation duty, the Optica sold to Air Foyle crashed near Ringwood in Hampshire, narrowly missing the town centre. 'The aircraft appeared to stall and dive'. Two policemen were killed. Comments from observers suggested that the cause was neither mechanical nor structural. The Civil Aviation Authority was reassuring: 'The crash makes no difference to the certificate of airworthiness. There is nothing to stop Edgley Aircraft continuing to make and deliver Opticas'.

The crash investigation report in August 1986 would exonerate the aircraft, but this would be too late to save Edgley Aircraft from receivership. Despite the company's statements there were no other firm orders for the aeroplane, and the crash caused interest in it to decline. The crash was a 'storm the company could not weather'.

The crash, it transpired, was 'not caused by structural or mechanical failure, or any flying control malfunction or jamming. The aircraft was serviceable immediately before the crash'.

The actual cause will never be known. One popular theory is that the photographer, feeling insecure during a steep turn (as people apparently often do), grabbed at something and interfered with the controls. The report also suggested that the pilot might

have been forced to descend by a partial loss of power arising from mishandling the fuel-tank selector switch – which it suggests could easily happen – or from some other cause. Not unnaturally, an incident like this causes people to speculate about the design and safety aspects. For example, the very slow loitering speed is a key selling point, but might it make the aircraft prone to stall in particular manoeuvres in certain wind conditions? If it is flying into a wind of 30–40 knots at a speed of 60 knots and turning very steeply it could end up with nearly 100 knots lifting one wing and next to nothing lifting the other.

In just the same way, questions are raised about designs which are particularly innovative. For example, the enclosed propeller, which is actually a fan, obtains high propulsive efficiency by being close to the rim of its cover, channelling all of the energy backwards rather than some sideways. The cowling has an abrasive lining because the fan blades touch it. While this may not be dangerous it will necessitate high manufacturing accuracy.

## Receivership

In October 1985 the directors called in a receiver (Cork Gully), whose aim was to find a buyer for the business and assets as a going concern. At the time 46 aircraft were being built and the company owed at least £1.5 million.

At the end of 1984 there had been the following debts:

| | £ |
|---|---|
| 15% debentures (due for repayment 1987–91) | 897,000 |
| 15-year bank loan (at 11/2% above base rate) | 434,750 |
| Leases and hire purchase | 170,250 |
| Total | 1,502,000 |

Against this the company had £2.3 million of tangible fixed assets (see Table 4). However, when the Statement of Affairs (under receivership) was eventually published the assets were actually worth less than £1 million, and the creditors (including the shareholders) were owed some £9 million.

*Table 4* Edgley Aircraft Ltd – tangible fixed assets at 30 November 1984

| Asset | Value £ |
|---|---|
| Land and buildings | |
| Freehold land and buildings | 392,777 |
| Long leasehold land | 311,938 |
| Jigs, plant, machinery and motor vehicles | 476,366 |
| Fixtures, fittings, tools and equipment | 435,996 |
| Aircraft | 215,037 |
| Drawings | 468,524 |
| Total: | 2,300,638 |

Receivership had resulted from three factors, essentially:

- high development costs
- the length of time taken to develop Optica
- the selling ability of the company, which arguably undermined the confidence of investors and bankers.

Against the 46 aircraft in production there were thought to be 'orders for 16 and potential orders for 100'. Receiver Christopher Barlow commented as follows: 'The figures suggest that the company was building aircraft in the hope that customers with options for additional machines would convert them into firm orders. It is unusual for an aircraft manufacturer to proceed so far ahead of firm orders given the high cost of shop floor production'.

In reality, it eventually transpired that there were not 16 definite orders. Inspiration had not been enough. Order, financial controls and proper business planning were all absent.

Barlow quickly shed 238 staff, including John Edgley and Bill Fraser, leaving 51 'core employees and management with knowledge of the Optica aircraft and shop floor procedures'. They were to concentrate on making and selling aircraft, financing future production from receipts. On survivor was Grenville Hodge, who had joined the company three weeks previously. Hodge would become the future managing director. The situation, however, remained precarious, and staff were employed on a 'one day's notice' basis.

## Under new ownership

After the receiver advertised the company for sale in October 1985, there were reputed to be four interested buyers, one of whom was William Purbrick through a management buy-out. In the end only one enquiry proved serious.

Alan Haikney started paying the Optica wage bill in November 1985 and concluded the purchase in January 1986. He paid £1 million for all the aircraft, buildings and machinery and was reportedly 'backed by overseas investors'.

Haikney (aged 52) was chairman of Aero Docks, which he had bought as a management buy-out from UBM builders' merchants in 1980. He had been, he said, 'learning fast about raising money in the City'. Aero Docks designed and supplied staging platforms for aircraft maintenance. Parts were subcontracted out and the company did its own construction and assembly, mainly overseas. It had a turnover of some £2 million, employed 15 people, and was run from Haikney's farm in Wiltshire, where he also produced wine.

Haikney aimed for sales of 20 aircraft in his first year, and was hoping to make a number of the reputed 16 orders real ones. He changed the name of the company to Optica Industries and quickly diversified into subcontract engineering activities. Employees regarded this as 'unskilled metal bashing', but something had to provide a cash flow and subsidize the continuing expenditure on the Optica.

After the purchase, the press reported a number of 'very serious' enquiries/orders. In June 1986 a Canadian distributor was reported to have bought four after seeing Optica at Expo '86 in Vancouver, and was considering an order for 16 more over three years to be sold throughout North America from Toronto. Including spares, the contract would be worth £2 million. By autumn 1986 an order from Thailand was recorded as definite, with serious interest in 18 other countries. A Norwegian contract for 24 aircraft was also mentioned. In reality, at the end of 1986 Optica Industries had delivered only one sale aircraft to Claymore Air Services of Bournemouth. This aeroplane was subsequently destroyed in the Old Sarum fire – it had been returned for servicing.

## The fire

In January 1987 a fire swept through the final assembly hangar, destroying eight aircraft and all of the jigs. The other hangar, where parts were manufactured, was not affected. Replacement of the aircraft would take at least four months, a long time for a firm that was still in difficulty. The workforce, 75 strong at the time, was said to be devastated. The police were convinced that the fire was arson, but this has never been either proved or disproved. Despite an appeal on the BBC's Crimewatch programme in February 1987, the fire has remained an unexplained mystery. Eventually Optica received a £3 million insurance payment.

## Brooklands Aerospace

After the fire Haikney decided to merge all of his business interests and call the new organization Brooklands Aerospace – Brooklands was the name of his farm. Haikney was fully committed to the Optica project, although the revenue that it generated represented only a small part of the total business. The company undertook subcontracting work for British Aerospace's BAe 146 (commuter jet) and Tornado bomber. In addition, spare parts were made for planes that were still in service but no longer being manufactured. Together these accounted for some 50% of the company's revenue. The ground maintenance platforms contributed a further third. Brooklands also made metal boxes for China, among other 'metal bashing' activities.

These various activities were still being used to fund developments with the Optica, which continued to face a dilemma. The aeroplane needed sales to prove that it was a success; at the same time it needed a track record of success before it would sell.

## Developments with the Optica

Neville Duke, the test pilot who had first broken the sound barrier, joined the company in 1987 to help with new developments. Over 40 modifications had been made since the crash and the plane was renamed the Optica Scout. The Hampshire Police continued their trials in a second rented plane (which they subsequently bought) and declared it an outstanding success. The plane would cruise for six hours without refuelling and was ideal for a number of surveillance activities. Traffic patrols were an obvious use. Football crowds (at Southampton) could be monitored before, during and after a match. Because Optica was quiet this was unobtrusive and in the main unnoticed by the fans. In other incidents it was used to track criminals – one was flushed out from undergrowth and arrested, for example. Hampshire Police recommended the Optica to other forces worldwide but the take-up rate was low.

A second plane was sold to Pinewood Studios of film work, and in March 1988 Brooklands announced a new Middle East distributorship. The distributor, who was convinced of Optica's potential for patrolling isolated borders and oil pipelines, bought one plane and took out an option on five per year for ten years. The price was still £140,000.

In the same year an Optica was used successfully for fire patrol duties in Yellowstone National Park, although the plane had yet to receive an American Certificate of Air Worthiness. Successful penetration of the American market could lead to huge orders.

Towards the end of the year Alan Haikney decided to retire and sold all of his shares in the business. Brooklands gained a new chairman, Alan Curtis, who was also chairman of Group Lotus. By this time Grenville Hodge was managing director of the aerospace activities. The production capacity was 120 aircraft per year, but Hodge commented that there was little hope of reaching that target in the next four years.

## Joint ventures

During 1988 Brooklands had entered a number of joint ventures and diversified further. An agreement with Aerospace Technologies of Australia enabled advanced electronic (including radar and thermal imaging) to be installed in the Optica, allowing for a second variant, the Optica Scoutmaster.

Brooklands acquired the rights to design and manufacture two new planes. The Fieldmaster had been designed by Norman Aeroplane, which was in receivership. Developed as an agricultural and fire-fighting aircraft, the Fieldmaster has a unique spraying system, integral within the wings, which allows for an extra-wide ground coverage, and a unique spray container tank which is fully integrated into the fuselage.

The second new plane was the Jindivik, a joint venture with its Australian designers. Jindivik is a remotely piloted jet which flies at 550 miles (885 kilometres) per hour and is used for military target practice. Brooklands had the rights to manufacture and sell throughout Europe.

In Autumn 1989 Brooklands would add a third aircraft, the Venture, an inexpensive two-seater civil trainer. A military version was also a real possibility. There is always demand for trainers, but like agricultural aircraft, the market is global and competitive.

## Renewed hopes

In January 1989 the City agreed a financial restructuring for Brooklands Aerospace, with Fleming Mercantile Investment Trust taking a substantial shareholding. The stated hope was a flotation by the mid-1990s. The workforce had expanded to 125 (all activities).

In July 1989 Kansas City Aviation Centre took out options for 132 aircraft over five years, a contract potentially worth US$22 million altogether. The planes would be used for surveillance work by police forces and the Drug Enforcement Agency. Certification in America was expected in August. The first deliveries would start in September, and an increase in the workforce was implied.

At this time there were just five Opticas in service and consequently this agreement was hailed as a major breakthrough.

## The second receivership

In March 1990 Brooklands Aerospace went into receivership, some £2 million in debt. Shortly afterwards the company was sold as a going concern to Lovaux Industries, a UK subsidiary of FLS. FLS is a Danish engineering conglomerate which, through a series of acquisitions, has become the largest independent provider of aircraft maintenance, modernization and rebuilding in Europe.

While Brooklands was happy to use its other activities to support the Optica, would the same be true with the new owner? Was there now a real chance that the Optica would simply become remembered as the brilliant idea that could not be marketed?

## Questions

1. Why did Optica Industries end up in receivership?
   What strategic changes did Brooklands Aerospace make?

2. What are the main strategic lessons from this case for small businesses?
   Given the decisions that were made at various times, was failure inevitable?

3. Was the Optica project ever really viable?

# C&J Clark

C&J Clark ('Clarks') is a long-established family company, based in the UK but well-known in the shoe industry around the world. By the late 1980s the company was in decline but has since been turned around with new strategic leadership. Both marketing and operational issues have been addressed. This case contains sufficient information for analysing and evaluating the relevant strategic issues, but readers are also encouraged to visit Clarks and rival shoe retailers to check out the latest designs and marketing strategies.

This case is copyright John L Thompson, 2000. It is for classroom discussion and should not be taken to reflect either effective or ineffective management.

## Introduction–the footwear market in the UK

At the end of the 1990s Clarks was UK market leader for shoes. Well-known as both a manufacturer and a retailer, the name Clarks is typically associated with children's shoes, especially among the older generations who 'grew up in Clark's sandals'. Now, of course, children are more keen to wear designer-name trainers. Over many years the company had become associated with sturdy and sensible shoes for adults as well as children, rather than high fashion shoes, although these are also included in the range. Sturdy, sensible shoes are still manufactured, but they have been relaunched with a different image and appeal. Clarks shoes are sold widely overseas, and increasingly they are made overseas. The company wants to be recognized as an 'international casual shoe company'.

The footwear market in the UK exceeded £5 billion annual sales for the first time in 1999. During the mid-late 1990s the growth rate had exceeded the prevailing rate of inflation. The highest growth was in children's shoes of all types, although these account for less than one-fifth of the market overall. Women's shoes account for 43% of sales revenue but 50% of the number of pairs bought. However, 75% of the shoes involved had been manufactured outside the UK, in both the Far East and other countries with relatively low labour costs.

In 2000 C&J Clark was 175 years old and still controlled by descendants of the founding family. A Clark has been strategic leader for most of the company's history, although this situation has

changed in recent years. Eighty per cent of the shares are owned by 500 family members and descendants, some of whom have a direct involvement with the company. Staff own a further 10% and institutional shareholders the remainder.

Table 1 shows market shares by manufacturer in 1999 and Table 2 provides details of retail distribution. Small, sometimes independent, businesses play a major role, as evidenced by the fact that the leading seven retailers account for just one-third of the market. Specialist manufacturers vary from those making high-quality shoes for adults (such as Charles Church) to those making rugged, waterproof outdoor footwear (Timberland) and children's wear (Start-rite). Most towns have at least one local independent store, often with a loyal customer trade. During the 1990s the popularity of trainers and other sports shoes, backed by heavy brand advertising, has grown dramatically, as has the popularity of shoes associated with designer names.

Taste and fashion changes have meant that the relative fortunes of different shoe retailers have changed.

*Table 1* Shoe sales by type of outlet, 1999

| Outlet | % |
| --- | --- |
| Specialist stores (both chains and independents) | 44 |
| Sports shops | 20 |
| Home shopping | 11 |
| Clothing stores (e.g. Next) | 8 |
| General stores | 7 |
| Department stores (including concessions) | 5 |

*Table 2*  Market shares, 1999 (Source: *Euromonitor*)

| Manufacturer | % |
| --- | --- |
| C&J Clark | 10.0 |
| Nike | 6.0 |
| Reebok | 5.0 |
| Marks and Spencer | 5.0 |
| Stylo | 4.5 |
| British Shoe Corporation | 2.0 |
| Adidas | 2.0 |

Some have improved, while others have declined markedly. However, at the same time, shoe manufacture in the UK has declined sharply. Some companies, like Clarks, have reduced their dependency on manufacture; others have simply closed down. One family company, based in Northamptonshire, home at one time to countless small and medium-sized manufacturers, has diversified imaginatively. When he inherited the family boot business, Steve Pateman realized that it was in long-term decline. Its fortunes have been changed dramatically as it has become one of the UK's leading manufacturers of boots and kinky leather products for the fetish-wear market.

## The growth of C&J Clark

The business began in 1825 when the founder, Cyrus Clark, began trading in sheepskin rugs in Street, Somerset, which remains home to the business to this day. The Clarks are a Quaker family and the business has always been paternalistic and, in some ways, benevolent to its workforce.

In 1828 Cyrus' brother, James, became an apprentice in the business and it was he who later used cut-offs from the rugs to make sheepskin slippers, which they called 'Brown Peters'. James became a full partner in 1833, hence the name C&J Clark. By this time socks and welted boots had been added to the product range. Together with the slippers they generated 30% of the company's revenue – until 1920 they were sold as Torbrand products. Most of the trade had grown by word of mouth.

In 1849 the company was experiencing trading difficulties and it began to use posters for advertising its products. On the verge of bankruptcy, Clarks exhibited at Prince Albert's Great Exhibition at Crystal Palace, where two prizes temporarily restored prosperity to the business. By the 1860s the company was once more nearly insolvent. Cyrus and James retired and William Stephens Clark took over as chairman. His contribution was to transform the company from a cottage industry to a mass-market shoemaker.

After the later death of Cyrus Clark the sheepskin business was moved to a separate company in nearby Glastonbury. New ranges and types of shoe followed, including (in 1893) a special range of hygienic boots and shoes, which followed the natural lines and shape of people's feet. Clarks was, by this time, the dominant employer in Street and the town was dependent upon its success. Interestingly, a coffee house, established earlier to dissuade workers from drinking, was turned into an inn which served beer. In 1903 Clarks opened a London showroom in Shaftesbury Avenue; the shoes were still made to order at this time. Five years later the family business was turned into a limited liability company.

Between 1900 and 1940 new materials and technologies were embraced and the manufacturing activities were able to benefit from economies of mass production. In 1920 a new production and distribution system allowed Clarks to despatch from stock upon receipt of an order. In 1920 the company used the brand name Clarks for the first time on its shoes, and soon afterwards began to produce women's fashion shoes which did not cover the whole ankle. Success throughout this period led to press advertising (1934) and to a number of small retail outlets, named Peter Lord (1937).

During World War II the factory switched over to the manufacture of aircraft components and torpedo parts. In 1942 Bancroft Clark succeeded his father, Roger, as chairman and, as soon as the war was over, declared that expansion would follow. One notable contribution from Bancroft, who remained in charge for 25 years, was the renowned foot gauge which measured both the width and length of the foot. This gave the company pre-eminence in children's shoes.

In the 1950s Clarks introduced their casual but smart Desert Boot, made out of soft suede leather, and then, in the 1960s, the Wallabee moccasin shoe, again in suede. Both of these designs are still popular today. In 1952 the name Clarks was used on retail outlets for the first time.

During the 1970s Clarks pioneered their cushioned polyurethane soles and spawned a range of shoes which again remains popular today – lightweight but strong, casual and semiformal shoes with springy soles which are both comfortable and shock absorbent. In 1967 Clarks bought Ravel, which made and sold fashionable shoes; and in 1980 also acquired K Shoes, based in Kendal, Cumbria, which remains as an independent label famous today for formal men's and women's shoes and lightweight casual shoes for women, known as Springers.

## The situation in 1990

C&J Clark prospered through the early 1980s and earned a record £35.7 million in pre-tax profits from sales of £604 million in 1986. The company was now established in Europe, America and Australia, where its products were popular. Some 60% of the shoes were manufactured in the UK; 40% were produced in Portugal, Italy and Brazil. The main brands were Clarks (mostly associated with children's and comfortable semiformal shoes), K (targeted at mature adults) and Ravel (high fashion shoes). But its fortunes then changed very quickly and both sales and profits fell towards the end of the decade.

As shown in Figure 1, the market leader at this time was British Shoe Corporation (BSC, owned by Sears) with a range of distinctive (but sometimes competing) retail outlets, including Curtess, Manfield, Saxone, Freeman Hardy Willis, Dolcis (good-quality, medium-priced stylish shoes for fashion-conscious youngsters) and Shoe City (a new warehouse-type operation in out-of-town shopping centres). BSC overall had a dominant position for low- and medium-price shoes for people up to middle age. High-price shoes for all ages were supplied by a host of independents including Ravel (owned by Clarks) and Cable and Co. (a new brand name invented by BSC in 1988

to gain introduction to this sector). Marks and Spencer was dominant with low-priced shoes for older people, leaving Clarks in a strong position with medium-priced shoes for a number of age groups.

However, the retail environment had been changing during the latter years of the 1980s:

- Sales had fallen as an economic recession took hold, but high-street property rents remained high.
- The market was much more competitive as an increasing number of imported brands was introduced and gained popularity.
- Customer tastes were changing, with casual shoes and trainers becoming increasingly popular.
- Market demographics were also changing, with fewer people in the younger age groups.

A concerned BSC introduced a number of strategic changes, designed in part to strengthen their position in the sector dominated by Clarks. Among other changes, the Manfield brand was consciously repositioned in the medium-priced older age groups. This required new store layouts and fittings, different ranges of shoes and a higher level of customer service. Thirty new outlets were opened in 1990 to complement the existing 850 concessions in department and fashion stores.

Family squabbles broke out inside Clarks as the company struggled to clarify a new strategic response. The company appeared to have 'boxed itself into a corner'. Its manufacturing costs were relatively expensive, making it relatively vulnerable to cheaper imports. As sales declined the company had to reduce its costs. Still with its Quaker traditions and still the dominant employer in Street, the company was reluctant to go down the redundancy route. Instead, the company sought to reduce its costs by using cheaper leathers and introducing simpler (easier-to-make) styles. The company, already with a 'traditional' image, was now seen as both dull and relatively expensive by many customers. The Danish company Ecco, which manufactured strong, comfortable, semiformal shoes in countries such as Portugal, was one new competitor which would take sales from Clarks during the 1990s.

In 1990 a new, external chairman, the first non-Clark, was recruited. Walter Dickson had been a

*Figure 1* Shoe retailing in the UK, late 1980s-segment domination. (Developed with the co-operation of British Shoe Corporation.)

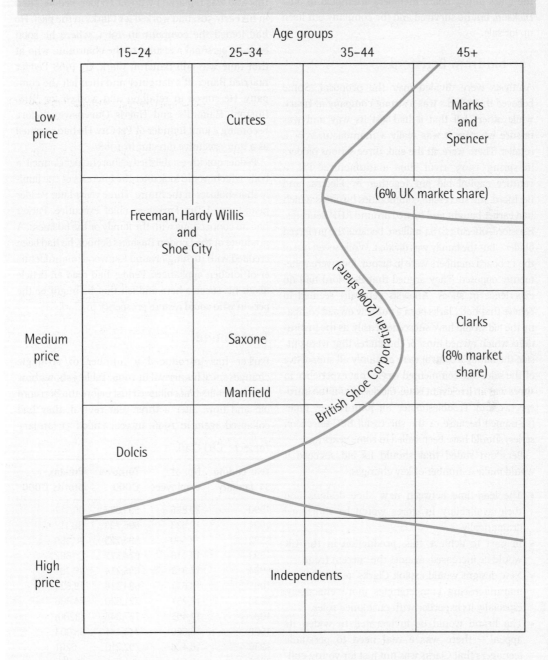

former chairman of Mars Europe and was recognized as a marketing expert. Two years later some of the Clark family board members attempted to oust Dickson, but he survived and the company put itself up for sale.

## The bid from Berisford

Analysts were divided over the proposal. Some believed that Clarks was a strong company at heart, while others felt that it had lost its way and was unsure whether it was really a manufacturer or a retailer. There were, in the end, three serious bidders in spring 1993: rival shoe manufacturer FII, a venture capital bid put together by Electra, and Berisford, the successful commodities business which had earlier bought and turned around RHP Bearings. Berisford, offering £184 million, became the preferred bidder – but the family was divided. While seven out of the 11 board members were in favour, four were vehemently opposed. They argued that Berisford had no experience in shoes. Analysts generally seemed to believe that had Clarks been a publicly owned company the bid would have succeeded easily, as the institutions which owned most of the shares that were outside the family's control were certainly all supportive of the sale. One commented wryly that experience in shoes was an irrelevant issue, Clarks was far too introspective and 'Troubleshooter' Sir John Harvey Jones (so-named because of the successful BBC television series) should have been called in some years ago.

Bersiford stated that should its bid succeed it would make a number of key changes:

- The lead-time between new shoe designs and their availability in stores would be shortened dramatically.
- In part to achieve this, production in the UK would be increased, against the current trend.
- New designs would exploit Clarks' technical and manufacturing competencies more effectively, especially its expertise with cushioned soles.
- The brand would be invigorated to widen its appeal – there was a real need to persuade teenagers that Clarks was not just for young children, for example.

In the end the bid failed and the board opted to remain independent. Dickson resigned shortly after this and was replaced by Roger Pedder. Pedder, then in his early 50s, had worked for Clarks in the past. He had joined the company in 1963, where he soon became personal assistant to the chairman, who at that time was still Bancroft Clark. In 1968 Pedder married Bancroft's daughter and then left the company. He stayed in retailing and worked for BHS, Burton, Halford's and Harris Queensway before becoming a joint founder of Pet City. He had rejoined as a non-executive director in 1988.

Pedder quickly established a Shareholder Council, a body which would look after the interests of the family shareholders in the future. Three years later Pedder head-hunted Tim Parker as chief executive. Parker had no connections with the family or the business. A graduate of the London Business School, he had been credited with turning around Kenwood, manufacturer of kitchen appliances. Pedder had read an article about his success here and felt that he might be the person who could restore prosperity to Clarks.

## Turnaround

Parker has introduced a number of strategic changes since his arrival in 1996. Table 3 shows how pre-tax profits had collapsed just before the Berisford bid and how, after a three-year revival, they had collapsed again in 1996. In year ended 31 January

*Table 3*  C&J Clark

| Year ending 31 January | No. of employees | Turnover £'000 | Pre-tax profits £'000 |
|---|---|---|---|
| 1990 | 20,835 | 599,927 | 30,317 |
| 1991 | 19,538 | 605,793 | 30,117 |
| 1992 | 19,550 | 594,223 | 20,389 |
| 1993 | 18,416 | 624,572 | 1687 |
| 1994 | 17,913 | 655,314 | 20,761 |
| 1995 | 18,631 | 684,318 | 19,623 |
| 1996 | 18,251 | 721,630 | 24,806 |
| 1997 | 17,405 | 727,345 | (3200) |
| 1998 | 16,620 | 743,141 | 35,003 |
| 1999 | 16,426 | 792,210 | 6261 |
| 2000 | 15,561 | 831,614 | 39,235 |

2001 both sales and profits were at record highs. In this year 38 million pairs of shoes were sold; the company was growing in a static market. However, the number of employees had declined as the proportion manufactured overseas had been increased. Specifically:

- Parker reduced, arguably culled, the existing team of managers. As well as taking out a complete layer, newcomers have been recruited to replace some of the others who left. There have also been internal promotions.
- He reduced the workforce worldwide. This included 25% of the workforce at the Street factory in Somerset. Parker dedicated some considerable time to visiting the factories and explaining what was happening.
- Some factories were shut completely and sold to the company which manufactures Doc Martens shoes and boots.
- The number of retail outlets was increased from 550 to 650 and every one was restyled with Clarks' new logo and new colours. The stores now have a different ambience – they no longer feel like an 'older person's store'. Worldwide there are almost 800 shops.
- Manufacturing in the UK has been reduced to just 25% of the total sold. Clarks was becoming more of a designer, wholesaler and retailer at the expense of manufacturing its own shoes. Clarks now owns eight factories, three in southwest England, three in northwest England and two in Portugal. Working conditions have been improved by Parker. Imported shoes are manufactured in Brazil, India, China, Romania and Vietnam.
- New designs have been introduced while older designs have been revamped and relaunched.
- New advertisements take a more 'tongue-in-cheek' approach. A typical magazine advertisement for ladies' boots features a large picture of the boots lying flat in their box. The main headline says: 'New boots and why you just have to have them'. Smaller illustrations are accompanied by the following copy: 'They'll keep your ankles warm', 'A box that big has to come in handy' and 'You won't have to shave your legs.'

- There is a website and on-line sales of selected products are planned for 2001. Clarks believes that there is a market for trainers but not shoes. People are less concerned about exact fit with trainers and are willing to adjust the thickness of the socks worn with them; in the case of shoes the issue of fit is much more critical.
- A shopping village outlet opened in the 1980s was sold to raise cash.

## The situation in 2000

*Clarks* is world leader for 'brown shoes' and shoe-care products and a major player in children's shoes. Table 2 showed that Clarks is overall market leader in the UK with 10% of sales – up 2% from 1990. The term 'brown shoes' represents casual shoes and loafers in the shoe industry; formal shoes are known as 'black' and trainers are 'white shoes'. The industry remains very fragmented and globally static. Sales are strong in the USA where the Clarks and Bostonian (men's fashion shoes) brands turn over £200 million a year and contribute 25% of the total profits – some 95% of the shoes sold in America are imported. The company is also particularly successful in Japan where its range of men's originals is very popular.

Clarks has a very wide range of practical (work) shoes, casuals, sandals and children's wear. They are not the highest price, but they are certainly not the cheapest. Of generally high quality, they represent value for money. The new image is focused on shoes that are fashionable and casual. The company claims that it offers individual designs, exceptional comfort, premium quality and expert service. Clarks' shoes are focused mainly on the 35–45 age group and the K brand on the over 50s.

There are five distinct ranges of women's shoes: formal, smart (with thicker soles), casual, boots, and Springers – semiformal casual shoes with soft soles sold under the K brand.

There are also five men's ranges: formal, smart, casual, originals, and waterproof (walking boots). The originals range includes designs from years ago which have been successfully relaunched. The Desert Boot (a lightweight lace-up boot made with thin, rugged suede leather and with crêpe soles) has become a fashion product, sported by media figures such as Oasis' Gallagher brothers. The Wallabee (a luxury soft suede lace-up moccasin shoe, again with a crêpe sole) was first introduced in the 1960s, a decade after the Desert Boot. The third main original is the Millcreek, another suede shoe with a crêpe sole, but this time a slip-on. The range competes effectively with designer fashion brands but sells at much lower prices – the first time that Clarks has been able to compete successfully in this particular sector.

There are separate children's ranges for boys and girls. These ranges comprise four age groups: first shoes, 2–4, 5–7, and 8 years and over, as well as a range of trainers with their own brand identity, Cica.

Excluding Nike and Reebok – manufacturers of trainers and sports shoes and which together with Adidas account for 13% of the UK market – *Marks and Spencer* follows Clarks with a 5% share, 1% less than its share in 1990. In 1999 the M&S profit margin on shoes was reported to be 6.6%, whereas a year earlier it had been 14.1%. The company had lost some of its international sales as a result of the high pound. It still retained a value-for-money image but it was introducing new designs for more fashion-conscious customers. *Stylo*, with 4.5% of the UK market, sells mainly through its chain of 250 Barratt stores and 350 ladies' shoe concessions in department stores.

The once-dominant British Shoe Corporation has seen its share tumble from 20% to 2% as Sears has divested brand after brand. Freeman Hardy Willis was sold in 1995, followed a year later by Saxone and Curtess and in 1997 by Shoe City and Dolcis. BSC had been overdependent upon that part of the market most affected by the growth and popularity of sportswear chains and clothing retailers such as Next and River Island, which have systematically added shoes to their range of products. BSC is now primarily the repositioned Manfield and its newer self-service format, Shoe Express, designed to provide convenience at low prices.

New retail names such as *Shoe* (targeted at young people) and *Dune* (high-fashion shoes at premium prices) have made an impact recently. Top (clothes) designer names are being attached to ranges of shoes, which are available in selected outlets and department store concessions. These include Pierce Fionda, DKNY, Patrick Cox and LK Bennett.

## The future

After the failed bid by Berisford and the formation of the Shareholder Council it was thought that the company might seek a flotation, but the family shareholders appear to have no inclination to relinquish their control at the moment. There is no longer any need to raise capital to fund expansion plans. There is, however, a rumour that Clarks might seek to acquire Shoe City from the Belgian retail group, Brantano, which bought it from BSC.

*C&J Clark: http://www.clarks.co.uk*

## Questions

1. Using Porter's five-forces model, how attractive do you think the shoe industry is? Apply the model to both manufacturing and retailing.

2. How does Clarks add value? How would you summarize the company's strategic (competitive) position in 1990? In 2000? Do you believe that Clarks is now in a much stronger position than it was ten years ago?

3. Evaluate the changes introduced by Parker in the last five years. To what extent do you think the current results can be attributed to these changes, and to what extent might they be the result of external circumstances?

4. If you were Tim Parker, what future strategies would you be considering? Is the family ownership a relative strength or a relative drawback?

# Polly Peck International

The Breaking of an Entrepreneur
This case study tells the story of the rise and fall of the entrepreneur Asil Nadir. From a textile industry base in northern Cyprus Nadir built a diversified corporate empire which also embraced foods and high-technology products. His downfall in 1993 involved an investigation by the UK Serious Fraud Office.

The case involves issues of management style, corporate governance and dishonesty.

The case was written by Dr Jim Gallagher. It is for classroom discussion and should not be taken to reflect either effective or ineffective management.

Copyright Dr JG Gallagher, Napier University, Edinburgh.

## Introduction

In the small hours of a cold May morning in 1993 a light aircraft took off from a deserted airfield in England. Its destination was the Continent and thence northern Cyprus. On board was Asil Nadir, the once powerful chairman and chief executive of the Polly Peck conglomerate. Polly Peck, a small textile company, had been transformed through growth, acquisition and diversification during the 1980s and had been the world's best performing share of the decade by multiplying its value by 1300 times. It had received the ultimate accolade by being admitted to the Financial Times Stock Exchange 100 Share Index during 1989 and by 1990 had a market capitalization of £1.6 billion.

From being fêted by both the commercial and political establishment, Nadir's reversal of fortune was such that he had become a wanted criminal on the run from the British Serious Fraud Office. Reflecting on the circumstances that led to this situation, it seemed that fact was indeed stranger than fiction.

As chairman and chief executive of Polly Peck, with 25% of its shares, Nadir had maintained total control of Polly Peck until it was placed in administration in 1990.

Born in Cyprus in 1941, Nadir spent his formative years in a volatile political cauldron where the British, Greeks and Turks coexisted uneasily. For much of the late 1960s and 1970s Nadir was closely involved in running the main family business, Wearwell, which had been set up in London in 1968 and floated on the stock exchange in 1972. Through his own cultural roots, political and social contacts, Asil Nadir rapidly recognized the opportunities offered in northern Cyprus and Turkey. Using both his connections and the cheap labour in Cyprus, Nadir was soon to become, on paper, a millionaire and gain valuable experience for what was to follow.

In 1974 northern Cyprus was invaded by Turkey, driving the Greek Cypriots into the southern part of the island. This partition of the island into a Turkish north and Greek south has never been recognized by the international community, but it was to prove to be an important part of Polly Peck's future and to provide complicated political overtones to Nadir's business life.

## Polly Peck

The purchase of Polly Peck gave an indication of the shrewd business sense and vision of Nadir. Polly Peck was originally a UK quoted, London-based textiles business controlled by the Zelker family. In February 1980, the Zelkers sold their 57% stake for £470,000, or 9 pence a share, to Restro, a Jersey-based company owned by Nadir. Within four months the share price had risen to 85 pence, giving it a value of £4.4 million.

Nadir's incessant hard work, ability to exploit opportunities and undeniable charm attracted many shareholders and helped the price of Polly Peck's shares to spiral upwards.

His strategy for Polly Peck was growth through acquisitions, mainly outside its traditional area of textiles. His first chairman's statement in the 1981 accounts refers to

> *enormous changes in your Company . . . dominated by the acquisition and start up of the packaging project in Northern Cyprus.*

Nadir recognized the opportunity to utilize the agriculturally rich northern part of Cyprus with its underdeveloped citrus groves. He had both personal and political connections in Turkey and he was encouraged to develop the opportunities that existed in northern Cyprus through tax-free incentives. In July 1980 through a rights issue he bought Unipac, a manufacturer of fruit packaging based in northern Cyprus, to launch Polly Peck's development in the food and agricultural business.

After a healthy expansion in the citrus fruit business in Cyprus, Nadir announced an electronics venture to build TV plants in Turkey and Egypt. The diversification of a textiles company, first into agricultural produce, then into a high-technology venture, seemed a strange development for the structure of Polly Peck. But Nadir seemed to have the right contacts and be able to spot a good business opportunity, as the TV venture in Turkey would prove to be.

Polly Peck acquired and set up businesses around the world, acquiring companies in the Far East, in textiles and electronics. Hong Kong and Taiwan were the first bases, but the purchase of Sansui gained Polly Peck a Japanese foothold and was seen as a particular coup.

The very successful food business based in Turkey and northern Cyprus was expanded to include acquisitions in Europe and the USA. This culminated in another coup for the company, the purchase of the well-known Del Monte Fresh Fruit business.

The business opportunities in Turkey and northern Cyprus proved irresistible to Asil Nadir as he moved into the leisure business around 1987, first by building a hotel in southern Turkey and then by making acquisitions in northern Cyprus.

Nadir was constantly on the look-out for new opportunities, although not all prospective deals came to fruition. In 1984, for example, a supposed deal with Daihatsu to produce cars in Turkey came to nothing. Nadir also wanted to buy his own bank (common among industrialists in Turkey) and the Ottoman bank interested him, although no purchase was made. He eventually achieved this ambition in the mid-1980s with the purchase of a small Turkish bank, Impex. Nevertheless, this growth through acquisition and diversification would be shown by the end of the decade to be a key strategy adopted by Nadir.

In the 1988 Annual Report and Accounts, Nadir stated:

> *We have clearly defined strategies for global growth which we pursue both organically and by acquisition.*

## Management structure and management changes

The evolution of the management structure of Polly Peck was complex and intricate. Interrelationships between the people involved in the structure played an important role in the changes that took place. They also influenced the actual acquisitions and diversifications that forced the structure to change.

Attempts were made to establish a hierarchical structure, outside professionals were brought in to help to reshape the management structure of the company, and substantial changes were made at board level, yet Nadir would not allow a structure to be created that would diminish his control over Polly Peck. There were often serious personality clashes between these proven successful professionals and Nadir. A succession of appointments and resignations took place at board level over the decade.

Nadir had many connections in northern Cyprus. It was through one of these contacts, Radar Reshad (a commercial officer in the Turkish Cypriot representative office in London) that the idea to invest in Cyprus emerged. At the time this was encouraged by the authorities in northern Cyprus through tax-free incentives, essentially as a result of the 1974 invasion of Cyprus by Turkey. Economic development of the northern part of Cyprus (occupied by Turkey) had not proceeded as expected and it was felt that Nadir was the ideal person (being the only Turkish Cypriot millionaire in London) to develop the potential in northern Cyprus.

In August 1981, Radar Reshad joined Polly Peck, where he remained until he resigned in January 1991. The first of many personality clashes in the management structure of Polly Peck appeared in 1982 when Raymond and Sybil Zelker resigned from the board of Polly Peck. There followed an acrimonious dispute over trade market agreements, which they finally lost to Nadir in December 1982. These signs of dissension would be repeated many times over the decade as many people found it impossible to cope with Nadir's autocratic, entrepreneurial style.

In 1982, Nadir diversified from Polly Peck's textile business into electronics, building a TV production facility in Turkey. Later, another diversification took place into spring-water bottling in Turkey. In 1983, a friend of Asil Nadir, Turgut Ozal, won the general election in Turkey. This led to the encouragement of free enterprise and trade liberalization in Turkey which provided tremendous opportunities for Polly Peck in that country.

Around this time, Brian Handicott, formally a general manager of Thorn EMI's International Division, joined Polly Peck and became commercial director. In 1983, Handicott and Mehmet Sakir set up the electronics operation, Vestel, in Turkey. Handicott was responsible for laying the foundations of the group's success in the electronics industry in Turkey in the second half of the 1980s.

A further diversification for Polly Peck was announced in May 1985 with the news that a hotel was to be built in Antalya in southern Turkey. This move into the leisure business was reinforced in August by the announcement of a deal regarding a hotel in northern Cyprus.

In April 1985, Richard Strong (finance) left the Polly Peck board, implying that Asil Nadir had not listened to his advice on cash flows and management structure. Two new non-executive directors, Neil Mills and Larry Tingle, were appointed.

In spring 1986, Handicott resigned his directorship of Polly Peck. This was caused by a confrontation with Nadir over a proposal by Handicott for a hierarchical structure for Polly Peck which would have made it more like other large companies. When the rest of the board failed to back him, Handicott approached the non-executive directors about possible improprieties. The allegations were rejected, and nothing leaked into the public domain about this incident, but Handicott resigned.

At this stage, although superficially there were the four divisions of food, electronics, textiles and other activities, Nadir still had total control over the major decisions affecting each division.

Other problems occurred among the directors when Polly Peck moved to new offices in Berkeley Square. Those members of the board who had not stood by Nadir in the Handicott affair (Ellis, Doshi and Reshad) were not invited to the new offices, and thus lost the benefit of daily contact with Nadir.

In Turkey, Handicott was replaced by Tahsin Karan. In the wake of Handicott's resignation came the resignation of Anil Doshi, the financial director, who was also linked with the attempted revolt against Nadir. Doshi's place was taken by David Fawcus, who was to remain with Polly Peck until January 1991.

In autumn 1987, Polly Peck began to recruit a new generation of managers with the skills needed by an international conglomerate. The new arrivals at the top of Polly Peck brought a financial and managerial sophistication not previously possessed by the company. Tony Reading joined Polly Peck in September 1987 as group managing director (a new post). He had previously been chief executive for manufacturing and engineering at BTR. Although he contributed a great amount to Polly Peck's image over the following two years, there were considerable tensions between his multinational corporation style and that of the existing executive directors who had worked for years in a different business culture, with few institutional and financial controls. In December 1987 Steven Breeze joined the board to run the consumer electronics division.

Personal relationships within the board of Polly Peck seemed to be in a state of continual turbulence. In May 1989 Nadir fired five staff while David Fawcus and Tony Reading were away from the office. This was without consultation, although it would affect Fawcus and Reading in their work. One of the five, Vi Jansen, was the corporate financial controller who had been working closely with David Fawcus on establishing corporate restraints and disciplines within Polly Peck. For Reading this was the final straw and he resigned at the beginning of June. Fawcus threatened to resign but actually stayed on.

The resignation of Tony Reading led to a major restructuring of Polly Peck, yet Nadir would still not allow a structure to be created that would diminish his control over Polly Peck. Nadir considered that he was not getting the full flow of information from the divisions and he decided to install six regional managers to ensure that decisions were taken rapidly and on the spot.

It became apparent that Polly Peck was being run as a business in two parts. Some of the subsidiaries had strong chief executives: Vestel and Tahsin Karan, Meyna and Fahrettin Otluoglu, Capetronics and Norbert Wirsching. The other parts depended on the constant flow of ideas and orders from Nadir. At this stage, it appeared that the company had reached a crossroads in its life, unsure in which direction to go. Rumours began to suggest that Nadir would take Polly Peck private.

By August 1989, Nadir had decided not to replace Tony Reading, but to divide the work among the chief executives of each of the newly formed divisions of Polly Peck: food, textiles, electronics and leisure. Radar Reshad was made head of the food division, Joe Harris in textiles, Norbert Wirsching in electronics and Tahsin Karan in leisure. At the same time Mark Ellis was appointed head of the new corporate development group in the company. Tim Wood was brought back as head of the investor relations department after Tony Reading's departure. Despite these changes, Polly Peck seemed to be moving back to a position where Nadir dominated the company.

Further changes took place on the board at the end of 1989, with Peter Compson becoming director of human resources and Brian Haycox becoming chief executive of Del Monte Fresh Fruit. Rumours increased that Nadir was planning a demerger of the group, with the food operations division being floated in New York and the Far East electronics operations being floated in Tokyo. It was also planned to float Vestel in Turkey. Polly Peck would become simply a holding company based in Switzerland.

Throughout the spring and summer of 1990, Nadir continued to look for new companies to buy or lines of business to go into. Standard Fruit and Vegetable (USA) was purchased in March and talks were undertaken with Peugeot to produce one of its car models in Turkey. By summer 1990, Polly Peck's board was advising Asil Nadir against further acquisitions. It was even proposed and approved by the board that Polly Peck should dispose of the leisure division and initiate a restructuring operation. The only flotation to take place was that of Vestel in Turkey, with 18% of the company being sold for $90 million.

A last major shake-up at board level was to involve David Fawcus being moved sideways to a new post of deputy chief executive and Reg Mogg becoming finance director.

However, the events of September/October 1990, including Nadir's abortive attempt to buy out the other shareholders, were to overtake many of these plans for a change in direction for Polly Peck.

## Company finance and performance

Polly Peck's phenomenal growth was accompanied by a complex web of financing arrangements.

On 14 February 1980, the Stock Exchange news agency reported that Restro Investments of Jersey, owned by Asil Nadir, was offering 9 pence a share for Polly Peck. By buying Polly Peck himself, rather than through a listed company, Nadir stood to make a greater personal gain if things went as planned. His offer of 9 pence was well above the value of 7.5 pence for Polly Peck shares on 19 February 1980, but within a short time the share price rose steeply, reaching 20 pence. This was to be the first of many unusual share price movements for Polly Peck. By 14 March, Restro had won its bid and owned 58% of the company.

Nadir's bid price had valued the company at £470,000. By June of that year, with a share price of 85 pence, the company was valued at £4.4 million.

On 8 July 1980 Nadir announced that Polly Peck would be making a £1.56 million two-for-five rights issue at 75 pence a share to buy Unipac. After a persuasive explanation of why Polly Peck should move into this area, the rights issue was 92.2% taken up by shareholders. This rights issue did not seem to check the rise in the Polly Peck share price, which soared by an extraordinary 2708% from 5.3 pence at the end of 1979 to 168 pence during 1980. Analysts could not explain the rationale behind this phenomenal rise.

Polly Peck was involved in another complex deal involving the purchase of Cornell Dresses. Initially, Azania Investments, a Jersey-based company owned by Asil Nadir, secured a commitment to buy 57% of Cornell's shares for 19 pence. However, the market price rose to 76 pence a week after news of the bid. In the end, Azania Investments did not buy Cornell, but transferred the option to Polly Peck. Polly Peck paid £570,000 for a company whose market value had reached £3.2 million.

By May 1981, the Polly Peck share price had risen to 385 pence, after the brokers L Messel had predicted profits of £10 million in 1981/82. The half-year results to 28 February were published in July 1981 and showed a slender profit of £51,779. The company, backed by analysts, predicted year-end profits of around £2 million. Sceptics wondered how a £5000 a month profit for the first 11 months of the financial 'year' (which was in this case a 16-month year) could be turned into a £400,000 a month profit for the final five months of the 'year'.

When the final results for Polly Peck were issued at the end of 1982, pre-tax profits had risen to £9.04 million. After this, Nadir announced Polly Peck's plans to diversify into an electronics venture by building a TV plant in Turkey. Although shareholders suspected that this might involve another rights issue, it did not prevent the share price rising £1.75 to £16.78.

The performance of Polly Peck during 1982 could only be described as remarkable. At the beginning of the year the share price had been 310 pence, but by the end of the year it was £25. When the annual report was published on 13 January 1983, the share price jumped to £27.50. What made this even more remarkable was the fact that Polly Peck's market value was £200 million, even though it only had assets worth £11.6 million and a turnover of £21 million. There had also been a change in stockholders from risk-taking private investors to institutional investors. Institutional investors held 84% of the stock not held by Nadir.

Although some people questioned the sustainability of the growth during 1982 and the validity of the profit figures, many were happy to accept apparently plausible reasons for the growth: tax advantages in Cyprus, vertical integration and new markets.

Early in 1983 a series of interrelated events caused the price of Polly Peck shares to crash. The Greeks had always claimed that Polly Peck's success in northern Cyprus depended on orange groves owned by the Greeks before the 1974 invasion. The Cyprus government declared that it was seriously considering including Polly Peck in a suit it was making against the Turks at the European Commission on Human Rights. Reports were also published that the Turkish Cypriot Ministry of Finance was trying to levy taxes on Unipac.

Amid this political and financial confusion, investors were unsure of the true facts. This was to prove the case throughout the 1980s as Polly Peck's accounts only gave indirect details of where in the group turnover and profits were obtained. Although currency translation problems were occurring at this time, they remained largely unrecognized or ignored, and it would only be later that the full impact of these problems would be exposed.

For whatever reasons, shareholders took fright and started selling heavily on 28 February 1983. The share price crashed from a high of £35.75 to touch £16 before other buyers took the price back up to £23.50. The company asked for a temporary suspension of its shares when its price had dropped again to £17.

The survival of Polly Peck at this stage depended on the support of its brokers L Messel, who stood by the profit forecast for the company of £25 million for 1982/83 and £42.5 million for the following year. Although many doubters were reassured, things were never quite the same at Polly Peck again. Some parts of the market never forgot or forgave the share price crash. However, by the middle of March, the share price was back at £22.

On 24 April the *Observer* published an article which, although largely ignored at the time, would reappear as an important indicator of potential problems in 1990. It revealed that the northern Cyprus operations were audited not by the group auditors, Stoy Hayward, but by a firm of local accountants, Erdal and Company. Another strange item was detected, which would only prove significant at a later stage. Gillard, the writer of the article, noted that Polly Peck's accounts had unusually high debts and prepayments. These had totalled over 50% of turnover and, at £10.6 million, exceeded profits.

Nadir circulated a statement refuting the allegations made in the newspaper report, but the share price dropped by £4 as a result of the article. There followed a lengthy series of legal battles between Polly Peck and the *Observer*, which eventually fizzled out some years later.

The half-year results published in May 1983 showed that turnover had more than doubled to £18.16 million, pre-tax profits were up 164% to £8.07 million and the interim dividend went up 42% to 9 pence. However, there were still doubters. The Lex column in the *Financial Times* was critical at the lack of a breakdown of how and where the profits had been achieved. During July, Nadir again had to defend Polly Peck against rumours that the Stock Exchange was investigating dealings in the company's shares.

By summer 1983, the share price had reached over £25. The publication of the year-end results showed pre-tax profits of £24.68 million, only fractionally below Messel's forecast of £25 million for the year. Although these appeared to be good results,

the stock market was not impressed. The shares dropped by £2 and then rose slightly to close at £24.12. The reason given was the lack of explanation as to where the profits had been achieved.

The recovery in the share price was helped by an announcement that Legal and General, a large insurance group, held over 5% of Polly Peck. This was followed in 1984 by Friends Provident acquiring over 5% of the company. Evidence of institutional involvement with Polly Peck helped to build the share price back up to £30.50.

At the end of 1983, £5 million was raised by placing 3% of the group's shares with an associate of Nadir. This was to help with development plans, without having to hold a rights issue. With shares trading at around £27, shares were to be split ten for one to make them more appealing to small shareholders. At the same time, the annual accounts were published, which were said to be much fuller and more informative than the previous accounts.

In May 1984 Nadir announced the take-over of Wearwell by Polly Peck. This was to be financed by offering 53 new Polly Peck shares for every 100 Wearwell shares, with an issue of £3 million of redeemable preference shares for the purpose, thus avoiding a cash call. The market reacted uneasily to this news and Polly Peck's price dropped by 24 pence to 289 pence. The summer saw continuous pressure on the share price even when the half-year results were published, showing an increase from £8.07 million a year earlier to £18.6 million.

Because of uncertainty as to how the profits had been achieved, the share price dropped over the summer, reaching 187 pence on 20 July. Two trips for fund managers of institutional investors to Turkey were arranged in August and September to boost confidence, and this helped to push the price back up to 235 pence. The 1984 profits were £50.4 million, up 68% from £29.9 million the year before, but below Messel's forecast of £60 million. Although the reported growth was astonishing, the share price fell by 12 pence to 227 pence.

Nadir was, yet again, disappointed by the market valuation of the company. Before the 1983 crash,

Polly Peck had price/earnings (*P/E*) ratios often above 30 and twice over 100. By the end of 1984 the *P/E* ratio had dropped to 4, even though a whole range of investments was due to come on-stream in 1985.

On 31 January 1985, Nadir surprised the market by announcing a rights issue for £42 million. This was the first time since the cash call in 1980 to set up Unipac's operations that shareholders had been asked for cash, although a little cash had been raised by private sales of newly issued shares. The claim was that the money was needed to fund expansions and improvements in Turkey and Cyprus.

This was an unusual rights issue, offering not ordinary shares, but a 9% convertible loan stock on the basis of £9 for every 220 shares (with a yield over four times that of the ordinary shares). It was followed by the announcement of a diversification for Polly Peck into leisure, with a planned 300-room hotel in Antalya in southern Turkey.

Although pre-tax profits increased by 32% from £21.36 million to £28.16 million when the interim profits for 1985 were published, Messel had been forecasting over £30 million. This caused the share price to remain static with the (*P/E*) ratio stuck at only 4, despite the fact that the dividend had been increased by 50% to 1.5 pence.

A further financial disaster for Polly Peck took place on 15 November 1985. Two weeks before the financial results were to be published, Messel stated that the forecasted £82 million pre-tax profits for the year would not be attained. Within hours the share price had dropped by 52 pence to 173 pence. When the final results were published on 2 December 1985, pre-tax profits for 1984/85 were worse than expected, only £61.1 million. This was explained as being due to a 44% depreciation of the Turkish lira against sterling in the second half of the year. In the heat of the moment, no one commented on the policy of charging exchange-rate losses to reserves rather than the profit and loss account.

The financial disasters of 1983 and 1985 were to have a serious effect on Polly Peck's ability to raise finance to buy or develop new businesses during 1986 and 1987. Banks were cautious about lending

money and shareholders did not like to be asked for cash from a company whose shares were underperforming.

In April 1987, Polly Peck resorted to a fairly unusual way of raising money. It placed new shares (the largest amount it was able to issue without going to the existing shareholders with a rights issue) with US investors by arranging for a dealing in American Depository Receipts. This raised over £20 million.

After the announcement of good half-year results in May 1987, the share price rose to 297 pence. Late in 1987 senior management was restructured and new people were brought in from industry and the City. This seemed welcome news to the market and the share price rose to 350 pence.

Two recruits, Tim Wood and David Stoddart, devised a new scheme to raise additional finance for Polly Peck. Swiss Fr 75 million was raised in five-year bonds guaranteed at 6% a year until 1992. Warburg Soditic led a consortium of 26 banks (only one of which was based in the UK) in the deal.

In performance terms, by the end of 1987, the company's profits had risen by 22% over the year to £86.2 million, although not all elements of the group had performed well. In addition, the stock-market crash of October 1987 took 100 pence off the share price.

Polly Peck was to continue raising finance during 1988 to fund further acquisitions. The favoured route seemed to be the unconventional. In February 1988 £75 million was raised in a syndicated loan through Credit Suisse–First Boston and 17 other banks. In April DM 100 million was raised in five-year bonds by Dans and Company, a German bank. In September another bond issue through Warburg Soditic raised Swiss Fr 125 million.

Many syndicates of European, Japanese and US banks backed Polly Peck, but few British banks were involved.

Another financial anomaly occurred in Polly Peck in 1988. For the second time it changed its year end from August to December.

In October 1988 Nadir felt that Polly Peck had recovered sufficiently and its image was strong enough to ask shareholders for cash in the form of a rights issue. Polly Peck asked for £133 million in a one-for-four issue, priced at 255 pence, well below the 317 pence opening price, so that the offer would be attractive to shareholders. Tim Wood had been worried about the amount of borrowing of small amounts from a wide number of banks, mainly from outside the UK. His concern was about the company's survival on such a high gearing without a fresh injection of equity capital to balance the bank borrowing. The rights issue brought the gearing down from the 135% it had been in September 1988 to 60%.

When the 1988 accounts were published, the figures were slightly above forecast with pre-tax profits of £144.1 million. A further anomaly was picked up in the financial accounts. The working capital had decreased by almost £100 million, when normally it should have grown. The accounts put this down to 'other variances', although it was probably due to currency problems, i.e. the weakness of the Turkish lira.

Rumours of a proposed buy-out of Polly Peck by Asil Nadir reached the City in July 1989. At that time the shares were valued at 279 pence with a *P/E* ratio of 6. The group had a market value of over £700 million. All other shareholders would need to be bought out and the borrowing would need to be refinanced. Tim Wood persuaded Nadir that the timing of the proposed buy-out was not right and the move was postponed.

In September 1989 the announcement of the Del Monte acquisition brought much-needed credibility to the group. But as would be discovered later, the financing of this purchase by 'ring fencing' would effectively keep Del Monte's finances separate from the rest of Polly Peck until the loans had been paid off. This was a condition imposed by Credit Suisse–First Boston on the £557 million purchase, which included a £283 million rights issue. The rest of the Polly Peck group would have no access to any of the funds generated by Del Monte until all loans involved in buying it had been paid back. No dividends would be transferred to the group from its profits and any dealings between

Polly Peck and Del Monte had to be carried out on a strictly formal basis, allowing the banks a full insight into what was happening. As David Pollock stated:

*Well, I suppose when you look back at that time it was a period of growth, Nadir had a charisma, an ability to motivate people. He had the ability to convince people, probably had a number of respectable businesses, was a big group, with names like Russell Hobbs and Del Monte Fruits and these were household names.*

Within seven weeks Polly Peck had announced the acquisition of a 51% stake in Sansui, the Japanese consumer electronics group, for £69 million. The acquisition of a brand name and potential synergy with Capetronics, Polly Peck's Taiwanese electronics business, were seen to offset the poor financial condition which Sansui was in at the time.

The purchase of Del Monte had raised gearing to 125% and the purchase of Sansui caused further financial problems. Since it would be inappropriate to ask UK shareholders for another cash call through a rights issue so close to the Del Monte deal, it was decided to place some shares with international investors in the form of a convertible preference share issue for £69 million.

In November 1989 Polly Peck finally moved out of the textiles business by selling off its Hong Kong textiles division for £38 million, which helped to reduce gearing, following the Del Monte and Sansui purchases, to 108%.

In May 1990 Nadir announced plans for a restructuring of the electronics division. Capetronics and Imperial would join the Sansui group, releasing £30 million in cash to Polly Peck. In addition, Polly Peck would increase its shareholding in Sansui from 51% to 70%.

In 1990 Polly Peck was given the accolade of being the best performing share of the 1980s. The share price climbed to 428 pence and the outlook for the company seemed bright.

Another financial deal was arranged for Swiss Fr 150 million with a rate of 8.75%, due to mature in

1997. Arrangements were being made to restructure the borrowing. Instead of using over 60 banks, the plan was to restrict borrowing to a much smaller banking group.

The 1989 accounts, published in March 1990, had shown encouraging news. Pre-tax profits had risen by 44% to £161.4 million, with half coming from acquisitions made during the year. More worrying was the fact that interest charges had more than doubled over the year to over £66 million and gearing was 103%, with debt up from £255 million in 1988 to £850 million.

Polly Peck made a further acquisition in March 1990 with the purchase of Standard Fruit and Vegetable (USA) for $30 million. This was paid for through a rights issue of new shares rather than cash. By 8 June Polly Peck shares were at 462 pence, the highest level they were to reach.

## The Serious Fraud Office

On Sunday 12 August 1990, Nadir announced that he wanted to take Polly Peck off the Stock Exchange by buying out the other shareholders. On hearing this news, the market did not know how to react. At first there was substantial buying of Polly Peck shares, causing the price to rise to 450 pence, before closing at 417 pence. On the following day the price dropped to 408 pence because of the uncertainty about where the money for the purchase was to come from.

A further shock came on Friday 17 August when Nadir announced his withdrawal of the buy-out offer, stating:

> I have received approaches from significant institutional and individual shareholders who indicated that they would not wish to see Polly Peck become a private company.

The effect on the share price was dramatic. It fell to 324 pence in an hour's trading. By the Tuesday of the following week the price was 310 pence. Newspaper reports over the weekend concerning suspect share dealings confused and complicated the issues. By the end of the month the price was down to 291 pence. On 17 August the Stock Exchange began an investigation into share-price movements during the days of the abortive bid. Worse for Nadir, however, was the prospect of an investigation by the Department of Trade and Industry (DTI).

During this critical time, Nadir maintained a calm, unworried demeanour. He published the interim results for Polly Peck early on 3 September, hoping that the good results would restore the company's credibility. The interim results showed that pre-tax profits had risen by 72% from £64.4 million to £110.5 million, and other figures published were equally impressive. However, the good results were unable to counterbalance the claims regarding the investigations into Polly Peck, and Nadir was unable to stem the rising concern among shareholders.

Although the market steadied a little, by 19 September the share price was down to 243 pence. A raid by the Serious Fraud Office (SFO) on South Audley Management, Nadir's property and personal financial interests management company, was to prove to be the final disaster for Polly Peck's share price. Thirty-six million shares were sold on 20 September before the board of Polly Peck requested that they be suspended at a price of 108 pence.

The loss of confidence by the banks made the cash-flow problem the most serious immediate problem. In early August Nadir had promised to deposit £25 million in London but he failed to do this. On 25 September, Polly Peck missed the first debt payment, and the whole future of a company that had been borrowing heavily was plunged into doubt.

Nadir's tenacity in the following weeks was obvious as he tried to arrange a rescue package for Polly Peck. He travelled to Turkey, northern Cyprus and the USA in an attempt to gain support, but without success. Although he tried to use his friendship with Turgut Ozal, the Turkish Prime Minister, to secure a politically inspired rescue package, this failed, along with his attempts to gain assistance from his lenders. In the 1983 crisis, the support of Messel had proved critical to the survival of the company. This time there would be no bailing out by the banks or other lenders. The complex financial issues and the inability of Nadir to obtain any cash from Cyprus finally led to Polly Peck being placed in administration on 26 October 1990.

On 15 December 1990 Nadir was arrested and charged on 70 counts of theft and false accounting. He was released on bail of £3.5 million, with his trial due to be held in 1993. By the time he fled to Cyprus these charges had been reduced to 13 counts, all of which related to dealings between Polly Peck and its subsidiary Unipac.

Almost a year after his initial arrest on 26 November 1991 Nadir was declared bankrupt having unsuccessfully used his fortune to support the price of Polly Peck's shares prior to their suspension.

## Currency mismatching

One of the major problems associated with the data contained in Polly Peck's published accounts relates to currency mismatching. This is caused when a large amount of money is borrowed in hard currency at, say, 7% per annum and is invested at a much higher rate of, say, 20% in a weak currency. The difference of 13% is brought into the accounts as a profit. However, the weak currency depreciates during the year by, say, 15%, but this is written off directly to the reserves in the balance sheet. The net result is that the published earnings each year appear much higher than is the case in reality.

In Polly Peck's case, the 1989 balance sheet showed guaranteed bonds (Swiss Francs and Deutschmarks) of £217.5 million at rates between 5.75 and 8.75%. However, inflation in Turkey, one of Polly Peck's main profit-generating areas, ranged from 24% in 1982 to 39% in 1983. The same accounts show 'exchange variances' of £46.4 million being deducted from reserves. In 1988 the figure was £182.4 million.

This was not a new phenomenon for Polly Peck. The 1983 accounts showed £5,196,233 written off for 'Exchange variances on overseas results'. The *Financial Times* highlighted these currency problems as early as 1 March 1983.

After the substantial share price drop in 1985, the policy of charging exchange rate losses to reserves rather than the profit and loss account was again highlighted, but no one appeared to take notice of this anomaly.

## Exaggerated profits

Although there may have been reason to suspect that reported profits from operations in Turkey and northern Cyprus were exaggerated, it was only some time after Polly Peck was taken into administration that the full story began to emerge.

When Meyna, Polly Peck's Turkish fruit business, was put up for sale some time after Polly Peck went into administration, it turned out that its sales were only one-fifth of what was claimed in the group accounts. Meyna's high reported contribution to Polly Peck's total reported profits belies the fact that it appeared to be a medium-sized business, with negligible exports, and about a 5% share of a highly competitive local market.

Polly Peck's administrators established from records at Polly Peck's London headquarters that Meyna had reported revenues of TL578 billion (£140 million) and trading profits of TL195 billion for the first six months of 1990, while the local management accounts revealed a much more modest performance. For the whole of 1990 Meyna's revenues totalled TL251 billion, and gross profit was just TL13 billion. Furthermore, Meyna's assets were valued at TL129 billion (£31 million), which is hard to reconcile with Turkish Treasury figures showing Meyna as the second largest UK capital investment; Vestel, PPI's Istanbul electronics subsidiary, was the largest.

Meyna was one of several Polly Peck subsidiaries whose reported performance did not tally with reality. Polly Peck's fruit exporter in northern Cyprus, Sunzest, was apparently supplying more oranges than the island's entire annual crop. Unipac, its packaging company, seems to have been producing more boxes than there was fruit to fill them. Strangely, the various trips organized for Polly Peck investors to northern Cyprus and Turkey did not seem to have come across any of this evidence.

However, perhaps other information in the published accounts should have raised some questions. The accounts show that profits from operations in the near and Middle East were consistently above 25%, and still providing two-thirds of group profits in 1989, at which time their contribution to turnover had fallen to 35%. The ratio of net purchase of tangible fixed assets to depreciation was also abnormally high. Stocks, debtors and work-in-progress all grew year by year to substantial levels, more than doubling between 1988 and 1989 alone; so did the number of days in debtors, creditors and stock. These figures never seem to have been checked.

## The auditors

Nadir deceived Polly Peck's auditors on at least one occasion for which there is evidence. He failed to disclose his interest in 1989 in Impexbank, a Turkish bank which was instrumental in channelling Polly Peck funds into his own personal and private business activities. The 1988 accounts of Polly Peck show that Nadir had an interest in both Impexbank, based in Istanbul, and the Industrial Bank of Cyprus (IBK). The 1989 accounts refer only to IBK. Shares in Impexbank, allegedly bought with Polly Peck money, were held by Nadir until 1991. Impexbank was used to channel at least £158 million of the £371 million that Nadir allegedly removed from Polly Peck between 1987 and 1990.

Nadir also said that he had no beneficial interest in the shares of AN Graphics, the Turkish printing and publishing company that had stakes in many of the Polly Peck Turkish businesses. Nadir attempted to gain control of AN Graphics shares just four days before Polly Peck went into administration.

The auditors can also be accused of not doing their jobs properly. There was supposedly a large amount of cash on deposit in northern Cyprus, and it was claimed that very high profits were generated in the region. However, Stoy Hayward, Polly Peck's group auditor, relied for the audit of these subsidiaries on Erdal and Company, a small local firm which it introduced to Horwath International, the network to which it is affiliated. Mr Paul Hipps, Stoy's senior partner, says that two partners and one or two managers went to northern Cyprus each year to examine Erdal's working papers, and sometimes visited Turkey. Stoy Hayward was apparently given no choice in selecting Erdal, which was chosen by Polly Peck, but it could have conducted its own audit on the Turkish and Cypriot subsidiaries, or qualified the Polly Peck accounts. It did neither.

Christopher Morris, joint administrator and a partner in Touche Ross, issued a writ against Stoy Hayward in December 1991, claiming damages for 'negligence and/or breach of contractual duty of care' in the preparation of Polly Peck's accounts.

## Misappropriation of funds

After Polly Peck went into administration, it appeared that there had been a large-scale misappropriation of funds. A *Financial Times* report in July 1993 gave a figure of 'as much as £565 million' being misappropriated from banks, bondholders and shareholders in the last few years before the collapse of Polly Peck. Nadir is alleged to have removed £371 million from Polly Peck, and at least a further £194 million remained unaccounted for. This was used to fund a wide range of Nadir's personal and business interests.

Most of the money seems to have come from more than £1 billion raised for Polly Peck in loans, rights issues and bond issues in the UK, Switzerland and other financial centres. The money was then switched, allegedly by Nadir and a small group of associates in London and northern Cyprus, in and out of a number of the group's bank accounts in several countries. It was apparently used to: buy about £100 million of Polly Peck shares through a series of Swiss and Jersey trusts; prop up loss-making businesses, principally in Turkey and Cyprus; buy hotels in Cyprus; help to purchase two stately homes in England; furnish his properties with valuable antiques; and create a printing and publishing empire in Turkey and Cyprus. All but £30 million of the £371 million was traced, but most appeared to have been frittered away. As David Pollock commented:

> The fact that the Serious Fraud Office were sniffing around the fact that the Inland Revenue were sniffing around somebody's private affairs and the dented confidence caused at that time resulted in some lenders demanding money back. It resulted in the share price falling such that some of Nadir's personal borrowings needed to be repaid because they were secured on his shareholdings. As the value of the shares fell, so the value of security fell the bankers called in some of those loans and there was a crisis which could not be resolved out of the groups existing cash resources which were weakened by sums misappropriated in previous years by Mr Nadir because you cannot have £400M disappearing without running into cash problems.

## Conspiracy?

Polly Peck directors were dismayed when the SFO leaked news of the raid on South Audley Management (SAM) while trading in Polly Peck shares was still going on. Subsequently, there seems to have been an undue delay in the suspension of Polly Peck shares by the Stock Exchange. It allegedly took three requests from Polly Peck's brokers before the shares were suspended. Concurrently, there was a news agency report of the assassination of Nadir, which added to the panic. Polly Peck directors asked the DTI to launch an investigation into events surrounding the share price collapse, but according to Nadir, they refused unless he agreed to pay them £1 million.

Was there a plot to foment panic on the market and cause a share price collapse? If so, who would have benefited? Who could have been behind it?

In response to an approach from Nadir, Michael Mates, the former Northern Ireland minister, took upon himself the task of defending Nadir. He repeated allegations of improper collusion between the SFO and the Internal Revenue, both of which were investigating Nadir. Elizabeth Forsyth, who ran Nadir's private financial affairs, is quoted as saying:

> The SFO had no evidence whatsoever to launch a raid on SAM. They found nothing there at all that related to Polly Peck, not that there was anything to find. The press were all tipped off about the raid. They must have known the effects a highly-publicised raid would have on Polly Peck shares.

It was alleged that Michael Allcock, an Inland Revenue investigator, first blew the whistle on Nadir by tipping off the Stock Exchange. Allcock had been investigating Nadir's personal tax affairs, and Nadir claimed that there were strong informal links between his unit and the Stock Exchange's surveillance unit, specializing in insider-dealing investigations from 1984 onwards. The Stock Exchange emphasized that its raids were based on information that they had been building up for several years, not only on last minute tip-offs from the Revenue.

Allcock, however, was subsequently jailed and lost his job in 1997 for taking bribes for turning a blind eye when investigating the tax affairs of some of the millionaire businessmen on his client list. He was the most senior Inland Revenue officer ever charged with corruption.

Nadir had also accused the Foreign Office of responsibility for the collapse of the last-minute Turkish rescue effort that ultimately forced Polly Peck International into administration in October 1990. He claimed that a credit package from Turkish state banks was ready to be signed when a telex message arrived from the Foreign Office which put an end to the package.

Further complaints from Nadir included the armed police presence at his return to Britain from his attempts to find a rescue package, and the fact that bail was set at a UK record of £3.5 million. He claimed that his private mail to and from his lawyers was opened, and the trustees in bankruptcy, escorted by the Metropolitan Police, took away documents needed in his defence.

In October 1992 Nadir was accused of plotting to bribe his trial judge. This accusation was found to be unsubstantiated and was thrown out. However, Nadir claimed that the SFO and Scotland Yard had set the plot up to discredit him.

In June 1993 Nadir further claimed that he had tapes of government ministers and officials which proved the existence of a conspiracy to bring down Polly Peck. Although no names or other details were forthcoming, Forsyth suggests that Nadir has tapes of the SFO and Scotland Yard officers outlining the bribery plot.

## Epilogue

In November 1994 Turkish Cypriot officials seized two of Nadir's hotels to recover accumulated tax debts and opened negotiations with the Polly Peck administrators to discuss access to Polly Peck assets and accounts.

## Questions

1. How would you evaluate Asil Nadir as an entrepreneur? How successful was he at overcoming setbacks?

2. Analyse and evaluate the growth of Polly Peck in terms of both its strategy and structure. What might have been the impact of tighter financial controls and earlier indications of the problems faced by the company?

3. Why did Polly Peck eventually fail? What issues of corporate governance are raised by this case? Was failure inevitable? Could the collapse have been prevented?

# Hanson (A)

The Hanson (A) case is divided into three sections:

1. The development of Hanson and the major acquisitions
   'Hansonizing': the Hanson strategy
2. Changes in the 1990s to the earlier strategy
   Non-events and failed acquisition attempts
3. A profile of Lord James Hanson.

The case stops in 1992 and invites discussion on the key issues that affect the future development prospects. Hanson (A) is particularly useful for provoking discussion on:

- diversification strategies and synergy
- acquisition and asset sales
- business objectives
- the contribution to the national economy of acquisitive diversifiers who split up companies.

Thus case was written in 1996 by John L Thompson. It is for classroom discussion and should not be taken to reflect either effective or ineffective management.

## Introduction

For the year ended 30 September 1992 Hanson plc reported the first ever decline in its pre-tax profits in nearly 30 years of trading. Exhibit 1 charts the growth of the company from 1965.

The fall has been attributed to two main causes. First, the costs of borrowing to acquire Beazer, the building company and the most recent (1991) of a long series of major acquisitions. Secondly, the world economic recession. Hanson is heavily involved in construction and basic industries in the USA and the UK. Exhibit 2 provides a summary of the main balance sheet and profit and loss data for the period 1988–1992, and also analyses Hanson's 1991–1992 results by activity, showing which sectors have shown increases and which ones have declined.

Hanson's considerable success has been based upon squeezing additional value from acquired assets, which have normally been underperforming companies bought at attractive prices. However, many of these businesses are in cyclical industries and consequently they offer few opportunities for growth during a recession.

The growth and success of Hanson plc has been created wholly by Lord James Hanson (chairman) and his partner, Lord Gordon White (the deputy chairman), who have worked together since the mid-1960s. In 1992 Hanson was 70 years of age, White a year younger. Both men indicated that they had no plans to retire for a number of years, but some arrangements for their succession have been put in place. Lord White works exclusively in America, controlling Hanson's US interests; Hanson splits his time between the UK and the USA but essentially runs the UK businesses.

It has been suggested that White was skilful at acquiring sleepy companies, while Hanson is expert at transforming them into immensely strong performers.

## Formation and early development

In 1964 James Hanson, then in his early 40s, was the controlling director of Oswald Tillotson, a distributor of commercial vehicles based in Yorkshire. Hanson had been born in Huddersfield, where his family ran a successful transport business, and he had trained as an accountant. Prior to Tillotson's he had run businesses in the UK and Canada.

In 1964 Tillotson was acquired by the Wiles Group, a recently quoted agricultural services busi-

*Exhibit 1*   Hanson (UK and USA)

| Year YE 30.9 | Sales (£m) | Profit before tax (£m) | Value of shareholders' funds (£m) |
|---|---|---|---|
| 1966 | 9.1 | 0.4 | 1.2 |
| 1967 | 11.8 | 0.6 | 1.8 |
| 1968 | 19.5 | 1.2 | 4.1 |
| 1969 | 48.5 | 2.2 | 5.3 |
| 1970 | 47.1 | 2.4 | 7.6 |
| 1971 | 28.8 | 2.9 | 7.7 |
| 1972 | 36.4 | 4.5 | 16.6 |
| 1973 | 51.7 | 8.2 | 31.1 |
| 1974 | 71.1 | 10.4 | 33.5 |
| 1975 | 75.7 | 12.1 | 48.6 |
| 1976 | 322.2 | 19.2 | 57.5 |
| 1977 | 477.4 | 24.4 | 67.2 |
| 1978 | 604.6 | 26.1 | 74.9 |
| 1979 | 658.0 | 31.2 | 107.0 |
| 1980 | 684.3 | 39.1 | 120.7 |
| 1981 | 855.9 | 49.7 | 165.1 |
| 1982 | 1148.3 | 60.4 | 188.5 |
| 1983 | 1484.0 | 91.1 | 428.9 |
| 1984 | 2382.3 | 169.1 | 410.3 |
| 1985 | 2674.5 | 252.8 | 1124.8 |
| 1986 | 3772.0 | 408.0 | |
| 1987 | 6682.0 | 741.0 | 1879.0 |
| 1988 | 7396.0 | 880.0 | 2339.0 |
| 1989 | 6998.0 | 1064.0 | 1086.0 |
| 1990 | 7153.0 | 1285.0 | 2834.0 |
| 1991 | 7691.0 | 1319.0 | 3325.0 |
| 1992 | 8798.0 | 1286.0 | 4224.0 |

ness, also based in Yorkshire. In 1965 Hanson became Chairman of Wiles, and he quickly began a long series of diversifications, acquisitions and divestments in Britain and the USA. The name of Wiles was changed to Hanson Trust in 1969, and some time later this was shortened to Hanson plc.

Exhibits 3 and 4 provide details of the major acquisitions in the UK and the USA, respectively.

Hanson and White had known each other for several years but their business partnership really began in 1963. Gordon White was then the owner of a printing company based in Hull, but he was frus-trated by the pressures of selling into a very competitive and diverse market. He fancied buying another company, but his resources were inadequate. Hanson introduced him to Lloyds Bank, who provided the necessary finance. Some time later White suggested that their business interests should be fused, and they duly were.

Hanson and White have worked together closely since the mid-1960s, and have jointly masterminded the growth and strategic development of the business. Initially, their investments and acquisitions were exclusively in the UK, but in 1973 the partners crossed the Atlantic. They have deliberately concentrated on English-speaking countries.

## The first acquisitions in the UK

Although Hanson's acquisitions have been in diverse industries, from the outset there was normally a strategic logic in the purchases. The strategy has, however, changed and evolved over time.

After Hanson acquired Scottish Land Development (1967) and Jack Olding (1969), and merged the two companies, they became the leading distributors of construction equipment in the UK. This strategy of acquiring related businesses in order to create critical mass, attain scale economies and build market share set a pattern which has been repeated in other industries.

Hanson entered the agriproducts (agricultural products) industry in 1968 when they acquired West of England Sack Holdings, but this has never become a major interest in the UK.

Hanson invested in the manufacturing of basic products for the first time also in 1968. They bought Butterly Brick, who were renowned for their high-quality facing bricks, and who had successfully developed technology for lowering costs in kiln operations. Butterly also made lightweight aggregates, materials which are mixed with cement to make concrete. After acquiring National Star Brick and Tile (1971), Castle Bricks (1972) and London Brick (1984), Hanson became the UK's leading brick manufacturer. During the 1980s Hanson built a strong position in the building materials industry in the USA.

**Exhibit 2** Hanson plc

| | Year ended 30.9 (£m) | | | | |
|---|---|---|---|---|---|
| | **1988** | **1989** | **1990** | **1991** | **1992** |
| **Extracted items from the balance sheet 1988–1992** | | | | | |
| Total fixed assets | 1476 | 2414 | 5057 | 6199 | 9146 |
| Investments | 178 | 957 | 704 | 429 | 191 |
| Current assets: | | | | | |
|   Stock and work-in-progress | 1071 | 988 | 984 | 992 | 1318 |
|   Debtors | 1227 | 1157 | 1126 | 1192 | 1441 |
|   Cash and investments | 3860 | 5309 | 6883 | 7771 | 8445 |
| Total current assets | 6158 | 7454 | 8993 | 9955 | 11,204 |
| Total current liabilities | 2463 | 3269 | 4226 | 4751 | 6386 |
| Net current assets | 3695 | 4185 | 4767 | 5204 | 4818 |
| Net assets | 5349 | 7556 | 10,528 | 11,832 | 14,155 |
| Share capital and reserves | 2339 | 1086 | 2834 | 3325 | 4224 |
| Long-term loans and provisions | 3010 | 6470 | 7694 | 8507 | 9931 |
| Total capital employed | 5349 | 7556 | 10,528 | 11,832 | 14,155 |
| **Extracted items from profit and loss account 1988–1992** | | | | | |
| Trading income | 7396 | 6998 | 7153 | 7691 | 8798 |
| Interest received | 373 | 531 | 856 | 941 | 844 |
| Interest charges | 287 | 330 | 638 | 741 | 777 |
| Published pre-tax profits | 880 | 1064 | 1285 | 1319 | 1286 |
| Less: published tax | 204 | 251 | 314 | 284 | 197 |
| Preference dividends | 8 | 2 | – | – | – |
| Ordinary dividends | 260 | 335 | 499 | 529 | 265 |
| Add: extraordinary items | 445 | 288 | 29 | 71 | – |
| Retained earnings | 853 | 764 | 501 | 577 | 824 |
| Published earnings per share (pence) | 17.46 | 20.66 | 20.28 | 21.55 | 22.62 |

**Hanson in 1992**

Sales: £8.8 billion (up 14%)      Pre-tax profits: £1.29 billion (down 2%)

**Geographical analysis**

| | Sales (£m) | Trading profits (£m) |
|---|---|---|
| UK | 4014 | 467 |
| USA | 3642 | 567 |
| Rest of world | 1055 | 78 |
| | 8711 | 1112 |

(Remaining sales and profits from discontinued operations)

*Exhibit 2   (Continued)*

| Main activities | Sales (£m) | Trading profit (£m) | Profit trend, 1991/92 |
|---|---|---|---|
| Industrial products (mainly USA) | | | |
| – Coal mining | 1011 | 157 | Down |
| – Chemicals | 543 | 116 | Down |
| – Materials handling | 258 | 42 | Down |
| – Gold mining | 106 | 29 | Down |
| – Others | 802 | 86 | Up |
| Consumer products | | | |
| – Imperial Tobacco (UK) | 2980 | 280 | Up |
| – Others (mainly USA) | 650 | 100 | Up |
| Building products | | | |
| – Aggregates | 1120 | 81 | Down |
| – Forestry and Lumber | 221 | 69 | Up |
| – Housebuilding | 338 | 45 | First profits |
| – Others | 677 | 72 | Up |

*Exhibit 3*   Hanson's major UK acquisitions

| Company | Date | Businesses | Cost (£m) | Value of disposals (£m) |
|---|---|---|---|---|
| Scottish Land Development | 1967 | Construction equipment distribution | 0.7 | |
| West of England Sack Holdings | 1968 | Agricultural sack hirers | 3.1 | |
| Butterley | 1968 | Brick manufacturing | 4.7 | |
| Jack Olding | 1969 | Construction equipment distribution | 1.7 | |
| National Star Brick & Tile | 1971 | Brick manufacturing | 1.4 | |
| Castle Brick | 1972 | Brick manufacturing | 2.7 | |
| BDH Engineers | 1973 | Engineering | 12.2 | 11.0 |
| Henry Compbell | 1978 | Linen and synthetic yarns | 4.9 | |
| Lindustries | 1979 | Linen and synthetic yarns + engineering and polymers | 27.0 | 49.3 (by 1990) |
| Berec | 1982 | Ever Ready batteries | 95.0 | 1983: $60 million* |
| United Gas Industries | 1982 | | 19.0 | |
| UDS | 1983 | Allders retailing, etc. | 260.0 | 263.1 |
| London Brick | 1984 | Brick manufacturing | 245.0 | 33.0 |
| Imperial Group | 1986 | Tobacco, foods, brewing and restaurants | 2800.0 | 2340.0 |
| Consolidated Gold Fields | 1989 | Mining | 3300.0 | 2654.0 |
| Beazer | 1991 | Building (including second-largest US aggregates business) | 351.4 | |

*The rest of Berec (later renamed British Ever Ready) was sold in 1992.

*Exhibit 4*    Hanson's major US acquisitions

| Company | Date | Businesses | Cost (£m) | Value of disposals (£m) |
|---|---|---|---|---|
| J Howard Smith | 1973 | Animal feedstuffs | 32.0 | |
| Carisbrook Industries | 1975 | Speciality textiles and machinery | 36.0 | 22.8 |
| Hygrade | 1976 | Meat processing and packing | 32.0 | 165.5 (by 1989) |
| Interstate United | 1977 | Food service and vending | 30.0 | 99.8 (by 1985) |
| Templon Spinning Mills | 1978 | Speciality textiles | 7.25 | |
| McDonough | 1981 | Foorwear, hand tools, building materials | 185.0 | 52.5 |
| US Industries | 1984 | Varied | 532.0 | 200.0 |
| SCM | 1986 | Office equipment (Smith-Corona) + paints, chemicals, foods | 930.0 | 1585.0 |
| Kaiser | 1987 | Cement | 250.0 | 274.0 |
| Kidde | 1987 | Conglomerate, including security systems, etc. | 1500.0 | 734.2 |
| Stuart Anderson | 1988 | Restaurants | 20.0 | 11.4 |
| Peabody | 1990 | Mining (coal) | 1200.0 | |
| Cavenham Forest Products | 1990 | Forestry, etc. | 1300.0* | |

*Cavenham was acquired in a swap arrangement for part of Consolidated Gold Fields (UK).

## The move to the USA

The first US purchase was J Howard Smith, an animal feedstuffs company, which Hanson re-named Seacoast Products. This was followed by the related acquisitions of Hygrade Food Products (meat processing) in 1975 and Interstate United in 1977. This company was active in food service, specifically serving meals in cafeterias in schools, factories and hospitals, and in vending machines.

The year 1975 saw a diversification into textiles. Carisbrook Industries, which manufactured speciality textiles and machinery, was followed by a series of related acquisitions on both sides of the Atlantic.

\* \* \* \*

Most of Hanson's early acquisitions were bought at favourable prices, often for a figure below the asset value of the business. Their post-purchase rationalization and cost-cutting strategies quickly generated an improved cash flow, which increased Hanson's profits and earnings per share, and helped to fund

further acquisitions. In the USA Hanson concentrated on companies that were happy to be bought out.

From the mid-1970s the acquisitions started to involve businesses that were already diversified and multiproduct. Hanson was always willing and happy to sell those parts of the business that did not fit with existing Hanson interests or appear to make strategic sense to him. He was also keen to divest the least profitable parts of the companies that he acquired, together with any businesses which offered little opportunity for adding further value and improving profits. Exhibits 3 and 4 include summary details of the money that Hanson has recouped from the various business and asset sales.

In the UK Hanson preferred to use new equity for his acquisitions, supported by the occasional rights issue and cash from asset sales. Cash was more normal in America.

## Selected major acquisitions

This section analyses a number of important Hanson acquisitions throughout the 1980s and into the 1990s. The hostile purchase of Imperial Group is looked at in greatest detail as it provides an excellent illustration of 'Hansonizing', as the Hanson strategy of the 1980s has been christened.

## McDonough

McDonough, bought for $185 million in 1981, spanned three quite different industries.

The Endicott Johnson subsidiary both imported and manufactured footwear, owning ten factories. The company had 689 shops and leased space in department stores across America, concentrating on the 'popular price' ranges. In addition, the company provided shoes to some 18,000 independent retailers.

McDonough also owned cement and ready-mix concrete businesses in Texas. These two activities were linked, with 35% of the cement sales going to the ready-mix business. The cement company contributed just 10% of McDonough's profits but Hanson sold it immediately for over $50 million.

The third interest was hand tools, with manufacturing based in West Virginia. The brand name was Ames and the products included lawn, garden and industrial tools. The business, which was over 200 years old, serviced independent distributors nationwide.

## Berec

Acquired in 1982 for £95 million, Berec was a battery manufacturer, and Hanson capitalized upon its well-known brand and renamed the company British Ever Ready. In 1980–81 Berec's pre-tax profits had fallen to £10.5 million from £17 million a year earlier – in 1977 they had peaked at £29 million. The company's main rival, Duracell, was developing new battery technology and gaining market share every year. Duracell was pioneering long-life batteries in ever smaller cases while Berec was still investing in new capital equipment to support increasingly obsolete technology.

Hanson's take-over bid prompted an acrimonious battle which featured hostile press advertising by both companies. After the acquisition Hanson cut Berec's head-office staff from 550 to 75, reduced the number of management layers from nine to three, and sold the research and development facilities and the Continental manufacturing plants to Duracell. These sales recouped $60 million. Over a longer period the blue-collar workforce was reduced by two thirds. Profits increased almost immediately. Research spending has been kept low and Duracell has been perceived to be more innovative and has strengthened its market dominance. Nevertheless, Ever Ready has successfully introduced Gold Seal batteries to compete with Duracell.

Hanson sold Ever Ready in April 1992 'to help finance further acquisitions'.

## UDS

UDS was a collection of retail chains bought for £260 million in 1983. Sequentially, most of the company, including John Collier and Richard Shops, has been sold, with the single exception of Allders, duty-free shops and department stores. Hanson recouped in excess of the £260 million purchase price, and Allders has always proved profitable.

## US Industries

This US conglomerate cost Hanson $532 million in 1984. The corporation consisted of 30 subsidiary companies and included the manufacture of equipment for the motor industry, building materials, lighting, furniture and furnishings, and clothing. Parts of the business have been sold in seven separate transactions between 1984 and 1990.

## Imperial Group

Hanson won control of Imperial Group in 1986 for £2.8 billion, its largest acquisition to date. The bid had been unwelcome to the Imperial Group directors, who had encouraged shareholders to accept a rival offer from white-knight bidder, United Biscuits. Imperial had fought the Hanson bid aggressively, using mass media advertising as well as direct communications with shareholders. Their theme was that Hanson's style of management was not so much 'hands off' (decentralized – see later) as 'sell off', and they quoted selected facts about the earlier Berec deal. Imperial advertisements featured the sale of the advanced projects division, Berec's major research and development facility, the sale of two European operations to a major competitor, the 'slashing' of capital expenditure by 50%, battery prices being increased by 33% over four years, well above the rate of inflation, 40% of the UK workforce being made redundant, and a 20% loss of market share between 1981 and 1985. The company was bought in 1982.

Shareholders, however, believed that the company's future would be safer in Hanson's hands. Imperial, like the other major tobacco companies, had diversified extensively as cigarette smoking declined in the face of adverse publicity and health scares. Arguably, they had diversified too much too quickly, and had stretched both their management and their cash. Howard Johnson in the USA (the hotel and restaurant chain) had proved a major drain on resources, appearing to require management skills that Imperial did not have. This business had already been sold earlier in the 1980s and, in fairness, the group was already being turned around by a new chief executive. Return on capital employed, which had hovered around 10% throughout most of the 1970s, had risen to 20% by the mid-1980s.

In the financial year ended October 1985 Imperial Group sales amounted to £4.92 billion with pre-tax profits of £235.7 million. Approximately half of the sales and half of the profits were contributed by the tobacco interests.

Hanson acquired the following businesses and brands when it bought the Group:

| | |
|---|---|
| Tobacco | The existing John Player and Wills businesses and including the Embassy, Golden Virginia and St. Bruno brands |
| Foods | Ross Frozen Foods, Young Seafoods, Golden Wonder Crisps, HP and Lea & Perrin Sauces |
| Brewing | Courage – including John Smith and Harp Lager |
| Hotels | Anchor Hotels |
| Restaurants | Happy Eater Roadhouses, Welcome Break Motorway Service Areas |
| Shops | Finlays Newsagents. |

## Divestments

In 1986 the remaining hotels and restaurants were sold to Forte (then Trusthouse Forte) for £186 million. The sale was subject to approval from the Monopolies and Mergers Commission, which investigated the effect of linking the Happy Eater chain and the Welcome Break Services with Forte's Little Chef restaurants.

Hanson maintains that brewing was the one activity he really intended to keep, but that he received an offer (from Elders IXL of Australia) 'he simply could not refuse' in the interests of his shareholders. Courage was sold for £1.4 billion in 1986.

Also in 1986 Hanson sold Golden Wonder to Dalgety for £87 million. £1.7 billion (out of a purchase price of £2.8 billion) was thus recouped in the year of purchase.

Two years later HP and Lea & Perrin were sold to the major French food group, BSN, for £199 million. The sale of Ross Frozen Foods and Young Seafoods brought in another £335 million.

After two years Hanson had recouped over £2 billion, and he still retained all of the tobacco interests. Under Imperial, tobacco had been run as two businesses, Players and Wills, with separate sales forces, factories and head offices (in Nottingham and Bristol, respectively). Hanson rationalized the business into one company, combining the sales and marketing and retaining just two from the existing five factories. There are now fewer brands. Since 1986 staffing has been reduced by 46% without any loss of output, and operating costs have fallen by 25%. Productivity and profits have increased significantly, but market share in the UK has declined. Limited investment in state-of-the-art manufacturing technology has been directed at making Imperial the lowest cost producer in Europe.

## SCM

The American conglomerate SCM proved to be another controversial purchase. The company cost $930 million in 1986. The acquisition was fought aggressively in America and legal actions were involved. Early disposals of pulp and paper, paints and foods businesses recovered $935 million in the year of purchase. By 1990 SCM divestments had earned $1.6 billion for Hanson.

After the initial divestments Hanson retained Smith-Corona typewriters and the profitable SCM specialist chemicals businesses. A majority stake in Smith-Corona was floated controversially in 1989. The share price collapsed shortly after the flotation as the company struggled against intensifying Japanese competition. Stockholder lawsuits ensued, and these took two years to settle. Lord Gordon White has insisted that the shares were priced appropriately and that the Japanese were dumping.

## Kaiser

After selling McDonough's cement business, Hanson bought Kaiser in March 1987 for $250 million. Kaiser was the fifth largest cement business in the USA, and market leader in California. Hanson has since sold a number of the Kaiser cement plants.

Northwest Terminals and Montana City Plant were sold for $50 million shortly after the acquisition. Hanson then agreed to sell a 42.8% stake in Kaiser's Indonesian cement company to Mitsubishi Mining and Cement of Japan. The October 1987 sale of the San Antonio (Texas) plant was followed in February 1988 by the sale of the Lucerne Valley Plant in southern California. This last sale was again to Mitsubishi and it recovered $195 million.

Hanson had again earned back more than the purchase price and still retained a key plant in Northern California. Hanson commented that it was holding on to plants which had contributed over half of Kaiser's 1986–87 profits.

## Consolidated Gold Fields/Cavenham Forest Products

Consolidated Gold Fields cost Hanson £3.3 billion in 1989, and the acquisition included a 49% stake in Newmont Mining, the largest gold producer in America, and the whole of Gold Fields, another US mining business. Hanson now owned more gold in the ground than any other company outside South Africa.

After the purchase Hanson flagged that he was not looking for any long-term involvement and that

he would be happy to sell any parts. Initial negotiations failed to result in any sales and some press articles speculated that the failure to recover a proportion of the investment might prove to be a limiting factor in Hanson's future development.

In October 1990 Hanson announced that it was swapping its stake in Newmont for Cavenham Forest Products, 85% of which was owned by Sir James Goldsmith. Goldsmith stated that he regarded the exchange as a long-term investment and an opportunity to retire from active business.

Cavenham comprised US timberland and sawmills together with oil and gas interests. Cavenham was valued at $1.3 billion, but as Goldsmith was himself renowned as an expert dealer in assets, it seemed unlikely that there would be any significant potential gain from selling off parts of the group. However, the company was profitable and enjoyed a sound cash flow. Moreover, Hanson's Newmont stake was estimated to be worth $300 million less than Cavenham's assets.

There have been further sales of Consolidated assets, and to date over £2.5 billion has been recouped.

## Peabody

When Hanson bought Consolidated Gold Fields, its Newmont Mining subsidiary already owned part of Peabody Coal, the second largest coal producer in America. Hanson developed an interest in this business and acquired the whole of Peabody before Newmont was traded.

In January 1993 Hanson agreed another swap arrangement, this time with Santa Fe Pacific, the US railroads and minerals group. The exchange involved Hanson's remaining gold-mining interests, specifically Gold Fields, which it had always wanted to divest, and Santa Fe's coal mining and aggregates businesses. The deal required approval from the US Internal Revenue Service. The coal mines would be amalgamated with Peabody, the aggregates business with Beazer.

Coal has become Hanson's fastest growing business interest and represents 30% of its capital employed.

> *Coal will continue to be an important long-term source of energy in the US and new technologies will increase its efficiency as a low-cost fuel.*
>
> (Lord White, January 1993)

## Beazer

Hanson paid £350 million in 1991 to buy the Beazer building and construction business in a friendly acquisition. However, it also took on debts of £1.1 billion. Servicing this debt had given Beazer cash-flow problems. The business, which included Koppers, the second largest aggregates company in the USA, fitted in well with Hanson's existing interests. Hanson was able to reduce Beazer's financing charges immediately and thereby improve its profitability. Long-term, Hanson hopes to benefit in both the UK and the USA when investment in building and the infrastructure goes up after the economic recession.

## The Hanson strategy

Throughout this period of growth Hanson's strategy has been based upon three essential principles:

(i) The key objective of a business is the maximization of shareholder value.
(ii) Many companies fail to do this, and are therefore run badly.
(iii) Such companies are often good buys because their assets can be made to create more value for shareholders.

Lord Hanson, interviewed in *The Treasurer* (June 1987), highlights three pillars in his company's success:

- Hanson has selected countries and businesses very carefully
- They have sought to identify the key individual(s) who are essential for the success of the company. They have then sought to instil in them Hanson's important financial disciplines and to motivate them to produce results, and
- They have looked after both their shareholders and their customers. Hanson argues: 'Look after these and everything else falls into place. You can raise shareholder capital, your businesses are healthy, you can borrow for expansion. At the same time your employees have confidence in the knowledge that their jobs are securely based'.

After acquisition Hanson's main target is unnecessary overheads and waste. It is, for example, usually quite straightforward either to close or to reduce the size of the existing head office of the newly acquired business. The directors of the business may or may not stay once Hanson has bought the company – if they do stay they will not be offered a seat on the main Hanson board and they will have to achieve Hanson's new targets and expectations. In general, Hanson believes that in the case of underperforming, sleepy companies, middle management is likely to be stronger than the most senior management, and that control of the business should be handed over to them.

## Acquisitions

A typical Hanson purchase will be characterized by recent poor results. Quite often these will feature high gross margins (indicating sound products or services which enjoy market demand) but a much reduced pre-tax profit figure resulting from high, and probably excessive, overheads and high interest charges.

Hanson also looks at the amount of capital employed in the business, relative to its turnover, arguing that in many cases some of this capital could be taken out or better utilized. A final indicator of a potentially good buy is a market position which does not reflect the potential suggested by the company's assets, brands and reputation.

Hanson maintains a small but permanently active 'tracking team' for evaluating the current progress and worth of a large number of possible future acquisitions. Part of the secret is knowing the right moment at which to strike, and being ready and able to act when the opportunity arises. One ex-member of this team is Greg Hutchings, who left Hanson in 1983 to become chief executive of the equally acquisitive F.H. Tomkins, the company which thwarted Hanson's bid for RHM in 1992.

Hanson believes that the strategy can be applied successfully in a wide range of industries, including services; and on the strength of this conviction Hanson has diversified into a number of unrelated areas. Earlier sections of this case showed how Hanson acquired businesses in construction, bricks, textiles, animal foods and meat processing, pulp, gold, coal and chemicals. For many years Hanson concentrated on consumer-orientated businesses in manufacturing, service and distribution. Cyclical businesses have also been attractive targets, but those that require expensive research and development with 'a prospect of a return sometime or never' (Lord Hanson) have been avoided.

The case has also described how Hanson divests companies and business units when they are not appropriate for their strategy. In the main, businesses in competitive industries, and those which require investment, are sold, and mature, slow-growth companies retained.

## The outcome

Exhibit 2 confirms that in the early 1990s the majority of Hanson's profits stemmed from mature industries. Despite the lack of growth potential in such mature industries, the restructuring strategy pursued by Hanson has generated a high and consistent growth in group profits.

It could also be argued that Hanson has avoided industries where they might not understand the key success factors. In particular, Lord White was anxious to avoid any real downside risk – where the risk of failure outweighs the benefits of success. Lord Hanson has suggested that White always looks for trouble with prospective deals, and that as a result the company has undoubtedly missed out on potentially good deals.

Earnings per share (the key measure for shareholders) are maximized when business units achieve the highest possible sustainable return on capital employed. Earnings per share can be improved by increasing returns from existing capital resources, or by maintaining earnings while reducing the capital employed to produce them. These themes explain the thinking behind the Hanson strategy.

Hanson, in common with certain other acquisitive diversifiers, is not necessarily committed to stay-ing in particular industries once the opportunities for increasing returns have been exploited. A restructuring strategy, like the one pursued by Hanson, dictates that businesses should be sold once their earnings cannot be increased any further. The money from their sale should be reinvested in companies with greater potential. Through most of the history of Hanson, profits in the acquired businesses have soared very quickly after purchase. Costs, workforces and investment programmes have been reduced as Hanson does not rely on organic growth within the businesses. Once profits stagnate, as for example they did at both Smith-Corona and Ever Ready, the companies are often available for sale.

Shareholders in companies such as Hanson expect to see constantly increasing returns and speedy turnarounds; and consequently Hanson is thought to take a prospective acquisition seriously only if the cost is realistically recoverable in under four years – from a mixture of asset sales and improved profits. In fact, Hanson expects the company to be profitable in the first year after purchase. Although earnings per share could be enhanced by preferring debt financing to increased equity, Hanson is fundamentally risk-averse and anxious to maintain a relatively low debt ratio.

Although Hanson seeks market share and critical mass in industries, in order to achieve economies of scale, it is not necessarily looking to be global players in these industries. Hanson has commented that he is not interested, for example, in being a major brick manufacturer in the USA or in having an involvement in garden tools in the UK.

## Structure and control

Structurally, therefore, the focus is on profit centres rather than products. Business units are decentralized and given 'demanding but realistic' targets to achieve. Hanson maintains only a small head office of around 20 staff who concentrate on policy and financial control. There are few layers of management and short lines of communication.

Managing directors of the businesses are given considerable independence as long as they achieve their agreed targets. 'Royal visits' to the factories from either Hanson or White are very rare. Capital investments in excess of £500 or $1000 have to be approved by either Hanson or White. Within these financial constraints businesses can adapt their competitive and functional strategies. There is a very strong emphasis on cash flow, and budgets are 'intentional rather than hopeful' – managers must intend to achieve them. Profits will be reinvested in the businesses that earn them, but only if they can produce further increases in profits. Hanson has a philosophy of 'earn before you spend'.

Weekly and monthly financial returns are sent to London (head office) for scrutiny, and each company holds a monthly board meeting. Budgets are produced initially in mid-Summer, and agreed with the main board, and they are then reviewed in the following February after four months' trading – the financial year runs from October to September. The revised targets are the ones that the companies and their managers *must* achieve.

Hanson motivates its managers with both a stick and a carrot. Unit managers are required to accept personal responsibility for achieving their targets and for the success of their business. 'Managers are not required to walk on water, but they are required to produce what they promised' (Lord Hanson, quoted in the *Financial Times*, 22 August 1990). If they exceed their budget targets they can earn substantial bonuses.

The UK and US arms of Hanson are run as separate businesses with separate treasuries. Different rules for borrowing and acquisition apply, with most US purchases being financed by debt, which is frequently secured against the value of the assets being acquired. The UK head office acts as a holding company. There are, however, very strong information flows between the USA and London.

### Taxation management

A final important aspect of Hanson's strategy and success has been an ability to manage company funds and transactions globally in such a way that tax is avoided (legally) as much as possible. Hanson is reputed to be a master at this. Between 1985 and 1994 Hanson paid, on average, 22% of its profits in UK corporation tax and its USA equivalent. The highest percentage over the period was 28% (in 1993); the lowest, 15% in 1992. The prevailing tax rates were 35% in the UK and 34% (plus State taxes) in the USA.

### A new strategy?

Some commentators have argued that Hanson 'cannot behave in the 1990s as it did in the 1980s', when it appeared to have a golden touch and built up a formidable reputation as well as a strong and successful business. There will be fewer opportunities to acquire and break-up companies; and consequently Hanson will have to focus on running the businesses it owns if it is to maintain profits growth.

In February 1992 Hanson announced that in the future the company would concentrate on running and expanding the group's core businesses and making further disposals of periphery activities. Hanson would no longer be a trader in assets, and instead would be dedicated to building and managing selected businesses.

By the early 1990s Hanson was involved in a variety of diverse industries, seven of which were designated core:

| UK | USA |
|---|---|
| *Core businesses* | *Core businesses* |
| Aggregates and bricks | Cement and |
| Tobacco | aggregates |
| | Chemicals |
| *Other businesses* | Coal mining |
| Food | Forestry |
| Textiles | Crane manufacture |
| Batteries (divested 1992) | (Grove) |
| Retailing | |
| | *Other businesses* |
| | Shoes |
| | Garden tools |
| | Electrical fittings and |
| | goods |

Hanson argued that its future strategy would involve further acquisitions of suitable companies which could be bolted on to existing core activities. The managing directors of the individual core businesses would be encouraged to follow the lead of Hanson head office, and seek out and cost potential buys. Justifiable organic growth might also be funded. In the past such internal investment has been rare. The other businesses would be retained, sold or floated off, the choice depending upon the opportunities for each one.

Although these changes have been implemented, Hanson has not switched over exclusively to the new strategy. Opportunistic acquisitions are still considered. In 1992, for example, Hanson bid for UK foods company Ranks Hovis McDougall. When challenged about how this fitted in to the newly declared strategy, Hanson commented that buying RHM was still consistent with the stated objective of maximizing the value of the business for its shareholders.

In addition, Hanson's chief executive in the UK, Derek Bonham, stated: '*Core* means a significant market sector which we think is capable of responding to our management style. It does not mean that such a business will never be sold, nor that the existing list of core businesses cannot be extended'.

Hanson's failure to acquire RHM provoked some analysts to comment that the company might be losing its touch. RHM was not Hanson's only recent disappointment.

## Non-events and failed acquisition attempts

In 1985 Hanson's £147 million bid for Powell Duffryn was rejected by that company's shareholders, and at this time such an occurrence was unusual. However, the situation began to change in 1990.

In 1990 Hanson expressed an interest in buying PowerGen from the UK government. PowerGen was the smaller of two electricity-generating companies to be created when the industry was privatized. Contrary to previous Hanson practice, electricity generating involves high technology supported by research and development. In addition, it was speculated that Hanson would have to adopt a much more hands-on style of management with Power-Gen. Had it bought the company, PowerGen would have constituted the largest business in the Hanson portfolio, but Hanson withdrew.

In 1992 Hanson also discussed buying at least part of the Canary Wharf development in London's Docklands, after the owners, Canadian company Olympia and York, went into receivership. Hanson again withdrew.

In between these two forays Hanson had bought a stake in ICI. In all three instances, but especially with ICI, Hanson's move had attracted considerable attention and publicity, much of it adverse.

## ICI – a bridge too far?

In May 1991 Hanson paid £240 million for a 2.8% shareholding in ICI. ICI is a global business in chemicals and pharmaceuticals. Once this was made public it fuelled an immediate controversy concerning whether Hanson intended to bid for the whole company, and what its longer-term intentions might be. It was acknowledged that ICI was underperforming and that more value could be squeezed from its assets. A combination of Hanson and ICI would, though, constitute a truly global force. Hanson quickly denied that a bid was in the offing, claiming that ICI's shares were priced attractively and that this was merely a strategic investment.

However, it was known that in 1988 Lord Hanson had approached ICI chairman Sir Denys Henderson and proposed that Hanson should acquire a 20% stake in ICI together with boardroom representation. This suggestion had been rejected. Since 1988 ICI's profits have declined, and Hanson believed that this was only partially the result of the economic recession.

Henderson opposed Hanson's intervention openly and vociferously. He complained that Hanson 'does not care about building businesses ... ICI is not a box of chocolates that can be unwrapped and sold off one-by-one'. ICI analysts and their advisers effectively turned Hanson's style and results inside-out in their defence against a possible bid, and the publicity created has probably tarnished the Hanson image, possibly for ever.

The speculation attracted interest and comment from various other stakeholders. The banking community questioned how Hanson could finance such an acquisition, speculating that it would require

£11 billion. Hanson had, at the time, £7 billion debts, but £7 billion in reserves and investments. Possibly additional borrowings of some £6 billion would be required. Hanson's assets would certainly support this, but it would leave the company very highly geared. Moreover, would the banks actually lend Hanson this amount of money? Acquiring ICI by issuing Hanson shares would certainly lead to a dilution of earnings.

The regulatory authorities would have to be involved, and probably the issue would be dealt with in Brussels by the European Commission rather than solely in the UK by the Monopolies and Mergers Commission. Trade unions called for the immediate involvement of the MMC in order to slow things down. Opposition Labour MPs demanded that the Government should express their opposition, but the Government was non-commital.

Other analysts commented that, like Power Gen, this would require a different style of management with a more involved head office. Nevertheless, few denied that ICI could benefit from Hanson's tight financial management for improving its efficiencies. Some asset sales would be inevitable if Hanson were to avoid a major involvement in the highly speculative, research-driven, pharmaceuticals industry.

Hanson never actually bid and later sold their shares for a substantial profit. ICI announced a major restructuring, involving splitting the corporation into two separate businesses (for details of this split see Minicase 19.2 in the main text).

## The bid for Ranks Hovis McDougall

Hanson made a hostile £780 million cash bid for RHM in October 1992. RHM is involved in milling, bakeries and grocery products. The company is the UK's second largest baker and it had already rationalized its bakeries in the face of intense competition.

Four years earlier RHM had successfully fought off a bid from a leading New Zealand bakery business. In 1989 a consortium involving Sir James Goldsmith became the company's largest shareholder with a 28.5% stake, but these shares had been sold in 1991.

Between 1988 and 1992 both sales and profits had declined, and arguably the company looked vulnerable with a depressed share price. Had Hanson timed it right? Hanson was bidding 220 pence per share. The current price was 175 pence, but three years earlier the shares were trading for 465 pence.

Despite their newly declared strategy it was assumed that Hanson would look to sell the RHM packaged grocery companies. When such businesses had been acquired with the purchases of Imperial and SCM they had been sold at the first suitable opportunity. In any case, if RHM could be acquired for a relatively low price the parts might well be worth more than the whole.

RHM opposed the Hanson bid, and after considering their response the RHM chairman declared an intention to split the company into three separate businesses, namely flourmilling and baking, grocery and speciality products and cakes (notably the Mr Kipling brand). RHM also announced the agreed purchase of a bakery business from Dalgety for £28 million. By this time the share price had risen to 246 pence. Hanson's reaction was that this confirmed that there really was strategic logic in what they did, but added that they felt RHM's approach to splitting up the company was 'clumsy'.

At the end of the same month a rival bidder appeared. FH Tomkins, run by Greg Hutchings, previously an acquisition specialist at Hanson, bid £935 million. Tomkins is another diversified conglomerate, whose portfolio includes Smith and Wesson handguns and lawnmowers. Early in November Hanson withdrew from the competition, only the second time it had ever lost a hostile take-over battle.

The *Financial Times* stated: 'Regarded as the consummate deal maker of the 1980s Hanson has failed to pull off a number of big deals in the 1990s'.

## Lord James Hanson

*Who is the man behind the business which is 'feared, loathed, admired and praised?'*
(*Financial Times*, 22 August 1990)

The company's head office overlooks the gardens of Buckingham Palace, and Hanson's own office is said to resemble a well-appointed living room. It is characterized by wood panelling, plush carpeting and shelves full of photographs of his family and friends. Easy listening music plays in the background. But this 'furnace' (as it has been described by Hanson executives) is the source of the energy and power which drives the company.

James Hanson was born in Huddersfield and, after military service, he initially joined his family transport business. When the haulage industry was nationalized in 1948 James crossed the Atlantic and, in partnership with his brother, founded Hanson Haulage in Canada. This business was sold in the early 1960s and James Hanson returned to Yorkshire to take a controlling interest in Oswald Tillotson, a distributor of commercial vehicles. The development of Hanson plc from this stage has already been described. James Hanson was knighted in 1976 and made a peer in 1983.

Hanson has been described as socially confident and charming, impeccably dressed and skilled at dealing with people. He is loyal to his employees and, in turn, inspires their loyalty. He has a temper, though, which is occasionally evident if he is challenged.

He is reported to be anxious that Hanson plc should behave ethically, and that it should enjoy a positive image and reputation. There have been instances where these concerns have been tested. For example, Hanson was once forced on to the defensive at an Annual General Meeting when it was highlighted that the company had invested £12 million in racehorses without shareholder approval. Lord White is a fanatical racegoer and Hanson plc, using the Ever Ready brand name, has sponsored the Derby.

Unlike Lord White, who has a high social profile, James Hanson has allegedly few interests outside work. Before he started Hanson in the 1960s he earned a reputation as something of a playboy, but for many years he has led a settled family life. He moves between his houses (in London, Berkshire, Los Angeles and Palm Springs), living in America for a considerable part of each year. Hanson was popular with Mrs Thatcher, but it has been said that their friendship cooled after he once chose to arrive at Chequers in his private helicopter.

Proud of his Yorkshire origins, Hanson says that in business he has been cautious and followed 'basic North-country business sense ... you do not over-borrow'. One measure of success that he jokes about is the fact that bankers now visit the company, whereas in the early days Hanson and White always had to visit the bank manager. Generally, Hanson is likely to buy businesses by spending its cash, and then borrowing to replenish the reserves. Hanson believes in borrowing money but always paying it back on time. Companies that succeed in doing this can always borrow more.

Hanson plc is unquestionably a very personal business which has always been dependent upon Lords Hanson and White, their long-standing friendship and their ability to work together. A former director has described the Hanson culture as 'a solar system, with everyone circling around the sun in the middle, James Hanson. Employees are encouraged to work within clear parameters and not to expect regular promotion'.

Lord Hanson believes that he has been a successful strategic leader because he has:

- ensured that he has stayed informed
- wanted to actually do things in business
- deployed his not inconsiderable energy into making things happen
- been able to inspire others to do things
- stayed responsive to change pressures.

## The future

James Hanson was 70 in January 1992, with Gordon White due to reach the same age in 1993. On his 69th birthday Hanson had announced that he and White intended to stay active in the company until 1997. Some commentators suggested that they believe in their own immortality and indispensability.

Succession, though, has not been wholly ignored. Hanson's son, Robert, is a main board member, together with the husband of one of Hanson's nieces. In 1992 a new chief executive post was created in the UK and filled by Derek Bonham. David

Clarke has acted as chief executive in the USA for some time.

But where does Hanson plc go next? The bottom line has always taken precedence over size, but companies such as Hanson grow primarily by constantly acquiring new businesses. However, as a take-over specialist grows ever larger, their targets also need to get bigger if they are to maintain any momentum. What size and type of business constituted a suitable acquisition for Hanson in the 1990s? Does this requirement explain the dalliance with ICI?

When profits fell for the first time in 1992, Hanson's share price, 40% above the FT all-share index in 1990, also fell to a premium of just 20%. If these trends were to continue any substantial acquisition funded by equity is likely to dilute earnings. However, the decline in profits and fortune may have been solely due to the recession, in which case Hanson's profits would bounce back up when the economy grew again. Others believe that Hanson and White have lost their way a little in recent years, although acknowledging that the Beazer purchase was 'classic Hanson'. These critics contend that Hanson and White will be unable to 'turn the clocks back to their glory days'.

Could Hanson plc conceivably become an acquisition and break-up target itself? Or will it always be able to find a suitable deal? Mainland Europe must offer new potential opportunities, especially with the single market in place. However, issues of corporate ownership and governance mean that friendly acquisitions are more likely than hostile take-overs to be a feature of a European expansion strategy.

## Questions

1. Describe and evaluate the key aspects of the Hanson strategy during the 1970s and 1980s.
   How did Hanson plc evolve through acquisition?
   Assess the strategic position at the end of the 1980s.

2. What are the limitations to this strategy?

3. Was the declared new strategy more appropriate for the 1990s?

4. Does 'Hansonizing' provide lessons for other companies?

5. Describe and assess Hanson's style of management.

6. If you were a shareholder in Hanson how would you evaluate the company's future prospects?

7. What contribution to the National economy does a company such as Hanson make?

# Hanson (B)

Hanson (B) is a continuation from the A case. It discusses the changes to the company and its corporate strategy after 1992.

It has been written to provoke discussion on four further important strategic issues:

- strategic lifecycles
- the diversification versus focus argument
- the rationale for the financial control style of corporate management
- strategic leadership succession.

This case was written in 1996 by John Thompson. It is for classroom discussion and should not be taken to reflect either effective or ineffective management.

## Introduction

For over 25 years from the mid-1960s, led by Lord Hanson in the UK and Lord White in the USA, Hanson grew relentlessly. The company's profits and share price continued to climb every year, and Hanson shares outperformed the FTSE All Share index. However, the company's fortunes changed in the early 1990s when Hanson suffered its first ever profits decline.

The graphs below (source: FT Extel) show how the FTSE All Share index grew by nearly 50% between 1990 and 1995, while Hanson shares declined by 3%. During 1995 the index grew by 15%; Hanson shares were now falling at a rate of 5%. Exhibits 1

and 2 provide a summary of the key Balance Sheet and Profit and Loss Account figures for the 1991–1995 period.

At the beginning of 1996 Hanson announced that the company was to be split into four separate businesses.

What had happened to the company which had successfully carried through 35 agreed acquisitions and six hostile take-overs – disposing of some 40 businesses and failing with 15 other hostile bids over the same 30-year period? Was there any convincing argument for retaining Hanson as a single Anglo-American entity? Was the diversified conglomerate strategy, practised superbly by Hanson, no longer appropriate? Or had Hanson individually run out of

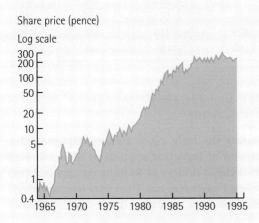

Share price (pence)
Log scale

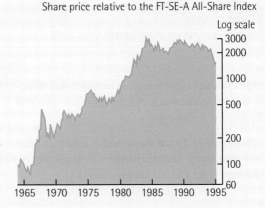

Share price relative to the FT-SE-A All-Share Index
Log scale

*Exhibit 1*   Hanson plc – extracted items from the balance sheet 1991–1995

| | Year ended 30.9 | | | | |
| | 1991 £m | 1992 £m | 1993 £m | 1994 £m | 1995 £m |
|---|---|---|---|---|---|
| Total fixed assets | 6199 | 9146 | 12,195 | 11,386 | 12,968 |
| Investments | 429 | 191 | 236 | 221 | 203 |
| Current assets | | | | | |
| – Stock and work-in-progress | 992 | 1318 | 1746 | 1184 | 1028 |
| – Debtors | 1192 | 1441 | 1813 | 1930 | 2015 |
| – Cash and investments | 7771 | 8445 | 8067 | 6815 | 7419 |
| Total current assets | 9955 | 11,204 | 11,626 | 9929 | 10,462 |
| Total current liabilities | 4751 | 6386 | 7065 | 6704 | 10,377 |
| Net current assets | 5204 | 4818 | 4561 | 3225 | 85 |
| Net assets | 11,832 | 14,155 | 16,992 | 14,832 | 13,256 |
| Share capital and reserves | 3325 | 4224 | 3953 | 4598 | 3623 |
| Long-term loans and provisions | 8507 | 9931 | 13,039 | 10,234 | 9633 |
| Total capital employed | 11,832 | 14,155 | 16,992 | 14,832 | 13,256 |

*Exhibit 2*   Hanson plc – extracted items from the profit and loss account 1991–1995

| | Year ended 30.9 | | | | |
| | 1991 £m | 1992 £m | 1993 £m | 1994 £m | 1995 £m |
|---|---|---|---|---|---|
| Trading income | 7691 | 8798 | 9760 | 11,199 | 11,390 |
| Interest received | 941 | 844 | 619 | 325 | 397 |
| Interest charges | 741 | 777 | 600 | 545 | 604 |
| Published pre-tax profits | 1319 | 1286 | 1016 | 1346 | 1275 |
| Less: published tax | 284 | 197 | 282 | 281 | 260 |
| ordinary dividends | 529 | 265 | 551 | 597 | 1181 |
| Retained earnings | 577 | 824 | 183 | 468 | (166) |
| Published earnings per share (pence) | 21.55 | 22.62 | 14.91 | 20.60 | 19.61 |

inspiration and opportunity? How much was strategic leadership an issue in the change of fortunes and the decision to demerge?

> *The purpose of life and the purpose of a job is to enjoy the adventure ... while the numbers are important, if business is not fun, it is not worth doing.*
>
> (Lord White of Hull, 1923–1995)

## The main strategic changes, 1993–1995

During the early 1990s Hanson implemented a number of important acquisitions while following its declared strategy of focusing on (and building) selected core businesses. There were several strategic disposals at the same time. It appeared that Hanson had regained its touch with a new sense of direction and a modified strategic approach.

## Acquisitions

In June 1993 Hanson bought a waste disposal business, *Econowaste*, from Tarmac. Econowaste was involved with waste-site management and waste haulage and it was to be incorporated into ARC, the quarrying business that Hanson had acquired with Cavenham Forest Products. Hanson was now the third largest landfill operator in the UK.

One month later Hanson bought the American company *Quantum Chemicals* for $3.2 billion, its largest ever American acquisition. The bid was a friendly one; and Quantum would join Hanson's SCM Chemicals business. Quantum is one of America's largest bulk chemical manufacturers, focusing on plastics products, but competing in nine distinct market segments. It holds two market leaderships, six second places and one third position in these nine segments.

Afterwards, the 'strike' was described as a 'classic Hanson deal' as it was concluded virtually at the end of a major recession in the chemicals industry. Consequently, the price was favourable to Hanson. Sales, prices and profits have all risen since 1993. Taking just one example, polyethylene prices rose gradually from 29 to 52 cents per pound (although more recently they have fallen back again) and it was claimed that Hanson's profits increased (or decreased) by $40 million for every one cent price change. Hanson has successfully refinanced Quantum's debts and reduced its interest charges, and invested selectively in a number of subsidiary activities.

In July 1994 there was another agreed bolt-on acquisition in the UK. *Scholes*, the UK electrical installation equipment manufacturer, was bought for £96.1 million to link with Crabtree, which it had acquired with Berec (Ever Ready) and retained when most of the rest of the Berec businesses had been divested. Analysts saw the acquisition as defensive, in the face of strengthening European competition in the UK market. Combined, Scholes and Crabtree would have a 23% share of the UK circuit protection

market, equal to that of the current market leader, the French company Schneider.

Hanson bought Exxon Coal's *Carter Mining* subsidiary for $360 million in October 1994. Carter would join Peabody Coal; both companies mine low-sulphur, clean-burning coal.

Hanson's energy interests were boosted in July 1995 when it bought the profitable electricity *distribution* company *Eastern Electricity*. Eastern was one of the largest RECs (regional electricity companies) to emerge from the privatization of the electricity industry in the UK. At an agreed price of £2.3 billion, it was Hanson's largest acquisition in the UK since Consolidated Gold Fields in 1989. It was the first major deal to be implemented by the new chief executive, Derek Bonham.

Eastern, led by a highly respected management team, brought with it a shareholding in the National Grid (which would have to be sold) and two gas-fired power stations. Eastern had diversified more than most of the other RECs, and was supplying gas to a range of industrial and commercial customers, including McDonald's. Hanson quickly expressed an interest in buying additional power stations from the electricity *generators*, particularly National Power.

## Geographical expansion

Hanson established an office in Hong Kong in March 1994, with the brief of searching out new opportunities in the Asia Pacific region. Previously, Hanson had concentrated almost exclusively on activities in the UK and America. Lord Hanson's son, Robert, then aged 33, was put in charge of the new venture. It was assumed that the most likely developments would be joint ventures for Peabody Coal, SCM Chemicals, Imperial Tobacco and Cavenham Forest Products.

Imperial Tobacco now has a joint venture production unit in China, and in 1995 Hanson began actively to pursue investment opportunities in power-generation projects in India, Indonesia and China.

## Disposals

Hanson continued to seek disposal opportunities for non-core businesses and when, in December 1993, 11 disparate companies were sold to a management buy-out team for £90 million, Hanson's earnings from corporate divestments in 1993 reached £250 million. The trend continued in the following year when, for example, Seven Seas, the UK vitamins manufacturer, was sold for £150 million.

In 1994 Hanson's house-building activities in the UK (Beazer) and USA were floated off as independent businesses to raise some £550 million.

Thirty-four assorted US businesses were demerged as an independent company, US Industries, in February 1995; the new head was David Clarke, who had been the chief executive of Hanson's operations in the USA and Lord White's apparent successor. These businesses had accounted for 17% of group turnover in 1994, and 15% of pre-tax profits. They included various household and leisure products, including bath and lighting goods, windows, automotive components, office furniture and shoes, as well as Hanson's remaining shareholding in Smith Corona office equipment.

Later in the same year Hanson announced its plans to float Suburban Propane, a subsidiary of Quantum, in the USA and to break up Cavenham Forest Products for sale in a number of lots. Altogether, these disposals should realize a further £1.5 billion.

## Outcomes

The various Hanson businesses performed with different levels of success in the 1990s. Coal mining saw profits fall in both 1992 and 1993 when there was a major coal strike in the USA. Profits doubled in the following year, but the trend was generally downwards. Profits for Hanson's total energy interests were boosted by the acquisition of Eastern Electricity.

Chemicals profits fell in 1992, stabilized in 1993 and grew in 1994 and 1995, especially after the acquisition of Quantum. They began to fall back again in early 1996 as another recession bit.

Tobacco profits have risen throughout the period; forestry products grew for three years but fell in 1995. Aggregates followed two years of falling profits with two years of growth.

The following table summarizes the situation in 1995:

| Activity | Turnover £m | Operating profits £m |
|---|---|---|
| Chemicals | 2020 | 591 |
| Tobacco | 3570 | 348 |
| Energy | 3500 | 460 |
| Bricks, aggregates and associated products | 2300 | 286 |

Structurally, Hanson included businesses which are important and valuable cash generators: aggregates and particularly tobacco. However, Hanson is also entrenched in industries which are notoriously cyclical: chemicals and natural resources. This raises two important questions. Which businesses were the cash generation supporting? And, given Hanson's long history of strong dividends, was investment capital being channelled to the most appropriate opportunities?

## Changes in strategic leadership

The 1992–1993 Annual Report clarified that Derek Bonham was the most likely candidate to succeed Lord Hanson as Chairman of Hanson plc when he stepped down; his retirement was being planned for early 1997, the year when he would be 75 years old. To this end, Bonham, who was 50 years old, was promoted to the position of deputy chairman; he had been the UK chief executive since April 1992.

In 1995 Christopher Collins, the husband of Lord Hanson's niece, became vice chairman of Hanson plc at the age of 55. At the same time, Hanson's son Robert was given the post relinquished by Collins, that of corporate development director.

The *Financial Times* reported that some investment managers 'were unhappy with the corporate structure ... the business was meeting a dead end ... succession was a problem ... Hanson Jr. was not the City's choice'.

Bill Landuyt, a 40-year-old American who was currently finance director for Hanson and based in the UK, returned to the USA in 1995 to replace David Clarke as head of US operations.

Clarke had been mentored by Lord White; he was seen as a similarly entrepreneurial deal-maker. Both Bonham and Landuyt were accountants, as was Lord Hanson by profession. The latest appointments were taken to reflect a general drift to internally driven growth with less reliance on the large acquisitions that had characterized Hanson in the 1980s, and which were proving to be increasingly difficult to find and implement in the 1990s.

The following comment sums up Hanson's new dilemma:

> *Hanson was an acquisition-driven company. The people who are the likely successors are not acquisition people – they are operating people. If Hanson remains in its current form, who will do the acquisition strategy?*

## The death of Lord White

When Lord White died in August 1995 his role had already been largely wound down to that of consultant to the company which he had helped to found and develop. The growth and prosperity of Hanson owed much to White, especially after he began the US operations in 1973. Under his stewardship and with his deal-making Hanson had become the largest foreign corporate investor in the USA. One obituary commented: 'the great White shark was able to merge his own unique deal-making instincts with an environment more favourable to predators than in any other era'.

## Plans to demerge

Five months after the death of Lord White, in January 1996, Lord Hanson announced his intention to split the corporation into four separate companies. Existing investors would receive shares in all the new businesses; clearer details of the demerger would emerge in the next few months. Had Hanson learned the benefits of demerger from the ICI/Zeneca split which followed Hanson's shareholding incursion into ICI – a foray which began a wave of hostile comment and publicity and which arguably tarnished the Hanson reputation permanently?

Lord Hanson argued that 'demerger is an exciting and radical move' and the *Financial Times* agreed. Commenting that this was 'as bold a move as any of Hanson's large take-overs', the FT quoted one large investor as saying: 'We always thought Lord Hanson would want to go out with a bang and this is the right thing to do for shareholders'.

Nevertheless, Hanson had always been expert at finding new opportunities for reducing waste and costs and for adding value to the businesses that it acquired. The four new businesses would have few opportunities for adding extra value. Moreover, would they each need a corporate head office, a 'luxury' that Hanson had been careful to restrict? Analysts also assumed that both debt costs and taxation rates would increase when the benefits of Hanson corporate ownership were lost. These had been important sources of competitive advantage for Hanson.

While suitable bolt-on acquisitions for each business might now be easier to find and integrate, the smaller companies might themselves be more vulnerable to take-over. The whole Hanson had seemed generally resistant to a hostile bid as it was accepted that any predator who attempted to buy Hanson and then divest Imperial Tobacco or the US chemicals businesses would face huge capital gains tax demands.

The US chemicals businesses would be the first to demerge; they would begin trading as an independent American company called Millennium Chemicals on 1 October 1996. The other businesses would follow systematically in the following few months. It was predicted that some £4 billion long-term loans would remain; these had to be allocated to the businesses. It appeared that they would be divided as follows: chemicals, £1.4 billion; tobacco and energy, £1.2 billion each; building activities, £0.2 billion.

The final section of this case briefly considers the prospects for the new companies.

## Millennium Chemicals

Very profitable in 1994 and 1995, the chemicals business was performing less well in the early months of 1996 with the onset of another industry recession. Growth was forecast again for 1997, however. The new chairman and chief executive of Millennium was to be Bill Landuyt.

In the main, Millennium comprises two different chemicals companies, SCM and Quantum, both of which are medium sized in their differently volatile sectors of the industry. Quantum specializes in plastics, and arguably has not invested in the latest technology for all its key markets. SCM's main product is titanium dioxide, which provides the white pigment for a variety of coatings products used in the paper and paints industries. Earlier in the 1990s this sector had been plagued by overcapacity, but a resurgence of demand had brought back the profits. SCM has invested in new technology and plant to become the second largest producer, behind Du Pont and ahead of ICI Tioxide. The third, and smallest, Millennium business is Gildco, a niche producer which makes turpentine-based fragrances and flavours.

## Imperial Tobacco

At face value Imperial Tobacco returned an operating profit of £348 million on a turnover of £3.57 billion in 1995, a rate of 9.7%. However, when excise duties are removed, turnover drops to £780 million, showing a profitability ratio of 45%. Given that the business employs capital of just £54 million, its return on capital employed is 650%. Derek Bonham was to be the new chairman; the chief executive would be Gareth Davis rather than Ron Fulford, who had been largely responsible for turning the business around and who had elected to retire.

Imperial Tobacco holds the number two spot in the UK market, but it has recently increased its sales force from 400 to 450 and is thought likely to replace Gallahers as the market leader. Hanson's main brands are JPS (John Player Specials) and Embassy; Gallahers, owned by American Brands, owns the Benson and Hedges and Silk Cut brands. Imperial has an estimated 38% share of the UK market which in aggregate terms is declining by approximately 2% per year.

Since it acquired the business, Hanson has dramatically improved its productivity (which trebled between 1987 and 1995) and made it the most efficient and lowest cost cigarette manufacturer in Europe. Nevertheless, it ranks only 22nd among world producers; BAT (British American Tobacco), the world leader and a company which, for historical reasons, does not manufacture in the UK, makes 20 times as many cigarettes.

Imperial's real growth prospects are outside the UK. The relative contribution of exports has grown from 5 to 15% in the 1990s. Western Europe, Eastern Europe and East Asia are all prospects for further expansion. Although Imperial has a joint venture in China it has yet to develop production plants overseas.

The current tax burden is just 11%; experts predict this will at least double once it is outside Hanson. Imperial could either become a take-over target or perhaps look to acquire another tobacco manufacturer. One possibility might be Gallahers if American Brands would sell it.

## Energy

The launch name for the energy businesses was still to be confirmed in summer 1996. However, it was clear that the company would have a joint listing in the UK and USA. Derek Bonham would again be the chairman and there would be joint chief executives, one for each main business.

Peabody is the world's largest private-sector coal manufacturer; its main uncertainty is the possibility of healthcare liabilities in the USA for black lung disease.

The profitable Eastern Electricity is seeking to expand its generating capacity to obtain synergy with its distribution activities. In 1996 it was awaiting the outcome of a Monopolies and Mergers Commission report concerning its desire to acquire power stations from National Power.

## Hanson (Building)

Hanson's bricks and aggregates businesses were the ones chosen to retain the Hanson name. Lord Hanson would chair the company until 1997, when he would be replaced by Christopher Collins. Andrew Dougal, who succeeded Bill Landuyt as

Hanson finance director, is the chief executive. The company inherited almost no debt and will again enjoy a joint UK/USA listing.

Hanson is the UK's largest brick manufacturer, with 30% of the market. Recently, it has been expanding into Europe with the acquisition of Belgium's leading brick company.

Hanson is one of the world's largest quarry operators, supplying rock, sand and gravel to the construction industries in the UK and the USA. ARC (second in the UK market behind Tarmac, and with an 18% share) has low overheads and is a cash generator along the lines of tobacco.

The new Hanson also inherited Grove, the world's leading manufacturer of cranes, Hanson Electrical, which manufactures a range of products from plugs to switchgear, and Hanson's 12.5% shareholding in National Grid – which it has to sell and which should yield in the order of £400 million. Grove and Hanson Electrical could be offered for sale, with the resulting income used to buy new aggregates businesses to seize market leadership.

*Hanson: http://www.hanson.com*
*Hanson plc: http://www.hansonplc.com*

## Questions

1. Did the acquisitions and disposals in the 1990s suggest that Hanson had rediscovered its deal-making skills? Did they fit Hanson's declared new strategy of concentrating on core activities?

2. Did the decision to change the structure of Hanson follow logically from the corporate strategy it was pursuing?
   How would you evaluate the prospects for the four new businesses?

3. Was the demerger decision the most appropriate for the company and its shareholders? Was it a defensive reaction to circumstances? Did it suggest that Lord Hanson was being astute, creative and proactive – or that maybe he simply did not want to leave behind the business that he had created?

4. Does the conglomerate diversification strategy have a future?

# Hanson (C)

Hanson (C) is a continuation from the B case. It discusses how the aggregates and building products business – the one to retain the Hanson name after the corporate split in 1997 – has developed and, in particular, its acquisition strategy. It has been written to enable a discussion on focused diversification and to encourage a debate on the differences between this business and the earlier conglomerate style of the original Hanson.

This case was written in 2000 by John L Thompson. It is for classroom discussion and should not be taken to reflect either effective or ineffective management.

## The corporate split

The four new businesses created from the original Hanson began trading independently on 24 February 1997. The businesses were: Imperial Tobacco, Millennium Chemicals, The Energy Group and Hanson (building products). US Industries had been formed earlier when a number of diverse US businesses was floated off as a separate venture. Shortly afterwards, both Hanson and Imperial Tobacco, the two shares being traded on the London Stock Exchange, retained a place in the Financial Times FTSE-100 Index (the index which tracks the share prices of the UK's largest 100 companies) despite being placed 101st and 103rd, respectively, in the actual capitalization rankings. Had the Hanson name been removed it would have been the first time ever in the company's history that it had not been a member of the index. In September 1997, however, Hanson was removed, only to regain its place just over a year later.

## The new Hanson

As planned by Lord Hanson, Christopher Collins took over as chairman. The new chief executive was Andrew Dougal; Jonathan Nicholls was recruited from Abbey National to be financial director.

Hanson quickly divested a number of unrelated (to its core building products) businesses, including Grove Cranes and Melody Radio, activities that it had retained when the old business was split. The sales raised £670 million. The main UK businesses in early 1997 were:

- bricks (including London and Butterley)
- ready-mix concrete
- aggregates, specifically crushed rock, sand and gravel (developed around ARC, Amalgamated Roadstone Corporation, acquired when Hanson acquired Consolidated Goldfields, its previous parent, in 1989).

The main business in the USA was aggregates and, in late 1997 and 1998, Hanson spent $300 million acquiring related US businesses in aggregates and concrete pipes. With the parallel divestments, net debt of £217 million was soon replaced by a cash surplus, which Hanson would use for further related acquisitions, mainly in the USA, but also in Europe and Asia wherever an appropriate business became available. Hanson declared that it would seek to spend some $300 million (£200 million) every year on acquisitions. Approximately 50% of the company's profits were being earned in the USA, 40% in the UK and the remaining 10% in Europe and Asia. Specific targets for acquisition would be bricks and aggregate recycling (including landfill) in the UK, and aggregates and concrete pipes in the USA.

The UK and US aggregates markets were very different. In the UK four companies, of which Hanson was one, controlled 70% of output. In the USA the top three added up to only an 18% share. Hanson, third largest, had 4.8%, Vulcan Materials 7.3% and Marlin Marietta 6.3%. All aimed to grow by acquisition in a very fragmented industry, and each would target certain geographical areas and seek local dominance. Because aggregates can only be moved cost effectively for some 50 miles (80 kilometres; and for ready-mix concrete the maximum distance is 15 miles or 24 kilometres) and the USA is a huge country, the industry had developed around over 5000 non-quoted companies, many of which were small, family companies which owned only one quarry. There were good acquisition opportunities, and the market was growing as substantial federal road- and bridge-building programmes were both underway and planned. The domestic house market was also booming. In the UK, however, the market was much flatter and, as a consequence, prices were tighter.

## Divisionalization

At the end of 1998 Hanson was restructured into three divisions. The divisional heads would have a much stronger corporate role than had been the case when Lord Hanson was strategic leader, to reflect the reality that Hanson was focused and no longer a diversified conglomerate. 'Hanson is no longer a buyer and seller of businesses' – Dougal.

The 49 US businesses were renamed Hanson Building Materials America. In Europe, 17 businesses, including ARC and excluding the brick companies, were renamed Hanson Quarry Products Europe. The brick companies were to be known as Hanson Brick Europe.

Each division would be set targets for long-term cash flow and internal rates of return. There would not be any specific intent to recover acquisition costs directly through short-term pricing decisions. There would also be targeted investment where it was appropriate, say where old equipment needed replacing and where increased productivity could lead to lower production costs.

In parallel with the new structure Hanson changed its logo. The previous logo – a composite of two tied ribbons based on the Union Jack and Stars and Stripes flags – had been used for 20 years. The new logo is a grid of nine squares which represent nine building blocks. They are in two colours such that the letter H can be picked out.

## Acquisitions

Hanson made 30 acquisitions worldwide in 1999. It began in January by acquiring a number of quarries in Malaysia – the start of the supply chain for aggregates – to supply the building industry in South Malaysia and Singapore. This move confirmed that Hanson would expand outside the UK and USA, although it intended its focus to remain there.

This was followed by the purchase of:

- the Jannock Brick Group, the second largest brick company in the USA, for the equivalent of £160 million
- an aggregates business in New York State, and
- a concrete pipe business in Ohio.

In November 1999 Hanson agreed an uncontested bid of £1.59 billion in cash and shares for Pioneer, one of Australia's leading aggregates businesses. Pioneer had expanded overseas such that only 38% of its assets were in Australia – 27% were in America, 20% in Europe and 15% in Asia. There was an obvious geographical overlap with Hanson and, indeed, in 1996, Pioneer had attempted to buy Hanson's building products activities. There were anticipated savings and synergy from the increased market share; with the acquisition, Hanson became the world's leading aggregate supplier and the second largest supplier of ready-mix concrete. In percentage terms this meant that Hanson controlled 19% of the market share controlled by the world's ten leading manufacturers of aggregates; the second largest had 16%. It now had 5% of the US market overall. For ready-mix cement Hanson controlled 15% of the market share controlled by the ten leading competitors, two-thirds the share of market leader, RMC. Dougal commented: 'This is not the start of a series of large transactions'.

By early 2000 Hanson's worldwide sales were broken down as follows:

| | |
|---|---|
| US | 38% |
| UK | 30% |
| Australia | 14% |
| Europe | 12% |
| Asia | 6% |

*Figure A1*   Hanson share price (----) relative to the FTSE All-Shares Index (—) from February 1997 to October 2000. (High: 626 pence, 22.6.99; low: 257 pence, 20.1.98; last: 329 pence, 10.10.00.) Source: Datastream.

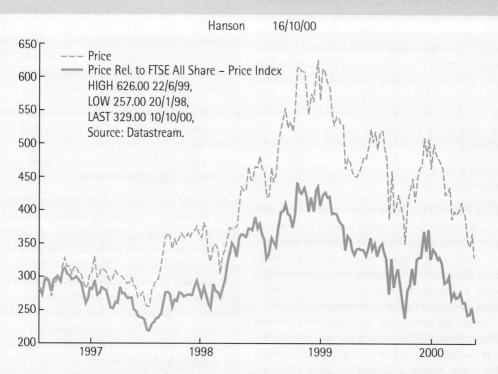

Hanson       16/10/00

Price
Price Rel. to FTSE All Share – Price Index
HIGH 626.00 22/6/99,
LOW 257.00 20/1/98,
LAST 329.00 10/10/00,
Source: Datastream.

Appendix 1 provides details of revenue and profits in 1998 and 1999 and Figure A1 tracks the Hanson share price against the FTSE all-shares index from the time of the corporate split to October 2000.

> Hanson: *http://www.hanson.com*
> Hanson plc: *http://www.hansonplc.com*

## Questions

1. Taking into account the nature of the building products industry worldwide and Hanson's stated intent, how would you evaluate the company's strategy since the corporate split in 1997?

2. Does the new divisionalized structure imply a change of corporate style?

*Appendix 1*  Hanson – revenue and profits for 1998 and 1999

**Year ending 31 December 1998**

| | |
|---|---|
| Total sales | £1.825 billion |
| Total sales excluding divestments | £1.59 billion |
| Operating profit | £260 million |
| Declared profit after interest and tax rebate | £356 million |

**Sales and profit by region and activity**

| | Sales | | Operating profits | |
|---|---|---|---|---|
| | £m | % of total | £m | % of total |
| US building materials | 770 | 48 | 129 | 50 |
| European quarries | 575 | 36 | 94 | 36 |
| European bricks | 199 | 13 | 35 | 13 |
| Rest of world | 46 | 3 | 2 | 1 |
| | 1590 | 100 | 260 | 100 |

**Year ending 31 December 1999**

| | |
|---|---|
| Total sales | £1.92 billion |
| Total sales of ongoing activities from 1998 | £1.779 billion |
| Sales contributed by acquisitions | £141 million |
| Operating profit | £332 million |
| Declared profit after interest and tax rebate | £334 million |

**Sales and profit by region and activity**

| | Sales | | Operating profits | |
|---|---|---|---|---|
| | £m | % of total | £m | % of total |
| US building materials | 1070 | 56 | 199 | 60 |
| European quarries | 604 | 31 | 97 | 29 |
| European bricks | 207 | 11 | 33 | 10 |
| Rest of world | 39 | 2 | 3 | 1 |
| | 1920 | 100 | 332 | 100 |

**Growth 1988–1999**

| | Sales | Operating profits |
|---|---|---|
| | % | % |
| US building materials | 39 | 54 |
| European quarries | 5 | 3 |
| European bricks | 4 | −6 |

# Glossary

**Acquisition** The purchase of one company by another, for either cash or equity in the parent. Sometimes the word *takeover* is preferred when the acquisition is hostile, and resisted by the company being bought. Similarly, *mergers* are when two companies simply *agree* to come together as one.

**Activities** Those things – acts and tasks – undertaken by an organization which, when aggregated, dictate the strength of a *strategic position*.

**Adaptive strategic change** Strategies that emerge and develop on an ongoing basis as companies learn of new environmental opportunities and threats and adapt (or respond) to competitive pressures.

**Adding value** Technically, the difference between the value of a firm's outputs and its inputs; the additional value is added through the deployment and effort of the organization's resources. Successful organizations will seek to add value to create outputs which are perceived as important by their customers. The *added value* or *supply chain* is the sequential set of activities from suppliers, through manufacturers and distributors which is required to bring products and services to the marketplace.

**Alliance (strategic alliance)** An agreement, preferably formalized, with another organization. The alliance might be with an important supplier, with a major distributor, or possibly with a competitor, say for joint research and development.

**Appropriability** The ability of an organization to ensure that at least some of the benefits earned from the value that it creates and adds comes back to the organization, rather than only benefiting others, such as suppliers, customers or even competitors.

**Architecture** A relational network involving either or both external linkages (see *alliance*) or internal linkages between managers in a company or businesses in a conglomerate. The supply chain is one such network. The main benefits concern information exchanges for the mutual gain of those involved, and *synergies* (see below) from interdependencies. Sometimes linked with reputation and innovation as key strategic resources for an organization.

**Backward (vertical) integration** The process by which a manufacturer acquires direct control over its inputs, such that it makes what it previously bought-in. See also *vertical integration*.

**Benchmarking** A process of comparative evaluation – of products, services and the performances of equipment and personnel. Sometimes companies attempt to benchmark their competitors; on other occasions they will benchmark those organizations which are seen as high performers.

**Branding** The additional value and reassurance provided to customers through the reputation of the business, represented by the strength and visibility of its brand name.

**Break-even** The level of activity where the total costs incurred in producing and selling a product or service – or pursuing a particular strategy – are equal to the total revenues generated.

**Business environment** See *environment*.

**Business ethics** The principles, standards and conduct that an organization practises – and sometimes states formally – for the way in which it deals with its people, its external stakeholders and environmental issues that arise.

**Business process re-engineering** The analysis and redesign of workflows and processes within organizations and between them (i.e. along the supply chain).

**Combination strategy** Term used where more than one discrete strategic alternative is pursued at the same time. Particularly relevant for a mixture of market penetration, market development and product development strategies; and invariably implies innovation.

**Competitive advantage** The ability of an organization to add more value for its customers than its rivals, and thus attain a position of relative advantage. The challenge is to sustain any advantage once achieved.

**Competitive strategy** The means by which organizations seek to achieve and sustain competitive advantage. Usually the result of distinctive *functional strategies*. There should be a competitive strategy for every product and service produced by the company.

**Competitor gap analysis** A comparison of the organization with its leading competitors in terms of their respective ability to satisfy key success factors. Ideally, this will involve an input from relevant customers.

**Concentration ratios** Normally the degree to which added value and/or turnover and/or assets in an industry are concentrated in the hands of a few suppliers. High concentration is reflected in monopoly and oligopoly industry structures. Sometimes measured in terms of aggregate output controlled by the largest companies in a country.

**Controls** Means by which progress against stated objectives and targets is measured and monitored, and changed as necessary.

**Core competencies** Distinctive skills, normally related to a product, service or technology, which can be used to create a competitive advantage. See also *strategic capability*. Together, they form key resources that assist an organization in being different from (and ideally superior to) its competitors.

**Corporate governance** The selection, role and responsibilities of the strategic leadership of the organization, their conduct and their relationships with internal and external stakeholders. Sometimes responsibility for overall strategy and ongoing operations will be separated.

**Corporate strategy** The overall strategy for a diversified or multiproduct/multi-service organization. Refers to the overall scope of the business in terms of products, services and geography.

**Cost leadership** The lowest cost producer in a market, after adjustments for quality differences. An important source of competitive advantage in either a market or a segment of a market. Specifically, the cost leader is the company that enjoys a cost advantage over its rivals through the management of its resources, and not simply because it produces the lowest quality.

**Cost of capital** The cost of capital employed to fund strategic initiatives, combining the rate of interest on debt and the cost of equity. The typical formula used is the weighted average cost of capital which encompasses the relative proportions of debt and equity. Normally should be lower than the dis-

counted rate of return from the investment or initiative – see *discounted cash flow*.

**Crisis management** How the organization (a) seeks to reduce the likelihood of, and (b) manages in the event of, a major disturbance which has the potential to damage the organization's assets or reputation. Some crises are the result of mismanagement or inadequate controls; others begin outside the organization and may be unavoidable.

**Critical mass** Relates to the actual and relative size of an organization in terms of its ability to be influential and powerful in its industry or environment.

**Culture** The values and norms of an organization, which determine its corporate behaviour and the behaviour of people within the organization.

**Decentralization/centralization** The extent to which authority, responsibility and accountability are devolved throughout the organization. Centralization should yield tight control; decentralization motivates managers and allows for speedier reactions to environmental change pressures.

**Delayering** The flattening of an organization structure by removing layers of management and administration.

**Demerger or divestment** Term used when an organization sells or spins off (or maybe even closes) a business or activity. Usually linked to a strategy of increased focus.

**Differentiation** Products and services are differentiated when customers perceive them to have distinctive properties that set them apart from their competitors.

**Directional policy matrix** A planning technique used to compare and contrast the relative competitive strengths of a portfolio of products and services produced by an organization. Used to help in evaluating their relative worth and investment potential.

**Discounted cash flow (DCF)** The sum of the projected cash returns or flows over a period of years from a strategic investment or initiative. Future figures are reduced (specifically, inflation is removed) to bring them into line with present values.

**Diversification** The extent of the differences between the various products and services in a company's portfolio (its range of activities). The products and services may be *related* through say marketing or technology, or *unrelated*, which normally implies that they require different management skills.

**Divestment** See *Demerger*.

**Divisionalization** A form of organization structure whereby activities are divided and separated on the basis of different products or services, or geographical territories.

**Dot.com companies** Organizations that have emerged as the power and potential of the Internet has been realized and exploited. Dot.com companies will normally trade over the Internet, but some are essentially service providers.

**Double-loop learning** An assessment of the continuing appropriateness and value of existing competitive positions and paradigms and the ability to create new competitive positions, ideally ahead of competitors. See also *single-loop learning*.

**Downsizing** Sometimes associated with business process re-engineering, downsizing occurs when organizations rationalize their product/service ranges and streamline their processes. People, in particular layers of management, are removed. See also *rightsizing*.

**E-commerce** Short for electronic commerce, and meaning trading over the Internet.

**E-markets** Markets is the term used for when buyers and sellers 'come together' to engineer an exchange. E-markets is the term used when this trading is via the Internet.

**Economies of scale** Cost savings accrued with high volume production, which enables lower unit production costs.

**Effectiveness** The ability of an organization to meet the demands and expectations of its various stakeholders, those individuals or groups with influence over the business. Sometimes known as 'doing the right things'.

**Efficiency** The sound management of resources to maximize the returns from them. Known as 'doing things right'.

**Emergent strategy** Term used to describe and explain strategies which emerge over time and often with an element of trial-and-error. Detailed implementation is not prescribed in advance. Some emergent strategies are *incremental changes* with learning as intended strategies are implemented. Other *adaptive strategies* are responses to new environmental opportunities and threats.

**Empowerment** Freeing people from a rigid regime of rules, controls and directives and allowing them to take responsibility for their own decisions and actions.

**Entrepreneur** Someone who perpetually creates and innovates to build something of recognized value around perceived opportunities.

**Entrepreneurial/visionary strategies** Strategies created by strong, visionary strategic leaders. Their successful implementation relies on an ability to persuade others of their merit.

**Environment** Everything and everyone outside the organization or organizational boundary – including competitors, customers, financiers, suppliers and government.

**E-V-R (environment-values-resources) congruence** The effective matching of an organization's resources (R) with the demands of its environment (E). A successful and sustained match has to be managed and frequently requires change; successfully achieving this depends on the organization's culture and values (V).

**Experience curve** The relationship between (reducing) unit costs and the total number of units ever produced of a product. Usually plotted as a graph, and often with a straight-line relationship on logarithmic axes. The percentage unit cost reduction holds steady every time output is doubled.

**Financial control** Term used to describe the form of control normally found in a *holding company* structure. Strategy creation is decentralized to independent business units which are required to meet agreed financial targets.

**Focus strategy** Concentration on one or a limited number of market segments or niches.

**Forward (vertical) integration** When an organization takes controls over aspects of its distribution, transport or direct selling. See also *vertical integration*.

**Functional strategies** The strategies for the various functions carried out by an organization, including marketing, production, financial management, information management, research and development, and human resource management. One or more functional strategies will typically be responsible for any distinctive competitive edge enjoyed by the company.

**Functional structure** A structure based around individual functions, such as production, sales and finance, all of which report to an identifiable managing director/chief executive.

**Generic strategies** The basic competitive strategies – based on cost leadership, differentiation and focus – which are open to any competitor in an industry, and which can be a source of competitive advantage.

**Global strategies** Strategies for companies which manufacture and market in several countries and/or continents.

Issues concern, for example, the location of manufacturing units and the extent to which control is centralized at a home base or decentralized on a local basis.

**Governance** The location of power and responsibility at the head of an organization. See *corporate governance*.

**Heartland** Term used to describe a cluster of businesses (in a multibusiness organization) which can be justifiably related and integrated to generate synergies.

**Holding company** A structure where the various businesses are seen as largely independent of each other and managed accordingly.

**Horizontal integration** The acquisition or merger of firms at the same stage in the supply chain. Such firms may be direct competitors or focus on different market segments.

**Implementation** See *strategy implementation*.

**Incremental strategic changes** Changes to intended (possibly planned) strategies as they are implemented. Result from ongoing learning and from changes in the environment or to forecast assumptions.

**Innovation** Changes to products, processes and services in an attempt to sharpen their competitiveness – through either cost reduction or improved distinctiveness. Strategically, it can apply to any part of a business.

**Intangible (strategic) resources** Resources which have no physical presence, but which can add real value for the organization. Reputation and technical knowledge would be typical examples.

**Intellectual capital** The hidden value (and capital) tied up in an organization's people which can set it apart from its competitors and be a valuable source of competitive advantage and future earnings. Difficult to quantify and value for the balance sheet. Linked to *knowledge*.

**Intended strategies** Prescribed strategies the organization intends to implement, albeit with incremental changes. Sometimes the result of (formal) strategic planning; sometimes the stated intent of the strategic leader. May be described alternatively as *prescriptive strategies*.

**Intrapreneurship** The process of internal entrepreneurship. Occurs when managers or other employees accept responsibility and actively champion new initiatives aimed at making a real difference.

**Joint venture** A form of strategic alliance where each partner takes a financial stake. This could be a shareholding in the other partner or the establishment of a separate, jointly owned, business.

**Just-in-time (JIT)** Systems or processes for ensuring that stocks or components are delivered just when and where they are needed, reducing the need for inventory.

**Key (or critical) success factors** Environmentally based factors which are crucial for competitive success. Simply, the things that an organization must be able to do well if it is to succeed.

**Knowledge** An amalgamation of experience, values, information, insight and strategic awareness – which goes beyond the notions of data and information. Retained, managed and exploited it can be a valuable source of competitive difference and advantage. See also *intellectual capital*.

**Leadership** See *strategic leader.*

**Learning organization** One which is capable of harnessing and spreading best practices, and where employees can learn from each other and from other organizations. The secret lies in open and effective communications networks.

**Leverage** The exploitation, by an organization, of its resources to their full extent. Often linked to the idea of *stretching resources*.

**Lifecycle** See *strategic lifecycle.*

**Liquidation** The closing down of a business, normally because it has failed. Typically a last resort, when a rescue or sale has either not been possible or not successful.

**Logical incrementalism** Term adopted by John B. Quinn to explain strategy creation in small, logical, incremental steps.

**Loose-tight properties** Term which explains the idea of tight central control over key strategies, policies, principles and values combined with delegated authority to subsidiary businesses and empowered managers.

**Machiavellian behaviour** Where individuals use power and influence to structure situations and events, and bring about outcomes, which are more in their own personal interests than those of the organization. Linked to *organizational politics*.

**Market development** Continuing with existing products and services but, and possibly with modifications and additions, seeking new market and new market segment opportunities.

**Market-driven strategy** Alternative term for *opportunity-driven strategy.*

**Market penetration** Persisting with existing products/services and existing customers and markets but accepting that continuous, incremental improvement is possible to strengthen the relevant strategic position. The assumption is that sales and revenue can be increased.

**Market segment(ation)** The use of particular marketing strategies to target identified and defined groups of customers.

**Mass marketing** Where one product (or service) is sold to all types of customer.

**Matrix organization** A multidivisional organization which seeks to link the various functional activities across the divisions, to achieve the synergy benefits of interdependency.

**Merger** See *acquisition.*

**Milestones** Interim targets which act as indicators or measures of progress in the pursuit of objectives and the implementation of strategies.

**Mission statement** A summary of the essential aim or purpose of the organization; its essential reason for being in business.

**Monopoly power** The relative power of an individual company in an industry. It does not follow that a dominant competitor will act against the best interests of customers and consumers, but it could be in a position to do so.

**Monopoly structure** Term for an industry with a dominant and very powerful competitor. Originally based on the idea of total control, competitive authorities around the world now consider a 25% market or asset share to be a basis for possible monopoly power.

**Multinational company** A company operating in several countries. See *global strategies.*

**Niche marketing** Concentration on a small, identifiable market segment with the aim of achieving dominance of the segment.

**Not-for-profit organization** Term used to describe an organization (such as a charity) that does not have profit as a fundamental objective. Such organizations will, however, have to achieve a cash surplus to survive.

**Objective** A short-term target or milestone with defined measurable achievements. A desired state and hoped-for level of success.

**Oligopoly structure** An industry dominated by a small group of competitors.

**Opportunity-driven strategy** Strategy creation and development that begins with an analysis of external environmental threats and opportunities. See also *resource-based strategy*.

**Organizational politics** The process by which individuals and groups utilize power and influence to obtain results. Politics can be used legitimately in the best interests of the organization, or illegitimately by people who put their own interests above those of the organization.

**Outsourcing** Procuring products and services from independent suppliers rather than producing them within the organization. Often linked to strategies of focusing on core competencies and capabilities.

**Paradigm** A recipe or model for linking together the component strands of a theory and identifying the inherent relationships, a competitive paradigm explains the underpinning logic of a competitive strategy or position.

**Parenting** The skills and capabilities used by a head office to manage and control a group of subsidiary business-es. The head office should be able to add value for the businesses, while the busi-nesses should, in turn, be able to add value for the whole organization.

**Performance indicators or measures** Quantifiable measures and subjective indicators of strategic and competitive success.

**PEST analysis** An analysis of the politi-cal, economic, social and technological factors in the external environment of an organization, which can affect its activities and performance.

**Plan** A statement of intent, generally linked to a programme of tactics for strategy implementation.

**Planning** See *strategic planning*.

**Planning gap** A planning technique which enables organizations to evalu-ate the potential for, and risk involved in, seeking to attain particular growth targets.

**Policies** Guidelines relating to deci-sions and approaches which support organizational efforts to achieve stated (intended) objectives. Can be at any level in the organization, and can range from mandatory regulations to recom-mended courses of action. They may or may not be written down formally.

**Portfolio analysis** Techniques for eval-uating the appropriate strategies for a range of (possibly diverse) business activities in a single organization. See *directional policy matrix*.

**Power** The potential or ability to do something or make something happen. Externally, it refers to the ability of an organization to influence and affect the actions of its external stakeholders. Internally, it concerns the relationships between people.

**Prescriptive strategies** See *intended strategies*.

**Product development** Developing addi-tional and normally related products and services to enhance the range available to existing customers and markets, and thereby increase sales and revenue.

**Profit** The difference between total revenues and total costs. Often profit is a fundamental objective of a manufac-turing or service business.

**Profitability** Financial ratios which look at profits generated in relation to the capital that has been employed to generate them. Two different ratios relate (a) trading profit (or profit before interest and tax) to total capital em-ployed (known as the return on capital employed) and (b) profit after interest and tax to shareholders' funds (known as the return on shareholders' funds).

**Public-sector organizations** Organizations controlled directly or indirectly by gov-ernment and/or dependent on govern-ment for a substantial proportion of their revenue. Includes local authori-ties, the National Health Service in the UK and the emergency services.

**Quality** Strategically, quality is con-cerned with the ability of an organiza-tion to 'do things right – first time and every time' for each customer. This includes internal customers (other departments in an organization) as well as external customers. *Total quality management* is the spreading of quality consciousness throughout the whole organization.

**Reputation** The strategic standing of an organization in the eyes of its cus-tomers and suppliers.

**Resource-based strategy** Strategy crea-tion built around the further exploita-tion of core competencies and strategic capabilities.

**Retrenchment** Strategy followed when an organization is experiencing diffi-culties and needs to cut costs and con-solidate its resources before seeking new ways to create and add value. Sometimes involves asset reduction (perhaps the sale of a business) and job losses.

**Rightsizing** Linked to downsizing, im-plies the reduction in staffing is to a level from which the organization can grow effectively. On occasions downsiz-ing can mean that strategically impor-tant skills and competencies are lost; rightsizing implies this is not the case.

**Risk management** The understanding where and how things can and might go wrong, appreciating the extent of any downside if things do go wrong, and putting in place strategies to deal with the risks either before or after their occurrence.

**Scenarios** Conceptual possibilities of future events and circumstances. Scenario planning involves using these to explore what might happen in order to help prepare managers for a wide range of eventualities and uncertain-ties in an unpredictable future environ-ment.

**Single-loop learning** The ability to improve a competitive position on an ongoing and continuous basis, acknowledging there is always the possibility of improvement. Sometimes the competitive paradigm itself has to be changed – see *double-loop learning*.

Small and medium enterprises (SMEs) Term used to embrace new and growing businesses, and those which (for any number of reasons) do not grow beyond a certain size.

Social responsibility Strategies and actions that can be seen to be in the wide and 'best' interests of society in general and the environment. Sometimes associated with the notion of mutual self-interest.

Stakeholders Any individual or group capable of affecting (and being affected by) the actions and performance of an organization.

Strategic awareness Appreciating the strategic position and relative success of the organization. Knowing how well it is doing, why and how – relative to its competitors – and appreciating the nature of the external environment and the extent of any need to change things.

Strategic thinking The ability of the organization (and its managers) to (a) synthesize the lessons from past experiences and to share the learning, (b) be aware of current positions, strengths and competencies and (c) clarify the way forward for the future.

Strategy The means by which organizations achieve (and seek to achieve) their objectives and purpose. There can be a strategy for each product and service, and for the organization as a whole.

Strategy creation Umbrella term for the formulation and choice of new strategies. Encapsulates direction from the strategic leader (or an entrepreneur), strategic planning, and emergent strategy. See: *emergent strategy; entrepreneurial strategies; strategic planning.*

Strategic alliance See *alliance.*

Strategic architecture See *architecture.*

Strategic business unit A discrete grouping within an organization with delegated responsibility for strategically managing a product, a service, or a particular group of products or services.

Strategic capability Process skills used to add value and create competitive advantage.

Strategic change Changes that take place over time to the strategies and objectives of the organization. Change can be gradual, emergent and evolutionary, or discontinuous, dramatic and revolutionary.

Strategic control A style of corporate control whereby the organization attempts to enjoy the benefits of delegation and decentralization with a portfolio of activities which, while diverse, is interdependent and capable of yielding synergies from co-operation.

Strategic issues Current and forthcoming developments inside and outside the organization which will impact upon the ability of the organization to pursue its mission and achieve its objectives.

Strategic leader Generic term used to describe a manager who is responsible for changes in the corporate strategy.

Strategic lifecycle The notion that strategies (like products and services) have finite lives. After some period of time they will need improving, changing or replacing.

Strategic management The process by which an organization establishes its objectives, formulates actions (strategies) designed to meet these objectives in the desired time-scale, implements the actions, and assesses progress and results.

Strategic planning *In strategy creation:* the systematic and formal creation of strategies – to be found in many organizations, and capable of making a very significant contribution in large,

multiactivity organizations. *In strategic control:* centralized control, most ideal where there is a limited range of core businesses.

Strategic positioning The chosen or realized relationship between the organization and its market. Clearly linked to competitive strategies and competitive advantage. The position itself is not a source of advantage, but the activities that underpin the position are.

Strategic regeneration (or renewal) Major and simultaneous changes to strategies, structures and styles of management.

Strategy implementation The processes through which the organization's chosen and intended strategies are made to happen.

Stretching resources The creative use of resources to add extra value for customers – through innovation and improved productivity.

Supply chain The linkage between an organization, its suppliers, its distributors and its customers.

Sustainable competitive advantage A sustained edge over competitors in an industry, usually achieved by first creating a valuable difference and then sustaining it with improvement and change.

SWOT analysis An analysis of an organization's strengths and weaknesses alongside the opportunities and threats present in the external environment.

Synergy Term used for the added value or additional benefits which ideally accrue from the linkage or fusion of two businesses, or from increased co-operation either between different parts of the same organization or between a company and its suppliers, distributors and customers. Internal co-operation may represent linkages between either different divisions or different functions.

Tactic Specific actions that follow on

from intended strategies but which can also form a foundation for emergent strategy.

Tangible resources The organization's physical resources, such as plant and equipment.

Transfer price Associated with the transfer of products, components or services between businesses in the same organization. A particularly important issue where there are considerable interdependencies between businesses. The (corporately) imposed or agreed transfer price can be of markedly different attractiveness to the

buying and selling businesses and can be a source of friction.

Turnaround strategy An attempt to find a new competitive position for a company in difficulty.

Value chain Framework for identifying (a) where value is added and (b) where costs are incurred. There is an internal value chain and one that embraces the complete supply chain. Internally, it embraces the key functions and activities.

Vertical integration Where firms directly enter those parts of the added value chain served by their suppliers or

distributors, the term used is vertical integration. To achieve the potential benefits of vertical integration (specifically synergy from co-operation) without acquiring a business which normally requires specialist and different skills, firms will look to establish strong alliances and networks.

Vision A statement or picture of the future standing of an organization. Linked to the mission or purpose, it embraces key values.

# Author Index